John A. Taylor

P9-ASG-024

THE COLLECTED SCIENTIFIC PAPERS OF
PAUL A. SAMUELSON

VOLUME I

THE COLLECTED SCIENTIFIC PAPERS OF PAUL A. SAMUELSON

Edited by Joseph E. Stiglitz

THE M.I.T. PRESS

Massachusetts Institute of Technology
Cambridge, Massachusetts, and London, England

See pages 763–771 for acknowledgments of previously published material.

Copyright © 1966
by
The Massachusetts Institute of Technology

All rights reserved. This book may not be reproduced, in whole or in part, in any form (except by reviewers for the public press), without written permission from the publishers.

Second Printing, June 1970

Third printing November 1972

ISBN 0 262 19021 4

Library of Congress Catalog Card Number: 65-28408
Printed in the United States of America

AUTHOR'S PREFACE

Over the years it has been suggested that I bring out some collected papers. As the supply of my reprints has become more and more exhausted, I have in principle become more and more impressed with the force of this argument. But I have always felt hesitant to interrupt current new research merely in order to reassemble old research. Now the matter has been taken out of my hands. The M.I.T. Press and kind colleagues have undertaken to do the job. Mr. Joseph Stiglitz, an able young graduate student, has agreed to do the minimum editing needed for such a collection.

My own preference was for as complete and unpretentious an assemblage as possible. I could not see why anyone else's research program should be interrupted by the arduous job of proofreading completely reset mathematical symbolism. As to selection of articles, the choice has been that of Mr. Stiglitz alone. A number of previously unpublished papers, such as the widely circulated RAND Memorandum on "Market Mechanisms and Maximization," have been included. My advice on selection was: When in doubt, include — of course excluding all nonscientific writing, such as periodic financial journalism for the *London Financial Times*, the *Nihon Keizai Shimbun*, and the *Washington Post*, and excluding most book reviews.

Personally, I should have preferred a simple chronological listing, so that any continuities of thought might reveal themselves. But wise friends, such as Professors Robert M. Solow and Charles P. Kindleberger, have prevailed upon me to agree to an arrangement by subject matter. Mr. Stiglitz has alone taken the responsibility for the selection and arrangement of articles. And I think he would be the first to admit that alternative classifications might have been made with equal advantage, since topics like Welfare Economics and International Trade, and indeed all of the topics of modern economics, are so interdependent as to defy any arbitrary classification.

I must confess that I have been tempted to make an editorial change here or there. This temptation I have resisted. In several places where an outright error of substance occurred, I have added correcting paragraphs that are clearly marked to be of 1965 vintage. When tempted to omit a particular article, I was taken aback to have a colleague say, "Why I thought that one of your most interesting pieces." Only one of the items included seems to me to express some bad temper, but I decided that to exclude it would be invidious and would also deprive the reader of the opportunity to judge whether, as I have sometimes heard it said, I have mellowed over the years.

Finally, my thanks go to Joseph Stiglitz for a difficult and thankless job well done. Since I have continued to write articles at a steady pace and since he cannot expect to stay young forever, Mr. Stiglitz has wisely decided to call a halt at the arbitrary date of late 1964. And high time, says my wife and fairest critic.

PAUL A. SAMUELSON

Cambridge, Massachusetts
September 1965

EDITOR'S PREFACE

These two volumes contain virtually all of Professor Paul A. Samuelson's contributions to economic theory through mid-1964. These articles have been collected from the economic journals, *Festschrifts*, and several books on current economic problems. A few of the articles were unpublished RAND Memoranda, and others were lectures.

The arrangement by topics has not been easy; some of the articles, or chapters, properly belong in several sections; some might be put most properly in sections of their own. A few of the final decisions had to be made somewhat arbitrarily. The parts are arranged into books of closely related subjects. Within the parts, the articles are arranged chronologically, except where several articles were very closely tied together. For instance, the 1963 article on the "Gains from International Trade Once Again" immediately follows the 1939 article "The Gains from International Trade." I hope that this arrangement will make the book more useful to the reader than a strictly chronological ordering. For those who prefer the latter, however, I have included in the acknowledgments a chronological list of the articles.

Although no major changes in text have been made, a number of minor corrections have been made. After several of the articles, a 1965 postscript has been inserted in which Professor Samuelson states his present position on these topics.

On some of the topics discussed, a more recent exposition will be found in *The Foundations of Economic Analysis* (Cambridge: Harvard University Press, 1948) by Professor Samuelson, and *Linear Programming and Economic Analysis* (New York: McGraw-Hill, 1958) by Robert Dorfman, Paul A. Samuelson, and Robert M. Solow.

JOSEPH E. STIGLITZ

Cambridge, Massachusetts
July 1965

Revised Contents from *The Collected Scientific Papers
of Paul A. Samuelson*. Published by
The M.I.T. Press. Copyright © 1966, by
The Massachusetts Institute of Technology

CONTENTS

Volume I

Book One

**Problems in Pure Theory: The Theory of Consumer's Behavior
and Capital Theory**

Contents

Contents

BOOK ONE

Problems in Pure Theory:
The Theory of Consumer's Behavior and Capital Theory

PART I

The Theory of Revealed Preference and Other Topics in
Nonstochastic Consumption Theory

1

A Note on the Pure Theory of Consumer's Behaviour

By P. A. SAMUELSON

FROM its very beginning the theory of consumer's choice has marched steadily towards greater generality, sloughing off at successive stages unnecessarily restrictive conditions. From the time of Gossen to our own day we have seen the removal of (*a*) the assumption of linearity of marginal utility ; (*b*) the assumption of independence of utilities ; (*c*) the assumption of the measurability of utility in a cardinal sense ; and (*d*) even the assumption of an integrable field of preference elements.

The discrediting of *utility* as a psychological concept robbed it of its only possible virtue as an *explanation* of human behaviour in other than a circular sense, revealing its emptiness as even a construction. As a result the most modern theory confines itself to an analysis of indifference elements, budgetary equilibrium being defined by equivalence of price ratios to respective indifference slopes.

Consistently applied, however, the modern criticism turns back on itself and cuts deeply. For just as we do not claim to know by introspection the behaviour of utility, many will argue we cannot know the behaviour of ratios of marginal utilities or of indifference directions.

Why should one believe in the *increasing rate of marginal substitution*, except in so far as it leads to the type of demand functions in the market which seem plausible ? Even on the advanced front we are confronted with this dilemma —either the argument with respect to indifference varieties is circular or to many people inadmissible (at least without further demonstration).

Hence, despite the fact that the notion of utility has been repudiated or ignored by modern theory, it is clear that much of even the most modern analysis shows vestigial traces of the utility concept. Thus, to any person not acquainted with the history of the subject, the exposition of the theory of consumer's behaviour in the formulation of Hicks and Allen[1] would seem indirect. The introduction and meaning of the marginal rate of substitution as an entity independent of any psychological, introspective implications would be, to say the least, ambiguous, and would seem an artificial convention in the explanation of price behaviour. (This would be particularly so in the many-commodity, non-integrable case.)

I propose, therefore, that we start anew in direct attack upon the problem, dropping off the last vestiges of the utility analysis. This does not preclude the introduction of utility by any who may care to do so, nor will it contradict the results attained by use of related constructs. It is merely that the analysis can be carried on more directly, and from a different set of postulates.

All that follows shall relate to an idealised individual— not necessarily, however, the rational *homo-economicus*. I assume in the beginning as known, i.e., empirically determinable under ideal conditions, the amounts of n economic goods which will be purchased per unit time by an individual faced with the prices of these goods and with a given total expenditure. It is assumed that prices are taken as given parameters not subject to influence by the individual.

Postulate I. Mathematically we assume as known the following single-valued functions :

$$\left. \begin{aligned} \psi_1 &= h^1(p_1, \ldots p_n, I) \\ &\vdots \\ \psi_n &= h^n(p_1, \ldots p_n, I) \end{aligned} \right\} \qquad (1.0)$$

subject to

$$\psi_1 p_1 + \psi_2 p_2 + \ldots \psi_n p_n = \sum_{i=1}^{n} \psi_i p_i = I \qquad (1.1)$$

Since we have $(n+1)$ equations and only n dependent variables, it is obvious that we may suppress one of the equations as redundant. We may rewrite our first assumption omitting the first equation in (1.0).

$$\left. \begin{aligned} \psi_i &= h^i(p_1, \ldots p_n, I) \qquad (i=2, \ldots n) \\ \sum_{i=1}^{n} \psi_i p_i &- I = 0 \end{aligned} \right\} \qquad (1.2)$$

---

[1] Hicks and Allen, "A Reconsideration of the Theory of Value," ECONOMICA, February and May, 1934.

4

Thus, confronted with a given set of prices and with a given income, our idealised individual will always choose the same set of goods. For mathematical convenience we assume that all our functions and their derivatives of the desired order are continuous with no singularities in the region under discussion.

Postulate II. We further assume that the consumer's behaviour is independent of the units in which prices are expressed. More specifically, if we multiply all prices and income by the same positive quantity, the amounts taken will remain the same.[1]

Mathematically our functions in set (1.2) are all homogeneous of order zero ; or

$$\left. \begin{aligned} &\psi_i = h^i(\lambda p_1, \ldots \lambda p_n, \lambda I) \quad (i=2, \ldots n) \\ &\sum_{i=1}^{n} \psi_i \lambda p_i - \lambda I = 0 \end{aligned} \right\} \quad (1.21)$$

Defining $\lambda = \dfrac{1}{p_1}$, these may be rewritten

$$\left. \begin{aligned} \psi_i &= h^i\left(1, \frac{p_2}{p_1}, \ldots \frac{p_n}{p_1}, \frac{I}{p_1}\right) \quad (i=2, \ldots n) \\ &= g^i\left(\frac{p_2}{p_1}, \ldots \frac{p_n}{p_1}, \frac{I}{p_1}\right) \quad (i=2, \ldots n) \\ \psi_1 &+ \sum_{i=2}^{n} \frac{p_i}{p_1} \psi_i - \frac{I}{p_1} = 0 \end{aligned} \right\} \quad (1.3)$$

This is equivalent to using p_1 as our *numéraire*, i.e., setting its price equal to unity.

Let us define $\beta_i = \dfrac{p_i}{p_1}$, $\quad (i=2, \ldots n)$ and $I^0 = \dfrac{I.}{p_1}$

We may rewrite (1.3) in the form

$$\left. \begin{aligned} &\psi_i = g^i(\beta_2, \ldots \beta_n, I^0) \quad (i=2, \ldots n) \\ &\psi_1 + \sum_{i=2}^{n} \beta_i \psi_i - I^0 = 0 \end{aligned} \right\} \quad (2.0)$$

Thus far we have not assumed that anything is known concerning the form or structural properties of our demand functions. Merely knowing that there will be a unique reaction to a given price and income situation puts no restrictions on that reaction. Fortunately, as I shall later

[1] This homogeneity assumption has been challenged by Mr. Keynes with respect to a different problem. For the pure theory of consumer's behaviour it is probably without objection. In any case it is always implicitly made.

show, it is possible to develop suitable restrictions so that our theory is more than formal.

Before doing so, it is convenient to develop certain additional relations. Substituting for I_i^0 its equivalent, we may rewrite set (2.0) in the following implicit form :

$$g^i(\beta_2, \ldots \beta_n, \psi_1 + \sum_{i=2}^{n} \beta_i \psi_i) - \psi_i = 0 \quad (i=2, \ldots n) \quad (3.0)$$

These are $(n-1)$ implicit functions involving $(2n-1)$ variables. Assuming that the conditions of the implicit function theorem are met in the region under discussion (and from later assumptions this will be likely), we may solve explicitly for the $(n-1)$ β's in terms of the n quantities ; i.e.,

$$\beta_i = \beta_i(\psi_1, \ldots \psi_n) \quad (i=2, \ldots n) \quad (4.0)$$

As before, nothing is known of the form of these functions in the absence of additional assumptions. It remains only to introduce some appropriate restriction to limit the form of our various functions.

To do so, I suggest the consideration of matters lying close to the modern theory of index numbers.

Let us consider an initial price and income situation.

$$(p_1, \ldots p_n, I)$$

Corresponding to this set there is a given set of consumer's goods bought.

$$(\psi_1, \ldots \psi_n)$$

Now consider a second set of prices and income.

$$(p_1', \ldots p_n', I')$$

and

$$(\psi_1', \ldots \psi_n')$$

I introduce a bracket notation to indicate the following sum :

$$[\psi p] = \psi_1 p_1 + \psi_2 p_2 + \ldots \psi_n p_n = \sum_{i=1}^{n} \psi_i p_i$$

or

$$[\psi p'] = \psi_1 p_1' + \psi_2 p_2' + \ldots \psi_n p_n' = \sum_{i=1}^{n} \psi_i p_i'$$

Suppose now that we combine the prices of the first position with the batch of goods bought in the second. The total cost of such a batch would be

$$[\psi' p] = \sum_{i=1}^{n} \psi_i' p_i \quad (5.0)$$

If this cost is less than or equal to the actual expenditure in the first period when the first batch of goods was actually bought, then it means that the individual could have purchased the second batch of goods with the price and income of the first situation, but did not choose to do so. That is, the first batch (ψ) was selected over (ψ'). We may express this symbolically by saying

$$[\psi'p] \leqq [\psi p] \qquad (5.11)$$

implies

$$(\psi') \ominus (\psi) \qquad (5.12)$$

The last symbol is merely an expression for the fact that the first batch was selected over the second. A reversal of the inequality sign could have the meaning that the second batch was selected over the first.

By analogous reasoning

$$[\psi p'] \leqq [\psi' p'] \qquad (5.21)$$

implies

$$(\psi) \ominus (\psi') \qquad (5.22)$$

By the usual rules of logic

$$(\psi) \overline{\ominus} (\psi') \qquad (5.31)$$

implies

$$[\psi p'] > [\psi' p'] \qquad (5.32)$$

since the negation of a consequence negates the antecedent.

Postulate III. I assume the following consistency in our idealised individual's behaviour. In any two price and income situations and corresponding quantities of consumer's goods given by equations (1.0) the individual must always behave consistently in the sense that (5.12) and (5.22) cannot hold simultaneously. Symbolically, we may write Postulate III

$$(\psi') \ominus (\psi) \qquad (6.01)$$

implies

$$(\psi) \overline{\ominus} (\psi') \qquad (6.02)$$

In words this means that if an individual selects batch one over batch two, he does not at the same time select two over one. The meaning of this is perfectly clear and will probably gain ready acquiescence. In any case the denial of this restriction would render invalid all of the former analysis of consumer's behaviour and the theory of index numbers as shown later.

Surprisingly enough, from this assumption and from this alone, it is possible to develop important restrictions on our demand functions.

Let us suppose

$$[\psi'p]=[\psi p] \qquad (7.01)$$

This implies from (5.11) and (5.12)

$$(\psi') \leqslant (\psi) \qquad (7.02)$$

which implies from (6.01) and (6.02)

$$(\psi) \lessgtr (\psi') \qquad (7.03)$$

which implies from (5.31) and (5.32)

$$[\psi p']>[\psi'p'] \qquad (7.04)$$

To summarise the argument

$$[\psi'p]=[\psi p] \qquad (7.01)$$

implies

$$[\psi p']>[\psi'p']^1 \qquad (7.04)$$

Without loss of generality let us write

$$\psi_i'=\psi_i+\triangle\psi_i; \quad p_i'=p_i+\triangle p_i$$

(7.01) and (7.04) become

$$[(\psi+\triangle\psi)p]=[\psi p] \qquad (8.01)$$

and

$$[\psi(p+\triangle p)]>[(\psi+\triangle\psi)(p+\triangle p)] \qquad (8.02)$$

Dropping the bracket notation

$$\sum_{i=1}^{n}(\psi_i+\triangle\psi_i)p_i=\sum_{i=1}^{n}\psi_ip_i \qquad (8.01)$$

$$\sum_{i=1}^{n}\psi_i(p_i+\triangle p_i)>\sum_{i=1}^{n}(\psi_i+\triangle\psi_i)(p_i+\triangle p_i) \qquad (8.02)$$

Setting the price of the first good equal to unity and using the notation previously defined

$$\psi_1+\triangle\psi_1+\sum_{i=2}^{n}(\psi_i+\triangle\psi_i)\beta_i=\psi_1+\sum_{i=2}^{n}\psi_i\beta_i \qquad (9.01)$$

$$\psi_1+\sum_{i=2}^{n}\psi_i(\beta_i+\triangle\beta_i)>\psi_1+\triangle\psi_1+\sum_{i=2}^{n}(\psi_i+\triangle\psi_i)(\beta_i+\triangle\beta_i)$$

$$(9.02)$$

[1] This means in the theory of index numbers that if the Laspeyres quantity index is equal to one, then the Paasche quantity index must be less than one. This provides a possible statistical check on the hypotheses underlying various index number studies.

By algebraic cancellation of terms this becomes

$$\triangle \psi_1 + \sum_{i=2}^{n} \beta_i \triangle \psi_i = 0 \qquad (10.01)$$

$$\triangle \psi_1 + \sum_{i=2}^{n} \beta_i \triangle \psi_i + \sum_{i=2}^{n} \triangle \psi_i \triangle \beta_i < 0 \qquad (10.02)$$

By substitution from the first of these expressions we may simplify the second.

$$\sum_{i=2}^{n} \triangle \psi_i \triangle \beta_i < 0 \qquad (10.03)$$

It will be noted that these are identically the conditions derived by Georgescu-Roegen in his admirable article,[1] conditions here derived exclusively from our three simple postulates. In our notation, however, the β_i stand for actual price ratios and not hypothetical indifference directions.

From now on we may parallel Georgescu-Roegen's mathematical analysis. Letting our second point approach the first we have the following condition holding in the limit :

$$d\psi_1 + \sum_{i=2}^{n} \beta_i d\psi_i = 0 \qquad (11.01)$$

$$\sum_{i=2}^{n} \sum_{j=1}^{n} \beta_{i,j} d\psi_i d\psi_j < 0 \qquad (11.02)$$

where $\beta_{i,j} = \dfrac{\partial \beta_i}{\partial \psi_j}$ in the functions defined in (4.0). These two conditions together imply, as Georgescu-Roegen has shown, that the following quadratic form be negative definite.

$$\sum_{i=2}^{n} \sum_{j=2}^{n} (\beta_{i,j} - \beta_j \beta_{i,1}) \xi_i \xi_j < 0 \qquad (12.0)$$

This requires that the principal minors beginning with the third of the following determinant be alternately negative and positive.

$$-\begin{vmatrix} 0 & 1 & \beta_2 & \ldots\ldots & \beta_n \\ 1 & 0 & \beta_{2,1} & \ldots\ldots & \beta_{n,1} \\ \beta_2 & \beta_{2,1} & 2\beta_{2,2} & \ldots\ldots & \beta_{2,n}+\beta_{n,2} \\ \cdot & \cdot & \cdot & & \cdot \\ \cdot & \cdot & \cdot & & \cdot \\ \cdot & \cdot & \cdot & & \cdot \\ \beta_n & \beta_{n,1} & \beta_{n,2}+\beta_{2,n} & \ldots & 2\beta_{n,n} \end{vmatrix} \qquad (12.01)$$

[1] "The Pure Theory of Consumer's Behaviour," *The Quarterly Journal of Economics*, Vol. L, August, 1936, pp. 545–593.

i.e.,

$$-\begin{vmatrix} 0 & 1 & \beta_2 \\ 1 & 0 & \beta_{2,1} \\ \beta_2 & \beta_{2,1} & 2\beta_{2,2} \end{vmatrix} < 0 \; ; \; -\begin{vmatrix} 0 & 1 & \beta_2 & \beta_3 \\ 1 & 0 & \beta_{2,1} & \beta_{3,1} \\ \beta_2 & \beta_{2,1} & 2\beta_{2,2} & \beta_{2,3}+\beta_{3,2} \\ \beta_3 & \beta_{3,1} & \beta_{3,2}+\beta_{2,3} & 2\beta_{3,3} \end{vmatrix} > 0 \quad (12.02)$$

In the absence of the assumption of integrability the quadratic form in (12.0) is not symmetrical, which apparently Allen overlooked in his exposition.

Concerning the question of integrability I have little to say. I cannot see that it is really an important problem, particularly if we are willing to dispense with the utility concept and its vestigial remnants. Thus, Georgescu-Roegen's demonstration of the spiral-like behaviour of indifference varieties projected upon the budget plane at the point of equilibrium, while acute and illuminating, in no way changes matters if the point of view advanced here is accepted. The only possible interest that integrability can have (except to those who have an historical attachment to the utility concept) would be in providing us with additional knowledge concerning a certain reciprocal relation, namely,

$$\beta_{i,j} - \beta_j\beta_{i,1} = \beta_{j,i} - \beta_i\beta_{j,1} \qquad (i,j=2, \ldots n) \qquad (13.0)$$

But it is this very implication which makes it doubtful and subject to refutation under ideal observational conditions, although I have little faith in any attempts to verify this statistically. I should strongly deny, however, that for a rational and consistent individual integrability is implied, except possibly as a matter of circular definition.

It remains now only to translate our restrictive conditions on the functions (4.0) into direct restrictions on our demand functions.[1] We may rewrite (8.01) and (8.02) in the form

$$\sum_{i=1}^{n} p_i d\psi_i = 0 \qquad\qquad (14.0)$$

$$\sum_{i=1}^{n} dp_i d\psi_i < 0 \qquad\qquad (14.1)$$

where not all dx_i vanish, i.e., where not all prices are allowed to vary in the same proportion.

From (1.0)

$$d\psi_i = \sum_{j=1}^{n} , h_j^i dp_j + h_I^i dI \qquad (i=1, \ldots n) \qquad (14.2)$$

[1] I should like to express my indebtedness to Mr. Rollin Bennett for his valuable aid in much that follows.

But

$$dI = \sum_{j=1}^{n} \psi_j dp_j + \sum_{j=1}^{n} p_j d\psi_j \qquad (14.3)$$

However from (14.0), this may be written

$$dI = \sum_{j=1}^{n} \psi_j dp_j \qquad (14.4)$$

Hence,

$$d\psi_i = \sum_{j=1}^{n} (b_j^i + b_I^i \psi_j) dp_j \qquad (i = 1, \ldots n) \qquad (14.5)$$

Therefore (14.1) becomes

$$\sum_{i=1}^{n} \sum_{j=1}^{n} (b_j^i + b_I^i \psi_j) dp_i dp_j < 0 \qquad (15.0)$$

for not all prices varying proportionately.

Defining[1]

$$\alpha_{ij} = b_j^i + b_I^i \psi_j + b_i^j + b_I^j \psi_i = \alpha_{ji} \qquad (15.1)$$

our direct conditions on the demand function are that the n^2 quadratic form be negative *semi-definite*[2]

$$\sum_{i=1}^{n} \sum_{j=1}^{n} \alpha_{ij} dp_i dp_j \leq 0 \qquad (16.0)$$

where the equality holds only for all prices changing in proportion. Because of our homogeneity condition, the n^2 determinant corresponding to this form vanishes identically,

$$| \alpha_{ij} | \equiv 0 \qquad (17.0)$$

Our final conditions are that every $(n-1)^2$ principal minor of this determinant must have been formed from the coefficients of an $(n-1)^2$ negative definite form. Briefly, it is necessary that the following minors alternate in sign for any ordering of variables:

$$\alpha_{ii} < 0; \quad \begin{vmatrix} \alpha_{ii} & \alpha_{ij} \\ \alpha_{ji} & \alpha_{jj} \end{vmatrix} > 0, {}_i \neq {}_j; \quad \begin{vmatrix} \alpha_{ii} & \alpha_{ij} & \alpha_{iK} \\ \alpha_{ji} & \alpha_{jj} & \alpha_{jK} \\ \alpha_{Ki} & \alpha_{jK} & \alpha_{KK} \end{vmatrix} < 0, {}_i \neq {}_j \neq {}_K \neq {}_i; \text{ etc. } (18.0)$$

Even if the approach outlined here is not accepted, these conditions are the direct restrictions imposed upon our demand function as the result of the usual stability or "concavity" conditions. The translation of these conditions into terms of elasticity coefficients of price and income is of course always possible, but is somewhat tedious and

---

[1] In the integrable case, the form will be already symmetrical.
[2] See M. Bocher, *Introduction to Higher Algebra*, p. 150.

is not given here. It is **my** feeling that much of the modern work has been rendered unnecessarily lengthy and involved because of a preoccupation with elasticity expressions, which are essentially redundant, since it is always possible to utilise a developed mathematical theory in expressing the conditions on the various partial derivatives directly. However, if this is desired, it is possible to make use of the following relationship derivable directly from the homogeneity assumption by Euler's Theorem :

$$N_{i1}+N_{i2}+ \ldots N_{in}+N_{iI}\equiv 0 \quad (i=1, \ldots n) \quad (19.0)$$

where the N's stand for elasticity coefficients.

In the case of two commodities our conditions take the following simple form :

$$\left. \begin{array}{l} N_{11}+N_{12}+N_{1I}=0 \\ N_{21}+N_{22}+N_{2I}=0 \end{array} \right\} \qquad (20.0)$$

and

$$\left. \begin{array}{l} N_{11}+k_1 N_{1I}<0 \\ N_{22}+k_2 N_{2I}<0 \end{array} \right\} \qquad (20.1)$$

where k represents the proportion of total income spent on the respective commodities.

Concerning definitions of complementarity, I have little to say. It is my personal opinion that the subject has received more attention than would seem justifiable. In other isomorphic equilibrium systems, e.g., the equations of analytic dynamics, or the Gibb's system of thermodynamic equilibrium, it is not felt to be necessary to define similar measures.

Historically, of course, the study of complementarity has been of great importance, since it was in the pursuance of this subject that the inconsistency in the thought of Pareto and the redundancy of the utility concept was revealed. Pedagogically, its introduction may be very desirable.

In concluding this exposition, it may be well to sound a warning. Woe to any who deny any one of the three postulates here ! For they are, of course, deducible as theorems from the conventional analysis. They are less restrictive than the usual set-up, and logically equivalent to the reformulation of Hicks and Allen. It is hoped, however, that the orientation given here is more directly based upon those elements which must be taken as *data* by economic science, and is more meaningful in its formulation. Even if this will not be granted, the results given in (18.0) are a useful extension of the restrictions in the older analysis, being directly related to the demand functions.

I have tried here to develop the theory of consumer's behaviour freed from any vestigial traces of the utility concept. In closing I should like to state my personal opinion that nothing said here in the field of consumer's behaviour affects in any way or touches upon at any point the problem of welfare economics, except in the sense of revealing the confusion in the traditional theory of these distinct subjects.

A Note on the Pure Theory of Consumer's Behaviour: An Addendum

In the February issue of this journal I suggested that the theory of consumer's behaviour could be founded on three postulates: (1) that the amount demanded of each commodity be a single valued function of all prices and income; (2) that this function be homogeneous of order zero in the variables prices and income, i.e., the simultaneous doubling of all prices and income must leave all quantities demanded invariant; (3) that the individual always behaves consistently in the sense that he should never "prefer" a first batch of goods to a second at the same time that he "prefers" the second to the first. "Preference" was defined in a special sense so that the mathematical statement of the third postulate was

$$\sum_{i=1}^{n} p_i^0(\psi_i^1 - \psi_i^0) \leqq 0 \text{ implies } \sum_{i=1}^{n} p_i^1(\psi_i^1 - \psi_i^0) < 0$$

where the points are distinct.

Since publication, I have discovered that this postulational base is redundant in the sense that postulates (1) and (2) are already implied in postulate (3), and hence may be omitted. In other words, postulate (3) alone is necessary and sufficient for all the developments in my note and, if the argument there is acceptable, for most of the empirical meaning of the utility analysis.

The proof that (1) and (2) are implied by (3) is very simple. Two separate proofs are not necessary.

Suppose an initial situation of prices and income and corresponding quantities $(p_1^0, \ldots, p_n^0, I^0)$ and $(\psi_1^0, \ldots, \psi_n^0)$. Suppose a second set of prices and income, each being respectively m times that of the previous situation, $(mp_1^0, \ldots, mp_n^0, mI^0)$ and $(\psi_1^1, \ldots, \psi_n^1)$. We wish to prove that

$$\psi_i^1 \equiv \psi_i^0 \qquad\qquad (i = 1, \ldots, n)$$

i.e., that the two batches of goods are identical in every respect.

From our hypothesis,

$$\sum_{i=1}^{n} p_i^0(\psi_i^1 - \psi_i^0) = 0$$

and
$$\sum_{i=1}^{n} p_i^1(\psi_i^1 - \psi_i^0) = m \sum_{i=1}^{n} p_i^0(\psi_i^1 - \psi_i^0) = 0.$$

This is a contradiction to postulate (3), and hence the two points cannot be distinct; i.e., they must be identical, and so our theorem is proved. For $m = 1$, postulate (1) emerges as a special case of postulate (2).

2

The Numerical Representation of Ordered Classifications and the Concept of Utility

1. A FEW years ago Dr. Lange initiated in this journal a series of discussions on the determinateness of the utility function.[1] Although admitting that no cardinal measure of utility was necessary for the description and rationalisation of market price-quantity behaviour, he felt that such a measure was of relevance to the problem of welfare economics. He went on to suggest a second postulate (in addition to the assumption that there exists an ordinal preference field) by means of which the utility function could be made " determinate."

2. As I shall try to indicate, Dr. Lange has not satisfactorily demonstrated that which he started out to prove. Before entering upon this, however, it is well to reconsider the relation between welfare economics and the cardinal measure of utility. Using the term "welfare economics" in its ordinary sense of comparisons between individuals, I believe the cardinal measure of utility is completely irrelevant to this problem. As Mr. Burk has shown in a recent article,[2] it is only necessary in order to make welfare judgments that we agree upon the definition of an ordinal function involving as variables the quantities of goods consumed by all individuals; and that even if we permit the individual's own preferences to " count," there is still no need for any cardinal measure of utility. Only those who consider general welfare as the algebraic sum of individual utilities require that utility be measurable in a cardinal sense. It is not only that we can get along without this cardinal concept, but literally nothing is added by its assumption.

3. Dr. Lange starts out to prove that from two postulates the measurability of utility is guaranteed. I shall state these postulates in my own language in order to avoid the merited charge of Mr. Phelps Brown that the question has been implicitly prejudged.

Postulate (1): Given any two combinations of consumer's goods $(x_1, y_1, z_1, \ldots)$ and $(x_2, y_2, z_2, \ldots)$, the consumer is able to state that one is " preferred " to the other or that they are equally " preferred." Further requirements of such an ordinal classification will be given later.

Postulate (2): Given any four combinations of consumer's goods $(x_1, y_1, z_1, \ldots), (x_2, y_2, z_2, \ldots), (x_3, y_3, z_3, \ldots), (x_4, y_4, z_4, \ldots)$, the individual is always able to place the movement from $(x_1, y_1, z_1, \ldots)$ to

[1] Lange, O., " The Determinateness of the Utility Function," REVIEW OF ECONOMIC STUDIES, June, 1934, pp. 218–25. " Notes on the Determinateness of the Utility Function," by Phelps Brown, Bernadelli, and Lange, REVIEW OF ECONOMIC STUDIES, October, 1937, pp. 66–77. Allen, R. G. D., " A Note on the Determinateness of the Utility Function," REVIEW OF ECONOMIC STUDIES, February, 1935, pp. 155–8.
[2] Burk, A., " A Reformulation of Certain Aspects of Welfare Economics," *Quarterly Journal of Economics*, February, 1938, pp. 310–34.

$(x_2, y_2, z_2, \ldots)$ in ordinal relationship to the movement from $(x_3, y_3, z_3, \ldots)$ to $(x_4, y_4, z_4, \ldots)$; i.e. one movement is " preferred " to the other, or they are equally " preferred."

Dr. Lange has not proved satisfactorily that from these two assumptions can be derived the cardinal measurability of utility (subject to a linear transformation involving scale and origin constants). Indeed, as we shall see, such a theorem is not valid.

4. What Dr. Lange has proved is the following much less interesting theorem : Given any numerical variable ϕ and a new variable F defined as a monotonic function of ϕ,

$$F = F(\phi) \text{ where } F'(\phi) > 0 \dots\dots\dots\dots\dots\dots\dots\dots\dots\dots\dots (1)$$

the respective differences of these two variables will be ordered in the same way if, and only if, F is a linear transformation of ϕ.

Given $\phi_1, \phi_2, \phi_3, \phi_4$, and corresponding $F(\phi_1), F(\phi_2), F(\phi_3), F(\phi_4)$, it will be true that

$$F(\phi_4) - F(\phi_3) \gtreqless F(\phi_2) - F(\phi_1) \dots\dots\dots\dots\dots\dots\dots\dots\dots (2)$$

whenever $\phi_4 - \phi_3 \gtreqless \phi_2 - \phi_1$, if and only if,

$$F = a + b\phi \dots\dots\dots\dots\dots\dots\dots\dots\dots\dots\dots\dots\dots\dots\dots\dots (3)$$

where a and b are constants.

The proof is simple. As a special case of (2) we have

$$F(\phi_2 + t) - F(\phi_1 + t) \equiv F(\phi_2) - F(\phi_1) \dots\dots\dots\dots\dots\dots\dots (4)$$

where ϕ_2, ϕ_1, and t take on arbitrary values. From the definition of a definite integral this may be rewritten

$$\int_{\phi_1}^{\phi_2} [F'(\phi + t) - F'(\phi)] d\phi \equiv 0 \equiv \int_{\phi_1}^{\phi_2} \int_0^t F''(\phi + t) dt \, d\phi \dots\dots\dots\dots (5)$$

In order that this expression vanish for arbitrary limits of integration, it is necessary that the integrand vanish identically, or

$$F''(\phi) \equiv 0 \dots\dots\dots\dots\dots\dots\dots\dots\dots\dots\dots\dots\dots\dots\dots\dots (6)$$

Therefore,

$$F = a + b\phi \dots\dots\dots\dots\dots\dots\dots\dots\dots\dots\dots\dots\dots\dots\dots\dots (3)$$

Thus, Dr. Lange has shown that if two utility indexes differ by more than a linear transformation, their differences cannot both be used as a numerical representation of the ordered terms of his second postulate. He has not shown that there exists even one utility index whose differences will perform this function. Indeed, it can be shown that in general none will exist.

5. To show this it is well to state abstractly the conditions under which we may legitimately describe an ordered classification by means of numerical

indexes. Consider a set of elements such that any two, A and B, can be placed in one of the following three mutually exclusive categories :

(a) A is " preferred " to B.
(b) B is " preferred " to A.
(c) A and B are equally " preferred."

In place of the word " preferred " anything may be inserted, such as A is " blank " to B.

Provided that the " transitivity " conditions, presently to be indicated, are met, we can construct a numerical index, N, corresponding to each element such that

$$N(A) \gtreqqless N(B) \quad \dots\dots\dots\dots\dots\dots\dots\dots\dots\dots\dots\dots\dots\dots\dots (7)$$

corresponds to the categories (a), (b), and (c) respectively. $F = F(N)$ will also serve as an index provided that

$$[F(N_2) - F(N_1)](N_2 - N_1) > 0.$$

For any numerical magnitudes the following transitivity conditions hold :

(1) $N_1 = N_2$ and $N_2 = N_3$
   implies $N_1 = N_3$
(2) $N_1 \geqq N_2$ and $N_2 > N_3$
   implies $N_1 > N_3$

In order that our numerical index should not involve us in a contradiction with the classification it represents it is necessary that our classification always result in similar relations.

(1) A equally preferred to B, and B equally preferred to C, must imply A equally preferred to C.
(2) A either preferred to B or equally preferred to B, and B preferred to C, must imply A preferred to C.

Provided only that these conditions are satisfied, a numerical representation is always possible. We might regard combinations of goods as our elements and the preferences of an individual as a rule for ordering them. There exists an infinity of numerical indexes which will serve to portray the facts implied by such an ordinal preference field. For convenience these may be taken as continuous and differentiable functions.

$$N = N(x,y,z, \, \dots) = N(X) \quad \dots\dots\dots\dots\dots\dots\dots\dots\dots\dots\dots\dots (8)$$

Also the following will serve

$$F = F(N) \text{ where } F'(N) > 0 \dots\dots\dots\dots\dots\dots\dots\dots\dots\dots\dots\dots (9)$$

Thus, we have a numerical representation for the facts indicated in Postulate (1).

For the facts of Postulate (2) a new index must be constructed which is a function of the end points of each movement.

$$G = G(x_1, y_1, z_1, \, \dots \, ; \, x_2, y_2, z_2, \, \dots) = G(X_1, X_2) \dots\dots\dots\dots (10)$$

This function is so constructed that

$$G(X_3, X_4) \gtreqqless G(X_1, X_2) \quad\dots\dots\dots\dots\dots\dots\dots\dots\dots\dots\dots\dots (\text{11})$$

corresponds respectively to the movement (X_3, X_4) more preferred than, less preferred than, equally preferred to the movement (X_1, X_2). Of course,

$$H = H(G) \text{ where } H'(G) > 0 \quad\dots\dots\dots\dots\dots\dots\dots\dots\dots\dots\dots (\text{12})$$

is also an index.

For convenience of terminology the numerical indexes constructed to relate ordinally combinations of goods as in Postulate (1) will be called indexes of the first kind. Ordinal indexes relating movements from one combination to another will be called indexes of the second kind.

The indexes of the second kind are not completely unrelated to those of the first kind. Thus, if we fix the initial point of a movement, then our index of the second kind regarded as a function of the end point alone as a variable must itself be capable of serving as an index of the first kind ; i.e. :

$$G(X_1, X) = F[\phi(X)] \quad\dots\dots\dots\dots\dots\dots\dots\dots\dots\dots\dots\dots (\text{13})$$

where F is some monotonic transformation.

6. Now under what conditions can one index of the second kind be written in the form suggested by Dr. Lange ; namely, as the difference between the values of an index of the first kind evaluated at the end and initial points of each movement ? That is, when will at least one cardinal index of the second kind be capable of representation in the form

$$G(X_1, X_2) = \phi(X_2) - \phi(X_1) \text{ ?} \quad\dots\dots\dots\dots\dots\dots\dots\dots\dots (\text{14})$$

Dr. Lange, it will be noted, implicitly assumes from the beginning that the individual orders movements according to the differences in " utility " involved in each movement.

Actually it can be shown that this is one possible representation if, and only if, there exists one cardinal index of the second kind for which the following functional equation holds :

$$G(X_1, X_2) + G(X_2, X_3) \equiv G(X_1, X_3) \quad\dots\dots\dots\dots\dots\dots\dots\dots (\text{15})$$

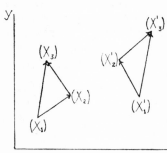

Figure I

In Fig. 1 I have indicated in the form of a vector triangle three movements corresponding to (X_1, X_2), (X_2, X_3), and (X_1, X_3). As a special case of (15) we have,

$$G(X, X) + G(X, X) \equiv G(X, X) \quad (\text{16})$$

Therefore,

$$G(X, X) \equiv 0 \quad\dots\dots\dots\dots\dots (\text{17})$$

i.e. the " distance " from a point to itself is zero.

Likewise,

$$G(X_1, X_2) + G(X_2, X_1) \equiv G(X_1, X_1)$$
$$\equiv 0 \dots\dots\dots\dots\dots\dots\dots (\text{18})$$

or

$$G(X_1, X_2) \equiv -G(X_2, X_1) \dots\dots\dots\dots\dots\dots\dots\dots\dots (19)$$

i.e. the " distance " from X_1 to X_2 is equal in magnitude, but opposite in sign, to the " distance " from X_2 to X_1.

Writing out (14) and (15) so as explicitly to introduce all consumer's goods as variables, we have

$$G(x_1, y_1, z_1, \dots ; x_2, y_2, z_2, \dots) = \phi(x_2, y_2, z_2, \dots)$$
$$-\phi(x_1, y_1, z_1, \dots) \dots\dots\dots\dots\dots\dots\dots\dots\dots (14')$$

and

$$G(x_1, y_1, z_1, \dots ; x_2, y_2, z_2, \dots) + G(x_2, y_2, z_2, \dots ; x_3, y_3, z_3, \dots)$$
$$\equiv G(x_1, y_1, z_1, \dots ; x_3, y_3, z_3, \dots) \dots\dots\dots\dots\dots (15')$$

The relationship (14') can easily be deduced from (15'). Differentiate (15') partially with respect to $x_1, y_1, z_1, \dots$ in turn to get

$$\frac{\partial}{\partial x_1} G(x_1, y_1, z_1, \dots ; x_2, y_2, z_2, \dots) \equiv \frac{\partial}{\partial x_1} G(x_1, y_1, z_1, \dots ; x_3, y_3, z_3, \dots)$$

$$\frac{\partial}{\partial y_1} G(x_1, y_1, z_1, \dots ; x_2, y_2, z_2, \dots) \equiv \frac{\partial}{\partial y_1} G(x_1, y_1, z_1, \dots ; x_3, y_3, z_3, \dots)$$

$$\frac{\partial}{\partial z_1} G(X_1, y_1, z_1, \dots ; x_2, y_2, z_2, \dots) \equiv \frac{\partial}{\partial z_1} G(x_1, y_1, z_1, \dots ; x_3, y_3, z_3, \dots)$$

$$\dots\dots\dots\dots\dots\dots\dots\dots\dots\dots\dots\dots\dots\dots\dots\dots\dots (20)$$

The left-hand members of these equations are evaluated as of the point (X_1, X_2); those on the right-hand side as of (X_1, X_3). Therefore, these partial derivatives must be constants with respect to $(x_2, y_2, z_2, \dots)$; i.e.

$$\frac{\partial^2 G}{\partial x_2 \partial x_1} = \frac{\partial^2 G}{\partial y_2 \partial y_1} = \frac{\partial^2 G}{\partial z_2 \partial x_1} = \dots \equiv 0$$

$$\frac{\partial^2 G}{\partial x_2 \partial y_1} = \frac{\partial^2 G}{\partial y_2 \partial y_1} = \frac{\partial^2 G}{\partial z_2 \partial y_1} = \dots \equiv 0$$

$$\frac{\partial^2 G}{\partial x_2 \partial z_1} = \frac{\partial^2 G}{\partial y_2 \partial z_1} = \frac{\partial^2 G}{\partial z_2 \partial z_1} = \dots \equiv 0$$

$$\dots\dots\dots\dots\dots\dots\dots\dots\dots\dots\dots\dots\dots\dots\dots\dots\dots (21)$$

The most general solution of the equations (21) can be written in the form

$$G(x_1, y_1, z_1, \dots ; x_2, y_2, z_2, \dots) = \theta(x_2, y_2, z_2, \dots) + \psi(x_1, y_1, z_1, \dots)$$
$$(22)$$

where θ and ψ are arbitrary functions. But from (17)

$$G(x, y, z, \dots ; x, y, z, \dots) \equiv 0$$

or $\quad \theta(x, y, z, \dots) + \psi(x, y, z, \dots) \equiv 0$

or $\quad \psi = -\theta \dots\dots\dots\dots\dots\dots\dots\dots\dots\dots\dots\dots\dots\dots (23)$

Therefore, our solution is

$$G(x_1, y_1, z_1, \ldots ; x_2, y_2, z_2, \ldots) = \theta(x_2, y_2, z_2, \ldots) - \theta(x_1, y_1, z_1, \ldots) \tag{24}$$

From (13) it is clear that θ is a cardinal index of the first kind.

At this point Dr. Lange's proof may be introduced to show that θ is unique, subject to scale and origin constants.

7. We have seen the crucial assumption necessary to substantiate Dr. Lange's thesis is expressed in the functional equation (15). What is the meaning of this condition in terms of the individual's ordinal classification of movements ? Can such a relationship in general be satisfied ? The answer is in the negative.

Among other things the relationship (15) contains the following implication : Given movements (X_1, X_2), (X'_1, X'_2) regarded as equally preferable, and movements (X_2, X_3), (X'_2, X'_3) regarded as equally preferable, equation (15) requires that (X_1, X_3) and (X'_1, X'_3) be necessarily regarded as equivalent. (See Fig. 1.) There is absolutely no a priori reason why the individual's preference scale of the second kind should obey this arbitrary restriction. Indeed, the chance that any one relationship drawn from an infinity of possible functional relationships should hold must be regarded as infinitely improbable.

8. Even in the singular case where the relationship (15) does hold, the uniqueness of any one utility index results merely from convention. While θ is the arithmetic difference of but one index, it is the " logarithmic difference " of another, the " exponential difference " of another, and in general the " Fth difference " of still another, where F is an arbitrary monotonic function. There would seem to be no particular reason for a favoured position to be granted to an index of the first kind whose arithmetic differences will serve as an index of the second kind.

9. In conclusion, I should like to express my agreement with Dr. Lange concerning the inconsistencies in the writings of the earlier mathematical economists.

Cambridge, Massachusetts.   PAUL A. SAMUELSON.

3

THE EMPIRICAL IMPLICATIONS OF
UTILITY ANALYSIS

By Paul A. Samuelson

I

IT IS MORE THAN HALF a century since the first formulations of utility analysis by Jevons, Menger, and Walras. In that time there has been much controversy for and against this concept.

Although much of the discussion has not gone beyond a quasi-philosophical defense or rejection of the utility concept, it is nevertheless possible to discern clear lines of development in the literature. First, there has been a steady tendency toward the removal of moral, utilitarian, welfare connotations from the concept. Secondly, there has been a progressive movement toward the rejection of hedonistic, introspective, psychological elements. These tendencies are evidenced by the names suggested to replace utility and satisfaction—ophélimité, desirability, wantability, etc.

The question arises as to what is left when all these elements are removed. Does not the whole utility analysis become *meaningless* in the operational sense of modern science? A meaningless theory according to this criterion is one which has no empirical implications by which it could conceivably be refuted under ideal empirical conditions. Thus, it is meaningless to ask whether the earth *really* moves around the sun rather than the sun around the earth, since no hypothesis with respect to the facts of celestial behavior is implied by either of these conventions. Is the same true of utility analysis? Has it no empirical implications for price-quantity behavior?

It is clear that in its early formulations it was thought to have very definite, even revolutionary, consequences for the analysis of price and value. Moreover, even today the instinct of the textbook writer is methodologically sound in his attempt to deduce the negatively sloping demand curve from the Weber-Fechner law and diminishing marginal utility; this does not alter the fact that the whole demonstration is hopelessly fallacious and illogical.

That some modern formulations of the utility concept are empty, circular, and meaningless in the above sense, is hardly open to doubt.[1] Consider, for example, a typical view as follows. (1) People act according to a plan; (2) a plan is how people act; (3) hence, people act as

[1] For an illuminating survey of the present status of utility theory see Alan R. Sweezy, "The Interpretation of Subjective Value Theory in the Writings of the Austrian Economists," *Review of Economic Studies*, Vol. 1, June, 1934, pp. 176–185.

they act. This last conclusion is devoid of empirical significance, being consistent with any and all kinds of behavior.

It is the purpose here to demonstrate that the utility analysis in its ordinary form does contain empirically meaningful implications by which it could be refuted. Whether the hypothesis with respect to price-quantity behavior implied in the utility analysis is fruitful or not is a question which lies outside the province of this paper. It is the sole purpose of this paper to finish a much-neglected task, that of squeezing out of the utility analysis its empirical implications for individual and group price-quantity behavior.

Only the most general assumptions are made: that there exists an ordinal preference field satisfying everywhere curvature conditions sufficient to insure a proper relative maximum under the constraint of a fixed total budget.

Mathematically, our ordinal preference field may be written as a function of the n commodities $(x_1, \cdots, x_n)$,

$$U = F[\phi(x_1, \cdots, x_n)], \qquad \frac{dF}{d\phi} > 0,$$

where ϕ represents any one utility index and U any other utility index.

For any particular utility index the curvature conditions sufficient for a relative maximum under the budgetary restraint

$$x_1 p_1 + x_2 p_2 + \cdots + x_n p_n = I$$

are known to be[2]

$$\sum_{i=1}^{n} \sum_{j=1}^{n} \frac{\partial^2 \phi}{\partial x_i \partial x_j} \xi_i \xi_j < 0,$$

for

$$\sum_{i=1}^{n} \frac{\partial \phi}{\partial x_i} \xi_i = 0, \qquad \text{not all } \xi\text{'s} = 0.$$

The restriction upon price-quantity behavior from which all our theorems will be derived will be indicated later.

[2] This condition is invariant under any transformation of the utility index, for

$$\frac{\partial^2 U}{\partial x_i \partial x_j} = F' \frac{\partial^2 \phi}{\partial x_i \partial x_j} + F'' \frac{\partial \phi}{\partial x_i} \frac{\partial \phi}{\partial x_j}.$$

Hence,

$$\sum_{i=1}^{n} \sum_{j=1}^{n} \left(F' \frac{\partial^2 \phi}{\partial x_i \partial x_j} + F'' \frac{\partial \phi}{\partial x_i} \frac{\partial \phi}{\partial x_j} \right) \xi_i \xi_j = F' \sum_{i=1}^{n} \sum_{j=1}^{n} \frac{\partial^2 \phi}{\partial x_i \partial x_j} \xi_i \xi_j$$

$$+ F'' \sum_{i=1}^{n} \sum_{j=1}^{n} \frac{\partial \phi}{\partial x_i} \frac{\partial \phi}{\partial x_j} \xi_i \xi_j.$$

But for $\sum_{i=1}^{n} \frac{\partial U}{\partial x_i} \xi_i = F' \sum_{i=1}^{n} \frac{\partial \phi}{\partial x_i} \xi_i = 0$ the second term vanishes, and

$$\sum_{i=1}^{n} \sum_{j=1}^{n} \frac{\partial^2 U}{\partial x_i \partial x_j} \xi_i \xi_j < 0 \qquad \text{for} \qquad \sum_{i=1}^{n} \frac{\partial U}{\partial x_i} \xi_i = 0.$$

II

It has long been recognized that under very general assumptions it is possible to rule out definitely many kinds of consumer's behavior in response to price changes. Barring changes in data (i.e., shifts in demand schedules), it was commonly believed that the quantity of product demanded by an individual or market would necessarily increase with a lowering of its price. For example, we have Marshall's dictum:

Every fall, however slight in the price of a commodity in general use, will, other things being equal, increase the total sales of it.[3]

This was felt to be implied by the diminishing marginal utility of the good, and conversely.[4]

More recent investigators such as Allen, Georgescu-Roegen, Hicks, Hotelling, Johnson, Schultz, and Slutsky have concerned themselves with the implications for consumer's behavior of the conventional utility- or indifference-curve assumptions.

Recently I proposed a new postulational base upon which to construct a theory of consumer's behavior.[5] It was there shown that from this starting point could be erected a theory which included all the elements of the previous analysis. There I expressed my opinion as to the advantages from a methodological point of view of such a reorientation. Completely without prejudice to such considerations I should like here to indicate the mathematical simplicities which suggested themselves from that investigation. That is to say, even within the framework of the ordinary utility- and indifference-curve assumptions it is believed to be possible to derive already known theorems quickly, and also to suggest new sets of conditions. Furthermore, by means of this approach the transition from individual- to market-demand functions is considerably expedited.

III

The essential advantages referred to above may be secured by writing the "stability" conditions for an individual implied in all utility- and indifference-curve analyses in the following simple form:[6]

$$(1) \qquad\qquad \sum_{i=1}^{n} \Delta p_i \Delta x_i < 0,$$

[3] A. Marshall, *Principles of Economics*, p. 98.

[4] One exception was recognized, however, and received the title of Giffen's Paradox.

[5] P. A. Samuelson, "New Foundations for the Pure Theory of Consumer's Behaviour," *Economica*, Vol. 5 (New Series), February, 1938, pp. 61–71.

[6] *Ibid.* Also Georgescu-Roegen, "The Pure Theory of Consumer's Behavior," *Quarterly Journal of Economics*, Vol. 50, August, 1936, pp. 545–593.

for

$$\sum_{i=1}^{n} p_i \Delta x_i = 0 \qquad \text{and not all } \Delta x_i = 0,$$

where $(x_1, \cdots, x_n)$ are respective consumer's goods and $(p_1, \cdots, p_n)$ their prices. More generally, we may include productive services sold by the individual as consumer's goods if we agree upon the convention of regarding services sold as the negative of commodities (services) bought.

By going through a limiting process, we may rewrite condition (1) as follows:

$$(2) \qquad \sum_{i=1}^{n} dp_i dx_i < 0,$$

for

$$\sum_{i=1}^{n} p_i dx_i = 0 \qquad \text{and not all } dx_i = 0.$$

It will be noted that only prices and quantities, observable phenomena, appear in these expressions.

From the condition that utility be a maximum, or that the individual be at a point of highest preference subject to a fixed total expenditure and given prices, it is possible to derive for any individual the following demand functions:

$$x_1 = h^1(p_1, \cdots, p_n, I),$$
$$x_2 = h^2(p_1, \cdots, p_n, I),$$

$$(3)$$

$$x_n = h^n(p_1, \cdots, p_n, I),$$

where

$$(4) \qquad I = \sum_{i=1}^{n} x_i p_i.$$

In fact, the whole object of the utility analysis is the attainment of these functions. It will be recalled from the ordinary rules of differential calculus that

$$(5) \qquad dx_i = \sum_{j=1}^{n} h_j{}^i dp_j + h_I{}^i dI, \qquad (i = 1, \cdots, n),$$

when

$$h_j{}^i = \frac{\partial x_i}{\partial p_j}$$

and

$$h_I{}^i = \frac{\partial x_i}{\partial I}.$$

24

Also

$$(6) \qquad dI = \sum_{i=1}^{n} x_i dp_i + \sum_{i=1}^{n} p_i dx_i.$$

Therefore, we may rewrite (5) as

$$(7) \qquad dx_i = \sum_{j=1}^{n} h_j{}^i dp_j + h_I{}^i \left(\sum_{j=1}^{n} x_j dp_j + \sum_{j=1}^{n} p_j dx_j \right).$$

But it is part of our hypothesis in (2) that

$$\sum_{j=1}^{n} p_j dx_j = 0.$$

Therefore, substituting in (2), we have

$$(8) \qquad \sum_{i=1}^{n} \sum_{j=1}^{n} (h_j{}^i + x_j h_I{}^i) dp_i dp_j < 0, \quad (i = 1, \cdots, n),$$

for not all $dx_i = 0$; or what comes to the same thing, for not all dp_i/p_i equal.

The condition expressed in (8) is a very simple one and has not to date, I believe, appeared in the literature. This quadratic form, symmetrical as a condition of integrability as pointed out by Slutsky, is semi-definite because of the homogeneity condition that doubling all prices and incomes leaves all quantities invariant. However, the quadratic form made up of any subset of $(n-1)$ variables must be negative definite. A necessary and sufficient condition that this be so is that the principal minors of order m of the following determinant have the sign $(-1)^m$. Let

$$\Delta = \left| \; h_j{}^i + x_j h_I{}^i \; \right|,$$

$$\Delta_{ij} = \begin{vmatrix} h_i{}^i + x_i h_I{}^i & h_j{}^i + x_j h_I{}^i \\ h_i{}^j + x_i h_I{}^j & h_j{}^j + x_j h_I{}^j \end{vmatrix} ; \text{ etc.}$$

Then

$$(9) \qquad\qquad (-1)^m \Delta_{i_\nu \cdots, i_m} > 0, \qquad\qquad m \leqq n - 1.$$

More specifically, we must have the following conditions:

$$(10) \qquad\qquad \frac{\partial x_i}{\partial p_i} + x_i \frac{\partial x_i}{\partial I} < 0,$$

$$(11) \qquad \left(\frac{\partial x_i}{\partial p_i} + x_i \frac{\partial x_i}{\partial I} \right) \left(\frac{\partial x_j}{\partial p_j} + x_j \frac{\partial x_j}{\partial I} \right) - \left(\frac{\partial x_i}{\partial p_j} + x_j \frac{\partial x_i}{\partial I} \right)^2 > 0, \quad \text{etc.}[7]$$

[7] Samuelson, loc. cit., p. 69.

It is not possible then to state that the elasticity of a good with respect to its own price must have an algebraically negative sign. This need not be so, provided that the income elasticity of demand be sufficiently negative, so that the whole term in (10) be less than zero.

These restrictions as developed thus far are seen to involve not only price elasticities of demand, but also the income elasticity of demand. However, from the condition that the demand functions in (3) be homogeneous of order zero, it will generally be true that the income elasticity of demand can be expressed in terms of price elasticities of demand, since a lowering of all prices is equivalent to an increase in money income. Indeed, from Euler's theorem on homogeneous functions:

$$(12) \qquad h_1{}^i p_1 + h_2{}^i p_2 + \cdots + h_n{}^i p_n = - h_I{}^i I, \qquad (i = 1, \cdots, n).$$

It should be possible, therefore, to develop restrictions on the demand functions relating only to price elasticities of demand. This can be done without making use of (12) directly as will be shown in the following discussion.

IV

Still considering only a single individual, let us regard his total income, I, as a constant and permit only prices to vary. Therefore,

$$(13) \qquad dI = \sum_{i=1}^{n} x_i dp_i + \sum_{i=1}^{n} p_i dx_i = 0.$$

Recalling from hypothesis (2) that

$$(14) \qquad \sum_{i=1}^{n} p_i dx_i = 0,$$

we have

$$(15) \qquad \sum_{i=1}^{n} x_i dp_i = 0$$

and

$$(16) \qquad \sum_{i=1}^{n} dp_i dx_i < 0,$$

not all $dx_i = 0$.

Setting I at its constant value $\bar{I}$, we may rewrite our demand functions of (3) as follows:

$$(17) \qquad x_i = h^i(p_1, \cdots, p_n, \bar{I}), \qquad (i = 1, \cdots, n),$$

where only $(p_1, \cdots, p_n)$ are regarded as variables.
Then

$$(18) \qquad dx_i = \sum_{j=1}^{n} h_j{}^i dp_j, \qquad (i = 1, \cdots, n),$$

and (16) becomes

(19)
$$\sum_{i=1}^{n} \sum_{j=1}^{n} h_j{}^i dp_i dp_j < 0,$$

for

$$\sum_{i=1}^{n} x_i dp_i = 0,$$

not all $dp_i = 0$.

In general,

(20)
$$h_j{}^i \neq h_i{}^j,$$

and so it is necessary to define a new symmetrical set of coefficients for this quadratic form:

(21)
$$\beta_{ij} = \frac{h_j{}^i + h_i{}^j}{2} = \beta_{ji}.$$

Thus we may rewrite (19) as

(22)
$$\sum_{i=1}^{n} \sum_{j=1}^{n} \beta_{ij} dp_i dp_j < 0,$$

for

$$\sum_{i=1}^{n} x_i dp_i = 0,$$

not all $dp_i = 0$.

Consider the following determinant:

(23)
$$D = \begin{vmatrix} & & & x_1 \\ & \beta_{ij} & & \cdot \\ & & & \cdot \\ & & & \cdot \\ & & & x_n \\ x_1 & \cdots & x_n & 0 \end{vmatrix}.$$

Let

(24)
$$D_{12} = \begin{vmatrix} \beta_{11} & \beta_{12} & x_1 \\ \beta_{21} & \beta_{22} & x_2 \\ x_1 & x_2 & 0 \end{vmatrix}, \qquad D_{123} = \begin{vmatrix} \beta_{11} & \beta_{12} & \beta_{13} & x_1 \\ \beta_{21} & \beta_{22} & \beta_{23} & x_2 \\ \beta_{31} & \beta_{32} & \beta_{33} & x_3 \\ x_1 & x_2 & x_3 & 0 \end{vmatrix},$$

and likewise for other combinations of subscripts.

Our conditions of (22) and (19) are that any one of the determinants $D_{i_1}, \ldots, {}_{i_{m-1}}$ must have the same sign as $(-1)^{m-1}$ where m is the order of the determinant involved; i.e.,

(25)
$$(-1)^{m-1} D_{i_1}, \ldots, {}_{i_{m-1}} > 0, \qquad\qquad m \leqq n + 1.$$

Specifically,

(26) $\qquad h_i{}^i(x_j)^2 - (h_j{}^i + h_i{}^j)x_jx_i + h_j{}^i(x_i)^2 < 0$

for any $i \neq j$, etc.

Professor Hotelling has developed similar conditions for the inverse of these demand functions.[8]

Consider the set of demand functions in (17):

$$x_i = h^i(p_1, \cdots, p_n, I), \qquad (i = 1, \cdots, n).$$

These are n equations in $2n$ unknowns. In general, it is possible to solve these inversely for the p's in terms of the x's as follows:

(27) $\qquad p_i = g^i(x_1, \cdots, x_n, I), \qquad (i = 1, \cdots, n).$

Therefore,

(28) $\qquad dp_i = \sum_{j=1}^{n} g_j^i dx_j, \qquad (i = 1, \cdots, n).$

We may rewrite, therefore, (16) as follows:

(29) $\qquad \sum_{i=1}^{n} \sum_{j=1}^{n} g_j{}^i dx_i dx_j < 0,$

for

$$\sum_{i=1}^{n} p_i dx_i = 0.$$

Defining

(30) $\qquad \gamma_{ij} = \dfrac{g_i{}^i + g_i{}^j}{2} = \gamma_{ji},$

we may rewrite (29) as

(31) $\qquad \sum_{i=1}^{n} \sum_{j=1}^{n} \gamma_{ij} dx_i dx_j < 0, \qquad \text{for} \quad \sum_{i=1}^{n} p_i dx_i = 0,$

not all $dx_i = 0$.

Consider the determinants

(32) $\qquad E = \begin{vmatrix} & & & p_1 \\ & \gamma_{ij} & & \vdots \\ & & & p_n \\ p_1 \cdots p_n & & & 0 \end{vmatrix}$

and

(33) $\qquad E_{ij} = \begin{vmatrix} \gamma_{ii} & \gamma_{ij} & p_i \\ \gamma_{ji} & \gamma_{jj} & p_j \\ p_i & p_j & 0 \end{vmatrix}, \text{ etc.}$

[8] H. Hotelling, "Demand Functions with Limited Budgets," ECONOMETRICA, Vol. 3, January, 1935, pp. 66–78.

Conditions (29) and (31) require that any of the determinants $E_{i_1, \cdots, i_{m-1}}$ must have the same sign as $(-1)^{m-1}$ where m is the order of the determinant involved; i.e.,[9]

$$(34) \qquad (-1)^{m-1}E_{i_1, \cdots, i_{m-1}} > 0, \qquad m \leqq n+1.$$

In one important case it is impossible to solve equations in (17) inversely for (27). This is in the case where total expenditure is equal to zero. It was this case where the total value of services rendered or of goods given up by an individual was just balanced by total value of goods consumed which received great attention from the older mathematical economists. Here (17) becomes

$$(35) \qquad x_i = h^i(p_1, \cdots, p_n, 0), \qquad (i = 1, \cdots, n).$$

Since these expressions are homogeneous of order zero, even when I is held constant at the level zero, the Jacobian

$$(36) \qquad J = |h_j{}^i| = 0, \qquad \text{for } I = 0,$$

and the inverse solution is not possible. This is clearly seen in Hotelling's presentation, where for $I = 0$, the functions in (27) become indeterminate. However, the conditions given here in (25) are still valid for this important case.

V

It remains now to consider relations between individual demand functions and the general demand functions for the whole market. Let us suppose we have s individuals in the market place and that the demand functions of the rth individual may be written

$$(37) \qquad {}^r x_i = {}^r h^i(p_1, \cdots, p_n, {}^r I), \qquad (i = 1, \cdots, n).$$

The total amount demanded of a good is equal to the sum of all individual amounts:

$$(38) \qquad X_i = {}^1 x_i + {}^2 x_i + \cdots + {}^s x_i = \sum_{r=1}^{s} {}^r x_i, \qquad (i = 1, \cdots, n).$$

Thus we may write the general demand functions as follows:

$$(39) \qquad X_i = H^i(p_1, \cdots, p_n, {}^1 I, \cdots, {}^s I), \qquad (i = 1, \cdots, n),$$

$$(40) \qquad = \sum_{r=1}^{s} {}^r h^i(p_1, \cdots, p_n, {}^r I).$$

It will be noted that the general amount of a commodity demanded is a function of all prices and the incomes of each and every person in the market place.

[9] *Ibid.*, p. 72.

Obviously,

$$(41) \qquad \frac{\partial X_i}{\partial p_j} = H_j{}^i = \sum_{r=1}^{s} {}^r h_j{}^i.$$

Let us consider first the conditions of Section IV, where all incomes are constant, i.e.,

$$(42) \qquad {}^r I = \overline{{}^r I}, \qquad (r = 1, \cdots, s).$$

Then

$$(43) \qquad {}^r x_i = {}^r h^i(p_1, \cdots, p_n, \overline{{}^r I}), \qquad (i = 1, \cdots, n),$$

and

$$(44) \qquad X_i = H^i(p_1, \cdots, p_n, \overline{{}^1 I}, \cdots \overline{{}^s I}),$$

$$(45) \qquad = \sum_{r=1}^{s} {}^r h^i(p_1, \cdots, p_n, \overline{{}^r I}).$$

For each individual,

$$(46) \qquad d({}^r I) = 0 = \sum_{i=1}^{n} {}^r x_i dp_i + \sum_{i=1}^{n} p_i d({}^r x_i).$$

And for

$$(47) \qquad \sum_{i=1}^{n} p_i d({}^r x_i) = 0$$

we have

$$(48) \qquad \sum_{i=1}^{n} {}^r x_i dp_i = 0$$

and

$$(49) \qquad \sum_{i=1}^{n} d({}^r x_i) dp_i < 0.$$

Since this holds for each, we may sum over all to get

$$(50) \qquad \sum_{i=1}^{n} dp_i \sum_{r=1}^{s} d({}^r x_i) = \sum_{i=1}^{n} dp_i dX_i < 0,$$

for

$$\sum_{i=1}^{n} X_i dp_i = 0 \quad \text{or} \quad \sum_{i=1}^{n} p_i dX_i = 0.$$

But, from (44),

$$(51) \qquad dX_i = \sum_{j=1}^{n} H_j{}^i dp_j,$$

and so (50) becomes

(52)
$$\sum_{i=1}^{n} \sum_{j=1}^{n} H_j{}^i dp_i dp_j < 0$$

for
$$\sum_{i=1}^{n} p_i dX_i = 0,$$

not all $dX_i = 0$,
or

(53)
$$\sum_{i=1}^{n} \sum_{j=1}^{n} \left(\frac{H_j{}^i + H_i{}^j}{2} \right) dp_i dp_j < 0,$$

for
$$\sum_{i=1}^{n} p_i dX_i = 0,$$

not all $dX_i = 0$.

Consider the determinants

(54)
$$F = \begin{vmatrix} \dfrac{H_j{}^i + H_i{}^j}{2} & \begin{matrix} X_1 \\ \cdot \\ \cdot \\ X_n \end{matrix} \\ X_1 \cdots X_n & 0 \end{vmatrix}$$

and

(55)
$$F_{ij} = \begin{vmatrix} H_i{}^i & \dfrac{H_j{}^i + H_i{}^j}{2} & X_i \\ \dfrac{H_j{}^i + H_i{}^j}{2} & H_j{}^j & X_j \\ X_i & X_j & 0 \end{vmatrix}, \text{ etc.}$$

Then every such determinant $F_{i_1}, \cdots, {}_{i_{m-1}}$ must have the same sign as $(-1)^{m-1}$; or

(56) $(-1)^{m-1} F_{i_1,\ldots,i_{m-1}} > 0,$ $m \leqq n + 1.$

Specifically,

(57) $H_i{}^i(X_j)^2 + H_j{}^j(X_i)^2 - (H_j{}^i + H_i{}^j)X_i X_j < 0,$ etc.

Of course this does *not* imply that partial-equilibrium demand curves must be negatively inclined. Furthermore, the analysis holds for all total (net) incomes equal to zero.

Professor Hotelling in his analysis of this same problem has indicated his belief that more rigid conditions can "with considerable probability be supposed to hold for total demand functions."[10] This may or may not be so, but it is not the part of mathematical deductive analysis to answer this question. Suffice it to point out contrary examples, such as negatively inclined supply schedules, etc.

One more point remains to be discussed, that of extending the conditions of Section III from individual to general demand schedules.

Recall that for each individual

$$(58) \qquad \sum_{i=1}^{n} \sum_{j=1}^{n} (^{r}h_{j}{}^{i} + {}^{r}x_{j}{}^{r}h_{I}{}^{i}) dp_{i} dp_{j} < 0, \qquad (r = 1, \cdots, s),$$

for not all prices changed proportionately. Summing with respect to all individuals, we get

$$(59) \qquad \sum_{i=1}^{n} \sum_{j=1}^{n} (H_{j}{}^{i} + \sum_{r=1}^{s} {}^{r}x_{j}{}^{r}h_{I}{}^{i}) dp_{i} dp_{j} < 0,$$

for not all prices changing proportionately. As before the integrability conditions require that these coefficients be symmetrical with respect to i and j.

Call

$$\alpha_{ij} = H_{j}{}^{i} + \sum_{r=1}^{s} (^{r}x_{j}{}^{r}h_{I}{}^{i}) = \alpha_{ji},$$

$$(60) \qquad B = |\ \alpha_{ij}\ |,$$

$$B_{ij} = \begin{vmatrix} \alpha_{ii} & \alpha_{ij} \\ \alpha_{ji} & \alpha_{jj} \end{vmatrix}; \text{ etc.}$$

Our final conditions are that each sub-determinant $B_{i_1, \ldots, i_m}$ have the sign $(-1)^m$, or

$$(61) \qquad (-1)^m B_{i_1, \ldots, i_m} > 0, \qquad m \leqq n - 1.$$

It will be readily recognized that there is no difficulty in deriving integrability conditions on the general demand functions. The difficulty is in deriving conditions which depend only upon price changes and changes in *total* income. That this is impossible follows from the impossibility, in general, of finding any functional relationship between amounts demanded and *total* income (as distinct from the specification of each and every individual's income). The problems which this entails must be reserved for consideration at a future time.

[10] *Ibid.*, p. 76.

VI

The value of any technique of analysis must depend pragmatically upon the fruits it yields. The easy derivation of conditions (9), (25), (34), (56), and (61) is submitted as evidence of the mathematical advantages of the approach here suggested.

In conclusion, a few remarks may be in order concerning the history of these conditions. Disregarding special unnecessarily restrictive assumptions made by particular authors (Marshall, Pareto, *et al.*), it is surprising how little fruit in the way of demand conditions the analysis of consumer's behavior has afforded. The conditions in (9) were developed for two commodities by W. E. Johnson in 1913.[11] (It may be of significance that these were first discovered by the indifference-curve approach.) Condition (10), one fragmentary part of the conditions in (9), was also pointed out by Slutsky in 1915.[12] Condition (34) was developed by Hotelling in 1935.[13] I am not aware that any of the other conditions have previously appeared in the literature.

Society of Fellows
   Harvard University
     Cambridge, Massachusetts

[11] W. E. Johnson, "The Pure Theory of Utility Curves," *Economic Journal*, Vol. 23, December, 1913, pp. 483–513.

[12] E. Slutsky, "Sulla Teoria del Bilancio del Consumatore," *Giornale degli Economisti*, Vol. 51, No. 1, pp. 1–26.

[13] Hotelling, *loc. cit.*

1965 POSTSCRIPT

All this is admirable up to Equation (50), except that (27) might have been written in the more explicit form $g^i(x_1, \cdots, x_n, I) \equiv IG^i(x_1, \cdots, x_n)$. To clarify restrictions of (49), (15), (19), replace dp_i always by $dp_i(t)/dt = p_i{}'$, where $P_i(t)$ represents the path of an indicated admissible variation; and note that, for the rth individual, when $[p_i(t), {}^rI(t)]$ satisfies

$$(46) \qquad 0 = {}^rI' = \sum_{i=1}^{n} p_i \, {}^rx_i{}' + \sum_{i=1}^{n} {}^rx_i \, p_i{}',$$

$$(47) \qquad \sum_{i=1}^{n} {}^rx_i \, p_i{}' = 0,$$

it is easily shown that utility remains constant and ${}^rU' = 0$. However, when the number of individuals with independent tastes is $s > n - 1$, (47) cannot be required simultaneously to hold for $r = 1, 2, \cdots, s$ individuals. Typically, it takes different price changes to leave different individuals on unchanged utility levels, and (47) could be saved from contradiction if rewritten in the trivial way with $p_i{}'$ replaced by ${}^rp_i{}'$. In any case (50) is false since

$$\sum_{r=1}^{s} \left[\sum_{i=1}^{n} {}^rx_i \, p_i{}' \right] = 0$$

does not imply that *each* of the bracketed expressions is simultaneously zero. Hence, Equations (50)–(57) lack validity and relevance: That every different man would need a different change in other prices (or in incomes) to compensate him for a change in P_i is what makes nonoperational in terms of observable market variables the "marginal indifference curve" of J. R. Hicks [*Review of Economic Studies*, XIII (1945–1946), pp. 68–74], and the form of the partial-equilibrium demand curve that M. Friedman [*Journal of Political Economy*, LVII (1949), pp. 463–495] attributes, unconvincingly in my reading, to Alfred Marshall. In post-1939 publications [for example, "Social Indifference Curves," *Quarterly Journal of Economics*, Vol. LXX, No. 1 (February 1956)], I have shown that to require that totals obey the Weak Axiom, in finite form or in the form of $\sum dp_i dX_i < 0$ for $\sum p_i dX_i = 0$, implies that all men have identical homothetic indifference contours, so that every dollar gets spent the same way, no matter whose hands it is in.

4

The End of Marginal Utility: A Note on Dr. Bernardelli's Article

By Paul A. Samuelson

Recently in this Journal,[1] Mr. H. Bernardelli advanced certain arguments purporting to resurrect the theory of marginal utility in a modified form. In particular, he suggested that the following three postulates

$$\text{I.} \quad \frac{\partial \phi(x_1, x_2, x_3, \ldots, x_n)}{\partial x_i} > 0$$

$$\text{II.} \quad \frac{\partial^2 \phi}{\partial x_i^2} < 0$$

and

$$\text{III.} \quad \frac{\partial^2 \phi}{\partial x_i \partial x_j} \text{ always definite in sign}$$

be replaced by an allegedly less objectionable set

$$\text{Ia.} \quad \frac{\partial f(x_1, x_2, x_3, \ldots, x_n; \ b_1, b_2, b_3, \ldots, b_n)}{\partial b_i} > 0$$

$$\text{IIa.} \quad \frac{\partial f(x_1, x_2, x_3, \ldots, x_n; \ 0, 0, \ldots, b_i, 0, \ldots 0)}{\partial x_i} < 0$$

$$\text{IIIa.} \quad \frac{\partial f(x_1, x_2, x_3, \ldots, x_n; \ 0, 0, \ldots, b_j, 0, \ldots, 0)}{\partial x_i}$$

always definite in sign, where

$$\phi = \phi(x_1, x_2, x_3, \ldots, x_n)$$

is one cardinal index of utility, and f is defined to be

$$f(x_1, x_2, \ldots, x_n; \ b_1, b_2, \ldots, b_n)$$
$$\equiv \sum_j \frac{\partial \phi}{\partial x_j} b_j + \tfrac{1}{2} \sum_{i,j} \frac{\partial^2 \phi}{\partial x_i \partial x_j} b_i b_j + \ldots \ +.$$

It is well known that Postulates II and III of the first set are not invariant under a monotonic transformation of the utility index of the form

$$\Phi = \Phi(\phi), \qquad \frac{d\Phi}{d\phi} > 0$$

It is this objectionable feature which the new definitions are believed to avoid. It is the intention here to indicate briefly that a more careful examination of the economic and mathematical implications of the new postulates must reveal that Postulates IIa and IIIa are

[1] H. Bernardelli: "The End of the Marginal Utility Theory?", Economica, May, 1938.

open to the same grave objections as II and III, and that far from clearing the way for the reintroduction of uniquely defined decreasing marginal utility and complementarity, the new definitions leave matters just where they were.

Concretely, it is easy to demonstrate that IIa and IIIa of the second set are *not* invariant under a monotonic renumbering of the indifference loci. The fact that they are invariant under Mr. Bernardelli's proposed monotonic transformation

$$\psi(f) \qquad\qquad \frac{d\psi}{df} > 0$$

is of no particular relevance to the economic problem of consumer's behaviour.

We may rewrite f in the obviously identical form

$$f(x_1, x_2, \ldots, x_n;\ h_1, h_2, \ldots, h_n)$$
$$\equiv \phi(x_1 + h_1, x_2 + h_2, \ldots, x_n + h_n) - \phi(x_1, x_2, \ldots, x_n)$$

Hence, corresponding to ϕ we have f; corresponding to Φ we have

$$F = \Phi(x_1 + h_1, x_2 + h_2, \ldots, x_n + h_n) - \Phi(x_1, x_2, \ldots, x_n)$$
$$= \Phi\big[\phi(x_1 + h_1, x_2 + h_2, \ldots, x_n + h_n)\big] - \Phi\big[\phi(x_1, x_2, \ldots, x_n)\big].$$

It remains only to compute the various coefficients of Ia, IIa and IIIa to determine the effect of this transformation upon them. Performing the indicated differentiations, we find

$$\frac{\partial F(x_1, x_2, \ldots, x_n;\ h_1, h_2, \ldots, h_n)}{\partial h_i} \equiv \frac{d\Phi}{d\phi} \cdot \frac{\partial f}{\partial h_i}$$

$$\frac{\partial F}{\partial x_i} \equiv \left(\overline{\frac{d\Phi}{d\phi}}\right)\frac{\partial f}{\partial x_i} + \int \frac{d^2\Phi}{d\phi^2}\ \underset{j}{\Sigma}\ \frac{\partial \phi}{\partial x_i}\frac{\partial \phi}{\partial x_j}\ dh_j$$

where $\left(\overline{\frac{d\Phi}{d\phi}}\right)$ indicates that this expression is to be evaluated at some point intermediate between $(x_1, x_2, \ldots, x_n, 0, 0, \ldots, 0)$ and $(x_1, x_2, \ldots, x_n, h_1, h_2, \ldots, h_n)$, and where the indicated line integral is taken between these same limits of integration. The above two expressions are valid for all values of the x's and h's, and hence for the special cases indicated in Ia, IIa, and IIIa.

Contemplation of these expressions reveals that the coefficient in Ia is invariant in sign under a monotonic transformation of utility index ; however, a suitable transformation can result in increasing marginal utility and contradictory complementarity due to the arbitrary element in the second term. Thus, the new definitions, IIa and IIIa, are open to precisely the same objections as the old ones. By working through the details of the example in Mr. Bernardelli's Appendix, one can verify the truth of these remarks.

I am very much afraid, therefore, that the answer is yes to Mr. Bernardelli's question, and that the text-books still need that rewriting which he hoped so much to avoid.

36

5

CONSTANCY OF THE MARGINAL UTILITY OF INCOME

PAUL A. SAMUELSON

Massachusetts Institute of Technology

I N THE theoretical and empirical literature on the theory of consumer's demand behavior one repeatedly encounters the hypothesis that the marginal utility of income or money can be assumed to be constant, or at least "sensibly" so.[1] As a result, many of the conclusions derived are of restricted validity; indeed, outright contradictions often emerge from this seemingly innocent assumption. It is proposed here to examine briefly, but exhaustively, the rigorous implications of the constancy of the marginal utility of income.

According to a well-known condition of equilibrium in the theory of consumer's behavior, a consumer with a given monetary income, I, confronted with respective prices, $(p_1, \cdots, p_n)$, of n goods, $(x_1, \cdots, x_n)$, will purchase each good up to the point where its marginal (degree of) utility is proportional to its price. Thus, in equilibrium

$$\phi_i(x_1, \cdots, x_n) = m_\phi p_i, \tag{1}$$

where ϕ_i represents the partial derivative with respect to the ith good of the cardinal index of utility, $\phi(x_1, \cdots, x_n)$, and m_ϕ is a factor of proportionality. This relation may be rewritten in the form

$$m_\phi = \frac{\phi_1(x_1, \cdots, x_n)}{p_1} = \frac{\phi_2(x_1, \cdots, x_n)}{p_2} = \cdots$$
$$= \frac{\phi_n(x_1, \cdots, x_n)}{p_n}. \tag{2}$$

This proposition is often translated to mean that in equilibrium the utility of the last dollar spent in every use must be equal; the value of this magnitude is m_ϕ and will be known hereafter as the

---

[1] Alfred Marshall, *Principles of Economics* (8th ed.; London, 1930); Vilfredo Pareto, *Manuel d'économie politique* (Paris, 1909), Appendix; Henry Schultz, *The Theory and Measurement of Demand* (Chicago: University of Chicago Press, 1938), chap. xviii; Milton Friedman, "Professor Pigou's Method for Measuring Elasticities of Demand from Budgetary Data," *Quarterly Journal of Economics*, L (1935), 151–63; A. C. Pigou, Milton Friedman, and N. Georgescu-Roegen, "Marginal Utility of Money and Elasticities of Demand," *Quarterly Journal of Economics*, L (1935), 532–39; E. B. Wilson, "Pareto versus Marshall," *Quarterly Journal of Economics*, LIII (1939), 645–49. See also P. A. Samuelson, *Foundations of Economic Analysis* (Cambridge: Harvard University Press, 1947), Ch. VII.

marginal utility of income for the cardinal utility index, ϕ. The subscript ϕ is appended in order to emphasize its dependence upon the particular choice of utility index. It will further depend upon the equilibrium position attained by the consumer; i.e., on the set of prices and income with which he is confronted. Given such prices and income, the consumer will select a given amount of each and every good. His demand functions can be written in the form

$$x_i = h^i (p_1, \cdots, p_n, I), \qquad (i = 1, \cdots, n) \tag{3}$$

where

$$\sum_{i=1}^{n} p_i x_i = I. \tag{4}$$

One feature of these demand functions should be noted. A simultaneous doubling of all prices and income will leave the individual with the same choice as between commodities and hence will leave unaffected the amount demanded of each good. More generally,

$$h^i (\lambda p_1, \cdots, \lambda p_n, \lambda I) = h^i (p_1, \cdots, p_n, I), \qquad (i = 1, \cdots, n) \tag{5}$$

where λ is any positive constant. Mathematically, the demand functions are homogeneous of order zero.

Thus, the marginal utility of income, as well as depending upon the particular cardinal index of utility selected, is also a function of all prices and income:

$$m_\phi = \frac{\phi_i [h^1 (p_1, \cdots, p_n, I), h^2 (p_1, \cdots, p_n, I), \cdots]}{p_i},$$
$$= m_\phi (p_1, \cdots, p_n, I). \tag{6}$$

DEPENDENCE UPON THE CHOICE OF UTILITY INDEX

It is well known that the demand functions or schedules of the consumer remain unaltered under any change of utility index. One may write the conditions of equilibrium so that they are independent of the choice of utility index, or even by the use of indifference varieties so that no index is employed. The last approach introduces the minor inconvenience of a notational asymmetry, but this is a small price to pay for the clarity of thought which the method often imparts.

The marginal utility of income does not possess this invariance. Let us consider a transformation of the utility index of the form

$$F = F [\phi (x_1, \cdots, x_n)] = F (x_1, \cdots, x_n), \tag{7}$$

where $F'(\phi) > 0$, and

$$F_i = F'\phi_i$$

$$F_{ij} = F'\phi_{ij} + F''\phi_i\phi_j .$$

(8)

Obviously,

$$m_F = \frac{F_i}{p_i} = \frac{F'(\phi)\phi_i}{p_i} = F'(\phi)m_\phi$$

$$= m_F(p_1, \cdots, p_n, I) .$$

(9)

In general, the change in this magnitude with respect to any parameter, say α, is also dependent upon the choice of utility index since

$$\frac{dm_F}{d\alpha} = \frac{d}{d\alpha}(F'm_\phi) = F'\frac{dm_\phi}{d\alpha} + F''m_\phi\frac{d\phi}{d\alpha} .$$

(10)

In our transformation of any utility index, no restriction can be placed upon $F''(\phi)$. Therefore, provided that $d\phi/d\alpha$ does not vanish, by an appropriate selection of utility index the rate of change in the marginal utility of income with respect to any parameter can be made to be of any arbitrary magnitude and sign. Thus, the change in the marginal utility of income with respect to a change in income, prices being constant, cannot be said to be unambiguously of any given sign. There exists an infinity of indexes for which it is of either algebraic sign at any position of equilibrium; at such a point an index can be found for which the value of this derivative is zero.

Care must be taken not to misinterpret these remarks. There need not, and in general there will not, exist any utility index for which this derivative vanishes at *every* level of income and all levels of prices. Moreover, in general there will not exist an index for which the marginal utility is constant with respect to two different parameters simultaneously. The force of these remarks will appear in the course of the argument.

There exists one particular compound change in price and income which does present an interesting invariance. Scrutiny of equation (10) reveals that

$$\frac{1}{m_F}\frac{dm_F}{d\alpha} = \frac{1}{m_\phi}\frac{dm_\phi}{d\alpha} = \frac{d\log m}{d\alpha} ,$$

(11)

provided that $d\phi/d\alpha = 0$. That is, *the logarithmic derivative of the marginal utility of income with respect to any parameter which leaves the level of utility unchanged is invariant under any transformation of utility index.* A compound change in any single price, p_i, accompanied by a change in I sufficiently great to leave the consumer at the same level of utility must necessarily fulfil this requirement. We should expect, therefore, to find the above coefficient invariant under such a "compensated price change."[2] This compensated price change can be written

$$\frac{1}{m_\phi}\frac{dm_\phi}{d\alpha} = \frac{1}{m_\phi}\left(\frac{\partial m_\phi}{\partial p_i} + x_i\frac{\partial m_\phi}{\partial I}\right). \tag{12}$$

Actually, by simple differentiation of equation (1), one can verify the following equivalence,[3]

$$\frac{1}{m_\phi}\left(\frac{\partial m_\phi}{\partial p_i} + x_i\frac{\partial m_\phi}{\partial I}\right) = -\frac{\partial x_i}{\partial I}. \qquad (i=1,2,\cdots,n) \tag{13}$$

The right-hand term, being a property of the demand functions, is independent of the choice of utility index so that our invariance is verified.

This also confirms the previous assertion that we cannot arbitrarily fix the sign of the change in the marginal utility of income with respect to both income and a given price, since these two must add up in a certain way (as given in eq. [13]) to a given number. Similarly, the change in the marginal utility of income with respect to each of two prices cannot be arbitrarily preassigned, since we can deduce from equation (13) the relation

$$\frac{1}{m_\phi}\left(\frac{\partial m_\phi}{\partial p_i}x_j - \frac{\partial m_\phi}{\partial p_j}x_i\right) = -\left(\frac{\partial x_i}{\partial I}x_j - \frac{\partial x_j}{\partial I}x_i\right). \tag{14}$$

The right-hand side of this equation cannot be altered by a transformation of the utility index.

In what follows reference will be made repeatedly to equation (13). It must be emphasized that it holds regardless of any assumptions of independence of utility, etc.

ALTERNATIVE INTERPRETATIONS OF CONSTANCY

The statement that the marginal utility of income is assumed to be constant is ambiguous.[4] With respect to what is it assumed to be constant? With respect to price changes? Income change? Or with respect to all of these?

---

[2] See Schultz, op. cit., pp. 41–46.
[3] Ibid., p. 40, eq. (3.15).
[4] One must be on guard against a superficial error. The fact that the marginal utility of income changes but slightly with respect to small changes in the variables under consideration does not imply that the rate of change of marginal utility with respect to these variables is small. The former proposition is a consequence simply of continuity and differentiability and holds for all functions possessing these properties.

Actually, it can be shown by simple mathematical argument that the latter cannot possibly hold. Recall that

$$m_\phi = m_\phi(p_1, p_2, \cdots, p_n, I) = \frac{\phi_i(x_1, x_2, \cdots; x_n)}{p_i}. \tag{15}$$

Consider a simultaneous doubling of all prices and income. This will leave the quantities of all goods unchanged and hence will not affect the numerator of the right-hand member. However, the denominator will be doubled. The total effect is to halve the marginal utility of income. Mathematically, m_ϕ is a homogeneous function of order minus one in the prices and income. As a consequence,

$$m_\phi(p_1, p_2, \cdots, p_n, I) = \lambda m_\phi(\lambda p_1, \lambda p_2, \cdots, \lambda p_n, \lambda I), \tag{16}$$

where λ is any positive constant. Applying Euler's theorem on homogeneous functions, we have the following identity:

$$-m_\phi \equiv \frac{\partial m_\phi}{\partial p_1} p_1 + \frac{\partial m_\phi}{\partial p_2} p_2 + \cdots + \frac{\partial m_\phi}{\partial p_n} p_n + \frac{\partial m_\phi}{\partial I} I. \tag{17}$$

Of course, m_ϕ, $p_1, \cdots, p_n$, I, all are positive quantities. Therefore, we cannot have simultaneously

$$\frac{\partial m_\phi}{\partial p_i} \equiv 0 \qquad (i = 1, 2, \cdots, n) \tag{18}$$

$$\frac{\partial m_\phi}{\partial I} \equiv 0,$$

else the right-hand sign of equation (17) would not add up to a negative quantity. This becomes even more clear if we divide (17) by m_ϕ to get the following expression involving dimensionless elasticity coefficients:

$$-1 \equiv \left(\frac{\partial m_\phi}{\partial p_1} \frac{p_1}{m_\phi}\right) + \cdots + \left(\frac{\partial m_\phi}{\partial p_n} \frac{p_n}{m_\phi}\right) + \left(\frac{\partial m_\phi}{\partial I} \frac{I}{m_\phi}\right) \tag{19}$$

The right-hand terms cannot all vanish and still add up to a -1.

How then shall we interpret constancy of the marginal utility of income? Knowingly or unknowingly, economists have formulated two distinct and alternative hypotheses under this heading. The first one involves the assumption that there exists an index of utility for which the marginal utility of income becomes independent of a change in any price, or

$$\frac{\partial m_\phi}{\partial p_i} \equiv 0. \qquad (i = 1, 2, \cdots, n) \tag{20}$$

As we have seen, this cannot possibly imply that the marginal utility of income is also constant with respect to income.

In introducing the second hypothesis attention is drawn to the fact that throughout I have repeatedly employed the term "marginal utility of *income*" rather than the "marginal utility of *money*." The latter is perhaps the term most commonly met in the literature. Not the least of its disadvantages is the fact that it suggests to the literally minded the second interpretation we are about to give.

As a preliminary it must be remembered that all demand functions and conditions of equilibrium depend upon *relative* prices and income. Very often writers arbitrarily equate the price of one good to unity, employing it as *numéraire*, or unit of reckoning, and referring to it as "money." It was only natural for such writers to conclude that constancy of the marginal utility of "money" meant constancy of the marginal utility of the good selected as *numéraire*.

Although Marshall does employ the term "marginal utility of money," there is no evidence that he had in mind this last interpretation.[5] In the first place, he rarely, if ever, employed the concept of a *numéraire*. Furthermore, he repeatedly states that the marginal utility of money decreases with income, which I shall later show to rule out the second hypothesis. He also insists that the marginal utility of money is to be associated with a flow of income rather than a stock of a commodity. This insistence is not conclusive proof but may be significant.

FIRST HYPOTHESIS

I turn then to the first or Marshallian hypothesis that the marginal utility of income is independent of price changes as expressed in equation (20). Obviously,

$$\frac{\partial m_\phi}{\partial p_i} \frac{p_i}{m_\phi} \equiv 0 \ . \qquad (i = 1, 2, \cdots, n) \tag{21}$$

Therefore, substituting into equation (19), we have

$$\frac{\partial m_\phi}{\partial I} \frac{I}{m_\phi} \equiv -1 \ . \tag{22}$$

[5] The only passages in the *Principles* which do suggest this interpretation are to be found in the Mathematical Appendix, Note XII. This argument, however, is borrowed from Edgeworth and other writers in order to establish the conclusion that market price is determinate. Against this may be cited pp. 95, 134–35, Mathematical Appendix, Note II, etc. In interpreting Marshall, it must be remembered that he regarded the constancy of the marginal utility of income as only "approximate." I shall follow out the rigorous implications of assuming this exactly; the closer is Marshall's approximation, the more nearly will the results coincide.

This says that the income elasticity of the marginal utility of income must be identically equal to minus unity. Therefore, we have

$$m_\phi = \frac{a}{I} , \tag{23}$$

where a is a constant. Mathematically, (23) is the only form that a homogeneous function of order -1 in a single variable can take. Equation (13) now becomes

$$\frac{\partial x_i}{\partial I} \frac{I}{x_i} \equiv - \frac{\partial m_\phi}{\partial I} \frac{I}{m_\phi} \equiv 1 . \qquad (i = 1, 2, \cdots, n) \tag{24}$$

In words, *the seemingly innocent assumption that there exists a utility index for which the marginal utility of income is constant with respect to price changes results in the empirical restriction of unitary income elasticities of demand, or that the consumption of each and every good is exactly proportional to income.* In this case the demand functions take the special form

$$x_i = I \psi^i (p_1, \cdots, p_n) \equiv I \lambda \psi^i (\lambda p_1, \cdots, \lambda p_n) . \tag{25}$$
$$(i = 1, 2, \cdots, n)$$

There is a vast amount of budgetary statistical data relating to income variations in consumption. As far as I know, every investigation contradicts flatly this basic assumption. Moreover, these relations do not hold approximately even in the neighborhood of a single point.[6]

Let us go still further and investigate the strict implications of imposing an additional Marshallian assumption, namely, that there exists a utility index which is the sum of the independent utilities of each good:

$$\phi (x_1, \cdots, x_n) = f_1 (x_1) + f_2 (x_2) + \cdots + f_n (x_n) . \tag{26}$$

Then

$$\frac{f'_i (x_i)}{p_i} = \frac{a}{I} . \tag{27}$$

---

[6] It is only in the empirically unimportant case of expenditure proportionality that the correct integrability conditions

$$\frac{\partial x_i}{\partial p_j} + x_j \frac{\partial x_i}{\partial I} \equiv \frac{\partial x_j}{\partial p_i} + x_i \frac{\partial x_j}{\partial I} \tag{1}$$

can be replaced by the special relations

$$\frac{\partial x_i}{\partial p_j} \equiv \frac{\partial x_j}{\partial p_i} . \tag{2}$$

Since the right-hand side of (27) does not contain $p_j (\neq p_i)$, the quantity demanded of the ith good must depend only upon its own price and income. Differentiating partially the budget equation with respect to p_j, we find

$$\frac{\partial I}{\partial p_j} = 0 = \sum_{i=1}^{n} p_i \frac{\partial x_i}{\partial p_j} + x_j . \tag{28}$$

Under the present independence of demand we derive

$$\frac{\partial x_j}{\partial p_j} \frac{p_j}{x_j} \equiv -1 . \qquad (j = 1, 2, \cdots, n) \tag{29}$$

In words, *the combined assumptions of constancy of the marginal utility of income and independence of utility imply that the elasticity of demand be always unity*. This together with the assumption that all demand functions be homogeneous of order zero requires that the demand functions take the special form

$$x_i = k_i \frac{I}{p_i} , \qquad (i = 1, 2, \cdots, n) \tag{30}$$

where the k's are constants equal to the fraction of income spent on each commodity.

Equation (27) can be rewritten

$$f'_i (k_i \frac{I}{p_i}) = a \frac{p_i}{I} . \tag{31}$$

Therefore,

$$f'_i (v) = \frac{a k_i}{v} , \tag{32}$$

or

$$f'_i (x_i) = \frac{a k_i}{x_i} . \qquad (i = 1, 2, \cdots, n) \tag{33}$$

Hence,

$$\phi = b + a (k_1 \log x_1 + k_2 \log x_2 + \cdots + k_n \log x_n) . \tag{34}$$

This result could also have been derived with the aid of the generalized form of Burk's theorem that expenditure proportionality plus independence of utilities restricts severely the indifference surfaces and utility indexes.[7]

As an illustration of the lack of invariance of the marginal utility

---

[7] A. Burk, "Real Income, Expenditure Proportionality, and Frisch's 'New Methods of Measuring Marginal Utility,'" *Review of Economic Studies*, IV, No. 1 (1936), 33–52.

of income the reader is invited to compute this magnitude for the transformed, equivalent utility index

$$F = B + A x_1^{k_1} x_2^{k_2} \cdots x_n^{k_n} . \tag{35}$$

It need hardly be said that no empirical observations justify the imposition of such a definite form upon the utility indexes of indifference surfaces and demand functions.

SUFFICIENCY CONDITIONS FOR CONSTANCY IN
THE FIRST SENSE

The introduction of the assumption of independence of utilities was in the nature of a digression designed to show the damage that may result from the addition of seemingly harmless and plausible hypotheses. I return now to the hypothesis of constancy of the marginal utility of income. We have seen that it implies (income) *expenditure proportionality.* Is this all? Are there perhaps still further hidden restrictions which more thorough investigation might reveal?

It is desirable to be able to answer definitely such questions. Fortunately, it can be proved that no further restrictions are implied by this hypothesis. This can be done once and for all by proving that the necessary conditions of equation (25) are also sufficient to insure the existence of a utility index in terms of which the marginal utility of income is constant with respect to price changes. The proof consists of a specification of the steps by means of which such an index can be constructed.

If expenditure proportionality holds, the indifference surface can be written in the following special form:

$$\frac{F'(\phi)\phi_i}{F'(\phi)\phi_j} = {}^j R^i (x_1, x_2, \cdots, x_n) = {}^j R^i (\lambda x_1, \lambda x_2, \cdots, \lambda x_n) ; \tag{36}$$

i.e., the slope functions are homogeneous of order zero. This being the case, a utility index can be found which is homogeneous of the first order in the quantities of goods,

$$\Phi = \Phi(x_1, x_2, \cdots, x_n) = \frac{1}{\lambda} \Phi(\lambda x_1, \lambda x_2, \cdots, \lambda x_n) . \tag{37}$$

In fact, the indifference surfaces can be "numbered" according to their respective distances from the origin along an arbitrary "spoke" going through the origin, and we will have such an index. In terms of this index the conditions of equilibrium can be written

$$\Phi_i = m_\Phi p_i . \quad (i = 1, 2, \cdots, n) \tag{38}$$

Multiplying each equation by x_i, respectively, and adding, we have

$$\sum_{i=1}^{n} \Phi_i x_i = m_\Phi \sum_{i=1}^{n} p_i x_i \ . \tag{39}$$

Because of the budget equation (4) and the fact that Φ obeys Euler's theorem for homogeneous functions of the first order, this can be written

$$m_\Phi = \frac{\Phi}{I} \ . \tag{40}$$

Consider the utility index, ϕ, defined as

$$\phi = b + a \log \Phi \ . \tag{41}$$

From equation (9) we find

$$m_\phi = \frac{a}{\Phi} m_\Phi = \frac{a}{I} \ , \tag{42}$$

which is identically equation (23). Hence, expenditure proportionality implies that a utility index can always be found for which the marginal utility of income is independent of prices. This completes the sufficiency proof and guarantees that there are no hidden additional implications of the assumption of constancy of the marginal utility of income in the Marshallian sense.

CONSTANCY OF THE MARGINAL UTILITY OF "MONEY"

I now turn to a brief analysis of the empirical implications of the second possible interpretation of constancy of the marginal utility of income.[8] According to this point of view, the marginal utility of some one good, which can be designated as *numéraire*, is constant with respect to changes in all *other* prices and income. Designating the *numéraire* as the first good, we have

$$\frac{\partial m_\phi}{\partial p_i} \equiv 0 \ ; \quad (i = 2, 3, \cdots, n)$$

$$\frac{\partial m_\phi}{\partial I} \equiv 0 \ . \tag{43}$$

Because m_ϕ is homogeneous of order -1 in all prices and income, we have

    [8] See Wilson, *op. cit.*; J. R. Hicks, *Value and Capital* (Oxford: Clarendon Press, 1939), pp. 38–41.

$$m_\phi \equiv \frac{a}{p_1} \, . \tag{44}$$

Substituting equations (43) into equation (13), we have

$$\frac{\partial x_i}{\partial I} \equiv 0 \, , \qquad (i = 2, 3, \cdots, n)$$

$$\frac{\partial x_1}{\partial I} \equiv -\frac{\partial m_\phi}{\partial p_1} \frac{1}{m_\phi} \equiv \frac{1}{p_1} \, . \tag{45}$$

The demand functions must take the special form[9]

$$x_i = G^i(p_1, \cdots, p_n) = G^i(\lambda p_1, \cdots, \lambda p_n) \, , \qquad (i = 2, 3, \cdots, n)$$

$$x_1 = \frac{I}{p_1} - \sum_{i=2}^{n} \frac{p_i}{p_1} G^i(p_1, \cdots, p_n) \, . \tag{46}$$

This means that any increase in income is spent completely on one commodity. It need hardly be said that all empirical budgetary studies show this hypothesis to be absurd.

As with the first hypothesis, I shall now prove the sufficiency of the necessary conditions of equations (46). Because of the homogeneity condition on the G's, the first $(n-1)$ equations can be solved to give the prices, $(p_2/p_1, \ p_3/p_1, \cdots, p_n/p_1)$ in terms of the goods, $(x_2, x_3, \cdots, x_n)$. These price ratios are independent of x_1, so the indifference curves take the special form

$$\frac{p_i}{p_1} = R^i(x_2, x_3, \cdots, x_n) \, . \qquad (i = 2, 3, \cdots, n) \tag{47}$$

The linear differential expression

$$adx_1 + \sum_{i=2}^{n} aR^i dx_i \, , \tag{48}$$

is an exact differential because the existence of at least one utility index implies

$$R_j{}^i - R_i{}^j \equiv R^j R_1{}^i - R^i R_1{}^j \equiv 0 \, . \tag{49}$$

Hence, a utility index exists of the form

$$\phi = b + ax_1 + a \sum_{i=2}^{n} \int_{c_i}^{x_i} R^i(x_2, \cdots, x_n) \, dx_i \, . \tag{50}$$

[9] Pigou appears to be in error in his belief that constancy of the marginal utility of income with respect to income implies infinite elasticity of demand. Equations (46) reveal no such implication.

For this index,

$$m_\phi = \frac{a}{p_1} \, ,$$

which is identically equal to equation (44). This proves the sufficiency of the conditions of equation (46).

As with the previous case, it is of interest to consider the simultaneous effects of the assumption of independence of utilities and constancy of the marginal utility of income. In this case, a utility index exists of the following form

$$\phi = b + ax_1 + f_2(x_2) + f_3(x_3) + \cdots + f_n(x_n) \, . \tag{51}$$

Hence,

$$m_\phi = \frac{f'_i(x_i)}{p_i} = \frac{a}{p_1} \, . \tag{52}$$

But

$$x_i = G^i\left(1 \, , \frac{p_2}{p_1} \, , \frac{p_3}{p_1} \, , \cdots \, , \frac{p_n}{p_1}\right) \tag{53}$$

so that

$$f'_i\left[G^i \left(1 \, , \frac{p_2}{p_1} \, , \frac{p_3}{p_1} \, , \cdots \, , \frac{p_n}{p_1}\right)\right] = a\frac{p_i}{p_1} \, . \tag{54}$$

Since the right-hand side does not involve (p_j/p_1) $(\neq p_i/p_1)$, neither can the left, requiring our demand curves to take the special form

$$x_i = G^i\left(\frac{p_i}{p_1}\right), \qquad (i = 2, 3, \cdots, n)$$

$$x_1 = \frac{I}{p_1} - \sum_{i=2}^{n} \frac{p_i}{p_1} G^i\left(\frac{p_i}{p_1}\right). \tag{55}$$

This does *not* imply unitary elasticity of demand, as some earlier writers have thought. In fact, unitary elasticity would lead to a contradiction. Of course, the restrictions imposed by the combined assumptions are even more incompatible with the facts of economic life.

CONSUMER'S SURPLUS AND ALLIED CONCEPTS

We have seen the empirical implications of the various hypotheses with respect to the strict constancy of the marginal utility of income and noted their incompatibility with statistical observations. It is desirable before concluding to indicate the effects of this analysis upon various constructions which depend for their validity upon the constancy of the marginal utility of income.

The first of these is Marshallian consumer's surplus. Before examining it in detail, let us consider the uses to which it is put. Among other things it is proposed as a measure of the gain (loss) of utility that results from a decrease (increase) in price of a single good. An attempt also has been made to apply it to the analysis of the burden involved in commodity taxation. It has been used to determine the maximum amount of revenue that a perfectly discriminating monopolist might exact from the consumer for a given amount of the good in question.

Since only an ordinal preference field is assumed in the theory of consumer's behavior, there is really little importance to be attached to any numerical measure of the gains from a price change. In particular, one cannot fruitfully compare the gain derived from a movement between two given price situations with the gain between two other price situations.[10] Moreover, all valid theorems relating to the burden of taxation can be stated independently of any numerical measure of utility change. We should not be greatly perturbed, therefore, if the concept of consumer's surplus should be found to be inadmissible. Its only advantage seems to lie in its easy two-dimensional representation.

Consider an initial price and income situation, $(p_1{}^a, \cdots, p_n{}^a, I^a)$, and the corresponding amount of goods purchased, $(x_1{}^a, \cdots, x_n{}^a)$. For any selected utility index, ϕ, there will also be a given amount of utility, $\phi(X^a)$. Suppose that a change is made in but one price, p_i, and income is left unchanged. There will be new amounts of every commodity, $(x_1{}^b, \cdots, x_n{}^b)$, and of utility, $\phi(X^b)$, corresponding to the new prices and income, $(p_1{}^b, \cdots, p_n{}^b, I^b)$, or $(p_1{}^a, p_2{}^a, \cdots, p_i{}^b, \cdots, p_n{}^a, I^a)$.

We are interested in the following magnitudes:

1.   The gain (loss) in utility resulting from the price change, or $\phi(X^b) - \phi(X^a)$.

2.   The area between the demand curve of the ith good and the p_i axis within the range of the price movement, or

$$- \int_{p_i{}^a}^{p_i{}^b} x_i \, dp_i \, .$$

3.   The amount by which the expenditure on the ith good in the new situation is exceeded by the maximum amount of money which

---

[10] One can, however, compare the gains derived from a change in the basic price situation with an alternative price change from the *same* basic situation, since this resolves itself into an *ordinal* comparison of the alternative new situations. The initial situation "cancels out" so to speak.

the consumer would be willing to pay for $x_i{}^b$ in preference to trading at the old set of prices. (This may be negative if we are dealing with a price increase rather than a decrease.) Call this E_{ab}.

4.   The change in income which will make trading at the new set of prices as attractive as trading at the old set of prices with the initial income. Call this $\varDelta I_{ab}$.

5.   The change in income which will make trading at the old set of prices as attractive as trading at the new set of prices with the initial income. Call this $\varDelta I'_{ab}$. [11]

According to the Marshallian doctrine of consumer's surplus, all five of these magnitudes are equal except for dimensional constants. We are explicitly warned, however, that this doctrine holds unqualifiedly only when the marginal utility of income is constant, and only if utilities are independent. I shall now examine the value of each of these magnitudes in four cases: (a) in the general unrestricted case of stable demand; (b) under the first interpretation of constancy of the marginal utility of income; (c) under the second hypothesis when the ith good is not the $num\acute{e}raire$; and (d) under the second hypothesis when the ith good itself has constant marginal utility of income. Only the most sketchy proofs will be indicated.

In the general case we have the following relations:

$$\phi(X^b) - \phi(X^a) = \int_{p_i{}^a}^{p_i{}^b} \left(\frac{d\phi}{dp_i}\right) dp_i = \int_{p_i{}^a}^{p_i{}^b} \sum_{j=1}^{n} \left(\frac{\partial\phi}{\partial x_j} \frac{\partial x_j}{\partial p_i}\right) dp_i$$

$$= \int_{p_i{}^a}^{p_i{}^b} m_\phi \sum_{j=1}^{n} \left(p_j \frac{\partial x_j}{\partial p_i}\right) dp_i = - \int_{p_i{}^a}^{p_i{}^b} m_\phi\, x_i\, dp_i . \qquad (56)$$

$$\varDelta I_{ab} = \max \left(\sum_{j=1}^{n} p_j{}^b x_j{}^b - \sum_{j=1}^{n} p_j{}^b x_j\right), \quad \text{where } \phi(X) = \phi(X^a), \qquad (57)$$

$$\geq \sum_{j=1}^{n} p_j{}^b (x_j{}^b - x_j{}^a), \qquad (58)$$

$$\geq \sum_{j=1}^{n} (p_j{}^a - p_j{}^b) x_j{}^a . \qquad (59)$$

If only the ith price changes, this becomes

$$\varDelta I_{ab} \geq (p_i{}^a - p_i{}^b) x_i{}^a . \qquad (60)$$

Similarly,

$$\varDelta I'_{ab} \leq \sum_{j=1}^{n} p_j{}^a (x_j{}^b - x_j{}^a) \qquad (61)$$

[11] Note that $\varDelta I_{ab} = -\varDelta I'_{ba}$; $\varDelta I'_{ab}$, but not $\varDelta I_{ab}$ nor E_{ab}, can exceed I.

$$\leqq \sum_{j=1}^{n} (p_j{}^a - p_j{}^b) x_j{}^b \tag{62}$$

and

$$\Delta I'_{ab} \leqq (p_i{}^a - p_i{}^b) x_i{}^b . \tag{63}$$

It is impossible in the general case[12] to determine the relative magnitude of ΔI_{ab} and $\Delta I'_{ab}$. Hence,

$$\Delta I_{ab} \gtreqless \Delta I'_{ab} . \tag{64}$$

It can be shown that

$$E_{ab} = - \int_{p_i{}^a}^{p_i{}^b} x_i dp_i + \int_{p_i{}^a}^{p_i{}^b} (\bar{p}_i - p_i) \frac{\partial x_i}{\partial p_i} \, dp_i , \tag{65}$$

where $\bar{p}_i$ is the price which would have to prevail for the consumer *freely* to select the batch of goods which he actually does consume when presented with an "all-or-none" offer by the perfectly discriminating monopolist. The first term on the right-hand side of equation (65) is the area under the demand curve. The second "correction" term may be of either sign.[13] It also follows from the definition of ΔI_{ab} that

$$\Delta I_{ab} \geqq E_{ab} . \tag{66}$$

In case (b) we find

$$E_{ab} < \Delta I_{ab} < \Delta I'_{ab} , \tag{67}$$

and

$$\frac{\phi(X^b) - \phi(X^a)}{m_\phi} = - \int_{p_i{}^a}^{p_i{}^b} x_i dp_i > E_{ab} .\,^{14} \tag{68}$$

The following relations must be satisfied in case (c) :

$$\frac{\phi(X^b) - \phi(X^a)}{m_\phi} = - \int_{p_i{}^a}^{p_i{}^b} x_i dp_i = E_{ab} = \Delta I_{ab} = \Delta I'_{ab} . \quad (i \neq 1) \tag{69}$$

[12] If we rule out the inferior good phenomenon so that demand is "normal,"

$$\Delta I_{ab} < \Delta I'_{ab} . \tag{1}$$

Actually,

$$\Delta I_{ab} - \Delta I'_{ab} = \int_{p_i{}^a}^{p_i{}^b} \{x_i(p_1{}^a, p_2{}^a, \dots, p_i, \dots p_n{}^a, \phi^b)$$
$$- x_i(p_1{}^a, p_2{}^a, \dots, p_i, \dots, p_n{}^a, \phi^a)\} dp_i .$$

[13] In the "normal" two-dimensional case it will be of negative sign; i.e., a perfectly discriminating monopolist will be able to exact less than the area under the demand curve from the consumer.

[14] The last of these inequalities will certainly hold in the two good case. I have not developed a satisfactory proof that it holds for the n-dimensional case.

Although this is not the Marshallian interpretation, consumer's surplus seems to be most justified in this case. However, the above equalities cannot hold simultaneously for every good.[15]

For case (d) we have the same relations as case (b); i.e., equations (67) and (68) must hold with the possible exception of the inequality referred to in a previous footnote.[16]

---

[15] Case (c) is *sufficient* to insure the equalities of eq. (69). Some of them may hold in other cases.

[16] It is of some interest to calculate these magnitudes in the *purest Marshallian case* when utilities are independent and the marginal utility of income is independent of price changes. Here we have for consumer's surplus

$$\frac{\phi(X^b) - \phi(X^a)}{m_\phi} = -\int_{p_i{}^a}^{p_i{}^b} x_i\, dp_i\,,$$

$$= k_i I \log \frac{p_i{}^a}{p_i{}^b} > 0\,, \quad p_i{}^a > p_i{}^b\,. \tag{1}$$

If we compute consumer's surplus from the origin, i.e., from the price at which the consumption of x_i is equal to zero, we find that consumer's surplus is infinite! That is

$$\lim_{p_i{}^a \to \infty} \log \frac{p_i{}^a}{p_i{}^b} = \infty\,. \tag{2}$$

Some writers regard consumer's surplus as being infinite but suggest that it may be made finite if measured from some minimum or subsistence level of the commodity in question. In the purest Marshallian case since the demand curve approaches the price axis asymptotically in such a way that the integral or area under the curve is divergent, there exists no such unique minimum level. Also

$$E_{ab} = I \left\{ 1 - \left(\frac{p_i{}^b}{p_i{}^a} \right)^{k_i/(1-k_i)} \right\} \leqq I\,, \tag{3}$$

$$\Delta I_{ab} = I \left\{ 1 - \left(\frac{p_i{}^b}{p_i{}^a} \right)^{k_i} \right\} \leqq I\,, \tag{4}$$

$$\Delta I'_{ab} = I \left\{ \left(\frac{p_i{}^a}{p_i{}^b} \right)^{k_i} - 1 \right\} > \Delta I_{ab}\,. \tag{5}$$

In the limit as $p_i{}^a$ goes to infinity we have

$$E_{ab} = I = \Delta I_{ab}\,, \tag{6}$$

$$\Delta I'_{ab} = \infty\,. \tag{7}$$

When the Marshallian assumptions are met perfectly, the area under the demand curve is not equal to the amount that a perfectly discriminating monopolist could exact from the consumer by an all or none offer—even though the marginal utility of income is constant!

HISTORICAL SUMMARY

In concluding I should like to touch briefly on the history of the discussion of the marginal utility of income. As cited earlier, Marshall assumed constancy in the first sense as a basis for his doctrine of consumer's surplus. He also employed constancy in the second sense to show that market price is determinate. It is amusing in this connection to notice that he did not feel it necessary to point out that the accidental determinateness of final price in this case is accompanied by complete indeterminateness in the quantity of one of the goods.

Pareto disliked the constancy of the marginal utility of income, although it is not possible to infer unambiguously from his *Manuel* in which sense he interpreted this. He clearly considers it to be constant with respect to $(n - 1)$ prices; since he does not differentiate with respect to the price of the *numéraire* good, either interpretation might hold. Throughout he deals only with the case of independent utilities. An incomplete derivation of the theorem of unitary price elasticity of demand for each good under these conditions suggests that it would be necessary to adopt the first interpretation.

Assuming marginal utility of income to be constant, utilities to be independent, and the proportion spent on each good to be small relative to the income elasticities of demand, Pigou suggested that the ratio of the price elasticities of demand of two goods is equal to the ratio of their respective income elasticities of demand.[17] The latter can be computed from budgetary studies. By the use of a theorem established by Friedman[18] it can be shown that this same conclusion follows from the second and third of these assumptions and is independent of the assumption of constancy of the marginal utility of income. It still seems to depend upon independence of utilities, the empirical implication of which I deal with in a forthcoming paper.

Aside from its use in connection with consumer's surplus, the main concern of writers has been to derive the negative slope of the demand curve by means of the assumption of constancy. For it is only when marginal utility of income is constant and utilities are independent that the slope of the demand curve can be derived from the behavior of the curve of marginal utility. In this case, the alleged law of diminishing marginal utility implies negatively sloping demand curves. We have seen here that the rigorous assumption of this relation for every good implies something much more definite; namely, unitary price and income elasticity of demand and vanishing cross-elasticities of demand.

[17] A. C. Pigou, *Economics of Welfare* (London, 1920), Appen. II.
[18] *Op. cit.*

6

Comparative Statics and the Logic of Economic Maximizing

I

Recently Professor George J. Stigler[1] made an interesting and startling calculation which showed that a scientist's definition of an adequate yearly diet for an adult economist could be bought in 1939 for $39.93 and in 1944 for $59.88. Taking the National Research Council's minimum standards seriously, and assuming that each nutritional element (calories, protein, calcium, iron, vitamin A, thiamine, riboflavin, niacin, ascorbic acid) could be regarded as *proportional* to the quantity of each food, Stigler was able to use Bureau of Labour Statistics' prices to make his calculations.

Mathematically, each unit of the ith of n goods $(X_1, X_2, \ldots X_i, \ldots X_n)$ is assumed to have $(A_{1i}, A_{2i}, \ldots, A_{mi})$ amounts of each of m nutritional elements $(A_1, \ldots A_m)$. That is, a quart of milk is assumed to have a certain number of calories, a certain amount of iron, etc. If the minimum standards of the National Research Council are $(\bar{A}_1, \bar{A}_2, \ldots, \bar{A}_m)$, then for an adequate diet, we must have the total of each element from all foods be at least equal to the prescribed minima ; or :

$$\sum_{i=1}^{n} A_{1i} X_i \geq \bar{A}_1$$
$$\sum_{i=1}^{n} A_{2i} X_i \geq \bar{A}_2 \quad \ldots\ldots\ldots\ldots\ldots\ldots\ldots\ldots\ldots\ldots\ldots\ldots\ldots\ldots(1)$$
$$\sum_{i=1}^{n} A_{mi} X_i \geq \bar{A}_m$$

Stigler assumes that a surplus of any element other than calories does no harm, which is approximately true and acceptable for present purposes.

Economically, we are to minimise the cost of an adequate diet. Thus :

$$C = P_1X_1 + P_2X_2 + \ldots + P_iX_i + \ldots + P_nX_n \qquad (2)$$

is to be a minimum subject to the above relations.

This is a wicked mathematical problem despite its seeming simplicity. The differential calculus does not help us much, because of the linearity of the cost expression and of the constraints ; moreover, the constraints may be inequalities rather than linear equalities. As a result, the minimum cost combination can be found only by systematic trial-and-error. And instead of the minimum point looking like the bottom of a hammock (with certain implied marginal or first derivative equalities), it looks like the bottom of a leaning step-ladder and can only be defined by inequalities.

Stigler's approximate solutions are given in the enclosed tables. That they are near to perfection is shown by the fact that the least-cost combination must certainly exceed the cheapest cost of securing any one single nutritional element.[2]

II

I do not wish at this time to go into the problem of how to find or to approximate the least-cost combination. I do want to point out a rather remarkable fact : *Without*

[1] George J. Stigler : " The Cost of Subsistence," from *Journal of Farm Economics*, Vol. XXVII, May, 1945, pp. 303–14.

[2] That is, the optimum C is greater than the maximum with respect to j of the minimum with respect to i of $P_i\bar{A}_j/A_{ji}$.

Minimum-Cost Annual Diets, August, 1939 *and* 1944.

Commodity	August, 1939		August, 1944	
	Quantity	Cost	Quantity	Cost
Evaporated Milk	57 cans	$3.84	—	—
Dried Navy Beans ..	285lb.	$16.80	—	—
Wheat Flour	370lb.	$13.33	535lb.	$34.53
Cabbage	111lb.	$4.11	107lb.	$5.23
Spinach	23lb.	$1.85	13lb.	$1.56
Pancake Flour	—	—	134lb.	$13.08
Pork Liver	—	—	25lb.	$5.48
Total Cost		$39.93		$59.88

knowing how to find the optimum cost combination in each of two price situations, we can nevertheless deduce how the optimal quantities must change in response to price changes. The method of attack, which depends only on simple arithmetic and logic, is a special application of a general technique that I have used repeatedly in the *Foundations of Economic Analysis.*[1]

In particular, we can rule out the possibility of Giffen's Paradox, wherein the amount consumed of a good increases as its price rises. Thus, we can definitely refute Stigler's conjecture :

" In this connection it is interesting to notice that the quantity of wheat flour is increased substantially between the two dates, although its price rose more than other eligible cereals. This is an artificial example of the Giffen paradox (of a positively-shaped demand curve.)" (p. 312).

Actually, Giffen's paradox is impossible in this case since " substitution effects " rather than " income effects " are involved.

The proof is simple and follows from the fundamental inequality implied in the definition of a least-cost combination. Let P^a and X^a represent respectively the first price situation and a resulting least-cost combination satisfying the adequate-diet criteria. Let P^b and X^b be the corresponding prices and optimal quantities in a second situation. Then obviously by definition of a least-cost combination.

$$\Sigma \ P^a X^b \geqslant \Sigma \ P^a X^a \dots\dots\dots\dots\dots\dots\dots\dots\dots\dots\dots\dots\dots (3)$$
$$\Sigma \ P^b X^a \geqslant \Sigma \ P^b X^b$$

Simply adding these two inequalities and rearranging terms, we get the interesting result :

$$\Sigma \ (P^b - P^a) \ (X^b - X^a) = \triangle P_1 \triangle X_1 + \triangle P_2 \triangle X_2 + \dots + \triangle P_n \triangle X_n \leqslant 0 \dots (4)$$

Obviously if only one price changes, say P_1, then the change in its quantity must be of opposite sign, because in this case we have :

$$\triangle P_1 \triangle X_1 + 0 + \dots + 0 \leqslant 0 \dots\dots\dots\dots\dots\dots\dots\dots\dots\dots\dots (5)$$

Therefore, strictly speaking, Giffen's Paradox cannot apply.

One small generalization of our results is possible. Suppose X^a and X^b are not necessarily *perfectly* optimum combinations. But suppose only that X^b is a better

[1] Particularly in Chapters 3, 4 and 5.

adjustment to P^b than the original X^a would be. And likewise that X^a is better adjusted to P^a than X^b would have been. (That is, we assume that the changed price situation has not had a favourable " shock " effect whereby the consumer is forced into doing what he should originally have been doing anyway). This is enough to give us the hypotheses of (3) and the results of (4) and (5).

III

I shall now turn from the problem of Stigler to a mathematically more intricate problem considered by Tintner and others.[1] Suppose a consumer has an infinitely large number of variables to determine, as in the case where he must determine the best way of spending his money over every instant of time. Then instead of his ordinal utility depending upon a large number of variables of the form $F(x_1, x_2, \ldots)$, it becomes a " functional " of the whole time shape of his consumption ; or

$$U = F\left[X_{t_0}^{t_1}(t)\right] \quad \dotfill \quad (6)$$

The total cost over time now becomes an integral rather than a sum. Neglecting the factor of interest (or including interest in with prices), this becomes :

$$C = \int_{t_0}^{t_1} P(t)\, X(t)\, dt \quad \dotfill \quad (7)$$

where the prices are known.

Formally, it is possible to state that C is at a minimum for a fixed level of U only when certain conditions on " functional derivatives " and prices are realised. But these do not get us very far, unless they help us to predict how $X(t)$ will change with a change in the time shape of $P(t)$. Unfortunately, this is not a case of definite quadratic forms and determinants. Mathematically, one would have to—through limiting processes or otherwise—develop a theory of integral equations, definite " kernels," and many other quite complicated relations—possibly involving an infinite number of unknowns.

This mathematical work has been done in part. It should be carried farther. But it is of interest to note that the same simple method that gave definite results in the Stigler case, will easily lead the reader to the corresponding result :

$$\int_{t_0}^{t_1} [P^b(t) - P^a(t)]\ [X^b(t) - X^a(t)]\ dt \leqslant 0, \quad \dotfill \quad (8)$$

for U constant.

This shows that the fundamental maximum-minimum conditions of economic life have intrinsically little to do with the formal techniques of the calculus or the equivalences of the literary " marginal analysis." In fact concentrating on marginal equivalances rather than on " secondary " (sic !) inequalities, obscures the important implied theorems of comparative statics-theorems whose enunciation is the sole *raison d'etre* of equilibrium analysis.

Cambridge, Massachusetts.   PAUL A. SAMUELSON.

[1] See the references in G. Tintner's *Henry Schultz Volume* essay (University of Chicago Press, 1942).

7

THE GRAPHIC DEPICTION OF ELASTICITY OF DEMAND

C. C. HOLT AND P. A. SAMUELSON

I. POINT ELASTICITY

THE present note describes a method for measuring and recognizing the elasticity of demand. The method is so simple that it must have been used by many teachers, but the writers have not been able to find any mention of it in the literature.

Marshall and other writers have shown how the elasticity of demand may be appraised graphically by comparing the lengths of certain line segments. This method suffers from one drawback. The human eye cannot easily determine when a given point exactly bisects a line, as it must in these methods whenever elastic and inelastic demands are to be identified. Moreover, none of these methods emphasizes sufficiently that elasticity and slope are not at all the same thing—except on double-log paper. The present method, based upon the comparison of parallel lines, at least partially remedies these deficiencies.

In Figure 1 we wish to measure the elasticity of demand at point A, or at least to recognize whether demand is elastic, inelastic, or of unitary elasticity. This is done in the following steps:

1. Draw the tangent to the demand curve at A.
2. Complete the total revenue rectangle at point A by drawing a broken horizontal price line from A to the price axis and by drawing in a broken vertical quantity line from A to the quantity axis.
3. Draw in the revenue rectangle diagonal traveling from northwest down to southeast.

Then the elasticity of demand is given by the ratio of the slope of the diagonal line to the slope of the tangent line. If the two lines are parallel, then the elasticity of demand is unitary. If the two lines tend to meet below and to the right, then demand is inelastic. If the two lines tend to meet above and to the left, then demand is elastic.[1]

This method emphasizes for the student and teacher that elasticity is not a slope but rather a comparison of slopes. Furthermore, the human eye can easily perceive the slightest deviation from a parallel condition. Finally, by the present method the student can easily recognize why every demand curve becomes infinitely elastic when so little is sold that the curve intersects the price axis.

II. ARC OR CHORD ELASTICITY

If we wish to measure the elasticity of demand not at a point but over a chord or an arc of finite length, a number of alternative definitions are possible. Despite the considerable number of papers written on this subject,[2] it is perhaps insufficiently realized that only one definition is satisfactory if the following simple (consistency) postulate is agreed upon: *that whenever two price-quantity situations lie along a curve of constant point*

[1] This may be simply proved from the definition of point elasticity as $-(dq/dp)(p/q)$ or as $-(p/q) \div (dp/dq)$. The numerator of the last expression is clearly nothing but the slope of the diagonal line. And the denominator is clearly the slope of the tangent line.

[2] A. Marshall, *Principles of Economics* (8th ed.), p. 102, n. 1, and "Mathematical Note III," p. 839; H. Dalton, *The Inequality of Income* (1920), p. 192; H. Schultz, *Statistical Laws of Demand and Supply with Special Reference to Sugar* (1928), p. 7; A. J. Nichol, "Measures of Average Elasticity of Demand," *Journal of Political Economy*, XXXIX (1931), 249, and "Further Note," *ibid.*, p. 658; A. P. Lerner, "The Diagrammatical Representation of the Elasticity of Demand," *Review of Economic Studies*, I (1933–34), 39, 229; R. G. D. Allen, "The Concept of Arc Elasticity of Demand," *Review of Economic Studies*, I (1933–34), 226.

elasticity, the arc elasticity of demand shall be equal to that constant value regardless of the size of the step. In that case, the only correct measure of arc elasticity of demand between any two points (q_1, p_1) and (q_2, p_2) is given by

$$-\frac{\Delta \log q}{\Delta \log p} = -\frac{\log q_2 - \log q_1}{\log p_2 - \log p_1}.$$

Graphically, this "true" elasticity is measured by the slope of the straight-line chord joining the two points plotted on double-log paper.

However, a number of teachers prefer not to use logarithms. In this case a number of makeshift definitions are possible which at least satisfy the above basic consistency postulate *along a line of constant total outlay* where point elasticity is always unitary.

Figure 2 shows two of the better known of these. If the elasticity of demand between A and B is to be measured, then the following steps are to be followed: (1) Instead of the instantaneous tangent to the curve, draw a straight-line chord connecting the two points in question. (2) Draw in the two total revenue rectangles corresponding to the two points in question. (3) Instead of drawing in diagonal lines within either of the two rectangles, rather draw a line connecting the upper left-hand corner of the *highest* price point with the lower right-hand corner of the *highest* quantity point. Or, as an alternative, connect the upper left-hand corner of the *lower* price situation with the lower right-hand corner of the *lower* quantity situation. (In terms of the diagram, connect either crosses or circles, but do not mix them up.) A third measure of arc elasticity will result from using the diagonal of a revenue rectangle drawn to a point midway between A and B.

Then just as point elasticity was given by a comparison of the rectangle's slope with the curve's slope, so arc elasticity is given by a comparison of either of the two indicated rectangle slopes with the slope along the chord AB.

If total outlay is the same in the two situations, both measures will indicate unitary elasticity of demand. If total outlay is

lower in the lower price situation, both will indicate elasticity of demand less than unity. But the two numerical measures will not be equal. Indeed, the first or "upper" measure will be greater than the "true" elasticity of demand, and the other measure will be smaller. If total outlay is larger at the lower price situation, both measures will be greater than unity; but now the second measure will be smaller numerically than the "true" measure and the first measure will be larger than the "true."

We may summarize these relations in two sentences: The first or "upper" measure of elasticity always lies between unity and the "true" elasticity. The "true" measure always lies between unity and the second "lower" measure.[3]

[3] The first or "upper" measure may be written symbolically as

$$E_u = -(\Delta q/\Delta p)\,(p_u/q_u),$$

where p_u and q_u refer to the larger of the two prices and quantities. The definition of the second or "lower" measure can easily be written down by analogy. Allen has objected to these Lerner definitions on the ground that, if the points are not treated asymmetrically in a mathematical sense, nevertheless they are treated asymmetrically in at least a *notational* sense. This objection will not hold up, since mathematicians often write for the maximum of two quantities the symmetrical, but rather lengthy, expression,

$$p_u = \tfrac{1}{2}(p_1 + p_2 + |p_2 - p_1|).$$

By changing the second plus sign to a minus sign, the smaller of two quantities can also be written in a symmetrical form.

If the "true" elasticity of demand is n, and if λ represents the fractional price decrease between the two situations, then it is not hard to show that

$$E_u = -(1 - \lambda^n) \div (1 - \lambda)$$

and

$$E_L = -\left(1 - \frac{1}{\lambda^n}\right) \div \left(1 - \frac{1}{\lambda}\right).$$

Also $E_L = E_u \lambda^{1-n}$. From these relations, it follows that as $\lambda \to 1$, $E_u \equiv n \equiv E_L$. Also, $E_L < n < E_u < 1$ whenever $n < 1$; and $1 < E_u < n < E_L$ whenever $n > 1$. The arithmetic mean of E_L and E_u approaches n extremely rapidly as $\lambda \to 1$, the difference being an infinitesimal of higher order. The same can be said for the third "midpoint" measure mentioned earlier.

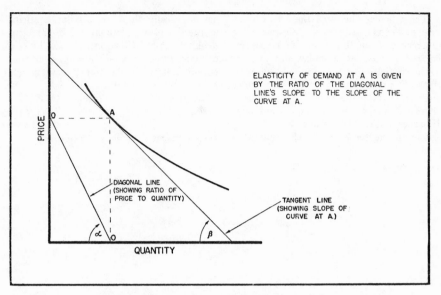

FIG. 1.—Graphic depiction of demand elasticity at a point

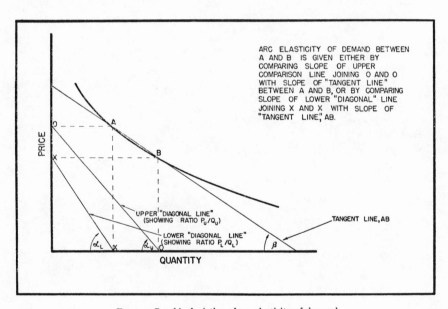

FIG. 2.—Graphic depiction of arc elasticity of demand

The difference between these two measures of arc elasticity and their respective divergences from the "true" or consistent logarithmic measure obviously increases (1) as the elasticity of demand in the two situations differs more and more from unity and (2) as the percentage size of the price change differs more and more from zero. However, both measures are "locally" consistent in the sense that each approaches asymptotically the correct point elasticity as the size of the price change becomes indefinitely small. However, this can be said of many measures which are not even consistent indicators of unitary elasticity; as, for example, the usual textbook definition in which one point or the other is taken as a base.

MASSACHUSETTS INSTITUTE OF TECHNOLOGY

8

Some Implications of "Linearity."[1]

Statisticians often make the assumption that various economic relations can be approximated, within a given range of observable data, by linear relationships. This is a perfectly proper procedure. As applied to the measurement of demand for good X_i in terms of prices $P_1, \ldots, P_n$ and income, r, this involves the customary Taylor's series approximation around any given point $(X_1^0, X_2^0, \ldots, X_n^0; P_1^0, P_2^0, \ldots, P_n^0, r^0)$;

or $X_i = X_i^0 + \left(\dfrac{\partial X_i}{\partial P_1}\right)^0 (P_1 - P_1^0) + \ldots + \left(\dfrac{\partial X_i}{\partial P_n}\right)^0 (P_n - P_n^0) + \left(\dfrac{\partial X_i}{\partial r}\right)^0 (r - r^0) +$

remainder. So long as the price and income changes are small, the remainder error term can often be neglected. The change in the cost of living, r, along an initial level of satisfaction, U^0, can be written down to an even higher order of approximation as:

$$r = r^0 + \sum_i X_i\ (P_i - P_i^0) + \frac{1}{2} \sum_j \sum_k \left(\frac{\partial X_k}{\partial P_j}\right)_{U^0} (P_k - P_k^0)\ (P_j - P_j^0) + \text{remainder}$$

where $\left(\dfrac{\partial X_k}{\partial P_j}\right)_{U^0} = \left(\dfrac{\partial X_j}{\partial P_k}\right)_{U^0} = \dfrac{\partial X_j}{\partial P_k} + X_k \dfrac{\partial X_j}{\partial r}$ are the Slutsky-Hicks compensated substitution terms. Without making stronger assumptions no better result can be stated.

No empirical limitations are implied by the above kind of "local" linearity assumption. The parameters $(\partial X_i/\partial P_j)^0$ and $(\partial X_i/\partial r)^0$ are actually functions of the initial point (X^0, P^0, r^0).

But the assumption[2] that:

$$X_i = \beta_i\ \gamma_1\ \frac{P_1}{P_i} + \ldots + \beta_i\ \gamma_n \frac{P_n}{P_i} - \gamma_i + \beta_i\ \frac{r}{P_i}$$

is not a local linearity assumption. It has numerous restrictive empirical implications; indeed, it is only because of these implications that the particular formula for measuring the cost of living emerges.

Some of the empirical implications may be briefly indicated. Suppose that at some point $\partial X_1/\partial P_2$ and $\partial X_1/\partial P_3$ were evaluated. Then instead of the ratio $(\partial X_4/\partial P_2) \div (\partial X_4/\partial P_3)$ being a variable to be determined by the facts, it and many other ratios would be frozen. Similarly, a person's cross-elasticity of demand, when poor, would have to be the same as when he is rich. Numerous other implied strait-jackets on the facts could be pointed out.

However, in this case, the full empirical implications can be neatly summarized in the following stringent empirical assumption:

(a) The consumer is assumed always to buy a *necessary set* of goods, $(\overline{X}_1, \overline{X}_2, \ldots, \overline{X}_n) = (-\gamma_1, -\gamma_2, \ldots, -\gamma_n)$;

(b) Any algebraic income left over after buying this necessary set is spent in constant proportions $(\beta_1, \beta_2, \ldots, \beta_n = 1 - \beta_2 - \ldots)$ on the various goods.

---

[1] Included in Cowles Commission Paper, New Series, No. 26.

[2] This is the fundamental equation of the Klein-Rubin paper, "A Constant-Utility Index of the Cost of Living," *The Review of Economic Studies*, Vol. XV (2), No. 38 (1947–1948), pp. 84–87. Together with the familiar Slutsky relations and the requirement that the demand functions be homogeneous of order zero in all prices and income, their strong linearity assumption —that each good is a strictly linear function of the ratio of other prices to its price and of income to its price—implies this fundamental equation.

This follows from rewriting our equation :

$$X_i = \Sigma \; \beta_i \; \gamma_j \; \frac{P_j}{P_i} - \gamma_i - \beta_i \; \frac{r}{P_i}$$

as

$$X_i = X_i + \frac{\beta_i \; (r - \Sigma \; P_k \; \overline{X}_k)}{P_i}$$

where $-\gamma_i$ has been replaced by X_i and where the expression in parenthesis is " super-numerary " income remaining after buying the necessary batch $(\overline{X}_1, \ldots, \overline{X}_n)$.

Immediately this explains the intuitive meaning of the cost-of-living formula. By itself, the necessary batch would imply a simple summation cost-of-living formula : $\Sigma \; P_i \overline{X}_i = - \Sigma \; P_i \gamma_i$. The proportionality of expenditure assumption, by itself, is known to lead to a weighted geometric mean formula for the cost of living : $\Pi P_i \beta^i$. Therefore, we get in this case a linear combination of the two, with the " constant of integration," C, being determined by the relative importance of necessary expenditure and supernumerary income.

By working with new variables $X_i = X_i - \overline{X}_i$, we also quickly see that the ordinal utility or preference field must be of the form :

$$U = F \; [\beta_1 \log X_1{}' + \ldots + \beta_n \log X_n{}']$$
$$= F \; [\beta_1 \log (X_1 - \overline{X}_1) + \ldots + \beta_n \log (\overline{X}_n - X_n)]$$

where F is any function with $F' > o$.

This is a highly restrictive empirical assumption, indeed. Such facts as are available concerning budgetary family data do not appear to be in accord with this hypothesis. Thus, on an indifference curve diagram, we do not find income expansion paths that are straight lines converging on a single focal point, as this theory requires.

In conclusion, the question may be asked as to the empirical observations needed to refute or verify the non-local linearity hypothesis under discussion. What kind and how many observations are needed to determine the n constants $\overline{X}_1, \ldots, \overline{X}_n$ and the $(n - 1)$ constants $(\beta_1, \ldots, \beta_{n-1})$? Each single price-quantity observation seems to imply $(n - 1)$ independent implicit equations for these parameters. One might hope, therefore, that just more than two independent price and income situations would be sufficient.

However, the problem is not this simple. The P's and γ's, taken together, are not involved in a linear fashion, since cross-products appear. A full answer would involve mathematical reasoning of more complexity. But whatever the requisite number of observations, be it 3, 4, or more, one single additional observation could be used to check the hypothesis.

As a matter of fact, without solving the mathematical question of the minimum number of observations needed to determine the parameters, we can still state various special ways of refuting the hypothesis in question. Thus, along any constant-price budget path, the β's are simply the marginal propensities to consume the different goods, and we can easily check on their constancy by means of three or more observations. With two points on each of a number of different budget lines, we can also check upon the constancy and uniformity of the β's. With pairs of points from three or more budget lines, we can check on the existence of a focal point of convergency of budgetary expansion paths.

If two points on the same budget path are available, it is obvious that the β's are all determined, and the X's are left indeterminate only upon a straight line, with only one degree of freedom left. A third point along the same straight line will not add to our information. But a single observation on a different budget line will, in a simple two commodity world, be just sufficient to determine the remaining degree of freedom of the X's. If there are more than two commodities, the problem is over-determined ; hence, with two points on one budget line and with a third different point, we could conveniently refute the assumed hypothesis of " linearity."

An important word of qualification should be added. All the above disregards the inevitable stochastical " errors " present in any empirical situation. Only if each observation were perfectly " exact " could the minimum number of observations described above be sufficient to test our hypothesis. No one would be so foolish as to think that three observations could tell us much about anything. In practice we should have to have numerous repeated independent observations in order to have confidence in our empirical inferences."

Cambridge, Mass.   P. A. SAMUELSON.

9

Consumption Theory in Terms of Revealed Preference

By Paul A. Samuelson

1. Introduction

A DECADE ago I suggested that the economic theory of consumer's behaviour can be largely built up on the notion of " revealed preference ". By comparing the costs of different combinations of goods at different relative price situations, we can infer whether a given batch of goods is preferred to another batch ; the individual guinea-pig, by his market behaviour, reveals his preference pattern—if there is such a consistent pattern.

Recently, Mr. Ian M. D. Little of Oxford University has made an important contribution to this field.[1] In addition to showing the changes in viewpoint that this theory may lead to, he has presented an ingenious proof that if enough judiciously selected price-quantity situations are available for two goods, we may define a locus which is the precise equivalent of the conventional indifference curve.

I should like, briefly, to present an alternative demonstration of this same result. While the proof is a direct one, it requires a little more mathematical reasoning than does his.

2. Observable Price Ratios and a Fundamental Differential Equation

If we confine ourselves to the case of two commodities, x and y, we could conceptually observe for any individual a number of price-quantity situations. Since only relative prices are assumed to matter, each observation consists of the triplet of numbers, $(p_x/p_y, x, y)$. By manipulating prices and income, we could cause the individual to come into equilibrium at any (x, y) point, at least within a given area. We may also make the simplifying assumption that one and only one price ratio can be associated with each combination of x and y. Theoretically, therefore, we could for any point (x, y) determine a unique p_x/p_y; or

$$(1) \qquad p_x/p_y = f(x, y)$$

where f is an observable function, assumed to be continuous and with continuous partial derivatives.[2]

---

[1] I. M. D. Little : "A Reformulation of the Theory of Consumers' Behaviour", *Oxford Economic Papers*, New Series, No. 1, January, 1949 ; P. A. Samuelson : *Foundations of Economic Analysis* (1947), Ch. V and VI ; P. A. Samuelson : "A Note on the Pure Theory of Consumer's Behaviour ; and an Addendum ", *Economica* (1938), Vol. V (New Series), pp. 61–71, 353–354.

[2] Mathematically, the above continuity assumptions are over-strict. Also, we shall make the unnecessarily strong assumption that in the region under discussion the price-quantity relations have the " simple concavity " property : $f(\partial f/\partial y) - (\partial f/\partial x) > 0$.

The central notion underlying the theory of revealed preference, and indeed the whole modern economic theory of index numbers, is very simple. Through any observed equilibrium point, A, draw the budget-equation straight line with arithmetical slope given by the observed price ratio. Then all combinations of goods on or within the budget line could have been bought in preference to what was

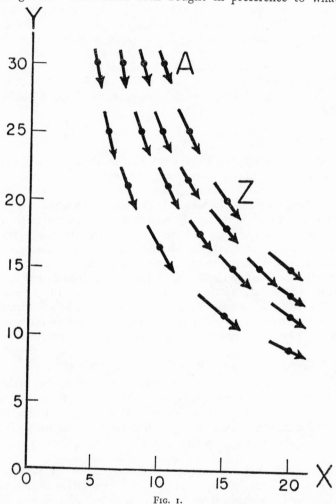

FIG. 1.

actually bought. But they weren't. Hence, they are all " revealed " to be inferior to A. No other line of reasoning is needed.

As yet we have no right to speak of " indifference ", and certainly no right to speak of " indifference slopes ". But nobody can object to our summarising our observable information graphically by drawing a little negative " slope element " at each x and y point, with numerical gradient equal to the price ratio in question.

This is shown in Figure 1 by the numerous little arrows. These little slopes are all that we choose to draw in of the budget lines which go through each point and the directional arrows are only drawn in to guide the eye. It is a well known observation of *Gestalt* psychology that the eye tends to discern smooth contour lines from such a representation, although strictly speaking, only a finite number of little line segments are depicted, and they do not for the most part run into each other.[1] (In the present illustration the contour lines have been taken to be the familiar rectangular hyperbolæ or unitary-elasticity curves and $f(x, y)$ takes the simple form $p_x/p_y = y/x$.)

There is an exact mathematical counterpart of this phenomenon of *Gestalt* psychology. Let us identify a little slope, dy/dx, with each price ratio, $-p_x/p_y$. Then, from (1), we have the simplest differential equation

$$(2) \qquad \frac{dy}{dx} = -f(x, y).$$

It is known mathematically that this defines a unique curve through any given point, and a (one-parameter) family of curves throughout the surrounding (x, y) plane. These solution curves (or " integral solutions " as they are often called) are such that when any one of them is substituted into the above differential equation, it will be found to satisfy that equation. Later we shall verify that these solution curves are the conventional " indifference curves " of modern economic theory. Also, and this is the novel part of the present paper, I shall show that these solution curves are in fact the limiting loci of revealed preference—or in Mr. Little's terminology they are the " behaviour curves " defined for specified initial points. This is our excuse for arbitrarily associating the differential equation system (2) with our observable pattern of prices and quantities summarised in (1).

3. The Cauchy-Lipschitz Process of Approximation

Mathematicians are able to establish rigorously the existence of solutions to the differential equations without having to rely upon the mind's eye as a primitive " differential-analyser " or " integrator ".[2] Also, mathematicians have devised rigorous methods for numerical solution of such equations to any desired (and recognisable) degree of accuracy.

It so happens that one of the simplest methods for proving the existence of, and numerically approximating, a solution is that called the " Cauchy-Lipschitz " method after the men who first made it

---

[1] Every student of elementary physics has dusted iron filings on a piece of paper suspended on a permanent magnet. The little filings become magnetised and orient themselves in a simple pattern. To the mind's eye these appear as " lines of force " of the magnetic field.

[2] The usual proof found in such intermediate texts as F. R. Moulton, *Differential Equations*, Ch. XII–XIII, is that of Picard's " method of successive approximations ". But the earlier rigorous proofs are by the Cauchy-Lipschitz method, which is very closely related to the economic theory of index numbers and revealed preference. See also, R. G. D. Allen, *Mathematical Analysis for Economists*, 1938, Ch. XVI.

rigorous, even though it really goes back to at least the time of Euler. In this method we approximate to our true solution curve by a connected series of straight line-segments, each line having the slope dictated by the differential equation *for the beginning point* of the straight line-segment in question. This means that our differential equation is not perfectly satisfied at all other points ; but if we make our line-segments numerous and short enough, the resulting error from the true solution can be made as small as we please.

Figure 2 illustrates the Cauchy-Lipschitz approximations to the true solution passing through the point A (10,30) and going from $x = 10$, to the vertical line $x = 15$. The top smooth curve is the true unitary-elasticity curve that we hope to approximate. The three lower broken-line curves are successive approximations, improving in accuracy as we move to higher curves.

Our crudest Cauchy-Lipschitz approximation is to use one line-segment for the whole interval. We pass a straight line through A with a slope equal to the little arrow at A, or equal to -3. This is nothing but the familiar budget line through the initial point A ; it intersects the vertical line $x = 15$, at the value $y = 15$ or at the point marked Z'.[1]

(Actually, from the economic theory of index numbers and consumer's choice, we know that this first crude approximation $Z' : (x, y) = (15, 15)$ clearly revealed itself to be " worse " than $(x, \hat{y}) = (10,30)$ —since the former was actually chosen over the latter even though both cost the same amount. This suggests that the Cauchy-Lipschitz process will always approach the true solution curve, or " indifference curve ", *from below*. This is in fact a general truth, as we are about to see.) Can we not get a better approximation to the correct solution than this crude straight line, AZ' ? Yes, if we use two line-segments instead of one. As before let us first proceed on a straight line through A with slope equal to A's little arrow. But let us travel on this line only two-fifths as far as before : to $x = 12$, rather than $x = 15$. This gives us a new point B' (12, 24), whose directional arrow is seen to have the slope of -2. Now, through B' we travel on a new straight line with this new slope ; and our second, better, approximation to the true value at $x = 15$, is given by the new intersection, Z'', with the vertical line, at the level $y = 18$. (The " true " value is obviously at Z on the smooth curve where y must equal 20 if we are to be on the hyperbola with the property $xy = 10 \times 30 = 15 \times 20$; and our second approximation has only $\frac{3}{5}$ the error of our first.)

The general procedure of the Cauchy-Lipschitz process is now clear. Suppose we divide the interval between $x = 10$ and $x = 15$ into 5 equal segments ; suppose we follow each straight line with slope equal to its initial arrow until we reach the end of the interval, and then begin a new straight line. Then as our numerical table shows, we get the still

[1] A Numerical Appendix gives the exact arithmetic underlying this and the following figure.

better approximation, $y = 19\frac{2}{7}$. In Figure 2, the broken line from A to Z''' shows our third approximation.

In the limit as we take enough sub-intervals so that the size of each line-segment becomes indefinitely small, we approach the true value of $y = 20$, and the same is true for the true value at any other x point. How do we know this? Because the pure mathematician assures us that this can be rigorously proved.

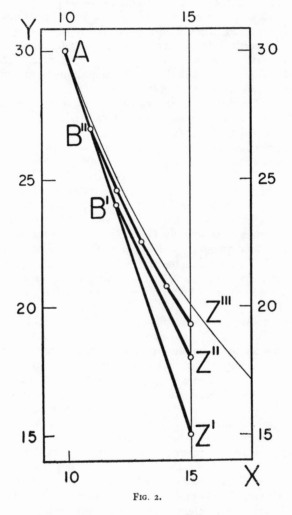

Fig. 2.

In economic terms, the individual is definitely going downhill along any one Cauchy-Lipschitz curve. For just as A was revealed to be better than Z', so also was it revealed to be better than B'. Note too that Z'' is on the budget line of B' and is hence revealed to be inferior to B', which already has been revealed to be worse than A. It follows that Z″ is worse than A.

By the same reasoning Z‴ on the third approximation curve is shown to be inferior to A, although it now takes four intermediate points to make this certain. It follows as a general rule : any Cauchy-Lipschitz path always leads to a final point worse than the initial. And strictly speaking, it is only as an infinite limit that we can hope to reveal the neutral case of " indifference " along the true solution curve to the differential equation.

4. An Indirect Proof of " Limiting Revelation of Indifference "

We have really proved only one thing so far : all points *below* the true mathematical solution passing through an initial point, A, are definitely " revealed to be worse " than A.

We have not rigorously proved that points falling on the solution contour curve are really " equal " to A. Indeed in terms of the strict algebra of " revealed preference " we have as yet no definition of what is meant by " equality " or " indifference ".

Still it would be a great step forward if we could definitely prove the following : all points *above* the true mathematical solution are definitely " revealed to be better " than A.

The next following section gives a direct proof of this fact by defining a new process which is similar to the Cauchy-Lipschitz process and which definitely approximates to the true integral solution *from above*. But it may be as well to digress in this section and show that by indirect reasoning like that of Mr. Little, we may establish the proposition that all points above the solution-contour are clearly better than A.

I shall only sketch the reasoning. Suppose we take any point just vertically above the point Z and regard it as our new initial point. The mathematician assures us that a new " higher " solution-contour goes through such a point. Let us construct a Cauchy-Lipschitz process leftward, or backwards. Then by using small enough line-segments we may approach indefinitely close to *that point vertically above A which lies on the new contour line above A's contour*. A will then have to lie below the leftward-moving Cauchy-Lipschitz curve, and is thus revealed to be worse than any new initial point lying above the old contour line. *Q.E.D.*

We may follow Mr. Little's terminology and give the name " behaviour line " to the unique curve which lies between the points definitely shown to be better than A, and those definitely shown to be worse than A. This happens to coincide with the mathematical solution to the differential equation, and we may care to give this contour line, by courtesy, the title of an indifference curve.[1]

---

[1] If our preference field does not have simple concavity—and why should it ?—we may observe cases where A is preferred to B at some times, and B to A at others. If this is a pattern of consistency and not of chaos, we could choose to regard A and B as " indifferent " under those circumstances. If the preference field has simple concavity, " indifference " will never explicitly reveal itself to us except as the results of an infinite limiting process.

5. A New Approximation Process from Above

Let me return now to the problem of defining a new approximating process, like the conventional Cauchy-Lipschitz process, but which : (1) approaches the mathematical solution from above rather than below, and which (2) definitely reveals the economic preference of the individual at every point.

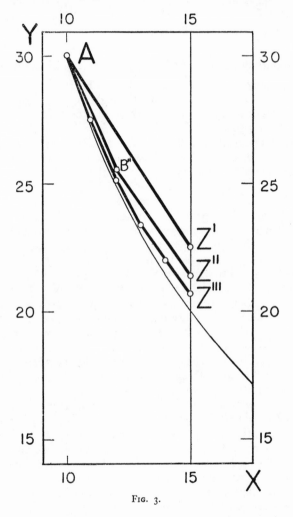

FIG. 3.

Our new process will consist of broken straight lines ; and in the limit these will become numerous enough to approach a smooth curve. But the slopes of the straight line-segments will not be given by their *initial* points, as in the Cauchy-Lipschitz process. Instead, the slope will be determined by the *final* point of the sub-interval's line-segment.

After the reader ponders over this for some time and considers its geometrical significance, he may feel that he is being swindled. How can we determine the slope at the line's final point, without first determining the final point ? But, how can we know the final point of the line unless its slope has already been determined ? Clearly, we are at something of a circular impasse. To determine the slope, we seem already to require the slope.

The way out of this dilemma is perfectly straightforward to anyone who has grasped the mathematical solution of a simultaneous equation. The logical circle is a virtuous rather than a vicious one. By solving the implied simultaneous equation, we cut through the problem of circular interdependence. And in this case we do not need an electronic computer to solve the implied equation. Our human guinea-pig, simply by following his own bent, inadvertently helps to solve our problem for us.

In Figure 3, we again begin with the initial point A. Again we wish to find the true solution for y at $x = 15$. Our first and crudest approximation will consist of one straight line. But its slope will be determined at the end of the interval and is initially unknown. Let us, therefore, through A swing a straight line through all possible angles. One and only one of these slopes will give us a line that is exactly tangent to one of the little arrows at the end of our interval. Let Z' be the point where our straight line is just tangent to an arrow lying in the vertical line. It corresponds to a y value of $22\frac{1}{2}$, which is above the true value of $y = 20$.

Economically speaking, when we rotate a straight " budget line " around an initial point A, and let the individual pick the best combination of goods in each situation, we trace out a so-called " offer curve ". This curve is not drawn in on the figure, but the point Z' is the intersection of the offer curve with the vertical line. It should be obvious from our earlier reasoning that Z' and any other point on the offer curve is revealed to be better than A, since any such equal-cost point is chosen over A.

So much for our crude first approximation. Let us try dividing the interval between $x = 10$ and $x = 15$ up into two sub-intervals so that two connected straight lines may be used. If we wish the first line to end at $x = 12$, we rotate our line through A until its final slope is just equal to the indicated little arrow (or price ratio) along the vertical line $x = 12$. For the simple hyperbolæ in question, where $-p_x/p_y = \frac{dy}{dx} = -y/x$, our straight line will be found to end at the point B'', whose (x, y) coordinates are $(12, 25\frac{4}{7})$ and whose arrow has a slope of just less than (-2).

We now begin at B'' as a new initial point and repeat the process by finding a new straight line over the interval from $x = 12$ to $x = 15$. Pivoting a line through all possible angles, we find tangency only at the point Z'', where $y = 21\frac{3}{7}$, which is still better approximation to the true value, $y = 20$.

The interested reader may easily verify that using more sub-intervals and intermediate points will bring us indefinitely close to the true solution-contour.[1] It is clear therefore that our new process brings us to the true solution in the limit, but unlike the Cauchy-Lipschitz process, it now approaches the solution from above. And we can use the word "above" in more than a geometrical sense. Along the new process lines, the individual is revealing himself to be getting better off. For just as A is inferior to Z', it is by the same reasoning inferior to B", which is likewise inferior to Z"; from which it follows that A is inferior to Z".

It should be clear, therefore, that no matter how many intermediate points there are in the new process, the consumer none the less reveals himself to be travelling uphill. It follows that every point above the mathematical contour line can reveal itself to be better than A.

6. CONCLUSION

This essentially completes the present demonstration. The mathematical contour lines defined by our differential equation have been proved to be the frontier between points revealed to be inferior to A, and points revealed to be superior. The points lying literally on a (concave) frontier locus can never themselves be revealed to be better or worse than A. If we wish, then, we may speak of them as being indifferent to A.

The whole theory of consumer's behaviour can thus be based upon operationally meaningful foundations in terms of revealed preference.[2]

---

[1] He may verify that using the points $x = 10, 11, 12, 13, 14, 15$ brings us to within $\frac{2}{3}$ of $y = 20$, as shown in the second table of the Numerical Appendix.

[2] The above remarks apply without qualification to two dimensional problems where the problem of "integrability" cannot appear. In the multidimensional case there still remain some problems, awaiting a solution for more than a decade now.

NUMERICAL APPENDIX

In the Cauchy-Lipschitz process, the straight line going from (x_0, y_0) to (x_1, y_1) is defined by the explicit equation

$$(a) \qquad y = y_0 - f(x_0, y_0)(x - x_0) = y_0 - \frac{y_0}{x_0}(x - x_0)$$

where $dy/dx = -f(x, y)$ is the differential equation requiring solution —in this case being $= -y/x$. The three approximations given in Figure 2 are derived numerically in the following table.

TABLE I. CAUCHY-LIPSCHITZ APPROXIMATION

x		y	$\dfrac{dy}{dx} = -f(x, y) = -\dfrac{y}{x}$	
	First Approximation			
10	initial point	30	$-30/10 =$	-3
15	$30 - 3(15 - 10) =$	15		
	Second Approximation			
10	initial point	30	$-30/10 =$	-3
12	$30 - 3(12 - 10) =$	24	$-24/12 =$	-2
15	$24 - 2(15 - 12) =$	18		
	Third Approximation			
10	initial point	30	$-30/10 =$	-3
11	$30 - 3(11 - 10) =$	27	$-27/11 =$	$-2\frac{5}{11}$
12	$27 - \dfrac{27}{11}(12 - 11) = \dfrac{270}{11} =$	$24\frac{6}{11}$	$-\dfrac{270}{(11)(12)} =$	$-2\frac{1}{22}$
13	$\dfrac{270}{11} - \dfrac{270}{(11)(12)}(13 - 12) = \dfrac{270}{12} =$	$22\frac{1}{2}$	$-\dfrac{270}{(12)(13)} =$	$-1\frac{19}{26}$
14	$\dfrac{270}{12} - \dfrac{270}{(12)(13)}(14 - 13) = \dfrac{270}{13} =$	$20\frac{10}{13}$	$-\dfrac{270}{(13)(14)} =$	$-1\frac{44}{91}$
15	$\dfrac{270}{13} - \dfrac{270}{(13)(14)}(15 - 14) = \dfrac{270}{14} =$	$19\frac{2}{7}$		

In the new process which approaches the true solution, $y = 300/x$, from above, the straight lines have their slopes determined by the final point of each interval, or by the implicit equation

$$(b) \qquad y_1 = y_0 - f(x_1, y_1)(x_1 - x_0).$$

In the case where $f(x, y) = y/x$, we have

$$y_1 = y_0 - \frac{y_1}{x_1}(x_1 - x_0) \quad \text{or}$$

$$y_1 = \frac{x_1}{2x_1 - x_0} y_0.$$

73

Our numerical approximations are given in the following table:

TABLE 2. NEW APPROXIMATING PROCESS

x_1	$y_1 = \dfrac{x_1}{2x_1 - x_0}(y_0)$	
	First Approximation	
10	initial point	30
15	$\dfrac{15}{2(15) - 10}(30)$	$= 22\frac{1}{2}$
	Second Approximation	
10	initial point	30
12	$\dfrac{12}{2(12) - 10}(30) =$	$\dfrac{180}{7} = 25\frac{4}{7}$
15	$\dfrac{15}{2(15) - 12}\dfrac{180}{7} =$	$\dfrac{150}{7} = 21\frac{3}{7}$
	Third Approximation	
10	initial point	30
11	$\dfrac{11}{2(11) - 10}(30) =$	$\dfrac{330}{12} = 27\frac{1}{2}$
12	$\dfrac{12}{2(12) - 11}\dfrac{330}{12} = \dfrac{12}{13}\dfrac{330}{12} =$	$\dfrac{330}{13} = 25\frac{5}{13}$
13	$\dfrac{13}{2(13) - 12}\dfrac{330}{13} = \dfrac{13}{14}\dfrac{330}{13} =$	$\dfrac{330}{14} = 23\frac{3}{7}$
14	$\dfrac{14}{2(14) - 13}\dfrac{330}{14} = \dfrac{14}{15}\dfrac{330}{14} =$	$\dfrac{330}{15} = 22$
15	$\dfrac{15}{2(15) - 14}\dfrac{330}{15} = \dfrac{15}{16}\dfrac{330}{15} =$	$\dfrac{330}{16} = 20\frac{5}{8}$

It may be mentioned that the third Cauchy-Lipschitz approximation satisfies the equation $270/x$ which is less than the true solution, $300/x$; and the third approximation of the new upper process satisfies the equation $330/x$, which happens to be equally in excess of the true solution.

74

10

The Problem of Integrability in Utility Theory[1]

By Paul A. Samuelson

1. Historical Survey of the Integrability Issue

A chapter in the history of utility theory has now been brought to a close by Mr. Houthakker's[2] important discussion of integrability. As far back as 1886, G. B. Antonelli[3] had noted that such a problem existed and seems to have given the correct " integrability conditions ". But to most economists this problem was first introduced by Irving Fisher's[4] 1892 study—perhaps the best of all doctoral dissertations in economics. Even here it is introduced pretty much as an afterthought so that it is no great wonder that Pareto's *Manuale di economica politica*[5] (1906) should have neglected this topic—even though Pareto was clearly aware of Fisher's work and had discussed integrability in journal articles as far back as 1893.

Vito Volterra[6] in his 1906 review of the *Manuale* performed one of the few services professional mathematicians have ever rendered to economic theory : he pointed out that when Pareto treats the case of three or more goods, his discussion of indifference directions is marred by the failure to recognise explicitly the integrability problem. Pareto admitted his mistake and discussed the problem a few

[1] Dedicated to the memory of Joseph A. Schumpeter, who had a lifelong interest in the logical foundations of utility theory.

[2] H. S. Houthakker: "Revealed Preference and the Utility Function", *Economica*, May 1950.

[3] G. B. Antonelli: *Teoria mathematica della economica politica*, Pisa (1886). This seems to be a rare item. I know of it only from the extension of Jevons' *Bibliography of mathematical economic writings*, and from the detailed reference by Wold in a paper later to be cited.

[4] Irving Fisher: "Mathematical Investigations in the Theory of Value and Prices", *Transactions of the Connecticut Academy*, Vol. IX, July 1892, and reproduced in a 1925 Yale Press edition, pp. 88–9. Recognition of non-integrability seems almost an afterthought in Fisher; since he uses his teacher, Gibbs' vector notation, Gibbs may have suggested the problem to him. If in 1892 Fisher was willing to entertain the hypothesis of non-integrability, it none the less seems that in all his later work he really believed in integrability.

[5] V. Pareto: *Manuale di economica politica*, Milan (1906). I have not checked the non-mathematical text to see whether Pareto had really neglected non-integrability completely.

[6] V. Volterra: Review of Pareto's *Manuale*, in *Giornale degli economisti*, Vol. 32 (2nd ser., 1906), pp. 296–301. Cf. Pareto's reply, *Ibid.*, Vol. 33, pp. 15–30.

months later in the same journal; most of this discussion is repeated in the improved French version, the *Manuel d'économie politique* (1909) and deals with the puzzling problem of "open and closed cycles" of consumption.[1] Professor E. B. Wilson,[2] when he reviewed the *Manuel* in 1912, expressed the opinion that the economist could throw out of court the integrability problem, however natural it might be for mathematicians to worry about it. He also expressed the interesting opinion that as a result of some remarks of J. Willard Gibbs, Yale's distinguished physicist, Fisher may have changed his mind concerning the admissibility of non-integrability.

W. E. Johnson's classic 1913 paper on utility[3] makes no mention of the integrability problem (nor for that matter of the work of Fisher and other important earlier writers). Eugen Slutsky[4] in his remarkable, but too little known, 1915 Italian article showed that the existence of an integrable utility surface had definite testable implications for cross-elasticities of individual's demand : i.e., a "compensated change" in the price of good i must have exactly the same effect on the quantity of j demanded as does a compensated change in the price of j have on the demand for i.

In his *Mathematical Groundwork of Economics* (1924) Professor A. L. Bowley does not, as far as I can see, anywhere deal with the problem of integrability. Professor G. C. Evans, an eminent mathematician, gives one of the most extensive discussions of this problem in *Mathematical Introduction to Economics* (1930).[5] Most of the arguments for non-integrability are contained in his treatment ; these will be discussed in some detail later.

———

We may now move into the modern era, which I arbitrarily date from R. G. D. Allen's foundation article of 1932.[6]

[1] V. Pareto : *Manuel d'économie politique*, Paris (1909) pp. 539–57, 249–51.

[2] Edwin B. Wilson, Review of Pareto's *Manuel*, in *Bulletin of the American Mathematical Society*, Vol. 18 (1912).

[3] W. E. Johnson : "Pure Theory of Utility Curves", *Economic Journal*, Vol. 23 (1913), pp. 483–513.

[4] E. Slutsky : "Sulla teoria de bilancio del consumatora," *Giornale degli economisti*, Vol. 51 (1915), pp. 1–26. See also R. G. D. Allen's description of this paper in *Review of Economic Studies*, Vol. 13 (1935–6), pp. 120–9.

[5] Ch. IX, pp. 119–22.

[6] R. G. D. Allen : "The Foundation of a Mathematical Theory of Exchange", *Economica*, Vol. 12 (1932), pp. 219–23. See also J. R. Hicks and R. G. D. Allen : "A Reconsideration of the Theory of Value", *Economica*, Vol. 14 (1934), I, pp. 52–76 and II, pp. 196–219 ; R. G. D. Allen : *Mathematical Analysis for Economists* (1937), pp. 438–42, 509–17.

This was a necessary preliminary for the later articles of Hicks-Allen and for their separate later writings. Allen was unacquainted with Slutsky's work but refers to most of the other important early writers. He entertains the hypothesis of non-integrability; and if I dare impute any differences to the separate components of the Hicks-Allen composite commodity, I would say that Hicks consistently rules out the non-integrability case, while Allen accepts it as the more general hypothesis. At least Allen in his 1932, 1934, and 1937 treatments deals at length with non-integrability, while Hicks in his 1934, 1937, and 1939 treatments goes out of his way to make it clear that he is against non-integrability.[1] Hicks-Allen also noted an empirical implication of integrability that is the inverse of the Slutsky reciprocity relation: under integrability, when tea is a substitute for coffee *vis-à-vis* a third commodity, then according to their same 1934 definition, coffee must be numerically equal as a substitute for tea.

As a partial digression, I should mention the 1932 work of Hotelling on the related problem of profit-maximisation by a firm *not* subject to a budgetary constraint.[2] Integrability conditions arise there which are related to, but distinct from, those that arise in the case of a consumer under budgetary constraint.[3] In this connection, the reader can be referred to Henry Schultz' 1937 book which gives an extensive discussion of the integrability question: while not itself an entirely satisfactory resolution of the problem, Schultz' pages give a very good summary of the uncertainties that pervade the literature.[4]

Professor Nicholas Georgescu-Roegen, now of Vanderbilt University, wrote in 1936 one of the most important

---

[1] J. R. Hicks: *Economica*, Vol. 14 (1934), p. 53; *Théorie mathématique de la valeur* (1937), p. 7; *Value and Capital* (1939), p. 19.

[2] H. Hotelling: "Edgeworth's Taxation Paradox and . . . Demand . . . Functions", *Journal of Political Economy*, Vol. 40 (1932), pp. 577–616.

[3] However, if we are willing to make very special assumptions of a good with constant marginal cardinal utility, we can write $U(x_1, \ldots, x_n) = x_1 + V(x_2, \ldots, x_n)$ for proper choice of units. This is to be a maximum subject to the budget constraint $1 . x_1 + p_2 x_2 + \ldots p_n x_n = I$; and thus, with income effects emasculated, the consumer can be thought of as maximising *without* constraint

$$V(x_2, \ldots, x_n) - p_2 x_2 - p_3 x_3 - \ldots - p_n x_n + I$$

which is precisely of the Hotelling 1932 form. (See pp. 592ff.) Later Hotelling addressed himself directly to the consumer problem and restated definitely some of the reciprocity conditions implied by integrability on the partial derivatives of price ratio functions of quantities of goods. H. Hotelling: "Demand Function with Limited Budgets", *Econometrica*, Vol. 3 (1935), pp. 66–78.

[4] H. Schultz: *Theory and Measurement of Demand* (1937), pp. 17–18, 575–81, 623ff. The bibliography is very complete.

clarifications of the problem of integrability and also of
the even more subtle problems of transitivity.[1]   Until
re-reading his article recently, I did not realise how much it
must have stimulated my own work on the subject, as
embodied in two 1938 articles and later.[2]

In 1943, Dr. Herman Wold of Uppsala University, Sweden,
wrote three illuminating articles on demand analysis entitled
" A Synthesis of Pure Demand Analysis ".[3]   Since these
appeared in a rather specialised journal and during wartime,
it is to be feared that they may suffer the neglect that was
long the fate of Slutsky's fundamental paper. I know in
my own case, although I was honoured with reprints, they
arrived at a time when I was temporarily out of economics ;
I am ashamed to say that I have only recently read them
after some correspondence with Mr. Houthakker ; and I
am even more ashamed of failure to cite these important
papers in my *Foundations of Economic Analysis* (1947).[4]

Although the above list of references cannot pretend to
be exhaustive,[5] it does bring us down to the present time
and to Mr. Houthakker's important contribution.

2. THE MEANING OF INTEGRABILITY : TWO-DIMENSIONAL CASE

I do not think there is any simple way of picturing
integrability conditions so that we can easily grasp their
meaning in common-sense intuitive terms. This is because
the picture must be in three-dimensional space at least,
and because it must concern itself with subtle " local "
conditions that slopes must obey. But I shall make the
attempt to convey a notion of what is involved. After this
is done, we shall be in a better position to appraise the
main arguments in favour of and against non-integrability.

[1] N. Georgescu-Roegen : " The Pure Theory of Consumer's Behaviour ", *Quarterly Journal of Economics*, Vol. 49 (1935–6), pp. 545–93.

[2] " A Note on the Pure Theory of Consumer's Behaviour ", *Economica*, Vol. 18 (1938), pp. 61–71, 353–4 ; " Empirical Implications of Utility Analysis ", *Econometrica*, Vol. 6 (1938) ; " Consumption Theory in Terms of Revealed Preference ", *Economica*, Vol. 28 (1948), pp. 243–53.

[3] H. Wold : " A Synthesis of Pure Demand Analysis ", I, II, III : *Skandinavisk Aktuarietidskrift* (1943), pp. 85–118, 221–63, (1944) pp. 69–120. See especially pp. 109ff. and pp. 78ff. The reference to Antonelli is on pp. 115 and 118.

[4] Ch. V.

[5] For example, there are papers by L. Court and R. Roy on related problems. Also there is a recent paper by de Ville which I know of only from a brief review by K. Arrow in *Mathematical Reviews*, 1947.

Let us begin in two dimensions where the problem of integrability does *not* arise. Imagine that you go to the south-west corner of a room. Look down at the floor, and let the corner be the origin from which goods x_1 and x_2 are to be measured. On the floor can then be traced the contour lines of indifference looking like Figure 1a. (The little arrows show the direction of preference of the indifference curves and are drawn perpendicular for convenience.) The same thing is pictured in Figure 1b, but as a consumer might *reveal* his preference field to us if we could observe his demand behaviour only externally. Thus, at point A

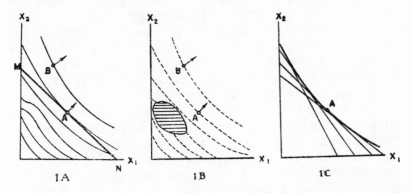

Let us begin

the consumer had his choice of all the points on the straight line MN. But he chose A, and we draw a little line through A with a slope equal to the price ratio $(-p_1/p_2)$ that brought him into equilibrium at A. Similarly at B or any other observed point we can draw a little " slope-element " (and if we like, a little arrow of preference) ; the budget lines whose price ratios determine the little slopes are, for simplicity, omitted. Figure 1c is another way of looking at the same problem. Any indifference curve, such as the one through A, can be thought of as the " envelope " or sheath of a family of budget lines, with only the heavy dark points being empirically observed.

It will be noted that any point where the indifference curves are convex rather than concave *cannot be observed in a competitive market*. (Cf. Fig. 1b.) Such points are shrouded in eternal darkness—unless we make our consumer a *monopsonist* and let him choose between goods lying on a very convex " budget curve " (along which he is affecting the prices of what he buys). In this monopsony case, we could still deduce the slope of the man's indifference curve from the slope of the curved constraint at the equilibrium point. The case of a Gallup-poll questioner who finds out the man's preference contours by giving him choices of every pair of goods is simply a limiting case of monopsony. And if we experiment sufficiently, we can always find a curved family of unique contours representing his ordinal preference field—if such a consistent field exists. Therefore, in this generalised monopsony we can behaviouristically identify the man's ordinal preference field if he has one.[1]

But I shall confine myself for simplicity to what will reveal itself under perfect competition and shall be concerned only with concave regions. In a recent article on " Consumption Theory in Terms of Revealed Preference ",[2] I discussed how the little slopes of Figure 1b can be mathematically integrated into the smooth contours of Figure 1a. If the little slope elements are made very small and very numerous, our mind's eye sees them as joining together into a one-parameter family of contours : it is as if iron filings on the floor line up to reveal the magnetic lines of force determined by a magnet under the floor. If the observed price ratio p_1/p_2 is given as the following continuous and differentiable function of the two goods, $B(x_1, x_2)$, then mathematical analysis assures us that the differential equation

(1) $dx_2/dx_1 = - B(x_1, x_2)$

gives rise to a unique family of curves as in Figure 1a. In two dimensions there is no integrability problem.

Before leaving the two-dimensional case, I should give preliminary warning concerning two red herrings that are confused with the integrability question. First, a consumer may be myopic in the sense that he does not know what his tastes are like in situations quite different from his customary position ; consequently his short-run demand behaviour may differ from the long-run " normal " behaviour

---

[1] In his last and most general formulation, *Encyclopédie des sciences mathématiques*, Tome I, Vol. IV, Fasc. 4 (1911), Pareto wished simply to assume that an individual's equilibrium choice would be given as an observable *functional* of every and any constraint offered him But Pareto did not sufficiently realise that the functionals so defined would have to be highly restricted so as to give consistent results and define a consistent ordinal preference field. See N. Georgescu-Roegen : " Note on a Proposition of Pareto ", *Quarterly Journal of Economics*, Vol. 49, 1934–5, pp. 706–14. Professor Kenneth Arrow of Stanford University in a set of as yet unpublished papers has given a formulation of such consistency conditions in terms of logical sets.

[2] *Economica*, November 1948, pp. 243–253.

which alone is our concern. But to be myopic means to be short-sighted—not zero-sighted or infinitesimal-sighted. We shall see in our multi-variable discussion that finite sight, however local, implies integrability; but the two-variable case drives home the irrelevancy of the problem of short-sightedness for the problem of integrability—since even if we choose to assume literally infinitesimal-sightedness, we still end up with a one-parameter family of contours and no integrability problem is possible.

Secondly, there is the related confusion between the " order of consumption " followed by a consumer and the " dependence of certain line integrals on the path " between two points. It must be emphasised that the paths along which I as an economic scientist choose to evaluate the man's preference have absolutely nothing to do with the order in which the human guinea-pig *consumes* the goods. I don't know whether he drinks his beer before his whisky or his whisky before his beer ; I don't know whether it even makes sense to say that he enjoys his shelter *before* rather than after he enjoys his food. Note too that in going from A to B the guinea-pig does *not* eat his way along the path, and in going from B to A regurgitate along the same path. Rather we should always regard the budget of goods at A as a steady flow of consumption per unit time, optimally patterned to the consumer's tastes. And the flow of consumption goods at B is again a steady flow long maintained. *The comparison of A and B* (and of intermediate points) *is a case of comparative statics*. We need not invade the privacy of the consumer's castle to concern ourselves with the minutiæ of his domestic arrangements.

I stress all these complications because they are complete irrelevancies. And yet they arise in the two-variable case where there is absolutely no integrability problem ! It should be absolutely clear, therefore, that the problem of " the order of consumption ", in the sense of the path along which the consumer actually moves behind the scenes of the market-place, has nothing to do with the problem of integrability versus non-integrability.

Pareto only confused the issue in his discussion of " open and closed cycles of consumption ". Actually, Pareto seems to end up with the conclusion that the consumer can be thought of as following optimal paths behind the scenes. From this he infers, if I understand his puzzling treatment, that there is no longer any ambiguity of path and therefore *integrability* is assured. This is all hopelessly confused: even if the consumer has definite and optimal domestic-housekeeping habits, we shall still have to *add* strong restrictions on his revealed-preference behaviour once we have more than two goods. To repeat, Pareto's primary confusion results from his identifying the paths of integration chosen by the economist-observer for statical comparisons with the behind-the-scenes programming of pleasures by the consumer.

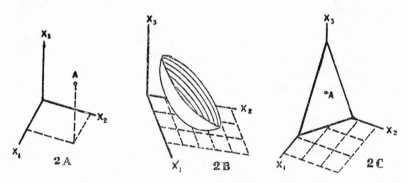

In our two-variable case we have already integrated our indifference elements and have arrived at indifference contours. To repeat again: no integrability problem is possible and no integrability conditions need be fulfilled.[1]

3. THE THREE-DIMENSIONAL PICTURE: THE INTEGRABLE CASE

When we bring a third good x_3 into the picture, we must use the altitude above the floor as the direction along which we measure the third good. Now we have three axes which meet in the south-west corner of our room. Along the lower edges of the wall, x_1 and x_2 are paced off as before. But the x_3 axis is measured along the vertical of the corner. Figure 2a shows the three axes. Any point in the room represents a combination of all three goods, as shown by A.

If we assume that the consumer has a consistent ordinal preference field, then we shall now have indifference *surfaces*, rather than indifference *curves*. How do these surfaces look? Rather like thin bowls inside of bowls, with the bottoms of

[1] See Mathematical Notes below.

the bowls pointing downward and south-westward toward the corner origin. As long as he moves on one bowl, the consumer is indifferent. As he moves toward " outside " bowls, nearer and nearer to the origin of zero consumption, he is worse off. As he moves away from the origin toward inner bowls, he is better off. Of course, this is all an imperfect picture : bowls are too thick, and umbrellas might be better.

Of course, any movement on an indifference surface will involve giving up something of one or more goods and taking on something of the other goods. Any movement off the surface and toward the origin involves a loss of ordinal satisfaction. Any movement off the surface in the opposite direction will involve a preferred move. If the consumer were free as a bird, he would want to get as far from the corner origin as possible, going upward and outward beyond the confines of the room and in the direction of bliss. But if we give him a limited money income, I, and prices of all goods, p_1, p_2, p_3, then he is not free as a bird. He cannot even move freely within the room. Instead he must stay inside the budget plane defined by

$$p_1 x_1 + p_2 x_2 + p_3 x_3 = I.$$

Figure 2c shows the limiting budget plane beyond which the consumer cannot go. If every good is desired by the consumer, he will never stay inside the budget plane but will instead choose to crawl on its surface seeking his most preferred position. If A is such an optimum position, at that point the budget plane will be touching but not crossing the highest attainable indifference surface ; hence there will be tangency, with the " bottom " of the indifference bowl just resting against the plane in the same way that a tea-cup rests against its saucer.

Of course, if income or prices change, then the budget planes will change and a new optimum point of tangency will be found[1] : thus we define the general demand functions showing how each good will depend on all prices and income.

Thus far I have sidestepped the problem of non-integrability by assuming it away. I have implicitly assumed that the consumer does have a *consistent ordinal preference field* : that he can always tell of any two situations either that A is

---

[1] If the indifference surfaces do not have the usually assumed curvature, the consumer may rush away from certain parts of the room ; he may even rush to one of the walls or floor and enjoy only a " generalised tangency ". This often happens, but need not be studied here.

Aa

" better than " B, or B better than A, or that they are indifferent ; and that his preferences among three or more situations are transitive in the sense that " if A is better than B and B better than C, then A is better than C ", etc. In short, I have assumed that indifference surfaces do exist. But need they ?

THE THREE-DIMENSIONAL CASE : NON-INTEGRABILITY

What is it that as scientists we are able actually to *observe* of a consumer who is in market equilibrium ? Only his demand functions in response to all possible prices and incomes. Or, in geometrical terms, all that we can observe are points like A which lie on an observable budget plane and which represent an optimum as compared to other points on or inside that plane. The reader will be tempted at this point to ask : " Just as we traced out indifference curves in the two-dimensional case as the envelope of carefully changed budget *lines*, can we not hope in the three-variable case to trace out the bowl-like indifference surfaces as the envelope of carefully changed budget *planes* ? " The answer must be worded cautiously : " Provided that the indifference surfaces exist, *yes* we can hope to trace them out in this way. But in the three-variable case there may not exist anything corresponding to such surfaces—unless certain extra restrictions are placed on the consumer's demand behaviour."

To investigate further the conditions of integrability and non-integrability, let us paint in just what it is that we can observe in our geometrical room. At any point such as A, we have the budget plane going through A ; our stage will get too cluttered up if we leave everything on it, so for simplicity we need at A indicate only a little " piece " of its budget plane. We need only indicate at A a little button, or better still a little thumb-tack, whose back or head lies in the budget plane and whose point tells us which is the " preferred " direction. At every observable point in our room there will be a little thumb-tack suspended in space ; its exact orientation in space is indicated by its point, or equally well by the head, which lies perpendicular to the point. Of course, the thumb-tack is just a non-rigorous way of picturing a little " planar element " determined at each point by the two price ratios at which equilibrium takes place : if we let x_3 be our *numéraire* or good whose price is taken as unity, then p_1/p_3 and p_2/p_3 will be assumed to be single-valued continuously differentiable functions[1] of x_1, x_2, x_3, written as $p_1/p_3 = B^1(x_1, x_2, x_3)$ and $p_2/p_3 = B^2(x_1, x_2, x_3)$.

Our little planar elements or thumb-tacks are often referred to as " marginal rates of substitution " between the goods in question, or as " little indifference elements ". It is said that so long as we take a "little" step on the surface of the thumb-tack, the consumer is just " indifferent "; if we step off the thumb-tack toward its point, the consumer is moving in a " preferred " direction ; finally, a move off the tack in the opposite direction is toward a " less-preferred " direction. In the present delicate investigation I must regard this as rather dangerous terminology. We have no right to regard our little elements as anything but shorthand ways of representing the observable price-ratios that give orientation to the observable budget plane passing through the observable optimum point. As behaviourists we have not yet earned the right to speak of " indifference " and " preference " ; and we certainly have no right to speak of " indifference directions for *infinitesimal* or *small* movements ", especially since the underlined words are by no means unambiguous or mutually equivalent.

But no one can stop us from asking a purely mathematical question : " Can we ' join together ' the little thumb-tacks to form bowl-like surfaces ? " This involves the purely mathematical properties of the partial differential equations

$$-\frac{\partial x_3}{\partial x_1} = B^1(x_1, x_2, x_3) \ , \ -\frac{\partial x_3}{\partial x_2} = B^2(x_1, x_2, x_3)$$

and of the so-called " total differential expression "

$$B^1(x_1, x_2, x_3)dx_1 + B^2(x_1, x_2, x_3)dx_2 + 1\ dx_3.$$

Can we define unique bowl-like surfaces by setting the last expression equal to zero ? The mathematicians know the answer to this,[2] but the meaning of their integrability conditions will not be understood until we investigate the geometrical picture further.

———

Few people can visualise well in three dimensions. And fewer still can correctly see what must be true about things

---

[1] We cannot in all cases invert our demand functions to express p's in terms of x's. But if appropriate " curvature assumptions " are made, this will be possible within certain regions. See Mathematical Notes below.

[2] See Mathematical Notes below.

infinitesimally close to each other. Therefore, few will be able to visualise the answer to the question of whether the thumb-tacks can be joined together to form surfaces. Let us therefore try to bring the matter down to two dimensions by the following device. Let us see what the planar elements or thumb-tacks look like *on any two-dimensional surface*. Let us put a thin wafer of wax in our room, bent so as to represent any desired surface. Now put in our whole field of thumb-tacks. Some tacks will not touch the wax surface ; but some will have to be pushed sideward into the wax so as to lie in their specified positions. Hence, our surface will be covered by the " tracks " of the planar elements.

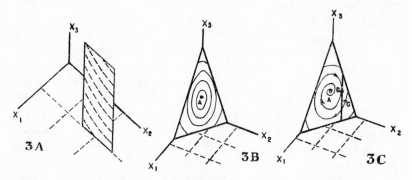

These tracks on the wax surface will look like the little line segments of the earlier two-dimensional picture. This is because the wax surface itself has only two rather than three dimensions.

Figure 3a, for example, shows how the little price ratios look on a plane which represents x_1 held constant, but with x_2 and x_3 varying. The little slope elements can obviously from our earlier two-dimension discussion always be joined together by the reader's eye to form a family of contours (which at this stage it would be dangerous to call indifference curves). In our remaining figures we shall assume that all such two-dimensional slope elements have been integrated into smooth contours. Figure 3b shows contour lines observed on a budget plane of a guinea-pig called Jeremy ; while 3c shows observations recorded by a scientist under similar conditions for a consumer called Gustav.[1]

[1] Of course, Jeremy need not be a hedonist of the Bentham type : he is the 20th century stream-lined version who believes only in *ordinal* utility ; and Gustav is more sophisticated than was the Cassel who rejected utility in favour of demand functions and nothing else, but was never fully aware of what he was thereby assuming or denying about empirical reality.

Note that at a point like A, where the planar thumb-tack is just tangent to our wax surface, we do not get a unique directional track, but instead get a dot with indeterminate direction. This remark will probably give the reader a hint as to how we might try to find indifference surfaces such as that pictured in Figure 2b. Why not cleverly bend a wax surface so that everywhere on it we get dots of indeterminate direction ? Professor Georgescu-Roegen in the 1936 article cited earlier was the first to show that this can indeed be done in the case of a consumer like Jeremy, whose tracks on any budget plane around an optimum point are always closed ellipse-like contours as in Figure 3b. *But it cannot be done for a consumer like Gustav who leaves spiral-like tracks on his budget planes* as in Figure 3c. This, then, is the geometrical meaning of the non-integrable case. Thus, by careful enough examination of the tracings left by a consumer's demand functions, we can determine whether he is a Jeremy or a Gustav.[1]

So-called Open and Closed Cycles

I shall return to the spiral-like contours left on the budget plane in the non-integrable case later and shall show how this provides us with an alternative proof to Mr. Houthakker's theorem that the " strong axiom of revealed preference " (whereby a consumer never reveals a contradiction of preference in any *chain·* of index number comparisons) definitely rules out non-integrability. But first I should like to use our geometrical model to throw light on Pareto's problem of open and closed cycles.

We have seen that Pareto confused the paths used by the scientist for comparative-statics comparisons with that actually followed by a consumer in consuming his goods. He did something else, less objectionable, but that I should like to avoid. He tried to define numerical or cardinal indexes of utility along such a path ; I on the other hand should like to remain in the objective realm of commodity space.[2]

With two goods there is no problem : every cycle is " closed " in the sense that Pareto can always find a utility index defined by an integral which returns to its old value

---

[1] See Mathematical Note 6 below.

[2] The present exposition, which was suggested to me by a reading of Houthakker's paper, was elegantly developed by Dr. Wold, *loc. cit.*, I, pp. 104–17.

once we get back to A. But with three or more goods, it may turn out that cycles are " open " : we pass from A to B and then back to A and our integral indicates to us that A is " better than itself ".[1]

That this phenomenon is independent of all cardinal utility considerations can be shown by Figure 4. We examine the contour lines traced in the wax by the little price-ratio planar elements. We have three wax surfaces

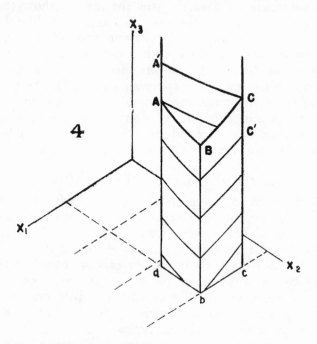

that form a kind of three-sided tower. (The old Flat-iron building in New York City was actually of this general shape.) One wall rises perpendicularly to the " street " ab ; another rises perpendicularly to the " street " bc. The third wall which is the back of the building could not be seen at all except that I have cut away part of the top to make it visible.

Instead of windows, there appears on each of our walls contour lines. I hesitate to call them " indifference curves ", but will do so, putting the expression in quotation marks. Let us start Gustav out at the point A. Let us hold x_1 constant and give him more x_2 ; to keep him on the same

[1] See Mathematical Note 4 below.

contour, we must take away something of x_3. Therefore, we move Gustav along the dark contour from A to B. Now we hold x_2 constant and decrease x_1; to keep Gustav indifferent we must then compensate him by increasing x_3, moving him along the dark contour BC. Likewise, by increasing x_1, decreasing x_2 and increasing x_3, we move him along the back wall, along the contour through C all the way to A'.

Gustav is obviously a rather strange chap. We have never crossed an " indifference " contour and yet we end up at the same amounts of x_1 and x_2 as at the beginning, *but with x_3 necessarily greater by the amount AA'* ! A man with such woolly preferences can be easily cheated. If Gustav would agree to our moving him anywhere along his " indifference " contours, we could take away x_3 from him by walking him around A'CBA, and we can continue the spiral downward until we have deprived him of indefinitely much x_3.[1]

This could not happen to a Jeremy. For him, A' and A will exactly coincide : such is the meaning of the integrability condition that his demand function must obey.[2]

But once again I must remind the reader that the paths followed, leading to open or closed cycles, have nothing to do with the process by which a consumer moves toward equilibrium or with the order of his personal consumption agenda.

REVEALED PREFERENCE AND INTEGRABILITY

We are now in a position to complete the programme begun a dozen years ago of arriving *at the full empirical implications for demand behaviour of the most general ordinal utility analysis*. My own work in this direction grew out of a remark made to me by Professor Haberler in his 1936 international trade seminar at Harvard. " How do you know indifference curves are concave ? " My quick retort was " Well, if they're not, your whole theory of index numbers is worthless ". Later I got to thinking about the implications of this answer (disregarding the fact that it

---

[1] This argument is really illegitimate : Gustav, not being a Jeremy, would have no reason to agree that we are free to move him along his " indifference " contours. The word " indifference " is probably *not* in his vocabulary.

[2] See Mathematical Note 5 below.

is not worded quite accurately). Being then full of Professor Leontief's analysis of indifference curves, I suddenly realised that we could dispense with almost all notions of utility : starting from a few logical axioms of demand consistency, I could derive the whole of the valid utility analysis as corollaries.

My fundamental axiom I borrowed from modern index-number theory. I shall call it (for reasons that will be obvious) the Weak Axiom of Consumer's Behaviour :

> Weak axiom : If at the price and income of situation A you could have bought the goods actually bought at a different point B and if you actually chose not to, then A is defined to be " revealed to be better than " B. The basic postulate is that B is never to reveal itself to be *also* " better than " A.

I soon realised that this could carry us almost all the way along the path of providing new foundations for utility theory.[1] But not quite all the way. The problem of integrability, it soon became obvious, could not yield to this weak axiom alone. I held up publication on the conjecture that if the axiom were strengthened to exclude non-contradictions of revealed preference for a chain of three or more situations, then non-integrability could indeed be excluded. At scientific meetings and in correspondence this problem was proposed, both to economists and mathematicians. But no proof was forthcoming for all these years, until Mr. Houthakker's paper arrived in the daily mail. Not only had he provided the missing proof, but in addition he had independently arrived at precisely the same strong axiom as I had hoped would save the day. To his paper which is such a model of logical elegance and compactness, the present historical treatment of the subject can hope to serve only as a supplement.

In words, the strong axiom can be worded roughly as follows :

> Strong axiom : If A reveals itself to be " better than " B, and if B reveals itself to be " better than " C, and if C reveals itself to be " better than " D, etc. . . . , then I extend the definition of "revealed preference" and say that A can be defined to be " revealed to be better

---

[1] For example, in a single step, one arrives at most of the properties of the Slutsky S matrix in the Mathematical Notes below.

than" Z, the last in the chain. In such cases it is postulated that Z must never *also* be revealed to be better than A.[1]

What Mr. Houthakker has shown is the following : Any Gustav, whose demand functions correspond to a non-integrable preference field, can be made to contradict the strong axiom. By judiciously varying prices and income, we can make him (on our strengthened definition of revealed preference) assert that A is better than Z and Z is at the same time better than A. Houthakker has shown how we should pick prices and income so as to reveal this contradiction. He has given us the long-sought test for integrability that can be formed in finite index-number terms, without need to estimate partial derivatives.

Figure 4 shows the same thing, but not so elegantly in that quantities and not prices are the independent variables. As Houthakker, Little and I have shown, we can pick a sequence of points very near to the path ABCA′ but lying just inferior to it, *along which the individual is asserting himself to be getting worse off.* We finally end up just below A′, but definitely above A—and it is obvious at this point that our consumer has revealed himself to have become " better off " since A′ and anything near it costs more than A. Here, we have a contradiction : the point between A and A′ is revealed to be *both better and worse* than A as a result of assuming non-integrability. Therefore, every cycle must be closed, and integrability is assured by our strong axiom. This is a variant of Houthakker's proof.

A second variant uses the spirals shown in Figure 3c. Just as there passed an optimal budget plane through A, so too there will pass an optimal budget plane through the point B. This will show up *on the original budget plane of A* as a line, tangent to B. Any point, like C which lies beyond this line on the side opposite to A, will lie *inside* the new budget plane and will reveal itself to cost less than B and thus be inferior to B. But we can find a sequence of points (such as C, D, E, . . . etc.) which hug near to the spiral

---

[1] I have glossed over a few delicate points. Thus, not all of the situations have to be different ones. Also, there is the question of how to handle two situations which at A's prices *cost the same*, but where A was chosen. If we rule out the possibility that B is " indifferent to A ", then we rule out some realistic cases of multiple equilibrium points. Even when B costs less than A at A's prices, in ruling that A is " better than B " we are making some implicit assumptions about the absence of " saturation-effects ". Throughout this paper I have dodged delicate problems of this sort, taking refuge in overly-strong assumptions about regularity of curvature. Since all this needs a definitive treatment, I must apologise for glossing over the difficulties.

through C but which march clockwise all the way around to just to the right of A and which always reveal themselves to be " worse than " C. But it is also clear that all points near to A can reveal themselves to be " better than " B. Thus, we have a point near A revealed to be both better and worse than C. This is our desired contradiction, and again we end up with the inadmissibility of non-integrability.

For purposes of identification, let us call a man a Paul if he satisfies the weak axiom for single-pair comparisons, whether or not he satisfies the strong axiom for any chain. Without going into next section's arguments concerning the merits of integrability v. non-integrability, this much seems clear to me : if a man is not a Jeremy with an integrable preference field, that is understandable ; but why should anyone be a semi-irrational Paul without going all the way and being a Gustav ? Or alternatively, why should an irrational Gustav make a bow in the direction of being consistent and stop short at being a Paul, refusing to take the final step toward becoming a Jeremy ? In short, I should expect there to be few Pauls reported by experienced observers.

Summary of Arguments for Non-Integrability

Let us now use the above analysis to appraise briefly the main arguments that have been advanced for non-integrability.

(1) There is the celebrated argument of Pareto, already mentioned, concerning the order of consumption and the question of open and closed cycles. Enough has been said already to indicate that I agree with the majority of writers that this is a confused discussion in at least the following respects : (a) comparative statics has little to do with the behind-the-scenes order of consuming; (b) even if the individual is presumed to follow the optimal order of consumption behind the scenes, there still remains the problem of integrability; (c) all of the problems raised in connection with the order of consumption arise just as essentially in the two-variable case where there is no problem of integrability[1] ; (d) there is the realistic possibility that the approach

---

[1] Thus, in G. C. Evans : op. cit., p. 121, the example of the carpenter who is not indifferent as to the order in which he renders services, receives wages, and consumes commodities would make as much (or little) sense if formulated in terms of two variables instead of three. On p. 120, this same author adds a new confusion : the path along which the line integral between two points is evaluated is called the path along which [market] exchanges take place.

to equilibrium may alter the final equilibrium point reached, because of irreversible *hysteresis* effects ; but again, this has nothing to do with the integrability problem.

(2) The second main argument for non-integrability involves the question of whether an individual may be able to form preferences in connection with so-called " small changes " even though he is incapable of making con- sistent choice judgments about far-away situations. There is indeed an air of realism about this observation, but as far as integrability is concerned this is also a complete red herring based upon logical confusion—at least such is my personal judgment after a careful re-reading of all the relevant literature. It is true that one cannot accurately predict how he would spend his income quantitatively if he became fabulously wealthy or extremely poor ; but the same would no doubt still be true if he consumed only two goods, and here the problem of integrability cannot arise.[1]

The most devastating weakness in this view is its failure to mean by *small* what the mathematician should mean by small in this context—namely, *finite* movements not greater than some specifiable amounts. The instant the movements become finite, however small, the integrability conditions (which are themselves of a " local character ") must become applicable or we cannot speak of local pre- ferences at all. If we try to get out of this dilemma by interpreting small to mean infinitesimally small in a rigorously defined sense, then the argument loses all its flavour of empirical realism.

I conclude this second issue by adding two red herrings of my own : (a) Georgescu-Roegen, Weber-Fechner, and others tell us that there is a " threshold effect " of per- ception which surrounds every situation in much the same way that static friction follows a particle on a rough table ; as Wicksell and others have recognised, this means that it is precisely for very *small* changes that the individual *cannot* have consistent preferences. (b) Since in the real as compared

---

[1] With hesitation, I question the opinions on this point of two such distinguished authorities as G. C. Evans and R. G. D. Allen. The former (*loc. cit.*) speaks of " infinitesimal loci of indifference " (p. 119) and of " small changes $dx_1, \ldots dx_n \ldots$ being made " (p. 122), and of an " approximate value function for small changes [which cannot, without extra assumptions, be extended] . . . beyond a merely local field ". In the cited 1937 publication, Allen assumes " that the individual has a scale of preferences for small changes from a given set of purchases . . . but this assumption . . . . does *not* imply that a complete scale of preferences exists. The consumer . . . need not be able to discriminate between widely different sets of purchases " (pp. 440-1).

to the idealised world, all goods are ultimately not divisible beyond certain quanta, what happens to the non-integrability argument based upon the rigorous interpretation of infinitesimals ? Leaving all levity aside, I must agree that it is only realistic, in the two-good or n-good case, to distinguish with Marshall between short-run and long-run preference behaviour—and for that matter between *ex ante* conjecture behaviour and *ex post* actual behaviour.

(*c*) There is the argument used ever since the time of Fisher, that *non-integrability* is the more *general* case of which integrable utility is but a *special* case. Since I have myself in the past stressed this point, I should like to make clear the sense in which I now think it valid. Generality pursued too avidly leads to emptiness. As scientists we must be willing to live dangerously. What we must seek is no inadmissible specialisations and no unnecessary generality. Newton did well to speak of the " inverse-square law of gravitation " rather than the " n^{th}-power law " ; at the same time, modern physicists do well to modify his law in the field of high-speed particles in favour of the more general Einstein relativity transformations.

As I now look at the matter, why should a Gustav, who has no mind to make up, so to speak, be expected not to be changing his demand behaviour constantly and capriciously ? In other words, where a man does not exhibit the behaviouristic traces of Jeremy-like consistent ordinal preferences, why should his demand have any *time invariance* ?

At least two answers might be given to this implicit defence of integrability as the only interesting hypothesis worth making. First, a man might display consistent demand behaviour through habit or crude rules-of-thumb *not consistent with an ordinal preference field*. Second, what is *a* man ? Or *a* consumer ? I am not so much concerned with the problem of Dr. Jekyll and Mr. Hyde, but with the problem of Dr. Jekyll and Mrs. Jekyll. Much consumption behaviour is *family* rather than *individual* behaviour. Now a family must be quite sophisticated indeed to end up with a consistent set of *collective* preferences : e.g., if they set up the rule that the wife will always spend 99 per cent (or 50 per cent.) of the income on her needs and the husband 1 per cent. (or 50 per cent.) on his quite different needs, this will *not* be consistent with an integrable set of price-ratio elements. Only if the family acts in terms of a Bergson Social Welfare Function will this condition result. But to explain this farther would take me into the frontier of research in welfare economics.[1]

(4) A last argument might be built up against non-integrability : if people lack the consistency of behaviour that integrability implies, then that attractive branch of individualistic welfare economics which says people's tastes should count loses most of its content ; hence, we should rule out non-integrability. I am afraid that this is an illegitimate intrusion of wishful thinking by the would-be political philosopher into the facts of life. If people do not behave as if it matters to them just what they consume, that is a weakness (but not necessarily a fatal one) for the Pareto-type compensationist new-welfare economics.[2] We must not bias our view of the facts to fit our wishes and prejudices, however pretty their pattern. On the other hand if integrability should turn out to be the best hypothesis to explain the empirical facts of the market-place, this makes a belief in individualistic ethics possible but still not mandatory. In the last analysis the definition of a welfare function is not an empirical problem.

In this connection it is interesting to note that Professor D. H. Robertson has put forward in his recent presidential address the view that Pareto and subsequent theorists were led through their fancy ·for fancy methods into a fanciful wild-goose chase in which they dethroned utility by the verbal act of giving new names to old terms—but that in recent years, Hicks and other devotees of the black arts of mathematical economics have completed the cycle and substantially returned to the common-sense orthodox utility views held all along (in quiet) by cooler heads, according to which utility is needed for welfare economics. I am not confident that I have correctly interpreted Robertson's meaning since his remarks were necessarily brief and purposely couched in charming ellipsis. But on the assumption that this is close to his intended meaning and that this one-fifth of his address was intended to be taken seriously, I must record some personal puzzlement.

In re-reading the cited thirty-odd basic papers of the last 60 years, I have not been able to discern trends of

---

[1] Cf. *Foundations of Economic Analysis* (1947), Ch. 8.
[2] See *Foundations*, pp. 219–28.

development along the lines of the propounded thesis. Nor am I aware that Hicks has anywhere in print reverted to a pre-Paretian position on utility; on the contrary, in 1939 Hicks independently arrived at an almost too-Paretian view of welfare economics. And other modern theorists (such as Lange, who once expressed the view that cardinal utility was unnecessary for demand studies but needed for welfare economics) were easily converted by Professor Bergson to the view that only ordinal comparisons are relevant.

However, Robertson can be interpreted to mean that the quest by Pareto and later writers for *non-integrable utility* was both factually unnecessary and destructive to much in welfare economics. Such a viewpoint on this more specialised and technical matter has its merits, and the present paper has the humble purpose of clarifying some of the issues.

———

We have now completed our main task. We know what it is that integrability implies, and what non-integrability implies : we know the full empirical implications on the demand functions of being a Jeremy or a Gustav. Deductive analysis can carry us no farther. Observation of reality must be the decisive test as to which hypothesis is the more fruitful—or whether neither is very fruitful.

MATHEMATICAL NOTES ON INTEGRABILITY

1. The observable n demand functions are assumed to be single-valued and continuously differentiable in terms of prices and income, of the form $x_k = D^k(p_1, p_2, \ldots, p_n, I)$. Changing all prices and income in the same proportion will, by hypothesis, cause no change in real quantities ; in consequence of this assumption of homogeneity of order zero, Euler's theorem tells us that the matrix $[D^k{}_j + D^j D^k{}_I]$ has a zero determinant—it being understood that subscripts stand for differentiation so that $D^k{}_j = \partial x_k / \partial p_j$, etc.

I now make the special additional hypothesis that these demand functions are *reversible* and can be inverted to express relative prices in terms of quantities. This will be assured in any local region around a point where the determinant of $[D^k{}_j]$ is not zero. A symmetrical representation of relative prices could be provided by defining new variables $(Q_1, \ldots, Q_n) = (p_1/I, \ldots, p_n/I)$. But it is more traditional to set the price of some *numéraire* good, say x_n, as 1, and to express income and all prices in terms of the nth price; hence, I define $[B_1, \ldots, B_{n-1}, 1] = [p_1/p_n, \ldots, p_{n-1}/p_n, 1]$, and after reversing our demand functions, we have the *observable price-ratio functions* (or marginal rates of substitution)

(1) $B_k = B^k(x_1, x_2, \ldots, x_n)$ $(k = 1, 2, \ldots, n-1)$

A similar function exists for I/p_n, which we might call $B_n = + B_1 x_1 + \ldots + B_{n-1} x_{n-1} + x_n$ after noting that there is no need to waste this symbol on p_n/p_n.

Our reversibility hypothesis can be expressed in terms of the Jacobian of the B's being non-zero. Specifically, let us define the matrix $\mathcal{J}_n$ to be the square matrix that results when we set $p_n = 1$ and exclude the nth price-column from $[D^k{}_j ;\ D^k{}_I]$. Then the interested reader can verify the following partitioned matrix identities.

(2) $$\mathcal{J}_n^{-1} = [B^k{}_j] = \begin{bmatrix} B^k{}_j & , & B^k{}_n \\ B^n{}_j & , & B^n{}_n \end{bmatrix}$$
$$= \begin{bmatrix} I & , & 0 \\ x_j & , & 1 \end{bmatrix} \begin{bmatrix} B^k{}_j & , & B^k{}_n \\ B^j & , & 1 \end{bmatrix}$$
$$= \begin{bmatrix} I & , & 0 \\ x_j & , & 1 \end{bmatrix} \begin{bmatrix} B^k{}_j - B^j B^k{}_n & , & B^k{}_n \\ 0 & , & 1 \end{bmatrix} \begin{bmatrix} I & , & 0 \\ B_j & , & 1 \end{bmatrix}$$

where I has 1's in its diagonals and 0's elsewhere and where the upper left-hand sub-matrix is always $(n-1)$ by $(n-1)$.

It is sufficient for reversibility in some small region around an observed point that the determinants of any one of these matrix products be non-zero. If we wish the B's to be reversible even when we hold some subset of x's constant, then the principal minors derived by striking out some of the first $(n-1)$ rows and columns must also be non-zero. The non-vanishing of all these principal minors throughout an extended domain will assure reversibility of our functions —not just locally—but throughout that domain.

97

2. So far nothing has been said about integrability conditions. Slutsky proved that if there does exist an integrable utility function $U = F[V(x_1, \ldots, x_n)]$ so that the B's can be written as the ratio of U_k/U_n, then the matrix

$$S = [s_{kj}] = \begin{bmatrix} D^k_{\ j} + D^j D^k_{\ I} \ , & D^k_{\ n} + D^n D^k_{\ I} \\ D^n_{\ j} + D^j D^n_{\ I} \ , & D^n_{\ n} + D^n D^n_{\ I} \end{bmatrix} = \begin{bmatrix} S_n \ , & s_{kn} \\ s_{nj} \ , & s_{nn} \end{bmatrix}$$

is *symmetric*, in consequence of the symmetry of the cross-derivatives, $U_{kj} = U_{jk}$. This is a singular matrix in virtue of the Euler-theorem relation $Sp = 0$; hence, the Slutsky integrability conditions involve only $(n-1)(n-2)/2$ *independent* conditions : e.g., the symmetry of the upper-left matrix, S_n, implies full symmetry.

Slutsky also showed that the elements of S are observable empirical invariant quantities, not dependent on the form of the arbitrary numerical indexes of utility. He interpreted the elements of S as *compensated* changes, for which ordinal utility is constant because the change in price is just offset by a change in money income. Slutsky showed that the diagonal or " own-elasticity " elements of S must be negative ; the off-diagonal elements provide the Slutsky-Schultz-Hicks definition of complementarity, which is of greatest qualitative richness only in the $n > 2$ case. It may be added that $-S$ is positive semi-definite, being of rank $n-1$, and with its principal minors being all positive. S constitutes the most important part of consumption theory.

Not only are the Slutsky integrability conditions necessary, they can be shown as well to be *sufficient* to insure integrability. By somewhat tedious manipulation, we can show that

$$(3) \qquad \begin{bmatrix} s_{kj} & D^k_{\ n} \\ s_{nj} & D^n_{\ n} \end{bmatrix} = \mathcal{J}_n \begin{bmatrix} I & 0 \\ x_j & I \end{bmatrix} \quad \text{or from (2)}$$

$$= \begin{bmatrix} I & 0 \\ B^j & I \end{bmatrix}^{-1} \begin{bmatrix} B^k_{\ j} - B^j B^k_{\ n} \ , & B^k_{\ n} \\ 0 & , & I \end{bmatrix}^{-1}$$

$$= \begin{bmatrix} [B^k_{\ j} - B^j B^k_{\ n}]^{-1} \ , & \Upsilon_k \\ Z_j & , & W \end{bmatrix}$$

where it is unnecessary to write out the expressions for the W, Υ and Z's.

If the Slutsky sub-matrix S_n is symmetric, then $[B^k_{\ j} - B^j B^k_{\ n}]^{-1}$ and $[B^k_{\ j} - B^j B^k_{\ n}]$ are symmetric. The symmetry of the last-written matrix we might call the Antonelli-Hicks-Allen conditions, since the former announced them in 1886 and the last two gave an interpretation of them in terms of symmetry of the Hicks-Allen (1934) defined measures of complementarity.[1]

3. These last conditions can now be related to the mathematicians' discussion of integrability. We associate with (1) the *partial differential equations*

$$-\frac{\partial x_n}{\partial x_j} = B^j(x_1, \ldots, x_n) \quad (j = 1, 2, \ldots, n-1),$$

and the *total differential equation*

$$B^1 dx_1 + B^2 dx_2 + \ldots + B^{n-1} dx_{n-1} + 1 dx_n = 0.$$

Any path in space along which the latter is satisfied might be termed an "indifference path", but with emphasis on the quotation marks; along such a path, we can replace the B's by any set of proportional functions

$$Q^1 dx_1 + Q^2 dx_2 + \ldots + Q^{n-1} dx_{n-1} + Q^n dx_n = 0$$

where Q^n is an arbitrary non-vanishing function and $Q^j = B^j Q^n$.

An expression like $\Sigma Q^k \, dx_k$ may be satisfactory as a *local* measure of preference, being positive when a "better" move is being made, being zero when there is "indifference", and negative when a "worse" move is being made. But its integral along any finite path between two points will *generally not* provide a consistent numerical indicator of ordinal preference—even if such a consistent preference field exists, and certainly not if such a field does not exist. Only if $\Sigma Q^k dx_k = dQ$, an *exact differential* with $Q^k = \partial Q / \partial x_k = Q_k$ and $Q_{kj} = Q_{jk}$, will such an integral be *always* the same for *different* paths between two specified end-points; and only in this case can we be sure that if we go from point A to point B by one path and return back to A by another path, the value of the integral will none the less be zero over the round trip, indicating that A is exactly as good as itself and not better.[2]

---

[1] In 1939 Hicks seems to have abandoned this definition in favour of the Slutsky-Schultz definitions. For $n = 3$, the results of either definition are *qualitatively* the same. For $n > 3$, this is not true. If we define all but the two goods in question to be a Hicksian composite commodity, then the Slutsky-Hicks definition can be cast in Hicks-Allen terminology. From this the specialist will gather that I no longer think that earlier criticisms of logical inconsistency between the text and appendix of *Value and Capital* are valid.

[2] The line-integral $\int \Sigma Q^k dx_k$ along a path between two points a and b is defined as the simple integral $\int [\Sigma Q^k (dx_k/dt)] \, dt$ where $x_k = x_k(t)$ is the equation of the path, and where the appropriate limits for t are understood. See, for example, E. B. Wilson : *Advanced Calculus*, Ch. XI and also Ch. X on partial differential equations.

The above condition on the cross-derivatives will rarely be met; but we can ask whether there is not some other set of functions proportional to the B's for which we do get an exact differential. For this to exist, we must be able to find a so-called integrating factor $i(x_1x_2, \ldots, x_n)$ such that

$$iQ^1dx_1 + \ldots + iQ^ndx_n = dV \quad \text{an exact differential.}$$

This is possible only if $V_{kj} = V_{jk}$, or if we have $n(n-1)/2$ conditions

$$(4) \qquad 0 = \frac{\partial(iQ^k)}{\partial x_j} - \frac{\partial(iQ^j)}{\partial x_k} = i_jQ^k - i_kQ^j + i(Q^k{}_j - Q^j{}_k) \quad j \neq k.$$

When we examine these conditions, they are seen not to be all independent. Also they are not conditions on the Q's alone but involve i and its partial derivatives, where i is a function not even known to exist. For any triplet of variables, say j, k, r, we can eliminate i and its derivatives by algebraic manipulation, to get the following relations on the Q's alone

$$(4)' \qquad 0 = Q^k(Q^j{}_r - Q^r{}_j) + Q^j(Q^r{}_k - Q^k{}_r) + Q^r(Q^k{}_j - Q^j{}_k)$$
$$, \quad j \neq k \neq r \neq j.$$

When $n = 2$, there are no integrability conditions; when $n = 3$, there is 1; when $n = 4$, we can write down 4 such conditions; and, in general, $n(n-1)(n-2)/6$ equations. But these are easily seen not to be all independent; at most $(n-1)(n-2)/2$ are independent and all the rest follow by algebraic manipulation.

A convenient way to get a set of independent conditions is to hold $r = n$, and work with $B^k = Q_k/Q_n$. Equation $(4)'$ then becomes

$$(4)'' \qquad B^k{}_j - B^jB^k{}_n = B^j{}_k - B^kB^j{}_n. \qquad n > k \neq j. < n.$$

But these are the Antonelli integrability conditions, already shown to be equivalent to the Slutsky symmetry conditions.[1]

4. It has been fairly easy to show that the above conditions are *necessary* if there is to be a family of integrable surfaces. They are also *sufficient* to guarantee the existence of such surfaces; but this is not so easy to show. We may, of course, always accept the guarantee of the pure mathematician that there is a general *existence theorem* on partial

---

[1] Jevons, Walras, and Marshall did not have to be concerned with the integrability problem primarily because they implicitly assumed it away, and because they assumed that the marginal utility of any good depends on its own quantity alone. In this case (4), $(4)'$, $(4)''$ are always satisfied.

differential equations assuring us that the above equations do define a family of integrating factors, i.

However, it may add to our intuitive grasp of the problem if I hastily sketch a method of actually constructing a single indifference surface. Let us start from any given point $(x_1^0, x_2^0, \ldots, x_n^0)$. Let us now make all but the last variable (x_n or x_3 as the case may be) move in a fixed ratio to moves in x_1; as we move x_1 from our beginning point, then $x_2 \ldots$ will move in this determined fashion; and now we require the last variable, x_n, to move as determined by

$$B^1 dx_1 + B^2 dx_2 + \ldots + 1 dx_n = 0$$

where

$$(x_k - x_k^0) = y_k(x_1 - x_1^0) \text{ or } X_k = y_k X_1 \ (k = 2, \ldots, n-1)$$

and where the y's are arbitrary proportionality constants.

In the three-dimensional case, we are swinging a vertical door whose vertical axis of hinging goes through the original point. When the door is at any angle, there is on its surface a unique " indifference " contour through the original point. If now we let the door swing through all angles, these indifference contours will sweep out a two-dimensional surface.

Analytically, for given y's, we can eliminate all the x's but x_1 and x_n, and end up with a differential equation for x_1 and x_n. This equation always has one solution through the initial point which we may write as follows

$$X_n = g(X_1; y_2, \ldots, y_{n-1})$$

where the y's are parameters. Now if we let the y's vary and recall the relation $X_k = y_k X_1$, we have defined a hyper-surface

$$(5) \qquad X_n = g(X_1; X_2/X_1, \ldots, X_{n-1}/X_1)$$

which of course goes through the original point and can be written in terms of the original small x's.

But will *any* movement along this relation satisfy $B^1 dx_1 + \ldots + dx_n = 0$? By tedious substitution, we find that the answer is generally *no*—unless the integrability conditions are satisfied, in which case the answer happens to be *yes*. Only in this case can we term our surface an *indifference* surface; and only in this case shall we arrive back at the same surface if we repeat the process starting out from any other point satisfying (5). For a description of this process, called Mayer's method, see any mathematical text such as Wilson's *Advanced Calculus, loc. cit.*

5. By similar reasoning, we can show that if the integrability conditions are *not* satisfied, there will always be " open cycles " as shown in Figure 4. Suppose the indifference movements there described, such as from A to B, always lie on a definite surface which can have but one value for x_n in terms of the other x's. Call this surface

$$x_n = G(x_1, x_2, \ldots, x_{n-1})$$

where of course

$$-\frac{\partial G}{\partial x_k} = B^k[x_1, x_2, \ldots, G(x_1, x_2, \ldots x_{n-1})].$$

Then

$$-dx_n = B^1[x_1, x_2, \ldots, G]dx_1 + B^2[x_1, x_2, \ldots, G]dx_2 + \ldots$$

would have to be an exact differential in $(x_1, \ldots, x_{n-1})$; hence, it is necessary that the cross-relations hold

$$(4)'' \quad B^k{}_j + B^k{}_n G_j = B^k{}_j - B^k{}_n B^j = B^j{}_k - B^j{}_n B^k = B^j{}_k + B^j{}_n G_k.$$

If these integrability conditions were not satisfied, we should have a contradiction to our assumption of an exact differential defining a surface yielding only closed cycles.

6. The Georgescu-Roegen demonstration that the contours on the budget-line planes of 3b and 3c are ellipses in the integrable case and spirals in the non-integrable case proceeds as follows. Setting all the x's constant but x_1, x_2, and x_3 or more generally x_n, then our budget plane is defined by

$$B_1{}^0 x_1 + B_2{}^0 x_2 + x_n = \text{constant} = C$$
$$B_1{}^0 dx_1 + B_2{}^0 dx_2 + dx_n = 0$$

where $B_k{}^0$ stands for the given constant prices; at the optimum point $(x_1{}^0, x_2{}^0, \ldots, x_n{}^0)$, of course, $B_k{}^0 = B^k(x_1{}^0, \ldots, x_n{}^0)$. The "indifference" contours on the budget plane must, after substitution, satisfy

$$B^1(x_1, \ldots, C - B_1{}^0 x_1 - B_2{}^0 x_2)dx_1 +$$
$$B^2(x_1, \ldots, C - B_1{}^0 x_1 - B_2{}^0 x_2) - B_1{}^0 dx_1 - B_2{}^0 dx_2 = 0$$

or $\quad W^1(X_1, X_2)dX_1 + W^2(X_1, X_2)dx_2 = 0$

where $X_k = x_k - x_k{}^0$, $W^k(x_1 - x_1{}^0, x_2 - x_2{}^0) = B^k(x_1, \ldots, C - B_1{}^0 x_1 - B_2{}^0 x_2)$

$$W^k{}_j = \frac{\partial W^k(0, 0)}{\partial x_j} = B^k{}_j - B^k{}_n B_j{}^0 = B^k{}_j - B^k{}_n B^j,$$
$$(j, k = 1, 2)$$

where it is understood that all partial derivatives are to be evaluated at the equilibrium point.

In the neighbourhood of the equilibrium point, the slope of the contour is determined by

$$(6) \qquad (W^1{}_1 X_1 + W^1{}_2 X_2 + \ldots) dX_1 + (W^2{}_1 X_1 + W^2{}_2 X^2 + \ldots) dX_2 = 0$$

with higher powers of the X's neglected. If $W^1{}_2 = W^2{}_1$, which in terms of the B's expresses our old integrability condition, this is an exact differential as it stands ; we immediately verify that

$$W^1{}_1 (X_1)^2 + 2 W^1{}_2 (X_1 X_2) + W^2{}_2 (X_2)^2 = \text{constant}$$

represents the contours of the budget plane. If the 2 by 2 determinant of $[W^k{}_j]$, which is essentially a principal minor in equation (2), is positive, we have concentric closed ellipses surrounding an extremum or *vortex point* as in Figure 3b. If the determinant is negative, we have a family of hyperbolæ surrounding a *saddle point*. If ordinal utility is at a maximum, the last case is ruled out.

If $W^1{}_2 \ne W^2{}_1$, then we shall have an infinite number of contours running into the singular point. If the above determinant is positive and the asymmetry limited in amount so as to satisfy the Allen (1937) generalised law of diminishing marginal rate of substitution, or my weak axiom, then

$$(7) \quad 0 > \sum_1^{n-1} dB^k dx_k \quad \text{along} \quad \sum_1^{n-1} B^k dx_k + dx_n = 0$$

and we shall have a *spiral point* as shown in Figure 3c. Another less interesting possibility will be a *nodal point* in which *all* the contours, orthogonal to the above case, run into the singular point from one or two directions. All of these cases are determined by the nature of the two roots of the characteristic equation of the W determinant, $m^2 + (W^1{}_2 - W^2{}_1) m + |W| = 0$. The economically interesting cases are when the middle term vanishes so as to yield pure imaginary roots, or does not vanish so as to yield complex numbers ; the real parts of the latter serve to damp down the closed elliptical sinusoidal motions into converging spirals. See L. Ford : *Differential Equations*, pp. 48–52.

7. There remains the troublesome question of what are the appropriate curvature (often miscalled " stability ") conditions to be assumed in the non-integrable case. In the integrable case where the consumer is at an interior

maximum point with the x's continuous and reversible functions of relative prices and income, the matrix

$$-[W^k{}_j] = -[B^k{}_j - B^k{}_n B^j] = -\left[\frac{\partial^2 x_n}{\partial x_j \partial x_k}\right] \text{ comp.}$$

must be positive definite, which in terms of (2) implies

(8) $\begin{vmatrix} -B^1{}_1 & -B^1{}_3 \\ -B^1 & -1 \end{vmatrix} > 0, \quad \begin{vmatrix} -B^1{}_1 & -B^1{}_2 & -B^1{}_3 \\ -B^2{}_1 & -B^2{}_2 & -B^2{}_3 \\ -B^1 & -B^2 & -1 \end{vmatrix} > 0,$ etc.

But when $W^k{}_j \ne W^j{}_k$, these last conditions are *not* equivalent to $-[W^k{}_j]$ being the coeficients of a positive definite quadratic form with

(9) $-W^1{}_1 > 0, \quad \begin{vmatrix} -W^1{}_1 & -\dfrac{W^1{}_2 + W^2{}_1}{2} \\ -\dfrac{W^2{}_1 + W^1{}_2}{2} & -W^2{}_2 \end{vmatrix} > 0,$ etc.

This was shown by Georgescu-Roegen, and in 1937 Allen pointed out how his 1934 conditions (8) should be strengthened to make (9) hold in the asymmetric case. Allen obviously prefers (9) to (8), because he postulates the generalised law of diminishing marginal rate of substitution indicated a few paragraphs ago.

But *why* should such a law hold for a Gustav who has no consistent scale of tastes ? Allen's argument seems to be postulational rather than persuasive, its only intuitive plausibility residing in the case of the integrable Jeremy. If all we demand is reversibility of demand—and I myself do not even demand that—then it is not clear but that the less " fully-developed " 1934 conditions are better than the 1937 conditions, even though the 1934 conditions are not invariant under linear commodity transformations.[1]

I am also a little puzzled by Wold's Theorem X, *op. cit.*, III, pp. 78–88. When this was cited in Mr. Houthakker's footnote as demonstrating that the assumptions of (1) homogeneous and (2) reversible demand functions were inconsistent with (3) non-integrability, I was aghast and ran to read Wold's paper—for such a result seemed miraculous. Interpreted literally, that theorem does seem to say that (1), (2), and (3) are " self-contradictory ". But this reading may arise from the English wording of the Swedish, for it

---

[1] Cf. Allen (1937), p. 516, with Allen (1934), p. 203. Even in the integrable case, I do not regard the usually assumed curvature conditions to be necessary nor do the arguments by which they are derived seem completely plausible. Cf. *Value and Capital*, p. 23.

is my interpretation from the proof that Wold really means to say that any *consumer* who obeys (1), (2), and (3) is behaving in a " self-contradictory " fashion from the standpoint of consistent ordinal preference. This is completely in line with what we should expect from non-integrability. When a scientist assumes (1), (2), and (3) it is not implied that *he* is being " self-contradictory ". I hope and trust that Wold and I would be in agreement that *reversibility as such* has nothing essential to do with *integrability*.

Massachusetts Institute of Technology,
Cambridge, Massachusetts.

11

Consumption Theorems
in Terms of Overcompensation rather than
Indifference Comparisons

By Paul A. Samuelson

To be of interest a scientific theory must have consequences. Upon hard-boiled examination, the theory of consumer's behaviour turns out not to be completely without interest. By this I mean: consumption theory does definitely have some refutable empirical implications. The prosaic deductive task of the economic theorist is to discern and state the consequences of economic theories.

In this paper I propose to deal with an extremely simple question : Under what conditions can we expect the quantity demanded by a consumer of a good to be inversely related to its price? This and related issues provide a good illustration of certain new methods of modern economic theory, and a testing of their powers.

I—The Fundamental Theorem of Consumption Theory

In its narrow version the theory of " revealed preference " confines itself to a finite set of observable price-quantity competitive demand data, and attempts to discover the full empirical implications of the hypothesis that the individual is consistent. The complete logical equivalence of this approach with the regular Pareto-Slutsky-Hicks-Arrow ordinal preference approach has essentially been established. So in principle there is nothing to choose between the formulations.[1]

There is, however, the question of convenience of different formulations. Revealed preference is a speedy way of deriving many of the fundamental finite inequalities (of index-number type) whose violation would constitute a definite refutation of the hypothesis of consistency. But it turns out that we cannot by revealed preference deduce the following : An increase in a good's price must, if income and other prices are held constant, decrease the amount of it demanded. Failure to deduce this simple and basic Marshallian proposition, we should indeed have to hold against any theory—if the proposition in question were true ! But the phenomenon of Giffen's Paradox reminds us that the Marshallian proposition is not a true theorem, and it is rather to a theory's credit than discredit if it refuses to enunciate a false theorem.

---

[1] J. R. Hicks, *Value and Capital;* P. A. Samuelson, *Foundations of Economic Analysis;* I. M. D. Little, *A Critique of Welfare Economics;* K. J. Arrow, *Social Choice and Individual Values;* H. S. Houthakker, " Revealed Preference and the Utility Function ", *Economica*, May 1950 ; P. A. Samuelson, " Consumption Theory in Terms of Revealed Preference " and " The Problem of Integrability in Utility Theory ", *Economica*, November 1948 and November 1950.

None the less, as a betting matter it is more likely than otherwise that a *ceteris paribus* change in one good's price will in fact lower its sale. As casual econometricians, this we know. Moreover, for about 40 years now—ever since the work of W. E. Johnson, Slutsky, Allen, and Hicks—we have known a condition under which such a bet on the truth of the Marshallian proposition would be 100 per cent. certain. Indeed, if I were asked to explain to a non-specialist the single most interesting result of the theory of consumer's behaviour, I should be tempted to cite the following valid theorem, which though not very exciting does have the modest merit of being true.

> *Fundamental Theorem of Consumption Theory.* Any good (simple or composite) that is known always to increase in demand when money income alone rises must definitely shrink in demand when its price alone rises.

Since as casual or systematic econometricians we know that most goods obey Engel's Laws corresponding to consumption increasing absolutely with increases in money income,[1] this Fundamental Theorem of consumption theory enables us to infer that most Marshallian price-elasticities of demand are definitely negative.

II—A WEAKNESS IN REVEALED PREFERENCE?

How shall we score the theory of revealed preference with respect to this Fundamental Theorem? I have already asserted the complete logical equivalence of revealed preference with any other valid version of (regular) consumption theory, and this must imply that revealed preference can deduce this theorem. But, in terms of convenience and directness, can revealed preference derive this result only by *first* converting itself into the more traditional Slutsky-like analysis of ordinal utility, utilising bordered matrixes, etc.? If this were the case, a legitimate point would be scored against the theory.

Actually, in the first 1938 article in which I discussed aspects of revealed preference,[2] one of the first and most direct deductions from the theory was to infer from the basic Weak Axiom

$$(1) \qquad\qquad \Sigma p_i \triangle q_i \leq 0 \text{ implies } \Sigma \triangle p_i \triangle q_i \leq 0$$

that $\left(\dfrac{\partial q_i}{\partial p_i} + q_i \dfrac{\partial q_i}{\partial I} \right)$ must be non-positive, which is the Slutsky-derived, partial derivative form of the Fundamental Theorem.

Also, in a 1951 lecture on "Integration of Demand Theory," Professor Hicks has elegantly shown how the finite inequality version of this Slutsky result can be derived from the simple consideration of batches of goods that are known to be " indifferent ". In his demonstration,

---

[1] To be pedantic, our exact requirement is that the quantity of the good in question can, with fixed prices, fall only if money income falls.
[2] P. A. Samuelson, " A Note on the Pure Theory of Consumer's Behaviour ", *Economica*, February 1938.

Hicks was able to dispense completely with the use of partial derivatives and the inversion of matrixes.[1] We may lighten the requirement that some goods (and ordinal satisfaction) be continuously divisible so as to guarantee the existence of situations indifferent to any given situation. Actually, for all situations *at least as good* as a specified level, any two observed points (q^1) and (q^2), which minimise the $\Sigma p^1 q$ and $\Sigma p^2 q$ needed to achieve the desired level, will satisfy $\Sigma(p^2 - p^1)(q^2 - q^1) \leq 0$. However, if we rigidly confine ourselves to the methodological straight-jacket of working only with a finite number of punch-cards of observed price-quantity data, derived from a regularly concave preference field, we shall never be able definitely to *identify* two situations $(q_1^1, \ldots, q_n^1)$ and $(q_1^2, \ldots, q_n^2)$ that are *indifferent*.[2] Therefore, the Hicks type of demonstration would have to be modified to meet the present conditions on the data.

My own methodological position is an eclectic one. I think it important to know what one can and cannot constructively accomplish with a finite set of data. But I see no reason in principle to eschew the use of constructions that involve indifference between various situations. And I should certainly say " So much the worse for the narrow version of revealed preference and for the methodological straight-jacket of working with a finite set of observable (p, q) data " if (1) the Fundamental Theorem (that positive income-elasticity implies negative price-elasticity) became a casualty of the approach or if (2) its derivation became indirect, tedious, and inelegant.[3]

But fortunately that is not at all the case. It is the simple purpose of this note to show that within the framework of the narrowest version of revealed preference the important Fundamental Theorem, stated above, can be directly demonstrated (*a*) in commonsense words, (*b*) by geometrical argument, (*c*) by general analytic proof.

[1] See also Richard Stone, *The Rôle of Measurement in Economics*, p. 17; my *Foundations of Economic Analysis*, pp. 69, 74.

[2] The cited works of Houthakker, Little, and myself show that revealed preference theory in its narrow sense can identify regular situations that are indifferent only by an *infinite* sequence of comparison points.

[3] A programme of remaining as far as is possible within the realm of a finite number of observations and deriving whatever true theorems we can is reminiscent of the views of the intuitionist school in mathematics. According to Kronecker, Brouwer, Weyl, and others of this school, an object exists only if we can give a method for constructing it. This serves to rule out many of the tempting extensions to infinite sets of the properties of finite sets, and seriously damages much of the body of accepted mathematics. The methodological issues are very deep, and recent work of Gödel and others on the impossibility of proving the consistency of a logical system from within itself have raised questions as to whether the Brouwer-established structures are " safer " than other parts of mathematics. See E. T. Bell, *Men of Mathematics* (New York, 1937), Paul Rosenbloom, *Elements of Math. Logic* (New York, 1950). The methodological issues involved in revealed preference are much less serious, and I should favour remaining within a narrow framework only for preliminary exploratory purposes—to see how far we can go; and when we have reached the limits of this approach, I should gladly relax it and go on to others. There is no reason to confine our consumer to choices of the form $\Sigma p^1 q \leq I^1$; a binary choice between any (q^1) *or* (q^2) is often legitimate, and this takes us to the traditional theory of ordinal preference, which is the broad version of *revealed* preference.

AI

III—LITERARY DEMONSTRATION AND GEOMETRICAL DEMONSTRATION

Suppose we increase to a consumer the price of tea alone and let him move to his new equilibrium in two stages. At the first stage we agree to give him enough extra money income to make it possible for him to continue buying *exactly* the same quantities of all goods. At worst he can choose to leave his consumption of tea and everything else unchanged and end up no worse off than before. In all likelihood

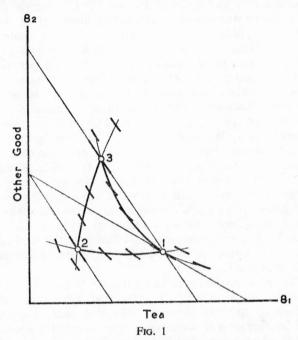

FIG. 1

The move along the price-consumption curve from 1 to 2 can be broken down into : (*a*) the " overcompensation effect " from 1 to 3, generated by pivoting a budget line through 1 until parallel with the budget line through 2 ; plus (*b*) the " income effect " along an Engel's curve from 3 to 2. If tea is a non-inferior good, 2 must lie to the west of 3 ; since 3 must be as good as 1, it cannot lie within 1's triangle of choice, and must therefore lie to the west of 1. Hence, 2 lies west of 1. *Q.E.D.*

he can in fact better himself by buying less of the now relatively dear tea, switching his purchases to more of other goods. In no case can it pay him now to buy more tea than before ; for if it were to pay now, it would certainly have more than paid to have made the switch when tea was less dear. So we know that at the end of the first stage he has —if anything—cut down on physical tea consumption.

Now in the second stage we leave tea relatively dear, but we take away from him the gift of extra income, leaving him in the end with only his original money income. Certainly, if tea is not an inferior good, cutting money income must never cause the consumer to buy more tea. So in the second stage, the consumer—if anything—again cuts down on physical tea consumption.

Combining the two stages, which is what we do when we increase the tea price alone while leaving income and all other prices constant, we find that tea consumption is debarred from rising—and for both of the reasons given in the two stages.

This completes the proof. Note that the second stage can legitimately be treated as a (real and money) " income effect ". But the first stage cannot literally be treated as a " substitution effect ", if we understand by this term the usual convention that the consumer undergoes no change in well-being. Any mandatory finite substitutions in the first stage can be expected to make the consumer definitely better off, shifting him to a higher indifference curve. Indeed, from the present standpoint of narrowest revealed preference, it is an absolute advantage that the consumer is not constrained to remain on the same level of indifference, since that is a requirement so hard to verify by price-quantity observations alone. We might dramatise this fact by replacing the words " substitution effect " with the more accurate description of the first stage—" overcompensation effect ". (To be sure, the magnitude of this gain is of a higher order of infinitesimal and for smooth contours will become vanishingly small relative to the shrinking size of the change in price. If we made our finite increase in price take place in many small steps, and after each such step made the needed overcompensation of income, then it can be shown that in the limit as the size of each step shrinks to zero we should approach movement along the indifference surface itself.)

It may be left to the reader to verify that in the case of a *seller* of an inferior good, we can similarly infer that raising its price will *never* reduce its quantity supplied. The legitimate *possibility* of a backward-bending or a forward-rising supply curve for a non-inferior good can also be verified. For a good on the verge of being bought or sold, we can deduce the desired Marshallian negative price effect. We can also easily verify that all arguments are fully applicable to the change in expenditure on a Hicksian composite commodity whose prices are constrained to all change in the same proportion.[1]

The diagram on page 4 gives a self-contained geometrical proof of the fundamental theorems.

IV—ANALYTIC PROOF IN GENERAL CASE

An analytic proof for any number of goods proceeds as follows. Write situation 1 as $(q_1^1, \ldots, q_n^1, p_1^1, \ldots, p_n^1, I^1 = \Sigma p^1 q^1)$ or (q^1, p^1, I^1).

[1] For the above arguments we have no need to make any continuity assumptions. Units of goods, price quotations, money income may all be discrete ; the man may find it difficult or *impossible* to spend all his money, and there may be no two batches of goods that are precisely indifferent ! The only assumption is that *availability* of more money income cannot make a man worse off.

Write 2 as $(q^2, p^2, I^2 = I^1)$ where $p_1^2 > p_1^1$ and all other p's are equal. Write 3 as $(q^3, p^3 \equiv p^2, I^3 = \Sigma p^2 q^1)$ so that it has the prices of 2 and enough income to buy (q^1).   In short

(2) $$\Sigma p^2 q^3 = \Sigma p^2 q^1 \geqq \Sigma p^1 q^1 = \Sigma p^2 q^2 \geqq \Sigma p^1 q^2,$$

where the equalities follow from our assumptions about incomes and the inequalities from our assumption that one price alone has definitely been increased and all q's are positive.

If the first good is debarred from being an inferior good, we see that by definition

$$\Sigma p^2 q^3 \geqq \Sigma p^2 q^2 \text{ implies } q_1^3 \geqq q_1^2 \quad (A).$$

Of course 1 can never be revealed to be better than 3, or this would contradict the latter's definition ; hence, from the Weak Axiom (1),

(3) $$\Sigma p^2 q^3 = \Sigma p^2 q^1 \text{ implies } \Sigma p^1 q^3 \geqq \Sigma p^1 q^1 ;$$

these last two relations by addition give

(4) $$\Sigma \ (p^2 - p^1)(q^3 - q^1) = (p_1^2 - p_1^1)(q_1^3 - q_1^1) + 0 + \ . \ . \ . \ + 0 \leqq 0,$$

or $\qquad\qquad q_1^1 \geqq q_1^3 \quad (B).$

Now adding (A) and (B) gives our desired result,[1] $q_1^1 \geqq q_1^2$.

V—UNDERCOMPENSATED CHANGES

The above literary, graphical, and analytic proofs are fully applicable to a *decrease* of prices as well as to an increase. For a price drop, the reader can easily prove the Fundamental Theorem by proceeding from point 2 to point 1 via (a) an overcompensated decrease in price in which income is *taken away* from him until he is left with enough to buy (q^2), and (b) via a restoration of the income which moves him eastward along the Engel's curve through 1.

However, our sense of symmetry suggests that we can say even more than all this. We should be able to duplicate all of our proofs for the case of overcompensated changes by considering the related case of " undercompensated " changes.   To define an undercompensated change, we raise the price of tea but then give the consumer enough extra income until he is buying at the new prices " a batch of goods that he could just barely have afforded to buy with his original income at the original prices ". In graphical terms, our man moves from 1 in Fig. 1 to the point (which the reader can pencil in with the label 4) where 2's Engel's curve intersects with 1's budget line. Obviously, this undercompensated change takes him to a new intermediate point that can never be better than the original point.   Why not ? Because by definition, this point could have been bought in preference to 1, but it was not.   The reader can easily prove that tea must go

[1] If a set of p's had all changed in the same proportion, and if the expenditure on the goods in question was debarred by hypothesis of non-inferiority from moving opposite to money income, we could have used a similar proof to show the necessity of negative price elasticity of such a Hicksian composite commodity. Also, I might mention that $I^1 \geqq \Sigma p^1 q^1$, as in the case where we can't spend all our money, would be admissible.

down in such an undercompensated change; i.e. 4 must lie to the west of 1. Hence, all the previous arguments are applicable.[1]

Anyone familiar with the theory of economic index numbers of the general Pigou-Staehle type will realise the dual rôle that the Laspeyre and Paasche index numbers play as upper and lower bounds. Hence, it will come as no surprise that running parallel with the case of over-compensation is a dual case of undercompensation. The former has certain trifling advantages over the latter, and for the sake of brevity I have given more attention to the case of overcompensation.

VI—Measuring Complementarity in Terms of Overcompensation

This finishes the main task of this note. I shall conclude by asserting briefly some related considerations.

1. The cross-effect upon one good of a small *overcompensated* (or *undercompensated*) change in the price of another good can provide a measure of complementarity and substitutability that has many of the properties of the Slutsky-Schultz-Hicks definition, and which approaches the latter in the limit as the changes become small.[2] (E.g. on this same definition if tea is locally a substitute for coffee, coffee must locally be a substitute for tea ; for all goods, substitutability must outweigh complementarity, so that with two goods, only local substitutes are possible, etc.)

2. The mathematical conditions of *integrability*[3] can be expounded in terms of overcompensated (or undercompensated) changes. Define the overcompensated demand locus

$$(5) \qquad q_i = D^i(p_1, \ldots, p_n, \Sigma p_k \, q_k^o) = F^i(p_1, \ldots, p_n)$$

where (q^o) refers to any given point $D(p^o, I^o)$. This represents a so-called " offer locus " which is tangential to the indifference surface at (q^o), lying outside it everywhere else. At (p^o, q^o), integrability conditions must be satisfied.

$$(6) \qquad \frac{\partial F^i(p_1^o, \ldots, p_n^o)}{\partial p_j} = \frac{\partial F^j(p_1^o, \ldots, p_n^o)}{\partial p_i} \qquad (i, j = 1, 2, \ldots, n).$$

[1] Analytically, we go from $(p^1; q^1, I^1)$ to $(p^2, q^2, I^2 = I^1)$ via $(p^4 \equiv p^2, q^4, I^4)$ where I^4 is just large enough to make $\Sigma p^1 q^4 = \Sigma p^1 q^1$. Using the fact that one price alone changes and the Weak Axiom, the reader should be able to prove $q_1^2 \leq q_1^1$.

[2] Overcompensated measures of complementarity have no particular advantages other than identifiability over ordinary substitutional definitions based on indifference. The overcompensated measure has one possible disadvantage : for finite changes in price that are large enough, it differs from the conventional measure by an " income term " that is always plus for superior goods and opposite for inferior goods ; for large price changes, this term normally works in the direction of substitutability rather than complementarity, even in the case where the usual Slutsky-Schultz-Hicks definition gives unchanging testimony for small and large price changes. The undercompensated measure will have opposite " bias ", their mean a " bias " that is a higher order of infinitesimal.

[3] See integrability article cited at the end of the first footnote, especially Figure 3, p. 366, in *Economica*, November, 1950.

For if they are not, it can be shown that the " indifference contours " on the surface of this offer locus will be spirals converging on (q°) rather than closed contours surrounding it, and we shall then always be able to find a chain of points contradicting the Houthakker Strong Axiom : i.e., we can find point A revealed to be better than B, which is revealed to be better than C, . . ., which is revealed to be better than Z, and then get the strange result that Z is revealed to be better than A, which has thereby indirectly been revealed to be better than itself.

Assuming smoothness, we can prove that the finite relations

$$(6)' \qquad \left(\frac{\triangle q_i}{\triangle p_j}\right) = \left(\frac{\triangle q_j}{\triangle p_i}\right)$$

should be more and more closely realised as the size of the over-compensated changes in each indicated single price becomes smaller and smaller.[1]

It has been demonstrated that the Strong Axiom exhausts the content of the regular theory of consumer's behaviour. An equivalent formulation would be the following requirements on the substitution or over-compensation matrix : (1) it must be symmetric and (2) it must be a negative semi-definite matrix, so that every *linear* composite good has an own-price term that is negative.

Within the narrow framework of relations refutable by a finite number of price-quantity observations, this last result is not entirely satisfactory. Without introducing approximations, or explicit assumptions about the magnitude of higher derivatives, we can never be certain that we have detected a large enough discrepancy to refute integrability. Why not ? Because we can never be sure that taking still smaller changes in prices will not lower the discrepancy. In practice, most of us will be willing to settle for approximate inferences, *faute*

---

[1] This can be seen by writing utility as a function of the overcompensating changes in prices or $U=U(q_1, \ldots) = U(F^1(p_1, \ldots, p_n), \ldots) = V(p_1, \ldots, p_n)$ with $[\partial V(p_1, \ldots, p_n)/\partial p_i]$ proportional to $(q_i - q_i^\circ)$ and vanishing at $p_i = p_i^\circ$. Hence, at p_i°, $[\partial(q_i - q_i^\circ)/\partial p_i]$ is proportional to $[\partial^2 V(p_1^\circ, \ldots, p_n^\circ)/\partial p_i \partial p_j]$, which is symmetric ; this last matrix is also negative semi-definite because the price ratios at (p°) give the lowest utility possible. Professor Hicks in the cited lecture has given an elegant generalisation of (6)' that holds in the limit for any three near-by points on the same indifference contour.

To handle the case of undercompensation, note that around any initial point, $q_1^\circ = D^i(p_1^\circ, \ldots, p_n^\circ, I^\circ)$, we can solve the implicit set of equations

$$\begin{cases} q_1 = D^i(p_1, \ldots, p_n, X) \\ \Sigma p_i^\circ D^i(p_1, \ldots, p_n, X) = \Sigma p_i^\circ q_i^\circ \end{cases}$$

for $q_1 = f^i(p_1, \ldots, p_n)$ and $X = X(p_1, \ldots, p_n)$; then it can be shown that for $U = U(q_1, \ldots) = U(f^1, \ldots) = W(p_1, \ldots, p_n)$, $[\partial f^i(p_1^\circ, \ldots, p_n^\circ)/\partial p_j] = [\partial^2 W/\partial p_i \partial p_j]$ is symmetric, and negative semi-definite by virtue of the fact that the price ratios at (p°) maximise U or W.

It can be shown that taking a mean of overcompensated and undercompensated changes—as e.g. $\frac{1}{2}[f(p_1, \ldots, p_n) + F(p_1, \ldots, p_n)]$—gives a change that agrees locally around (p°) with an indifference change up to derivatives of still higher order: such a locus osculates the indifference surface so as to have not only the same slope but also the same curvature.

de mieux. But if we wish (p, q) data to provide an exact refutation, we must fall back on the search for a finite chain contradicting the Strong Axiom of revealed preferences ; thanks to the work of Houthakker, Wold, Ville, and others, we know that every non-integrable preference field will display such a contradiction to the investigator who is patient enough to take enough observations close enough together.

But how many observations is " enough " and how close is " close enough " ? For a long time I have been trying to find a theorem stating the minimum number of situations that will serve to refute a non-integrable preference field in n dimensions. I have had no success. If my confidence in my powers were greater, I should be tempted to conjecture that the needed number cannot be specified in advance but will depend upon the magnitude of higher partial derivatives. Light on this open question would be welcome.

M.I.T., Cambridge, U.S.A.

PART II

Stochastic Models of Consumer's Behavior

12

Probability and the Attempts to Measure Utility

Paul A. Samuelson

Massachusetts Institute of
Technology Cambridge, Massachusetts

1. By the 1890's Pareto and Irving Fisher came to realize that the *cardinal* measurability of utility postulated by earlier economic theorists such as Bentham and Edgeworth could be dispensed with in favor of purely *ordinal* utility dealing only with more or less. To the modern theorist cardinal utility is irrelevant both for the positive explanation of demand behavior and for normative welfare economics.

Nonetheless, a few still engage in the parlor-game of devising assumptions which define a unique measure of cardinal utility. This can be done by a variety of different tricks, with the most common ones involving an arbitrary assumption of *additive* utility functions. One of the oldest of these procedures has recently come into vogue again ; it involves an attempt to identify a utility function by observing the response of the consumer to probability situations. Only in special empirical cases is this procedure valid ; and even in the narrow class of cases where not invalid, it is only of limited theoretical interest except as a convenient way of unifying the description of the consumer's *ordinal* behavior with respect to gambling and insurance. ⸰ In the following I have stated my views on this matter rather dogmatically so as to provide a broad target for discussion and criticism.

2. Bernoulli and Marshall[1] argued that if utility grows linearly with income (margi-

nal utility being constant) then people will risk a 50 per cent chance of a $1 loss if compensated by an equal chance of a $1 gain. On the other hand, if the law of diminishing marginal utility holds, it will be necessary to compensate people for such a risk of loss by the chance of a larger gain. Peoples' reactions to gambling can thus not only reveal the qualitative behavior of marginal utility, but the exact *quantitative* properties of the utility function as well.[2]

1) A. Marshall, *Principles of Economics*, 8th ed., pp. 135, 842-3. Also see M. Friedman and L. J. Savage, "The Utility Analysis of Choices Involving Risk," *Journal of Political Economy*, Vol. 54 (1948) pp. 279-304 for valuable discussion and further references. J. v. Neumann and O. Morgenstern, *Theory of Games and Economic Behavior*, (Prinston, 1944 and 1947) has given the theory a rigorous axiomatic basis. Neither Daniel Bernoulli nor Marshall can be credited with particularly original contributions, but their names have become associated with their theory.

2) Except for scale and origin constants, a determinate function $U=f(x)=\int_0^x f'(s)ds$ can be defined by an infinity of *different* experimental set-ups. E.g. around any income level x_0, we can observe the empirical relation between a 1/2 chance of a loss of h and the 1/2 chance of a compensatory gain, g; this function $g=g(h;x_0)$ determines $f'(x)$ in all but scale. Or for any two income levels, x_1 and x_2 surrounding x_0, there will be an observable unique probability of x_1, p, that will leave the man indifferent as compared to a sure and certain x_0; call this observed function, $p(x_1, x_2; x_0)$. From it too we can determine $f'(x)$. A third method is to study the limiting behavior of $2[g(h;x_0)-h]/h^2$ as h goes to 0. This defines $\partial^2 g/\partial h^2$, which can be shown to equal $-2f''(x_0)/f'(x_0)$; and from this we can easily get the elasticity of the marginal utility function and (by integration over x_0) its complete shape. An infinity of other similar experiments can be devised ; and except in an unlikely special empirical case, each method can be expected to yield a *different* utility function.

Some of the gross facts about gambling for some people are consistent with this theory—e.g. the classical case of a man who never gambles at mathematically fair odds and who pays to be hedged by insurance. But the perfectly possible case of a man who refuses fair small bets at all income levels and yet buys lottery tickets can be handled only by going beyond this simple theory. As yet I know of no empirical predictions that this theory has suggested which have turned out to be (1) valid and (2) novel or inexplicable without this special theory. I may also record the personal view that the sociology of gambling is infinitely richer than this particular theory permits : There is as much to be learned about gambling from Dostoyevsky as from Pascal.

3. My present purpose, however, is not to examine the factual basis of the Bernoulli-Marshall theory of numerical utility, but to show its arbitrariness at the logical level. Moreover, I shall not criticise its gravest defect of bypassing the basic philosophical problem of induction : No philosopher has yet provided the bridge between purely deductive mathematical probability (combinatorial analysis, set and measure theory) and the empirical problem of making a finite number of decisions. Mathematicians, properly, ignore this problem and confine themselves with defining procedures which will be optimal if followed an infinite number of times under ideally defined conditions. But whether I should risk my only child's life in an operation, or believe a witness in court, or back a certain horse or investment project—on these questions mathematical probability gives little counsel.

This basic problem is not peculiar to the Bernoulli-Marshall theory, so I too shall bypass it here and grant that probabilities p_1,

$p_2 \cdots$ of income levels $x_1, x_2 \cdots$, have a meaning and relevance to the individual's single decisions. More specifically, given any two situations

A $\quad x_1{}^a, x_2{}^a \cdots;\ p_1{}^a, p_2{}^a \cdots$

B $\quad x_1{}^b, x_2{}^b \cdots;\ p_1{}^b, p_2{}^b \cdots$

with $\sum p = 1$, I assume the individual can always decide whether A is worse than B, or B is worse than A, or A and B are indifferent.[3]

In effect, this means that we can define an indefinite number of numerical indexes or indicators of ordinal preference, of the form

$$V(x_1, x_2, \cdots;\ p_1, p_2, \cdots)$$
or $\quad W(V) = W(x_1, x_2, \cdots;\ p_1, p_2, \cdots)$

with A worse than B implying $V(A) < V(B)$, A indifferent to B implying $V(A) = V(B)$, and with $W(V)$ any one-directional function or renumbering. The indifference loci determined by V or W held constant are empirically identifiable by behavioristic experiments.

For the sake of keeping the exposition simple we may postulate continuity and differentiability of the functions. What properties can we expect of this ordinal preference pattern showing reactions to risk ? Unless we confine ourselves to relatively " rational " men, very few *a priori* restrictions can be placed on the data. And if we do agree to confine ourselves to " rational " men, then there is danger of ending up with completely tautological semantic results that entirely depend upon what we choose to read into the word " rationality." Thus, we might end up with the fatuity : " Rational men fulfill the Bernoulli-Marshall conditions, because that is the definition of rationality."

3) Moreover, I assume that this has all the properties of consistent ordinal preference : e.g. A worse than B, and B worse than C, means A worse than C, and similar transitivity relations.

Actually, there is no need to descend to this level of inanity. Certain " reasonable " properties of the V or W functions can be hypothesized.* For example, in the simple case of only two income situations, where $p_1 = 1 - p_2 = p$, our indifference contours are defined by surfaces

$$W[V(x_1, x_2; \; p)] = \text{constant}$$

in the (x_1, x_2, p) space. There is no harm in confining ourselves to the region in which $x_1 \geq x_2$, so that we can always think of p as the probability of the *larger* of the two incomes, with $1 - p$ the other probability.

Then the obviously reasonable requirements on the preference pattern are as follows :

Basis Hypothesis : An increase in any of the three variables, x_1 or x_2, or p, will tend to lead to higher preference.

Thus, raising one of the incomes and changing nothing else will certainly give the man a new situation that has everything the previous situation had, and *something additional* too. Or increasing the probability of a larger income at the expense of a smaller one should certainly make him better off. Only in the limiting case where the two incomes are equal will changes in p be of complete indifference.

The task of the empirical statistician is to record for the human guinea-pig the exact form of this one-parameter family of indifference-surfaces. Aside from the Basic Hypothesis he has no legitimate right to expect these surfaces to satisfy any special laws. Needless to say he has no right to expect that the behavior of the surfaces in one part of the space dictates how they *must* behave in any other part of the space —

any more than we have a right to extrapolate from a poor man's consumption of tea what his consumption of yachts *must* be when he is rich.

4. The Bernoulli-Marshall theory can be easily shown to involve not-easily-recognized special arbitrary assumption about the family of indifference surfaces—namely that all of the surfaces *everywhere* can be determined by heroic extrapolation, from the behavior of their partial derivatives upon an *arbitrary curve in space.*[4]

In my judgment this is nonsense. The most rational man I ever met, whom I shall

4) The earlier footnote dealing with three out of an infinity of ways of identifying $V = \int_0^z f'(s)\,ds$ provides examples. A geometrical way of stating the Bernoulli-Marshall straight-jacket is as follows: for fixed $(x_1^\alpha, x_2^\alpha; \; p^\alpha)$, the relation $W(x_1, x_2; \; p^\alpha) = W(x_1^\alpha, x_2^\alpha; \; p^\alpha)$ defines a horizontal indifference curve in space. There will always exist a mutual stretching of the axes, $x_i = f(x_i)$ which will make *this* curve a straight line. But only in the Bernolli-Marshall curve will this stretching make *all the surfaces satisfy arbitrary relations* $p x_1 + (1-p) x_2 = \text{con-}$ stant, with all horizontal indifference curves becoming perfectly straight lines.

Necessary and sufficient conditions for the empirical data to be of the B-M form can be written in many equivalent ways. One operationally meaningful procedure is to define.

$G = \log(1-p) - \log p + \log(-\partial x_2/\partial x_1)$ $v = \text{constant}$
Then

$$\frac{\partial G}{\partial p} \equiv 0, \quad \frac{\partial^2 G}{\partial x_1 \partial x_2} \equiv 0, \quad G(x_1, x_2) \equiv -G(x_2 x_1)$$

are together necessary and sufficient conditions : of course,

$$G(x_1, x_2) = \log f'(x_2) = \log f'(x_1)$$
$$= \int_{x_1}^{x_2} [d \log f'(x)/dx] dx.$$

Prof. Jacob Marschak of Chicago has worked out some further conditions that must be satisfied when there are more than two income situations. My colleague, Prof. Robert L. Bishop, has worked out a variety of consistency conditions that follow from B-M theory. I have also been informed by Prof. William J. Baumol of Princeton that he has unpublished criticisms of the B-M theory.

---

* Even this hypothesis appears to me to be inconsistent with the rich sociology of gambling and risk-taking.

call Ysidro, determined his own ordinal preference pattern and found that it satisfied the exact equation of the well known " ideal index "

$$W = W[(p_1\psi_1 + p_2\psi_2)^{\frac{1}{2}}(p_1\psi_1^{-1} + p_2\psi_2^{-1})^{-\frac{1}{2}}]$$

where $p_1 + p_2 = 1$, and $W'(V)$ is an arbitrary positive function.[5] When told that he did not satisfy all of the v. Newmann-Morgenstern axioms,[6] he replied that he thought it more rational to satisfy his preferences and let the axioms satisfy themselves. Once the empirical implications of the v. Neumann-Morgenstern axioms are understood, their arbitrariness and that of the Bernoulli-Marshall theory stands revealed.

The history of statistical theory is replete with cases where writers have postulated innocent-seeming restrictions and achieved far-reaching and arbitrary results. The great Gauss himself provided two examples which he came later to regret : He once thought an ideal " mean " should be a symmetric and continuously differentiable function which (1) grows by a if each observation grows by a, and which (2) is multiplied by a scale factor, b, when each observation is so multiplied. This leads to the arithmetic mean as the ideal statistic, a highly arbitrary result that stayed in many text-books for a century. Similarly, he made an error in calculating a maximum likelihood statistic and ended up, in effect, defining the " ideal curve of error " as that function for which the arithmetic mean is a maximum-likelihood statistic. He might have achieved the same

gratuitous result as cheaply by defining the " perfect " error function as that one for which $\sum x/n$ and $\sum(x - \sum x/n)^2/n$ are independently distributed. Some text-book writers have also followed Clerk Maxwell's similar-type proof of the normal curve based on arbitrarily postulated invariances under axis-rotations of coordinates. Eddington has recently carried this ancient art of *a priori* reasoning even further. If only the data knew what men know, planets might move in perfect circles and incomes might be distributed along Pareto curves.

5. Why did such a plausible theory of utility maximizing lead to such implausible— if not down-right nonsensical—results ? I suppose the answer lies in the fact that it is not really a very plausible theory once you examine it carefully. Those who are familiar with the magic by which Irving Fisher, Frisch, and Samuelson were able to put the rabbit of cardinal utility into their hats[7]

---

5) Ysidro's father and mother had B-W functions, but he inherited a blend of them which is *not* such a function.

6) J. v. Neumann and O. Morgenstern, *Theory of Games and Economic Behavior*, 2nd ed., 1947, pp. 17-31, and Appendix. See my appendix for more details. In the future I hope to give a more lengthy survey of these axioms.

7) Irving Fisher, " A Statistical Method for Measuring ' Marginal Utility ' and Testing the Justice of a progressive Income Tax " in *Economic Essays in Honor of John Bates Clark* (1927). R. Frisch, " New methods of Measuring Marginal Utility," *Beiträge zur ökonomischen Theorie*, no. 3 (1932). These involve an " additive " assumption in the field of budgetary consumption data. Still another type of additive assumption in utilities over time—along the lines of Böhm-Bawerk's first ground for interest because of expected increases of future income—permits a unique measurement of conventionally-defined cardinal utility ; see P. A. Samuelson, " A Note on the Measurement of Utility," *Review of Economic Studies*, Vol. 4, (1937), pp. 155-61, where some, but not all, of the empirical implications of this procedure are indicated. A not-at-all-obvious " independence assumption " can be shown to give v. Neumann and Morgenstern their results. Readers interested in cardinality of utility will find technical writings of Bishop, Vickrey, Lange, Bernardelli, Lerner, Armstrong, Zeuthen, *et al* of interest. Cf. K. Menger " Das Unsicherheitsmoment in der Wertlehre," *Zeitschrift für Nationalökonomie*, Vol. 5 (1934) pp. 458-85, *especially* 481 ff.

easily recognize that the use of an *arithmetic mean* involves an arbitrary *additive* assumption. Why not the median? Or some other type of mean? Many of these, but not all, would negate the Bernoulli-Marshall theory.

I think the acceptance of "mathematical expectation of utility" or its "arithmetic mean" was an unthinking carryover from the mathematical theory of the law of large numbers as applied to asymptotic processes. Suppose two gamblers each have an infinite amount of money or credit and they gamble together at "potentially fair odds" and infinite number of times, or a very large number of times; suppose one of them acts to maximize the arithmetic mean of his money winnings (*not* of their utility:) and the other maximizes something different. Then as the length of play grows, the probability *approaches in the limit* unity that the first man's winnings will exceed any prescribed number. For finite sequences, however long they may be, the basic philosophical problem remains; and even for infinite sequences, the theory seems already to have assumed away any change in marginal

utility by its assumption of infinite wealth. Where money is concerned, the additive assumption of the arithmetic mean has an inherent rationale, because *coins are added to coins* in forming a stock of wealth. But to assume that there is *a utility bank in which people make deposits and withdrawals over time* is not only implausible nonsense, but comes close to begging the issue.

A possible limited valid use of the Bernoulli-Marshall methods is in the smoothing of imperfectly observed parts of the surfaces; this is quite different from using them for extrapolation to unobserved parts of the space. Unfortunately, existing experimental techniques seem too crude to make the most interesting tests of all—namely, the extent to which the Bernoulli-Marshall specializations are invalid or valid.*

---

* And even if there should turn out to be a non-empty class of people for whom these special relations hold, we must not forget that it is their *ordinal* behavior that is of interest; there is no special significance to be attached to the convention of calling the special index of utility $V = pf(x_1) + (1-p)f(x_2)$ the true measure of utility: $W(V) = f^{-1}(V)$ has the interesting property $W(x, x; p) = x$, but it too has no privileged status as numbering of ordinal utility.

APPENDIX

I suspect that I must be quite confused in my interpretation of the logical basis of the v. Neumann-Morgenstern and Friedman-Savage theories since so many eminent mathematicians and economists rarely go wrong in the field of pure deduction. I am a little fearful, therefore, to confess that I regard both systems to be unacceptable, and as far as I can see not even consistent between themselves.

Friedman and Savage (*op. cit* pp. 287-8) base their whole logical case on the following:

[α] "The hypothesis that is proposed for rationalizing the behavior just summarized can be stated compactly as follows: In choosing among alternatives open to it, whether or not these alternatives involve risk, a consumer unit (generally a family, sometimes an individual) behaves as if (a) it had a consistent set of preferences; (b) these preferences could be completely described by a function attaching a numerical value—to be designated "utility"—to alternatives each of which is regarded as certain; (c) its objective were to make its expected utility as large as possible. [β] It is the contribution of von Neumann and Morgenstern to have shown that an alternative statement of the same hypothesis is: An individual chooses in accordance with a system of preferences which has the following properties:

1. The system is complete and consistent; that is an individual can tell which of two objects he prefers or whether he is indifferent between them, and if he does not prefer C to B and does not prefer B to A, then he does not prefer C to A. (In this context, the word 'object' includes combinations of objects with stated probabilities; for example, if A and B are objects, a 40-60 chance of A or B is also an object.)

2. Any object which is a combination of other objects with stated probabilities is never preferred to every one of these other objects, nor is every one of them ever preferred to the combination.

3. If the object A is prefered to the object B and B to the object C, there will be some probability combination of A and C such that the individual is indifferent between it and B " [Two footnotes omitted by me.]

To me [α] is completely arbitrary and inadmissable, while [β] appears quite acceptable and rather harmless. Indeed my continuity assumptions plus the Basic Hypothesis on the V and $W(V)$ functions, which I shall call [γ], seem to me to be equivalent to [β], except for a few technical details concerning the overstringency of my differentiability conditions. Ysidro's function I believe satisfies [β] but not [α].

Yet Friedman and Savage believe that v. Neumann and Morgenstern have shown the complete equivalence of [α] and [β]. The complete axioms of v. Neumann and Morgenstern (*Theory of Games*, pp. 26-7) are too long to quote here; let us call them [δ]. In the sense in which [δ] is logically equivalent to [α], it must also be unacceptable to me. Therefore, I must doubt that both [β] ≡[δ] and [δ]≡[α] are true.

How can I account for all my strange views? The most likely explanation is that I am simply confused. But assuming the contrary, let me record the suggestion that the v. Neumann-Morgenstern axioms, in the sense that they are equivalent to [β] and in the sense that they are economically acceptable, are *not* equivalent to [α]. How have the authors of the *Theory of Games* deceived themselves as to the inevitability of their demonstration of the measurability of utility—if it should turn out that they are wrong?

My tentative guess is as follows: they have not made a simple error in logic, but have implicitly added a hidden and unacceptable premise to their axioms. The empirical content of their axioms can be translated into the terminology of ordinal utility, $W = W[V(x; p)]$, and they then become unobjectionable. In this purely ordinal context, let us call the axioms [δ]′ rather* than

---

* In terms of their axioms 3: A to 3: C, I think [δ]′ would read
A: There exists $V(x_1, x_2\cdots; p_1, p_2,\cdots)$ and $W(V)$ functions which satisfy the usual transitivity relations.
B: The W and V functions have appropriate continuity properties, and $\partial V/\partial x_i > 0$; $\dfrac{\partial V/\partial x_i}{\partial V/\partial x_j} - 1$ has the sign of $(x_i - x_j)$.
C: V is symmetrical and depends only on the final income sitution, no matter how the lottery tickets and probabilities are compounded.
On this definition [β]≡[γ]≡[δ]′≢[δ]≡[α], as I hope to show in a later paper.

[δ]. I believe there to be a world of difference between [∂] and [δ]'.

Whatever the logical validity and economic admissibility of the complete v. Neumann-Morgenstern axioms, the preliminary literary discussion leading up to these axioms appears open to objections. For example, the authors follow the excellent example of Pareto, Bowley, and Lange and argue that if we can always *ordinally* relate any two *changes in well-being*, then we can define a *cardinal* measure of well-being or utility. Thus, if I cannot go beyond statements of the type : ." I like Paris better than London, and I like New York better than Chicago," then only *ordinal* utility statements are possible. But if I can make statements like the following : " I like Paris as much better than London as I like New York better than Chicago," then a numerical scale of utility can be defined.

Now there are some subtle difficulties with this type of argument and certain implicit assumptions must be made if the result is to follow.* But let us waive these subtleties and for the moment grant the

* See O. Lange, " The Determinateness of the Utility Function," *Review of Economic Studies*, Vol. 1 (1934), pp. 218-25 and later articles appearing in the same journal over the next five years by R.G. D. Allen, Phelps Brown, Bernardelli, Lange, and Samuelson. F. Alt published in the Zeitschrift für Nationalökonomie (1936) an axiomatic treatment of a similar problem.

authours this convention that *the cardinal utility to me of Rome is exactly half way between that of London and Paris if I am indifferent between the certain prospect of going to Rome and a (.5, .5) chance of going to London or Paris*. This has been shown by my colleague Prof. Robert L. Bishop *not* to define a satisfactory scale of utility in the general case. Only in the very special Bernoulli-Marshall case will a unique self-consistent scale be defined. If the validity of the " Bishop-effect " is granted, then the authors appear in this part of their discussion to have begged the question at issue.

To see why their procedure leads to contradictory scales, suppose that they have found five situations that are equally spaced in their defined metric.

milk   *wine*   tea   *fruit juice*   coffee

This means that a certain and sure cup of tea is equally attractive to a (.5, .5) chance of getting a cup of fruit juice or of wine; and so forth for the other items. Now let us exclude the italicized intermediate items so that we have the sequence

milk   tea   coffee

For a general surface such as is described in this paper, will it be necessarily true that tea is then " half way " between milk and coffee ?

The answer is " no, not necessarily," as Prof. Bishop has shown. I hope he will publish his discussion at some later date.

1965 POSTSCRIPT

Soon after this paper appeared, I changed my mind about its contents as a result of correspondence with L. J. Savage, then of Chicago but now at Yale, and as a result of the fundamental reformulation of stochastic utility theory by Professor Jacob Marschak (who, I seem to recall, enjoyed many discussions on this topic with Herman Rubin). In particular, everything said in the present paper deserves to be said if one is unwilling to posit what I have called the "Independence Axiom" in my two 1951 papers on the subject. Then the Ysidro ordinal indicator, $(\Sigma P_j X_j)^{1/2}(\Sigma P_j X_j^{-1})^{-1/2}$, which is indeed inconsistent with any Bernoulli-Neumann ordinal indicator of the form $\Sigma P_j U(X_j)$, is admissible. But as Savage pointed out to me in a 1950 letter, duplicating a similar argument that had been made by Frank P. Ramsey prior to 1930, if I behave like an Ysidro, I can, so to speak, make book against myself and end up making — or shall I say losing? — money!

Suppose indifference between the options on lottery tickets, \$2 certain or (\$1, \$4) with respective probabilities $(1/2, 1/2)$, necessarily implies indifference among each of these and any composite lottery ticket which is a probability blend of them — namely (\$2, \$1, \$4) with respective probabilities $(1 - p, p/2, p/2)$. Agreeing to this necessitous implication is equivalent to positing what I elsewhere call the basic "Independence Axiom" of additivity. Stipulating it rules out the Ysidro function, and any ordinal function that cannot be put into the form $W[\Sigma P_j U(X_j)]$, $W'[\,.\,] > 0$; it also rules out, by postulation, the Bishop effect discussed in the Appendix. Von Neumann, in the last edition of the *Theory of Games* published before his death, seems to have rejected my criticism of the axiom system of stochastic utility in that book. However, I believe most readers will agree that Edmond Malinvaud, "Note on von Neumann-Morgenstern's Strong Independence Axiom," *Econometrica*, Vol. 20 (October 1952), p. 679, did successfully verify my suggestion that von Neumann and Morgenstern inadvertently slipped the important Independence Axiom into their "zeroth axiom" by which the entities of their system are defined.

There is another point about welfare economics. For the last few years I have come to regret the last sentence of this paper's first paragraph, specifically: "To the modern theorist cardinal utility is irrelevant both for the positive explanation of demand behavior and for normative welfare economics." This recantation came from my rediscovering (the hard way!) a basic theorem that had been first enunciated in John C. Harsanyi, "Cardinal Welfare, Individualistic Ethics, and Interpersonal Comparisons of Utility," *Journal of Political Economy*, Vol. 63 (August 1955), pp. 309–321. To understand it, define $X^j = (X_1^j, X_2^j, \cdots)$ as the vector of consumption goods of the jth man, $U^j(X^j)$ as an ordinal indicator of utility for him, and $W(X^1, X^2, \cdots X^j, \cdots)$ as a Bergson social welfare function. So far there is no need to utilize individuals' ordinal utility notions like $U^j(X^j)$ or $F^j[U^j(X_j)]$. But suppose W is an individualistic social welfare function. Then Bergson insists that we be able to posit the following "tree property": $W(X^1, X^2, \cdots) \equiv f[U^1(X^1), U^2(X^2), \cdots]$. This says, "In nonstochastic situations, if every man thinks he is better off, then social welfare is necessarily better off." Now make a new step forward and stipulate an "individualistic *ex ante* social welfare function," which says, "If all men think *ex ante* that a particular prospect makes them better off, then the *ex ante* individualistic social welfare function is necessarily (ordinally) higher." Add to this the same regularity Independence Axiom, which holds for each man, and posit it for the social welfare function. Just as it follows that each regular *ex ante* U^j can be put in the probabilistic form $\Sigma_i P_i u^j\{X^j(i)\}$ where $u^j = F^j[U^j\{X^j\}]$ represents the Bernoulli-Neumann cardinal utility whose first moment is maximized and where P_i represents the probability of the ith "state of the world" in which $X = [X^1(i), X^2(i), \cdots]$, so must the *ex ante* social welfare function (that satisfies the probabilistic independent axiom) be capable of being written in the form $\Sigma P_i w[u^1\{X^1(i)\}, u^2\{X^2(i)\}, \cdots]$. If also it is *ex ante* individualistic with the tree property, we must in the end have

$$\sum_i P_i w[u^1\{X^1(i)\}, u^2\{X^2(i)\}, \cdots] \equiv f\left[\sum_i P_i u^1\{X^1(i)\}, \sum_i P_i u^2\{X^2(i)\}, \cdots\right].$$

If we posit smooth differentiability for the functions w and f, the equivalent functional equation

$$\sum_i P_i w(y_i^1, y_i^2, \cdots) \equiv f\left[\sum_i P_i y_i^1, \sum_i P_i y_i^2, \cdots\right]$$

can easily be shown to have as necessary solutions

$$f[Y^1, Y^2, \cdots] = A^1 Y^1 + A^2 Y^2 + \cdots,$$
$$w[Z^1, Z^2, \cdots] = A^1 Z^1 + A^2 Z^2 + \cdots,$$

leading to the final additive form for the "individualistic (regular) *ex ante* social welfare" function

$$w = A^1 u^1(X^1) + A^2 u^2(X^2) + \cdots, A^j > 0.$$

From 1938 to around 1960, overlooking these Harsanyi probability implications, I thought that functions like

$$[1/2\, u^1(X^1) + 1/2\, u^2(X^2)]^{1/2}\,[1/2\, u^1(X^1)^{-1} + 1/2\, u^2(X^2)^{-1}]^{-1/2},$$

which *cannot* be put into additive form, were admissible Bergson social welfare functions. Although I should hate to agree that people's *ex ante* probability judgments are *always* to be accepted (as, for example, when people are inveterate gamblers of their food money), these probability considerations have caused me to change my views in an important way.

For those who like logical paradoxes, let me point out that one does seem involved here. The additive form, written out in nonvector, nonstochastic form,

$$w = A^1 u^1(x_1^1, x_2^1, \cdots) + A^2 u^2(x_1^2, x_2^2, \cdots) + \cdots,$$

has the ordinal implication

$$\frac{\partial}{\partial x_k^2} \frac{\partial w/\partial x_i^1}{\partial w/\partial x_j^1} \equiv 0,$$

for all i, j, k. This strong observable implication for a purely nonstochastic case follows, apparently, from the mere *contemplation* of the *possibility* of a stochastic situation involving probabilities $(P_1, P_2, \cdots)$ even if there were no probability variations at all possible in actual fact! That is, suppose the actual world under view involves only $(P_1, P_2, \cdots) \equiv (1, 0, \cdots)$, the possibility that the P's *could* be fractional — even though they are not — puts restrictions on the $(1, 0, \cdots)$ case.

13

UTILITY, PREFERENCE, AND PROBABILITY[1]

INTRODUCTION

For brevity, we may give the name Bernoulli utility theory to the notion that a rational individual, confronted with different "income-situations" $(X_1, X_2, \cdots, X_n)$, each with respective mutually exclusive nonnegative probabilities $(x_1, x_2, \cdots, x_n = 1 - x_1 - \cdots - x_{n-1})$, chooses among them *as if* he were trying to maximize $u = \Sigma x_1 p(X_1)$, where $p(X_1)$ is a conceptually observable function, unique up to a linear transformation involving arbitrary scale and origin constants. A long line of writers before and since Bernoulli have believed in such a formulation: for example, the famous "moral expectation" solution to the St. Petersburg paradox; the proofs of Jeremy Bentham that gambling is bad and insurance is good, and the similar better-known proofs of Marshall's *Principles*; the recent revival by von Neumann and Morgenstern of similar cardinal utility notions in connection with game theory; the empirical inferences and hypotheses of Törnqvist, Friedman-Savage, and Mosteller; the theoretical reformulations by Nash, Marschak, Savage, Dalkey, and the present author; the rediscovery of Frank Ramsey's foundations for probability, the work of Finetti, and the modern Wald-like theories of efficient statistical decision making. There have also been criticisms of this theory by Knight, Shackle, Baumol, R. L. Bishop, Allais, the present author, and many others. A useful

[1]Brief abstract of a paper given before the conference on "Les fondements et applications de la théorie du risque en économétrie," May 1952.

survey giving references to most of the important papers is that of K. J. Arrow, *Econometrica*, Vol. 19 (October 1951), pp. 404–437.

Partly through the patient good offices of Savage, my own earlier opposition to the theory has been modified. From the standpoint of explaining *actual behavior* of men on this planet, the Bernoulli utility hypothesis appears to me to be of rather trifling significance. Even since I have become sympathetic toward the theory, I have not been able to find any confirmation of the theory's aspects that are special and (therefore) interesting. In saying this I am not using the perfectionist standards by which we could easily discredit any part of economic theory — such as the theory of nonstochastic indifference curves, or the maximization of profits. I am making all the generous allowances and abstractions that are needed to leave those theories with a residue of explanatory interest.

Part of the reason why actual economic and sociological behavior in the presence of uncertainty escapes the net of the Bernoulli utility hypothesis lies in the complexity of the probability inferences that must be made and in the implied calculations. If this were all, in time we might find a growth of use of Bernoulli methods by professional statisticians, and *their* empirical behavior might become partially interpretable in terms of the Bernoulli hypothesis. But part, and probably the largest part, of human behavior is probably intrinsically and inescapably different from the utility hypothesis, precisely because the things it denies — pleasures of gambling or of uncertainty, love of danger, taboos, etc. — are sociologically and economically important for Homo sapiens.

If we turn from the *empirical* validity of the theory, what can we say about its *normative* significance? Even if imperfect humans don't behave in the way it prescribes, *oughtn't* they to? I do not wish to be dogmatic on this point, since it is still in need of much further searching examination. But, as yet, I have not seen any demonstrations of the theory's normative properties. Most of the suggested demonstrations seem either (1) to beg the question; or (2) to boil down to an exhortation to people to be "consistent" or "elegant," which raises questions presently to be discussed; or (3) to invoke one or another of the large number "limit theorems," so that the man who does not follow the theory will, over a large number of repeated decisions, be "probably" bested by the man who does follow the theory. This last type of argument is very important as a defense of statistical procedures of the Fisher-Neyman type, since these are shown to have asymptotic efficiency; but it completely, in my view, fails to meet the basic philosophical problem of how one reacts to a single event or to a single compound event consisting of a *finite* (albeit very long) sequence. What is at stake is the epsilon of divergence of probability from one, which is inevitably present in any finite sample. Where the hole of the doughnut is what is in question, one only obscures the issue by taking for an expository example a doughnut with a very small hole.

Almost the least important part of the problem — especially once it has been clarified — is the purely *deductive* analysis of various axiomatic foundations for the Bernoulli utility theory. Here good mathematical analysis should remove all disagreements. It is true that there still seems to remain something of a shroud of mystery about the interpretation of the Neumann-Morgenstern axiomatic system, and it is perhaps something of mathematical scandal that this should still be the case at this late date. (I have heard one mathematician in almost the same breath describe the *Games* axiom $3:C:b$ as a (redundant?) truism of combinatorial probability and as a questionable hypothesis; other literary summaries of the content of these axioms have been given which need not lead to Bernoulli utility.)

In recent years, Nash, Marschak, myself, and others have in effect turned away from the particular *Games* axiomatic formulation and have replaced it by what I shall describe as "a complete ordering of probability-income situations, involving no necessary connection with cardinal utility, but where the complete ordering satisfies a *strong independence assumption*": this turns out essentially to imply the complete Bernoulli utility theory. (If one tries to find the axiom or subset of axioms of the *Games* formulation that corresponds to this independence assumption, one seems almost to look in vain; I suspect that the key to this paradox rests in the fact that the crucial assumption of von Neumann and Morgenstern is not in any one of their axioms from 1 to n but rather "in" their "zeroth" axiom or preliminary entities and concepts in terms of which the axioms are couched; some mathematician should clear this all up.)

After two different logical formulations have been found to be equivalent to each other and to meet the tests of logical consistence, completeness, and lack of redundancy, we must in a deeper sense be indifferent between them. Nonetheless, one formulation may for extralogical reasons be preferable to the other. The approach to ordinal preference via the strong independence axiom to be given later can only be superficially different from an outright axiom that there exists a cardinal utility whose weighted-arithmetic-mean or first moment the individual tries to maximize. The argument that one formulation is more intrinsically plausible or elegant than the other is impressive, but it has only a stopgap significance and will not really stand up once we have *familiarized* ourselves with the logical identities involved. There is, perhaps, the attractive feature to the formulation in terms of the independence axiom that some of the empirical, testable, operationally meaningful implications of the Bernoulli theory are prominently displayed from the very beginning to the eye of both the uninitiated and the initiated.

Within the purely *deductive* realm of any problem, no real disagreements can persist. If someone wishes to make stronger or weaker axioms than I do, and if he correctly translates his results into other propositions and theorems, I have no way of establishing the deductive supremacy of my system over his. Just as there is no arguing about tastes, there is, from the purely deductive side, no arguing about axioms.

Having successively stripped the Bernoulli theory of its (1) *empirical,* (2) *normative,* and (3) *deductive* supremacy, what have I left to justify its interest and importance? In what sense have I recanted from my position of a few years ago?[2] As I expressed the matter at the September 1950 meetings of the Econometric Society, held in conjunction with the International Congress of Mathematics, the new significance of the Bernoulli theory to me is of an *aesthetic* and *semantic* character. The problem that I have in mind is not how people behave, nor how they ought to behave, nor what axiomatic systems logicians should formulate and analyze. It is rather the following: Given the ancient usages with respect to how a "rational man" behaves, and given the modern economist's reduction of the rational behavior concept down to little more than "consistent" preference behavior, what strength of axioms most "naturally" fits in with usage?

Prior to 1950, I felt that it seemed most appropriate to assume that the individual had transitive preferences among probability-income situations, and to assume a few weak restrictions on these preferences (for example, increasing the probability of a big prize at the expense of a smaller prize must make a lottery ticket more attractive). I felt that any further strengthening of axioms involved jumping across a natural discontinuity from an aesthetic and semantic standpoint. Others might care to make the jump, but I felt no need or desire to do so. However, since the summer of 1950, I was converted to the view that consistency of ordinal preference with respect to mutually exclusive *ex ante* probabilities should be naturally construed to include the *fundamental independence axiom.* In the field of nonstochastic choice, independence assumptions with their additive implications represent the usual trick by which cardinal utility is defined. I felt, and still feel, that such assumptions there have little empirical, normative, logical, or semantic-aesthetic support. But without pretending that I have settled notions concerning the philosophical foundations of *probability,* I am inclined to think that in this realm independence is a natural if not inevitable concept.

Thus far, I have not explicitly written down the nature of the fundamental independence assumption. The remainder of this paper is devoted

[2] "Probability and the Attempts to Measure Utility," *Economic Review,* Tokyo University of Commerce (Hitotsubashi University), Vol. 1 (July 1950), pp. 167–173, English and Japanese translations.

to a brief sketch of what now seems to me as the best theoretical formulation of ordinal preference.

Axioms of Ordinal Preference in Probability Situations

0.1. Definition of 100-Per-Cent-Certain Income Situations.

As in nonstochastic theory, the individual can be thought of as choosing between different amounts of money expendable at constant prices: for example, I prefer \$10 to \$5 today, or I prefer \$5 today spendable at New York City prices to \$10 spendable at Washington prices. Or, instead of dealing with money, we can deal with a market basket of goods, whose composition is defined, so that I can speak of preferring 5 baskets of bread and wine to 4 baskets of bread and wine. Or, more generally, the certain-income situations may not be represented as one-dimensional scalars, but rather as many-component vectors. Such a vector consists of a specified numerical amount of *each* of m economic goods and services, but can be written by the single letter X, or X_1 or X_2 or Y, etc. To underline the fact that the income situations are 100 per cent certain, we could insist on writing these as $(X; 1)$ or $(X_1; 1)$ or $(X_2; 1)$ or $(Y; 1)$, with probabilities always being written to the right of the semicolon. Needless to say, the ordinary nonstochastic theory of consumers' behavior is defined in terms of these *certain* entities.

0.2. Definition of Simple Probability-Income-Situations or "Lottery Tickets"

Suppose the individual faces or chooses the prospect of getting *either* the certain-income situation X_1, or X_2, or $\cdots X_n$ with the defined mutually exclusive nonnegative probabilities $x_1, x_2, \cdots, x_n = 1 - x_1 - \cdots - x_{n-1}$. We call this prospect a probability-income situation and write it as $(X_1, X_2, \cdots, X_n; x_1, x_2, \cdots, x_n)$; or for short $(X; x)$; or, where there will be no confusion, as either (X) or (x). Examples of such lottery tickets or income-probability situations would be (\$5, \$10; .1, .9) or (5 bread and 3 wine, 4 bread and 7 wine; .2, .8). The first of these lottery tickets can also be written as (\$10, \$5; .9, .1) or as (\$1, \$5, \$10; 0, .1, .9) or even as (\$5, \$10, \$5; .03, .9, .07). It is clear, therefore, that the representation of a lottery ticket may not be unique; we could, but shall not, specify conventions to eliminate ambiguity — for example, gather together all *identical* prizes and pool their respective probabilities, or iit prizes with zero probabilities, etc. Often it is convenient to list before the semicolon *all* the prizes (assumed denumerable) that could ever occur; if this convention is followed, any probability-income situation can be denoted by its probabilities $x_1, \cdots, x_n$ alone, and the X_i may be omitted. If we wish to work with probability densities and general probability distributions, Stieltjes integrals and other notations may be convenient.

0.3. Definition of Super- or Compound-Probability-Income-Situations

It is easy to imagine super-lottery tickets whose prizes are not certain-income situations but rather are themselves lottery tickets. Thus, consider the situation, written in terms of our notation as $((X; x), (Y; y);$ $.1, .9)$; clearly, more general situations can be easily written out. *Associated* with every super- or compound-lottery ticket is an ordinary lottery ticket as defined in Section 0.2. This ordinary lottery ticket is defined exclusively in terms of the definitions of probabilities and the classical algebraic combinatorial laws of probability. Thus, associated with

$$((X_1, X_2, \cdots; x_1, x_2, \cdots), (Y_1, Y_2, \cdots; y_1, y_2, \cdots),$$
$$(Z_1, \cdots; z_1, \cdots), \cdots; a, b, c, \cdots),$$

where $a + b + c + \cdots = 1$, we have by the usual laws of composition of probability the associated simple income-probability situation

$$(X_1, X_2, \cdots, Y_1, Y_2, \cdots, Z_1, Z_2, \cdots;$$
$$ax_1, ax_2, \cdots, by_1, by_2, \cdots, cz_1, cz_2, \cdots),$$

where the probabilities beyond the semicolon necessarily add up to unity. Of course, if some of the X's equal some of the Y's or Z's, we can coalesce some of the probabilities. Actually, as mentioned earlier, we can by use of enough zero probabilities ensure that $X_i = Y_i = Z_i$ in every case; hence the simple income-probability situation associated with any such compound income-probability situation can be written

$$(X_1, X_2, \cdots; ax_1 + by_1 + cz_1 + \cdots, ax_2 + by_2 + cz_2 + \cdots, \cdots)$$

and the capital letters to the left of the semicolon might be omitted if no misunderstanding would arise.

Note that the simple ticket "associated" with every compound ticket is defined completely in terms of classical algebra and has in it no assumption as yet about human behavior or preference. Note too that the case of compound-compound lottery tickets gives rise to no new problems: all compound tickets of any order have associated with them a simple lottery ticket.

Axiom I of Complete Ordering: The individual under discussion is assumed to have a set of ordinal preferences or a complete ordering of all income-probability situations; and these preferences can be defined (with suitable assumptions concerning continuity and differentiability) in terms of the simple income-probability situations associated with any compound income-probability situation.

If we use the symbol R to mean "at least as good as," this means the individual can say of any two situations $(X; x)$ and $(Y; y)$:

$$\text{Either} \quad (X; x) \; R \; (Y; y) \quad \text{or} \quad (Y; y) \; R \; (X; x)$$

and of any three situations:

$$(X; x) \; R \; (Y; y) \quad \text{and} \quad (Y; y) \; R \; (Z; z) \quad \text{implies} \quad (X, x) \; R \; (Z; z).$$

Since minimum continuity assumptions are of no interest to us, we may replace the preceding assumptions by the single assumption that there exists a continuously differentiable function of the arguments $x_1, x_2, \cdots,$

$$U = U(X_1, X_2, \cdots; x_1, x_2, \cdots)$$

such that

$$U(X; x) \geqq U(Y; y) \quad \text{if and only if} \quad (X; x) \; R \; (Y; y).$$

Because the number system is transitive, no further assumptions are needed. Of course, any monotonic function of U will also be a perfectly good utility-indicator, and there is no privileged index out of the infinity of possible indicators.

Note that many of the difficulties involved in "the pleasure of gambling" and "joy in competitive gamesmanship" are already begged away by Axiom I's insistence that the *form* of a compound lottery is of no significance. This is a definite nonmathematical assumption about human behavior.

Axiom II of Strong Independence: For any three income-probability situations and probability a,

$$(X; x) \; R \; (Y; y) \quad \text{if and only if} \quad ((X; x), (Z; z); a, 1 - a)$$
$$R \; ((Y; y), (Z; z); a, 1 - a)$$

This says that using the same probability to combine each of two prizes with a third prize should have no "contaminating" effects upon the ordering of those two original prizes. This is the crucial independence assumption. Its validity must depend upon the primary notion of *ex ante* probabilities that are "mutually exclusive."

Several writers are willing to accept this axiom without question and seem to feel no need for justifying it. I must confess that I feel such a need to justify it and must go through some such argument as the following: Suppose you admit that $(X; x)$ is at least as good as $(Y; y)$. Now imagine two alternative compound lottery tickets that will each give you with probability $1 - a$ the same lottery ticket $(Z; z)$. Then if on the first draw $(Z; z)$ turns up, there is nothing to choose between the two. However, with probability a, the second compound ticket gives as a prize $(Y; y)$, whereas the first gives as a prize $(X; x)$. Then *no matter whether* $(Z; z)$ *is or is not drawn*, the first lottery ticket must be at least as good as the second. A similar argument can be made for the concepts of "definitely not as good as" and "indifferent to"; we could split up Axiom II into two separate axioms dealing with strong preference and indifference, but it is convenient to let the words "if and only if" in Axiom II express the same results.

This completes the axiom system and there remains the purely deductive task of utilizing our continuity assumptions (or certain lighter assumptions) to show that there exists a monotonic function of $U(X; x)$ which can be written in the special additive moral expectation form of Bernoulli:

$$u = u(u(X; x)) = x_1 p(X_1) + x_2 p(X_2) + \cdots.$$

Our proof can be briefly sketched. A direct consequence of Axiom II is the following

> THEOREM 1. Suppose that any lottery ticket $(X_1, X_2, \cdots;$ $x_1, x_2, \cdots)$ can be partitioned into a compound lottery ticket of the form $((A), (B), \cdots; a, b, \cdots)$, and suppose that there exist other lottery tickets $(A)', (B)', \cdots$, which are respectively indifferent to $(A), (B), \cdots$. Then in *all* preference relations, we may replace $(X; x)$ by $((A)', (B)', \cdots; a, b, \cdots)$.

Let us now consider a domain of situations containing a "best" and "worst" income situation, M and N, so that

$$(M; 1) \ R \ (X; x) \quad \text{and} \quad (X; x) \ R \ (N; 1), \quad \text{for all} \quad (X; x)$$

If $(N; 1) \ R \ (M; 1)$, we have the trivial case where all situations are equivalent and there is no more to say. If N, the worst situation, is definitely worse than M, the best situation, and if all other $(X; x)$ were indifferent to one of these extremes, we would have the scarcely less trivial case of but two levels of satisfaction. The Bernoulli theory covers these two trivial cases, but it begins to have interest only in the case where there are at least three distinct levels of ordinal satisfaction.

In the present domain, by our last theorem we may completely summarize all our information about any $(X_i; 1)$ by replacing it with

$$(M, N; p, 1 - p) \quad \text{indifferent to} \quad (X_i; 1).$$

Because of our assumption that the preference relations are *continuous* in the probability arguments, the preceding implicit equation necessarily has at least one solution for p; except in the trivial case of a single level of satisfaction, this solution will be unique and could be behavioristically determined by interrogation or by a choice experiment. We may write it as $p(X_i; M, N)$ or briefly as $p(X_i)$ or p_{X_i}. By exactly the same reasoning, we can combine this result with Theorem 1 and replace any probability-income situation $(X_1, X_2, \cdots; x_1, x_2, \cdots)$ with

$$((M, N; p_{X_1}, 1 - p_{X_1}), (M, N; p_{X_2}, 1 - p_{X_2}), \cdots; x_1, x_2, \cdots);$$

this last can be translated by the combinatorial law of Section 0.3 so that we have the following theorem.

THEOREM 2: $(M, N; x_1 p_{X_1} + x_2 p_{X_2} + \cdots, x_1(1 - p_{X_1}) + x_2(1 - p_{X_2}) + \cdots)$ can replace $(X_1, X_2, \cdots; x_1, x_2, \cdots)$ in *every* preference relation.

Hence, with M and N given, the size of the probability of M in the preceding is alone a complete indicator of the desirability of $(X; x)$, since the greater the probability of a better prize at the expense of a worse prize, the better the resulting ticket. We may write out the probability of M indicator of the desirability of $(X; x)$ in the Bernoulli form

$$u = x_1 p_{X_1} + x_2 p_{X_2} + \cdots = x_1 p(X_1; M, N) + x_2 p(X_2; M, N) + \cdots.$$

This completes our proof. Note that there is nothing necessarily unobjective or introspective or unobservable about the cardinal measure $p(X; M, N)$. Like every small-letter symbol used in this paper, it represents a probability that could be observed behavioristically under proper conditions. Note, too, that M and N enter as parameters in the measure of Bernoulli utility; but their function is simply to fix scale and origin, the two constants at our disposal in the linear indicator of utility. Indeed, the reader can easily verify that widening the limits of our domain to $(M'; 1) R (M; 1)$ and $(N; 1) R (N'; 1)$ gives us $p(X; M', N')$ such that

$$p(X; M, N) \equiv \frac{p(X; M', N') - p(N; M', N')}{p(M; M', N') - p(N; M', N')}.$$

This identity is a theorem for all situations which define a nonnegative p that is not greater than 1. If we wish to, we can adopt a *convention* so as to give a meaning to $p(X; M, N)$ when X lies *outside* the range of M and N. If $(X) R (M)$, we substitute $X = M', N = N'$ into the above identity to get

$$1 \leqq p(X; M, N) = \frac{1}{p(M; X, N)}.$$

If $(N) R (X)$, we substitute $M = M'$ and $X = N'$ into the identity to get

$$0 \geqq p(X; M, N) = \frac{-p(N; M, X)}{1 - p(N; M, X)}.$$

A few remarks about the problem of cardinal utility may be in order. The individual in question may or may not be introspectively aware of the p function; in any case, he acts *as if* he were maximizing its first moment. Actually, anyone rational enough to be consistent in this respect would probably be clever enough to sense the importance of binary-probability comparisons that define p, and he would probably find it convenient to do his "taste calculations" in terms of this simplest form. In no other sense is the linear-additive utility indicator privileged. Nor does such a measure have any interpersonal welfare ethical implications. Finally, if for 100-per-cent-certain situations referring to, say, food and clothing and shelter, there should happen to exist an additive utility indicator of the form $U = F(\text{food}) + G(\text{clothing}) + H(\text{shelter})$, such a utility scale could differ completely from the utility scale defined by probability. In other words $p(\text{food, clothing, shelter})$ would generally have *non*-vanishing cross-derivatives, and would have to be written as $p = W(U)$ where $W''(U) \neq 0$.

Suppose that the "pleasure of gambling," "love of danger," "joy of expert gamesmanship" cause Axiom I to be falsified, because the form of the compound lottery ticket provides the essence of the person's motivation. It would be formally possible to redefine what we mean by the prizes $(X_1, X_2, \cdots)$ so that the *process* of arriving at them, and not just their final value, will be regarded as ends. Then, in terms of the newly defined prizes (which would include the color of the gaming tables, the time-period of suspense, etc.), the axioms might again hold. But this formal victory must not be given too much weight: its simplicity, and therefore its empirical content, may be largely gone, and it may have in it as many degrees of freedom as the facts to be explained. If this should turn out to be the case, we can dispense with it or use it as we please; but what we must not do is to let our theoretical predispositions warp our view of the richness of actual empirical behavior and cause us to neglect the very real importance of the elements that characterize human behavior even though they elude our axioms.

14

PROBABILITY, UTILITY, AND THE INDEPENDENCE AXIOM

BY PAUL A. SAMUELSON

1. WITH EVER fewer exceptions, modern economic theorists believe that the nonstochastic theory of consumers preference need not be *cardinal*; everything of interest and relevance in the theory can be expressed in purely *ordinal* terms. In the empirically special case where the number of goods can be partitioned into two separate constellations such that changes in the members of one constellation have zero effect on marginal rates of substitution between all members of the other set, it does happen to be possible to define a measure of additive cardinal utility (unique except for scale and origin constants). But even in this special case of "independence" (as far as I know never empirically validated), there is no special interest in this cardinal measure rather than in any other.

2. When we come to a theory of consumers' preference in stochastic situations, the basic methodology is the same. We are alone interested in the "more or less" ordinal relations that determine how the consumer will choose between one uncertain prospect with its "probable prizes" and any other specified uncertain prospect. The notion of personal probability evaluations now becomes important. There has been much disputation in the philosophical and mathematical literature concerning the nature and relevance of probability concepts to induction. Recently, Ramsey, de Finetti, and Savage have worked out an interesting theory of what I might term "consistent ordinal reactions to uncertainty situations." The upshot of their consistency conditions on the consumer is that his numerical or cardinal probabilities and numerical or cardinal utilities can be said to be uniquely and simultaneously defined, with the numerical probabilities satisfying the usual algebraic laws.[1] If a person is to be "consistent" in dealing with "*mutually-exclusive*" outcomes, we find ourselves postulating for him "strong independence conditions" in the uncertainty realm of the type that we regard as empirically absurd in the nonstochastic realm. It is these strong independence conditions that create the existence of certain special or canonical indexes of utility and probability that are *additive*.

The problem of simultaneously axiomatizing utility and probability is quite complex and goes beyond economics into the province of statistical inference. For the present purpose, I should like to simplify the exposition by assuming without discussion that the primitive notion of

[ED. NOTE: The above is one of several related contributions published in this issue. Reference should be made to the editorial note which appears on page 661.]

[1] Nevertheless, as they emphasize, it is important to realize that this is a purely ordinal theory and the same facts can be completely described without using privileged numerical indicators of utility or probability.

numerical probability is well defined and applicable to our consumers. For further discussion of what is being postulated here without question, I must refer the reader to the forthcoming book by L. J. Savage, which will represent a landmark in the history of probability theory.

3. Suppose we represent one hundred per cent certain outcomes or prizes by $(X_1 ; 1)$, $(X_2 ; 1)$, $\cdots$, where each X_i represents a sum of money income spendable at specified prices, or where X_i is a vector specifying a market basket of definite quantities of a number of different goods. Then the indifference curve analysis of ordinary nonstochastic theory gives us a transitive ordering (or "complete" ordering) of all possible $(X_i ; 1)$.

By a *simple income-probability-situation* we mean a lottery ticket of prizes $(X_1 , X_2 , \cdots , X_n)$ each respectively expected with mutually-exclusive nonnegative numerical probabilities $(x_1 , \cdots , x_n)$, where $x_1 + x_2 + \cdots + x_n = 1$. Write this income-probability-situation as $(X_1 , X_2 , \cdots , X_n ; x_1 , x_2 , \cdots , x_n)$ with the order of the pair of variables $(X_i ; x_i)$ being unimportant; or for short as $(X; x)$ or (X). Absolutely certain events, such as $(X_1 ; 1)$, are obvious special cases of one-prize lottery tickets.

Warning: what constitutes a prize is a tricky concept. When I go to a casino, I go not alone for the dollar prizes but also for the pleasures of gaming—for the soft lights and sweet music. In such cases, the X's should be complicated vectors embodying *all* these elements. We shall see that this may raise serious operational problems for the applicability of the theory to be outlined.

4. By a *compound income-probability-situation*, we mean a lottery ticket whose prizes are lottery tickets: e.g., $[(X_1 , X_2 ; \frac{1}{2}, \frac{1}{2}), (X_3 , X_1 ; \frac{1}{4}, \frac{3}{4}); \frac{2}{3}, \frac{1}{3}]$.

By the *associated income-probability-situation* to any compound income-probability-situation, we mean that simple lottery ticket whose prizes are all the possible prizes of the compound lottery ticket, each evaluated with the compound probabilities that the classical algebra of probability defines. Simple algebra permits us to calculate every associated lottery ticket: e.g., the above case has associated with it $(Y$ $X_2 , X_3 ; \frac{2}{3} \frac{1}{2} + \frac{1}{3} \frac{3}{4}, \frac{2}{3} \frac{1}{2}, \frac{1}{3} \frac{1}{4})$. Generally, any two compound prizes such as $[(X_1 , X_2 , \cdots ; x_1 , x_2 , \cdots), (Y_1 , Y_2 , \cdots ; y_1 , y_2 , \cdots), \cdots ; a, b, \cdots]$ can be replaced by $[(X_1 , X_2 , \cdots , Y_1 , Y_2 , \cdots ; ax_1 , ax_2 , \cdots , by_1 , by_2 , \cdots) \cdots ; a + b, \cdots]$ and if this is done repeatedly, after a finite number of steps a unique *associated* ticket will be defined for every compound ticket.

It is important to emphasize that this is purely a definition of the term associated income-probability-situation or lottery ticket. And only alegbra, not human behavior, is involved in this definition.

5. Now turn to hypotheses or postulates on human behavior. It is

perhaps natural to expect that a reasonable or coherent man should be able to give a transitive-ordinal ranking of every compound probability-income-situation that confronts him. This could be made a first axiom.

But some might argue that, *provided we properly* define the prizes $X_1, \cdots$, etc., so that they include all elements of gamesmanship and pleasures of gambling *per se*, a stronger assumption can be made: namely, every compound situation can be replaced by its associated situation and all rankings made in terms of associated situations alone. (Warning: from an operational viewpoint, the definition of prizes may become slippery.) In my Paris exposition,* I combined the assumptions of this and the previous paragraphs into what I called Axiom I.

AXIOM I OF COMPLETE ORDERING: *All situations can be completely ordered and in terms of their associated prizes alone. (This ordering may be further assumed to be continuous in the probabilities $x_1, x_2, \cdots$.)*

Axiom I is not innocent or weak and it is as far as some theorists will go. Prior to 1950, I hestitated to go much farther. But much brooding over the magic words "mutually-exclusive" convinced me that there was much to be said for a further "strong independence axiom." This may be loosely paraphrased[2] as follows:

AXIOM II (STRONG INDEPENDENCE): *If lottery ticket $(A)_1$ is (as good or) better than $(B)_1$, and lottery ticket $(A)_2$ is (as good or) better than $(B)_2$, then an even chance of getting $(A)_1$ or $(A)_2$ is (as good or) better than an even chance of getting $(B)_1$ or $(B)_2$.*

6. The reason why this is plausible is spelled out in the paragraph quoted by Dr. Manne from my Paris exposition. This is simply a version of what Dr. Savage calls the "sure-thing principle." Whether heads or tails comes up, the A lottery ticket is better than the B lottery ticket; hence, it is reasonable to say that the compound (A) ticket is definitely better than the compound (B).

It is this independence axiom that is crucial for the Bernoulli-Savage theory of maximization of expected cardinal utility, and which is the concern of the present symposium. Within the stochastic realm, independence has a legitimacy that it does not have in the nonstochastic realm. Why? Because either heads *or* tails must come up: if one comes up, the other cannot; so there is no reason why the choice between $(A)_1$ and $(B)_1$ should be "contaminated" by the choice between $(A)_2$

---

[2] This differs trivially from the Paris version in which $(A)_2$ and $(B)_2$ were both equal to an arbitrary (C) and where an even chance was replaced by an arbitrary positive probability.

* Reprinted as "Utility, Preference, and Probability."

and $(B)_2$.[3] How different this is as compared to the two blends of gasoline, where we must reckon with physical and chemical interactions.

7. The above represents a very condensed description of what must be assumed if we want to end up with behavior describable by the individual's acting *as if* he were maximizing the Bernoulli expected cardinal-utility magnitude $x_1u(X_1) + x_2u(X_2) + \cdots + x_nu(X_n)$. I have omitted my brief Paris proof that the axioms do lead to this result, and other interpretations. The ground is now prepared to discuss Professor Wold's interesting questions.

8. Wold has very correctly described the *lack* of independence between wine and milk that holds in the nonstochastic realm: more specifically, in the realm of a single decision as to what stationary plateau of weekly wine and milk drinking I should choose over the next n years.

If the independence axiom of the probability theory somehow negated this lack of independence in the nonstochastic realm, I should quickly agree to drop it as illegitimate. But, according to my interpretation, independence in probability situations puts *no* restriction whatsoever upon the dependence or independence that holds in the nonstochastic situation. Thus, suppose the wine-milk indifference curves were describable by the nonindependence-satisfying function,

$$f = \text{wine}^2 + \text{wine} \cdot \text{milk} + \text{milk}^4.$$

No monotonic transformation of this utility indicator, of the form $F(f)$, can result in an F that is an additive sum of a milk and wine function. Yet if we have the lottery tickets consisting of a fifty–fifty chance of ten wine and twenty milk *or* eight wine and four milk, and compare it with a thirty–seventy chance of eleven wine and seventeen milk *or* zero wine and fifteen milk, our Bernoulli comparison of mathematical expectation will be between

$$.5u(10^2 + 10 \cdot 20 + 20^4) + .5u(8^2 + 8 \cdot 4 + 4^4)$$

and

$$.3u(11^2 + 11 \cdot 17 + 17^4) + .7u(0^2 + 0 \cdot 15 + 15^4)$$

[3] Around 1950, Marschak, Dalkey, Nash, and others independently recognized the crucial importance of the independence axiom. Prior to this the Neumann-Morgenstern axioms had puzzled many economists, including myself. A number of interpretations of those axioms, much like the Manne octane example, had seemed to fulfill the spirit of those axioms and yet to *not* lead to additive cardinal utility. Marschak, I, and no doubt others had come to suspect that the independence axiom had been implicitly assumed in the pre-axiom concepts of the *Games* discussion. At the Paris conference, M. Malinvaud presented me with a confirmation of this suspicion. This has been reproduced as a note following this article.

where $u(f)$ represents a unique $F(f)$ except for origin and scale parameters. Note that $F(f)$ is not additive in *its* components, but $x_1 F(f_1) + x_2 F(f_2) + \cdots$ is additive over the *alternative* probability situations.[4] Note too that if (a wine, b milk) and (c wine, d milk) should be indifferent, the independence axiom does tell us that an x-to-$(1-x)$ chance of getting these prizes is also indifferent to them. But it does *not* tell us that $[xa + (1-x)c$ wine, $xb + (1-x)d$ milk] is indifferent to them.

9. The above applies to *single* probability decisions: how I choose between a lottery ticket giving me tomorrow's market basket of wine and milk; or how I choose between a lottery ticket giving me next year's stationary plateaus of weekly wine and milk consumption. Wold, quite properly, wishes to go beyond single event decisions to series of repeated discussions either (i) of a nonstochastic nature, or (ii) of a probability character.

To handle the nonstochastic case (i), we might list consumption of wine, milk, and each other good *for every time period*. Thus, our indifference map would refer to the space of variables (wine$_1$, milk$_1$, $\cdots$, wine$_2$, milk$_2$, $\cdots$, wine$_t$, milk$_t$, $\cdots$): the dimensions of this space are Nr in number, where N is the number of time periods and r the number of goods. A rational consumer can presumably give a transitive ordering of every such point. The amount of wine I drank yesterday and will drink tomorrow can be expected to have effects upon my today's indifference slope between wine and milk. For this reason, neither Wold nor I would care to treat the preference over time as if it could be written as a sum of independent daily utilities. We should be content with any ordinal indicator f written as a function of all the variables. Given specified constraints, the consumer can decide on action that maximizes his ordinal utility, f.[5]

---

[4] I have purposely avoided couching the above discussion in terms of money or in terms of a one-dimensional vector of income; instead I have used the convenient wine-milk example of Professor Wold. But, if my argument is acceptable, it will be seen to apply no less to multi-component consumption vectors than to money itself or to any other single-vector concept of income. Actually, because we must approach the conventional nonstochastic indifference curves as all probabilities but one go to zero, it is clear that $u(X)$, which might be written as $u(X^1, X^2, \cdots, X^r)$ if there are r components to the X vector, can always be written in the special form $u(X) \equiv F[f(X^1, X^2, \cdots, X^r)]$, so that f or any monotonic renumbering does gather into one summary scalar the full preference content of the vector X.

[5] If storage over time is permissible, and if we consider consumption of repeated periods, it is sometimes possible to prove that (8)'s last linear-combination vector is no worse than the original two. In other words, storage can sometimes negate the existence of wrongly-curved indifference curves. Also, if we consider additions to our inventories of stored wine and milk that are "very small" relative to our total inventory, the indifference curves plotted with the

10. The above nonstochastic dynamic formulation permits a critique of the beer-milk example of Manne. If our time periods are short enough, the consumer may decide to consume one of them at a time: his observed temporal consumption stream may be of the form (0 beer, K_t milk), (J_{t+1} beer, 0 milk), etc., because it is such a pattern that happens to maximize his ordinal utility function, f. This fact of one-at-a-time consumption does not carry the implication that f can be written in terms of additive independent functions of dated beer and dated milk. On the contrary, my relative desire for beer now generally depends upon how much beer and milk I consumed in the past and will consume in the future.

These considerations should also help to dispose of a similar argument made to me by a student at Nuffield College. He asked whether consumption of (a wine, b milk) rather than (c wine, d milk) is not a choice among "mutually exclusive" events to which an independence argument could be applied like that in the probability situation. Neither in the single event nor dynamic temporal context does such a use of the words mutually exclusive have the same meaning and implications, as an attempt to frame axioms will, I think, show.

11. The above dynamic formulation also permits me to register my agreement with Wold's rejection of the ambiguous Paretian arguments concerning integrability conditions and order of consumption paths. In connection with single events or steady plateaus of consumption, Pareto's discussion seems confused. Yet there is no reason why the theory of consumers behavior, either in its stochastic or in its nonstochastic form, should *necessarily* confine its attention to steady levels of consumption. If we want to go behind the yearly totals, and have a theory of consumption in the summertime and consumption in the wintertime and consumption in spring and consumption in fall, there is nothing to prevent us from doing so. Similarly, if we want to, we can investigate the difference between a man's Saturday night behavior and his behavior the rest of the week. Indeed, it is usually without interest to the economist but not forbidden him to study the order in which at one meal a man consumes wine, fish, meat, coffee, and dessert. According to the tastes of most people, this order is not a matter of indifference and there exists an ordinal preference theory that explains a man's actual temporal behavior. But from the standpoint of demand as it would be seen by a chain of grocery stores, the economist is usually

---

additions on the axes may be approximately straight lines over a range. But this is the result of the additivity postulate of storage and not of the probability independence axiom. Originally, I tended to regard such a phenomenon as a *reductio ad absurdum*, but I now recognize that it may be legitimate under certain postulated dynamic conditions.

uninterested in such details—they make no essential difference and he can neglect them in his analysis. Note, however, that I do hypothesize integrability conditions and transitivity in the enlarged Nr dimensional space, in agreement with Wold.

12. Now for the first time, let us subject the consumer to *repeated* probability choices. These must be specified in detail: e.g., he can each day barter for a lottery ticket with various wine and milk prizes, it being assumed that he knows his previous period's consumption and lottery outcomes; or alternatively, we might assume that he must commit himself at the beginning to all of his lottery decisions of every future day, not knowing in making his Wednesday decision, the outcome of his Tuesday's decision. Assumption about storability of goods must also be spelled out in detail. Assumptions about how long it takes for my present wine orgy to wear off so that I again am eager for wine will have been supplied by the indifference curves in the Nr space as summarized by the f function.

Once all of these details have been spelled out, the consumer can in advance specify what his *strategy* will be so as to cover all possible actual outcomes of chance and decision problems. Readers of the *Theory of Games* will understand what I mean by such a complete strategy. For each such strategy, there will in principle result *definite probabilities* for all possible points in the complete space. Assuming for simplicity that only integral consumption amounts will ever come up, we can in principle choose so as to maximize sums of the additive form $x_1 u(f_1) + x_2 u(f_2) + \cdots$, where each f_i refers to expressions of the form $f(X_i)$, with X being a vector of Nr integral components.[6]

13. I might summarize all of the above arguments as follows: the independence axiom must always be applied to a definite set of entities— e.g., (1) single-event money prizes, (2) single-event vectors of goods, (3) single-event money prizes *cum* gaming and suspense feelings, (4) stationary plateaus of money or of goods-vectors, (5) alternative time profiles of goods, with or without associated suspense sensations, etc. The independence axiom then has implications and restrictions upon choices among such entities; but, strictly speaking, it need not impose restrictions upon some different (and perhaps simpler) set of entities. Thus, if the entities of (5) above are the correct ones, we cannot necessarily make inferences about decisions dealing with information on (1) alone.

I wish at the same time to express agreement with Wold's uneasiness with such a formalistic defense of the axioms: a few more such victories

---

[6] All this holds even if the consumer is given so many repeated choices and such great opportunities for storage that various forms of the law of large numbers or limit theorems become applicable. If this is the case, so much the better.

might indeed result in disaster, caught between the Scylla and Charybdis of theoretical formulation and operational empirical hypothesis formation. It is for this reason that I have throughout this discussion given much more emphasis than in the main body of my Paris paper to the *operational* aspects of the axioms.

In what dimensional space are we "really" operating? If every time you find my axiom falsified, I tell you to go to a space of still higher dimensions, you can legitimately regard my theories as irrefutable and meaningless. However, I am not so completely pessimistic. I think that Savage or any adherent of the Bernoulli theory—and I count myself as one of its fellow travelers—can hope some day to accomplish the following: he may succeed in finding a significant range of human behavior that can to a satisfactory degree of approximation be accounted for by the Bernoulli concepts as applied to a finite, specifiable, and convenient set of delimited entities.

14. From my own direct and indirect observations, I am satisfied that a large fraction of the sociology of gambling and risk taking will never significantly be discernible in terms of money prizes alone, as distinct from elements of suspense and gamesmanship. On the other hand, when it comes to a public corporation's hiring a statistical quality control expert, I suspect that such elements of suspense will receive minor weight; and in time, as the implications of the axioms become realized, we may find an increasing proportion of that kind of behavior approximating to the axioms.

Even here, as experiments by Professor Bishop and others show, we have a task of recognizing the proper entities of the theory. Professor E. C. Brown refused an outrageously favorable bet that Bishop offered him, but said he would take it provided he could make a hundred such bets. (We shall also want to know where Brown could sell to a hundred friends an equal sharing in his one hundred bets: for in that case, he would be utilizing James Bernoulli rather than nephew Daniel Bernoulli.) When someone observes my present action, he may be observing not my reaction to the present gain and loss, but rather my lifelong habit with respect to betting. This makes a difference in interpreting my behavior and in inferring my utility.

15. Having blown cold concerning the theory, I should like to conclude by again blowing hot. It is desirable, though not mandatory, that opponents of the Bernoulli theory should make a direct attack upon the independence axiom. Thus, in dealing with compound lotteries with prizes of the form $(A)_1$ or $(A)_2$ and $(B)_1$ or $(B)_2$, you might explicitly introduce some time interval between drawings, so that suspense elements might enter to contaminate the choices; etc.

Reasons like this impress me as valid causes of deviation from any simply expressed independence postulate. But in the absence of such complications, I don't see why a "reasonable" man should not be willing —in Manne's words—to repeat firmly over and over again that the events faced are mutually exclusive.[7]

It is true that you can surprise an unwary reasonable man by getting him to commit himself on how he feels towards a small chance of losing his life, and then usually trick him into revealing a violation of the independence axiom. But if he understands the theory and is given a couple of years to brood over his answers, he will discover that no indifference curves satisfying Axiom I will continue to appear "reasonable" to him and be "consistent" with his answer. In short: it is anything but a casual thing to have and know one's complete ordering or set of indifference curves; and if you ask a casual question, you must expect to get a casual answer.

16. My closing admission reverses the story of the farmer who regarded everyone in the world as crazy but himself and his wife, and who sometimes wasn't sure about her. I sometimes feel that Savage and I are the only ones in the world who will give a consistent Bernoulli answer to questionnaires of the type that Professor Allais has been circulating—but I am often not too sure about my own consistency.

Massachusetts Institute of Technology

[7] In the Paris oral discussion, I added a plausible explanation of the independence axiom by giving the man options to have his choice of $(A)_i$ or $(B)_i$. If $(A)_i$ will always be definitely picked over $(B)_i$, this joint option is assumed worth only what $(A)_i$ is worth and is definitely better than $(B)_i$. If this is postulated within all compounds, the independence axiom comes out as a theorem.

15

THE ST. PETERSBURG PARADOX AS A DIVERGENT DOUBLE LIMIT*

BY PAUL A. SAMUELSON

1. OFTEN, to analyze a paradox is to dispel it. The St. Petersburg Paradox, in which Paul refuses to pay Peter the extraordinarily high price that ordinary calculation of mathematical expectation of money-gain computes for the privilege of Paul's receiving 2^i ducats if heads first appears at the i-th toss of a fair coin, made an important contribution to the history of philosophy and probability. It dramatized the fact that men feel they value money losses and gains at something different from their expected or arithmetic-mean values. Had all Pauls not already instinctively felt this, they would not have recoiled in shock from the prospect of paying Peter the infinite true mathematical odds, but it took the formulation of the problem by Cramer, Bernoulli, and others to rationalize what men already felt.[1]

Now it may be cogently argued that a long series of—say 1 billion—coin tosses is really sufficient to drive home the point that rational men maximize their "moral expectation" (i.e., expected value of utility of wealth) rather than maximizing their simple "money expectation". And yet, how much more dramatic is infinity than any large finite number!

A present-day savant might grant the eye-opening service rendered by the St. Petersburg Paradox and still argue that it has by now done its work, and that—like most of the scaffoldings used to construct the edifice called the modern mind—it can now be dispensed with. Accepting the fact that each man acts as if he has an ultimately bounded utility function, or finite wealth and limited borrowing power, or only a finite life span in which to toss coins, such sophisticates argue that the St. Petersburg Paradox can never arise in real life. *Paul will never be willing to give as much as Peter will demand for such a contract; and hence the indicated activity will take place at the equilibrium level of zero intensity.* Zero cancels out infinity, so to speak.

2. I do not disagree with this line of argument. But I propose to

* Manuscript received July, 14, 1959.

[1] I. Todhunter, *History of the Mathematical Theory of Probability* (New York: Chelsea, 1949) p. 220 gives a good account of the early discussions.

show here that the essence of the paradox—its infinity—remains even after we take into account the fact that marginal utility of money is not a constant. For, as (i) we make the constant size of the stake at each coin toss, y, get smaller and smaller, and (ii) let the stipulated number, n, of coin tosses get larger and larger, we find that the value, v, which *any* rational Paul will in real life pay for the privilege of playing becomes indefinitely large in ratio to the size of the stakes. That is, v/y must go to infinity as y goes to zero.

3. To avoid the non-operational concept of an infinity of tosses, I consider a finite game of n tosses: if heads never comes up, as will happen with probability 2^{-n}, Peter returns the value v Paul has paid him and all bets are off; if heads first turns up at the i-th toss, Peter pays Paul 2^i times the agreed stakes-parameter y. (I.e., y = one ducat, one dollar, one dime, or any stipulated positive amount.) To calculate v, the maximum that Paul will pay for the privilege of playing the game, we find what expected value of his utility $\sum_1^n 2^{-i} U(x - v + y2^i) + 2^{-n} U(x)$ will equal the certain utility $U(x)$ of not playing at all, thereby leaving him indifferent whether or not to play.

4. This is summarized in the following mathematical theorem about a double limit.

THEOREM: *Let utility be a smooth function of money so that* $U(X)$, $U'(X)$, $U''(X)$, *are continuous functions for* $X \geqq 0$; *Let* $U'(X) \geqq 0$; *and at* $X = x$ *where* $U'(x) > 0$, *let* $v = V(n, y; x)$ *be defined by the following implicit equation*

$$U(x) = \frac{1}{2} U(x - v + y2) + \frac{1}{4} U(x - v + y4) + \cdots$$

$$+ \frac{1}{2^n} U(x - v + y2^n) + \frac{1}{2^n} U(x) .$$

Then

$$\lim_{n \to \infty} \lim_{y \to 0} \frac{V(n, y; x)}{y} = \lim_{y \to 0} \lim_{n \to \infty} \frac{V(n, y; x)}{y} = \infty .$$

The intuitive proof of this is simple for the economist. As the size of the stake goes to zero, the marginal utility of money becomes sensibly constant so that the traditional formulation of ordinary expected value of money becomes applicable,[2] with

[2] Professor Robert M. Solow points out that for any prizes $(yZ_1, yZ_2, \cdots, yZ_n)$, occurring with respective probabilities $(p_1, p_2, \cdots, p_n)$, v/y will in the limit always equal the expected value of Z, $E(Z) = \sum p_i Z_i$. Later I refer to this as Solow's Theorem.

$$v = \frac{2}{2}y + \frac{4}{4}y + \frac{8}{8}y + \cdots + \frac{2^n}{2^n}y + \cdots = \infty \ .$$

In real life, mathematicians should perhaps have recognized that at most one can lay down one's all for anything, so that $v \leq x$. But the infinity paradox remains in that as $x \to \infty$, the maximizer of mere money gain will pay his all regardless of how large that all becomes!

For a mathematical proof of the Theorem, we note that since $V(n, 0; x) = 0$,

$$\lim_{n \to \infty} \lim_{y \to 0} \frac{V(n, y; x)}{y} = \lim_{n \to \infty} \lim_{y \to 0} \frac{\partial V(n, y; x)}{\partial y}$$

$$(1) \qquad = \lim_{n \to \infty} \frac{\sum_1^n 2^{-i} U'(x - v + y2^i)2^i}{\sum_1^n 2^{-i} U'(x - v + y2^i)} \Bigg|_{y=0} \qquad \begin{array}{l} \text{by differentiation of our} \\ \text{implicit equation,} \end{array}$$

$$= \lim_{n \to \infty} \frac{\sum_1^n 1}{\sum_1^n 2^{-i}} = \lim_{n \to \infty} \frac{n}{1 - 2^{-n}} = \infty \ .$$

To prove the divergence of the double limit taken in the reverse order, note that with $V(n, 0; x) \equiv 0$ for all n and x, $V(\infty, 0; x) = 0$. Now consider $V(\infty, y; x)$ for any small y. If it is infinite, *a fortiori* our double limit is divergent. If it is finite, the limiting V/y must equal the limiting value of $\partial V/\partial y$ as $y \to 0$. Where $V(\infty, y; x)$ is finite,

$$(2) \qquad \frac{\partial V(\infty, y; x)}{\partial y} = \frac{\sum_1^\infty U'(x - v + y2^i)}{\sum_1^\infty 2^{-i} U'(x - v + y2^i)} \ .$$

But if v is finite, the denominator must be finite, since for $X \geq$ some A, $U'(X) \leq$ some B, and the denominator is dominated by a convergent geometric series. The numerator, however, must as $y \to 0$ approach $U'(x) \lim_{n \to \infty} n = \infty$[3].

---

[3] Professor Solow has contributed the following somewhat stronger result: The *general* double limit holds, entirely independently of the path along which the limits are taken,

$$\lim_{\substack{n \to \infty \\ y \to 0}} \frac{V}{y} = \infty, \text{ or equivalently } \lim_{\substack{n \to \infty \\ y \to 0}} \frac{y}{V(n, y; x)} = 0 \ .$$

This follows from results already deduced, supplemented by some slightly more delicate considerations. Consider first

$$\lim_{n \to \infty} \frac{y}{V(n, y; x)}$$

as a function of y (x is fixed). If we give this function the value 0 at $y = 0$, the arguments already made show it to be a continuous function of y in a closed interval

A geometrical description of our result may be of interest. Suppose $V(\infty, y; x)$ is plotted against the size of the stake y for any fixed wealth x. Then the original St. Petersburg paradox consisted of the recognition that V would be infinite for all positive y for an "expected-money" maximizer. But Bernoulli and others "resolved" the paradox by showing that an "expected-utility" maximizer, whose utility function was sufficiently well behaved, would have a finite $V(\infty, y; x)$ function for all y and, incidentally, one that begins at the origin.

What the present paper shows is essentially the following: even in the case where $V(\infty, y; x)$ is finite and enters the origin, it must enter the origin at a limiting 90° vertical angle—a strong result but not one that is, on reflection, paradoxical.

GENERALIZATION BEYOND CASE OF MORAL EXPECTATION MAXIMIZER

5. In concluding, I should like to indicate that the validity of our limit does not depend upon the willingness of a rational man to act so as to maximize moral expectation, i.e., to maximize the first moment of the utility of the possible outcomes $\sum p_i U(X_i)$ where $(X_1, X_2, \cdots;$ $p_1, p_2, \cdots)$ represent the possible outcomes known to occur, with respective probabilities $(p_1, p_2, \cdots)$. There are persuasive reasons why a "rational man" might out of a sense of consistency alone wish to maximize such a moral expectation, as Marschak, Savage and Ramsey have shown[4]. But even if he does not so act, provided only that he maximizes an ordinal utility indicator $W(X_1, X_2, \cdots; p_1, p_2)$ that is smooth enough to have continuous second partial derivatives, our infinite limit for v/y will hold. The heuristic reasoning to demonstrate this follows.

6. Suppose Paul maximizes an ordinal utility function $W(X_1, X_2, \cdots;$ $p_1, p_2, \cdots)$, such as $(\sum P_i X_i)^{1/2}(\sum P_i X_i^{-1})^{-3/2}$, which cannot be put into the additive form $\sum P_i U(X_i)$. Purely as a notational matter $(X_1, X_2, X_3, \cdots; p_1, p_2, p_3, \cdots)$ is the same thing as $(X_2, X_3, \cdots;$ $p_1 + p_2, p_3, \cdots)$ if $X_1 = X_2$. So with W twice differentiable,

$0 \leq y \leq y^*$, and the limit of a sequence of continuous functions. Moreover, consideration of the game itself shows that $V(n, y; x)$ is a monotone increasing with n, so that y/V is decreasing. By Dini's Theorem on the convergence of monotone sequences of functions, $\lim_{n \to \infty} y/V$ exists uniformly. In turn, this uniform convergence together with what is proved about the repeated limits guarantees that the double limit

$$\lim_{\substack{n \to \infty \\ y \to 0}} \frac{y}{V} = 0.$$

4 Jacob Marschak, "Rational Behavior, Uncertain Prospects, and Measurable Utility," *Econometrica* Vol. 18, 1950, p. 111; L. J. Savage, *Foundations of Statistics* (New York: Wiley, 1954); F. P. Ramsey, *Foundations of Mathematics* (London: Routledge and Kegan Paul, 1930), Ch. VII.

(3) $\lim_{X_1 \to X_2} W(X_1, X_2, X_3, \cdots; p_1, p_2, p_3, \cdots) = W(X_2, X_3, \cdots; p_1 + p_2, p_3, \cdots)$,

from which it will be shown that for all X's close enough together, we can approximate W by the linear expression

(4) $$W = W(\overline{X}; 1) + \frac{\partial W(\overline{X}; 1)}{\partial X} \sum_{1}^{n} p_i(X_i - \overline{X}) .$$

7. This last expression asserts the fundamental result that the general case of any smooth maximizer will become indistinguishable from the case of a moral-expectation-maximizer (a "Bernoulli") or of a money-expectation-maximizer (a "Pascal") as the range of uncertainty of the outcomes shrinks toward zero. This has its good and bad implications. A bad implication is the fact that we cannot hope to distinguish between a "Bernoulli," a "Pascal," or a (smooth!) "Dostoevsky" by experiments that involve small dispersions (one evening's gamblings?).

A good implication is the fact that we can hope to determine a guinea pig's subjective or personal probabilities about particular contingent events by observing his betting behavior connected with such events when the prize and penalties associated with those events are "small." Ramsey and others have suggested this possible operational method for approximating to personal probabilities; and our present result demonstrates that this method of "revealed preference," generalized to become a method of "revealed personal probabilities," does not depend upon the assumption that the observed person maximizes the first moment of a utility function.[5]

---

[5] F. P. Ramsey, op. cit., p. 176. As many scholars have observed, there is a dilemma in all small-prize experiments. If we make the prize small enough to minimize the changing marginal utilities (cardinal or ordinal), we may destroy the motivation of the guinea pig to reveal to us his true opinions. (He may be too uninterested to do the mental work to find his opinion; he may spite us; etc.) Indeed, operationally, who dares assert that his "opinion" exists if it is not in principle observable? This may be a social science analogue to the Heisenberg "uncertainty principle" in quantum physics. Just as we must throw light on a small object to see it and if it is small enough must thereby inevitably distort the object by our observational process, so we must to motivate a human guinea pig shower him with finite dispersion, whose effect may be to change his marginal utilities and contaminate his revealed probabilities. In principle, we can move to large scale dispersion experiments: thus, to determine whether Paul thinks rain more probable for July 4 than fair weather, let us threaten him with death if his guess is wrong and then observe which forecast he makes. Such "destructive tests" are expensive, even in these days of foundation philanthropy. Also, as Ramsey's p. 177 discussion of "ethically neutral" entities shows, we must be sure that the pig does not think that dying on a rainy day sends him to Paradise; for such a belief would violate the implicit independence assumption we make in separating out a man's probability beliefs from his evaluation of outcomes.

To prove (4), we shall show that (3) implies

$$(5) \quad \frac{\partial W(X, X, \cdots, X; p_1, p_2, \cdots, p_n)}{\partial X_i} = \frac{\partial W(X; 1)}{\partial X} p_i \quad (i = 1, 2, \cdots, n) \, .$$

This important identity is most easily proved for rational p_i, but then by continuity considerations above can be extended to all real p_i. We suppose $p_i = m_i / \sum m_j = m_i / m$ and rewrite W in terms of m rather than n arguments,

$$(6) \quad W\left(X, X, \cdots, X; \frac{m_1}{m}, \cdots, \frac{m_n}{m}\right) = W\left(X, X, \cdots, X; \frac{1}{m}, \frac{1}{m}, \cdots, \frac{1}{m}\right)$$

where $m = m_1 + \cdots + m_n \geqq n$. By symmetry

$$\frac{\partial W\left(X, X, \cdots, X; \frac{1}{m}, \cdots, \frac{1}{m}\right)}{\partial X_j} = \frac{\partial W\left(X, X, \cdots, X; \frac{1}{m}, \cdots, \frac{1}{m}\right)}{\partial X_1}$$

$$(j = 2, \cdots, m)$$

and since changing one X_i on the left of (6) is like changing m_i X's on the right,

$$\frac{\partial W\left(X, \cdots, X; \frac{m_1}{m}, \cdots, \frac{m_n}{m}\right)}{\partial X_i} = m_i \frac{\partial W\left(X, \cdots, X; \frac{1}{m}, \cdots, \frac{1}{m}\right)}{\partial X}$$

$$= \frac{m_i}{m} \frac{\partial W(X; 1)}{\partial X} \, .$$

This proves (5) for all rational probabilities; and hence for all continuously differentiable W functions a similar relation holds for all real probabilities.

Relation (4) follows[6] directly from (5) if we use the Taylor's expansion

$$W(X_1, X_2, \cdots; p_1, p_2, \cdots) =$$
$$W[\overline{X} + (X_1 - \overline{X}), \overline{X} + (X_2 - \overline{X}), \cdots; p_1, p_2, \cdots]$$

$$= W(\overline{X}; 1) + \frac{\partial W(\overline{X}; 1)}{\partial X} \sum_{1}^{n} p_j (X_j - \overline{X}) + \cdots$$

[6] The above heuristic argument needs amplification. Specifically, if W is a functional of a probability distribution $P(X)$, where $\int_0^\infty dP(X) = 1$, then the existence of functional derivatives of order two of W at any point where $P(X)$ is varied should be shown to make W capable of being approximated in some sense by the linear expression $\alpha + \beta \int_0^\infty (X - A) dP(X)$ so long as $P(X)$ is in a close region of $H(X - A)$, where $H(t) = 1$ for $t > 0$, $H(t) = 0$ for $t \leqq 0$. The limits of the approximation should be rigorously established.

8. We can now prove the divergence of our double limit v/y, where $v = V(n, y; x)$ is defined by solving the implicit equation

$$(7) \qquad W(x; 1) = W(x - v + y2, x - v + y2^2, \cdots,$$
$$x - v + y2^n, x; 2^{-1}, 2^{-2}, \cdots, 2^{-n}, 2^{-n}) .$$

If $V(\infty, y; x)$ is infinite for all small y around x, our infinite limit for v/y is proved. If $V(\infty, y; x)$ is finite, since $V(\infty, 0; x) = 0$, the limit for v/y equals the limit for $\partial V/\partial y$. But

$$\frac{\partial V}{\partial y} = \frac{\sum_{1}^{n} 2^i \frac{\partial W}{\partial X_i}}{\sum_{1}^{n} \frac{\partial W}{\partial X_i}} .$$

It follows from (5) that as $y \to 0$ and all the X_i's coalesce to x,

$$\frac{\partial V}{\partial y} \to \frac{\sum_{1}^{n} 2^i 2^{-i}}{\sum_{1}^{n} 2^{-i}} .$$

Hence, $\lim_{n \to \infty} \lim_{y \to 0} \dfrac{\partial V}{\partial y} = \lim_{n \to \infty} \dfrac{n}{1 - 2^{-n}} = \infty .$

The order of these limits can be reversed by the same arguments used in the moral expectation case. Solow's Theorem—that for any probabilities $(p_1, \cdots, p_n)$, as the size of the stakes parameter y goes to zero, v/y equals the expected money gain $E(Z) = \sum p_i Z_i$, where $x - v + yZ_i$ represents the outcome of money price yZ_i occurring with probability p_i—also holds in the more general case.

Massachusetts Institute of Technology, U. S. A.

16

RISK AND UNCERTAINTY:
A FALLACY OF LARGE NUMBERS [1]

Experience shows that while a single event may have a probability spread, a large repetition of independent single events gives a greater approach toward certainty. This corresponds to the mathematically provable Law of Large Numbers of James Bernoulli. This valid property of large numbers is often given an invalid interpretation. Thus people say an insurance company reduces its risk by increasing the number of ships it insures. Or they refuse to accept a mathematically favorable bet, but agree to a large enough repetition of such bets: e. g., believing it is almost a sure thing that there will be a million heads when two million symmetric coins are tossed even though it is highly uncertain there will be one head out of two coins tossed. The correct relationship (that an insurer reduces total risk by *subdividing*) is pointed out and a strong theorem is proved: that a person whose utility schedule prevents him from ever taking a specific favorable bet when offered only once can never rationally take a large sequence of such fair bets, if expected utility is maximized. The intransitivity of alternative decision criteria-such as selecting out of any two situations that one which will more probably leave you better off-is also demonstrated.

1. INTRODUCTION. - « There is safety in numbers. » So people tell one. But is there ? And in what possible sense ?

The issue is of some importance for economic behavior. Is it true that an insurance company *reduces* its risk by *doubling* the number of ships it insures ? Can one distinguish between risk and uncertainty by supposing that the former can count on some remorseless cancelling out of actuarial risks ?

To throw light on a facet of this problem, I shall formulate and prove a theorem that should dispel one fallacy of wide currency.

2. A TEST OF VALOR. - S. Ulam, already a distinguished mathematician when we were Junior Fellows together at Harvard a quarter century ago, once said: « I define a coward as someone who will not bet when you offer him two-to-one odds and let him choose *his* side.»

With the centuries-old St. Petersburg Paradox in my mind, I pedantically corrected him: « You mean will not make a *sufficiently small* bet (so that the change in the marginal utility of money [2] will not contaminate his choice). »

3. A GUINEA PIG SPEAKS. - Recalling this conversation, a few years ago I offered some lunch colleagues to bet each $200 to $100 that the side of a coin *they* specified would not appear at the first toss. One distingui-

---

[1] See the article of M. B. De Finetti, " La decisione nell' incertezza, " in *Scientia*, April-May 1963, p. 61.
[2] I might have quibbled that the chap could have a corner in his Bernoulli-Ramsey-Neumann utility function at his initial point, and thus escape the charge of cowardice or (even worse) irrationality. This, however, would have been a quibble since Ulam could move him from the corner by giving him a dollar and then test his "courage." As for the "St. Petersburg Paradox," see footnote 2, Section 5.

shed scholar - who lays no claim to advanced mathematical skills - gave the following answer:

« I won't bet because I would feel the $100 loss more than the $200 gain. But I'll take you on if you promise to let me make 100 such bets».

What was behind this interesting answer ? He, and many others, have given something like the following explanation. « One toss is not enough to make it reasonably sure that the law of averages will turn out in my favor. But in a hundred tosses of a coin, the law of large numbers will make it a darn good bet. I am, so to speak, virtually sure to come out ahead in such a sequence, and that is why I accept the sequence while rejecting the single toss. »

4. MAXIMUM LOSS AND PROBABLE LOSS. - What are we to think about this answer ? Here are a few observations.

a) If it hurts much to lose $100, it must certainly hurt to lose 100 x $100 = $10,000. Yet there is a distinct *possibility* of so extreme a loss. Granted that the probability of so long a run of repetitions is, by most numerical calculations, extremely low: less than 1 in a million (or $1/2^{100}$); still, if a person is already at the very minimum of subsistence, with a marginal utility of income that becomes practically infinite for any loss, he might act like a minimaxer[1] and eschew options that could involve any losses at all. [Note: increasing the sequence from n = 100 to n = 1,000 or n ➡ ∞ , will obviously not tempt such a minimaxer - even though the probability of any loss becomes gigantically tiny].

b) Shifting your focus from the maximum possible loss (which grows in full proportion to the length of the sequence), you may calculate the probability of making no loss at all. For the single toss, it is of course one-half. For 100 tosses, it is the probability of getting 34 or more correct heads (or, alternatively, tails) in 100 tosses. By the usual binomial calculation and normal approximation,[2] this probability of making a gain is found to be very large, $P_{100} = .99+$. If this has not reduced the probability of a loss by enough, it is evident that by increasing n from 100 to some larger number will succeed in reducing the probability of a loss to as low as you want to prescribe in advance.

c) Indeed, James Bernoulli's so-called Law of Large Numbers guarantees you this: « Suppose I offer you favorable odds at each toss so that your mathematical expectation of gain is k per cent in terms of the money you put at risk in each toss. Then you can choose a long-enough sequence of tosses to make the probability as near as you like to one that your earnings will be indefinitely near k per cent return on the total money you put at risk ».

---

[1] In the literature of statistical decision making, a minimaxer is defined as one who acts so as to insure that his maximum possible loss is at a minimum.

[2] I assume the coin is a reasonably new one. If it has developed some bias toward landing on one side, and if prior experimentation leads you to prefer one side to bet on, you can hope to do even better than as given above. Note: for definiteness I assume that when you decide to bet on a sequence of tosses, you are held to the full contract and cannot opt out in midstream; nor can you learn the coin's bias in the early tosses, since you are told immediately the result of your 100-toss play.

5. Irrationality of compounding a mistake. - The « virtual certainty » of making a large gain must at first glance seem a powerful argument in favor of the decision to contract for a long sequence of favorable bets. But should it be, when we recall that virtual certainty cannot be complete certainty and realize that the improbable loss will be very great indeed if it does occur ?

If a person is concerned with maximizing the expected or average value of the utility of all possible outcomes[1] and my colleague assures me that he wants to stand with Daniel Bernoulli, Bentham, Ramsey, v. Neumann, Marschak, and Savage on this basic issue - it is simply not sufficient to look at the probability of a gain alone. *Each outcome must have its utility reckoned at the appropriate probability; and when this is done it will be found that no sequence is acceptable if each of its single plays is not acceptable.* This is a basic theorem.

One dramatic way of seeing this is to go back to the St. Petersburg Paradox itself. No matter how high a price my colleague agreed to pay to engage in this classic game, the probability will approach one that he will come out as much ahead as he cares to specify in advance.[2]

6. An alternative axiom system of maximizing probabilities. No slave can serve two independent masters. If one is an expected-utility-maximizer he cannot generally be a maximizer of the probability of some gain. However, economists ought to give serious attention to the merits of various alternative axiom systems. Here is one that, at first glance, has superficial attractiveness.

Axiom: In choosing between two decisions, *A* and *B*, select that one which will more probably leave you better off. *I.e.*, select *A* over *B* if it is more probable that the gain given by *A* is larger than that on *B*, or, in formulae:

$$\text{Prob}\left\{ \text{ A's gain} > \text{B's gain} \right\} > \frac{1}{2}$$

[abbreviate the above to A > B].

Similarly with respect to any pair of (A, B, C, D, ...).

In terms of the above system, call *A* agreeing to bet on one toss; B deciding not to toss at all; and C agreeing to a long sequence of tosses. Then clearly,

$$A = B, \ C > B, \ C > A \,.$$

So my friend's decision to accept the long sequence turns out to agree with this axiom system. However, if D is the decision to accept a sequence of two tosses, my friend said he would not undertake it; and yet, in this

---

[1] *I. e.*, he acts to maximize $U = p_1 U_1 + p_2 U_2 + \ldots + p_n U_n$, where U_i represents the utility of each possible outcome and p_i represents its respective probability.

[2] The « Paradox » (Daniel Bernoulli, St. Petersburg, 1738) says, that turnig a coin until head appears for the first time, and to get S1, or 2, 4, ..., 2^{n-1}, ... according to the number of turns required, is a favorable bet no matter how large the amount to be paid for it. To avoid such a paradox, D. Bernoulli suggested dealing with the utilities rather than with money values (that is, with a concave scale with diminishing increments). To get rid of any initial infinity in the problem, see the modified sequence of finite tosses for the Petersburg situation in P. A. Samuelson, *The St. Petersburg Paradox as a Divergent Double Limit* « International Economic Review » Vol. 1, N. 1, January, 1960), pp. 31-37.

system, $D > B$. Moreover, call E the decision to accept the following bet: you win a million dollars with probability .51 but lose a million with probability .49. Few could accept such a bet; and of those who could, few would. Yet in this axiom system $E > B$.

There is a further fatal objection to this axiom system. It need not satisfy transitivity relations among 3 or more choices. Thus, it is quite possible to have $X > Y$, $Y > Z$ and $Z > X$.

One example is enough to show this pathological possibility. Let X be a situation that is a shade more likely to give you a small gain rather than a large loss. By this axiom system you will prefer it to the Situation Y, which gives you no chance of a gain or loss. And you will prefer Y to Situation Z, which makes it a shade more likely that you will receive a small loss rather than a large gain. But now let us compare Z and X. Instead of acting transitively, you will prefer Z to X for the simple reason that Z will give you the better outcome in every situation except the one in which simultaneously the respective outcomes would be the small gain and the small loss, a compound event whose probability is not much more than about one-quarter (equal to the product of two independent probabilities that are respectively just above one-half).

7. PROOF THAT UNFAIRNESS CAN ONLY BREED UNFAIRNESS. - After the above digression, there remains the task to prove the basic theorem already enunciated.

Theorem. If at each income or wealth level within a range, the expected utility of a certain investment or bet is worse than abstention, then no sequence of such independent ventures (that leaves one within the specified range of income) can have a favorable expected utility.

Thus, if you would always refuse to take favorable odds on a single toss, you must rationally refuse to participate in any (finite) sequence of such tosses.

The logic of the proof can be briefly indicated. If you will not accept one toss, you cannot accept two - since the latter could be thought of as consisting of the (unwise) decision to accept one plus the open decision to accept a second. Even if you were stuck with the first outcome, you would cut your further (utility) losses and refuse the terminal throw. By extending the reasoning from 2 to $3 = 2 + 1$, ..., and from n-1 to n, we rule out any sequence at all.[1]

---

[1] Mathematically, if you start at a known utility U_t, the probability of ending after *one* venture with at least U_{t+1} can be written as $F(U_{t+1}, U_t)$. By hypothesis, in the utility metric each toss is an unfair game (even though it may be more than fair game in the money metric). Or

$$E(U_{t+1}/U_t) = \int_{-\infty}^{\infty} U_{t+1}\, dF(U_{t+1}, U_t) \ U < t.$$

It is an easy theorem that repeated (identical and independent) fair games yield a fair game; and repeated unfair games yield an unfair game. Specifically, the probability of getting at least $U_{t+k} = X$, after starting out with $U_t = Y$ and playing a sequence of k games, is given by

$$F_k(X, Y) = F(X, Y)^* F_{k-1}(X, Y) = \ldots = F(X, Y)^* F(X, Y)^* \ldots {}^* F(X, Y), \quad \text{where}$$

$F(X, Y)^* G(X, Y)$ is the integral $\int_{-\infty}^{\infty} F(X, S)\, dG(S, Y)$. And, if $\int_{-\infty}^{\infty} X dF(X, Y) < Y$

then necessarily $\int_{-\infty}^{\infty} X\, dF_2(X, Y) < Y$ and $\ldots \int_{-\infty}^{\infty} X\, dF_k(X, Y) < Y$.

8. CONCLUSIONS. - Now that I have demonstrated the fallacy that there is safety in numbers - that actuarial risks must allegedly cancel out in the sense relevant for investment decisions - a few general remarks may be in order.

Firstly, when an insurance company doubles the number of ships it insures, it does also double the range of its possible losses or gains. (This does not deny that it reduces the probability of its losses.) If at the same time that it doubles the pool of its risks, it doubles the number of its owners, it has indeed left the maximum possible loss per owner unchanged; but - and this is the germ of truth in the expression « there is safety in numbers » - the insurance company has now succeeded in reducing the probability of each loss; the gain to each owner now becomes a more certain one.

In short, it is not so much by *adding* new risks as by *subdividing* risks among more people that insurance companies reduce the risk of each. To see this, do not double or change at all the original number of ships insured by the company; but let each owner sell half his shares to each new owner. Then the risk of loss to each owner per dollar now in the company will have indeed been reduced.

Undoubtedly this is what my colleague really had in mind. In refusing a bet of $100 against $200, he should not then have specified a sequence of 100 such bets. That is adding risks. He should have asked to subdivide the risk and asked for a sequence of 100 bets, each of which was 100th as big (or $1 against $2). If the *money* odds are favorable and if we can subdivide the bets enough, any expected-utility-maximizer can be coaxed into a favorable-odds bet - for the obvious reason that the utility function's curvature becomes more and more negligible in a sufficiently limited range around any initial position. For sufficiently small bets we get more-than-a-fair game in the utility space, and my basic theorem goes nicely into reverse.[1]

Secondly, and finally, some economists have tried to distinguish between risk and uncertainty in the belief that actuarial probabilities can reduce risk to « virtual » certainty. The limit laws of probability grind fine but they do not grind that exceeding fine. I suspect there is often confusion between two similar-sounding situations. One is the case where the owner of a lottery has sold out *all* the tickets; the buyers of the tickets then face some kind of risky uncertainty, but the owner has completely cancelled out his risks whatever the draw may show - which is not a case of risk as against uncertainty, but really reflects a case of certainty without any risks at all. Another case is that in which the management of Monte Carlo or of the « numbers game » do business with their customers. The management makes sure that the odds are in their favor; but they can never make *sure* that a run of luck will not go against them and break the house (even though they can reduce this probability of ruin to a *positive* fraction).

In every actuarial situation of mathematical probability, no matter

---

[1] Cf. my cited 1960 paper. I should warn against undue extrapolation of my theorem. It does not say one must always refuse a sequence if one refuses a single venture: if, at higher income levels the single tosses become acceptable, and at lower levels the penalty of losses does not become infinite, there might well be a long sequence that is optional.

how large the numbers in the sample, we are left with a finite sample: in the appropriate limit law of probability there will necessarily be left an epsilon of uncertainty even in so-called risk situations. As Gertrude Stein never said: Epsilon ain't zero. This virtual remark has great importance for the attempt to create a difference of kind between risk and uncertainty in the economics of investment and decision-making.

P. A. SAMUELSON

Cambridge, Massachusetts Institute of Technology.

PART III

The Pure Theory of Capital and Growth

17

SOME ASPECTS OF
THE PURE THEORY OF CAPITAL

SUMMARY

Definition of an investment account, 469. — Relationships between capitalized value, depreciation, and income holding at all times under any rate of discount, 470. — Necessary equality between capital invested and value of investment account derived by capitalization, 474.— Definition and derivation of internal rate of interest; its relation to market rate, 475. — Identification under ideal conditions of market value of investment account with capitalized value, 477.— Problem of optimum determination of variables; maximization of internal rate vs. maximization of present value of assets, 478.— Demonstration that all principles remain invariant under a varying interest rate, 483.— Mathematical appendix I, 488.— Mathematical appendix II, 492.

Recent discussion has brought into renewed prominence those problems in General Economic Theory and Business Cycle Analysis in which time is involved. And yet, even in the Pure Theory of the subject, there is still an absence of that universal agreement on fundamentals which characterizes the timeless analysis. It is proposed here to apply relatively elementary mathematical analysis to a certain restricted field of the problem, in order to establish the validity of certain general principles upon which there can be little disagreement. I follow the path blazed by Mr. Boulding[1] and investigate the Pure Theory of the Single Investment under somewhat more general conditions than those which he imposes in his treatment.

It is not necessary to give a rigorous definition of what constitutes a Single Investment Account, since I wish to leave the analysis in as general a form as possible. The Single Investment Account consists of a stream of *net* income, given as a function of time, defined on some interval of time. At each instant of time, on the interval under consideration, the net income [positive or negative] is uniquely determined.

1. K. E. Boulding, "The Theory of the Single Investment," Quarterly Journal of Economics, May, 1935.

Mathematically, I take as given the following function

$$N = N(t) \qquad 0 \leqq t \leqq b \qquad (1)$$

where 0 and b represent the boundaries of the interval of time under consideration.

How this income arises and is delimited need not here concern us. Suffice it to define the Single Investment Account as a Source to which income is unequivocally imputed. It is to be noted that the Income stream is a rate, a flow of dollars per unit time.

If we assume any given rate of interest,[2] the capitalized value at time t of this income stream will be uniquely determined, consisting of the integrated [summed] income stream, reduced to present values by discounting with the given interest rate. Thus, value is given as a function of time and the rate of interest by the following well-known formula:

$$V = V(t,r) = \int_t^b N(x) e^{r(t-x)} dx \qquad (3)$$

where r is the rate of interest [continuously compounded] and x is a variable of integration.

As a special case, we have the initial value of the investment account, i.e., the value at time 0, given as follows:

$$V(0, r) = \int_0^b N(x) e^{-rx} dx \qquad (4)$$

The initial value will be different for each interest rate assumed.

2. Purely for mathematical convenience, I shall employ the force of interest in all that follows. This is equivalent to that rate of interest which, if continuously compounded, would make funds grow at the same rate as they actually do when compounding is made at finite intervals. The relationship between r, the continuously compounded rate of interest [force of interest] and the rate of interest, i, compounded per unit of time is as follows:

$$r = \log_e (1+i) \qquad (2)$$

Thus, there is a one to one correspondence between these rates, and both increase or decrease together. By this device, we can avoid the use of troublesome finite differences and summations, and instead bring the powerful tools of the differential and integral Calculus to bear upon these problems. This will simplify the proofs, and the reader may readily verify for himself that this involves no loss of generality.

Still assuming r to be given, we define the rate of appreciation [depreciation] as the rate of gain [loss] of value with respect to time, or

$$\frac{\partial V}{\partial t} = rV(t) - N(t) \tag{5}$$

We may also consider the following variations of this equation

$$N(t) = rV(t) - \frac{\partial V}{\partial t} \tag{6}$$

$$r \equiv \frac{N(t) + \dfrac{\partial V}{\partial t}}{V(t)} \tag{7}$$

Now purely as a matter of formal definition of what is meant by value, depreciation, and return on value, the following relationships hold for all rates of interest, positive or negative: The rate of depreciation at any instant of time is equal to the difference between net income and the return on value of the Investment Account at that instant of time. This is equivalent to saying that net income includes return on given value of investment plus rate of depreciation.

I emphasize again the fact that these are in no sense market values or market rates of interest, but values defined for any rate of interest or discount. If we assume ideal conditions, that there is a market rate of interest at which all can borrow or lend in unlimited amounts, that all incomes are clearly imputable and perfectly certain, that all individuals behave perfectly rationally, that all markets are perfect and frictionless, then our purely formal relationships will have their counterpart in "real" market values. Note that in our ideal conditions I do not include those of stationariness, i.e., that all income streams are constant or periodic. In the present section we are discussing relationships which hold with a constant rate of interest, but as I shall show later, we may dispense with this assumption and consider the case where the interest rate itself is an unrestricted function of time, and show that all our relationships still remain invariant. In fact the case of a constant rate of interest falls in as one special case under this more general heading.

In the case that net income is constant and perpetual, by performing the integration indicated in (3), we find that

$$r \equiv \frac{N}{V} \qquad (8)$$

That is to say, if value remains constant, the rate of depreciation becomes equal to zero from equation (6), and the *rate of interest may be expressed as the ratio between perpetual net income and value*. That this is so follows from our purely formal definition, and from the properties of the exponential function or infinite geometric series. That the interest rate is merely this [or "really" this!] does not at all follow. Furthermore, the fact that the difference between net income and return on investment equals a residuum of money which could be invested in order to provide a sum of money for replacement, in no way implies that this money, even under ideal conditions, will be so used. To say that after allowance for depreciation [appreciation], all net incomes are *virtually* put on a perpetual basis is to put emphasis on the relation given by equation (6); but the difference implied by the word virtually may be extremely important from some points of view. If there were such a sinking fund, it would properly fall into a separate account. Of course the addition of these two accounts would result in a constant income stream and a constant joint value. Moreover, from a social point of view, even if we admit behavior on the part of all individuals which will result in a [foreseen] fall or rise in the rate of interest, all our invariances will remain, even tho there is a presumption in favor of a general change in the sum of values of all income accounts in the same direction. In other words, I am under no compulsion here to discuss the meaning of capital as a quantity, or the meaning of maintenance, growth, or decline of such a magnitude.

Let us now consider the change in value resulting at any instant of time from a change in the rate of interest, r.

$$\frac{\partial V}{\partial r} = \int_{t}^{b} (t-x)N(x)e^{r(t-x)}dx \qquad (9)$$

It will be seen that there is sort of a weighting of discounted income by the time elapsing until that income is realized in order to arrive at the algebraic value of this rate of change. If "on the whole" negative incomes are realized during the earlier times, and positive net incomes during the later periods of time, then the sign of this term will be negative. That is to say, the value of the asset account will be larger the smaller the rate of interest. If the contrary case holds, the change will be opposite in sign.

Now, in order to develop as general a theory as possible, I assume that there are no restrictions on our income stream function. Writers who have had in mind certain types of assets have usually insisted that the investment account must be of the first class mentioned in the preceding paragraph, or at least, that the undiscounted sum of all income should be positive, in order, to use Mr. Boulding's phrase, that the investment be "absolutely" profitable. It would be easy to multiply examples of investment accounts, defined in our loose sense, in which this would not be so — in which (to borrow another concept recently developed by Mr. Boulding)[3] the *time spread* of the investment account is negative.

Since we leave our income function unrestricted we may have

$$\frac{\partial V}{\partial r} \gtreqless 0 \tag{10}$$

depending upon the income function under discussion and the particular values of r and t. This means, of course, that, everything else being given, r may not be a single valued function of V. That is, there may be more than one value of r which will yield the same value for the investment account at any given time.

Let us now establish another relationship which must hold at each instant of time for *any* given rate of interest. Let the initial value of the investment account $[V(0, r)]$ be the capitalized value of the income stream subsequent to the time 0.

3. K. E. Boulding, "Time and Investment," *Economica*, May, 1936.

Similarly, the value at any time t is given by capitalizing the income stream subsequent to time t, at the given rate of interest. That is to say,

$$V(0, r) = \int_0^b N(x)e^{-rx}dx \qquad (11)$$

$$V(t, r) = \int_t^b N(x)e^{r(t-x)}dx \qquad (12)$$

Let the *capital invested* in the income account up to the time t, be the income stream at all times previous to t, with algebraic sign reversed, compounded up to time t at the given rate of interest, plus the original value of the investment account compounded up to time t at the given rate of interest. Thus

$$c(t) = V(0, r)e^{rt} + \int_0^t -N(x)e^{r(t-x)}dx \qquad (13)$$

I shall now show that *for any given rate of interest, positive or negative, the value of capital invested, as above defined, is at all times equal to the value of the investment account, regarded as a capitalization of subsequent income.*

The proof is simple. From the fundamental theorems relating to the limits of integration we have the following identity for all values of t

$$V(0, r) = \int_0^b N(x)e^{-rx}dx = \int_0^t N(x)e^{-rx}dx + \int_t^b N(x)e^{-rx}dx \qquad (14)$$

Rewrite (14) as follows:

$$V(0, r) + \int_0^t -N(x)e^{-rx}dx = \int_t^b N(x)e^{-rx}dx \qquad (15)$$

Now multiply through both sides of the equation by e^{rt}, and we have our desired relationship.

$$V(0, r) + \int_0^t -N(x)e^{r(t-x)}dx \equiv \int_t^b N(x)e^{r(t-x)}dx \qquad (16)$$

Again, this relationship holds purely as a matter of formal definition, for any given rate of interest, or as I shall show later for a varying rate of interest.

I come now to the concept of the *internal* rate of interest (or return) of an investment account. While not an entirely new concept, it has been thoroughly discussed by Mr. Boulding in "The Theory of the Single Investment," *QSE*, May 1935.

The initial value of our investment account is given in equation (11) as a function of the rate of interest (discount), since it is a capitalization of the discounted income stream. For each rate of interest, r, there will be a determinate initial value. *The internal rate of interest is that rate [if it exists] corresponding to which, the initial value of the investment account is equal to zero.* Setting the initial value equal to zero, we have the following implicit equation for r. The value $\bar{r}$ which satisfies this equation is defined as the internal rate of interest. Thus,

$$V(0, \bar{r}) = 0. \tag{17}$$

Of course, in the absence of restrictions on our income function, there may be no value which satisfies this equation [e.g., the value of an income stream which is always positive, can never be equal to zero]. On the other hand, as pointed out before, r, may not be a single valued function of V, and so there may be a multiplicity of solutions of this equation.[4]

4. This integral equation may be solved in a number of ways. Mr. Boulding in his Economica article has presented one method which essentially is a method of iteration. Another method, making use of the statistical moments of the income account regarded as a kind of frequency distribution, is here suggested.

Expand the exponential term in a Taylor's series

$$e^{-rx} = 1 - rx + \frac{r^2 x^2}{2!} + \cdots + (-1)^n \frac{r^n x^n}{n!} + \cdots$$

Then

$$\int_0^b N(x)e^{-rx}dx = \int_0^b N(x)dx - r\int_0^b xN(x)dx + \cdots + (-1)^n \frac{r^n}{n!}$$
$$\int_0^b x^n N(x)dx + \cdots$$

Define

$$U_n = \frac{\int_0^b x^n N(x)dx}{\int_0^b N(x)dx}$$

Now solving our original equation for r is equivalent to solving the following polynomial, where any degree of approximation may be achieved by retaining more and more terms.

$$0 = 1 - U_1 r + \frac{U_2 r^2}{2!} + \cdots$$

This polynomial may be solved by any of the usual methods, Horner's method, Newton's method, or any other method. The multiplicity of roots of this polynomial should not be confused with that of the original equation.

See Whittaker and Robinson, Calculus of Observations, Ch. VII.

As I have remarked, this notion is not a new one. It appears, altho not always explicitly, in almost everybody's analysis *at the margin*. Indeed, Mr. Keynes' marginal efficiency of capital will be recognized as being essentially the internal rate of interest applied to a particular kind of an investment account, notably a fixed asset.[5]

The internal rate of interest, here defined, is of course not the same thing as the market rate of interest. *By the market rate of interest, I shall mean that rate at which each can borrow or lend in unlimited amounts.* At first I shall assume that the interest rate is a constant during the time under discussion, but shall later consider the more general case of a varying rate of interest. I assume throughout ideal conditions — perfect markets, complete foresight in the sense of an absence of Uncertainty.

I must first make clear that even under these ideal conditions, we are not by definition making the internal rate of interest equal to the market rate of interest [external rate]. As Mr. Boulding has pointed out, the internal rate of interest is in a real sense internal to the investment account, and is given as soon as the income stream of the account is given. I have purposely left the definition of an income account without restrictions. I shall later show that under our ideal conditions, all market valuations must be made at the market rate of interest. If this were equal to the internal rate of interest, this would imply that as a matter of definition, the "original" value of all investment accounts would be zero. But here we are not pretending to start at the beginning [sic] of time when all values are zero by definition. Rather our original time is arbitrarily chosen. We break into the system at any convenient point. Under our ideal conditions, all

---

5. Here our income stream contains an initial negative item (E), representing the cost in the market of the new asset, and a subsequent income stream. The marginal efficiency of capital is that rate of interest which equates discounted value of subsequent income to initial cost. That is, we solve

$$\int_0^b N(x)e^{-rx}dx + E = 0$$

for r. This is equivalent to our previous definition of the internal rate of interest.

future income must be imputable to present income accounts [sources of that future income]. All potential income must be capitalized. That is to say, we start with institutional property rights. Each income account "belongs" to some "person." We may even have income accounts with initial negative values if past contractual obligations exist.[6]

Under the ideal conditions we have assumed, it is not difficult to show that at any instant of time the value of every investment account is unequivocally determined. *The value of the account will necessarily be given by integration of the income stream, discounted at the market rate of interest.* The economic implementation of this law follows from the behavior of individuals in the market place. For should the market price of the account, the price at which it can be either bought or sold, be higher than its capitalized value, it would pay the owner to sell it and lend out the resulting sum of money at the current rate of interest. But note that nobody would be willing to pay any price for it above its capitalized value since he can always do better with his money elsewhere. Thus, its price cannot exceed its capitalized value. A similar argument shows that it cannot have a lower price. Hence its market value is identically its capitalized value.

It is of course true that in the real world the value of any investment account is not so unambiguously determined. This is due to a multiplicity of aberrations from ideal condi-

6. Of course we might still tautologically make the internal rate equal to the external rate by defining the original values of the investment account as part of our income stream. That is, the owner "puts in" the original value of the investment account into the investment. This has its advantages from several points of view and certain invariances emerge (see equation 16). But, and this is the crucial point, we must know the external rate and then compute the original value from it residually, in order to alter our income stream tautologically, so that our internal rate is brought to equality with the external rate. So defined, the income stream is not given, but depends upon the market interest rate.

Of course at the "margin," the external and internal rates will be necessarily equal. But the problem of giving a complete determination of the interest rate involves a specification of *sufficient* conditions to determine where the margin shall fall. This obviously lies outside of the province of this discussion.

tions. In the first place there is always the problem of Uncertainty. Waiving this, there is still the problem of imputation of income. In the absence of perfect divisibility there may be difficulty in separation of income attributable to a particular accounting unit, which difficulty may necessitate the lumping together of accounts, e.g., "going concern valuations." Despite this, and for reasons which it is not part of our present task to elucidate, there may still remain a problem of imputation. Furthermore, there is no perfect loan market in which all can lend or borrow in unlimited amounts at a fixed rate of interest. This is of course partly a subcase under the heading of Uncertainty but deserves special notice in this connection. In general, each decision-making entity has a certain characteristic position with respect to the loan market, and can borrow or lend in varying amounts at varying costs. Therefore, for purposes of allocating funds between different uses, it may legitimately employ internal valuations of its own. But the basis for distinction here is the "obstacle" under which the firm must carry out its financial operations. The rate of internal discount, in this sense, must never be confused with the internal rate of interest in our previous use of the term.

Let me emphasize that under our ideal conditions the "correct" valuations are capitalizations at the market rate of interest, the rate at which all can borrow or lend in unlimited quantities. Note that these valuations will in general be different from those arrived at by capitalizing at the internal rate of interest. That is to say,

$$V(0, r^0) \neq V(0, \bar{r})$$
$$\text{for } r^0 \neq \bar{r} \tag{18}$$

where $\bar{r}$ is the internal rate of interest, and r^0 is the market rate of interest.

Thus far, we have been taking our income stream as a given. To stop with this assumption would be to neglect an important aspect of our problem. More generally, it will be conceded that the income stream depends upon a multitude of parameters, each representing a relevant economic variable or condition. Some of these will be taken as outside the control of the firm, but some will be within the power of the decision-making owner of the investment account to fix in value.[7] For example, the account may refer to a productive process selling some commodity, and it is the problem of the entrepreneur to determine the "best" amounts of output, so-called inputs, etc., subject to certain given market and technological conditions. [Of course in the general case these parameters may be functions of time. Still more generally, income may be a functional of these parameters. That is to say, it may be necessary to know the value of these magnitudes at all previous times before the income at any one time is determinable. For the present we confine ourselves to the simpler case where the entrepreneur need only select the best value of these parameters once and for all.]

Mathematically, we have given the following function

$$N = N(a_1, \cdots a_n, \beta_1, \cdots \beta_m, t) \tag{19}$$

where the a's refer to the variables subject to control by the firm, and where the β's are outside the control of the firm. Hereafter, we may take the β's as givens, and so disregard them.

Now what general principles shall the firm employ in determining the best values of the variables under its control? As Mr. Boulding has suggested, it should not select these parameters so as to maximize its income during any small subinterval of time, nor indeed to maximize its absolute [undiscounted] income over time. What then shall be maximized?

Mr. Boulding has presented his answer to this problem, and it may be well to quote from him at this point:

... Thus, bound up in the very structure of any net revenue series there is a rate of return which pertains to it, and which can be calculated if we know all the terms of the net revenue series *and nothing else.*

We must now enunciate the central proposition of this argument, which is that the *magnitude which the perfectly rational and perfectly foreseeing investor wishes to maximize is this internal rate of return,* if we are considering policy as it affects not merely a single year but the life of the investment as a whole. It is clear that the investor will not want to

7. We neglect here certain indeterminacies arising out of quasi-duopolistic situations.

maximize the net revenue of a particular year at the expense of the net revenues of other years — indeed, the way to maximize the net revenue of a particular year is to liquidate the investment as quickly as possible! It is also clear on reflection that it is not the total excess of positive over negative net revenues that is to be maximized; this would assume that the investor is indifferent as to the date at which these surplus net revenues occurred. It is in fact the "rate of profit" in the classical terminology, the rate of return over the whole period of the enterprise, that is the real measure of its profitability and it is this which we have to maximize.[8] (Italics mine.)

Mathematically, we may represent his solution as follows, considering for simplicity that there is only one parameter

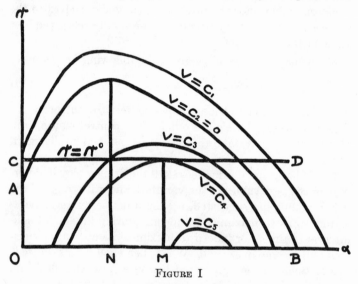

FIGURE I

whose value is to be determined: We may write initial value [or value at any given time] as a function of a and the rate of interest.

$$V = \varphi(a, r) = \int_0^b N(a, x)e^{-rx}dx \qquad (20)$$

For any preassigned value of V we get an implicit relationship between r and a. That is to say, there is a locus of combinations of a and r which will yield any given Value. For a

8. Quarterly Journal of Economics, May, 1935, p. 482.

different given V, there will be a new locus. Thus we get a family of curves, each representing a kind of Value-indifference curve. (See Fig. I) Consider now the curve AB which corresponds to

$$V = 0 = \varphi(a, r) \tag{21}$$

Given any value of a there is some value of r, which reduces the Value to zero. That is to say, there is a different internal rate of interest for each a. Mr. Boulding's solution is for the entrepreneur to select that value of a which yields the greatest internal rate of interest.

Along AB, we have

$$\frac{d\bar{r}}{da} = \frac{-\dfrac{\partial \varphi}{\partial a}}{\dfrac{\partial \varphi}{\partial r}} \tag{22}$$

At a maximum value for $\bar{r}$, we must have

$$\frac{d\bar{r}}{da} = 0 \tag{23}$$

and hence Mr. Boulding requires that

$$\frac{\partial \varphi(a, \bar{r})}{\partial a} = 0 \tag{24}$$

This equation together with (21) will determine Mr. Boulding's optimum value. It is essentially this method which Mr. Boulding has used in his illustrative example.

It is my purpose here to try to demonstrate that Mr. Boulding's criterion, that rational behavior implies the maximization of the internal rate of interest, is incorrect. Would it be unfair at the outset to suggest that in Mr. Boulding's exposition, it is a pure assumption, not a deduction from other propositions? The discarding of other fallacious criteria does not constitute a demonstration that this one is true.

It is my contention that under our ideal conditions the proper principle is clear, and that it is an old one in the literature of the subject. Moreover, it may be deduced from other considerations. Briefly this principle is as follows: *Given an interest rate at which all can lend or borrow* [r^0] *each entrepreneur will select that value of the variable under his control which maximizes the present value of the investment account, the present value being computed by capitalization of the income stream at the market rate of interest.* This follows from the fact that under our ideal conditions, the investment account necessarily has a market value equal to the capitalized value, and is equivalent to an equal money sum, *and a larger initial sum of money is always to be preferred to a smaller one.*

Mathematically, my solution is as follows: Value is a function of a and r^0. Since the entrepreneur must under our assumptions take the rate of interest as given, he varies a so as to maximize Value. This is equivalent to setting the following conditions on his behavior.

$$\frac{\partial \varphi(a,\, r^0)}{\partial a} = 0 = \int_0^b \frac{\partial N}{\partial a}\, e^{-r^0 x}\, dx \qquad (25)$$

This equation together with certain sufficiency conditions imposed on the higher derivatives will provide us with the optimum value of the variable. Graphically, the entrepreneur moves along CD, until it becomes tangent to one of the value contour lines. At this point he will be realizing the maximum possible value under the imposed conditions. The optimum value of a will be OM as contrasted with Mr. Boulding's optimum value of ON.

That his solution will yield different results from mine [in general], should be obvious from the following statement of his conditions and mine. For the maximum internal rate of interest not equal to the market rate of interest, the value of a which satisfies

$$\frac{\partial \varphi(a,\, r^0)}{\partial a} = 0 \qquad (25)$$

will be different [in general] from that which satisfies

$$\varphi(a,\, \bar{r}) = 0 \qquad (21)$$

$$\frac{\partial \varphi(a,\, \bar{r})}{\partial a} = 0 \qquad (23).$$

Of course special cases are conceivable in which we might accidentally get the same results by the different methods. But in any case as a matter of principle his method would be wrong.[9]

In the mathematical appendix I have taken up at greater length the illustrative example presented by Mr. Boulding to show how much my results differ from his. It is only just to add that my previous discussion constitutes a criticism of only one part of Mr. Boulding's theoretical structure, and that all students of the subject must remain under heavy obligations to him for his service in turning the discussion into a more fruitful channel.

Thus far, I have been treating the rate of interest as a constant with respect to time. This has been a serious limitation upon the generality and applicability of the theory. In order to assume that this is possible, we must assume stationary conditions in the loan market. This explains, I think, why so much of the previous work in capital theory has been predicated on a stationary society in which there is no capital accumulation. Not only is this a highly abstract assumption to be forced to make, but from the point of view of some theories, there is a contradiction in a positive rate of interest and equilibrium in the accumulation market. Clearly it is desirable to free our theory from such an assumption.

It is my purpose to show that we can abandon this assumption and still leave our results intact. I still assume ideal conditions in the sense that Uncertainty is absent, but I do not assume stationariness.[1] I shall show, moreover, that the case when the interest rate is a constant is just one special case in the more general analysis.

9. A further consideration of equation (25) gives us an interesting result. Using the differential notation

$$\int_0^b \left\{ \frac{\partial N}{\partial a}\, da \right\} e^{-rx} dx = 0$$

We may interpret this as saying that at the "margin," the addition of value is reduced to zero, that is to say for the marginal increment, the internal rate [the rate which reduces the marginal increment of value to zero] is equal to the market rate.

1. Cf. F. H. Knight, Risk, Uncertainty, and Profit, pp. 35, 36.

Let us suppose now that the interest rate [continuously compounded as before] is itself a function of time

$$r = r[t] \qquad 0 \leq t \leq b \qquad (26)$$

At any instant of time, all will be able to borrow or lend in unlimited amounts at the rate indicated by this function. Actually, every transaction will have some time duration. Depending upon the length of time of the transaction, there will be a different *average* rate of interest at which any person can borrow or lend. The limiting value of this average rate of interest, as the time interval becomes shorter and shorter, is the instantaneous rate of interest.

The relationship between the average rate of interest ρ between any two values of t [say 0 and t] and the instantaneous rate of interest r, on this time interval is a perfectly definite one and is given by the following equation:

$$\rho(t) = \frac{\int_0^t r(t)dt}{t} \qquad (27)$$

The reader will note that the instantaneous rate bears the same relationship to the average rate, as a marginal cost [revenue] curve bears to an average cost [revenue] curve. In the case that the average rate is a constant, so too will be the instantaneous rate, and they will be equal to each other. Thus in our previous section we had no need to distinguish between the two. Since the average rate may always be derived from the instantaneous one in all that follows, we shall confine our attention to the instantaneous rate.

Now from the fact that all can lend in unlimited amounts at the rate of interest given as a function of time in (26), it follows that any initial amount of money, $P[0]$ will grow according to the following law:

$$P(t) = P(0)e^{\int_0^t r(\epsilon)d\epsilon} \qquad (28)$$

where ϵ is a variable of integration.

Likewise, the value at time 0, $[P(0, t)]$ of any amount of money at time t, $[P(t)]$, is as follows:

$$P(0, t) = P(t)e^{-\int_0^t r(\epsilon)d\epsilon} = P(t)e^{\int_t^0 r(\epsilon)d\epsilon} \qquad (29)$$

As before, let the income stream of the investment account be

$$N = N(t) \qquad\qquad 0 \leqq t \leqq b \tag{30}$$

Then the value of the income account at any time t is uniquely determined by the following formula.

$$V(t) = \int_t^b N(x) e^{\int_x^t r(\epsilon)d\epsilon} dx \tag{31}$$

This is the capitalized value of future income, capitalized at a varying rate of interest; and under our ideal conditions, market value can neither rise above, nor fall below this figure.

[Note that where the interest rate is a constant, V may be taken as a function of this constant, i.e., it is a function of a point. But where r is a function of time, V is a functional of the time shape of interest, i.e., it is a so-called function of a line.]

It is easy to demonstrate that in the case where the interest rate is taken as a constant, this formula degenerates into our old one given in the previous section. For a constant r,

$$\int_x^t r(\epsilon)d\epsilon = r \int_x^t d\epsilon = r(t-x) \tag{32}$$

and we have our previous result given in (3).

$$V(t) = \int_t^b N(x) e^{r(t-x)} dx \tag{3}$$

Furthermore, we may differentiate value with respect to time in order to get the rate of appreciation [depreciation]. To do this we follow the usual rules for differentiating a definite integral with respect to a parameter.[2]

Thus

$$V'(t) = \int_t^b N(x)\{r(t)\} e^{\int_x^t r(\epsilon)d\epsilon} dx - N(t) \tag{33}$$

or finally

$$V'(t) = r(t)V(t) - N(t) \tag{34}$$

The importance and generality of this relationship can hardly be sufficiently stressed. For it is exactly the same relationship as held with a constant rate of interest, which is

2. Cf. E. B. Wilson, Advanced Calculus, pp. 283–284.

in fact a special case of this formulation. Even with a varying rate of interest, net income in our definition of the term contains a return on value of investment and also an amount equal to rate of depreciation. As algebraic variants of this relationship we get

$$N(t) = r(t)V(t) - V'(t) \tag{35}$$

$$r(t) \equiv \frac{N(t) + V'(t)}{V(t)} \tag{36}$$

It must be remembered again that the last equation is a formal identity, arising out of our definition of value under our ideal conditions, and will not in general be sufficient to "determine" the rate of interest.

From a contemplation of this equation, we see that a constant perpetual income will not necessarily maintain a constant value. If the rate of interest is expected to rise or fall monotonically, the value of such a perpetual income will decrease or increase. On the other hand, maintenance of a constant value will not provide a constant income under a varying rate of interest.[3] Changes in value arising out of changes in the interest rate would not fall out of the province of our theory as long as such fall in the rate of interest is foreseen. We relegate to the theory of Obsolescence only unforeseen changes.

I shall now develop my other relations under these more general conditions. Defining the *capital invested* in the investment account exactly as before, but this time using a variable rate of interest, we have the following mathematical equation for this concept.

$$c(t) = V(0)e^{\int_0^t r(\epsilon)d\epsilon} + \int_0^t -N(x)e^{\int_x^t r(\epsilon)d\epsilon} dx \tag{37}$$

Recalling that value at time t is as follows

$$V(t) = \int_t^b N(x)e^{\int_x^t r(\epsilon)d\epsilon} dx \tag{31}$$

3. If the value of such an investment account is to be finite, the interest rate may fall asymptotically to zero, but only at a certain rate of convergence. In real life, the existence of assets with a perpetual net imputed yield [land, etc.] would be expected therefore to have an influence in determining the rate at which the interest rate could *approach* zero.

it is easy to show that they are identically equal for all values of t. The proof is as follows:

$$V(0) = \int_0^t N(x) e^{\int_x^0 r(\epsilon)d\epsilon} dx + \int_t^b N(x) e^{\int_x^0 r(\epsilon)d\epsilon} dx \quad (38)$$

Multiplying both sides by $e^{\int_0^t r(\epsilon)d\epsilon}$, and transposing, we have our required result.

$$V(0)e^{\int_0^t r(\epsilon)d\epsilon} + \int_0^t -N(x) e^{\int_x^0 r(\epsilon)d\epsilon + \int_0^t r(\epsilon)d\epsilon} dx$$

$$= \int_t^b N(x) e^{\int_x^0 r(\epsilon)d\epsilon + \int_0^t r(\epsilon)d\epsilon} dx$$

or

$$V(0)e^{\int_0^t r(\epsilon)d\epsilon} + \int_0^t -N(x) e^{\int_x^t r(\epsilon)d\epsilon} dx \equiv \int_t^b N(x) e^{\int_x^t r(\epsilon)d\epsilon} dx \quad (39)$$

Thus, the time shape of interest being given and income being known, the capital invested up to any time is always equal to the value of the account at that time, the value being a capitalization of subsequent income. Again, the case for a constant rate of interest is just a special instance deducible from this more general relationship.

It is well to point out that altho these relationships hold merely as a matter of formal definition, under ideal conditions, they will "really" hold in the market place since there are always efficacious economic forces tending to bring them about.

Since the concept of the internal rate of interest is independent of the market rate of interest, being dependent only upon the income stream, even in a world where the market rate of interest is a variable with time, the internal rate of interest would still be a clear-cut concept with definite meaning. But again I should be prepared to argue that it has no relevance to the problem of rational behavior. As before the proper principle remains the same. Each entrepreneur behaves so as to maximize the present capitalized [using the market rate of interest] value of the investment account. In Mathematical Appendix II, I have worked out Mr. Boulding's illustrative example under our general conditions.

In stating the above relationships, I have attempted to

present that which must be obviously true, almost as a matter of formal logic. Once there is general agreement on these fundamentals, the ground may be clear for investigation of realistic conditions, where ideal conditions are never perfectly realized.

MATHEMATICAL APPENDIX I

It has been suggested by Mr. Keynes[4] and others, that even under ideal conditions there are other rates of interest than the money rate of interest. Actually, there is a rate of interest expressed in terms of any commodity, and there are at least as many rates of interest as there are commodities. This has raised the question whether there is anything primary about the money rate of interest, and whether our results would be changed if we computed in terms of other rates of interest. Concerning the first question, I shall give no answer, but shall attempt to show that *under ideal conditions*, the rates of interest expressed in different commodity terms are all rigidly connected to each other and to the money rate of interest. *Furthermore, I shall demonstrate that under such conditions, all decisions remain invariant with respect to any change in the commodity which is used as our measure of value.* That such a change in our units should not cause any change in results should seem probable from certain common sense considerations, but since the question has been raised I shall attempt to give a mathematical demonstration of this result.

I shall first give a mathematical definition of the rate of interest expressed in terms of money which will permit of generalization to the rate of interest defined in terms of any other commodity. Suppose the money rate of interest $[r_1]$ is given as a function of time.

$$r_1 = r_1(t) \tag{1}$$

The value at time 0 of a dollar at time t is given as follows:

$$\Pi_1(0, t) = 1 \cdot e^{\int_t^0 r_1(\epsilon) d\epsilon} \tag{2}$$

4. J. M. Keynes, *General Theory of Employment, Interest and Money*, Ch. 17.

Converting to natural logs, we have

$$\log_e \Pi_1(0,\,t) = \int_t^0 r_1(\epsilon)d\epsilon \qquad (3)$$

Multiply through by minus one, and then differentiate both sides with respect to t, and we get

$$r_1(t) = -\frac{\partial \log \Pi_1(0,\,t)}{\partial t} \qquad (4)$$

Thus the money rate of interest at time t may be expressed as the negative of the logarithmic [percentage] rate of change in the *present* value of a dollar at time t.

Similarly, I define the rate of interest expressed in terms of the jth commodity as the negative of the logarithmic rate of change in present value of a unit of that commodity at time t; i.e.,

$$r_j(t) = -\frac{\partial \log \Pi_j(0,\,t)}{\partial t} \qquad (5)$$

where $r_j[t]$ is the rate of interest expressed in terms of the jth commodity, and where $\Pi_j[0,\,t]$ is the present value of a unit of commodity j at time t. It will later become apparent that this is precisely the same definition of the rate of interest expressed in terms of any commodity as Mr. Keynes and others have had in mind.

I shall now relate the commodity rate of interest, so defined, to the money rate of interest. Under our ideal conditions, the price of the jth commodity is given as the following function of time

$$p_j = p_j(t) \qquad (6)$$

Now Uncertainty being absent, and the money rate of interest being given [i.e., the rate at which all can borrow or lend funds in unlimited amounts], there is a definite relation which must hold between Π_j and p_j, due to the rational behavior of individuals in the market place. *The present value of a future unit of any good is the amount of money which must be set aside today in order to yield an amount of money equal to its price at that future date.* This must be true independently of any possibility of carryover of the commodity, since a violation of this condition would inevitably bring into play forces which would reëstablish this relationship. Symbolically

$$\Pi_j(0,\ t) = p_j(t)\, e^{\int_t^0 r_1(\epsilon)d\epsilon} \tag{7}$$

Again taking the natural logarithm of both sides, we get

$$\log \Pi_j(0,\ t) = \log\ p_j(t) + \int_t^0 r_1(\epsilon)d\epsilon \tag{8}$$

Now if we differentiate with respect to time and rearrange terms we have

$$r_1(t) = -\ \frac{\partial \log \Pi_j(0,\ t)}{\partial t} + \frac{d \log\ p_j(t)}{dt} \tag{9}$$

Recalling the definition of the commodity rate of interest in (5) we get the following relationship between the money rate of interest and all the commodity rates of interest.

$$r_1(t) = r_2(t) + \frac{d \log\ p_2(t)}{dt} = \cdots r_j(t) + \frac{d \log\ p_j(t)}{dt} \tag{10}$$

In the case of a stationary economy where all prices remain constant we have

$$\frac{d \log\ p_j(t)}{dt} = \frac{dp_j(t)}{dt}\ \frac{1}{p_j(t)} = 0 \tag{11}$$

and so all the rates of interest are identical. If we have differential price movements this will of course not be so. Moreover, given a sharp enough price drop, we could have commodity rates of interest as large negatively as we choose.

I shall now show that expressing all values in terms of any commodity leaves all results invariant. Deflating all net income by the price of the jth commodity, we have for our new income stream

$$N_j(a,\ t) = \frac{N_1(a,\ t)}{p_j(t)} \tag{12}$$

where a is any parameter which the firm can influence. Capitalizing this income stream, using the jth commodity rate of

interest for discounting, we get the present value of the investment account in terms of the jth commodity.

$$V_j(0, a) = \int_0^b N_j(a, x) e^{\int_x^0 r_j(\epsilon) d\epsilon} dx \tag{13}$$

But

$$r_j(t) = r_1(t) - \frac{d \log p_j(t)}{dt} \tag{10}$$

$$N_j(a, t) = \frac{N_1(a, t)}{p_j(t)} \tag{12}$$

Hence

$$V_j(0, a) = \int_0^b \frac{N_1(a, x)}{p_j(x)} e^{\int_x^0 r_1(\epsilon) d\epsilon - \int_x^0 d \log p_j(\epsilon)} dx$$

$$= \int_0^b \frac{N_1(a, x)}{p_j(x)} \frac{p_j(x)}{p_j(0)} e^{\int_x^0 r_1(\epsilon) d\epsilon} dx$$

$$= \frac{1}{p_j(0)} V_1(0, a) \tag{14}$$

In other words, the capitalized value expressed in terms of
any commodity is equal to the capitalized value expressed in
money terms divided by a dimensional constant. This
dimensional constant [factor of proportionality] is, as we
should have expected, the present price of the jth commodity.
Of course, we may use any point in time as the "present"
time, so our results would just as well hold for every instant
of time.

This result, that capitalized value expressed in terms of
any commodity is always proportional to capitalized value
expressed in terms of money is crucial to our argument. *For
since these two expressions differ only by a factor of proportionality, the value of a which maximizes the one, will be the same
as that which maximizes the other.* Thus, as we should have
expected, all decisions remain unchanged by the method of
calculation.

Actually we might go Mr. Keynes one better and use any
arbitrary function of time as a deflating factor, defining a
corresponding rate of interest in consistence with such a

transformation. We might, for example, use some market basket or composite commodity index, the course of the tides in the Bay of Fundy, or any other arbitrary basis for our dimensional change without at all altering our results.[5]

From the standpoint of my analysis here, the only difference between money and other commodities is that money is the commodity whose price is always equal to unity, by definition. In this discussion, I have been able to neglect the obvious fact that there are also other essential differences which may be relevant for other problems.

MATHEMATICAL APPENDIX II

It is proposed to work out the illustrative example given by Mr. Boulding, first to show how my results would differ from his; second, and this is the more important reason, to place emphasis upon an approach which comes directly to grips with some of the problems of time. The usual method in analyzing similar problems in which time is involved has been to use indirect methods, which convert the problem into an equivalent timeless one. It cannot be denied that this may yield the correct answer in particular cases, where such constructions are possible. But such methods are lacking in generality, and divert attention from the essential distinctiveness of the problem.

I assume, without committing myself as to its reality, that product at any time is a given function of two factors of production [inputs], and the elapsed time since they were invested. Thus

$$q = q(a, b, \theta) \tag{1}$$

5. Of course fixed assets themselves are commodities bought and sold. It is important to distinguish the rate of interest expressed in terms of such a commodity from the yield [marginal efficiency, etc.] of such a commodity. The former is merely a function of the change in price of new fixed assets and has no necessary connection with its net productivity in any sense of the term. For example, the former may be negative at the same time that it pays to buy the asset.

It may be well to point out that we have taken all prices as known. Of course purely from the standpoint of intertemporal equilibrium in the market place, there will be certain restrictions on the behavior of the price of a commodity as a function of time, due to qualities peculiar to each commodity [durability, possibility of carryover, etc.]. These things are of no concern to us here.

where θ is the elapsed time between input and output. I make the usual assumptions with respect to continuity of this function and its partial derivatives. I assume that the price of each factor of production is given to the firm as is the price of its finished good.

I also assume a market rate of interest at which all can lend or borrow in unlimited amounts as follows:

$$r = r(t) \tag{2}$$

We must now investigate the income stream which would result from such a productive process. If we start our inputs at time 0, and continue them in varying amounts up to time b, we shall have certain costs coming due on the interval of time 0 to b, depending in amount upon the quantities of the factors of production used at any instant of time. Selecting the initial amount of time for which we shall leave the inputs in the productive process, we shall have sales and revenue starting at that time. Moreover, revenues will continue past the time b, since inputs at time b will not "mature" until a later date. It remains only to write down our actual revenue and outlay as functions of time, to take their difference to get the net income at any instant of time. This net income will depend on our choice of inputs as function of time, and our period of investment as function of time. My method is to capitalize this net income, using the market rate of interest, and then to select each input, period of investment, at every instant of time, which maximizes the present value of the investment account so defined. [The reader who has grasped the essentials of this analysis will understand at once why I do not include as costs any interest charges on capital invested, etc. That this would involve double counting should be obvious from the logic of my analysis.]

For convenience, we break up our net income stream into three parts, and capitalize it, using the variable market rate of interest:

$$V = \int_0^\theta -\{p_a a + p_b b\} e^{\int_x^0 r(\epsilon)d\epsilon} \, dx + \int_\theta^b \{pq - p_a a - p_b b\} e^{\int_x^0 r(\epsilon)d\epsilon} dx$$
$$+ \int_b^{b+\theta} pq e^{\int_x^0 r(\epsilon)d\epsilon} dx \tag{3}$$

Now we algebraically rearrange terms:

$$V = \int_0^b - \{ p_a a(x) + p_b b(x) \} \, e^{\int_x^0 r(\epsilon)d\epsilon} dx + \int_\theta^{b+\theta} pq(x) e^{\int_x^0 r(\epsilon)d\epsilon} dx$$

$$(4)$$

For reasons which may not be apparent, we shall transform our variable of integration in the second integral. The reader will at least be able to satisfy himself that this is a legitimate mathematical procedure, which will not change the value of the expression. Our transformation is to introduce a new variable of integration defined as follows:

$$u = x - \theta \tag{5}$$

We may rewrite our second integral as follows:

$$\int_\theta^{b+\theta} pq(x) e^{\int_x^0 r(\epsilon)d\epsilon} dx = \int_0^b pq(u+\theta) e^{\int_{u+\theta}^u r(\epsilon)d\epsilon + \int_u^0 r(\epsilon)d\epsilon} du \quad (6)$$

Now introducing a uniform notation for the variables of integration in the two integrals, we get the following expression for our present value:

$$V = \int_0^b \{ pq(t+\theta) e^{\int_{t+\theta}^t r(\epsilon)d\epsilon} - p_a a(t) - p_b b(t) \} \, e^{\int_t^0 r(\epsilon)d\epsilon} dt \quad (7)$$

The economic interpretation of our transformation was essentially the "stepping back" of revenues [output] to the costs [inputs], which gave rise to them.

Let us now write our results in as general a form as possible in order to see what the mathematical requirements for a maximum of present value are. We may write present value as equal to the following integral:

$$V = \int_0^b G[\bar{q}(t+\theta), \, \bar{r}(t), \, a(t), \, b(t), \, \theta(t)] dt \tag{8}$$

Now in this expression, our independent variables are the unbarred terms

$$a(t), b(t), \theta(t)$$

The interest rate must be taken as a given, and output is a given as soon as our inputs and period of investment are known. Our problem is to determine the following functions of time, in order that the integral given by equation (8) be maximized:

$$a = a(t)$$
$$b = b(t) \tag{9}$$
$$\theta = \theta(t)$$

From the elementary theory of the Calculus of Variations, we know that a first necessary condition for a maximum of such an integral requires that the following Euler differential equations be satisfied:

$$\left. \begin{aligned} \frac{\partial G}{\partial a} &\equiv 0 \\ \frac{\partial G}{\partial b} &\equiv 0 \\ \frac{\partial G}{\partial \theta} &\equiv 0 \end{aligned} \right\} 0 \leqq t \leqq b \tag{10}$$

In terms of our specific functions, this imposes the following relations on our problem.

$$\left. \begin{aligned} p_a &\equiv p\frac{\partial q}{\partial a} e^{\int_{t+\theta}^{t} r(\epsilon)d\epsilon} \\ p_b &\equiv p\frac{\partial q}{\partial b} e^{\int_{t+\theta}^{t} r(\epsilon)d\epsilon} \\ r(t+\theta) &\equiv \frac{\partial \log q(t+\theta)}{\partial \theta} \end{aligned} \right\} 0 \leqq t \leqq b \tag{11}$$

These are, of course, the well-known discounted marginal productivity theorems of Professor Taussig and Wicksell. We note here that in case the rate of interest varies it will pay to change the optimum values of output and investment period at each instant of time. For a constant market rate, (11) becomes

$$p_a \equiv p\frac{\partial q}{\partial a} e^{-r_0\theta}$$

$$p_b \equiv p\frac{\partial q}{\partial a}e^{-r^0\theta} \tag{12}$$

$$r^0 \equiv \frac{\partial \log q}{\partial \theta}$$

In the case that the market rate of interest is a constant with respect to time, the optimum values will be constants. But my optimum values will be different from Mr. Boulding's. For he discounts marginal productivities at the internal rate of interest, while I discount them at the market rate of interest.

It is the implication of Mr. Boulding's method that entrepreneurs would behave exactly the same in the face of a given set of alternatives, regardless of any given market rate of interest. Moreover, if the market rate of interest is a variable, they would still not make corresponding changes in their behavior.

In the case that the market rate of interest is a constant and the internal rate of interest is equal to it, then the initial value of the investment account is zero. Moreover, if we step back revenues to the same time that costs are incurred, and include interest as a cost we find that

$$pq = p_a a e^{\bar{r}\theta} + p_b b e^{\bar{r}\theta} \tag{13}$$

In other words, if we convert our analysis to a timeless [or instantaneous rate of flow] basis, this implies that the rate of instantaneous profit is equal to zero. Now it may be that in the presence of free entry into the industry [absence of institutional advantage], profits will be forced down to zero. But this will not be due to the deliberate behavior of the firm. Rather will it be due to changes in our outside parameters [price of product, cost elements] which are beyond the power of the firm. Unless my whole analysis is wrong, to argue as Mr. Boulding does in this case would be just like arguing that in timeless production firms *seek* to produce at minimum average cost, just because under atomistic competition they are forced to do so.

PAUL A. SAMUELSON.

HARVARD UNIVERSITY

18

THE RATE OF INTEREST UNDER IDEAL CONDITIONS

SUMMARY

Implications of Ideal Conditions, 286.— Entrepreneurial behavior with a given rate of interest, 287.— Individual behavior with a given rate of interest, 290.— The identity between Saving and Investment, 292.— The determination of the rate of interest, 295.— Distinguishable components of the process of capital growth, 296.— The assumption of perfect certainty, 297.

In discussing the determination of a price in a purely competitive market it is convenient to divide the analysis into two stages. First, we assume a price and show how any individual would act if confronted with that price. At this level of analysis it is assumed that no (one) individual can affect the price; that it is a *given*. In the second stage, however, it is necessary to show how all together determine that equilibrium price with which each as an individual is confronted. This same method of analysis may be applied fruitfully to the problem of the rate of interest, whatever theory of capital is held. It is convenient and meaningful to discuss, first, the behavior of enterprises and households when confronted with a given rate of interest or a given set of rates of interest, present and future. After this is done it may be possible to show how such behavior tends to establish a unique rate of interest, or at least that there is only one rate of interest compatible with such reactions.

In a previous paper[1] I discussed the behavior of an enterprise under ideal conditions of certainty, when confronted with a given rate of interest at which it could borrow or lend in unlimited amounts. It was argued there that the norm towards which behavior tended was the maximization of present value of the assets of the enterprise, where all valuations are computed by discounting at the above rate all future algebraic net revenues, no allowance being made for capital change. I should like here to carry the analysis further in an attempt to indicate some of the forces which help to determine the market rate of interest at which all can borrow or lend under ideal conditions.

At the beginning admittedly restrictive assumptions are made. It is assumed that all net revenues are perfectly foreseen,

1. "Some Aspects of the Pure Theory of Capital," Quarterly Journal of Economics, May, 1937, p. 469.

and that all markets are perfect and frictionless. Consequently there is, in effect, only one kind of asset, all incomes being equally safe, and only one rate of interest at each instant of time. In order to avoid the difficult problem of the function of a cash balance in such a liquid world, we assume either a perfect clearing system in which there is a unit of account for the reckoning of prices but no medium of exchange; or, alternatively, we assume that the medium of exchange consists of perfectly liquid and convertible interest-bearing assets. At first glance it might seem as if we have assumed away the rate of interest as a result of such abstraction, but, as will appear later, many of the problems of capital theory still remain under these ideal conditions. In any case, it is hoped that the analysis of this simplified system may serve as a useful introduction to more complex reality.

Entrepreneurial Behavior with a Given Rate of Interest

At the beginning it is well to discuss certain simple necessary conditions of equilibrium in our ideal market, where each individual is too unimportant to affect the interest rate appreciably. From my previous analysis it is clear that for every investment account (opportunity) we must have the following relationship:[2]

$$r(t)\ v(t) = n(t) + v'(t) \tag{1}$$

where $n(t)$ is the net revenue from the process under consideration; $v(t)$, the value of the investment; $v'(t)$, the rate of appreciation of the investment; and $r(t)$ is the rate of interest.

That is to say, every investment opportunity must bring in the same rate of return, equal, moreover, to the market rate of interest at which all can borrow or lend in unlimited amounts. This does not mean that each equal investment will be yielding up the same amount of money revenue per unit time. Those investments which are rising in value will be yielding revenues smaller by just enough to equalize the rate of return to the market rate of interest — in other words, dividends may be small because of plowed-back earnings. On the other hand, any investment which is depreciating in value will yield a compensatory larger revenue. Thus under our ideal conditions the owners of a mine in the process of being exhausted will necessarily receive an excess of dividend

2. Ibid., pp. 471, 485, 486.

equivalent to the rate of depletion. As a practical illustration of this principle, we have the case of a rising security market in which the rate of actual dividends paid bears a small ratio to the market value of the securities. Despite this fact, investors are quite willing to borrow money on call at high rates of interest. Equilibrium is only possible in these conditions because of the anticipation of investors that there will be an appreciable rise in value of the securities bought.[3]

This condition is not a mere mathematical property of the exponential function. It is a necessary condition of equilibrium, the economic implementation of which arises from the fact that its violation will bring into immediate play arbitrage movements sufficient to establish it again.[4]

Furthermore, it was seen that the maximization of the present value of each investment implies that for every continuously variable decision the following conditions must hold at the margin:

$$\frac{\partial V}{\partial a} = \int_0^b \frac{\partial N}{\partial a} e^{-rx} dx \qquad (2)$$

where a is any variable which the enterprise is free to determine, e.g., output, price, etc.[5] This condition corresponds to the theorem in the timeless analysis that the marginal cost of any (continuously variable) decision must be equal at the point of equilibrium (stopping) to the marginal revenue. Similarly here, at the point of equilibrium the rate at which present value is being increased by any move or decision must be just balanced by the ensuing rate of decrease of present value.

This condition, it should be noted, is maintained as a result of adjustment of parameters of action (decisions) to any given rate of interest. It is not in itself sufficient to determine the rate of interest, any more than the marginal productivity of a worker can be said to determine the wage rate. Only in conjunction with other conditions is it possible to get a set of mutually interdependent relations sufficient to determine the rate of interest.

3. It is not correct to say that all investments are "placed on a perpetual income basis," since a perpetual constant income may vary in value with foreseen changes in the rate of interest. It would be better to say that all investments are placed on a *constant value basis*.

4. Quarterly Journal of Economics, May, 1937, p. 477.

5. This is Irving Fisher's condition that the marginal rate of return over cost must be equal to the rate of interest.

This last theorem is not to be interpreted as being identical with the statement of Mr. Keynes that the marginal efficiency of capital tends to be equal to the rate of interest. What Mr. Keynes means by marginal efficiency is not really a marginal concept in our sense of the term. It is the (average) *rate of return over cost* applied to a "marginal" investment; i.e., an investment which by definition is earning an internal rate of return just equal to the rate of interest.[6] The difference can be brought out by an analogy to price in an ideal competitive market. It is one thing to say that, for every firm which can continuously vary its output, price must be equal to marginal cost. It is quite another thing, and perhaps just a bit old-fashioned, to say that price equals the average cost of the "marginal" firm, i.e., the firm which by definition can just cover its average costs. The distinction between the intensive and extensive margins is of course involved.

This theorem has been stated in very general terms so as to apply to any maximum problem, and I believe rightly so. Too many writers have concentrated upon specific applications of it, under the impression that they were expounding *the* theory of capital. A case in point is the Jevons — Böhm-Bawerk length of the period of productions. Now it is conceivable that certain special technical processes might be found in which the production of a specific commodity might be linked up in some way with a period of production or turnover in some technical sense. In such a case this variable, like any other one, would be varied up to the point of equality of marginal rates of addition and subtraction to present value of assets. But it is a far cry from this to the view that all society is a huge sausage machine, and that the rate of interest is merely the marginal net productivity of lengthening the period of production. The fallacy of misplaced concreteness is certainly involved in the reckless application of a simplified model to the interpretation of the real world.[7] Other special cases of this general formulation are found in the Taussig-Wicksell discounted marginal productivity theorems. Recently Mr. Hicks and Mr. Hart have developed these special relations at some length.

6. J. M. Keynes, The General Theory of Employment, Interest, and Money, Ch. 11.

7. Of course in practice the term "increased roundaboutness of production" is so vague in definition as to be harmless, being practically synonymous with capitalistic, specialized, complex, or technical production. It is only when more specific content is given to the term that it becomes inadmissible.

But these are by no means exhaustive. The problem of investment and business organizations cannot be reduced to such simple type processes. It is extremely difficult to find in reality even reasonably good examples of such production relations, much less explain by them the bulk of economic activity. Actually the possible forms of investment and productive relationships are multifarious. It is almost impossible to formulate a production function of wide applicability. Moreover, investment is not necessarily of a technical kind. A heavy advertising campaign, a price reduction whose full effect can register only after a period of time, these are all investment activities which give rise to imputable income and asset value. Furthermore, much investment activity is neither continuous nor periodic and may be essentially irreversible. Hence our virtual-displacement analysis cannot always apply.

From all this it follows that nothing definite can be said about the effect of a change in the rate of interest on asset value. In general, different optimal behavior is to be expected. Even in the absence of such change in behavior, it is not necessarily true that asset value will increase with a lowering of the rate of interest, altho this would, of course, be true in the case of a positive income stream. In general, it is to be presumed that the lower the rate of interest, the more "capital" will be employed in any process, i.e., the larger will be the present asset value, optimally determined.[8]

BEHAVIOR OF INDIVIDUALS CONFRONTED WITH A RATE OF INTEREST

It is convenient to consider separately the behavior of individuals or families, because in real life there is a similar institutional cleavage. Modern specialized life tends to segmentalize thought patterns, so that the same man thinks differently as an entrepreneur and as a consumer. Moreover, our economic organization is such that enterprises (corporations, et cetera) stand apart, linked to the public only through banks and security exchanges. Furthermore, it is demonstrable that under our ideal conditions rational economic behavior on the part of the entrepreneur is independent of his own preferences as to time of consumption.[9]

8. It is interesting to note here that it is perfectly possible for a particular productive process to be in equilibrium at a zero rate of interest, even tho there is "superiority of present goods over future goods in a technical sense," provided only that the future selling price of that good be lower than the present.
9. This follows from the fact that the maximization of present value of

It has been customary to lay considerable stress upon psychological, hedonistic aspects of individual behavior with regard to saving. Among the older economists emphasis was placed upon the disutility aspects of abstinence and waiting. At the end of the nineteenth century the fashion turned more towards the analysis of the utilities of consumption through time. It is possible, I think, so to state the matter that these approaches come to very much the same thing. However, I do not think that much is to be gained from this approach.[1]

Starting from a few elemental facts concerning our civilization, it is clear that individuals are born into families and remain dependent for a number of years. There follows a period of earning power during which income may be rising, falling, or remaining constant, and usually a twilight period of decreased earnings or even no earnings. Altho particular families may show non-synchronized "replacement waves," i.e., distinct generations, barring wars and epidemics, the age distribution of all society tends towards a more or less constant form. If the clan were the form of communal organization, it is conceivable that children and old people might be supported solely by the current earnings of the active members. Because of the break between generations and the growing tendency for each generation to keep its own books, except in the case of bringing up children, there is a considerable holding of assets by individuals in anticipation of a period of dependency. Even tho some savings are being used up as others are made, it does not follow that these items cancel out. On the contrary, there is a gap between the time of purchase of assets by any one family and their liquidation, and so even tho the process may be synchronized from the viewpoint of all society, still the result is a large group of assets always held. Obviously the inflow-tank-outflow analogy suggests itself here. It is probable that a considerable proportion of asset holding in the form of life insurance policies and savings accounts is of this kind. The magnitude of such a pool can be visualized in part by considering the size of the proposed Old Age Reserve Fund established to provide minimum old age benefits.

assets results in an equivalent (money) sum immediately. This can then be spent in any way and at any time, according to the tastes of the individual.

1. I have indicated elsewhere what can be done in a mathematical way with such hypotheses. This was intended only as an axiomatic experiment, an intellectual curiosity, which served to reveal to my own satisfaction the arbi-

Of course, it is impossible to discuss the behavior of households with respect to asset holding without reference to the distribution of income and amount of assets already held. From the fragmentary evidence which we possess, it appears that the size of asset holding and estates at death of members of the lower class is extremely low.[2] On the other hand, as we go into the highest income brackets, the artificiality of the convention of maximization of consumption utility over time becomes more and more evident. Asset holding and increasing one's asset holding become ends in themselves. It is very difficult to distinguish between the consumption of the "services" of a diamond and those of a gilt-edged security. In the middle income groups there would seem to be a tendency toward the development of a more or less automatic saving plan in the attempt to maintain or improve an accustomed standard of life, this being modified of course by the state of the business cycle. On the whole it is probable that the rate of yield of assets, the rate of interest, is only a minor element among many in determining the rate of change of asset holding by individuals.[3] The cultural values of modern society are such that there would presumably be asset accumulation at any rate of interest.

As Professor Knight has pointed out, it is a peculiarity of our legal and social customs that the revenues from personal services are not capitalized and sold. As a result it serves no useful purpose to consider each family as owning its future discounted earnings. However, under ideal conditions, the possibility of any person's borrowing on the basis of earning prospects would serve to modify considerably the differences presented by this case, just as it would where land is under entail.

The Identity Between Savings and Investment

It is well to consider certain aggregated identities which result from my definition of terms and of ideal conditions of certainty. The results will, I think, differ in at least one important respect from the views recently expressed by Mr. Keynes.

trariness of the assumptions and the barrenness of the results. See "A Note on the Measurement of Utility," Review of Economic Studies, Vol. IV, No. II.

2. Still, as Professor Viner has pointed out, it is to be remembered that on balance the low income groups are creditors rather than debtors, since many possess savings accounts and few are in a position to borrow money.

3. It is even possible to construct cases with conditions equivalent to a negative rate of interest on *all* assets. Even under these circumstances, there might very well be accumulation and increased asset holding.

Let

$N(t) \equiv \Sigma n(t)$ be the algebraic sum of all net revenues per unit time accruing to all capitalized sources of income;

$C(t) \equiv \Sigma c(t)$ be the algebraic sum of all non-capitalized revenues;

$S(t)$ be the amount of total sales from enterprises to consumers per unit time;

$V(t) \equiv \Sigma v(t)$ be the algebraic sum of all asset values in the system, liabilities being treated as negative assets in order to avoid double counting.

$V'(t) \equiv \Sigma v'(t)$ be the rate of change of total assets per unit time.

For each asset, we have

$$n(t) \equiv r(t)\ v(t) - v'(t) \tag{1}$$

Hence by addition, we have

$$\Sigma n(t) \equiv r(t)\ \Sigma v(t) - \Sigma v'(t) \tag{3}$$
$$\text{or}\quad N(t) \equiv r(t)\ V(t) - V'(t) \tag{4}$$
$$\text{or}\quad V'(t) \equiv r(t)\ V(t) - N(t) \tag{5}$$

This last term I define as the rate of Investment per unit time, i.e., the rate of increase of total asset value for the whole economy.

From the standpoint of all enterprise, when inter-entrepreneurial exchanges are cancelled out, the total return to capitalized sources is equal to the difference between total sales and the return to non-capitalized sources.

$$N(t) \equiv S(t) - C(t) \tag{6}$$

From the standpoint of each consumer all revenue received from capitalized or non-capitalized sources must be disposed of, either through consumption or through accumulation of asset value, which looked at from the standpoint of the consumer I call Savings, $B(t)$.

$$I(t) \equiv C(t) + r(t)\ V(t) \equiv S(t) + B(t) \tag{7}$$

Combining (5) and (6) , we have

$$V'(t) \equiv r(t)\ V(t) - [S(t) - C(t)] \tag{8}$$

But from (7)

$$S(t) - C(t) \equiv r(t)\ V(t) - B(t) \tag{9}$$

Hence,

$$V'(t) \equiv r(t)\ V(t) - r(t)\ V(t) + B(t) \tag{10}$$

or

$$V'(t) \equiv B(t) \tag{11}$$

This identity between Saving and Investment results as a

matter of definition of these terms under ideal conditions. Being such an identity and not a condition of equilibrium, it cannot possibly help to determine the level of the rate of interest or level of income.

In the recent theory of Mr. Keynes is to be found a similar identity between Saving and Investment, but with an important difference in the definition of Investment. By an argument, which I believe to rest upon a subtle fallacy, Mr. Keynes identifies Investment, defined primarily as above, with the rate of production of *new* capital equipment expressed in value terms. He expresses this as follows in Chapter 7 of the *General Theory:*

"Thus, assuming that income in the popular sense corresponds to my net income, aggregate investment in the popular sense coincides with my definition of net investment, namely the net addition to all kinds of capital equipment, after allowing for those changes in the value of the old capital equipment which are taken into account in reckoning net income." (p. 75)

". . . since exchanges of old investments necessarily cancel out." (p. 75)

"But no one can save without acquiring an asset, whether it be cash or a debt or capital-goods; and no one can acquire an asset which he did not previously possess, unless *either* an asset of equal value is newly produced *or* someone else parts with an asset of that value which he previously had. In the first alternative there is a corresponding new investment; in the second alternative someone else must be dis-saving an equal sum." (pp.81–2)

"It follows that the aggregate savings of the first individual and of others taken together must necessarily be equal to the amount of current investment." (p. 82)

My interpretation of this argument is, in summary, as follows: any increase in aggregate asset value must be equal to the value of *new* assets created, since the sale of old assets necessarily cancels out. If this interpretation be correct, it is, I think, demonstrably clear that Mr. Keynes has become enmeshed in Zeno's paradox of motion. It is, of course, true that there are two sides to every transaction, and that there must be a corresponding buyer to each seller. It is further true that the value of sale must be equal to the value of purchase. But it is not true, and this would be necessary for the soundness of Mr. Keynes' argument, that over an interval of time the value of an existing asset cannot change or cannot be changing. It is only by concentrating upon the "instant" of sale that the cancelling out emerges.

Altho the use of any consistent method of accounting accruals will illustrate the point, I prefer to consider a special case where this is brought out strongly. Suppose only one kind of asset to exist in fixed amount (say land, government bonds, etc.). Furthermore, suppose all persons to be identical in every respect, including asset holding. Now imagine all suddenly to place a higher value on each unit of this asset. Its price will rise, total asset value will increase, and there will be investment in my sense, altho no transactions have taken place and no new capital equipment has emerged. It is investment in this sense which will be identical with savings. By working with time rates of increase of asset value, instead of concentrating upon periodic, discrete transactions, it is easy to avoid the apparent contradiction of simultaneous motion and fixity of position.[4]

THE DETERMINATION OF THE RATE OF INTEREST

It is possible now to combine the results of our previous analysis, in order to throw light on the determination of the rate of interest. No pretense is made at specifying complete necessary and sufficient conditions, since this would involve the discussion of general equilibrium in all its complexity; rather, emphasis is placed upon strategically relevant factors. More precisely, we are interested in the determination of the rate of interest over time. Since no emphasis is placed here on any fundamental rate of time-discount, on any level of "effective desire to save," on any broad margin or constant supply price of saving, there is no presumption of a tendency towards any normal or asymptotic rate.

In the first instance, for convenience of exposition, I break time up into discrete periods and discuss the determination of the rate of interest in each. All rates of interest and all asset holding of previous periods are taken as *data* when considering any given period. Like a never-ending chain, the values of the variables of each period proceed from those of the previous, and in turn become the determinants of the succeeding periods. This being so, *the interest rate which will be established in any period must be such as to equilibrate the total asset holding of all individuals (households, invest-*

4. As is later maintained, it is doubtful whether any theoretically unambiguous meaning can be given to the concept of a quantity of new capital equipment in a physical sense. Such an attempt would involve the vexing problem of the dimensionality of capital in a real sense.

ors) and the total assets of all enterprises, optimally determined for each rate of interest.[5]

Irreversible, *hysteresis* effects being disregarded, there will be a certain total aggregate asset value, V, optimally determined by all enterprises for each rate of interest, r;

$$V = D(r) \qquad (12)$$

For each rate of interest and for any given period t, there will be a certain amount of assets which all households will be willing to hold:

$$V = S^t(r) \qquad (13)$$

In general, these relations are assumed to be such as to determine a unique rate of interest.[6] For each period we have such relations, and so the course of the interest rate is determined for the whole interval of time under consideration.[7]

It will be noted that the present approach does not require any definition of *capital* as a physical quantity. The persistent attempts in the literature to find such a quantity, besides being totally unnecessary for the determination of the rate of interest, have actually served to conceal differences in the components of "capital growth" which are analytically distinguishable. These

5. Since the previous level of total assets is taken as a given, it is immaterial whether we use as variables the addition to previous total assets or the new level of total assets, since these differ by only a constant.

6. As stated previously, it is to be expected that total assets provided by entrepreneurs will vary inversely with the rate of interest; the lower the rate of interest, the larger total asset value. The total assets which households wish to hold will probably not vary much with the rate of interest — at least not under ideal conditions of certainty. However, this inelasticity is not to be confused with the inelastic supply of capital in some physical sense assumed by many writers. To avoid confusion, I have not employed the terminology of supply and demand.

7. An alternative method of exposition is possible which avoids the use of discrete periods. As before, the total optimal value of all assets is a decreasing function of the rate of interest:

$$V = D(r) \ or \ r = g(V) \qquad (14)$$

For each of n individuals the rate of saving, increase of asset holding, may be regarded as a function of the rate of interest and the existing amount of assets held:

$$dv_i/dt = S_i(v_i, r) \qquad (i = 1, \ldots n) \qquad (15)$$

By substitution from (14) this becomes

$$dv_i/dt = S_i[v_i, g(V)] \qquad (i = 1, \ldots n) \qquad (16)$$

Recalling that total asset value is the sum of that held by all individuals, and prescribing initial conditions, this set of differential equations is in general sufficient to determine the rate of interest over time:

$$r = \ddot{r}(t) \qquad (17)$$

differences can only be indicated sketchily here by specifying certain strong type cases illustrating the various processes. The first of these is the bidding up of asset values with no necessary change in money coupons, resulting in a lowering of the rate of interest. This could go on in a community in which all physical assets were perfectly fixed in amount and in which there could not possibly be real physical investment in any sense. The second component, emphasized most strongly by older economists, is the creation of new and more physical assets or equipment, resulting in greater potentialities for consumers' goods output. More recently attention has been drawn to the process of investment as forming a source of demand for factors of production. There remains the problem of the interactions of these processes in connection with the secular development of an economy and the oscillations of the Trade Cycle.

THE ASSUMPTION OF PERFECT CERTAINTY

I have assumed throughout *perfect certainty* as an analytic device. I fully recognize that it is philosophically impossible to deduce behavior on the part of perfectly rational individuals which will guarantee that this condition be fulfilled, since the behavior of each individual forms the obstacle or *liason* under which all other individuals act, and reciprocally. It is an admittedly singular case when all people do behave in a manner which fulfills the hypothetical expectations in terms of which they have behaved. But there is no contradiction involved in the assumption; such cases need not exist, but they *could* exist. It has long been customary in economic science to consider such singular cases, and it is my belief that the clear working out of this one may prove to be a useful and illuminating introduction to more complex reality.

PAUL A. SAMUELSON.

SOCIETY OF FELLOWS,
HARVARD UNIVERSITY

19

DYNAMICS, STATICS, AND THE STATIONARY STATE

PAUL A. SAMUELSON
Massachusetts Institute of Technology

I

UNTIL now, much of dynamical economic analysis has been concerned with the business cycle. This may seem so natural as to be hardly worthy of explicit comment. Nevertheless, it was not inevitable; and if in the future the business cycle, as we have known it, should undergo extreme modifications, a need for dynamical analysis in connection with many economic problems would still exist. Thus, we should still need a theory of the path by which a given market approaches its equilibrium position, not for sake of the theory alone, but for the information that such knowledge throws upon the direction of displacement of the new equilibrium position as well.[1]

In comparatively recent times, significant advances have been made in analytical dynamics. A rigorous differentiation between statics and stationariness, between dynamics and history, is now possible. The present essay attempts, first, to elucidate the nature of these concepts and to contrast them with some other prevalent usages of the terms; and, second, by means of the concepts to go back to analyze the very important notion of the *circular flow*. In doing so, I am not attempting to improve upon what I consider a logically consistent argument, but rather am endeavoring to amplify the discussion at critical points where confusion has arisen.

II

Often in the writings of economists the words "dynamic" and "static" are used as nothing more than synonyms for good and bad, realistic and unrealistic, simple and complex. We damn another man's theory by terming it static, and advertise our own by calling it dynamic. Ex-

amples of this are too plentiful to require citation.

Some writers attempt to distinguish between statics and dynamics by analogy with what they understand to be the relationship in theoretical physics. That this is a fruitful and suggestive line of approach cannot be doubted. But it is too much to suppose that very many economists have the technical knowledge necessary to handle the formal properties of analytical dynamics. Consequently, they become bogged down in the search for economic concepts corresponding to mass, energy, inertia, momentum, force, and space. A case in point is Professor Frank Knight's otherwise stimulating essay on *Statics and Dynamics*.[2]

It is certainly true, notably in the writings of Marshall,[3] that economists have made use of biological as well as of mechanical analogies, in which evolution and organic growth is used as the antithesis to statical equilibrium analysis. In general the results seem to have been disappointing; viz., the haziness involved in Marshall's treatment of decreasing cost. And if one examines the more exact biological sciences, one looks in vain for any new weapon, secret or otherwise, for discovering scientific truths. If the bloodstream is capable of a simple, abstract, rigorous description in terms of the usual laws of physical thermodynamics, so much the better; if not, one must be content with more complicated, unwieldy explanations. Indeed, according to the late L. J. Henderson the very notion of a stable equilibrium, so characteristic of physical theory, was actually

---

[1] This truth is summarized in what I have called the *correspondence principle*, which points out the intimate connection between the purely *dynamical* aspects of a system and its *comparative statical* properties. See P. A. Samuelson, "The Stability of Equilibrium, I and II," *Econometrica*, IX (1941), pp. 97–120; X (1942), pp. 1–25.

[2] Chapter VI of *The Ethics of Competition* (New York, 1935). This is an English translation of an article in *Zeitschrift für Nationalökonomie* for 1930.

[3] See the references to *statical method* and *biology* in the Index to the eighth edition of the *Principles*. In none of his writings does Marshall show more than a passing familiarity, such as might be expected of any intelligent layman, of the biological notions of his time. Therefore, he could not be expected to have discerned the lasting truths from the fashions of the moment. Nevertheless, writing at the time that he did, it was inevitable that he should have been influenced, if not convinced, by the Spencerian doctrines popular at the end of the nineteenth century.

first observed empirically in connection with the resistance of the human body to disease, and formulated by the ancients as the well-known *vix medicatrix naturae*.[4]

Nor should the problems encountered in the biological field be considered necessarily more complex and less subject to simple formulation than those in the physical field. Few biological sciences are less "exact" than meteorology, which must certainly be included in the physical sciences.[5] Here, simple and abstract theories spun out from a few assumptions are likely to be inferior to the intuitive hunches of experienced practitioners, but this is only a reflection of the present primitive state of the subject. New truths are ascertained in the same way as in more advanced subjects, and it is to be hoped that rule of thumb may be replaced by more exact and unambiguous formulations.[6]

III

Leaving aside all analogies with other fields, there has necessarily been within the main corpus of economic theory a preoccupation with dynamics, if only implicitly. The Classical economists from Smith through Mill had theories of the long-run movements of population and accumulation.[7] J. B. Clark rigidly separated the static from the dynamic in his thought.[8] (Other examples could be multi-

[4] See J. A. Schumpeter, *The Theory of Economic Development* (Cambridge, Mass., 1934, English edition), Preface, p. xi, for Mill's notions of statics and dynamics and their intellectual origins.

[5] Of course, it can be said that experimentation is not possible in meteorology as in other physical sciences. But what about astronomy, in some ways the most exact of all, in which no experimentation is possible?

[6] In discussing the limitations of mathematical methods in economics, Professor Viner expresses the belief that the biological character of the subject, so to speak, makes such methods of limited applicability. By this I take him to mean that the subject is complex and difficult, not that any fundamentally different methods of investigation are required. See "Marshall's Economics, the Man and His Times," *American Economic Review*, XXXI (1941), pp. 223–36.

Gustav Cassel in his *Fundamental Thoughts in Economics*, Chapter I, considers Economic Dynamics to be a third stage of analysis, following a pure Static Economy and a "quasi-static" Uniformly Progressive Economy.

[7] See L. Robbins, "On a Certain Ambiguity in the Conception of Stationary Equilibrium," *Economic Journal*, XL (1930), pp. 194–214.

[8] J. M. Clark has wished to carry on where his father left off, to construct a dynamics which would supplement statics. See J. M. Clark, *A Preface to Social Economics* (New York, 1936).

plied.) Clark's celebrated static state and the "circular flow" of Professor Schumpeter raise a rather vexing point of terminology — the relation of static to stationary — now cleared up more or less to the satisfaction of everybody by Professor Frisch.

Stationary is a descriptive term characterizing the behavior of an economic variable over time; it usually implies constancy, but is occasionally generalized to include behavior periodically repetitive over time. Used in this sense, the motion of a dynamical system may be stationary: e.g., the behavior of a pendulum satisfying Newton's Laws of Motion, but subject to no disturbance and hence remaining at rest; or the behavior of national income after a change in investment has given rise to dwindling transient geometric progressions of the usual "block-diagram" character.

Statical then refers to the form and structure of the postulated laws determining the behavior of the system. An equilibrium defined as the intersection of a pair of curves would be statical. Ordinarily, it is "timeless" in that nothing is specified concerning the duration of the process, but it may very well be defined as holding over time. A simple statical system as defined above would also have the property of being stationary; but as we shall see in a moment, statical systems can be devised which are not stationary over time.

In defining the term *dynamical*, at least two possibilities suggest themselves. First, it may be defined as a general term including statical as a special rather degenerate case. Or on the other hand, it may be defined as the totality of all systems which are *not* statical. Much may be said for the first alternative; the second, however, brings out some points of controversy in the literature and will be discussed here. This decision involves no point of substance, since only verbal problems of definition are involved.

We may say that *a system is dynamical if its behavior over time is determined by functional equations in which "variables at different points of time" are involved in an "essential" way.* This formulation is to be attributed to Professor Frisch.[9] Special examples of such systems

[9] Ragnar Frisch, "On the Notion of Equilibrium and Disequilibrium," *Review of Economic Studies*, III (1935–36), pp. 100–106.

are those defined by *difference* equations, i.e., those involving a variable and its lagged values; integral equations in which the preceding values of the variable enter in a "continuous" way. By a liberal interpretation of the circumlocution "variable at a different point of time," we may bring differential equations under the definition, remembering that differential coefficients characterize the behavior of a function in the neighborhood of a point. Mixed types and more general functionals are included.

Attention is called to the fact that variables at different points of time must enter into the problem in an *essential* way. Thus, a system involving a rate of production per unit time, i.e., a time derivative, may yet be statical. This is because the variable of which the rate is the time derivative may have no economic significance. It can be interpreted as the cumulated amount of production from the beginning of time or from an initial date; no significant economic process depends upon this variable. The necessity for the present insistence may be apprehended if it is realized that every variable can be written as the derivative of something, namely its own integral. Moreover, a system may be pseudo-dynamic in the sense that formal manipulation of it permits us to reduce it to statical form. Unless, therefore, we reserve the designation dynamics for systems which involve economically significant variables at different points of time in an *irremovable* way, we shall find that no non-dynamic systems exist.

According to the present definition the historical movement of a system may not be dynamical. If one year the crop is high because of favorable weather, the next year low, and so forth, the system will be statical even though not stationary. The same is true of a system showing continuous growth or trend, if the secular movement is taken as a datum and if the system adapts itself instantaneously.[10]

On the other hand, a truly dynamical system may be completely non-historical or causal, in the sense that its behavior depends only upon its initial conditions *and the time which has elapsed*, the calendar date not entering into the process. For many purposes, it is necessary to work with systems which are both historical and dynamical. The impact of technological change upon the economic system is a case in point. Technological change may be taken as a historical datum, to which the economic system reacts non-instantaneously or in a dynamic fashion. Another instance is provided by a business cycle of a regular periodic character, which results from impressing an oscillatory outside force upon a mechanism with an intrinsic (damped) period of its own.

We may distinguish, then, four distinct cases made up of all possible combinations of static-dynamic and historical-causal:

1. Static and stationary
2. Static and historical
3. Dynamic and causal (non-historical)[11]
4. Dynamic and historical

Almost all systems can be placed in one of these categories; and, depending upon the point of view or purpose at hand, the analysis may be formulated so as to put a given system arbitrarily in one category rather than another. Thus, if a system is very heavily damped so that it approaches its equilibrium value extremely rapidly, its dynamic features may be passed over in order to simplify the analysis.

Or a system which is causal from a very broad viewpoint may be regarded as historical if certain movements are taken as unexplained data for purposes of the argument. (In fact, every historical system is to be regarded as an *incomplete* causal system.) To a meteorologist-economist a business cycle caused by weather disturbances and sunspots would constitute a causal process. But ordinarily the economist is willing to regard the causation as unilateral and to adopt a division of labor in which he does not study astronomy but considers his job as done when he has pushed economic analysis to a "non-economic" cause.[12] However, there is nothing sacred about the conventional bound-

---

[10] I conceive Henry Moore's moving equilibrium to be of this statical type, although the movements around the secular trend are dynamic in character. H. L. Moore, *Synthetic Economics* (New York, 1929).

[11] The notion of causation in a closed interdependent system is exceedingly slippery and ambiguous. As used here, a system is said to be causal if from an initial configuration it determines its own behavior over time. While it is not appropriate to say that one subset of variables causes another to move, it is permissible to speak of a change in a given parameter or datum as causing changes in the system or in its behavior over time.

[12] J. A. Schumpeter, *Theory of Economic Development*, Chapter I.

aries of economics; if the cycle were meteorological in origin, economists would branch out in that direction, just as in our day a political theory of fiscal policy is necessary if one is to understand empirical economic phenomena.

In his recent book *Value and Capital*,[13] Professor Hicks has given an exceedingly simple definition of dynamics: "I call Economic Statics those parts of economic theory where we do not trouble about dating; Economic Dynamics those parts where every quantity must be dated" (p. 115).

In terms of the above four categories this definition is overly general and insufficiently precise. The second category consisting of historically moving static equilibria would certainly require dating of the variables, but it would not thereby become dynamic. My objection is to his definition, not to his practice, for many of the systems which he analyzes are in the strict sense dynamic.[14]

IV

We are now in a position to utilize the above concepts to analyze the famous notion of the stationary state, which received its highest expression in the first chapter of Professor Schumpeter's classic.[15] Upon rereading this chapter once again I have been struck by the degree to which the exposition is poetic in form. It is like a parable, and its wisdom lies between, as much as within, the lines.

It is, above all, clear that the *stationary* state is not *statical*. The recurring economic processes take place in time, and decisions are made with respect to variables at different points of time. Although the process is repetitive and "synchronized," there is not simultaneity between the application of inputs and the appearance of their imputable output.[16] The circular flow is a stationary solution of a dynamical

process. If once established it would repeat itself. Moreover, the equilibrium is stable in the sense that, once disturbed from equilibrium, the system would move over time so as to approach it again asymptotically. It does not matter for the purpose at hand that empirically new inventions will be forthcoming so as to prevent the system from remaining at rest, nor that ideally the system will only approach equilibrium asymptotically and never reach it.

Simply to fix ideas the system may be compared with a pendulum moving in a viscous fluid. If disturbed by a shock, it will depart from the equilibrium position; but its motion will be damped by the dissipation of energy due to the "friction" resulting from its passage through the viscous fluid. Strictly speaking, even if all shocks were to cease, the system would never regain the equilibrium position, although it would approach indefinitely close to that position.

In the essay referred to above, Professor Robbins pointed out that economists who write on the stationary or static state (between which he does not distinguish) differ in their assumptions. Some simply postulate fixity of the amounts of the productive factors; others postulate fixity of the supply schedules of the productive factors, with stationary behavior of the amounts of the factors emerging along with the fixity of all of the unknowns of the solution as a consequence of the conditions of equilibrium which make the system determinate. Professor Robbins expressed the belief that J. B. Clark belonged to the first group. He goes on to argue that the same is true of Professor Schumpeter, and that because of this fact there is a serious flaw in his theory of interest.[17]

It is clear that Professor Schumpeter's theory of a zero rate of interest in a stationary circular flow economy could be dispensed with, and no great harm would be done to his theory of the cycle or of development. Instead of tending to rebound to a zero rate, the interest rate would tend, after a period of innovation, to return to some other rate, alleged to represent an intrinsic rate of time preference or impatience, or any other broad margin which the ingenuity of an economist can devise. Nevertheless, his interest rate theory has received a large share of the attention of critics.

---

[13] J. R. Hicks, *Value and Capital* (Oxford, 1939).

[14] One wide class of processes cannot easily be brought under my classification; viz., stochastical processes. The initial idea of such processes seems to be due to G. U. Yule. See the references to the works of Yule, Slutsky, and Frisch in H. Wold, *A Study in the Analysis of Stationary Time Series* (Uppsala, Sweden, 1938).

[15] I do not know, however, to what extent Professor Schumpeter would agree with the following remarks.

[16] This does not imply that capital can be measured by any time period of production, or that there is any meaning or significance to any average period of production.

[17] Robbins, *op. cit.*, pp. 211–14.

Therefore, an examination of Professor Robbins' argument, to see whether or not there is an intrinsic flaw in the assumption of a zero rate of interest, is not unimportant. Our answer may be stated in advance: Professor Robbins is wrong, economically, mathematically, and logically. His argument may be briefly summarized. If in the circular flow the amount of capital is to be constant with the rate of interest zero, it must be shown that this is consistent with the motivated activity of the people whose actions will make the amount of capital remain constant. But this is impossible since some bait will be necessary to prevent people from consuming their capital, or from attempting to do so. Thus, he says:

"Why should labour and the use of material factors be devoted to the maintenance of the produced means of production if no net remuneration is forthcoming?" (p. 212) . . . "For if there were no yield to the use of capital (no *reinertrag*), there would be no reason to refrain from consuming it" (p. 213). . . . "It is in short, *an* interest rate, which, other things being given, keeps the stationary state stationary — the rate at which it does not pay to turn income into capital or capital into income" (p. 213).

I may note in the first place that this argument is distinct and quite independent from other criticisms of the zero interest rate, such as that of Professor Knight which is discussed below.

In the second place, a detailed structural analysis of the argument will show it to be an incomplete demonstration. At every step the controversial point at issue is begged. Why should capital be maintained at a zero rate of interest? Why should it not? If *an* [Robbins' italics] interest rate is needed to keep the stationary state stationary, why should it not be a zero rate? In the economic literature we are quite accustomed to an *entrepreneur faisant ni benefice ni perte* and who is yet maximizing his profits. It is often necessary to keep running just in order to stand still! And so here, in this quite different connection, part of the problem is to see whether or not it is impossible for a rational being to refrain from eating up his capital at a zero rate of interest.

Now, of course, one cannot prove the possibility of a zero rate by such verbal circumlocutions as these any more than Professor Robbins could demonstrate his thesis by the same methods. Economic theory, fortunately, can put a matter like the present one to a decisive test. For a question of fact is not being debated, but rather a question of logical possibility and necessity emerging from a particular set of agreed-upon axioms.

Let us assume, therefore, a condition of perfect certainty and an economy consisting of one or more individuals. We further assume, since otherwise the discussion can end before it starts, that there is no intrinsic rate of time preference.[18] We need not speculate as to whether or not this implies infinite life expectations for the individual, for his family, etc., etc., since in any case we are not concerned here with the realism or the usefulness of the argument. For our purposes it is convenient to adopt the quite *arbitrary* assumption that utility is a given function of income in each period; more specifically, that it is the same function at each instant of time and that the individual acts so as to maximize the sum of utilities thus defined over all future time.[19]

Actually, this seems to be Professor Schumpeter's assumption.[20] Probably today he would be less likely to read normative, or ethical, significance into this assumption, and would be less likely to regard deviations from it as reflecting irrationality. On the other hand, although perhaps only as a coincidence, this assumption is nearer the modern tendency to regard savings as taking place institutionally and quasi-automatically for reasons of power, insecurity, etc., and only secondarily as a result of a weighing of present and future consumption preferences. Thus, time preference theories are rather at a discount these days; indeed, many would go further than Professor Schumpeter and expect *attempts* to make positive accumulations even at a zero or negative rate of interest.

---

[18] The observational significance of the concept of time preference is rarely discussed in the literature, and need not concern us here.

[19] Hicks, Tintner, and others have discussed the problem of consumers' behavior over time under much less restrictive assumptions. See particularly numerous articles by the latter in *Econometrica* of the last half a dozen years. In the *Review of Economic Studies*, IV (1937), I discuss some of these issues under the title, "A Note on Measurement of Utility," pp. 155–61.

[20] *Theory of Economic Development*, p. 35, *passim*.

Our problem now becomes a simple mathematical exercise. We assume one or more individuals with fixed incomes throughout the future, with diminishing marginal utility, operating under conditions of perfect certainty so that by borrowing or lending at a zero rate of interest they can modify their consumption streams over time. How will such individuals behave? Will they borrow, that is eat up their capital, so as to have more consumption now; will the absence of any net yield make them unwilling to refrain from consumption out of capital? [21] Professor Robbins would have to answer *yes*.

But he may be shown to be wrong. The question may be treated mathematically as a simple iso-perimetric problem in the Calculus of Variations, or as a problem in many variables. The fact that an infinite set of variables is involved (consumption over all future periods) provides no real difficulty. In fact, intuition without mathematics leads to the same result. The substitution, on even terms, of future consumption for present, would never pay if in the original situation one planned to consume evenly over time. For the increment of future consumption would add marginal units of utility which are lower simply because they are superimposed upon existing income. On the other hand, because of diminishing utility, the subtractions from present income would result in greater losses of utility because of the smallness of present income. Only an even distribution of income over time is optimal, if the rate of interest is zero, and if there is no time preference. This means no decumulation of capital, and a similar argument shows that there would be no accumulation.

This is an example of a commonly encountered fallacy. Literary writers often become enmeshed in the notion of the infinitesimal involved in the intensive margin. Because the marginal unit "just pays" with no surplus of satisfaction, it does not follow that it will be a matter of indifference whether the marginal unit is secured or not. On the contrary, any

other action would result in less satisfaction. The fact that the price of wheat in Chicago exceeds its price in Kansas City by the amount of transportation cost does not mean that no wheat will flow between the two cities, nor that an indeterminate amount will flow, but rather that precisely the necessary amount to keep prices in this relation will flow. And so with the problem at hand. A rate of interest other than zero would result in behavior tending to lower it, so that the only equilibrium level would be at a zero rate.

This concludes the refutation of Professor Robbins' belief that there is a contradiction in the existence of a zero rate of interest in the circular flow economy. In justice to him, however, we should admit that the reasoning in the *Theory of Economic Development* is rather obscure at this point. Thus, Professor Schumpeter is correct in his insistence that the abstinence necessary to start a given capitalistic process is different from that necessary to keep it in existence once the process is *synchronized* (p. 39). Still, is it not misleading to say, "Whatever may be the nature of waiting, it is certainly not an element of the economic process which we are here considering, because the circular flow, once established, leaves no gap between outlay or productive effort and the satisfaction of wants. Both are, following Professor Clark's conclusive expression, automatically synchronized. . . . I emphasize once more outlay and return are *automatically* synchronized with one another under the accelerating and retarding influence of profit and loss" (p. 38)?

Here Professor Schumpeter appeals to one of the most doubtful features of the Clarkian system, and if we were to take his statement at face value, he would indeed be open to the objections of Professor Robbins. True, capital is constant in the circular flow, but only because of the inadmissibility of virtual deviations from this condition, and not as a matter of definition. In our own day Professor Knight has fallen into the same error of regarding synchronization as a methodologically necessary axiom, rather than as a deduced condition of equilibrium. I am not an adherent of the neo-Austrian capital theory, but on this point I think that Professor Hayek is definitely in the

[21] Alternatively, one can consider an economy in which the decisions made by people with respect to present and future consumption are not financial market decisions, but real production ones. Would Robinson Crusoe, if constituted as above, drink up his wine stores without laying down more, simply because at the margin there was no net yield?

right, just as years ago Bohm-Bawerk was correct in his polemic against Clark.[22]

That Professor Schumpeter does not rely upon a synchronization which begs the question is clear from a passage in which he deduces the constancy of capital: "In the normal circular flow one has not periodically to withstand a temptation to instantaneous production, because one would *immediately* fare worse by succumbing" (p. 38). What he means to say is that in the circular flow one *does* have periodically to withstand the temptation to eat up one's capital, but that a balancing of advantages will motivate one to resist the temptation every time. Moreover, the word immediately, which Professor Schumpeter italicized, should preferably be omitted, since one is harmed at once in only an indirect sense. In a direct sense, one can go along consuming at a higher clip if one is willing to dip into capital. But, of course, at a later date the reverse will be the case; only the current reckoning of the utility which one will enjoy over all time is immediately reduced in amount.

Again a few pages later (p. 45 *passim*), the fact of motivated constancy and synchronization is so stretched in meaning as to lead to a denial of the existence of a stock of goods in process which is being turned over, and maintained, or which could be consumed. This is no more convincing than the related arguments of Professor Knight: (1) that it is methodologically necessary to regard increments to capital as being set aside in perpetuity; and (2) that furthermore in all modern communities capital is growing and is not invested; and, for any who are still not convinced, (3) that it is impossible to disinvest capital anyway. Argument (1) begs the question at issue; while (2) and (3) are questions of fact, of which the former is irrelevant. In this connection, it is not without interest that Professor Knight's dicta on the impossibility of capital disinvestment were reaching a crescendo in the early thirties, precisely at a time when the number of automobiles and the stock of unused mileage embodied therein were decreasing, when the average age of all machine tools was increasing, when capital facilities of almost all kinds were being used

[22] What I regard as Professor Knight's definite, and unnecessary, error on this point in no way invalidates his criticisms of the period of production concept.

in excess of replacement; in short, when capital disinvestment was taking place in the United States at a considerable rate.[23] In any case, we should want a general theory of capital which is applicable to non-progressive as well as progressive societies. And in the present writer's opinion, it is a mistake to think that the cessation of growth of capital, or even the introduction of a small amount of decrease, would result in a radically different rate of interest and analysis for explaining it.

We have shown that there is no logical inconsistency in Professor Schumpeter's theory of interest on the side of supply. On the contrary, the strict assumption of absence of time preference implies no decumulation at a zero rate of interest, and no cessation of accumulation at any positive rate of interest.

V

We may now turn to objections from the demand or productivity side. After all, our previous argument has not shown that the rate of interest will be zero, but rather that, if it is not zero, there will be disequilibrium in the sense of a continuation of accumulation. In fact, we may reverse Professor Robbins' previous assertion; *it is the existence of a zero rate of interest which keeps the stationary state stationary*. Perhaps the system will not approach this equilibrium state, i.e., the position of equilibrium may not be a stable one. Of much less importance, but still worthy of notice, is the possibility that the system may

[23] See S. Kuznets, *National Income and Capital Formation, 1919–1938* (New York, 1937). Now that we are at war, it will be part of deliberate social policy to divert resources from maintaining civilian capital intact, thereby considerably augmenting our national war potential. Knight regards capital as a familiar bottled drink cooling machine, in which the bottles pass through a tube surrounded by ice. A warm bottle is forced into one end and this moves every bottle in the tube so that a cold one comes out the other end. An initial number of bottles must be invested before a cold bottle is available; after this minimum number of bottles, for each one added, a cold one comes out the other end. The process is synchronized, and one may neglect if one wishes the "bottles in process." If one should now wish to disinvest, disappointment will arise. For as soon as one stops adding bottles at one end, no more come out the other. The bottles in the tube are irretrievably lost — unless of course one can take the contraption apart, or unless one cheats the machine by putting in an empty bottle at one end!

Of course, there are some processes like this, but they are only a few of many special cases. There is no need to erect a theory of capital on this basis, particularly as there is no analytic necessity or convenience for so doing.

approach but never *reach* the stable stationary equilibrium state.

I must confess to a lack of knowledge of the relevant German literature, but I should expect Bohm-Bawerk, Professor Schumpeter's teacher, to have been a little uneasy with the Schumpeterian theory. The former might have wondered whether interest could fall to zero while the third of the celebrated grounds for interest still persisted: namely, "the productivity of roundabout means of production," or if one wishes to avoid period of production concepts, simply the existence of a technical net productivity of capital.

If this point were raised, Professor Schumpeter would simply point out that the question was being begged, and counter with a point-blank denial of its validity in the stationary state.[24] Or so I should have thought he would. But in one place, in connection with goods which are said to increase "automatically" (herds, seed-corn, etc.), he is willing to entertain the possibility, although correctly stating that much of the gross return should really have expenses deducted from it before the net return is computed. At this point, he definitely, in my opinion, takes the wrong way out. In an analogous, but quite distinct case, of wine which improves with age, he correctly points out that the physical transformation is of no consequence, that there would be imputed back to the grape the full value of the wine, providing that the rate of interest were zero. Even under the latter condition, equilibrium would be possible for reasons similar to those discussed above under the heading of supply.[25]

But the case where a good undergoes a percentage rate of increase per unit-time in terms of identical units is quite different. Equilibrium at a zero rate of interest and constant prices would be quite impossible. It would pay anyone to borrow, at a zero rate, buy some of this magic substance, hold it while it increases, and sell it at a handsome profit. Hence there could not have been equilibrium in the first place.

Schumpeter's assertion that imputation will take care of even this case and leave nothing to interest is not satisfactory. He says, ". . . for the crop and the herds are certainly dependent

upon seed-corn and breeding cattle, and the latter must therefore be valued according to the values of the former. . . . Their price would be equal to the price of the product imputed to them." Now there is nothing which contradicts the usual notion of equilibrium in the assertion that a gallon of green wine is worth as much as a gallon of mature wine — any more than there would be a contradiction in the statement that wheat sells for as much in Kansas City as it does in Chicago, there being no cost of transportation between them. But it is definitely in contradiction to the usual notion of equilibrium to state that the price of corn is constant over time, and yet one hundred units of corn are today worth as much as one hundred and ten bushels are worth tomorrow. But this is what is implied in the Schumpeterian assertion that there will be reflected in today's corn the full value of tomorrow's output stemming from it.

I may put the matter in another way. By hypothesis, corn has an own-rate of interest different from zero, namely equal to its percentage rate of increase per unit time. The notion of an own rate, or real rate other than a money rate, is associated with the names of Thornton, Marshall, Wicksell, Sraffa, and above all Fisher. Equilibrium coexistent with a zero money rate of interest would be possible only if prices violated the constancy postulated of the stationary state. If capital in general had a continuing, real, net, own productivity, the money rate of interest could be zero only if prices were falling at a percentage rate equal to that of the productivity. It is not without interest in this connection that the value of perpetual *real* income streams would be finite even with a zero rate of interest, the undiscounted sum converging. This shows by the way, if it is not already self-evident, that the third ground of Bohm-Bawerk, even if it existed in real terms, would not necessarily imply a positive rate of interest on money.

From these remarks it must be clear that Professor Schumpeter does not really want to take this way out. (We shall consider what would seem to be the more correct resolution of the difficulty in a moment.) Here and at other places a reader may sense an element of circularity in the argument. Actually if one takes the argument as a whole, such is not the

[24] *Theory of Economic Development*, Chapter V.
[25] *Ibid.*, pp. 170–71.

case, as we shall see. But at isolated points the charge of circularity can perhaps be sustained. Too much is attributed to a vaguely defined process of "imputation," which is asserted to cause the full value of the product to be decomposable into the original factors, land and labor. I refer the reader to the discussion around page thirty of Professor Schumpeter's volume. Occasionally it is suggested that the maximization of profits will bring about the necessary arbitrage. That this is not directly the case can be seen from the fact, well explained in his Chapter V, that no attempts to maximize profits will wipe out interest if there should really be time preference.[26]

If Professor Schumpeter had not been under the necessity of keeping the discussion from becoming overlong, he would no doubt have developed at greater length the analysis of the dynamical path by which equilibrium is approached. But, of course, the stationary state was only preparatory to his real purpose, and he could not have known in advance that his theory of interest would prove such a stumbling block to his readers.

Not only would the analysis of the approach to equilibrium be of value for its own sake, but, at the same time, it would have enabled him to banish his concern over the danger of proving the existence of interest after circularly assuming its existence.[27] Historically, his concern with the problem of circularity is bound up with his belief that one must first decide whether or not interest will exist, and then what its numerical value will be; that the qualitative problem of the "essence" of interest must precede the quantitative problem.

[26] It would have been better if the Walras in Schumpeter had been able to dominate the Bohm-Bawerk in him. He might have avoided then completely what seems to me the utterly false problem of imputation. There simply is no problem of dividing up social product among cooperating factors. Of course, J. B. Clark and the Austrians always wrestled with it, but that tells us nothing about its truth or falsity as a problem. Walras and Pareto quite properly considered it as only a problem of pricing the factors of production as well as finished goods. This involves showing how every firm and family unit will behave when confronted with a given set of prices, and how all together determine the prices with which each as a small individual is faced.

[27] Thus on p. 35 of the *Theory of Economic Development* he says: "No possibility of investing savings at interest exists — for if we were to grant this we should assume the element of interest beforehand and come dangerously near to circular reasoning."

These preoccupations seem a little strange in an admirer of the mathematical school of economists, since in mathematical analysis "almost all" circles of reasoning turn out to be "virtuous" rather than "vicious." With reference to the problems at hand, if one believes in the necessity of a zero rate of interest, one gladly invites an opponent to assume that the rate of interest is not zero; i.e., he is given enough rope to hang himself. The assumption is shown to lead to a contradiction, constituting a perfectly valid, albeit indirect, proof of the original proposition. On the other hand, if one were able to produce supply and demand conditions showing that the rate of interest would always stay at ten per cent, it would not be necessary to question further concerning the essence of the phenomena.

The key to these paradoxes lies in the fact that while every great economist changes the thought of his day, he also reacts to it and selects for emphasis the problems acutely discussed by his colleagues. We must not forget the dualism mentioned above that Professor Schumpeter stems from the Austrian School as well as the Mathematical School. That he was in way of being the *enfant terrible* of the Austrians only adds to the plausibility of this interpretation.

Let us then break into an historical process in which technological change has recently taken place. According to anybody's theory, a positive rate of interest may exist. Arbitrage will tend to equalize the net yield on all assets, so that the same rate of interest will be charged upon purely consumption loans, and the same return will be earned even in those lines of endeavor where there has been no technological change. Nobody expects that the current rate will necessarily be maintained in perpetuity. Therefore, in calculating the net return which is to be equalized, the yield is *not* converted into the equivalent perpetual yield, but rather the yield is reckoned only after making algebraic correction for changes in asset values.[28] Under the assumption which we now make explicit, that all technological change ceases, we

[28] Contrast Professor Knight's statement, ". . . the correct standard of comparison is that of a perpetual income of a given size with the value of the wealth yielding such an income" (*op. cit.*, p. 258), with my paper, "Some Aspects of the Pure Theory of Capital," *Quarterly Journal of Economics*, LI (1937), pp. 469–96.

shall see that the interest rate will fall through time. Under conditions of perfect certainty, this would be realized by all interested parties, so that it would be very inconsistent of them to think that a five per cent interest rate between this period and the next would imply a perpetual realization of an equivalent annuity on the same principal.

In the short run, capital will be simply what it is. The limitation in its amount in a certain sense explains its net yield in the short run. But with the utility assumptions of earlier passages, in which utility is not subject to psychological discount for time, at the positive rate of interest positive net savings would take place. There is no paradox in the assertion that in the short run capital is constant, and at the same time is showing an (instantaneous) rate of growth. Over time, the cumulation of this rate of capital formation will result in ever increasing capital, however defined. Even if capital is constructed with the use of the services of both labor and capital goods, if we assume a stationary population and the usual "laws" of proportions and returns, this will necessarily imply a diminution of the net yield of the increased stock of capital goods. And so the rate of interest will fall over time.[29]

Will the process end at any positive rate of interest? Professor Schumpeter would answer, no; and I believe his reasoning would proceed along the indicated lines. As stated the argument can hardly be controverted. Technological development may produce a positive rate of interest, but after it ceases, only time preference can keep the rate up. Actually, a rigorous mathematical demonstration of the proposition under simplified conditions is provided by Ramsey's brilliant article on Savings.[30] This is far from being inconsistent with what I understand to be Professor Knight's theory of interest.

The real difficulty which Professor Knight and other theorists find with the Schumpeterian interest theory lies in the passage to the limit. Does the rate of interest reach zero, or simply approach it? The argument is one about asymptotes and limits. Such processes are notorious breeders of paradoxes, but should yield to careful rigorous mathematical analysis.

The few words that follow attempt to discuss some of the problems involved in the limiting process. Because the problem is not a real one, the discussion must necessarily seem unreal. For Professor Schumpeter does not believe that the rate of zero becomes zero in real life, nor even that there is any secular tendency for interest to fall. We have seen above that Schumpeter's theories of development and of the cycle would be unaltered in essentials if there were a non-zero rate toward which interest were tending. Similarly, these theories would require no modifications if interest simply approached a zero rate without ever reaching this limit.

Professor Knight's objections on the demand side relate to the question of whether or not the limit could *conceptually* be reached, and must be given only the importance which this whole question deserves.[31] I say *conceptually* because the mathematical treatment of Ramsey deals with a case where the rate of interest *could* become zero; but, in fact, a rational maximizing individual would only find it optimal to increase his capital at a decreasing rate so as to approach a zero rate rather than ever reach it. The Ramsey argument also shows that *without logical inconsistency the rate of interest can become zero without all goods becoming free*, as has been denied by Professor Knight and his disciple Stigler.

[29] Numerous models of simplified kinds of capital processes can be brought in to illustrate the process. One may define point input and point output processes for which the crudest Austrian period of production concepts become correct. Or we may neglect all circulating capital in favor of fixed capital goods. Finally, the process may feed back on itself in the sense that so-called produced goods of production may themselves contribute to produce their own kind. Nor need any special concern be shown for the division of productive factors into "original," produced, or permanent categories. All of these considerations acquire importance in terms of realistic appraisals of concrete historical processes such as do not concern us here. However, even from this standpoint it is important to keep factual and logical questions rigidly distinguishable.

[30] F. P. Ramsey, "A Mathematical Theory of Saving,"

Economic Journal, XXXVII (1928), pp. 543–59. Note particularly that a rational maximizer would act so as to reduce interest only gradually over time, rather than precipitously.

[31] They are summarized in the sentences: ". . . Schumpeter assumes that the rate [of interest] is zero. It is difficult to see the reasons for this assumption: there is no limit to the use of capital even in the absence of new inventions, although the rate of return would of course fall indefinitely low as investment proceeded." (*Ethics of Competition*, p. 257.)

The significant Knightian objection rests upon the purely factual, technical question as to the nature of the "absolute" returns to capital. If we write "Product" as a function of "Labor" and "Capital," does this function attain a maximum for a finite value of C as of a fixed value of L? The argument is one about the horizon, from its nature incapable of a significant answer. The following remarks must therefore be taken with a grain of salt.

I believe that Bohm-Bawerk was in error in thinking that the methods of technologically advanced economies are more "roundabout" than those of simpler communities. The word in quotations is used too often as a synonym for complexity and efficiency. That a pun is involved is hidden by mistaken allusion to the amount of "roundaboutness" and abstinence which would be involved in an attempt to rebuild our technical structure from scratch. Today, our machines for the purpose of building machines are so efficient that less, rather than more, "waiting" may be tied up in stock of capital goods.

I further believe that society's greatest stock of productive capital inherited from the past is knowledge, not capital goods. If the last century had seen current rates of savings less by *ninety per cent* than actually occurred, but accompanied by a *quadrupling* of the community's resources devoted to scientific and engineering research, we might today have a much more productive industrial structure. The piling up of capital is itself not very productive. With a moratorium on further acquisitions of knowledge, no amount of capital could raise the level of national income to the equivalent of very many times the present American potential. This view would seem to be at variance with that of Professor Knight. For him, diminishing returns set in very slowly. I repeat that these are difficult questions of technology, upon which neither he nor I as economists can lay any special claim to knowledge.

Of course, all resources which have a perpetual net rental yield per unit-time give rise to certain difficulties once the rate of interest becomes literally zero. Their capitalized value increases indefinitely as the rate of interest becomes a smaller positive number, and the expression for capitalized value has a mathematical "pole" for interest equal to zero. But

if people really had no time preference, because they lived forever or otherwise, they clearly would never part with the title to such a perpetual income stream for any finite price, however high. Of course, these perpetual assets might exchange in terms of each other at finite ratios; e.g., two acres of land of a given grade equal to twice the value of one acre. Actually, in feudal societies in which the clan is expected to continue indefinitely, one would as soon sell the children as the family acres. These mores are reflected in the legal form of *entail*. I see no reason why Professor Schumpeter should object to the statement that the value of such assets is infinite; i.e., in strict mathematical terms, higher than any preassigned positive number.[32]

I may summarize the above discussion briefly as follows: (1) It is a matter of only esoteric interest whether the rate of interest reaches zero, or approaches it asymptotically. As Ramsey has shown, even if technological conditions make it possible that capital should have a strictly zero net productivity beyond a certain point, utility motives would require that this point only be approached asymptotically. (2) It is an equally esoteric technological question as to whether Knight is right in his belief that a maximum output, even if approached, is never attained for a finite value of capital. For purposes of the business cycle, it is of the greatest importance to know whether or not there is a broad margin of capital opportunities, but this is a factual rather than an *a priori* question. (3) If the infinite value of permanent assets in a zero interest rate economy seems anomalous, the paradox springs from the unreal character of the assumption that men maximize utility in terms of an infinite horizon. It is questionable whether the whole process of saving is illuminated by the attempts to explain it in terms of adjusting consumption streams over time. (4) My own preference is not to reify the limit by asking what really happens at a zero rate of interest, but rather to concentrate upon the dynamic path toward this limiting condition. But much may be said, nevertheless, for the dramatic value of Professor Schumpeter's expository device.

---

[32] If correct, this obviates Professor Schumpeter's necessity of denying that value of assets is reckoned by summation of income streams over time. (*Development*, p. 166.)

20

A Note on Measurement of Utility

THE possibility of measuring the marginal utility of income from budgetary studies and market behaviour has been investigated by many writers.[1] In this note a possible alternative method, resting upon different assumptions, is presented, not so much in the hope of furthering inductive investigation in these matters as of bringing out certain theoretical relations between the variables under consideration.

In order to arrive inductively at the measurement of utility, essentially a subjective quantity, it is necessary to place the individual (*homo economicus*) whose scale is sought under certain ideal circumstances where his observable behaviour will render open to *unambiguous* inference the form of the function which he is conceived of as maximising.

As has long been known, the behaviour of an individual in the market, when confronted with various price combinations and under limitations of various incomes, is not in itself sufficient to determine the form of his utility function, but can only give us at best a system of indifference loci to which an infinite number of utility indexes might have given rise, integrability conditions being met.[2]

Under the following four assumptions, it is believed possible to arrive theoretically at a precise measure of the marginal utility of *money income* to an individual whose tastes maintain a certain invariance throughout the time under consideration, and during which time the prices of all goods remain constant.[3]

---

[1] Cf. Irving Fisher, . . . *Econ. Essays in Honor of J. B. Clark* ; R. Frisch, *New Methods of Measuring Marginal Utility.*

[2] To arrive at a unique measure of utility certain extra assumptions must be made in order to select a particular scale out of the infinitude of possible scales. We might assume, for example, that our utility function must be an additive function of the utilities corresponding to each commodity. This in turn involves an axiom (definition) and an hypothesis. The hypothesis, subject to refutation by the statistical data, is that such an additive function could possibly have given rise to the observable behaviour. The other assumption consists in *defining* that additive function, subject to freedom of a scale constant and choice of origin, as *the* utility function, in preference to any monotonic function of this additive function. This definition, like any other, is axiomatic and not subject to verification or refutation.

The choice of such an additive function can hardly be defended as a first approximation. The fact that any multiple valued function may be expanded in a Taylor series, certain terms of which form an additive function in the many variables, does not justify our assuming such a function to fit the data over an extended range, any more than we may fit a straight line to a single valued function because in the neighbourhood of any point the function may be approximated by its tangent. Moreover, if we consider the possible uses or mis-uses to which our results might be put, it is likely that we may be interested in the very properties of the function, from which we have already abstracted, else our original indifference field would have sufficed.

[3] The marginal utility of income derived will hold only for a given set of prices. This limitation is inherent in the problem, since the concept has meaning only with reference to a fixed set of prices. Moreover, we could have easily considered the expenditure on each commodity over time, and thus have solved for the marginal utility of each commodity as a function of all the variables without making any assumptions as to independence. Under assumptions analogous to the usual integrability conditions, we could then go directly to the utility function in terms of all commodities. However, this would have added to the elaborateness of our equations without introducing any results of additional analytical interest.

It may be noted here, that marginal utility of money income as here defined will *not* in general be identical with marginal utility of money income as defined by other writers.

---

1. *Utility is uniquely measurable as, in consequence, is marginal utility.* A fixed set of prices being given, variations of income will define a path along which we may measure the marginal utility of money income. It is the form of this function which we are trying to determine. Utility (U) of income (x) is regarded as a time flow, a rate per unit-time. Marginal (degree of) utility is the rate of utility per dollar (X), per unit of time with dimension $(UX^{-1}T^{-1})$. Mathematically

$$U = U(x) \dots\dots\dots\dots\dots\dots\dots\dots\dots\dots\dots\dots\dots\dots \quad (1)$$

where x representing money income per unit-time is of dimension (XT^{-1}).

2. *During any specified period of time, the individual behaves so as to maximise the sum of all future utilities, they being reduced to comparable magnitudes by suitable time discounting.* This is in the nature of an axiom, or definition, not subject to proof in any empirical sense, since any and all types of observable behaviour might conceivably result from such an assumption. Mathematically, the following integral is to be made a maximum subject to side conditions to be imposed later :

$$J = \int_0^b V(x, t)dt \dots\dots\dots\dots\dots\dots\dots\dots\dots\dots\dots\dots \quad (2)$$

where the beginning of the time period under consideration is taken as the origin along the time scale, and where b represents the end of this time period, here taken as finite.

3. *The individual discounts future utilities in some simple regular fashion which is known to us.* For simplicity, we assume in the first instance that the rate of discount of future utilities is a constant. This constant might of course be such that there is no time preference whatsoever, or even a premium on future utilities. This third assumption, unlike the previous two, is in the nature of an hypothesis, subject to refutation by the observable facts, i.e. refutation in the sense of proved inconsistency with the previous axioms. Moreover, this assumption, added to the previous ones, serves to limit our marginal utility function to a sub-class of all possible functions, from which sub-class it will be possible to identify a unique utility function. The arbitrariness of these assumptions is again stressed mathematically :

$$V(x, t) = U(x)e^{-\pi t} \dots\dots\dots\dots\dots\dots\dots\dots\dots\dots\dots\dots \quad (3)$$

where π bears the following familiar relationship to the rate of discount (positive or negative) p, here assumed to be constant :

$$\pi = \log e(1+p) \dots\dots\dots\dots\dots\dots\dots\dots\dots\dots\dots\dots \quad (3.1)$$

In accordance with this assumption we may re-write equation (2) as follows :

$$J = \int_0^b U(x)e^{-\pi t}\, dt \dots\dots\dots\dots\dots\dots\dots\dots\dots\dots\dots \quad (4)$$

(4) We define an ideal set of experimental conditions under which the individual under observation must act. The individual is given an initial sum of money (S), upon which he may draw at will. All money not drawn upon bears interest, compounded at a given rate. Moreover, the individual must so allocate his expenditures that there be no balance left at the end of the

period. Mathematically, we may state this as the imposition of the following isoparametrical side condition on the previous functional to be made a maximum :

$$S = \int_0^b x(t)e^{-rt}\, dt \quad \dots\dots\dots\dots\dots\dots\dots\dots\dots\dots\dots\dots \quad (5)$$

where r corresponds to the return on the unused balance.

Given these assumptions, it is possible to state certain necessary conditions between the time shape of income expenditure, an observable phenomenon, and the marginal utility of money income. Without knowing the form of the utility function itself, we can state on *a priori* mathematical grounds these relationships. Later from the actual observable shape of the income expenditure as a function of time, we shall be able to deduce the actual shape of the utility function, invariant except for a linear transformation, i.e. scale and origin constants.

In order to simplify the exposition of the necessary conditions of a maximum of (3), subject to the side conditions (4), we may avail ourselves of a Lagrange multiplier λ, and reduce our problem to the equivalent one of maximising the following functional :

$$\int_0^b U(x)e^{-\pi t}dt - \lambda[\int_0^b x(t)e^{-rt}dt - S] \quad \dots\dots\dots\dots\dots\dots\dots \quad (4')$$

A necessary condition that this functional be a maximum, may be secured heuristically by disregarding the integral signs, and differentiating with respect to x, treating it as an independent variable. This yields us the following Euler-necessary condition for a maximum : [1]

$$U'(x)e^{-\pi t} - \lambda\, e^{-rt} = 0 \dots\dots\dots\dots\dots\dots\dots\dots\dots\dots\dots\dots \quad (6)$$

where $U'(x)$ represents the marginal utility of income. We may re-write this as follows :

$$U'(x) = \lambda e^{(\pi - r)t} \dots\dots\dots\dots\dots\dots\dots\dots\dots\dots\dots\dots\dots \quad (6')$$

Here we have the precise way in which marginal utility will vary through time under the assumptions we have made. In 6 and 6', λ is a constant depending upon the original amount of money S, and the actual unit in terms of which utility is reckoned. From 6', we can solve explicitly for x as a function of t providing that we know the form of the utility function. On the other hand, and this is the object of our search, if we know x as a function of t, we can always arrive at the form of the utility function.

Now, by observing the results of our experiment (i.e. the behaviour of the individual in the allocation of his expenditures over time), we arrive at an empirical function between x and t as follows :

$$x = \bar{f}(t) \dots\dots\dots\dots\dots\dots\dots\dots\dots\dots\dots\dots\dots\dots\dots\dots \quad (7)$$

---

[1] For the purpose of this paper it does not seem advisable to go into the problem of providing additional necessary conditions or sufficiency conditions. At a later point, where relevant, notice will be taken of another necessary condition. Furthermore, in what follows we should treat all functions as if single-valued. Where this is unjustified, the argument may be easily modified.

where the bar over the function indicates that it is one whose form is known to us. We may re-write equation (7) in the following manner :

$$t = \bar{q}(x) \quad \dots\dots\dots\dots\dots\dots\dots\dots\dots\dots\dots\dots\dots\dots\dots\dots\dots (7')$$

where $\bar{q}$ is the inverse function of $\bar{f}$ and is known to us.

Now we may substitute $7'$ in $6'$ and get the following unambiguous expression for our marginal utility function :

$$U'(x) = \lambda e^{(\pi-r)\bar{q}(x)} \quad \dots\dots\dots\dots\dots\dots\dots\dots\dots\dots\dots\dots\dots\dots (8)$$

By simple integration we may easily come to the form of the utility function as follows :

$$U(x) = \lambda \int_C e^{(\pi-r)\bar{q}(x)}dx \quad \dots\dots\dots\dots\dots\dots\dots\dots\dots\dots\dots\dots\dots (8')$$

where C indicates the limits of integration to be taken, subject to the condition that this expression be finite.

Our main quest is now over. It remains only to investigate the relationships which our analysis may reveal, and to discuss the serious limitations of our approach. For this purpose it is most useful to consider the following dimensionless elasticity expression between marginal utility and income :

$$E_{u'x} = E = xU''(x)/U'(x) \quad \dots\dots\dots\dots\dots\dots\dots\dots\dots\dots\dots\dots (9)$$

Differentiating (6') with respect to x we get

$$U''(x) = (\pi-r)e^{(\pi-r)t}dt/dx \quad \pi \neq r \quad \dots\dots\dots\dots\dots\dots\dots\dots\dots (10)$$

Therefore, by substitution of (10) in (9),

$$E = x(\pi-r)dt/dx \quad \pi \neq r \quad \dots\dots\dots\dots\dots\dots\dots\dots\dots\dots\dots (11)$$

In equation (11) we have presented in most convenient form the relations which must hold between our functions in consistence with our assumptions. In general, economists assume on *a priori* grounds that marginal utility decreases with income in a monotonic manner. Moreover, in terms of our previous assumptions we can definitely state as a secondary necessary condition for a relative maximum, that marginal utility be *not* an increasing function of income in a neighbourhood of the equilibrium expenditures at each instant of time. Hence, x being of necessity a positive number we have the following condition :

$$(\pi-r)dt/dx < 0 \quad \pi \neq r \quad \dots\dots\dots\dots\dots\dots\dots\dots\dots\dots\dots\dots (12)$$

Thus, each of the terms in (12) must be of opposite signs. We may say then that whenever the individual's subjective rate of utility discount is greater (less) than the rate of interest at which he can borrow or lend unlimited amounts, he will allocate his income over some finite period of time in a decreasing (increasing) function of time. This, of course, is consistent with our common sense, intuitional judgments. In the case that these two rates are equal we know immediately from (6') that marginal utility is a constant throughout time, and hence income must be spent at a constant rate. Here our experiment gives us but one point on the marginal utility function. In order to arrive at its form over an interval we must introduce another interest rate. This suggests a possible way to determine experimentally the value of π, i.e.

by determining for which value of r the rate of money expenditure is a constant.

It may be well to point out that when the interest rate equals the rate of time discount the individual will *not* be conserving the value of his capital assets, in the sense that net saving will be zero. Rather will he be eating up his capital in such a way that it will provide him a steady income over the finite period under consideration (life of the individual, lifespan plus lifespan of immediate heirs, etc.). Only if the individual is maximising such a function over an infinite period of time, i.e. when the rate of amortisation of capital value is zero, will his capital assets remain constant in value in the sense that net savings (investment) are equal to zero.

In the case where the " individual " is maximising such an integral over an infinite period of time, the interest rate being conceived of as remaining constant, we may take the initial amount of money possessed by the " individual " as the discounted value of all the future net yields of all the services (property or human) to which the " individual " has legal claim (uncertainty being assumed absent). In this abstract case, the " individual " would always be increasing the net value of his assets, i.e. be always saving, so long as the interest rate exceeds his rate of discount of utility. The opposite proposition may be formulated for the case in which the rate of utility discount exceeds the perpetual rate of interest. We assume here that the interest rate is taken as a datum by the individual.[1]

Our task now is to indicate briefly the serious limitations of the previous kind of analysis, which almost certainly vitiate it even from a theoretical point of view. In the first place, it is completely arbitrary to assume that the individual behaves so as to maximise an integral of the form envisaged in (2). This involves the assumption that at every instant of time the individual's satisfaction depends only upon the consumption at that time, and that, furthermore, the individual tries to maximise the sum of instantaneous satisfactions reduced to some comparable base by time discount. As has been suggested,[2] we might assume that the individual maximises an integral which contains not only consumption per unit time but also the rate of change of consumption per unit time, and higher derivatives. This is more general in the sense that it includes our assumption as a special case, but still would seem arbitrary. A more general formulation of the problem might conceive of the individual's behaving so as to maximise a *functional* of various time shapes of consumption through time. Mathematically, we might conceive of a *functional* utility index as follows :

$$J = \underset{a}{\overset{b}{Z}}(x\,t) \dots\dots\dots\dots\dots\dots\dots\dots\dots\dots\dots\dots\dots\dots (13)$$

or, slightly more generally :

$$F = F(J) \dots\dots\dots\dots\dots\dots\dots\dots\dots\dots\dots\dots\dots\dots (14)$$

---

[1] It may be well to note here the brilliant article by the late F. P. Ramsey on kindred subjects : " A Mathematical Theory of Savings," *Economic Journal*, 1928.
[2] Gerhard Tintner : " A Note on Distribution of Income Over Time," *Econometrica*, V, IV, pp. 60–66.

where $F(J)$ indicates any monotonic transformation of J. This would include as a special case the integrals studied in the Calculus of Variations.[1]

Moreover, and this is the important theoretical implication, there is almost nothing that we can say concerning such a functional on *a priori* grounds. Since we could only know it by its effects, there would seem to be little value in the concept, since it can hardly be argued that it would serve as a convenient construction in simplifying our analysis in view of the inaccessability of such theory to students without an advanced knowledge of mathematics.

A less important point to be noted is the fact that our equations hold only for an individual who is deciding at the beginning of the period how he will allocate his expenditures over the period. Actually, however, as the individual moves along in time there is a sort of perspective phenomenon in that his view of the future in relation to his instantaneous time position remains invariant, rather than his evaluation of any particular year (e.g. 1940). This relativity effect is expressed in the behaviour of men who make irrevocable trusts, in the taking out of life insurance as a compulsory savings measure, etc. The particular results we have reached are not subject to criticism on this score, having been carefully selected so as to take care of this provision. Contemplation of our particular equations will reveal that the results are unchanged even if the individual always discounts from the existing point of time rather than from the beginning of the period. He will still make at each instant the same decision with respect to expenditure as he would have, if at the beginning of the period he were to decide on his expenditure for the whole period. But the fact that this is so is in itself, a presumption that individuals do not behave in terms of our functions.

Moreover, in the analysis of the supply of savings, it is extremely doubtful whether we can learn much from considering such an economic man, whose tastes remain unchanged, who seeks to maximise some functional of consumption alone, in a perfect world, where all things are certain and synchronised. For in any case such a functional would have to be dependent upon certain parameters which are socially determined ; " effective " desire for social prestige, length of human life, life cycle of individual economic activity, corporate structure, institutional banking and investment structure, etc. In general, there is strong reason to believe that changes in such parameters are not of an equilibrating nature. Even to generalise concerning these can only be done in terms of a theory of " history " (in itself almost a contradiction in terms). In any case, this would seem to lie in the region which Marshall termed Economic Biology, where the powerful tools of mathematical abstraction will little serve our turn, and direct study of such institutional data would seem in order.

In what way have our assumptions enabled us to arrive at a particular measure of utility rather than merely one index of utility ? Reflection as to

---

[1] If functional theory is to be applied to this problem, it would seem preferable to confine the discussion, at least in the preliminary stages, to functionals which have functional derivatives at every point, i.e. functionals of continuity zero. Cf. Volterra : *Theory of Functionals*. This would seem preferable on economic and mathematical grounds. Such procedure would exclude the integrals discussed by Tintner (ibid.), but would, on the other hand, be much wider than the kind of integral depicted in (2).

the meaning of our Assumption Two, that the individual seeks to maximise an integral of the kind envisaged in (2), will reveal that the individual must make preferences in the Utility dimension itself, that is to say, we must invoke Pareto's Postulate Two, which relates to the possibility of ordering *differences* in utility by the individual.[1] The advantage of our experiment is that it compels the individual to make just such judgments. Thus, with postulates one and two being fulfilled, it is to be expected that utility is uniquely measurable.[2]

In conclusion, any connection between utility as discussed here and any welfare concept is disavowed. The idea that the results of such a statistical investigation could have any influence upon ethical judgments of policy is one which deserves the impatience of modern economists.

Cambridge, Mass.   PAUL A. SAMUELSON.

[1] Cf. O. Lange : " The Determinateness of the Utility Function," REVIEW OF ECONOMIC STUDIES, V. I, pp. 218, 225.

[2] Professor Leontief has pointed out to me that this method may be compared with the usual method of deriving demand or supply curves from knowledge of the shifts of these functions through time. Here, it was assumed that we know the shifts of the utility function through time (rate of time discount). This, together with our side conditions and maximisation conditions, enables us to go back from our observed income expenditure function of time, to the utility function itself.

21

AN EXACT CONSUMPTION-LOAN MODEL OF INTEREST WITH OR WITHOUT THE SOCIAL CONTRIVANCE OF MONEY*

PAUL A. SAMUELSON
Massachusetts Institute of Technology

M Y FIRST published paper[1] has come of age, and at a time when the subjects it dealt with have come back into fashion. It developed the equilibrium conditions for a rational consumer's lifetime consumption-saving pattern, a problem more recently given by Harrod the useful name of "hump saving" but which Landry, Böhm-Bawerk, Fisher, and others had touched on long before my time.[2] It dealt only with a single individual and did not discuss the mutual determination by all individuals of the

market interest rates which each man had to accept parametrically as given to him.

Now I should like to give a complete general equilibrium solution to the determination of the time-shape of interest rates. This sounds easy, but actually it is very hard, so hard that I shall have to make drastic simplifications in order to arrive at exact results. For while Böhm and Fisher have given us the essential insights into the pure theory of interest, neither they nor other writers seem to have grappled with the following tough problem: in order to define an equilibrium path of interest in a perfect capital market endowed with *perfect certainty*, you have to determine *all* interest rates between now and the end of time; every finite time period points beyond itself!

Some interesting mathematical boundary problems, a little like those in the modern theories of dynamic programming, result from this analysis. And the way is paved for a rigorous attack on a simple model involving money as a store of value and a medium of exchange. My essay concludes with some provocative

* Research aid from the Ford Foundation is gratefully acknowledged.

[1] "A Note on Measurement of Utility," *Review of Economic Studies*, IV (1937), 155–61.

[2] As an undergraduate student of Paul Douglas at Chicago, I was struck by the fact that we might, from the marginal utility schedule of consumptions, deduce saving behavior exactly in the same way that we might deduce gambling behavior. Realizing that, watching the consumer's gambling responses to varying odds, we could deduce his numerical marginal utilities, it occurred to me that, by watching the consumer's saving responses to varying interest rates, we might similarly measure his marginal utilities, and thus the paper was born. (I knew and pointed out, p. 155, n. 2; p. 160, that such a cardinal measurement of utility hinged on a certain refutable "independence" hypothesis.)

remarks about the field of social collusions, a subject of vital importance for political economy and of great analytical interest to the modern theorist.

THE PROBLEM STATED

Let us assume that men enter the labor market at about the age of twenty. They work for forty-five years or so and then live for fifteen years in retirement. (As children they are part of their parents' consumptions, and we take no note of them.) Naturally, they want to consume in their old age, and, in the absence of comprehensive social security—an institution which has important bearing on interest rates and saving—men will want to consume less than they produce during their working years so that they can consume something in the years when they produce nothing.

If there were only Robinson Crusoe, he would hope to put by some durable goods which could be drawn on in his old age. He would, so to speak, want to trade with Mother Nature current consumption goods in return for future consumption goods. And if goods kept perfectly, he could at worst always make the trade through time on a one-to-one basis, and we could say that the interest rate was zero ($i = 0$). If goods kept imperfectly, like ice or radium, Crusoe might have to face a negative real interest rate, $i < 0$. If goods were like rabbits or yeast, reproducing without supervision at compound interest, he would face a positive rate of interest, $i > 0$. This last case is usually considered to be technologically the most realistic one: that is, machines and round-about processes (rather than rabbits) are considered to have a "net productivity," and this is taken to be brute fact. (Böhm himself, after bitterly criticizing naïve productivity theorists and criticizing

Thünen and others for assuming such a fact, ends up with his own celebrated third cause for interest, which also asserts the fact of net productivity. Contrary to much methodological discussion, there is nothing circular about assuming brute facts—that is all we can do; we certainly cannot deduce them, although, admittedly, we can hope by experience to refute falsely alleged facts.)

For the present purpose, I shall make the extreme assumption that nothing will keep at all. Thus no intertemporal trade with Nature is possible (that is, for all such exchanges we would have $i = -1!$). If Crusoe were alone, he would obviously die at the beginning of his retirement years.

But we live in a world where new generations are always coming along. Formerly we used to support our parents in their old age. That is now out of fashion. But cannot men during their productive years give up some of their product to bribe other men to support them in their retirement years? Thus, forty-year-old A gives some of his product to twenty-year-old B, so that when A gets to be seventy-five he can receive some of the product that B is then producing.

Our problem, then, is this: In a stationary population (or, alternatively, one growing in any prescribed fashion) what will be the intertemporal terms of trade or interest rates that will spring up spontaneously in ideally competitive markets?

SIMPLIFYING ASSUMPTIONS

To make progress, let us make convenient assumptions. Break each life up into thirds: men produce one unit of product in period 1 and one unit in period 2; in period 3 they retire and produce nothing. (No one dies in midstream.)

In specifying consumption preferences,

I suppose that each man's tastes can be summarized by an ordinal utility function of the consumptions of the three periods of his life: $U = U(C_1, C_2, C_3)$. This is the same in every generation and has the usual regular indifference-curve concavities, but for much of the argument nothing is said about whether, subjectively, men systematically discount future consumptions or satisfactions. (Thus Böhm's second cause of interest may or may not be operative; it could even be reversed, men being supposed to overvalue the future!)

In addition to ignoring Böhm's second cause of systematic time preference, I am in a sense also denying or reversing his first cause of interest, in that we are *not* supposing that society is getting more prosperous as time passes or that any single man can expect to be more prosperous at a later date in his life, since, on the contrary, during his years of retirement he must look forward to producing even less than during his working years.

Finally, recall our assumption that no goods keep, no trade with Nature being possible, and hence Böhm's third technological cause of interest is being denied.

Under these assumptions, what will be the equilibrium time path of interest rates?

INDIVIDUAL SAVING FUNCTIONS

The simplest case to tackle to answer this question is that of a stationary population, which has always been stationary in numbers and will always be stationary. This ideal case sidesteps the difficult "planning-until-infinity" aspect of the problem. In it births are given by $B_t = B$, the same constant for all positive and negative t.

Now consider any time t. There are B men of age one, B men of age two, and B retired men of age three. Since each

producer produces 1 unit, total product is $B + B$. Now, for convenience of symbols, let $R_t = 1/(1 + i_t)$ be the discount rate between goods (chocolates) of period t traded for chocolates of the next period, $t + 1$. Thus, if $R_t = 0.5$, you must promise me two chocolates tomorrow to get me to part with one chocolate today, the interest rate being 100 per cent per period. If $R_t = 1$, the interest rate is zero, and tomorrow's chocolates cost 1.0 of today's. If $R_t > 1$, say $R_t = 1.5$, the interest rate is negative, and one future chocolate costs 1.5 of today's. (Clearly, R_t is the price of tomorrow's chocolates expressed in terms of today's chocolates as numeraire.)

We seek the equilibrium levels of . . . R_t, R_{t+1}, . . . , that will clear the competitive markets in which present and future goods exchange against each other.

At time t each man who is beginning his life faces[3] the budget equation,

$$C_1 + C_2 R_t + C_3 R_t R_{t+1} \tag{1}$$
$$= 1 + 1 R_t + 0 R_t R_{t+1} .$$

This merely says that the total discounted value of his life's consumptions must equal the discounted value of his productions. Subject to this constraint, he will, for each given R_t and R_{t+1}, determine an optimal (C_1, C_2, C_3) to maximize $U(C_1, C_2, C_3)$, which we can summarize by the "demand" functions,

$$C_i = C_i(R_t, R_{t+1}) \qquad (i = 1, 2, 3) . \tag{2}$$

---

[3] I rule out, as I did explicitly in my 1937 paper (p.160), the Ulysses-Strotz-Allais phenomenon whereby time perspective distorts present decisions planned for the future from later actual decisions. Thus, if at the end of period 1 his ordinal preference follows $V(C_1, C_2, C_3)$ rather than $U(C_1, C_2, C_3)$, I am assuming $(\partial V/\partial C_i)/(\partial V/\partial C_j) \equiv (\partial U/\partial C_i)/(\partial U/\partial C_j)$. Hence all later decisions will ratify earlier plans. For a valuable discussion of this problem see R. H. Strotz, "Myopia and Inconsistency in Dynamic Utility Maximization," *Review of Economic Studies*, XXIII (1956), 165–80.

It might be convenient for us to work with "net" or "excess demands" of each man: these are the algebraic differences between what a man consumes and what he produces. Net demands in this sense are the negative of what men usually call "saving," and, in deference to capital theory, I shall work with such "net saving" as defined by

$$S_1 = S_1(R_t, R_{t+1}) = 1 - C_1(R_t, R_{t+1}),$$

$$S_2 = S_2(R_t, R_{t+1}) = 1 - C_2(R_t, R_{t+1}), \quad (3)$$

$$S_3 = S_3(R_t, R_{t+1}) = 0 - C_3(R_t, R_{t+1}).$$

In old age presumably S_3 is negative, matched by positive youthful saving, so as to satisfy for all (R_t, R_{t+1}) the budget identity,

$$S_1(R_t, R_{t+1}) + R_t S_2(R_t, R_{t+1})$$
$$+ R_t R_{t+1} S_3(R_t, R_{t+1}) = 0. \quad (4)$$

Of course, these functions are subject to all the restrictions of modern consumption theory of the ordinal utility or revealed preference type. Thus, with consumption in every period being a "superior good," we can infer that $\partial C_3 / \partial R_{t+1} < 0$ and $\partial S_3 / \partial R_{t+1} > 0$. (This says that raising the interest rate earned on savings carried over into retirement must increase retirement consumption.) We cannot unambiguously deduce the sign of $\partial S_1 / \partial R_t$ and other terms, for the reasons implicit in modern consumption theory.

We can similarly work out the saving functions for men born a period later, which will be of the form $S_i(R_{t+1}, R_{t+2})$, etc., containing, of course, the later interest rates they will face—likewise for earlier interest rates facing men born earlier. Finally, our fundamental condition of clearing the market is this: Total net saving for the community must cancel out to zero in every period. (Remember that no goods keep and that real net investment is impossible, all loans being "consumption" loans.)

At any time t there exist B_t men of the first period, B_{t-1} men of the second period, and B_{t-2} men of the third period. The sum of their savings gives us the fundamental equilibrium condition:

$$0 = B_t S_1(R_t, R_{t+1}) + B_{t-1} S_2(R_{t-1}, R_t)$$
$$+ B_{t-2} S_3(R_{t-2}, R_{t-1}), \quad (5)$$

for every t. Note that in S_2 we have the interest rates of one earlier period than in S_1, and in S_3 we have still earlier interest rates (in fact, interest rates that are, at time t, already history and no longer to be determined.)

We have such an equation for every t, and if we take any finite stretch of time and write out the equilibrium conditions, we always find them containing discount rates from before the finite period and discount rates from afterward. We never seem to get enough equations: lengthening our time period turns out always to add as many new unknowns as it supplies equations, as will be spelled out later in equations (14).

THE STATIONARY CASE

We can try to cut the Gordian knot by our special assumption of stationariness, namely,

$$\ldots B_{t-1} = B_t = B_{t+1} = \ldots$$

$$= B, \text{ a given constant for all time}$$
$$\ldots R_{t-1} = R_t = R_{t+1} = \ldots \quad (6)$$

$$= R, \text{ the unknown discount rate.}$$

The first of these is a demographic datum; the second assumption of non-changing interest rates is a conjecture whose consistency we must explore and verify.

Now substituting relations (6) in equation (5), we get one equilibrium equation to determine our one unknown R, namely,

$$0 = BS_1(R, R) + BS_2(R, R)$$
$$+ BS_3(R, R) . \tag{7}$$

By inspection, we recognize a solution of equation (7) to be $R = 1$, or $i = 0$: that is, zero interest must be one equilibrium rate under our conditions.[4]

Why? Because

$$B[S_1(1, 1) + 1S_2(1, 1) + 1S_3(1, 1)] = 0$$

by virtue of the budget identity (4).

Can a common-sense explanation of this somewhat striking result be given? Let me try. In a stationary system everyone goes through the same life-cycle, albeit at different times. Giving over goods now to an older man is figuratively giving over goods to *yourself* when old. At what rate does one give over goods to one's later self? At $R > 1$, or $R < 1$, or $R = 1$? To answer this, note that a chocolate today *is* a chocolate today, and when middle-aged A today gives over a chocolate to old B, there is a one-to-one *physical* transfer of chocolates, none melting in the transfer and none sticking to the hands of a broker. So, heuristically, we see that the hypothetical "transfer *through time*" of the chocolates must be at $R = 1$ with the interest rate i exactly zero.

Note that this result is quite independent of whether or not people have a systematic subjective preference for present consumption over future. Why? Because we have assumed that if *anyone* has such a systematic preference, *everyone* has such a systematic preference. There is no one any different in the system, no outsider—so to speak—to exact

a positive interest rate from the impatient consumers.[5]

A BIOLOGICAL THEORY OF INTEREST AND POPULATION GROWTH

A zero rate of population growth was seen to be consistent with a zero rate of interest for a consumption-loan world. I now turn to the case of a population growing exponentially or geometrically. Now

$$B_t = B(1 + m)^t, \quad \text{with}$$

$$B_{t+1} = (1 + m)B_t = (1 + m)^2 B_{t-1} \dots .$$

For $m > 0$, we have growth; for $m < 0$, decay; for $m = 0$, our previous case of a stationary population. As before, we suppose

$$\dots R_{t-1} = R_t = R_{t+1} = \dots$$

$$= R, \text{ a constant through time.}$$

Now our clearing-of-the-market equation is

$$0 = B(1 + m)^t S_1(R, R)$$
$$+ B(1 + m)^{t-1} S_2(R, R) \tag{8}$$
$$+ B(1 + m)^{t-2} S_3(R, R) ;$$

or, cancelling $B(1 + m)^t$, we have

$$0 = S_1(R, R) + (1 + m)^{-1} S_2(R, R)$$
$$+ (1 + m)^{-2} S_3(R, R) . \tag{9}$$

Recalling our budget identity (4), we realize $R = (1 + m)^{-1}$ or $i = m$ is one root satisfying the equation, giving

$$0 = S_1(R, R) + RS_2(R, R) + R^2 S_3(R, R) .$$

We have therefore established the following paradoxical result:

[4] We shall see that $R = 1$ is not the only root of equation (7) and that there are multiple equilibriums.

[5] If productive opportunities were to exist, Mother Nature would operate as an important outsider, with whom trade could take place, and our conclusion would be modified. But recall our strong postulate that such technological opportunities are non-existent.

THEOREM: Every geometrically growing consumption-loan economy has an equilibrium market rate of interest exactly equal to its biological percentage growth rate.

Thus, if the net reproductive rate gives a population growth of 15 per cent per period, $i = 0.15$ is the corresponding market rate of interest. If, as in Sweden or Ireland, $m < 0$ and population decays, the market rate of interest will be negative, with $i < 0$ and $R > 1$!

OPTIMUM PROPERTY OF THE BIOLOGICAL INTEREST RATE

The equality of the market rate of interest in a pure consumption-loan world to the rate of population growth was deduced solely from mechanically finding a root of the supply-demand equations that clear the market. Experience often confirms what faith avers: that competitive market relations achieve some kind of an optimum.

Does the saving-consumption pattern given by $S_1(R, R)$, $S_2(R, R)$, $S_3(R, R)$, where $R = 1/(1 + m)$, represent some kind of a social optimum? One would guess that, if it does maximize something, this equilibrium pattern probably maximizes the "lifetime (ordinal) well-being of a representative person, subject to the resources available to him (and to every other representative man) over his lifetime." Or, what seems virtually the same thing, consider a cross-sectional family or clan that has an unchanging age distribution because the group remains in statistical equilibrium, though individuals are born and die. Such a clan will divide its available resources to maximize a welfare function differing only in scale from each man's utility function and will achieve the same result as the biological growth rate.

To test this optimality conjecture, first stick to the stationary population

case. The representative man is thought to maximize $U(C_1, C_2, C_3)$, subject to

$$C_1 + C_2 + C_3 = 1 + 1, \quad (10)$$

$1 + 1$ being the lifetime product available to each man. The solution to this technocratic welfare problem (free in its formulation and solution of all mention of prices or interest rates) requires

$$\frac{\partial U / \partial C_2}{\partial U / \partial C_1} = \frac{\partial U / \partial C_3}{\partial U / \partial C_1}. \quad (11)$$

But this formulation is seen to be identical with that of a single maximizing man facing market discount rates $R_1 = R_2 = 1$. Hence the solution of equations (10) and (11) is exactly that given earlier by equation (3): that is, our present welfare problem has, for its optimality solution,

$$1 - C_1 = S_1(1, 1),$$
$$1 - C_2 = S_2(1, 1),$$
$$0 - C_3 = S_3(1, 1).$$

Now that we have verified our conjecture for the stationary $m = 0$ case, we can prove it for population growing like $B(1 + m)^t$, where $m \gtrless 0$. As before, we maximize $U(C_1, C_2, C_3)$ for the representative man. But what resources are now available to him? Recall that in a growing population the age distribution is permanently skewed in favor of the younger productive ages: society and each clan has an age distribution proportional to $[1, 1/(1 + m), 1/(1 + m)^2]$ and has therefore a per capita output to divide in consumption among the three age classes satisfying

$$C_1 + \frac{1}{1 + m} C_2 + \frac{1}{(1 + m)^2} C_3$$
$$= 1 + \frac{1}{1 + m}. \quad (12)$$

By following a representative man throughout his life and remembering that there are always $(1 + m)^{-1}$ just older than he and $(1 + m)^{-2}$ two periods older, we derive this same "budget" or availibility equation. Subject to equation (12), we maximize $U(C_1, C_2, C_3)$ and necessarily end up with the same conditions as would a competitor facing the biological market interest rate $R_1 = R_2 = 1/(1 + m)$: namely,

$$1 - C_1 = S_1(R, R),$$

$$1 - C_2 = S_2(R, R),$$

$$0 - C_3 = S_3(R, R), \qquad (13)$$

$$R = \frac{1}{1 + m}.$$

Hence the identity of the social optimality conditions and the biological market interest theory has been demonstrated.[6]

COMMON-SENSE EXPLANATION OF
BIOLOGICAL MARKET INTEREST
RATE

Productivity theorists have always related interest to the biological habits of rabbits and cows. And Gustav Cassel long ago developed a striking (but rather nonsensical) biological theory relating

[6] If U has the usual quasi-concavity, this social optimum will be unique—whether U does or does not have the time-symmetry that is sometimes (for concreteness) assumed in later arguments. Not only will the representative man's utility U be maximized, but so will the "total" of social utility enjoyed over a long period of time: specifically, the divergence from attainable bliss

$$[U(C_1, C_2, C_3) - U^*] + [U(C_1, C_2, C_3)$$

$$- U^*] + \dots$$

over all time will be miminized, where U^* is the utility achieved when $R_1 = 1 = R_2$ and $S_i = S_i(1, 1)$. This theorem may require that we use an ordinal utility indicator that is concave in the C_i, as it is always open to us to do.

Of course, this entire footnote and the related text need obvious modifications if $m \neq 0$.

interest to the life-expectancy of men of means and their alleged propensity to go from maintaining capital to the buying of annuities at an allegedly critical positive i. I seem to be the first, outside a slave economy, to develop a biological theory of interest relating it to the reproductivity of human mothers.

Is there a common-sense market explanation of this (to me at least) astonishing result? I suppose it would go like this: in a growing population men of twenty outnumber men of forty; and retired men are outnumbered by workers more than in the ratio of the work span to the retirement span. With more workers to support them, the aged live better than in the stationary state—the excess being positive interest on their savings.

Such an explanation cannot be deemed entirely convincing. Outside of social security and family altruism, the aged have no claims on the young: cold and selfish competitive markets will not teleologically respect the old; the aged will get only what supply and demand impute to them.

So we might try another more detailed explanation. Recall that men of forty or of period 2 bargain with men of twenty or period 1, trying to bribe the latter to provide them with consumption in their retirement. (Men of over sixty-five or of period 3 can make fresh bargains with no one: after retirement it is too late for them to try to provide for their old age.) In a growing population there are more period 1 men for period 2 men to bargain with; this presumably confers a competitive advantage on period 2 men, the manifestation of it being the positive interest rate.

So might go the explanation. It is at least superficially plausible, and it does qualitatively suggest a positive interest rate when population is growing, although perhaps it falls short of explaining the remarkable quantitative identity between the growth rates of interest and of population.

THE INFINITY PARADOX REVEALED

But will the explanation survive rigorous scrutiny? Is it true, in a growing or in a stationary population, that twenty-year-olds are, in fact, overconsuming so that the middle-aged can provide for their retirement? Specifically, in the stationary case where $R = 1$, is it necessarily true that $S_1(1, 1) < 0$? Study of $U(C_1, C_2, C_3)$ shows how doubtful such a general result would be; thus, if there is no systematic subjective time preference so that U is a function *symmetric* in its arguments, it would be easy to show that $C_1 = C_2 = C_3 = \frac{2}{3}$, with $S_1(1, 1) = S_2(1, 1) = +\frac{1}{3}$ and $S_3(1, 1) = -\frac{2}{3}$. Contrary to our scenario, the middle-aged are *not* turning over to the young what the young will later make good to them in retirement support.

THE TWO-PERIOD CASE

The paradox is delineated more clearly if we suppose but two equal periods of life—work and retirement. Now it becomes *impossible* for *any* worker to find a worker younger than himself to be bribed to support him in old age. Whatever the trend of births, there is but one equilibrium saving pattern possible: during working years, consumption equals product and saving is zero; the same during the brutish years of retirement. What equilibrium interest rate, or R, will prevail? Since no transactions take place, $R = 0/0$, so to speak, and appears rather indeterminate—and rather academic. However, if men desperately want *some* consumption at *all* times, only $R = \infty$ can be regarded as the (virtual) equilibrium rate, with interest equal to -100 per cent per period.[7]

We think we know the right answer just given in the two-period case. Let us test our previous mathematical methods. Now our equations are much as before and can be summarized by:

Maximize $U(C_1, C_2) = U(1 - S_1, 0 - S_2)$

subject to $S_1 + R_t S_2 = 0$.

The resulting saving functions, $S_1(R_t)$ and $S_2(R_t)$, are subject to the budget identity,

$$S_1(R_t) + R_t S_2(R_t) \equiv 0 \text{ for all } R_t. \quad (4')$$

Clearing the market requires

$$0 = B_t S_1(R_t) + B_{t-1} S_2(R_{t-1}) \quad \text{for} \quad (5')$$
$$t = 0, \pm 1, \pm 2, \ldots.$$

If $B_t = B(1 + m)^t$ and $R_t = R_{t+1} = \ldots = R$, our final equation becomes

$$0 = B\left[S_1(R) + \frac{1}{1 + m} S_2(R)\right]. \quad (8')$$

The budget equation $(4')$ assures us that equation $(8')$ has a solution:

$$R = \frac{1}{1 + m} \quad \text{or} \quad m = i.$$

$$\text{with} \quad 0 < S_1(R) = -RS_2(R).$$

So the two-period mathematics appears to give us the same answer as before—a biological rate of interest equal to the rate of population growth.

Yet we earlier deduced that *there can be no voluntary saving in a two-period world*. Instead of $S_1 > 0$, we must have $S_1 = 0 = S_2$ with $R = +\infty$. How can we reconcile this with the mathematics?

---

[7] A later numerical example, where $U = \log C_1 + \log C_2 + \log C_3$, shows that cases can arise where no positive R, however large, will clear the market. I adopt the harmless convention of setting $R = \infty$ in every case, even if the limit as $R \to \infty$ does not wipe out the discrepancy between supply and demand.

We substitute $S_1 = 0 = S_2$ in equation (5′) or equation (8′), and indeed this does satisfy the clearing-of-the-market equation. Apparently our one equilibrium equation in our one unknown R has more than a single solution! And the relevant one for a free market is *not* that given by our biological or demographic theory of interest, even though our earlier social optimality argument does perfectly fit the two-period case.

THE PARADOX CONTEMPLATED

The transparent two-period case alerts us to the possibility that in the three-period (or n-period) case, the fundamental equation of supply and demand may have multiple solutions. And, indeed, it does.[8] We see that

$$\lim_{R \to \infty} S_1(R, R) = -\infty$$

is indeed a valid mathematical solution. This raises the following questions:

Is a condition of no saving with dismal retirement consumption and interest rate of -100 per cent per period thinkable as the economically correct equilibrium for a free market?

Surely, the non-myopic middle-aged will do almost anything to make retirement consumption, C_3 non-zero?[9]

One might conjecture that the fact that, in the three-period model, workers can always find younger workers to bargain with is a crucial difference from the two-period case.[10] To investigate the

[8] There is nothing surprising about multiple solutions in economics: not infrequently income effects make possible other intersections, including the possibility of an infinite number where demand and supply curves coincide.

[9] Before answering these questions, it would be well to decide what the word "surely" in the previous sentence means. Surely, no sentence beginning with the word "surely" can validly contain a question mark at its end? However, one paradox is enough for one article, and I shall stick to my economist's last.

problem, we must drop the assumption of a population that is, always has been, and always will be stationary (or exponentially growing or exponentially decaying). For within that ambiguous context $R = 1(R < 1,\ R > 1)$ was indeed an impeccable solution, in the sense that no one can point to a violated equilibrium condition. (Exactly the same can be said of the two-period case, even though we "know" the impeccable solution is economically nonsense.)

We must give mankind a beginning. So, once upon a time, B men were born into the labor force. Then B more. Then B more. Until what? Until . . . ? Or until no more men are born? Must we give mankind an end as well as a beginning? Even the Lord rested after the beginning, so let us tackle one problem at a time and keep births forever constant. Our equilibrium equations, with the constant B's omitted, now become

$$S_1(R_1, R_2) + 0 + 0 = 0\,,$$

$$S_2(R_1, R_2) + S_1(R_2, R_3) + 0 = 0\,,$$

$$S_3(R_1, R_2) + S_2(R_2, R_3)$$
$$+ S_1(R_3, R_4) = 0\,,$$

$$S_3(R_2, R_3) + S_2(R_3, R_4) \qquad (14)$$
$$+ S_1(R_4, R_5) = 0\,,$$

$$\cdot\ \cdot\ \cdot\ \cdot\ \cdot\ \cdot\ \cdot\ \cdot\ \cdot\ \cdot\ \cdot\ \cdot\ \cdot\ \cdot\,,$$

$$S_3(R_{t-2}, R_{t-1}) + S_2(R_{t-1}, R_t)$$
$$+ S_1(R_t, R_{t+1}) = 0\,,$$

$$\cdot\ \cdot\ \cdot\ \cdot\ \cdot\ \cdot\ \cdot\ \cdot\ \cdot\ \cdot\ \cdot\ \cdot\ \cdot\ \cdot\ \cdot$$

We feel that $S_1 \equiv 0 \equiv S_2 \equiv S_3$, while a mathematical solution, is not the economically relevant one. Since $S_1(1, 1)$, $S_2(1, 1)$, and $S_3(1, 1)$ do satisfy the last

[10] By introducing overlap between workers of different ages, the three-period model is essentially equivalent to a general n-period model or to the continuous-time model of real life.

of the written equations, we dare hope[11] that the Invisible Hand will ultimately work its way to the socially optimal biological-interest configuration—or that the solution to equation (14) satisfies

$$\lim_{t \to \infty} R_t = 1, \quad S_i(R_t, R_{t+1})$$

$$= S_i(1, 1), \quad (i = 1, 2, 3) . \tag{15}$$

THE IMPOSSIBILITY THEOREM

But have we any right to hope that the free market will even ultimately approach the specified social optimum? Does not the two-period case rob us of hope? Will not all the trade that the three-period case makes possible consist of middle-aged period 2 people giving consumption to young period 1 people in return for getting consumption back from them one period later? Do not such voluntary mutual-aid compacts suggest that, if R_t does approach a limit x, it must be such as to make $S_1(x, x) < 0$? Whereas, for many men[12] not too subject to systematic preference for the present over the future (not too affected by Böhm's second cause of interest), we expect $S_1(1, 1) > 0$.

A colleague, whose conjectures are

[11] Our confidence in this would be enhanced if the linear difference equation relating small deviations $r_t = R_t - 1$ had characteristic roots all less than 1 in absolute value. Thus $a_0 r_{t+3} + a_1 r_{t+2} + a_2 r_{t+1} + a_3 r_t = 0$, where the a_i are given in terms of the $S_i(R_t, R_{t+1})$ functions and their partial derivatives, evaluated at $R_t = 1 R_{t+1}$. Logically, this would be neither quite necessary nor sufficient: not sufficient, since the initial R_0, R_1, R_2 might be so far from 1 as to make the linear approximations irrelevant; not necessary, since, with one root less than unity in absolute value, we might ride in toward $R = 1$ on a razor's edge. In any case, as our later numerical example shows, our hope is a vain one.

[12] There is admittedly some econometric evidence that many young adults do dissave, to acquire assets and for other reasons. Some modifications of exposition would have to be made to allow for this.

often better than many people's theorems, has suggested to me that in the three-period or n-period case I am taking too bilateral a view of trade. We might end up with $S_1 > 0$ and encounter no contradictions to voluntary trade by virtue of the fact that young men trade with *anyone* in the market: they do not know or care that all or part of the motive for trade with them comes from the desire of the middle-aged to provide for retirement. The present young are content to be trading with the present old (or, for that matter, with the unborn or dead): all they care about is that their trades take place at the quoted market prices; and, if some kind of triangular or multilateral offsetting among the generations can take place and result in $S_1(R_t, R_{t+1})$ positive and becoming closer and closer to $S_1(1, 1) > 0$, why cannot this happen?

I, too, found the multilateral notion appealing. But the following considerations—of a type I do not recall seeing treated anywhere—suggest to me that the ultimate approach to $R = 1$ and $S_1(1, 1) > 0$ is quite impossible.

List all men from the beginning to time t. All the voluntary trades ever made must be mutually advantageous. If A gives something to B and B does nothing for A directly in return, we know B must be doing something for some C, who does do something good for A. (Of course, C might be more than one man, and there might be many-linked connections within C.)

Now consider a time when $S_1(R_t, R_{t+1})$ has become positive, with $S_2(R_{t-1}, R_t)$ also positive. Young man A is then giving goods to old man B. Young man A expects something in return and will actually two periods later be getting goods from someone. From whom? It certainly cannot be directly from B: B will be dead then. Let it be from someone called C. Can B ever do anything good for such a C, or have in the past done so? No. B only has produce during his first two periods of life, and all the good he can do anyone must be to people who were born before him or just after him. That *never* includes C. So the postulated pattern of $S_1 > 0$ is logically impossible in a free market: and hence $R_t = 1 = R_{t+1}$, as an exact or approximate relation, is impossible. (Note that, for some special pattern of time preference, the competitive solution *might* coincide with the "biological optimum.")

A NUMERICAL EXAMPLE

A concrete case will illustrate all this. The purest Marshallian case of unitary price and income elasticities can be characterized by $U = \log C_1 + \log C_2 + \log C_3$, where all systematic time preference is replaced by *symmetry*.

A maximum of

$$\sum_1^3 \log C_i \text{ subject to} \tag{16}$$
$$C_1 + R_1 C_2 + R_1 R_2 C_3 = 1 + R_1$$

implies

$$R_1 = \frac{\partial U / \partial C_2}{\partial U / \partial C_1} = \frac{1/C_2}{1/C_1},$$

$$R_1 R_2 = \frac{\partial U / \partial C_3}{\partial U / \partial C_1} = \frac{1/C_3}{1/C_1};$$

and, after combining this with the budget equation, we end up with saving functions,

$$S_1(R_1, R_2) = \frac{2}{3} - \frac{R_1}{3},$$

$$S_2(R_1, R_2) = \frac{2}{3} - \frac{1}{3R_1}, \tag{17}$$

$$S_3(R_1, R_2) = 0 - \frac{1}{3R_1 R_2} - \frac{1}{3R_2}.$$

Equations (14) now take the form

$$\frac{2}{3} - \frac{R_1}{3} + 0 + 0 = 0,$$

$$\frac{2}{3} - \frac{1}{3R_1} + \left(\frac{2}{3} - \frac{R_2}{3}\right) + 0 = 0,$$

$$-\frac{1}{3R_1 R_2} - \frac{1}{3R_2} + \left(\frac{2}{3} - \frac{1}{3R_2}\right)$$
$$+ \left(\frac{2}{3} - \frac{R_3}{3}\right) = 0,$$

$$\left(-\frac{1}{3R_2 R_3} - \frac{1}{3R_3}\right) + \left(\frac{2}{3} - \frac{1}{3R_3}\right) \tag{18}$$
$$+ \left(\frac{2}{3} - \frac{R_4}{3}\right) = 0,$$

$$\cdots \cdots \cdots$$

$$\left(-\frac{1}{3R_{t-1} R_{t-2}} - \frac{1}{3R_{t-1}}\right)$$
$$+ \left(\frac{2}{3} - \frac{1}{3R_{t-1}}\right) + \left(\frac{2}{3} - \frac{R_t}{3}\right) = 0,$$

$$\cdots \cdots \cdots$$

Aside from initial conditions, this can be written in the recursive form,

$$R_t = 4 - \frac{1}{R_{t-1} R_{t-2}} - \frac{2}{R_{t-1}}. \tag{19}$$

Note that $\partial S_3(R_1, R_2) \equiv 0$ made our third-order difference equation degenerate into a second-order difference equation.

If we expand the last equation around $R_{t-2} = 1 = R_{t-1}$, retaining only linear terms and working in terms of deviations from the equilibrium level, $r_t = R_t - 1$, we get the recursive system,

$$r_{t+2} = 3r_{t+1} + r_t. \tag{20}$$

which obviously explodes away from $r = 0$ and $R = 1$ for all small perturbations from such an equilibrium. This confirms our proof that the *social optimum configuration can never here be reached by the competitive market, or even be approached in ever so long a time.*

Where does the solution to (18) eventually go? Its first few R's are numerically calculated to be $[R_1, R_2, R_3, \ldots] = [2, 3\frac{1}{2}, 3\frac{2}{7}, \ldots]$. It is plain that the limiting R_t exceeds 1; hence a negative interest rate i is being approached by oscillations. Substituting $R_{t+2} = R_{t+1} = R_t = x$ in equation (19), we get the following cubic equation to solve for possible equilibrium levels:[13]

$$x = 4 - \frac{1}{x^2} - \frac{2}{x} \quad \text{or}$$

$$ \tag{21} $$

$$x^3 - 4x^2 + 2x + 1 = 0 .$$

We know that $x = 1$, the irrelevant optimal level, is one root; so, dividing it out, we end up with

$$(x - 1)(x^2 - 3x - 1) = 0 .$$

Solving the quadratic, we have

$$x = \frac{3 \pm \sqrt{9 + 4}}{2}$$

or

$$x = \frac{3}{2} + \frac{\sqrt{13}}{2} = 3.3028 \text{ approx.}$$

for the asymptote approached by the free competitive market. The other root, $(3 - \sqrt{13})/2$, corresponds to a negative R, which is economically meaningless, in that it implies that the more we give up of today's consumption, the more we must give up of tomorrow's.

Our meaningful positive root, $R = 3.303$, corresponds to an ultimate negative interest rate,

$$i = \frac{1 - R}{R} = -\frac{2.303}{3.303} ,$$

[13] Martin J. Bailey has pointed out to me that the budget equation and the clearing-of-the-market equations do, in the stationary state, imply $S_1 = RS_3$ whenever $R \neq 1$, a fact which can be used to give an alternative demonstration of possible equilibrium values.

which implies that consumption loans lose about two-thirds of their principal in one period. This is here the competitive price to avoid retirement starvation.[14]

RECAPITULATION

The task of giving an exact description of a pure consumption-loan interest model is finished. We end up, in the stationary population case, with a negative market interest rate, rather than with the biological zero interest rate corresponding to the social optimum for the representative man. This was proved by the impossibility theorem and verified by an arithmetic example.

A corresponding result will hold for changing population where $m \gtrless 0$. The actual competitive market rate i_m will always be negative and always less than the biological optimality rate m.[15] And

[14] In other examples, this competitive solution would not deviate so much from the $i = m$ biological optimum. But it is important to realize that solutions to equations (14) that come from quasi-concave utility functions—with or without systematic time preference—*cannot* be counted on to approach asymptotically the biological optimum configuration of equation (13).

In this case the linear approximation gives for $r_t = R_t - 3.297$ the recursion relation

$$r_{t+2} = \frac{1}{(3.297)^3} r_{t+1} + \frac{2}{(3.297)^2} r_t .$$

This difference equation has roots easily shown to be less than 1 in absolute value, so the local stability of our competitive equilibrium is assured.

[15] Writing $\lambda = 1/(1 + m)$, our recursion relation (14) becomes

$$0 = S_1 (R_t, R_{t+1}) + \lambda S_2 (R_{t-1}, R_t)$$

$$+ \lambda^2 S_3 (R_{t-2}, R_{t-1}) .$$

For the case where $U = \Sigma \log C_i$, our recursion relation (18) becomes

$$R_t = 2(1 + \lambda) - \frac{\lambda^2}{R_{t-1}R_{t-2}} - \frac{\lambda^2}{R_{t-1}} - \frac{\lambda}{R_{t-1}} .$$

Then $x = R_t = R_{t-1} = R_{t-2}$ gives a cubic equation with biological root corresponding to $x = \lambda$ and

increasing the productive years relative to the retirement years of zero product would undoubtedly still leave us with a negative interest rate, albeit one that climbs ever closer to zero.

Is this negative interest rate a hard-to-believe result? Not, I think, when one recalls our extreme and purposely unrealistic assumptions. With Böhm's third technological reason for interest ruled out by assumption, with his second reason involving systematic preference for the present soft-pedaled, and with his first reason reversed (that is, with people expecting to be *poorer* in the future), we should perhaps have been surprised if the market rate had not turned out negative.

Yet, aside from giving the general biological optimum interest rate, our model is an instructive one for a number of reasons.

1. It shows us what interest rates would be implied if the "hump saving" process were acting alone in a world devoid of systematic time preference.[16]

2. It incidentally confirms what modern theorists showed long ago but what is still occasionally denied in the literature, that a zero or negative interest rate is in no sense a *logically* contradictory thing, however bizarre may be the *em-pirical* hypotheses that entail a zero or negative rate.

3. It may help us a little to isolate the effects of adding one by one, or together, (*a*) technological investment possibilities, (*b*) innovations that secularly raise productivity and real incomes, (*c*) strong biases toward present goods and against future goods, (*d*) governmental laws and more general collusions than are envisaged in simple laissez faire markets, or (*e*) various aspects of uncertainty. To be sure, other orderings of analysis would also be possible; and these separate processes interact, with the whole not the simple sum of its parts.

4. It points up a fundamental and intrinsic deficiency in a free pricing system, namely, that free pricing gets you on the Pareto-efficiency frontier but by itself has no tendency to get you to positions on the frontier that are ethically optimal in terms of a social welfare function; only by social collusions—of tax, expenditure, fiat, or other type—can an ethical observer hope to end up where he wants to be. (This obvious and ancient point is related to 3*d* above.)

5. The present model enables us to see one "function" of money from a new slant—as a social compact that can provide optimal old age social security. (This is also related to 3*d* above.)

For the rest of this essay, I shall develop aspects of the last two of these themes.

SOCIAL COMPACTS AND THE OPTIMUM

If each man insists on a *quid pro quo*, we apparently continue until the end of time, with each worse off than in the social optimum, biological interest case. Yet how easy it is by a simple change in the rules of the game to get to the optimum. Let mankind enter into a Hobbes-Rousseau social contract in which the

---

$i = m$. The relevant competitive market root is given by

$$x = \frac{2+\lambda}{2} + \sqrt{\frac{(2+\lambda)^2 + 4\lambda}{2}}.$$

Where $m = 0$, $\lambda = 1$, we have $x = 3.303$; for $m \to \infty$, $\lambda \to 0$, $x \to 2$ and $i \to -\frac{1}{2}$; for $m \to -1$, $\lambda \to \infty$, $x \to \infty$ and $i \to -1$. Thus the market rate of interest is always between -1 and $-\frac{1}{2}$, growing as m grows, in agreement with the small husk of truth in our earlier "common-sense explanation."

[16] T. Ophir, of the Massachusetts Institute of Technology and Hebrew University, Jerusalem, has done unpublished work showing how systematic time preference will tend to alter the equilibrium interest rate pattern.

young are assured of their retirement subsistence if they will today support the aged, such support to be guaranteed by a draft on the yet-unborn. Then the social optimum can be achieved within one lifetime, and our equations (14) will become

$$S_1(1, 1) + S_2(1, 1) + S_3(1, 1) = 0$$

from $t = 3$ on.

We economists have been told[17] that what we are to economize on is love or altruism, this being a scarce good in our imperfect world. True enough, in the sense that we want what there is to go as far as possible. But it is also the task of political economy to point out where common rules in the form of self-imposed fiats can attain higher positions on the social welfare functions prescribed for us by ethical observers.

The Golden Rule or Kant's Categorical Imperative (enjoining like people to follow the common pattern that makes each best off) are often not self-enforcing: if all but one obey, the one may gain selfish advantage by disobeying—which is where the sheriff comes in: *we* politically invoke force on *ourselves*, attempting to make an unstable equilibrium a stable one.[18]

Once social coercion or contracting is admitted into the picture, the present problem disappears. The reluctance of the young to give to the old what the old can never themselves directly or indirectly repay is overcome. Yet the young never suffer, since their successors come under the same requirement. Everybody ends better off. It is as simple as that.[19]

[17] D. H. Robertson, *What Does the Economist Maximize?* (a keynote address at the Columbia bicentennial celebrations, May, 1954), published by the Trustees of the University in the *Proceedings of the Conference, 1955* (New York: Doubleday & Co.) and reprinted as chap. ix in D. H. Robertson, *Economic Commentaries* (London: Staples, 1956).

The economics of social collusions is a rich field for analysis, involving fascinating predictive and normative properties. Thus, when society *acts as if* it were maximizing certain functions, we can predict the effect upon equilibrium of specified exogenous disturbances. And certain patterns of thought appropriate to a single mind become appropriate,

[18] Now, admittedly, there is usually lacking in the real world the axis of symmetry needed to make all this an easy process. In a formulation elsewhere, I have shown some of the requirements for an optimal theory of public expenditure of the Sax-Wicksell-Lindahl-Musgrave-Bowen type, and the failure of the usual voting and signaling mechanisms to converge to an optimum solution (see "The Pure Theory of Public Expenditure," *Review of Economics and Statistics*, XXXVI [November, 1954], 387–89, and "Diagrammatic Exposition of Public Expenditure," *ibid.*, XXXVII [November, 1955], 350–56). Such a model is poles apart from the pure case in which Walrasian laissez faire happens to be optimal. I should be prepared to argue that a good deal of what is important and interesting in the real world lies between these extreme poles, perhaps in between in the sense of displaying properties that are a blending of the polar properties. But such discussion must await another time.

[19] How can the competitive configuration with negative interest rates be altered to everyone's advantage? Does not this deny the Pareto optimality of perfect competition, which is the least (and most) we can expect from it? Here we encounter one more paradox, which no doubt arises from the "infinity" aspect of our model. If we assume a large finite span to the human race—say 1 million generations—then the final few generations face the equations

$$S_1(R_{T-1}, \infty) + S_2(R_{T-2}, R_{T-1})$$
$$+ S_3(R_{T-3}, R_{T-2}) = 0,$$
$$S_2(R_{T-1}, \infty) + S_3(R_{T-2}, R_{T-1}) + 0 = 0,$$
$$S_3(R_{T-1}, \infty) + 0 + 0 = 0,$$

$$\text{where} \quad T = 1,000,000.$$

If we depart from the negative interest rate pattern, the final young will be cheated by the demise of the human race. Should such a cheating of one generation 30 million years from now perpetually condemn society to a suboptimal configuration? Perfect competition shrugs its shoulders at such a question and (not improperly) sticks to its Pareto optimality.

even though we reject the notion of a group mind. (Example: developed social security could give rise to the same bias toward increasing population that exists among farmers and close family groups, where children are wanted as a means of old age support.)

The economics of collusion provides an important field of study for the theorist. Such collusions can be important elements of strength in the struggle for existence. Reverence for life, in the Schweitzer sense of respecting ants and flowers, might be a handicap in the Darwinian struggle for existence. (And, since the reverencer tends to disappear, the ants may not be helped much in the long run.) But culture in which altruism abounds—because men do not think to behave like atomistic competitors or because men have by custom and law entered into binding social contracts—may have great survival and expansion powers.

An essay could be written on the welfare state as a complicated device for self- or reinsurance. (From this view, the graduated income tax becomes in part a device for reducing *ex ante* variance.) That the Protestant Ethic should have been instrumental in creating individualistic capitalism one may accept; but that it should stop there is not necessarily plausible.[20] What made Jeremy Bentham a Benthamite in 1800, one suspects, might in 1900 have made him a Fabian (and do we not see a lot in common in the personalities of James Mill and Friedrich Engels?).

Much as you and I may dislike government "interferences" in economic life, we must face the positive fact that the moti-

vations for higher living standards that a free market channels into Walrasian equilibrium when the special conditions for that pattern happen to be favorable —these same motivations often lead to social collusions and myriad uses of the apparatus of the state. For good or evil, these may not be aberrations from laissez faire, but theorems entailed by its intrinsic axioms.

CONCLUSION: MONEY AS A SOCIAL CONTRIVANCE

Let me conclude by applying all these considerations to an analysis of the role of money in our consumption-loan world. In it nothing kept. All ice melted, and so did all chocolates. (If non-depletable land existed, it must have been superabundant.) Workers could not carry goods over into their retirement years.

There is no arguing with Nature. But what is to stop man—or rather men— from printing oblongs of paper or stamping circles of shell. These units of money can keep.[21] (Even if ink fades, this could be true.) With ideal clearing arrangements, money as a medium of exchange might have little function. But remember that a money medium of exchange is itself a rather efficient clearing arrangement.

So suppose men officially through the state, or unofficially through custom, make a grand consensus on the use of these greenbacks as a money of exchange. Now the young and middle-aged do have something to hold and to carry over into their retirement years. And note this: as long as the new current generations of

---

[20] Recall the Myrdal thesis that the austere planned economies of Europe are Protestant, the Catholic countries being individualistic.

[21] I have been asked whether introducing durable money does not violate my fiat against durable goods and trades with Nature. All that I must insist on is that the new durable moneys (or records) be themselves quite worthless for consumption. The essence of them as money is that they are valued only for what they will fetch in exchange.

workers do not repudiate the old money, this gives workers of one epoch a claim on workers of a later epoch, even though no real *quid pro quo* (other than money) is possible.

We then find this remarkable fact: without legislating social security or entering into elaborate social compacts, society by using money will go from the non-optimal negative-interest-rate configuration to the optimal biological-interest-rate configuration. How does this happen? I shall try to give only a sketchy account that does not pretend to be rigorous.

Take the stationary population case with $m = 0$. With total money M constant and the flow of goods constant, the price level can be expected very soon to level off and be constant. The productive invest their hump savings in currency; in their old age they disinvest this currency, turning it over to the productive workers in return for sustenance.

With population growing like $(1 + m)^t$, output will come to grow at that rate. Fixed M will come to mean prices falling like $1/(1 + m)^t$. Each dollar saved today will thus yield a *real* rate of interest of exactly m per period—just what the biological social-optimality configuration calls for. Similarly, when $m < 0$ and population falls, rising prices will create the desired negative real rate of interest equal to m.

In short, the use of money can itself be regarded as a social compact.[22] When economists say that one of the functions of money is to act as a store of wealth and that one of money's desirable properties is constancy of value (as measured by constancy of average prices), we are entitled to ask: How do you know this? Why *should* prices be stable? On what tablets is that injunction written? Perhaps the function of money, if it is to serve as an optimal store of wealth, is so to change in its value as to create that optimal pattern of lifetime saving which could otherwise be established only by alternative social contrivances.[23]

I do not pretend to pass judgment on the policies related to all this. But I do suggest for economists' further research the difficult analysis of capital models which grapple with the fact that each and every today is followed by a tomorrow.

[22] In terms of immediate self-interest the existing productive workers should perhaps unilaterally repudiate the money upon which the aged hope to live in retirement. (Compare the Russian and Belgium calling-in of currencies.) So a continuing social compact is required. (Compare, too, current inflationary trends which do give the old less purchasing power than many of them had counted on.)

[23] Conversely, with satisfactory social security programs, the necessity for having secular stable prices so that the retired are taken care of can be lightened. Even after extreme inflations, social security programs can re-create themselves anew astride the community's indestructible real tax base.

22

REPLY

PAUL A. SAMUELSON

Massachusetts Institute of Technology

BECAUSE Professor Lerner has made so many important contributions to modern economics, I am pleased to welcome his entrance into the discussion of some of the problems raised by my analysis of an exact consumption-loan interest model under the abstract condition that no goods can be preserved physically through time. Such a dynamic problem, involving as it does the infinity of time and the almost philosophical problems raised by the presence or absence of "perfect certainty," is to me one of the most difficult in all economics, and I regard my own paper as a first tentative effort in a field that needs much cultivation.

For both these reasons I should not have felt too much chagrin if it were pointed out that I had made a boner in the course of my mathematical and logical discussion. It would not have been my first, and, considering the difficulties of the subject matter, I should have been able to find my consolations. But after reading Lerner's paper twice, I remain stubbornly convinced that my only plea to the crime he charges me with is "Not guilty."

Specifically, the biological rate of interest,

which is equal to the rate of growth of a population that always follows an exponential law, seems to me, upon re-examination, definitely to have the optimality property that I asserted for it and that I proved about it: *it does give every representative man in such a society a lifetime consumption profile that he would prefer over any other one available to him and everyone else.* (This theorem does not assert that there are not other definitions of an optimum in terms of which the biological interest rate represents a deviation.)

Lerner says and resays many things that we can both agree with completely, and the only real issue between us that I can discern is whether or not my biological interest rate has the optimality property that I asserted for it. Of course, even if it should prove that I am right in my contention, it may well be that I should be ashamed of myself for having been so unclear in my exposition as to have led at least one astute economist into a misunderstanding of my meaning. And I might wish to reproach myself, too, that I had not anticipated Lerner's discussion of a quite different meaning of an "optimum" and had not related the two quite different concepts.

I shall try here briefly to clarify these issues.

II

To simplify the exposition of the issue under contention, I can here confine myself to the two-dimensional case in which each identical person works one period of his life producing one unit and then lives an equal length of time in total retirement. For the reasons given in my paper, such a simplification to fewer than three periods of life would not have been legitimate in my general discussion, but I believe it will do no harm here. It has the advantage of being graphable, and if the denial that the biological interest rate has the stipulated optimality property is right, I shall be just as guilty of logical error in the two-period case as in any other.

As before, I assume that the representative man has an ordinal utility preference field for the consumptions of the two periods of his life that can be written in the form $U = U(C_1, C_2)$; this has the usual convexity properties on its indifference curves, two of which are drawn in Figure 1. I need make no special assumptions about time preference; but, to sharpen the issues, Figure 1 is drawn with the special property that

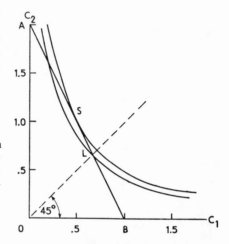

FIG. 1.—The biological interest rate at S gives each man a higher utility level than does the L point of equal C's and zero interest rate.

there is no systematic time preference for present over future or vice versa, the indifference contours being symmetric about the 45° line of equal C's. Although in all realistic problems involving time, one must be prepared for a substantive divergence between *ex ante* preferences and *ex post* evaluations, for the present purpose we can waive the difficulty and rule out all "myopia" effects of the Böhm-Strotz type.

My last heroic abstraction is the assumption of a population of identical men that has always grown and will always grow at an algebraic percentage rate of m per period, its total number being proportional to $(1 + m)^t$, where m positive means compound interest growth, m zero means stationary population, and m a negative fraction means radioactive decay. This idealization of an infinite past and future is central to my discussion, and it divorces matters not only from realism but also from some of the more simple forms of intuitive reasoning.

III

My paper chose to confine itself to the case in which there are no social compacts and the case in which the use of money is the only social compact. However, I have no wish or need to rule out other forms of social contrivances. So I am very glad to introduce lump-sum taxes and transfers

TABLE 1

ALTERNATIVE FEASIBLE ALLOTMENTS
(PER CAPITA)

Workers, C_1.....	1	$\frac{2}{3}$	$\frac{1}{2}$*	$\frac{1}{3}$	0
Retired, C_2.....	0	$\frac{2}{3}$	1*	$\frac{4}{3}$	2

* Optimal solution for $U(C_1, C_2) = \log C_1 + \log C_2$.

(or pensions) that are coercive programs introduced by unanimous vote of the identical individuals upon themselves. Such a pension-tax device could be used, without reference to any use of money, to realize the biological interest rate or any other configuration, and it permits us to scan all feasible configurations to appraise whatever optimality properties they may have.[1]

For definiteness, imagine a population doubling every period, so that $m = 1$ and so that there are always twice as many people in the first period of work as in the second period of retirement. By suitable tax and pension plans we can divide the existing production of goods in any proportions we like between the workers and the retired. How much per head of each class is possible? By giving no consumption to

[1] I daresay that I could think of still other social contrivances besides money or pensions that might be used to arrive at any feasible point in Fig. 1. In particular, I stand my ground that the biological interest rate $i = m$ is a statical *market* rate of interest: i.e., the statical excess-demand-for-saving curve does cross the vertical axis of equilibrium at $i = m$, even if, from a dynamic viewpoint, that may represent an unstable equilibrium. This was shown by my equations (9) and (8′) and is affirmable from the present diagram.

the retired, the representative worker can have his C_1 be the 1 he produces. At the other extreme, by giving none to workers, we could give the retired a C_2 per capita of 2, there being two workers for every retired man. In between these two extreme cases, there exist an infinity of intermediate linear combinations, of which Table 1 shows but a few.

The equation of this special kind of "budget equation" for society is, of course,

$$2C_1 + 1C_2 = 2 ,$$

or

$$(1+m) C_1 + 1C_2 = (1+m) 1 ,$$

for the reasons that were made clear in the discussion of my equation (12).

The heavy line AB in Figure 1 depicts this special social "budget equation." Its absolute slope is 2—or $(1+m)$ in the general case, being a negative 45° line if $m = 0$ and even flatter if population is actually declining.

IV

Now "the kind of a social optimum" that I conceived of was in the spirit of Kant's Categorical Imperative: *What common rule or configuration would, if it were to be established for every representative man by universal (self-imposed) fiat, lead each representative man to the highest point on his preference field?*

Note that I have not presumed that utility is numerically measurable. On that I need not pronounce. Nor have I had to resort to adding the utilities of different minds, the utility of today's worker to that of today's oldster (or of today's other worker). I am working completely on the typical individual's level, letting his preferences be the relevant norms in terms of which the optimality theorem is to be stated. This does not deny others, or me, the right to consider at another time the maximization of some quite different social welfare function.

In terms of Table 1, what configuration for (C_1, C_2) that is to be enjoyed by *every* individual from the beginning to the end of time will represent the maximum of his ("lifetime") $U(C_1, C_2)$? This depends on the form of his indifference curves: if they are the rectangular hyperbolas shown in Figure 1, corresponding to my illustrative case of logarithmic utility $U(C_1, C_2) = \log C_1 + \log C_2$, the starred configuration,

$$C_1 = \frac{1}{2}, \quad C_2 = 1, \quad i = m = 1,$$

is the optimal answer to the problem I posed.[2]

This is seen in Figure 1 by the tangency of the budget line AB to the highest indifference contour at the "Samuelson" point S. Note the contrast of this S point with the "Lerner" point L, where i = 0, $C_1 = C_2$. As described in my previous footnote, such a Lerner point maximizes an interpersonal summed current utility that is not depicted on my representative individual's lifetime diagram.

What the diagram does show is that a society which has always been, and will always be, organized on the basis of Lerner's optimality prescription will yield for every man that ever lives a *lower* position of lifetime well-being (as each man evaluates his own well-being *ex ante*) than will a society organized on my optimality prescription. I do not say my biological optimum is better than his, for I am not donning the mantle of an ethical prescriber. But I do say that my optimality point has the properties asserted and proved for it—in my original paper and again here.

V

Those who have had trouble in grasping my theorem and its limitations may impute to me an error I never made. They may argue: "A chocolate is a chocolate is a chocolate. At any one time society moves on a negative 45° substitution line. Samuel-

[2] Lerner puts "the" optimum at $(C_1, C_2) = (\frac{2}{3}, \frac{2}{3})$, which is the solution to a quite different mathematical maximizing problem:

Subject to $2C_1 + C_2 = 2$,

maximize today's total cardinal utility of society got by adding every living man's current utility, i.e.,

Maximize $2U(C_1) + 1U(C_2)$.

Ask a different question, and you get a different answer. Because $2 + 3 = 5$, it does not follow that I err in stating that $2 + 2 = 4$.

son's steeper 'social budget equation' AB is a myth, a fable, a fairy tale, a pretense, a slip in logic in which meaningless consumption substitutions *across time* between a man and himself when old are confused for solid contemporaneous substitutions."

I shamelessly deny all the charges. Not for a moment have I forgotten that a chocolate is a chocolate and that physical goods are, by hypothesis, completely perishable. It is precisely for the reason that all contemporaneous transfers between young and old must be along the negative 45° line that when we consider the consumption profile available to the representative man over time, we must use a steeper line. For next period's retirement consumption must come out of next period's product, produced by more numerous others. For the representative-man Categorical-Imperative maximum problem, the alternatives depicted by AB *are* the relevant ones by virtue of the postulated symmetries, and no critic should for a moment confuse cross-sectional identities with lifetime relations. My earlier discussion of equation (27) and the "kind of social optimum" achieved by the biological interest rate seems to me to stand up completely to any criticism that can be made against its logic.[3]

VI

Without committing myself to the strict Benthamite assumption needed to justify adding cardinal utilities across persons of different ages, let me try to resolve the following paradox that has arisen: A Lerner policy, which maximizes at each period society's total current utility, results in everyone's always being worse off over his life than he would have been in the biological optimum. Since society's utility is the sum

[3] The case of a declining population where $m < 0$, say, where $(1 + m) = \frac{1}{2}$, I leave to the interested reader. He can show that the Lerner configuration gives every man $U = \log \frac{1}{3} + \log \frac{1}{3} = \log \frac{1}{9}$ over his lifetime, while my biological optimum gives him $U = \log \frac{1}{2} + \log \frac{1}{4} = \log (\frac{1}{8}) > \log \frac{1}{9}$. Also, in the three-period case where numbers double every period, the biological optimum gives each man log $\frac{1}{2} + \log 1 + \log 2 = \log 1 > 3 \log \frac{2}{3}$, the Lerner optimum.

of every individual's, how is this contradiction possible?

The source of the paradox lies, of course, in the *infinity* that my model postulates. Therein lies the only fairy tale I plead guilty of. In the case of a growing population, society's total of utility over all time is a *divergent* infinite sum. Frank Ramsey, or a mathematician, would call this an "improper" problem—not thereby implying a breach in etiquette in considering it.

Still the Benthamite policy of $C_1 = C_2$ at every time and $i = 0$ will *in every period* give more *total social utility* than will any other policy. This I do not deny and have never denied. Nor need I in this case worry about the problem that bothered such Benthamites as Sidgwick and Edgeworth— Should we maximize individual utility per head or total utility of the universe?—for population is already prescribed in my problem.

If we were to reckon the total of social utility enjoyed throughout all the past, the Benthamite can calculate this as a convergent infinite sum in the case of a growing exponential population. Suppose he were to alter the ground rules of my model and ask: "What configuration imposed on all will give us the maximum social utility *already* enjoyed up to this prescribed time and which we are anxious to have maximized on the supposition that society were to be wound up at this instant?" My answer to this problem, and Lerner's answer, would be the Lerner optimum configuration of $C_1 = C_2$, $i = 0$.

True, all the individuals who have *completed* their lifetimes have been worse off than in the Samuelson configuration. But in an exponentially growing population, the single-period present has finite weight compared to the summed infinite past! (In the case of a population that doubles every period, the workers now alive equal in number *all* the people who have ever retired and are twice as numerous as all those who have already died.) So if we were to alter the rules of the game and now wind up society abruptly, the utility enjoyed today by the workers who are not going to

live to enjoy any utility in the last part of their lives would be so great on the Benthamite solution as to more than compensate for the lower living standards of all those who have ever died or are now about to die naturally.

All this quite reminds us of other paradoxes-of-the-infinite associated with growing exponentials. I refer to the Ruml pay-as-you-go plan paradox: if taxable income grows exponentially, forgiving last year's tax and collecting this year's tax contemporaneously will not lose the Treasury any cash revenues but will, on the contrary, for the rest of time increase Treasury revenues. The same mathematics is involved in the Domar paradox of accelerated depreciation: such a policy is not so much an interest-free loan to an ever growing firm as it is a "permanent gift."

To repeat my resolution of the paradoxical fact that maximizing each man's completed-life utility differs in an exponential process from maximizing total social utility: under the last policy, the extra utility enjoyed by the current young who have *incomplete* lives outweighs the loss to those with completed lives.[4]

VII

In defending the logic of my own exposition, I hope I shall not be construed as belittling Lerner's contribution. Who knows, if I read his paper a third time, I might become convinced of the errors of my way.

---

[4] Mathematically, let $B_t = (1 + m)^t$ and $U = U_1(C_1) + U_2(C_2)$. The social utility enjoyed by society *up to time t* under any stationary (C_1, C_2) configuration is

$$SU_t = [(1 + m)^t U_1 (C_1)]$$
$$+ [U_1 (C_1) + U_2 (C_2)] [(1 + m)^{t-1}$$
$$+ (1 + m)^{t-2} + \ldots]$$
$$= \frac{(1 + m)^t}{m} [(1 + m) U_1 (C_1)$$
$$+ U_2 (C_2)] ;$$

and, subject to the budget equation

$$(1 + m) C_1 + C_2 = (1 + m) ,$$

this is at its maximum, as Lerner and one of my earlier footnotes show, when $C_1 = C_2$ and $i = 0$.

The first expression in brackets represents the crucially growing terminal utility of those with incomplete lives.

23

INFINITY, UNANIMITY, AND SINGULARITY: A REPLY[1]

PAUL A. SAMUELSON

Massachusetts Institute of Technology

Some years ago at the Boston Christmas meetings I gave a rather innocuous talk on the uses of mathematics in economics. When it was over, my friend Robert Bishop met an old teacher of mine and asked him how he liked the talk. "I didn't like it," was the reply. When interrogated as to what it was he did not like about it, he stated: "Well, it wasn't so much what Samuelson said as what I knew he was thinking."

I suspect that most of the very interesting criticisms of my consumption-loan paper stem more from an extrapolation of what was alleged to have been in my mind than from a literal reading of my logical and mathematical theorems. But there has been sufficient discussion raised by my paper—in print and by correspondence with some of our leading economists—to suggest that the last word has not yet been said on the subject.

In particular, I welcome the chance to discuss the point raised by Meckling[2] as to whether the multiple solution to the statical equilibrium, in the form of my biological interest rate, incorrectly translates the "facts" of my model. In terms of the distinctions I am accustomed to make between statical—dynamical and stable—unstable equilibrium solutions, I do not feel impelled to alter my formulation. But there is an interesting semantic difference involved here, and I shall not presume to be dogmatic.

Because this reply must be briefer than I should like, it may fail to indicate the full measure of my great respect for the quality of Meckling's reasoning.

I

Let me first note that the last part of Meckling's discussion coincides for the most part with the analytical point of Lerner: namely, that what I have proved to be "optimal" for the representative individual in a population that has always been (and will always be) exponentially changing will cease to be valid if there is the danger or cer-

[1] Appreciation to the Ford Foundation for research aid is gratefully acknowledged.

[2] W. H. Meckling, "An Exact Consumption-Loan Model of Interest: A Comment," pp. 72–76 above.

tainty that the exponential process will change to some other mode of population growth.[3] This is not, properly understood, a criticism of my theorem, which clearly stated the hypothesis under which its optimality conclusion was true. The resulting paradoxes of my theorem stem from the infinity of time at the beginning and its infinity at the end. I announced these paradoxes but am not morally responsible for their existence and as a messenger do not deserve to have my head chopped off for bringing the news. Still, I must affirm that Lerner and Meckling render valuable service in calling attention to the difficulties on the side of "realism" involved in the assumption of an ever exponential process.[4]

Quite apart from defense or attack of my model, this part of the discussion raises a question very important for sociology and policy. When diminishing returns is not pressing on a society so that it is quite capable of exponential growth, the Darwinian process of each representative individual's seeking his own well-being may cause certain habits and institutions to be formed; for example, because parents can maximize *their* old age security by having many children, such a habit may be formed. And, so long as the exponential is possible, there may be no apparent harm or even inequity in this. But diminishing returns may be slowly at work, even though not apparent as a response to each atomistic individual's behavior; and, in any case, diminishing returns may later come strongly into play. There must then eventually result a modi-

fication of the conditions of the exponential. Now, aside from the resulting interpersonal equity problem between the generations, there may well be the noteworthy problem of "cultural lag," in which the modes of behavior of one epoch are painfully clung to even after the time for them is past.

II

While Meckling and Lerner are agreed on the analytic point dealing with the cessation of exponential growth, they are quite at odds on the appropriate policy for a stationary state. Lerner is for redistributing incomes from young to old to equalize each man's marginal (social and individual) utility. I judge Meckling to be somewhat hostile to this Benthamite solution, essentially on these grounds: *introducing such a redistributive scheme into a society that will not always remain stationary must hurt at least one man, so such a scheme cannot be unanimously voted in.* (The italicized words are not Meckling's, but they do represent a valid theorem that was already implicit in my paper and which can be proved by the consideration that a competitive solution arising between a *finite* number of men is Pareto-optimal and that any departure from it must hurt at least one man.)

Neither Bentham nor Lerner would be deterred by this objection. They are for the redistribution because it will add to their defined total of social utility, not worrying unduly that it will hurt some and help others provided that those who are helped add more to the total utility than those who are hurt.[5]

This is an ancient debate that can be judged only in terms of the social welfare function brought to it by the judger. So there is no need for me to pronounce on it. There is, though, one aspect of the welfare question that is related to the recursive time nature of my analytical discussion and was

---

[3] While Lerner balks at the prospect of perpetual exponential growth, if only for the reason that in cosmologist Lerner's view the universe is finite, it is interesting that Meckling balks at the thought of an ever stationary process. I myself would balk most strongly at the case of $m < 1$ and exponential decay, for that means, so to speak, that once upon a time there was an infinite population.

[4] In "Intertemporal Price Equilibrium: A Prologue to the Theory of Speculation," *Weltwirtschaftliches Archiv*, LXXIX (1957), 215–16, I had already called attention to the self-perpetuating "swindle" aspect of a continuing exponential process.

[5] The point that redistribution may not properly go all the way if it has adverse effects on efficiency and involves "deadweight loss" is so obvious that I relegate it to a footnote.

already commented on in footnote 19 of my original paper.

Laissez faire competitive pricing will, teleologically speaking, condemn a society to a negative interest-rate configuration that leaves, say, thousands of generations at a sub-Bentham optimum in order that the single terminal generation's property rights not be infringed. Now it would be wrong to think that these thousands of generations could transfer goods so as to bribe the terminal generation into a move nearer toward the Benthamite zero-interest optimum—for the negative interest-rate configuration is Pareto-optimal for any finite collection of people.[6] But even those who think the simple adding of Bentham utilities rather näive may be likely, as the time for which society exists grows larger and larger, to favor a move toward the zero-interest configuration. This result could be formulated in terms of a rigorous theorem, but I shall here take the time only to word it loosely: Any welfare function that makes social welfare a function of the separate commensurate welfares of different individuals will, if it gives no preponderate weight to the welfare of any one generation of men, achieve its optimum nearer and nearer the zero-interest configuration as the length of society's existence grows larger and larger. The proof would go something like this: If one is still large relative to thousands, it is smaller relative to millions, or billions, etc. (Note that this hypothesis

[6] Here and earlier I pedantically append the words "for a finite collection of people" because in the case of the infinite collection involved in the abstraction of a forever stationary or exponential population a comparison of the biological interest rate with a stationary negative interest rate shows that *each* person is better off in the former state. In the artificial case of an infinite collection, the rules of Pareto optimality have to be reformulated—a fact which was to me one of the most surprising outcomes of my paper.

Incidentally, since the Bentham point is a competitive equilibrium after lump-sum redistribution has taken place, no separate proof of its Pareto-optimality is needed; and one must, of course, choose between different Pareto-optimal points in terms of one's social welfare function.

rules out the discontinuity that would be involved in the possible assumption that any one soul has a unique right and sanctity.)

III

I now turn to a quite different issue from that of optimality questions and the problems created by dropping the assumption of the infinity of future time for our society. The first two-thirds of Meckling's comment has little overlap with Lerner's discussion. Formally, it might be characterized as worrying about what happens, not when we drop the infinity assumption concerning the future, but when we question the infinity assumption with respect to the indefinite past.

Everyone is agreed that a negative interest rate, $1 < R = 1/(1 + i)$, will give a *statical* equilibrium solution to the competitive equations of supply and demand for all cases where there is no systematic subjective preference for the future over the present. What is at issue is whether my biological interest rate, which in the case of a stationary population implies zero interest with $R = 1$, is also a *statical* equilibrium interest rate. This I assert. This Meckling questions.

I have italicized the word "statical" because it is in terms of a strict definition of this concept that all of my discussion has been formulated. Using the word in the strict sense in which I have always used it, I reaffirm that $R = 1$ is a statical equilibrium—which is not to deny that someone else is not free to alter his definitions, provided that we all understand the differences in our terminology.

By a statical equilibrium price, I mean one which, *if it had ever been established and without regard to the dynamic process by which it was established*, would clear the market and would continue to clear the market. Thus an intersection of supply and demand curves in a dynamically stable way represents a statical equilibrium; so too does an intersection of such curves in a dynamically unstable way—that is, an intersection which, if dynamically disturbed, would be run away from by the system in all subsequent time, and one which could never have been dynamically established.[7] While the determination of the dynamic stability and behavior of a system will involve the solution of various functional equations in time (differential, difference, or integral equations), the determination of statical equilibrium points will usually involve the timeless solution of ordinary algebraic or implicit equations for their roots.

By definition I mean (and have always meant) by the set of statical solutions for R to the interest model the set of all roots of the following relations:

$$S_1(R,R) + S_2(R,R) + S_3(R,R) = 0 \quad (1)$$

$$S_1(R,R) + RS_2(R,R) + R^2 S_3(R,R) \equiv 0 \quad (2)$$

where the last is an identity in R reflecting the fact that the S_i functions are not independent. These are, respectively, relations (4) and (5) of my original paper applied to the statical equilibrium problem as on page 471 of that paper. They are also essentially equations (6) and (3) of Meckling.

One infers on sight that $R = 1$ is indeed a root of the equation system (1) and (2), a formal truth that has not so much to do with the "economic facts" of my model but is concerned only with the deductive properties of my strict definition of what constitutes statical equilibrium. The fact that $R = 1$ is a root independently of the form of man's utility function is, as Meckling suggests, a remarkable one. But, rather than causing us to deny the truth that $R = 1$ is a root, this remarkable fact merely adds to our appreciation of the remarkable nature of the biological interest rate. At least that has always been my reaction to it.

To relate all this to Meckling's discussion, let us combine my (1) an d(2) above as follows: multiply (1) by R and subtract it from (2). After rearrangement this gives

[7] See my *Foundations of Economic Analysis* (Cambridge, Mass.: Harvard University Press, 1949), Part II, for a discussion of dynamics and statics.

$$(1-R) S_1(R,R) = (1-R) RS_3(R,R). \quad (3)$$

This is almost the Bailey formula given in my footnote 13 and denoted by Meckling's equation (8). Almost but not quite. For the factor $(1-R)$ has not yet been canceled from both sides of (3). As Bailey and I pointed out, on the proviso that $R \neq 1$, we can perform such a cancellation to get

$$S_1(R,R) = RS_3(R,R) \quad (3')$$

which is Meckling's (8).

Now it is true that any root of (3') is a root of the system (1)−(2), but not vice versa. Only if we adjoin to (3') the relation

$$(1-R) = 0 \quad (3'')$$

can we say that (3') and (3'') give *all* the roots of (1)−(2) or of, what is the same thing, the legitimate (3).

Pointing out this singular case where $R = 1$ would imply division by zero, and illegitimate cancellation is not a pedantic quibble but is at the heart of the matter. Here is an analogy: When we factor the quadratic equation $x^2 - 1 = 0$ (into $(x+1)(x-1) = 0$, we would illegitimately lose the root $x = -1$ were we to cancel $(x+1)$ and end up with $(x-1) = 0$ and $x = +1$ as the alleged full solution.[8]

[8] Analogies prove nothing, but here is one that seems analytically exact. You have a pump with a dry leather valve. There are two statical equilibriums possible: one with zero output of water; another where somehow you get some initial water to "prime" the pump and which is followed by a steady capacity flow. I have argued that you cannot exclude the latter equilibrium as a *statical* equilibrium.

A similar phenomenon turns up in Neumann-Leontief dynamic input-output systems. Let labor be exogenously given by $L(t) \equiv L$, a prescribed constant. And let machines and labor, $K(t)$ and L, produce machines one period later according to the Douglas production function $K(t+1) = L^{.75}K(t)^{.25}$, and in no other way. Then there are two statical equilibriums: $K(t) \equiv 0$ and $K(\infty) = 1 \cdot L$. From initial conditions $K(0) = 0$, only the zero level can be reached because, without a beginning machine, nothing can be produced. But from any positive

IV

It would be absurd for me to imagine that Meckling is not fully aware of the above algebraic facts. Rather, I suspect, is he concerned with a different concept of statical equilibrium than the one I have strictly defined. From my definition the Meckling situation $S_1(1, 1) = -1$, where the young consume in the first period of life all their lifetime income, is odd but quite compatible with statical equilibrium—whereas Meckling thinks it logically absurd, presumably on the grounds that the *first* generation of human beings could never have overconsumed in this fashion because there could not have been anyone else around to provide them with the surplus consumers' goods beyond what they had themselves produced. But the problem of how a statical equilibrium could ever have gotten started is not germane to the issue of whether it is in truth a statical equilibrium, however relevant it is for dynamic stability. If you came upon a system which had somehow gotten into the equilibrium $S_1(1, 1) = -1 = -S_2(1, 1) - S_3(1, 1)$, you would find that it would persist in that situation, with the dissaving of older groups always exactly clearing the auctioneer's surplus of first-period saving.[9]

In my strict vision of a statical equilibrium, I envisage an auctioneer who clears markets. There is no bilateralization of exchange: specific individuals do not contract with other specific living individuals; all contract impersonally with the central clearing mechanism, whose only duty is to find an over-all meshing of net *totals*. If, at a profile

initial $K(0)$, $K(t) \to 1 \cdot L$ as $t \to \infty$. (The fourth-degree algebraic equation for statical equilibrium yields two other complex equilibriums $L[-1 \pm \sqrt{3}i]/2$, but they are economically meaningless.)

[9] Incidentally, some correspondents have written to me that, while the biological interest rate—here $R = 1$—is determined independently of tastes, the "distribution of income" is not. But this is as one should expect: it does not mean that the distribution of income is undetermined at $R = 1$ but rather that it is well determined *after* we know tastes and have the specified saving functions $S_i(1, 1)$.

of constant interest rates now and in the future, total positive loans add up to total negative loans so that net savings are zero—and if this situation can *thereafter* repeat itself—I call that interest rate a statical equilibrium one. Whether others prefer to use some other definitions does not matter much, provided we and scholars generally understand the senses in which the words are used.

But there is a more substantive issue here relevant to welfare economics. Most readers have interpreted my analysis to have uncovered a defect in the competitive pricing mechanism of laissez faire in terms of conceivable optima. However, in denying that my biological optimum is a statical equilibrium, a critic is in danger of going too far and losing sight of the following important technical fact: after there had been an appropriate *initial* interference with a laissez faire regime—perhaps involving transient fiats and algebraic lump-sum payments—the laissez faire mechanism of clearing the market of net loans could be counted on to realize the biological optimum in all subsequent periods. (This is not to deny that the biological optimum is dynamically unrealizable by itself, starting from scratch and without interference.)

Leaving the question of purely statical equilibrium, one can agree with Meckling that $R = 1$ is not a stable equilibrium that will be dynamically approached starting from scratch. But this fact must not be considered as a point against me. For that is precisely what I demonstrate in my paper: my Impossibility Theorem, stability analysis, two-period discussion, and numerical example aimed to bring out precisely the important fact of life that a negative interest rate with $R > 1$ could be expected to prevail under laissez faire competition.

It is to the "dynamic" issue that Meckling has made a real contribution. And I must take off my hat to him for having shown how the Bailey approach of (3′) above can throw new light on the asymptotic level of interest that will be approached by a system starting from scratch and thereafter being stationary. The following discussion will follow his lead and try to advance the matter a little farther.

Our dynamic equations starting from the beginning are

$$S_1(R_1, R_2) + 0 + 0 = 0$$
$$S_2(R_1, R_2) + S_1(R_2, R_3) + 0 = 0 \quad (4a)$$

. . . .

$$S_3(R_{t-2}, R_{t-1}) + S_2(R_{t-1}, R_t)$$
$$+ S_1(R_t, R_{t+1}) = 0 \quad (4b)$$

. . . .

Relation (4b) is a third-order difference equation, which holds for all integral $t \geq 3$, and (4a) represents the initial or boundary condition needed to help make the system as a whole determine a unique solution for all the future.

Now, as we have seen, to determine all the stationary solutions of (4b) alone, we substitute into it $R_t \equiv R$ and get the roots of both (3') and (3''). But that does not mean that the combined determinate system will approach *both* of these asymptotes. Actually, it can at most approach one of them; and, except in the case of my special numerical example, we must leave it as an open question whether *either* statical R will be approached asymptotically by the solution to (4). What Meckling has cleverly shown is that the complete system (4) can, if it approaches any asymptote, approach only that R which is a root of (3').

To give an illuminating variant of his inductive proof, use the budget identity

$$S_1(R_{t-1}, R_t) + R_{t-1} S_2(R_{t-1}, R_t)$$
$$+ R_{t-1} R_t S_3(R_{t-1}, R_t) \equiv 0$$

to eliminate the S_2 function from (4). The resulting form of (4) can be written

$$S_1(R_1, R_2) = 0$$
$$[S_1(R_2, R_3) - R_2 S_3(R_1, R_2)] = 0 \quad (4a')$$

. . . .

$$[S_1(R_t, R_{t+1}) - R_t S_3(R_{t-1}, R_t)]$$
$$= \frac{1}{R_{t-1}}[S_1(R_{t-1}, R_t) \quad (4b')$$
$$- R_{t-1} S_3(R_{t-2}, R_{t-1})].$$

Now it will be convenient to regard the expression in square brackets as a new symbol

$$Y_t = [S_1(R_t, R_{t+1}) - R_t S_3(R_{t-1}, R_t)]$$
$$= f(R_{t+1}, R_t, R_{t-1}), \quad (5)$$

which is a specified function of three adjacent periods' interest rates. In terms of this symbol, (4) becomes

$$S_1(R_1, R_2) = 0$$
$$Y_2 = 0 \quad (4a'')$$

. . . .

$$Y_t = \frac{1}{R_{t-1}} Y_{t-1}. \quad (4b'')$$

. . . .

From (4b'') alone it is evident that $Y_3 = (1/R_2)Y_2$, $Y_4 = (1/R_2 R_o)Y_2$, . . . , and, generally,

$$Y_t = \frac{1}{R_{t-1}R_{t-2}\ldots R_3 R_2} Y_2. \quad (6)$$

Hence the initial condition that $Y_2 = 0$ means that all subsequent Y's must vanish. So $Y_t \equiv 0$ might be called an invariant of the motion defined by the complete (4). Thus Meckling has in effect shown that, for the special initial conditions of (4a) or (4a''), our interest rates must satisfy the simpler second-order difference relation

$$[S_1(R_t, R_{t+1}) - R_t S_3(R_{t-1}, R_t)] \equiv 0. \quad (7)$$

And now, as Meckling observes, the only possible stationary asymptote for (4) must satisfy the earlier Bailey relation

$$[S_1(R, R) - R S_3(R, R)] = 0. \quad (3')$$

Without subtracting from the worth of the Meckling analysis of the dynamic behavior of my (4), I must point out the singular razor's-edge nature of this general result.

Were one to vary the initial conditions of (4a) ever so little, one would lose the $Y_2 = 0$ property upon which the Meckling invariant depended. Thus it would have been perfectly permissible for me to have started off the stationary population gradually, with the first generation's being *half* the size of all subsequent ones. This would give as an alternative to (4a)

$$\tfrac{1}{2}S_1(R_1, R_2) = 0$$

$$\tfrac{1}{2}S_2(R_1, R_2) + 1 \cdot S_1(R_2, R_3) = 0 ,$$

which in turn implies

$$Y_2 = [S_1(R_2, R_3) - R_2 S_3(R_1, R_2)]$$

$$= -\tfrac{1}{2}R_2 S_3(R_1, R_2) ,$$

which is generally *not* zero. So we lost our invariant $Y_t \equiv 0$; and more difficult analysis is needed.[10]

V

Since it is open season for criticism of my paper, I may perhaps be permitted to add some of my own.[11] In particular, I reproach myself that I did not sufficiently emphasize the perplexing analytical problem introduced by an infinite horizon, foreseen with certainty.

It ought to be strongly noted that the dynamic system (4) above is in a sense an indeterminate or undetermined system. Why? Because while (4b) is a third-order difference equation, yet (4a) contains only two initial conditions. This is one less initial

[10] If we could be sure that all R's exceed a number greater than unity—and in the absence of strong preference for the future there is some presumption of this—we could use (6) to deduce that $Y_\infty = 0$ and that (3') holds asymptotically.

[11] Some minor typographical errors and slips in my original paper have been kindly pointed out by T. Ophir: in my equation (1), p. 469, R_ϵ should be R_t; in p. 469, n. 3, $\partial U/\partial C$ should be $\partial U/\partial C_i$; at the middle of p. 470, the inequalities should read $\partial C_3/\partial R_{t+1} < 0$ and $\partial S_3/\partial R_{t+1} > 0$, with "lowering" replaced by "raising"; on p. 475, for the log formula, $S_1(R, R)$ as $R \to \infty$ approaches $-\infty$ and not the conventional value of zero; at top of p. 478 the approach to a negative-interest equilibrium should be emphasized as "oscillatory"; throughout p. 478 and elsewhere, the sequence of numbers .297 should be replaced by .303 or .3028.

condition than is needed for the system to determine its interest rates recursively as it goes along.

The above important fact was, perhaps, masked by my numerical example of additive logarithmic utilities.[12] The fact that this case involved no systematic time preference seems unobjectionable: it thereby enabled us to separate out the effect of systematic time preference from the effect of foreseen changes in one's current income status. But, to use a familiar word, $U = \Sigma \log C_i$ was "singular" in that it led to isoelasticity and to the degenerate result that $S_1(R_{t-1}, R_t)$, first period saving, was independent of last period's interest rate R_t. Thus equation (18) degenerated into a second-order difference equation that could develop its own time path recursively out of its previous behavior—a fact that was of advantage for easy computation but of disadvantage for showing the essentials of futurity.

What do you need to make our general dynamic system determinate? You need a terminal condition in the future—at the *end* of (relevant) time, so to speak. To know today's interest rate we have to know tomorrow's interest rate, because that helps determine today's saving on the part of the young. Inductively, then, today's interest rate is determined simultaneously with—and not prior to—*all* subsequent interest rates. Our difference equations are not so much causal as teleological.

If the end of time is soon, the matter is simple. Thus suppose you know the human race will become extinct after three generations have lived. Then (4) becomes

$$S_1(R_1, R_2) + 0 + 0 = 0$$

$$S_2(R_1, R_2) + S_1(R_2, R_3) + 0 = 0$$

$$S_3(R_1, R_2) + S_2(R_2, R_3)$$
$$+ S_1(R_3, R_4) = 0 \tag{8}$$

$$S_3(R_2, R_3) + S_2(R_3, R_4) = 0$$

$$S_3(R_3, R_4) = 0 ,$$

[12] Equations (18), p. 477, of my original paper.

which is four equations for four unknowns. One is tempted to guess that, as the number of generations in (8) grows large, the interest profile will most of the time remain nearer and nearer to the stable equilibrium of (3′).

But, realism aside, what about (4) as it stands, a system that will never be wound up? We have no natural right-hand terminal equation. An infinity of future expected profiles of $\{R_t\}$ will justify an infinity of possible values for today's R_1![13] A Ponzi swindle, the critics will say.

---

[13] The theory of speculation given in the cited 1957 *Weltwirtschaftliches Archiv* paper encountered this same dilemma. But heavy storage charges for goods usually terminates the interdependence after a finite number of time periods, greatly simplifying the analysis.

While I cannot pretend to provide a definitive solution to the problem, I might hazard a guess. As is done in the mathematics of wave mechanics, we might adjoin as our right-hand boundary condition the limit requirement

$$\lim_{t \to \infty} R_t = R \qquad (9)$$

The economic rationale for this would go somewhat as follows: our equilibrium pattern should not forever live off of its own expectations but rather should be such as to be capable of being wound up at any time. But I doubt that a condition like (9) will produce determinateness. And so I am left with a final paradox that should be cleared up by someone: a perpetual competitive system seems to be an indeterminate one.

24

BALANCED GROWTH UNDER CONSTANT RETURNS TO SCALE[1]

By Robert M. Solow and Paul A. Samuelson

The recent literature of long-run economic dynamics pays particular attention to the existence and stability of moving equilibrium paths characterized by steady compound-interest growth. In both aggregative and many-sector models the assumption is usually made that inputs are combined in fixed proportions. The present paper lifts this restriction and studies the steady-growth potentialities of a more general many-industry system which is closed in the sense that all of each period's output is plowed back as input in the next period.

1. INTRODUCTION

SYSTEMS of linear fixed-proportion production functions, or input-output models, were proposed by Walras and Wieser, revived by Leontief, and have recently been studied intensively. The capacity of such idealized economic systems for steady balanced growth was first explored in the well-known paper of von Neumann [12] and more recently by Samuelson [10] and Georgescu-Roegen [4, Chapter 4]. By balanced growth (or decay) we mean a state of affairs in which the output of each commodity increases (or decreases) by a constant percentage per unit of time, the mutual proportions in which commodities are produced remaining constant. The economy changes only in scale, but not in composition.

The object of this paper is to consider balanced growth properties in a way which will be more or less familiar to economists who are used to the formulation of dynamic models in terms of difference equations. In so doing, we replace the hypothesis of fixed proportions by the more general one that production functions are homogeneous of first degree. Thus we retain constant returns to scale, but permit continuous substitution of inputs. Our difference equations become nonlinear, but remain fairly simple.

On the other hand, we suppose all optimization and allocation problems to have been solved in one way or another. We do not question what happens inside the economic sausage grinder; we simply observe that inputs flow into the economy and outputs appear. Since the economy is assumed to be closed (with labor "produced" by consumption), all outputs become the inputs of the next period. Thus, it is as if we had a single joint production process with continuously variable proportions.

2. JOINT PRODUCTION WITH VARIABLE PROPORTIONS

In our formulation, a production process corresponds to the possibility of transforming present amounts a_1, a_2, $\cdots$, a_n of n perfectly defined

---

[1] An earlier version of Sections 1–8 of this paper was read by R. M. Solow at the Santa Monica meeting of the Econometric Society, August 1951.

commodities into definite and nonsubstitutive amounts b_1 , b_2 , $\cdots$, b_n . If the nth commodity is a nondepreciating capital good, then we simply enter $a_n = b_n$. It is assumed that amounts λa_1 , λa_2 , $\cdots$, λa_n of inputs will produce λb_1 , λb_2 , $\cdots$, λb_n of outputs, i.e., there are constant returns to scale. In linear programming the ratios $a_1 : a_2 : \cdots : a_n$ are fixed for each process, and optimization consists of determining which processes will be operated and with what intensities. We bypass this last question, drop the fixed-proportion assumption, and simply require that $b_1 = H^1(a_1 , \cdots , a_n)$, $b_2 = H^2(a_1 , \cdots , a_n)$, $\cdots$, $b_n = H^n(a_1 , \cdots , a_n)$; where any proportions of inputs are permitted, and the functions H^i are all homogeneous of the first degree.

In a completely closed economy, outputs become inputs one unit of time later and this fact gives us the causal system of nonlinear difference equations

$$(1) \qquad X_i(t + 1) = H^i[X_1(t), X_2(t) , \cdots , X_n(t)] \qquad (i = 1, \cdots , n),$$

where $X_i(t)$ is the output of the ith commodity in period t.

One other stipulated property of the H^i will be used later. As production functions, we suppose them to be continuous and monotonic nondecreasing functions of each argument; as one or more inputs are increased, other things being equal, no output can fall. For simplicity we rule out saturation cases and assume the functions to be strictly increasing; this implies among other things that so long as some inputs are positive, some of every output will be produced.[2] If the production functions are smooth enough to have marginal productivities, these latter are positive.

3. BALANCED GROWTH

This is not the only interpretation which can be given to the fundamental difference equations (1). Another possibility is to think of

[2] This restriction is somewhat stronger than it might at first seem. It implies, for instance, that if we start with a positive amount of one input, say bananas, then all other inputs and commodities would be produced from it in nonzero amounts. This could probably be weakened to require only that from bananas alone we could produce, say, bananas and labor in the next period; that from bananas and labor alone we could produce in one period bananas, labor, and something else; and so on until after at most n periods all commodities could be made available. This weaker property is analogous to indecomposability in linear systems [11]. The purpose of assumptions like this is to assure that there exists an equilibrium state with positive output of all commodities. Otherwise further considerations might apply only to one or more subsets of commodities. A concrete example of a system (1) satisfying these assumptions might be:

$$X_1(t + 1) = a_{11}X_1(t) + a_{12}X_2(t) + p_1 X_1(t)^{q_1} X_2(t)^{1-q_1},$$

$$X_2(t + 1) = a_{21}X_1(t) + a_{22}X_2(t) + p_2 X_1(t)^{q_2} X_2(t)^{1-q_2},$$

where a_{ij} , p_i , q_i , $1 - q_i$ are all positive. The linear part is needed to provide positive partial derivatives everywhere.

$X_i(t)$ as the size of a population in the ith age (or other) group. The increasing functions H^i would then represent combined fertility-mortality schedules.[3] We also remark that (1) generalizes systems of linear difference equations, all of whose coefficients are positive as studied by Chipman, Goodwin, Metzler, and others [11].

Balanced growth has been defined to mean $X_i(t + 1) = \lambda X_i(t)$ for each i and for some positive constant λ. This in turn implies, if we consider only integral values of t, that

$$(2) \qquad X_i(t) = x V_i \lambda^t \qquad (i = 1, \cdots, n);$$

and since the $X_i(t)$ are essentially positive, we must be able to choose the x, V_1, $\cdots$, V_n all positive. Inserting (2) in (1) and using the homogeneity of H^i gives

$$(3) \qquad \lambda V_i = H^i(V_1, \cdots, V_n) \qquad (i = 1, \cdots, n).$$

The constant x can be adjusted to insure that $\sum_{j=1}^n V_j = 1$, and we suppose this done.

Thus, finding a balanced growth solution (2) to the difference equations is reduced to solving the nonlinear eigenvector problem (3) with positive λ, V_1, $\cdots$, V_n. This will determine the proportions $V_1 : V_2 : \cdots : V_n$ in which output may grow or decay steadily.

4. EXISTENCE OF A BALANCED GROWTH PATH

The existence of a solution to (3), and thus the possibility of balanced growth in (1), is not immediately apparent, but can be proved as follows. The vectors $V = (V_1, \cdots, V_n)$ with, let us recall, $V_i \geqslant 0$, $\sum V_j = 1$, define a closed simplex in Euclidean n-space. Consider the points $y = (y_1, \cdots, y_n)$ determined by

$$y_i = \frac{H^i(V_1, \cdots, V_n)}{\sum_{j=1}^n H^j(V_1, \cdots, V_n)} \qquad (i = 1, \cdots, n).$$

Clearly $y_i \geqslant 0$, $\sum y_j = 1$, so that we have here a continuous mapping of the closed simplex into itself. According to the fixed-point theorem

---

[3] $X_i(t)$ may refer to age groups of each sex, with the H's involving nuptiality behavior. In some such cases, however, the monotonicity assumption may become unrealistic.

There is an extensive literature on the growth of animal and human populations, to which the interested reader may refer. Rather than give a complete bibliography here we refer to the following few papers, each of which contains numerous further references: (see [7], [8], [1], and [3]). The theory of random processes also runs somewhat parallel to our development (see [2]). Most of the works referred to here deal with linear problems.

of Brouwer [**6,** p. 117], such a mapping has a fixed-point. That is, there is at least one vector V^* carried into itself by this transformation of coordinates. For this vector V^* we can write

$$V_i^* \sum_i H^j(V_1^*, \cdots, V_n^*) = H^i(V_1^*, \cdots, V_n^*) \qquad (i = 1, \cdots, n).$$

Thus V^* is a solution to our problem, with $\lambda = \sum_i H^j(V_1^*, \cdots, V_n^*)$. For proper initial conditions, a steady geometric growth or decay is always possible for systems of homogeneous production functions. Should output once find itself in the proportion $V_1^* : V_2^* : \cdots : V_n^*$ it will remain in these proportions, and be multiplied by the factor λ each new unit of time. It follows from the stipulated properties of the H^i functions that every component of the equilibrium vector V^* is strictly positive.

5. PROOF OF UNIQUENESS OF GROWTH RATE

So far we have been concerned only with the existence of a steady-growth solution and its accompanying magnification factor λ. May there be more than one such solution? Not if the functions H^i are monotonic.

This is especially easy to see when $n = 2$. Let us suppose the contrary, that there exist two growth rates λ and μ with eigenvectors (V_1, V_2) and (U_1, U_2) respectively. This means we have

$$\lambda V_i = H^i(V_1, V_2) \qquad (i = 1, 2),$$

$$\mu U_i = H^i(U_1, U_2) \qquad (i = 1, 2);$$

and using the homogeneity property,

$$\lambda = H^1\left(1, \frac{V_2}{V_1}\right) = H^2\left(\frac{V_1}{V_2}, 1\right),$$

$$\mu = H^1\left(1, \frac{U_2}{U_1}\right) = H^2\left(\frac{U_1}{U_2}, 1\right).$$

Then $\lambda > \mu$ would imply, since we are assuming the H^i to be monotonically increasing functions, that $V_2/V_1 > U_2/U_1$ and also $V_1/V_2 > U_1/U_2$. This contradiction shows that λ cannot be greater than μ. By symmetry it cannot be less. Hence λ is unique.

For general n, a different line of proof is easier. We recall that $A_i \geqslant B_i$ for all i implies that $H^i(A_1, \cdots, A_n) \geqslant H^i(B_1, \cdots, B_n)$ for all i. Now suppose there exist vectors of positive components, U and V, such that

$$\lambda V_i = H^i(V_1, \cdots, V_n),$$

$$\mu U_i = H^i(U_1, \cdots, U_n), \qquad (i = 1, \cdots, n).$$

$$\sum_j U_j = \sum_j V_j = 1,$$

It is clear from the homogeneity of the H^i that U and V are not proportional if $\lambda \neq \mu$. There obviously exists a positive constant M so large that $V_i/M \leqslant U_i$ for each i. Then by the monotonicity assumption

$$\frac{\lambda V_i}{M} = H^i\left(\frac{V_1}{M}, \cdots, \frac{V_n}{M}\right) \leqslant H^i(U_1, \cdots, U_n) = \mu U_i;$$

and again

$$\frac{\lambda^2 V_i}{M} = H^i\left(\frac{\lambda V_1}{M}, \cdots, \frac{\lambda V_n}{M}\right) \leqslant H^i(\mu U_1, \cdots, \mu U_n) = \mu^2 U_i;$$

and by induction $\lambda^N(V_i/M) \leqslant \mu^N U_i$ for every i and every N. Since the larger exponential must ultimately dominate, this implies that $\lambda \leqslant \mu$. By an exactly symmetrical argument $\lambda \geqslant \mu$, and hence $\lambda = \mu$. Thus, there is only one possible rate of balanced growth.

6. PROOF OF UNIQUENESS OF PROPORTIONS

There is still one more uniqueness question to be answered. Is it possible that a rate of steady growth λ should be compatible with more than one set of proportions $V_1:V_2:\cdots:V_n$? Is there more than one composition of outputs capable of steady growth? Here again the answer is no. For if there were, we would have

$$\lambda V_i = H^i(V_1, \cdots, V_n),$$
$$\lambda U_i = H^i(U_1, \cdots, U_n),$$

and thus

$$H^1(1, V_2/V_1, \cdots, V_n/V_1) = H^1(1, U_2/U_1, \cdots, U_n/U_1),$$
$$H^2(V_1/V_2, 1, \cdots, V_n/V_2) = H^2(U_1/U_2, 1, \cdots, U_n/U_2),$$
$$\cdots\cdots\cdots\cdots\cdots\cdots\cdots\cdots\cdots\cdots\cdots\cdots\cdots\cdots$$
$$H^n(V_1/V_n, V_2/V_n, \cdots, 1) = H^n(U_1/U_n, U_2/U_n, \cdots, 1).$$

If U and V are not simply proportional, the assumed monotonicity tells us that in each of the above equations there must be at least one $V_i/V_j < U_i/U_j$ and at least one $V_k/V_j > U_k/U_j$. Suppose $V_2/V_1 < U_2/U_1$. Then in the second equation $V_1/V_2 > U_1/U_2$, and so, say, $V_3/V_2 < U_3/U_2$. Now this implies $V_3/V_2 \cdot V_2/V_1 = V_3/V_1 < U_3/U_2 \cdot U_2/U_1 = U_3/U_1$. Thus $V_1/V_3 > U_1/U_3$, $V_2/V_3 > U_2/U_3$, and in the third equation we must have, say, $V_4/V_3 < U_4/U_3$. This is enough to guarantee that $V_k/V_4 > U_k/U_4$ for $k = 1, 2, 3$. Proceeding in this way we will find $V_1/V_n > U_1/U_n$, $V_2/V_n > U_2/U_n$, $\cdots$, $V_{n-1}/V_n > U_{n-1}/U_n$ and this contradicts the last equation above. Thus U and V are proportional.

7. BOUNDS ON THE GROWTH RATE

Our result so far is that under the assumption of strict monotonicity of the functions H^i, there is only one possible rate of geometric growth or decay, and only one composition of output capable of growth or decay at this constant geometric rate. This uniqueness of the magnification factor λ means, disregarding the razor's edge of a stationary system, that a system is capable either of balanced growth or of balanced decay but never of both. Which will it be? When can we say whether λ will be greater or less than unity? Certainly without detailed knowledge of the functions H^i only very crude statements can be made, for λ is a characteristic of the entire structure of the system.

We are not entirely at a loss, however. One simple estimate is available. Under our assumptions, which are in accord with economic meaning, the transformation (1) maps the nonnegative hyperoctant into itself: outputs are always positive or zero. Suppose, in addition, the functions H^i are such that there exists a vector $(V_1, \cdots, V_n)$ with the property that for each i and for some positive constant c, $H^i(V_1, \cdots, V_n) \geqslant cV_i$. This means that there is a certain composition of output which, in one time period, is transformed into a new output in which the contribution of each commodity is multiplied by a factor *at least* equal to c. We can then conclude that the steady growth rate λ is *at least* equal to c. In intuitive terms this theorem[4] says that if the economy can increase output by, say, at least five per cent for each commodity and maybe more for some, then it can certainly increase all outputs in proportion at a rate not less than five per cent a year. As a corollary, if a simple system of the kind studied can increase every component of output in one year, then it is not capable of balanced decay but only of balanced growth. A similar upper-bound on the rate of growth can be found.

Another byproduct of this theorem is a characterization of the unique rate of steady growth λ. It is the largest positive number c with the property that there exists a positive vector V such that $H^i(V) \geqslant cV_i$ for every i. An alternative characterization can be found by using Euler's

---

[4] The statement in the text is a specialization of the following theorem of Krein and Rutman [5, p. 115]: A homogeneous, completely continuous operator c-monotone with respect to K, has in K a characteristic vector which corresponds to a positive characteristic number not less than c.

This theorem is proved for operators in a Banach space, which we specialize to Euclidean n-space. An operator A is defined to be homogeneous if $A(\lambda x) = \lambda A(x)$ for all $\lambda \geqslant 0$, completely continuous if it maps closed sets into compact sets, c-monotone with respect to a cone K if $x \leqslant y$ (vector inequality) implies $A(x) \leqslant A(y)$ and if there exists a vector u in K such that $A(u) \geqslant cu$. The nonnegative hyperoctant plays the role of the cone K. Actually, for the simple special case that we need, a quite elementary proof can be given.

theorem[5] in (3) to obtain

$$\lambda V_i = \sum_{j=1}^{n} H_j^i(V_1^*, \cdots, V_n^*) V_j^*,$$

so that λ is the unique real positive characteristic root of the Jacobian $J = [H_j^i(V^*)]$ to which corresponds a positive eigenvector. For this and other properties of Frobenius matrices like J with positive elements see [11] and the literature referred to there.

8. STABILITY OF PROPORTIONS

A second important circle of questions concerns the stability of the balanced growth solution. We know that if outputs should ever find themselves in the proportions $V_1^* : V_2^* : \cdots : V_n^*$, they will remain so. But if the system is *slightly* disturbed from this special path, will forces be set in action that tend to restore the original motion? This is the question of stability in the small of the solutions (2) of (1). Or more strongly: If the system (1) is started from *arbitrary* positive initial conditions, will a balanced growth time path (2) tend eventually to be established? This is stability in the large, and includes stability in the small.

Fairly straightforward calculations show that a sufficient condition for stability in the small of the solution (2) is that all the characteristic roots of $J'J$ be less than one, provided the H^i functions have bounded second derivatives. This type of sufficient condition is known in the linear case [9].

But this is not much of an advance. Smallness of the characteristic roots of $J'J$ will tend to be associated with smallness of the roots of J, and therefore (see end of preceding section) with balanced decay. Hence the case of balanced growth cannot be fruitfully handled by the above condition. This is, after all, only natural. In the case where the system is expanding geometrically, one unit of output lost in the distant past could have been the progenitor of an ever-growing quantity of output lost since that time. This is especially clear if, as suggested earlier, we think of $X_i(t)$ as being the size of a population in the ith age group. Now suppose one mother had been subtracted from the population many generations ago. If the population is expanding geometrically in the Malthusian manner, the number of potential descendants would also be increasing approximately geometrically. The loss in potential population attributable to the past disturbance would be increasing, not de-

---

[5] To do this requires that the H^i be differentiable, something which we have not assumed and do not need except for certain minor side results in Section 10 below. Where derivatives are not defined, the slopes of supporting hyperplanes of the H^i surfaces can be used to state a generalized Euler's theorem.

creasing. The steady-growth solution cannot be stable in the absolute sense that changes in initial conditions have effects ultimately damping to zero.

What we might expect, however, is that the equilibrium *relative* age distribution might tend to reestablish itself; that the population might tend to resume its geometrical expansion at the rate λ. In our notation, we might expect that the proportions $V_1^* : V_2^* : \cdots : V_n^*$ will be asymptotically regained and the system will asymptotically again expand at the rate λ, as a result of some initial conditions other than the original ones. This is in fact the case, and in the next section we will show that the system (1) is stable in this relative sense, and, moreover, stable *in the large*. In other words, from any arbitrary positive initial conditions, the equations (1) eventually generate steady growth in the unique proportions V^* and rate λ.

9. PROOF OF RELATIVE STABILITY IN THE LARGE

Let $X_i(t)$ be generated by the system (1) from positive initial conditions. In mathematical terms our object is to show that

$$(4) \qquad \lim_{t \to \infty} \frac{X_i(t)}{V_i^* \lambda^t} = \text{constant} = x \qquad (i = 1, \cdots, n)$$

where V_i^* and λ have their usual meanings and x is a constant depending on the initial conditions or last arbitrary displacement, but independent of i [see (2)].

Define

$$x_i(t) = \frac{X_i(t)}{V_i^* \lambda^t},$$

and substitute into (1) to obtain

$$V_i^* \lambda^{t+1} x_i(t + 1) = H^i[V_1^* \lambda^t x_1(t), \cdots, V_n^* \lambda^t x_n(t)].$$

By use of the homogeneity property this becomes

$$
\begin{aligned}
(5) \quad x_i(t + 1) &= H^i\left[\frac{V_1^*}{V_i^* \lambda} x_1(t), \cdots, \frac{V_n^*}{V_i^* \lambda} x_n(t)\right] \qquad (i = 1, \cdots, n) \\
&= G^i[x_1(t), \cdots, x_n(t)]
\end{aligned}
$$

where the G^i functions are *means* with the easily verifiable properties:

$$
\begin{aligned}
&G^i(1, \cdots, 1) = 1, \\
(6) \quad &G^i(mx_1, \cdots, mx_n) = mG^i(x_1, \cdots, x_n), \qquad\qquad m \geqslant 0, \\
&G^i(x, \cdots, x) = x, \qquad\qquad\qquad\qquad\qquad (i = 1, \cdots, n) \\
&G^i \text{ is strictly increasing, like } H^i,
\end{aligned}
$$

min $(x_1, \cdots, x_n) \leqslant G^i(x_1, \cdots, x_n) \leqslant$ max $(x_1, \cdots, x_n)$, with the equality signs holding if, and only if, all the x's are equal.

In the trivial case where $x_1(0) = x_2(0) = \cdots = x_n(0) = x$, the balanced growth proportions are already established and we have automatically $x_i(t) = x$, confirming (4).

Now define the two sequences $\{m(t)\} = \{\min [x_1(t), \cdots, x_n(t)]\}$ and $\{M(t)\} = \{\max [x_1(t), \cdots, x_n(t)]\}$. From (5) and (6) we have, $m(t + 1) = \min \{G^1[x_1(t), \cdots, x_n(t)], \cdots, G^n[x_1(t), \cdots, x_n(t)]\} \geqslant m(t)$, the equality sign holding only in the trivial case that $x_1(t) = \cdots = x_n(t)$.

By an identical argument, we prove that $M(t)$ is a never-increasing sequence, and is, in fact, strictly decreasing except in the trivial case of equal initial conditions. Thus the two limits exist:

$$\lim_{t \to \infty} m(t) = m^* \leqslant M(0),$$

$$\lim_{t \to \infty} M(t) = M^* \geqslant m(0).$$

Clearly $M^* \geqslant m^*$, and it only remains to show that $M^* = m^*$. Suppose the contrary, that $M^* - m^* = \Delta > 0$. Given any small positive number ϵ, we can find a $T = T(\epsilon)$ so large that for $t \geqslant T$, $m(t) \geqslant m^* - \epsilon$. Now let $m_1 = m_1(\epsilon)$ be the smallest of the n^2 numbers $G^i(M^*, m^* - \epsilon, \cdots, m^* - \epsilon)$, $G^i(m^* - \epsilon, M^*, m^* - \epsilon, \cdots, m^* - \epsilon)$, $\cdots$, $G^i(m^* - \epsilon, \cdots, m^* - \epsilon, M^*)$, $(i = 1, 2, \cdots, n)$. If, as has been assumed, $M^* > m^*$, we will have $m_1(0) > m^*$, by (6). Consider $m(T + 1)$. This quantity will surely be larger than $m_1(\epsilon)$, since $M^* < M(T)$ and M^* appear in place of the $x_k(T) = M(T)$ in at least one of the above G^i functions, while also $m^* - \epsilon \leqslant x_j(T)$, $j = 1, \cdots, n$, so that for each i at least one of the above G^i has each of its arguments less than the corresponding component of the vector $[X_1(T), \cdots, X_n(T)]$. Hence $m(T + 1) \geqslant m_1(\epsilon)$ and if we let ϵ tend to zero (and hence T tend to infinity), we get finally,

$$m^* = \lim m(T + 1) \geqslant \lim m_1(\epsilon) = m_1(0) > m^*,$$

a contradiction. Hence $M^* = m^*$.

We have

$$m(t) \leqslant x_i(t) \leqslant M(t) \qquad (i = 1, \cdots, n),$$

and

$$\lim_{t \to \infty} m(t) = \lim_{t \to \infty} M(t) = m^* = M^* = x.$$

Hence

$$\lim_{t \to \infty} x_i(t) = x \qquad (i = 1, \cdots, n),$$

and from the definition

$$\lim_{t \to \infty} \frac{X_i(t)}{V_i^* \lambda^t} = x \qquad (i = 1, \cdots, n);$$

i.e., for any initial conditions, the X's eventually grow like $xV_i^*\lambda^t$, which completes the proof.

10. SUFFICIENT CONDITIONS FOR RELATIVE STABILITY IN THE SMALL

Stability in the large, which we have just verified, implies the stability in the small of the balanced growth proportions. There is thus no further independent interest in the latter. But a necessary condition for stability in the small is that the characteristic roots of certain linearized difference equations should not exceed unity in absolute value. Thus the proof of the preceding section gives us gratis certain theorems on matrices, which we record for completeness.

The intensive variables or proportions $V_i(t)$ are defined by

$$V_i(t) = \frac{X_i(t)}{\sum X_j(t)} \qquad (i = 1, \cdots, n).$$

Substituting in (1) and using once more the homogeneity of the H^i we find that the $V_i(t)$ satisfy the difference equations

$$(7) \quad V_i(t+1) = \frac{H^i[V_1(t), \cdots, V_n(t)]}{\sum H^j[V_1(t), \cdots, V_n(t)]} = Q^i[V_1(t), \cdots, V_n(t)],$$

where the Q^i are now homogeneous of zero degree. The now familiar balanced-growth proportions are obtained by putting $V_i(t+1) = V_i(t) = V_i^*$ in (7), and the existence and uniqueness of V^* is assured. Our stability proof tells us that from any initial conditions $V_1(0), \cdots,$ $V_n(0)$, all positive and such that $\sum V_j(0) = 1$, the equations (7) generate sequences $V_i(t)$ such that $\lim_{t \to \infty} V_i(t) = V_i^*, i = 1, \cdots, n$. Hence (7) is stable under small disturbances. This implies that if we consider the linear approximations to (7), $V(t+1) = QV(t)$, the matrix Q has all its characteristic roots less than or equal to unity in absolute value.

Now Q is simply[6] the Jacobian $[\partial Q^i / \partial V_j]$ evaluated at the equilibrium point V^*. Simple calculation and use of the fixed-point equation show that

$$Q_j^i = \frac{\partial Q^i}{\partial V_j} = \frac{H_j^i}{\sum H^k} - \frac{H^i \sum_k H_j^k}{(\sum H^k)^2} = \frac{H_j^i - V_i^* \sum_k H_j^k}{\sum H^k},$$

[6] We are now assuming the H^i to be continuously differentiable.

all evaluated at V^*. Incidentally, it is easily seen that $\sum_{i=1}^{n} Q_j^i = 0$, so that Q will not be a matrix of nonnegative elements. If $\bar{V}$ represents the matrix with V_1, V_2, $\cdots$, V_n down the main diagonal and zeros elsewhere and if 1 is the matrix with unity in every place, $Q = (1/\sum H^k)\{J - \bar{V}1J\} = (1/\sum H^k)\{I - \bar{V}1\}J$. J is the Jacobian (H_j^i) introduced in Section 7.

As a result of our stability proof we have the proposition:[7] if H^1, $\cdots$, H^n are homogeneous functions of first degree with positive partial derivatives and V^* is the solution of (3), then all the characteristic roots of $(1/\sum H^k)\{I - \bar{V}1\}J$ are less than or equal to one in modulus. Another way of saying this is that $\{I - \bar{V}1\}J$ has all its roots less than or equal to $\sum H^k(V^*)$ in modulus. Note that $\sum H^k(V^*)$ is the unique λ satisfying (3).

Since the characteristic equation is unaltered if we change the order of a product, $\{I - \bar{V}1\}J$ has the same roots as $J\{I - \bar{V}1\}$, the (i, j) element of which is simply $H_j^i(V^*) - H^i(V^*)$. Hence, none of the roots of this matrix exceed $\sum H^k(V^*) = \lambda$ in absolute value.

It is interesting that in these stability equations the Hessian matrices (H_{ij}^k) play no role; only first partial derivatives count. Thus, in this model, stability is entirely independent of the presence or absence of diminishing marginal returns.

11. DIFFERENTIAL-EQUATIONS ANALOGUES

Essentially the same methods and results carry over to differential equations

$$(8) \qquad \dot{Y}_i = F^i[Y_1(t), \cdots, Y_n(t)] \qquad (i = 1, \cdots, n),$$

where the functions F^i are homogeneous of first degree with positive partial derivatives. Substitution of $Y_i(t) = cu_i e^{\lambda t}$ leads to the eigenvalue problem

$$(9) \qquad \lambda u_i = F^i(u_1, \cdots, u_n),$$

where we can choose $\sum u_i = 1$. Our earlier results yield the existence and uniqueness of the positive constants $(\lambda, u_1, \cdots, u_n)$.[8]

To prove the relative stability in the large of the balanced growth solution $Y_i = cu_i e^{\lambda t}$, we define as before

[7] We could have dealt similarly with any positively-weighted sum of the V's, or, what is the same thing, made a dimensional transformation of the original variables.

[8] Note that since λ is positive, cases of balanced decay require different arguments. The true analogue in differential equations would be systems like $\dot{Y}_i = F^i(Y) - Y_i$, where F_j is positive so that the matrix $(F_j^i - \delta_{ij})$ has positive elements everywhere, or else has the Minkowski-like property of having all its off-diagonal elements positive.

$$y_i(t) = \frac{Y_i(t)}{u_i \, e^{\lambda t}}, \qquad \dot{Y}_i = u_i \, e^{\lambda t}(\lambda y_i + \dot{y}_i)$$

and find

(10)
$$\dot{y}_i = F^i\left(\frac{u_1}{u_i}\, y_1, \cdots, \frac{u_n}{u_i}\, y_n\right) - \lambda y_i.$$

Let $m(t) = \min_i[y_i(t)]$. If at time t, $m(t) = y_k(t)$, we have

$$\dot{y}_k = F^k\left(\frac{u_1}{u_k}\, y_1, \cdots, \frac{u_n}{u_k}\, y_n\right) - \lambda y_k$$

$$= \frac{y_k}{u_k}\, F^k\left(u_1 \frac{y_1}{y_k}, \cdots, u_n \frac{y_n}{y_k}\right) - \lambda y_k$$

$$> \frac{y_k}{u_k}\, \lambda u_k - \lambda y_k = 0$$

by the monotonicity of F^k and the fact that $y_i/y_k \geqslant 1$ with inequality holding at least once. Thus $m(t)$ is bounded above [by $M(0)$] and increasing, and approaches a limit m^*. An analogous argument shows that $M(t) = \max_i[y_i(t)]$ has a limit M^*. It is not hard to show, by an argument much like that used in Section 9, that $M^* = m^*$, so that $y_i(t) \to y$ for every i. Thus the balanced growth solution is stable in the large.

As before we can define the intensive variables $Z_i = Y_i/\sum Y_j$ which satisfy the normalized equations $\dot{Z}_i = F^i(Z_1, \cdots, Z_n) - Z_i\sum F^k(Z_1, \cdots, Z_n)$. Relative equilibrium (i.e., a stable set of proportions Z_i) requires $\dot{Z}_i = 0$, or $Z_i^*\sum F^k(Z^*) = F^i(Z^*)$. Such an equilibrium exists and is unique and stable in the large. The matrix of the approximating linear equations in Z is

$$J_1 = \left(F_j^i - Z_i^* \sum_k F_j^k - \delta_{ij} \sum_k F^k\right),$$

all evaluated at Z^*. We conclude that all the characteristic roots of J_1 have nonpositive real parts.

Massachusetts Institute of Technology

REFERENCES

[1] FELLER, W., "On the Integral Equation of Renewal Theory," *Annals of Mathematical Statistics*, Vol. 12, 1941, pp. 243–267.

[2] ———— *Probability Theory and Its Applications*, Vol. 1, New York: John Wiley and Sons, 1950, pp. 307–363.

[3] HARRIS, T. E., "Branching Processes," *Annals of Mathematical Statistics*, Vol. 19, 1948, pp. 474–494.

[4] KOOPMANS, T., ed., *Activity Analysis of Production and Allocation*, New York: John Wiley and Sons, 1951, pp. 98–115.

[5] KREIN, M. AND S. RUTMAN, *Linear Operators Leaving Invariant a Cone in a Banach Space*, 1948, Translation No. 26 of American Mathematical Association Translation Series, 1950.

[6] LEFSCHETZ, S., *Introduction to Topology*, Princeton: Princeton University Press, 1949.

[7] LESLIE, P. H., "On the Use of Matrices in Certain Population Mathematics," *Biometrika*, Vol. 33, Nov., 1945, pp. 183–212, and Vol 35, Dec., 1948, pp. 213–245.

[8] LOTKA, A. J., *Théorie analytique des associations biologiques*, 2e Partie, Paris: Hermann, 1939, 149 pp.

[9] SAMUELSON, P., *Foundations of Economic Analysis*, Cambridge: Harvard University Press, 1947, p 438.

[10] ————— *Market Mechanisms and Maximization*, Part III, unpublished RAND Corporation Memorandum.

[11] SOLOW, R., "On the Structure of Linear Models," ECONOMETRICA, Vol. 20, No. 1, 1952, pp. 29–46.

[12] VON NEUMANN, J., "A Model of General Economic Equilibrium," *Review of Economic Studies*, Vol. 13, No. 1, 1945–1946, p. 1–9.

25

A COMPLETE CAPITAL MODEL INVOLVING HETEROGENEOUS CAPITAL GOODS

By PAUL A. SAMUELSON AND ROBERT M. SOLOW

I. INTRODUCTION AND REVIEW

Long ago Frank Ramsey[1] gave a complete capital model involving a single homogeneous capital good. By this model economists could test the consistency of their literary theorizing about capital, and could establish important propositions like the following:

> A zero rate of interest is possible in an economic model even though consumption goods remain scarce and nonfree; and in a model where all consumption goods are free, there may still be a determinate positive own rate of interest.

None the less economists have often been suspicious about a one-capital-good theory of interest. And properly so since the real world involves a great variety of heterogeneous capital goods. The present paper therefore generalizes the Ramsey capital model to any number of capital goods. The resulting mathematical problem turns out to have some intrinsically intricate transversality or end conditions that will probably be of importance in many dynamic programming problems. And one of the by-products of our intense logical analysis will be the following very important implication:

> Even though there is no such thing as a single abstract capital substance that transmutes itself from one machine form to another like a restless reincarnating soul, the rigorous investigation of a heterogeneous capital-goods model shows that over extended periods of time an economic society can in a perfectly straightforward way reconstruct the composition of its diverse capital goods so that there may remain great heuristic value in

1. F. P. Ramsey, "A Mathematical Theory of Saving," *Economic Journal*, XXXVIII (Dec. 1928), 543–59.

the simpler J. B. Clark-Ramsey models of abstract capital substance.

In review, Ramsey's problem is the following:

(1)   Maximize $J(b) = \int_0^\infty U(C)\,dt$ subject to

$$C(t) + \frac{dS}{dt} = f(S)$$

$$S(0) = b$$

where

$$0 = U(A) > U(C) \text{ for } 0 < C < A \leqslant \infty,$$

$$0 < f(S) < f(a) \text{ for } b \leqslant S < a \leqslant \infty.$$

In words, society maximizes the (undiscounted) integral of all future utilities of consumption, subject to the fact that the sum of current consumption and of current capital formation is limited by what the current capital stock can produce. (We hold labor constant, and can therefore ignore it; also, with Ramsey, we assume the overly-strong "diminishing returns" conditions $U''(C) < 0$ and $f''(S) < 0$.)

In (1) either A or a is assumed to be finite, so that the improper integral will converge. (Even here, discount factors or truncating $t = \infty$ to $t = T$ would, as Ramsey knew, give a well-determined problem.)

Ramsey distinguishes two different "bliss points" depending upon whether (α) utility or (β) production is first satiated:

(α) If $A \leqslant f(a)$, he maximizes our formulated (1).

(β) If $A > f(a)$, he replaces $U(C)$ by $U(C) - U(f(a))$ in the maximum problem, thereby keeping the improper integral finite without use of any mathematically-motivated discount factor. (We shall assume U has so been normalized if this case applies.)

The following necessary Euler conditions must hold if

$$J = \int_0^\infty U(f(S) - \dot{S})\,dt$$

is to have a maximum value:

(2) $\dfrac{d}{dt}\{- U'\} = U'f'$ or

(3) $U + U'\dot{S} = \text{constant}.$

Since the integrand is independent of time, Equation (3) follows from (2), where dashes represent differentiations with respect to the indicated arguments and dots represent time derivatives. Since $\dot{S}$ must go to zero as bliss is asymptotically approached, obviously the constant in (3) must, as our transversality condition, vanish; i.e., the horizontal line in the (t,S) plane corresponding to S at the bliss level represents our variable-end-point condition.

To derive this transversality condition more simply, note that if $b <$ the S level producing bliss, and there is no minimum subsistence level of C at which U' becomes infinite, it can be shown that it always pays to move toward bliss by saving and $\dot{S} > 0$ must always hold. This being the case, change from t to S as independent variable and determine $\dot{S} = g(S)$ to maximize

$$(4) \qquad J = \int_b^{a^*} \frac{U(f(S) - \dot{S})}{\dot{S}}\, dS,$$

where a^* is the bliss level for S. Hence

$$(5) \qquad \frac{\partial}{\partial \dot{S}}\left\{\frac{U}{\dot{S}}\right\} = 0 = \frac{-\dot{S}U' - U}{\dot{S}^2}.$$

The vanishing of the last numerator is seen to be equivalent to (3), and the further secondary condition

$$(6) \qquad \frac{\partial^2}{\partial \dot{S}^2}\left\{\frac{U}{\dot{S}}\right\} = \frac{U + \dot{S}U' + \dot{S}^2 U''}{\dot{S}^3}$$

$$= 0 + \frac{U''}{\dot{S}} < 0$$

guarantees that our stationary value does correspond to a true local maximum. (It is interesting that the diminishing returns condition $f'' < 0$ is of little relevance.)

II. MANY-GOODS MODEL

Now let utility depend on consumption of many goods so that

$$(7) \qquad U(C_1, \ldots, C_n) < U(A_1, \ldots, A_n) = 0 \text{ for } \sum_1^n |C_i - A_i| > 0$$

with $\left[\dfrac{\partial^2 U}{\partial C_i \partial C_j}\right]$ neg. def. everywhere.

Let production conditions be defined by the general transformation relation

$$C_1 + \dot{S}_1 = f(S_1, \ldots, S_n; C_2 + \dot{S}_2, \ldots, C_n + \dot{S}_n)$$

263

where

$$\left[\frac{\partial^2 f}{\partial C_i \partial C_j}\right] \text{ is neg. def.}$$

In what follows we will adopt the following simplified notation. Vectors like $(C_1, \ldots, C_n)$ and $(\dot{S}_1, \ldots, \dot{S}_n)$ will be written as C and $\dot{S}$. Since sometimes the first commodity will play a special role, we will sometimes use the same notation to represent the truncated vector: thus on occasion S will stand for $(S_2, \ldots, S_n)$. In most cases the context will indicate what is meant. If confusion is possible, we will write $(S_1, \ldots, S_n)$ as (S_1, S). Thus the last, unnumbered, equation will appear as

$$C_1 + \dot{S}_1 = f(S; C + \dot{S}).$$

First, let us suppose that saturation of production cannot take place, and that

(8) $$\frac{\partial f}{\partial S_i} \geqslant \epsilon > 0 \qquad\qquad (i = 1, 2, \ldots, n)$$

$$\frac{\partial f}{\partial C_i} \leqslant -\epsilon < 0 \qquad\qquad (i = 2, \ldots, n).$$

Our generalized problem now becomes

Maximize $J(b) = J(b_1, \ldots, b_n) = \displaystyle\int_0^\infty U(C)dt$ subject to

(9) $$f(S; C + \dot{S}) - C_1 - \dot{S}_1 = 0$$
$$S_i(0) = b_i \qquad\qquad (i = 1, \ldots, n).$$

That this infinite integral does admit of a finite solution follows from the fact that if initially capitals are so plentiful that

(10) $$f(b_1, \ldots b_n; A_2, \ldots, A_n) - A_1 \geqslant 0,$$

one can at worst throw away the redundant capitals and set $(C_1, \ldots, C_n) = (A_1, \ldots, A_n)$, thus achieving a zero value for J. If (10) is untrue, then by freezing $(C_1, \ldots, C_n)$ at values of (B_i) such that

$$f(b; B) - B_1 > 0,$$

we can make $\dot{S}_1 = \dot{S}_2 = \ldots = \dot{S}_n > 0$, and after a sufficiently long finite time of capital formation, we can have (10) realized. Hence, the integral vanishes from then on and J is shown to be a finite negative number.

In the second case, where production satiation comes before

utility satiation, we can modify the integrand as in the one-good case and have a well-determined finite integral. Thus, let

maximum $U(C)$ subject to

(11) $f(S;C) - C_1 = 0$

have a unique solution in which

$(S_i) = (a_i^*)$ and $(C_i) = (A_i^*)$ with

(12) $f(a^*;A^*) - A_1^* = 0$

$U(A^*) \leqslant U(A) = 0.$

$$\frac{\partial f^*}{\partial S_i} = 0 \qquad\qquad (i = 1, \ldots, n).$$

$$\frac{\dfrac{\partial U^*}{\partial C_i}}{\dfrac{\partial U^*}{\partial U_1}} = \frac{\partial f^*}{\partial C_i} \qquad\qquad (i = 2, \ldots, n).$$

Then our fundamental maximum problem (9) remains the same but with integrand $U(C) - U(A^*)$ rather than with integrand $U(C) = U(C) - U(A)$.

The finiteness of the new J easily follows: If $(b_1, \ldots, b_n)$ all exceed or equal $(a_1^*, \ldots, a_n^*)$, J is obviously zero. If one or more $b_i < a_i^*$, we could freeze consumptions at some low levels and by making $\dot{S}_1 = \dot{S}_2 = \ldots \dot{S}_n = > 0$, can in finite time make every $S_i \geqslant a_i^*$, thus assuring a finite value to J. The optimum J will be even better.

III. EULER NECESSARY CONDITIONS

Substituting our production relation into the integrand, we reformulate our problem:

(13)   Maximize $J(b) = \displaystyle\int_0^\infty U(f(S;C + \dot{S}) - \dot{S}_1, C_2, \ldots, C_n)dt$

$S_i(0) = b_i \qquad\qquad (i = 1, \ldots, n).$

The Euler necessary conditions for a regular maximum are seen to be

(14a) $\dfrac{\partial U}{\partial C_i} + \dfrac{\partial U}{\partial C_1} \cdot \dfrac{\partial f}{\partial C_i} = 0 \qquad\qquad (i = 2, \ldots, n)$

265

(14b) $\dfrac{d}{dt}\left\{-\dfrac{\partial U}{\partial C_1}\right\} = \dfrac{\partial U}{\partial C_1}\dfrac{\partial f}{\partial S_1}$

(14c) $\dfrac{d}{dt}\left\{\dfrac{\partial U}{\partial C_1}\dfrac{\partial f}{\partial C_i}\right\} = \dfrac{\partial U}{\partial C_1}\dfrac{\partial f}{\partial S_i}$ $(i = 2, \ldots ,n)$.

The first set (14a) have the usual economic interpretation — that any two goods must have subjective marginal rates of substitution equal to their instantaneous technological marginal rates of substitution. Using (14a), we could eliminate all C's as explicit variables, throwing each good's equation in (14c) into exactly the same form as (14b) with $-\partial U/\partial C_i$ in the brackets of (14c).

Alternatively, we can use (14a) to eliminate $(C_2, \ldots ,C_n)$ from the integrand of (13), writing

$$\underset{\{C_i\}}{\text{Max}}\; U(f(S;\dot{S} + C) - S_1, \ldots ,C_n) = U^*(S,\dot{S}),$$

$$\frac{\partial U}{\partial S_i} = \frac{\partial U^*}{\partial S_i},\; \frac{\partial U}{\partial \dot{S}_i} = \frac{\partial U^*}{\partial \dot{S}_i} \qquad (i = 1,2, \ldots ,n)$$

where the C's in U are made to satisfy (14a) so as to afford maximum U.

Then

$$J(b) = \text{Max}\int_0^\infty U^*(S;\dot{S})dt \quad \text{subject to}$$

$$S_i(0) = b_i \qquad\qquad (i = 1,2, \ldots ,n).$$

The Euler conditions of this new formulation express (14) in the more symmetrical form

(15) $\dfrac{d}{dt}\dfrac{\partial U^*}{\partial \dot{S}_i} = \dfrac{\partial U^*}{\partial S_i}$ $(i = 1, \ldots ,n)$,

which, because U and U^* are independent of t, must already imply

(15)′ $U^* - \overset{n}{\underset{1}{\Sigma}}\dfrac{\partial U^*}{\partial \dot{S}_i}\dot{S}_i = \text{constant} = U - \overset{n}{\underset{1}{\Sigma}}\dfrac{\partial U}{\partial \dot{S}_i}\dot{S}_i.$

Equation (15)′ is already implied by (14), as well as by (14a) and (15).

Equations (15) or (14) are dynamic ones. They boil down to n second-order differential equations in the n unknown capital paths $S_i(t)$; and even with the n initial capitals (b_i) prescribed, we still lack n terminal or transversality conditions. These must be determined from the condition that J be a maximum.

Before examining end conditions, we shall establish some useful intermediate expressions. For prescribed time T, and any feasible end conditions

$$S_i(0) = b_i, \ S_i(T) = a_i \qquad\qquad (i = 1, \ldots, n)$$

the maximum of $\int_0^T U^*(S; \dot{S}) \, dt$ is assumed to exist and can be written

(16a) $\quad K(T; b_1, \ldots, b_n; a_1, \ldots, a_n)$

$$= \int_0^T U^*(S_1(t), \ldots, S_n(t), \dot{S}_1(t), \ldots, \dot{S}_n(t)) dt$$

(16b) $\quad \dfrac{\partial K}{\partial a_i} = \dfrac{\partial U^*(a_1, \ldots, a_n, \dot{S}_1(T), \ldots, \dot{S}_n(T))}{\partial \dot{S}_i} = \dfrac{\partial U^*(a, \dot{S}^a)}{\partial \dot{S}_i},$

for short,

(16c) $\quad \dfrac{\partial K}{\partial T} = U^*(a, \dot{S}^a) - \overset{n}{\underset{1}{\Sigma}} \dfrac{\partial U^*(a, \dot{S}^a)}{\partial \dot{S}_j} \dot{S}_j^a$

(16d) $\quad K(T; b; a) \equiv -K(-T; a; b)$

(16e) $\quad \dfrac{\partial K}{\partial b_i} = - \dfrac{\partial U^*(b, \dot{S}^b)}{\partial \dot{S}_i}$

where it is understood that $S_i(t)$, $\dot{S}_i(t)$ are evaluated along the extremals of (15) that satisfy the prescribed end conditions. Equations (16b), (16c) and (16e) are what Carathéodory[2] calls the "fundamental relations of the calculus of variations" and may be assumed established. They could also be written in terms of $\partial U/\partial \dot{S}_i$ for arguments satisfying (14). With U^* not involving T explicitly we can add

(16f) $\quad - \dfrac{\partial K}{\partial T} = - U^*(b, \dot{S}^b) + \overset{n}{\underset{1}{\Sigma}} \dfrac{\partial U^*(b, \dot{S}^b)}{\partial \dot{S}_j} \dot{S}_j^b;$

the equivalence of (16f) and (16c) is an alternative way of establishing the constancy of (15)′ everywhere along an extremal.

Now consider an optimal path that does have the proper end conditions to give us the maximal $J(b_1, \ldots, b_n)$. From the initial point (b_i) to any intermediate point (a_i) reached a finite time T later, we must by definition have

$$J(b) = K(T; b; a) + J(a).$$

2. C. Carathéodory, *Variationsrechnung und Partielle Differentialgleichungen erster Ordnung* (Leipzig, 1935), chap. 12.

It is necessary therefore that the point (a_i) be reached in optimal time or that K be a maximum with respect to T; or that

$$(15)'' \quad 0 = \frac{\partial K(T;b;a)}{\partial T} = U^*(a,\dot{S}^a) - \sum_1^n \frac{\partial U^*(a,\dot{S}^a)}{\partial \dot{S}_j} \dot{S}_j^a$$

for any two points (b,a) joined by an optimal path. This assures us that the constant in $(15)'$ or $(16c)$ is indeed zero. (In words, this argument asserts that in going to any capital state, we go there by a path and in a time period so as to maximize our integral of utility in getting there.)

This universal transversality condition $(15)''$ we already met in the Ramsey one-good case. But in the many-goods case we must add still further transversality conditions to get a determinate system.

IV. CASE OF SATIATED PRODUCTION

The simpler case to examine is that just mentioned in (12) where $(S_i) = (a_i^*)$ satiates production and further capitals cannot add to output. It is clear that all optimal paths must approach this satiation point (a_i^*) in the end; for any path that stays away from (a_i^*) can certainly in a long enough time be bettered.

We can also show that (a_i^*) will be approached asymptotically rather than ever be reached in finite time. For if we got to bliss by finite time, T, from then on we would certainly stay there, with $S_i(T + t) = a_i^*$. Now in a reversible variational system there can be only one extremal through a point like $(S_i,\dot{S}_i,T + t) = (a_i^*,0,T + t)$. Since with u smoothly differentiable and $[\partial^2 U/\partial \dot{S}_i\, \partial \dot{S}_j]$ nonsingular, the extremal can have no corners, that one must be $S_i(t) \equiv a_i^*$ for all t. Such a path certainly cannot go through an initial sub-bliss point (b_i). Thus, we deduce that the approaching motion must never reach (a_i^*) in finite time.

While $\dot{S}_i \to 0$ as $t \to \infty$ and $S_i(t) \to a_i^*$, the ratios $\dot{S}_i/\dot{S}_1$ will be determinate for each optimal path from any prescribed initial point (b_i). Figure I shows the optimal paths branching backward from (a_i^*) or α. Through a specified point (b_i) or β, the path $\beta\alpha$ is the optimum, with a determinate limiting slope at α. Running transversally to the family of extremals that fan backward from α is the family of contours of $J(b_1, \ldots ,b_n)$, which form concentric contours around the bliss point $J(a_1^*, \ldots ,a_n^*) = 0$. As will be shown later, the integrations which give us the extremal paths also give us the transversal J slopes.

To get the optimal paths analytically, we can solve (14) or (15) for

$$S_i(0) = b_i, \; S_i(T) = a_i^* \qquad\qquad (i = 1,2, \ldots ,n),$$

which for large finite T will have a unique solution. Now let $T \to \infty$ to get the correct optimal solution.

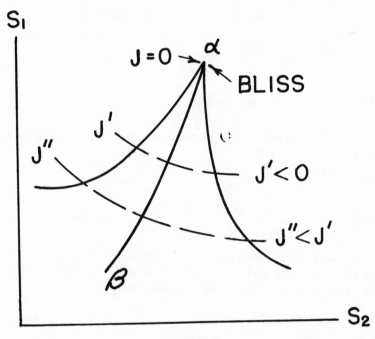

FIGURE I

An alternative method will be useful for the following section and is reminiscent of Ramsey's transformation from t to S_1 as independent variable. If $\dot{S}_1 \neq 0$ along the optimal path, we can convert our maximum problem into either of the two following equivalent ones:

$$(17) \qquad \text{Maximize } J(b_1, \ldots ,b_n) = \int_{b_1}^{a_1^*} \dot{S}_1^{-1} U^*(S_1, S_2(S_1), \ldots ,S_n(S_1),$$

$$\dot{S}_1, \dot{S}_1 \dot{S}_2', \ldots ,\dot{S}_1 S_n')dS_1$$

$$S_i(b_1) = b_i \;\; , \quad S_i(a_1^*) = a_i^* \quad (i = 2, \ldots ,n)$$

where $S_i' = dS_i/dS_1 = S_i'(S_1)$.

Or

(18)   Maximize $J(b_1, \ldots, b_n) = \int_{b_1}^{a_1{}^*} L(S_1, S_2(S_1), \ldots, S_n(S_1), S_2{}'(S_1),$

$$\ldots, S_n{}'(S_1))dS_1$$

$$S_i(b_1) = b_i \quad , \quad S_i(a_1{}^*) = a_i{}^* \quad (i = 2, \ldots, n)$$

where

$$L(S_1, S_2, \ldots, S_n, S_2{}', \ldots, S_n{}') = \underset{\dot{S}_1}{\text{Max}}\ \dot{S}_1^{-1}U^*(S_1, S_2, \ldots, S_n,$$
$$\dot{S}_1, \dot{S}_1 S_2{}', \ldots, \dot{S}_1 S_n{}')$$

$$\frac{\partial L}{\partial S_i} = \dot{S}_1^{-1}\ \frac{\partial U^*}{\partial S_i} = \dot{S}_1^{-1}\ \frac{\partial U}{\partial S_i} \qquad (i = 1, 2, \ldots, n)$$

(19) $\dfrac{\partial L}{\partial S_i{}'} = \dfrac{\partial U^*}{\partial \dot{S}_i} = \dfrac{\partial U}{\partial \dot{S}_i}$

The Euler equations for (17) are equivalent to (14) and take the form

(20a) $\dot{S}_1 \dfrac{\partial U^*}{\partial \dot{S}_1} + \dot{S}_1 S_2{}' \dfrac{\partial U^*}{\partial \dot{S}_2} + \ldots + \dot{S}_1 \dot{S}_n{}' \dfrac{\partial U^*}{\partial \dot{S}_n} - U^* = 0$

(20b) $\dot{S}_1\ \dfrac{d}{dS_1} \dfrac{\partial U^*}{\partial \dot{S}_i} = \dfrac{\partial U^*}{\partial S_i} \qquad\qquad (i = 2, \ldots, n).$

By itself (20a) is seen to be equivalent to (15)″. Using (20a) to express $\dot{S}_1 = \dot{S}_1(S_1)$ and substituting into (20b) verifies for us the Euler equations that (18) directly implies, namely

(21) $\dfrac{d}{dS_1} \dfrac{\partial L}{\partial S_i{}'} = \dfrac{\partial L}{\partial S_i} \qquad\qquad (i = 2, \ldots, n).$

Given the boundary conditions

$$S_i(b_1) = b_i \quad , \quad S_i(a_1{}^*) = a_i{}^* \qquad (i = 2, \ldots, n)$$

(21) can now be solved for the optimal path, with t determined by

(22) $t(S_1) = \displaystyle\int_{b_1}^{S_1} \dfrac{ds_1}{\dot{S}_1(s_1)}$

and with $t(a_1{}^*) = \infty$. Computationally, it is probably best to integrate (21) backwards from $(a_i{}^*)$ for all possible $S_i{}'(a_1{}^*)$ until one finds the right path passing through the prescribed initial point (b_i). Then (20a) will determine $\dot{S}_1$ and (22) t; finally (14a) will determine the C's.

That the extremals do represent a maximum is assured by the

"diminishing returns" condition on U and on f. With

(23) $\left[\dfrac{\partial^2 U}{\partial C_i \partial C_j}\right]$ and $\left[\dfrac{\partial^2 f}{\partial C_i \partial C_j}\right]$ each neg. def.

the Legendre secondary conditions for (14e) or (21) are satisfied.[3] This assures us that the extremals are truly minimizing — at least between close enough together time periods. This by itself does not rule out conjugate points; but our earlier argument concerning the finiteness of J rules out any such pathologies, and thus assures us that the two-period boundary conditions can be satisfied by our differential equations.

The whole optimal path can now be summarized

$$S_i(t) = \sigma_i(t, b_1, \ldots, b_n; a^*)$$

$$\dot{S}_i(t) = \frac{\partial \sigma_i(t, b_1, \ldots, b_n; a^*)}{\partial t}$$

(24) $\qquad\qquad\qquad\qquad\qquad\qquad (i = 1, 2, \ldots, n)$

$$C_i(t) = \gamma_i(t, b_1, \ldots, b_n; a^*)$$

$$\dot{S}_i(0) = \frac{\partial \sigma\ (0, b_1, \ldots, b_n; a^*)}{\partial t}$$

$$C_i(0) = \gamma_i(0, b_1, \ldots, b_n; a^*)$$

where the previously given equations determine the σ_i and γ_i functions uniquely for each prescribed U and f function. The last two expressions of (24) give the decision rules that tell the system exactly how to invest and consume at each state of capital (b_i) it finds itself.

V. Physical Analogy of Small Vibrations

In conservative dynamics, the path of a particle is given by extremals of the integral $\int_0^t L\,dt$ where $L = T - V = 1/2\ \Sigma\Sigma a_{kj}$ $(S_1, \ldots, S_n)\dot{S}_k \dot{S}_j - V(S_1, \ldots, S_n)$, with $[a_{kj}]$ positive definite. A stable vibration is realized around a point $(S_k) = (0)$ where the potential energy function V is at a minimum, with $V(0, \ldots, 0)$ $< V(S_1, \ldots, S_n) = V(0, \ldots, 0) + 1/2\ \Sigma\Sigma\ V_{kj}^0 S_k S_j + \ldots$, where higher powers of S are neglected and $[V_{kj}^0]$ is positive definite.

3. The economist often encounters cases where the law of diminishing returns is violated. And even in cases where diminishing returns prevail there may be no solutions to (14) or (16), the maximum being one of boundary type. An example is $f = (S_1 + S_2) - (1 + r)(C_2 + \dot{S}_2)$. For $r \neq 0$, we must recognize the limits $\dot{S}_i + C_i \gtrless 0$, and possibly $\dot{S}_i \gtrless \alpha_i$ and look for boundary solutions.

The Euler extremals then yield simple harmonic solutions for small oscillations — namely

$$(25) \qquad S_k(t) = \Sigma A_{kj} e^{i\lambda_j t} + \Sigma B_{kj} e^{-i\lambda_j t}$$

where the λ^2's are the negative roots of the determinantal polynomial $| a_{kj}^0 \lambda^2 + V_{kj}^0 |$, and the A's and B's are conjugate complex constants dependent on the initial conditions. Though the motion is "stable" — in the sense of being limited in amplitude and of periodically returning toward the equilibrium level — we know that the extremals minimize the integral $\int_0^t L dt$ only for small values of t. For $t > \pi/\lambda_j$, the extremals have gone through a conjugate point and the true motion merely renders the integral *stationary* rather than truly *minimizing* it. (Actually, the integral can be made indefinitely negative.)

Our economic problem is like the unconventional case of a point of maximum rather than minimum potential energy — as e.g., a stiff pendulum with its bob upright. Touch it with a molecule and it departs ever further from the unstable equilibrium point. This is because $V(0, \ldots, 0) > V(S_1, \ldots, S_n) = V(0, \ldots 0) + 1/2 \Sigma\Sigma V_{kj}^0 S_i S_j + \ldots$ with $[V_{kj}^0]$ now negative definite and with $| a_{kj}^0 \lambda^2 + V_{kj}^0 |$ having all positive roots. Now the solution becomes

$$(26) \qquad S_k(t) = \Sigma A_{kj} e^{\lambda_j t} + \Sigma B_{kj} e^{-\lambda_j t}$$

with no conjugate points possible. For any point near the equilibrium there will be one special set of initial velocities such that all the A's will vanish, and the resulting motion will asymptotically approach the equilibrium level. This special motion — and only it — will truly minimize the Hamilton-Lagrange integral over *all* time. Such a motion would be unstable with respect to any exogenous shocks or displacements, but if an intelligence bent on truly minimizing Hamilton's integral guided the pendulum, it could re-aim the pendulum so as to seek a true minimum. This re-aiming is, so to speak, what an optimizing society is constantly doing.

Figures IIa and IIb show the motions. In IIa, the point a represents a minimum of the potential energy function, and the vibrations represent clockwise closed motions around a. The motions can be regarded as contours of equal total energy (i.e., potential plus kinetic energy, or contours of the Hamiltonian function $H(S_i, p_i)$ $= \Sigma \dot{S}_i p_i - L$, with $p_i = \partial L / \partial \dot{S}_i$).

In IIb, the point a represents a maximum of the potential energy function (and a is the saddlepoint of the Hamiltonian energy function). Now every point near a moves ultimately away from a except for points along one diagonal razor's edge, which approach a asymptotically. (It is of interest to note that the contours of IIa, without arrows, are qualitatively like the contours of L when H is like IIb. Dually, when H is like IIa, the L contours are like IIb, as the requisite Legendre transformations will confirm.)

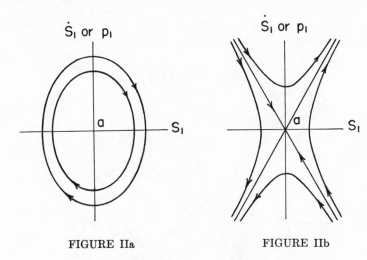

FIGURE IIa   FIGURE IIb

VI. CASE OF UTILITY SATIATION

The case of production satiation, which economists recognize to be the Schumpeter stationary state where all capitals have a zero net productivity, proved simple because it provided a unique endpoint in the $(S_1, \ldots, S_n)$ space. In the present case of utility satiation, there at first appears to be no natural single target point to aim for. At first glance all we can see is that our optimal path must approach one of the infinity of points defined by $(S_i) = (a_i)$ where

$$(27) \qquad U(A_1, A) = 0 \quad , \quad f(a; A) - A_1 = 0$$

with $\partial f / \partial S_i > 0$ and $J(a) = 0$. For if one of these points were not approached, the path could certainly be bettered. And by the reasoning of Section IV, such a point must not be reached in finite time.[4]

Figure III shows the locus defined by (27), EF, where $(S_i) = (a_i)$ is just great enough to yield the bliss level of consumption $U(A) = 0$.

---

4. In the utility satiation case, $[\partial^2 U / \partial \dot{S}_i \partial \dot{S}_j]$ becomes singular where $U = 0$; the no-corner argument of the earlier footnote must be replaced by a more delicate argument.

Were we to begin at a point on *EF* like α' or α'' or α, just staying there would certainly be an optimal path. Therefore, one might be tempted to guess that from an initial point just southwest of α', one would proceed to α', thus aiming at a different point on the *EF* locus from each different initial point (b_i). The first of us actually made this erroneous conjecture, but it turns out that *no matter where the initial nonbliss point (b_i) is, one aims at a unique bliss point α on the EF locus!* Thus, the utility-satiation case turns out to have the same single-end-point condition as did the capital-satiated case.

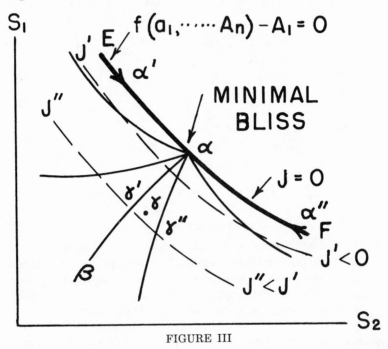

FIGURE III

The special target point α, which as before we may designate by (a_i^*), is one of the set satisfying *EF* or (27). But it differs from any other such (a_i) point in that from every other such point the system is capable of moving to either side of *EF*. Thus, from α' we can enjoy maximal utility while doing one of four things: (a) standing still; (b) moving above *EF*; (c) moving below *EF*; (d) moving along *EF* toward α at a determinate rate. Of these four policies, the first and last are both optimal, while moving off *EF* will give us less than the bliss level of utility. (If we can throw away some goods, moving above *EF* will do us no harm; and with *n* goods *EF* is a hyper-surface along which we can move in many directions.)

What is true at α' is also true at any other ordinary point like α''. At such points we are at bliss, so to speak, "with something to spare." By disinvesting in one capital and adding to another we can beat our way from α' toward α or from α'' toward α.

At one peculiar point α or $(a_i{}^*)$ we are, so to speak, at bliss with nothing to spare. Only policies (a) and (c) are there possible; no movement along *EF* is possible. Indeed this property defines our Minimal Bliss point a^*, which can be characterized in the following way. Consider the expression

$$(28) \qquad \Phi\,(a;\dot{S}) = \sum_{1}^{n} \frac{\partial f(a;A)}{\partial a_j}\,\dot{S}_j$$

where always

$$f(a;A + \dot{S}) - A_1 - \dot{S}_1 = 0$$
$$(28)'$$
$$f(a;A) - A_1 = 0;$$

this Φ is a weighted sum of net investments, with weights equal to the marginal productivities or rentals, measured in units of C_1. It represents a kind of measure of the total increment in the rental of all capitals that is attainable when we start at bliss and pay attention to production constraints. Given any point (a_i) it is natural to ask for the maximum of $\Phi\,(a;\dot{S})$ as we vary the $\dot{S}_j$ subject to $(28)'$. At the Minimal Bliss point a^*, this maximal value will be zero. At other bliss points the maximum value of Φ will be positive. Note that at Minimal Bliss, the maximal value of Φ is achieved with all $\dot{S}_j = 0$; no pattern of capital formation will increase total rentals in terms of C_1.

Thus we have a minimax interpretation of the Minimal Bliss point a^*:[5]

$$(29) \qquad 0 = \Phi\,(a^*;0) = \underset{a}{\text{Min}}\ \underset{S}{\text{Max}}\ \Phi\,(a;\dot{S}).$$

Here for the first time we must use a diminishing returns assumption on the capitals, that the Hessian of f be negative definite in the full input-negative output space.

5. In earlier work by the authors it is shown that a^* is the only point of maximal steady consumption where capitals are efficiently stabilized. At all other (a_i) points one could freeze consumption and, by cleverly selecting algebraic rates of capital formation, end up after a finite time with more of all capitals. At a^* all own-rates of interest will be equal, and a condition like the later (37)

Upon reflection it will perhaps seem plausible that from every sub-bliss point β, the rational path to take is one that gets to Minimal Bliss. We can think of an ordinary bliss point like α' as being in "unstable equilibrium." We can in time push it along EF toward α. It will then not seem surprising that any sub-bliss point near α' will be headed down toward α. Thus in Figure III the optimal paths, such as $\beta\alpha$, are all shown fanning backward from α, looking much like Figure II's production-satiation spider web, but with the J contours now kept from being closed contours by the presence of the EF bliss locus where $J = 0$.

One analytical way to get the optimum path through any (b_i) is to take the limit as finite T grows. Thus, from (16a)

$$(30) \qquad J(b) = \underset{\{T, a_i\}}{\mathrm{Max}}\ K(T;b;a)$$

where it is understood that the (a_i) satisfy $f(a_1, a; A) - A_1 = 0$. But we know that $T = \infty$ at the optimum so that

$$(31) \qquad J(b) = \underset{T \to \infty}{\lim}\ \underset{\{a_i\}}{\mathrm{Max}}\ K(T;b;a)$$

$$= \underset{T \to \infty}{\lim}\ K(T;b;a(T,b))$$

where $a(T;b)$ is short for the optimal end-point for each (T,b).

Now we shall show that

$$(32) \qquad \underset{T \to \infty}{\lim}\ a_i(T;b) = a_i^* \qquad\qquad (i = 1, \ldots, n)$$

independently of b.

For each T, the maximum of K in (30) requires

$$(33) \qquad \frac{\dfrac{\partial K(T;b;a)}{\partial a_i}}{\dfrac{\partial K(T;b;a)}{\partial a_1}} = \frac{\dfrac{\partial f(a;A)}{\partial a_i}}{\dfrac{\partial f(a;A)}{\partial a_1}} \qquad\qquad (i = 2, \ldots, n).$$

But "fundamental relations" like (16) permit us to rewrite the left-hand side of (33) as

$$(34) \qquad \frac{\dfrac{\partial U}{\partial \dot{S}_i}}{\dfrac{\partial U}{\partial \dot{S}_1}} = \frac{\dfrac{\partial U}{\partial C_1} \dfrac{\partial f}{\partial \dot{S}_i}}{-\dfrac{\partial U}{\partial C_1}} = -\frac{\partial f}{\partial \dot{S}_i}$$

will have to hold. See R. Dorfman, R. M. Solow, and P. A. Samuelson, *Linear Programming and Economic Analysis*, a RAND Corporation monograph to be published by McGraw-Hill in 1957, chap. 12.

where in U and f the arguments $(a, \dot{S}^a, C^a)$ are evaluated at the end of the extremal. Even at $U = 0$, where $\partial U / \partial C_1 = 0$, (34) is valid. Hence, our transversality conditions are

$$(35) \qquad -\frac{\partial f(a; \dot{C}^a + S^a)}{\partial \dot{S}_i} = \frac{\dfrac{\partial f(a; A)}{\partial S_i}}{\dfrac{\partial f(a; A)}{\partial S_1}}$$

Now for finite T, we do not know the terminal $\dot{C}_i^a + \dot{S}_i^a$ until we have solved our problem and integrated the correct extremal. But we have already established that as $T \to \infty$, $\dot{S}_i^a \to 0$ and $C_i^a \to A_i$ — which is to say that a bliss point is approached. Hence, as $T \to \infty$, the target (a_i) must satisfy the basic equations

$$(36) \qquad -\frac{\partial f(a; A)}{\partial \dot{S}_i} = \frac{\dfrac{\partial f(a; A)}{\partial S_i}}{\dfrac{\partial f(a; A)}{\partial S_1}} \qquad\qquad (i = 2, \ldots, n)$$

$$f(a; A) - A_1 = 0.$$

These are remarkable relations. That they do not contain T explicitly is not surprising since they were derived for $T \to \infty$. But that they do not contain (b_i) shows that their defined target point, which we have called the point of Minimal Bliss (a_i^*), is a unique point aimed at by all *initial* states. The n equations (36) are sufficient to determine the n unknown co-ordinates of (a_i^*) and our diminishing returns assumptions suffice to make the solution a unique one. Relations (36) are precisely those needed to achieve the minimax of (28) and (29).

VII. Practical Computation

Even though we have our end-point, we shall not find it convenient to integrate through infinite time. As in Section IV, we find it convenient to work in the $(S_1, S_2, \ldots, S_n)$ space alone, using the L function of (19) and integrating the Euler equations (21) between (b_i) and (a_i^*) as in our earlier problem. (The fact that in the utility satiation case L has a singular matrix $[\partial^2 L / \partial S_i{}' \partial S_j{}']$ at bliss points where $J = U = 0$ will not matter.)

Transversality conditions like (35) could be written in terms of derivatives of L. Such conditions would have some singular properties, being solvable only for $(a_i{}^*)$ and leading to different $S_i{}'(a_i{}^*)$ depending upon the initial point. Discussion of this topic is omitted, since it would only establish what we already have demonstrated — that $(a_i{}^*)$ is always our target.

In Figure III as in Figure I it is well to work backward from $(a_i{}^*)$. A good guess of a path, say $\alpha\beta$, should take us close to any specified initial point, γ: when we get to a nearby point, like γ', its slope is a good approximation to the desired policy-rule at γ. If a better solution is wanted, we try another path gauged to move "closer" to γ than γ' turned out to do. If a point on the new path is "closer," its slope will be a better approximation.

Actually, given two nearby paths, one can hope to get a still better approximation. On the new path $\alpha\beta'$, pick a point γ'' that is exactly the same J distance away from α as is γ': i.e., integrate until $J(\gamma'') = J(\gamma') \doteq J(\gamma)$. Then, from the "fundamental relations," $\partial U^*/\partial \dot{S}_i$ or $\partial L/\partial S_i{}'$ will give us the transverse J-contour slopes at γ' and γ'', permitting a third-degree interpolation of the J contour through γ' and γ''. At a point on this contour near γ, the known numerical slopes $\partial J/\partial b_i$ can be used to get a still more accurate guess at $(\dot{S}_i)$: i.e., invert

$$(37) \qquad -\frac{\partial J}{\partial b_i} = \frac{\partial U^*(b, \dot{S}^b)}{\partial \dot{S}_i} \qquad\qquad (i = 1, \ldots, n)$$

to get a better approximation

$$(38) \qquad \dot{S}^b{}_i = Q_i\left(b, -\frac{\partial J}{\partial b}\right) \qquad\qquad (i = 1, \ldots, n).$$

Equations (38) or (37) are useful in giving exact policy rules if the J function should happen to be known, as in the case where a central agency has computed it by integrating (21) once and for all for every extremal through $(a_i{}^*)$. Then decentralized decision-makers could use (38) to get day by day programs. In the next section further methods will be suggested.

VIII. Hamiltonian Formulation

Our generalized Ramsey problem is now solved. The solution is quite straightforward, even though tedious because of the need to integrate the Euler differential equations.

We shall now briefly review some of the fashionable Hamiltonian formalisms that are often used in the physics and mathematics literature to describe variational problems. The computational advantage of these is not evident, since the resulting partial differential equations are in practice usually solvable only by integrating the Euler differential equations or their canonical equivalents. Rather than deal with U and U^*, we shall confine ourselves to the slightly simpler L formulation in (S_i) space.

First, define new conjugate variables or "generalized momenta"

$$(39) \qquad \frac{\partial L(S_1, S_2, \ldots, S_n, S_2', \ldots, S_n')}{\partial S_i'} = p_i, \qquad (i = 2, \ldots, n).$$

Since $[\partial^2 L / \partial S_i' \partial S_j']$ is definite at all sub-bliss points because of the maximum character of the problem, we can always invert these equations to get

$$(39)' \qquad S_i' = Q_i(S_1, S_2, \ldots, S_n, p_2, \ldots, p_n), \qquad (i = 2, \ldots, n).$$

We now define the Hamiltonian function

$$(40) \qquad H(S_1, S_2, \ldots, \dot{S}_n, p_2, \ldots, p_n)$$

$$= \overset{n}{\underset{2}{\Sigma}} \, p_j Q_j(S,p) - L(S, Q_2(S,p), \ldots, Q_n(S,p))$$

which can be shown to be "dual" to L through the Legendre transformation just described. Either H or L can be used as single functions to "store" all the "information" of the problem.

One easily verifies

$$(41a) \qquad -\frac{\partial H}{\partial S_i} = \frac{\partial L}{\partial S_i} \qquad\qquad (i = 1, 2, \ldots, n)$$

$$(41b) \qquad \frac{\partial H}{\partial p_j} = Q_j = S_j' \qquad\qquad (j = 2, \ldots, n).$$

These last and our Euler conditions now give us the $2(n - 1)$ first-order "canonical" differential equations in the $2(n - 1)$ independent variables $(S_2, \ldots, S_n, p_2, \ldots, p_n)$:

$$\frac{dS_j}{dS_1} = \frac{\partial H(S,p)}{\partial p_j}$$

$$(42) \qquad\qquad\qquad\qquad\qquad\qquad (j = 2, \ldots, n)$$

$$\frac{dp_j}{dS_1} = -\frac{\partial H(S,p)}{\partial S_j}.$$

Solving these canonical equations is one way, but usually not an essentially easier numerical method, of solving the Euler differential equations.[6]

Of course

$$\frac{dH}{dS_1} = \sum_2^n \frac{\partial H}{\partial S_j} \frac{dS_j}{dS_1} + \sum_2^n \frac{dH}{\partial p_j} \frac{dp_j}{\partial S_1} + \frac{\partial H}{\partial S_1} = \sum_2^n \left(\frac{\partial H}{\partial S_j} \frac{\partial H}{\partial p_j} - \frac{\partial H}{\partial p_j} \frac{\partial H}{\partial S_j} \right)$$

$$+ \frac{\partial H}{\partial S_1} = \frac{\partial H}{\partial S_1}$$

This "total energy" expression does not vanish along an optimal path: our economic system is truly time-free, but after we convert to S_1 as the independent variable it becomes "nonconservative" with S_1 usually entering explicitly into L and H.

We now define a W function

(43) $$W(b,a) = \operatorname*{Max}_T K(T:b;a;) = \int_{b_1}^{a_1} L dS_1, \text{ with } L \text{ evaluated}$$

along the extremals between

$$S_i(b_1) = b_i \text{ and } S_i(a_1) = a_i \qquad\qquad (i = 2, \ldots, n).$$

The fundamental relations which gave us (16) and (35) also give

$$\frac{\partial W}{\partial a_i} = \frac{\partial L(a,a')}{\partial S_i'} = p_i \qquad\qquad (i = 2, \ldots, n)$$

(44)

$$\frac{\partial U}{\partial a_1} = L - \sum_2^n a_j' \frac{\partial L}{\partial S_j'} = -H(a,p)$$

where $a' = (a_2', \ldots, a_n')$ and $p = (p_2, \ldots, p_n)$ are respectively the extremals' slopes and momenta.

We can combine these last relations into a single nonlinear first-order partial differential equation for the W function, namely

(45) $$\frac{\partial W}{\partial a_1} + H\left(a_1, \ldots, a_n, \frac{\partial W}{\partial a_2}, \ldots, \frac{\partial W}{\partial a_n} \right) = 0.$$

6. E.g., writing $d/dS_1 \{\partial L/\partial S_i\} - \partial L/\partial S_i = \Sigma a_{ij} S_j'' - M_i = 0$ where $[a_{ij}] = [\partial L/\partial S_i' \partial S_j']$, we can write $S_i'' = N_i(S_1, S_2, \ldots, S_n, S_2', \ldots, S_n')$ where $N_i = [a_{ij}]^{-1} M_i$. We need not invert $[a_{ij}]$ everywhere, but only along the path of integration where it changes only gradually and can often be swiftly approximated by iteration.

This Hamilton-Jacobi equation is a necessary condition that W must satisfy. It becomes a sufficient condition only when we adjoin the boundary conditions

$$W(b,a) = 0 \text{ when } a_i = b_i \qquad (i = 1, \ldots, n)$$

(46)
$$\frac{dW}{dS_1} = \lim_{h \to 0} \frac{W(b_1, \ldots, b_n, b_1 + h, b_2 + hb_2', \ldots, b_n + hb_n')}{h}$$
$$\equiv L(b_1, \ldots, b_n, b_2', \ldots, b_n')$$

for arbitrary prescribed $(b_2', \ldots, b_n')$.

Hamilton was led to his partial differential equation for mechanical systems by analogy to his formulation of the variational properties of an optical wave system. Equation (45) enables us to interpret the transverse W or J contours of Figure II. Just as the wave front of light emanating from a point can by Huyghens' Principle be thought of as the envelope of circular light rays going out from each new point, so can J'' be regarded as the envelope of $\int L dt$ contours emanating backward in all directions from each point beyond α, with each new point being a new source of backward rays.

For arbitrary b, (45) and (46) do define a unique function $W(b,a)$. But it is an illusion to think that (45) and (46) have computational advantages; for in most practical cases the only way to solve the Hamilton-Jacobi partial differential equation is by the method of characteristics, which is precisely equivalent to integrating the Euler differential equations. (Hamilton himself for the most part evaluated his principal function J by integrating the Euler equations. Incidentally the derivation of the partial differential equation (45) is quite independent of the Hamilton canonical formulation (42), being dependent only on the fundamental relations (44) and the Legendre transformation (39)–(40). Hamilton was the first to derive the canonical equations, though Lagrange and Poisson seem to have come close to them; still Hamilton does not appear to have attached great significance to them.)

This much can be said for an approach based upon evaluating the W function. Like L and H, W is a function of about $2n$ variables which completely "stores" or contains all the "information" of the problem. Thus if a bomb destroyed all but knowledge of W, we could deduce from it L or H and all the extremals and policy rules. Moreover W, unlike L or H, permits us to find the extremals by purely analytical acts of evaluating derivatives and inverting functions, there being no further need to integrate differential equations once W is known.

Thus, given W for all values of b — which is a tall order — we can find the extremal paths by solving the following equations

$$(47) \qquad \frac{\partial W(b,S)}{\partial b_j} = - p_j^b, \text{ fixed constants} \qquad (j = 2, \ldots, n)$$

to get

$$(48) \qquad S_i = \varphi_i(S_1; b_1, \ldots, b_n, p_2^b, \ldots, p_n^b) \qquad (i = 2, \ldots, n)$$

the equation for the extremals through (b_i) · with prescribed initial momenta $(p_2^b, \ldots, p_n^b)$. Jacobi improved on Hamilton by showing how any n parameter complete solution to (45) whether it satisfies (46) or not, can be used to determine the extremals.

Thus let a complete solution to (45) alone be $V(a_1, \ldots, a_n, c_2, \ldots, c_n) + c_1$. Jacobi showed that the $2(n-1)$ equations

$$\frac{\partial V}{\partial c_i} = - \beta_i$$

$$\frac{\partial V}{\partial a_i} = p_i \qquad\qquad (i = 2, \ldots, n)$$

can be solved for $(a_2, \ldots, a_n, p_2, \ldots, p_n)$ in terms of a_1 and the constants $(c_2, \ldots, c_n, \beta_2, \ldots, \beta_n)$. These functions can easily be shown to satisfy the canonical equations (42) and hence do define extremals.

Hamilton's editors, Conway and McConnell[7] have shown that any complete solution of (45) $V(a_1, \ldots, a_n, c_2, \ldots, c_n) + c_1$ can be converted into Hamilton's special solution W, as follows. Set

$$(49a) \qquad w = V(a_1, \ldots, a_n, c_2, \ldots, c_n) - V(b_1, \ldots, b_n, c_2, \ldots, c_n)$$

$$(49b) \qquad \frac{\partial w}{\partial c_i} = 0 \qquad\qquad (i = 2, \ldots, n).$$

Using (49b) to eliminate the c's and substituting into (49a) gives us the envelope $w(b_1, \ldots, b_n, a_1, \ldots, a_n)$ which can be shown to satisfy (45) and (46), and hence to be our desired W function.

However, when we leave the realm of simple textbook examples and special functions, the Jacobi improvements do not advance us much since a complete solution to (45) can usually be found only by tedious integration of $2(n-1)$ first-order differential equations or the equivalent. It is possible, though, that the use of the W function

7. A. W. Conway and A. J. McConnell (ed.), *Mathematical Papers of Sir William Rowan Hamilton*, Vol. II, *Dynamics* (Cambridge, 1940), Editors' Appendix, Note 2.

might have administrative conveniences: W might be computed by a research department, not because its computation saves labor, but because its information can be conveniently turned over to the line officials who currently make decisions at each given state of the system $(b_1, \ldots, b_n)$ or $(S_1, \ldots, S_n)$.

To arrive at possibly helpful forms for W, we first note that $W(b,a)$ must satisfy partial differential equations with respect to the b's very similar to those satisfied with respect to the a's. Corresponding to (44) and (45) we have

$$(50a) \qquad \frac{\partial W}{\partial b_i} = -\frac{\partial L(b,b')}{\partial \dot{S}_i} = -p_i \qquad\qquad (i = 2, \ldots, n)$$

$$(50b) \qquad \frac{\partial W}{\partial b_1} = -\left(L - \sum_2^n b_j' \frac{\partial L}{\partial S_j'}\right) = +H(b,p)$$

and

$$(51) \qquad -\frac{\partial W}{\partial b_1} + H\left(b_1, \ldots, b_n, -\frac{\partial W}{\partial b_2}, \ldots, -\frac{\partial W}{\partial b_n}\right) = 0$$

where the (b_i') are initial derivatives. The proof of this is as before, but follows even more directly from the fact that

$$(52) \qquad W(b,a) = \int_{b_1}^{a_1} L dS_1 = -\int_{a_1}^{b_1} L dS_1 = -W(a,b),$$

so that (44) and (45) are seen to imply (50) and (51).

IX. Pay-off in Terms of Initial State

The above Hamiltonian theory is standard for fixed end-points. We must now develop it to take into account the special transversality and end conditions of the problem. Instead of wanting our pay-off integral W as a function of the $2n$ variables $(b_1, \ldots, b_n, a_1, \ldots, a_n)$, we want it in terms of the initial state $(b_1, \ldots, b_n)$ alone: i.e., we want our original $J(b_1, \ldots, b_n)$ function.

From earlier sections we know

$$(53) \qquad J(b_1, \ldots, b_h) = W(b,a^*).$$

Of course,

$$(54) \qquad \frac{\partial J(b)}{\partial b_i} = \frac{\partial W(b,a^*)}{\partial b_i} \qquad\qquad (i = 1, 2, \ldots, n).$$

Equations (54) tell us that J must satisfy the same Hamilton-Jacobi partial differential equation (51) that W satisfied. Thus, $J(b)$ must satisfy

$$(55) \qquad -\frac{\partial J}{\partial b_1} + H\left(b_1, \ldots, b_n, -\frac{\partial J}{\partial b_2}, \ldots, -\frac{\partial J}{\partial b_n}\right) = 0.$$

If J were known, we have seen already in (37) and (38) that we could get the policy rules at each (b_i) point from

$$(56) \qquad p_{i,}^b = -\frac{\partial J(b)}{\delta b_i} \qquad\qquad (i = 2, \ldots, n)$$

$$(57) \qquad S_i'(b_1) = Q_i(b, p^b)$$

where the Q functions come from (38) or from solving (37).

As an alternative to solving (37), we could use the known J function in the following way:

$$\frac{d}{dS_1}\frac{\partial J}{\partial b_i} = -\frac{d}{dS_1}p_i^b = \frac{\partial H\left(b_1, \ldots, b_n, -\dfrac{\partial J}{\partial b_2}, \ldots, -\dfrac{\partial J}{\partial b_n}\right)}{\partial S_i}$$

from (57) and the canonical equations. Hence,

$$(58) \qquad \sum_2^n \frac{\partial^2 J}{\partial b_i \partial b_j} S_j'(S_1) = \frac{\partial H\left(b_1, \ldots, b_n, -\dfrac{\partial J}{\partial b_{2i}}, \ldots, -\dfrac{\partial J}{\partial b_n}\right)}{\partial S_i} - \frac{\partial^2 J}{\partial b_i \partial b_1}$$

$$(i = 2, \ldots, n).$$

These are $(n - 1)$ *linear* equations for the slopes, involving nothing worse than differentiations of the known J and H functions. This seems to avoid inverting the functions in (37); but to have found the H function would probably already have involved inverting (37), so (58) is of illusory advantage except possibly in connection with decentralization of decision-making.

A known J can give us our decision rules for S' in still another, equivalent way. Construct an excess function as follows:

$$(59) \qquad E(S_1, \ldots, S_n, S_2', \ldots, S_n') = L(S_1, \ldots, S_n, S_2', \ldots, S_n')$$
$$- \sum_2^n \frac{\partial J}{\partial S_j} S_j' - \frac{\partial J}{\partial S_1}.$$

Then the proper (S_i') are those which maximize E, achieving $E = 0$. Similarly, working in terms of t as independent variable, we could define

$$(60) \qquad E(S_1, \ldots, S_n; \dot{S}_1, \ldots, \dot{S}_n, C_2, \ldots, C_n) = U - \sum_1^n \frac{\partial J}{\partial S_j} \dot{S}_j - 0,$$

and our decision rules are given by the $(\dot{S}_i, C_i)$ that realize the maximum $E = 0$ for any prescribed (S_i). This formulation is a slight adaptation of the Carathéodory[8] principle that extremals of a field represent "paths of steepest descent."

But suppose we do not yet know the J function. By itself (55) is a necessary but not a sufficient condition to determine J. We must adjoin to (55) the boundary conditions like (46) where J vanishes at (a_i^*). I.e.,

(61)
$$J(a_1^*, a_2^*, \ldots, a_n^*) = 0$$

$$\lim_{h \to 0} \frac{J(a_1^* - h, a_2^* - hS_2', \ldots, a_n^* - hS_n')}{-h}$$

$$\equiv -L(a_1^*, \ldots, a_n^*, S_2', \ldots, S_n')$$

for arbitrary (S_i').

The combined conditions (56) and (61) give a problem in first-order partial differential equations, and existence theorems assure us of a unique J solution.

X. CONCLUSION

The logical structure of a complete capital model is provided by the present discussion. However our completed analysis has made no use of Lagrangian multipliers $[\mu_j(t)]$, instead using constraints to eliminate redundant variables. Greater symmetry as among goods would have been retained by use of such Lagrangian multipliers. Moreover, these multipliers could be given the usual economic interpretations in terms of "shadow prices" or "dual variables." It would also be possible to give price interpretations to the Hamiltonian momenta $[p_i(t)]$.

Various easy generalizations of our basic assumptions are possible. Thus we could easily rewrite $C_1 = f(S_1, \ldots, S_n; C_2 + \dot{S}_2, \ldots, C_n + \dot{S}_n) - \dot{S}_1$ as $C_1 = f(S_1, \ldots, S_n; \dot{S}_1 \dot{S}_2, \ldots, \dot{S}_n; C_2, \ldots, C_n)$ or even as a general vanishing implicit function of all these variables. More important, we could replace the $\int U dt$ functional to be maximized by a more realistic functional not having the independently-additive utilities of a simple integral. Our Euler differential equations would no longer be valid; but interestingly enough, there will remain valid intertemporal efficiency conditions, which are implied by the Euler equations, but which are independent of all the terms in the Euler expression involving the U function.[9]

8. *Op. cit.*, p. 250.
9. See R. Dorfman, R. Solow, and P. A. Samuelson, *op. cit.* for a different derivation of these intertemporal efficiency conditions.

Various specializations of the foregoing analysis are also possible as e.g., the important case where the production function f is homogeneous of the first degree. The Leontief-Koopmans-von Neumann case of dynamic *linear* finite-activities analysis can also be considered, only here we must replace the Euler equalities by more general differential *inequations*. Finally, replacing continuous time by discrete time, integrals by sums, and derivatives by differences would bring us back to the discrete case from which Euler deduced his extremal condition as a limit, but no one seems to have worked out the full Hamiltonian theory for this discrete case.

PAUL A. SAMUELSON
ROBERT M. SOLOW
MASSACHUSETTS INSTITUTE OF TECHNOLOGY

26

Efficient Paths of Capital Accumulation in Terms of the Calculus of Variations

PAUL A. SAMUELSON
Massachusetts Institute of Technology

1. Introduction

In the case of discrete time, Dorfman, Samuelson, and Solow [4] showed that efficient paths of capital accumulation lead to radiating tangency conditions for envelope frontiers which are formally reminiscent of Huyghens' Principle in physics. When discrete time is replaced by flows in continuous time, similar relations must prevail; but now the problem has to be formulated in terms of the standard calculus of variations.

The present paper briefly presents the theory appropriate for the continuous-time case. We shall consider only what might be called the classically regular case: variational equalities, like those of the ordinary calculus, are given rather than the more general inequalities of linear and non-linear programming. Also, we shall not fully explore the dual variables or shadow prices that are implied by the maximum problem.

2. Maximizing Conditions

Let $[S_1(t), S_2(t), \cdots, S_n(t)]$ represent the magnitude of n capital stocks at each time; their time derivatives, or net capital formations, can then be written as $[\dot{S}_1(t), \cdots, \dot{S}_n(t)]$. Finally, let there be n consumption flows over time written as $[C_1(t), \cdots, C_n(t)]$.

We take as given an instantaneous production function f that is a homogeneous function of the first degree.[1] Consider

$$(1) \qquad \dot{S}_1(t) = f[S_1(t), S_2(t), \cdots; \dot{S}_2(t) + C_2(t) \cdots] - C_1(t),$$

The present paper is a revised version of an appendix written for [4] but eventually not used there. An independent treatment of this same subject was drafted by Robert M. Solow. To him, the RAND Corporation, and the Ford Foundation go my thanks.

[1] Relation (1) is the continuous analog of (12-2) of [4]; it was already given in [6, p. 539]. We could dispense with the adding of C_i to $\dot{S}_i$, replacing (1) by $\dot{S}_1 = f(S_1, \cdots, S_n; \dot{S}_2, \cdots, \dot{S}_n; C_1, \cdots, C_n)$. Also, we could lighten the homogeneity assumption, replacing it simply by convexity requirements on f.

with

$$\frac{\partial f}{\partial S_1} > 0, \quad \frac{\partial f}{\partial S_i} > 0, \quad \frac{\partial f}{\partial \dot{S}_i} < 0 \qquad (i = 2, \cdots, n) \,,$$

and with

$$\begin{bmatrix} \dfrac{\partial^2 f}{\partial S_i \partial S_j} & \dfrac{\partial^2 f}{\partial S_i \partial \dot{S}_j} \\[2ex] \dfrac{\partial^2 f}{\partial \dot{S}_i \partial S_j} & \dfrac{\partial^2 f}{\partial \dot{S}_i \partial \dot{S}_j} \end{bmatrix} \qquad (i, j = 2, \cdots, n) \,,$$

a negative definite $[2(n-1)]^2$ matrix.

Subject to equation (1), where the $C_i(t)$ are prescribed functions on $t^0 \leqq t \leqq t^1$, and to the conditions

(2)
$$S_i(t^0) = S_i^0 > 0 \quad (i = 1, \cdots, n),$$
$$S_i(t^1) = S_i^1 > 0 \quad (i = 2, \cdots, n), \text{ where } t^1 > t^0,$$

we are to maximize

(2′)
$$S_1(t^1) - S_1(t^0) = \int_{t^0}^{t^1} \dot{S}_1(t) \, dt \,.$$

We set up the Lagrangian expression

(3)
$$\int_{t^0}^{t^1} \varPhi(S_1, S_2, \cdots ; \dot{S}_1, \dot{S}_2, \cdots ; \lambda) \, dt \,,$$

where

$$\varPhi = \dot{S}_1(t) + \lambda(t)\{f[S_1(t), \cdots ; \dot{S}_2(t) + C_2(t), \cdots] - \dot{S}_1(t) - C_1(t)\} \,,$$

and treat each $S_i(t)$ *as if* independently variable. This yields the Euler differential equations necessary for a maximum:

$$\frac{d}{dt} \frac{\partial \varPhi}{\partial \dot{S}_i} - \frac{\partial \varPhi}{\partial S_i} = 0 \qquad (i = 1, \cdots, n) \,,$$

or

$$\frac{d}{dt}\{1 - \lambda(t)\} = \lambda(t) \frac{\partial f(S_1, S_2, \cdots ; \dot{S}_2 + C_2, \cdots)}{\partial S_1} \,,$$

(4)
$$\frac{d}{dt}\left\{ \lambda(t) \frac{\partial f(S_1, S_2, \cdots ; \dot{S}_2 + C_2, \cdots)}{\partial \dot{S}_i} \right\}$$

$$= \lambda(t) \frac{\partial f(S_1, S_2, \cdots ; \dot{S}_2 + C_2, \cdots)}{\partial S_i} \qquad (i = 2, \cdots, n) \,,$$

$$\dot{S}_1 = f(S_1, S_2, \cdots ; \dot{S}_2 + C_2, \cdots) - C_1 \,.$$

We can eliminate the Lagrangian multiplier from (4) to get the fundamental efficiency conditions[2]

(5)

$$\frac{d}{dt}\frac{\partial f}{\partial \dot{S}_i} = \frac{\partial f}{\partial S_i} + \frac{\partial f}{\partial S_1}\frac{\partial f}{\partial \dot{S}_i} \quad (i = 2, \cdots, n)$$

$$\dot{S}_1 = f(S_1, S_2, \cdots ; \dot{S}_2 + C_2, \cdots) - C_1$$

Also

(5′)
$$\frac{-d\lambda(t)}{\lambda(t)dt} = \frac{\partial f(S_1, S_2, \cdots ; \dot{S}_2 + C_2, \cdots)}{\partial S_1}.$$

Since $\partial \dot{S}_1/\partial S_1 = \partial f/\partial S_1$ is an own rate of interest in terms of S_1, equation (5′) relates λ to a discounting function.

An economic interpretation of our fundamental efficiency conditions (5) can be given in terms of market prices or dual variables. Let the own rate of interest in terms of the ith commodity be $r_i = \partial \dot{S}_i/\partial S_i = -(\partial f/\partial S_i)/(\partial f/\partial \dot{S}_i)$; and note that $p_i = -\partial \dot{S}_1/\partial \dot{S}_i$ represents the price ratio of the ith flow commodity expressed in terms of the first flow commodity as *numéraire*. Then a little manipulation converts (5) into $r_1 = r_i + (1/p_i)(dp_i/dt)$, where $(i = 2, \cdots, n)$, which is the fundamental relationship that must hold between various own rates of interest.[3]

3. Envelopes and Efficient Paths

Because of our definite Hessian in the constraints on (1), equations (3) and (5) do ensure a true maximum to our problem.[4] We can write the resulting maximum S_1^1 in the form

(6)
$$S_1^1 = E(t^1 ; S_2^1, \cdots, S_n^1 ; t^0 ; S_1^0, \cdots, S_n^0 ; C),$$

where C stands for all the consumption time functions.

One could show from (1) and (4) that

(7a)
$$\frac{\partial E}{\partial S_1^0} > 0, \quad \frac{\partial E}{\partial S_i^0} > 0, \quad \frac{\partial E}{\partial S_i^1} < 0 \quad (i = 2, \cdots, n)$$

and that

---

[2] The fundamental relations (5) were already implicit in the extremal equations (14) of [6]. Just as the necessary conditions of the narrow "New Welfare Economics" are those conditions derivable by eliminating from the complete optimality conditions all expressions involving a social welfare function, so will eliminating all forms of utility U from the cited (14) lead to the present (5).

[3] See [5, p. 490, eq. (10)] and [4, pp. 317–22].

[4] The Legendre-Clebsch definiteness of $[\partial^2 f/\partial \dot{S}_i \partial \dot{S}_j]$ suffices only to establish the existence of a maximum in a region *sufficiently near* to the initial point at t^0. But the definiteness of the whole Hessian matrix enables one to rule out conjugate points and to prove that a maximum exists in the large.

(7b)
$$
\begin{bmatrix}
\dfrac{\partial^2 E}{\partial S_i^1 \partial S_j^1} & \dfrac{\partial^2 E}{\partial S_i^1 \partial S_j^0} \\[3mm]
\dfrac{\partial^2 E}{\partial S_i^0 \partial S_j^1} & \dfrac{\partial^2 E}{\partial S_i^0 \partial S_j^0}
\end{bmatrix}
\qquad (i, j = 2, \cdots, n)
$$

is negative definite.

In the special von Neumann case, in which all C's are zero (or are fixed proportions of outputs), equation (6) will be a homogeneous function of the first degree in the S's because of the similar property of f. Because f does not involve t explicitly, E will then involve t^1 and t^0 only in the form of their difference $t^1 - t^0$.

Of course, in all of the above relations, the first variable S_1 or $\dot{S}_1$ is really *any* variable, so that the asymmetry of results is purely notational.

The differential equations (5) can be solved explicitly for efficient time paths once we have prescribed initial $[S_1^0, \cdots, S_n^0]$ and $[\dot{S}_2^0, \cdots, \dot{S}_n^0]$. Once we have arbitrarily prescribed $\lambda(t^0) = \lambda^0$, the set of relations (5) and (5') can be solved explicitly. Thus

(8)
$$
S_i(t) = S^i(t; t^0; S_1^0, \cdots, S_n^0; \dot{S}_2^0, \cdots, \dot{S}_n^0; C) \qquad (i = 1, \cdots, n),
$$
$$
\lambda(t) = \lambda^0 M(t; t^0; S_1^0, \cdots, S_n^0; \dot{S}_2^0, \cdots, \dot{S}_n^0; C).
$$

These solutions are known to exist because, after the left-hand side of (4) or (5) has been differentiated with respect to time, the indicated definiteness of our $[\partial^2 f / \partial \dot{S}_i \partial \dot{S}_j]$ matrix assures us that we can solve explicitly for

$$
\ddot{S}_i = R^i(S_1, S_2, \cdots; \dot{S}_1 + C_1, \dot{S}_2 + C_2, \cdots) - \dot{C}_i \qquad (i = 2, \cdots, n),
$$

(9)
$$
\dot{S}_1 = f(S_1, S_2, \cdots; \dot{S}_2 + C_2, \cdots) - C_1,
$$

$$
\dot{\lambda} = -\lambda \frac{\partial f(S_1, \cdots; \dot{S}_2 + C_2, \cdots)}{\partial S_1},
$$

and this system of the $2n$th order is known to be solvable for the $2n$-parameter family of functions given in (8).

For $t = t_1$ and for varying parameters $[\dot{S}_2^0, \cdots, \dot{S}_n^0]$ and fixed $[t_0; S_1^0, \cdots, S_n^0]$, the first n relations in (8) are the parametric equations of our envelope E function given in (6).

It is also clear from applying fundamental existence theorems (9) that there exists a single solution through $(t^0, S_1^0, \cdots, S_n^0)$ and any nearby point $(t^1, S_2^1, \cdots, S_n^1)$; actually

(10)
$$
S_i(t) = J^i(t; t^0; S_1^0, \cdots, S_n^0; S_2^1, \cdots, S_n^1; t^1; C) \qquad (i = 1, \cdots, n).
$$

For $t = t^1$ the first of these equations is again essentially our envelope relation (6).

In the case $C_i \equiv 0$, equation (10) becomes

(10')
$$
S_i(t) = J^i(t - t^0; S_1^0, \cdots, S_n^0; S_2^1, \cdots, S_n^1) \qquad (i = 1, \cdots, n).
$$

4. Transversality and Equivalence of Flow and Stock Prices

We may now prove that the slopes of the envelope function (6) are related to the slopes of the f function (1) by the transversality relation

$$\frac{\partial E}{\partial S_i^1} = f_{\dot{S}_i}(S_1^1, S_2^1, \cdots ; \dot{S}_2^1 + C_2^1, \cdots) \qquad (i = 2, \cdots, n),$$

(11)
$$\frac{\partial E}{\partial t^1} = f(S_1^1, S_2^1, \cdots ; \dot{S}_2^1 + C_2^1, \cdots) - C_1$$

$$- \sum_{j=2}^{n} f_{\dot{S}_j}(S_1^1, S_2^1, \cdots ; \dot{S}_2^1 + C_2^1, \cdots)\dot{S}_j^1,$$

where $(\dot{S}_2^1, \cdots, \dot{S}_n^1)$ are evaluated so as to satisfy (4) or (5) and subscripts to functions indicate partial differentiation.

Once the first set of these relations is proved, the last follows immediately from the relations

$$\frac{dE}{dt} = \frac{\partial E}{\partial t} + \sum_{i=2}^{n} \frac{\partial E}{\partial S_i^1}\dot{S}_i^1 = \dot{S}_1 = f - \dot{C}_1.$$

To prove the first set, we note

(12)
$$\frac{\partial E}{\partial S_i^1} = \int_{t^0}^{t^1} \left\{ \sum_{i,j=1}^{n} \frac{\partial \Phi}{\partial S_j} \frac{\partial J^j}{\partial S_i^1} + \sum_{i,j=1}^{n} \frac{\partial \Phi}{\partial \dot{S}_j} \frac{\partial \dot{J}^j}{\partial S_i^1} + \frac{\partial \Phi \partial \lambda}{\partial \lambda \partial S_i^1} \right\} dt$$

$$= \int_{t^0}^{t^1} \left\{ \sum_{i,j=1}^{n} \frac{\partial \Phi}{\partial S_j} \frac{\partial J^j}{\partial S_i^1} + \sum_{i,j=1}^{n} \frac{\partial \Phi}{\partial \dot{S}_j} \frac{\partial \dot{J}^j}{\partial S_i^1} + 0 \right\} dt,$$

by virtue of Φ's definition in (3)

$$= \int_{t^0}^{t^1} \frac{d}{dt} \left\{ \sum_{i,j=1}^{n} \frac{\partial \Phi}{\partial \dot{S}_j} \frac{\partial J^j}{\partial S_i^1} \right\} dt,$$

by virtue of the fact that the J functions satisfy the Euler conditions (4)

$$= \left\{ (1 - \lambda)\frac{\partial J^1}{\partial S_i^1} + \sum_{i,j=2}^{n} \lambda f_{\dot{S}_j}\frac{\partial J^j}{\partial S_i^1} \right\}\Bigg|_{t^0}^{t^1}.$$

But note that by definition in (10)

(13)
$$\frac{\partial J^1(t^1; t^0; S_1^0, S_2^0, \cdots ; S_2^1, \cdots ; t^1; C)}{\partial S_i^1} = \frac{\partial E}{\partial S_i^1},$$

$$\frac{\partial J^j(t^1; t^0; S_1^0, S_2^0, \cdots ; S_2^1, \cdots ; t^1; C)}{\partial S_i^1} = \begin{cases} 1 \text{ if } j = i \\ 0 \text{ if } j \neq i, \end{cases}$$

and hence we have proved

$$\frac{\partial E}{\partial S_i^1} = (1 - \lambda)\frac{\partial E}{\partial S_i^1} + \lambda f_{\dot{S}_i}(S_1^1, S_2^1, \cdots ; \dot{S}_2^1 + C_2, \cdots)$$

$$= f_{\dot{S}_i}(S_1^1, S_2^1, \cdots ; \dot{S}_2^1 + C_2^1, \cdots) \qquad (i = 2, \cdots, n),$$

which is (11).

These transversality conditions have an economic meaning. As a comparison of Figures 1 and 2 shows, they imply that at every point along a developing efficient path, the price ratios of capital stocks $[S_i(t)]$ must be exactly the same as the price ratios of flows $[\dot{S}_i]$: i.e.,

(14) $$p_i = -\frac{\partial \dot{S}_1}{\partial \dot{S}_i} = -\frac{\partial S_1}{\partial S_i} \qquad (i = 2, \cdots, n).$$

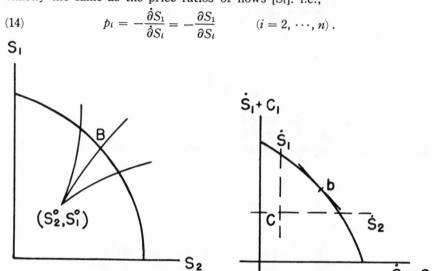

Figure 1   Figure 2

Figure 1 depicts the growth of capital stocks along alternative efficient paths streaming out from an initial endowment point, and the resulting envelope frontier, attainable at t^1. Figure 2 shows the instantaneous flow outputs at t^1. Point b here corresponds to point B in Figure 1; and our transversality result implies that the slope of f at b is exactly the same as the slope of the envelope at B in Figure 1. (One could show that the path through B is a curve of "steepest descent" in the sense of Carathéodory[5] and maximizes the growth in value of all capital stocks, evaluated at B's prices.)

The relations (7) show that our envelope is a convex function. This can be proved from the definiteness of the Hessian matrix of f. Or it can be deduced from the fact that any linear combination of feasible points $[S_1^1, \cdots, S_n^1]^a$ and $[S_1^1, \cdots, S_n^1]^b$ is also feasible. In particular, $q[S_i^1]^a + (1-q)[S_i^1]^b$ $(0 < q < 1)$ is feasible.

Because E is convex, we can give an equivalent reformulation of our maximum problem that treats all the capitals symmetrically. For prescribed positive numbers $(K_1, \cdots, K_n)$,

(15)   maximize

$$\int_{t^0}^{t^1} \sum_{j=1}^{n} K_j \dot{S}_j(t) \, dt$$

---

[5] See Bliss [3, pp. 77–80]; also see Samuelson and Solow [6, pp. 560–61] and Bellman [1, chap. 9].

subject to known functions

$$C_i(t), S_i(t^0) = S_i^0 > 0 \qquad (i = 1, 2, \cdots, n) ,$$

$$f(S_1, S_2, \cdots, \dot{S}_2 + C_2, \cdots) - \dot{S}_1 - C_1 = 0 .$$

The necessary conditions (4) or (5) must then hold. Transversality conditions provide us with our end conditions,

(16) $$-\frac{K_i}{K_1} = f_{\dot{S}_i}(S_1^1, S_2^1, \cdots ; \dot{S}_2^1 + C_2^1, \cdots) \qquad (i = 2, \cdots, n) ,$$

which make our previous solution determinate. By varying the K's through all positive combinations, we can generate any efficient path we want:

(17) $$S_i(t) = Q^i(t; t^0; S_1^0, \cdots, S_n^0; K_1, \cdots, K_n; t^1; C) \qquad (i = 1, 2, \cdots, n) .$$

For $t = t^1$ and K's varying, these are parametric equations for the envelope function; of course, $n - 1$ ratios of the K's alone are needed.

5. Maintainable Consumption Levels[6]

If at $[S_i^1]$ we were to change our minds and set all net capital formations equal to zero, $\dot{S}_i^1 = 0$, we could produce in perpetuity a given vector of consumptions. Thus when we are at B in Figure 1 we could produce in Figure 2 the locus of indicated consumptions—including, of course, the consumption of b. But such a way of "maintaining capital intact" would presumably be inefficient; the ensuing net national product would not be maximal and could be improved on in terms of every consumption.

This can be seen from the extremal equations (5). A steady state with fixed $[S_i]$ and $[C_i]$ would imply $df_{\dot{S}_i}/dt = 0$ or

(18) $$f_{S_i} + f_{\dot{S}_i} f_{S_1} = 0 \qquad (i = 2, \cdots, n) .$$

Coming into B with motion will presumably mean that (18) is violated. In this case we can improve on consumptions, as in Figure 12-5 of [4], by disinvesting in one or more capital stocks until (18) is satisfied. If these $n - 1$ equations can be inverted[7] to solve for the C's in terms of the S stocks, we have arrived at the efficient maintainable consumption vector—which will presumably be northeast of b. Of course, the resulting functions

(19) $$C_i = C^i(S_1, S_2, \cdots, S_n) \qquad (i = 1, \cdots, n)$$

will be homogeneous of the first degree if f is—as would be any inverse of (19).

6. Von Neumann Mode of Maximum Balanced Growth

By definition, a balanced-growth state is one for which $\dot{S}_i(t)/S_i(t) = m$

---

[6] This material duplicates the discrete-time discussion of [4, chap. 12, secs. 2–7].

[7] Whether or not the authors of [4] were right in saying that "the law of diminishing returns assures us" that such a set can be inverted (p. 324) I must now regard as an open question.

$(i = 1, \cdots, n)$. With consumption zero, substituting into (1) gives the following implicit equation for m:

(20) $mS_1 = f(S_1, S_2, \cdots ; S_2 m, \cdots)$.

Because $\sum f_{\dot{s}_j} S_j - S_1 < 0$, we can solve (20) uniquely for

(21) $m = m(S_1, S_2, \cdots, S_n)$.

Of all these values for m there will be a maximum rate of balanced growth, reached for

(22) $$\frac{\partial m}{\partial S_i} = 0 \qquad (i = 1, \cdots, n) .$$

From the equivalence of (20) and (21), this implies

(22') $f_{S_1} - m = 0, \quad f_{S_i} + f_{\dot{s}_i} m = 0 = f_{S_i} + f_{\dot{s}_i} f_{S_1} \quad (i = 2, \cdots, n)$.

At any initial point satisfying (22) or (22'), with S_1 held constant, the $(n-1)^2$ Hessian $[\partial^2 m / \partial S_i \partial S_j]$ is proportional element for element to

(23) $[f_{S_i S_j} + 2m f_{\dot{s}_i S_j} + m^2 f_{\dot{s}_i \dot{s}_j}]$,

which from (1) is certainly negative definite. Hence we know that m does achieve a unique maximum von Neumann rate of balanced growth m^*, corresponding to the von Neumann configuration or mode $[S_1^*, S_2^*, \cdots, S_n^*]$ of (22'), where only ratios count.

Examination of (22') shows that the von Neumann mode $[S_i^*]$ does satisfy the efficiency conditions of (5). It is the only balanced growth configuration that is efficient; all slower rates of balanced growth are themselves inefficient paths. Note that this section, for the first time, uses the homogeneity property of f.

For the discrete-time case, the so-called "turnpike theorem" was enunciated. This asserts that if the goal of maximization is far enough ahead, one will want to travel very near to the von Neumann mode of balanced growth. The economic common sense of this is evident, but it would be well to have a general proof for the continuous-time case. The remaining two sections will deal with this and related matters.

7. Alternative Formulation in Terms of Minimum Time[8]

We have seen two different efficiency formulations: at the beginning of Section 1, we maximized terminal S_1 for other terminal stocks being given; at the end of Section 4, we maximized a value-weighted sum of terminal

---

[8] The mathematics of this paper bears a striking similarity to that of classical mechanics. In particular, the Principle of Least Action is derived by minimizing an integral subject to a constant-energy constraint like (1). Hamilton's Principle, however, works with no side constraint; and it is known that the constraint in the least-action formulation can be eliminated by redefining time very much as we define it in the present section.

S's. A third, non-linear, formulation (only mentioned here) would be to fix terminal ratios $S_i/S_1 = a_i$ and then to maximize the scale parameter β in $S_i = \beta a_i$.

For the "closed-system case," where $C_i(t) \equiv 0$ and the system is capable in every efficient path of positive $[\dot{S}_i]$ for all capitals, we can give a fourth formulation. We rewrite our production relation (1) in the equivalent form

$$(24) \qquad \dot{S}_1 = f(S_1, S_2, \cdots; \dot{S}_2, \cdots) = f\left(S_1, S_2, \cdots; \frac{dS_2}{dS_1}\dot{S}_1, \cdots\right).$$

Equation (24) can be regarded as an implicit equation for $\dot{S}_1$ or for $dt/dS_1 = 1/\dot{S}_1$. It, like (20), can always be solved explicitly in the form

$$(25) \qquad \frac{dt}{dS_1} = L\left(S_1, S_2, \cdots; \frac{dS_2}{dS_1}, \cdots\right), \qquad \frac{\partial L}{\partial S_i} > 0 .$$

Because doubling $(S_1, S_2, \cdots; \dot{S}_1, \dot{S}_2, \cdots)$ leaves (1) satisfied, the function in (25) must clearly be homogeneous of order -1 in $(S_1, \cdots, S_n)$: i.e., other things being equal, doubling every S will halve the amount of time needed to achieve a (small) increment of capital.

An efficient path has the property of going between a prescribed initial and a prescribed terminal capital position in a *minimum of time*. For were this not so, we could find a better path that takes less time, and by utilizing the remaining time to produce more of every capital, we would successfully contradict the hypothesis that the original path is efficient.

Hence, we can define efficient paths by a new formulation, equivalent to (2′) and (15):

(26)   minimize

$$\int_{t^0}^{t^1} dt = \int_{s_1^0}^{s_1^1} L\left(S_1, S_2(S_1), \cdots; \frac{dS_2(S_1)}{dS_1}, \cdots\right) dS_1 ,$$

subject to $S_i(S_1^0) = S_i^0$ and $S_i(S_1^1) = S_i^1$ $(i = 2, \cdots, n)$.

This is a standard problem in the calculus of variations, free of all constraints. Necessary conditions for its solution are the Euler differential equations

$$(27) \qquad \frac{d}{dS_1}\frac{\partial L}{\partial S_i'} - \frac{\partial L}{\partial S_i} = 0 \qquad (i = 2, \cdots, n) ,$$

where $S_i' = dS_i/dt$. These efficiency conditions must of course be equivalent to (5), and under our stipulated conditions can be solved to give efficient paths

$$(28) \qquad \begin{aligned} S_i(S_1) &= \theta^i(S_1 ; S_1^0, \cdots, S_n^0 ; S_1^1, \cdots, S_n^1) \qquad (i = 2, \cdots, n) , \\ t(S_1) &= \theta^0(S_1 ; S_1^0, \cdots, S_n^0 ; S_1^1, \cdots, S_n^1), \end{aligned}$$

where the last equation is derived from integrating (25) after (27) has been solved for the first set of solutions. Then with $t'(S_1)$ and $\dot{S}_1$ positive, equations (28) can be converted into equations (10′), which are completely equivalent.

Our new formulation has the virtue of being free of all constraints on the capitals. It has the drawback of not being applicable when arbitrary time paths of consumption are present. It is applicable, however, with appropriate modifications, if consumptions are all proportional to total outputs.

Further minor modifications are in order if the new analysis is to be applicable to cases in which negative investments occur. Thus if $\dot{S}_1$ changes sign, we can use some parameter other than S_1 as our independent variable: e.g., write $S_i = S_i(u)$ and $t = t(u)$, and solve

$$S_1 = \frac{dS_1}{du} \bigg/ t'(u) = f\left[S_1, S_2, \cdots; \frac{dS_2}{du} \bigg/ t'(u), \cdots\right]$$

explicitly for $t'(u) = \bar{L}[S_1(u), S_2(u), \cdots; S_1'(u), S_2'(u), \cdots]$. Now minimize

(29) $$\int_0^1 t'(u)\, du = \int_0^1 \bar{L}\, du \quad \text{for } S_i(0) = S_i^0,\ S_i(1) = S_i^1 \quad (i = 1, \cdots, n)\,.$$

An alternative device to get around investments that change sign is to define new variables $[s_i(t)] = [S_i(t)e^{ht}]$. Then for h sufficiently large, $[\dot{s}_i]$ will always be positive.

8. Catenary Motions Near a Saddle-Point

Returning to the monotone case, we can proceed to prove the stated property of the von Neumann mode of maximum balanced growth. Intuition suggests that if we start from any arbitrary initial capital configuration $[S_i^0]$ and efficiently aim at a new configuration $[S_i^1]$ that is "far away," we should approach arbitarily close to the von Neumann mode for much of the time.

To handle the general case of n goods, we find it convenient to transform slightly the variables in (26), (27), and (28). Thus, consider the non-singular transformation

$$x_1 = \log S_1,$$

(30) $$x_i = \log \frac{S_i}{S_1}, \qquad x_i' = \frac{dx_i}{dx_1} = \frac{dS_i}{dS_1}\frac{S_1}{S_i} - 1 \qquad (i = 2, \cdots, n)\,,$$

$$L\left(S_1, S_2, \cdots; \frac{dS_2}{dS_1}, \cdots\right)dS_1 = L(1, e^{x_2}, \cdots; 1 + x_2'e^{x_2}, \cdots)dx_1\,.$$

Now our minimum problem becomes:

(26′)   minimize

$$\int_{x_1^0}^{x_1^1} F[x_2(x_1), \cdots; x_2'(x_1), \cdots]\, dx_1$$

for $x_i(x_1^0) = x_i^0,\ x_i(x_1^1) = x_i^1\ (i = 2, \cdots, n)\,,$

where the function F is defined in terms of the function L in (30) and is seen, because of our original homogeneity assumption, *not* to involve x_1 explicitly.

The Euler necessary conditions for the minimum become

$$(27')\quad \frac{d}{dx_1}\frac{\partial F(x_2,\cdots;x_2',\cdots)}{\partial x_i'}-\frac{\partial F(x_2,\cdots;x_2',\cdots)}{\partial x_i}=0\qquad (i=2,\cdots,n).$$

We shall now deduce the special properties of the function defined by (27'). Since equations (4) and (5), or (27), are known because of the definiteness of (1) to yield a unique extremum, one infers that

$$(31)\qquad \left[\frac{\partial^2 F}{\partial x_i'\partial x_j'}\right]\text{ is everywhere positive definite .}$$

From (30) we see that any balanced growth path, with $\dot{S}_i(t)=mS_i(t)$, corresponds to $x_i(x_1)\equiv x_i^*$, which are constants. Also $x_i'(x_1)\equiv 0$. In order that the von Neumann balanced growth $[S_1^*,S_2^*,\cdots,S_n^*]$ be truly optimal, we must then have the minimum conditions

$$F(x_2^*,\cdots,x_n^*;0,0,\cdots,0)<F(x_2,\cdots,x_n;0,0,\cdots,0)$$

for any $[x_i]$ other than $[x_i^*]$. Thus, corresponding to the maximum conditions (22) and (22'), we have the minimum conditions

$$(32)\qquad \frac{\partial F(x_2^*,\cdots,x_n^*;0,0,\cdots,0)}{\partial x_i}=0\qquad (i=2,\cdots,n),$$

$$\left[\frac{\partial^2 F(x_2^*,\cdots,x_n^*;0,0,\cdots,0)}{\partial x_i\partial x_j}\right]\text{ positive definite.}$$

Now we proved earlier that the von Neumann motion is an efficient path. It follows that the fixed point

$$(x_1,x_2,\cdots;x_2',\cdots)=(x_1^*,x_2^*,\cdots,x_n^*;0,0,\cdots,0)$$

must satisfy the efficiency conditions (27'). With F independent of x_1, this can be shown to imply

$$(33)\qquad \frac{\partial F(x_2^*,\cdots,x_n^*;0,0,\cdots,0)}{\partial x_i'}=0\qquad (i=2,\cdots,n).$$

Now it is a classical fact that any "variational or Hamiltonian system" of the type depicted in (26') has special behavior properties at any one of its singular points. In particular, if we consider the linearized part of (27') near the singular points, its characteristic numbers are known from a theorem of Poincaré to occur in pairs of opposite sign: $+\lambda_1, -\lambda_1, +\lambda_2, -\lambda_2,$ etc.[9] In this case the λ's are real, a fact that leads to the desired catenary motions around a saddle-point (shown in [4, fig. 12–9]).

To see this, we may briefly go through the usual "small vibrations" analysis of the motions in the neighborhood of the equilibrium point. Expanding (27') in a Taylor's series around the singular point and neglecting higher-power terms gives, after some cancellations,

---

[9] See Birkhoff [2, pp. 74–78].

(34)
$$\sum_{i,j=2}^{n} \frac{\partial^2 F^*}{\partial x_i' \partial x_j'}(x_j - x_j^*)'' - \sum_{i,j=2}^{n} \frac{\partial^2 F^*}{\partial x_i \partial x_j}(x_j - x_j^*) = 0 ,$$

whose characteristic numbers are given by

(35)
$$\det\left[\frac{\partial^2 F^*}{\partial x_i' \partial x_j'}\lambda^2 - \frac{\partial^2 F^*}{\partial x_i \partial x_j} \right] = 0 = \Delta(\lambda^2) .$$

From the positive definiteness conditions of (31) and (32) we know that all the λ^2 are *real* and positive, and hence their square roots correspond to equal and opposite-signed real numbers.

This demonstrates that $F(x_2, \cdots, x_n; x_2', \cdots, x_n')$ has a saddle-point at the von Neumann mode $(x_2^*, \cdots, x_n^*; 0, 0, \cdots, 0)$. All the motions *near* this mode must therefore have special "asymptotic" properties. Economic intuition suggests that the local result proved here must also hold in the large; but this must remain an open question.

REFERENCES

[1] BELLMAN, R. *Dynamic Programming*, Princeton, N.J.: Princeton University Press, 1957.

[2] BIRKHOFF, G. D. *Dynamical Systems*, New York: American Mathematical Society, 1927.

[3] BLISS, G. A. *Lectures on the Calculus of Variations*, Chicago: University of Chicago Press, 1946.

[4] DORFMAN, R., P. A. SAMUELSON, and R. M. SOLOW. *Linear Programming and Economic Analysis*, New York: McGraw-Hill, 1958.

[5] SAMUELSON, P. A. "Some Aspects of the Pure Theory of Capital," *Quarterly Journal of Economics*, **51** (1937), 469-96.

[6] SAMUELSON, P. A., and R. M. SOLOW. "A Complete Capital Model Involving Heterogeneous Capital Goods," *Quarterly Journal of Economics*, **70** (1956), 537-62.

27

THE EVALUATION OF 'SOCIAL INCOME': CAPITAL FORMATION AND WEALTH

BY

PAUL A. SAMUELSON
Massachusetts Institute of Technology

I. INTRODUCTION

AN earlier paper [1] dealt with problems of interpreting aggregate data on production and consumption. The present paper explores theoretical problems raised for national income calculation by investment, technological change, and uncertainty windfalls. It purposely works with simple and strong models so that the intrinsic difficulties will not be obscured by observational difficulties of detail. Government expenditure and taxes are throughout ignored.

The simplest neo-classical capital model is that of Ramsey. In my version, it assumes a fixed amount L of 'primary' factor that I shall call labour, but that could also be interpreted as unaugmentable land or a composite of natural resources and labour. A homogeneous flow of gross product called $\dot{Y}$ per unit time is produced by labour and by a physically homogeneous stock of capital K according to the production function

$$\dot{Y} = F(K, L), \tag{1}$$

which obeys the classical laws of constant-returns-to-scale and diminishing returns to variations in capital unaccompanied by any change in labour.

The current flow of product is assumed to be allocable [2] between (i) current consumption flow of product $\dot{C}$ and (ii) gross capital formation per unit time of capital, which I call $\dot{K}$: or

$$\dot{Y} = \dot{C} + \dot{K} = F(K, L). \tag{2}$$

To arrive at (iii) net capital formation, dK/dt, we must subtract from gross births of capital the current rate of capital deaths, called D

---

[1] P. A. Samuelson, 'Evaluation of Real National Income', *Oxford Economic Papers* (New Series), 1950, pp. 1-29.

[2] Equation (2) has assumed for simplicity (what is dropped in Fig. 3) that the consumer and capital goods industries always use labour and capital in the same proportions.

to refer to current rate of depreciation or capital consumption. If capital of all ages is to be really homogeneous, we must assume that depreciation involves the physical destruction of capital at a rate independent of age and proportional to the existing total stock of capital. This involves a life table for any given stock of capital showing a radioactive rate of decay in an exponential fashion.

We can summarize our capital consumption postulate in the relations

$$\dot{D} = mK$$

$$\frac{dK}{dt} = \dot{K} - \dot{D} = \dot{K} - mK, \tag{3}$$

where m is a positive constant representing the percentage rate per unit time of capital depreciation. The average length of life of capital will then be $1/m$.

We may now summarize our net national product flow $\dot{y}$ and its allocation between consumption and net capital formation as follows:

$$\dot{y} = \dot{Y} - \dot{D} = F(K, L) - mK$$

$$= \dot{C} + \frac{dK}{dt} = f(K, L) \tag{4}$$

where the new net product f function is defined by (4).

II. NET VERSUS GROSS CAPITAL FORMATION

The above relations between net and gross national product and gross and net capital formation are the familiar ones met with in the literature of national income. Within the framework of a purely theoretical model such as this one, I believe that we should certainly prefer net national product, NNP, to gross national product, GNP, if we were forced to choose between them. This is somewhat the reverse of the position taken by many official statisticians, and so let me dispose of three arguments used to favour the gross concept.

First, there is the argument that estimates of depreciation are conceptually and statistically inaccurate so that $\dot{Y}$ is more accurate than $\dot{y} = \dot{Y} - \dot{D}$. Within our simple model, we know precisely what depreciation is and so for our present purpose this argument can be provisionally ruled out of order.

Second, there is the argument that GNP gives a better measure than does NNP of the maximum consumption sprint that an economy could make by consuming its capital in time of future war or emergency. If we are speaking *ex post* of an emergency economy, the recorded level of consumption $\dot{C}$ does tell us how much it has been consuming for peace and war and no further measure is needed. If consumption exceeds NNP, the positive difference does accurately measure the rate of recorded capital disinvestment. If the level of gross capital formation was recorded to be zero, then the emergency consumption did indeed equal the whole of the recorded GNP.

None the less, it is misleading to apply a *present* non-emergency level of GNP in forming an estimate of *future* emergency consumption potential. Once we recognize that depreciation depends on intensity of use as well as on mere passage of time, we realize that future emergency consumption is not limited by *present* GNP but rather by the maximum future GNP that the system can squeeze out through more intensive using-up of its capital.

This means that the size of GNP producible at any time with given technology, capital and labour is *not* a solid figure ; it depends on our volition and is what we make it ; it is in this respect unlike NNP whose maximum value we cannot better without somehow getting more inputs or changing production functions. A striking example of my contention is the strong case where all capital is like a storage battery or an inventory of chocolates. In any very short period, our rate of chocolate or electricity consumption can be as great as we wish provided only we run down our capital fast enough. This means that we can in any emergency period think of our decisions as increasing m, the force of mortality of capital, to any desired level. As a result, the level of emergency consumption — and emergency GNP — can be much greater than the usual peace-time GNP.[1]

Our summarizing equations (4), in writing $\dot{y} = f(K, L)$, seem to assume implicitly that m is a given technical constant which is not one of the economic unknowns of our problem. This seems to imply that we recognize depreciation due to the passage of time but deny the existence of depreciation due to service or to 'user cost'. Actually, I am willing to entertain the assumption that current gross production can be increased by deferring maintenance and increasing intensity of capital use as measured by m. Thus, we can write $\dot{Y} = F(K, L, m)$; but we do suppose that for each given L and K,

---

[1] Our model has not distinguished between (i) inventory or circulating capital and (ii) fixed capital or capitalized items. The accountant arbitrarily uses one year or some other criterion to determine which way any item is treated. The result of a change in such an arbitrary decision is an arbitrary change in the level of GNP as we double count more or less in the total. However, and this is one of the most important arguments for NNP, the net magnitude remains invariant under changes in accounting conventions. Incidentally, with inventories *not* capitalized, we definitely can have $\dot{C} > GNP$ because gross investment $\dot{K}$, inclusive of negative inventory change, can be negative. Thus, emergency GNP computed along official lines does not correctly measure maximum emergency consumption. Nor does it give much insight into the range of feasible time profiles of emergency consumption.

there has already been selected an optimal intensity m so as to maximize net product, $\dot{y} = F(K, L, m) - mK$, as determined by the condition

$$\frac{\partial \dot{y}}{\partial m} = 0 = \frac{\partial F(K, L, m)}{\partial m} - K. \tag{5}$$

We assume that this optimum value of m has been determined and substituted into $F(K, L, m) - mK$, which can therefore be written as our function of K and L alone, $f(K, L)$.[1]

A third argument favouring a gross rather than net product figure proceeds as follows : new capital is progressively of better quality than old, so that net product calculated by the subtraction of all depreciation and obsolescence does not yield an ideal measure 'based on the principle of keeping intact the physical productivity of the capital goods in some kind of welfare sense'.[2] The next section's separate argument will deal with problems of technological change and uncertainty leading to quality changes. Within our simple theoretical model, depreciation is correctly calculable with no obsolescence problems arising. So we have no reason to think that our gross product $\dot{Y}$ is a better approximation to true net product than is our exact net product $\dot{y}$ itself.

III. QUALITY CHANGES AND CAPITAL GAINS

The 1935 debate between Pigou and Hayek as to the meaning of maintaining capital intact can be pointed-up by an extension of our simple model. Suppose in addition to K a new capital good K_2 is

[1] If war makes us want $\dot{C} > \dot{y}$, we at first find it advantageous to stay with our optimal peace-time m. The excess $\dot{C} - \dot{y}$ is at first matched by positive $D - \dot{K}$, and the old optimal m gives us the minimum of disinvestment of capital compatible with our emergency consumption needs. However, after consumption goals have been so increased as to make $\dot{K} = 0$, we cannot on most interpretations imagine making *gross* investment actually negative. But from now on we let $\dot{C} = F(K, L, m)$ with $dK/dt = -mK$; and by increasing the intensity with which capital is used still further, we can further increase current consumption. But with m varying from its optimal peace-time value, we meet the following paradox : to enjoy high sprints of consumption, we greatly increase GNP, deliberately letting NNP as measured by $f = F - mK$ (slightly) decrease. The paradox is resolved when we reflect that $\dot{C}$ can only be added algebraically on a one-to-one basis to dK/dt in a meaningful valuation provided society really can achieve 1 extra $\dot{C}$ for each extra unit of disinvestment. When $\partial f/\partial m = (\partial F/\partial m) - K \neq 0$, because we have exceeded the optimal peace-time m, each new unit of $\dot{C}$ really costs (and is worth) more than each sacrificed unit of capital formation : so a correct emergency NNP would be computed by giving greater than unity weight to $\dot{C}$ relative to dK/dt ; and this new correct measure would not be sub-maximal in the emergency sprint. (See Fig. 2's curvature beyond d for an illustration of all this.)
[2] Quoted from Richard Ruggles, 'Concepts, Sources, and Methods of United States National Income Accounts', *Econometrica*, 1952, pp. 469-70, by E. F. Denison, 'Quality Change, Capital Consumption, and Net Capital Formation', *National Bureau Conference on Research in Income and Wealth*, October 9-11, 1953.

discovered which has twice K's productivity in *every* use but which is produced by exactly the same production function as K (same costs) and with the same life expectancy as K. Then we get

$$\dot{C} + \dot{K} + \dot{K_2} = F(K + 2K_2, L)$$

$$\dot{K} = \frac{dK}{dt} + mK \geq 0, \quad \dot{K_2} = \frac{dK_2}{dt} + mK_2 \geq 0.$$

Competition will immediately insure that $\dot{K} = 0$ as the old capital good becomes 'obsolete' in the sense that its current value at once drops to half its cost of reproduction : its algebraic net investment will be $dK/dt = -mK$ for ever afterwards.

How shall we write NNP (i) ever afterwards ; (ii) before the new K_2 is at all known ; and (iii) the 'instant' or period it becomes known ? We have already given the answer to (ii) in (4) — but if the new K_2 were 'suspected' in advance but not known as to exact date of its invention and form, what would the answer be ? Question (iii) involves the issue of what financial revaluation you wish to put in NNP or GNP. The important question (i) would seem best answered by going from the indisputable relation

$$\dot{C} + 1\frac{dK_2}{dt} + \tfrac{1}{2}\frac{dK}{dt} = F(K + 2K_2, L) - mK_2 - m\tfrac{1}{2}K$$

$$= g(K + 2K_2, L), \quad \frac{dK}{dt} = -mK,$$

to the definition

$$NNP = \dot{y} = \dot{Y} - 1\dot{D_2} - \tfrac{1}{2}\dot{D}. \tag{6}$$

Operational difficulties of statistical measurement aside, my solution may be more nearly akin to Hayek's than Pigou's (or Denison's) : the depreciation I subtract from GNP to get NNP evaluates the physical capital being used up not at its historic (bygone) production cost, nor at its current reproduction cost if it is in fact not being produced, but at its current competitively-bid used market price.[1] Note that the post-invention NNP has risen, whatever it may be supposed to have done in the transition when learning the 'bad news' of the new invention was causing anguish and revaluations by owners of old K. The immediate post-invention GNP has not changed at all, even though society's 'prospects' are now

[1] Suppose in a decade better K_2 is replacing K but with $dK_2/dt = -dK/dt$ so that the national income statistician is registering zero capital formation. Then using my measure of capital formation $\tfrac{1}{2}dK/dt + 1 dK_2/dt$, positive capital formation is really going on. Add the value integral of this over the decade to initial $\tfrac{1}{2}K + 1K_2$ and call the result V. Then the new product will be given by $F(2V, L)$, reflecting a higher GNP, and where the factor 2 must be written in the old production function to portray correctly the new production possibilities.

definitely improved. While the physical capital-output ratio K/f will at first remain constant, the value capital-output ratio pK/f will immediately halve ; the incremental capital-output ratio, in the relevant form $[\partial(dK_2/dt)/\partial K_2]^{-1}$ will be half that of the old $[\partial(dK/dt)/\partial K]^{-1}$ as the interest rate doubles.

IV. FACTOR PAYMENT IMPUTATION OF PRODUCT

I have assumed conditions most favourable to viable competition — namely constant returns to scale. Therefore, competitive pricing of the services of labour and capital can in the absence of uncertainty be relied on to create a state of zero (excess profits) and a price of consumption and investment flow exactly equal to unit cost of production as measured by the sum of wages and capital rents per unit· of product. Thus

$$p\dot{y} = p\left(\dot{C} + \frac{dK}{dt}\right) = wL + rK, \tag{7}$$

where (p, w, r) are respectively (i) the price (in money or any other *numeraire*) of current flow of output, whether consumption output or equivalent investment output ; (ii) the wage of labour per unit time, which is to say the rent per unit time for the services of human population ; and (iii) the rent per unit time for the use of capital K, it being understood that the capital is returned intact to its owner — or what is the same thing that the gross rental rate R has subtracted from it an allowance for depreciation before the capital owner can reckon his net rental r. This means we can write down a factor payment breakdown of gross national product as follows :

$$p\dot{Y} = p(\dot{C} + \dot{K}) = p(\dot{y} + \dot{D}) = p\left(\dot{C} + \frac{dK}{dt} + \dot{D}\right) \tag{7}'$$
$$= wL + RK.$$

In our simple theoretical model, the rents of all factors can be immediately recognized as equivalent to the value of their marginal products. Thus, on a net and gross basis, we have

$$r = p\frac{\partial f(K, L)}{\partial K}$$

$$R = p\frac{\partial F(K, L)}{\partial K} = p\frac{\partial f(K, L)}{\partial K} + pm = r + mp \tag{8}$$

$$w = p\frac{\partial f(K, L)}{\partial L} = p\frac{\partial F(K, L)}{\partial L}.$$

These relations show us that the subtraction from gross rent R to get net rent r equals the percentage depreciation of capital per unit time m multiplied by the price of capital p : i.e. $R - mp = r$ in our model.

Euler's theorem on homogeneous functions is of course applicable under our neo-classical assumptions of constant returns to scale ; this assures us of the compatibility of the exhaustion of product assumptions of (7) and (7)' with the marginal productivity equivalences of (8).

Table 1 gives a symbolic presentation of the usual two views of national income or product : on the left-hand side we have the cost

TABLE 1

Factor Payments or Cost		Flow of Product	
'Profits'	0		
+ Wage Rents	$wL = p\dfrac{\partial f}{\partial L}L$	Consumption Product	pC
+ Capital Net Rents	$rK = p\dfrac{\partial f}{\partial K}K$	+ Net Capital Formation	$p\dfrac{dK}{dt}$
Total of Net National Income or Product	$wL + rK = pf$	Total of Net National Product	$p\left(C + \dfrac{dK}{dt}\right) = pf$
+ Depreciation or Capital Consumption	$pmK = pD$	+ Difference between Gross and Net Capital Formation	$p\left(\dot{K} - \dfrac{dK}{dt}\right) = pmK$
Total Gross National Product	$wL + RK = pF$	Total Gross National Product	$p(\dot{K} + C) = pF$

or factor payment view ; on the right-hand side, the flow of consumption and investment product.

The above view regards value of product as being composed on the cost side completely of current factor rents : rents for use of the stock of capital ; rents for the use of stocks of primary factors, in our case human population. Rents for the use of physical capital goods are commonly met in modern economies, so this corresponds to usual usage. More bizarre is the appellation 'rents' for what is usually called wages. But reflection shows that under most systems of jurisprudence, human population is the one factor that *cannot* be bought outright : unless slavery is permitted, labour services must be rented.[1]

[1] Because we assume a fixed total of L, no problems of depreciation of human capital here arise. But even in a steady population, if we let individuals die and be

However, if the factor labour could be capitalized and titles to labour transferred, we could calculate the total value of all stocks of factors, including such primary factors. The total value of net product could now be regarded not as total factor *rents* but rather as total *interest* on the capitalized factor wealth (account being taken of 'capital gains' magnitudes).

Because labour is usually not capitalized, we can on the left side of Table 1 leave in wage rents. At the same time we may replace capital rents by interest on the capitalized value of physical capital assets.[1]

But where do we get (*a*) the instantaneous interest rate per unit time *i*, and (*b*) the capitalized value of the physical capital K?

One advantage of our simple capital model is the ease with which it can answer these questions. As long as there is positive gross capital formation going on, so that $\dot{K}>0$ and both $\dot{C}$ and $\dot{K}$ are being simultaneously produced, the current market price p quoted for consumption and investment flows provides us also with the current value of the stock of capital K. We are in the following fortunate position : *A current reproduction cost of the capital that is being produced always gives us an unambiguous market value for all capital.*

We can now work backwards : what interest rate *i* will multiply into the value of capital pK to get us the same non-wage net rental income as does rK? Clearly, we must have

$$i = \frac{rK}{pK} = \frac{r}{p} = \frac{\partial f(K, L)}{\partial K}, \tag{9}$$

where the last marginal productivity relation comes from our earlier derived equations (8). Among the factor payments on the left-hand side of Table 1, we can now replace rents of capital goods rK by the equivalent interest return on value of capital $i(pK)$.

born and if we do not define our units as clans that maintain the same age distribution, there does arise for the individual problems of valuation of lifetime earnings and of depreciation. A so-called 'personal income tax' that treats the perpetual earnings of securities the same as the earnings of a doctor or actor in the prime of life chooses to ignore a substantive difference.

[1] Adding some rents to some interest may seem illogical. If so, current statistical practice is still more illogical. Even the items that can all be capitalized are treated either as rents or as interest depending upon the accidental institutional form in which families happen to choose to hold titles to the productive assets used by business. An even greater heterogeneity is introduced by lumping together into corporate or unincorporated enterprise 'profit' a *mélange* of implicit wages, rent, or interest earned on owner-supplied factors and various returns that result from lack of 'perfection' in all economic markets. Of course, the statisticians are not to be criticized because the world happens to depart from simplified conditions. (See my p. 48 footnote for the demonstration that factor rents differ from interest by a fundamental 'capital gains' term.)

V. OWN-RATES OF INTEREST AND PRICE CHANGES

A rate of interest is a pure number per unit of time. How then can (9) make i equal a physical marginal productivity ? If we rewrite $\partial f/\partial K$ in the form $\partial(dK/dt)/\partial K$, we recognize that the dimensionality K cancels out, leaving us with a pure number per unit of time. We can interpret $\partial f/\partial K$ as an 'own-rate-of-interest' *in natura* : it gives the 'net productivity of capital', the rate at which extra capital stock can produce extra rate of growth of *itself*.[1]

So long as the price of capital goods is constant over time, the own-rate-of-interest i is the same thing as the prevailing rate of interest on money loans i_m. Thornton, Marshall, Wicksell, Fisher, Keynes, and others have known that the own-rate and the money rate of interest must diverge by a term equal to the percentage price change of the good in terms of which the own-rate is measured. Thus,[2] equilibrium requires that

$$i_m = i + \frac{dp}{pdt}. \tag{10}$$

This says : When the price of K is rising in a foreseen way, the money rate of interest will exceed the own-rate of interest by the foreseen percentage rate of price inflation.

Statisticians are alert to the possibility that general price changes may introduce revaluations into their measured profits. Under conditions of certainty, price changes will necessarily introduce themselves into contractual interest as well. Under these conditions, a typical firm that owns physical capital financed completely by borrowed money can 'afford' to pay the prevailing high market rate of interest only by reckoning as an addition to its current sale receipts a capital revaluation term equal to $K(dp/dt)$. The resulting augmented total of calculated 'receipts' will just equal its wage-rent payments plus money-interest payments, leaving it contented with zero residual 'profits'.

If the statistician accepts such income statements and consolidates them for all businesses, he will arrive at a total greater than the NNP of Table 1 whenever prices are rising in a foreseen fashion. This total will then be $p\dot{y} + K(dp/dt)$. If he tries to eliminate this

[1] If all the fruits of capital were ploughed back into investment, $i = \partial f/\partial K$ would measure the slope of product growth plotted against capital : i.e. $i = (df/dt)/(dK/dt) = (d\dot{y}/dK)$ if $\dot{C} = 0$; it is then K''/K' the slope (or percentage rate of growth) of net investment plotted against time on semi-log paper. Whether or not $\dot{C} = 0$, i is the reciprocal of the marginal capital-output ratio $\partial K/\partial f(K, L)$.

[2] See P. A. Samuelson, 'Some Aspects of the Pure Theory of Capital', *Quarterly Journal of Economics*, May 1937, pp. 469-96, particularly equation (10) of Math. Appendix I.

element of capital revaluation, he can do so only by refusing to count in the $K(dp/dt)$ receipt that the firm has been relying on in determining its prudent borrowing. Only if the statistician adopts the rule that firms are making 'negative residual profits' equal to their current cash deficit $p\dot{y} - wL - i_m pK$ will he be able to get the left-hand factor payment side of Table 1 to add up to the same total as the right-hand side. It will no doubt come as a surprise to the firms to learn that when they are just breaking even according to their prudent calculations, they are really enjoying negative adjusted profits. Yet unless a firm is selling off some of its physical capital to families, it cannot 'realize' the capital revaluation term and will be having to do new borrowing to finance its cash deficit. If the rentier families try to spend all their money interest on consumption, they will find it necessary to reduce their ownership of physical capital.

Three facts require emphasis. Although we speak here of capital gains, there is nothing of the 'windfall' character in them ; they are completely foreseen and counted on in validating all decisions. Secondly, these capital gains are not necessarily temporary or 'non-recurring', or unmaintainable. On the contrary, if the balanced rate of inflation were known to last for a century, the capital gains would occur in every year.

Thirdly, different kinds of assets and contracts must all create the same instantaneous yield per unit of time, equal in money to i_m times capitalized market value V ; but each different contract will have this common yield made up in different proportions of (a) current coupon receipt or dividend and (b) capital appreciation. In a perfect capital market, the fundamental identity between current net receipts N, value V, and interest i_m is

$$i_m = \frac{N}{V} + \frac{dV}{V dt} \tag{11}$$

holding for all assets.[1] This means that a $2\frac{1}{2}$ per cent coupon bond maturing in 1970 will sell at a discount compared with a 5 per cent coupon maturing in 1970. The changing amount of the discount is such that their yields are equal in every period. The U.S. and U.K. governments treat much of the yield of the old discount bond as so-called capital gain and tax it more lightly or not at all : the national income statistician must not — at least under conditions of certainty — make this same mistake.

The price changes discussed in the last few paragraphs have all been of a generally inflationary type, with consumption goods changing in price by the same amount as physical capital goods.

[1] *Ibid.* p. 471, equations (7).

However, if we widen our model so that there are many kinds of capital goods, it is easy to produce cases where the mere accumulation of capital depresses interest rates and raises capital prices relatively to consumption good prices. Investors can then truly feel that their capital gains increase their command over consumption goods.

VI. EQUALITY OF CAPITALIZED VALUE AND REPRODUCTION COST

We have deduced a market price for all physical capital from reproduction cost. Is this necessarily consistent with its value as calculated in Irving Fisher's way by summing *present discounted values* of all future receipts ? The answer can be shown to be, Yes.

Employing money units for all valuations, we must use the compound interest formulas appropriate to instantaneous interest rates that *change* according to the foreseen function $i_m(t)$. Then [1] value of K at $t = t^0$ is

$$V = \int_{t^0}^{\infty} r(t) \exp\left[-\int_{t^0}^{t} i_m(T)dT \right] dt$$

$$= \int_{t^0}^{\infty} \frac{\partial f[K(t), L]}{\partial K} p(t) \exp\left[-\int_{t^0}^{t} \frac{\partial f[K(T), L]}{\partial K} dT - \int_{t^0}^{t} \frac{d \log p(T)}{dT} dT \right] dt$$

$$= p(t^0) \int_{t^0}^{\infty} \frac{\partial f[K(t), L]}{\partial K} \exp\left[-\int_{t^0}^{t} \frac{\partial f[K(T), L]}{\partial K} dT \right] dt \qquad (12)$$

$$= p(t^0) \int_{0}^{\infty} e^{-x}\, dx$$

$$= p(t^0).$$

The proof in (12) of the equivalence between capital's reproduction cost and present discounted value has made use of our earlier (8) relating rent and marginal value productivity and of (10) relating money interest to the own-rate $\partial f/\partial K$.

VII. SUMMARY OF SIMPLEST CAPITAL MODEL

Figs. 1 and 2 summarize the salient features of the simplest capital model. With primary factors L fixed, Fig. 1 shows the level of Net National Product ($\dot{y}$) producible by each level of capital (K).

[1] See P. A. Samuelson, 'Some Aspects of the Pure Theory of Capital', *Quarterly Journal of Economics*, May 1937, p. 485, equations (31).

On the vertical axis, the brackets indicate the factor payment break-down between (i) the imputed rental share of capital, $K(\partial f/\partial K) = Kr$, which has been shown to be equal to the interest return on capitalized value of capital or reproduction cost, and (ii) the imputed wage or rent return to labour and other primary factors.

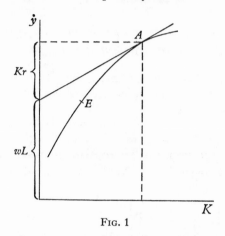

FIG. 1

Fig. 2 shows the production possibility curve, depicting society's alternative choices between current consumption ($\dot{C}$) and net capital formation (dK/dt). The production possibility schedule is a straight

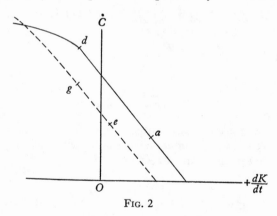

FIG. 2

line with $-45°$ slope because of the special assumption that consumption flows and capital formation are infinitely substitutable from the production viewpoint. This is true even when net capital formation becomes negative, as capital depreciation exceeds gross capital formation. However, beyond the point d, where gross capital

310

formation is zero, further expansion of consumption at the expense of investment is possible only by heavily milking capital ; therefore, the curve becomes convex from above, as shown.[1]

VIII. IS INCOME CONSUMPTION ?

We may now dispose of a terminological question of purely historical interest. Irving Fisher, perhaps the shrewdest single writer in the field of capital theory, always insisted on defining income so that it is identical with 'benefits', i.e. with 'consumption', or with psychic utility of consumption.

Thus, compare in Figs. 1 and 2 the situation prevailing at A and a with the situation that prevailed some time earlier at E and e. In the elapsed time, net saving and investment has increased the stock of capital from the point E to the point A. The flow of producible output, which we have called $\dot{y}$ or Net National Product, is also seen in Fig. 1 to have been increased. In Fig. 2, the $-45°$ line ad is north-east of the parallel line ge : at the later date more consumption *and* more investment are *possible* than at the early date.

The usual definition of income implicitly assumed by us until now, and associated with the names of Haig and Marshall, would say that income has increased over time. Irving Fisher would object, saying, 'Earnings have indeed increased ; but since income ought to be defined so as to be synonymous with consumption, we must determine where society is on the two schedules before passing judgment. If in the early period, society was at the point marked e, and later at a enjoying less consumption than at e, then we must conclude that income (i.e. consumption) has fallen.'

Few have followed Fisher in his terminology.[2] More popular is

[1] Our earlier footnote to equation (5) covers this case. Mathematically, maximum $\dot{C}$ does equal $f(K, L) - dK/dt$ so long as $dK/dt \geq -mK$. But if we want still more $\dot{C}$, we must maximize with respect to m, $F(K, L, m) - mK - dK/dt$ subject to $dK/dt = -mK$. And this gives $\dot{C} = F(K, L, m)$, $dK/dt = -mK$ as the parametric equations of the curve north-west of d, defined for m greater than the value satisfying (5). (From now on I treat p as unity.)

[2] Arguments as to what income really is remind one of the ancient pseudo-question : 'How do we know that Uranus is really Uranus ?' The problem becomes important only when Fisher insists that an income tax should tax what he chooses to call 'income' rather than what he chooses to call 'earnings'. The substantive merits of a consumption spending tax as against an earnings tax should not be appraised in such purely semantic terms, nor even in terms of the semantic question of whether the latter involves 'double taxation' of current earnings as well as the later fruits of those earnings. Single taxation has no unambiguous meaning, and double taxation may be no more objectionable than heavier 'single' taxation. To be sure, A. C. Pigou (*Public Finance*, Part II, ch. x) and others have correctly insisted that a consumption tax uniform throughout time *may* involve less dead-weight distortion of saving-investment decisions than an equivalent earnings tax, which is a substantive rather than a philological point.

the definition of Haig, which defines income as 'net accretion to . . . economic power' (including whatever part of the accretion is used for consumption).

The Haig-Marshall definition of income can be defended by one who admits that consumption is the ultimate end of economic activity. In our simple model, the Haig-Marshall definition measures the economy's *current power to consume* if it wishes to do so. The amount that it can consume in this period, without impairing its capital and destroying its power to consume in the future,[1] is indicated in Fig. 2 by the vertical intercept of the $-45°$ line. In the later period, society could, if it wanted to, consume more than it could in the earlier period ; regardless therefore of how much it actually chooses to consume in either period, the Haig-Marshall definition says that income is higher in the later period.

Note that in our simple model, one $-45°$ line is definitely out-and-beyond the other. Hence, we could alter the Haig-Marshall definition in many ways and still come out with the same answer. Thus, if we defined income as a maximum net capital formation possible if consumption were zero, we would be using the horizontal intercept as our measure and would come out with exactly the same qualitative and quantitative comparisons. The same would be true if we generalized the definition and defined income as an arbitrarily weighted sum of producible consumption and investment.

Fig. 3 for the first time depicts an alternative capital model, where capital formation and consumption flow are not infinitely substitutable. Instead, as we desire more current consumption, we must sacrifice even more investment at the margin. How would (i) Fisher, (ii) Haig-Marshall, (iii) Hicks, or (iv) an income statistician, compare and measure income at *a* and *b* in Fig. 3 ?

Fisher would find consumption higher at *b* than *a* and would therefore say income was higher at *b*.

Some statisticians would, I think, tend to measure incomes by the vertical intercepts of the tangent lines through *a* and *b*. On their definition, *b* would involve more income than *a*. The statistician might defend his measure as being most nearly in accord with the Haig-Marshall definition : Add in the 'value' of consumption goods and net capital formation.

(iii) Neither Haig nor Marshall have told us exactly how they would evaluate and compare *a* and *b* in Fig. 3. Certainly some economic statisticians would interpret them as follows : Money

---

[1] J. R. Hicks, *Value and Capital* (1939 and 1946), in effect defines income as the maximum level of permanently maintainable consumption. Capital is required to be maintained intact only so that consumption can be permanently maintained.

national income is meaningless ; you must deflate the money figures and reduce things to constant dollars. To deflate, apply the price ratios of *b* to the *a* situation and compare with *b* ; alternatively, apply the price ratios of *a* to the *b* situation and compare with *a*. If both tests give the same answer — and in Fig. 3 they will, because *a* lies outside of *b* on straight lines parallel to the tangent at either *a* or at *b* — then you can be sure that one situation has 'more income' than the other. If these Laspeyre and Paasche tests disagree, reserve judgment or split the difference depending upon your temperament.

(iv) Others (e.g. Hicks of the earlier footnote) want to measure income by comparing the vertical intercepts of the curved production possibility schedules passing respectively through *a* and *b*. This is

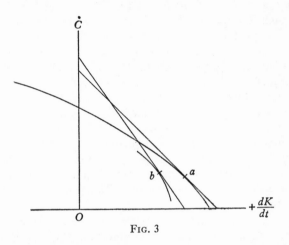

Fig. 3

certainly one attractive interpretation of the spirit behind Haig and Marshall. The practical statistician might despair of so defining income : using market prices and quantities, he could conceivably apply any of the other definitions ; but this one would be non-observable to him. An economy that has historically been doing positive investment will not, in the absence of gigantic controlled social experiments, reveal what its full consumption potentialities really are.[1]

Fig. 3 has been drawn in such a way that the intercept of the curve through *b* might conceivably fall outside or inside the intercept of the curve through *a*. A statistician, who cannot command society

[1] Occasionally, by lucky accident, we may infer something about the relative positions of the intercepts : thus, if *a* were north of the vertical intercept of *b*'s *tangent* line, we could infer, from convexity of the curves, that the *a*'s intercept was north of *b*'s.

to perform controlled experiments, could observe the points *a* and *b* and their slopes, but could not observe the shapes of the curves away from these points.

Why did not the problem of making investment goods dK/dt and consumption goods $\dot{C}$ commensurable arise earlier, in Fig. 2 and in our first capital model ? It did not because of our arbitrary simplification which made dK/dt and $\dot{C}$ infinitely substitutable along a $-45°$ line. We can always tell unambiguously how much nearer to or farther from the origin one parallel line is than another.

Actually the problem did arise in our model in a concealed way. In Fig. 2 the production *loci* cease to be $-45°$ straight lines when consumption becomes so great that we rapidly milk capital. To the left of the points *d* and *g*, the *loci* in Fig. 2 are curved. I have drawn them in such a way that the *loci* cross, showing the *ge locus* to be capable of a greater emergency consumption sprint than is the *da locus*, even though the latter *locus* generally lies outside the former. Every statistician, Haig-Marshall, Hicks, or anybody else, would have been inclined to judge income to be higher in the latter situation than in the former. However, if we defined income as 'capacity to produce emergency consumption' — and why shouldn't we ? — income along the broken curve will be the higher.

Our dilemma is now well depicted. The simplest economic model involves two current variables, consumption and investment. A measure of national income is one variable. How can we fully summarize a doublet of numbers by a single number ?

You might answer :

'Even in a Crusoe static one-period world, an economy involves more than one variable : e.g. bread and wine. We boil these down into a single measure of income by (i) taking certain linear sums of their values, using as coefficients in the summation one or another situation's relative prices. This often gives a good approximation to (ii) the indifference-curve ordinal welfare evaluation of bread and wine to Crusoe, or to (iii) the production potentialities of the economies being compared, as measured by the 'distance' outward from the origin that their respective production possibility schedules lie. See Samuelson's lengthy and complex discussion in the *Oxford Economic Papers* of the index-number problems and dilemmas involved and references there to the work of Pigou, Hicks, Kuznets, and others.

'Why not apply the same index-number reasoning to the simple dynamic model, combining investment and consumption in the same way as you combine bread and wine in the static model ?'

I am forced to answer that this suggestion will not do. We do not ordinarily think of capital formation, dK/dt, as being desired for its own sake. I am anxious that the U.S. should have plenty of pig-iron and machinery, not because I care about them, but only inasmuch as they later permit me to have more bread, wine or defensive guns.

To see that our earlier methods fail, consider the strong case shown in Fig. 4*b*, where the situation containing *a* is 'clearly better' than the situation containing *b* in that more of both consumption *and* net investment is possible in the first situation. (Fig. 4*b* consists solely of −45° lines, but if the *loci* were curved, only trifling modifications in my argument would be called for.)

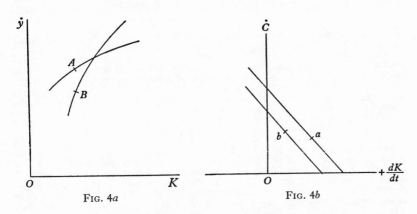

FIG. 4*a*   FIG. 4*b*

Fig. 4*a* shows the two different production functions of two different societies whose national products we are interested in comparing. That Society *B* produces less *currently* than Society *A* is shown by both diagrams.

If $\dot{C}$ and dK/dt were ultimate goods that could be treated like bread and wine, no one could stop us from conceptually drawing in indifference curves on Fig. 4*b* with points of tangency at *a* and *b*. Supposing the social indifference curves to be regularly convex, who could deny (i) that the point *a* is 'better' than *b* according to either society's valuation or (ii) that the production potentialities of *A* are uniformly 'better' than those of *B*? If $\dot{C}$ and dK/dt were replaced by bread and wine, we could be sure that citizens in *B* would gladly trade places with citizens in *A*.

Can we make the same inference in this dynamic context? Following the Hicks [1] interpretation, we should certainly have to

---

[1] The earlier reference to Hicks should not be construed as a criticism of him. His *Value and Capital* discussion is directed *against* the income concept, and his formulation of income as 'level of consumption flow permanently attainable'

argue that income is higher in *A* — as measured by its high vertical intercept depicting level of permanently maintained consumption.

But note that neither in Society *A* nor Society *B* is the representative citizen choosing to maintain capital intact : in both cases he is doing net saving and increasing the society's capacity to consume. One might be tempted to give preference-weighting to dK/dt as well as $\dot{C}$ and conclude that both citizens would feel that point *a* is better than point *b*.

However, Fig. 4a shows that no such inference is justified. It may be legitimate for us to regard the $\dot{C}$ of one society as consisting of the same consumption good(s) as for the other, or at least as being capable of being made commensurable through the use of each

reflects the typical definition of his predecessors. See, e.g., F. Hayek, 'Maintenance of Capital', *Economica*, August 1935, and a long chain of earlier writers.

Incidentally, if positive saving will always go on and if the capital marginal productivity curve will always be inelastic, then the capitalistic class as a whole can count on no above-zero level of permanent consumption. So some might argue that their net income is throughout literally zero. Or supposing that there existed one, essential, irreplaceable, exhaustible resource, then society as a whole might be regarded as having zero net income.

If labour (or better still land) in $f(K, L)$ were perpetual and capitalizable, and if it were known that positive dK/dt were going to take place at some definite rate, then the interest rate would fall. This would not affect the value of each unit of *K* since its net rental would fall in the same measure ; but it is definitely not true that the unit value of all assets could not rise. Actually the capitalized value of *L*, the price of the asset labour or $P_L L$, would go up for two reasons : more *K* will raise the rent of *L* ; and lower interest means less discounting of future rentals. So the total asset value of society (measured in $\dot{C}$ and *K* units) will be rising through time. At any moment what is the total interest yield on these assets ? It is $[K\partial f/\partial K+0]+[L\partial f/\partial L+d\log P_L/dt]$ where the last term comes from (11)'s statement about capital revaluations. This total exceeds *f* by the last revaluation term. Now actually, after we have subtracted from this expression the dK/dt that the *K* owners have decided to save, the remainder will *not* be truly available for consumption — since the whole expression does exceed $f=\dot{C}+dK/dt$ by the 'spurious' revaluation term.

A simple example may show that NNP regarded as $f(K, L)$ *cannot* be regarded as the interest yield on any meaningful capital value magnitude, but must instead be corrected by a capital gains term. Suppose *f* is such that primary *L* is redundant until *K* reaches some larger magnitude than today's *K*. Then all of current *f* or $\dot{y}$ goes as rent on scarce *K*. But suppose dK/dt is going on and we are known to be reaching the time when capital's net productivity falls to a new plateau at half its previous level. After that time, primary *L* will command a positive rental, which will be right now capitalized in the markets for *L*. Since the days of those revenues are approaching, P_L will *now* be rising in a known way. Equation (11) shows that this foreseen capital gain must be taxed if we are to treat investors in land the same way we treat investors in *K* ; but if we do this, our base for the income tax is $(rK+0)+(0+Ld\log P_L/dt)=\dot{y}+$ an irremovable capital gains term.

[In a trivial sense $\dot{C}(t)+dK(t)/dt=\lambda(t)\ K(t)$, where λ is the *average* productivity of capital $f(K, L)/K$. So K can be trivially regarded as the present discounted value of all future consumption, the rate of discount being not the interest rate $i(t)$ — the *marginal* productivity of capital goods — but $\lambda(t)$ — the *average* productivity of capital goods. It is only in this trivial sense that income $\dot{y}$ can be regarded as the interest fruit λ on the reproducible goods of society *K*. Such a formulation imputes, in a way that is meaningless from the market or social viewpoint, all production to *K* alone. Such a non-labour, non-land theory of value has little relevance.]

society's indifference contours. But what is the commensurability of dK/dt in the two situations ? Unit by unit they both have current unit opportunity costs in terms of the (commensurable) $\dot{C}$ of the two societies. True, but what of that ? Society A's capital is subject to much faster diminishing returns *in the future*. Very soon, at the rate both are saving, will Society B forge ahead of Society A.

If you asked Citizen B which he would rather live in, he might reply : 'My society is currently poorer, but I prefer it to A.'

If you asked Citizen A which he would rather live in, he might reply : 'B's technology is currently poorer than mine, as measured by the half-dozen earlier proposals of Haig-Marshall, Fisher and others, but I too would prefer it to my own society.'

For note that Fisher's current consumption, as measured in Fig. 4b by the latitudes of b and a, is just as bad as a measure of welfare as is any Haig-Marshall or statistical definition. Current consumption in Society A exceeds that in B, yet both citizens agree on the welfare primacy of B !

How do we know that both citizens prefer B ? To answer 'Both have told us so' is superficial, and causes us to rephrase the question : 'How does each know that he prefers the set-up of B to that of A ?'

His answer would be : 'I consider my ordinal preferences between present-day consumption and consumption *of all future dates*. I perceive that B, with its more slowly declining productivity curve for capital, permits me to enjoy a time-profile of consumption that lies definitely higher on my indifference contours than does any time-profile of consumption feasible in A.'

The question is resolved in terms of the indifference contours plotted in what space ? The $\dot{C}$ and dK/dt two-dimensional space ? Definitely not. Rather, *in the space of all present and future consumption* ! Reverting to discrete time periods with future consumptions given by $[C_0, C_1, C_2, ..., C_t, ...]$ we envisage the citizen as choosing, from the feasible menus of consumption implicit in Fig. 4a's two technologies, the time-profile of $[C_0, C_1, ...]$ he likes best.[1]

One might feel that this formulation makes our task all the more impossible. Given three time-periods, we seek to evaluate and summarize in a single variable — index of welfare — a triplet of numbers. Given n future periods, we seek to reduce to a single number an n-tuple of variables.

---

[1] If we stay with the continuous model, we must set up an ordinal index that is a 'functional' of the whole time-profile of $\dot{C}(t)$ from now to as far in the future as is relevant. The value *sums* of our later discussion would then be written as *integrals*. If we truncate the time-horizon, we must subjectively evaluate $(C_0, C_1, ..., C_t, S_t)$ where S_t is the terminal vector of society's capital.

However, things are not really so bad. Even in the one-period statical case, we really have thousands of different goods. Having 3 or n times as many consumption goods does not particularly add to our theoretical complexity. To the extent that we can set up meaningful statical index-number comparisons — and the reader of my earlier paper will remember how delicate and complex this procedure is — we can also set up meaningful comparisons of time-profiles of consumption. That is, we can do so on our heroic assumptions of foresight of the future and transitive ordinal tastes.

What we need for our index-number comparisons are market-price ratios reflecting intertemporal substitution choices : i.e. we need interest rates and future money or relative prices. With competitive market prices and quantities given, we can hope to set up index-number comparisons that will sometimes tell us (i) whether the consumption profile of A is better or worse than that of B in the estimation of a consistent set of ordinal preferences, or (ii) whether the consumption profile of one of the situations is capable of being bettered *in respect of every good and every time-period* by the other situation.

Irving Fisher, if this were all explained to him, would break in with the remarks, 'You have cast scorn on my semantic suggestions that current consumption be called current income. Instead you have embraced as a definition of income what I call current earnings and what Haig, Marshall, and most legislators (wrongly) call income. You have then gone on to show that no interpretation of such an income concept can be given a meaningful welfare connotation. (And in all honesty I must add that you have also shown that my own income concept of current consumption cannot be given the desired welfare interpretation.)

'None the less, you are now veering toward another of my important concepts. What you really seem to be proposing as your welfare measure is something close to what I (and others) call *wealth*. By wealth I mean the present discounted value of all future *consumption* (and not, mind you, the present discounted value of future earnings or Haig-Marshall income).'

Fisher would be right. Our rigorous search for a meaningful welfare concept has led to a rejection of all *current* income concepts and has ended up with something close to wealth.

Specifically, in complete analogy with the statical one-period case, we shall want to set up the rather complex index-number comparisons of the following types.

For simplicity, we work with discrete time-periods $(0, 1, ..., t, ...)$. Let the consumption of each time-period be made up of the total expenditure on m different goods of each period, evaluated at market prices. Thus

$$C(t) = p_1(t)q_1(t) + p_2(t)q_2(t) + \ldots + p_m(t)q_m(t) = \Sigma p(t)q(t),$$

for $t = 0, 1, \ldots$, etc. Again for simplicity, let $p_1(t)$ always be unity, the first consumption good being our *numeraire*. Let i_t be the interest rate of the tth period expressed in terms of the *numeraire* good.

Then wealth in any situation is defined as

$$W = \frac{C(0)}{1} + \frac{C(1)}{1+i_1} + \frac{C(2)}{(1+i_1)(1+i_2)} + \frac{C(3)}{(1+i_1)(1+i_2)(1+i_3)} + \ldots \tag{13}$$

$$= \sum_{t=0}^{\infty} \{\beta(t)\Sigma p(t)q(t)\},$$

where

$$\beta(0) = 1, \ \beta(1) = (1+i_1)^{-1}, \ldots, \beta(t) = \{(1+i_1)(1+i_2)\ldots(1+i_t)\}^{-1}.$$

More compactly, we can call each good at each different time a different good, letting capital Q's represent such goods. The relevant prices of these goods are their discounted prices: thus, if Q_{999} corresponds to $q_{13}(17)$, its relevant price is $\beta(17)p_{13}(17)$, which we may write as P_{999}. Then we may rewrite wealth compactly as,

$$W = P_1 Q_1 + P_2 Q_2 + \ldots = \Sigma PQ.$$

The wealth in Situation A is of course $\Sigma P^a Q^a$. The wealth in Situation B is $\Sigma P^b Q^b$. Clearly, there is no meaning in comparing the *money* wealth of one situation (i.e. time and place) with that of another situation. Even if our money or *numeraire* consists of the same initial period's consumption good, a comparison of $\Sigma P^b Q^b \gtreqless \Sigma P^a Q^a$ is meaningless.

It is not meaningless to compare the Q's of one situation with those of another provided we use the *same prices* and *interest rates* in the comparison. Thus

$$\Sigma P^b Q^b > \Sigma P^b Q^a \text{ or } \Sigma P^b(Q^b - Q^a) > 0 \tag{14}$$

does tell us that the real wealth in B is preferable (according to the tastes and time-preferences prevailing in B) to the time-profile of goods available in A. The reader can provide the similar, alternative interpretation in the case that $\Sigma P^a Q^a > \Sigma P^a Q^b$.[1]

[1] If we had observed $\Sigma P^b Q^b < \Sigma P^b Q^a$, we could have concluded something about B's capacity to produce consumption: namely, B was not capable of producing what A was actually enjoying. This and other statements made here can be verified to follow from the analysis of my cited 1950 paper.

IX. THE TRUE NATURE OF THE COMPARISONS

Our comparisons are not of wealth directly, but of wealth-like magnitudes. I must stress and restress that although they offer no difficulties in theoretical principle as compared with the statical case, the national income statistician is very far from having even an approximation to the data needed for these comparisons. A vital difficulty is the hard and unchangeable fact of uncertainty. Futures markets might enable us to salvage something even in the presence of uncertainty ; but futures markets are themselves of little quantitative importance in present-day economies.

This may sound pessimistic. After all we do have estimates of national wealth. Could not a magnitude like $\Sigma P^a Q^a$ be approximated by summing the capitalized value of productive factors ? [1] In theory, yes. We could similarly approximate from market valuations the actual wealth in B, $\Sigma P^b Q^b$.

But none of this is any help. We have agreed that the only meaningful comparisons are not those of the type between $\Sigma P^b Q^b$ and $\Sigma P^a Q^a$, but rather those of mixed type involving $\Sigma P^a Q^b$ and $\Sigma P^b Q^a$ in comparison with the actual wealths. I know of no way of even approximating from market valuations of factors what the values of consumption quantities Q^a at P^b prices would be.

We are left with the pessimistic conclusion that there is so much 'futurity' in any welfare evaluation of any dynamic situation as to make it exceedingly difficult for the statistician to approximate to the proper wealth comparisons. Reflection shows that this is inherent in the nature of things. An appraisal of an economy's situation does involve implicitly or explicitly an appraisal of its future prospects. The current consumption or earnings of the present instant are as nothing against the prospect of the near and far future.

In real life, all decisions are decisions about wealth. Closely examined, no decisions appear to be in terms of current instantaneous magnitudes. If we use as our income period the present minute or day, this truth becomes more obvious. It is only the calendar year, which some accountants and primitive aborigines sometimes regard as fundamental, that blinds us to this fact.

Adam Smith is often these days criticized for writing about the

---

[1] Note that labour or other primary factors must be included in the capitalized total : otherwise we may miss a full three-quarters of it. Note too that ordinal disutility of labour or other factors is not taken account of in the total as stated : but in principle, we can introduce inputs as negative outputs ; this could reduce the new total $\Sigma P^a Q^a$ to zero or less, but the comparison $\Sigma P^a Q^a \gtrless \Sigma P^a Q^b$ remains valid.

wealth of nations and not about their incomes. But the present discussion reveals that he was (inadvertently ?) right. Indeed it is revealing, from the present viewpoint to go back and read Professor Pigou's discussion of this point in *Wealth and Welfare* (1912) and, since 1920, in *The Economics of Welfare*. I cannot do better than quote verbatim his argument concerning proper definition of national dividend or income.

'The major part of this volume, however, is concerned . . . with causation. The general form of our questions will be : "What effect on economic welfare as a whole is produced by such and such a cause operating on the economic circumstances of 1920 ?" Now it is agreed that the cause operates through the dividend, and that direct statements of its effects must refer to the dividend. Let us consider, therefore, the results that follow from the adoption of those two conceptions respectively. On Fisher's follower's plan, we have to set down the difference made by the cause to the dividend, not merely of 1920, but of every year following 1920 ; for, if the cause induces new savings, it is only through a statement covering all subsequent years that its effect on the dividend, as conceived by Fisher's follower, can be properly estimated. Thus, on his showing, if a large new factory is built in 1920, not the capital establishment of that factory, but only the flow of services rendered by it in 1920, should be reckoned in the dividend of 1920 ; and the aggregate effects of the creation of the factory cannot be measured without reference to the national dividend of a long series of years. On Marshall's plan this inconvenient elaboration is dispensed with. When we have stated the effect produced on the dividend, in his sense, for the year 1920, we have implicitly included the effects, so far as they can be anticipated, on the consumption both of 1920 and of all subsequent years ; for these effects are reflected back in the capital establishment provided for the factory. The *immediate* effect on consumption is measured by the alteration in the 1920 dividend as conceived by Fisher's follower. But it is through total consumption, and not through immediate consumption, that economic welfare and economic causes are linked together. Consequently, Marshall's definition of the *national dividend* is likely, on the whole, to prove more useful than the other, and I propose in what follows to adopt it.' [1]

[1] A. C. Pigou, *The Economics of Welfare* (Fourth edition, 1932, London), pp. 36-7. I have omitted earlier passages in which Professor Pigou admits that Fisher's (current) consumption concept of income (i) gives a better objective index of correlation with 'economic welfare which a community obtains over a long

Careful reading of Professor Pigou's argument suggests to me that it does establish the following point. (i) Current consumption does *not* fully reflect the welfare effects of policies now being initiated. (ii) It is necessary, even though difficult, to consider effects on future consumption (suitably discounted ?) ; i.e. welfare changes are to be measured by wealth changes.

So far, this is all in accord with the results of the present investigation, which was led to wealth rather than income as the *desideratum* for the economic theorist. But Professor Pigou goes on to conclude : (iii) adding the rate of net capital formation to the rate of consumption does adequately measure the sought-for wealth. This does not, in my tentative judgment, follow ; and from the standpoint of the many important subjects discussed in *The Economics of Welfare*, it seems to me it would have been better to eschew both Fisher and Haig-Marshall income and to ask how any given policy change will increase the *wealth* of the nation.

I think this becomes clearer if one concentrates on the wording : 'What effect on economic welfare . . . is produced by . . . a cause *operating on the economic circumstances of 1920* ?' Why confine the question to the time period that I have italicized ? To make the point clearer, suppose we transform our time-dimensions and concentrate on 'The economic circumstances of the minute of noon, July 4th, 1920', or the 'circumstances of the Twentieth Century'. Are we to let dimensional change alter our substantive decision ? Are we to regard the calendar year as a privileged set of units ?

Page through the rest of Pigou's great book. Ask the important questions he asks, such as : Should factories be permitted to burn noxious chemicals in crowded cities ? Would it pay the community to introduce a given device for reducing smoke nuisance ? Should decreasing-cost industries be subsidized ?

To a cardinal hedonist like Professor Pigou or an ordinalist like myself, these questions are truly answerable only in terms of effects upon objective or subjective wealth. If the consumption prospect *over all relevant time* that every person can envisage will be deemed better after a given policy change than before, then it is a good one. Only by remote chance can such questions be answered by considering

series of years' and (ii) is more relevant to a country's temporary war-time potential. My earlier critical remarks concerning our ability to infer the latter potential from normal *ex post* income data will be seen to apply even more to Fisher's current-consumption concept than to the Haig-Marshall concept. As to the community's obtaining welfare over a long period of years, this seems to me to apply some 'interpretation' of utility over a period of time (on an *ex ante* or *ex post* basis ?) and to very clearly relate to what Fisher would have to consider dimensionally and conceptually a wealth or stock item rather than what he defines as his income flow per unit time.

Haig-Marshall definitions of current income; and in the singular cases where this is possible, we will know it to be so only by making the correct wealth calculation.

Note that my reformulation in terms of wealth rids us of a fundamental difficulty. My proposal requires us, in making policy judgments, to answer if we can that Situation A is better, worse or indifferent to Situation B. The current income concepts try in some sense to measure finite changes, or rates of change, of a wealth-like [1] magnitude between, say, A, the January 1, 1920, date and B, the January 1, 1921, date. Similarly, 1922 income measures some kind of change between C, the January 1, 1922, date and D, the January 1, 1923, date.

If the theorist gives his *imprimatur* to an income concept, who can blame the statistician for comparing 1922 real income with 1920 real income? But this is not methodologically like comparing Paris and London — or the Twentieth and the Thirteenth Centuries. Such questions usually turn out to mean : 'Given the choice, would you prefer to live in Paris or London?' 'Or live now or then?'

Comparing 1922 and 1920 income is more like asking the quite different and usually uninteresting question : 'Do you like Paris as much better than London as you like Salt Lake City better than Fresno?' [2] On the other hand, comparing the consumption prospects over all time subsequent to 1920 with those subsequent to 1922 does involve a wealth index-number problem and is comparable to a simple comparison of London and Paris. It is like Coué's statement : 'Every day in every way I'm getting better and better'. It does not involve the conceptually less interesting statement : 'Every day I'm getting better at an increasing rate'.[3]

[1] The shocking looseness of the Haig definition of income as the 'accretion to wealth' between two periods is of course to be modified — as I did earlier — to take into account consumption of the period in question. Therefore, I term the magnitude of which income can be regarded as the difference not wealth but a wealth-like magnitude. Dimensionally these are the same, and in the limiting case of zero consumption they would be numerically identical.

[2] The occasion for answering such a question scarcely ever arises. If forced to answer such a question, there are an unlimited number of assumptions and considerations by which one could give an answer rather than be burned at the stake. I should warn the reader that the ordinal fact that I am indifferent between (i) living in Salt Lake City, (ii) living in London, and (iii) a lottery ticket that with probability one-half determines whether I live in Paris or Fresno, *is an ordinal fact* about my reactions to stochastic situations. He misunderstands the Ramsey–Finetti–Savage–Neumann theories of subjective probability and utility who thinks that this approach verifies or refutes the views of an introspective arithmetical hedonist, even though it may be convenient to say that London and Salt Lake City have equal utilities that are half-way between the utilities of Paris and Fresno.

[3] Many of us do look at production statistics to determine whether a nation is accelerating in its physical indexes. We even redouble our efforts when the rate of growth falls below past average values. But this reflects an empirical inference about engineering and other potentialities, not any opinion about psychic geiger-counters.

X. SUMMARY

The present investigation can be briefly summarized :

1. When we work with simple and exact models, in which no extraneous statistical difficulties of measurement could arise, we find that the only valid approximation to a measure of welfare comes from computing *wealth-like* magnitudes not income magnitudes (of the Haig, Fisher or any other type).

2. In the absence of perfect certainty, the futures prices needed for making the requisite wealth-like comparisons are simply unavailable. So it would be difficult to make operational the theorist's desired measures. But operational practicality aside, if the theorist specifies in detail the dynamic technology of his model, he will meet none of the pitfalls that come from an attempt to summarize his model by various crude aggregations. The contradictions that result from over-crude aggregation should never be confused with the technical relations that hold at the firm and family level or with the market capitalizations which hold in competitive security and asset markets.

28

Parable and Realism in Capital Theory: The Surrogate Production Function[1]

I. INTRODUCTION

Repeatedly in writings and lectures I have insisted that capital theory can be rigorously developed without using any Clark-like concept of aggregate "capital", instead relying upon a complete analysis of a great variety of heterogeneous physical capital goods and processes through time. Such an analysis leans heavily on the tools of modern linear and more general programming and might therefore be called neo-neo-classical. It takes the view that if we are to understand the trends in how incomes are distributed among different kinds of labor and different kinds of property owners, both in the aggregate and in the detailed composition, then studies of changing technologies, human and natural resources availabilities, taste patterns, and all the other matters of *micro*economics are likely to be very important.

This general viewpoint has been referred to, and not with complete admiration, as the "MIT school". And I do stand by it as the best tool for the description and understanding of economic reality, and for policy formulation and calculated guesses about the future.

At the same time in various places I have subjected to detailed exposition certain simplified models involving only a few factors of production. Because of a Gresham's Law that operates in economics, one's easier expositions get more readers than one's harder. And it is partly for this reason that such simple models or parables do, I think, have considerable heuristic value in giving insights into the fundamentals of interest theory in all its complexities.

It is the case, I believe, that Robert Solow and I have pretty much the same general views in this matter, having arrived independently and together at the same general conclusions. But Solow, in the interest of empirical measurements and approximation, has been willing occasionally to drop his rigorous insistence upon a complex-heterogeneous-capital programming model; instead, by heroic abstraction, he has carried forward the seminal work of Paul H. Douglas on estimating a single production function for society and has had a tremendous influence on analysts of statistical trends in the important macroaggregates of our economy. One might almost say that there are two Solows—the orthodox priest of the MIT school and the busman on a holiday who operates brilliantly and without inhibitions in the rough-and-ready realm of empirical heuristics. Just as red wine and white wine are both good, so are both Solows of vintage quality. But if I were forced to choose between red and white wine, I for one would reveal a preference for the red.

[1] Dedicated to Joan Robinson on the occasion of her memorable 1961 visit to MIT. (Acknowledgment, non-incriminating, to the Ford Foundation for research finance is gratefully made.)

But must there always be a need for mutually exclusive choice? Cannot each in its place be useful? What I propose to do here is to show that a new concept, the " Surrogate Production Function," can provide *some* rationalization for the validity of the simple J. B. Clark parables which pretend there is a single thing called " capital " that can be put into a single production function and along with labor will produce total output (of a homogeneous good or of some desired market-basket of goods). In so doing, I may also be providing some extenuations for Solow's holiday high-spirits.

When I tried to explain all this in correspondence with my good friend Nicholas Kaldor (the chap who likes to talk about a " stylized "—i.e., non-rigorous but suggestive—description of a modern economy), he replied with the amiable gibe: " You are trying to pretend that J. B. Clark can be defended as ' stylized ' Samuelson." That is much what I want to argue here. I shall use the new tools of the Surrogate Production Function[1] and Surrogate Capital to show how we can sometimes predict exactly how certain quite complicated heterogeneous capital models will behave by treating them *as if* they had come from a simple generating production function (even when we know they did not *really* come from such a function).

I must not overstate my case. There are many realistic capital models where many o the tricks developed here will not work: later I give instances.

II. Heterogeneous Capitals Model of the Linear Programming Type

I begin with a concrete model in which there are a great variety of capital goods: call them alpha, beta, . . . , 999 or anything else and think of each as co-operating with a fixed crew of workers and being as specific as you like to one kind of use. Assuming for simplicity that society produces only one kind of homogeneous final output, we can regard the use of each kind of physical good as a separate linear programming activity and can adhere to the most extreme assumption of fixed-proportions (involving L-shaped isoquants of the Leontief-type). Constant returns to scale is assumed throughout, but it is understood that concrete capital goods depreciate only gradually over time and that society cannot convert one kind of good into another except by the slow device of refusing to replace one kind and alternatively producing more of the other.

One need never speak of *the* production function, but rather should speak of a great number of separate production functions, which correspond to each activity and which need have no smooth substitutability properties. All the technology of the economy could be summarized in a whole book of such production functions, each page giving the blueprint for a particular activity. Technological change can be handled easily by adding new options and blue prints to the book, but for simplicity I shall assume that technical knowledge does not change.

Finally it is enough to assume that there is but one " primary " or non-producible factor of production, which we might as well call labor (or a dose of labor and land). All other inputs and outputs are producible by the technologies specified in the blue prints.

Along with our returns assumptions we stipulate the perfect knowledge condition appropriate to a perfectly competitive market, one which lacks monopolistic or monopsonistic domination. Alternatively we can think of this as a completely planned state

---

[1] One might call this the As-if Production Function.

that organizes itself for Pareto-optimality by explicit or implicit use of Lerner-Lange pricing (equivalent to the shadow-price dual variables of a linear programming problem).

III. The Fundamental Factor-Price Frontier

Given the stage directions of our system it acts out its own scenario just as a logical system develops its own theorems once its axioms are specified.

A first simple question is this: What various stationary or steady states are possible? Upon detailed reflection, one will agree that the system can " end up " in a great variety of states in which the real wage of labor and the interest rate per annum (or, what is the same thing with our stipulation of no uncertainty, the percentage rate of profit) are determined. Once they are determined, all equilibrium machine rentals, valuations, commodity prices and all the rest are uniquely determined (provided, as in the usual discussion of " substitution theorems," we rule out the influence of the composition of demand on such joint products as wool and mutton or new taxi rides and old.)

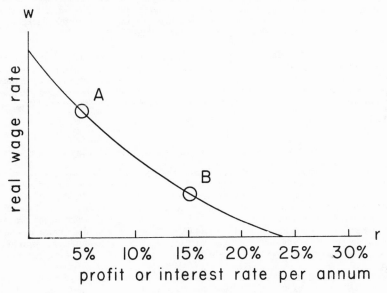

FIGURE 1.
The Factor Price Frontier

Fig. 1 portrays the steady state configurations of equilibrium real wage and interest rate. At *A* society has, so to speak, been able to afford such " time-intensive " or " mechanized " processes as to produce a high real wage for workers and a low rate of interest or profit return. At *B*, the rate of interest is so high that society can afford only to use such direct processes as yield a low real wage. There is always a tradeoff between the wage and profit level: in the absence of innovation both cannot go up; and whatever the pattern of innovation, both cannot go down, since a simultaneous declining rate of profit and an immiserization of the wage earner would be arithmetically impossible in the stipulated technology. A good name for this fundamental tradeoff relation would be the Factor-price Frontier. A number of writers (v. Thünen, J. Robinson, P. Samuelson, P. Sraffa, . . .) have indicated the existence of such a frontier for various capital models, and I shall not here venture to discuss its properties in detail, save to say that it will have non-positive slope and (in the most general case) be of any curvature.

If two economies have each a different book of technical blue prints, they will have different Frontiers. Thus, an effective technological change will shift the Frontier north-eastward, permitting higher real wage rates at the same profit rate, or higher profit rates at the same real wage, or higher rates of both. One could try to define a technological change as " neutral " or otherwise in terms of the way it shifts this Frontier, but I shall not stop to discuss that question.

Can two economies with different technologies (i.e. different sets of blue prints) have exactly the same Frontier? Certainly it would be most unlikely for such a rare coincidence to happen; but it is not impossible. (Thus, imagine the planet Mars where there exist unicorns that do the work of horses, or where there are even more subtle background differences that yet end up with the same final wage-profit equilibria.)

In the singular case where two economies have exactly the same Factor-price Frontier, however they may be different in the background, we can treat them as equivalent in so far as predictions about their long-run interest and wage rate properties are concerned. And, what may be more useful, if two economies have approximately the same Frontiers within a given range, we can use either one to predict the long-run properties of the other in that range.

IV. A SPECIAL MODEL OF HETEROGENEOUS PHYSICAL CAPITALS

All that has been said up until now is completely general, holding rigorously for any constant-returns-to-scale technology no matter how complicated are the technological processes and resulting book of blue prints. But now I want to consider a special subclass of realistic cases, to present certain valid results that hold rigorously for such models. Obviously, it would serve no purpose here to consider a model in which there were not diverse physical capital goods. And it would evade the issue to consider a model in which the capital goods, were not highly specific to one use and to one combination of co-operating labor. None of these issues will be dodged in the slightest.

In particular, I assume that any one capital good, call it alpha, looks entirely different from a second beta capital good. Thus, think of one as a plow; another as a machine tool or loom, or as a much more " mechanized " plow. No alchemist can turn one capital good into the other. Alpha needs labor to work with it in a fixed proportion: more than its critical proportion of labor will yield nothing extra; more of the critical proportion of alpha will itself, with labor constant, yield nothing extra; take away either input, while holding the other input at the previously proper proportion, and you lose *all* the product that has resulted from the combined dose of the two inputs. Just as alpha and labor can produce final output, it is assumed that they too can produce a flow of new alpha machines. I shall here assume that the same proportion of inputs is used in the consumption-goods and alpha-goods industries, with full warning that this is a drastically simplifying assumption whose limitations will be commented on later.   Since alpha, like any other capital goods, will depreciate through time, we can reckon its net capital formation only after its physical depreciation has been made good or allowed for.   To keep the alpha good homogeneous independently of age, one has to assume a force of mortality independent of age (or an exponential life table).   This means that physical depreciation is always directly proportional to the physical stock of alpha, K_α: Depreciation equals δ_α times K_α, where the average length of life of alpha is the reciprocal of the δ_α factor.[1]

The same general assumptions are to hold for capital goods beta, gamma, . . ., etc. Each works with its peculiar proportion of labor, and can produce our market-basket flow of finished goods.   Each can produce its own gross capital formation, and depending upon its peculiar length of life, we can reckon its physical depreciation and physical rate of net capital formation of the type $\dot{K}_\beta$.   The present model, however, does not require any of beta to help in producing alpha, nor vice versa.   Warning is given that this is a deliberate over-simplification of reality.

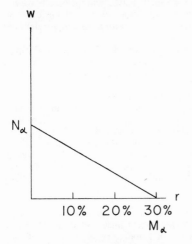

FIGURE 2a.
The Frontier for Alpha.

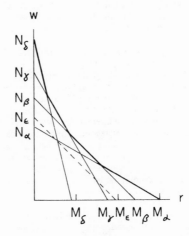

FIGURE 2b.
The Optimal Frontier for Alpha, Beta, . . .

What would the Factor-price Frontier look like if there were only the one physical capital, K_α?   Fig. 2a shows it as a straight line $M_\alpha N_\alpha$.

The horizontal intercept, M_α, gives that maximal profit rate which would be possible if labor were a redundant and free good.   Thus, from our techncial coefficient of the amount

---

[1] In linear programming terminology, we have two activities: one uses a certain amount of L and K_α as inputs to produce a certain amount of final product; the second activity uses L and K_α in the same proportions to produce a certain number of units of new (gross) alpha capital goods G_α—and by convention we may choose as our unit for alpha capital goods just that amount which uses the same inputs as would the production of one unit of final consumption output.   Needless to say, to produce one unit of *net* capital

formation of alpha, $\dot{K}_\alpha = dK_\alpha/dt$, requires additional inputs large enough to make good depreciation:

i.e., $\dot{K}_\alpha = G_\alpha - \delta_\alpha K_\alpha$.

of alpha needed to produce a unit of itself, we can compute the fastest rate at which alpha can make itself grow. Call this, say, 40 per cent per annum. But if alpha has only a 10 year average life, we have to subtract 10 per cent for depreciation to get the maximum self-growth and profit rate of 30 per cent at M_α.

The vertical intercept, N_α, gives the highest productivity of labor on the supposition that the profit or interest rate is zero. The magnitude of this long run real wage, $w = W/P$, is completely determined from the technical input coefficient alone : if less direct labor were needed to produce a unit of consumption and alpha output, w would rise; it would rise if, *ceteris paribus*, the machine became longer lived; and it would rise if less alpha were needed directly to produce consumption Q or the gross capital formation G_α.

Why is the Frontier a straight line between these two intercepts? The answer is traced to our fixed-proportions postulate.[1] With no substitutability possible, there can be no " deepening of capital," and every stationary state produces exactly the same output related to the size of total labor employed. Hence, when labor's relative share of net product falls from all to one-half, its real wage must exactly halve; and the percentage rate of profit (or " own-interest "), will rise to half its maximum rate. Applying the same reasoning to all other fractional division of shares, we end up with a perfectly straight line

Fig. 2b shows the various straight line Frontiers that would hold for physical capital goods, alpha, beta, gamma, . . . , etc. Each is characterized by its technologically-derivable intercept coefficients of the N and M type. These are all calculated from the postulated book of blue prints specifying the model. Note that beta is a more " round-about, mechanized time-intensive " process than alpha. What do such terms mean? This, and no more than this: alpha will be used at very high interest or profit rates in preference to beta; but if the interest rate were lower, below 10 per cent, society would let alpha wear out and put all its resources into the gross capital formation of beta. Likewise gamma is more " time-intensive " than beta. And so it goes in the table and diagram. (Note too that process epsilon will never be used in a stationary state; once beta has been invented, it will never pay workers, capitalists, or planners to start any new epsilon investments since epsilon is dominated by beta from the (*a*) wage, (*b*) profit, and (*c*) technocratic productivity viewpoints.)

With all the different capital goods available, stationary equilibrium is possible only on the north-east frontier or " envelope " of all the straight lines. Planners, electronic computers, and arbitragers will be led, as if by a Visible Hand, to ensure that. The heavy curve in 2b shows the resulting Factor-price Frontier defined by the whole set of technical blue prints. This Frontier consists of straight lines and corner points, which can initially be characterized as follows:

On any straight line segment, only the process corresponding to that line is being used (Query: Can you easily read off relative shares?)

At any corner point, there is a blending of two adjacent processes, relative shares there characterizing each process separately. Geometrically, we can say that the corner has all the slopes between the limiting slopes of each separate process; each blending gives rise to one of these intermediate slopes, and from that slope we can infer the relative shares for society as a whole as an average of relative shares in the component processes.

[1] If more (less) alpha relative to labor were needed to produce itself than to produce consumption output, the Frontier would be convex to the origin (concave to the origin).

V. The Frontier and Relative Factor Shares

If one believed the over-praised statement of Ricardo that " Political Economy . . . should rather be called an enquiry into the laws which determine the division of the produce of industry amongst the classes who concur in its formation," the Factor-price Frontier would be among the most important concepts in this economic model. For, the Frontier can (in the special diverse-goods model of the previous section) give us more information than merely what the wage and profit rates will be at any point. Improbable as it may first seem to be, it is a fact that the behaviour of stationary equilibria *in the neighborhood* of a particular equilibrium point will completely determine the possible level(s) of relative factor shares in total output *at* that point itself. It is as if going from New York to its suburbs were necessary and sufficient to tell us the unseen properties of New York City itself.

Specifically, how do we infer the relative shares of wages and of property income at a point like *A*, when we know only the *rates* of wages and interest there.   If *A* is at a point

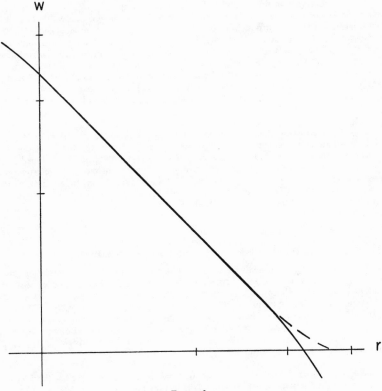

FIGURE 3.
Double-Log Frontier.

where the curve is smooth and cornerless, we need simply calculate its ordinary Marshallian elasticity, E, there: if E is unity, the wage bill and interest bill are each half of total net national product. If E is inelastic and less than unity, labor gets less than half of the total product. If, as is more realistic for modern nations, the curve has an elasticity at A of around 3, then labor's share is three times that of property and labor gets three-fourths of the total.

Since elasticity rather than slope is crucial, it will obviously be useful to plot the Frontier on double-log paper, as in Fig. 3. No longer must it have the usual convexity-from-below property of Fig. 2. On the depicted straight-line stretch, we have the elasticity of substitution equal to unity (much like the Cobb-Douglas case); above and below that range the double-log Frontier is concave from below, indicating elasticity of substitution less than unity (which studies of different countries suggest may be the more realistic case). If the dotted alternative held, elasticity of substitution could be greater than unity and as the wage rate fell the relative share of labor could actually rise.

Our assumption of a finite number of heterogeneous physical capital goods makes it impossible that the Frontier should be an iso-elastic curve of the type that would be implied by a single Cobb-Douglas production function of labor and a single homogeneous physical capital good of great plasticity of form and use. Actually, if there are a finite number of alternative capital goods and activity techniques, the Factor-price Frontier will have corners.[1] At such points, the elasticity coefficient is defined within a limited range of values (corresponding to all the slopes between the limiting slopes to the left and right of the point in question). At such corner points, a limited range of relative shares must be possible, depending upon the relative proportions of labor and non-labor inputs that can coexist there.

I shall not give here the mathematical proofs of all these assertions about elasticity and factor shares, and yet simple literary reasoning may at first be insufficient to convince the reader of the truth of what I have been saying. An interesting point developed in the next sections is that even in our discrete-activity fixed-coefficient model of heterogeneous physical capital goods, the factor prices (wage and interest rates) can still be given various long-run marginalism (i.e., partial derivative) interpretations. And all this without our ever having to pretend there is any quantitative aggregate of homogeneous " capital " that itself truly produces anything.

VI. THE EXACT MODEL OF THE CLARK-RAMSEY PARABLE

Now let us forget our realistic book of blueprints. Instead suppose labor and a homogeneous capital jelly (*physical* not dollar jelly!) produce a flow of homogeneous net national product, which can consist of consumption goods or of net capital (*i.e.* jelly) formation, the two being infinitely substitutable (in the long run, or possibly even in the short run) on a one-for-one basis. The resulting production function obeys constant returns to scale and may have smooth substitutability and well-behaved marginal-productivity partial derivatives. Such a Ramsey model, if it held, could justify all of Solow's statistical manipulations with full rigor.

As is well known, labor's share is given by total labor times its marginal productivity. The marginal productivity of capital (jelly) tells us how much a unit of the stock of capital

---

[1] On double-log paper the Frontier will consist of arches joining in cusps.

can add to its own rate of capital formation per unit time: the result is the (own) rate of profit or interest, a pure number per unit time like ·06 or ·18 per annum. It would even be 1·5 per annum if society could earn 150 per cent per year on its productive investments.

Since only factor proportions count, Fig. 4a shows the different real wages and profit rates that would have to prevail at each level of capital-labor intensities in accordance with the law of diminishing returns. To get the Factor-price Frontier, we simply plot the magnitude of the upper curve against that of the lower, with the result shown in Fig. 4b.

Note how generally similar are the Frontiers of Fig. 2b and Fig. 4b, even though the former has been *rigorously* derived from a definitely *heterogeneous* capital-goods model and the latter from the neoclassical fairy tale. Indeed if we invent the right fairy tale, we can come as close as we like to duplicating the true blue-print reality in all its complexity. The approximating neoclassical production function is my new concept of the Surrogate Production Function.

But what is the interpretation of the capital jelly *J* that all this presupposes? This can be called the Surrogate (Homogeneous) Capital that gives exactly the same result as does the shifting collection of diverse physical capital goods in our more realistic model of Sections IV and V. How can the quantity of Surrogate Capital *J* be computed at each stationary equilibrium situation in the Ramsey-Clark neo-classical model? Merely by calculating the slope of the Factor-price Frontier at each and every point and multiplying it by the easily measurable labor at that point. (See the appendix, Note 1.)

There is still another way of calculating (or verifying) the magnitude of the Surrogate capital that is to go into the Surrogate Production Function that will predict all behavior. In any situation, there will be an observed market (or shadow) interest rate, and observed total output, and an observed labor share. The residual share of property, when capitalized at the observed interest or profit rate must, under our postulated absence of uncertainty, be equal exactly to the balance sheet value of heterogeneous capital goods, where each is evaluated at its well-determined equilibrium market price as established by spirited bidding of numerous suppliers and demanders. Call this observable national aggregate *V* and recall that, at the market rate of profit or interest, it yields the non-labor share. But the same is true of Surrogate Capital J. So, under our postulations, one can rigorously estimate *J* by

$$J \equiv V \equiv P_\alpha K_\alpha + P_\beta K_\beta + \cdots,$$

where the equilibrium market (*numeraire*) prices of the heterogeneous physical capitals are weights that most definitely do change as the real wage and interest rate are higher along the Factor-price Frontier.[1]

VII. CONCLUSION

I trust the above shows that simple neoclassical capital models in a rigorous and specifiable sense can be regarded as the stylized version of a certain quasirealistic MIT

---

[1] While I come to defend Solow, not criticize him, this shows he might better have used a current-weighted index number of capital (measured in terms of *numeraire* units) rather than the available fixed-weight indexes that purport to measure relevant real capital. The resulting bias ought to be roughly calculable.

model of diverse heterogeneous capital goods' processes. But it is well to emphasize that a full blown realistic MIT model cannot be so simply summarized.[1]

Cambridge, Mass.   PAUL A. SAMUELSON.

BRIEF NOTES

1. Let Q = Consumption goods + net capital formation = $C + \dfrac{dJ}{dt}$

(1) $\qquad = F(L, J) \equiv LF\left(1, \dfrac{J}{L}\right) \equiv LF\left(\dfrac{J}{L}\right)$

(2) real wage $= w = \dfrac{\partial Q}{\partial L} = F\left(\dfrac{J}{L}\right) - \dfrac{J}{L} F'\left(\dfrac{J}{L}\right)$

(3) r = instantaneous interest (or profit) rate per annum

$$= \frac{\partial Q}{\partial J} = \frac{\partial(dJ/dt)}{\partial J} = F'\left(\frac{J}{L}\right)$$

Equations (2) and (3) are parameteric equations for the Frontier,[2] whose slope satisfies the basic duality relation

$$\frac{dw}{dr} = \frac{dw/d(J/L)}{dr/d(J/L)} = \frac{F' - F' - \dfrac{J}{L}F''}{F''} = -\frac{J}{L} \; .$$

Elasticity $= -\dfrac{wdr}{rdw} \equiv \dfrac{(w\,L)}{(rJ)}$ = ratio of relative shares. *Q.E.D.*

2. Suppose for some reason we pretended factor J were not directly observable to us. It could still be the case that all the intensive magnitudes Q/L, r, w would be uniquely inferrable if any one of them were specified; and from the technical relation between any two of these, we could deduce the other relations and could also deduce the production function and any other relations that do involve J or any intensive ratios it can enter into.

---

[1] I am grateful to Professor Piero A. Garegani of Rome, formerly of Cambridge University and in 1961-2 a visiting Rockefeller Fellow at MIT, for saving me from asserting the false conjecture that my extreme assumption of equi-proportional inputs in the consumption and machine trades could be lightened and still leave one with many of the Surrogate propositions. I hope he will publish his note showing why the Surrogate case is so special.

[2] Consider any homogeneous production function of the first degree, and involving any number of inputs $Q = Q(x_1, \ldots, x_n) \equiv m^{-1}Q(mx_1, \ldots, mx_n)$, $m > 0$. The usual returns assumptions are that $1 \geqslant Q(x_1, \ldots, x_n)$ defines a convex set; in the most " regular", smooth case this means that the singular hessian matrix $[\partial^2 Q/\partial x_i \partial x_j]$ be negative semi-definite of rank $n - 1$. We can easily define its Factor Price Frontier, by writing down the *minimum unit cost* function $c(w_1, \ldots, w_n) = \underset{\{x_j\}}{\text{Min}} (\overset{n}{\underset{1}{\Sigma}} w_j x_j)/Q(x_1, \ldots, x_n)$.

This is a " dual " function to Q, with the same homogeneity and convexity properties. For any number of factors, the convex-to-the-origin Real-Factor-Price Frontier is defined by $1 = c(w_1, \ldots, w_n)$, possessing the duality properties $\partial w_i/\partial w_j = -x_j/x_i$ and $-Ew_i/Ew_j = (w_j x_j)/(w_i x_i)$, relative factor shares.

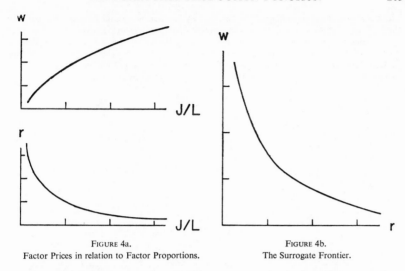

FIGURE 4a.

Factor Prices in relation to Factor Proportions.

FIGURE 4b.

The Surrogate Frontier.

Now the relations among w, r and Q/L that prevail for Section IV's quasi-realistic complete system of heterogeneous capital goods can—by extensions of modern linear and concave programming methods—be shown to have the same formal properties as does the parable system. (Note: this is not an approximation but a rigorous equivalence.) This perhaps justifies the Surrogate Production Function as a useful summarising device.

3. If Q is not a single product or a fixed-composition dose of goods, relative price ratios will generally change as the profit and real wage rates change. This is the fatal flaw in a simple labor theory of value, as Ricardo's critics kept reminding him and as he himself realized. One would have thought he would cut his losses, but he persisted in thinking his theory could be defended as some kind of a useful approximation. I cut my losses and offer the Surrogate Function only as a dramatic model to show that mere *physical* heterogeneity need not lead to qualitatively new behavior patterns.

4. This Surrogate case gives another example where a labor theory of value can help to make the analysis more complicated. Faced with a heterogeneous model in which there are terrible index number problems involved in measuring any aggregate, some modern economists fall back in despair on wage units as a best approximation for measurement, including the measurement of some kind of an aggregate of capital itself. The present model, in which we know rigorously exactly where we are at each stage illustrates how treacherous the use of wage units may be, and how they create *unnecessary* complications to the problem. Thus, let J be measured in its own jelly units, or in the case of our heterogeneous alpha, beta, gamma, . . . stationary state model in terms of its Surrogate Capital units—which is equivalent to using various relative market price valuations divided by the unit of output as a *numeraire*, and where the reader will have missed the point of this article if he does not realize that no viciously circular logical process is involved. Fig. 5a shows that the usual shape of a returns curve will hold if we plot Q against J, with labor held constant and with the perfect understanding that the composition of alpha, beta, . . . will have taken form in consistence with the conditions of stationary equilibrium. But

Fig. 5b shows the consequence of deflating J by the real wage and plotting the result on the horizontal axis.   Note that the usual shape of the returns curve—and even the notion of a single-valued function—has now been lost by the gratuitous act of deflating by real wages.   (The dotted curves of the two figures show the same treacherous behavior of wage units in the simplest neoclassical case of the logically possible kind of versatile physical capital that is capable of being used with varying proportions of labor.)

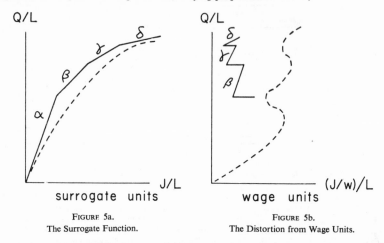

FIGURE 5a.

The Surrogate Function.

FIGURE 5b.

The Distortion from Wage Units.

5.   Once relative commodity prices change, we lose our single real wage rate and must define a different real wage rate $(w/P_1, w/P_2, \ldots)$ for each final good 1, 2, ... with price of $P_1, P_2, \ldots$ Each will be a function of the pure profit rate r defining its industry's Frontier; but must each be a declining function?

At first one is tempted to ask: while raising the profit rate certainly must lower the real wage in terms of a good that has a longer-than-average period of production, can it not possibly raise the real wage of a very short-lived good?

The answer, in our Section IV model, can be shown to be, No.   Since every good involves some finite time in its production, raising the interest rate must lower the real wage expressed in terms of each and every good.   Here is a brief sketch of a proof.

With no joint products, my 1960 generalized substitution theorem (in the Åkerman *Festschrift*) assures us that the price pattern at any profit rate is independent of final demand. And so for any one good we can always assume that it alone is produced—which brings us back to the already settled one-good case.   *Q.E.D.*

6.   The following analysis shows how to derive the Factor-price Frontiers in the general case when the proportions of inputs in various consumption- and capital-goods industries are not necessarily alike.   For any possible process, such as alpha or gamma, let a_c and a_k represent the labor requirements per unit flow of consumption- and capital-goods output respectively; let b_c and b_k represent respectively the needed capital-goods inputs for the same purposes; and let δ represent the depreciation factor as before.   Then the following cost-of-production equations must hold.

$$P_k = a_k W + b_k(r + \delta)P_k$$
$$P_c = a_c W + b_c(r + \delta)P_k$$

These can be easily solved to give P_c/P_k whenever the profit rate r is specified[1]; with r specified, the real wage rates W/P_c and W/P_k can be also easily determined. Alternatively, if either of these real wage rates is specified, we can solve the above equations to get the profit rate and all the other price ratios. (In the special case where $P_k = P_c$, $a_c = a_k$, $b_c = b_k$, from the first equation alone we can get $W/P_c = [1 - b_k(r + \delta)]/a_k$ and Fig. 2b.)

Note that the above equations also are valid in a neoclassical model in which there is a versatile homogeneous capital (call it K or J), which combines smoothly with labor in each of the two industries. The only difference is that the a and b coefficients are no longer a finite set of constants but instead become smooth functions of the ratio $(W/P_k) / (r + \delta)$. Since the above equations are intensive ones, independent of the composition of output, it will be clear that the same industry Frontiers will be valid for states of *balanced* exponential growth or decay and not merely for stationary states in which no widening of capital-cum-labor is permitted. However, when the system is growing exponentially, a different over-all social capital-output ratio will hold at the same profit-wage point if the machine industry needs relatively less or more of machines than does the consumption industry. This shows that the slope and elasticity of any one Frontier does *not* in the general case give relative factors and shares.[2]

7. Can wage and profit rates be given a " marginal productivity " interpretation in our realistic blue-print economy? Yes, as dual variables even though Surrogate or other capital aggregates are eschewed. Thus, let

$$\ldots, r_{t-1}, \ w_{t-1}, \ r_t, w_t, \ \ldots$$

represent equilibrium market prices corresponding to the following production-possibility schedule for society

$$T(\ldots, C_{t-1}, C_t, C_{t+1}, C_{t-1}, \ldots; \ldots) = 0$$

where the dots beyond the final semi-colon refer to initial and terminal stocks of *all* physical capital goods. Then necessarily

$$(1 + r_t) = - \frac{\partial C_{t+1}}{\partial C_t}$$

$$w_t = \frac{\partial C_t}{\partial L_t}$$

[1] In an unpublished paper, I have shown how such equations provide a powerful generalization of the Factor-Price-Equalisation theorem. With appropriate a/b intensities and non-specialization, equalisation by trade of goods prices will equalize the interest rate r and not merely the rentals of machines; of course, all this without any flows of investment funds at all!

[2] If true joint-costs are present, the Non-substitution theorem fails. There will then be no simple trade-off between r and w independent of the composition of demands for C and J, and no Real Wage-Interest Rate frontier curve definable. Example: the social transformation function $(C^2 + J^2)^{1/2} = (LJ)^{1/2}$ can yield as equilibrium profit-wage configurations *any* point in the 2-dimensional quadrant of Fig. 4b that lies *beyond* a certain rectangular hyperbola, if only we make the composition of final demand for consumption and investment appropriate!

If the market (or State) has the foresight to price correctly only for very short periods and if there are very few alternative activities and techniques, this transformation locus can have very sharp corners and the range of possible slopes or marginal productivities may be wide; hence the above equalities become non-narrow inequalities, which are then of limited predictive value.

8.   Historical comments.   The dual relations of Note 1 is an easy extension of Wicksteed's 1896 exposition of homogeneous production functions, and will surprise no reader of the works on indirect or dual utility functions by Hotelling, L. Court, R. Roy, Houthakker, Samuelson, and others over the last 30 years.

The Frontier itself is implied in Joan Robinson's book on Marx and by von Thünen. Sraffa gives a version of it in his 1960 book, based upon reasearches of the earlier 35 years. Before my own article on Marx (1957) I know of no explicit reference to its properties. Relevant also are my earlier papers on Ricardo, factor-price equalisation, simple and generalized substitution theorems, LeChatelier principles and the Legendre transformations of thermodynamic and general minimum systems.

The J. B. Clark parable was given rigorous form in Frank Ramsey's 1928 production function.   Solow, Tobin, Meade, Phelps, Uzawa, Swan and I have written extensively on related and generalized models.   Joan Robinson has properly questioned the Clark model's realism and relevance, and Nicholas Kaldor is even more scathing in rejecting neoclassical production functions.   Simple Harrod-Domar models are often interpretable in terms of a fixed-proportion homogeneous function.

PART IV

On Ricardo and Marx

29

WAGES AND INTEREST: A MODERN DISSECTION OF MARXIAN ECONOMIC MODELS

By Paul A. Samuelson*

Modern economic analysis can throw light on the ancient problems of Ricardo and Marx. Neither of these gave a logically complete description of factor and goods pricing in the simplest case where land is free and where labor and intermediate capital goods applied today produce output after one period of time according to a constant-returns-to-scale production function. I propose to analyze such a simple economy, and then compare it with their formulations.

Just as the utilitarian Bentham was called "Paley without hell-fire," Marx can be classified by the modern theorist as "Ricardo without diminishing returns." The present treatment is part of a longer study of Ricardo-like systems. It makes no attempt to do justice to the many noneconomic and imperfect-competition aspects of Marx's thought, but takes seriously his belief that he was baring the inner workings of competitive capitalism.

Technological Assumptions. Assume two industries. Industry I produces homogeneous physical machines or raw materials called K (for physical capital). Industry II produces homogeneous consumption goods called Y. Production in both industries requires homogeneous labor $L_1 + L_2 = L$ and physical capital $K_1 + K_2 = K$ today, with output appearing one period later. Or:

$$
(1) \quad
\begin{aligned}
K^{t+1} &= F(L_1{}^t, K_1{}^t) & L_1{}^t + L_2{}^t &\leq L^t \\
Y^{t+1} &= f(L_2{}^t, K_2{}^t) & K_1{}^t + K_2{}^t &\leq K^t,
\end{aligned}
$$

where the inequalities reflect the fact that one input may be redundant in supply.

Marx is supposed to have thought the production functions F and f in (1) to be of the fixed-coefficient type rather than of the smooth J. B. Clark type. So in this case we can[1] replace the functions of (1)

---

* The author is professor of economics at the Massachusetts Institute of Technology.

[1] For this and other facts about linear programming and modern economic theory, see R. Dorfman, R. M. Solow, and P. A. Samuelson, *Linear Programming and Economic Analysis* (New York, 1957), particularly Ch. 11. It is shown there that the functions F and f can be written in the form:

$$
\text{Minimum of } (L_i{}^t/a_i, K_i{}^t/b_i).
$$

by the logically equivalent relations:

$$L_1{}^t \leqq a_1 K^{t+1} \qquad K_1{}^t \leqq b_1 K^{t+1}$$
$$L_2{}^t \leqq a_2 Y^{t+1} \qquad K_2{}^t \leqq b_2 Y^{t+1},$$

where $(a_1, b_1; a_2, b_2)$ are the positive technical production coefficients characterizing the fixed-proportion constant-returns-to-scale production functions.

The system's production possibilities can be summarized by

(2)
$$a_1 K^{t+1} + a_2 Y^{t+1} \leqq L^t$$
$$b_1 K^{t+1} + b_2 Y^{t+1} \leqq K^t.$$

These relations are portrayed in Figures 1a and 1b. In Figure 1a, the straight lines correspond to the two equations of (2) with inputs L^t and K^t given. The corner A of the production-possibility locus will move northwest or southeast when one of the inputs is increased. Figure 1b shows the equations of (2), but with outputs K^{t+1} and Y^{t+1} specified: if an output rises, the corner A' of society's input-requirement locus $RA'S$ will move northeast.

The relative prices of outputs K^{t+1} and Y^{t+1}, $(p_2/p_1)^{t+1}$, must equal the absolute slope of the NAM locus at the production point actually observed. The relative prices of inputs L^t and K^t, $(w/p_1)^t$, where w is the wage of labor, can be any nonnegative number because the corner A' in Figure 1b can have a straight line of any slope tangent to it.

I. Stationary Conditions

Simple Reproduction. Under stationary conditions, or slowly chang-

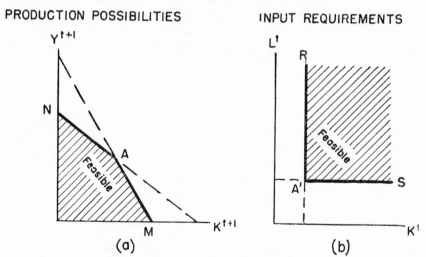

FIGURE 1. NAM shows goods producible with given inputs. $RA'S$ shows inputs needed to produce specified outputs.

ing conditions, the capital stock K^t will accommodate itself to the supply of labor L^t, which is assumed to be fixed, so that we shall be at a corner A rather than at a point on NA or AM where one of the inputs would be redundant and therefore free. Hence, p_1, w, and p_2 will all be strictly positive. These prices, or their ratios, need not be constant through time but may be slowly changing—probably in a rather predictable way.

The model of "simple reproduction," in which all variables repeat themselves over time, is the natural starting place for an exact analysis. In this case we replace (2) by:

$$L^t = L^{t+1} = \cdots = L$$
$$K^t = K^{t+1} = \cdots = K$$
$$Y^t = Y^{t+1} = \cdots = Y$$

(3)
$$a_1 K + a_2 Y = L$$
$$b_1 K + b_2 Y = K;$$

or solving, by:

(4)
$$Y = \frac{1 - b_1}{a_2(1 - b_1) + a_1 b_2} L$$

$$K = \frac{b_2}{a_2(1 - b_1) + a_1 b_2} L$$

where labor supply L^t is taken as given at the L level. Being the only factor nonaugmentable in the long run, labor plays a pivotal role: all other magnitudes are proportional to it. The national product NP can be expressed in labor units simply as L; in consumption-good units NP is given by Y in the first equation of (4). Production of K goes into gross product; but K being an intermediate good needed to produce final consumption goods, it is not included in stationary NP.[2]

Prices, Wages, Interest. Though prices and wages are constant under repetitive stationary conditions, this does not mean that production is timeless or that intermediate products just now produced by labor and machines will exchange one for one against themselves when

---

[2] Ricardo made quite different assumptions about L. He assumed a Malthus-like subsistence wage level at which any number of workers would be produced and reproduced. Such subsistence wages he treated as intermediate product—like hay being fed to horses or coal to furnaces; hence Ricardo's net product would be mine minus wages. Marx assumed actual L used to be less than available L because of the existence of a "reserve army of the unemployed." He would interpret L in (4) then as actual L and would have to add this magnitude as a further unknown variable of the system. A new equation is then needed. The Marxian literature relates the size of the reserve army to labor-saving innovations, depressions, and migration but does not appear to contain a determinate quantitative equation to explain why it is as large as it is, why it is not larger than it is.

"ripened" one period from now—or one for one against finished goods produced today from last period's inputs. The fundamental factor relating unripened product today to ripened product one period from now is the market interest rate r (or what Ricardo and Marx would call the rate of profit, a pure percentage per period).

If the interest rate were $r = .05$ per period, then 100 finished units of Y (or of K) would today trade in the competitive market for 105 unfinished units of Y (or of K) just produced by current labor and capital goods. Free competition among producers, investors, owners of labor, and owners of capital goods will insure the following unit cost-of-production equations:

(5)
$$p_1 = (wa_1 + p_1 b_1)(1 + r)$$
$$p_2 = (wa_2 + p_1 b_2)(1 + r).$$

The first of these equations is directly solvable for p_1/w; and substituting the result into the second, we get the following explicit solution to (5) in terms of $(a_1, b_1; a_2, b_2; r)$:

(6)
$$\frac{p_1}{w} = \frac{a_1(1 + r)}{1 - b_1(1 + r)}$$
$$\frac{p_2}{w} = \frac{a_2(1 + r)[1 - b_1(1 + r)] + a_1(1 + r)b_2(1 + r)}{1 - b_1(1 + r)}.$$

The reciprocal of the last of these is the real wage expressed in terms of consumption goods. If interest were zero, this expression would equal the full productivity of labor in producing consumption goods, as given in the first equation of (4). But of course (4) refers only to steady states of output and input, paying no attention to the time lag between inputs and outputs. Only under special, and unrealistic, market assumptions can the competitive supply and demand relations be expected to ignore these timing relations: if supply and demand among investors and consumers yields a positive r, then workers will receive their "discounted" productivity. This means many things to many writers: exploitation to some, to others merely that workers (and machine-owners) receive their full *undiscounted* productivities in terms of the intermediate product that they *now* produce. Because of the workers' supply and demand for ripe and unripe products, and the corresponding supply and demand of those who own consumption or capital goods, the market rate of interest r is what it is. And being what it is, costs and prices and incomes are what they are.

Note too that the price ratio between any two goods, such as $p_2/w \div p_1/w$ in (6), or between either of these and any third good, will *not* be proportional to their embodied labor contents as given in the first equation of (4) and the corresponding equation derivable for

K in terms of L_1 alone.[3] Exchange values would precisely be given by such labor contents if interest or profit were zero. (Remember we have also conveniently banished all land rents from existence.) This mathematical fact will not be of comfort to one looking for a labor theory of value as a base point for a theory of labor exploitation; the proportionality of market price to labor content applies validly only when surplus value is zero and not worth talking about!

When interest is positive, a change in its magnitude will change all relative prices, a hard fact that Ricardo never could square with his desire to find an absolute measure of value based upon labor. And even had Marx lived to write a fourth or fortieth volume of *Capital*, he could not have altered this arithmetic obstacle to the relevance of his labor theory of value.

The Tableau Économique. For each stationary state based on L and r, we can combine the prices of (6) and the quantities of (4) to get the Quesnay-Marx-Leontief money-flow matrix. Of course, we must reverse the Marxian emphasis, beginning with market exchange values rather than labor values because that is what the market that determines people's incomes and goods' prices begins (and ends!) with. We get:

$$(7) \qquad \begin{aligned} p_1 K &= (wL_1 + p_1K_1)(1 + r) \\ p_2 Y &= (wL_2 + p_1K_2)(1 + r). \end{aligned}$$

Write p_1K_1 as the Marxian "constant capital" C_1, wL_1 as "variable capital" V_1, and the difference between Industry-I receipts and the sum of these as "surplus value" S_1. Define C_2, V_2, S_2 for the second industry likewise. Then by definition (7) can be rewritten:

$$(8) \qquad \begin{aligned} p_1 K &= C_1 + V_1 + S_1 \\ p_2 Y &= C_2 + V_2 + S_2. \end{aligned}$$

Such a relation would be valid even if positive accumulation were taking place, with $\Delta K = K^{t+1} - K^t > O$, and (7)'s $K = K_1 + K_2 + \Delta K$. If simple reproduction is assumed, with $K = K_1 + K_2$, then it is easy to derive the Marxian condition for simple reproduction.[4]

$$(9) \qquad\qquad C_2 = V_1 + S_1$$

However, the supposition made in *Capital*, Vol. I, of equal rates of surplus value in different industries, $S_1/V_1 = S_2/V_2$, is seen to be gen-

---

[3] If we write $\Delta K = K^{t+1} - K^t$ as the net production of physical capital, over and above what is used up as intermediate product in production ("depreciation"), then the steady-state production-possibility equation of final goods producible for each L may be shown to be given by:

$$a_1(1 - b_1)^{-1}\Delta K + [a_2 + a_1(1 + b_1)^{-1}b_2]Y = L.$$

[4] P. M. Sweezy, *The Theory of Capitalist Development* (New York, 1942), p. 77. This seems by all odds the best book on Marxian economics.

erally untrue. By (6)-(8), we find:

(10)
$$\frac{S_1}{V_1} = \frac{r(wa_1 + p_1b_1)}{wa_1} = r + r\frac{p_1}{w}\frac{b_1}{a_1} = \frac{r}{1 - b_1(1 + r)}$$

$$\frac{S_2}{V_2} = \frac{r(wa_2 + p_1b_2)}{wa_2} = r + r\frac{p_1}{w}\frac{b_2}{a_2} = \frac{S_1}{V_1} + r\frac{p_1}{w}\left(\frac{b_2}{a_2} - \frac{b_1}{a_1}\right).$$

It would be a fortuitous selection of $(a_1, b_1; a_2, b_2)$—namely that for which $b_1/a_1 = b_2/a_2$—that would make these equal when both are not zero. However, the situation is a little better than Marx's critics have realized: for if the "organic composition of capital" happened to be the same for different industries at one interest rate, then it would have to be the same for all values of r.

Table I shows the simple reproduction model in the Leontief tableau form of input-output money flows. Each industry is listed in rows and in columns. Thus, the column of Industry I gives the dollar production

TABLE I.—SIMPLE REPRODUCTION, LEONTIEF-STYLE

Industries	I	II	Final Products	Gross Product Totals
I	p_1K_1	p_1K_2	0	Σ
II	0	0	p_2V^*	Σ^*
Value Added { Wages	wL_1	wL_2		Σ } Σ^*
Value Added { Interest	$r(wL_1+p_1K_1)$	$r(wL_2+p_1K_2)$		Σ }
Gross Costs	Σ	Σ^*	Σ^*	$\Sigma\Sigma$

costs it pays out. The row indicates where Industry I sells its products. Above and to the left of the broken lines are the intermediate-goods flows; then on the right comes the value of final output, and below come the value-added cost items (excluding, of course, all depreciation). The starred quantities represent national product, as final commodity flow or equivalent factor costs. The sums of rows or columns are indicated by Σ, and the $\Sigma\Sigma$ checks the identity of all the table items to the gross sum of column sums and to the gross sum of row sums. As a condition of stationariness, $\Delta K = O$ in row I's third column: hence (9)'s identity between p_1K_2 and the value-added items of column I.

To be stressed is the fact that our table is limited by more than the tautological accounting identities: having committed ourselves to equations (1)-(6), we must make each entry in the table directly proportional to total labor L, with a proportionality coefficient that is an easily determined function of $(a_1, b_1; a_2, b_2; r)$ and nothing else. I leave the working out of such coefficients to the reader, since they are important only for Marx's special two-industry circular model. Later we shall see how the coefficients vary for each percentage rate of growth of the system.

A Digression on the "Transformation" Problem. Marx seems never to have quite mastered the purely technological implications of his simplest models. It is idle to speculate whether his Volume II analysis of circular flows might not have been more fruitful if he had not misled himself by Volume I's attempted labor theory. After all, we don't expect in 1860 to find 1960 models. But later scholars surely would have made progress faster in this field if they had subjected the labor theory to careful analysis rather than spent so much time in what must seem to a critic as sterile apologetics.

One honest attempt to analyze the relations between exchange values and labor values beyond the unsatisfactory state left by the posthumous Volume III is associated with the names of Bortkiewicz, Sweezy, and Winternitz.[5] Yet the present *exact* analysis of this model suggests that this so-called "transformation problem" is rather pointless. Equations (6)-(7) determine all market magnitudes in terms of $(a_1, b_1; a_2, b_2; r; L)$. Using the definitions implicit in (8), we can then evaluate all the Marxian expressions as functions of these same variables. Logically this transformation goes from exchange values to Marxian-defined values—not vice versa! This is because exchange values are solidly based on equations (5)-(6), as Ricardo, Smith, and all modern economists would agree. There is no similar solid ground to be found in the Marxian labor theory of value; a model based on equal rates of surplus value is like a made-up nursery tale, of no particular relevance to the ascertainable facts of the simple competitive model (nor to the facts, for that matter, of the Chamberlin monopolistic competition models or the models of developing and oscillating capitalism).

Many Marxians have thought it a virtue of the labor theory of value that it "explains its deviations" from the market-price theory. If so it shares this virtue with every theory, however nonsensical: for

[5] See Sweezy, *op. cit.*, Ch. 7 for discussion and references. Also, L. von Bortkiewicz, "On the Correction of Marx's Fundamental Theoretical Construction in the Third Volume of *Capital*," transl. by Sweezy from the July 1907 *Jahrbücher für Nationalökonomie und Statistik* and given as an appendix in Sweezy's English edition of Böhm-Bawerk's critique of Marx and Hilferding's rejoinder: *Karl Marx and the Close of His System* (New York, 1949). J. Winternitz, "Value and Prices: A Solution of the so-called Transformation Problem," *Econ. Jour.*, June 1948, LVIII, 276-80. R. L. Meek, *Studies in the Labour Theory of Value* (London, 1956), pp. 189-200, discusses this problem and gives reference to later *Econ. Jour.* writings.

truth always equals "error plus a deviation"; and while I should prefer to say that Euclid's geometry explains the deviations between it and my daughter's geometry rather than vice versa, I would not go to the guillotine over such a semantic issue. A quite different defence of the Volume I detour is the historical argument that prices *once* were in accord with Volume I's labor theory, but just as Volume III evolved from Volume I so did the capitalistic system outgrow the simple labor theory: ontogeny repeating phylogeny may be accurate biology, but a respect for the facts of history and anthropology stands in the way of this hypothesis. There is finally Marx's own view that the labor theory of Volume I is needed to "determine" or "explain" the *aggregate* of surplus value, with the bourgeois theories of Volume III having the mundane task of settling the details of how the determined aggregate is to be *allocated* among the different industries. Actually, in the competitive Marxian model defined by equations (1) and the following, there can be no prior determination of the aggregate: the whole is the sum of its (admittedly nonindependent) parts and all the pricing relations are simultaneously determined.[6]

I have not the space to deal with the defensive argument that Volume I's labor theory is a (needed or unneeded?) simplifying first approximation. Modern science and economics abound with simplifying first approximations, but one readily admits their inferiority to second approximations and drops them when challenged. Moreover, to my mind, the only legitimate first approximation would be that of Smith

---

[6] Maurice Dobb, *On Economic Theory and Socialism* (London, 1955), Chapter 17, deals with the transformation problem. Dobb, as does Sweezy, seems to feel that Bortkiewicz came to criticize Marx but in effect ended up justifying him by showing that labor's wage was determined after a "deduction" and by arguing as follows: "If . . . the rate of profit in no way depends on the condition of production of those goods which do not enter into real wages, then the origin of profit must clearly be sought in the wage-relationships and not in the ability of capital to increase production." (L. von Bortkiewicz, "Value and Price in the Marxian System," English transl. in *International Economic Papers No. 2* [1952], p. 33). I do not see that the Bortkiewicz "deduction" or "withholding" theory of wages differs essentially from the conventional "discounted" productivity theories here analyzed and subscribed to by Taussig, Wicksell, Böhm-Bawerk, and non-Austrians. Adding a nonwage-good sector with its new (a,b) coefficients and adhering to horizontal labor-supply conditions which fix the real wage, we may find it true that all three industries can come into stationary equilibrium and with r determinable from (6) or (11) quite independently of the new (a,b) coefficients. But how does this make anyone prefer Volume I to Volume III or to any modern bourgeois theory?

Without going into the social relations of the past or future, any economist can see these implications of competitive market prices. (He can also see that the (b_1,b_2) coefficients reflecting the productivity of capital *do* affect r; and he can envisage a case where Industry III alone, by virtue of having $a_3 = 0$ and $b_3 < 1$ will determine its own-rate of profit by itself, and he will realize that if this new r differs from that of (11) what must give is not bourgeois economic theory or the capitalistic institutional economy but rather the assumption of stationary relative prices!)

and Ricardo in which the labor theory is first introduced with zero surplus value or profits (as in Ricardian comparative advantage examples) but is then to be dropped as unrealistic. Volume I's first approximation of equal positive rates of surplus value, S_i/V_i, is not a simplifying assumption but rather—to the extent it contradicts equal profits rates $S_i/(V_i + C_i)$—a complicating detour. Marxolaters, to use Shaw's term, should heed the basic economic precept valid in all societies: Cut your losses!

II. *Incompatibility of Falling Profit and Falling Real Wage*

Falling Real Wage or Falling Rate of Profit? We now have the equipment to answer an unresolved problem of the Marxian literature. Is there a law of the declining rate of profit as time goes on? Ricardo and Sir Edward West in 1815 showed that the answer is, Definitely yes, if you assume Malthusian reproduction of labor matches the capital accumulation that is applied to scarce land. The law of diminishing returns applied to land then guarantees that profit, or interest, should fall.

Marx, having in most of his work ruled out such rising rent considerations, explicitly rejects this explanation of falling profits. Moreover, Marx was like Malthus and older economists in not bothering to distinguish between technological changes and changes within a given production function. This does not mean that for him a postulated secular econometric law meant that literally what it prophesied would indeed happen; for, like Malthus and others, he often spoke of "tendencies," and in such a way that we hardly know how to decide when he was wrong—and hence when he was right!

From a tautology relating the profit rate r to society's rate of surplus value $\Sigma S/\Sigma V$ and its organic composition of capital $\Sigma C/\Sigma V$, Marx deduced the tautology that higher values of the latter, the former being held constant, would necessarily mean that r falls. Sweezy, Joan Robinson, and most analysts of Marx have rightly, I think, criticized this arbitrary *ceteris paribus* type of argument. The rate of surplus value is a purely derived concept about which little can be said in advance until we already know what is happening to the (a, b) technological coefficients and the supply-demand relations for labor and interest loans. Instead therefore we must tackle directly the question of what accumulation will tend to do to r, basing ourselves on the actual behavior equations of competitive capitalism.

First though, we should note a contradiction in Marx's thinking that analysts have pointed out. Along with the "law of the falling rate of profit," Marxian economists often speak of the "law of the falling (or constant) real wage of labor." Some Marxians have even thought that the important fruit of *Capital*'s peculiar definitions has been this law of the "immiseration" of the working classes, with the rich getting richer the poor poorer, and with nothing to be done about it until capitalism becomes so senile and cycle-ridden as to lead inevitably to a revolutionary transformation into socialism or communism. The facts of economic history have, of course, not dealt kindly with this law. And Marx himself did not adhere to it at all times. But he perhaps didn't fully realize the inconsistency of his two inevitable laws. As Joan Robinson points out: "Marx can only demonstrate a falling tendency in profits by abandoning his argument that real wages tend to be constant."[7] Our model is well-designed to show this.

Specifically, with specified (a, b) coefficients if attempts to accumulate did succeed in bringing profit r down to a lower plateau, the real wage would have to be higher—and by a quantitative amount to be predicted from our second formula of (6), namely

$$(11) \qquad \frac{w}{p_2} = \frac{1 - b_1(1 + r)}{a_2(1 + r)[1 - b_1(1 + r)] + a_1(1 + r)b_2(1 + r)}.$$

This rational function grows as the interest or profit rate falls, reaching its maximum when r reaches its zero level.

A Theorem about Technological Change under Perfect Competition. This wage-profit relation is derived, not from the orthodox model involving smooth marginal productivities, but from the simplest fixed-coefficients model that Marx seems often to have had in mind.[8] It does rest though on fixed technology as given by the (a, b) coefficients. Since Marx admits technological change into his system, doesn't *my*

---

[7] Joan Robinson, *An Essay on Marxian Economics* (London, 1942), p. 42. Also, Sweezy, *op. cit.*, Ch. 6.

[8] J. Robinson, *op. cit.*, p. 43 demonstrates the orthodox case, making implicit use of a smooth two-factor homogeneous production function. Her next page's numerical example, suggesting that with a fixed real wage r *might* fall, is inconsistent with such a model, no matter how "very sharply" the marginal productivity of capital is assumed to fall; forgotten is the fact that when increased capital to labor leaves the real wage constant, decreased labor to capital *must* leave the profit rate constant too; actually, for all changes within a smooth or unsmooth homogeneous production function, Δ(real wage) equals $-\lambda\Delta$(profit rate), where λ is an intermediate positive capital/labor ratio.

Recently William Fellner, "Marxian Hypotheses and Observable Trends under Capitalism: A 'Modernized' Interpretation," *Econ. Jour.*, Mar. 1957, LXVII, 16-25, argues that a two-factor, homogeneous production function, zero-monopoly world can have its real-wage marginal productivity and its profit marginal productivity simultaneously fall— provided a sufficiently labor-saving invention has intervened. Fellner's conclusion is inconsistent with my theorem: competition would keep the invention he envisages from ever becoming exclusively dominant. The rest of Fellner's excellent paper is quite unaffected by his pp. 20-21 discussion of this point, which in any case no longer represents his opinion on the subject. Since writing this paper, I note H. D. Dickinson, "The Falling Rate of Profit in Marxian Economics," *Rev. Econ. Stud.*, Feb. 1957, XXIV, 120-31, deals with a similar topic, attempting to use the Marxian C, V, S, categories. The sharp contrast with the present treatment is worthy of note.

argument that falling r with given (a, b) coefficients implies rising real wage w/p_2 become irrelevant? In the competitive model, I believe not completely.

For technological change is itself subject to *some* laws. A technical improvement must be an improvement or it will not be introduced in a perfect-competition market economy: Marx cannot repeal the valid part of Adam Smith's law of the Invisible Hand, for its validity depends only on the existence of numerous avaricious competitors. To illustrate, imagine an old set of coefficients $(a_1, b_1; a_2, b_2; r)$ and a new possible set $(a_1', b_1'; a_2', b_2'; r')$. Then if $r' < r$ and if the new technology will actually win its way in a competitive market over the old, I assert the theorem that *the new steady-state real wage $(w/p_2)'$ must be greater than the old real wage.*[9]

This is straightforwardly provable by the mathematics of linear programming. It will become intuitively clear if one considers the special Ricardian case where $b_1 = 0$ and no circular complications can arise from the fact that it takes machines (K_1) to make machines (K). Remember that in a perfectly competitive market it really doesn't matter who hires whom: so have labor hire "capital," paying the new market interest rate $r' < r$; then labor could always use the old technology and paying less than r get better than the old real wage. If labor does not do this, it must be because it can now do even better than better.[10]

If my result or my argument seems paradoxical, remember that perfect competition—like Christianity—will be found to be very paradoxical if ever it is universally tried. And remember too that Marx has made the unrealistic assumption that everything except labor is reproducible in the long run. If he had abandoned his labor-theory-of-value concepts and from the beginning built on the patent fact that natural resources too are productive (in the unemotive sense that if the U.S.A. or U.S.S.R. didn't have them, its product would be less), then the possibility of having profit and wages both fall would have to

[9] Rewriting (11) as $w/p_2 = \Phi(r;a,b)$, and now letting (a,b) be variable as a result of technological change, the competitive Invisible Hand can be proved to select (a,b) so that $w/p_2 = \Phi(r) = $ maximum of $\Phi(r;a,b)$ with respect to (a,b). Similarly, $r = \Phi^{-1}(w/p_2)$ $= $ maximum of $\Phi^{-1}(w/p_2;a,b)$ with respect to (a,b). Always $\Phi'(r) < 0$. I believe this to be a new theorem. Of course, it is a prosaic mathematical fact not a Dr. Pangloss teleology.

[10] The argument holds even if capitalists do all the hiring, provided only that workers go where they get highest w and competing capitalists do what gives highest profits. If $b_1 > 0$, the argument needs some amplification because workers have to hire some of the old-type K_1 to carry through the old-type activities and for quite a while the rents of the K's might be adverse to labor; also we could not be sure of being able to settle down to a steady state in two periods when $b_1 > 0$. The stated theorem remains valid though. (Note that with $b_1 > 0$, there *must* have been other ways of producing or getting K, else the system could never have gotten started and could never recreate any K if it were all bombed out—or if, like passenger pigeons or dodo birds, K once became extinct.)

be admitted. He would also have been in a better position to explain why some people are very rich indeed and why some countries are more prosperous than others.

Causality and History. Faced with two contradictory dogmas, what are we to do? Decide that the capitalistic system is doomed to contradiction, and that when the irresistible force meets the immovable object there will ensue an inconceivable disturbance—with communism peeking up through the revolution's ruins? This is the "pathetic fallacy" —in which the observer imputes to Nature his mental states—with a vengeance.

Instead, of course, we jettison one (at least!) of the dogmas. Which one? I nominate the law of the declining (or constant) real wage for the junk pile, and note with interest that modern Marxians increasingly turn to that part of the sacred writings more consistent with last century's tremendous rise in workers' real wage rates.[11]

It would be unsafe to predict an actual secular decline in interest or profit rates in that most economists—notably Schumpeter and Irving Fisher—have emphasized how technological change may raise sagging interest rates, just as plucking a violin string restores its dissipating energies. Moreover, interest rates have historically oscillated in such a way as to lead many economists to the view that there is a fundamental law of constancy of the interest rate. (Taussig, *e.g.,* tried to frame a theory of a horizontal savings schedule to explain this alleged constancy.)

None the less it is of some import to know what would be the effect of attempts to accumulate capital at a rate greater than labor supply increases, *on the assumption of unchanged technology.* For such an inquiry can throw light on the tendencies upon which technological changes of a labor-saving, capital-saving, or neutral character have to be superimposed. Within the framework of my simple two-sector fixed-coefficients model, the resulting analysis will be seen to be at least a little like the despised wage-fund doctrines of Smith, McCulloch, and the Mills.

III. *Steady Growth*

The Expanded-Reproduction Model. Apparently Marx did not have the time to perfect his "expanded reproduction" model in which investment and growth take place. Modern techniques make such analysis a simple task. I retain the fixed-proportions assumption and take up the natural case where, instead of being geared to a stationary level, the economic system is geared to steady growth. This necessarily

[11] See for example, discussion of this topic in *Econ. Rev.* (Tokyo), Jan. 1957, VIII, particularly 21-25.

means steady geometric or exponential growth at uniform percentage rates: no other time-path is possible if many variables and their rates of change are to remain in constant proportions. Such a geometric progression has the further property that relative contemporaneous prices and relative intertemporal prices can be constant along it.

Our production conditions (1) and (2) remain applicable. So do our cost-of-production conditions (5)-(6). But now our simple-reproduction equations (3)-(4) must be replaced by their equivalent relations corresponding to each percentage rate of growth m per period. Now:

$$K^{t+1} = (1 + m)K^t = \cdots = (1 + m)^t K^o$$

$$L^{t+1} = (1 + m)L^t = \cdots = (1 + m)^t L^o$$

(12)

$$a_1(1 + m)K^t + a_2 Y^{t+1} = L^t$$

$$b_1(1 + m)K^t + b_2 Y^{t+1} = K^t,$$

where I have substituted for K^{t+1} its indicated value in terms of K^t and have omitted all inequalities by virtue of the assumption that the system is geared to its rate of growth with no excess capacities of men or machines. Just as we solved the static (3) for (4), we can solve the last two equations of (12) explicitly to get

$$Y^{t+1} = \frac{1 - b_1(1 + m)}{a_2[1 - b_1(1 + m)] + a_1 b_2(1 + m)} L^t$$

(13)

$$K^t = \frac{b_2}{a_2[1 - b_1(1 + m)] + a_1 b_2(1 + m)} L^t.$$

The first of these coefficients has a slight similarity to the expression for the real wage in (11) or (6). In (11) and (6) the positive interest factor r acted to blow up, so to speak, every input requirement a_i or b_i into $a_i(1 + r)$ and $b_i(1 + r)$. Here the positive growth rate m acts to blow up b_1 and a_1 into $b_1(1 + m)$ and $a_1(1 + m)$, but b_2 and a_2 are quite unaffected.[12]

Table II presents the moving equilibrium. Except for $p_1 \Delta K$, which is equal to $m p_1(K_1 + K_2)$, it looks like the earlier Table I. National product is now given by fewer starred sums Σ^*, and this must equal the sum of all the value-added items. No longer does the condition for simple reproduction, $p_1 K_2 = w L_1 + r(w L_1 + p_1 K_1)$ as in (9), hold. Also the precise dollar magnitudes are now definitely weighted toward more importance to Industry I, since we now spend more of our available final incomes on capital growth: the exact quantitative magni-

---

[12] In the closed von Neumann model of dynamic equilibrium, characterized by constant-returns-to-scale and everything plowed back into the system, m and r turn out to be identical. This is not such a system and the possible relations are $m \gtrless r$.

TABLE II.—STEADY-GROWTH EXPANDED-REPRODUCTION, LEONTIEF-STYLE

Industries		I	II	Final Products	Gross Product Totals
I		p_1K_1	p_1K_2	$p_1\Delta K$	Σ
II		0	0	p_2Y	Σ
Value Added	Wages	wL_1	wL_2		Σ
	Interest	$r(wL_1+p_1K_1)$	$r(wL_2+p_1K_2)$		Σ
Gross Costs		Σ	Σ	Σ^*	$\Sigma\Sigma$

tudes are given by functions of the $(a_1, b_1; a_2, b_2; r; m)$ coefficients and are easily computed from equations (6) and (13).

In the next period our tableau would look like that of this period, but with all magnitudes blown up by the common factor $(1 + m)$; and so forth with each succeeding period. Hence, such a steady-growth progression *could* go on forever if only the same behavior rules continue to prevail. (The only restriction on the possible rate of growth is that $1 - b_1(1 + m) > 0$ or $0 \leqq m < (1 - b_1)/b_1$ so that all indicated ratios shall exist and keep all our variables positive. A similar restriction $1 - b_1(1 + r) > 0$ had to hold for r. Otherwise production of capital goods K could never have paid.)

I have said nothing about the saving habits of wage or interest earners that would give rise to the analyzed growth rate m. Certainly if each group saved a constant proportion of its income at all times, say σ_w for workers and σ_r for interest receivers, we could solve for the only "warranted rate of growth" m that is compatible with these properties. (Of course, to assume that L^t is always available at the resulting geometric rate is tantamount to postulating a "natural rate of growth" equal to whatever warranted rate results.)[13]

The solution for m in terms of σ_w and σ_r is more complicated than one might at first think. Obviously, the distribution of income depends upon the interest rate r, postulated to go along with the given $(a_1, b_1; a_2, b_2)$ technical coefficients. Call the fractions of income going to wages and interest k_w and $k_r = 1 - k_w$. Then the community's average propensity to save must be

$$\sigma = k_w\sigma_w + k_r\sigma_r = k_w(\sigma_w - \sigma_r) + \sigma_r;$$

and we see that this will be the higher the higher is the income of the relatively more thrifty interest receivers.

What we may not realize is that the distribution of income coeffi-

[13] These terminologies will be recognized as those of the modern Harrod-Domar growth models.

cients, besides being functions of the interest rate r, are also functions of the unknown m growth rate as well; indeed the ratio of total capital asset value to income, the so-called "accelerator" coefficient β, which is needed along with σ to define the warranted rate of growth, is itself a function of m (as well as of r). So the equation defining the warranted rate of growth:

$$m = \frac{\sigma}{\beta} \qquad \text{or } \beta m - \sigma = 0$$

must, even for given (a, b) coefficients, be written in the implicit-equation form:

(14) $\qquad m = \dfrac{\sigma(r; m)}{\beta(r; m)}, \qquad \text{or } \beta(r, m)m - \sigma(r, m) = 0.$

Why do the accelerator and the distribution-of-income coefficients depend on m as well as on r? First, because the relative share of wages will differ generally in Industries I and II, and each different growth rate gives a different relative importance to the capital-goods and consumption industries. Our equations permit us to compute the exact effects for each $(a_1, b_1; a_2, b_2; r; m)$ coefficients. Second, and related to the above, each different r will change the dollar (or consumption-good or labor-hour) total of asset value to which the yield r is applied. The equation:

Total interest return $= r$ (total asset value)

(15) $\qquad\qquad\qquad = r(wL_1 + wL_2 + p_1K_1 + p_1K_2)$

$\qquad\qquad\qquad = r[A(a_1,b_1; a_2, b_2; r; m)wL],$

where A is a function determinable from our earlier equations and where the bracketed expression represents total asset value.

Our whole problem then has a determinate solution quite free of any of the dilemmas of "capital metaphysics." All is grounded in hard technological fact and hard competitive-market fact: there are circular relations between interest and asset value, but they are virtuous circles not vicious ones.[14]

IV. *Changing Factor Proportions and Prices*

The Law of the Rising Rate of Profit. So long as labor and the sys-

---

[14] The case where profit receivers have $\sigma_r = 1$ and workers have $\sigma_w = 0$, however econometrically unrealistic, is a special case of the above analysis. Were $\sigma_w > \sigma_r$, the logic of the system would be little changed. Of course, with $\sigma_w = \sigma_r$, the distribution of income would become irrelevant and the analysis slightly simplified. Also, in the singular case earlier mentioned, where $a_1/b_1 = a_2/b_2$ and labor-values are proportional to prices, k_w and k_r are independent of m and the analysis becomes even more simple; but to assume away differences in the organic composition of capital is to ignore one relevant factor in the distribution of income.

tem are geared to grow at the same rate, there is no need for profit or interest to change. But if labor grows at a faster percentage rate than does "capital," our equilibrium conditions become inconsistent. Something has to give. What?

One definite possibility is for labor to become redundant and—if it has no reservation price or real cost of staying fit to work—its wage will have to fall. Fall how far? Adhering to the extreme assumption of fixed-coefficient production functions as given in (1) and what follows, we recognize that the real wage becomes literally zero. Kill off one of the now superfluous man-hours and you have outputs unchanged: so the competitive market will impute a zero wage to all manhours. Mathematically, the inequality will now hold in the first relation of (2); and since all subsequent equations were based on the equality in this relationship, all must now be replaced by new relations. *E.g.*, cost-of-production now requires:

$$
\begin{aligned}
p_1{}^{t+1} &= b_1 p_1{}^t (1 + r^t) + a_1 0 \\
p_2{}^{t+1} &= b_2 p_1{}^t (1 + r^t) + a_2 0;
\end{aligned}
$$

(16)

and if prices are to be constant through time with $p_i{}^{t+1} = p_i{}^t$, we must have

$$
1 + r = \frac{1}{b_1}
$$

(17)

$$
\frac{p_2}{p_1} = b_2 (1 + r) = \frac{b_2}{b_1}.
$$

These show that the interest rate, which is now interpretable as the own-rate and net-reproductive-rate of machines, must, so long as any of them are being produced, be determinable by technology alone quite independently of all time preferences; and that the terms of trade between consumer goods and machines now depends only on technology, and more specifically only on machine requirements as given by the b's with the a requirements of free labor now being irrelevant.

We can now reckon the national product from the first equation of (12). The following must all hold:

$$
b_1 K^{t+1} + b_2 Y^{t+1} = K^t
$$

$$
b_1 \Delta K + b_2 Y^{t+1} = (1 - b_1) K^t
$$

(18)

$$
\frac{b_1}{1 - b_1} \Delta K + \frac{b_2}{1 - b_1} Y^{t+1} = 1 \cdot K^t
$$

$$
\frac{p_1}{p_2} \Delta K + 1 \cdot Y^{t+1} = r \left(\frac{p_1}{p_2} K^t \right).
$$

The next-to-the-last of these shows the total value of final products expressed in machine *numeraire* units. The last equation shows on the left side the total value of final products expressed in consumer-good *numeraire* units. The right side, which was derived by using the relations (17), shows that the national product is equal from the cost side to interest on value of machines alone. This is natural enough since wages are zero and must have a zero share of total income.[15]

In this case where capital goods have ceased growing as fast as labor, the rate of profit has risen to become all of the product. So bizarre a result came from the bizarre assumption of fixed coefficients. If there were many alternative techniques, a faster growth of labor than capital would imply rising interest or profit rates and falling real wages, but not a zero wage with profits getting all.[16]

Even in the extreme case of fixed-proportions technology, a zero wage is one possibility: indeed a quite likely one. But it is not the only possibility. As long as the organic compositions of the two industries differ, by shifting demand toward that industry with relatively high labor requirements—as measured by higher a_i/b_i—we could put off the evil day of labor redundancy and zero wage. There is no Invisible Hand, though, which inevitably leads the system to this demand shift: the reduction in the relative price of the labor-intensive good need not coax out much more physical demand for it. In any case, if labor really grows at a faster geometric rate than capital, labor must inevitably become more plentiful relative to capital than either industry could employ and must ultimately become free.

How Profits Fall. The case where capital grows more rapidly than labor is perhaps more true to Western life. In order to see what happens when people try to accumulate faster than the labor supply, consider the special instance where labor is completely stationary and yet savers would like to accumulate. This special case, where the natural rate of growth of the system is given by $m = 0$, does not differ in its qualitative features from any case where m is positive but less than the warranted percentage rate at which capitalists would like to have the system grow.

---

[15] If capitalists saved all, with $\sigma_r = 1$, and if they received all the income, with $k_r = 1$, then the system's actual rate of growth would be $m = r = (1 - b_1)^{-1}$, which would prevail so long as available labor grew even more rapidly and stayed freely available. It would involve a certain amount of implicit theorizing to argue that this actually would happen in a model in which laborer's-consumption was tied to subsistence and had already been included by convention in the b (rather than a) coefficients; but such a mode of arguing would not be logically wrong, however unrealistic these econometric assumptions might be regarded.

[16] The simplest neoclassical model is one where $Y + (dK/dt) = Q(K,L)$, Q being a homogeneous function of the first degree with partial derivatives ("marginal productivities") Q_L and Q_K. The diminishing-returns condition $\partial^2 Q/\partial L^2 = Q_{LL} < 0$ implies that a rising trend in L/K entails a rising trend in $r = Q_K$ and a falling trend in $w = Q_L$.

The Marxian model with fixed coefficients presents some quite patho-logical features. For if the attempt to accumulate were to cause physi-cal machines K to grow relative to fixed labor L, the machines would become redundant in supply and their rents would fall immediately to zero.[17] The most obvious case in which this would have to happen in-stantaneously is that in which the organic compositions of capital are equal: $b_1/a_1 = b_2/a_2 = b/a$. The instant K/L exceeded b/a, K would become free, with $(p_1/w)^t = 0 = (p_1/p_2)^t$. We should then have:

(19) $$p_2^{t+1} = w^t a_2 (1 + r^t).$$

No production of future K would take place unless it covered its pro-duction costs; so only so much would take place as could match the b/a machine-labor ratio. Industry I would therefore contract so as no longer to produce K^{t+1} in excess of La/b. Industry II would temporarily produce more consumption goods: whether these would end up con-sumed by workers or capitalists would depend on the interest rate and price configuration prevailing at the end of the next period.

A similar but slightly more complicated analysis would handle the case where $b_1/a_1 \neq b_2/a_2$. In every case should the attempt to save cause a disproportionate temporary growth in K, K would become free. This does not imply euthanasia of the capitalist class, not even temporarily. For as (19) shows, interest would still be received on "advances" to workers. Machines are only one type of capital asset. Goods in process are another.[18]

Had the attempt to save forced K rents to zero, it could only be the result of a miscalculation: competitive future prices could not have been correctly quoted in the market place. To be sure, competitive capitalists have no crystal ball picturing the exact future and mistakes have often been made. But once K had become free, it could never stay

[17] There is the possibility, mentioned in the last section, that shifts in product-demand-mix toward the industry using more of the excessively-supplied factor might absorb its extra supply—at least for a while. Thus the cheapening of the machine-intensive good might meet a sufficiently elastic demand for that good to keep both factors nonredundant. But note that this shift could not carry us back to the stationary-state simple-reproduc-tion configuration of Table I with the same price ratios and interest rate prevailing and the same zero net investment prevailing, because our hypothesis is that people are no longer content to refrain from saving in that situation. And growth of K at ever so small an exponential rate faster than labor's growth rate would inevitably make it a free good in finite time.

In this pathological model labor might collusively wipe out all K rents by producing one redundant unit of K. But only temporarily. Production of K will subsequently con-tract. In this model, collusion of all owners of K could limit its supply and wipe out wages. However, if any one unit of K escaped from the cartel, it and collusive labor could eventually reproduce any needed K outside the cartel.

[18] Such intermediate goods are probably a better description of capital than the old view of capital as the historic, now gone, food that was advanced to workers. The latter double-counts if we add it to the former; by itself, the latter undercounts in that interest is also earned on outlays for factors other than labor.

free and continue to be produced. Curtailment of its production by Industry I would undoubtedly take place. One could even try to construct a cobweb-like business cycle theory of intermittent over- and underproduction of capital goods; certainly, though, a two-sector fixed-coefficients model has such special features as to make the result rather unrealistic.

What then is the equilibrium time-path that is consistent with stationary L and attempts to accumulate? The fixed-coefficient Marxian model makes all "real" accumulation quite impossible: there can be *no* technical "deepening of capital" in it. Does this mean that the profit rate r cannot fall? No. Why should it mean this? If I wish to save, for my old age or to enhance my power, why should I be led to desist from trying to do so by the consideration that the system is incapable of using new investment? Rather will I continue to try to save, to try to buy up existing assets.

Thus, suppose I earn income from K rents, or from interest return on goods in process, or from selling goods for more than I paid in wages and rent in producing them, or for that matter merely from my wages. Then instead of spending all this income on current consumption goods Y, I may *try* to hire labor or machines for next period's production, giving up so to speak my consumption allotment to owners of those factors.

Now what is it which guarantees that there will be owners of such factors willing to hire them out in the amount that investors wish to employ them? Of course, it is the competitive pricing mechanism that causes all markets to be cleared.[18a] Crudely, you can say that the interest rate r^t falls enough to eliminate any excess in the value of what people want to save and invest over the value of factors available to them; contrariwise, if the wish to save and invest is lagging, the present factor prices p_1^t and w^t will be depressed relative to future goods' prices p_1^{t+1} and p_2^t and the competitive rate of interest (or of profit) will be bid up very high. It is crude to speak of the interest rate r^t as alone providing equilibration: actually it is the whole pattern of present and future prices $(p_1^t, p_2^t, w^t; p_1^{t+1}, p_2^{t+1}, w^{t+1})$.

In the special case where the urge to accumulate is modest and steady, the profit rate r^t could be steadily falling as a result of this process, but at so slow a rate as to permit relative prices $(p_1/w)^t$ and $(p_2/w)^t$ to remain practically constant over time.[19] Then our cost-of-

---

[18a] See later sections for some qualifying remarks concerning "effective demand."

[19] I make a point of considering a slow change in r^t because the actual interest change in each period will cause changes in (p_2/p_1) and (p_2/w) and create revaluations and money windfalls. With relative prices changing, we no longer have equality of "own-interest-rates" and (5)-(6) need obvious modifications. By assuming $(r^{t+1} - r^t)$ always very small, we make these revaluation-effects small and ignorable.

production equations (5)-(6) would still be valid but are to be written with a slowly falling r^t in them. The steady attempt to accumulate leads to no physical accumulation of K or anything else; rather it causes an upward valuation of existing input prices relative to output prices, which is the same thing as a reduction in the profit rate r^t. Some savers may now succeed in hiring additional inputs $(K_1^t, K_2^t, L_1^t, L_2^t)$ but, if they do, it is because other capitalists become content at the new interest rate and price pattern to hire less. If all capitalists are exactly alike, they merely bid up factor prices and bid down profit rates.

What has all this attempted accumulation done to real wages? With lower r^t in equations (5)-(6), and in particular in the last line of (6), we see that less is being "discounted" from labor's ("gross") productivity. Real wages have been rising. If, at the lower interest rate, net accumulation should now cease, the real wage going to the unchanged labor supply will not fall back to its previous level but will stay at the higher plateau forever.

Each capitalist in trying to save and increase his own profits ends up killing off the total of profits in favor of the workers. This extreme phenomenon results from the extreme assumption of fixed-coefficients with implied zero marginal-productivity to all further machines or changes in the roundaboutness of production. Yet something of what happens in this case will also hold in a more realistic case of multiple production techniques. As attempted saving lowers interest rates it lowers the discounting of real wages; but in the more neoclassical case, employers will not lose all that workers gain, the difference coming from the extra product producible from "deepening of capital" (*i.e.*, producible from the new complex of physical capital goods brought into existence by the pricing changes induced by the attempt to save).[20]

All this makes clear that the technical (a, b) coefficients and the competitive cost-of-production equations are insufficient to determine all our variables: we need further equations of supply and demand, as *e.g.* ordinal utility conditions showing how workers and interest receivers allocate their consumption expenditures among different goods. But even the latter consumption demand equations are not enough: the rate of interest r^t would still not be determined.[21] We need saving-investment propensities, and propensities to hold and add to earning assets to complete the system.

[20] See Figures 2b and 2c for elucidation of the many-techniques case.

[21] If labor is assumed always to be on a horizontal long-run supply schedule at a "subsistence real wage w/p_2," then (6) or (11) would alone determine r. But prescribing employment L leaves r and w/p_2 still to be determined.

The next sections show the wage-fundlike character of this competitive process.

V. *Wage-Fund Notions*

Perhaps the expression "wage fund" should be avoided altogether as conjuring up too many ghosts and as being too hopelessly ambiguous. Sometimes the wage fund meant merely sums of money "destined" for wage payments, whatever the word "destined" is supposed to mean. Sometimes it meant inventories of finished consumption goods "destined" for workers, and to some writers supposedly consisting of different consumption items than more elegant capitalists would deign to consume. Sometimes it meant a numerator of "all capital," which in some ill-described fashion got divided by the denominator of population number to give as an arithmetic quotient the real wage per capita. Finally in F. W. Taussig's resurrection, *Wages and Capital* (1896), the wage-fund doctrine merely becomes a reminder that production does take time and that men do not consume unfinished goods, with the implication of a certain short-run inexpansibility in the consumption goods available to the community (to nonworkers as well as workers).[22]

In connection with the present two-sector model, it is superficial to split consumption Y^t into two parts, Y^* "destined" for workers and Y^{**} destined for capitalists, and then to write down the trivial identities:

$$(1 - \sigma_w)w^t L^t = p_2{}^t(Y^t - Y^{**}) = p_2{}^t Y^*$$

(20)
$$\left(\frac{w}{p_2}\right)^t = \frac{(Y^t - Y^{**})/(1 - \sigma_w)}{L^t}.$$

Except possibly for L^t, none of the right-hand variables are given constants. In the shortest run itself, when we are realistic enough to introduce inventories into our model, we see that not even total consumption Y^t is unilaterally given. And suppose it were: still, in anything but the shortest run, decisions could be made to cause it to change.

What does need emphasizing is the fact that in every run the supply-demand decisions of workers, of old capitalists, of new investors are

---

[22] In its most rigid form, the wage-fund doctrine implied that unionized or ununionized workers face a short-run aggregate demand schedule of exactly unitary elasticity. This neglects the short-run possibility of using up finished-goods inventories faster than the usual rate, and tells nothing about the longer-run demand elasticity, which could be on either side of unity. In its weakest form, it suggests that the demand for labor is not perfectly inelastic and that the demand curve's rightward and upward shift induced by accumulation *may* be slowed down by concerted measures to raise present wage levels at the expense of thrifty capitalists.

needed to give us determinate equations for our set of present and future prices (p_1^t, p_2^t, w^t, p_1^{t+1}, p_2^{t+1}, r^t, . . . etc.). Taussig was quite right in pointing out that the Malthus red herring of a (very-long-run) horizontal supply schedule of labor at the "[conventional] subsistence level" kept Ricardo, J. S. Mill, and most of the Classicals—but not the aging Malthus!—from perceiving how undetermined and implicit was their theory of current wage determination and pricing. Marx's reserve army is in some ways an even redder herring that deflects attention from the missing supply-demand relations.

Here I shall simply sketch in a superficial way the process determining wages, surplus values or interest, and goods pricing. We start out with a given K^t owned by its owners, with a given L^t perhaps to be taken as a demographic parameter. Today's Y^t we suppose to be given by past decisions, and we overlook changes in short-term inventories of consumer goods. The system has a history of prices and wages. This period's market must determine decisions on how much of (K_1^t, L_1^t, K_2^t, L_2^t) are to be hired to produce next period's (K^{t+1}, Y^{t+1}). The competitive market does this through determining now (p_1^t, p_2^t, w^t; r^t). Simultaneously a set of notions about future prices (p_1^{t+1}, p_2^{t+1}) are formed and in terms of these relative prices, employers make decisions. If goods were homogeneous, undoubtedly a futures market would spring up to register and resolve differences of expectations about future prices; but if this did not happen, our theory would still be valid after certain easy alterations.

The "profits" of employers are, retroactively reckoned, determined by comparing $p_1^t K^t$ and $p_2^t Y^t$ with their past wage and machine costs. The profits resulting from today's decisions will similarly be known in the next period. In tranquil times, the *ex ante* hopes for profit and *ex post* realized profits will not differ too much; but differences that do develop will be noted in the market and will influence later decisions in the obvious direction.

"Net or excess demands" for (Y^t, K^t; K_1^t, L_1^t, K_2^t, L_2^t) will be determinate interdependent functions of (w^t, p_1^t, p_2^t; p_1^{t+1}, p_2^{t+1}; r^t; . . . etc.). Our number of independent equations is equal to the number of unknowns, with only price ratios being determinable until we specify enough about the supply and demand conditions for a circulating medium (*e.g.*, given gold coins; or minable gold; or paper currency issued by the State according to specified behavior rules; or stipulated banking practices).

My fixed-coefficient Marxian model, in the absence of technical innovations altering the (a, b) coefficients, would probably be characterized by attempted accumulation whenever r^t is high. As we have seen, this would cause r^t to be falling; with no physical deepening of capital possible, capitalists would lose in income what workers gain, which might slow up the accumulation process and which later could even cause it to cease. (If we assume that interest and profit rates are quite high, we can perhaps avoid some of the effective-demand problems that arise from the temptation to hoard money when interest rates are very low.)

Where alternative (a, b) techniques exist, lower r^t will induce adaptations in technique. These adaptations can be expected usually to slow down the drop in total interest income. Does this mean that the real wage will grow less rapidly? If lower r^t induces irreversible (a, b) changes of a so-called "labor-saving" type, the rise in real wage could indeed be slowed down or even be wiped out; and if this were to happen, the fall in r^t would have been converted into a subsequent rise in r^t, interest rising more than the drop in total wages. However, any change to a new (a, b), which now pays only because r^t is lower, will produce a higher real wage for each r^t than would the old (a, b); but if the demand for "capital" is sufficiently elastic or sufficiently little inelastic, induced technical changes might slow up the rate of fall of r^t so much as to cause the real wage to rise more slowly than it would under a single technique. I suspect, but cannot prove conclusively, that a Marxian who takes seriously the fixed-coefficient single-technique case is selecting the very model in which improvement of labor's share of the total income would be easiest within the framework of an unchanged-technology capitalism.

Life's Libretto: One Technique or Many? The case of a single fixed-coefficient technique is a very peculiar one indeed. Increase labor by epsilon and its share of the product may go from 100 per cent to zero! The later neoclassical economists would consider this as the extreme case of a marginal product curve for labor that is infinitely steep over a wide range: confront so steep a curve with a coinciding infinitely-steep supply curve of labor, and you have indeed created an indeterminate equilibrium wage with all the scope for collective bargaining and class power struggles that you could want.

Perhaps Karl Marx really had such a technology in mind. Perhaps not. It may be reasonable to believe that Marx, like Ricardo and other early writers, and unlike modern neoclassicists, never explicitly thought about what properties of the production function (a concept not yet explicitly defined or named) he wished to posit. It would be reading into him things that he would not recognize to claim a smooth production function with infinite substitution possibilities. On the other hand, he speaks again and again of alternative techniques. While many of these clearly depict technological change in the production function rather than movement within one function, the fact that the old methods are still known along with the new shows that Marx and Ricardo definitely envisage the existence of more than one technique. (Both Ricardo and Marx write of technical changes induced by price changes and adapted to changed price ratios; neither rules out the possibility that if the old price ratios were restored, the old technique might again become more economical.)

Whether or not Marx would resent being interpreted as a believer in a fixed-coefficient single-technique world, I should resent on behalf of the real world any such description. Go into any machine plant, pick up any engineering catalogue, study the books of physics and the histories of industrial processes, and you will see the variety of different ways of doing anything. If fixed Leontief coefficients (a_i, b_i) had characterized the world, it could never have got started. If the world has changed, the old processes are still remembered. Changing prices will induce accommodating changes in techniques. Perhaps the bookish economist will reply, "Foul! You are bringing in nonstatical, nonreversible changes." To this the realistic observer of the world will shrug his shoulders and answer, "So much the worse for a statical one-technique theory, or for that matter for any statical theory of production: but if we are to approximate reality by quasistatical tools, the more realistic production function to use is one with numerous alternative techniques, quite different in their input combinations and intensities."

We must not be put off by the bogey-man query: "Do you think that God created the earth with smooth Wicksteed homogeneous production functions involving a few aggregative factors, Socially Necessary Labor, Efficiency-unit Land, and Catch-all Dollar Capital?" To deny such a belief is not to confirm a belief in fixed-coefficients. A more realistic interpretation of actuality will recognize the existence of a large, perhaps finite, number of alternative techniques. The modern theory of linear programming permits the economist to handle these analytically; but even if we ivory-tower observers could not easily handle the analysis of many techniques, it would be another case of the Pathetic Fallacy to think that the actors in the real world will desist from making jig-saw puzzle substitutions because we economists can't easily analyze them.

John Jay Chapman once said that a visitor to this world would find its people behaving more like the people in a Verdi opera than in an Emerson essay. So if a visitor from Mars insisted upon a grandiose simplification of the economic system—instead of using the less dramatic methods of Walras, Chamberlin, and Keynes—I think he'd be safer in positing an aggregative production function of the Clark-Wicksteed type than one of the Leontief-Walras type.[23]

VI. *The Reserve Army of the Unemployed*

I shall conclude my dissection by investigating whether the existence of a reserve army of the unemployed can do the powerful things Marxians have claimed for it. Can it lower real wages to subsistence? Can it lower real wages below the marginal product of the last man when all the unemployed are put to work? Can it lower real wages below the marginal product of the first man of the reserve army when put to work?

Such questions must not be answered in simple terms. First, we shall have to specify exactly what monetary assumptions we are making; what institutional assumptions with respect to unionism, labor mobility, interpersonal differentials in skills and zealousness; what microeconomic assumptions about the mix of demand; etc. I shall not attempt to deal with these intricacies but will for the sake of the argument walk along the road with the simple Marxian aggregative models, making drastically simplifying assumptions.

Thus I assume two industries: Industry I producing capital goods and Industry II producing consumption goods. I go along with the simplifying assumption that machines and chocolates are produced with the same organic compositions of labor and capital goods; and that all capital is used up in one period so that the Marxian "constant capital" concept is easiest to handle. I assume the unemployed workers are as zealous and able as the employed. I assume away monopsony and monopoly to see where cruel competition will lead.

How do the unemployed depress real wages? If the unemployed are away at a distance and unable to offer their services, they will have no effect on money or real wages. It is by offering to work for less, and only by so doing, that they can depress money wages. The employer cannot get his workers to accept a cut merely by talking about the threat of replacing them by the unemployed; he will get the cut only if experience has taught the workers that this is not an empty threat. If men out of work do offer to work for less, the money wage cannot remain stationary in a perfectly competitive labor market. The money wage will fall and continue to fall until no more excluded men bid it down. I stress these banalities because so much Marxian literature seems to regard the mere *existence* of the unemployed (or of the

---

[23] I speak here of the first-edition Walras. In his second-edition *Éléments*, Walras had the system select among a number of different techniques to minimize costs; and in his third edition, he considered the infinite-substitution homogeneous production function case. Leontief, it must be said, never meant that his fixed coefficients be applied to gross aggregates.

"disguised unemployed") as itself a reason for competitive wages to fall. The natural question to ask then is this: "What is the effect on wages after the unemployed have been employed? How much have they depressed money and real wages?" Today, thanks to Keynes and others, we know that this is a complicated question. Falling money wages need not mean falling real wages if prices are made to fall as much. Indeed, waiving favorable Pigou-Keynes effects resulting from increased real balances induced by the price-wage decline, we can construct models of hyperdeflation in which money wages push down prices indefinitely with unemployment never disappearing and real wages not necessarily changing. Had Marx used a reserve army of the unemployed as a reason for falling *money* wages, one could better understand the logic of his system.

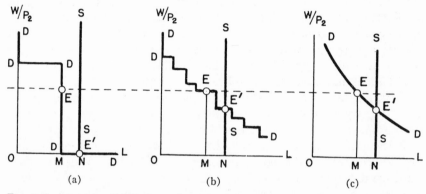

FIG. 2. In every case DD is "aggregate real demand for labor," SS is total labor force available for work, MN is the "reserve army of the unemployed," and E' the real wage when reserve army has disappeared.

To isolate the effects the unemployed have on real as against money wages, let's make the unrealistic supposition that they can bargain institutionally in terms of real wages—in terms of consumer goods or Ricardian corn. Then under the equal-organic-composition assumptions of our two-sector model, the "aggregative demand curve for labor in terms of wage goods" would be given by the discounted-marginal-physical-product curve of labor for either industry, the consumer-goods curve being exactly the same as the discounted-marginal-product curve in the capital goods industry once we have scaled the products so that they are 1-to-1 producible with the same labor and machine inputs.[24]

[24] The reader may make his own effective-demand assumptions to make this compatible with his theory of income determination. Thus, a good Keynesian will probably prefer to assume that aggressive government fiscal policy operates to offset any incipient deflationary or inflationary gaps threatened at full employment by nonintersecting saving and investment schedules. Some may give an active offsetting role to the central bank. Still others may be unaware or may deny that a problem could arise.

Figures 2a, 2b, and 2c show the resulting aggregative real demand for labor in the single-technique case, the many-technique case, and the infinitely-many-techniques neoclassical case. In every case, the unemployed reserve army of NM is made about 10 per cent of the labor force. Depending upon the technical elasticity of the marginal-product curve, the reserve army could reduce real wages by different amounts—but in Figures 2b and 2c wages can be reduced only by the reserve army's shrinking in size. The wage level E' in the three diagrams represents the lowest that real wages could fall when the reserve army had done its worst and become indistinguishable from the army of the employed. Would any competent observer of U.S.A., U.K., or U.S.S.R. technology believe that 10 per cent more men could not in any way be employed without making the last man incapable of adding much to product?[25]

The question is not whether in the shortest run, before employers knew they were to employ more and had made the necessary adjustments, marginal products might not fall greatly. Of course, they might fall. To get me to hire more workers in the next minute or day might require a great reduction in real wages. But let this happen for a few days or for months and years. Spurred by the ridiculously low real wages, employers will make needed adjustments and if we insist upon letting the real wage fall to absorb the unemployed in the long run, the equilibrium long-run wage will be at E' along the long-run marginal product curve *after* adjustments are made.[26]

I conclude from this way of looking at the problem that the strongest competition among the unemployed, the employed, and the employers will—when it has done its worst and depressed real wages enough to wipe out the unemployed—fail in modern western societies to depress real wages to anything like the subsistence level, instead bringing it down at worst to the (quite high) discounted marginal

[25] Writing in the 1860's, Marx could with some excuse think that real wages might fall to a subsistence level. A Marxian acquainted with the statistics of real wages in modern Western economies has no such excuse.

[26] A simple set of mathematical equations describing the content of Fig. 2c would be:

$$Y + (dK/dt) = Q(L,K), \quad dK/dt = \sigma_w(LQ_L) + \sigma_r(KQ_K),$$

with government expenditure or aggressive central bank policy assuring that (dK/dt) is always such as to take up the resources not required for consumption. With fixed K, we can compute the reduction in real wage resulting from ΔL of the unemployed becoming employed, as follows: new real wage $= w + \Delta w = \partial Q(L + \Delta L,K)/\partial L$, and with $\Delta w/w$ equal to $[Q_{LL}L/Q](\Delta L/L)$, where the bracketed expression is the "reciprocal of the elasticity" of the marginal product curve at some intermediate point. Note that for given K and L, w is here quite independent of σ_w and σ_r. If we drop Marx's equal-organic-composition-of-capital assumption, this will no longer be true and the analysis has to be expanded.

product of labor at the level of employment equal to 100 per cent of the available labor force. Such a wage-floor is not only very high in the most advanced capitalistic society, but the bulk of the statistical evidence of economic history and the qualitative evidence concerning scientific invention and capital formation suggest as well that this wage-floor is advancing dynamically from year to year, decade to decade, at a rate that doubles perhaps about every 30 years.

VII. *Some Conclusions*

I have dealt with Karl Marx the economist, not Marx the philosopher of history and revolution. A minor Post-Ricardian, Marx was an autodidact cut off in his lifetime from competent criticism and stimulus. In applying to the models of Ricardo and Marx modern tools of analysis, I hope we are violating no rules of etiquette and in no way trying to suggest we are cleverer than they were!

What then is the verdict of the present dissection? Our post-mortem suggests the following conclusions:

1. Marx did do original work in analyzing patterns of circular interdependency among industries. Such work gains few converts and is not very helpful in promoting revolution or counterreactions. But like all pioneering effort it deserves the commendation of later craftsmen, and it deserves further development. There is half-truth in Schumpeter's adaptation of Clemenceau: "Marxian economics is too hard to be left to the Marxians." Only half, because the present paper is seen to involve little worse than school algebra and to be well within the frontier of modern economic theory.

2. Marx's labor theory of value of *Capital*, Volume I, does appear to have been a detour and an unnecessary one for the understanding of the behavior of competitive capitalism. The admittedly important analysis of imperfect or monopolistic competition is helped little or none at all by the "surplus-value" approach. That Böhm-Bawerk, Wicksteed, and Pareto were essentially right in their critiques of Marx seems borne out by the present investigation of the Marxian model.

3. I have concentrated, however, not on the problem raised for the pricing of many different goods by the unnecessary Marx-Ricardo labor-value assumptions. Instead I have concentrated on the more-neglected implications for relative goods-factor pricing of the Marxian surplus-value notations and notions. The present logical analysis suggests that the Marxian notions do not achieve the desired goal of "explaining the laws of motion or of development of the capitalistic system."

If it were true that the rich get richer the poor poorer, the distribution of income more skewed against labor and in favor of profit,[27] the two-sector models here analyzed would provide no particular hint of this. Indeed, writing in 1860 and being aware of the Industrial Revolution going on, an economist who took those models seriously should have (i) expected technological change to lower the (a, b) coefficients, (ii) should have expected the odds to favor a strong increase in real wages, the only exception arising from an extreme "bias" of inventions toward the extreme labor-saving type (a phenomenon *not* particularly sugested by the pre-1860 data known to financial journalists or men-of-affairs, nor particularly suggested by any a priori reasonings about the model or about the nature of technology).

I blame no one for failing to foresee the trends in the century after his death. But one can be forgiven for insisting upon the established fact that real wages in Germany, England, and America did rise more or less proportionately with total product from 1857 to 1957. To have been judged lucky by economic historians, Marx should have phrased a theory to explain the approximate constancy of wage's relative share of the national product, not the secular decline of this relative share. His actual models, we have seen, were perhaps better than he: for gifted with hindsight, we see that they contain in them no tendency for real wages to fall or to lag particularly behind the growth of output.

Nor do such models throw much light on the secular trends in the degree of imperfection of competition or on the propensity of the system to oscillate or stagnate. But all that is another story.

[27] We know little about the secular trends of the inequality of the personal distribution of income, as measured by Pareto's coefficient or by Gini's parameter describing the Lorenz curve. Pareto himself thought he had established a natural law of constancy of income inequality, independent of all public policies and institutional frameworks. The empirical basis for this generalization was never very impressive. The bulk of the available evidence, in fact, suggests that as capitalism has developed the Pareto coefficient has moved towards greater equality: whereas underdeveloped countries did, and do, show Pareto coefficients around 1.3, we find in developed countries Pareto coefficients of 2.0 for income before taxes and 2.2 after taxes. See J. Tinbergen, "On the Theory of Income Distribution," *Weltwirtschaftliches Archiv*, 1956, LXXVII, 156-57. Modern economics has no grandiose explanations to offer, but it can contribute to an analysis of the relevant forces at work.

30

Wages and Interest—A Modern Dissection of Marxian Economic Models: Reply

I must assert agreement with the view that my paper on Marxian economic models did not do justice to Marx's own formulations of the issues treated. Nor was it ever intended to undertake such a task, whose extreme difficulty can be illustrated by the following topic.

What did Marx really think would happen to the real wage under capitalism with its alleged falling rate of profit? Some scholars (e.g., Jürgen Kuczynski) believe Marx proved that the real wage would fall and claim by empirical statistical observation to verify this law of immiserization of the proletariat; other scholars (such as Maurice Dobb, perhaps?) seem to argue that, with exceptions, this was Marx's view about competitive capitalism but that it came to be falsified by historical reality primarily because of the growth in political and economic powers of trade unions and the working class; still other scholars (notably Thomas Sowell in the March 1960 issue of this *Review*) argue with considerable persuasiveness that in his major economic writings, Marx did not conclude that the real wage per hour or day would decline under competitive capitalism. I claim no competence or interest in such doctrinal history.

Of the many uses we can make of the past, one—but certainly not the only one—is to reask some of the questions older writers posed and to provide them with answers in terms of modern analytical methods and terminology. The Marx-like or Ricardo-like model I described could be stripped of all proper names and could as well be described thus: a simple model involving labor, unlimited land, producible circulating- and fixed-capital items; and involving competition-consistent technology.

From the present methodological slant, it may not be presumptuous to wonder what would be Marx's comment on my 1957 model and analysis. I suspect with Gottheil that he might disagree often with my reasonings. Although Marx is not here to speak for himself, it is a legitimate question to ask whether my conclusions can stand up to the objections which seem implicit in Marxian reasonings and categories, and I am grateful to Gottheil for having raised specific queries for further consideration.

Query 1. If Marx and I agree it is unthinkable for production not to take time, which is the more appropriate behavior equation of competitive capitalism: mine, in which unripened spring product sells at a discount to finished autumn product (corresponding to a market-determined positive interest or profit rate); or the view quotable from Gottheil, "according to Marx . . . intermediate product will exchange one for one against *themselves* when ripened— if they contain the same quantity of labor . . ."?

That a modern theorist will agree that my position is the one appropriate to competition seems to admit of little doubt.

Query 2. If an improvement in technology becomes known to one or more producers, and even if they realize that after they have used it for some time competitive imitation will deprive them of their temporary "monopoly" profits, is it possible for the new equilibrium to involve a lower interest (or profit) rate *and* a lower real wage rate? My 1957 answer was categorically No: if the innovation is competitively viable, it *must* either raise the real wage, the interest rate, or both. This theorem I hold to be valid whether there are fixed or variable coefficients of production; and I may remind readers that I have no great liking for the usual narrow interpretation of Ricardo and Marx which imputes to them a rigid fixed-coefficient assumption.

Gottheil seems to suggest that if Marx were here today he could *validly* put forward behavior equations other than mine which would negate my theorem. This I bluntly deny. Whether or not factor supplies react to their changing market prices, whether or not technological innovation is induced by factor-price changes so as to counteract initial price changes (as Marx, Hicks, and Fellner have argued), any new equilibrium that is truly characterized by a lower interest rate $r' < r$, must by the same kind of reasoning that makes two plus two equal four, be characterized by a higher real wage $(w/p_2)' > (w/p_2)$; and if in the short or longer run we have the old and the new technologies persisting side by side, then the computed average profit and wage rate cannot both go down.

If Joan Robinson and I are wrong in this contention, we are dead wrong, it not being an issue upon which two contradictory opinions can be legitimately held. And no reasoned defense of the opposing view have I yet seen.

In standing my ground, I hope I am not contradicting Professor Gottheil or any one else but rather am clarifying the methodological background to the earlier discussion.

* The author is professor of economics at the Massachusetts Institute of Technology.

31

A MODERN TREATMENT OF THE RICARDIAN ECONOMY:*
I. THE PRICING OF GOODS AND OF LABOR
AND LAND SERVICES

By PAUL A. SAMUELSON

INTRODUCTION

1. One fool can ask more questions than twelve wise men can answer. And so can one wise man. David Ricardo propounded a number of what we today should call linear programming problems. Except in the simplest cases he was not able to give complete and correct answers. Yet, despite a number of false conjectures, he did intuitively perceive properties of the equilibrium configuration which he probably could not have rigorously proved.

I intend to cast a few of his problems in today's symbolism. To avoid arguments over what Ricardo himself "meant" or understood, I shall describe Ricardo-*like* models. The reader can easily modify my assumptions to correspond more closely to what he regards as Ricardo's. I shall not try to relate systematically modern terminology to Ricardo's, even though a good deal of the apparent novelty of his valid conclusions arises primarily from the special way he used words of many meanings.

This is not intended to be an exercise in piety. Nor a debunking commando raid. If our researches prove that "chimeras" are chimeras — that invariable standards of value and absolute values cannot be accurately defined once Ricardo has left his simplest and singular cases — it is only what David Ricardo himself already real-

* Grateful acknowledgment is made to the Ford Foundation for research assistance.

ized.[1] What modern theory and mathematics can add is closure: an assertion of nonexistence can be given definite meaning and proved once and for all.

2. They can also demonstrate what one would have thought Ricardo and other clever economists would have long since discovered, that basic difficulties for a labor theory of value come from the theory of differential rent as much as from problems of the organic composition of capital. By going to an extensive margin, one cannot really "get rid of land as a factor of production and of rent as a determining element of cost and exchange value." For the extensive margin is itself a variable, to be determined like any other equilibrium variable as part of the theorist's explicit task. And a shift — say in the pattern of landlords' consumption — can be expected to change the extensive margin and thus to vary the relative labor costs of the different goods at these margins. Moreover, it can be expected to vary them *in a systematic way,* namely the systematic way predicted by those critics of the one-factor labor theory who seek to replace it by a multi-factor neoclassical theory of economic production and distribution.

The use of mathematics can also produce some amusing conclusions. Thus, a *long-run* Ricardian system involving subsistence wages and *homogeneous* land, can have applied to it the sentence "Labor is the cause and measure of exchangeable value . . . ," but with "Labor" struck out and "Land" put in its place. Goods can be shown to exchange in proportion to their mathematically definable "embodied" land content, with land services providing us something like an "invariable standard of value" in terms of which "absolute values" can be measured with perfect accuracy. And all this will hold regardless of inequalities in (i) the organic composition of capital, (ii) the time intensities of different processes, or (iii) the proportions of direct land used in different productive processes.

In a sense the Physiocrats were right after all — if you can make the special long-run econometric assumptions that Ricardo seems often to do!

This significant result is a particular application and a generalization of the "substitutability theorem of one-factor Leontief systems" that Professor Georgescu-Roegen and I separately discovered in 1949.[2]

1. See the Editor's Introduction to the Sraffa edition of Ricardo's *Principles,* particularly pp. xl–xlix. All references hereafter to *Principles* will refer to the Sraffa edition. References to other volumes of the Sraffa edition of Ricardo's works will be given as Ricardo, *Works* with the Roman numeral volume number and page reference.
2. See T. Koopmans (ed.), *Activity Analysis of Production and Allocation*

3. The present paper is divided into two main parts, with an appendix on differential rent sandwiched in between. Except in the appendix, I rarely go beyond school arithmetic and mathematics; but the student of modern theory will recognize the underlying skeleton of mathematical economics. Part II is distinguished from the earlier sections by its explicit treatment of the problems of time and capital in the Ricardian system.[3]

In the Beginning

4. Before good land was scarce or capital goods dreamed of, life was simple and fitted a one-primary-factor theory. Smith, Ricardo, and for that matter the prewar Leontief, would call this single factor "labor." But we can work with any single factor: labor, or land, or a dose of labor-land-shovels, or simply any given total x. If each of n goods — deer, beaver, . . . , or $y_1, . . . , y_n$ — is producible at constant returns to scale in terms of the respective factor input $x_1, . . . , x_n$ applied to it, our production functions can be written

$$(1) \qquad y_1 = \frac{1}{a_1} x_1, y_2 = \frac{1}{a_2} x_2, . . . , y_n = \frac{1}{a_n} x_n,$$

where the "coefficients of production" $(a_1, . . . , a_n)$ are all positive.

Our production-possibility (or opportunity cost!) schedule becomes

$$(2) \qquad x_1 + . . . + x_n = a_1 y_1 + . . . + a_n y_n \leqslant x$$

for all non-negative x's and y's. Figure I shows the two-good picture.

Technology is here favorable to viable perfect competition in which men trade with each other and with nature at determinate price ratios as follows:

$$(3) \qquad p_1 \leqslant w a_1, p_2 \leqslant w a_2, . . . , p_n \leqslant w a_n,$$

where w is the wage of the single factor x. It is understood that an inequality holding implies that the respective $y_i = 0 = x_i$: i.e., each good's price = factor cost of production whenever a good is produced,

(New York: Wiley, 1951), Chap. VII-X. See too the expository RAND monograph, Robert Dorfman, Paul A. Samuelson and Robert M. Solow, *Linear Programming and Economic Analysis* (New York: McGraw-Hill, 1958), Chaps. 9 and 10. Hereafter this book is referred to as *L.P.E.A.*

3. Further material that could have gone into this paper on Ricardo, I found convenient to gather together in a related paper on Marx. See P. A. Samuelson, "Wages and Interest: A Modern Dissection of Marxian Economic Models," *The American Economic Review*, XLVII (Dec. 1957), 884–912.

but may fall short of it when the industry shuts down. (In Figure I note the broken-line price sloped at the intercepts.)

Thus, if we know y_1 and y_2 are produced and y_3 and y_4 are not, we can from technology alone predict

$$\frac{p_2}{p_1} = \frac{a_2}{a_1}, \quad \frac{p_3}{p_1} \lessgtr \frac{a_3}{a_1}, \quad \frac{p_4}{p_1} \lessgtr \frac{a_4}{a_1}, \quad \frac{p_4}{p_3} \gtrless \frac{a_4}{a_3}.$$

5. Critics and defendants of the labor theory of value have overlooked the following fact: the operational significance of a one-factor hypothesis lies in the powerful predictive value that it gives to *technology alone*. A spy can memorize only the numbers $(a_1, a_2, \ldots, a_n, x)$ and he knows most of what there is to know about such an economy. Most, but not all. Demand considerations, and whatever subjective

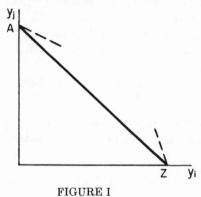

FIGURE I

functions that lie behind them, also are needed to give us the actual breakdown of attainable physical consumption.

Even beyond this, there is a more subtle reliance on demand implied by (3). Both blades of the Marshallian scissors must indeed be cutting. Not until demand (with supply) is brought in to assure $y_i > 0$, can we infer $p_i = wa_i$. To have a full equilibrium solution for $(y_1, \ldots, y_n, x_1, \ldots, x_n, p_1/w, \ldots, p_n/w)$ the classicists would have had to develop a full theory of consumption to supplement their theory of technology. Even to have a determinate theory of $(p_1/w, \ldots, p_n/w)$, they needed an implicit demand theory — as they recognized in regarding "value-in-use" as a *qualitative necessary condition* for market value.

6. Note that in relations (3) the single-factor constant-cost model need assume nothing about the subjective or other supply conditions of the single factor. We could have an inelastic supply of labor x,

with all wages being true economic rents and with all relative prices being determined by an opportunity-cost doctrine orthodox enough to delight any Austrian. The possibility of a prescribed total of x shows that a labor-cost doctrine need not have anything to do with psychic disutility or with indifference curves between work and goods.

Philip Wicksteed in his attack[4] on the Marxian labor cost doctrine was therefore perhaps unnecessarily subtle. He could have pointed out the unrealistic technology — for today's USSR or USA and for nineteenth century Europe — of a one-factor economy. This criticism granted, economists' shop talk about value as being derived from utility rather than disutility, or about the need to take demand into account in describing prices, would have been somewhat redundant. Were this technological criticism denied, most of what the modern economist considers significant in a one-factor theory would stand up against Wicksteed's criticisms.

THE EXPANDING UNIVERSE

7. The classical economists did have a "real cost" theory, which in Ricardo's day was still primarily a population theory concerning the reproducibility-at-constant-returns of people. If there were a single necessity corn, y_1, which each unit of labor had to have in amount c_1, then total labor would grow, stand still, or decrease depending upon the difference between actual subsistence per head y_1/x_1 and needed subsistence c_1: i.e.,

(4)
$$\frac{1}{x_1}\frac{dx_1}{dt} \underset{<}{\overset{>}{=}} 0 \text{ depending on whether } \frac{y_1}{x_1} = \frac{1}{a_1} \underset{<}{\overset{>}{=}} c_1.$$

If $1 - c_1 a_1 < 0$, the population in question will have become extinct. If $1 - c_1 a_1 = 0$, population is in neutral equilibrium.[5]

The case of $1 - c_1 a_1 > 0$ was thought by Malthus to be the most realistic one: in it nature originally provided more than what was needed for life, giving rise to a geometric rate of population growth on a virgin continent. This process would continue indefinitely, were it not for the ultimate limitation on land and the implied operation of the law of diminishing returns.[6]

4. P. H. Wicksteed, *The Common Sense of Political Economy*, Vol. II contains a reprint of his 1884 article, *Das Kapital, A Criticism*. This actually converted Bernard Shaw from Marxism to Jevonsism! P. M. Sweezy, *The Theory of Capitalist Development* (New York: Oxford University Press, 1942), pp. 46–47 cogently argues that under the postulated simple conditions supply and demand will agree with the labor theory of value.

5. The first Leontief system was a closed one and postulated such a vanishing of the matrix $[1 - c_1 a_1]$. W. W. Leontief, *Structure of the American Economy* (New York: Oxford University Press, 1951), p. 47.

6. The nonspecialist may skip the next section at a first reading.

8. In terms of linear programming, the system (1)–(4) can be thought to act as if it were trying to maximize the surplus of product over needed cost of reproducing labor: i.e., as if it were to

(5)   maximize $Z = y_1 - c_1 x_1$ subject to

$$a_1 y_1 - x_1 \leqslant 0, \ x_1 \geqslant 0, \ y_1 \geqslant 0.$$

This implies $Z = y_1 - c_1 x_1 \leqslant x_1 \left(\dfrac{1}{a_1} - c_1 \right)$; hence ignoring any

scarcity of land, the solutions to this problem obviously are

(6) $(Z, x_1, y_1) = (0,0,0)$, if $1 - c_1 a_1 < 0$

             $= (0, x, x_a = c, x)$ for any $x > 0$, if $1 - c_1 a_1 = 0$

             $= (\infty, \infty, \infty)$, if $1 - c_1 a_1 > 0$.

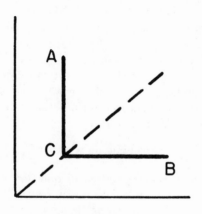

FIGURE II

Land ignored, the last case, of course, has no stationary finite solution and represents the exploding Malthusian exponential, which may be moderated into a Verhulst-Pearl logistic or related form only after the limitation of land ceases to be neglectable.

9. Mr. Kaldor[7] has stated that Marx differed essentially from Ricardo in regarding many goods other than "corn" as necessary parts of a minimum standard of living. Actually Ricardo often insisted upon the point that workers required many different goods; and even if he had not, the mathematical picture would be little

7. Nicholas Kaldor, "Alternative Theories of Distribution," *Review of Economic Studies*, XXIII (1955–56), 87.

changed by our introducing such a variety of necessities. We simply stipulate that the worker requires $(c_1, c_2, \ldots, c_n)$ of the different goods for his subsistence wage. In Figure II, the indifference curve corresponding to the minimum of subsistence is ACB, and goods being non-free, the man will always end up at $C(c_1, \ldots, c_n)$, the corner of the L-shaped indifference curve.

We now can think of a composite good consisting of $(c_1, \ldots, c_n)$ of the n goods. Its labor requirements per unit must then be $c_1a_1 + c_2a_2 + \ldots + c_na_n$, and if population is to be capable of growth (retardation, neutral stability), we must have as our criterion $\Sigma c_j a_j > 1$ (or < 1, or $= 1$). The interesting case is where $1 - \Sigma c_j a_j > 0$, which is the generalization of our earlier one-good condition $1 - c_1a_1 > 0$.[8]

Scarcity of Land and Positive Rent

10. Exponential growth of men must finally use up finite territory. The labor constraint

$$a_1y_1 + \ldots + a_ny_n \leqslant x$$

must then be explicitly augmented by a land constraint

(7) $b_1y_1 + \ldots + b_ny_n \leqslant L,$

where b_i represents the minimum positive land required *along with* a_i units of labor to produce one unit of y_i and L is the supply of available homogeneous land.

For L sufficiently large relative to x, this constraint could previously be ignored, since (7)'s inequality would necessarily have held. But when all superfluous L disappears, many things begin to happen.

Competition among laborers will make positive rent for land's services spring up. Goods' costs will now have a non-wage component, with this result: the existence of scarce land has destroyed the simple labor theory of value. (Figure III now contains, in addition to Figure I's labor constraint AB, the new straight line BC depicting equation (7)'s land constraint. The resulting production

8. The condition $1 - \Sigma c_j\, a_j > 0$ which implies explosion of a closed Malthus v. Neumann system that plows all its superfluous consumption back into itself as invested input, is precisely the 1949 Hawkins-Simon condition for an open statical Leontief system to be capable of positive final consumption and to possess all positive solutions for prices and quantities. See *L.P.E.A.*, p. 215. It would be easy to generalize the above analysis to the case where the base indifference curve allows of substitution — as, e.g., where workers need calories from *any* source.

possibility schedule is *ABC*, with cost and price ratios of produced goods being anywhere from the slope of *AB* to *BC* *depending upon the pattern of demand.*[9]

11. When rent on good land is bid up high enough, this will drive laborers to inferior lands if such exist. The postulated existence of many grades of land, of course, permitted Ricardo to phrase a differential theory of rent that compared the productivity of labor on good land with its productivity on free land just at the "extensive margin," the difference being the numerical measure of good land's rent.[1]

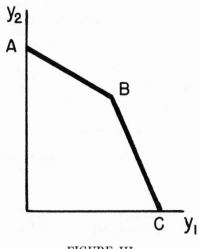

FIGURE III

However, aside from his extensive-margin theory of rent, Ricardo also had a differential theory of rent based upon the "internal margin." This internal, differential theory is very much in the spirit of the later 1890 neoclassical smooth substitutability theories of J. B. Clark, Wicksteed, and the third-edition Walras. In particular

9. Beginning students of economics today learn in their first week that the transformation terms between a labor-intensive and a land-intensive good vary with demand. See P. A. Samuelson, *Economics: An Introductory Analysis* (4th ed.; New York: McGraw-Hill, 1958), pp. 22–23; yet in reading a thousand pages on the labor theory of value, I can remember but one author who comes close to emphasizing that land — and not merely capital — vitiates a simple labor theory and that no tricks with no-rent marginal land can change this. See Lionel Robbins, *Robert Torrens and the Evolution of Classical Economics* (London: Macmillan, 1958), p. 237 *passim*.

1. In the Appendix on Differential Rent, I investigate the linear programming problems raised by several grades of land, confining the text for the most part to the case of homogeneous land.

Ricardo did not fall into the trap that caught some of his unwary followers: he did not believe that the existence of a single grade of land would, simply because it made the differential rent measurement between good and marginal land impossible, cause rent to vanish; he knew that scarcity of homogeneous land would create positive rent.

Indeed, even before replying to Say's criticism alleging the non-existence of the extensive margin in contemporaneous Western Europe, Ricardo had insisted that rent could be measured differentially *on every piece* of homogeneous land. In this connection, Ricardo is thinking of varying the doses of labor (and capital, which I temporarily ignore) applied to the same valuable land. The last profitable dose of labor will add to product just what it cost, and so Ricardo speaks of it as the unit of labor "that pays no rent." Thus, in modern terminology, the total of rent is measured by the difference between the product of all labor units and what labor at the intensive margin produces.[2]

RESIDUAL RENT TO HOMOGENEOUS LAND

12. Interestingly enough, if we refuse to let Ricardo have the smooth assumptions of later neoclassical theory, his internal, differential rent formulation fails.[3] In other words, Ricardo's differential method could not handle the simplest of all technological cases, where all land is alike and where a_i and b_i are fixed non-substitutable coefficients. (I omitted labels from Figure II's axes so that it can do double duty and depict the L-shaped isoquants implied here when

2. I recall Professor Viner's lectures of a quarter of a century ago in which he pointed out that the extensive and intensive margin is the literary man's substitute for the mathematically rigorous calculus concepts of partial derivatives. Ricardo, without knowing it, is setting up the smooth homogeneous production function $y_i = Q_i(x_i, L_i)$, where $1 = Q_i(a_i, b_i)$ gives the substitutable relations between the labor and land coefficients. Ricardo assumes workers are hired at the given wage up to the point where the last worker is just worth his real wage: i.e., $w/p_i = \partial Q_i/\partial x_i$. Hence residual rent (in goods per acre) = total product/acre minus total wages/acre = $Q_i/L_i - (x_i \partial Q_i/\partial L_i)/L_i$. Euler's theorem implies that this also equals land's marginal physical product, a fact that Wicksteed knew and that J. B. Clark perhaps took too much for granted.

3. When I speak of Ricardo's rent theory, I really mean the rent theory that Sir Edward West and Malthus independently published in 1815 and that Ricardo later elaborated on. See the Editor's remarks, Ricardo, *Works*, IV, 6–7. I have too little knowledge in these doctrinal matters to make confident assertions; but it is my impression that Ricardo's 1817 *Principles* puts more stress on the quantitative differential aspect of rent involving comparisons of different grades of land than did West and Malthus or than did Ricardo's *An Essay on the Influence of a Low Price of Corn on the Profits of Stock*, which was written in 1815 under the direct stimulus of the Malthus and West writings. At the very beginning of that *Essay* (*Works*, IV, 10), Ricardo quotes a residual-rent formulation of Malthus precisely like that offered in this present section.

we deny substitutability.)   For in this case, when all homogeneous land is used there is no labor "that pays no rent" from which Ricardo can measure differential rent.

None the less this simplest long-run Ricardian model does have a determinate solution, which is intuitively fairly obvious.   To see the solution, first consider a corn-labor-land economy.   Labor grows in the long run until it is in a determinate ratio to land.   (Namely, until there is just enough labor to use up all the land in co-operative production — until $x_1/L_1 = a_1/b_1$.)   Now think of this dose of labor-land as producing total corn product.   Labor's wage is fixed in corn at the conventional subsistence level c_1.   So we know what labor is paid.   What's left over is the rent of land.   It's as simple as that.[4]

There is a vulgar prejudice against a "residual" theory of distribution.   It would be well-taken if directed at a theory that explains wages as what's left over after land gets paid and *simultaneously* explains rent as what's left over after labor gets paid.   Such a theory is no theory at all, being one equation for two unknowns.   However, there is absolutely nothing unrigorous about a theory that "explains" *one* factor's share as a residual from well-determined other factors' shares.   (Incidentally, rent can be simultaneously thought of as a residual or as a marginal product.)

A Numerical Example

13. The simple Ricardian economy is completely characterized by its a,b,c technological coefficients and the amount L of its unaugmentable land.   Figure IV shows an exact numerical model for the following econometric constants:

$$a_1 = .1 \text{ men per ton of corn}$$
$$b_1 = 50 \text{ acres per ton of corn}$$
$$c_1 = 4 \text{ tons of corn per man}$$
$$L = 1 \text{ million acres.}$$

A million acres needs 2,000 men $(=L/[a_1/b_1])$ to work it.   Together they produce 20,000 $(=L/b_1)$ tons of corn, of which 8,000 $(=c_1\ 2,000)$ tons must be fed as fodder to labor, leaving *produit net* of 12,000 tons in all for land or rent of .012 corn tons per acre.

4. Actually, a dynamic theory of the stability of the long-run equilibrium would recognize oscillations around this level — incidentally in conformity with ecologists' observations of the struggle for biologic survival.   Letting the variable factor grow until it hits up against the ceiling of a vanished "reserve army" of unemployed *land*, we might try to construct a "crisis" theory in the later Marxian manner.

The whole area in Figure IV measures gross corn product. The horizontal long-run labor supply curve SS splits this total gross product into the two subrectangles of intermediate wage product and *produit net* or residual rent. The share of wages to total gross product is c_1a_1; the relative share of rent $1 - c_1a_1$. If labor comes to need more corn, c_1 rises and the absolute and relative share of rent must fall. If labor becomes more efficient, a_1 decreases and the absolute and relative shares of rent rise. If land becomes more efficient, b_1

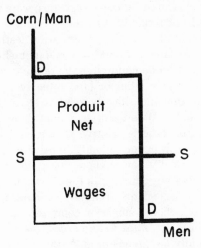

FIGURE IV

drops and there is an increase in population, wages, and total rent, with relative shares unaffected.

14. That land is the measure and "creator" of all products in the long-run Ricardian system is shown by the fact that doubling L will exactly double the width of all rectangles; halving L will halve the width of all rectangles. Land is the source of wage's gross product, the source of total product, the source of rent's net product. Labor, to be sure, is needed as a co-operating input, but being reproducible within the system it can be regarded simply as "congealed" or "embodied" corn. Even this is an understatement. We shall see that corn itself can be thought of as *congealed or embodied land*, and so labor too can be regarded in the last analysis as embodied land! When a modern uses words like "embodied," "congealed," "decomposable," he is employing figures of speech for a prosaic mathematical fact. Needless to say no deep philosophical or ethical significance is implied. Beyond the important implication of eco-

nomic fact and meaningful predictive hypothesis, the present-day economist finds only boring pseudo-questions.

THE CASE OF MANY GOODS AND HOMOGENEOUS LAND

15. The full significance of the "land theory of value" being expounded here can be grasped only after contemplating the many-good case. It would then be a miracle if the direct land and labor requirements, as measured by the a_i/b_i ratios, were the same in every industry. Would not difficulties in the "organic composition" (not of capital but) of land and labor necessarily destroy the invariant relation of price to land content? Would not shifts in landlords' pattern of consumption demand alter the relative costs and prices of goods that are relatively labor or land intensive? And won't such shifts in landlords' demand alter the relative share of wages and rent in the total product? Won't shifts of final demand toward labor-intensive goods raise labor's relative shares, and by lowering rent cause substitutions toward more land-intensive methods?

The answer to every one of these questions is, No. So long as technology and labor's requirements for subsistence, as measured by its $(c_1, c_2, \ldots, c_n)$ coefficients, remain unchanged, *the total of rent* (measured in terms of any single or composite good or in terms of purchaseable labor hours) *must remain exactly the same!* And the terms of trade between any two goods produced must remain unaltered by any shift in the composition of landlord demand. (I say landlord demand because a constant-cost concept of population leaves labor demand no longer free.)

Why these sweeping and possibly paradoxical sounding assertions? Because in this long-run system labor, corn, velvets, deer, beaver, and everything can be decomposed into embodied land — and nothing else! It is nonsense to say that corn is more land-intensive than velvets. For all goods are 100 per cent land intensive when you take into account the indirect land needed to grow the labor foods needed for velvet and corn production.

16. Perhaps Frank Knight, and others, will feel there is a vicious circle here, arguing: "It takes corn to make men, and it takes men (and land) to make corn. Neither corn nor men can be considered antecedent to the other." We need not quarrel with this temporal relationship, nor attempt to argue that a fertile island without men will soon or ever populate itself with people. Still as Leontief has shown, the logical circle is a virtuous one and the unique solution to the problem comes from *solving simultaneously* the algebraic equa-

tions relating the variables.[5] This statical simultaneous-equation solution can be interpreted to give prices equal to embodied land content, and can be interpreted in terms of a hypothetical multiplier chain going back infinitely in time.

17. The deepest insight into these analytic facts will come from the standard matrix methods of the Leontief input-output system. However, for the nonspecialist I shall first give an elementary algebraic statement of the one-good case, and then an equivalent treatment of the n-good case but using a single composite cost-of-living commodity.

The price of corn p_1 must equal its labor plus rent costs of production. And the wage w must just buy c_1 wants of corn. Depicting rent per acre by r, this gives us two independent equations for (p_1, w, r):

$$(8) \quad \begin{matrix} p_1 = wa_1 + rb_1 \\ w = p_1 c_1 \end{matrix} \quad \text{or} \quad \begin{matrix} p_1/r = b_1(1 - c_1 a_1)^{-1} \\ w/r = c_1 b_1 (1 - c_1 a_1)^{-1}. \end{matrix}$$

Clearly the ratios $(p_1/r, w/r)$ are uniquely determined, not the absolute level of prices. Working with ratios to r is equivalent to using land as our *numeraire*, expressing all other prices in terms of embodied land.

18. We can give a symbolic picture in the form of an infinite multiplier[6] of the decomposition of corn's price into its direct land content and into the land needed to produce the corn to produce the labor to produce the corn, etc., back to the "beginning of time." Recalling the converging infinite geometric expansion for any fractional $h, 1/(1 - h) = (1 - h)^{-1} = 1 + h + h^2 + \ldots + h^n + \ldots$, we rewrite

$$(9) \quad \frac{p_1}{r} = b_1(1 - c_1 a_1)^{-1} = b_1[1 + c_1 a_1 + (c_1 a_1)^2 + \ldots + (c_1 a_1)^n + \ldots]$$

$$= b_1 + b_1(c_1 a_1) + b_1(c_1 a_1)^2 + \ldots + b_1(c_1 a_1)^n + \ldots \quad .$$

Here b_1 is the direct land cost per unit of corn; $b_1 c_1 a_1$ is the direct land cost of the corn needed for the direct labor; and so forth in a series

5. Leontief, *op.cit.*, Part II. Marx in *Capital*, Vol. II had already introduced a model of two sectors involving circular interdependence more sophisticated than that of the simple hierarchical Austrian models in which the stages of production can be uniquely ordered in terms of their "earliness or lateness." Professor Adolph Lowe has called my attention to a neglected discussion of these matters, F. A. Burchardt, "Die Schemata des stationären Kreislaufs bei Böhm-Bawerk und Marx," *Weltwirtschaftliches Archiv*, Kiel, Vol. 34 (1931), pp. 525–64 and Vol. 35 (1932), pp. 116–76. See also the reference in *L.P.E.A.*, p. 234, to Hugh Gaitskell's 1938 notes.

6. See *L.P.E.A.*, p. 253.

that has a convergent sum by virtue of the Hawkins-Simon-Malthus assumption that $c_1 a_1 < 1$.

19. Turning to the many-good case, we have equations just like (8) but more numerous.

$$p_1 = wa_1 + rb_1$$
$$p_2 = wa_2 + rb_2$$

(10)   .   .   .

$$p_n = wa_n + rb_n$$
$$w = p_1 c_1 + p_2 c_2 + \ldots + p_n c_n.$$

These are $(n + 1)$ equations for the $(n + 2)$ unknowns $(p_1, \ldots, p_n, w, r)$. Hence, we can solve for the $(n + 1)$ price ratios $(p_1/r, \ldots, p_n/r, w/r)$. The simplest way to solve is to multiply the first equation by c_1, the second by c_2, the nth by c_n; then add these all together, getting

$$w = \sum_1^n p_j c_j = w(\sum_1^n c_j a_j) + r(\sum_1^n c_j b_j), \quad \text{or}$$

(11) $$\frac{w}{r} = (\Sigma c_j b_j)(1 - \Sigma c_j a_j)^{-1}.$$

But this is just like the w/r expression in (8), except that it involves many c's. It can be easily interpreted in terms of a composite market-basket of subsistence, with $\Sigma c_j a_j$ and $\Sigma c_j b_j$ the labor and land requirements of a unit of the composite good.

Knowing w/r, we easily substitute (11) into (10) to get our final solution in terms of land's value alone

$$w/r = (\Sigma c_j b_j)(1 - \Sigma c_j a_j)^{-1}$$
(12) $$p_1/r = (\Sigma c_j b_j)(1 - \Sigma c_j a_j)^{-1} a_1 + b_1$$

. . . .

$$p_n/r = (\Sigma c_j b_j)(1 - \Sigma c_j a_j)^{-1} a_n + b_n.$$

Our mathematical decomposition is now complete. We can leave to the reader the infinite multiplier expansion of $(1 - \Sigma c_j a_j)^{-1}$ in (12) with its interpretation in terms of direct and indirect land requirements.

20. In concluding this section, I might mention that the price ratios of (12) enable us to write down the production possibility schedule of *produit net*, available for any given L. The straight line in Figure I will still serve, if we reinterpret its axes to refer not to gross production $(y_1, y_2, \ldots)$ but to each of these minus workers' consumptions; or $(Y_1, Y_2, \ldots) = (y_1 - c_1 x, y_2 - c_2 x, \ldots)$. Also the

locus is drawn up with L held constant but with population x changing *mutatis mutandis* whenever landlord demand is shifted toward goods "directly labor intensive." It is the absolute level of rent that is completely fixed when (L,a,b,c) are all given. The absolute level of total wages will vary with population variations induced by changes in the composition of landlord demand; but in the long run, the real wage expressed in terms of our $(c_1,c_2, \ldots)$ composite commodity will be unchanged. Such fixity of the real wage does not in a many-good model imply fixity of labor's total share or relative share of the gross produce.

The new relation corresponding in our land economy to Equation (2)'s simple labor economy is

$$(13) \qquad \frac{p_1}{r} Y_1 + \frac{p_2}{r} Y_2 + \ldots + \frac{p_n}{r} Y_n = L,$$

the (p/r)'s being given by (12).[7]

The Leontief-Ricardo Tableau

21. Labor being an output as well as an input in the classical system, we can summarize the economy by a Leontief matrix that lists in columns each good's input requirements.

LEONTIEF-RICARDO MATRIX

Inputs	1 corn	2 velvets	Outputs ...	n zebras	$n+1$ labor	Landlord consumptions
1 corn	0	0	...	0	c_1	Y_1
2 velvets	0	0	...	0	c_2	Y_2
.	.	.		.	.	.
.	.	.		.	.	.
.	.	.		.	.	.
n zebras	0	0	...	0	c_n	Y_n
$n+1$ labor	a_1	a_2	...	a_n	0	0
land	b_1	b_2	...	b_n	0	

Note that each good requires labor and land, as shown in the last two rows. (Leontief would also add circular requirements of *other goods*

7. It could easily be shown that each final composition of landlord demand (Y_i) determines a unique amount of x and a unique relative share of wage to rents. The final average share of wages will then depend on how demand patterns weigh the different final goods Y_i. I.e., $x = \alpha_1 Y_1 + \ldots + \alpha_n Y_n$, where the α's depend only on the (a,b,c) coefficients. It follows that wx/rL is a simple rational function of the Y's, which are themselves constrained by (13).

as raw materials, but we follow Ricardo and put in zeros.) Labor requires goods as shown by the $(c_1, \ldots, c_n)$ column; for luxuries, $c_i = 0$. Land is below the line because in the "open Leontief system" it is unproducible, being a primary factor. Landlord consumption is also exogenous and is to the right of the line.[8]

22. Now we can rewrite in matrix form the cost of production equations (10),

(14)

$$[p_1, \ldots, p_n, w] = [p_1, \ldots, p_n, w] \begin{bmatrix} 0 & \ldots & 0 & c_1 \\ 0 & \ldots & 0 & c_2 \\ \cdot & & \cdot & \cdot \\ \cdot & & \cdot & \cdot \\ \cdot & & \cdot & \cdot \\ 0 & \ldots & 0 & c_n \\ a_1 & \ldots & a_n & 0 \end{bmatrix} + r[b_1, \ldots, b_n, 0]$$

Letting A be the indicated $(n + 1) \cdot (n + 1)$ matrix, $B = [b_1, \ldots, b_n, 0]$ and $P = [p_1/r, \ldots, p_n/r, w/r]$ we can rewrite (14) in matrix terms as

(15)

$$P = PA + B$$

$$P = B[I - A]^{-1} = B[I + A + A^2 + \ldots]$$
$$= B + BA + BA^2 + \ldots \ .$$

The last multiplier chain (of Gaitskell type) has the advantage of giving labor's price as well as goods' prices in terms of direct and indirect needed land. All such prices are determined by the full land costs of (12) or (14). Also, the gross outputs $[y_1, \ldots, y_n, x]$ can by similar algebra be written as the following column vector

(16) $$[I - A]^{-1}Y = Y + AY + A^2Y + \ldots$$

which is the so-called Leontief-Cornfield infinite multiplier chain of input requirements.

NON-SUBSTITUTABILITY EVEN WHERE SUBSTITUTABILITY IS POSSIBLE

23. We can now leave the simple case of fixed (a_i, b_i) input coefficients. As mentioned, Ricardo himself varies the inputs applied to a unit of land in the later neoclassical manner. I can now apply the "substitutability theorem" to show that *even though there are possibilities for substitution, the long-run one-factor Ricardo system need experience no substitutions.*

8. The next section can be skipped by the nonspecialist.

This already cited theorem has been proved by Georgescu-Roegen, Koopmans, Arrow, and myself and need not here be repeated.[9] It will be enough to indicate its implication in the corn-labor-land case. Figure Va shows the fixed-coefficient L-shaped isoquants of Figure II replaced by solid isoquants admitting of *alternative* (a_1, b_1) combinations. Figure Vb shows the long-run SS labor supply curve determining a unique real wage: the residue for rent is given by the triangle SER, total wages by $OMES$, and total product by $OMER$.

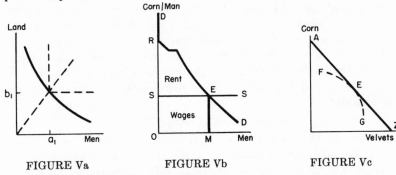

FIGURE Va   FIGURE Vb   FIGURE Vc

Note that Ricardo's differential formula for rent measured from the intensive margin E is now directly valid, and gives us the SER area. Note too that land now becomes scarce and expensive long before labor reaches its subsistence size.[1] The long-run constancy of the real wage because of the horizontal SS is crucial. It means that in Figure Va we shall always be at the same slope of the isoquant and hence we must remain at the point (a_1, b_1) with no observed substitutions in the long run; and the same would be true for (a_2, b_2) on a similar diagram for good 2.

24. Figure Vc adds insight into the far-reaching nature of the "substitutability theorem" — or more exactly, the "non-substitutability theorem." A simple argument can show why the transformation curve between two goods cannot be curved as in the dotted FEG curve, but must instead be a straight line as in AEZ or Figure I. For by giving up our right to substitute and remaining at (a_1, b_1) in Figure Va, we can always deduce from the earlier fixed-coefficients discussion that a straight-line relation through E is feasible: let us call this AEZ and note that this is simply the graph of (13). Obvi-

9. See *L.P.E.A.*, pp. 224–26, 248–52.
1. In such a world of smooth substitution it might be harder to devise a plausible "crisis" theory dependent on a reserve army of land suddenly disappearing. Cf. the earlier footnote on a crisis theory.

ously, if every frontier point of the transformation curve has a feasible straight line going through it, the transformation schedule must be a straight line.[2]

To conclude: in a one-factor world there is never any leverage for substitution; a rise in rents raises the cost of labor and of all potentially substitutable factors. (We shall later see that, with the long-run interest rate unchanged, a rise in rents also raises proportionately the price of every machine and every other input.)

25. Of course, one obvious qualification is in order. Ricardo and Smith would probably have admitted that the relative prices of joint products — of venison and deer skin, for example — would have to be determined by a demand theory and not from labor or land costs alone. One wonders why they did not worry more about this "jointness," which every student of Walrasian equilibrium knows to be an intrinsic part of the actual pricing relations among diverse factors and goods.[3]

SUMMARY AND CONCLUSION

26. We have seen that a simple labor theory of value is a valid general equilibrium formulation in the special case where land and capital are assumed to be ignorable. The importance of such a classical theory is not in its emphasis upon real costs and psychic disutility — there need not be such an emphasis; nor is its importance in catering to the metaphysician's desire for an "absolute" standard of value. Rather is the simple labor theory of importance because it *permits of a wide class of predictions concerning price behavior from a knowledge of technology alone.* This does not deny that demand conditions operate as well as production conditions. They, of course, do. But many of the technical predictions of the theory have a wide range of validity independently of sweeping changes in demand conditions. To be sure, if we insist upon a full description of the system, we must even in this simplest classical case invoke the full equations of general equilibrium.

27. Students of the classical theory have always recognized that the presence of capital and time created real difficulties for a simple labor theory of value. But, along with Ricardo, they have been under the illusion that land and rent could be avoided as a genuine difficulty

2. That the curve cannot be concave from above already is implied by the classical law of constant returns to scale and addibility of separate productions.

3. When we come to speak of fixed capital, joint products *must* be in the picture: a new machine produces corn *and* old machines. Hence, a needed condition for the usual substitutability theorem will be denied. The theorem will be saved, though, when we generalize it to cover cases of joint intermediate products that are never used by two separate industries.

by going to the external margin where labor works with free no-rent land and thus provides all the costs of commodity production. This is definitely an illusion; and it would indeed be remarkable if by introducing the complication of lands of many different grades, Ricardo and the classicists could simplify the equilibrium problem rather than complicating it.

Actually, raising the problem of many grades of land at once raises an equilibrium problem that Ricardo never explicitly faced up to. Although he was one of the formulators of the theory of comparative cost designed to explain the international division of labor (which was itself an early example of modern linear programming!), Ricardo did not recognize that an exactly similar problem was raised for the domestic division of labor: on which land of which grade will corn rather than potatoes be raised — and so forth? I am relegating to the Appendix the discussion of this important problem which, as far as I know, has been virtually overlooked by all writers since Ricardo's time with the sole exception of the later cited paper of Ragnar Frisch.[4]

28. Having demolished labor as an absolute standard of value, we can turn Ricardo upside down and find in his simplest long-run model a "land theory of value." This physiocratic interpretation of the Ricardian system comes from the special assumption that labor is reproducible — like any other good — at constant costs. Were

---

4. Figure III and its accompanying footnote demonstrated the inadmissibility of a simple labor theory once homogeneous land came into the picture. The device of going to the internal margin and concentrating on the outputs produced by the last increments of labor which pay no rent fails to work for the following mathematical reason: our cost of production for such a last unit becomes $p_i = w(\partial Q_i / \partial x_i)$. But the expressions in parentheses are now not hard technological constants or parameters; instead they are varying unknowns of the problem whose values have to be determined by the general equilibrium pattern of supply and demand. Professor Viner, in his 1930 *Economica* review of Edwin Cannan's, *A Review of Economic Theory* partially defends Ricardo's labor theory of value by use of the above marginal identity. This review is reprinted in J. Viner, *The Long View and the Short* (Glencoe, Ill.: Free Press, 1958), pp. 400–1. But, as Viner knows, a similar identity holds for land and shovels, and no one is interested in such a verbalistic shovel theory of value — particularly since the "constants" in it are economic variables whose new values we must determine every time demand shifts. (I wish I had given this answer on Viner's final examination a quarter of a century ago!)

As the Appendix shows, the same variability holds in the case of the extensive margin. Thus, in the simplest case where there are two grades of land, a change in the composition of landlord demand in the direction of the good which uses relatively much of the good land will finally lead to recourse to the second grade of land. At that new extensive margin, we are on a new straight-line segment — like *BC* rather than *AB* in Figure III. So no predictability of prices independently of demand is possible in the extensive margin case either.

there then but one homogeneous grade of land, we could in the manner of the Leontief system decompose the costs of every good — luxuries, wage goods, and even that intermediate good called labor itself — into its direct and indirect land content.

The substitutability theorem of modern input-óutput guarantees that even though technological substitutions are possible in such a one-primary-factor economy, they in fact never need be made. All other factors being the indirect product of land, there is never any leverage possible for relative-price change and substitution.

True, this decomposition into embodied land involves an infinite-chain multiplier; but its sum is definitely convergent, as can be shown by simple algebra or matrix methods familiar to students of input-output. Or, if we like we can avoid the multiplier chain completely, instead solving simultaneous equations for all prices in terms of land alone.

Land, being the only primary (i.e., nonproducible) item in this simplest model, has imputed to it — either as a residual or as a marginal product — all the net product of the system. As Ricardo well knew, it is scarcity and bottlenecks that give rise to value.

As the Physiocrats and classicists were aware, this central importance of land would have vast implications for public policy and taxation.

After the appendix on differential rent, Part II will grapple explicitly with the complications introduced by capital goods and time into the simplest Ricardian system. Provided we are willing to go along with the extreme classical assumption that in the long run the minimum interest rate is determined by an infinitely elastic supply schedule that is like the long-run supply schedule of labor, we shall find that an extension of the substitutability theorem will apply and that a decompilation of all value magnitudes into land alone will still be possible.

APPENDIX: THEORY OF DIFFERENTIAL RENT

INTRODUCTION

1. In the body of this paper I have shown that scarce land — even of one grade and in the absence of interest complications — destroys the possibility of a labor theory of value. Instead, under the special Ricardian longest-run assumptions, a single grade of land would itself provide a simple "land theory of value," based upon all prices equal to mathematically definable "embodied land."

In this Appendix, I examine the complications raised by the

existence of many grades of land. The resulting theory is even more damaging to a labor theory of value, and in fact destroys my own simple "land theory of value." Though the theory of differential rent is straightforward, I have not been able to find a rigorous treatment of it in the old or new literature.[1] And when we examine its main outlines, we see how illusory is Ricardo's belief that an extensive margin enabled him to "get rid" of rent and land as complications and how odd it is that this fact was not long ago pointed out in the strongest terms by economists.

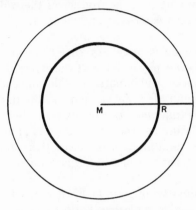

FIGURE VI

One-Good Case of Corn

2. Figure VI uses Thünen-like concentric circles to depict smooth differences in land quality (but ignores the transportation costs upon which Thünen based his location theory). The most fertile land is at the center M. The first unit of labor (I ignore capital in this Appendix for simplicity of exposition) will be applied to M. Then additional land will be applied in widening circles around M.

If all the land around M were equally fertile, labor would at first be applied at the same density around M in widening circles. Of course, doubling total labor x will not double the radius of the circle:

1. Since completing this Appendix, I have had pointed out to me by Paul Rosenstein-Rodan, a pioneering discussion of this problem, Ragnar Frisch, "Einige Punkte einer Preistheorie mit Boden und Arbeit als Produktionsfaktoren," *Zeitschrift für Nationalökonomie*, III (Sept. 25, 1931), 62–163.

Frisch, fifteen years before the development of linear programming, had properly formulated this problem, discovered many aspects of its solution, and rigorously analyzed the few-goods few-lands fixed-coefficient case, and outlined important aspects of the general problem. As Schumpeter would have said, "A remarkable performance!"

it will double the area; and since area is proportional to the square of the radius, doubling x will increase the radius MN by about 40 per cent. (Recall $\sqrt{2} = 1.4+$.)   Only after top-fertile land became scarce would land cease to be a free factor and begin to command positive market rent.

If we assume that land's fertility drops continuously after leaving the center M, then the fact that labor applied at M begins to yield diminishing marginal products implies that labor will spread in concentric circles around M.   Fertile land at M will from the beginning yield positive rent.   At the frontier of the widening concentric circle we face no-rent external-marginal land; labor working there pays no rent.

A modern economist would say that labor anywhere inside the circle receives the same pay as labor at the external margin, and that the competitive market will impute to inside land exactly its marginal product if that magnitude is definable by a smooth constant-returns-to-scale production function.   But in any case, the modern economist can agree with Ricardo that the rent on good land must *also* equal the difference between total product produced there and what the labor *there* (and on the frontier!) has to be paid under competitive wage determination.

3. Only a minority of writers have noticed that there is an ambiguity in the usual formulation that says: Good land's rent equals the difference between what labor (and "capital") produce on it and what "they" would produce at the external margin.   It is forgotten that if one man and one plow till one good acre, there is no particular reason to think that one man and one plow will also be tilling an acre of frontier no-rent land.   One man might be tilling five acres of such land, or one-fifth of an acre; and he might find it most economical to use two plows and one drill in doing so.   In short, there is a good deal of "implicit theorizing" in the classical account of how factors are to be allocated and compared on different lands, with Adam Smith's Invisible Hand being relied on to provide the determining equations that the conscientious economic scientist ought explicitly to provide.

Since I have agreed to ignore the complications due to use of capital goods, I can sidestep the plow-drill problem for now.   But we must face up to the question of how we optimally combine labor with land.

4. First, what do we mean by saying that land declines in fertility as we move on the radius away from the center M?   Do we mean that less corn will in fact be produced *per acre* at each outlying point than will be produced per acre at M?   No; not necessarily.   It could well

happen that the poor land *toward* the frontier *has* to be cultivated more *intensively* and in such a way as to give us more corn y_1 per acre.

To study this problem write down the constant-returns-to-scale production function relating corn output at R to labor and land there. It is convenient to relate output per acre, called $y_1(R)$, to labor per acre, called $x_1(R)$ and to total number of land acres devoted to corn at R_1 called $L_1(R)$. Then

(1A) $\quad y_1(R) = \dfrac{f_1[x_1(R)L_1(R),L_1(R);R]}{L_1(R)}$

$\qquad\qquad = f_1[x_1(R),1;R],$

where the marginal physical productivity of labor and land are given by the partial derivatives $\partial f_1/\partial x_1(R)$ and $\partial f_1/\partial L_1(R)$ respectively and where f_1 is a homogeneous function of the first degree in terms of its labor and land inputs.

To say that the quality of land decreases as the radius R increases is to say that labor's *beginning* average or marginal productivity, $\partial f_1[0,1;R]/\partial x_1(R)$, is a diminishing function of R: hence land at larger R will be used only after diminishing returns has reduced labor's marginal productivity on land at smaller R.

We can proceed to relate the technical coefficients, a_1 and b_1, defined in the text as the needed inputs of labor and land per unit of corn output, to the production function. Now a_1 and b_1 become functions of $R,a_1(R)$ and $b_1(R)$, which are connected by the relations:

(2A) $\quad b_1(R) = \dfrac{1}{y_1(R)} \,, a_1(R) = \dfrac{x_1(R)}{y_1(R)}$

$\qquad\quad 1 = f_1[a_1(R),b_1(R);R].$

This last relation will look like the cornered isoquants of the text's Figure II if we have fixed coefficients, or like the smoother isoquants of Figure Va if we have variable coefficients.

The requirement coefficient $a_1(R)$ is simply the reciprocal of labor's average productivity; and if we assume zero labor produces zero output, average and marginal productivities are equal when labor is initially applied. Hence, the initial $a_1(R)$ is the reciprocal of $\partial f_1[0,1;R]/\partial x_1(R)$ and we can replace our definition of the criterion for a decline in land's quality by the following equivalent one: To say land declines in quality with R is to say that the initial needed amount of labor per unit of output, $a_1(R)$, is a rising function of R.

5. At first one is tempted to think of land at the frontier as being used in a very extensive rather than intensive way. That this is not

universally true is shown by working through the case of fixed coefficients, where $a_1(R)$ and $b_1(R)$ are technically given. How then will labor and output be determined at each R? I.e., what will the equilibrium profile of $y_1(R)$ be for each available total labor x?

For each given x, labor will be applied up to a variable frontier R^* that is determined by solving the implicit equation:

(3A) $$2\pi \int_0^{R^*} a_1(R)y_1(R)RdR = 2\pi \int_0^{R^*} \frac{a_1(R)}{b_1(R)} RdR = x,$$

which is a single equation solvable for the unknown R^* in terms of x. (The 2π and RdR factors in the integrals come from the geometric relation between circular area and radius: i.e., from the analytical facts $\int_0^{2\pi} d\theta = 2\pi$, $dA = RdRd\theta$.) For $R > R^*$, production will be zero with $y_1(R) \equiv 0 \equiv x_1(R)$.

All this is no accident but follows from the solution of the following mathematical problem: Pick that non-negative $y_1(R)$ function which maximizes total output

$$y_1 = 2\pi \int_0^{\infty} y_1(R) \, RdR, \text{ subject to}$$

(4A) $$2\pi \int_0^{\infty} a_1(R)y_1(R) \, RdR \leq x$$

$$y_1(R) \leq \frac{1}{b_1(R)} .$$

For $a_1(R)$, a rising function, the optimal solution will necessarily entail $y_1(R)$'s vanishing beyond the cut-off point R^* of (3A).

Now what is the resulting intensity of cultivation? Measured in men/acre it is given by $a_1(R)/b_1(R)$. If $b_1(R)$ rises more slowly with R than $a_1(R)$ — as certainly can happen — then $a_1(R)/b_1(R)$ will increase with R and we see that frontier land will be more intensively tilled by labor. (E.g., suppose bad land is very weedy and requires much manual stooping.)

6. The variable-coefficient case, which Ricardo thought more realistic when considering varying doses applied to land, is a little more complicated. The mathematical problem (4A) still holds; but now $a_1(R)$ and $b_1(R)$ are not technologically given but are to be determined by the solution to the maximum problem, subject only to the production-function relation connecting them in (2A).

Intuitively, the economist realizes that in the smooth case where marginal productivities $\partial f_1/\partial x_1(R)$ exist, our solution must satisfy (3A) and (2A) and also equality of labor's marginal productivity everywhere that labor is used.

To see all this we have to set up the calculus of variations problem.

Maximize $y_1 = y_1(x) = 2\pi \int_0^\infty f_1[x_1(R),1;R] \, R dR$ subject to

(5A) $$2\pi \int_0^\infty x_1(R) \, R dR \leqq x, \; x_1(R) \geqq 0.$$

By use of a Lagrange multiplier $\lambda = w/p_1$, we derive the conditions of equilibrium

(6A)
$$\frac{\partial f_1[x_1(R),1;R]}{\partial x_1(R)} = w/p_1, \; R \leqq R^*$$
$$< w/p_1, \; R > R^*$$
$$\frac{w}{p_1} = \frac{\partial f_1[0,1;R^*]}{\partial x_1(R)} = \frac{dy_1(x)}{dx}$$
$$2\pi \int_0^{R^*} x_1(R) \, R dR = x$$

with the economic laws of returns giving us the Legendre condition $\partial^2 f_1/\partial x_1{}^2 < 0$ and the Jacobi and Weierstrass conditions sufficient to assure a true maximum.[2]

At each R we can define a unique land rent $r(R)$ satisfying

(7A) $$\frac{r(R)}{p_1} = \frac{\partial f_1[x_1(R),1;R]}{\partial L_1(R)} = \frac{1}{b_1(R)} - \frac{a_1(R)}{b_1(R)} \frac{w}{p_1} \, , \; R \leqq R^*$$
$$\frac{r(R)}{p_1} \equiv 0 \qquad\qquad\qquad , \; R \geqq R^*.$$

For R just below R^*, rent will necessarily decline with R; but well inside the frontier, there is the possibility that rent could at times rise with R.

As kind of a "dual problem" to (5A), we could derive the conditions (7A) as the solution to the *minimum* problem

2. Cf. G. A. Bliss, *Lectures on the Calculus of Variations* (University of Chicago Press, 1946).

$$\text{Subject to} \frac{r(R)}{p_1} \geqq \frac{1}{b_1(R)} - \frac{a_1(R)}{b_1(R)} \frac{w}{p_1} \qquad\qquad R \geqq 0$$

$$1 = f_1[a_1(R), b_1(R); R]$$

pick non-negative $r(R)/p_1$ and w/p_1 to minimize

(8A)
$$y_1{}^* = 2\pi \int_0^\infty \frac{r(R)}{p_1} R\,dR + \frac{w}{p_1} x$$

$$= y_1(x).$$

Let us summarize the resulting equilibrium of the corn-labor-land economy. An external observer who merely recorded the total of corn y_1 produced for each total of labor x would see a marginal product curve $dy_1(x)/dx$ such as mn in Figure VII. This is indis-

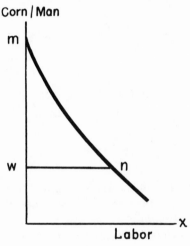

FIGURE VII

tinguishable from the case of homogeneous land. The only generalization possible is that the absolute total of rent — measured in corn by the residual triangle mnw — always goes up as total labor x grows. But nothing at all can be predicted about labor's relative share, whether it will be a small or large fraction of the total or how it will change with extra labor. The writings of the classical economists are replete with false statements on these delicate questions of relative shares.

Of course, if the supply of labor is determined by a horizontal long-run SS curve through wn in the Ricardian fashion, we have a complete theory. Or alternative supply conditions could be postulated.

RENTS IN THE MULTI-GOOD, MULTI-LAND ECONOMY

7. We now must consider the case of more than one good, where $y_1, y_2 \ldots$ are to be produced. For each point R on a radius in Figure VI, we are now given a production function for each different good, as in (1A). Such a production function will for the ith good give us the possible relations between $a_i(R)$ and $b_i(R)$, just as in (2A). In all we have

$$y_i(R) = f_i[x_i(R), 1; R] \qquad (i = 1, 2, \ldots)$$

(9A) $$1 = f_i[a_i(R), b_i(R); R].$$

What pattern of cultivation will now follow for each given total of labor x? It could happen that the production functions for $i = 1$ and $i = 2$ differ only in scale. In this singular case, corn and velvets would be produced *indifferently anywhere* in the circle of cultivation. Figure VIII shows the pie-wedge possibilities; but local polka dots of corn and velvets would be as good. The reason for the indifference

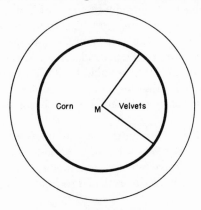

FIGURE VIII

is that corn and velvet, once scales have been rectified, are essentially the same good with a production possibility curve for each x being a negatively-sloped straight line.

The pie-wedge case of Figure VIII has the merit that both goods can be said to be producible at the external margin, with their price ratios being determinable from their external-margin wage costs alone.

8. But we must face up to the fact that it is terribly unrealistic to suppose that all qualities of land are *equally* good or bad in the production of *every* good. Sandy land good for cucumbers is terrible for rice. To each scarcity of labor and each pattern of commodity

demand, there will be an elaborate set of comparative advantage conditions needed to determine the optimal geometric pattern of cultivation.

David Ricardo is rightly given great credit for his origination of the theory of comparative cost in international trade. I find it therefore a little paradoxical that he failed to see how within a region — where labor is fully mobile and lands have differential qualities — there arises a difficult economic problem of resource allocation. Not only did he leave the equilibrium conditions implicit, but he quite failed to see that the new set-up is fatal to his "embodied labor" theories.

For now with two or more lands having different comparative advantages for two or more goods, the production possibility between y_1 and y_2 — say corn and velvets — will be concave to the origin as in Figure Vc's broken curve *FEG*. Having dropped the assumption of homogeneous land, and even if still adhering to Ricardo's long-run assumptions of constant reproduction cost of labor, we no longer can end up with the straight line transformation curve — of Figures I and Vc. Each change in the pattern of landlord demand must change the relative labor contents of corn and velvets at the external margins (if such can be found), and presumably at all other locations as well both in physical and value terms. The classical attempt to deduce and predict price ratios from labor alone becomes a mathematical impossibility.[3]

I propose to give the mathematical solution to the many-land case, not merely to buttress the criticism made of long-dead Ricardo, but for the constructive reason that modern location theories are greatly in need of further theoretical development.

LINEAR PROGRAMMING FORMULATION

9. I first consider the case of m finite grades of land, in fixed amounts $[L(1), L(2), \ldots, L(j), \ldots, L(m)]$. After that the case of an infinity of grades can be heuristically summarized. As before I begin with the simple case where $a_i(j)$ and $b_i(j)$ are fixed, technologically-given coefficients for each industry on each land.

To deduce the production possibility locus of $(y_1, y_2, \ldots, y_n)$ for each available x, it is most convenient to think of specifying the

---

3. The same criticism holds also for Marx, but he at least had the grace to assume away land explicitly thereby avoiding Ricardo's logical error and being guilty only of the misdemeanor of unrealism. To explain actual production — under capitalism or communism, between nations or sub-regions — the Marxian theory must become neoclassical!

outputs (y_i) and then to seek to minimize the needed total labor x, subject to the prescribed technology. This gives us the following linear programming problem: Subject to

$$y_1(1) + y_1(2) + \ldots + y_1(m) \geqq y_1$$
$$y_2(1) + y_2(2) + \ldots + y_2(m) \geqq y_2$$

$$y_n(1) + y_n(2) + \ldots + y_n(m) \geqq y_n,$$
$$\text{all } y_i(j) \geqq 0$$
$$b_1(1)y_1(1) + b_2(1)y_2(1) + \ldots + b_n(1)y_n(1) \leqq L(1)$$
$$b_1(2)y_1(2) + b_2(2)y_2(2) + \ldots + b_n(2)y_n(2) \leqq L(2)$$

$$b_1(m)y_1(m) + b_2(m)y_2(m) + \ldots + b_n(m)y_n(m) \leqq L(m),$$

(10A)   minimize

$$x = \sum_{i=1}^{n} \sum_{j=1}^{m} a_i(j)y_i(j)$$

$$= X[y_1, \ldots, y_n; L(1), \ldots, L(m)].$$

Provided the specified outputs are not more than the specified lands can produce, this will be a proper linear programming problem with a determinate solution assured. The resulting optimal pattern of production $[y_i(j)]$ can be converted into the optimal pattern of labor allocation $[x_i(j)] = [a_i(j)y_i(j)]$. Many of the grades of land, such as $L(k)$ say, may not be used at all or may be used incompletely: in that case the inequality $\Sigma y_i(k) < L(k)$ will hold, and such land will be redundant with its rent $r(k) = 0$. If a grade of land is used some, it may have to be used for only one good or it may have to be used for more than one good. (If $m < n$, more than one good will have to be produced by *some* grade of land, the exact geographical pattern being indifferent. Recognizing transport costs hitherto ignored will get rid of many of the inessential geographical indeterminacies.)

10. Now exactly how are prices p_i/w and land rents expressed in wage units $r(j)$ determined? Ricardo would probably have recognized the cost-of-production inequalities

(11A) $\dfrac{p_i}{w} \leqq a_i(j) + r(j)b_i(j)$ $(i = 1, \ldots, n; j = 1, \ldots, m)$,

with an inequality for any i and j implying that nothing of the ith good is to be produced on the jth land. But he could not from these have deduced prices and rents, since there is an infinity of possible solutions.

Of course, if he could have found for any good a no-rent land on which it was produced, he would then know its price. And then he could infer, residually or "differentially," the rent of any other land where it was also produced. Moreover, he could also infer the prices of any other good produced on lands whose rents he had thus deduced. Proceeding in this chain-like way (along a "mathematical tree") he could hope to determine still other land rents, namely those on which were also produced the further goods whose prices had just been inferred, etc., etc.

I say Ricardo could have done all this. But I don't recall that he ever did explicitly do so or fully realized the complicated nature of the problem that was to be solved. Moreover, even had he been able to pursue the above complicated reasonings, he would still not be out of the woods. For there could easily remain goods and lands which are never related by an indirect chain to any of the goods and lands whose prices and rents have been determined. To see this, we have only to consider the simple case where *no* lands actually used turn out to have zero rents. The Ricardian differential method based upon an extensive margin then breaks down completely.

To be sure, as we already have seen, Ricardo thought of coefficients as being variable on each intra-marginal unit of land: hence, he claimed to determine such land's rent by a differential measurement between what all labor applied to it produces and what the last unit of labor (the one at the internal margin that "pays no rent") produces; this is precisely what we should today call the land's marginal physical product valued at output's market price. But the simplest case of all, the case of fixed coefficients, Ricardo could apparently not solve by such methods.[4]

11. Is the failure intrinsic? No, it is not. The modern technique of linear programming gives us the optimal solution in a straightforward manner. The challenge of Cairnes — What economic truth was ever derived or ever will be derived by the mathematical method — has been answered hundreds of times in subsequent years. Here is a further striking case where a literary problem, old in Cairnes's time, could not be rigorously solved until the development a decade ago of the "duality theorem" of linear programming. Of course, could we confront Cairnes with this fulfillment of his challenge, he would

4. A reader might wonder whether Ricardo's comparative advantage analysis applied within a country (*Principles*, p. 136 footnote) might not be used to solve this problem. It cannot. Working out the comparative advantage of $L(j)$ and $L(k)$ in corn and velvets by comparing $b_1(j)/b_2(j)$ and $b_1(k)/b_2(k)$ gives no valid clue to the optimal pattern, nor would $a_1(j)/a_2(j)$ and $a_1(k)/a_2(k)$ comparisons.

probably dismiss the whole problem as a trivial one and besides, *after* he had grasped its solution, he might regard it as obvious. There are some competitions you just can't win!

12. The definitive solution for the ratios of prices, rents, and wage comes from solving a maximum problem in linear programming that is the so-called "dual" to the minimum problem of (10A). Until this decade, no economist of literary or mathematical persuasion realized that just as the ideal competitive system acts so as to get as much outputs with as little inputs as is possible, so does it act as if it were trying to maximize the factor return to the minimized input. This sounds obvious, when stated, but its meaning is not at all obvious and to fail to realize this is to convict one's self of superficiality.

Specifically, subject to the nm price inequalities of (11A)

$$\frac{p_i}{w} - r(j)b_i(j) \leqq a_i(j) \qquad (i = 1, \ldots, n; j = 1, \ldots, m),$$

we are to pick non-negative $[p_1/w, \ldots, p_n/w; r(1), \ldots, r(m)]$ to

$$\text{(12A) maximize } x^* = \frac{p_1}{w} y_1 + \frac{p_2}{w} y_2 + \ldots + \frac{p_n}{w} y_n - r(1)L(1)$$

$$- r(2)L(2) - \ldots - r(m)L(m).$$

The duality theorem tells us that the maximal $x^* = X[y_1, \ldots, y_n; L(1), \ldots, L(m)]$ must be the same in magnitude as the minimized labor of the original problem. We can regard x^* as a maximized total wage return, measured in labor hours; or multiplying through by w, as maximized total wage return in any wage units; or dividing through by p_i/w, as the real wage return measured in the ith good as *numeraire*. Lest anyone think the formulation gives any comfort to those who hanker for a labor theory of value, I must point out that instead of minimizing labor we could have minimized any grade of good land and formulated our dual problem in such terms.

I should add that the formulation (12A) provides a solution to the over-and-under determinacy problem raised in 1932 concerning the Walras-Cassel fixed-coefficients production equations.[5]

13. From the $x = X[y_1, \ldots, L(m)]$ function of our original problem (10A) alone, we can define prices and rents without the dual formulation. It can be mathematically shown that

$$\frac{\partial X[y_1, \ldots; \ldots L(m)]}{\partial y_i} = \frac{p_i}{w} \qquad (i = 1, \ldots, n)$$

5. See *L.P.E.A.*, Chap. 13.

$$(13A) \quad -\frac{\partial X[y_1, \ldots ; \ldots L(m)]}{\partial L(j)} = \frac{r(j)}{w} \qquad (j = 1, \ldots, m).$$

Total rent

$$= \sum_1^m \frac{r(j)}{w} L(j) = -X[y_1, \ldots ; \ldots L(m)] + \sum_1^n y_i \frac{\partial X[y_1, \ldots ; \ldots, L(m)]}{\partial y_i},$$

where Euler's theorem on homogeneous functions of the first degree has become applicable to $X[y_1, \ldots ; \ldots, L(m)]$ by virtue of our constant-returns-to-scale assumptions.

Again, with or without Ricardian assumptions of long-run constant real wages, the relative shares of total wages and rent will be dependent on the pattern of consumption demand. And it is no longer true that an increase in labor must always increase the absolute total of rent: only if all y_i are increased in proportion can we be sure that absolute land rent then rises, and even here the *relative* distribution of income can move in either direction or stand still.

14. The time has come to consider the variable-coefficient case favored both by Ricardo and later neoclassical economists. The minimum problem (10A) still stands, but the a's and b's are no longer given constants, being instead related by the mn production relations

$$(14A) \quad 1 = f_i[a_i(j), b_i(j); j] \qquad (i = 1, \ldots, n; j = 1, \ldots, m).$$

Unless each production function admits of but a finite number of alternative activities, such a minimum problem is no longer strictly a linear programming problem; but it will have a determinate solution.

In the infinite-activity case where the production functions everywhere have second partial derivatives, the full conditions of equilibrium can be defined in terms of marginal productivity inequalities. Combining the theory of nonlinear programming[6] with the spirit of neoclassical economics, we can reformulate the augmented (10A) and (12A) problem in terms of a saddlepoint requirement. Thus, the "labor" expression

$$(15A) \quad \Phi = \sum_{i=1}^n \sum_{j=1}^m x_i(j) + \sum_{i=1}^n \frac{p_i}{w}\left\{ y_i - \sum_{j=1}^m f_i[x_i(j), L_i(j); j] \right\}$$
$$+ \sum_{i=1}^m \frac{r(j)}{w}\left\{ \sum_{i=1}^n L_i(j) - L(j) \right\}$$

must be at a *minimum* with respect to the output-input variables $[x_i(j), L_i(j)]$ and at a *maximum* with respect to the price-rent variables $[p_i/w, r(j)/w]$.

6. See *L.P.E.A.*, Chap. 8.

This implies firstly that the bracket expressions are all non-positive; and that, if a particular bracket expression is not zero, its price or rent coefficient must be zero and must correspond to a free output or input.

Secondly, the saddlepoint condition implies the following marginal productivity conditions, derived from differentiating Φ:

(16A)
$$1 \geqq \frac{p_i}{w} \frac{\partial f_i[x_i(j),L_i(j);j]}{\partial x_i(j)}$$

$$(i = 1, \ldots, n \, ; j = 1, \ldots, m)$$

$$\frac{r(j)}{w} \geqq \frac{p_i}{w} \frac{\partial f_i[x_i(j), L_i(j);j]}{\partial L_i(j)},$$

it being understood that an inequality rather than equality implies in each case that the output or input in question is zero. The classical laws of diminishing returns will guarantee the convexity needed to assure genuine maximum and minimum conditions.

Ricardo's intensive-margin differential measurement of rent using the last unit of labor that pays no rent does point in the direction of the correct conditions (16A). But we see how much implicit theorizing there remains in his formulation.

15. We can dispense with the assumption that marginal productivities $\partial f_i/\partial x_i(j)$ and $\partial f_i/L_i(j)$ exist everywhere. In fact an interesting case is provided by the assumption that each industry has only a finite number of different $[a_i(j),b_i(j)]$ possibilities on each land. (Of course, "mixtures" of these provide an infinite gradation of possibilities.) Such a case is easily converted into a standard linear programming problem by defining non-negative activity levels $[y_i(j)';y_i(j)''; \ldots]$ corresponding to each possible $[a_i(j)',b_i(j)'; a_i(j)'', b_i(j)''; \ldots]$ technical method. Then the conditions of (10A),

$$\sum_j y_i(j) \geqq y_i, \sum_i b_i(j) \, y_i(j) \leqq L(j), \underset{ij}{\sum\sum} a_i(j) \, y_i(j) \text{ a minimum,}$$

now simply become
Subject to

$$\sum_j y_i(j)' + \sum_j y_i(j)'' + \ldots \geqq y_i \qquad (i = 1, \ldots, n)$$

$$\sum_i b_i(j)' \, y_i(j)' + \sum_i b_i(j)'' \, y_i(j)'' + \ldots \leqq L(j), \; (j = 1, \ldots, m)$$

pick non-negative variables $[y_i(j)', y_i(j)'', \ldots]$ to minimize

(17A) $\quad x = \underset{ij}{\sum\sum} a_i(j)' \, y_i(j)' + \underset{ij}{\sum\sum} a_i(j)'' \, y_i(j)'' + \ldots,$

a standard linear programming problem.[7]

7. Alternatively in (10A), we can regard n as greater than the number of distinct goods by the number of alternative ways of producing actual goods. So

In the limit as the number of alternative activities becomes infinite, we can approach as close as we like to the smooth neoclassical marginal productivities.

17. The theory of rent will be complete if I sketch the corresponding treatment when land takes on a continuum of different fertilities. Our discussion can be quite brief because the assumed circular patterns now become quite artificial: a point M where corn is most efficiently produced is not likely also to be the point where velvets are first to be produced; so relations that depend on a radius R are no longer worthy of detailed mathematical analysis.

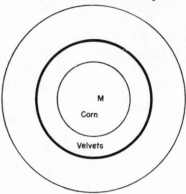

FIGURE IX

I shall go directly to the smooth variable-coefficient case. The formulation (15A) suggests how we should generalize the one-good continuum formulation (5A). Now let (u,v) be generalized space co-ordinates, with each point of space giving a "density" production function for each good.

Now we set up a saddlepoint labor expression like Φ of (15A), but replacing Σ_1^m everywhere by a double integral over the (u,v) space, $\int\int \ldots dudv$. The conditions of equilibrium will, disregarding all transport costs, everywhere be

$$\frac{p_i}{w}\frac{\partial f_i[\quad ;u,v]}{\partial x_i} \leq 1 \qquad (i = 1, \ldots, n)$$

(18A)
$$\frac{p_i}{w}\frac{\partial f_i[\quad ;u,v]}{\partial L_i} \leq \frac{r(u,v)}{w},$$

the condition $\Sigma y_i(j) \geq y_i$ can now be added for all y_i produced by different methods but really representing the same goods. Subject then to the new conditions, we solve the problem in the (10A) form, interpreting the result in terms of optimal methods to be used. It may be noted that no industry ever has to use more than two different methods on any one spot at any one time.

it being understood that an inequality for an i at some point means that nothing of good i is produced there.

Thünen-like circles of production are shown in Figure IX. Presumably certain lands will be definitely better for some goods than for others — depending on the changing pattern of demand.

The only significant difference between the case of finite and infinite land varieties is the likelihood that the finite case will produce corners in the $X(y_1, \ldots, y_n)$ function. In either case, in terms of suitably generalized partial derivatives, total rent is given by $-X + \Sigma y_i \partial X / \partial y_i$, a function rising as all y's rise in proportion but with few other predictable properties.

MASSACHUSETTS INSTITUTE OF TECHNOLOGY

32

A MODERN TREATMENT OF THE RICARDIAN ECONOMY:

II. CAPITAL AND INTEREST ASPECTS OF THE PRICING PROCESS

By PAUL A. SAMUELSON

BACK TO THE BEGINNING

28. Part I has neglected the role of time in the productive process. To this I now turn.

Both Smith and Ricardo speak in parables when they refer to an earlier golden age when land rent and interest can be neglected. There never was such a golden age in human history; but we are entitled to think of this device as an ancient form of the method of successive approximations, in which one first assumes very simple models before introducing various complications into them.

The way we got rid of the complication of land rent at the beginning of Part I is really different from the way we might hope to get rid of the complication of interest. In Part I we began by assuming that good land is so superabundant that its rent is free and can be neglected. Certainly one can imagine a Europe peopled by so few cavemen as to make this a logical possibility. But can we imagine an early age in which all production relationships take place in an instant, so that time is perfectly ignorable? I do not think we can. Production operations must always have taken place over a period of time.

An alternative formulation would be to assume that our early system is "time saturated." By this I mean that so much accumulation had taken place in the system's past as to have driven the interest rate down to zero or to a negligible level. It is then still true that outputs become available after inputs in time; but the market place is supposed to evaluate these time differences as if they were unimportant. What about this interpretation? I do not think that any classical economist would have been such a utopian antediluvian as

408

to have imagined that ever in the golden past capital was superabundant in the same sense as land might have been superabundant.
(Recall that Smith uses the words *"before* stock had accumulated.")
And certainly such a model would not provide a convenient spring-
board for the study of the effects of accumulation in lowering the
interest rate.

We must instead, I think, imagine a golden age which was not
very golden — one in which life was short and brutish, in very part
because of the extreme shortage of capital. In such a world we might
still hope to be able to neglect interest at a first approximation provided the interest rate were so high as to force the system into using
very short-lived projects exclusively. (Alternatively, we may turn
back the clock of technology and envisage a system with only very
short-lived processes available to it.) If all the delay periods in the
system are sufficiently short — say of the magnitude of a day rather
than a year — then even if the interest rate is quite high expressed
as a rate per annum, interest per day and the relative share of interest
in the total may be so small as to be at first neglectable. And so if
we persist with the assumption of free land, the simple labor theory
of value may serve as a good approximation, as in Figure I of Part I.

29. When, however, we leave the realm of parables and nursery
tales, the phenomenon of interest or profit[1] does raise its head and
we must take it explicitly into account.

As accumulation lowers the interest rate, time-consuming processes which previously had not paid will now become worthwhile.
This the classical economists, along with any observers of technology,
would presumably have recognized[2] even if they did not explicitly
foresee a Böhm-Bawerkian model in which some dimension of time
intensity can be continuously varied so as to increase the outputs of
primary inputs. Still another way that more time consuming processes become relevant is through the process of irreversible techno-

---

1. Profit in the real world consists (1) partly of implicit wages, paid for the
services provided by the entrepreneur himself (including management services);
(2) partly of monopoly returns to "contrived scarcities," and imperfectly competitive situations; (3) partly of the *ex ante* and *ex post* rewards to uncertainty
bearing; and (4) partly of the "surplus" residual or rents paid to factors in
inelastic supply. Assuming perfect competition and sidestepping the important
problems connected with uncertainty, we need not distinguish implicit factor
returns from explicit factor returns and we can strictly identify the profit rate
with the pure interest rate.

2. That Ricardo was aware of substitution possibilities induced by changes
in factor costs is shown by passages like the following: "Now if the wages of labour
rise 10 per cent . . . , he will no longer hesitate, but will at once purchase the
machine . . ." David Ricardo, *Works*, Sraffa ed., I, 61. Any who attribute to
Ricardo a fixed-proportions model do him an injustice.

logical change and invention, even though the older economists were not so meticulous as moderns in separating out reversible, induced changes from irreversible changes of exogenous or induced type.

Time and Interest

30. We now no longer ignore the fact that labor and land do not instantaneously produce outputs. Ricardo, following Smith and the Physiocrats, thinks of each worker (and each acre, if land is scarce) as engaged in moving raw materials towards completion — "adding value" we would say today. But the worker needs finished consumption goods today and ordinarily does not want to be paid out of the *ultimate* finished fruits of his today's labor. The employer "advances" to the worker finished consumption goods; such a primitive "wage fund" theory regards these advances as "capital" and supposes wages today to be limited by the magnitude of the available finished wage goods "destined" to be paid out as wages. The men (and acres) receive today less than their tomorrow's fruits. The capitalist or entrepreneur receives the difference as profit or interest on the money value of the capital he has advanced.

In brief, employers hire current men and acres and now pay them money wages and rents. These factors push the employer's inventory of unfinished goods towards completion, and when the goods are finished the employer sells them. Under free entry and absence of uncertainty, competition ensures that the employer earns the market rate of interest (per annum or per day) on the value of his goods in process as determined in the auction markets for unfinished or finished goods. Per year or per day the money flow of society's final product (finished consumption goods plus net capital formation) exceeds the sum of wages (and rents) by the interest return of capitalists.[3]

31. Some may say that workers (and landlords) are "exploited" by the "interest discounting" of their ("ultimate") productivity entailed by the lapse of time between inputs and outputs. Others may say that workers are free to be paid in their current unfinished products without any discount; but such unfinished products, when the workers now try to sell them, would be found to have a market price lower than the price of finished goods — lower by exactly the

---

3. If land is not free, its rent can also be regarded as the interest return on land's capitalized market value. Though one saver can "invest" in land by buying part of the limited supply from some seller, society cannot create more of the inelastically-supplied original and indestructible land. Operationally, it would be hard to separate improvements in land that are like other capital projects from the original supply of land.

amount of interest that the workers could earn on their sale proceeds in the time between now and completion.[4] Such people argue that there is no "exploitation" here, no more than in the case of a Kansas landlord who gets the full Kansas value of his land's marginal product, which naturally involves a discounting of the full Chicago value for the transport cost across space.

There is no need here to go into the welfare economics of the problem. Those who approve or disapprove both recognize (1) that a positive market rate of interest coupled with the fact (2) that it takes months to change grape juice to wine means that interest receivers will share in the gross or net output of the economy. Of course, if the interest rate were lower, if corn grew faster, if nature were kinder, if brains were better and muscles harder — in short if pies were bigger and others' shares less, the world and things would be different!

32. The above section deals only with circulating capital: i.e., with productive processes in which labor transforms one material into another. Ricardo was also familiar with the kind of fixed capital represented by a machine. Fixed capital working with labor and materials produces new materials *and* also produces as a by-product (slightly older) fixed capital. Such is the modern distinction between fixed and circulating capital. There is no implication, as Ricardo at first may have thought, that the durability of fixed capital is necessarily greater than that of circulating capital: wine or redwood trees may be circulating capital while a brief candle may be fixed capital. Both circulating and fixed capital, which are not to be confused with Marx's variable and constant capital, create insuperable difficulties for an exact labor theory of value — as Ricardo well knew.

FAILURE OF THE LABOR THEORY

33. The simplest model to show that relative exchange values cannot be predicted from the labor theory of value alone is the following. Let there be two goods as before, y_1 and y_2. Let each require a_1 and a_2 of labor per unit; and let the land requirements b_1 and b_2 be neglectable because land is so abundant as to be free. But now assume, as Jevons later was to do, that inputs in the two industries produce their outputs exactly θ_1 and θ_2 periods later, respectively.

4. For simplicity I here neglect possible needed later factor inputs; these can be taken account of in an obvious manner. See also my "Wages and Interest: A Modern Dissection of Marxian Economic Models," *American Economic Review*, XLVII (Dec. 1957), 884–912.

Then if i is the interest rate per period, the steady-state cost of production equations for prices become

$$(17) \qquad p_1 = wa_1(1 + i)^{\theta_1} \qquad\qquad p_2 = wa_2(1 + i)^{\theta_2},$$

with

$$(18) \qquad \frac{p_2}{p_1} = \frac{a_2}{a_1}(1 + i)^{\theta_2 - \theta_1}.$$

From the embodied labor coefficients a_i alone, we can no longer predict unchanging relative prices — except in the singular cases where the time intensities of the industries are exactly equal, $\theta_1 = \theta_2$; or where the interest rate i is literally zero.

When he came to write his *Principles*, Ricardo realized this. But instead of cutting his losses,[5] he continued to toy with standards of durability that involved one year periods or that represented the social average. And he was even under the illusion[6] that he was making great improvements on Adam Smith's pragmatic doctrine that price equals the sum of all costs of production. (To have done that he would have had to anticipate Leon Walras's doctrine of general equilibrium, which made sure that it had enough equations to determine *all* the constituents of price.)

34. In (18) a change in the profit rate will vary the price ratios between goods of different durability. This change in the interest rate is associated with what Ricardo[7] calls an opposite change in "wages," meaning by this not as one might at first think, money wages, but rather real wages. (This effect can be seen from regarding the first equation in (17) as determining the price of corn, the sole wage good: then the real wage $w/p_1 = 1/a_1(1 + i)^{\theta_1}$, an inverse function of the interest rate i.)

Ricardo is again wrong to think that he can neglect effects of these changes on rent by going to the external margin where no rent is paid. A change in the interest rate or real wage can be presumed to change the location of the extensive margin. Because he insufficiently realized this, Ricardo repeatedly set up too sharp an opposition between wages and interest, not sufficiently realizing that the problem is really a three-factor one.

5. As he was tempted to do in his famous 1820 letter to McCulloch, *Works*, I, xxxix, xl.
6. *Works*, I, xxxvi, xxxvii.
7. *Works*, I, xxxviii, 53, 56–63, 66.

A Simple Corn Economy

35. We have been using the interest rate before explicitly introducing the conditions needed to determine it. The time has come to try to come to grips with this problem. Rather than beginning with the complex case of many goods, I shall first follow the example of West and Ricardo and concentrate on the one-good example of corn. How does the fact that there must be a passage of time between inputs and outputs affect wages, rent, interest, and the distribution of income? Insight is provided by the simplest example where corn, y_1, appears one period ($\theta_1 = 1$) after the application of labor, x_1, and homogeneous land L_1.

As in Sections 7–17 of Part I of this paper, all the technological facts are summarized by the (a_1, b_1) technical coefficients giving the needed amounts of labor and land per unit of corn. (These coefficients may be taken as technically given, or we may wish to assume the variable-coefficient case in which more a_1 may be substituted smoothly for less b_1.) We can complete the system by specifying c_1, the number of units of corn needed by each man to insure that the labor supply will be exactly reproduced.

We saw that $1 - c_1 a_1 < 0$ would imply that population becomes extinct. The interesting case is where land is still free and $1 - c_1 a_1 > 0$. Statically, this implies a "contradiction." Corn cannot sell for its labor cost simultaneously with labor selling for its corn cost, since $1 - c_1 a_1 > 0$ implies the incompatibility of the two cost-of-production equations

$$(19) \qquad p_1 = a_1 w \text{ and } w = c_1 p_1.$$

Which relation must give? Actually, both of them must be made non-statical to take account of the dynamic dating implicit in the problem.

The Special Timeless Case

36. If corn output were producible instantaneously but periods of human gestation were nine months and periods of infancy were measured in decades, then undoubtedly under competition the first equation would be valid and the one to be jettisoned would be the second equation: so long as land continued superabundant, the Ricardo-Malthus subsistence real wage would be irrelevant to the higher actual market real wage. Workers could earn "surplus rent over subsistence" or surplus quasi-rent. Surplus rent on what? On their temporary scarcity! Biological factors and the height of the

real wage above subsistence would determine the geometric rate of population and output growth.

But what about the long run? So long as land remains abundant, no matter how long the run this state of affairs with real wage equal to $1/a_1$ could continue forever. (West, better perhaps than Ricardo, realized that in America wages had remained and were remaining higher than subsistence.) What has to give in (19) is the assumption of equilibrium or stationariness of population, no other contradiction occurring. Let us be clear about this: with land free and production instantaneous, there is no possibility of exploiting labor or depriving men of their full product; they need only move to the frontier. Only by withholding from labor something it needs for production can you get it to share with you the total produce. And then *whose* produce it is that is being shared becomes a welfare-economics or semantic question.[8]

THE EXTREME TORRENS-RICARDO CASE

38. It is unrealistic to get around (19)'s contradiction by making corn production instantaneous. Instead of holding the first equation and dropping the second, Ricardo followed Torrens in tending to neglect the long time period it would take for population to bring the real wage back to the conventional-subsistence level. This is in accordance with his tendency to treat long-run relations as if they held in the shorter run and also represents a one-sided resolution of (19)'s contradiction.

However unrealistic is such a practice, it does provide us with an instructive, extreme case. Now the second equation of (19) is assumed to hold instantaneously, but the lag in time between labor input and corn output is explicitly introduced. Still keeping land superabundant with rent free and keeping $\theta_1 = 1$, we now write (19) as

---

8. We have already seen how the ultimate scarcity of homogeneous or heterogeneous land and the law of diminishing returns would, in a zero-interest or timeless system, cause population to grow until the new a_1 coefficient at the external (or speaking loosely, at the intensive) margin will be such as to just satisfy $1 - c_1 a_1 = 0$. Hence, at such margins (19)'s costs of production of corn and of people are consistent. *Men on the margin* then do work twelve hours per day, and twelve hours per day is just enough to produce *their* subsistence. Men on good land, or the hypothetical first men applied to good land, will in working twelve hours produce their own subsistence and, let's say, an equal amount of produce for landlords. To say that such men produce in six hours *their own* subsistence and work six hours producing *surplus value* for the landlord is always my privilege: but little insight into the laws of motion of the system or its distribution is provided by such a formulation.

(20) $p_1 = w_1 a_1 (1 + i),\ w_1 = c_1 p_1;\ \text{or } 1 + i = \dfrac{1}{c_1 a_1}.$

The rate of interest is now determinable from the (a_1, c_1) coefficients alone!

This is what Ricardo had in mind already in 1813, before the Malthus-West rent theory of 1814 had been published. Ricardo believed that only the limitation on land could explain a falling rate of profit: for if one could always tack on new islands to the existing England, accumulation would spend itself in expanding the scale of population and production with no law of diminishing returns ever coming into play. Neither West nor Ricardo would have believed in Marx's falling rate of profit — on the basis of Marx's usual willingness to ignore rent and to postulate an inexhaustible reserve army of the unemployed.

39. Though Ricardo had many children, one often wonders whether he knew the biological facts of life, so content is he with the assumption that labor will *soon* adjust to its long-run horizontal wage at the subsistence level. Actually, it is unrealistic and inconsistent to make either one of the equations in (19) hold as if it referred to a timeless adjustment. As in equation (4) of Part I, any discrepancy in the equalities of (19) will act as an "error signal" to set up certain dynamic adjustment processes both in the creation of people and of goods: thus, the percentage rate of population growth might be a rising function of the discrepancy of the real wage and the subsistence level; and each greater profit discrepancy between market price and labor cost alone might be expected to give rise to a greater rate of capital accumulation.

I shall not stop to write down a specific model of these dynamic processes. But the general outline of the results is reasonably clear and can be related to the discussion in my cited paper on Marx.

First, it would probably be most natural to assume that some accumulation is going on. This is spending itself in population increase — in a widening of capital. The real wage is above the subsistence-reproduction level by enough to coax out the described rate of endogenous labor increase. The interest rate is positive but less than the $1/a_1 c_1$ level appropriate to instantaneous population growth, the remainder being what has been referred to as the quasi-rent to labor's temporary (but recurring) scarcity.

The above process *could* go along in a geometric or exponential steady state, with only scale expanding and with unchanging wage and profit rates. But Ricardo is wrong to think that in the absence of land shortage the profit rate cannot permanently possibly fall. It can. Provided the propensity to save out of interest income is sufficiently large relative to the requirements for extensive growth of the system, there may actually be a deepening of capital. Capitalists will be trying to save more than mere growth in scale is using; this means they will be bidding among themselves for existing labor, thereby raising the real wage, and undermining the profit rate, and in all probability finding that more roundabout processes now pay. This drop in the profit rate could go on forever. But it is unlikely, so the classicists thought, to bring the profit rate down below a critical equilibrium level. This asymptotic equilibrium level for i will be reached when interest has fallen low, enough to reduce the incomes of savers enough to call forth from them a pace of accumulation no larger than can be absorbed in mere duplication of population and scale.[9]

LAND SCARCITY AND FALLING INTEREST

40. For Ricardo and West a dynamic model which neglects scarcity of land is like a whodunit without a corpse. How does the using up of all the available best land affect the pattern of development? We have seen that as more and more men work on the best land their marginal returns decline; this can be expressed by saying that some kind of an intensive marginal a_1 coefficient goes up, which is the reason why recourse may also be had to poorer qualities of land; and if lands are of continuous grades of quality, we can also concentrate on the extensive marginal a_1, which corresponds to the high labor requirements on that piece of land which is just worth cultivating when you have to pay no rent for it at all.

With a_1 no longer a constant but now a variable over an indefinite range, Ricardo no longer has a determinate formula for the interest rate in terms of technological coefficients alone. (The matter is even worse if large θ_1's can be substituted for smaller a_1's at the margin.) But he correctly felt that the process of accumulation would entail a steadily falling profit rate and higher rent as land became more intensively cultivated and commanded higher rents. As we have seen he rather exaggerated the speed with which real wages would revert to their conventional-subsistence level, and we

9. The critical level might be reached from below, with i rising as accumulation belatedly catches up with population increase. The critical steady state might be at a profit rate so low as to kill off all accumulation and growth. Indeed once scarce land is taken into account, most classical economists would expect accumulation to lead eventually to an interest rate at the floor determined by capital's long-run "subsistence" level of supply, as we shall see.

can cling to the Smith notion that, depending upon how fast accumulation is causing the system to advance, real wages will remain somewhat above the subsistence level.

For intramarginal and marginal lands respectively, we can write down the formulas

$$(21) \qquad p_1 = (wa_1' + rb_1')\,(1 + i)^{\theta_1'}, \qquad p_1 = wa_1''(1 + i)^{\theta_1''}.$$

But even if we knew the real wage to be $1/c_1$, these are not sufficient equations to determine the interest rate, there being a suitable a_1'' to satisfy the last equation for *any* interest rate. Again, we face the fact that the external and internal margins vary in direct response to drops in the interest rate — as Ricardo well realized.

41. The classical economists never did write down an explicit model to determine in each moving short run the level of interest and of the other variables of the system. We cannot criticize them too harshly for this in that the neoclassical economists also — save in very special cases — failed to write down explicit models which determined rigorously the time shape of interest and other variables. These failures seem due to the intrinsic difficulty of getting into two- or few-dimensional diagrams the complexity of the real world's vectors of diverse capital goods and time processes.

Most of the classicists spoke vaguely of some kind of a capital stock or wage fund. By analogy with what happens when you increase the quantity of something so apparently concrete as land or labor, they felt that accumulation of more of this capital stuff would bring down its price — the profit or interest rate. Qualitatively, these vague notions do, I think, lead to the correct insights into the dynamics of a developing, competitive system. But we must not be under any illusion that such notions go far beyond the language of parable.[1]

However, the problem of the storyteller must not be confused with the action of the market place. In the real world engineers combine inputs over time to produce outputs. And merchants and consumers buy and sell securities and goods in various markets. Were it not for imperfections of competition — whose intrinsic difficulties for the analyst are tied up with the *uncertainty of the future* — we could write down in great detail the full set of equations for all the

---

1. Jevons, Böhm-Bawerk, Wicksell and others carried the parable farther. See also Robert Dorfman, Paul A. Samuelson, and Robert M. Solow, *Linear Programming and Economic Analysis* (New York: McGraw-Hill, 1958), Chaps. 11, 12; and P. A. Samuelson and R. M. Solow, "A Complete Capital Model Involving Heterogeneous Capital Goods," this *Journal*, LXX (Nov. 1956), 537–62.

diverse micro-processes that are going on. We would talk of the interest rate for each period along with a host of other intertemporal price ratios. We might also talk of capital asset values, as determined in competitive market places, and as might be added by the recording statistician. But no market would directly hinge on such a defined capital aggregate, and our rigorous theory of interest and general equilibrium could eschew completely the use of any homogeneous aggregate of capital. Thus, we could hope to sidestep completely the index number problem that every social aggregate, including Capital with a capital C, is known to involve intrinsically.

A LONG-RUN, CONSTANT FLOOR FOR INTEREST

42. One of the reasons the classical economists had so weak a theory for short-run interest and wages was that they had so strong a long-run theory. If you believed, as Ricardo somehow did, that wages would soon settle down to their floor as determined by a long-run horizontal schedule of supply, what was the point in elaborating a theory to explain the ephemeral deviations from this level? The same, but to lesser degree, might be said of the long-run level of interest. Ricardo is not so explicit as John Stuart Mill and other classicists, but he does at times come close to the notion of a horizontal long-run supply curve for interest like that for wages. Thus, he says

"Long indeed before this period [of zero interest rate], the very low rate of profits will have arrested all accumulation . . .

"I have already said, that long before this state . . . , there would be no motive for accumulation; for no one accumulates but with a view to make accumulation productive. . . . *The farmer and manufacturer can no more live without profit, than the labourer without wages.* Their motive for accumulation . . . will cease altogether when their profits are so low as not to afford them an adequate compensation for their trouble, and the risk which they must necessarily encounter in employing their capital productively."[2]

43. For the purpose, therefore, of seeing how my land theory of value can be extended to a Ricardian system involving time, I shall interpret the system as literally having a long-run SS schedule for interest like the one shown in Figure IV for wages. Above that critical interest rate accumulation will be taking place; below it, decumulation will be taking place so as to restore it; at it, there will be a stationary equilibrium.

2. *Works*, I, 120, 122; my italics. The last sentence might possibly be interpreted as being compatible with a zero interest rate, once we allow for wages of management and *ex post* losses. It might also open the door to an equilibrium with Keynesian stagnation rather than full employment.

We have then in addition to our (a,b,c) coefficients one new important constant — the long-run interest rate. Let us label this $i = d$. And we must now turn back from a simple one-good economy involving corn alone to a many-good model. The total of homogeneous land, L, is also taken as a given.

The Land Theory Restated

44. Under the postulated conditions, it then follows that my "Ricardian land theory of value" remains intact in the long run.

1. All long-run magnitudes remain directly proportional to the supply of land L.

2. The prices of all goods produced (final and intermediate) and the wage rate all remain in determinate ratio to the rent rate r, *independently of the quantitative pattern of consumption demand.*

3. While the absolute level of total rent or *produit net* depends only on the a,b,c,d coefficients independently of the composition of consumption demand, the absolute and relative sizes of the gross returns to wages and interest will depend upon the quantitative pattern of landlord and capitalist consumption demand.

45. To see all this I suggest we consider a three-good example. Let y_1 (corn) and y_2 (velvets) involve only circulating capital in their production; but follow Ricardo in letting y_2 have, say, twice the time interval that y_1 has between first application of land and labor and ultimate product. (I.e., $\theta_2 = 2\theta_1 = 2$.) Finally, let y_3 (gold) require in addition to labor and land (and one time interval for their action to take effect) also fixed capital in the form of a machine (and one time interval for its co-operative action with land and labor to take effect).

This simple three-good case presents all the complicating difficulties that rightly bothered Ricardo. It involves circulating capital of different degrees of durability. And it involves fixed as well as circulating capital. (Indeed, since the third industry uses new and old machines, we really have a fourth industry that produces machines.)

I now proceed to write down the cost-of-production relations of this system, in order of their simplicity.

(22)

$$
\begin{array}{ll}
\text{(i)} & w = p_1 c_1 \\
\text{(ii)} & p_1 = (wa_1 + rb_1)(1 + d) \\
\text{(iii)} & p_2 = (wa_2 + rb_2)(1 + d)^2 \\[2pt]
\hline \\[-6pt]
\text{(iv)} & p_0 = (wa_0 + rb_0)(1 + d) \\
\text{(v)} & p_3 + e_3 p_0' = (wa_3 + rb_3 + p_0 f_3)(1 + d) \\
\text{(vi)} & p_3 = (wa_3' + rb_3' + p_0' g_3')(1 + d)
\end{array}
$$

The first equation is Ricardo's long-run corn theory of the real wage. The second gives corn's cost of production, as in (17). Before going any farther, we can solve equations (i) and (ii) by simple substitution to determine in terms of the given (a,b,c,d) coefficients the corn level of rent, or corn's price in terms of rent. I leave this to the reader.

Now consider the first three equations alone. By themselves they are enough conditions to enable us to solve for $(w/r, p_1/r, p_2/r)$ in terms of the (a,b,c,d) coefficients alone.

The last three equations are more complicated because they involve the use of fixed capital. Thus, they introduce the unknown price of a new machine, p_0, as determined in (iv) by its cost of production. More complicated is (v), which gives the cost of the third good, gold's p_3; but now it takes f_3 units of the new machine along with labor and land to make gold; and as a by-product, so to speak, the process also leaves us with e_3 old machines, each worth an unknown price p_0'. The last equation gives the same p_3 for gold produced with old machines.

In all we have six equations to determine the six unknowns $(w/r, p_1/r, p_2/r, p_0/r, p_0'/r, p_3/r)$; and provided that (generalized) Hawkins-Simon conditions are satisfied, these will determine unique positive solutions. What is important to emphasize is that *if the primary factors returns (r,d) are given us, the resulting pattern of prices is quite independent of the mix of consumption demand.* Equations (22) make this quite clear in the case of fixed (a,b,c,e,f,θ) coefficients. But even if there were a finite, or infinite, set of substitutable processes in (ii)–(vi), a change in consumers' demand for corn, velvets, or gold would not make any new substitutions profitable.

46. A sketchy proof is given in P. A. Samuelson, "Prices of Factors and Goods In General Equilibrium,"[3] But it needs to be modified to take account of the joint production inherent in (v). Ordinarily, jointness of production will rule out the "substitutability theorem." Thus, if people wanted to consume old machines directly, as well as use them to produce gold, a shift in tastes towards such old machines would tend to raise the price p_0', and probably to lower p_3. Mathematically, new (a,b,e,f) coefficients would be substituted. Or if these were fixed, the last equation would become an inequality once it became too expensive to use old machines to produce gold; but in the production of gold with new machines, it is gold which, so to speak, now becomes the by-product to the production of such valued old machines that are now highly in demand. However, when

3. *Review of Economic Studies*, XXI (1953–54), 19.

we rule out the possibility that machines are anything but intermediate goods, each belonging solely to one consumers good industry, the substitutability theorem is saved.

Recall Section 25's qualification concerning joint consumer goods, venison and deer skin. Similarly, if corn stalks were used in gold production, or if old gold machines were used to produce velvets, the substitutability theorem would be lost. For it to be valid, all jointness must be *within* each vertically integrated single consumer good.

47. *Net product* for society would be proportional to land L. Since there is no accumulation, net product would equal the gross value of all consumers goods minus the goods consumed by laborers and by interest receivers. Why define net product so? In post-Ricardian language, because there is no consumer's or producer's surplus enjoyed by laborers or capitalists, their returns just being enough to cover their costs.

The equation for net product would be

$$(23) \qquad \frac{p_1}{r} Y_1 + \frac{p_2}{r} Y_2 + \frac{p_3}{r} Y_3 = L$$

where the p's come from (22).

While the total value of net product is unaffected by changes in the mix of (Y_i) demand, the total of wages and of interest-bearing capital will definitely depend on that mix. Thus, if landlords (or capitalists) want more labor-intensive goods, the short-run rise in wages will be wiped out by a permanent increase in population, with the typical man ending up no better off than before. Likewise, if final demand moves towards capital-intensive goods, the total interest return and capital value will permanently rise but the return per dollar, d, will stay the same by hypothesis.

A Final Word

49. After examining Ricardo-like models, what feeling are we left with? Were the classical economists fools? Were they gods? What were they?

I for one am left with mixed feelings. Ricardo's logical skills have been, I think, somewhat exaggerated.[4] But they were very considerable. He would have made a most excellent modern economist! Despite though the high native abilities of the ancients, we have advanced a long way ahead of their discussions. Poor as our

4. If Ricardo has been overrated, Smith has in our day perhaps been underrated. I mean as a theorist.

knowledge and insights are, they are way ahead of those of our predecessors.

In particular we are more humble. They declared so many things to be necessarily so that we today recognize as not having to be so. This is, in a sense, a step backward. How exciting to be able to assert definitely that invention of a machine cannot do this and must do that! But, alas, dull as it may be, the modern theorist must face the facts of life — the infinite multiplicity of patterns that can emerge in actuality. Good, advanced theory must be the antidote for overly-simple, intuitive theory.

MASSACHUSETTS INSTITUTE OF TECHNOLOGY

BOOK TWO

Topics in Mathematical Economics

PART V

Essays on Linear Programming and Economic Analysis

33

MARKET MECHANISMS AND MAXIMIZATION[1]

Since at least the time of Adam Smith and Cournot, economic theory has been concerned with maximum and minimum problems. Modern "neoclassical marginalism" represents the culmination of this interest.

In comparatively recent times, mathematicians concerned with complex problems of internal planning of the U.S. Air Force or other large units have developed a set of theories and procedures closely related to the maximum problems of economic theory. The name of this technical field is "linear programming." Within the U.S. Air Force and outside, considerable progress has been made on the mathematical theory of linear programming and on its practical application to administrative problems. But to most economists it remains only a name, if indeed they have heard of it at all.

The following study has one primary purpose — to provide an exposition of linear programming that students of economic theory can understand and can relate to the existing body of economic theory. I assume only a minimum of mathematical knowledge on the part of the reader.

I have benefited from reading unpublished memoranda of Tjalling Koopmans of the Cowles Commission, George Dantzig of Project SCOOP. At RAND I am indebted to George W. Brown and others.

[1]This chapter was originally published as two research memoranda (Parts I and II on March 28, 1949, and Part III on June 29, 1949) by the RAND Corporation, Santa Monica, California.

I. The Theory of Comparative Advantage

Introduction

Professional economists are often impressed with the efficiency of a price system in realizing prescribed goals. A whole technical literature of "welfare economics" dealing with this subject has grown up; and there even exists a school of thought that would "play the game of competition" in order to solve the complex problems of a completely planned socialist state.

In the last year interest in linear programming has grown, within the Air Force and elsewhere. But just as many people have been speaking prose all their lives without knowing it, so for centuries have problems of linear programming been presenting themselves for solution.

The question therefore arises: In the new branch of "linear programming" will there be any computational methods suggested by pursuing the logic of a market mechanism? This study is an attempt to explore certain aspects of the problem, beginning with an analysis of the well-known "theory of comparative advantage."

International Comparative Advantage

More than a century ago the English economist David Ricardo outlined a simple theory to explain the actual pattern of international trade and to proclaim its benefits to all participating countries. A traditional numerical example (somewhat simplified) is of the following form: Portugal can divert resources from food to clothing production and in effect convert one unit of food into one unit of clothing; England, on the other hand, can convert one unit of food into two units of clothing.

Almost certainly Portugal will specialize completely in food, England completely in clothing. England will export clothing in exchange for food imports, the "terms of trade" (or barter price ratio) being almost certainly somewhere between one-food-for-one-clothing and one-food-for-two-clothing. Both countries will be better off than if they do not specialize. World production will be "optimal."

These four economic conclusions are really nothing but mathematical truisms or theorems within the field of linear programming. Mathematically, we may consider any one country — say England — to be subject to a linear relation ("production possibility" curve) of the type shown in Figure 1. Thus

$$(1) \qquad 2x_1 + x_2 \leq C, \qquad\qquad x_1 \geq 0, x_2 \geq 0$$

If there exists an international price ratio, p_1/p_2, somewhere between 1 and 2, at which it can convert food into clothing, the real value of England's National Product (expressed in clothing units) may be written as

(2) $\qquad Z = \left(\dfrac{p_1}{p_2}\right) x_1 + x_2 \quad$ or, say, $\quad Z = 1.5x_1 + x_2$

The problem is to maximize National Product, NP, subject to the technical production-possibility curve of England. Or, mathematically, to maximize a linear sum of the form (2) subject to a linear inequality of the form (1). This is a typical problem of linear programming.

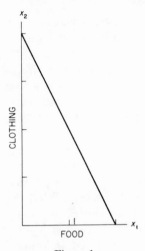

Figure 1

Graphical or numerical experimentation will soon convince one that the highest NP will be reached only when $x_1 = 0$, $x_2 = C$, and $Z =$ NP $= C$.[2] Any other solution will lead to lower NP. Thus, if unemployment is allowed to develop so that England is *inside* its production-possibility curve, NP will suffer. Or if it should specialize on the wrong commodity, food, then NP will turn out to be only $.75C = (1.5/2.0)C$.

The reader may easily verify that for Portugal the best production

---

[2]This may be seen by superimposing on Figure 1 *contour lines of equal NP*. These will be a family of parallel lines all with a slope of (p_1/p_2); these parallel lines will be flatter than the single production-possibility line of Figure 1, because the price ratio is less than 2. We want to get up to the highest NP line, which we can do only by climbing northwest along the production-possibility line until we reach the X_2 intercept, where food production is zero. If negative numbers are allowed, we would want to continue moving northwest indefinitely. This is what happens in an arbitrage situation where two powerful and rich agencies try to maintain different relative price ratios between the same pair of commodities. In this case, little chaps named Gresham who are on their toes can make a lot of money, buying cheap and selling dear and repeating the process indefinitely — or rather until one of the agencies runs out of one of the goods or changes its mind about its price pegging. Buying and selling introduces negative as well as positive numbers. But in linear programming, all variables must usually be nonnegative.

pattern, when p_1/p_2 is greater than 1, involves zero clothing production and complete specialization on food. Only in that way will she maximize her NP:

$$(3) \qquad Z' = 1.5x_1' + x_2' = \left(\frac{p_1}{p_2}\right) x_1' + x_2'$$

subject to

$$x_1' + x_2' \le C'$$

The Mathematical Problem

Under atomistic competition, where there are numerous competing firms in each country, all this will come about automatically without the conscious deliberation or intervention of any planning body. But there is nothing very surprising about this. After all, we have been describing a commercial situation, and it is very natural that we should have had to use commercial and economic language in doing so. There was nothing shadowy or contrived about the prices used, p_1/p_2; they were real and concrete.

However, fingers were made before forks, and we can imagine this situation as it might appear to a naïve scientist from Mars who had never heard about prices and competitive private enterprise. He might still ask the noncommercial question: What is the "optimal" pattern of world production of food and clothing between England and Portugal? If he was acute, the Martian scientist would be troubled by his own question, particularly by the word in quotation marks — "optimal." Optimal in what sense? Certainly not — as we have already agreed — in the sense of money value, since this is a precommercial stage of world history. The scientist might be tempted to consider evaluating food and clothing by their "intrinsic worth"; but unless he had been contaminated by a course in heavy German philosophy, he would soon realize that this is an undefinable concept for food and clothing in a world where some people are more like peacocks and others more like gluttons.

An omniscient Martian would soon settle for a more modest definition of the optimum. He would say "I don't know how the final choice between food and clothing is to be made, whether English millionaires will have the greatest say, or the United Nations Commission on Living Standards. But it is my job as a production expert to give *the world the best menu from which to choose*. Or in other words, for each specified amount of any one good — say food — I must make sure that the production of the other good is as large as possible."

In saying this, the scientist has unwittingly defined a definite class of problems in linear programming. Prices as such have nothing to do with the problem, although — like Voltaire's God — it may be desirable to invent them if they do not exist! To the economist, at least, it will seem natural to introduce a system of "shadow" or accounting prices or some sort of system of numerical points. If such shadow prices are really useful, then it follows that many problems of linear programming may benefit on the computational side from a process of imitating the market mechanism.

But first let us write down the mathematical problem that the scientist has posed for himself. He wants (a) to maximize the total of clothing production in Portugal and England, subject to (b) a prescribed total of food, and subject to (c) the two linear production-possibility constraints of the two countries, and where (d) all quantities must by their nature not be negative numbers. Mathematically,

$$Z = X_2 = x_2 + x_2{}'$$

is to be a maximum subject to

$$x_1 + x_1{}' \geq X_1$$

(4) $$2x_1 + x_2 \leq C,$$

$$x_1{}' + x_2{}' \leq C' \quad \text{and} \quad x_1 \geq 0,\, x_2 \geq 0,\, x_1{}' \geq 0,\, x_2{}' \geq 0$$

This is a typical problem of linear programming, which is defined as the problem of maximizing one linear relation subject to a number of linear inequalities.

Note that with C and C' being given, there will be a different best Z (or X_2) for each prescribed X_1. Actually our economic intuition — if pushed far enough — tells us that the resulting "menu" or world production-possibility curve looks like that shown in Figure 2.

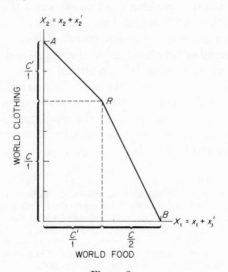

Figure 2

The flatter of the two line segments has a slope of -1, equal to Portugal's food-clothing technical ratio; the steeper segment has a slope of -2, corresponding to the similar technical ratio for England. The absolute maximum of X_2 (corresponding to zero X_1) occurs at A, where all resources in both countries are used to produce X_2 alone, giving us (from the technical relations) $C/1 + C'/1$ of clothing. The maximum of food comes at B, where all resources in both countries are going to food, and yielding in all $C/2 + C'/1$ of food.

The critical corner-point on the $X_2 - X_1$ curve occurs at R, where England is specializing completely on clothing and Portugal on food. It might be called the "Ricardo point," since it is there that the classical theory of comparative advantage tells us we will *almost* certainly end up.[3]

There is another remarkable economic feature of our final so-called "world opportunity cost relation between food and clothing." The curve is a *concave* one: In economic terminology, the "marginal opportunity cost" of converting one good into the other is increasing as we want more of any one good. Or, more accurately, it is *nondecreasing*, since along any one of the line segments it is constant, neither increasing or decreasing. But between line segments it is strongly increasing, a result that may seem at first surprising in view of the so-called constant cost assumptions of the classical theory of comparative advantages.

Economic and mathematical importance attaches to the concept of marginal cost as defined by $(- dX_2/dX_1)$, the absolute slope of our curve. To the left of the Ricardo point this is exactly equal to one of the technical coefficients of the problem, that of Portugal. To the right, it is equal to the corresponding coefficient of England. At the critical point R it is, strictly speaking, undefined, since the right-hand and left-hand limits that define a mathematical derivative are different. We may adopt the convention whereby marginal cost at such a point is defined as any number between the limiting right- and left-hand slopes. A similar problem arises in defining marginal cost at the limiting intercept points where the curve hits the axes. It is natural and convenient to define MC at such a point as the upper intercept on the X_2 axis, A, as any number equal to or less than the absolute right-hand slope at that point; that is, MC is one or any number *less* than one. Similarly, at the lower intercept the MC or slope is any number equal to or *greater* than 2.[4]

---

[3]The classical economists recognize that the word "almost" is needed in order to take account of the possibility that the final market price ratio might be at the *limit* of the range of differing comparative costs instead of *within* the range. This case was considered especially likely if one country was big compared with the other. In such cases, where the final price ratio settles at the cost ratio of one of the countries, production within that country would be indeterminate. The actual result will have to be dictated by the final pattern of international demand.

[4]We define MC at any point on the curve as the numerical slope of any straight

Economic Considerations

An economic theorist who is used to thinking of problems in terms of market situations will immediately be struck by a rather remarkable fact: The purely technical concept of MC or slope, which could be arrived at from the pure logic of the maximum problem without reference to prices or markets, does behave remarkably like a market price ratio. His economic intuition tells him:

1. When $1 < p_1/p_2 < 2$, each country will specialize on its best product, and the world will in fact be at the Ricardo point where $1 \leq MC \leq 2$.

2. When $p_1/p_2 < 1$ (or > 2), both countries will specialize completely on the same product, and the world will actually be at one (or the other) intercept with $MC \leq 1$ (or ≥ 2).

3. When $p_1/p_2 = 1$ (or $= 2$), we will actually be anywhere on one (or the other) of the two line segments with MC, if uniquely defined, being $= 1$ (or $= 2$).

Not only does a market price ratio have the properties of world MC, but by creating a shadow price ratio even where none existed and playing the game of competition, we could end up at any specific point of the final optimal locus. Moreover, in the special case of this problem where the production conditions in the two countries are independent, the problem of decision-making can be in a certain sense decentralized and partitioned into separate parts.

Shadow Prices

Thus, if we invent a parameter λ which is to play the role of a shadow price, p_1/p_2, we can split our original maximum problem into two quasi-separate ones. Instead of maximizing

I. $\qquad Z = x_2 + x_2'$

subject to

$$x_1 + x_1' \geq X_1$$
$$2x_1 + x_2 \leq C, \qquad\qquad x_1 \geq 0, x_2 \geq 0$$
$$x_1' + x_2' \leq C', \qquad\qquad x_1' \geq 0, x_2' \geq 0$$

let us separately maximize

II. $\qquad z = \lambda x_1 + x_2$

---

line that "touches" but does not "cut" the curve at that point, i.e., the slope of a line that never lies inside the curve, but does touch it at the point in question, or the slope of a "supporting plane."

subject to

$$2x_1 + x_2 \leq C, \qquad\qquad x_1 \geq 0, x_2 \geq 0$$

and

II'. $\quad z' = \lambda x_1' + x_2'$

subject to

$$x_1' + x_2' \leq C', \qquad\qquad x_1' \geq 0, x_2' \geq 0$$

There is some choice of λ for which separate optimal solutions to the latter problems, II and II', do add up to the optimal solution to I for any X_1. Also, it is clear that solving both II and II' is equivalent to solving the world problem of maximizing

$$Z = z + z' = \lambda(x_1 + x_1') + (x_2 + x_2')$$

subject to

I'. $\quad 2x_1 + x_2 \leq C, \qquad\qquad x_1 \geq 0, x_2 \geq 0$

$\qquad x_1' + x_2' \leq C', \qquad\qquad x_1' \geq 0, x_2' \geq 0$

To arrive at an optimal point (on our $X_2 - X_1$ locus) of each of the following types:

(a) At the upper or X_2 intercept, A
(b) On the upper flat-line segment, AR
(c) At the Ricardo point, R
(d) On the lower steep-line segment, RB
(e) At the lower or X_1 intercept, B,

we must have

(a) $\lambda \leq 1$
(b) $\lambda = 1$
(c) $1 \leq \lambda \leq 2$
(d) $\lambda = 2$
(e) $2 \leq \lambda$

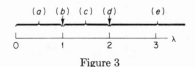

Figure 3

As λ grows from small to large, X_1 goes from nothing to the maximum, always at the expense of X_2.

Internal Shadow Prices

From an economist's viewpoint the problem can be decentralized even further. Consider the maximum problem within any one of the countries, such as England. A central planning board could issue shut-down orders so as to maximize

$$z = \lambda x_1 + x_2$$

subject to

$$2x_1 + x_2 \leq C, \qquad\qquad x_1 \geq 0, x_2 \geq 0$$

But, alternatively, we might abolish all planning agents and think of food and clothing industries each made up of a myriad of small inde-pendent firms. They incur costs and earn revenues from the sale of their products. This they do by converting resources into products. So far we have not spoken much about the character of the resources involved (labor as in Ricardo's theory, etc.). But it will be obvious on reflection that C is a sort of measure of total resources that can be parceled out to the various firms in the two industries, provided that all the little c's provided to the firms must add up to not more than C. Also, the pro-duction function of, say, the 999th food producer is of the form

$$x_{1,\ 999} \leq \tfrac{1}{2}\, c_{1,\ 999}$$

and the corresponding production function of the 77th clothing firm is

$$x_{2,\ 77} \leq c_{2,\ 77}$$

where total output of England's food is the sum of all food firms' output

$$X_1 = x_{1,\ 1} + \cdots + x_{1,\ 999} + \cdots$$

and total England's clothing is

$$X_2 = x_{2,\ 1} + \cdots + x_{2,\ 77} + \cdots$$

and where, so to speak, the total of all resources used by all firms cannot exceed the total of all resources available in the country; or where

$$C \geq c_{1,\ 1} + \cdots + c_{1,\ 999} + \cdots \text{ plus } c_{2,\ 1} + \cdots + c_{2,\ 77} + \cdots$$

Note too that England's grand production-possibility curve as given earlier in Figure 1 or Equation (1) is simply an aggregation of these individual firm production relations.

One minor point should be noted. Why is there an inequality in the production functions? This is because a firm may be inefficient and not be getting as much product as known technology permits. It must be shown that such inefficient behavior — which is clearly inconsistent with a final optimum — will in fact be heavily penalized by a competitive market and thus be eliminated. The similar inequality with respect to the sum of the c's, which would imply wasteful unemployment of avail-able resources, will also turn out to be prohibited by a perfect market mechanism.

To the Martian with world vision, λ is a shadow price constructed for a purpose; to the domestic English planners interested in maximizing the value of English NP, as in II, λ is a real enough external price, or barter ratio at which goods can be converted into each other by international trade. The time has now arrived for the English planners to introduce some new shadow prices, or internal accounting point-prices, of the following form.

Establish the following three shadow prices:

λ_1 = price of food = λ
λ_2 = price of clothing = 1 by convention[5]
λ_3 = price of resources, C

Then for any food producer, say the 999th, the profit statement

$$\text{Total Revenue} - \text{Total Cost} = \lambda_1 x_{1,\,999} - \lambda_3 c_{1,\,999}$$

and the "profitability per unit of output" will be

$$\pi_{1,\,999} = \lambda - \lambda_3 \frac{c_{1,\,999}}{x_{1,\,999}} \leq \lambda - \lambda_3 2$$

from the production function for food.

Similarly, for the 77th clothing producer, unit profits are

$$\pi_{2,\,77} = 1 - \lambda_3 \frac{c_{2,\,77}}{x_{2,\,77}} \leq 1 - \lambda_3$$

In these profit expressions, we may omit the inequality signs whenever we are speaking of most-efficient producers. How shall the prices of resources be determined? At first let us suppose that there is an all-powerful Office of Price Administration that will use high intelligence to solve this problem, but that once the best price has been established we shall try to rely on the quasi-automatic response of competing firms to determine appropriate output as quantities.

The planning authorities will probably set up some such rule of behavior for firms as follows:

(a) If you make losses, you must contract your scale of operations until finally you go out of business.

(b) If you make positive profits, you may (and hence will) expand your scale of operations at some positive rate.

(c) If you just break even with zero profits, let us for the moment say you stand pat at any existing level of activity.

[5]The price of food has here been arbitrarily set equal to the given international price, λ. This step could be deduced as a theorem by creating a third class of firms that are arbitraging exporters or importers. But this is so obvious a result that I have short-circuited the exposition and simply assumed this step. It is clear in any case that only the ratios of the λ's are important.

In terms of this rule, there are certain obvious things that the OPA must do in setting the best price or wage for resources. At the least, λ_3 must be set so as *not to lead to positive profits anywhere in the system* — in other words, set so high that even the most-efficient producers in clothing and food are unable to realize surplus profits. This means we must have

$$\pi_{1,\,999} = \lambda - 2\lambda_3 \leq 0 \cdots \quad \text{or} \quad \lambda_3 \geq \frac{\lambda}{2}$$

$$\pi_{2,\,77} = 1 - \lambda_3 \leq 0, \text{ etc.,} \quad \text{or} \quad \lambda_3 \geq 1$$

It will be noted that there is no longer an inequality sign accompanying the left-hand equality signs in such a profit expression. This is because we are considering the profitability of the most-efficient producers of food and clothing; not even they are permitted to have (excess) profits.

Our specified conditions determine a minimum below which λ_3 must not go, but they do not rule out still higher shadow prices. However, it is reasonable to add the further condition that *profits are not to be every-where negative* — that they are to be *somewhere* zero. Otherwise, no firms could stay permanently in business and the total of resources used would be zero, and all production and income would also be zero.

If the equality sign must hold for at least one of our profit expressions, it follows logically that

$$\lambda_3 = \frac{\lambda}{2} \text{ or } 1, \text{ whichever is greater}$$

$$= \text{Max}\left(\frac{\lambda}{2},\, 1\right)$$

This means that if $\lambda = 1.5$, as in our earlier example, we must set our shadow price equal to Max $(3/4, 1)$ or to 1. This yields negative profits for all food firms and zero profits for all most-efficient clothing firms; profits for inefficient food firms are always negative.

If our extreme price ratio should be $\lambda = 4$, then $\lambda_3 = \text{Max}\,(2, 1) = 2$, and it is clothing that has negative profits. Only in the critical case where $\lambda = 2$ will both industries be capable of simultaneous operation.

Our OPA has solved its price problem satisfactorily. But there is one major difficulty about our set-up when it comes to determining the exact quantities of resources and output. This difficulty is a consequence of the extreme constant-cost assumption involved in all simple versions of linear programming, assumptions that put the word "linear" into the name of the subject. At our final best price, firms are not forced all to contract or all to expand indefinitely. Efficient firms in the proper industry are permitted to have a large or small output. But there is nothing driving them in total toward 100 per cent use of society's resources, neither more nor less. The atomistic firms are suspended in a kind of *neutral* equilibrium: they have no incentive to do other than what they are doing. Profit considerations neither encourage nor discourage them from doing what society desires.

At the very last stage OPA must call upon the WPB (War Production Board) for a few mild direct quantity fiats. Once the proper prices have been promulgated by the pricing authorities, the production authority does not have to use much intelligence; but it does have to use a little. It must lead the neutral (efficient) producers — by their mustaches so to speak — to use up exactly 100 per cent of the available resources.

If the actual amount of total resources currently in use at time t is called $C(t)$, then

$$C(t) = c_{1,\,1} + \cdots + c_{1,\,999} + \cdots$$

plus

$$c_{2,\,1} + \cdots + c_{2,\,77} + \cdots$$

The WPB must make sure that

$$C(t) = C$$

if a true optimum is to be reached, and it must have the intelligence to recognize this condition.

Automatic Determination of Price and Quantity

Actually, it seems reasonable to expect that a market mechanism can be set up which, more or less automatically and without the use of centralized intelligence or planning, will simultaneously determine both the best price and quantity.

Imagine an auctioneer (or ticker tape) that causes λ_3 to grow whenever total resources used, $C(t)$, exceeds the available amount of C (thought of as being the average amount available over a longer period of time when no temporary stockpiles of resources can be drawn upon). Suppose the market price automatically falls at a rate proportional to any deficiency of $C(t)$ below C. When there is exactly full employment and $C(t) = C$, then price is constant and $d\lambda_3/dt$ is zero.

Dynamically, this means that we have the following law of growth or decay of price:

$$\alpha \frac{d\lambda_3}{dt} = [C(t) - C] + \cdots$$

where α is a positive proportionality factor or time constant, and where any nonlinear powers of $[C(t) - C]$ have been neglected.

To make our system completely automatic and self-generating, we need to have some law of growth for $C(t)$. Our earlier rule that firms have to follow provides us with such a law. Whenever λ_3 went above the level at which efficient firms could anywhere make profits, firms contracted their use of resources. When λ_3 fell below said critical level, the growth of resources in use was made to be proportional to this deficiency of price. In crude mathematical terms, we have in effect

$$-\beta \frac{dC(t)}{dt} = [\lambda_3 - \lambda_3{}^0] + \cdots$$

where $\lambda_3{}^0$ is the (as yet unknown) equilibrium value [which will turn out to be Max $(\lambda/2, 1)$], where higher powers of the term in brackets can be neglected, and where β is a positive proportionality factor.[6]

Our combined dynamic equations form a determinate system. Any initial price and quantity situation $[C(t), \lambda_3(t)]$ will generate its own laws of motion over time, according to the relations

$$\alpha \frac{d\lambda_3}{dt} = [C(t) - C], \lambda_3(t) \geq 0$$

$$-\beta \frac{dC(t)}{dt} = [\lambda_3 - \lambda_3{}^0], C(t) \geq 0$$

If price of resources or the wage stays too high, profits will be negative, and employment will be dropping; as employment drops below the full-employment level, the wage will begin to fall; finally profits will be positive, and employment will begin to grow rather than fall; it then may — and actually will — overshoot the full-employment level, and we are off on another oscillatory cycle around the equilibrium position.

It is a fairly obvious that the system can never come to rest except at the equilibrium levels $(C, \lambda_3{}^0)$. It is also fairly obvious from the arrows in Figure 4a that the system will oscillate around the equilibrium. (For example, when we have both shadow wage and employment above their equilibrium levels, the wage will be still rising, and employment will be falling — as shown by the arrows pointing northwest in the Quadrant I above and to the right of the equilibrium point, E; and so forth, for Quadrants II, III, and IV.)

It is not at all obvious whether the system will finally settle down to rest, or oscillate ever more explosively, or just wobble back and forth in an undamped and unexplosive "conservative" fashion. Actually, as Figure 4b shows, the system will behave like a frictionless pendulum and wobble indefinitely without growing or declining in amplitude. If we start out near enough to the equilibrium, the averages of our variables over time will be very near to the correct values; this is because the

[6]Strictly speaking, our constant-cost assumptions leave the specified relation undefined for $\lambda_3 - \lambda_3{}^0 = 0$. It will not matter if we have the firms with zero profits stand pat, because in any case profits will be exactly zero for only an instant and not long enough for them to have changed their operations appreciably. Note that implicit "inertia" assumptions are involved in all of the postulated dynamic laws.

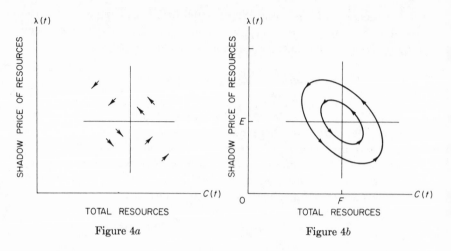

Figure 4a   Figure 4b

concentric ellipse that the system travels along will then be a very small one.

Actual market systems often behave something like the one just described, as modified by speculation and other factors.[7] But I am not so much concerned with the realism of this description of actual markets or with the feasibility of playing the game of shadow prices to solve actual administrative problems. Rather I am trying in this study to elucidate the theory of linear programming and to see whether economic intuition suggests any computational methods for the solution of purely mathematical problems of linear programming. The next section of this study explores the matter further by means of an extended discussion of a problem involving the minimum-adequate-diet problem, which involved many more variables.

II. The Cheapest-Adequate-Diet Problem

In the first part of this study the simplest Ricardian theory of comparative advantage was shown to be a typical problem in the new field of "linear programming." Some tentative explorations into the role of real and shadow prices were indicated. The successive steps in the analysis were suggested in a natural way by a post-mortem of familiar and well-understood market situations.

It would seem desirable now to apply the suggested mode of attack

---

[7]In the next section, dealing with minimum cost of an adequate diet, I shall show how certain kinds of speculation may actually cause the system to damp down to the correct equilibrium. It should be noted that in many setups more than 100 per cent of full employment is impossible, so that the oscillations are asymmetrical.

to a quite different problem of purely internal planning at the technical or biological level, where shadow prices play no obvious role. Finding the cheapest diet that meets prescribed nutritional standards provides such a problem. It has been studied by Stigler and others[8] and represents a good pedagogical case study in the field of linear programming.

Statement of the Problem

Health standards. The National Research Council (NRC) has set forward a table purporting to show, on the basis of present scientific knowledge, the minimum (annual) amounts of different nutritional elements — calories, niacin, vitamin D, etc. — that a typical adult should have. Opinions change rapidly in this field, and no claim can be made for great accuracy in such a specification. Moreover, the penalties for having less than these amounts are known only for extreme cases of unbalanced diets; and furthermore, too much of some elements, such as calories, may be as harmful as too little. But for our purposes we may take the information as definitive and write it symbolically as in Table I.

Table I

Minimum Nutritional Elements

1	2	3	...	i	...	m
C_1	C_2	C_3	...	C_i	...	C_m

Nutritional composition of foods. Our second bit of information comes from biologists and chemists. It analyzes the nutritional content of a large number of common foods (cooked in some agreed-upon way). We may call these foods, measured in their appropriate units, X_1, X_2, $\cdots$, X_n. We shall make the (somewhat doubtful) assumption that there is a constant amount of each nutritional element in *each* unit of any given food; so that if 10 units of X_1 gives us 100 calories, 20 units will give us 200, and 100 units will give us 1,000 calories — all this independently of the other X's that are being simultaneously consumed. This "constant-return-to-scale" and "independence" assumption helps to keep the problem within the simpler realms of linear programming theory. It also permits us to summarize our second type of information in Table II.

In words, the amount of the 3rd nutritional element contained in the 7th commodity is a_{37}. If we think of one slice of toast as having 50 calories, we could say $a_{\text{calories, toast}} = 50$ (calories per slice), etc.

[8]G. J. Stigler, "The Cost of Subsistence," *Journal of Farm Economics*, Vol. XXVII (1945), pp. 303–314; also an earlier unpublished memo by Jerome Cornfield.

P. A. Samuelson, "Comparative Statics and the Logic of Economic Maximizing," *Review of Economic Studies*, Vol. XIV (1946–1947), pp. 41–43.

Table II

Nutritional Content of Various Commodities, per Unit

Nutritional Element	Commodities							Minimum Standards
	X_1	X_2	X_3	...	X_k	...	X_n	
Element 1	a_{11}	a_{12}	a_{13}	...	a_{1k}	...	a_{1n}	C_1
Element 2	a_{21}	a_{22}	a_{23}	...	a_{2k}	...	a_{2n}	C_2
...	...	...	...	...	...	...	...	...
Element i	a_{i1}	a_{i2}	a_{i3}	...	a_{ik}	...	a_{in}	C_i
...	...	...	...	...	...	...	...	...
Element m	a_{m1}	a_{m2}	a_{m3}	...	a_{mk}	...	a_{mn}	C_m

Usually the number of goods will be much greater than the known number of nutritional elements, so that $n > m$. But this need not be the case; indeed, it would not be the case on a desert island or for a community subject to many taboos. So long as we can find one food that contains something of a given prescribed element, it is clear that the given standard of nutrition can somehow be reached. (This means that we must not have *all* the a's equal to zero in any row). Ordinarily, the prescribed standard of nutrition $(C_1, C_2, \cdots, C_i, \cdots, C_m)$ can be reached and surpassed in a variety of different ways or diets; but the different diets will not all be equally tasty or cheap.

How do we test whether a given diet, say,

$$(X_1, X_2, \cdots, X_k, \cdots, X_n) = (100, 550, \cdots, 3.5, \cdots, 25{,}000)$$

is adequate? We must test each nutritional element in turn. Since each unit of the first good contains a_{11} units of the first element, we get, all together, $a_{11}X_1$ of such an element from the first good. Similarly, we get $a_{12}X_2$ of this first element from the second good. We must compare the sum of this element *from all goods in the diet* with the prescribed minimum C_1, to make sure that

$$a_{11}X_1 + a_{12}X_2 + \cdots + a_{1k}X_k + \cdots + a_{1n}X_n \geq C_1$$

and, similarly, for the second element we must have

$$a_{21}X_1 + a_{22}X_2 + \cdots + a_{2k}X_k + \cdots + a_{2n}X_n \geq C_2$$

and so forth, for the ith or mth element.

We have not yet introduced the cost of food into the picture, but when we do, it will become apparent that it is desirable not to have to pay for any excess consumption of food. In the preceding equations we should like — if possible — to have the equality signs hold rather than the inequalities. But this will not always be possible, as an ambitious dietician might discover after trying to find a diet that *exactly* reaches the prescribed standard in every respect. And even where it is, in fact, possible, she will discover that it is an exceedingly difficult arithmetical feat to find such an exact diet. Moreover, and this may surprise her still more, it may turn out to be most economical *not* to follow such an exact diet, since there will often turn out to be a cheaper diet that overshoots the mark in some respect.

To show that an exact diet may be impossible, consider the case where every food contains more than twice as much of the first element as of the second; and suppose that the NRC asks for equal amounts of the two elements. Obviously, the guinea pig must eventually consume an excess of the first element if he is to have enough of the second element.[9]

Where there are many "varied" foods, a number of different exact diets may exist. But the dietician will feel frustrated in her attempt to find out by trial and error. If she adds more meat to make up a deficit of protein, she may create an excess of calories, and she finds herself constantly in the position of the old lady, who in picking up one bundle drops several others.

In some cases her search for an exact diet would be a relatively easy one. Suppose there exist "pure foods" that consist solely of each of the nutritional elements. Thus a concentrate of Vitamin D would be a commodity with the convenient property of containing nothing else; in its vertical column in Table II, there would be zeros everywhere except in the Vitamin D row. If such a pure food or concentrate existed for every element, an exact diet could be easily concocted from these pure elements alone; or such pure elements could be added in the easily recognized necessary amounts to supplement any diet that fell anywhere within the prescribed standards. Such pure foods are commercially available in many cases, but as everyone knows, they are usually quite expensive, so that it is usually cheaper to sacrifice exactness and get some excess of cheaper foods.[10]

The NRC standards refer to an average normal person. It is easy to imagine cases where, because of disease or other reasons, the prescribed standards must be altered and where the category of permitted foods might be greatly narrowed. This might even lead to an impossible situation in which all the equations could not be satisfied. Thus a patient suffering from certain digestive disturbances might require large amounts of fats; but if he is at the same time suffering from a circulatory disorder that cannot tolerate fats, there may still be found a starchy diet that will meet the situation. However, if a disorder of the pancreas is also

[9] In this case the matrix a is such that the equation $ax = C$ does not have a non-negative solution in the variables, x. This may be because a is of rank less than m, or because the solution yields negative x's.

[10] If we could imagine that there existed a continuous range of meats, say, with all gradations of calorie-protein ratios, then some of the earlier-mentioned difficulties in finding an exact diet would be obviated. This shows that where many "varied" foods are available, an "almost exact" diet can be fairly easily approximated.

present, there may be no known resolution of the incompatible biological demands, with the final outcome obvious and unpleasant.

Because I am interested in the deductive aspects of linear programming, I do not wish to go further into the biological relevance of the simplified linear relations assumed in this problem. But one of the big bottlenecks in the fruitful application of linear programming is the problem of setting up hypotheses which are in reasonable agreement with empirical reality and in filling in the postulated numerical constants. I suspect that a competent student of nutrition, who carefully examined the laboratory procedures for isolating vitamins and determining food contents, could show that a person would be ill-advised to take Tables I and II at their face value. In picking a best diet on the basis of such data, he might inadvertently aid science in isolating new vitamins, sacrificing his health in the attempt.

Economic price data. Thus far, no mention has been made of the economic costs, in terms of dollars, of the various diets. In theory we can hope to get from the Bureau of Labor Statistics (BLS) data on the prices of the different goods, such as might be indicated in Table III.

Table III

Price (per Unit) of Different Goods

Number or Name of Commodity	X_1	X_2	...	X_k	...	X_n
Price (per Unit)	P_1	P_2	...	P_k	...	P_n

For any given diet $(x_1, x_2, \cdots, x_n)$, the total cost would be easily calculated as the sum of the costs of each of the n goods (it being understood that in any one diet only a few of the possible array of foods would appear, the rest having zero weight). Mathematically, the total dollar cost of a diet would be

$$Z = P_1 x_1 + P_2 x_2 + \cdots + P_k x_k + \cdots + P_n x_n$$

We may state the full problem as that of minimizing this last sum subject to the m basic inequalities which guarantee that the minimum of each nutritional element is in fact secured. That is,

(5) $$Z = P_1 x_1 + \cdots + P_n x_n$$

is to be a minimum subject to

$$a_{11}x_1 + \cdots + a_{1n}x_n \geq C_1 \qquad\qquad x_1 \geq 0$$

and

$$a_{21}x_1 + \cdots + a_{2n}x_n \geq C_2 \qquad\qquad x_2 \geq 0$$
$$\cdots \qquad\qquad\qquad\qquad \cdots$$
$$a_{m1}x_1 + \cdots + a_{mn}x_n \geq C_m \qquad\qquad x_n \geq 0$$

It is clear that every such problem has a least-cost solution which will be realized by one or more optimal diets. It is also clear that information contained in Tables I, II, and III uniquely defines the problem and can be summarized by the following shorthand description of the data:

$$
(6) \quad
\begin{bmatrix}
a_{11} & a_{12} & \cdots & a_{1k} & \cdots & a_{1n} & C_1 \\
a_{21} & a_{22} & \cdots & a_{2k} & \cdots & a_{2n} & C_2 \\
\cdot & \cdot & & \cdot & & \cdot & \cdot \\
a_{m1} & a_{m2} & \cdots & a_{mk} & \cdots & a_{mn} & C_m \\
P_1 & P_2 & \cdots & P_k & \cdots & P_n &
\end{bmatrix}
\quad \text{or} \quad
\begin{bmatrix}
a & C \\
P &
\end{bmatrix}
$$

A Numerical Example

A simple hypothetical example will illustrate the nature of the problem. Assume only two nutritional elements, 1 and 2, or "calories" and "vitamins," with $(C_1, C_2) = (700, 400)$. Assume that there are 5 foods; let the first, X_1, contain only calories as given by a coefficient $a_{11} = 1$, with a_{21} being zero; let the second, X_2, contain only vitamins as indicated by a given $a_{22} = 1$, with a_{12} being zero; let the third good be like the first in that it contains only calories so that $a_{13} = 1$ and $a_{23} = 0$; let the fourth good contain something of both elements, and where for simplicity we can define our nutritional elements' units so that a_{41} and a_{42} are equal to each other and to unity; and finally let the fifth good possess relatively twice as many calories compared with vitamins as does the fourth good so that $a_{25} = 1$ and $a_{15} = 2$. Finally, we must assume some prices to make the problem complete; thus let $(P_1, P_2, P_3, P_4, P_5) = (2, 20, 3, 11, 12)$, where all prices are in dollars per unit.

Our numerical data can be summarized in Table IV. Our problem is to find a best diet $(x_1, x_2, \cdots, x_5)$ and the least cost, Z, as indicated by the question mark.

Table IV

Comparison of Costs and Nutritional Elements

	Goods					*Standards*						
Calories	a_{11}	a_{12}	a_{13}	a_{14}	a_{15}	C_1 =	1	0	1	1	2	700
Vitamins	a_{21}	a_{22}	a_{23}	a_{24}	a_{25}	C_2	0	1	0	1	1	400
Prices	P_1	P_2	P_3	P_4	P_5	Z	2	20	3	11	12	?

If one tackled this problem by trial and error, by luck or good judgment, one would finally find that (1) the cheapest Z is 4700. It happens that (2) this can be reached in only one way: by the diet $(x_1, x_2, x_3, x_4, x_5) = (0, 0, 0, 100, 300)$, with nothing of the first three goods being bought. Note that (3) there are only as many goods bought as there are

443

nutritional elements. The rest are zero. Finally, it happens that (4) this "best diet" is also an "exact" one, yielding no surplus of either element.

How are these answers arrived at? For the moment such questions may be deferred. Let us first ascertain how general our results are. Is our first conclusion, of a single best Z, universally true in linear programming? The answer is "yes" for all well-behaved problems. If there are two different Z's, one would be better than the other. Moreover, the set of admissible X's in linear programming is often — but not always — made a closed one, so that Z can never be made indefinitely better but will remain within a definite bound, which will, in fact, be reached for some set of X's. It may be remarked that in the present problem Z is to be at a minimum, whereas in the previous discussion of comparative advantage Z was to be at a maximum. These are essentially the same mathematical problem.

But our second conclusion — that the X's are unique — is not universally true. Often the best Z will be reached by a number of alternative X's, quite possibly by an infinite number of such. For example, suppose that the first three goods had been given extremely cheap prices compared with the last two. Obviously, the best diet would be found among the first three goods. But suppose good X_1 and good X_3, which are exactly alike, were given equally low prices. Then the best way of getting our calories could involve any one of an infinite number of combinations of X_1 and X_3, providing only that their sum adds up to 700.

In this last case our final diet might involve three goods instead of only two. But even in this case there could be no harm in setting either X_1 or X_3 to zero and achieving the best Z with *as few goods as there are nutritional elements.* This suggests a general proposition in the field of linear programming:

> THEOREM: In a linear minimum or maximum problem involving n variables (i.e., x's) and m inequalities (i.e., C's), the number of nonzero x's will never have to be greater than m.

This general statement of our third conclusion will have to be proved later. Note that the theorem would not help much if m were greater than n, as can happen in many problems. Note too that we may sometimes have more than this number of zeros. A simple example will show this possibility. Suppose the price of X_4 were extremely low compared with all other prices; then it stands to reason that all of our required calories and vitamins can be bought most cheaply by purchasing 700 units of X_4, and buying a single good would be the best way to get two elements.[11]

---

[11]The reader may be tempted to stretch the theorem to cover this case. He may argue that for this example we can forget about vitamins, since C_2 is no bottleneck. In effect, then, we have only 1 rather than 2 effective constraints and a new $m = 1$

The last example shows that our best diets will not always be exact, so that our fourth conclusion is not generally true. Often some of the m side conditions or constraints will turn out *not* to be binding; however, they cannot be thrown away, because for other prices or standards they may become binding. It is intuitively clear that changing any C_i — such as increasing the calorie requirements — will cause a definite change in the best Z; but it is also clear that changing a nonbinding C will have zero effect on Z, until it begins to be binding. The rates of change of the form (dZ/dC_i) are in the nature of *marginal costs* and will be found to have an important economic and mathematical significance, related to "shadow prices" and so-called "Lagrangian multipliers."

Possible Methods of Attack

Random trial and error. Let us now examine various possible ways of trying to solve our minimum problem. The first and simplest method consists of aimlessly trying different diets in the hope that the best one will soon be found. This is clearly a hopeless method, even if only an approximate solution is desired. The number of possibilities is endless, and in any case if we should happen to stumble on the best solution, we might never be aware of its optimal properties.

Use of elementary calculus. An economist of any sophistication is accustomed to solving maximum or minimum problems by moving his variables until "marginal something" is just balanced by "marginal something else," or until "marginal net something" is zero. This corresponds in the language of calculus to "differentiating the quantity to be minimized, Z, with respect to the independent variables, which are X's, and then setting the resulting expression equal to zero." It is hoped that this gives enough equations to determine the optimal point uniquely.

Obviously, this method cannot be used in problems of linear programming. In the first place if we differentiate a linear sum

$$Z = P_1 x_1 + P_2 x_2 + \cdots + P_n x_n$$

with respect to any variable such as x_1, we get

$$\frac{\partial Z}{\partial x_1} = P_1$$

which is either never zero or always zero and does not give us determining equations for the x's. If it made any sense to regard x_1 as an independent variable, the obvious information given by such a derivative would be the following: You will always lower Z by decreasing x_1 indefinitely,

---

can be substituted for $m = 2$. But there are many problems involved in defining such a new m that are glossed over in this discussion. It should be emphasized that m is the number of inequalities or "possible equalities," not the actual number of equalities that turn out to be satisfied.

P_1 being positive; or if P_1 is negative, by increasing x_1 indefinitely; or if $P_1 = 0$, the value of x_1 is indifferent.

Determining free variables. But there is a more serious objection to the procedure of simple differentiation. A variable like x_1 is far from being independent; it is constrained in a number of different ways. In the first place, no quantity of good consumed can be negative so that $x_1 \geq 0$. This tells us that even in the strange case where x_1 is not subject to constraint, we would not wish to decrease x_1 indefinitely, but only to zero; and our equilibrium condition would be stated, not by a derivative set equal to zero, but by an inequality.

Even this is a gross oversimplification, since x_1 is not free to move over the range of positive numbers independently of the other x's. Our constraints — minimum calories and vitamins in this problem, maximum domestic production possibilities in the theory of comparative advantage — link up the x's. This is not peculiar to linear programming. It also arises in well-behaved problems of economics, such as the problem of maximizing a consumer utility

(7) $\qquad U = U(x_1, x_2, \cdots, x_n)$

subject to the "budget equation"

$$P_1 x_1 + P_2 x_2 + \cdots + P_n x_n = I$$

where I is the prescribed maximum total expenditure. There should really be a symbol $<$ before the I, but this is usually omitted, since it is obvious that short of the point of satiation the consumer will not let purchasing power go to waste.

The x's are clearly not all independent. If all but the last one, x_n, are prescribed, then the latter is determined by the budget equation. It is rational — and in this simple example easy — to "eliminate" x_n as an independent variable by substituting into U the value of

$$x_n = \frac{I}{P_n} - \frac{P_1}{P_n} x_1 - \frac{P_2}{P_n} x_2 - \cdots - \frac{P_{n-1}}{P_n} x_{n-1}$$

as determined by the budget equation.

This gives us U as a function of only $(n - 1)$ x's, and all of them are free and independent variables; or

$$U = U\left(x_1, x_2, \cdots, x_{n-1}, \frac{I}{P_n} - \frac{P_1}{P_2} x_1 - \cdots - \frac{P_{n-1}}{P_n} x_{n-1}\right)$$

Now we may differentiate U with respect to each of the independent x's, holding the other x's constant but implicitly letting x_n vary in accordance with the constraint. This gives us for any x, such as x_1, the equation

$$\left(\frac{\partial U}{\partial x_1}\right)_{\substack{\text{other } x\text{'s except} \\ x_n \text{ constant}}} = \frac{\partial U}{\partial x_1} - \frac{\partial U}{\partial x_n} \frac{P_1}{P_n}$$

Now if we set all these partial derivatives simultaneously equal to zero and if U has the well-behaved concavity properties usually assumed — law of diminishing (relative, ordinal) marginal utility, etc. — this defines a unique optimum. In words, the optimum is characterized by "marginal utilities proportional to respective prices."

In linear programming the side conditions or constraints are all linear. This would seem to be a great advantage, since it is often difficult or impossible to solve nonlinear relations for "dependent variables" that we wish to "eliminate" from our Z function. The advantage of linearity in the constraints is partly illusory. It is rendered nugatory by the appearance of the innocent-looking inequality sign, $>$, in these side conditions. We cannot be sure in advance that we shall be able to find, or shall want to find, an exact diet. This means that some of the side conditions will *not* have the equality sign holding, and in such cases we shall not be able to use those linear side conditions to eliminate variables. Unfortunately, we are not told in advance which side conditions will be "binding" (i.e., which ones will have equality signs) and which will be "nonbinding." We must find this out the hard way.

Occasionally economic intuition will tell us which we can disregard. Thus, imagine a rich man who has no thought of the future. Suppose he has a certain sum of money that he may spend during a war year. But suppose the government forces him to pay ration points for everything he buys, and suppose it sets the ration points equal in value to the dollar prices of the goods he buys. Further suppose that the government gives him fewer ration points than he has dollars. He must now maximize his utility subject to two budget constraints: a dollar and a ration-point limitation. But it is obvious in this case that the dollar constraint is redundant. It is physically impossible for him to spend more dollars than ration points; and since we have assumed *no* future use for the dollars, it is clear that they may be disregarded. The interested reader may verify that in this case the consumer's equilibrium involves "marginal utilities proportional to ration points," etc.[12]

Even in the simplest problem of rationing, economic intuition usually cannot be relied upon to give information as to which equalities will or will not be effective. Thus, suppose that ration points set for each good are *not* proportional to quoted prices. Then it is quite possible that a given consumer will be able — if he wants to — to spend the total of both his dollars and his ration points. But will he always want to? The case of a rich diabetic during sugar rationing shows that the answer is no; dollars and not points may be binding. The case of a rich glutton pro-

[12]See P. A. Samuelson, *Foundations of Economic Analysis* (Cambridge, Mass.: Harvard University Press, 1947), pp. 163–171, for further treatment and references. In recent years, A. Henderson and H. Makower have discussed similar issues in the *Review of Economic Studies*. The particular example here discussed is related to the proposal for wartime "expenditure control."

vides an opposite example, where points and not dollars are binding.[13]

As we shall see presently, there is a formal artifice by which we can get rid of *all* the inequality signs—that is, by defining new variables such as "unused" dollars, "unused" ration points, "excess" calories, etc. Of course, this does not avoid the question as to which of these new variables will turn out to be zero.

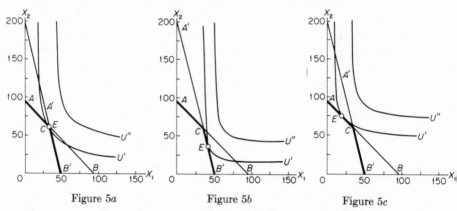

Figure 5a	Figure 5b	Figure 5c

The lines AB and $A'B'$ represent the dollar and ration-point budget equations respectively. The heavy locus ACB' represents the locus available to the consumer, since the "scarcest currency" is always the bottleneck. In Figure 5a, this locus touches but does not cross the highest indifference curve at C. In Figure 5b, this phenomenon occurs along CB', where dollars are redundant; in Figure 5c, the ration points are redundant. When there are only two x's and when both constraints are known to be binding, there is no room left for maximizing behavior; only when there are more goods does the problem become interesting.

But for the moment let us suppose that we know which of the constraints will be binding.[14] Let them be $r < m$ in number. How do we proceed to use these equations in order to eliminate redundant variables and arrive at a set of independent variables? We may first illustrate by the rather trivial case where $r = 1$ and there is only one constraint. Suppose that we can forget vitamins and have only this calorie side condition:

$$a_{11}x_1 + a_{12}x_2 + a_{13}x_3 + a_{14}x_4 + a_{15}x_5$$
$$= 1x_1 + 0x_2 + 1x_3 + 1x_4 + 2x_5 = 700$$

[13]Imagine a consumer confronted by dollar prices $(P_1, P_2) = (1, 1)$ and with dollar income $I = 95$; let him be faced by point prices $(P_1', P_2') = (4, 1)$ and with total points to spend $I' = 200$. He can buy $(X_1, X_2) = (35, 60)$ if he spends all his points and dollars. In Figure 5a, he would choose to do so; but in Figures 5b and 5c, he would let either dollars or ration points go to waste.

[14]In the calorie-vitamin numerical example, I have already indicated that the best solution happens to involve both constraints, and we may imagine a problem in which an umpire had provided us with this information. In other problems we might imagine setting up in turn the hypothesis that all possible combinations of sets of inequalities will hold. This would involve considering 2^m possible cases, a fierce number when m is large.

448

We can use this equation to solve for any variable except x_2, which has a zero coefficient. Suppose we decide to eliminate x_5 as redundant; then we solve for it and substitute into our cost data to get

$$Z = P_1 x_1 + P_2 x_2 + \cdots + P_5 x_5 = 2x_1 + 20x_2 + 3x_3 + 11x_4 + 12x_5$$

$$= P_1 x_1 + P_2 x_2 + \cdots + P_5 \left(\frac{C_1 - a_{11}x_1 - a_{12}x_2 - \cdots - a_{14}x_4}{a_{15}} \right)$$

$$= \left(P_1 - \frac{a_{11}}{a_{15}} P_5 \right) x_1 + \left(P_2 - \frac{a_{12}}{a_{15}} P_5 \right) x_2 + \cdots$$

$$+ \left(P_4 - \frac{a_{14}}{a_{15}} P_5 \right) x_4 + \text{constant}$$

$$= (2 - 6)x_1 + (20 - 0)x_2 + (2 - 6)x_3 + (11 - 6)x_4 + \text{constant}$$

$$= -4x_1 + 20x_2 - 3x_3 + 5x_4 + \text{constant}$$

Our cost function has now been expressed in terms of one less variable than we had originally. But, presumably, these four variables are now free to move independently over all positive values.

How should we optimally adjust x_2? Because it has a positive coefficient, it is clear that $(\partial Z / \partial x_2) = 20 > 0$, and every increase in x_2 sends up costs. Therefore, we go into reverse and reduce x_2 in order to effect savings. This we continue until we reach the limit $x_2 = 0$. Exactly the same can be said for x_4, which has a positive coefficient.

So far, so good. But applying the same reasoning to the other x's leads to a perplexing situation: x_1 and x_3 have negative coefficients, and it would seem that increasing them indefinitely would be in order. This is surely absurd. Or is it? Will increasing x_1 and/or x_3 cause the total of calories to become excessive, and therefore be a foolish procedure? No, it will not; it will not, because x_5 is always being reduced so as to keep total calories equal to 700 equal to C_1. That is the meaning of our earlier substitution.

In disposing of one objection we encounter another. If x_1 and x_3 are increased enough, x_5 will ultimately become a negative number, which it is not permitted to do. If we could regard foods as bundles of calories and could "convert" x_1 and x_3 into x_5, and then could *sell* (as well as buy) x_5 in unlimited amounts at $P_5 = 12$, then it would indeed be optimal to increase x_1 and x_3 indefinitely at the expense of x_5. But all this is not possible; in our problem no x can ever become negative. This means that x_1 and x_3 can be increased only until x_5 is zero; from that point on, if we increase x_1, we must decrease x_3 and vice versa. This means that, with x_2 and x_4 being already set equal to zero, and with x_1 and x_3 being made so large as to set x_5 equal to zero, we are finally left with the following choices for x_1 and x_3:

$$\frac{1}{2} x_1 + \frac{1}{2} x_3 - \frac{700}{2} = x_5 = 0 \quad \text{or} \quad x_1 = -x_3 + 700$$

We substitute this into Z to get

$$
\begin{aligned}
Z &= P_1 x_1 + P_3 x_3 = 2x_1 + 3x_3 \\
&= P_1(-x_3 + 700) + P_3 x_3 = (P_3 - P_1) x_3 + \text{constant} \\
&= 1x_3 + \text{constant}
\end{aligned}
$$

Since x_3 is now our remaining free variable and since it has a positive coefficient, we shall realize economies by making it as small as possible. When x_3 is set equal to zero, then obviously — from the above relation between x_1 and x_3, or from the original calorie constraint — we must have $x_1 = 700$.

At long last we have our optimal diet: $(x_1, x_2, x_3, x_4, x_5) = (700, 0, 0, 0, 0)$. As we had reason to expect earlier, where there is only one effective constraint, there must be only one nonzero variable.

An intuitive economist might have arrived at this result almost immediately. He is used to working with the concept "marginal utility of the (last) dollar spent on each commodity." In this problem, he would replace utility by calories and look for the most calories per dollar, or for the maximum of

$$
(8) \qquad \frac{a_{11}}{P_1} = \frac{1}{2}, \frac{a_{12}}{P_2} = 0, \frac{a_{13}}{P_3} = \frac{1}{3}, \frac{a_{14}}{P_4} = \frac{1}{11}, \frac{a_{15}}{P_5} = \frac{2}{12}
$$

Clearly, x_1 is the cheapest way of getting calories. It is too bad that this simple device will not solve more complicated problems.

As a matter of fact, the more tedious method of substitution outlined earlier can follow many paths. With good luck we might have picked a path that would have gotten us our solution in almost a single step. Suppose we had used our calorie relations to solve for x_1 rather than x_5. Then our cost would have turned out to be

$$
Z = \left(P_2 - \frac{a_{12}}{a_{11}} P_1 \right) x_2 + \left(P_3 - \frac{a_{13}}{a_{11}} P_1 \right) x_3
$$

$$
+ \left(P_4 - \frac{a_{14}}{a_{11}} P_1 \right) x_4 + \left(P_5 - \frac{a_{15}}{a_{11}} P_1 \right) x_5 + \text{constant}
$$

$$
= 20x_2 + 1x_3 + 10x_4 + 8x_5 + \text{constant}
$$

All the coefficients of the variables are positive; each variable is best set equal to zero; from our constraint we find that $x_1 = 700$. Hindsight always helps.

We have labored hard to get the best solution. The only trouble with our solution is that *it is wrong*. We have already been informed that the best diet for our original problem is $(x_1, x_2, x_3, x_4, x_5) = (0, 0, 0, 100,$

300). What is lacking about $(700, 0, 0, 0, 0)$? Clearly, it yields the correct calories, but it fails to yield the specified amount of vitamins. It is definitely the cheapest diet under the assumption made that only the calorie constraint would be binding. But this was a gratuitous assumption that we had no right to make, as can be verified by seeing whether the full conditions of the problem are satisfied.

Our work has not been entirely in vain. We have not solved our original problem, but we have given the correct answer to some other questions. We have the best solution to the problem where vitamins are of no importance. (Or, alternatively, if the first food, x_1, contained a great many vitamins so that a_{21} were very large instead of being zero and so that we could be sure that the vitamin requirements would be more than satisfied, then our solution would be a correct one.)

There is one further virtue to our solution to the problem where only calories count. It gives us a *lower bound* to the best obtainable cost. If calories alone cost at least the amount $700 \times 2 = 1400$, then a diet adequate in every respect must cost that much or more.[15]

The main purpose of this discussion was, however, expository. When only one constraint is binding, the problem of elimination by substitution is at its simplest, and the logic of the process is revealed most clearly.

We may recapitulate just what was done in this process:

1. We found an expression for one of the dependent variables by using our constraint.

2. We substituted this expression into our Z sum wherever the dependent variable appeared, thus *eliminating* the dependent variable from our Z sum.

3. The remaining variables were *not* perfectly free to move as they pleased. When one became zero, it hit an inflexible stop. Worse than that, when a movement of the independent variables caused the elimi-

---

[15]Thus, our optimal Z must be at least as great as the cheapest way of buying calories alone: or

$$Z \geq \operatorname*{Min}_{i} \frac{P_i C_1}{a_{1i}}$$

This must equally be true with respect to vitamins or any other element: or

$$Z \geq \operatorname*{Min}_{i} \frac{P_i C_k}{a_{ki}} \text{ where } k = 1, 2, \cdots, m$$

The best of these lower bounds is given then by

$$Z \geq \operatorname*{Max}_{k} \operatorname*{Min}_{i} \frac{P_i C_k}{a_{ki}}$$

In these expressions $\operatorname*{Max}_{k}$ means "maximum with respect to k" and similarly for $\operatorname*{Min}_{i}$. Note finally that if some of the a's in our problem could be negative, this line of reasoning would fail.

nated dependent variables to hit zero, we again ran into an inflexible wall and could at best move along that wall.

4. But our minimizing procedure, within these constraints, was logically simple. We kept repeating firmly to ourselves: "Every day in every way, we must be getting better and better. We just keep moving, so long as we are moving *down* the cost trail." Specifically, when we had chosen to eliminate x_5, we then moved to $x_2 = 0$ because the positive coefficient of x_2 meant that this would be a downward direction; then we moved further downward by setting $x_4 = 0$. Since x_1 and x_3 had negative coefficients, our next downward move involved increasing one or both of them; this went on until we hit the "geometrical plane or wall" represented by

$$x_2 = x_4 = x_5 = 0 = \frac{C_1}{a_{15}} - \frac{a_{11}}{a_{15}} x_1 - \frac{a_{13}}{a_{15}} x_3$$

We proceeded to edge our way along this wall in a downward direction by decreasing x_3, which had a positive coefficient in the expression for Z defined in terms of x_3 along this final wall. If x_3's coefficient had been negative instead of positive, we would have increased it at the expense of x_1, up to the $C_1 = 700$ limit. If its coefficient had been zero, any point on the wall would have been indifferently good.

So much for the process of elimination of dependent variables when there is only one constraint. If there are two or more constraints, the logic of the process is unchanged; but the numerical steps are considerably more tedious. Let us illustrate by examining briefly our simple calorie-vitamin problem, where we have been told that both constraints are, in fact, to be binding. Here we have two effective constraints, and so we can eliminate two variables. Actually, in this case, except for x_1 and x_3 we can eliminate *any* two variables from the numerical relations

$$1x_1 + 0x_2 + 1x_3 + 1x_4 + 2x_5 = 700$$

$$0x_1 + 1x_2 + 0x_3 + 1x_4 + 1x_5 = 400$$

Applying the methods of high-school or more advanced algebra, we will soon find that it is much easier to eliminate the "pure" variables, x_1 and x_2 or x_3 and x_2, than any other pair. In fact, to express x_4 and x_5 in terms of the remaining variables involves solving two simultaneous equations (or as a mathematician would say, "inverting a matrix"). This is logically easy to do but tedious in practice.

Let us therefore agree to eliminate x_1 and x_2 to get

$$x_1 = 700 - 1x_3 - 1x_4 - 2x_5$$

$$x_2 = 400 - 0x_3 - 1x_4 - 1x_5$$

We now substitute these into our cost expression

$$Z = \sum_1^5 P_i x_i = 2x_1 + 20x_2 + 3x_3 + 11x_4 + 12x_5$$

$$= 2(700 - 1x_3 - 1x_4 - 2x_5)$$
$$+ 20(400 - 1x_4 - 1x_5) + 3x_3 + 11x_4 + 12x_5$$
$$= (-2 + 3)x_3 + (-2 - 20 + 11)x_4 + (-4 - 20 + 12)x_5$$
$$= 1x_3 - 11x_4 - 12x_5$$

Because x_3 has a positive coefficient (or "*net* cost"), we must obviously reduce it to zero. Just as clearly, the negative coefficients of x_4 and x_5 mean we must increase them *at the expense of* x_1 *and* x_2. But x_1 and x_2 can never be reduced below zero. When they both reach zero, x_4 and x_5 take on the values $(100, 300)$, which we earlier said were the best values.[16]

In the general case where we know there are r ($\leq m$ and $\leq n$) independent and consistent binding constraints, we can always eliminate r variables and substitute for them in the Z expression. The resulting expression for Z will be defined in terms of the remaining $n - r$ quasi-free variables; and depending on their coefficients, we can proceed to find some $n - r$ variables that can be set equal to zero. The final values of the nonzero variables can be found by solving our r effective equations. If and only if we have selected the right set of effective constraints, the whole process will be consistent.

To picture this process in terms of higher geometry is conceptually very helpful but will be reserved for a later section.

Use of Lagrangian multipliers. In ordinary well-behaved maximum or minimum problems, there is a well-known artifice, due to Lagrange, for dealing with side conditions or constraints. If we have

$$(9) \qquad Z = F_0(x_1, x_2, \cdots, x_n)$$

to be a minimum subject to

$$F_1(x_1, x_2, \cdots, x_n) = 0$$
$$F_2(x_1, x_2, \cdots, x_n) = 0$$
$$\cdots \qquad \cdots \qquad \cdots \qquad \qquad m \leq n$$
$$F_m(x_1, x_2, \cdots, x_n) = 0$$

the trick is to form the Lagrangian expression

$$G = \lambda_0 F_0 + \lambda_1 F_1 + \cdots + \lambda_m F_m = G(x_1, x_2, \cdots, x_n; \lambda_0, \lambda_1, \cdots, \lambda_m)$$

where λ_0 may be set equal to one, and where the other λ's are "undetermined multipliers." Usually it is said, "We have added nothing to the

---

[16]To be rigorous, we must verify that *both* x_1 and x_2 should be forced to zero levels. If we had eliminated x_4 and x_5, the resulting coefficients of x_1, x_2, x_3 would all be positive, providing roundabout verification of what can be directly shown.

F_0." But we next are told to treat the x's "as if they were independent variables," and we end up with the minimum conditions

$$(10) \qquad \frac{\partial G}{\partial x_i} = \lambda_0 \frac{\partial F_0}{\partial x_i} + \lambda_1 \frac{\partial F_1}{\partial x_i} + \cdots + \lambda_m \frac{\partial F_m}{\partial x_i} = 0$$

$$(i = 1, 2, \cdots, n)$$

We can eliminate the λ's and end up with $(n - m)$ minimizing equations involving the partial derivatives of the F's.

This is purely a formal trick, whose sole justification lies in the fact that it rapidly gives us what other rigorous methods assure us are the true first-order minimum conditions. But it is *not* true that $G(x_1, \cdots, x_n; \lambda_0, \lambda_1, \cdots, \lambda_m)$ is necessarily at a relative minimum with respect to freely variable x's, even when the correct λ's are prescribed. And the correct secondary conditions on the higher partial derivatives are much more complicated than the usual textbook treatment would ever suggest.

For linear programming, we already know that most minimum conditions involve boundary inequalities rather than vanishing derivatives. Therefore, the Lagrangian device is still more in need of justification. Actually, it is closely related to "shadow prices" and can be a suggestive method. But here only a brief outline of its possible application can be indicated.

Given

$$Z = \sum_{k=1}^{n} B_k x_k$$

to be a minimum subject to

$$(11) \qquad \sum_{k=1}^{n} a_{ik} x_k - C_k \geq 0 \qquad \left(i = 1, 2, \cdots, m \gtrless n \right)$$

$$x_j \geq 0 \qquad (j = 1, 2, \cdots, n)$$

We form the Lagrangian expression

$$(12) \qquad G = Z + \lambda_1 \left(\sum_{k=1}^{n} a_{1_k} x_k - C_1 \right)$$

$$+ \lambda_2 \left(\sum_{k=1}^{n} a_{2_k} x_k - C_2 \right) + \cdots$$

$$= \sum_{k=1}^{n} B_k x_k + \sum_{i=1}^{m} \sum_{k=1}^{n} a_{ik} \lambda_i x_k - \sum_{i=1}^{m} C_i \lambda_i$$

$$= \sum_{i=0}^{m} \sum_{k=0}^{n} a_{ik} \lambda_i x_k = G(x_0, x_1, \cdots, x_n; \lambda_0, \lambda_1, \cdots, \lambda_m)$$

where $\lambda_0 = 1$, $x_0 = -1$, $a_{0k} = B_k$, $a_{i0} = C_i$. Here G is a so-called bilinear form. If it is to be at a minimum with respect to the x's, for suitably constant λ's, we must have certain equalities or inequalities holding for

$$\frac{\partial G}{\partial x_j} = B_j + \sum_{i=1}^{m} a_{ij}\lambda_i$$

As yet this tells us not very much. We suspect that wherever a constraint is not binding, the corresponding λ will be zero. This being the case, we can determine unique λ's by the equations

$$(13) \qquad \frac{\partial G}{\partial x_j} = 0 = B_j + \sum_{i=1}^{m} a_{ij}\lambda_i$$

where j represents the subscript of any of the r nonzero x's, and where i is the subscript of any of the r effective constraints. For all other x's, we must have negative profitability, or

$$(13)' \qquad \frac{\partial G}{\partial x_j} = B_j + \sum_{i=1}^{m} a_{ij}\lambda_i \geq 0$$

But all this is as yet conjecture, based upon an analogy with shadow prices (these being the λ's, except for sign) and "unit profitability" $\left(\text{being } \dfrac{\partial G}{\partial x_j}, \text{ except for sign} \right)$. It may be said that our G function is closely related to similar bilinear forms introduced by von Neumann in his article on economics and the book on the theory of games.[17]

Intuitive Economic Considerations

For the moment, let us abandon a direct mathematical attack and investigate whether any common-sense hunches can suggest a new line of action. If only one constraint, such as calories, were involved, it would seem natural to concentrate on finding a food with the "lowest cost per calorie" or "greatest number of calories per dollar." Let us try to define the concept of "profit" a little more formally so that it will conveniently handle more complicated cases. This will involve the concept of "shadow prices," or accounting prices created for the purpose of solving our minimum problem.

When a consumers' advisory committee says that "spinach is a good buy this week," it probably means that the housewife can get a lot of iron for her cash outlay, and other elements as well. But how can we evaluate and compare the vitamin content of the spinach with its iron content? One rule of thumb would be to give a certain number of points to each nutritional element, so that a dollar spent on spinach is thought of as buying us some number of points in the form of calories plus some

[17]J. von Neumann, "A Model of General Equilibrium," *Review of Economic Studies*, Vol. XIII (1945–1946), pp. 1–9, a translation of an earlier German work dating back to the 1930's; J. von Neumann and O. Morgenstern, *The Theory of Games and Economic Behavior* (2nd edition; Princeton: Princeton University Press, 1947).

number of points derived from its iron content plus the points derived from its other elements. It would seem reasonable only to buy foods which give us the maximum number of points per dollar, avoiding all other foods.

This rule would give us a definite answer to our problem. But we cannot apply it until we know how to score our different elements (calories, vitamins, etc.) in terms of points. If calories are "dirt cheap" or so plentiful that we are sure to get enough of them, we obviously will have to stay away from buying expensive starchy foods. This is because they will have a low total "point score," or "profitability" if we prefer to use that term. On the other hand, it may turn out that calories are the expensive bottleneck and each calorie should be awarded a high number of points relative to what is awarded to each vitamin. But how can we know what relative point evaluation to give the different elements?

An economist well versed in utility theory might hope to be able to reduce all the different elements down to comparable "nutrition utiles." He might try to draw up a curve showing the different combinations of calories and vitamins that give the human guinea pig the same "level of nutritional well being." In Figure 6a, such an "indifference contour" is drawn up for vitamins and calories. Our economist would infer from the steep slope of the curve that many calorie units have the same point value as one vitamin unit.

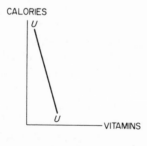

Figure 6a

Economist's attempt to define relative evaluation of calories and vitamins by nutritional indifference contour.

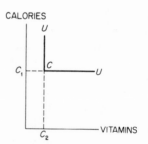

Figure 6b

Biologist's contour of minimum needs.

All this is illegitimate. The NRC has defined basic nutritional requirements, and *each* of these elements must attain its minimum level. In economic terms our correct indifference contour looks like Figure 6b. We must get to point C, and anything above or to the right of that point is irrelevant. The slope at C, is anything between zero and infinity, so once again we are at sea as to how to award points, or how to set shadow prices for calories and vitamins. It is no good to describe what to do on the assumption that so much C_1 can be substituted for so much C_2. This is not the problem set to us.[18]

For our original problem it would seem only reasonable to expect the relative point values of calories and vitamins to vary with commodity market prices rather than to be natural physiological (or psychological) constants. To find the appropriate shadow price or points in any problem will not be easy. This should not discourage us so much as to lead us to abandon the present line of attack.

The Simple Case of "Pure" Foods

Suppose we tackle a rather simple problem first — that in which all foods are "pure" foods, each containing something of one nutritional element and nothing of all others. Thus, x_1 may have only calories, x_2 only vitamins, x_3 perhaps only calories (but not necessarily with the same number as x_1 or with the same market price), etc. In this pure-foods case our problem obviously breaks up into m different, independent, simple problems. Among all the calorie foods we select that one which most cheaply gives us our calorie requirements. Similarly, we make our selection among the pure foods containing only iron for the cheapest way of buying iron. Our final cost of an optimal diet is the sum of the cost of getting calories *and each* of the other elements.

Let us consider calories alone. For this purpose we might as well number all the pure calorie foods $x_1, x_2, x_3, \cdots$ with market prices $P_1, P_2, P_3, \cdots$ and with unit calorie contents $a_{11}, a_{12}, a_{13}, \cdots$. We must minimize

$$(14) \qquad Z = P_1 x_1 + P_2 x_2 + \cdots$$

subject to

$$a_{11}x_1 + a_{12}x_2 + \cdots \geq C_1$$
$$x_1 \geq 0, x_2 \geq 0, \cdots$$

[18]If we could consider some linear relation between the C's as equally satisfactory, our problem would become a different (and much simpler) problem in linear programming. We would minimize

$$\sum_{i=1}^{n} P_i x_i$$

subject to the *single* constraint

$$K_1 \sum_{j=1}^{n} a_{1j}x_j + K_2 \sum_{j=1}^{n} a_{2j}x_j + \cdots = A_1 x_1$$
$$+ \cdots + A_n x_n \geq C = K_1 C_1 + \cdots + K_m C_m$$

where the K's are the substitution ratios (or relative points) of the respective elements. We would only have to compare A_i/P_i, the "final net utiles per dollar" yielded by the ith commodity, and pick the highest value. Presumably, one food would be enough if the K's were really constants (as they are usually assumed not to be in economics).

We could get our answer by simply picking the greatest of a_{11}/P_1, a_{12}/P_2, etc., and concentrating on the corresponding food.

It will turn out to be a little more convenient to define a shadow price for calories. Let this be called y_1. As yet, we do not know its value (in dollars per calories). The "unit profitability" of any food can be thought of as dollars of calorie revenue it brings in minus its cash cost per unit, or as

$$\pi_1 = a_{11}y_1 - P_1$$
$$\pi_2 = a_{12}y_1 - P_2$$
$$\cdot \ \cdot \ \cdot \ \cdot \ \cdot \ \cdot \ \cdot \ \cdot$$
$$\pi_i = a_{1i}y_1 - P_i$$
$$\cdot \ \cdot \ \cdot \ \cdot \ \cdot \ \cdot \ \cdot$$

These are definite numbers once y_1 is given a definite value. At first glance, one might suppose that we should pick the largest of these profitability numbers and get our calories from the corresponding food. But a second look will convince us that this is not a valid procedure. If one food cost twice as much as another and had twice as many calories, its profitability would be twice as great; but there would be no advantage whatever in choosing one good over the other.

Our profitabilities have to be put on a per-dollar basis if they are to be comparable. We could work with

$$\frac{\pi_1}{P_1} = \frac{a_{11}}{P_1} y_1 - 1$$
$$\cdot \ \cdot \ \cdot \ \cdot \ \cdot \ \cdot \ \cdot \ \cdot$$
$$\frac{\pi_i}{P_i} = \frac{a_{1i}}{P_i} y_1 - 1$$
$$\cdot \ \cdot \ \cdot \ \cdot \ \cdot \ \cdot \ \cdot \ \cdot$$

The greatest of these would give us our cheapest food. For any positive y_1, or calorie shadow price, this would be the same thing as picking the greatest a_{1i}/P_i, or number of calories per dollar, which was our earlier approach.

Let us suppose that the kth food is the best one, so that

$$\frac{a_{1k}}{P_k} \geq \frac{a_{1i}}{P_i} \qquad (i \neq k)$$

Our best calorie diet is

$$\left(X_1, X_2, \cdots, X_k, \cdots, X_i, \cdots \right) = \left(0, 0, \cdots, \frac{C_1}{a_{1k}}, \cdots, 0, \cdots \right)$$

and its cost is

$$Z = 0 + 0 + \cdots + P_k \frac{C_1}{a_{1k}} + \cdots + 0 + \cdots$$

Obviously, the (cheapest) extra or marginal cost of increasing our calorie requirements from C_1 to $C_1 + 1$ units would be

$$MC_1 = \frac{P_k}{a_{1k}}(C_1 + 1) - \frac{P_k}{a_{1k}}C_1 = \frac{P_k}{a_{1k}} = \frac{\partial Z}{\partial C_1}$$

The *cost* of calories — and note that I do *not* say the *worth* of calories — would seem to be given by P_k/a_{1k}. It seems natural therefore to say that this is the proper (shadow) price of calories, or

$$y_1 = \operatorname*{Min}_i \frac{P_i}{a_{1i}} = \frac{\partial Z}{\partial C_1} = MC_1$$

With our shadow price now determined, we can go back and look at our original profit figures $\pi_1, \pi_2, \cdots$, etc. Our objection to them — that they are not on a per-dollar basis — now disappears. In every case the profits are negative except in the case of our very cheapest calorie source, x_k. Thus

$$\pi_1 = a_{11}y_1 - P_1 \leq 0$$

$$\pi_2 = a_{12}y_1 - P_2 \leq 0$$

$$\cdot \quad \cdot \quad \cdot \quad \cdot \quad \cdot \quad \cdot \quad \cdot \quad \cdot \quad \cdot$$

$$\pi_k = a_{1k}y_1 - P_k = 0$$

$$\cdot \quad \cdot \quad \cdot \quad \cdot \quad \cdot \quad \cdot \quad \cdot \quad \cdot \quad \cdot$$

$$\pi_i = a_{1i}y_1 - P_i \leq 0$$

If the unusual should happen and some other good also had exactly zero profit, then it would be a matter of indifference as to how we divided our calorie expenditure between the cheap good and x_k.

In effect, we have determined the highest possible price for calories that is possible. Or more accurately, the highest possible calorie price compatible with some good in the system "breaking even." All other nonoptimal goods will show a loss. In order to solve a minimum problem (lowest cost from selecting best x's), we have in effect chosen to solve a maximum problem (highest price for calories). This is similar to the result of my earlier examination of comparative advantage as a problem in linear programming. Then, in order to get the x's that would give *maximum* national income or product, it was necessary to find the price of shadows that would yield *minimum* income (or cost outlay).

Is there any advantage in trying to solve a problem of best quantities by replacing it by a hardly less difficult price problem in linear programming? Thus our correct y_1 is the solution of

$$(14)' \qquad Z' = C_1 y_1$$

to be a maximum subject to

$$a_{11}y_1 \leq P_1$$

$$a_{12}y_1 \leq P_2 \qquad\qquad (y_1 \geq 0)$$

$$\cdots\cdots$$

$$a_{1i}y_1 \leq P_i$$

Whether there is any advantage to this indirect approach or not, it well illustrates an important theoretical point: the "principle of duality."

To each minimum problem in the x's of the form

(15) $\qquad Z = \sum_{j=1}^{n} P_j x_j$

to be a minimum subject to

$$\sum_{j=1}^{n} a_{kj}x_j \geq C_k \qquad\qquad (k = 1, 2, \cdots, m)$$

$$x_j \geq 0 \qquad\qquad (j = 1, 2, \cdots, n)$$

there corresponds a dual maximum problem of the form

(15)' $\qquad Z' = \sum_{k=1}^{m} C_k y_k$

to be a maximum subject to

$$\sum_{k=1}^{m} a_{kj}y_k \leq P_j \qquad\qquad (j = 1, 2, \cdots, n)$$

$$y_k \geq 0 \qquad\qquad (k = 1, 2, \cdots, m)$$

Note that everything has been transposed or "turned on its side." This duality is remarkable. Even more remarkable is the fact that the best (maximum) Z' turns out to be equal to the best (minimum) Z. And any nonoptimal Z' will be algebraically less than any Z (optimal or not).

We must reserve judgment as to whether shadow prices are at all helpful. But at the moment it looks rather discouraging, since to find the right shadow prices appears to be just as difficult a problem in linear programming as to find the right quantities. In fact, the thoughtful reader should be still more discouraged by the proposed method. Let us call the task of finding the best quantities "problem 1" and the task of finding the best prices "problem 2." The penetrating reader will say, "You tell me to solve problem 1 by first solving an equally difficult problem 2. By the same reasoning, I should try to solve problem 2 by a method of — so to speak — shadow prices to shadow prices, or by an equally difficult problem 3."

All this looks like an infinite regress. And if our critic is still more acute, he will claim that it involves a vicious circle. For after you have "turned a problem on its side" to get a second problem, when you then turn that problem on its side, you end up, not with a new third problem, but rather with your first problem back again. If problem 2 is "dual" to problem 1, then 1 is also dual to 2. We seem almost to be perpetrating the swindle: "Solve a problem by solving it, and waste a little time on the way."

There is some merit in this contention. Unless we can reverse the doctrine "divide and conquer" to make it read "expand your problem and conquer," we shall have gained nothing by using prices. Our hope must be that solving the two dual problems simultaneously will have some advantages over solving each separately.

All that we have established in the pure-calorie-foods case also holds for the vitamins-pure-food case and for any other pure foods. Let me recapitulate what we have established:

1. We can define the profitability of any pure food in terms of dollars per unit, that is, the $\pi_1, \pi_2, \cdots$.
2. To do this we must first know the (shadow) price of the nutritional elements, that is, the y_1 per calories, the y_2 per vitamins, $\cdots, y_m$, etc.
3. The shadow prices have a number of properties:

   (a) They are in dollars per unit of each nutritional element.
   (b) They represent marginal costs, that is, the least cost of an extra prescribed unit of the element in question.
   (c) They must be such as to make profits negative for a category of goods — namely, those goods that are not bought at all.
   (d) They must be such as to make profits zero for any good that is bought in positive quantities.
   (e) Their values are, in economic jargon, "derived demands" and depend on the prices of the goods $(P_1, \cdots, P_n)$, on the food contents (a_{ij}), and (possibly) on the specified requirements $(C_1, \cdots, C_m)$.
   (f) The shadow prices $(y_1, \cdots, y_m)$ are the solution of the "dual" or "transpose" problem to our original problem. They give us the maximum amount of what might be called "economic rent" that can be imputed to the nutritional elements; and the sum total of optimal rents must add up to exactly the same value as the total optimal cost of foods.[19]

[19]The interested reader can verify all this by working out our earlier arithmetical example of calories and vitamins on the assumption that only the goods x_1, x_2, x_3 can be bought. The data and solution are, respectively,

$$\left[\begin{array}{c|c} a & C \\ \hline P & Z \end{array}\right] = \left[\begin{array}{ccc|c} 1 & 0 & 1 & 700 \\ 0 & 1 & 0 & 400 \\ 2 & 20 & 3 & ? \end{array}\right], \qquad \begin{array}{c} (x_1, x_2, x_3) = (700, 400, 0) \\ (y_1, y_2) = (2, 20) \end{array}$$

$$2(700) + 20(400) = 9400 = Z = Z' = 700(2) + 400(20)$$

General Case of Mixed Commodities

The conclusions just given were developed for the almost trivial case of pure goods, where no food had more than one nutritional element. It so happens that they remain substantially unchanged if we consider the more realistic and complicated case where foods are mixtures of many elements. A slightly more complicated argument is necessary to demonstrate this; at the same time, the actual task of finding a best diet is also slightly more complex.

To handle the case of foods which contain more than one element, let us think of any such commodity as a package containing these different components. Thus a package of mixed nuts contains so many almonds, filberts, peanuts, and so forth. Likewise, in our earlier 5-variable arithmetic example, x_4 was a package of one calorie and one vitamin unit; x_5 was a package of two calories and one vitamin unit.

Let us suppose that there were some way of costlessly decomposing any commodity into its different elements. Then the price of any food, say P_5, must be just equal to the value of its components, where each is evaluated at its shadow price, $y_1, y_2, \cdots$, etc. Were this not so, an excess profit would be possible, and eventually in a competitive market the price of the elements would have to change so as to bring this about, in much the same way as the price of pork comes into relation to the price of corn over the long run.

Thus, for any good that is actually ever bought and sold, we must end up with

$$P_k = a_{1k}y_1 + a_{2k}y_2 + \cdots + a_{mk}y_m$$

or what is the same thing, with

$$\pi_k = a_{1k}y_1 + a_{2k}y_2 + \cdots + a_{mk}y_m - P_k = 0$$

Profitability must finally be equal to zero. More precisely, profitability must be zero if it is rational to buy the food at all. If a food is nonoptimal, then its profitability will have to be negative. Thus if x_i is *not* a good buy, we will have

$$\pi_i = a_{1i}y_1 + a_{2i}y_2 + \cdots + a_{mi}y_m - P_i < 0$$

In Table V let us revert to our 5-variable example. Our unknowns are the best diet and its cost, and also the correct shadow prices for vitamins and calories. We happen to have been told that the best diet is $(0, 0, 0, 100, 300)$. It can also be revealed that the correct shadow prices for calories and vitamins are $(y_1, y_2) = (1, 10)$. How can we find this out for ourselves? And what good is this last information once we have acquired it?

Table V

NRC Requirements and Shadow Prices of Best Diet

	x_1	x_2	x_3	x_4	x_5	NRC Requirements	Shadow Price
Calories	1	0	1	1	2	700	?
Vitamins	0	1	0	1	1	400	?
Prices	2	20	3	11	12	$Z = ?$	
Best Diet	?	?	?	?	?		

To find it out for ourselves, we might set down this rule:

Find shadow prices which permit no positive profits anywhere in the system and which permit zero profits somewhere in the system.

This rule certainly will help us to eliminate a number of price configurations. Thus we could never have the vitamin price greater than 20 because that would make

$$\pi_2 = 1y_2 - 20 > 0$$

Likewise, we could never have the price of calories greater than 2 since that would make π_1 greater than zero. We might simply examine all of our profit figures, and try all combinations of the y's until we finally obtain the following pattern of profits:

(16) $\qquad \pi_1 = a_{11}y_1 + \cdots + a_{m1}y_m - P_1 \leq 0$

$$\cdot \ \cdot \ \cdot \ \cdot \ \cdot \ \cdot \ \cdot \ \cdot \ \cdot \ \cdot \ \cdot \ \cdot \ \cdot \ \cdot \ \cdot \ \cdot \ \cdot \ \cdot$$

$$\pi_n = a_{n1}y_1 + \cdots + a_{mn}y_m - P_n \leq 0$$

and where the equality sign holds at least once.

After much lucky experimentation, we might be lucky enough to hit upon the combination $(y_1, y_2) = (1, 10)$, which results in

$$\pi_1 = 1(1) + 0(10) - 2 = -1 < 0$$

$$\pi_2 = 0(1) + 1(10) - 20 = -10 < 0$$

$$\pi_3 = 1(1) + 0(10) - 3 = -2 < 0$$

$$\pi_4 = 1(1) + 1(10) - 11 = 0$$

$$\pi_5 = 2(1) + 1(10) - 12 = 0$$

We might conclude that our rule had led us to the true equilibrium prices. But this is too hasty a conclusion. Perhaps there are other lucky guesses for the y's that would also give us a pattern of profits compatible with the rule stated earlier. Even worse, our result seems to be independent of the C's prescribed by the NRC; we certainly have not used the C's in applying the rule or calculating profits.

Our darkest suspicions are confirmed when we happen to try any of the following price combinations:

$$(y_1, y_2) = (0, 11) \qquad A$$

or $\qquad\qquad\qquad (1, 10) \qquad B$

or $\qquad\qquad\qquad (2, 8) \qquad C$

or $\qquad\qquad\qquad (2, 0) \qquad D$

We have already seen that B satisfies our profit rule. The reader may verify that any of these other points also gives profits which are nowhere positive. Thus, he will find that for D,

$$(\pi_1, \pi_2, \pi_3, \pi_4, \pi_5) = (0, -20, -1, -9, -8)$$

Our rule leads not to one solution but to four solutions. Actually, the multiplicity of price patterns is much greater. It is infinite. Any weighted average of the prices in A and B, or in B and C, or in C and D, also satisfies our rule. For example, the point $(y_1, y_2) = (1.3, 9.4)$, which is $3/10$ of the way between B and C, gives a profit pattern whose algebraic signs are $(-, -, -, -, 0)$, etc.

All this is summarized in Figure 7. The lines $\pi_1 - \pi_1, \cdots, \pi_5 - \pi_5$ represent the combinations of the shadow prices that will make each good show zero profitability. The "pure goods," x_1, x_2, and x_3, all yield

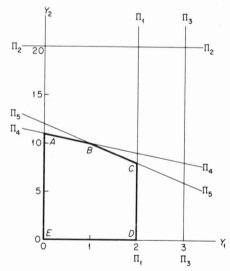

Figure 7

east-west or north-south lines. The mixed goods have profit boundaries that slope downward depending upon the mixture of calories and vitamins.

Our rule of no positive profits means we must always be below or to the left of every line. Also, shadow prices cannot be negative; thus, in all, our profitability rule constrains us to the five-sided area $ABCDE$.

Our rule of no positive profits certainly needs amplification. So long as we had only one constraint — as in the simple theory of comparative advantage — the rule worked out satisfactorily. But now that we have two (or more) constraints, the rule gives us too many possible sets of equilibrium prices. What we seem to need in Figure 7 is a "best" direction to aim toward. And intuitively one feels that this best direction can be supplied only by a knowledge of the C's, or minimum nutritional requirements.

How can we generalize our rule so as to introduce the C's and lead to the relevant equilibrium price pattern? A clue is provided by a market analogy. Suppose that there are middlemen who buy the mixed foods and decompose them into their elements, selling the resulting pure calories, pure vitamins, etc. The (shadow) prices offered to middlemen for the elements must be such as to leave them with no (excess) profits even when they handle only the optimal foods, and with negative profits if they are rash enough to handle uneconomical goods. So far, so good, but this carries us no farther than our previous rule, which we saw needed amplification.

Our more complete rule for setting shadow prices can now be formulated as the following:

> Consistently with there being no positive profits anywhere in the system, set the y prices so that a *maximum* of total dollar revenue is realized from all the total required elements. (In economic jargon, the equilibrium prices must maximize the sum total of imputed or "derived" rents.)

The total revenue from all elements is the sum of calorie revenue, $C_1 y_1$, plus vitamin revenue, $C_2 y_2$, $\cdots$, and so forth. Hence, our procedure for setting shadow prices may be stated mathematically as follows:

$$(17) \qquad Z' = C_1 y_1 + \cdots + C_m y_m$$

is to be a maximum subject to

$$a_{11} y_1 + a_{21} y_2 + \cdots + a_{m1} y_m \leq P_1$$
$$a_{12} y_1 + a_{22} y_2 + \cdots + a_{m2} y_m \leq P_2$$
$$a_{1n} y_1 + a_{2n} y_2 + \cdots + a_{mn} y_m \leq P_n$$
$$y_1 \geq 0, y_2 \geq 0, \cdots y_m \geq 0$$

A minimum-cost problem has been turned into a maximum-rent problem! A quantities problem has been turned into a prices problem! This is the remarkable duality feature, discovered by von Neumann and other mathematicians but quite consistent with economic reasoning. Thus we should expect the national income ("rents") paid to factors to equal in a simple economic system the value of national output sold; or (maximum) $Z' =$ (minimum) Z.

Let us apply our generalized rule to see whether it does select the correct one from the four consistent price patterns: $(0, 11)$, $(1, 10)$, $(2, 8)$, $(2, 0)$. Our four different totals of rents are

$$Z' = C_1 y_1 + C_2 y_2 = 700 y_1 + 400 y_2$$

$$= 700 \ (0) + 400 \ (11) = 400, \quad A$$

or

$$= 700 \ (1) + 400 \ (10) = 4700, \quad B$$

or

$$= 700 \ (2) + 400 \ (8) \ = 4600, \quad C$$

or

$$= 700 \ (2) + 400 \ (0) \ = 1400, \quad D$$

Clearly, the second case, B, represents the true optimum or maximum Z', which does equal the minimum $Z = 4700$ that we have seen earlier.[20]

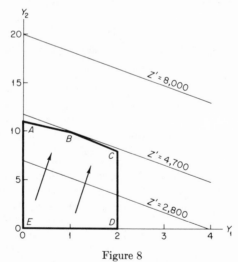

Figure 8

Figure 8 indicates the same solution for optimal prices. We are free to move in $ABCDE$ so as to maximize Z'. Contours of equal Z' are given by parallel lines with absolute slopes $C_1/C_2 = 700/400$. The arrows

[20] $ABCDE$ is a convex contour. It follows, as common sense will confirm, that raising calorie requirements will — if anything — raise the shadow price of calories.

(perpendicular to the contour) indicate the direction in which our optimum lies. Clearly, the best place to end up is at B, where $Z' = 4700$; anywhere else will give a lower Z'; only at B will the broken line ABC be touching (but not crossing) the highest Z' contour.

If we imagine an Office of Price Administration (OPA) that tries to find the best prices by the deliberate use of intelligence, its task is now finished. It has posed for itself a prices-maximum problem in linear programming, rather than the quantities-minimum problem that a War Production Board (WPB) might formulate. If the OPA mathematicians are omniscient, they will have found the best solution to this dual problem and set prices accordingly.

Determining Quantities by Use of Prices

Let us imagine that we have somehow been given the solution to our dual problem and know the correct set of (shadow) prices. We can use them immediately in two ways. First, we may directly compute the minimum cost of the best diet *even before we know the composition of that diet!* The minimum cost, Z, has been shown to be equal to the maximum rents, $Z' = \sum C_i y_i$ ($= 4700$ in our arithmetic example).

Second, we now know what the marginal costs of specifying one extra calorie unit or other nutritional element will be. These marginal costs are nothing but our shadow prices:[21]

$$(18) \qquad MC_1 = y_1 = \left(\frac{dZ}{dC_1}\right); \cdots; MC_i = y_i = \left(\frac{dZ}{dC_i}\right), \cdots$$

But most important of all, once the OPA or anyone else has given us best shadow prices, we can use this information to select deliberately the best quantities in the diet. Or we can set up quasi-automatic little market units and mechanisms which will eventually approach the best solution.

Given the best prices — for example $(y_1, y_2) = (1, 10)$ in our problem — we know that at least all but m of our goods can be regarded as unprofitable and their quantities set equal to zero. Thus, for $(y_1, y_2) = (1, 10)$, we have $(\pi_1, \pi_2, \pi_3, \pi_4, \pi_5) = (-, -, -, 0, 0)$, so that our best diet will be $(X_1, X_2, X_3, X_4, X_5) = (0, 0, 0, X_4?, X_5?)$. Because there are only two elements, calories and vitamins, we can concentrate on only two foods, in this case X_4 and X_5. We must select the precise amount of

---

[21]As mentioned earlier, the Lagrangian multipliers, λ_i, and the prices, y_i, are essentially the same thing. In ordinary well-behaved nonlinear maximum problems a general theorem assures us that the derivatives of the form $\partial Z/\partial C_i$ are exactly equal to the Lagrangian multiplier, λ_i. See Samuelson, *Foundations of Economic Analysis, op. cit.*, p. 132. It is remarkable that in the boundary maxima of linear programming the λ's have the same property. Also, when a C_k is not binding, $\lambda_k = 0$, just as MC_k obviously should be too. By direct differentiation of $Z' = Z\sum C_k y_k$, we find $(\partial Z'/\partial C_k) = y_k =$ (strangely enough) (dZ/dC_k).

these two foods so as to achieve our nutritional constraints. These constraints are also 2 (or m) in number, so that we have enough equations to determine our two unknowns.

Our general procedure is as follows:

> Suppose we know our best prices. They are m in number at most; but some prices may be zero, so that we may have only $r \leq m$ effective constraints. This means there will be some r economical goods that will exactly satisfy the effective constraints. We solve these r equations for exact values of the r economical X's.

The process of solving simultaneous equations is straightforward but very tedious to do even in a mathematics laboratory. How do people ordinarily solve the problem of not starving to death or becoming malnourished? In part, they are taught good habits; those taught very bad habits may have died out long ago. In part, there is some physiological evidence that Nature's evolutionary development has resulted in built-in "thermostats" of hunger and appetite so that when an animal has eaten too little salt over a period of time, it "hankers for" and seeks out salt.

In a crude way, it is as if there is a dynamic mechanism tending to make the animal seek foods containing much of the missing element. If we call $C_i(t)$ the amount of the ith nutritional element that the animal is currently getting, and if C_i is the amount it needs for good health, then specific hunger causes $dC_i(t)/dt$ to be negative whenever $C_i(t) - C_i$ is positive, and vice versa. In this way, over time, the animal obtains on the average a tolerable if not optimal diet.

The exact solution to our arithmetic problem is to determine the amounts of X_4 and X_5 from our calorie and our vitamin equations, or from

$$1X_4 + 2X_5 = 700$$
$$1X_4 + 1X_5 = 400$$
or $$X_4 = 100, X_5 = 300$$

as substitution or elementary algebra will verify.[22]

[22]A sophisticated economist might notice in this problem that it would be possible to define certain composite commodities, or market baskets of X_4 and X_5, which, if properly weighted, would be found to consist entirely of calories and entirely of vitamins. He would have to be sophisticated because the relative weights could not be positive numbers. I cannot buy X_4 and X_5 and put them into a basket and hope that there will be only vitamins in the basket. But if I *buy 2 units of X_4 and sell 1 unit of X_5*, I will finally get one unit of vitamins and nothing else! My market basket or composite commodity has weights $(+2, -1)$. Similarly, to get pure calories, I must buy 1 of X_5 and sell 1 of X_4; this would leave me with one calorie unit and nothing else.

What is the market cost or price of each of these composite commodities or constructed "pure" foods? For the vitamin basket it is twice the price of X_4

The reader may verify that if the NRC set the vitamin requirement $C_2 = 0$, then a best set of prices would be $(y_1, y_2) = (2, 0)$, and we would have only X_1, a nonzero quantity.[23] We would solve for the exact X_1, by the $r = 1$ equation system:

$$1X_1 = 700$$

or

$$X_1 = 700$$

Simultaneous, Automatic Solutions of the Dual Problems

We have explored a great many aspects of the general problem of linear programming. We have seen that to find equilibrium prices is just as hard as to find the equilibrium quantities directly. The task of a central price board is no less difficult than that of a central production board. The intelligence and data needed are very great.

This is somewhat disappointing. But to economists like A. P. Lerner or O. Lange,[24] who have advocated the use of pricing systems even in a socialist state, there is still one important saving feature. They believe that an automatic market mechanism can be set up that will minimize the need for central authority and intelligence and will *simultaneously* solve *both* the price and quantity problems. The executives who run the different factories will take prices as given and according to profitability will expand or contract their operations. Prices themselves will not be determined by slide-rule boys in OPA, but will be determined so as to "clear the market" or equalize total supplies and demands. Gradually, by successive approximations the system — it is hoped — will settle down to the optimum configuration.

At the end of the first part of this study, which deals with linear programming and international theory, we saw that a similar procedure

---

minus once the price of X_5, or $2(11) - 1(12) = 10$. For the calories, it is the net algebraic cost of the foods in the second basket or $+1(12) - 1(11) = 1$. It is not surprising that we have ended up with $(1, 10)$, already seen to be the shadow prices (y_1, y_2) and (MC_1, MC_2).

The reader may be referred to Samuelson, *Foundations of Economic Analysis*, *op. cit.*, pp. 135–146, for a discussion of such composite commodities and the laws of their price formation.

[23]At $C_2 = 0$, MC_2 is ambiguous and ill-defined. This is because $(y_1, y_2) = (2, h)$ are solutions to our dual problem for all $0 \leq h \leq 8$. This means that $0 \leq MC_2 \leq 8$. Our best direction in Figure 8 is eastward and the line segment CD represents the set of optimal prices for our dual problem. The point C, itself, is not truly a correct point for our original problem since it falsely tells us that X_4 shows a zero profit and can be bought. In the most general case of m constraints, even when we have best prices, care is necessary in selecting the proper sets of variables (x's) and equations (constraints).

[24]See A. P. Lerner, *Economics of Control* (New York: Macmillan, 1946); O. Lange, "On the Economic Theory of Socialism," in B. E. Lippincott, editor, *On the Economic Theory of Socialism*, by Oskar Lange and Fred M. Taylor (Minneapolis, Minn.: University of Minnesota Press, 1938).

could be envisaged in the case of comparative advantage. In the diet problem, can we also set up mechanisms that will automatically give us both prices and quantities?

The answer seems to be in the affirmative. It is, in a sense, easier to define dynamic processes that give us quantities and prices at the same time than it is to get either alone.

A procedure that will seem reasonable to an economist is the following:

1. Let the value of any x_i grow at a rate that is proportional to its profitability, π_i, where this is computed as described earlier in terms of any initial set of shadow prices.

Let x_i decrease if profits are negative, at a rate proportional to these losses — but with the proviso that when any $x_i = 0$, it can fall no further.

2. Our rule for prices is similar. Let the shadow price of any nutritional element, say y_j, diminish whenever the total of that element forthcoming is greater than the minimum prescribed C_j, subject to the proviso that no price can be negative. Similarly, when there is a deficiency of any element, then let its price grow at a rate proportional to the deficiency.

These rules define our system's movement over time starting with any nonnegative x's and y's. Let us call $C_j(t)$ the total of the jth element being yielded by the system's current X values, so the $[C_j(t) - C_j] = c_j(t)$ is the "algebraic excess" of the jth element. Then, mathematically, our two rules state that

$$(19) \qquad \alpha_1 \frac{dx_1}{dt} = \pi_1, \ \cdots, \ \alpha_n \frac{dx_n}{dt} = \pi_n$$

$$\text{with } x_1 \geq 0, \ \cdots, x_n \geq 0$$

and

$$(19)' \qquad -\beta_1 \frac{dy_1}{dt} = c_1, \ \cdots, \ -\beta_m \frac{dy_m}{dt} = c_m$$

$$\text{with } y_1 \geq 0, \ \cdots, y_m \geq 0$$

and where the α's and β's are positive proportionality time constants.

The system can settle down and come to rest only if profits are everywhere zero for all goods that are not themselves zero, and if "excesses" are everywhere zero for all elements whose prices are not zero. For all zero y's and x's the corresponding excesses are positive and the profits are negative.

The economic common sense of all this is something like the following: Too low shadow prices will yield high profits and great expansion of quantities; but expansion of quantities will flood the market with excessive supplies and cause prices to fall; this in turn will choke off the excess by diminishing output; and the system will oscillate around its equilibrium values.

Note that I do not say the system will necessarily settle down. Actually, for this system it will tend to oscillate in nondamped but also nonexplosive oscillations, rather like a pendulum in a "conservative" physical system without friction.[25]

A little intelligent speculation or foresight can be expected to cause the system actually to settle down. I would conjecture that if we subtract something from profits whenever there are great general surpluses of elements and make the growth rate, dx_i/dt, proportional to profits so adjusted rather than to π_i, then the system will finally damp down. Since some excesses are optimal — those for which the y's are zero — this will tend to bias our solution. But this bias can be avoided if we make sure that our correction to profits are only for "unwanted" excesses and are of the form

$$\alpha_i \frac{dx_i}{dt} = \pi_i - \sum_{j=1}^{m} K_{ij} c_j y_j$$

where the K's are nonnegative proportionality time constants.

Likewise, it makes economic sense to add still more dampening, if we wish to do so, by causing the growth of prices to be reduced whenever profits are "generally" too great.

Our final dynamic system might be something like this:

$$\alpha_i \frac{dx_i}{dt} = \pi_i - \sum_{j=1}^{m} K_{ij} c_j y_j \qquad (i = 1, 2, \cdots, n)$$

with $x_i \geq 0$

$$-\beta_j \frac{dy_j}{dt} = c_j + \sum_{i=1}^{n} M_{ji} \pi_i x_i \qquad (j = 1, 2, \cdots, m)$$

with $y_j \geq 0$

where the M's, like the K's, are nonnegative time constants.

Later I hope to return to a mathematical consideration of the problems dealt with here.

III. Dynamics and Linear Programming

Introduction

The preceding sections of this study dealt with the statical problem of international comparative advantage and with the statical problem of a cheapest adequate diet. This section provides a simple introduction to the dynamic problems of maximizing like those which von Neumann

[25]If we start the system out with a very good approximate guess to the true solution $(y_1^0, \cdots, y_m^0, x_1^0, \cdots, x_m^0)$, then the time averages of $[y_j(t), x_i(t)]$ will closely approximate the values $[y_j^0, x_i^0]$. Any bias will vanish with our initial error.

471

and Dantzig have investigated.[26] Leontief has also been extending his input-output studies in this direction. I should also mention that within the realm of economic theory — particularly capital theory — there has been a voluminous literature on related subjects.

The Simplest Case of a Single Dynamic Process

Consider the simplest possible case where a single commodity — chocolates, rabbits, gold coins, or simply output — can be used at time t as an input to produce itself as an output at time $t + 1$. The output at any time $t + 1$ can be split into two parts: consumption or $C(t + 1)$, and input for the next period's output or $x(t + 1)$. Our production function at any time period may be written in the simplest linear form as

$$(20) \qquad C(t + 1) + x(t + 1) \leq ax(t)$$

where the left-hand side is total output, and where a is a given technical constant, and where the inequality is included in recognition of the fact that people might by stupidity get less output than is technically feasible. Note that the *linear* character of the production relation means we assume "constant returns to scale."

If at time $t = 0$ we start out with K units of our good, then at that time, our choice between consumption then and consumption for the future is given by

$$C(0) + x(0) \leq K$$

and if we are maximizing, the inequality can be dropped.

Our choice for period $t = 1$ is given by

$$C(1) + x(1) \leq ax(0) \leq a[K - C(0)]$$

Similarly, for the 2nd period, our choice is

$$C(2) + x(2) \leq ax(1) \leq a\{a[K - C(0)] - C(1)\}$$

or in general, for any period, we can verify the formula

$$C(n) + x(n) \leq a^n K - a^n C(0) - a^{n-1} C(1) - \cdots - aC(n - 1)$$

The economist who remembers his formula for present discounted value of an income stream will be able to think of a as $(1 + \text{interest rate})$ and of the productive process as a bank that pays this rate of compound interest on all deposits; he will recognize the preceding formula as saying that the amount in the bank today is the cumulated value of the original deposit minus the cumulated value of all consumption withdrawals. This

[26]J. von Neumann, "A Model of General Equilibrium," *Review of Economic Studies*, Vol. XIII (1945–1946); G. B. Dantzig, *Programming of Interdependent Activities II: Mathematical Model*, LPC-105.

formula can also be written in the equivalent alternative form

$$(21) \qquad K \geq C(0) + \frac{C(1)}{a} + \frac{C(2)}{a^2} + \cdots + \frac{C(n)}{a^n} + \frac{x(n)}{a^n}$$

and if $a > 1$, this can be extended to be a convergent infinite series.

Such a relation is an optimal one: it gives us the maximum amount of consumption for *any* period as of specified initial and terminal amounts of output and as of prescribed amounts of consumption for *all* other periods. It gives us the "menu" of consumption possibilities that we can choose between. Figure 9 illustrates this locus of "efficient points" in the simple case of the two variables $C(0)$ and $C(1)$.

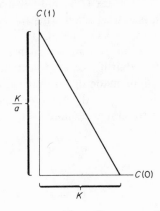

Figure 9

The "marginal rate of substitution" between any two consumptions is always a constant, namely

$$(22) \qquad MRS_{ij} = -\frac{\partial C(i)}{\partial C(j)} = a^{i-j}$$

It was very easy in this case to get to the optimum. We simply decided never to waste any unconsumed output but to put it all back into the productive process. Can we justify this procedure by means of the statical theory of linear programming outlined earlier? We can. Dynamic processes can be regarded as interesting special cases of static ones.

A single productive process will involve, over a long enough period of time, an indefinitely large number of variables. The production relation (1) is not one equation: it is as many equations as we have time periods; and there are as many variables, $x(0)$, $x(1)$, $x(2)$, $x(3)$, $\cdots$, $x(n)$ $\cdots$, as we care to consider. Let us keep matters simple and consider $t = 0, 1, 2, 3, 4$ only, and let us seek to maximize $C(3)$ with K, $C(0)$, $C(1)$, $C(2)$, $C(4)$, and $x(4)$ all being arbitrarily prescribed.

Subject to

$$x(0) \leq K - C(0)$$

$$x(1) - ax(0) \leq -C(1)$$

$$x(2) - ax(1) \qquad \leq -C(2)$$

$$-ax(3) \qquad\qquad \leq -C(4) - x(4)$$

we wish to maximize

(23) $\quad Z = C(3) = B_3 x(3) + B_2 x(2) + B_1 x(1) + B_0 x(0)$
$\qquad\quad = 1x(3) - ax(2) + 0 + 0$

We shall be at the maximum $C(3)$ only if every inequality sign is discarded. The remarkable thing about this solution is that it does not change as we change the values of $C(0)$, $C(1)$, $\cdots$, etc., something that would be surprising were our system not such a simple one. A related singular feature is the fact that if we were to extend our sequence beyond $t = 4$, the efficient decisions made up to that point would be invariant. This is associated with the special character that our static matrices take when they belong to simple dynamic sequences. The matrix is of the form

$$
\begin{matrix}
\cdot & \cdot & 0 & 0 & 0 & 1 \\
\cdot & \cdot & 0 & 0 & 1 & -a \\
\cdot & \cdot & 0 & 1 & -a & 0 \\
\cdot & \cdot & \cdot & \cdot & \cdot & \cdot
\end{matrix}
$$

and it builds downward and to the left without any feedback influences on the earlier inequalities.

One remark will relate our simple system to von Neumann's processes. He assumes that all output is used to produce further outputs so that

$$0 = C(0) = C(1) = \cdots = C(t) = \cdots$$

In this case our system grows in a geometric progression

(24) $\quad x(t) = Ka^t$

with a maximum percentage rate of growth given by

(25) $\quad \dfrac{x(t + 1)}{x(t)} = a$

We should expect prices to play a role in dynamic sequences like that in the two earlier sections. Specifically, we should guess that the price ratio between the output of two periods would be equal to the marginal rate of substitution between the outputs of those periods. Let us set

$p(0)$ equal to 1 and work with the initial period's output as our unit of value. Then we should guess from (22) that

$$(26) \qquad -\frac{\partial C(0)}{\partial C(t)} = \frac{p(t)}{p(0)} = a^{-t}$$

$$(27) \qquad \frac{p(t+1)}{p(t)} = a^{-1}$$

To verify this, let us seek for a set of (shadow) prices that will make profits zero on all the processes used. On a typical process, we invest one unit of $x(t)$ worth $p(t)$ and get in return output worth $p(t+1)a$. Our profit is defined as

$$(28) \qquad \pi(t) \le p(t+1)a - p(t)$$

This must be zero for every t, so that the price relations of (27) immediately follow.

The economic theorist will recognize (28) as the formula for *present discounted value*, and the p's as ("own") rates of interest and discount. The formal similarity between equations (24) and (25) and equations (26) and (27) is another instance of the duality between prices and quantities that has been discussed earlier.

The Case of Alternative Processes

The case of a single process is almost trivial from the standpoint of linear programming and maximizing decisions. Scarcely any intelligent choices had to be made. Consider therefore a slightly more interesting case, but still an exceedingly simple one. Suppose that we can allocate the unconsumed output of any period as inputs to either of two productive processes. Let $x_1(t)$ be the input to the first process, and let $a_1 x_1(t)$ be the maximum output resulting in the following period; likewise, let $x_2(t)$ be the second process' input and $a_2 x_2(t)$ its output in the following period. Note that we have two production functions; but we can add the identical outputs of the processes and allocate the total between consumption $C(t+1)$ and the two inputs for the *following* period's production to get the relation:

$$(29) \qquad C(t+1) + x_1(t+1) + x_2(t+1) \le a_1 x_1(t) + a_2 x_2(t)$$

This is the generalization of our first equation; and as in the case of a single process, we suspect that the inequality signs can be dropped in any optimal process.

But now if we start with initial output

$$C(0) + x_1(0) + x_2(0) = K$$

the resulting process does not give us a unique choice among the consumptions of different periods. Depending upon how we decide to determine $x_1(t)$ and $x_2(t)$ at each stage, we shall get a different menu of consumption choices. How do we resolve this ambiguity? By the same principle as before: *With initial and final outputs being given us, and with all but one consumption item being given us, we must try to maximize that remaining consumption item.*

The solution is intuitively obvious — as obvious as the answer to this question: If two banks offer you different interest rates on your bank balances, how should you invest your money? Only in the bank that gives you the higher interest rate is the obvious answer. Similarly, if $a_1 > a_2$, then we never allocate any input to the second process; and our solution is exactly as in the case of a single process, but with a subscript 1 on all the earlier a symbols. Thus,

$$0 = x_2(0) = x_2(1) = x_2(2) = \cdots = x_2(t) = \cdots$$

(30) $$K \geq C(0) + \frac{C(1)}{a_1} + \frac{C(2)}{a_1{}^2} + \cdots + \frac{C(t)}{a_1{}^t} + \frac{x_1(t)}{a_1{}^t}$$

$$p(t+1) = a_1{}^{-1}p(t)$$

where the p's are the prices of the output of any period. Note the negative profitability of ever using any $x_2(t)$ as given by

$$\pi_2(t) = p(t+1)a_2 - p(t) = (a_2 - a_1)p(t+1) < 0$$

As in the single process, we get a geometric progression if all "consumption" is zero and all output is plowed back into the business. We also get the von Neumann dual relations

(31) $$\begin{cases} \text{Max } \dfrac{x(t+1)}{x(t)} = a_1 = \max\,[a_1, a_2] \\[4mm] \text{Min } \dfrac{p(t+1)}{p(t)} = a_1{}^{-1} = \min\,[a_1{}^{-1}, a_2{}^{-1}] \end{cases}$$

Note that in this special case, as in the single-process case, the system can go instantly into its maximal rate of growth regardless of how we start it off. This will not be generally true. Note too that three or more alternative processes, with defined $a_1, a_2, a_3, \cdots$, would be subject to the same rule: select the process with the highest a (i.e., the highest "net reproductive rate" or "rate of interest *in natura*").

The More General Case of Transient Unbalance

The two cases considered so far have had the special property of always being in a constant relative price configuration: regardless of the pattern of desired consumption, the same price ratios have prevailed over time; and regardless of the initial endowments of the various commodities, the system can generate itself at a stable geometric rate. In more general systems this will not be the case. An example of joint production will make this clear.

Suppose that a unit of the first commodity, x_1, will reproduce itself by tripling in every period. Suppose that at the same time it produces as a by-product a unit of a second product, x_2. Assume that x_2 can also reproduce itself by doubling every period, so that there are two separate ways of getting x_2. As before, assume that the output of any good may be consumed in any period or can be used as input for the next period's output. Mathematically, our equations are

$$(32) \quad \begin{cases} C_1(t+1) + x_1(t+1) \le 3x_1(t) \\ C_2(t+1) + x_2(t+1) \le 1x_1(t) + 2x_2(t) \end{cases}$$

How will the system grow if there is no consumption? Suppose we start out with no x_1 and one unit of x_2, so that $[x_1(0), x_2(0)] = [0, 1]$. In the next period x_2 will double, so we have $[x_1(1), x_2(1)] = [0, 2]$. This will be followed by $[0, 4]$, $[0, 8]$, $(0, 16]$, $\cdots$, $[0, 2^t]$, which is obviously a steady geometric progression.

But suppose we had started with one unit of each good, with $[1, 1]$. The x_1 will triple itself, and provide $1x_2$ as a by-product. The x_2 unit will double itself. All together we shall have $[3, 3]$. Similarly, in the next periods we shall have $[9, 9]$, $[27, 27]$, $\cdots$, $[3^t, 3^t]$. Again we have a steady geometric progression but with a tripling per period instead of a doubling.

Suppose we start with any amounts of the two goods — say $[1, 10]$. The obvious way to handle this is to decompose it into our previous two cases: into $[1, 1]$ + nine $[0, 1]$. Does the result grow at a tripling rate or a doubling rate? The answer is neither, but somewhere in between; after a long period of time the tripling items become overwhelmingly great compared to the doubling ones, so that in the limit the strongest geometric progression dominates. The interested reader may easily work out the case $[10, 1]$ and show that x_2 will at first grow at more than a tripling rate.

Let us bring consumption back into the picture. What are our choices between, say, $C_1(1)$ and $C_2(1)$? Or between $C_1(2)$ and $C_2(2)$? Or between $C_1(t)$ and $C_2(t)$? Or between $C_1(0)$ and $C_2(2)$? The answer now depends upon our initial values. In Figure 10a, I have assumed that

$$x_1(0) = K_1 = 1$$
$$x_2(0) = K_2 = 0$$

and have indicated the consumption menus at $t = 0, 1, 2, 3$ (on the postulate that consumption at other rates is zero).

Figure 10b shows the substitution relations between $C_2(t)$ and $C_1(0)$

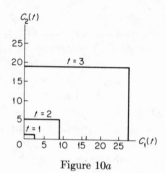

Figure 10a

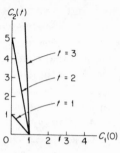

Figure 10b

under the same conditions. Note that the price ratio $p_2(t)/p_1(0) = [-\partial C_1(0)/\partial C_2(t)]$ is steadily dropping in the sequence $1, 5^{-1}, 19^{-1}, \cdots, (3^t - 2^t)^{-1}, \cdots$, which is no longer a simple geometric sequence, except asymptotically.

Mathematically, we must always have

$$(33) \quad \begin{cases} x_1(t) \leq K_1 3^t - C_1(0)3^t - C_1(1)3^{t-1} - \cdots - C_1(t) \\ x_2(t) \leq K_2 2^t - C_2(0)2^t - \cdots - C_2(t) \\ \qquad\qquad + [K_1 - C_1(0)](3^t - 2^t) - C_1(1)(3^{t-1} - 2^{t-1}) \\ \qquad\qquad\qquad\qquad\qquad - \cdots - 1C_1(t - 1) \end{cases}$$

One rather subtle point should be mentioned. Figures 10a and 10b and price formulas hold on the assumption that we are choosing between $C_2(t)$ and $C_1(0)$ not giving a hang about *future* consumption and inputs. Let us also prescribe some future inputs, $x_2(t + 1)$, $x_2(t + 2)$, $\cdots$, etc. If these are prescribed low enough, then our formulas may still hold. But if we insist on their being still higher, then the effective menu between $C_1(0)$ and $C_2(t)$ will change. Thus if $x_2(t + k)$ is made high enough to be the limiting factor, then the effective MRS between $C_1(0)$ and $C_2(t)$ will be

$$(34) \qquad \left[-\frac{\partial C_1(0)}{\partial C_2(t)}\right]_{t+k} = \frac{2^k}{3^{t+k} - 2^{t+k}} \leq \frac{1}{3^t - 2^t}$$

This can be verified by differentiation of the formula for $x_2(t + k)$ in (33).

The important thing to notice about this third case is the fact that constant costs no longer hold. According to the patterns of $C_1(t)$ and $C_2(t)$ that we specify, there will be different rates at which the different consumption items can be substituted one for the other. After digressing in the next section I shall return to this point again.

Exceptions to Steady-State Growth

In every case so far, setting consumption at zero has resulted ultimately in an approach to a state of steady maximal growth. Must this always be the case? The answer is, clearly, no. Two different examples will be of interest.

Suppose rabbits obey the production function

$$x_1(t+1) = 100x_1(t)$$

and cheese obeys the production function

$$x_2(t+1) = 2x_2(t)$$

The production functions are entirely independent and lead to two different "own rates of interest" and two different rates of growth. Obviously, the price of rabbits must deteriorate over time relative to the price of cheese.[27]

A more interesting example of no approach to a limiting steady growth is one in which tomorrow's chickens, $x_2(t+1)$, grow out of today's eggs, $x_1(t)$, which in turn have grown out of yesterday's chickens. Our relations are

$$x_1(t+1) = ax_2(t), \ x_2(t+1) = bx_1(t)$$

and the development over time is

$$\begin{cases} x_1(2t) = (ab)^t x_1(0) \\ x_1(2t+1) = (ab)^t a x_2(0) \end{cases}$$

$$\begin{cases} x_2(2t) = (ab)^t x_2(0) \\ x_2(2t+1) = (ab)^t b x_1(0) \end{cases}$$

The ratio of $x_i(t+1)/x_i(t)$ oscillates every other time, varying in the pattern a, b, a, b, a, b, $\cdots$, etc. The price ratios also show this every-other-time oscillation.

The mathematical reason for this is simple. The matrix iteration

$$x(t+1) = Ax(t)$$

will have a "dominant mode" or "characteristic vector" corresponding to the characteristic root of A with the greatest absolute value or modulus. If every element a_{ij} of A is positive, this dominant root must be real and positive. Hence, if we start from arbitrary positive values of the vector $x(t)$, we shall approach in the limit a geometric progression

$$x(t) = \lambda^t K$$

[27]In a sense we might consider

$$x_1(t) = K100^t$$
$$x_2(t) = 0, \qquad \frac{p_1(t)}{p_2(t)} = 0$$

a limiting steady-growth motion.

where K represents a vector with all positive constants and λ is the dominant characteristic root.

The present chicken-egg example is one on the border where no a_{ij} is negative but all diagonal elements are zero. The characteristic roots are given by

$$\begin{vmatrix} 0 - \lambda & a \\ b & 0 - \lambda \end{vmatrix} = \lambda^2 - ab = 0, \text{ or } \lambda = \pm \sqrt{ab}$$

The negative one of these two roots has as large a modulus as the positive one, and hence there is no dominance. Our earlier solution can be written in the form

$$x_1(t) = \frac{x_1(0) + ax_2(0)}{2} (+ \sqrt{ab})^t + \frac{x_1(0) - ax_2(0)}{2} (- \sqrt{ab})^t, \text{ etc.}$$

Neither term shrinks in relative importance, and the sum oscillates.

Before leaving the barnyard, let us consider the closely related Malthusian theory of population. Without preventive checks or the positive check of inadequate food, population might double every generation. Malthus argued that food could not also grow at such a fast rate, so that checks would operate to prevent a doubling every generation. Some of his early critics argued that food consisted of animals and plants and that these also grew by nature in a geometric progression. Granting this for the moment, we may still deny that the geometric rate of growth of subsistence need be at the same rate as for humans — namely a doubling every quarter century or so. There are two possibilities: subsistence may grow — while it is drawn on to feed man at the level he is accustomed to — at a faster rate or a slower rate than man himself. It is quite clear that the component of *slowest* growth will set the pace for the whole.[28] If shmoos double every century instead of every quarter century, then positive checks will keep man's growth rate down to that of shmoos. But if man can make subsistence grow so as to double in less than every quarter century, then men will be the bottleneck.

---

[28]Bateman and others have studied chains of radioactive substances in which ultimately the slowest disintegrating substance sets the pace for all. The system can be written in terms of a triangular matrix

$$\frac{dx}{dt} = ax(t), \qquad\qquad a_{ij} = 0 \quad \text{for} \quad j > i$$

[*1965 Postscript:* If an output X_1 grows out of input X_2 or input X_3, the linear equation $X_1 = a_1 X_2 + a_3 X_3$ might hold. But if X_1 requires X_2 *and* X_3, we have $X_1 = \text{Min}[X_2/a_2, X_3/a_3]$. Difference equations of the form $X_i(t + 1) = F^i[X_1(t)/a_{1i}, \cdots, X_n(t)/a_{ni}]$, $(i = 1, \cdots, n)$, $a_{ij} > 0$ will for all positive $X_i(0)$ approach in the limit a positive exponential motion: $X_i(t) \to C_i \lambda^t$, $C_i > 0$, $0 < \lambda \lessgtr 1$, where (λ, C_i) depend on the a_{ij} coefficients λ being diminished by any increase in any a_{ij}.

In point of fact, Malthus based his theory on the assumption that inorganic natural resources — "land" — were limited and could not grow in effectiveness in a geometric ratio. The zero own-rate-of-growth of land would set the pace for organic food and for man, so that a stationary population would be reached in a technologically stationary society.

Simple von Neumann Processes

In this section I shall try to shed some expository light on von Neumann's elegant model of general equilibrium. For simplicity, I shall consider the case of just two commodities, and I shall rule out the not-too-interesting case of joint production; both of these limitations can be removed if one wants to do so. In other respects, I shall generalize beyond the von Neumann assumptions: first, consumption need not be zero with all outputs fed back into the system as inputs for its further growth; second, the production function can be assumed to be perfectly general, involving continuous substitutability of inputs (or, in von Neumann's terminology, an infinite number of alternative processes).

We start out at time t with a first good that can be consumed or can be used as input for the next period's production. The procedure is similar for a second good. But now we assume that each good's total input must be broken down and allocated to the production of each of the next period's two goods. Let $C_i(t)$ be the consumption of the ith good; let $X_i(t)$ be the total amount available of the ith good out of previous period's production; let $x_{1i}(t)$ be the amount of the ith good allocated as input to the production of tomorrow's $X_1(t+1)$; and let $x_{2i}(t)$ be the ith input allocated to produce the good $X_2(t+1)$. Our results can be summarized as shown in Table VI. As a matter of notation, let us use small $x_i(t)$ to represent the total of inputs or

$$C_i(t) + x_i(t) = C_i(t) + \sum_{j=1}^{2} x_{ji}(t) \leq X_i(t)$$

We now add the technological assumptions that specify how much of each good can be produced in $t+1$ on the basis of all possible inputs used for that good at t. These production functions can be written as

(35) $\begin{cases} X_1(t+1) = F_1[x_{11}(t), x_{12}(t)] \\ X_2(t+1) = F_2[x_{21}(t), x_{22}(t)] \end{cases}$

where each of these equations corresponds to a *row* in the Table VI.

So far, we have assumed nothing about the form of the F functions. Leontief usually assumes that output depends linearly upon a combined dose of fixed-proportion inputs so that whenever one input is in greater

Table VI

Input Allocation of Goods

	First Good	Second Good
Allocation to Production of $X_1(t+1)$	$x_{11}(t)$	$x_{12}(t)$
	$+$	$+$
Allocation to Production of $X_2(t+1)$	$x_{21}(t)$	$x_{22}(t)$
	$+$	$+$
Allocation to Consumption	$C_1(t)$	$C_2(t)$
Total of Good Available	$\leq X_1(t)$	$\leq X_2(t)$

than the critical proportion, its marginal productivity is zero. Dr. von Neumann makes a similar but slightly more general assumption: for him there may be more than one critical fixed-proportion dose that will yield output. Figure 11*a* shows the equal-product contours for Leontief: if both inputs are increased together along the broken line, output increases proportionally; but increasing any one input beyond this critical proportion leads to no increase in product.

In Figure 11*b*, the points *A*, *B*, *C*, and *D* represent four different possible processes by which one unit of output can be produced from the two inputs. Each such point is like *A* in the Leontief model. But it is now quite obvious that we can forget about the point *C* that corresponds to the third process, P_3. This is because it requires more of *both* inputs to produce the same output as the point *D* can produce; the fourth process, B_4, is always better than the third. The point *B*, corresponding to the second process, can also be disregarded, but the reason is not so obvious. If we assume constant-returns-to-scale, as von Neumann does, then by some judicious weighting of the first and fourth processes, P_1 and P_4, we can end up wherever we please on the straight line between *A* and *D*. For example, if we mix P_4 and P_1 in the ratio of 7 to 13, we shall get our one unit of $X_1(t+1)$ with a 15 per cent saving of both inputs as compared to P_2 and the point *B*, as indicated by a comparison of *E* and *B* in Figure 11*b*.

Figure 11*c* shows a general production function with variable proportions. Were we not making the assumption of constant-returns-to-scale and insisting on the definition of a production function as giving "the maximum amount of output for available amounts of inputs," we should have to admit the possibility of convex as well as concave contours.

Contours of $X_1(t+1)$

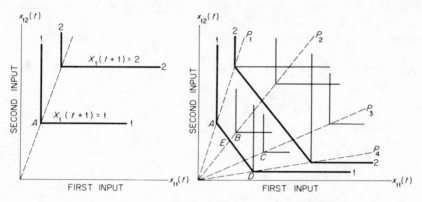

Figure 11a

Leontief Production Function

Figure 11b

Von Neumann Production Function

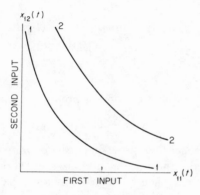

Figure 11c

General Production Function

Let us now consider the dynamic development of our system. We can combine our Table VI and Equation (35) to get

$$(36) \quad \begin{cases} C_1(t+1) + x_1(t+1) \leq X_1(t+1) = F_1[x_{11}(t), x_{12}(t)] \\ C_2(t+1) + x_2(t+1) \leq X_2(t+1) = F_2[x_{21}(t), x_{22}(t)] \end{cases}$$

If we start out with initial outputs $X_i(t)$, and if we specify the final outputs $X_i(n)$, and if we specify all but one of the consumptions $C_i(t)$, then that last consumption must be made maximal.

On the other hand, if we set all consumptions equal to zero, our system can grow. But there is not a unique method of growth: we may at each stage choose to have much X_1 or much X_2, and this will result in an infinite variety of developing patterns. Nonetheless, whatever pattern we finally choose, it must have the following property: we must never follow a pattern of production that would permit us to find another pattern that is superior in terms of every good; any permissible pattern must give us the maximum amount of $X_2(t + 1)$, for specified $X_1(t + 1)$, $X_1(t)$, and $X_2(t)$.

At any time t, we must so select $x_{11}(t)$, $x_{12}(t)$, $x_{21}(t)$, and $x_{22}(t)$ so as to make

$$Z = X_2(t + 1) = F_2[x_{21}(t), x_{22}(t)]$$

a maximum subject to

$$(37) \quad \begin{cases} F_1[x_{11}(t), x_{12}(t)] \geq X_1(t + 1) \\ x_{11}(t) + x_{21}(t) \leq x_1(t) \\ x_{12}(t) + x_{22}(t) \leq x_2(t) \end{cases}$$

The condition for the optimum — if no inputs are zero and the derivatives exist — is

$$(38) \quad \frac{\dfrac{\partial F_1[x_{11}(t), x_{12}(t)]}{\partial x_{11}(t)}}{\dfrac{\partial F_1[x_{11}(t), x_{12}(t)]}{\partial x_{12}(t)}} = \frac{\dfrac{\partial F_2[x_{21}(t), x_{22}(t)]}{\partial x_{21}(t)}}{\dfrac{\partial F_2[x_{21}(t), x_{22}(t)]}{\partial x_{22}(t)}}$$

This will give us an optimal relation or production menu of the form

$$(39) \quad X_2(t + 1) = M[X_1(t + 1); x_1(t), x_2(t)]$$

This function is homogeneous of the first order because of our assumption about returns-to-scale, and can be normalized by working with one unit of the first input; it can then be depicted as a one-parameter family of curves.

Figure 12a shows the typical P-P ("production-possibility") curve for the general case of continuously varying production functions like that of Figure 11c. Note the nonconvexity of the curves and their noncrossing.

The heavy black curve in Figure 12b shows the P-P curve for a Leontief-type structure. The two parallel families of lines show the possibilities if varying amounts of each one of the inputs were the limiting factor. Each line is labeled by a number representing the available amount of $X_1(t)$ or $X_2(t)$, as the case may be. Knowing both these numbers and hence the relevant two lines, we derive our heavy black P-P curve by following *whichever curve is inside*. The result will usually have a ("concave") corner, and away from there one of the inputs will have a zero marginal productivity.

The von Neumann case is a little more complicated. In Figure 12c, I have drawn two P-P curves of the Leontief type: they are ABC and DEF, respectively. Anyone who has followed the earlier reasoning concerning

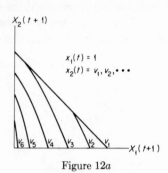

Figure 12a

General Production-Possibility Function

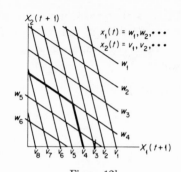

Figure 12b

Leontief P-P Curve

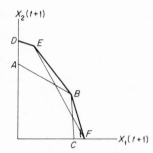

Figure 12c

Von Neumann P-P Curve

Figure 11c will easily convince himself that the resultant optimal P-P curve is the heavy dark *DEBF* curve. Even in more complicated cases, we must always end up with a concave polygon.

Another aspect of the crucial P-P Equation (39) is illuminated by the following question: Our outputs $X_1(t + 1)$ and $X_2(t + 1)$ having been specified, what combinations of $x_1(t)$ and $x_2(t)$ are possible? Figures 13a, 13b, and 13c exemplify the answer to our question.

With or without the use of prices, the economist will readily perceive that any optimum pattern over time must at least satisfy the following conditions at every instant of time:

(40)
$$\frac{\dfrac{\partial U}{\partial C_1(t)}}{\dfrac{\partial U}{\partial C_2(t)}} = \frac{\partial M[X_1(t); x_1(t - 1), x_2(t - 1)]}{\partial X_1(t)}$$

$$= \frac{\dfrac{\partial M[X_1(t + 1); x_1(t), x_2(t)]}{\partial x_1(t)}}{\dfrac{\partial M[X_1(t + 1); x_1(t), x_2(t)]}{\partial x_2(t)}}$$

485

This says that there must be equality between the marginal rates of substitution of (1) the consumer, (2) the production of today's goods from yesterday's inputs, and (3) the use of today's inputs for tomorrow's outputs.

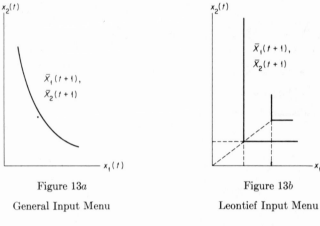

Figure 13*a*	Figure 13*b*
General Input Menu	Leontief Input Menu

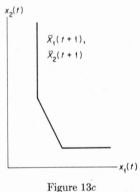

Figure 13*c*

Von Neumann Input Menu

Consumers' tastes are no business of ours in the present study, but the other relationship can be given a simple and fairly obvious interpretation in terms of maximizing. To keep the argument simple, and without materially affecting our results, let us suppose all consumption to be zero. Let us start out with $X_1(0)$, $X_2(0)$ and ask the following questions:

1. How do we get the best menu at $t = 1$?
2. Disregarding $t = 1$, how do we get the best menu at time $t = 2$?
3. Disregarding all intermediate times, how do we get the best menu at time $t = n$?

The first of these three questions has been answered by Equation (39). The second can be shown to have its answer given by the last part of (40). Curiously enough, if the second question is properly answered at every stage of time, then the third will already be answered, even though the second is only the special case of the third where $n = 2$.

The third question is the general one, and we may phrase it mathematically as follows. Maximize

$$Z = X_2(n) = M[X_1(n); x_1(n-1), x_2(n-1)]$$

subject to

(41) $\qquad M[X_1(t); x_1(t-1), x_2(t-1)] - X_2(t) \geq 0$
$$(t = 1, 2, \cdots, n-1)$$

when $X_1(0)$, $X_2(0)$, and $X_1(n)$ are all constants. If all of the functions are differentiable and our maximum is an interior one, then the theory of constrained maxima implies

(40)′ $\qquad \dfrac{\partial M[X_1(t+1); x_1(t), x_2(t)]}{\partial X_1(t+1)}$

$$= \dfrac{\dfrac{\partial M[X_1(t); x_1(t-1), x_2(t-1)]}{\partial x_1(t-1)}}{\dfrac{\partial M[X_1(t); x_1(t-1), x_2(t-1)]}{\partial x_2(t-1)}}$$
$$(t = 1, 2, \cdots, n-1)$$

But this is only a repetition of the condition that must hold when $n = 2$, that is, Equation (40). The interested reader can draw a graph to show how the optimal relation

$$X_2(t+2) = M_2[X_1(t+2); x_1(t), x_2(t)]$$

is the envelope of the M curves corresponding to each point on M itself.

One final point needs more exploration. Let us define

(42) $\qquad X_2(t+n) = M_n[X_1(t+n); x_1(t), x_2(t)]$

as the optimum menu resulting from the solution to (41). What, then, are the properties of the function

(43) $\qquad X_2 = M_n[X_1; x_1, x_2]$

as n increases? The answer is probably related very closely to the special "equilibrium solution" to von Neumann's system.

The Equilibrium Mode or Configuration

By an equilibrium position of such a dynamic system, von Neumann means a condition of steady self-generated growth in which all ratios of extensive magnitudes are constant. As usual, he is assuming that there is no "consumption," but rather that everything is fed back into the system to make it grow. Not only is there to be steady geometric growth but the equilibrium rate of growth is defined to be the *maximum* possible rate of balanced growth.

This may be illustrated by the two-variable system $X_2 = M[X_1; x_1, x_2]$. Since only ratios matter, we may work with the (λ, v) variables defined as follows:

Set, for all t,

$$(44) \qquad \begin{cases} x_1(t) = 1, \dfrac{x_2(t)}{x_1(t)} = v(t) \\[2ex] \dfrac{X_1(t+1)}{x_1(t)} = \lambda(t), \dfrac{X_2(t+1)}{X_1(t+1)} = v(t+1) \end{cases}$$

and now if we agree to keep proportions constant through time, or $v(t+1) = v(t) = v$, then we can eliminate all datings and simply work with

$$(44)' \qquad x_1 = 1, \frac{x_2}{x_1} = v, \frac{X_1}{x_1} = \frac{X_2}{x_2} = \lambda, \begin{cases} X_1 = \lambda \\ X_2 = v\lambda \end{cases}$$

Now (39) can be written as

$$(39)' \qquad v\lambda = M[\lambda; 1, v]$$

This is an implicit relation between λ and v. It tells us what balanced rate of growth, λ, in all variables is possible when we start with an arbitrary proportion v between our two goods. It can be solved to show the greatest λ possible as a function of v, or

$$(39)'' \qquad \lambda = \lambda(v)$$

Under normal economic assumptions,[29] this function, showing all the efficient producible situations, will yield a maximum λ^*; that is, for some $v = v^*, \lambda^* = \lambda(v^*) \geq \lambda(v)$. We may call λ^* the von Neumann dominant root of our system and $(1, v^*)$ the equilibrium mode or configuration of our system. This is an important concept.

Among other things, it tells us that if we start out with $X_1(0) = 1$, $X_2(0) = v^*$, the system can, with no consumption goods taken away from it, grow in the steady geometric progression $X_1(t) = (\lambda^*)^t, X_2(t) = v(\lambda^*)^t$. This will eventually outstrip any lesser geometric rate of growth.

---

[29]One must be wary of singular cases where the marginal productivities of sets of the factors and goods are identically zero so that the system splits up into disconnected parts.

If our implicit relation (39)′ is properly differentiable, we may find the optimum λ^* by setting $(d\lambda/dv)$ equal to zero; hence, at $\lambda = \lambda^*$,

$$
(45) \qquad -\frac{d\lambda}{dv} = \frac{\lambda - \dfrac{\partial M[\lambda; 1, v]}{\partial v}}{v - \dfrac{\partial M[\lambda; 1, v]}{\partial \lambda}}
$$

This can be interpreted as a remarkable equivalence between the rate of growth and own marginal productivities: at the optimum λ^*, we have

$$
(45)' \qquad \lambda^* = \frac{\partial X_2}{\partial x_2} = \frac{\partial X_1}{\partial x_1}
$$

where the first of these identities follows directly from (45) and the second from considerations of the symmetry between the two variables or from the homogeneity properties of the $M[X_1; x_1, x_2]$ function.

Let us return to the interpretation of the optimal rate of growth λ^*. Growth in the equilibrium mode will ultimately surpass any other rate of balanced growth. This suggests that if we start with any factor proportion $v \neq v^*$, it will still pay us if we are investing *for the very far future* to get into (or near) the equilibrium mode. At worst, we can do this by throwing away some of whichever factor is initially redundant as compared to v^*; and at best we can obviously make some use of the redundant factor.

This suggests the following conjecture. Consider

$$
(43)' \qquad X_2(n) = M_n[X_1(n); x_1(0), x_2(0)]
$$

for fixed x_1, x_2, $X_2(n)/X_1(n)$. As n grows, so will X_2 and X_1, and we should expect X_2 and X_1 ultimately to approach the geometric rate of growth $(\lambda^*)^n$. But, clearly, at first v would not be near v^* but would ease in gently toward v^*. And it is also clear that if we prescribe $X_1(n)$ and want the maximum $X_2(n)$, then as we finally get near n, it will pay to leave v^* even if we are already there or near there.

One would conjecture, therefore, that beginning with $v_0 \neq v^*$ and ending with $X_2(n)/X_1(n) = v_n \neq v^*$, the optimal time path of v would look something like Figure 14 for large n. As n gets large, the average v should approach v^*.

The exact meaning of the intrinsic growth potential of a system, or its von Neumann dominant root, which is the same thing, is a little hard to grasp at first. A few examples may help to clarify the concept.

If we had a single self-generating variable as in Equation (20), then the technical coefficient a would itself be the dominant root. This is an almost trivially simple case.

The Leontief fixed-coefficient case is more interesting. Figure 12b shows that the production-possibility curve is defined by two straight

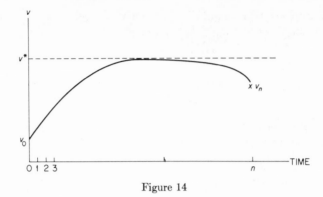

Figure 14

lines

$$(46) \quad \begin{cases} a_{11}X_1 + a_{12}X_2 \le x_1 \\ a_{21}X_1 + a_{22}X_2 \le x_2 \end{cases}$$

for every t, where the a's are positive technical constants defined by the relations

$$(47) \quad \begin{cases} x_{ij}(t) \ge a_{ij}X_j(t) \\ \sum x_{ij}(t) = X_i(t) \end{cases} \qquad (i, j = 1, 2)$$

To eliminate the irrelevant scale factors, we prefer to work with the (λ, v) variables defined by (44). We can now write (46) in terms of λ and v to get

$$(46)' \quad \begin{cases} a_{11}\lambda + a_{12}v\lambda \le 1 \\ a_{21}\lambda + a_{22}v\lambda \le v \end{cases}$$

this being derived by dividing each equation through by x_1 and using the definition of (44).

We can easily rearrange $(46)'$ to get the following limits for λ:

$$(46)'' \quad \begin{cases} \lambda \le \dfrac{1}{a_{11} + a_{12}v} \\ \lambda \le \dfrac{v}{a_{21} + a_{22}v} \end{cases}$$

The general shapes of these two bounding functions of v can be clearly inferred. For v near zero, the left-hand function is rising from the level zero; for large v, it ultimately approaches the level $1/a_{22}$. The right-hand function begins at $1/a_{11}$ and ultimately ends up at zero. The two functions must intersect at some positive v as is shown in Figure 15. This value of v will finally become the optimal one, v^*, for which λ takes on its maximal value, λ^*. Since λ is restricted in Figure 15 to lie in the shaded area, it follows directly from the monotone character of the

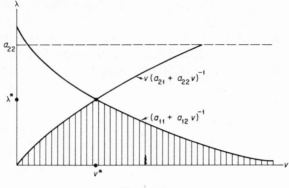

Figure 15

two bounding functions that the intersection point gives the maximum λ. This point also corresponds to the intersection corner point in Figure 12b.

This is in line with economic intuition, since at any other point one input is essentially a free good; and one would hardly expect an optimum combination of factors designed to yield a maximum rate of balanced growth to be one in which one of the factors is worthless and redundant; the economist intuitively sees that by producing less of the redundant factor he can improve the situation, and hence he expects a corner intersection point to be optimal.

The mathematician also has an interpretation of our (λ^*, v^*) configuration. For this simple 2×2 case, it is the ordinary *characteristic root* and *vector* of the $[a_{ij}]^{-1}$ matrix. Thus

$$
\left.
\begin{aligned}
a_{11}1 + a_{12}v &= \frac{1}{\lambda}1 \\[2mm]
a_{21}1 + a_{22}v &= \frac{1}{\lambda}
\end{aligned}
\right\} , \quad \text{and} \quad
\begin{vmatrix}
a_{11} - \dfrac{1}{\lambda}a_{12} & \\[2mm]
a_{21} & a_{22} - \dfrac{1}{\lambda}
\end{vmatrix}
= 0
$$

is the definition of the characteristic root λ and vector $(1, v)$ of the inverse of the a matrix. Thus, von Neumann roots are generalizations to systems of inequalities of the algebraic notion of the characteristic roots of a matrix.[30]

When consumption enters the picture, Equation (40) is still valid once we carefully distinguish between $X_i(t)$ and $x_i(t)$. But the von Neumann steady-state solution may lose its economic significance, even asymptotically.

[30]Just as in game theory, where an algebraic kernel of the game matrix yields optimal solutions, I should expect here that for general von Neumann dynamic systems there is some subset of rows and columns for which the dominant algebraic characteristic roots do yield the intrinsic growth rate of the system. But to find the "kernel" of the system often involves much of the programming computational work.

One is almost tempted to summarize the dispute between Schumpeter, who thinks of every static system as ultimately approaching a zero rate of interest, and Knight, who denies this possibility, as a dispute over whether $\lambda^* = 1$ or $\lambda^* > 1$. But this is an oversimplification and begins to lead us into some fundamental questions concerning the conservation of energy and the second law of thermodynamics.

34

LINEAR PROGRAMMING AND ECONOMIC THEORY[1]

Introduction

Anyone who is familiar with both economic theory and linear programming must admit that linear programming has been one of the
most exciting developments in economic theory of recent years. A glance
at the economic journals shows that a fairly extensive literature has
already accumulated, even though the subject is scarcely old enough
chronologically to go to kindergarten. Outside the realm of economics,
there appear numerous linear programming articles in magazines of
applied business practice and in more purely mathematical journals.
But even these publications do not tell the whole story, since a veritable
gusher of unpublished research papers on the theory and application of
linear programming seems to pour out every month.

This conference itself testifies to the widespread interest in the subject.
And periodic conferences like this one, and like the original June 1949
conference in Chicago, provide convenient bench marks to measure our
progress. The Washington Conference on Inequalities and Programming
of June 1951 showed that the theory of linear programming had been
extended in the previous two years; and it, of course, revealed the
tremendous quantitative expansion of applications. Similarly, just

[1]This paper was originally published as part of the *Proceedings of the Second
Symposium in Linear Programming* of the National Bureau of Standards and the
United States Air Force, January 27–29, 1955. It was reprinted by the Department
of Economics and Social Science, M.I.T., as No. 34, Series 1, of Publications in
Social Science.

reading over the advance titles of the papers at this conference acquaints one with the further advances of the last few years.

Ordinally, therefore, we can truthfully say: Every day, in every way, we are getting better and better.

For the purpose of decision making, ordinal comparisons are usually alone relevant. But if I were to digress momentarily to make an odious quasi-cardinal comparison, frankness would compel me to make this statement: The proceedings of the 1949 conference on linear programming, *Activity Analysis of Production and Allocation* — which Tjalling Koopmans so beautifully edited — is the volume on my bookshelf that I find myself most often referring to; the primary advance recorded in the subsequent 1951 conference seemed to have been chiefly in the (no doubt important) field of computation and in the extension of applications. It is too soon to tell whether this same phenomenon of "diminishing returns" will be discernible in a numerical appraisal of the advance this conference will record.

Let me hasten to qualify this remark. Even at the risk of seeming to contradict the famous J. M. Clark aphorism that "everything but intelligence is subject to the law of diminishing returns," we must recognize that most conscious direction of scientific research must be toward pushing it along paths of diminishing returns. So there should be nothing discouraging in my comparison. More than that: my evaluation should stand as a tribute to the fundamental work of the late 1940's rather than as a denigration of subsequent developments. Finally, I have given an economic theorist's subjective evaluation. I can readily imagine that according to the indifference curves of some applied mathematicians, the subject is just now beginning for the first time to become really interesting.

Sources of Inspiration for Linear Programming

The richness of linear programming for the economic theorist can be illustrated by the dilemma that we have been facing in preparing an expository RAND monograph aimed to introduce the nonspecialist economist to the subject. Some years ago I prepared some introductory chapters, written from the general viewpoint of the economist. But with each passing month the projected outline grew and grew in length. This was not because of any desire to make the treatment comprehensive, but rather simply a reflection of the many interesting topics where economic theory and linear programming overlap. I began to feel like Tristram Shandy, who, you will recall, took several years to write up the first three weeks of his life. To make the series converge to a finite sum, Professors Robert Dorfman and Robert Solow have joined the project, but they too have had to face its tendency to grow out of bounds.

What are some of the important areas where economic theory and linear programming overlap? I think that we cannot do better than to list the four sources of inspiration for linear programming given by Professor Koopmans in his introduction to the *Activity Analysis* book. These are as follows:

1. The recognition in the early 1930's by such Continental economists as Neisser, Von Stackelberg, Zeuthen, Schlesinger, von Neumann, and Wald that the simple Cassel version of Walrasian general equilibrium could not be adequately appraised by an uncritical counting of the number of its equations and the number of its unknowns.

2. The "new welfare economics" in the various versions of Lerner, Bergson, Kaldor, Hicks, Samuelson, Lange, and Arrow, which threw new light on the earlier writings of Smith, Walras, von Wieser, Marshall, Pareto, Barone, Pigou, von Mises, and Fred Taylor.

3. The interindustry input-output theories and measurements of Leontief, Evans, and Hoffenberg; and the related multisector analysis of Keynes, Harrod, William Salant, Machlup, Metzler, Solow, Goodwin, and Chipman.

4. The specific programming and optimizing problems raised by defense and military problems — and, more generally, the numerous optimizing problems that business firms have always had to solve in their quest for profits and survival. (The Cornfield-Stigler diet problem and the Hitchcock-Koopmans-Kantorovich transportation problem might be put in this category.)

I think to these four sources of inspiration should be added at least five more, even though only the last two of these are primarily economic in nature.

5. The interrelations between linear programming and the theory of games of Borel, von Neumann, R. A. Fisher, and Morgenstern.

6. The foundations of the Wald statistical decision theory, casting new light on the Fisher and Neyman-Pearson theories of statistics; and the related foundations of personal probability and decision making of the Ramsey-Savage type.

7. The purely mathematical interest of Minkowski, Weyl, Bonnesen and Fenchel, and a host of other mathematicians in various aspects of the theory of convex sets and of topology generally.

8. Within the area of economic maximizing problems, theorists during the last couple of decades had begun to concentrate on the *inequalities* that characterize a maximum rather than on the first-derivative equivalences that happen to describe certain smooth interior maximum points. The economic theories of index numbers, of revealed preference, of Le Chatelier principles — all these are examples of this trend antedating the birth of linear programming.

9. Finally, in the economic theories of arbitrage, speculation, location, and rationing there have from the earliest days been recognized to enter problems of *inequalities;* since these problems have not always been formulated as maximum or as general equilibrium problems, I have added them as a category separate from the earlier categories. (The names of Ricardo, Cournot, Scitovsky, de Graaf, and other economists could be mentioned in this regard.)

Theoretical Insights Provided by Linear Programming

If you examine the listed ways that economic theory has inspired linear programming, you may superficially infer that the process has been one of unilateral causation from economics to programming. Inasmuch as economic theory antedates linear programming as a formal discipline of study and research, this is in a sense natural and to be expected. However, you may not infer that programming is the inferior activity even where it has taken its problems directly from ancient economic theory. Often, the economist has had the important but vastly easier task of asking certain questions; and the linear programming expert has often been able to answer these questions — in some cases to give answers to them for the first time.

I have been racking my brain to see if I could think of any converse examples — where linear programming has raised new and important questions for the economic theorist that he had not previously thought about. I have not, offhand, been able to produce any, and I hope that some economist or mathematician will provide us with some such examples for discussion.[2]

[2]In the oral discussion on this paper, Dr. Martin Beckmann suggested that linear programming had raised a number of interesting questions for the theorist of locational problems. And as I shall argue later, many of the general mathematical tools that are needed for linear programming — such as convex sets, fixed-point theorems, saddlepoints — turn out to be extremely useful to the modern mathematical economist.

Upon reflection, I must admit that linear programming has succeeded in tackling empirically many of the general problems that the theorist had always talked about. Thus, the economist speaks glibly of a multiproduct firm as having a cost function dependent upon all its outputs and as reaching equilibrium when it equates each product's marginal revenue to its marginal cost. Work of Cooper, Charnes, Manne, Henderson, Schlaifer, and others has given concrete applications to what might otherwise remain in the category of "empty boxes."

When Dr. George Dantzig asked me in the oral discussion why economic theorists are so "uninterested" in linear programming applications, I replied: "Theorists are congenitally a little bored with concrete applications. They prefer to consider the general qualitative aspects of things rather than themselves to become interested in the quantitative details of, say, the oil industry's multiple products. Moreover, the theorist often suspects that the linear programmer grinds out an exact solution to a rather idealized approximation to the true reality — so that in any case only the qualitative direction of changes can be inferred from the programming results." Upon reflection, I feel that parts of my answer are indefensible. The theorist *should*

Does this failure to supply questions for the economic theorist imply that linear programming is, from his selfish point of view, sterile? Not at all. Programming theory has not only provided the theorist with many answers to his questions. It has also provided him with fairly rigorous proofs for some of his theorems — or as the purist would say — for some of his conjectures. Even more important, it has provided him with feedback insights into the fundaments of his subject.

Thus, the modern economist had, prior to the birth of linear programming as a recognizable separate entity, attained a fair understanding of the nature of a pricing mechanism for the attainment of various welfare-economics optima. In other words, he had made considerable progress beyond Adam Smith's notion of the invisible hand, toward a deeper understanding of what that notion involved. Nonetheless, no one who understands both economic theory and programming theory is likely to deny that the latter's fundamental duality theorems have added to his understanding of the pricing mechanism and its limitations.

Existence of Competitive Equilibrium

During this conference, Professors Harold Kuhn, a mathematician, and Lionel McKenzie, an economist, are scheduled to discuss the problem which I listed as one of the first sources of inspiration for linear programming. Until Wald's proof came along, economists had no rigorous demonstration of the existence of competitive equilibrium. Indeed, some incautious formulations of the Walrasian system, such as that of Cassel, gave rise to long-unnoticed contradictions and difficulties. The keen literary economist — and he does exist — always realized that the way out of these contradictions came from making some factors free and then dropping the requirement that all of a free factor be employed, which is precisely the mathematician's final resolving of the paradox. (Also during this conference, Professor Georgescu-Roegen, a keen literary as well as mathematical economist, will interpret the economic history of Rumania in terms of such a redundancy of labor; the Dutch economist Valk offered a similar hypothesis to explain depression unemployment, and my colleagues at the M.I.T. Center for International Studies, Dr. Rosenstein-Rodan and Dr. Eckaus, have suggested similar interpretations to explain the redundancy of labor in modern Italy.)

---

be interested in concrete applications — if they are valid. Also, if businessmen come increasingly to use linear programming techniques — even when not valid — then the theorist must take this fact into account in describing their behavior, in the same way that he takes into account the systematic aberrations of widely used accounting techniques. This does not mean that every economic theorist must himself specialize in solving problems of internal administration for firms or other maximizing units: such applications, when they become coherent enough, will tend to move outside the narrow discipline of economics in the same way that accounting and technology have done.

The nature of the difficulty with the Cassel system is easy to see from the following two sets of equations:

$$(1) \qquad \sum_1^n a_{ij}X_j = V_i \qquad\qquad\qquad (i = 1, 2, \cdots, m)$$

$$(2) \qquad \sum_1^m a_{ji}W_i = P_j \qquad\qquad\qquad (j = 1, 2, \cdots, n)$$

where X's are n outputs with P's their competitive market prices, and V's are m factor inputs and W's their market factor prices, and where a_{ij} are specified nonnegative fixed coefficients of production. Equations (1) say that all factors are used up, and Equations (2) say that all goods sell at their unit costs of production, with competition grinding out all profits or surpluses.

Even with $n \neq m$, there is nothing contradictory about (1) and (2) until the theorist goes on to make the assumption that the factor supplies, as given by the right-hand V's in (1) can be arbitrarily specified, at the same time that the commodity prices on the right of (2) are all arbitrarily specified. Usually, we think of the number of goods as exceeding the number of factors, so $n > m$. This means that the set (1) is *underdetermined*, with $(n - m)$ X's being capable of taking on arbitrary values.

This is troublesome, but not logically contradictory. However, look at (2). With all P's arbitrarily specifiable, we have n conditions on $m < n$ unknown W's. So (2) is *overdetermined*, possessing no solution. The degree of its overdeterminacy is, so to speak, $n - m$.

How was this basic irreconcilability overlooked? In part, because theorists counted the total number of unknowns in (1) and (2), which worked out to be $n + m$ and found them equal to the total number of equations in (1) and (2), also $n + m$. So to speak, they unknowingly canceled out the underdeterminacy of (1) taken by itself against the overdeterminacy of (2) taken by itself. This is logically illegitimate. This is also shown by the mathematical fact that the determinant

$$\begin{vmatrix} a_{11}a_{12} & \cdots & a_{1n} & 0 & \cdots & 0 \\ \cdot & & \cdot & \cdot & & \cdot \\ \cdot & & \cdot & \cdot & & \cdot \\ \cdot & & \cdot & \cdot & & \cdot \\ a_{m1}a_{m2} & \cdots & a_{mn} & 0 & \cdots & 0 \\ 0 & \cdots & \cdots & 0 & a_{11} & \cdots & a_{m1} \\ \cdot & & & \cdot & \cdot & & \cdot \\ \cdot & & & \cdot & \cdot & & \cdot \\ \cdot & & & \cdot & \cdot & & \cdot \\ 0 & \cdots & \cdots & 0 & a_{1n} & \cdots & a_{mn} \end{vmatrix} = 0 \text{ if } m \neq n$$

as Laplace's development shows.

Economists like Wieser and Fred Taylor had avoided this difficulty by assuming that m equals n. However, this does not avoid the difficulty; it only postpones the logical contradiction. For, in the first place, even with $n = m$, there is no reason at all why the a_{ij} matrix should not be singular: why shouldn't two goods use exactly the same proportion of inputs? If the theorist objects that this is equivalent to defining them as the same goods and therefore reducing n to one below m, he is simply admitting that there is a logical difficulty.

Let us, for the purpose of the argument, suppose that Nature is kind and does give us a nonsingular square matrix of a's. Except in the trivial case where each good requires but one factor which is unique to it, (1) and (2)'s determinate solution for each prescribed set of positive V's and P's cannot have the property of always avoiding negative values. That is, we can easily specify arbitrary positive values of the V's and P's which cause one or more of our economic unknowns to be negative. (This follows from simple economic reasoning if we supply the factors in proportions more extreme than any good uses; or it can be proved by the mathematical fact that a nonsingular matrix of nonnegative coefficients that is not a diagonal matrix must have negative elements in its inverse, so that $a^{-1}V$ can for appropriate choice of positive V's be made to have one or more negative elements.)

Economists eventually learned all this, and if they had been numerically minded, they might have learned this even earlier. But one way that they had of resolving any such difficulties was to deny one of the postulates giving rise to the trouble: why keep insisting that the factor supplies V_i could be prescribed at arbitrary levels? Why keep insisting that any competitive prices could be prescribed? Alternatively, why not prescribe that only those prices compatible with cost of production are possible? And only those factor supplies that can all be used?

Thus, we may still be able to avoid logical inconsistency by insisting on the equalities of (1) and (2) but letting *all* variables be unknowns — not just half the variables. Thus, we have $n + m$ equations binding $2(n + m)$ unknowns, and there need be no overdeterminacy. There is, of course, underdeterminacy, but we feel that we can add taste or demand equations and disutility or factor supply equations that will serve to determine our system.

But do we know this? The economist feels intuitively that this is so; yet the mathematician will require proof of the Wald or other type. I shall briefly sketch the elements of such a proof, making slightly stronger assumptions than Wald does. But since I believe his assumptions are overstrong, from the economic viewpoint, there will not really be much difference between my assumptions and those of Wald and Schlesinger.[3]

[3]Wald assumes that market demand functions relating totals bought by everybody satisfy what we today call the "Weak Axiom" of preference theory. Such an axiom

First, assume that there is a single Robinson Crusoe with regularly convex indifference curves describable by a smooth ordinal indicator $U(X_1 \cdots, X_n) = U(X)$ with this property: if $U(A) = U(B)$, then $U(\frac{1}{2}A + \frac{1}{2}B) \geq U(A) = U(B)$. The substitution ratios

$$\frac{\partial U/\partial X_i}{\partial U/\partial X_j}$$

are determinate functions $f_{ij}(X)$ of the goods consumed, independently of the utility indicator. Finally, assume that Crusoe is indifferent as to how much of each V_j he supplies between 0 and $\bar{V}_j$, where the latter are prescribed positive numbers.

These conditions will be sufficient to define *a* competitive equilibrium, which will maximize

$$U(X_1, \cdots, X_n)$$

subject to

$$(3) \qquad \sum_1^n a_{ij}X_j \leq \bar{V}_i \qquad\qquad (i = 1, \cdots, m)$$

Writing the resulting maximized value of U as $F(\bar{V}_1, \cdots, \bar{V}_m)$, we can determine the resulting factor prices W_j as proportional to $\partial F/\partial \bar{V}_j$, and prices P_i will be proportional to $\partial U/\partial X_i$, and will satisfy a set of relations just like (2) but with inequalities inserted to take account of the possibility that for goods not produced, price may exceed unit cost of production. Wald does admit the existence of inequalities in (1), but following Schlesinger he makes the unnecessarily restrictive assumption that if any X_i is zero, the resulting level of well-being is less than it is for any point at which all X's are positive: this ensures that every X_i is positive and that all the equalities hold in (2). Since uniqueness is arbitrary, I do not follow Wald in assuming that the rank of a is m; it can be anything.

Time does not permit me to dwell on the naturalness of the fixed-point types of proof of the existence of competitive equilibrium. To some these may seem like rather sophisticated mathematical tools for the economist to be using; but to my mind, they do strikingly capture the economist's intuitive feeling that equilibrium intersections must exist

---

holds for a single individual, but it is arbitrary to assume it holds for the market totals. Many plausible examples can be given of this fact. In another paper, I have proved that something like this — and more — would hold in a "good society" where incomes are always optimally redistributed so as to maximize a social welfare function. Such a good society acts like a single individual — so we might as well from the beginning talk of Robinson Crusoe. Note that McKenzie's proof of existence is free from this limitation; but he rightly abandons Wald's attempt to prove what is untrue of competitive equilibrium generally — namely uniqueness of equilibrium.

if all the supply and demand functions have the appropriate continuity properties.

I heartily approve of the gentlemen's agreements that are made about continuity so that these beautiful theorems and proofs can be brought in. Nonetheless, from the strict economics of the case, we must be prepared to encounter phenomena that lead away from the existence of an equilibrium. Here is a simple example. Man A has indifference curves for two goods that are like rectangular hyperbolas. So far, so good. But Man B has indifference curves in terms of his consumption of those same goods which are like quarter circles, or at least are very slightly convex from above. This denies the usual textbook convexity, but what does B care about that! Now let us start each man out with a given endowment of both goods, and derive the resulting competitive supply and demand curves. Man A's will be of the normal continuous type. But Man B's demand curve will defy the continuity axiom of Wald or McKenzie. Figure 1 shows how the resulting demand curve may "have a hole in it" and make the existence of competitive equilibrium impossible. (The reader might imagine a servo that drives prices up when demand exceeds supply, and argue that some kind of statistical averaging out occurs at what would be the equilibrium intersection of the continuous curve drawn from A to B to C to D.)

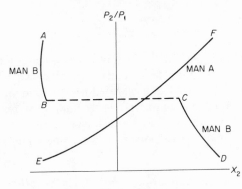

Figure 1

The Power of Advanced Methods

Advanced mathematical methods are usually considered more difficult than elementary ones. The reverse is often the case. I shall conclude with an example that illustrates enormous simplification of the mathematical economist's technical task that results when he uses a few of the concepts of inequality and convexity rather than the intricate tools of the advanced calculus (such as Jacobians, Hessians, bordered determinants, definite quadratic forms).

First, consider the classical law of diminishing returns as applied to a smooth production function involving many variables. Such a function is usually assumed to be homogeneous of the first degree, so that

$$y = g(x_1, \cdots, x_n) = g(x) = g(\lambda x)/\lambda \qquad \lambda > 0$$

(4) $$g(x) \equiv \sum_1^n x_j \frac{\partial g}{\partial x_j}$$

$$\sum_1^n \frac{\partial^2 g}{\partial x_i \partial x_j} x_j \equiv 0$$

so that

$$H = \left[\frac{\partial^2 g}{\partial x_i \partial x_j} \right] = H'$$

is a singular matrix. To the assumption of constant-returns-to-scale is added the usual assumption of "diminishing returns to disproportionate changes." The mathematical economist summarizes this by requiring H to be negative semidefinite, usually of rank $n - 1$.

All this is expressed with more economical assumptions and exposition by the two requirements

(5a) $$y = g(x) = g(\lambda x)/\lambda \qquad \lambda > 0$$

(5b) $$g(x + z) \geqq g(x) + g(z)$$

Indeed, we could dispense with the first of these conditions if we modify the second so as to require the equality sign when $[x_i] = \alpha[z_i]$.

From (5a) and (5b) we can easily deduce the fundamental concavity of the equal-product contours that is so important for classical competitive theory and for nonlinear and linear programming: in words, a point halfway between two points on the same contour can never lie below that contour. Or

$$g(a) = g(b) \text{ implies } g(\tfrac{1}{2}a + \tfrac{1}{2}b) \geqq g(a) = g(b)$$

Proof:

$$g(\tfrac{1}{2}a + \tfrac{1}{2}b) = \tfrac{1}{2}g(a + b) \geqq \frac{g(a) + g(b)}{2}$$

a relation which holds even if $g(a) \neq g(b)$.[4]

Without any modification, (5b) by itself serves to rule out decreasing returns to scale. (Mathematical proof: $g(2x) \geqq 2g(x)$ for all x does imply

[4]The reader might tediously prove this from (4) by bordering the Hessian H by $\partial g/\partial x_i$; or by solving $y = g(x_1, \cdots, x_n)$ for $x_1 = G(x_2, \cdots, x_n; y)$ and proving the positive-definiteness of the $(n - 1)^2$ Hessian $[\partial^2 G/\partial x_i \partial x_j] = [\partial B_{i1}/\partial x_j - B_{j1}\partial B_{i1}/\partial x_1]$ where $B_{i1} = -(\partial g/\partial x_i)/(\partial g/\partial x_1)$ for $i > 1$.

$g(\lambda x) \geq \lambda g(x)$ for all $\lambda > 0$.) [*1965 Note:* This proof needs modification.] The common sense of this is important for economics. If we can always at worst get the sum of independent production activities, increasing scale can never lower unit returns. This means that antitrust policy cannot rely on diseconomies of large-scale production to police competition if the different parts of General Motors are always capable of desisting from contaminating each other.

Both ($5a$) and ($5b$) are hypotheses that can be falsified by reality; they are hence not provable by logic. Yet ($5b$) will seem to many economists to have greater empirical plausibility than the more special assumption of constant returns to scale. It is, therefore, worth pointing out the disastrous analytic consequences both for linear programming and for the usual versions of nonlinear programming if ($5b$) is affirmed and ($5a$) denied. We cannot then be sure that the equal-product contours have the classically postulated convexity needed for competitive equilibrium and needed to ensure that a local maximum is indeed a maximum in the large.

A single example will make this clear: $g = x_1^2 + x_2^2$ satisfies ($5b$) but does not have the convexity property $g(a) = g(b) \geq g(\frac{1}{2}a + \frac{1}{2}b)$, as can be seen from the quarter-circle product contours. (Note that $g = \sqrt{x_1^2 + x_2^2}$ has the same contours and does satisfy ($5a$); hence, it could not satisfy ($5b$) — and does not. If $g = \sqrt{x_1^2 + x_2^2}$ is technologically feasible and our final production function $g^*(x_1, x_2)$ is required to satisfy ($5b$), then $g^*(x_1, x_2) \geq \sqrt{x_1^2} + \sqrt{x_2^2} = x_1 + x_2$, and will in fact equal $x_1 + x_2$, which will be the economically relevant production function.)

Here is an important final theorem with many applications. To prove it by manipulation of bordered Hessians would be tedious indeed.

THEOREM: Let $U = f(x_1, \cdots, x_n) = f(x)$ have the property: $f(a) = f(b)$ implies $f(\frac{1}{2}a + \frac{1}{2}b) \geq f(a)$; and let m functions $g_i(x_1, \cdots, x_n) = g_i(x)$ each have the properties

$$g_i(\lambda x) = \lambda g_i(x)$$

$$g_i(x + z) \geq g_i(x) + g_i(z),$$

and let $U = f(x)$ to be a maximum subject to

$$g_i(x) \geq Y_i \qquad\qquad (i = 1, \cdots, m)$$

attain a maximum equal to $U = F(Y_1, \cdots, Y_m) = F(Y)$. Then, F has the same property as f, namely $F(A) = F(B)$ implies $F(\frac{1}{2}A + \frac{1}{2}B) \geq F(A) = F(B)$.

Proof: Suppose $f(a) = F(A) = f(b) = F(B)$ with $g_i(a) \geq A$ and $g_i(b) \geq B$. Then $\frac{1}{2}a + \frac{1}{2}b$ is a feasible point in that $g_i(\frac{1}{2}a + \frac{1}{2}b) = \frac{1}{2}g_i(a + b) \geq$

$\dfrac{g_i(a)}{2} + \dfrac{g_i(b)}{2} = \dfrac{A + B}{2}.$ Certainly $f(\tfrac{1}{2}a + \tfrac{1}{2}b) \geqq f(a) = f(b) = F(A) = F(B)$ by hypothesis, and since the optimal value $F(\tfrac{1}{2}A + \tfrac{1}{2}B) \geqq f(\tfrac{1}{2}a + \tfrac{1}{2}b)$, our theorem is proved.

Special cases of this theorem are the following:

(i) The efficient production-possibility frontier relating total outputs and inputs must be a convex set if each production satisfies the classical returns law. (Set

$$g_i = F_i(V_{1i}, \cdots, V_{mi}) - \sum_1^n V_{ij}$$

to prove this.)

(ii) In my equations (3), $U = F(V_1, \cdots, V_n) = F(V)$ has the stipulated convexity property.

(iii) The beautiful Hicks theorem that composite goods have regularly shaped indifference contours follows if we set $g_1 = P_1 x_1 + \cdots + P_r x_r$, $g_2 = P_{r+1} x_{r+1} + \cdots + P_k x_k, \cdots$, etc.

Lest the power of these methods betray us into ignoring the non-convexity that may occur in the real world, let me end with a valid inequality of revealed preference that holds even when we deny the convexity of the indifference curves needed for the preceding theorems. Whatever the shape of $U = f(x_1, \cdots, x_n)$, truly minimizing

$$\sum_1^n P_j x_j$$

subject to $f(x) \geqq \bar{U}$ will give us $x_i = \phi_i(P_1, \cdots, P_n)$ with the property $\sum \Delta x_j \, \Delta P_j \geqq 0$ — a result in revealed preference that is true even when many local maxima have to be painfully eliminated from the optimal solution. Other important examples in the realm of decreasing cost industries arise to plague the linear programmer and impatient economist.

35

Frank Knight's Theorem in Linear Programming

Paul A. Samuelson

Massachusetts Institute of Technology, Cambridge, Massachusetts, USA

With 3 Figures

A quarter of a century ago Frank Knight showed that there exists some kind of a relation between the Walras-Wieser pricing theory involving technically fixed coefficients of production and the more conventional modern Walras-Clark pricing theory in which the coefficients of production are variable and are to be determined by least-cost or so-called marginal productivity conditions[1]. The exact meaning, and therefore significance, of this relationship is not easy to determine. However, the recently developed theory of linear programming enables us greatly to generalize the Knight result, to simplify its proof, and perhaps to appraise its significance. The recently discussed problem of equalization of factor prices as a result of free trade in commodities turns out to be closely related to the Knight problem[2].

I.

Knight assumes in effect n goods $Q_1, Q_2, \ldots, Q_n$ produced by means of an equal number of factors or inputs $V_1, \ldots, V_r$, where $r = n$ in our

---

[1] F. H. Knight: A Note on Professor Clark's illustration of Marginal Productivity. Journal of Political Economy, *XXXIII* (1925), 550—3; F. M. Taylor: Principles of Economics (8th ed., 1923), Ch. XXX; G. J. Stigler: Production and Distribution Theories, 166—71, 178. Early in the 1930's numerous economists, such as Schlesinger, Neisser, v. Stackelberg, Wald, v. Neumann, Zeuthen, Hicks, and Schultz concerned themselves with problems of determinacy of the Walras-Wieser-Cassel system of production. The present paper dates back to a 1950 RAND memorandum; for subsequent references see R. Dorfman, R. M. Solow, P. A. Samuelson: Linear Programming and Economic Analysis (1958), Ch. 13.

[2] E. Heckscher: The Effect of Foreign Trade on the Distribution of Income, translated from a Swedish article appearing in the Ekonomisk Tidskrift, *XXI* (1919), 497—512 and appearing as Ch. 13 of Readings in the Theory of International Trade (1933), Part I, Appendix I; P. A. Samuelson: International Trade and the Equalisation of Factor Prices. Economic Journal, *LVIII* (1948), 163—84; P. A. Samuelson: International Factor-Price Equalisation Once Again. Economic Journal, *LVIX* (1949), 182—97.

initial discussion. The total of each input such as V_j is allocated among the n industries, so that for every non-free input $V_j = \sum\limits_{i=1}^{n} V_{ij}$, where the first subscript always relates to the good and the second to the input. Initially we assume with Knight that commodity prices $p_1, \ldots, p_n$ are prescribed arbitrary constants determined somehow by domestic or international demands. The prices of the inputs, $w_1, \ldots, w_r$, are unknowns and in the eyes of Wieser the chief task of the theory was to determine them. Walras in the 1870's and Wieser in the 1880's assumed that the requirements of the jth input to produce one unit of the ith good was in every case a constant given by technology and not capable of being adapted to different relative factor prices. Hence the $n\,r$ constants, a_{ij}, are given to us. Finally, perfect competition is assumed to prevail.

Clearly the p's will have to be equal to the unit costs of production, which are immediately to be calculated from the w's and the a's according to

$$p_i = \sum_{j=1}^{r} a_{ij} w_j \qquad i = 1, 2, \ldots, n \qquad (1)$$

strictly speaking we should add a less than sign to each equation to take account of the possibility that price might fall short of cost for any good not produced at all.

Also it is clear from the fact that the inputs in all industries add up to the available total V's, and from the fact that $a_{ij} = V_{ij}/Q_i$, that total outputs and total inputs are simply related by the a's:

$$V_j = \sum_{i=1}^{n} Q_i a_{ij} \qquad j = 1, 2, \ldots, r \qquad (2)$$

Again we must note that in the case of a factor whose $w = 0$, the equality sign can be supplemented by a greater-than sign, since unemployment of a free factor is without significance.

Knight's theorem can now be briefly stated: *An increase in any input, V_j, will — with p's and other V's constant — be increasing the value of the total national product $\sum\limits_{i} p_i Q_i$ at a rate equal to the wage of V_j, or w_j.*

Most of the arithmetic and algebraic manipulations used to demonstrate this result are designed to prove something that most economists are apt to regard as self-evident: namely, the equivalence of the value of total product with the value of the total factor-income, or $\sum\limits_{i} p_i Q_i = \sum\limits_{k} w_k V_k$. In modern discussions of national income the value equivalence between total product and total factor income is taken as a tautology (stemming from the definition of „profit"). But there is no harm in checking on its consistency with the other relations that hold under perfect competition.

If we add to this equivalence the statement that so long as the p's do not change then the w's also do not change, then it is immediately clear that the change in $\sum\limits_i p_i Q_i$ when V_j alone changes is nothing but the change in $\sum\limits_k w_k V_k$, or even in $w_j V_j$ alone. Hence, the rate at which total product or factor-income changes with each change in an input cannot be other than its wage.

There remains only the details of a rigorous proof. Clearly if $n = r$ and a is a non-singular matrix then w's are immediately determined from (1) by inverting the equations (1), or in matrix terms by $w = a^{-1} p$. Without going to the trouble of inverting any matrix, we easily prove the value equivalence of total product and total factor income by multiplying each equation in (1) by the corresponding Q_i and summing, and by at the same time multiplying each equation in (2) by the corresponding w_j and summing, to get *in both cases* $\sum\limits_i \sum Q_i a_{ij} w_j$.

II.

What is the significance of the Knight theorem? Does it say more than that so long as the wage rate is a constant, increasing the total of labor must increase the total wage bill at a rate equal to the wage, so that the average cost of this factor is the same thing as its marginal cost? If there is nothing more to be said than that, economists cannot find it very interesting. Such a surface relation by itself does not seem capable of showing any significant relation between the Walras-Wieser „net productivity" theory and the Walras-Clark „marginal productivity"; nor will any reconciliation of Wieser's productivity principle with the vaguely-worded „loss-principle" of Carl Menger be of much interest if its content is simply the equivalence of the two ways of looking at national product.

I imagine that something more than this was intended. In any case, it can be said that both the cases of fixed a's and of continuously variable and substitutable a's constitute instances of the general theory of linear programming and that certain theorems are shared in common between them. Hence, we can generalize Knight's result in a number of directions.

Consider for example what happens as we add more and more V_j to Knight's system. We are told its w_j will not change. But surely there will come a point beyond which increasing V_j will make it a free factor and send its wage to zero, even though all the p's remain constant. Beyond this point, increasing V_j will have what effect on national product? Obviously, none. But now its wage is zero and something like Knight's theorem still seems to hold. This can hardly be an accident. But note that with this factor free, we now have only $n - 1$ rather than n factors of production[3]. Hence, a theorem like Knight's seems still to

---

[3] We lose the jth equation in (2) so that now this gives us more unknowns than equations. It is clear what must happen: along the lines of the Ricardian theory of comparative advantage, competition will cause the country to specialize on the $n - 1$ goods that maximize its value of total product; in the singular case

hold when we relax his requirement of an equal number of inputs and outputs.

To go to the case of more factors than goods is even more interesting. Now there are less equations in (1) than unknowns so that the factor prices *may* not be uniquely determined by the commodity prices. It all depends on the V's in relationship to the given technology. Perhaps most often we can expect the V's to be such that at least $r - n$ factors are free; hence, concentrating on the rest, we can treat this as a case of equal goods and factors. But there will be interesting singular endowments of the V's that will cause the various w's to be indifferently determined within broad ranges. (Thus one good produced by two inputs will result usually in one of the inputs being superabundant relative to the technical requirements, so that the other input gets all the product. But if the two inputs happen to be originally supplied in ratios just equal to the ratios of their a's, then the wage of any one is indeterminate, being anything from 0 to 100 per cent of the total product.)

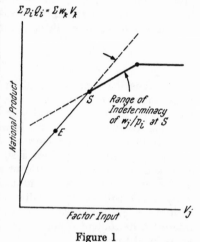

Figure 1

This provides a severe test of the general theorem. In such a singular case what happens as we increase a V_j whose wage is indeterminate? Our suspicion would be that the partial derivative of total product with respect to V_j is undefined, there being a corner in the relationship at such a singular point as in Figure 1 at S. The „right-hand limiting slope" for an increase in V_j beyond the singular point would be the new determinate wage *after* the new V_j has been added; likewise the „left-hand derivative" would be the wage that would result after we have taken away some of V_j. The range of indeterminacy of w_j at the singular point would be the range of indeterminacy between these two limits.

This suspicion is completely verified by the rigorous analysis of what is called „dual-problem" in linear programming. We may paraphrase Adam Smith by saying that there is an „invisible hand" that leads a competitive system and the economic theorist to the theorems of linear programming.

This particular dual problem of linear programming may be briefly indicated. With p's and V's, and a's prescribed, the competitive system will act as if to *maximize*

---

where the prescribed price ratios happen to coincide with cost ratios, there may be a range of indifference. Note that the phenomenon of specialization is quite likely to take place before any particular factor becomes free.

Nat'l Product $= p_1 Q_1 + \ldots + p_n Q_n$ subject to the r conditions

$$a_{11} Q_1 + a_{21} Q_2 + \ldots + a_{n1} Q_n \leqq V_1$$
$$a_{r1} Q_1 + a_{r2} Q_2 + \ldots + a_{nr} Q_n \leqq V_r, \qquad \text{A}$$

all Q's non-negative.

Note that there is no mention of factor prices or w's in this problem.

But it can be shown that along with this problem, there goes a closely related so-called „dual problem" of minimizing the total expense or factor payments imputable from the given commodity prices: or to *minimize*

Nat'l Expense $= V_1 w_1 + \ldots + V_r w_r$ subject to the n conditions

$$a_{11} w_1 + a_{12} w_2 + \ldots + a_{1r} w_r \geqq p_1$$
$$a_{n1} w_1 + a_{n2} w_2 + \ldots + a_{nr} w_r \geqq p_r, \qquad \text{A}$$

all w's non-negative.

It is shown in linear programming, and the economist will readily believe it, that the maximum national product is perfectly determinate and so is the minimum national expense; moreoever, they must both be equal. This holds true regardless of whether $n \geqq r$. It will even hold true if we generalize the problem by assuming with Fred Taylor and other economists that within any industry we can choose between alternative sets of a's; or for that matter if we go all the way with Walras, Wicksteed, and J. B. Clark and assume a single continuous differentiable relationship between the a's in any one industry so that an infinite number of different methods or activities can be substituted for any given activity or set of a's. Thus a result like Knight's must also hold in the case of the most general marginal productivity theory.

III.

But we shall prove both too much and too little if we examine only effects on value of total product or value of total wage bill under a regime of frozen commodity prices. The equivalence of the two ways of looking at national income must always prevail; but in the conventional marginal productivity theory, more interesting physical relationships also hold, and this *regardless of any changes in the p's* that will be induced within a general equilibrium system by a change in total factor input.

Suppose we take the viewpoint of an observer of all society who is quite uninterested in the petty details of cost-accounting within each industry and who has no particular interest in the intra-industry marginal productivity conditions that lie behind the derived demands for all the factors of production. There are still some partial derivatives, slopes, or marginal physical productivities that he might be interested in. With given V's, it is clear that society has at best a given „menu" or „production-possibility locus" of possible Q's open to it; or with given Q's, society at its best must still have a certain minimum list of requirements of the V's compatible with such production.

Let a given V_j now increase, other V's held constant. It will depend upon the intricate workings out of the general equilibrium system to determine what the final effects will be on all p's and w's, and Q's to say nothing of the allocation of the latter among different individuals. Certainly we can usually expect all p's and w's to change.

Yet our observer can ask himself this „virtual" question. With the extra available V_j, what is the extra amount of Q_i that society *could* produce if a decision were made to leave all the other Q's constant? We may indicate this as a partial derivative, $Q^i{}_{Vj}$, which will depend of course on the level of prescribed V's and Q's and (with technology given and optimal production conditions always being understood) on nothing else.

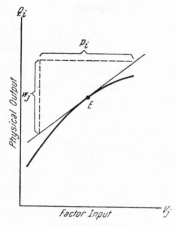

Now it is easy to show that this purely physical quasi-social marginal productivity is equal under ideal competition to the real wage rate of V_j in terms of the good Q_i, or to the actual w_j/p_i that would prevail in the market place. This is shown in Figure 2 whose physical magnitude should not be confused with the *value* magnitude of Figure 1. The slope at any point such as E must exactly equal the real wage w_j/p_i.

Figure 2

We can scarcely hope to find such a sharply defined result in the case where coefficients of production are not continuously substitutable for each other. Indeed at first glance it will seem as if there is no corresponding theorem to be found in such a case. One is tempted to think that for any configuration of the V's there is only one possible configuration for the Q's, so that an increase in a given V_j must have a determinate effect on *all* the Q's, making it impossible to hold all but one constant. At least this would seem to be so in Knight's case where equations (2) give us as many relations between the V's and Q's as there are Q's. But our earlier discussion of the inequalities that must be added to all of our equations (to take account of what will actually happen in a competitive market when some of the factors become free or when some of the goods are not produced at all) shows that this is not true. In increase of a V_j can be fully employed in adding to the production of one Q_i alone, even if that does cause some of the factors to change in value to the extent of becoming free goods[4].

---

[4] The production possibility schedule, or what is called in linear programming the „efficiency locus" will in the case of continuously differentiable marginal productivities be a smoothly convex curve in a $Q_i - Q_j$ diagram. In the case of fixed coefficients of production or of a finite number of activities, the curve will consist of broken straight lines intersecting in corners of indeterminate slope, but of the same convexity.

Figure 3 shows how Q_i can be expected to vary when we change V_j and hold other V's and Q's constant. Again we have a generally covex locus, but it now consists of intersecting straight lines which meet in corners of indeterminate slope.

A bold conjecture suggests itself: just as in the Walras-Clark continuous case of marginal productivities, so in the Walras-Wieser case of fixed coefficients of production (or for that matter in the case where a finite number of alternative methods can be chosen from) *there will be a definite relationship between the slope $Q^i{}_{V_j}$ and the real wage w_j/p_i.*

But of course we must take care to allow for the corners of indeterminate slope that will now occur. We must distinguish between the „left-hand slope" for a loss of a factor and the „right-hand slope" pertaining to an addition to a factor beyond such a singular point. Any numerical value lying within this range may be defined as the „generalized slope or partial derivative" at that point. In case an ordinary derivative does exist, the limits narrow down to a definite value equal to the ordinary derivative; consequently, our general case includes the conventional special case.

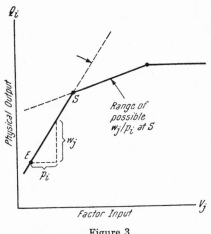

Figure 3

The definite theorem can now be stated: *The real wage that can prevail under competition will always be equal to the generalized partial derivative $Q^i{}_{V_j}$.*

We must guard against a possible misunderstanding. Suppose the system is at a singular point such as S in Figure 3: such a case will often be the rule rather than the exception. One might at first be tempted to think that the wage must be indeterminate within the indicated ambiguity of slope. This is incorrect. Wages are determined by the full conditions of general equilibrium, and not by technological conditions alone, whether these technological conditions be of a marginal productivity type or of the Walras-Wieser type. Often the supplies of the factors will depend upon all commodity and factor prices and the household's demands for goods will depend upon the same variables in such a way as to lead to unique p's and w's even at a singular point like that at S in Figure 3. The range of indeterminacy shown there is *not* the range of indeterminacy that must prevail in the market. All that we can say is that whatever determinate wage that can prevail in the market and whatever the range of indeterminacy that can prevail in the market, there must never emerge a wage that lies *outside* the range of indeterminacy prescribed by technology alone (as in Figure 3). Also, it should be emphasized that in the real world there may often emerge zones of indifference, but no *essential* indeterminacy can ever take place in a properly constructed theory. Either the indeterminacy does not matter or an enlarged theory can be found to explain what does actually take place.

More important than this general relationship between real wage rates and the partial derivatives of societies production-possibility or efficiency locus is the recognition that in a world characterized everywhere by constant-returns-to-scale technology, a general pricing system is one way of making sure that society has reached its efficiency locus and not remained inside it. This is the extra insight that the „duality principle" of linear programming has added to the teleology implied in Smith's „invisible hand". It is interesting that modern welfare economics clearly apprehended this before the birth of linear programming as a formal discipline[5].

IV.

In conclusion I should like to call attention to the relationship of all this to the recently discussed question of the extent to which perfect international mobility of commodities is a substitute for perfect international mobility of the factors of production. In equations (1) for the case of equal number of goods and factors, commodity prices seem to determine factor prices completely and independently of the total supplies of factors in the country involved. It is rather surprising that no economist until Heckscher in 1919 seems to have anticipated the view that in many cases free trade would have effects as important as free migration of factors. Heckscher's 1919 discussion is, in fact, first worked out in terms of fixed coefficients of production, and leads to the complete equalization of factor prices rather than to the necessarily-incomplete equalization claimed by Heckscher's follower Ohlin. I gather that Heckscher himself formed the opinion that as soon as the coefficients become variable, as in the Walras-Clark theory, then the equalization will not go all the way. As a result of recent discussion, it is agreed, I believe, that full equalization will still take place so long as the number of goods commonly produced in the two countries is at least as great as the number of factors, and provided the intensities of use of the different factors by the different goods is sufficiently „different" (in relationship to the differences in regional factor endowments)[6].

---

[5] Cf. for example, the well-known work of Pareto, Lerner, and others. Incidentally, the parametric-pricing theories of atomistic competition or of Lerner-Lange decentralized planners playing the game of competition show us how the Knight theorem on values are to be interpreted when the p's are actually changing rather than constants. We must consider the virtual movement that assumes fixed prices, and then the identity of national product and national factor expense gives us the Knight result in every case. This identity, by the way, is a consequence of constant-returns-to-scale assumptions and there exists in linear programming a generalized form of Euler's theorem on homogeneous functions.

[6] A set of sufficient conditions that will guarantee a unique one-to-one relation between commodity prices and factor prices even when the a's are functions of factor-prices rather than constants is as follows: let there be a naturally-ordered set of principal minors of the a matrix that in no case change sign.

PART VI

Nonsubstitution Theorems

36

ABSTRACT OF A THEOREM CONCERNING SUBSTITUTABILITY IN OPEN LEONTIEF MODELS

By Paul A. Samuelson

Leontief [1941, 1946a] assumes that total production of each of n outputs, $x_1, \cdots, x_n$, is divided up into final outputs, $C_1, \cdots, C_n$, and into inputs used to help produce (with labor) all the inputs. Hence, for all i,

$$x_i = C_i + \sum_{j=1}^{n} x_{ji} \qquad (i = 1, 2, \cdots, n).$$

Labor, the $(n + 1)$th good, can be thought of as the sole "primary factor" or "nonproduced good," and its given total is allocated among all the different industries as follows:

$$x_{n+1} = 0 + \sum_{j=1}^{n} x_{j, n+1}.$$

Note that joint products are ruled out, so the x_{ji}'s are functionally independent.

Since Leontief works with so-called "fixed" coefficients of production, it is usually thought that he must try to approximate reality by a produc-

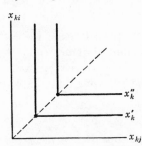

FIGURE 1a—Equal output curves for x_k with fixed coefficients.

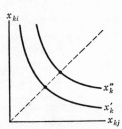

FIGURE 1b—General equal output curves for x_k.

tion function of the form shown in Figure 1a, rather than of the more general form admitting of substitution as shown in Figure 1b. Actually, *all* his theory in its present form is compatible with the more general case of substitutability. With labor the only primary factor, *all desirable substitutions have already been made by the competitive market*, and no variation in the composition of final output or in the total quantity of labor will give rise to price change or substitution. Only the circled points in Figure 1b will ever be observed. The following discussion shows that this is a property of the efficiency frontier always reached under competition.

1. Let each good be subject to a production function, homogeneous of the first order,

$$(1) \qquad x_i = F_i(x_{i1}, x_{i2}, \cdots, x_{i, n+1}) = mF_i\left(\frac{x_{i1}}{m}, \cdots, \frac{x_{i, n+1}}{m}\right).$$

Our equilibrium requires that any C, such as C_1, be at a maximum subject to fixed values of total labor, x_{n+1}, and all other C's; that is,

$$C_1 = F_1(x_{11}, x_{12}, \cdots, x_{1, n+1}) - \sum_{j=1}^{n} x_{j1}$$

is to be a maximum subject to

$$(2) \qquad F_i(x_{i1}, x_{i2}, \cdots, x_{i, n+1}) - \sum_{j=1}^{n} x_{ji} = C_i \qquad (i = 2, 3, \cdots, n),$$

$$0 - \sum_{j=1}^{n} x_{j, n+1} = -x_{n+1},$$

where F_{n+1}, the amount of labor produced, can be set equal to zero. We have the $n(n + 1)$ variables of the form x_{ij} to determine. We assume that with a finite amount of labor some finite quantity of each good is producible.

2. Because of homogeneity or constant returns to scale, the coefficients of production, $a_{ij} = x_{ij}/x_i$, are not constants but are connected by a relation of the form $F_i(a_{i1}, a_{i2}, \cdots, a_{i, n+1}) = 1$. Except for scale, this is shown in Figure 1b. Nevertheless, the following remarkable theorem holds:

THEOREM: *Regardless of the assigned values of $C_2, C_3, \cdots, C_n, x_{n+1}$, the optimal coefficients of production will always assume the same constant values, and the resulting production-possibility schedule for society will be of the simple linear form*

$$K_1 C_1 + K_2 C_2 + \cdots + K_n C_n = x_{n+1},$$

where the K's are constants independent of the C's and x_{n+1}. It is also true that relative prices of the form P_i/P_j will be similar constants.

PROOF: Form the Lagrangian expression

$$(3) \quad \lambda_1 C_1 + \lambda_2 (F_2 - \sum_{j=1}^{n} x_{j2} - C_2) + \lambda_3 (F_3 - \sum_{j=1}^{n} x_{j3} - C_3) + \cdots ,$$

and differentiate it with respect to each x_{jk}, treating the λ's as undetermined multipliers with $\lambda_1 = 1$. This gives us

$$(4) \quad \lambda_i \frac{\partial F_i}{\partial x_{ij}} - \lambda_j = 0 \quad (i = 1, 2, \cdots, n; j = 1, 2, \cdots, n + 1).$$

We can eliminate the λ's to get the equations [1]

$$(5) \quad \frac{\partial F_1}{\partial x_{11}} = 1, \quad \frac{\partial F_1}{\partial x_{1i}} \frac{\partial F_i}{\partial x_{ij}} - \frac{\partial F_1}{\partial x_{1j}} = 0 \quad \begin{array}{l} (i = 2, \cdots, n; \\ j = 1, 2, \cdots, n + 1). \end{array}$$

There are, by (5), $1 + (n - 1)(n + 1)$ equations to determine our $n(n + 1)$ variables x_{ij}. Their economic significance in terms of prices or equivalent marginal rates of substitution is easily expressed. The missing n equations are supplied by the specified C's and x_{n+1}. It may be added that, if we admitted the case of joint production, this simple elimination of the λ's would not be possible.

Since each of the F-functions is homogeneous of order one, each of our partial derivatives must be homogeneous of order zero (i.e., the economic assumption of constant returns to scale implies that all marginal productivities depend on the *proportions* of the inputs alone). Hence the set of equations in (5) may be written so that instead of their involving $(n^2 + n)$ x_{ij}'s they involve only the n^2 proportions of inputs of the form $b_{ij} = x_{ij}/x_{i, n+1}$, where i and j now range only from 1 to n.

Equation (5) determines all the proportions, b_{ij}, independently of the C's and x_{n+1}. With proportions always being invariant, it follows that we observe only one invariant set of "coefficients of production," a_{ij}, and the remaining assertions of the theorem are clearly implied.[2]

3. All the above is valid on the assumption that the partial derivatives of equations (5) exist everywhere and define a unique interior solution to

---

[1] Because of the necessary convexity of the F's, each of whose Hessian is required to be negative semidefinite, these necessary first order equations for a maximum are also sufficient. If some x_{ij} does not appear at all in F_i, then we drop the corresponding equation in (4), replacing it by $x_{ij} = 0$. We also make obvious modifications in (5). If a good uses no labor, we must modify our use of b's in a simple and inessential fashion.

[2] I have assumed that the price ratios are the same thing as (marginal) cost ratios, as indeed they will be if something of both goods in question is being produced.

(5). In the usual problems of linear programming, where only a finite number of activities are considered, the functions have corners at which the partial derivatives are undefined, and the optimum solution is defined by boundary inequalities rather than interior equalities of the partial derivatives. Also, we must consider the possibility that more than one set of values satisfy equations (5).

Nonetheless, the theorem remains true; a change in the bill of goods, $C_1, \cdots, C_n$, cannot make substitution profitable, and the frontier of efficiency points remains linear. A sketch of a brief but rigorous proof is as follows: [3]

First, we accept the easily proved fact that the efficiency frontier defined by our maximum problem must be a convex set in consequence of our strong homogeneity assumptions. We then show that through *any* efficient point there passes a linear hyperplane of feasible points. It must follow that the frontier locus is itself a linear hyperplane, for, if it anywhere had a corner or a curved surface, it would be impossible for us to find a hyperplane of feasible points going on all sides of the efficient point in question.

The only problem is to show that through any efficient point, $(C_1^0, C_2^0, \cdots, C_n^0, x_{n+1}^0)$, there does go a hyperplane of feasible points,

$$\sum_1^n \alpha_i(C_i - C_i^0) = x_{n+1} - x_{n+1}^0,$$

for some constant α's. Suppose that there really were absolute constant a_{ij}'s. Then it is a well-known property of Leontief systems [Leontief, 1941, 1946a] that the bill of goods is constrained to follow a linear hyperplane by the equations

$$C_i = x_i - \sum_1^n a_{ji}x_j \qquad (i = 1, 2, \cdots, n),$$

$$-x_{n+1} = -\sum_1^n a_{j, n+1}x_j.$$

Consider now an actual efficient point $(C_1^0, C_2^0, \cdots, C_n^0, x_{n+1}^0)$ being produced in the general case of Figure 1b by (x_{ij}^0). These quantities implicitly define a set (a_{ij}^0). Although it may not be obvious that it is *efficient* to stick to these fixed coefficients, the result will certainly be *feasible*. Hence there does exist a set of feasible points along a hyperplane through (C^0, x_{n+1}^0), and the theorem follows.

[3] I believe this argument is closely related to the more elaborate argument of Koopmans [VIII].

Less heuristically, we can easily show that

$$C_i = F_i(t_i x_{i1}, t_i x_{i2}, \cdots) - \sum_1^n x_{ki} t_k,$$

$$-x_{n+1} = -\sum_1^n x^0_{k,\, n+1} t_k,$$

define, because of the homogeneity property of the F_i, linear parametric equations in terms of the t's; for all the t's equal to one we get $(C^0_1, \cdots, C^0_n, x^0_{n+1})$, and for all nearby t's we get feasible points on a linear hyperplane.

37

PAUL A. SAMUELSON

A New Theorem on Nonsubstitution

Simple-minded people often say that raising wage rates will cause machines or "capital" to be substituted for labor. More sophisticated folk have wondered a little about this argument, asking: "If the rise in wage rates is a general one that bears as much on workers in the machine industries as it does on workers elsewhere, why will not the cost of machines and of their services rise by the same percentage amount as the rise in wages, thereby giving rise to no leverage conducive to substitution?"

I.

The acceptable answer to a question like this must, of course, depend upon the economic model that is envisaged. If one works with a no-joint-products constant-returns-to-scale model in which all effects of time are nonexistent or ignorable, and postulates a single primary factor of production labor, then the only conclusion possible is this:

All goods can be regarded as "congealed labor"; all prices are equal to the sum of direct labor costs ("live" labor) and indirect labor costs ("dead" labor). Raising the money wage must result in an exactly proportionate rise in every price including the price of machinery and its rental rates per unit time. So there cannot be any leverage for effective substitution induced by such a wage rise: even if technological possibilities for substitution were possible, they would never come into play. Moreover, so long as there is but the one primary factor of production labor, it is quite impossible within the framework of a given technology to stipulate any exogenous increase in the real wage: the real wage is already endogenously determined, and if one persists in prescribing a higher real wage rate than the critical endogenous one ,the result would be to shut down all activities completely and to render the stipulated real wage meaningless. (Example: suppose neo-Malthusians teach people to insist on a real wage higher than can be produced; then human race disappears, and zero, zero/zero equilibrium results.)

All the above is rather obvious in the special Austrian production structure where goods can be put into "early and late stages": bread is made with labor and flour; flour is made with labor and wheat; wheat is made with labor alone. Then a good at any stage can be decomposed into the total labor in all previous stages in a finite number of steps. It is self-evident that there will be no play for substitution and that the production-possibility curve relating any two finished goods (bread and circuses) will be a simple straight line. So long as something of both goods is demanded, their relative prices can be predicted from technology alone. (It is this technological predictability, rather than vague philosophical implications, which constitutes what it is that would be interesting about a simple labor theory of value, a conclusion that seems to have been rather overlooked in the literature.)

When one turns from a simple Austrian hierarchy of production stages to a Marx-Leontief model in which any stage can use an input of any other, so that none can be said to be "early" and none "late", the problem is a more complex one. Actually, it can be shown that everything said about the Austrian model remains valid for such a general whirlpool model. But it was not until 1949, when N. Georgescu-Roegen and P. Samuelson independently formulated and proved the "substitutability theorem", that this was established. After such a theorem has been stated it may indeed seem obvious; but this is the fate of all truth and one has to keep reminding oneself that *ex ante* isn't *ex post*. As Maugham said about an unforgettable Mondrian painting, "It looks as though you had only to take a ruler, a tube of black paint and a tube of red, and you could do the thing yourself. Try!"

II.

Still ignoring all time relations, one must make certain evident qualifications when confronted by two or more primary factors. Thus where homogeneous labor and land are the two primary factors, raising the money or real wage of labor relative to land is indeed possible: it will raise the relative prices of all goods that are "relatively labor intensive" relative to other goods; and raising the wage will most definitely cause land to be substituted (both "directly" and "indirectly") for labor, so that the system can end up with a lower total-labor to total-land ratio and with a higher real wage that has grown, so to speak, at the expense of a reduced real land rental. Now the predictability of relative factor and commodity prices from technology alone is no longer possible. The production-possibility curve between two goods, such as bread and circuses, will certainly look convex from above, save in the singular case where both goods happened to be of "equal factor intensity"; and a change in consumer demand toward any good can be expected to raise its relative price, so that one must introduce full knowledge about preferences to make any kind of guess about prices. (All the above is as true of Marx-Leontief as of Austrian structures.)

What is true of two primary factors is broadly true of more than two, as in the case where the real wage is raised in a model that has two kinds of homogeneous land. (Some subtle mathematical differences I here ignore.)

III.

Still ignoring all time relations, I want to call attention to a rather interesting mathematical or logical fact. No matter how many "primary" factors there may be, suppose we stipulate that all but one of them are available at fixed factor prices (in money, or better still relative to the unknown price of the unique factor, which we can call labor). Then with only a little difficulty one can show that all pricing relations are predictable from knowledge of the money wage rate alone; all real factor returns, including that of labor, are now predictable from technology alone; all net production-possibility relations between any two consumable goods are perfectly straight lines, whose slopes are given in terms of the "embodied" labor in them.[1]

---

[1] My friend, Robert Solow, reminds me that the use of the expression "'primary' factor" is a rather strained one in this context. For, factors that are available in unlimited amounts at a fixed remuneration can conveniently be thought of as items that are producible, so to speak, in a simple technological way; hence, they can be thought of as *not* being primary factors; hence, with there being truly only one primary factor, we are back to a simple one-factor theory of value; and, thus, the mathematical phenomenon of this section will be intuitively plausible by analogy with the simplest one-factor model.

I ought to add that the concept of the "net production-possibility" relation is one that needs a nice interpretation. The goods in it are *not* the gross totals of goods producible by the system; rather they are the net totals actually available to the owners of the one truly primary factor; and such net totals come after we have carefully subtracted from the gross productions of society those amounts that must go to the productive factors stipulated to be available at constant factor prices. My later discussions and diagrams will elaborate on this. (Note: no one should

This remarkable fact appears implicitly in a number of my papers of the 1950's. It will suffice to cite the Samuelson-Ricardo-Turgot theorem that all relations in simple Ricardo-like models can be expressed in terms of a pure *"land* theory of value". This theorem might have surprised two of its god-parents; but when we recall the classical notion that people are producible and reproducible at constant real wage rates (and that the same is true about "capital" and the long-run interest rate), then it is evident that only land is the bottleneck in the model and that all magnitudes become proportional to a definable embodied land computation. To any historian of tax theories this Physiocratic theory of Ricardo should, upon reflection, come as no great shock.

IV.

Now we must come to grips with the problem of time. Production does take place in time; inputs do precede outputs. And time does cost money; or more precisely the use of money or resources through time does require an interest payment in any competitive model where there is a positive rate of interest.

Economists often simplify the problem and try to talk of primary factors like labor and land, *and* some *other* aggregative factor called "capital". All this, it bears repeating, is but a figure of speech. What we observe in life are concrete factors and goods and their services: the wheat inventories of millers; flour; wrapped and unwrapped bread, in the shop or delivered to the home; grape juice, fermented wine, and mellowed vintages; roads in the process of being built and roads in the process of being used and worn out; prenatal machines, just-born machines, senile machines. In *perfect* competitive markets no one has doubts concerning the market valuations of all such assets (including quasi-imperishable land), and no one can stop the contented merchant from adding up his asset values, or prevent the national statistician from adding up his estimates of the community's wealth. Such computed value totals, it need hardly be said, cannot be fed into production functions, kicked, or leaned against.

confuse gross and net as used here with their usage by the national income statistician. If double counting of depreciation were included in my model, then a still grosser concept of product would have to be employed. My use of "net" is in the sense of the Physiocrats *"net produit"*, generalized beyond their application to land alone.)

The great neoclassical writers, such as Wicksell and Clark, realized all this. But some, especially Clark, liked to spin the parable of a composite generalized capital factor, whose magnitude C could somehow be treated in production functions like other factors, even though it merely represented an abstraction from the diversity of concrete "capital goods" which represented reality. Just as the wage and rent are the factor prices of labor and land, the interest rate is the return to abstract capital. Other economists, up until the present day, have never ceased to be uneasy about such abstractions; and some in our own day, like J. Robinson, have spent a good deal of time in deploring the practice.

In arriving at sums of asset values, the economist must realize that various market magnitudes – such as the interest rate – are involved. These interest rates are part of what a theory of capital has to explain, and so there may seem to be something of a vicious circle involved in use of any abstract capital concept. In theoretical economics, one realizes that circular interdependences do always exist and that equilibrium configurations are defined from finding the simultaneous solution to sets of circularly dependent equations or logical conditions. So many circles in economics are virtuous ones rather than vicious ones. (Thus, if there were but one homogeneous physical capital good, the fact that its capitalized value depends upon the interest rate and that the size and rate of growth of the physical capital stock depends upon people's patterns of thrift and consumption through alleged interest rate and wealth effects, involves reciprocal circularity, but that does not vitiate a simultaneous equation solution of capital and interest in such a model.)

In a quasi-realistic world of many different physical capital goods, a proper description of its operations must be in terms of its technological properties. For this reason modern theorists – or perhaps I had better merely speak for one member of the so-called "MIT school" – insist upon working with "capital models" that involve detailed vectors of capital goods, in which there is any finite number of different capital goods (each defined in terms of its *physical* properties) or even an infinite number of such goods. Then any resulting pattern of interest rates and other equilibrium magnitudes will work themselves out. For those with the appropriate mathematical technique or imagination, the result is not only manageable but in addition all its general properties can be inferred. (Sraffa's belatedly published book on commodity production, which eschewes use of all magnitudes that cannot be invariantly defined prior to any confrontation with market forces, is thus completely within the MIT tradition – or, more fairly, some of us have been Sraffian without realizing it.)

V.

But let us return to Clark's realm of parable and nursery tale. We ask of such a story not whether it is literally true but whether it is well told – not in the sense of being elegantly narrated but in the sense of conveying some important insight into reality. There is, I suggest, a certain sense in which the Clark parable is an interesting one.

First, and least important, the parable would be literally true in a greatly simplified model in which there was indeed but a single homogeneous capital good. This makes it a useful pedagogical device. But at a deeper level such a defense suffers from the technical likelihood that no single capital good has the complete substitutability properties so dear to the Clark kind of neoclassical writer: While it is not impossible that there should be a single equipment that could be smoothly combined with other factors in all proportions (as in a Cobb-Douglas production function), still it is not very likely.

Second, there is the neoclassical perception that, as specific capital equipments wear out, their replacement funds can be used to channel resources into building different kinds of equipment more appropriate to the new pattern of demand. So to speak, physical capital transforms itself into a new form – while allegedly some kind of magnitude of abstract capital jelly is being maintained in total quantity. The last part of this sentence is, of course, pure metaphor, but the first part is literal truth, a description of what does happen in real life.

Third, there is a deeper sense underlying the metaphor and parable that can be brought out by asking the following specific question: What happens in real life and in a Clark parable when two communities start out with exactly the same endowments of land and labor and physical capital goods, but one cuts down on its current consumption of all goods and uses its resources to create more of all varieties of physical capital goods?

Using the Clark model the economist would easily predict the following: More consumption and other goods will be producible at a later date in the "accumulating" economy. Real wages will rise. Profit rates (which are indistinguishable from interest rates if uncertainty and technological innovation are abstracted from) will fall. Land will sell at more years' purchase. Consumption loans, if they exist, will carry a lower interest rate.

So goes the usual neoclassical process in which "capital is deepened". But, and this is the point of the current section, precisely the same thing can be expected in a capital-goods-vector model in which absolutely no use is made of any abstract notion of aggregative capital. Curtailed consumption causes production possibilities to rise. The market-imputed factor prices of primary factors also rise. The rate of interest (or its whole structure) declines through time. Moreover, in most such elaborated models that seem like realistic engineering studies of production, the rate at which interest rates fall is *not* cataclysmically fast – as would be the outcome in oversimplified models where there is but a single production function with limited-substitution properties.

While honesty requires me to improve on Voltaire by saying that "History is a fable, *not* agreed upon", it also compels one to admit that there is *something* to the Clark fable when we want to describe the process of accumulation under capitalism or communism.

VI.

All the above involve questions of judgment and taste. If I am deemed wrong in claiming some merit to the oversimplified parable of an abstract capital, I shall cheerfully agree. The modern theorist has no real need for such childish devices and, in any case, should not be permitted to use them until he has shown he can rigorously formulate his theories completely without them.

I now leave the concept of an abstract capital factor of production that is used along with a primary factor like labor; and I leave the quarrelsome realm of approximation behind and proceed to the realm of exact analysis. What I shall now show is the following theorem:

> *Although it be rigorously impossible in a labor and multi-capital-good model to reduce matters to a two-factor labor and capital model, it is nonetheless completely possible to reduce everything rigorously down to a real wage and single interest-rate model. While capital goods involve millions of different dimensions, the whole problem yet can be rigorously boiled down to the two-dimensional realm of wage and interest.*

The remarkable nature of this can be indicated by an example. At the Corfu September 1958 International Economic Meeting on capital, Kaldor made the point that the interesting differences between rich and poor countries lay in the differences in "horizontal" rather than "vertical" price relations. By horizontal, he meant such facts as that in a poor country the relative rental of a machine in relation to prevailing wages might be many times the rental of that same machine in the rich country. Such horizontal differences in prices he regarded as different from, and more important than, the fact that the rich country allegedly had a higher capital-output ratio and a lower interest rate – or any of the other vertical relations so beloved of neoclassical writers concerned with the conventional deepening of capital.

Without trying to diagnose reality, which involves great differences in natural resources between countries, great differences in technology or effective technology, and great differences in achieved capital formation, we can subject the Kaldor distinctions to rigorous analysis within a well-defined model, where labor is nonproducible but where every kind of capital good is producible by labor and other capital goods. In equilibrium how can such a model look in a given state of invention and knowledge?

If the Kaldor separation of horizontal from vertical relationships were a valid one, then my indented paragraph would be completely false. And, as we shall see, if my assertion is true, then the Kaldor distinction will not hold up within the framework of a rigidly defined model where all the relationships are firmly understood.

For in two such societies, there can be differences in real wages and in horizontal price relationships if, *and only if*, there is a difference in the interest rate. It is such a difference in the interest rate that creates the usual differences in *vertical* relations (not perhaps a happy adjective but a useful one if Kaldor were right). Thus, when the rich country with the high real wage uses much machinery of a certain type, it must certainly be the case that the net rentals for the use of such machines are low enough relative to going wage rates to induce such methods; but this *horizontal* fact will, in such models, be merely the pale reflection of the changed interest rate that gives us the clue to the costs of producing and using any one of the infinite set of different capital goods that are potentially producible. Homer, I mean Kaldor, nodded.

VII.

All this leads up to the new and general substitution, or what is of course more accurate, nonsubstitution theorem. It says something like the following:

"In a model where one primary factor (labor) is non-producible, where there are myriad capital goods of all types producible by known constant-returns-to-scale technologies, let us suppose there is a change in the money wage rate. In the short run when the stocks of the various capital goods are fixed, there will, of course, be a substitution against labor and the quasi-rents to non-labor factors will fall, their falling being a necessary condition for the transient rise in real rates. In all likelihood the interest rate or pattern of interest rates will in the short run move downward. If, however, one performs the experiment under long-run conditions, stipulating that all the adjustments of various types of capital goods take place until in the new equilibrium the old interest rate reasserts itself, then the increase in the real wage will have been transient and will have disappeared. If the money wage rate is permanently higher, then all other price relationships will be permanently higher in the same percentage degree. More remarkably, even if the initial disturbance is not that of a stipulated change in the wage rate but rather a stipulated change in the pattern of demand for end-goods such as bread and circuses or specific capital formations, the net production-possibility relations will in the long run, under the stipulation of a resorted interest rate, be perfectly straight lines, whose slopes represent predictable unchanged price ratios that are interpretable as 'embodied labor-*cum*-interest' parameters".

VIII.

The accompanying figure well illustrates the relations involved. Let food on the vertical axis be producible with labor alone; to introduce the element of time most simply, suppose there is a one-period delay between the input of one unit of labor and the output of one unit of food. Let clothing on the vertical axis be produced by labor alone – one labor now produces one of clothing a period from now; but to admit of a little technological substitutability, let's follow Jevons and Böhm-Bawerk and assume that one labor now can alternatively produce two of clothing if we let it ripen for two periods.

The line AB represents the (gross) production-possibility locus for

528

society if we ignore the roundabout option for clothing. It refers to the steady state and tells us how much of the two goods society can have in each period with a fixed amount of labor (regardless of the process by which society is able to get into that steady state). Because, and only because, the two industries have the same periods of production (or "organic compositions of capital"), their relative price ratios will be the same as the slope of AB, being proportional to their respective labor contents. Because of our choice of units, this will be a one/one ratio. If we use units of labor as our *numéraire*, the price of food in wage units will be *more* than 1.0, depending on how high the interest rate is for one period; but by the same token the price of clothing will be equally in excess of its 1.0 labor content and the ratio of the two goods' prices will have interest cancelled out from it.[2] It is special cases like this that adherents of a labor theory of value can rely on to save their theory, since changes in the interest rate would then not affect relative prices (even though they would affect real wages in the opposite direction).

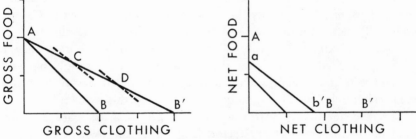

Figs. 1 and 2.

Gross production-possibilities are shown by AB and AB', depending on the interest rate. Actual market price ratios are given by the parallel broken-line slopes at C or D, such slopes becoming steeper as the interest rate rises. Such slopes are parallel to the ab' net production-possibility locus giving goods actually available to labor after capitalists have received the stipulated interest rate on whatever total of capital value will be appropriate for each stipulated point on ab'. Raising interest rate will shift ab' downward and steepen it as less of the "capital-intensive" good becomes available; if no substitutions beyond that of AB are possible, the equal "time intensities" of the goods will result in parallel further shifts of the net curve because of the coincidental equal intensity assumption needed to validate the simple labor theory of value.

[2] To isolate the returns to "effort" as against "waiting", I make the usual assumption that wages are payable at the beginning of each period.

The line AB' shows the greater production possibilities made possible if the interest rate gets low enough to induce clothing producers to use the more efficient, roundabout technical option. Again the slope of this line represents the ratio of labor contents alone, it being flatter than before because the labor content per unit of clothing is now less. What about market price ratio of clothing to food? This will now depend on the interest rate. The steeper broken-line slope at a point like C shows that clothing's actual price relative to food will be greater than its relative labor content alone because the greater roundaboutness of its production makes it involve more interest. A rise in the interest rate would make this broken-line slope steeper and steeper (until when it became as steep as the old AB line the roundabout clothing option would no longer pay). This fact that relative goods prices are distorted by changes in interest is, of course, fatal to any simple labor theory of value – as Ricardo and his friends realised only too well.

One of the implications of the general nonsubstitution theorem is this: No matter whether society chooses to end up at C or D or anywhere else on AB', the broken-line slope measuring relative commodity prices will be exactly the same as anywhere else *so long as the interest rate is the same.* That is why the slope at D is parallel to that at C, and both will change together if, *and only if,* the interest rate changes.

I do not extend the broken-line segments into "contours of equal ('gross') national product", for the reason that society simply has not the choice to move along such a contour. After reflection on the technological stipulations of the model, one will find this evident.

The second figure portrays the net products that are actually available to the one primary factor, labor, after the owners of all the capital goods have been paid off at the stipulated interest rate. This *net* production-possibility locus is inside the gross locus AB' for the obvious reason that positive interest means that some of the gross product goes to non-laborers. Note the striking fact that the net locus is a straight line; and note the even more remarkable implication of my theorem that the slope of the straight line is exactly parallel to the broken-line slopes in the earlier figure. These slopes do reflect actual competitive market prices, and they are precisely interpretable as "embodied labor-*cum*-interest" parameters. From technology and the interest rate alone, *and completely without regard to the demand considerations that lead workers to end up at one point or another on the net locus,* such slope and price relations can be accurately predicted as constants. (It will be seen, too, that the values of such constants are quite independent of how the interest receivers are supposed to spend their incomes.)

Just how can the net locus be derived from the gross one? If the fixed interest rate were earned on a fixed total value of capital, then non-labor claim on gross outputs would be strictly constant. Subtracting a constant amount of food and clothing from AB' would give a reduced locus, but one with the same slope. Hence, a fixed claim of interest receivers is quite incompatible with the process in which laborers, with interest fixed, choose to vary their relative consumptions of food and clothing. What will happen is the following:

If laborers were to increase their relative demand for clothing, the total of capital value upon which the fixed interest rate is earned must go up. Recall that the more roundabout process is being used in clothing. Hence the total value of what has to be subtracted from gross production must go up. Hence, less is indeed left for workers than would be shown by a locus whose slope remained as flat as before. Since the locus must fall off more steeply, we do see intuitively that the net locus has the slope given by relating actual market prices.[3]

IX.

The above nonsubstitution theorem will be seen to include the 1949 theorem as that special case where the stipulated interest rate is zero, as in a timeless system or a "capital-saturated" system. Its importance lies not in the fact that in actual long-run situations one has much reason to expect that accumulation and rearrangement of capital goods will proceed until the previous interest rate has been restored. The time is long past when one takes seriously Ricardo, Cassel, Pigou notions of a basic long-run interest rate determined by special time preferences or anything else. The point of the theorem is to show that any changes that do take place in the equilibrium relations *must*, in the

[3] To test his understanding of this terse exposition, the reader can assume an increase in interest rate small enough to keep us on AB'. Now the net locus in the second diagram will become *flatter* and shift inward. The reader can show that when interest is raised enough to make the two-period clothing method uneconomical, the resulting net locus will be well inside the AB line but now it will have exactly the slope of that line. Further increases in the interest rate must cause the locus to shift indefinitely inward, but from now on in the strictly parallel fashion imposed by the assumption of coincidental equal organic compositions of capital in the two industries.

absence of technological change, be associated with the change in the interest rate and nothing else!

Let me illustrate with a bizarre example. Suppose the Soviet Union had about the same primary factors, labor and natural resources, as the United States – actually not too unrealistic an assumption. Suppose by virtue of free trade or anything else that capital could move so as to equalise interest rates in the two continents and that the same knowledge of nature were open to all. Then after all adjustments had been made there would be quite comparable real wages and all other possibilities in the two places. Be it noted that this is quite consistent with the Clark parable, but that the "capital" which moves in the previous sentence is not at all any mysterious abstract capital jelly nor need it be every or any kind of capital good that moves. All that is required for the truth of my bizarre example is that the Soviet Union have truly open to it the same interest rate at which everything can be had – not merely gold, rubles or dollars but anything – including "abstract purchasing power". (This last expression is a metaphor that can be given specific meanings.) In passing I might mention that this has a relevance to the Heckscher–Ohlin–Lerner–Samuelson theorems about equalisation of factor prices by international trade. Under really idealized conditions of returns and free movement of knowledge and credit, the only persisting differences in geographical specialisation and welfare would have to be attributable to the facts of economic geography and nothing else – to differences in human and natural resources. Without such primary differences the specialisation and factor-intensity-reversals which vitiate complete equalisation cannot come permanently into play.

X.

In real life can increases in wage induce substitution of machinery for labor? Our answer can now be given.

"An increase in money wages can increase real wages at the expense of other primary factors of production, such as land; except in special technical conditions, there will usually be a substitution of such other factors for labor. In the short run, the existing stocks of machinery behave very much like primary factors, earning Marshallian quasi-rents rather than classical rents. Hence gains at the expense of machine returns and substitution are certainly possible and even likely in the short run. Ignoring other primary factors and assuming certain return conditions, one sees that even the short-run change in real wages and factor substitutions are only possible because the effective equilibrium interest rate has been jarred from its previous level. Should it happen that subsequent accumulation or adjustments of composition of capital goods were to lead back to the previous interest rate, then there could indeed be no lasting substitution of 'capital' for labor and no change in real wages not attributable to technological change. To use Kaldor's terminology, in the stipulated models horizontal and vertical price relationships are uniquely related to each other. To use Wicksell – Böhm-Bawerk terminology, the degree of roundaboutness of production can be affected by wage change only in the degree that this has produced interest rate change. It is nonsensical to say that a change in wage rate, with the other factor return, interest, held constant, will lead to some kind of 'lengthening' of the period of production as (the same?) capital can now provide more roundabout methods for the new (smaller?) number of workers."

XI.

Our model and results have important applications in connection with the problem of automation and technical change generally. The naive scientist assumes without thinking that robots and automatic machines must naturally depress real wages of human labor. This view must be more carefully formulated.

No one doubts that automation could change the terms of trade between different kinds of primary factors. Will the modern computer raise or depress the relative returns to persons with high I.Q.? In principle, either effect is possible. Though many amateur economists make pronouncements that artificial intelligence will compete away the rents to human intelligence, the presumption is by no means clear. Thus, what does it take to train men who can maintain delicate mechanisms? Stupid people might conceivably gain or lose in relative position in such a new age of automation; a priori reasoning will not take us far in a matter like this. Likewise, a trend to automation could raise the returns to certain rare raw materials that are peculiarly useful in connection with such mechanisms; but it is by no means clear that such effects are likely to be substantial.

Aside from any changes in relative remunerations of labor and other primary factors, there is the question of whether technical change could increase the return to "capital" at the expense of the return to labor.

Treating all primary factors as one homogeneous class dubbed labor, we can infer from the present discussions that there is essentially only one way that the real wage could be harmed by technological improvements. Only if the innovation were to bid up the interest rate to a critical degree could labor conceivably be hurt by it. I say by a considerable degree because an increase in the interest rate that was very small relative to the improvement in productivity would definitely raise the real wage. It could definitely raise the relative share of labor in the total national income. Likewise, if the new technology is sooner or later accompanied by a drop in interest rate, then the equilibrium real wage must definitely have risen. One must resist any temptation to assert that the relative share of labor must also have risen, since it is quite possible that the lower interest rate will be applied to a larger total of capital value; in a rigorous capital-goods model, one must be wary of making any statement about the total of capital as having been preserved throughout the process of a changing technology.

That kind of technological change which is associated with the name "automation" probably receives more dramatic attention than it deserves. The cold statistics do not seem to proclaim any great "second industrial revolution". Still economists ought not to be spoil-sports. If scientists like to prattle about automation, we should agreeably go along with the gag. In this spirit, let us ask the final question: Suppose society learns how to make robots that are very close substitutes for man himself? What will the effect of that be on real wages paid to man?

At least in the short run, this must depend on just what it takes to make a robot. If it takes a man alone, then the extra product of the first robots may have to be imputed back to man himself. (Of course, if it takes 40 years of a man's life to make one robot, which will duplicate him but be senile in less than 40 years, such robots will not be economical.) But after we have got over the hurdle of the first robot, from now on a robot can make a robot. What are the consequences of this for the real wage of man (and for robots)? On the assumption that no other technical change takes place except the ability to make good man substitutes, we can indicate the answer.

Call the number of robots that one man (or robot) can make in his (its) working life x: then x is the net reproductive rate, so to speak, of robots, and from that rate per generation we can hope to infer the robot per-year reproductive rate. If this exceeds the previous interest (or profit) rate, then ultimately the real wage of a man will have to fall.

However, so long as the interest rate stays as low as it has sometimes been, real wages cannot fall below what they were in such periods.

All the above was on the assumption that human labor was the only primary factor. When we take into account limitation of land and natural resources, we realise that the growth of men and robots relative to land will force up land rents relative to wages. Diminishing returns will set in and the reproductive rate of robots will fall. Assuming that robots are easier to produce than babies, the final equilibrium must be even stranger than the dire Malthusian one: equilibrium will take place with wages at the subsistence rate for robots, with mankind having become virtually extinct. I say virtually extinct because in the end there will still remain the class of humans called landlords and capitalists: this class could consist of a single family, or if society runs itself in that direction, it could be the whole human race of property owners. It is owners of mere skills who will be extinct. In such an epoch the authority of parents will at last come back into its own.

HISTORICAL NOTES

The beginning arguments must be prehistoric. In recent times they are perhaps best known through the famous 1933 *Economic Journal* review by G. F. Shove of J. R. Hicks, *Theory of Wages* (1932); but American economists were already familiar with the fact that a change in interest was the necessary condition for substitution because of a long string of articles in the *American Economic Review*, initiated by H. Gordon Hayes (1923) and followed by C. O. Fisher (1923), Hayes (1923), L. A. Morrison (1924), M. A. Gerhart (1924), F. D. Graham (1926), W. Wissler (1927), G. E. Bigge (1927); P. H. Douglas, *Theory of Wages* (1933) inadequately refutes Hayes. My teacher and friend, Jacob Viner, had pointed out to me certain inadequacies in Ricardo's discussion of similar matters, an item which future editors might still elaborate on.

The recent book by Piero Sraffa, *Production of Commodities by Means of Commodities* (Cambridge, 1960), gives results arrived at in the 1920s that bear on the present discussion. Though this "Prelude to a Critique of Economic Theory" presents results that are compatible with marginalist theory or certain modern generalisations of that theory of the linear programming type, we have no right to indict Sraffa for being a marginalist. Material relevant to the present discussion might be found in R. Dorfman, P. A. Samuelson, R. M. Solow, *Linear Programming and Economic Analysis* (1958) and my recent papers on factor price equalisation, Ricardo, and Marx: *Review of Economic Studies* (1953), *Quarterly Journal of Economics* (1956), *American Economic Review* (1957). For the 1949 substitution theorem, see T. C. Koopmans (ed.), *Activity Analysis of Production and Allocation* (1951), chapters by P. Samuelson, T. C. Koopmans, K. J. Arrow, and N. Georgescu-Roegen.

The Austrian model stems from Menger, Böhm-Bawerk, Wicksell, Hayek, and others; the Marxian model of whirlpools of production from *Capital*, v. II; various Leontief generalisations of input-outputs are summarised in W. W. Leontief, *Structure of the American Economy* (1939) and *Studies in the Structure of the American Economy* (1953). Joan Robinson's views are given in *The Accumulation of Capital* (1956), other contemporaneous writings, and also, I believe, in correspondence with R. M. Solow, from whose numerous writings on capital theory I have benefited much. My interpretation of N. Kaldor's oral remarks at Corfu may reflect my misunderstanding and not his intention; I extend my apologies if I have nodded. No doubt his intention was to criticize the realism of assumptions like mine.

Mathematical programmers in the armed services and followers of v. Neumann have recognised that fixed capital goods imply joint-production (in which a new machine and labor produce as byproducts cigarettes and slightly older machines, as Ricardo's friend Torrens would have agreed). The 1949 substitution theorem, however, can lack validity when joint-products are admitted into the discussion. So with the general theorem here. However, as I indicated in my Ricardo papers, the kind of jointness of production involved in machinery will not vitiate the result if we confine our attention to the alternative production possibilities of end-products that are not jointly produced. To clarify this, note that the production-possibility schedule between wool and mutton is not a straight line even in the case of a labor theory of value, for the reason that they are joint products. Similarly if people want to choose between consuming the services of new and old cars, it will be evident that their joint-production relations make a straight-line choice impossible. The conclusion is quite opposite in the case of a choice between consumable grape juice and consumable wine, as the careful reader will be able to discern. Still, and this is the point, if food is produced by ovens, labor, and wheat and if clothing is produced by sewing machines, labor and wool, it can still be rigorously true that the production-possibility relation between end-product food and end-product clothing can be a straight line, with relative prices that are parameters predictable from technology alone.

Mention should be made of the fact that I have generally talked about a single interest rate. This is legitimate for purposes of comparative statics when we compare two alternative situations of equilibrium in which relative prices remain reasonably stable and all "own rates of interest" are identical. Solow, M. Morishima, and I have carried through researches in the more general case where relative price changes are foreseeable and anticipated capital gains must be taken account of in the conditions for profit equalisation everywhere.

PART VII

Some Metaeconomic Propositions:
Comparative Statics, Dynamics, and the Structure of Minimum Equilibrium Systems

38

THE STABILITY OF EQUILIBRIUM: COMPARATIVE STATICS AND DYNAMICS*

By Paul A. Samuelson

INTRODUCTION

It was an achievement of the first magnitude for the older mathematical economists to have shown that the number of independent and consistent economic relations was in a wide variety of cases sufficient to determine the equilibrium values of unknown economic prices and quantities. Since their life spans were only of finite duration, it was natural that they should have stopped short at this stage of counting equations and unknowns. It remains to be explained, however, why in the first quarter of the twentieth century economists should have been content with what was after all only preliminary spade work containing in itself (at least explicitly) few *meaningful* theorems of observational significance such as could even ideally be empirically refuted under any conceivable circumstances.

It is the task of comparative statics to show the determination of the equilibrium values of given variables (unknowns) under postulated conditions (functional relationships) with various data (parameters) being specified. Thus, in the simplest case of a partial-equilibrium market for a single commodity, the two independent relations of supply and demand, each drawn up with other prices and institutional data being taken as given, determine by their intersection the equilibrium quantities of the unknown price and quantity sold. If no more than this could be said, the economist would be truly vulnerable to the gibe that he is only a parrot taught to say "supply and demand." Simply to know that there are efficacious "laws" determining equilibrium tells us nothing of the character of these laws. In order for the analysis to be useful it must provide information concerning the way in which our equilibrium quantities will change as a result of changes in the parameters taken as independent data.

In the above illustration let us consider "tastes" as a changing parameter influencing only the demand curve. Will an increase in demand raise or lower price? Clearly the statement that, before and after the assumed change, price is determined by the intersection of supply and demand gives us no answer to the problem. Nothing can be said concerning the movement of the intersection point of *any* two

* Reprinted from *Econometrica*, Vol. 9, No. 2 (April 1941). With slight modifications, this and the following two articles appear as Chapters IX through XI in *Foundations of Economic Analysis* (Cambridge: Harvard University Press, 1947).

plane curves as one of them shifts. And yet most economists would argue that in a wide variety of circumstances this question can be given a definite answer—namely that price will increase.

How is this conclusion derived? For few commodities have we detailed quantitative empirical information concerning the exact forms of the supply and demand curves even in the neighborhood of the equilibrium point. Not only would large amounts of time and money be necessary to get such information, but in many cases it is on principle impossible to derive useful empirical information concerning what would happen if virtual changes in price confronted the demanders or the suppliers.

This is a typical problem confronting the economist: in the absence of precise quantitative data he must infer analytically the qualitative direction of movement of a complex system. What little success he has hitherto achieved can be classified in large part under two headings: (1) theorems proceeding from the assumption of maximizing behavior on the part of firms or individuals, and (2) stability conditions relating to the interaction between economic units. Although inadequately explored until comparatively recently, the first type of conditions is best known and will not be dealt with here except incidentally. As will become evident later, however, from certain points of view they can be fitted in as special cases of the second set. It is the central task of this paper to show how the problem of stability of equilibrium is intimately tied up with the problem of deriving fruitful theorems in comparative statics.

COMPARATIVE STATICS

The problem may be approached in full generality by considering n unknown variables $(x_1, \cdots, x_n)$ whose equilibrium values are to be determined for preassigned values of a parameter, α. We assume n independent and consistent, continuously differentiable implicit relations involving some or all of the unknowns and the parameter α; or

(1) $$f^i(x_1, \cdots, x_n, \alpha) = 0, \qquad i = 1, \cdots, n.$$

These determine a set of equilibrium values[1]

(2) $$x_i^{\,o} = g_i(\alpha).$$

We wish to determine the sign of

(3) $$\frac{dx_i^{\,o}}{d\alpha} = g_i{}'(\alpha).$$

---

[1] If for a given value of $\alpha = \alpha_1$, there exists a solution $(x_1^o, \cdots, x_n^o)$, and if the matrix $\|\partial f^i/\partial x_j\|$ is of rank n in a neighborhood of (x^o), then by the implicit-function theorem equations (2) represent single-valued continuously differentiable functions in a sufficiently small neighborhood of (α_1, x^o).

Differentiating (1) totally with respect to α, we can express this a_s

$$(4) \qquad \frac{dx_i^o}{d\alpha} = - \frac{\sum_{i=1}^{n} f_\alpha{}^i \Delta_{ji}}{\Delta},$$

where the subscripts indicate partial differentiation,

$$\Delta = \begin{vmatrix} f_1{}^1 & f_2{}^1 & \cdots & f_n{}^1 \\ f_1{}^2 & f_2{}^2 & \cdots & f_n{}^2 \\ \cdot & \cdot & \cdots & \cdot \\ f_1{}^n & f_2{}^n & \cdots & f_n{}^n \end{vmatrix} = | f_i{}^i |,$$

and Δ_{ji} is the cofactor of the element in the jth row and ith column of Δ.

Unless some a priori restrictions are placed upon the nature of the elements involved in these determinants, no useful theorems can be derived. Each unknown derivative depends upon an $n(n+1)$ infinity of possible values. If the various determinants were expanded out, a sum of $n!$ terms would appear in the denominator and in the numerator. Regarded simply as chance drawings taken at random from a hat, the probability that the signs of these would all agree would go rapidly to zero as the number of variables increased. Fortunately, as will be shown, the analysis of the stability of equilibrium will aid in evaluating these complicated expressions.

In the simple example of supply and demand alluded to above our unknowns are (p, q), and our equilibrium system can be written:

$$(5) \qquad \begin{cases} q - D(p, \alpha) = 0, & D_\alpha > 0, D_p < 0, \\ q - S(p) = 0, \end{cases}$$

where α is a parameter of shift representing "taste" and D_p is usually assumed to be less than zero. Also

$$(6) \qquad \frac{dp^o}{d\alpha} = D_\alpha{}^o \frac{1}{S_p{}^o - D_p{}^o},$$

$$(7) \qquad \frac{dq^o}{d\alpha} = D_\alpha{}^o \frac{S_p{}^o}{S_p{}^o - D_p{}^o}.$$

Whether or not price will increase when demand increases is seen to depend upon the algebraic difference between the slopes (referred to the price axis) of the demand and supply curves at the equilibrium point. Quantity will increase only if the slope of the supply curve is of the same sign as this algebraic difference. If the system is stable in the sense of Walras, it can be shown that the supply curve must have a greater algebraic slope than the demand curve so that price will necessarily increase; the change in quantity is necessarily of ambiguous sign depending upon whether the supply curve is positively inclined or so-called "backward-rising."[2]

STABILITY AND DYNAMICS

Before deriving explicitly the Walrasian stability conditions referred to above, I turn to a discussion of the meaning of a stable equilibrium. This will be found to presuppose a theory of dynamics, namely a theory which determines the behavior through time of all variables from arbitrary initial conditions. If we have given n variables $[x_1(t), \cdots, x_n(t)]$, and n functional equations of the general form

$$(8) \qquad F^i[\overset{t}{\underset{-\infty}{x_1(\tau)}}, \overset{t}{\underset{-\infty}{x_2(\tau)}}, \cdots, \overset{t}{\underset{-\infty}{x_n(\tau)}}, t] = 0, \qquad i = 1, \cdots, n,$$

then their behavior is determined once certain initial conditions are specified.[3] Examples of functional equation systems are given by sets of differential, difference, mixed differential-difference, integral, integro-differential, and still more general systems. Following the excellent terminology of Professor Frisch,[4] stationary or equilibrium values of the variables are given by the set of constants $(x_1^o, \cdots, x_n^o)$ which satisfy these equations identically, or

[2] The distinction suggested by Mr. Kahn between "forward-falling" and "backward-rising" negatively inclined supply curves while suggestive does not rest upon a dynamic analysis of the attainment of equilibrium and so does not adequately come to grips with the problem in all its complexity. Cf. R. F. Kahn, "The Elasticity of Substitution and the Relative Share of a Factor," *Review of Economic Studies*, October, 1933, pp. 72–78; also N. Kaldor, "A Classificatory Note on the Determinateness of Equilibrium," *Review of Economic Studies*, 1933, p. 122–136.

The suggestion of Professor Viner that the latter type of curve gives the maximum amount forthcoming at a given price while the former does not will receive amplification in the course of this argument.

[3] What constitute initial conditions depends upon the nature of the functional equations. For differential systems only values of the co-ordinates, velocities, and higher derivatives at some initial time need be specified. For difference equations defined only for integral values of t the same is true, where differences replace derivatives. In the general case values of the variables over a continuous time interval, possibly stretching back to $-\infty$, are required to constitute a complete set of initial conditions.

[4] R. Frisch, "On the Notion of Equilibrium and Disequilibrium," *Review of Economic Studies*, February, 1936.

(9)
$$F^i\left[\underset{-\infty}{\overset{t}{x_1^\circ}},\ \underset{-\infty}{\overset{t}{x_2^\circ}},\ \cdots,\ \underset{-\infty}{\overset{t}{x_n^\circ}},\ t\right] = 0,[5] \qquad i = 1,\ \cdots,\ n.$$

If the system has *always* been in equilibrium up until time t_o, it will subsequently continue in equilibrium. However, the equilibrium values $(x_1^\circ,\ \cdots,\ x_n^\circ)$ may be attained or even be maintained for a finite period of time, and yet because of generalized dynamical "inertia" it need not (and in general will not) remain in equilibrium subsequently, but may well "overshoot" the mark.

The equilibrium position possesses *perfect stability of the first kind* if from any initial conditions all the variables approach their equilibrium values in the limit as time becomes infinite; i.e., if

(10)
$$\lim_{t \to \infty} x_i(t) = x_i^\circ,$$

regardless of the initial conditions. Alternatively, it is sometimes stated that an equilibrium is stable if a displacement from equilibrium is followed by a return to equilibrium. A displacement is equivalent to an arbitrary change in the initial conditions and is possible only if some of our functional equations are momentarily relaxed or if our system is enlarged to include impressed forces or shocks.

Stability of the first kind *in the small* exists if for sufficiently small displacements the equilibrium is stable. Stability in the small is contained within perfect stability but not vice versa. A system may be stable for small finite displacements but not for large displacements. Nevertheless, stability in the small is a necessary condition for perfect stability and will be analyzed here in greatest detail.

It should be pointed out that no conservative dynamical system of the type met in theoretical physics possesses stability of the first kind. If one displaces a frictionless pendulum, it will oscillate endlessly around the position of stable equilibrium.[6] Its motion is bounded, however, and it never remains on one side of the equilibrium position for more than a finite time interval. Such behavior may be characterized as *stability of the second kind* or as stability in the second sense. As before, a distinction can be made between stability of the second kind in

---

[5] Of course, such a set need not exist. Thus, the simple system

$$\frac{dx}{dt} = e^x - x$$

has no stationary equilibrium values since $e^x - x = 0$ has no real roots. Similarly, $dx/dt = 1$ defines no stationary equilibrium position.

[6] A dynamical system into which friction is introduced via a dissipation function may enjoy stability of the first kind. On these and kindred matters see G. D. Birkhoff, *Dynamical Systems*.

the small and complete stability of the second kind. For the most part in the present investigation I shall be concerned with the problem of stability of the first kind.

The equations of comparative statics are then a special case of the general dynamic analysis. They can indeed be discussed abstracting completely from dynamical analysis. In the history of mechanics, the theory of statics was developed before the dynamical problem was even formulated. But the problem of stability of equilibrium cannot be discussed except with reference to dynamical considerations, however implicit and rudimentary.[7] We find ourselves confronted with this paradox: in order for the comparative-statics analysis to yield fruitful results, we must first develop a theory of dynamics.[8] This is completely aside from the other uses of dynamic analysis as in the studies of fluctuations, trends, etc. I turn now to some illustrations of these propositions.

i. In the literary explanations of the process by which supply and demand are equated, the assumption is usually made that if at any price demand exceeds supply, price will rise; if supply exceeds demand, price will fall. Let us state this more precisely as follows:

$$(11) \qquad \dot{p} = \frac{dp}{dt} = H(q_D - q_S) = H[D(p, \alpha) - S(p)],$$

where $H(0) = 0$, and $H' > 0$.

In the neighborhood of the equilibrium point this can be expanded in the form (if H is analytic):

$$(12) \qquad \dot{p} = \lambda(D_p{}^o - S_p{}^o)(p - p^o) + \cdots,$$

where $\lambda = (H')^o > 0$, and where terms involving higher powers of $(p - p^o)$ are omitted. The solution of this simple differential equation for initial price $\bar{p}$ at time zero can be written at sight:

$$(13) \qquad p(t) = p^o + (\bar{p} - p^o)e^{\lambda(D_p{}^o - S_p{}^o)t}.$$

If the equilibrium is to be stable,

$$(14) \qquad \lim_{t \to \infty} p(t) = p^o.$$

This is possible if, and only if,

---

[7] This is seen to be involved in the virtual-work analysis and in the minimum-potential-energy condition characteristic of a stable statical ("stationary") equilibrium position.

[8] The point made here is not to be confused with the commonplace criticism of comparative statics that it does not do what it is not aimed to do, namely describe the transition paths between equilibria.

(15) $$D_p{}^o - S_p{}^o \leqq 0.$$

If in what follows we rule out neutral equilibrium in the large and in the small, the equality sign may be omitted so that

(16) $$D_p{}^o - S_p{}^o < 0.$$

If the supply curve is positively inclined, this will be realized. If it is negatively inclined, it must be less steep (referred to the price axis) than the demand curve. If our stability conditions are realized, the problem originally proposed is answered. Price must rise when demand increases.

ii. These so-called Walrasian stability conditions are not necessarily the only ones.[9] If alternative dynamic models are postulated, completely different conditions are deduced, which in turn lead to alternative theorems in comparative statics.

Thus, in Marshall's long-run theory of normal price the quantity supplied is assumed to adjust itself comparatively slowly. If "demand price" exceeds "supply price," the quantity supplied will increase. Preserving our notation of equations (5), remembering that quantity rather than price is regarded as the independent variable, and neglecting higher-order terms, we have the following differential equation

(17) $$\dot{q} = k\left(\frac{1}{D_p{}^o} - \frac{1}{S_p{}^o}\right)(q - q^o), \qquad k > 0$$

whose solution is

(18) $$q(t) = q^o + (\bar{q} - q^o)e^{k(1/D_p{}^o - 1/S_p{}^o)t}.$$

If the equilibrium is to be stable,

(19) $$\frac{1}{D_p{}^o} - \frac{1}{S_p{}^o} = \frac{1}{D_p{}^o}\frac{S_p{}^o - D_p{}^o}{S_p{}^o} < 0 \cdot$$

i.e., the demand-curve slope referred to the quantity axis is less algebraically than that of the supply curve. Since the demand curve is negatively inclined,

(20) $$\frac{S_p{}^o}{S_p{}^o - D_p{}^o} > 0.$$

Referring back to equations (7), we see that Marshallian stability con-

[9] An historical error is involved in the identification of the above stability conditions with Walras in alleged contrast to those of Marshall which are shortly to be discussed. Actually as far back as in the *Pure Theory of Foreign Trade* Marshall defined stable equilibrium, in which a so-called backward rising supply curve was involved, exactly as in the Walrasian case.

ditions require that quantity increases when demand increases in every case, while the change in price is necessarily ambiguous depending upon the algebraic sign of the supply curve's slope.

It is to be pointed out that this forward-falling supply curve is not a true supply curve in the sense of the amount forthcoming at each hypothetical price, although it is a true supply curve in the sense of being the locus of price-quantity points traced out by fluctuations in *sufficiently steep* demand curves. As such it is a reversible long-run relation.

iii. Still another dynamic model may be considered. It has been held that for some commodities supply reacts to price only after a given time lag, while price adjusts itself almost instantaneously. This leads to the familiar cobweb phenomenon. Using the same notation, our dynamic model takes the form of the following difference equations,

$$
(21) \qquad \begin{aligned} q_t &= S(p_{t-1}), \\ q_t &= D(p_t, \alpha). \end{aligned}
$$

In the neighborhood of equilibrium

$$
(22) \qquad (q_t - q_0) = \left(\frac{S_p{}^o}{D_p{}^o}\right)(q_{t-1} - q^o)
$$

with the solution

$$
(23) \qquad q_t = q^o + (\bar{q} - q^o)\left(\frac{S_p{}^o}{D_p{}^o}\right)^t.
$$

Stability requires that

$$
(24) \qquad \left|\frac{S_p{}^o}{D_p{}^o}\right| < 1.
$$

If the supply curve is positively inclined, it must be steeper absolutely than is the demand curve, reference being made to the quantity axis. In this case the approach to equilibrium is of a damped oscillatory nature, every other observation being on one side of the equilibrium value.

If the supply curve is negatively inclined, it must be steeper referred to the quantity axis than is the demand curve, precisely as in the case of Walrasian stability. The approach to equilibrium is asymptotic. As in the Walrasian case, we can deduce the theorem in comparative statics that price will necessarily increase even though the change in quantity is indefinite.

It is to be noted that a first-order difference equation is richer in solution than the corresponding first-order differential equation. Not only does it admit of oscillatory solutions, but the stability conditions relate to the absolute value of the root of an equation, implying two distinct inequalities. Remembering that $D_p{}^o$ is negative, the inequality of (24) can be written

$$D_p{}^o < S_p{}^o < - D_p{}^o.$$

The new inequality tells us that any increase in output as a result of an increase in demand cannot be so large as the increase in output resulting from an "equivalent" increase in supply.

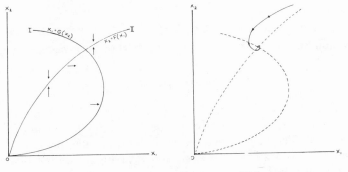

Figure 1   Figure 2

iv. Still a fourth dynamical model that has been considered is that of Marshall in the *Pure Theory of Foreign Trade*. Let Figure 1 represent the familiar offer curves of two trading bodies (suppliers and demanders) respectively. Equilibrium is attained at the intersection (not necessarily unique) of two such curves. If equilibrium is displaced, country I is to act in such a way as to change the amount of x_1 in the horizontal direction of its offer curve (as indicated by the pointed horizontal arrows. Similarly country II adjusts x_2 vertically in the direction of its offer curve. Mathematically,

(25)
$$\dot{x}_1 = H_1[G(x_2) - x_1],$$
$$\dot{x}_2 = H_2[F(x_1) - x_2],$$

where $H_i' > 0$, $H_i(0) = 0$, and G $(x_2) - x_1 = 0$, $F(x_1) - x_2 = 0$ represent the statical offer curves of countries I and II respectively. If units are properly chosen, the following system of differential equations will hold in the neighborhood of equilibrium,

(26)
$$\dot{x}_1 = - (x_1 - x_1{}^o) + (G')^o(x_2 - x_2{}^o),$$
$$\dot{x}_2 = (F')^o(x_1 - x_1{}^o) - (x_2 - x_2{}^o).$$

The solution takes the form:

$$(27) \qquad \begin{aligned} x_1(t) &= x_1{}^o + k_{11}e^{\lambda_1 t} + k_{12}e^{\lambda_2 t}, \\ x_2(t) &= x_2{}^o + k_{21}e^{\lambda_1 t} + k_{22}e^{\lambda_2 t}, \end{aligned}$$

where the k's depend upon the initial values $(\bar{x}_1, \bar{x}_2)$ and the λ's are roots of the characteristic equation

$$(28) \qquad D(\lambda) = \begin{vmatrix} -1 - \lambda & (G')^o \\ (F')^o & -1 - \lambda \end{vmatrix} = 0.$$

Clearly

$$(29) \qquad \lambda = -1 \pm \sqrt{(G')^o(F')^o}.$$

The equilibrium will be stable if the real part of λ is necessarily negative, or

$$(30) \qquad R(\lambda) < 0.$$

If both $(G')^o$ and $(F')^o$ are of opposite sign (e.g., if one has an elastic demand, the other an inelastic demand), this condition will necessarily be satisfied. The solution will be oscillatory, but damped, approaching equilibrium in a spiral as shown above in Figure 2, and obeying an equation of the form

$$(31) \qquad x_i = x_i{}^o + e^{-t}(a_i \sin \theta t + b_i \cos \theta t), \qquad i = 1, 2.$$

If both are positive, however (each with elastic demands),

$$(32) \qquad \sqrt{(G')^o(F')^o} < 1,$$

$$(33) \qquad (G')^o(F')^o < 1,$$

and

$$(34) \qquad (G')^o < \frac{1}{(F')^o}.$$

In terms of the slopes of both offer curves referred to the x_1 axis

$$(35) \qquad \left(\frac{dx_2}{dx_1}\right)_I > \left(\frac{dx_2}{dx_1}\right)_{II}.$$

The equilibrium is approached asymptotically.

If both curves are negatively inclined, stability requires

$$(36) \qquad \left(\frac{dx_2}{dx_1}\right)_I < \left(\frac{dx_2}{dx_1}\right)_{II}.$$

Clearly, the general condition when the curves are of like sign can be written

(37)
$$\left|\frac{dx_2}{dx_1}\right|_{\mathrm{I}} > \left|\frac{dx_2}{dx_1}\right|_{\mathrm{II}},$$

and the approach to equilibrium will in every case be asymptotic.[10] The stability conditions derived here will be found, if translated into terms of supply and demand curves rather than offer curves, to imply differing and inconsistent conditions from those of the preceding cases.

v. In the four cases considered I have been concerned with problems of stability of the first kind. Following a suggestion of Dr. Francis Dresch of the University of California, let us suppose that price falls not when the instantaneous supply exceeds demand, but only when accumulated stocks exceed some normal value, Q^o, or

(38) $\qquad \dot{p} = \lambda(Q^o - Q) + \cdots = \lambda Q^o - \lambda \int_0^t (q_S - q_D)dt, \qquad \lambda > 0,$

since the stock equals the accumulated difference between the amount produced and the amount consumed. Differentiating with respect to t, neglecting terms of higher power, and adhering to our previous notation, we have

(39) $\qquad\qquad \ddot{p} = (D_{p^o} - S_{p^o})(p - p^o),$

whose solution is

(40) $\qquad\qquad p(t) = p^o + c_1 e^{(\sqrt{D_{p^o} - S_{p^o}})t} + c_2 e^{-(\sqrt{D_{p^o} - S_{p^o}})t},$

the c's depending upon the initial price and price change.

Only if

(41) $\qquad\qquad\qquad D_{p^o} - S_{p^o} < 0,$

can explosive behavior be avoided. If the above inequality is realized, however, the square root will be a pure imaginary number so that the solution takes the form of an undamped harmonic:

(42) $\quad p(t) = b_1 \cos \sqrt{S_{p^o} - D_{p^o}}\, t + b_2 \sin \sqrt{S_{p^o} - D_{p^o}}\, t + p^o.$

Thus, if we require our second-order differential equation to have at least stability of the second kind, we come to the same theorems in comparative statics as in case i.

There is at least one serious objection to assuming a nondamped

[10] Somewhat paradoxically, in this case positions of stable equilibrium need not be separated by positions of unstable equilibrium because of the possibility of complex roots.

system of this kind. If there are superimposed upon our system random shocks or errors, these will tend to accumulate so that the expected amplitude of the cycles will increase with time. This is well illustrated by the familiar Brownian movement of large molecules under the impact of random collisions. The molecule "takes a random walk," and its mean variance increases with the observation time.[11] Before adopting a similar hypothesis in economic analysis, some statistical evidence of its possible validity should be adduced.[12]

We have now surveyed five different dynamic setups and related stability conditions, all referring to a simple one-commodity market. Except possibly for cases iv and v, all are mathematically trivial. Unaided intuition or simple geometrical methods serve to reveal sufficient conditions for stability. They are of significance, however, because each has played an important part in the history of economic science; and precisely because of their simplicity, they provide a useful illustration of the general principle involved. In the following sections I shall be concerned with more complex problems.

THE STABILITY OF MULTIPLE MARKETS

While it might be more elegant at this stage to develop formally for general systems the fundamental principles illustrated thus far, our

---

[11] Random shocks are not necessarily to be regarded as a nuisance. In their absence friction might imprison the system at some fixed level other than the "true" equilibrium level (friction being disregarded). Often random shocks serve to insure the realization of *average* values nearly equal to the equilibrium ones, just as iron filings placed upon a piece of paper over a magnet assume the lines of force of the magnetic field when gently tapped.

[12] One can avoid an undamped system by assuming that price tends to fall not only when stocks are large, but also when current supply exceeds current demand; i.e., when stocks tend to accumulate. Then we have

$$\dot{p} = \alpha\left[Q^o - \int_0^t (q_S - q_D)dt \right] - \beta(q_S - q_D)$$

or

$$\ddot{p} = \alpha(D_{p^o} - S_{p^o})p + \beta(D_{p^o} - S_{p^o})\dot{p}, \qquad \alpha, \beta > 0.$$

The equilibrium is stable only if

$$R(\lambda) < 0,$$

or if $\lambda < 0$, where

$$\lambda^2 - \beta(D_{p^o} - S_{p^o})\lambda - \alpha(D_{p^o} - S_{p^o}) = 0,$$

or if

$$D_{p^o} - S_{p^o} < 0.$$

This agrees with the condition of case i and the one just derived. In fact, each of these is a special case when one of the coefficients vanishes. For intermediate values, the solutions range continuously between damped harmonic motion and exponential approach to equilibrium.

foregoing discussion provides a very convenient opening for an examination of a problem which has received considerable attention lately at the hands of Professor Hicks. In *Value and Capital*, Chapter VIII and Mathematical Appendix, §21, he has attempted to generalize to any number of markets the stability conditions of a single market. The method of approach is postulational; stability conditions are not deduced from a dynamic model except implicitly.[13] Propositions which are deduced here as theorems are assumed as definitions of stability.

For a single market, according to Professor Hicks, equilibrium is stable if an increase in demand raises price. (This rules out in the beginning cases ii and iv.) For multiple markets equilibrium is *imperfectly* stable if an increase in demand for a single good raises its price after all other prices have adjusted themselves; the equilibrium is *perfectly* stable if an increased demand for a good raises its price even when *any* subset of other prices is arbitrarily held constant (by means of a relaxation of other equilibrium conditions).

To test the necessity or sufficiency of these criteria in terms of a more fundamental definition of stability of equilibrium let us make a natural generalization of the Walrasian conditions of the following form: the price of any good will fall if its supply exceeds its demand, *these each being regarded as functions of all other prices.*

Mathematically,

$$\dot{p}_i = - H(q_S{}^i - q_D{}^i)$$
$$= - H\left[q_S{}^i(p_1, \cdots, p_n) - q_D{}^i(p_1, \cdots, p_n)\right]$$

$$(43) \qquad = \sum_{j=1}^{n} a_{ij}{}^o(p_j - p_j{}^o) + \cdots,$$

where

$$(44) \quad 0 = q_S{}^i(p_1, \cdots, p_n) - q_D{}^i(p_1, \cdots, p_n) = - a_i(p_1, \cdots, p_n)$$

represent statical equations of supply and demand, $a_{ij}{}^o$ represents the partial derivative of a_i with respect to the jth price evaluated at the equilibrium set of prices. In general, $a_{ij}{}^o \neq a_{ji}{}^o$.[14] It is instructive to

[13] It is true that on page 70 a hint of a dynamical process creeps into the discussion. The approach to equilibrium seems to be regarded as taking place in finite steps at discrete intervals of time; i.e., in accordance with certain difference equations. Correctly stated, this argument would not lead to essentially different stability conditions from my system of differential equations discussed below, as the later general discussion will disclose.

[14] If the demand and supply were each drawn up with reference to firms maximizing profit, well-known integrability conditions would guarantee this equivalence. On the consumer's side there need be no such equivalence, and if we

consider first, however, the symmetrical case (such as characterizes markets made up exclusively of entrepreneurs). The solution of equations (43) can be written

$$(45) \qquad p_i(t) = p_i{}^o + \sum_{j=1}^{n} k_{ij} e^{\lambda_j t},$$

where $(\lambda_1, \cdots, \lambda_n)$ are latent roots of the characteristic equation and

$$(46) \qquad f(\lambda) = \begin{vmatrix} a_{11}{}^o - \lambda & a_{12}{}^o & \cdots a_{1n}{}^o \\ a_{21}{}^o & a_{22}{}^o - \lambda & a_{2n}{}^o \\ \cdots\cdots\cdots\cdots\cdots\cdots\cdots\cdots\cdots \\ a_{n1}{}^o & a_{n2}{}^o & \cdots a_{nn}{}^o - \lambda \end{vmatrix}$$

$$= \left| a - \lambda I \right| = \left| a_{ij}{}^o - \lambda \delta_{ij} \right| = 0,$$

the k's depend upon the matrix a and upon the initial conditions.[15] As before, stability requires $R(\lambda_j) < 0$.

By a well-known theorem of Hermitian matrices, in the symmetrical case all the roots are necessarily real. If the equilibrium is to be stable, they must all be negative. According to a classical theorem, this is possible if and only if a is the matrix of a negative definite quadratic form; i.e., only if all principal minors alternate in sign as follows:

$$(47) \qquad \left| a_{ii}{}^o \right| < 0; \quad \begin{vmatrix} a_{ii}{}^o & a_{ij}{}^o \\ a_{ji}{}^o & a_{jj}{}^o \end{vmatrix} > 0; \quad \begin{vmatrix} a_{ii}{}^o & a_{ij}{}^o & a_{ik}{}^o \\ a_{ji}{}^o & a_{jj}{}^o & a_{jk}{}^o \\ a_{ki}{}^o & a_{kj}{}^o & a_{kk}{}^o \end{vmatrix} < 0,$$

$$i \neq j \neq k \neq i.$$

Any ratio of the form

---

consider a consumer whose total purchases balance his total sale of productive services, such an equality for every combination of goods and services would, strictly interpreted, lead to an absurdity; it would imply expenditure proportionality and, hence, zero consumption of every good and zero offering of every service! For the general demand or supply function we need not expect a cancelling off of "income effects" since individuals usually face firms in consumption and factor markets. Contrast in this connection Hicks' views, Chapters V and VIII.

[15] If the roots are not distinct, polynomial terms of the form $te^{\lambda t}, t^2 e^{\lambda t}, \cdots, t^s e^{\lambda t}$ appear where $(s+1)$ is the multiplicity of a repeated root. In any case the problem of stability depends only upon the λ's and is unaffected by such multipliers since the exponential always governs the asymptotic behavior of the solution whenever dampening does occur.

$$
(48) \qquad
\frac{
\begin{vmatrix}
1 & 0 & \cdots & 0 \\
0 & a_{jj}{}^{o} & \cdots & a_{jk}{}^{o} \\
\cdot & \cdot & \cdots & \cdot \\
0 & a_{kj}{}^{o} & \cdots & a_{kk}{}^{o}
\end{vmatrix}
}{
\begin{vmatrix}
a_{ii}{}^{o} & a_{ij}{}^{o} & \cdots & a_{ik}{}^{o} \\
a_{ji}{}^{o} & a_{jj}{}^{o} & \cdots & a_{jk}{}^{o} \\
\cdot & \cdot & \cdots & \cdot \\
a_{ki}{}^{o} & a_{kj}{}^{o} & \cdots & a_{kk}{}^{o}
\end{vmatrix}
}
$$

is necessarily negative in sign. But such ratios are precisely equal to the change in the price of the ith good with respect to a unit increase in its own supply when appropriate subsets of other prices are held constant, so that for this case the stability criteria of Professor Hicks are seen to be correct theorems. In the symmetrical case more than this can be said: *Imperfect stability in the Hicks sense necessarily implies perfect stability and conversely.* Imperfect stability involves the same n inequalities as does perfect stability, no more and no less.

Where perfect symmetry is not present (and in business-cycle analysis it is almost always absent), the Hicks criteria are not at all necessary conditions and in many cases not sufficient.[16] A system may possess stability of the first kind even though neither *perfectly* nor *imperfectly* stable in Hicks' sense. I suspect but have not yet devised a proof to show that perfect stability is a sufficient condition for stability

---

[16] A word of warning may be in order concerning Hicks' indiscriminate use of either prices or quantities as independent variables. This leads to contradictory definitions of complementarity in the literary discussion on page 44 and the mathematical definitions on page 311, the inconsistency between which can lead to opposite signs. Such an interchange of independent variables (as between the literary definition of stability on page 63 and the mathematical conditions on 315 and 325) is particularly important where nonsymmetrical matrices are concerned. Does

$$
(49) \qquad \frac{dx_i}{dp_i} < 0, \qquad
\begin{vmatrix}
\dfrac{dx_i}{dp_i} & \dfrac{dx_i}{dp_j} \\[2ex]
\dfrac{dx_j}{dp_i} & \dfrac{dx_j}{dp_j}
\end{vmatrix} < 0, \cdots \qquad \text{where} \qquad \frac{dx_i}{dp_j} \neq \frac{dx_j}{dp_i},
$$

imply

$$
(50) \qquad \frac{dp_i}{dx_i} < 0, \qquad
\begin{vmatrix}
\dfrac{dp_i}{dx_i} & \dfrac{dp_i}{dx_j} \\[2ex]
\dfrac{dp_j}{dx_i} & \dfrac{dp_j}{dx_j}
\end{vmatrix} > 0, \cdots ?
$$

Even with symmetry the product $(dp_i/dx_j)(dx_i/dp_j)$ need not be of positive sign if more than two variables are involved.

of the first kind.*In any case it is too strict a condition, while the requirement of imperfect stability is not strict enough; only in the case of symmetry do these limits converge. Why any system should be expected to possess *perfect* stability, or why an economist should be interested in this property is by no means clear. Not working with an explicit dynamical model, Professor Hicks probably argued by analogy from well-known maximum conditions, whereby a maximum must hold for arbitrary displacements and through any transformation of variables. As a result, some variables may be made constants, and with respect to the remaining arbitrary subsets the definiteness of various quadratic forms must be insured. On the other hand, in terms of a truly dynamic process the equilibrium must be stable for arbitrary initial conditions or displacements and for arbitrary nonsingular transformations of variables, but *not* necessarily for arbitrary modifications of the dynamic equations of motion such as are involved in the Hicks procedure of holding subsets of other prices constant (by violating or relaxing true dynamical relations). In principle the Hicks procedure is clearly wrong, although in some empirical cases it may be useful to make the hypothesis that the equilibrium is stable even without the "equilibrating" action of some variable which may be arbitrarily held constant. (In connection with the Keynesian model later discussed, an example of this is presented.)

To summarize: for every case true necessary and sufficient stability conditions are that $R(\lambda_j) < 0$, where λ_j represents the latent roots of the matrix a. This is not equivalent to the Hicks conditions.[17]

Before leaving the problem of stable multiple markets, I should like to sketch the effect of the introduction of stocks and its relevance to stability of the second kind. Let price fall not when current supply exceeds current demand, but when existing stocks (accumulated over time from the divergence of current production and consumption) exceed an equilibrium amount. Then neglecting terms of higher powers, we write

---

[17] The following illustrations bear this out: The system

$$(51) \quad \begin{aligned} \dot{p}_1 &= -2p_1 + 4p_2, \\ \dot{p}_2 &= -p_1 + p_2, \end{aligned}$$

possesses stability of the first kind, but is neither perfectly nor imperfectly stable. The system

$$(52) \quad \begin{aligned} \dot{p}_1 &= p_1 - p_2, \\ \dot{p}_2 &= -2p_1 + p_2, \end{aligned}$$

is imperfectly stable, but departs ever further from equilibrium.

* *Ed. note:* For proof that Hicksian perfect stability is not sufficient for dynamic stability, see "The Relation between Hicksian Stability and True Dynamic Stability," in the following chapter.

$$\dot{p}_i = Q_i^o - \int_0^t (q_S - q_D)d\tau = Q_i^o + \int_0^t \sum_{j=1}^n a_{ij}{}^o(p_j - p_j^o)d\tau + \cdots$$

or

$$(53) \qquad \ddot{p}_i = \sum_{j=1}^n a_{ij}{}^o(p_j - p_j^o) + \cdots ,$$

whose solution takes the form

$$(54) \qquad p_i(t) = p_i^o + \sum_{j=1}^n (k_{ij}e^{\sqrt{\lambda_j}\,t} + h_{ij}e^{-\sqrt{\lambda_j}\,t})$$

where $|a_{ij}{}^o - \lambda_j\delta_{ij}| = 0$, and where for unrepeated roots the k's and the h's are constant depending upon initial conditions. Clearly the motion will be explosive and undamped unless $\sqrt{\lambda_j}$ are all pure imaginary numbers; i.e., unless λ_j is real and negative.

If the system is symmetrical, this clearly leads to the same conditions as those for stability of the first kind. If not symmetrical, the substitution of second derivatives everywhere for first derivatives (through the hypothesis of dependence upon accumulated stocks rather than instantaneous flows) implies more rigid conditions upon the coefficients to insure stability of the second kind than were previously required to insure stability of the first kind. This is of course because of the requirement that the roots be real as well as negative.[18]

ANALYSIS OF THE KEYNESIAN SYSTEM

Up until now I have considered examples drawn from the field of economic theory. The techniques used there are of even more fruitful applicability to problems of business cycles. To illustrate this I shall analyze in some detail the simple Keynesian model as outlined in the *General Theory*. Various writers, such as Meade, Hicks, and Lange, have developed explicitly in mathematical form the meaning of the Keynesian system.[19] The three fundamental relationships stressed by

[18] One could consider the generalization of the intermediate hypothesis of footnote 12 where price change depends upon stocks and flows, namely,

$$(55) \qquad \ddot{p}_i = \sum_{j=1}^n a_{ij}{}^o \lfloor \alpha\dot{p}_j + \beta(p_j - p_j^o) \rfloor, \qquad \begin{aligned} \alpha &> 0, \\ \beta &> 0. \end{aligned}$$

If stable for $\beta > 0$, $\alpha = 0$, and also for $\beta = 0$, $\alpha > 0$, it can perhaps be proved to be stable for all intermediate cases.

[19] J. E. Meade, "A Simplified Model of Mr. Keynes' System," *Review of Economic Studies*, February, 1937, pp. 98–107; J. R. Hicks, "Mr. Keynes and the 'Classics'; A Suggested Interpretation," ECONOMETRICA, Vol. 5, 1937, pp. 147–159; Oskar Lange, "The Rate of Interest and the Optimum Propensity to Consume," *Economica*, 1938, pp. 12–32.

Keynes are (1) *the consumption function* relating consumption (and hence savings-investment) to income, and for generality to the interest rate as well; (2) *the marginal efficiency of capital* relating *net* investment to the interest rate and to the level of income (as of a fixed level of capital equipment, fixed for the short period under investigation); (3) *the schedule of liquidity preference* relating the existing amount of money to the interest rate and the level of income.

Mathematically, these may be written as follows:

$$(56) \qquad C(i, Y) - Y + I = -\alpha,$$

$$(57) \qquad F(i, Y) - I = -\beta,$$

$$(58) \qquad L(i, Y) = M,$$

where i, Y, I stand respectively for the interest rate, income, and investment; C, F, L stand respectively for the consumption function, the marginal-efficiency-of-capital schedule, and the schedule of liquidity preference. M stands for the existing amount of money, taken as a parameter; α is a general parameter representing an upward shift in the propensity-to-consume schedule; similarly as the parameter β increases, the marginal-efficiency schedule shifts upward.

We have three relations to determine the three unknowns in terms of three parameters, viz.:

$$i = i(\alpha, \beta, M),$$
$$(59) \qquad Y = Y(\alpha, \beta, M),$$
$$I = I(\alpha, \beta, M).$$

As explained in the first section of this paper, the usefulness of the Keynesian equilibrium system lies in the light it throws upon the way our unknowns will change as a result of changes in data. More specifically, what are the signs of

$$\frac{di}{d\alpha}, \quad \frac{dY}{d\alpha}, \quad \frac{dI}{d\alpha},$$

$$\frac{di}{d\beta}, \quad \frac{dY}{d\beta}, \quad \frac{dI}{d\beta},$$

$$\frac{di}{dM}, \quad \frac{dY}{dM}, \quad \frac{dI}{dM}?$$

Differentiating totally with respect to our parameters and evaluating the resulting linear equations, we find

$$\frac{di}{d\alpha} = \frac{-L_Y}{\Delta}, \quad \frac{dY}{d\alpha} = \frac{L_i}{\Delta}, \quad \frac{dI}{d\alpha} = \frac{F_Y L_i - F_i L_Y}{\Delta},$$

$$\frac{di}{d\beta} = \frac{-L_Y}{\Delta}, \quad \frac{dY}{d\beta} = \frac{L_i}{\Delta}, \quad \frac{dI}{d\beta} = \frac{(1 - C_Y)L_i + C_i L_Y}{\Delta},$$

(60)

$$\frac{di}{dM} = \frac{1 - C_Y - F_Y}{\Delta}, \quad \frac{dY}{dM} = \frac{F_i + C_i}{\Delta},$$

$$\frac{dI}{dM} = \frac{F_Y(F_i + C_i) + (1 - C_Y - F_Y)F_i}{\Delta},$$

where

(61) $\quad \Delta = \begin{vmatrix} C_i & C_Y - 1 & 1 \\ F_i & F_Y & -1 \\ L_i & L_Y & 0 \end{vmatrix} = L_Y(F_i + C_i) + L_i(1 - C_Y - F_Y).$

On the basis of a priori, intuitive, empirical experience the following assumptions are usually made:

(62) $\qquad C_Y > 0, \quad F_Y > 0, \quad F_i < 0, \quad L_Y > 0, \quad L_i < 0,$

while

$$C_i \gtrless 0$$

and is usually assumed in modern discussions to be of minor quantitative importance.

In order to evaluate our nine derivatives we must be able to determine unambiguously the signs of all numerators as well as the common denominator, Δ. Δ consists of five terms, two of which are of positive sign, two of negative sign, and one ambiguous. On the basis of deductive analysis along strictly statical lines nothing can be inferred concerning its sign. Moreover, even if the sign of Δ were determined, all but four of the nine would be found to have numerators of indeterminable sign.

This is a typical case. If we are to derive useful theorems, we must clearly proceed to a consideration of a more general dynamic system which includes the stationary Keynesian analysis as a special case. This can be done in a variety of alternative ways. I shall consider two, the first of which is based upon a differential system and yields quite definite results.

Case 1. Let us assume as before that the second and third relations of marginal efficiency and liquidity preference work themselves out in so short a time that they can be regarded as holding instantaneously. Let us assume, however, that I now represents "intended" investment, and this magnitude equals savings-investment only in equilibrium, i.e., when all the variables take on stationary values. If, however, because of some change, consumption (say) should suddenly increase, national income not having a chance to change, actual savings-investment would fall short of "intended" investment because of inventory reduction, etc. Consequently, income would tend to rise. Similarly an excess of actual savings-investment over intended investment would tend to make income fall. Mathematically, this hypothesis may be stated as follows: *the rate of change of income is proportional to the difference between intended savings-investment and actual savings-investment.* The discussion here is unrelated to the controversy over the equality of savings and investment despite possible appearances to the contrary. The superficial resemblance between my formulation and the Robertson-Ohlin identities whereby the difference between investment and savings is the time difference of income should not mislead the careful reader.

Equations (56), (57), and (58) are replaced by the dynamical ones:

$$(63) \qquad \dot{Y} = I - [Y - C(i, Y) - \alpha],$$

$$(64) \qquad 0 = F(i, Y) - I + \beta,$$

$$(65) \qquad 0 = L(i, Y) - M.$$

The solution of these is of the form:

$$(66) \qquad \begin{aligned} Y &= Y^o + a_1 e^{\lambda t}, \\ i &= i^o + a_2 e^{\lambda t}, \\ I &= I^o + a_3 e^{\lambda t}, \end{aligned}$$

where

$$(67) \qquad \Delta(\lambda) = \begin{vmatrix} C_i & C_Y - 1 - \lambda & 1 \\ F_i & F_Y & -1 \\ L_i & L_Y & 0 \end{vmatrix} = \Delta + \lambda L_i = 0.$$

The equilibrium is stable only if

$$(68) \qquad \lambda = -\frac{\Delta}{L_i} < 0.$$

But $L_i < 0$; therefore,

$$(69) \qquad \Delta < 0$$

unambiguously.

This establishes four theorems: an increased marginal efficiency of capital will (1) raise interest rates and (2) raise income; an increased propensity to consume will (3) raise interest rates and (4) raise income. But how will the creation of new money affect interest rates? This can be answered by considering more stringent stability conditions. Let us suppose that the interest rate were kept constant (say) by appropriate central bank action. This assumption is equivalent to dropping the liquidity preference equation (65) and treating i as a constant in the remaining equations. If the equilibrium is stable under these conditions, we must have

$$(70) \qquad \begin{vmatrix} C_Y - 1 - \lambda & 1 \\ F_Y & -1 \end{vmatrix} = 0 = (1 - C_Y - F_Y) + \lambda,$$

or

$$(71) \qquad\qquad -\lambda = (1 - F_Y - C_Y) > 0.$$

This leads to another important theorem: (5) *the marginal propensity to consume plus the marginal propensity to invest cannot exceed unity or the system will be unstable* (as of a fixed interest rate).[20] It also tells us (6) that an increase in the amount of money must, *ceteris paribus*, lower interest rates.

We are left with four ambiguities of sign. Two of them depend upon the fact that savings may vary in any direction with respect to a change in interest rates. If we assume that normally savings out of a given income increase with the interest rate, or, if they do decrease, do so not so much as does investment, then three more theorems become true: an increase in the amount of money (7) increases income and (8) increases investment; (9) an increase in the marginal-efficiency schedule increases investment. There remains a final ambiguous term. What is the effect upon investment of an increased propensity to consume? This is seen to be essentially ambiguous depending upon the quantitative strengths of the liquidity-preference slopes and the marginal-efficiency slopes. As income increases, money becomes tight because of the need for financing more transactions. This tends to depress investment. As an offset, the increase in income tends to increase investment through the marginal propensity to invest. Which effect will be the stronger cannot be decided on a priori grounds.

[20] If we take investment also as an independent parameter (say through government action), we lose equation (57) and have for stability the condition

$$| C_Y - 1 - \lambda | = (C_Y - 1) - \lambda = 0,$$
$$\lambda = C_Y - 1 < 0,$$

or that *the marginal propensity to consume must be less than one.* But this is weaker than the previous condition in view of the fact that the marginal propensity to invest is assumed positive.

PAUL A. SAMUELSON

I have prepared a 3×3 classification indicating the signs of the nine terms. All but four have definite signs. Of these four, one is essentially ambiguous as indicated by a question mark. The remaining three show under question marks their normal, presumptive signs.

	i	Y	I
Increase in propensity to consume	α	$+$	$+$	?
Increase in marginal efficiency of capital	β	$+$	$+$	$\frac{?}{+}$
Increase in amount of money	M	$-$	$\frac{?}{+}$	$\frac{?}{+}$

Case 2. I now turn to a system based on a difference equation. It is founded upon considerations similar to these underlying the Kahn-Clark multiplier block diagrams, and for this reason alone is worth consideration. In addition, the analytical contrasts between differential and difference systems is brought out. Reversing the order of the previous exposition, let us take investment as an independent parameter and the interest rate as a constant. Let consumption be a given function of income during the preceding period of time:

$$(72) \qquad C_t = C(\bar{\imath}, Y_{t-1}) = C(Y_{t-1}).$$

What properties must this function satisfy if the equilibrium is to be stable? Income clearly equals consumption plus investment:

$$(73) \qquad Y_t = C_t + I_t.$$

Recalling that investment is treated as a constant, $\bar{I}$, and using the consumption relation, we find

$$(74) \qquad Y_t = C(Y_{t-1}) + \bar{I},$$

or, to a first approximation,

$$(75) \qquad (Y_t - Y^o) = C_{Y^o}(Y_{t-1} - Y^o),$$

where

$$(76) \qquad Y^o = C(Y^o) + \bar{I}$$

is the equilibrium level of income for investment equal to $\bar{I}$.

The solution of this difference equation takes the form

$$(77) \qquad Y_t = Y^o + K(C_{Y^o})^t$$

and is stable only if

$$(78) \qquad |C_{Y^o}| < 1$$

or

$$(79) \qquad\qquad -1 < C_{Y^o} < 1. \quad [21]$$

While the marginal propensity to consume is usually assumed to be positive, it need not be so, and still the equilibrium can be a stable one. Even if it lies between zero and minus one, it is interesting to observe that the "multiplier" is positive since

$$(80) \qquad\qquad \frac{dY^o}{dI} = \frac{1}{1 - C_{Y^o}} > 0,$$

but less than unity because of negative "secondary" effects.

Let us now drop the assumption that investment is a datum, although keeping the interest rate constant. Our dynamic system is of the form

$$(81) \qquad\qquad C(i, Y_{t-1}) - Y_t + I_t = 0,$$

$$(82) \qquad\qquad F(i, \dot{Y}_t) - I_t = 0,$$

and the equilibrium is stable only if

$$(83) \qquad\qquad |\lambda| = \left| \frac{C_Y}{1 - F_Y} \right| < 1,$$

or

$$(84) \qquad\qquad -|1 - F_Y| < C_Y < |1 - F_Y|.$$

Now if the marginal propensity to invest is less than unity $(1 - F_Y > 0)$,[22] this leads to essentially the same stability conditions as before, namely the marginal propensity to consume plus the marginal propensity to invest must be less than unity $(C_Y + F_Y < 1)$. But, and this is paradoxical, if the marginal propensity to invest is sufficiently large, i.e., greater than $+2$, the marginal propensity to consume may exceed unity, and yet the equilibrium will be stable! Moreover, beyond a certain critical value the larger the marginal propensity to invest, the more stable is the system.

If we now consider the system in which none of the variables are taken as given, namely

[21] This inequality is in effect the formal justification of Keynes' reply to those criticizing his fundamental law, that the burden of proof lay upon them to explain why, if their allegations were correct, the economic system was not hopelessly unstable. See the passages quoted from a letter of Keynes in E. W. Gilboy, "The Propensity to Consume: Reply," *Quarterly Journal of Economics*, August, 1939, p. 634. While fundamentally correct, Keynes does overlook the possibility of other stabilizers such as the marginal propensity to invest, interest rate, etc.

[22] In the marginal-efficiency relation I have made investment depend upon income, which itself includes investment. Other writers, notably Lange (*op. cit.*), have made it depend only upon consumption. The result is indifferent since they can be shown to be equivalent. If, however, it is assumed that $dI/dC > 0$, the marginal propensity to invest, $dI/dY = (dI/dC)/[1 + (dI/dC)]$, cannot exceed unity.

$$C(i_t, Y_{t-1}) - Y_t + I_t = 0,$$
(85)
$$F(i_t, Y_t) - I_t = 0,$$
$$L(i_t, Y_t) - M = 0,$$

stability requires that

(86)
$$|\lambda| = \left| \frac{L_i C_Y}{\Delta + L_i C_Y} \right| < 1.$$

In what may be termed the normal case, where the marginal propensity to invest is less than unity, this requires as before that

(87) $\Delta < 0,$

and immediately all the eight determinations of sign of Case 1 become correct.

In the unusual, but possible, case where

(88) $1 - F_Y < 0 < C_Y < (F_Y - 1) - \dfrac{L_Y}{L_i}(F_i + C_i)$

the equilibrium will be stable, but the signs of our 3×3 table now are as follows:

	i	Y	I
α	−	−	?
β	−	−	?
M	−	?	?

In words, the only theorem which remains true under all circumstances is that an increase in the amount of money must lower interest rates if the equilibrium is stable.

This example illustrates the additional complexities which systems based upon difference equations involve. In a later analytic treatment some of the reasons for this will be explained.

The examples here adduced serve, I hope, to illustrate the light which dynamical analysis sheds upon comparative statics. Problems in theory and business cycles of any complexity will almost surely require similar analytic treatment if useful and meaningful theorems are to be derived. In a later paper I examine in more detail formal mathematical aspects of the problem.

Massachusetts Institute of Technology

39

THE RELATION BETWEEN HICKSIAN STABILITY AND TRUE DYNAMIC STABILITY

By Paul A. Samuelson

I

In *Value and Capital*,[1] Professor Hicks introduces the concept of *imperfect* stability to describe the case where an increase in demand for a given good causes a rise in the price of that good after all other prices have been adjusted to the new circumstance. *Perfect* stability, he uses to characterize an economic system in which an increase in demand for a good will increase its price, where any subset of other markets have their prices adjusted, and where the remaining markets have fixed prices which are not adjusted.

Previously,[2] I pointed out that these stability conditions were essentially statical in character, and were not derived from explicit dynamical considerations, but rather from a particular extension to many variables of the one variable case. At that time, by means of simple numerical exceptions, I showed that imperfect stability was neither necessary nor sufficient for dynamic stability. It was also shown by means of an example that perfect stability was *not* a necessary condition. However, despite some efforts, I was unable to produce an example that was perfectly stable in the Hicksian sense, and that yet gave rise to instability. I was moved by this failure to conjecture that Hicksian *perfect* stability, even if it was not a necessary condition, would nevertheless be a sufficient condition. Off and on for some years I have tried to prove this conjecture, but with no success.

I now find this conjecture to be false. Like imperfect stability, perfect stability is neither necessary nor sufficient for true dynamic stability. It is the purpose of this note to present a counter-example that illustrates the falsity of the conjecture. I am much indebted to Dr. W. Hurewicz for the example in question.

II

Mathematically, the conjecture may be summarized in the *proposition* that a matrix whose principal minors are all positive must have latent or characteristic roots whose real parts are all positive.[3]

---

[1] J. R. Hicks, *Value and Capital*, Oxford, 1939, Chapter 5.

[2] P. A. Samuelson, "The Stability of Equilibrium; Comparative Statics and Dynamics," Econometrica, Vol. 9, April, 1941, pp. 111–112.

[3] For stability we are ordinarily concerned with negative rather than positive real parts, and with principal minors that oscillate in sign rather than remaining positive. However, by changing signs everywhere in the matrix, we may avoid the

Consider the 4×4 matrix

$$\begin{bmatrix} \epsilon & 1 & 0 & 0 \\ 0 & \epsilon & 1 & 0 \\ 0 & 0 & \epsilon & 1 \\ -1 & +1 & -1 & +1+\epsilon \end{bmatrix}.$$

For ϵ any positive number, the reader may verify that all of its principal minors are positive. He may also verify that its characteristic equation is given by

$$P(x) = Q(x - \epsilon) = (x - \epsilon)^4 - (x - \epsilon)^3 + (x - \epsilon)^2 - (x - \epsilon) + 1 = 0$$

It can also be immediately verified that

$$Q(y) = \frac{y^5 + 1}{y + 1},$$

so that the roots of Q are four of the five complex roots of minus unity, or $-\cos 72° \pm i \sin 72°$, $\cos 36° \pm i \sin 36°$. The latent roots of the matrix differ from these by ϵ, and if we make ϵ a small number between zero and $\cos 72°$, we shall have two latent roots whose real parts are negative. This disproves the conjecture.

Massachusetts Institute of Technology

---

awkwardness of having to distinguish between odd- and even-order minors. In economic terms, this means simply working with the expression "excess supply" rather than "excess demand," and concentrating upon the partial derivatives of these with respect to price.

40

THE STABILITY OF EQUILIBRIUM: LINEAR AND NONLINEAR SYSTEMS

By Paul A. Samuelson

INTRODUCTION

In a previous paper[1] it was pointed out that there exists an intimate formal dependence between comparative statics and dynamics. To my knowledge this had not previously been explicitly enunciated in the economic literature, and for lack of a better name I shall refer to it as the *Correspondence Principle*. It is the purpose here to probe more deeply into its analytical character, and also to show its two-way nature: not only can the investigation of the dynamic stability of a system yield fruitful theorems in statical analysis, but also known properties of a (comparative) statical system can be utilized to derive information concerning the dynamic properties of a system.

An understanding of this principle is all the more important at a time when pure economic theory has undergone a revolution of thought —from statical to dynamical modes. While many earlier foreshadowings can be found in the literature, we may date this upheaval from the publication of Ragnar Frisch's Cassel Volume essay of only a decade ago. The resulting change in outlook can be compared to that of the transition from classical to quantum mechanics. And just as in the field of physics it was well that the relationship between the old and the new theories could be in part clarified, so in our field a similar investigation seems in order.

Before entering, however, upon these unavoidably technical matters, a few *obiter dicta* concerning the fundamental differences between statical and dynamical systems may be in order. Conceived broadly, a dynamical system might be regarded as any set of functional equations which together with initial conditions (in the most general sense) determine as solutions certain unknowns in function of time. According to this definition timeless, statical systems are simply degenerate special cases in which the functional equations take on simple forms and determine as solutions functions of time which are identically constants. We may, however, define a dynamical system more narrowly so that it

---

[1] "The Stability of Equilibrium: Comparative Statics and Dynamics," Econometrica, Vol. 9, April, 1941, pp. 97–120.

will not be regarded as truly dynamic if the functional equations involve only variables "of the same instant of time," containing time, if at all, only as a parameter.[2] This excludes the customary statical systems of the "historical" as well as the timeless variety.[3] It is possible, however, that certain subsets of the solutions of the dynamical equations are defined by equations which are structurally identical with those which define a statical system. [Thus the stationary solution of a time-sequence analysis, say of the multiplier-block-diagram variety, may be determined by a formula exactly like that of a timeless, instantaneous system.] This constitutes a second possible mutual orientation of statical and dynamical systems.

From still a third point of view a statical system can be looked upon as *the limiting case of a heavily damped dynamical system.* Thus any statical equation

$$f(x) = 0$$

which admits a unique solution x^o can be related to a dynamical system of the form

$$f\{x_t + \Delta(x_t - x^o)\} = 0.$$

This yields directly the equivalent linear difference equation

$$x_t + \Delta(x_t - x^o) = x^o,$$

or

$$x_{t+1} = x^o.$$

Thus, whatever the initial magnitude of x, at the next "instant" the system always takes on its correct statical value. This generalizes easily to systems of more than one variable.

In the following I deal with interrelationships between statics and dynamics which largely fall under the second of the three headings here discussed.

FUNCTIONAL EQUATIONS AND STATIONARY SOLUTIONS

Starting out with n functional equations which constitute a dynamical system involving n unknown functions $\{x_1(t), \cdots, x_n(t)\}$, but not time explicitly,

[2] Ragnar Frisch, "On the Notion of Equilibrium and Disequilibrium," *Review of Economic Studies*, Vol. 3, February, 1936, pp. 100–105.

[3] In an unpublished manuscript I deal at some length with the distinction between complete causal systems and historical or incomplete causal ones, also with the closely related topic of the generalization of the notion of stationary equilibrium to systems involving time explicitly.

(1) $$F^i\{\underset{-\infty}{\overset{t}{x_1(\tau)}}, \underset{-\infty}{\overset{t}{x_2(\tau)}}, \cdots, \underset{-\infty}{\overset{t}{x_n(\tau)}}\} \equiv 0, \qquad i = 1, \cdots, n,$$

we define a stationary solution $(x_1^0, \cdots, x_n^0)$ as one for which

(2) $$F^i\{\underset{-\infty}{\overset{t}{x_1^0}}, \underset{-\infty}{\overset{t}{x_2^0}}, \cdots, \underset{-\infty}{\overset{t}{x_n^0}}\} \equiv 0.$$

These last equations correspond to a set of ordinary statical functions in n variables $(x_1, \cdots, x_n)$:

(3) $$f^i(x_1, \cdots, x_n) = 0, \qquad i = 1, \cdots, n,$$

where of course

(4) $$f^i(x_1^0, \cdots, x_n^0) = 0, \qquad i = 1, \cdots, n.$$

The types of functional equations which have been most studied are those defined by differential equations, difference equations, and integral equations, and mixed varieties. The first of these possesses the most highly developed theory and provides valuable examples of various principles. Since economic observations consist essentially of series defined for integral values of time, the second category of difference equations is perhaps of greatest interest to the theoretical economist.

The above classes of functional equations have this much in common: they can all be written as the limit of an infinite set of equations in an infinite number of unknowns. However, it is not customary to write a system of differential equations in the form (1); but by use of the singular Dirac δ function defined to make the following identity formally true,

(5) $$f(x) = \int_{-\infty}^{\infty} \delta(a - x)f(a)da,$$

any linear differential equation can be written as an integral equation. Similarly any integral equation of the form

(6) $$B(t) + \int_0^{\infty} k(a)B(t - a)da = 0,$$

where B is analytic and k possesses finite moments of all orders, can be written as a differential equation of infinite order, namely,

(7) $$B(t) + \sum_0^{\infty} c_i B^i(t) = 0,$$

where

(8) $$c_i = \frac{(-1)^i \int_0^{\infty} k(a)a^i da}{i!}.$$

Difference equations and mixed types can also be regarded as differential equations of infinite order; by the use of the Dirac function or by extension of the definition of integration, they can equally well be represented as integral equations. In the following treatment I shall investigate formal identities, being little concerned with problems of convergence, and leaving more rigorous proofs for another occasion. There is ample precedent and pragmatic justification for this procedure in all applied sciences.

The greatest attention will be paid to systems of differential equations and systems of difference equations. Without loss of generality these can be written in the following *normal* form:[4]

$$(10) \qquad \frac{dx_i}{dt} = f^i(x_1, \cdots, x_n), \qquad i = 1, \cdots, n,$$

and

$$(11) \qquad \Delta x_i(t) = g^i\{x_1(t), \cdots, x_n(t)\},$$

or

$$(12) \qquad x_i(t+1) = G^i\{x_1(t), \cdots, x_n(t)\} = x_i + g^i.$$

If not already in this form they can be so transformed by the introduction of new variables.

For the stationary solutions,

$$(13) \qquad \frac{dx_i}{dt} = 0 = f^i(x_1, \cdots, x_n), \qquad i = 1, \cdots, n,$$

or

$$(14) \qquad \Delta x_i = 0 = g^i(x_1, \cdots, x_n) = G^i - x_i, \qquad i = 1, \cdots, n.$$

LINEAR AND NONLINEAR SYSTEMS

Up until now most economists have concerned themselves with linear systems, not because of any belief that the facts were so simple, but rather because of the mathematical difficulties involved in nonlinear systems. This is understandable and excusable since all thought advances in small steps. Nevertheless, from the standpoint of a study of industrial fluctuations this can be a rather serious limitation. [Thus,

---

[4] Systems of Volterra linear integral equations with Poisson kernels of the form

$$(9) \qquad x_i(t) = \phi_i(t) + \sum_1^n \int_{-\infty}^t K_{ij}(t - \epsilon)x_j(\epsilon)d\epsilon, \qquad i = 1, \cdots, n,$$

are also of interest. Unfortunately, the theory of nonlinear integral equations is only fragmentary.

in a linear system the amplitude of fluctuation depends upon the initial displacement; no intrinsic amplitude—as between full employment and zero employment—is involved. The attempt to introduce such a fixed amplitude in a linear system by the device of determining coefficients so that there will be neither dampened nor explosive solutions appears to be misdirected. As pointed out in the previous paper, page 108, the stochastical dispersion of the system increases indefinitely. Related to this is the fact that this does not yield a unique amplitude, but one which depends linearly upon initial conditions.]

If we insist that a system be linear and that it do not involve time explicitly, then for differential and difference systems we are restricted to the case of constant coefficients. This type is mathematically simple, and exact solutions are known. But a high price is paid for this simplicity in terms of special assumptions which must be made.

THE NONLINEAR DIFFERENTIAL EQUATION IN ONE VARIABLE

Nevertheless, I shall show that the problem of stability of equilibrium, if not that of macrodynamic business-cycle analysis, depends formally in an important way upon the solution of linear systems. This may be illustrated by a simple differential equation in one variable.

$$(15) \qquad \frac{dX}{at} = \dot{X} = f(X) = A_0 + A_1 X + A_2 X^2 + \cdots,$$

where f is analytic and expressible as a power series. This equation presents no difficulties of solution since by a single quadrature it may be solved; namely,

$$(16) \qquad t - t_0 = \int_h^X \frac{dX}{f(X)} = F(X).$$

Let us suppose a "simple" stationary solution $X = X^o$ exists so that

$$(17) \qquad \begin{aligned} f(X^o) &= 0, \\ f'(X^o) &\neq 0. \end{aligned}$$

Then the transformation of variables

$$(18) \qquad x = X - X^o$$

transforms (15) into the form

$$(19) \quad \dot{x} = f(x + X^o) = \frac{\sum_1^n f^i(X^o) x^i}{i!} = 0 + a_1 x + a_2 x^2 + \cdots,$$

where a constant term is no longer involved, and a_1 does not vanish.

Then we can assert:

THEOREM I. *A formal solution of the differential equation (19) can be written as an infinite power series in the solution of the simple linear system*

$$(20) \qquad\qquad\qquad \dot{x} = a_1 x,$$

or

$$(21) \qquad x(t) = \sum_{1}^{\infty} c_i \{g_1(\alpha, t)\}^i = \sum_{1}^{\infty} c_i \{\alpha e^{a_1 t}\}^i,$$

where α is a constant depending upon initial conditions.[5]

That this holds formally (i.e., without regard to the question of convergence) can be shown by substitution. Thus,

$$(22) \qquad \dot{x} = a_1 \sum_{1}^{\infty} i c_i g_1{}^i = \sum_{1}^{\infty} a_j \left\{ \sum_{1}^{\infty} c_k g_1{}^k \right\}^j.$$

Expanding out and equating coefficients of the same degree in g_1, we find that each c can be determined in succession from the a's and all previous c's.

$$c_1 = 1,$$

$$c_2 = \frac{2a_2 c_1}{a_1} .$$

$$\cdots\cdots ,$$

$$(23) \qquad\qquad\qquad \cdots\cdots ,$$

$$\cdots\cdots ,$$

$$c_n = M(c_{n-1}, \ldots, c_1).$$

[Equation (15) before transformation to the form not involving a constant term can in a similar fashion be formally solved by an infinite power series in the solution of the equation

$$(24) \qquad\qquad\qquad \dot{x} = a_0,$$

or

$$(25) \qquad x = \sum_{1}^{\infty} K_i g_0{}^i(t, \alpha) = \sum_{1}^{\infty} K_i \{a_0 t + \alpha\}^i.$$

But this is only the conventional power-series solution in t and tells

---

[5] E. Picard, *Traité d'Analyse*, Vol. III, p. 185; G. D. Birkhoff, *Dynamical Systems*, Chapter 3.

us nothing about the stability of the system; every term taken by itself goes to infinity regardless of the a's, although the infinite sum need not.]

It is well known that such a series as that in the exponentials is convergent for absolute values of α sufficiently small in a time interval sufficiently small. But if the system possesses first-order stability,[6] i.e., if $a_1 < 0$, then the series will converge for all values of t between t^o and $+\infty$ since $\left| e^{a_1 t i} \right|$ is decreasing with time, approaching zero in the limit. Since each term approaches this limit, then

$$(26) \qquad \lim_{t \to \infty} x(t, \alpha) = 0.$$

Therefore, if the system possesses first-order stability, it necessarily possesses stability in the small. It is to be emphasized that this is an *exact* solution in which no terms are considered to be of an order of smallness and ignorable. Likewise, if the system possesses first-order instability, it must be unstable in the small. However, the system may be in neutral first-order equilibrium, and possess either stability or instability in the small. In this case a_1 vanishes, and we must consider the stability of the nonvanishing term of lowest degree. This will be done later. We may state our results as follows:

THEOREM II: (*a*) *First-order stability is a sufficient condition for stability in the small.* (*b*) *The absence of first-order instability is a necessary condition for stability in the small.*

EXAMPLE: LOGISTIC LAW

We may illustrate the above principles by considering the simplest nonlinear system

$$(27) \qquad \dot{X} = A_0 + A_1 X + A_2 X^2,$$

where

$$(28) \qquad A_1^2 - 4A_0 A_2 > 0$$

if there are to be any "simple" stationary solutions.

Without essential loss of generality, we may by linear transformation of X involving only translation and scale change, and by scale change in t, bring the above system into the form

$$(29) \qquad \dot{x} = x(1 - x).$$

The equation

$$(30) \qquad x - x^2 = 0$$

---

[6] Not to be confused with stability of the first kind, a concept employed in my previous paper.

has roots 0 and 1, each of which represents a stationary state. The above differential equation will be recognized as one which is satisfied by the Verhulst-Pearl-Reed logistic law, according to which percentage changes in a variable fall off linearly with the magnitude of that variable, approaching a limit asymptotically. The above equation, however, is slightly more general since it admits of solutions which are not S-shaped.

By quadrature its general solution is found to be of the form

$$(31) \qquad x = \frac{1}{1 + Ke^{-t}},$$

where K is a parameter determined by the initial value of x at time zero according to the formula

$$(32) \qquad K = \frac{1}{x(0)} - 1.$$

For $K=0$ we have the stationary solution

$$(33) \qquad x(t) \equiv 1,$$

and for $K = \infty$ we have the stationary solution

$$(34) \qquad x(t) \equiv 0.$$

It can be easily verified that the latter stationary level is unstable, while the stationary level of unity is approached asymptotically by all adjacent motions. We may classify all possible initial conditions as follows:

$$(35) \quad \begin{aligned} &+ 1 \leqq x(0) \leqq \infty, & -1 < K \leqq 0, & \left.\right\} \; \lim_{t \to \infty} x(t) = 1; \\ &\; 0 < x(0) \leqq 1, & 0 \leqq K < + \infty, & \\ &\quad\;\; x(0) = 0, & K = \infty, & \quad x \equiv 0; \\ &-\infty < x(0) < 0, & -\infty < K < -1, & \quad \lim_{t \to \infty} x(t) = -\infty. \end{aligned}$$

Let us now apply our expansion theorem to this problem.[7] Expanding around the zero equilibrium point, and determining the c coefficients, we readily find

$$(36) \; x = \alpha e^t - \{\alpha e^t\}^2 + \{\alpha e^t\}^3 - \{\alpha e^t\}^4 + \cdots = \sum_1^\infty (-1)^{i-1}\{\alpha e^t\}^i.$$

For given values of t and sufficiently small values of α this is readily seen to be a convergent series equal to the geometric series expansion of

[7] Cf. A. J. Lotka, *Elements of Physical Biology*, pp. 64–68.

$$(37) \qquad \frac{\alpha e^t}{1 + \alpha e^t} = \frac{1}{1 + \dfrac{1}{\alpha} e^{-t}} \cdot$$

But for large values of t

$$(38) \qquad |\alpha e^t| > 1,$$

and the series diverges. This confirms our expectation that the zero equilibrium level is unstable.

The transformation

$$(39) \qquad y = x - 1$$

enables us to apply our expansion theorem to the determination of the stability of the other equilibrium level. Our differential equation becomes

$$(40) \qquad \dot{y} = -y + y^2,$$

and in the new variable the equilibrium level equals zero. Determining the c's by substitution as before, we find

$$(41) \qquad y(t) = -\{Ke^{-t}\} + \{Ke^{-t}\}^2 - \{Ke^{-t}\}^3 + \{Ke^{-t}\}^4 - \cdots$$
$$= \sum_1^\infty (-1)^i \{Ke^{-t}\}^i.$$

This will be recognized as the formal expansion of

$$(42) \qquad y = \frac{1}{1 + Ke^{-t}} - 1.$$

For small values of K and nonnegative values of t, this converges uniformly, and each term goes to zero as time becomes infinite. Thus, the equilibrium is stable in the small.

This example also throws light on the domain of convergence of the series of exponentials. It is easy to see from the exact solution of (31) that the stationary level ($y=0$, $x=1$) is stable for all positive displacements from equilibrium [i.e., $y(0)>0$, $x(0)>1$], and also for all negative displacements which are less than unity in absolute value $[-1 < y(0) < 0,\ 0 < x(0) < 1]$. But the series expansion of (41) is convergent only for $|K| < 1$, or for $[-\frac{1}{2} < y(0) < +\infty,\ \frac{1}{2} < x(0) < \infty]$.[8] Thus, its

[8] The expansion breaks down at the level at which the curve has an inflection point; i.e., where

$$\ddot{y}(t) = 0 = f'\{y(t)\}\dot{y}.$$

I venture the conjecture, completely unverified, that this may be a general phenomenon.

domain of convergence is smaller than the region of true stability. It provides only a lower limit which is not generally at the same time an upper limit to the region of stability.

In Figure 1 is depicted the solution of this equation for all possible initial conditions $x(0)$. The stationary level of unity is seen to be stable; that of zero unstable. The diagram brings out one feature not yet mentioned. The lower and upper branches each approach an asymptote

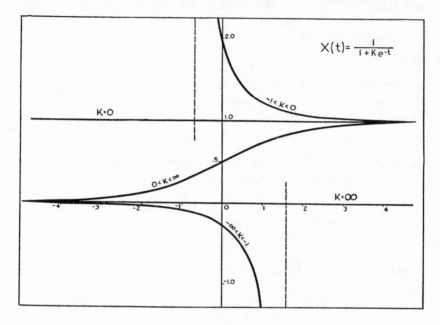

for finite values of t. This means that for negative displacements around the zero level the system recedes from equilibrium at an infinite rate of speed after some finite time has elapsed. For the upper branch it may be loosely said that the system approaches equilibrium after "coming in from infinity at an infinite velocity."

This example also suggests what is doubtless a valid "separation" theorem. *Points of stable equilibrium (in the small) are separated by points of definitely unstable equilibrium; and vice versa.* (In the interpretation of this, stable or unstable equilibrium may be of higher order so long as positions of one-sided stability-instability are ignored.)

THE PROBLEM OF HIGHER-ORDER STABILITY

Thus far I have considered only "simple" stationary states; i.e., those with power-series expressions in which the first-degree term does not vanish. I now turn to "degenerate" stationary states, those corresponding to multiple roots of the equation

(43) $$\dot{X} = 0 = f(X),$$

where

(44) $$\frac{d^i f(X^o)}{dX^i} = 0, \quad i = 0, \cdots, n - 1; n \geqq 2.$$

In the neighborhood of such a root the differential equation takes the form

(45) $$\dot{x} = a_n x^n + a_{n+1} x^{n+1} + \cdots,$$

where

$$n \geqq 2.$$

The solution of the equation

(46) $$\dot{x} = a_n x^n,$$

where higher powers are neglected, can be expected by analogy with the previous case to dominate the remaining terms for sufficiently small initial displacements of equilibrium. In the investigation of simple systems this was analytically deduced (viz., Theorems I and II); for higher-order systems this conjecture has not been verified, but is doubtless true. We wish to investigate, therefore, the stability of solutions of equation (46). If they are all stable (unstable), we shall say that the equilibrium position in question possesses nth-order stability (instability).

By elementary methods of integration we can find the exact solution to (46); thus

(47)
$$x^{-n} dx = a_n dt,$$
$$x^{1-n} = (1 - n) a_n t + x(0)^{1-n}.$$

To solve explicitly for x two cases arise depending upon whether n is odd or even.

(48)
$$x(t) = \frac{1}{\left\{ a_n(1 - n)t + x(0)^{1-n} \right\}^{1/(n-1)}} \qquad \text{for } n \text{ even};$$

$$x(t) = \pm \frac{1}{\left\{ a_n(1 - n)t + x(0)^{1-n} \right\}^{1/(n-1)}}, \qquad \text{for } n \text{ odd};$$

where the appropriate sign is to be taken so that x satisfies the initial condition $x = x(0)$. Both cases may be subsumed under the heading

$$(49) \qquad x(t) = \{ \operatorname{sgn} x(0) \}^n \, \frac{1}{\{ a_n (1 - n)t + x(0)^{1-n} \}^{1/(n-1)}} \, .$$

Clearly if n is even, $(n-1)$ is odd. Therefore, the second term within the brackets takes on either sign depending upon whether the initial displacement is plus or minus. Consequently, regardless of the sign of a_n, for some value of t, and for some displacement, the denominator will vanish, which means that x becomes infinite, and the equilibrium is not stable. Actually for n even the equilibrium possesses one-sided stability-instability. If $x(0)$ is of the same sign as a_n, the motion will be unstable; if $x(0)$ is of opposite sign to a_n, it will be stable. Thus, we have one-sided stability-instability.

If n is odd, then the second term of the denominator is always positive. If, and only if, a_n is negative (so that the first term is positive) will the denominator stay of the same sign and approach infinity as t approaches infinity. Hence, we have the following:

THEOREM III: *If the first nonvanishing coefficient is odd and negative, the system is stable in the small; if the first nonvanishing coefficient is odd and positive, the system is unstable. If the first nonvanishing term is even, the system possesses one-sided stability-instability.*

This presents a strong analogy to the necessary secondary conditions for a maximum. Write the differential equation

$$(50) \qquad \dot{X} = f(X) = F'(X),$$

where

$$F(X) = \int_a^X f(X) dX.$$

Then the following sums up the results achieved:

THEOREM IV: (a) *If $F(X^\circ)$ affords a relative maximum to F, then X° is a stationary solution of the differential equation and possesses stability in the small; and conversely.*

(b) *If $F(X^\circ)$ affords a relative minimum to F, then X° is an unstable equilibrium level.*

(c) *If X° is a stationary value of $F(X^\circ)$ which is not an extremum, then the system possesses one-sided stability-instability. Alternatively, if F assumes a stationary value, and $F' = f$ assumes an extremum value, the equilibrium is stable-unstable.*

(d) *If $F'(X)$ vanishes identically, the equilibrium is neutral.*

This possibility of linking up the problem of stability with a statical maximum problem is but one special aspect of the *Correspondence Principle*, and one to which we shall have occasion to refer again.

The meaning of one-sided stability-instability may not be intuitively obvious; fortunately a simple well-known economic example may be used to illustrate it. According to Malthus population would increase, decrease, or remain stationary depending upon the per capita level of subsistence (real income, food, etc.). Let X = total population, S = per capita real income. Then the percentage rate of growth of the population is an increasing function of the level of subsistence, passing from negative values to positive values at some "minimum level of subsistence," S^o. Mathematically,

$$(51) \qquad \frac{1}{X}\frac{dX}{dt} = \psi(S),$$

where

$$\psi'(S) > 0, \ \psi(S^o) = 0.$$

But the level of income (production) depends itself upon the level of population (labor) as of given capital, land, and technology. Moreover, Malthus implicitly and explicitly assumed the law of diminishing (per capita) returns. Thus,

$$(52) \qquad S = \phi(X), \ \phi'(X) < 0.$$

This last relationship enables us to eliminate S as a variable and to express the rate of growth of the population in terms of itself.

$$(53) \qquad \frac{1}{X}\frac{dX}{dt} = \psi\{\phi(X)\} = f(X),$$

where

$$f' = \psi'\phi' < 0,$$

and a stationary level X^o corresponds to

$$(54) \qquad f(X^o) = \psi(S^o) = 0.$$

The equilibrium is stable because $f'(X^o) < 0$. If the population exceeds the equilibrium level, each family will receive less than the subsistence level, and the population will decline. If it falls below the equilibrium level (through war, etc.), the average income will be high, and the population will increase. In Figure 2 the minimum level of subsistence is shown by MM'. Below this level population will decrease as shown by the long arrow; above this level it will increase as shown by the other long arrow. R'R is the returns curve, and the intersection E_1 represents a position of stable equilibrium as shown by the short directed arrows.

More modern theory suggests the possibility that there may be increasing returns in the early stages. In this case there may be two inter-

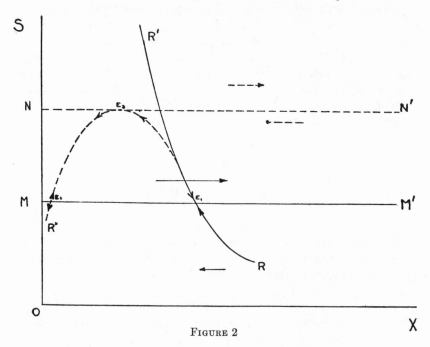

FIGURE 2

sections between the returns curve and the minimum subsistence level, yielding two points of equilibrium. In the diagram the new returns curve is $R''R$, and the new intersection point is E_2. The new equilibrium point is unstable since here

$$(55) \qquad f' = \psi'\phi' > 0.$$

If population falls below this level, it will become extinct since as returns fall off, so does population, etc., etc.

About a decade ago the theory of an optimum population achieved a certain vogue. According to one form of this theory, at some intermediate point average returns would be at a maximum. If by education one could raise the minimum standard of comfort insisted upon by all families to this maximum level, then population would reach this optimum equilibrium level. Without entering upon the merits or demerits of the scheme, I should like to point out that such an equilibrium level possesses one-sided stability-instability. For displacements from equilibrium towards a larger population it is stable, since such a movement lowers returns and causes population to decrease towards equilibrium. But for negative displacements of population it is unstable, since these also lower returns and cause population to decrease still more until the point of extinction is reached. In Figure 2 the minimum level of subsistence (comfort) is irreversibly pushed up by education exactly to NN' so that its intersection, E_3, with $R''R$ represents a maximum of per capita real income. The arrows indicate the one-sided nature of the equilibrium point.

Analytically,

$$(56) \qquad\qquad f' = 0,$$

and the first nonvanishing derivative is even and negative. Thus, f is at an extremum, and Theorem IV, (c), applies. The equilibrium is one-sided.[9]

SYSTEMS OF EQUATIONS IN n VARIABLES

Definition: The system of n differential equations

$$(57) \quad \dot{x}_i = f^i(x_1, \cdots, x_n) = \sum_j a_{ij} x_j + \sum_{j,k} a_{ijk} x_j x_k + \cdots, i = 1, \cdots, n,$$

where all summations range from 1 to n, will be said to possess a *simple* stationary solution $(0, \cdots, 0)$ providing that the matrix (a_{ij}) possesses n (distinct, nonvanishing) roots $(\lambda_1, \cdots, \lambda_n)$, which are *not* connected by a linear commensurability relation of the form

$$(58) \qquad\qquad i_1\lambda_1 + i_2\lambda_2 + \cdots + i_n\lambda_n = 0$$

for any set of integers $i_1, \cdots, i_n$, not all zero.

In this case a fundamental set of solutions of the equations involving only linear terms

$$(59) \qquad\qquad \dot{x}_i = \sum_{j=1}^{n} a_{ij}x_j$$

can be written in the form

$$(60) \qquad\qquad \alpha_1 e^{\lambda_1 t}, \; \alpha_2 e^{\lambda_2 t}, \; \cdots, \; \alpha_n e^{\lambda_n t},$$

where the λ's are the latent roots of the matrix (a_{ij}) or roots of the secular equation

[9] I need not warn the reader against the lack of realism of the above theories in light of modern demographic trends. For large parts of Western Europe and North America where *net and gross reproduction rates* are low, perhaps no level of real income can lead to a stationary population. Moreover, these rates may fall with increasing real income; this, however, is presumably an irreversible effect.

$$(61)\ D(\lambda) = \begin{vmatrix} a_{11}-\lambda & a_{12} & \cdots & a_{1n} \\ a_{21} & a_{22}-\lambda & \cdots & a_{2n} \\ \cdot & \cdot & & \cdot \\ \cdot & \cdot & & \cdot \\ \cdot & \cdot & & \cdot \\ a_{n1} & a_{n2} & \cdots & a_{nn}-\lambda \end{vmatrix} = (\lambda_1-\lambda)(\lambda_2-\lambda)\cdots(\lambda_n-\lambda).$$

Then we have the following theorem:[10]

THEOREM V: *A formal solution of the set of differential equations is provided by a power series in the solutions of the first-order equations; i.e.,*

$$(62) \qquad \begin{aligned} y_i &= g^{i}(\alpha_1 e^{\lambda_1 t},\ \alpha_2 e^{\lambda_2 t},\ \cdots,\ \alpha_n e^{\lambda_n t}) \\ &= \sum_{i} c_{ij}(\alpha_j e^{\lambda_j t}) + \sum_{i,k} c_{ijk}\alpha_k\alpha_j e^{(\lambda_n+\lambda_k)t} + \cdots. \end{aligned}$$

By formal substitution this can be verified, remembering that the non-commensurability relationship (58) is satisfied. Each set of c's can be determined in terms of previous sets and the known a's.

The matrix **a** may have (pairs of) complex roots, corresponding for linear systems to damped or undamped sine-cosine terms. The system will be said to have first-order stability if the real parts of all roots, real or complex, are all negative, since this will imply damped motion (exponential or harmonic) of the linear system. An important part of the stability problem is the determination of necessary or sufficient conditions that all real parts are negative, and this will be dealt with in another paper.

Here I should like to mention the generalization of Theorem II.

THEOREM VI: (a) *First-order stability is a sufficient condition for stability in the small;* (b) *the absence of first-order instability is a necessary condition for stability in the small.*

This follows because the series (62) can be shown to converge for all values of t and values of α sufficiently small if all the real parts are negative. Since it converges for limited values of α and t, and since all terms are decreasing in absolute magnitude, it consequently never ceases to converge.

A stationary equilibrium position is not "simple" if a commensurability relationship of the form mentioned holds. Even if such a relationship does exist, the above theorem is valid providing there are no zero roots. If no roots vanish, linear commensurability relations introduce into the infinite power series terms of the form

[10] Cf. Picard, *op. cit.*; Birkhoff, *op. cit,*

$$(63) \qquad p_n(t)e^{(i_1\lambda_1 + \cdots + i_k\lambda_k + \cdots)t},$$

where $p_n(t)$ is a polynomial. If the real parts of all λ's are negative, the exponential will dominate, and the solution will still be stable.

Zero roots or ones whose real parts are zero, i.e., pure imaginaries, cause greater difficulties since stability in the small becomes dependent upon terms of higher degree. I am not aware that this has been completely analyzed in the mathematical literature except for special cases. I shall not, therefore, enter upon the problem except to prove a *general* theorem relating to those many variable systems associated with the maximum of some function.

Before doing so I may summarize briefly the results achieved so far as follows: Stability in the small of a nonlinear system of differential equations depends except in singular cases upon the stability of a linear system. This dependence can be rigorously defined and does *not* involve a dubious neglect of the squares of small quantities, etc.

THE STABILITY OF A STATIONARY POSITION
WHICH IS ALSO A MAXIMUM

If $(X_1^o, \cdots, X_n^o)$ yields a proper relative maximum to a twice differentiable function $F(X_1, \cdots, X_n)$, then it is not hard to show by the theorem of the mean that

$$(64) \qquad \frac{\partial F}{\partial X_i} = F_i(X_1^o, \cdots, X_n^o) = 0, \qquad i = 1, \cdots, n,$$

and

$$(65) \quad F_1(X_1, \cdots, X_n)(X_1 - X_1^o) + F_2(X_1, \cdots, X_n)(X_2 - X_2^o) + \cdots < 0$$

for values of X sufficiently close to X^o, but distinct from it.

Suppose we are given a system of differential equations

$$(66) \qquad \frac{dX_i}{dt} = f^i(X_1, \cdots, X_n) = F_i(X_1, \cdots, X_n).$$

Only special differential systems can be so written. Unfortunately space does not permit a discussion of necessary and sufficient conditions satisfied by such special systems.

THEOREM VII: $(X_1^o, \cdots, X_n^o)$ *is a stationary solution for the above system, and it is stable in the small.*

Transforming the equilibrium point to the origin $(0, \cdots, 0)$, we have

$$(67) \qquad \frac{dx_i}{dt} = F_i(X_1^o + x_1, \cdots, X_n^o + x_n),$$

and $\sum_1^n F_i x_i < 0$ for sufficiently small nonzero values of x.

Multiplying the first equation of (67) by x_1, the second by x_2, etc., and summing we find

$$(68) \qquad \sum_1^n x_i \frac{dx_i}{dt} = \frac{d}{dt} \left\{ \sum_1^n \frac{x_i^2}{2} \right\} = \sum_1^n F_i x_i < 0.$$

For sufficiently small values of x, the sum of squares is decreasing. Hence, as t goes to infinity, it approaches a limit which cannot be different from zero. If

$$(69) \qquad \lim_{t \to \infty} (x_1^2 + x_2^2 + \cdots + x_n^2) = 0,$$

then

$$(70) \qquad \lim_{t \to \infty} x_1 = 0, \quad \lim_{t \to \infty} x_2 = 0, \quad \cdots, \quad \lim_{t \to \infty} x_n = 0.$$

Hence, the equilibrium is stable. A relative proper minimum yields definitely unstable equilibrium, while a nonextremum stationary value yields stability-instability.

This theorem, while not applicable to all differential equations, is nevertheless very important for economic systems. Within its scope it is exceedingly general since it does not require that the f's be analytic, and it covers simultaneously the stability of first and higher orders.

THE DIFFERENCE EQUATION IN ONE VARIABLE

The problem of differential systems has been analyzed in a fairly complete manner, and we must now turn to systems of difference equations, which are perhaps of even greater importance for economic theory. The simplest case is provided by the general nonlinear difference equation in one variable

$$(71) \qquad X(t + 1) = f\{X(t)\},$$

or

$$(72) \qquad \Delta X(t) = g\{X(t)\} = f - X(t).$$

So simple is this equation that we can indicate its solution graphically, showing on one diagram all possible types of qualitative behavior in the neighborhood of an equilibrium position. In Figure 3 two functions are plotted—one relating the succeeding value of X (vertical axis) to the given value of X (horizontal axis); the other is simply a 45° line.

The solution of our equation for any initial condition is shown by broken lines running between these two functions in the indicated fashion. Any initial value $X(t)$ leads to a new value $X(t+1)$ indicated by running up vertically to the curve $f\{X(t)\}$; this new value must be transferred to the abscissa in order to derive its successor. This is affected by moving horizontally to the 45° line; a vertical movement yields the next value, and so the process goes. Stationary equilibrium positions are defined by the intersection of the f function and the 45° line, or analytically by roots of the equation

$$(73) \qquad\qquad f(X) - X = 0.$$

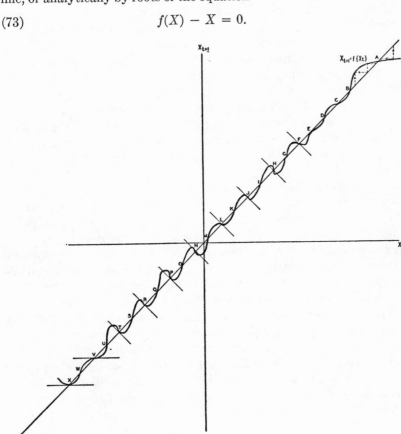

FIGURE 3

The diagram illustrates what are essentially all possible types of equilibria. Twenty-four points of equilibrium are indicated, but only sixteen represent qualitatively different kinds of equilibrium, eight being duplicates. Point A represents a position of equilibrium, stable in the small. Displacement in either direction results in an asymptotic return to equilibrium. Point B represents unstable equilibrium; displacement is followed by an ever-increasing one-way disequilibrating movement. C represents a position of stable equilibrium, differing from

A in that it has first-order neutrality and has only high-order stability. D possesses first-order neutrality, but high-order instability; therefore, it is unstable in the small, and the recession from equilibrium is monotonic. E has first-order neutrality, but its next nonvanishing derivative is even. Consequently, it has one-sided stability-instability.

Thus far we have met only equilibria like those of the one-variable differential system. That the single difference equation is richer in types of equilibria is illustrated by the variety still to come. F possesses first-order stability, and hence is stable in the small. Unlike A the approach to equilibrium is not monotonic, but rather by means of damped oscillations of period two. G represents simply a position of neutral equilibrium in the small, possessing first- and high-order neutrality. The system stays wherever it is put. H differs from F only in that the equilibrium is unstable, the divergence from equilibrium being along explosive oscillations, I is simply a duplication of B, as are K, M, O, Q, S, U, and W.

J represents a position of neutral equilibrium. The system oscillates with constant amplitude around this position. [In physics this would be called stable equilibrium. In the terminology of the previous paper, it has stability of the second kind—not to be confused with second- or high-order stability.] L like J possesses first-order neutrality, but unlike J has high-order stability. Equilibrium is approached by damped oscillations. N also has first-order neutrality, but possesses high-order instability of an oscillatory nature. P and R like L and N possess high-order, oscillatory stability and instability, respectively, but analytically differ slightly. T possesses oscillatory neutrality of all orders, and hence is neutral in the small. It can be thought of as including J as a special case. Finally, V and X, while they possess first-order stability, are analytically of singular type and should be differentiated. The former has monotonic stability, the latter oscillatory stability.

The following classification may clarify the possible types.

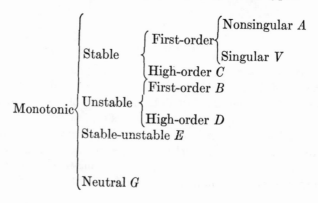

$$\text{Oscillatory} \begin{cases} \text{Stable} \begin{cases} \text{First-order} \begin{cases} \text{Nonsingular } F \\ \text{Singular } X \end{cases} \\ \text{High-order} \begin{cases} \text{Type 1 } L \\ \text{Type 2 } P \end{cases} \end{cases} \\ \text{Unstable} \begin{cases} \text{First-order } H \\ \text{High-order} \begin{cases} \text{Type 1 } N \\ \text{Type 2 } R \end{cases} \end{cases} \\ \text{Neutral } J, T \end{cases}$$

We discriminate analytically between the sixteen cases depending upon the first and higher derivatives of $f(X)$. The first subdivision between monotonic and oscillatory hinges upon whether $f'(X)$ is positive or negative. Within the monotonic classification we have first-order stability if f' is less than unity, and first-order instability if f' is greater than unity. If f' equals unity, we have first-order neutrality and must proceed to higher derivatives. If all these derivatives vanish, we have true neutrality in the small. If the first nonvanishing derivative is odd and positive, we have high-order stability; if odd and negative, we have high-order instability. If the first nonvanishing higher derivative is even, we have one-sided stability-instability.

Within the oscillatory classification things are even more complicated. If f' is less than unity in absolute value, we have first-order stability; if greater than unity in absolute value, we have first-order instability. If $f' = -1$, then we must proceed to higher derivatives. Should all of these vanish, we have neutral oscillatory equilibrium (J). More generally, if all odd higher derivatives vanish, the equilibrium is neutral and oscillatory as in T. When $f' = -1$, and the first nonvanishing derivative is odd and positive, the equilibrium possesses high-order oscillatory stability; if odd and negative, the equilibrium possesses high-order oscillatory instability. When $f' = -1$, and the first nonvanishing derivative is even, then we go on to consider the first nonvanishing odd derivative. As in the previous cases, we have stability or instability depending upon whether this is negative or positive.

Finally, we are confronted with the singular cases when $f' = 0$. If the next nonvanishing derivative is odd and positive, we have monotonic stability; if odd and negative, or if even and of any sign, we have stable oscillatory equilibrium. If all derivatives vanish, the equilibrium is perfectly stable as indicated in the first section of this paper; when displaced, the system returns "instantly" to equilibrium and does not merely approach equilibrium asymptotically.

A few remarks 'may be in order concerning the qualitative behavior of a first-order system from any initial condition. It could no doubt be shown that it must do one of the following: (a) go off to infinity; (b) approach an equilibrium level; or (c) approach a periodic motion of some finite period. If it is reversible, that is, if $f(X)$ is not only single-valued but admits of a single-valued inverse, then the only periodic motion possible under heading (c) is one of period two. It does not fall within the scope of the present paper to investigate the meaning of the stability of motions more general than stationary equilibrium levels. When this is done, it will be found no doubt that there exist valid "separation" theorems concerning the ordering of stable and unstable periodic motions. The necessity because of continuity (Rolle's theorem, etc.) of duplicating certain equilibrium points in the above diagram provides a hint at such relationships.

ANALYTIC SOLUTION

As with the differential equation systems an exact solution of the general nonlinear analytic difference equation can be indicated. Let

$$(74) \qquad x(t+1) = a_1 x(t) + a_2 x(t)^2 + a_3 x(t)^3 + \cdots,$$

or

$$(75) \qquad \Delta x(t) = (a_1 - 1)x(t) + a_2 x(t)^2 + a_3 x(t)^3 + \cdots.$$

We rule out cases where the first-degree term vanishes in either of these expressions; and we rule out all cases of singular and neutral first-order equilibrium so that $a_1 \neq 1$, 0, or -1.

A formal solution of this is given by a power series in the solution of the simpler linear equation

$$(76) \qquad \begin{aligned} x(t+1) &= a_1 x(t), \\ \Delta x(t) &= (a_1 - 1)x(t). \end{aligned}$$

Let

$$(77) \qquad g_1(t) = \alpha a_1{}^t.$$

THEOREM VIII: *A formal solution to (74) is provided by*

$$(78) \qquad x(t) = c_1\{\alpha a_1{}^t\} + c_2\{\alpha a_1{}^t\}^2 + c_3\{\alpha a_1{}^t\}^3 + \cdots.$$

This may be verified by formal substitution provided that $a_1 \neq 1$, 0, or -1. Each c is obtainable in terms of all previous c's and the known a's.

More generally, we are given n difference equations in normal form

$$(79) \qquad x_i(t+1) = \sum_j a_{ij}x_j(t) + \sum_{j,k} a_{ijk}x_j(t)x_k(t) + \cdots,$$

where the latent roots of $\mathbf{a}$, $(\lambda_1, \cdots, \lambda_n)$, are never equal in absolute value to zero or one, and where there exist no linear commensurability relations of the form

$$(80) \qquad m_1 \log \lambda_1 + m_2 \log \lambda_2 + \cdots + m_n \log \lambda_n = 0,$$

for m's integers not all vanishing. Then

THEOREM IX: *A formal solution to the system of difference equations is given by an ascending power series in the solutions of the linear system*

$$(81) \qquad x_i(t+1) = \sum_j a_{ij}x_j(t),$$

or

$$(82) \qquad x_i(t) = \theta^i(\alpha_1\lambda_1{}^t, \cdots, \alpha_n\lambda_n{}^t)$$
$$= \sum_j c_{ij}\{\alpha_j\lambda_j{}^t\} + \sum_{j,k} c_{ijk}\{\alpha_j\lambda_j{}^t\}\{\alpha_k\lambda_k{}^t\} + \cdots.$$

Each set of c's can be determined by formal substitution from all previous sets and the known a's. If some of the roots are multiple, or if a linear commensurability relation of type (80) does hold, there will probably exist a similar power-series solution augmented by terms with polynomial multipliers in t, provided always that the absolute value of all roots equals neither zero nor one.

All of the remarks of earlier sections concerning convergence of such series apply. We must remember, however, that first-order stability of a difference-equation system implies

$$(83) \qquad |\lambda_i| < 1,$$

and conversely. The following theorem is easily derived along now familiar lines.

THEOREM X: *For a difference-equation system first-order stability is a sufficient condition for stability in the small, and the absence of first-order instability is a necessary condition.*

Space does not permit me to illustrate the above remarks with an economic example, such as would be provided by the familiar cobweb theorem applied to nonlinear supply and demand curves.

OTHER FUNCTIONAL EQUATIONS

While this has not been verified, one can hazard the conjecture that more general nonlinear functional equations can in the neighborhood of an equilibrium point be expressed as a power series in solutions of the simpler linear systems. Thus, under suitable assumptions functional equations can be written in the Taylor-like expansion

$$X_i(t) + F^i\{X_1^t(\tau), \cdots, X_n^t(\tau)\}$$
$$\underset{-\infty}{} \qquad \underset{-\infty}{}$$

(84)
$$= \{X_i(t) - X_i^\circ\} + \sum_j \int_{-\infty}^t K_{ij}(t - \tau)\{X_j(\tau) - X_j^\circ\}d\tau$$

$$+ \sum_{j,s} \int_{-\infty}^t \int_{-\infty}^t K_{ijs}(t - \tau_1, t - \tau_2)\{X_j(\tau_1) - X_j^\circ\}$$
$$\cdot \{X_s(\tau_2) - X_s^\circ\}d\tau_1 d\tau_2 + \cdots,$$

where K_{ij}, K_{ijs} represent first and second functional derivatives respectively. The linear system

(85) $$X_i(t) - X_i^\circ + \sum_j \int_{-\infty}^t K_{ij}(t - \tau)\{X_j(\tau) - X_j^\circ\}d\tau = 0$$

is known to have solutions of the form

(86) $$X_i(t) - X_i^\circ = \sum_1^\infty \alpha_{ij}e^{\lambda_j t},$$

where the λ's are infinite roots of the transcendental equation

(87) $$D(\lambda) = \left| \delta_{ij} + \int_0^\infty K_{ij}(v)e^{-\lambda v}dv \right| = 0.$$

In population analysis single integral equations of this type play an important part, and the solution in terms of an infinite number of exponentials has been called by A. J. Lotka[11] the Hertz-Herglotz solution of these equations. It can perhaps be shown that an infinite power series in the infinite solutions of the linear system will provide a solution for the nonlinear case.

Similarly mixed equations of the type

(88) $$y'(t) = f\{y(t), y(t - \theta)\}$$

may be expressible in terms of the Frisch-Holme linear equation

(89) $$y'(t) = ay(t) + by(t - \theta).$$

As in the preceding integral equation, boundary or initial conditions for this equation necessarily involve an arbitrary function over an in-

---

[11] For an excellent bibliography of applications see A. J. Lotka, "A Contribution to the Theory of Industrial Replacement," *Annals of Mathematical Statistics*, June, 1939.

terval, and hence the exponential solutions must be infinite in number so that an arbitrary function can be expanded in terms of them. [The same would be true of difference equations not solely defined for integral values of t. Arbitrary periodic functions would enter into the solution, and these would be expressible in the Fourier infinite exponential series.] This raises problems of doubly infinite series and cannot be entered upon here.

CONCLUSION

It has been the purpose of this paper to show that the investigation of linear systems is, except in singular cases, sufficient to determine the stability of a system. The singular cases of first-order neutrality will be encountered in relatively few instances since they form a nowhere-dense set in the totality of all possible functional equations. Nevertheless, the problem of high-order stability and neutrality must be investigated at least once, and this has been done for differential- and difference equation systems in one variable.

Having established the importance of the analysis of first-order stability, I shall in the near future deal at some length with the problem of defining conditions under which this will be guaranteed, and with the mutual interrelations between dynamics and statics as formulated in the *Correspondence Principle*.

Massachusetts Institute of Technology

41

DYNAMIC PROCESS ANALYSIS

Paul A. Samuelson

I. Introduction

THE geometric progressions of the Malthus population theories and the concern of the classical economists with the approach toward a stationary state remind us that dynamic analysis is not new in economics. Nevertheless, it is fair to say that not until the second quarter of this century has there been great progress in working out the specific quantitative development of dynamic processes.

In a literary and intuitive way, the economist of a score of years ago was acquainted with such dynamic models as J. M. Clark's "principle of acceleration," or with the Aftalion theory of business oscillations resulting from the lagged over-response of output to previous capital formation —a process which its formulator compared to the successive over- and under-heating of a room that results when the fuel we add to the fire at one moment gives rise to heat at a later time.

Numerous other instances of rudimentary dynamics prior to, say, 1925 could be given in the related field of economic price theory. Marshallian and Walrasian notions of stable and unstable demand-supply intersections provide a class of examples. However, if we look for pre-1925 examples of dynamic processes in the third great area of their present-day prominence—i.e., in the field of "income analysis" rather than business cycle or price theory—we shall not fare so well; since, with the honorable exception of Knut Wicksell, economists had scarcely come to recognize this as a problem distinct from that of business fluctuations.

In the last two decades, progress in dynamics erupted on many fronts. Frisch, Roos, Tinbergen, Kalecki, and many others[1] began to formulate mathematical models that give rise to cycles of varying periodicity and amplitude.

[1] See the valuable summary of much of this discussion in J. Tinbergen, "Annual Survey: Quantitative Business Cycle Theory," *Econometrica*, July 1935, III, pp. 241–308; R. Frisch, "Propagation Problems and Impulse Problems in Dynamic Economics," *Economic Essays in Honour of Gustav Cassel* (London, 1933), pp. 171–206; M. Kalecki, "A Macrodynamic Theory of Business Cycles," *Econometrica*, July 1935, III, pp. 327–344; C. F. Roos, "A Mathematical Theory of Price and Production Fluctuations and Economic Crises," *Journal of Political Economy*, October 1930, XXXVIII, pp. 501–522.

In the general field of income analysis, Robertson, Keynes, Haberler, Kahn, Harrod, Marschak, Hansen, and Machlup were among the many writers in English who placed stress on dynamic processes; on the Continent the whole of the "neo-Wicksellian" school, particularly the Swedish economists Myrdal, Ohlin, Lindahl, and Lundberg, stressed this mode of thinking.[2]

And in more recent years, Metzler, Goodwin, Smithies, Haavelmo, Koopmans, Klein, Hicks, Lange, Tintner, Domar, the present writer, and many others[3] have elaborated upon further dynamic models which study the stability and fluctuating deviations around any defined equilibrium and which straddle the three fields of cycles, price theory, and income determination.

II. NATURE OF DYNAMICS

Since almost any problem in economics has been, or can be, treated dynamically, it is clear that the only thing that different dynamic studies have in common is their *method*. And since the formal methods involved in dynamics are usually numerical and mathematical, the ordinary student of economics frequently finds himself shut out from an understand-

[2] D. H. Robertson, *Essays in Monetary Theory* (London, 1946), Ch. IV, "Saving and Hoarding," reprinted from the 1933 *Economic Journal*; J. M. Keynes, *The General Theory of Employment, Interest and Money* (New York, 1936); G. Haberler, *Prosperity and Depression* (New York, 1946); R. F. Kahn, "The Relation of Home Investment to Unemployment," *Economic Journal*, June 1931, XLI, pp. 173–198; R. F. Harrod, *The Trade Cycle: An Essay* (Oxford, 1936); A. H. Hansen, *Fiscal Policy and Business Cycles* (New York, 1941); F. Machlup, *International Trade and the National Income Multiplier* (Philadelphia, 1943); J. Marschak, "Identity and Stability in Economics: A Survey," *Econometrica*, January 1942, X, pp. 61–74; Bertil Ohlin, "Some Notes on the Stockholm Theory of Saving and Investment," reprinted from the 1937 *Economic Journal* in *Readings in Business Cycle Theory* (Philadelphia, 1944), pp. 87–130; G. Myrdal, *Monetary Equilibrium* (London, 1939); E. Lundberg, *Studies in the Theory of Economic Expansion* (London, 1937); E. Lindahl, *Studies in the Theory of Money and Capital* (New York, 1939).

[3] L. A. Metzler, "Underemployment Equilibrium in International Trade," *Econometrica*, April 1942, X, pp. 97–112; *idem*, "The Transfer Problem Reconsidered," *Journal of Political Economy*, June 1942, L, pp. 397–414; R. M. Goodwin, "Innovations and the Irregularity of Economic Cycles," *Review of Economic Statistics*, May 1946, XXVIII, pp. 95–104; A. Smithies, "Process Analysis and Equilibrium Analysis," *Econometrica*, January 1942, X, pp. 26–38; T. Haavelmo, *The Probability Approach in Econometrics*, supplement to *Econometrica*, July 1944, XII; T. Koopmans, "The Logic of Economic Business Cycle Research," *Journal of Political Economy*, April 1941, XLIX, pp. 157–181; L. R. Klein, *Economic Fluctuations in the United States, 1921–41*, 2nd draft (Chicago, 1947; Cowles Commission); J. R. Hicks, *Value and Capital* (Oxford, 1939); O. Lange, *Price Flexibility and Employment* (Bloomington, 1944); G. Tintner, "A 'Simple' Theory of Business Fluctuations," *Econometrica*, July–October 1942, X, pp. 317–320; E. Domar, "Capital Expansion, Rate of Growth, and Employment," *ibid.*, April 1946, XIV, pp. 137–148; P. A. Samuelson, *Foundations of Economic Analysis* (Cambridge, Mass., 1947), Part II.

ing of much of the modern discussions—unless he is willing to put in a fair amount of concentrated effort in mastering the rudiments of the dynamic method.

Statics and dynamics differ in many ways, so that the investigator must develop new ways of looking at things in a dynamic world. For instance, consider such a classic illustration of logical fallacy as: "I'm glad I don't like olives, because if I liked them I'd eat them—and I hate them." Statically, this is nonsensical, a complete fallacy. But from a dynamical viewpoint, this same argument can be modified to explain why a person at times eats olives and at others does not.[4]

Statics concerns itself with the simultaneous and instantaneous or timeless determination of economic variables by mutually interdependent relations. Even a historically changing world may be treated statically, each of its changing positions being treated as successive states of static equilibrium. A "still" cameraman could capture in a cross-cut photo all that was relevant to such a world; and the printed picture would be the same whether the previous or subsequent positions of the system were subject to rapid or to negligible change.

It is the essence of dynamics that *economic variables at different points of time are functionally related*; or what is the same thing, that *there are functional relationships between economic variables and their rates of change, their "velocities," "accelerations,"* or higher *"derivatives of derivatives."* It is important to note that each such dynamic system generates its own behavior over time, either as an autonomous response to a set of "initial conditions," or as a response to some changing external conditions. This feature of self-generating development over time is the crux of every dynamic process.[5]

Most dynamic economic processes fall into one of two categories: (a) discrete processes, treated in "period analysis," and (b) continuous processes involving flows, treated in "rate analysis." In mathematical terms, period analysis falls under the category of "difference equations," while rate analysis involves "differential equations."[6] The choice between period

---

[4] Similarly, there is the beautiful example of static economic fallacy presented in D. H. Henderson's *Supply and Demand*, in which the novice economist is tempted to argue that a tax will cause price to rise, but at the higher price demand will fall off so that price will fall, . . . etc. But from a dynamic viewpoint, one must admit the possibility of cobweb oscillation not so very different from those just described.

[5] See the author's *Foundations of Economic Analysis*.

[6] By a differential equation, mathematicians mean a relationship holding between the value of a function and its various derivatives; for example,

$$\frac{d^3y(t)}{dt^3} = f\left[y(t), \frac{dy(t)}{dt}, \frac{d^2y(t)}{dt^2}\right]$$

is a differential equation—of the sort called third order, involving as it does derivatives up to the third derivative. If we add to this differential equation the "initial values" of

or rate analysis is usually one of convenience, since by taking periods of short enough duration we can approximate to rates and can neglect the interrelations within the period.

Period analysis lends itself to exposition in terms of simple arithmetic examples rather than the more complex mathematics of differential equations. But really to understand these numerical examples, one must still study the elements of "difference equations," which are closely analogous to differential equations. Period analysis has the disadvantage that in speaking of investment or income of a period, one often loses sight of the "per unit time" dimensionality of these concepts; rate or flow analysis, on the other hand, is not so likely to suppress the time dimensionality.[7]

III. OUTLINE OF THE DISCUSSION

The nature of dynamic processes can best be appreciated from a study of concrete examples. Moreover, if one agrees that the common core of dynamic process analysis consists of its formal *method*, and recognizes the intrinsic technical difficulties of that method, then the advantages of a case treatment of the subject are reinforced.

For these reasons, I have confined my survey to an elucidation of half a dozen different general models or cases, each illustrating some important economic problem. Cases I and II, dealing with compound-interest exponential growth at discrete and continuous stages respectively, are presented for the insight they give into the simple mathematics of the problem. Case III, dealing with some relationships between the stock of capital and the flows of investment and income, provides insight into "rate" as distinct from "period" analysis. Case IV is concerned with the familiar dynamic multiplier response of income to a continued stream of new investment. Case V illustrates in a quantitative way the well-known qualitative properties of the cobweb cycle. In conclusion, there follows a

---

the function and its first two derivatives, we have a well-determined differential equation system which will generate its own behavior over all subsequent time.

By a difference equation, mathematicians mean a relationship holding between the value of a function at a number of different time points; for example,

$$y(t + 3) = f[y(t), y(t + 1), y(t + 2)]$$

is a difference equation of the third order. If we prescribe the initial values $y(0)$, $y(1)$, and $y(2)$, the system generates its own subsequent behavior. The name "difference equation" comes from the fact that "different" time periods are involved and also from the fact that such relations may be rewritten in an alternative—but equivalent—form involving "finite differences" of the form

$$\Delta y(t) = y(t + 1) - y(t), \Delta^2 y(t) = \Delta[\Delta y(t)], \text{ etc.}$$

[7] Nevertheless, it would be a mistake to think that all flow analysis is necessarily dynamic. In a static Marshallian wheat-market equilibrium, the quantities sold are stationary flows per unit time, but the system may still be regarded as static.

brief summary of the significance of past accomplishments in this field for future developments of economic science.

In order to free the bulk of the discussion from mathematics of any complexity, I have confined to the Appendix a brief treatment of dynamic processes involving more than one period.

CASE I. COMPOUND INTEREST AT DISCRETE INTERVALS

Perhaps the oldest dynamic process that economists have handled rigorously involves the growth of an initial sum of money invested and reinvested at compound interest. The value at the end of t periods—called $V(t)$—of an initial principal, V_0, is given by[8]

$$V(t) = (1 + i)^t V_0 \qquad (1)$$

where i is the rate of interest per period of compounding. This familiar solution is an instance of a "geometric progression or exponential term multiplied by a scale factor"—and is of the general form $M^t K$.

Now the essential thing about a sum invested at compound interest is the fact that its *value at one period is always proportional to its value at a previous period.* In mathematical terms, this is described by saying that $V(t)$ satisfies a simple "difference equation"; namely

$$\begin{cases} V(t + 1) = (1 + i)\, V(t) \\ V(0) = V_0 \end{cases} \qquad (2)$$

In other words, the sequence generates its own growth, once we give it the "initial condition," V_0, to start it off—as is shown in detail in the following table:

t	0	1	2	. . .	t	t + 1	. . .	∞
$V(t)$	V_0	$(1 + i)\, V_0$	$(1 + i)^2 V_0$	. . .	$(1 + i)^t V_0$	$(1 + i)\, V(t)$	. . .	∞

This self-generating property is characteristic of all dynamic processes. Let us therefore summarize and generalize what we have learned:

(1) The simplest dynamic process for any variable, $X(t)$, is that generated by a difference equation system of the general form

$$\begin{cases} X(t + 1) = a\, X(t) \\ X(0) = X_0 \end{cases}$$

---

[8] Throughout this paper the notation for any variable, X, at time 0, 1, . . ., t, t + 1, . . . is given by $X(0)$, $X(1)$, . . ., $X(t)$, $X(t + 1)$, ... The initial values of an economic variable when regarded as constants are denoted with subscripts

(2) We suspect that its solution over all subsequent time is given by a geometric progression or exponential expression of the form

$$X(t) = M^t K$$

We also suspect that the constant, K, depends only on the initial condition, X_0; and that the constant, M, depends only on the constant, a, in the difference equation.

(3) These suspicions are verified once we experimentally try $M^t K$ wherever $X(t)$ appears in the difference equation. This gives us

$$M^{t+1} K = a M^t K$$
$$M^0 K = X_0$$

Cancelling the $M^t K$ from both sides of the first equation, we find

$$M = a$$
$$K = X_0$$

(4) Therefore, the solution to the difference equation

$$X(t+1) = a X(t)$$
$$X(0) = X_0 \tag{3}$$

is always given by

$$X(t) = a^t X_0 \tag{4}$$

In the compound-interest case, $a = 1 + i$, and the solution grows at a very rapid rate. If the interest rate were a negative fraction, then the value of our principal would ultimately decay away to nothing, after the fashion of a disintegrating radioactive material. This is because *a* would then be a fraction less than one, and any fraction when raised to higher and higher powers becomes smaller and smaller and ultimately approaches zero.

Already our simple mathematical analysis reveals one possibility that goes beyond the compound interest example. What if *a* itself is negative? Then obviously we get an oscillation, with every other year being alternately negative and positive. For example, when $a = -2$ and $X_0 = 10$, our sequence becomes an "explosive oscillation": $+10$, -20, $+40$, -80, $+160$, -320, . . ., or $(-2)^t$ 10. But if $a = -\frac{1}{2}$, we get a decaying oscillation of the form: $+10$, -5, $+2.5$, -1.25, $+.625$, . . . ,

---

as follows: $X(0) = X_0$, $X(1) = X_1$, etc. Structural coefficients such as the marginal propensity to consume or the "relation coefficient" in the Acceleration Principle are represented respectively by such letters as a and β. Small a's are often used for structural coefficients in the general case.

or $(-\frac{1}{2})^t$ 10. This every-other-period oscillation will later be seen to be important in connection with the cobweb cycle.

Later, in Case IV we shall study the case of a repeated stream of investment which causes income to grow to a new "multiplied" level. But already we have seen how the simpler case of a single non-repeated impulse of investment is to be handled.

Let us make the conventional assumption that "today's" extra consumption, $C(t)$, is always some fixed fraction—say $\frac{3}{4}$—of yesterday's extra disposable income, $Y(t-1)$. Then, in the initial period of a single impulse of investment of spending, extra consumption is still zero and extra income is equal to the single pulse of investment spending, I_0. In subsequent periods after investment has disappeared, income is equal to consumption, which in turn is a fixed fraction of previous income. Thus, we have the difference equation system

$$\begin{cases} Y(t) = C(t) + o = \frac{3}{4} Y(t-1), \text{ or } Y(t+1) = \frac{3}{4} Y(t) \\ Y(o) = o + I_0 \end{cases} \quad (5)$$

Obviously, therefore, the resulting pattern of income is the decaying geometrical progression

t	o	1	2	. . .	t	t + 1	. . .	∞
$Y(t)$	I_0	$\frac{3}{4} I_0$	$(\frac{3}{4})^2 I_0$	. . .	$(\frac{3}{4})^t I_0$	$\frac{3}{4} Y(t)$	. . .	o

Another example illustrates the rate of price increase as a result of a wartime inflationary gap. Suppose the government is willing to release only k_1 per cent of full-employment production for civilian use; and suppose that families and businesses insist upon spending on civilian goods $k_2 > k_1$ per cent of their full-employment real income. Let us define our time units so that there is a lag of one period between receipt of civilian income and its expenditure. Then the impasse can only be circumvented by having prices bid up in each period by just enough to ration out the goods released for civilian use. The excess spending of "yesterday's" income is handled by letting prices rise enough to induce "forced saving."

The growth rate of prices can be shown[9] to be proportional to $\left(\dfrac{k_2}{k_1}\right)^t$.

This says that the rate of price inflation is increased by a shortened expenditure lag and by large government use of resources relative to voluntary saving.

---

[9] T. Koopmans, "The Dynamics of Inflation," *Review of Economic Statistics*, May 1942, XXIV, pp. 53–65. See also J. M. Keynes, *How to Pay for the War* (London, 1940), and the later "inflationary gap" discussions.

CASE II. CONTINUOUS COMPOUNDING AND DIFFERENTIAL
EQUATION RATE ANALYSIS

So far we have been concerned with "period analysis" over discrete time. In contradistinction, rate analysis concerns itself with flows, with instantaneous rates of change, with speeds, or in calculus terms, with derivatives. These "differential equation" procedures are closely related to the "difference equation" procedures of period analysis.

To see this, let us return to the compound interest example. Suppose the rate of interest were 100 per cent per annum so that $1 + i = 1 + 1 = 2$. Then the value of an asset would double every year, or grow like the progression 2^t.

What if a bank now offered us 50 per cent interest compounded every 6 months? or 33⅓ per cent compounded every 4 months? or 1/100 per cent compounded every 1/n of a year? Because of interest earned on interest within the year, we should obviously find ourselves successively better off. But no matter how indefinitely small the period of compounding becomes, we shall never find ourselves better off by more than an important limiting value. It will be found that 100 per cent interest *compounded instantaneously* causes a principal to grow at the rate of $(2.71828..)^t$ or $(1+1.71828..)^t$—or in words, at the same rate as 171.828.. per cent compounded only once a year.

The important number 2.71828.. is called by mathematicians e (after Euler, and because it is the basic "exponential" number).[10] It bridges the

---

[10] Mathematically,
$$e = \lim_{n \to \infty} \left(1 + \frac{1}{n}\right)^n = 1 + \frac{(1)}{1} + \frac{(1)^2}{1 \cdot 2} + \frac{(1)^3}{1 \cdot 2 \cdot 3} + \cdots + \frac{(1)^s}{1 \cdot 2 \cdot 3 \cdots s} + \cdots$$
and also we have the "magic series"
$$e^t = 1 + \frac{(t)}{1} + \frac{(t)^2}{1 \cdot 2} + \cdots + \frac{(t)^s}{1 \cdot 2 \cdots s} + \cdots$$
Using the simplest rules for differentiating a power, the reader can easily deduce from this series the remarkable fact that e^t is its own first derivative. Also that the proportional rate of change of e^{mt} is m. Even without expressing e^t as a series, we can see that it is the only function of t that has a derivative equal to itself. More generally, let us ask for the function whose derivative is proportional to itself, or which satisfies the differential equation.
$$\frac{dx(t)}{dt} = m\,x(t)$$
$$x(o) = x_0$$
where m is any constant.
We may rewrite this as
$$\frac{dx}{x} = m\,dt$$
or, since percentage and logarithmic changes are the same thing, as
$$d \log_e x = m\,dt;$$

gap between discrete difference equation analysis and continuous differential equation analysis.

Let us now summarize our conclusions:

(1) Any process which grows continuously at a constant instantaneous percentage rate, m—i.e., which satisfies the differential equation

$$\frac{1}{y(t)}\frac{dy(t)}{dt} = m \quad or \quad \frac{dy(t)}{dt} = m\,y(t) \tag{6}$$

—has for its solution the exponential expression

$$y(t) = (2.71828 . .)^{mt}\,y_0 = e^{mt}y_0$$

where y_0 is the initial value of the process.

(2) An interest rate of i per year compounded once a year grows like $(1+i)^t$. But when compounded instantaneously, a percentage rate of i per year gives rise to the faster growth rate of e^{it} or $[(2.718 . .)^i]^t$. When i is very near to zero, the expressions for instantaneous and discrete compounding are not very far apart.[11]

(3) Thus, just as $X(t) = M^t\,X_0$ is the solution of the simplest *difference* equation, so is $x(t) = e^{mt}\,x_0$ the corresponding solution of the simplest *differential* equation of continuous growth. And just as $-1<M<1$ leads to a decaying, settling-down solution, so does m<0 lead to a stable solution. When m is negative the rapidly growing exponential term is thrown into the denominator, and the solution decays away to the stable

---

and, taking the indefinite integral of both sides (which is just the opposite of differentiation), we have

$$d \log_e x = mdt,$$
$$\int \log_e x = \int mt + K$$

Taking anti-logs of both sides, we get

$$x = e^{mt}\,e^K = e^{mt}\,K'$$

We may easily determine the constant K' from the initial condition

$$x(0) = K'\,e^0 = x_0$$

or

$$K' = x_0 \quad and$$
$$x(t) = e^{mt}\,x_0$$

is our solution.

[11] There is also some *instantaneous* rate of interest, called ?, which will give the same growth rate as will *i* compounded *once per annum*. This is defined by the equation

$$e^? = (1 + i)$$

But, in mathematical language, the power to which e must be raised to equal $(1 + i)$ is called the "natural logarithm of $(1 + i)$" and therefore we can write

$$? = \log_e (1 + i)$$

because, by definition

$$e^? = e^{\log_e (1+i)} = (1 + i)$$

The exponentials and logarithms are like man and wife; they are opposites in the same sense that P and Q are opposites along a demand curve. If we run up to the curve $y = e^t$ vertically from the horizontal axis and read off the vertical ordinate, we have the exponential function $y = e^t$. If we pick a y value and run horizontally over the curve and read off the corresponding t value, we have the natural logarithm of y, or $t = \log_e y$.

equilibrium level. Likewise $|M| > 1$ and $m > 0$ lead to explosive instability, or to growth at an exponential rate.

CASE III. CAPITAL FORMATION, CAPITAL, AND INCOME[12]

Let us illustrate the case of continuous growth by a number of examples. If we write the stock of capital as $K(t)$, then net investment, $I(t)$, is nothing but the derivative or rate of increase of $K(t)$, $\dfrac{dK(t)}{dt}$. Under what conditions will investment be always proportional to the stock of capital? The answer is simple:

$$\frac{dK(t)}{dt} = mK(t) \tag{8}$$

only when $K(t) = e^{mt} K_0$ and when $\dfrac{dK(t)}{dt} = e^{mt} (mK_0)$ $$= e^{mt} I_0 \tag{9}$$

Only in the case of steady exponential growth can the proportion between a stock and a flow be maintained.

Similarly, as Domar has shown, the public debt and its rate of change, the deficit, will remain proportional to income if, and only if, all three magnitudes are growing or decaying at a compound-interest or exponential rate. Or, as numerous writers have shown, births and deaths and the relative number of people in different age groups can only remain invariant if population is rising or falling at an exponential rate.

A more complicated problem has been posed by Harrod and Domar. What are the conditions of economic expansion which will cause (a) capital, $K(t)$, and income, $Y(t)$, to grow *proportionally* and at such a rate that (b) investment, $I(t)$ or $\dfrac{dK(t)}{dt}$, will be equal to the exact fraction of income, a, that people try to save at full employment? Writers on the acceleration principle often use the letter β to denote the ratio between the capital stock and flow of income.

In symbols

$$K(t) = \beta Y(t)$$
$$I(t) = \frac{dK(t)}{dt} = aY(t) \tag{10}$$

---

[12] E. D. Domar, *op. cit.*; also *idem*, "The 'Burden of the Debt' and National Income," *American Economic Review*, December 1944, XXXIV, pp. 798–827; and R. F. Harrod, "An Essay in Dynamic Theory," *Economic Journal*, March 1939, XLIX, pp. 14–33.

Hence

$$\frac{dK(t)}{dt} = \left(\frac{a}{\beta}\right) K(t)$$

implying that

$$K(t) = e^{\frac{\alpha}{\beta}t} K_0$$

$$I(t) = \frac{dK(t)}{dt} = \left(\frac{a}{\beta}\right) e^{\frac{\alpha}{\beta}t} K_0 = e^{\frac{\alpha}{\beta}t} I_0 \qquad (11)$$

$$Y(t) = e^{\frac{\alpha}{\beta}t} Y_0$$

In words, the smaller is the ratio of capital to income, β, and the greater is the fraction of income saved, a, the faster must the economic top keep spinning if full employment is to be maintained from growth factors alone. The following table shows, for different values of a and β, the indicated necessary rate of dynamic growth if full employment is to be self-maintained.

"NEEDED" RATE OF GROWTH UNDER VARIOUS CONDITIONS
(in % per year)

Saving Proportion, a	"Relation" of Capital to Annual Income, β			
	½	1	4	10
0%	0	0	0	0
10%	20	10	2½	1
20%	40	20	5	2

So far, our flow analysis of investment and capital has yielded only exponential growth trends. However, it is easy to illustrate a decay toward a stationary position of equilibrium. We have only to suppose that the level of investment, $I(t)$, becomes positive whenever the level of capital, $K(t)$, is below a crucial equilibrium level, $\overline{K}$; and investment is negative whenever capital exceeds that equilibrium level. (The level of $\overline{K}$, we may assume, depends on the interest rate, income, and the state of technology.)

In simplest terms, let I be proportional to $[\overline{K} - K(t)]$, called $- [k(t)]$ or

$$I(t) = -m [K(t) - \overline{K}] = -m \, k(t)$$

But since

$$\frac{dK(t)}{dt} = \frac{d[K(t) - \overline{K}]}{dt} = \frac{dK(t)}{dt} - o = I(t)$$

we have

$$\frac{dk(t)}{dt} = -m\,k(t) \qquad\qquad (12)$$

and

$$k(t) = e^{-mt}\,k_0 \qquad\qquad (13)$$

so that the deviation, $k(t)$, approaches zero, and $K(t)$ approaches in the long run to $\overline{K}$.

Cyclical oscillations will occur if an excess of capital, rather than leading to negative investment, instead leads to a "deceleration" of the algebraic rate of investment. In this case

$$\frac{dI}{dt} = -m\,k(t) \qquad\qquad (14)$$

or

$$\frac{d}{dt}\left[\frac{dk(t)}{dt}\right] = \frac{d^2k(t)}{dt^2} = -m\,k(t) \qquad\qquad (15)$$

Thus, the rate of investment will decrease algebraically in proportion to the amount of excess capital.

As is shown in the Appendix, such a system gives rise to sinusoidal oscillations around the equilibrium—oscillations which are exactly like those of a pendulum. Intuitively, we can glimpse this as follows: Suppose capital is growing, and it pushes through its equilibrium level. Its inertia causes it to overshoot the mark, because the positive level of investment is only gradually tapering off. But after capital has grown to a critical peak, its decelerating effects finally cause investment to become negative. Capital is now returning toward its equilibrium level at an increasing rate. It passes through the equilibrium level with negative investment at its peak rate. Now there is a downward over-shoot, which lasts until the gradual acceleration of investment, due to capital shortage, causes investment to become positive—at which point capital has reached its trough and has begun to revive. And so forth.

CASE IV. THE MULTIPLICATION OF A STREAM OF INVESTMENT

R. F. Kahn, J. M. Clark, J. M. Keynes, Fritz Machlup, and others have analyzed the case whereby a new plateau of income will—after a spending lag—lead to a new higher plateau of investment.[13] Instead of the single impulse of investment discussed earlier, we now have a constant stream of new impulses, and after we have superimposed their effects, we finally build up to a new steady state. This takes time because extra consumption at time t, $C(t)$, is supposed to be a fraction, a, of extra disposable income at time $t - 1$, $Y(t - 1)$.

Mathematically, we always have the income identity

$$Y(t + 1) = C(t + 1) + I(t + 1)$$

and now after the new steady level of investment spending begins at time $t = 0$, $I(t) = \overline{I}$, so that

$$Y(t + 1) = C(t + 1) + \overline{I} = aY(t) + \overline{I} \qquad (16)$$
$$Y(0) = \overline{I}$$

This is a difference equation which generates its own solution. But something new has been added; the constant investment term, $\overline{I}$, means that the solution will not be a geometric progression decaying away to zero, as in the case of the response to a single pulse of spending. Instead, the system will grow so as to "decay away" to a new equilibrium plateau of income. Our solution can be thought of as consisting of two parts: a "new equilibrium component" and a temporary transient; or

$$Y(t) = \overline{Y} - M^t K$$

where $\overline{Y}$ is the new stationary equilibrium level of (extra) income, and where $M^t K$ is called a "transient" because it will finally disappear as a subtraction from the new income level.

After some experimentation, one will find it wise to work with deviations from the new equilibrium income level, $\overline{Y}$. That is, we define $y(t) = Y(t) - \overline{Y}$, even though we don't know yet what $\overline{Y}$ is—except that if we put $\overline{Y}$ into our system it must repeat itself. Therefore

$$\text{Let } Y(t) = \overline{Y}$$
$$Y(t + 1) = \overline{Y}$$

---

[13] R. F. Kahn, op. cit.; J. M. Clark, The Economics of Planning Public Works (Washington, 1935); J. M. Keynes, The Means to Prosperity (New York, 1933); F. Machlup,

and

$$Y(t + 1) = aY(t) + \bar{I} \text{ becomes } \bar{Y} = a\bar{Y} + \bar{I} \qquad (17)$$

or

$$\bar{Y} = \frac{1}{1 - a}\bar{I}$$

Obviously, $1/(1 - a)$ is the ultimate "multiplier," and it can always be solved for statically by forgetting the time subscripts on the Y's, and solving our dynamic equations for a timeless or stationary income level.

What happens now if we put $Y(t) - \bar{Y} = Y(t) - \frac{1}{1 - a}\bar{I} = y(t)$ in our basic dynamic equation? The stationary income level terms will then just cancel out the stationary level of new spending, and we will be left with

$$[Y(t) - \bar{Y}] = a[Y(t - 1) - \bar{Y}]$$
$$Y(o) - \bar{Y} = \bar{I} - \frac{1}{1 - a}\bar{I} = -\frac{a}{1 - a}\bar{I}$$

or with

$$y(t + 1) = ay(t)$$
$$y(o) = \frac{-a}{1 - a}\bar{I}$$

But this is a simple difference equation with the simple geometric progression solution:

$$y(t) = -a^t\left(\frac{a}{1 - a}\bar{I}\right)$$

so that our final solution for $Y(t)$ becomes

$$Y(t) = \frac{1}{1 - a}\bar{I} - a^t\left(\frac{a}{1 - a}\bar{I}\right)$$

Therefore, if $o < a < 1$, Y will climb from $\bar{I}$ dollars up indefinitely close to $\bar{I}/(1 - a)$ dollars. The following table provides a quick summary of the results reached thus far in the analysis of a constant stream of investment.

"Period Analysis and Multiplier Theory," reprinted from the 1939 *Quarterly Journal of Economics* in *Readings in Business Cycle Theory*, pp. 203–234.

t	0	1	2	...	t	$t+1$	...	∞
$Y(t)$	$(1)\bar{I}$	$(1+a)\bar{I}$	$(1+a+a^2)\bar{I}$	...	$(1+a+a^2+\cdots+a^t)\bar{I}$ $=\dfrac{1-a^{t+1}}{1-a}\bar{I}$		...	$\dfrac{1}{1-a}\bar{I}$
$Y(t)-Y(\infty)$	$(1)\bar{I}-\dfrac{\bar{I}}{1-a}$ $=-1\left(\dfrac{a}{1-a}\right)\bar{I}$	$(1+a)\bar{I}-\dfrac{1}{1-a}\bar{I}$ $=-a\left(\dfrac{a}{1-a}\right)\bar{I}$		...	$\dfrac{1}{1-a}\bar{I}-a^t\left(\dfrac{a}{1-a}\right)\bar{I}$	$aY(t)+\bar{I}$	...	0
$=y(t)$	$=-1\left(\dfrac{a}{1-a}\right)\bar{I}$		$-a^2\left(\dfrac{a}{1-a}\right)\bar{I}$	...	$-a^t\left(\dfrac{a}{1-a}\right)\bar{I}$	$ay(t)+0$	...	

We may summarize the general mathematical case as follows: Suppose that instead of a simple difference equation of the form

$$X(t+1) = a X(t)$$
$$X(o) = X_0$$

we have a constant term as well, or

$$X(t+1) = a X(t) + A$$
$$X(o) = X_0 \qquad (18)$$

Then our solution consists of two terms: a "steady state" solution, $\overline{X}$, plus a "transient" of the form $M^t K$, or,

$$X(t) = \overline{X} + M^t K$$

where $\overline{X}$ is found by substituting X with no time subscripts in both sides of the equation and then solving statically to get

$$\overline{X} = \frac{1}{1-a} A \qquad (19)$$

and where $M^t K$ depicts the deviations from equilibrium

$$x(t) = X(t) - \overline{X} = X(t) - \frac{1}{1-a} A$$

satisfying the simple difference equation

$$x(t+1) = a x(t)$$
$$x(o) = X_0 - \frac{1}{1-a} A \qquad (20)$$

Hence, our full final solution[14] becomes

$$X(t) = \frac{1}{1-a} A + a^t \left(X_0 - \frac{A}{1-a} \right) \qquad (21)$$

It may be remarked that X_0 will often equal A, if previously the system has been in equilibrium at zero.

If a is less than one in absolute value, and only then, will the solution settle down to a new equilibrium level. Otherwise it will explode.

---

[14] In the special "resonant" case where $a = 1$, no stationary solution exists. In this case the solution grows steadily according to the law $X(t) = X_0 + At$, as can be verified by taking the limit as $a \to 1$ of the general expression (21).

CASE V. COBWEB CYCLES[15]

An example that throws light on the nature of business cycles as well as on the requirements for a stable equilibrium is that of the familiar cobweb phenomenon. This is a beautiful case because its formal difficulties are so slight, and yet at the same time it illuminates the basic problems so clearly.

We make the usual assumption that the demand curve relates this period's price, $P(t)$, to this period's quantity, $Q(t)$. But this period's

Table 1

$Q(t)$	Demand Relationship $P(t)$	Supply Relationship $P(t-1)$
0	200	50
30	170	65
50	150	75
60	140	80
70	130	85
80	120	90
90	110	95
100†	100†	100†
110	90	105
120	80	110
121	79	118
122	78	126
123	77	134
124	76	142
125	75	150
126	74	158
127	73	166
128	72	174
129	71	182
130	70	190

† Equilibrium level.

[15] For references, see M. Ezekiel, "The Cobweb Theorem," reprinted from the 1938 *Quarterly Journal of Economics* in *Readings in Business Cycle Theory*, pp. 422–442. The definitive treatment of non-linearity is that of W. Leontief, "Verzögerte Angebots-anpassung und Partielles Gleichgewicht," *Zeitschrift für Nationalökonomie*, 1934, V, pp. 670–676.

quantity supplied, Q(t), is assumed to be a determinate function of last period's market price, P(t − 1). The length of our time period is that between seasons of a crop, or between the starting of the productive process and the pouring of goods onto the market.

For simplicity, let us suppose that $\overline{P} = 100$ and $\overline{Q} = 100$ represents the unique point of intersection of the assumed supply and demand relations. Obviously, this is the only equilibrium level which will be self-maintaining through time if once established. But is it a stable equilibrium in the sense that a disturbance—such as might be caused by bad weather—will be followed by a return to equilibrium level? Or will P and Q depart ever further from equilibrium if once disturbed? In any case, what are the laws of motion of the system when out of equilibrium?

To make matters simple, let us assume a linear demand relation of the sort that each one-unit increase in quantity is followed by a one-unit decrease in the price for which it will sell. If Q(t) goes from 100 to 100 + h, then P(t) will go from 100 down to 100 − h.

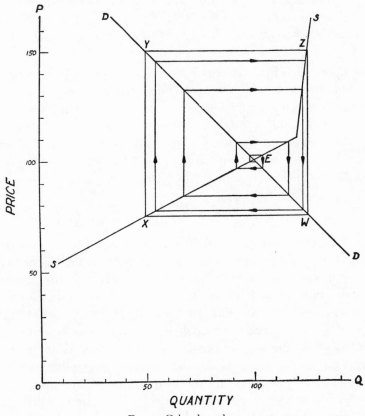

FIG. 1. Cobweb cycles.

Our assumption about supply will be a little more interesting. First, let us suppose that each one-unit increase in P(t) will be followed in the next year by a two-unit change in quantity supplied, Q(t + 1). But to add variety to the problem, let us suppose that this 2Q for 1P relation holds only for price changes between $50 and $110, and that at all higher prices there is so much cost resistance to further expansion of output that there is only 1/8 of a unit change in Q(t + 1) for each unit change in P(t).

Figure 1 depicts our demand-supply relations, D-D and S-S. Table 1 illustrates the same numerically for selected numbers, between which the reader can linearly interpolate.

Because the supply curve consists of two straight lines intersecting in a corner, we have a curvilinear rather than a linear system. And, as we shall see, this introduces new richness into the problem that will make possible something that is important for the study of business cycles—namely, a theory of the unique amplitude of *cyclical* fluctuations.

Let us now experiment with our model. If we start out with Q(o) = 100, obviously P(o) = 100, Q(1) = 100, P(1) = 100, ... and so forth. This equilibrium state is depicted for Q in Figure 2 by the horizontal line $\overline{Q}$.

But suppose that for some reason we started out with Q one unit above the equilibrium, so that Q(o) = 101. Then from our demand curve, P(o) = 99; but next year's supply will subsequently fall short of 100 by 2 units, or Q(1) = 98, and P(1) = 102. It is easy to show—as in columns 2 and 3 of Table 2—that our Q's and P's begin to depart ever further from the equilibrium level in an explosively oscillatory way according to the formula.

$$Q(t) = 100 + (-2)^t [Q(o) - \overline{Q}]$$
$$P(t) = 100 - (-2)^t [Q(o) - \overline{Q}] = 100 + (-2)^t [P(o) - \overline{P}] \quad (22)$$

The geometric rate of oscillatory explosion is $(-2)^t$ because the numerical slope of the supply curve is twice as flat as that of the demand curve. If the condition were reversed, the solution would spiral in toward the stable equilibrium level at the rate of $(-\frac{1}{2})^t$. If the slopes were exactly equal in absolute value, then we would have a sort of "neutral equilibrium," with motion around it in closed boxes whose dimensions depend only on the size of the initial disturbance. With no further disturbances, the cycles would not be changing in amplitude, but there would still be no possibility of a theory of a unique amplitude.

But let us not forget the curvilinearity of our system. All the above holds only so long as P remains below $110. Above this figure, our

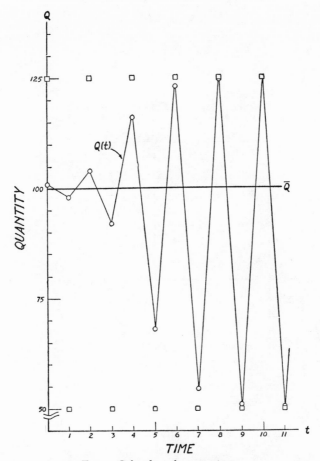

FIG. 2. Cobweb cycles over time.

simple geometric progressions no longer hold. This is shown in Table 2, beyond the time, $t = 5$.

Because of non-linearity, the simple pattern of our sonnet is ruptured, but there remains rhyme and reason in our verse. First, it is clear from the figures that the oscillation of price and quantity continues, but no longer at such an explosive rate. Indeed, Figure 1 shows that the oscillation is growing until it approaches the "box" YZWX. For if Q ever reached 125 or fell to 50, it would subsequently go round and round the box forever. If ever Q exceeded this range, it would spiral back toward the YZWX box. In actuality, without a new disturbance, Q and P can never quite reach the promised land of the box, but will approach indefinitely close toward it.

We may conclude that in a non-linear system, there may occur certain special periodic motions. These cycles with definite amplitudes can be

Table 2

COBWEB CYCLE AWAY FROM EQUILIBRIUM
AND TOWARD A STABLE PERIODIC BOX MOTION

Time	Quantity	Price	New Era Time	Periodic Box Motions		$Q - Q^*$	$P - P^*$
t	Q	P	$t' = t-6$	Q^*	P^*	q	p
0	101	99					
1	98	102					
2	104	96					
3	92	108					
4	116	84					
5	68	132					
6	$122\frac{3}{4}$	$77\frac{1}{4}$	0	125	75	$-2\frac{1}{4} = -\frac{9}{4}$	$+2\frac{1}{4}$
7	$54\frac{1}{2}$	$145\frac{1}{2}$	1	50	150	$+4\frac{1}{2} = \frac{9}{2}$	$-4\frac{1}{2}$
8	$124\frac{7}{16}$	$75\frac{9}{16}$	2	125	75	$-\frac{9}{16} = -(\frac{1}{4})\frac{9}{4}$	$+\frac{9}{16}$
9	$51\frac{1}{8}$	$148\frac{7}{8}$	3	50	150	$1\frac{1}{8} = (\frac{1}{4})\frac{9}{2}$	$-1\frac{1}{8}$
10	$124\frac{55}{64}$	$75\frac{9}{64}$	4	125	75	$-\frac{9}{64} = -(\frac{1}{4})^2\frac{9}{4}$	$+\frac{9}{64}$
11	$50\frac{9}{32}$	$149\frac{23}{32}$	5	50	150	$\frac{9}{32} = (\frac{1}{4})^2\frac{9}{2}$	$-\frac{9}{32}$
...							
$2t-12$	$125+q(t)$	$75+p(t)$	$2t'$	125	75	$-\frac{1}{8}q(2t'-1)$ $= -(\frac{1}{4})''\frac{9}{4}$	$-q(2t')$
$2t-11$	$50+q(t)$	$150+p(t)$	$2t'+1$	50	150	$-2q(2t') = (\frac{1}{4})''\frac{9}{2}$	$-q(2t'+1)$
...							
2∞	125	75	2∞	125	75	0	0
$2\infty+1$	50	150	$2\infty+1$	50	150	0	0

thought of as "generalized equilibrium states," which may be stable or unstable. As Leontief has shown in the cited article, there may even be boxes within boxes, alternately stable and unstable.

Let us take a further step. What are the quantitative laws of approach to the periodic box motion YZWX, or to $[Q^*(t), P^*(t)] = [50,150]$; $[125,75]$; $[50,150]$; $[125,75]$; etc.?[16]

Previously when we were interested in the behavior of our system around the equilibrium point $(\overline{Q}, \overline{P}) = (100, 100)$, our crucial variables were the deviations $[Q(t) - \overline{Q}]$ and $[P(t) - \overline{P}]$. Similarly, now we are interested in the deviations around the periodic box motions $[Q^*(t), P^*(t)]$. It is convenient, therefore, to work from now on with the new deviations

$$q(t) = Q(t) - Q^*(t)$$
$$p(t) = P(t) - P^*(t) \qquad (23)$$

Also, like Mussolini, Lenin, Napoleon, and the Church, we find it convenient to begin to count our time periods from the date of introduction of the revolutionary non-linearity—so that our new t' will be o when the old t was 6. Columns 4–8 have been added to Table 2 to show the new era data.

If we look at our table, it becomes clear that the deviations from the box are approaching zero. It is less obvious, but careful attention will show that the numerical value of each odd-year quantity deviation is going downhill in a geometric progression, and the same is true of each even-year quantity deviation. But the two rates of decay are quite different, that of the even years being like $-\frac{3}{4}, ., -(\frac{1}{4})\frac{3}{4}, ., -(\frac{1}{4})^2\frac{3}{4}, .;$ the odd years being like $\frac{1}{2}, ., (\frac{1}{4})\frac{1}{2}, ., (\frac{1}{4})^2\frac{1}{2}, \ldots$.

It is exactly as if our deviations satisfied the difference equation system

$$q(t' + 1) = M\, q(t')$$
$$q(o) = -\frac{3}{4} \qquad (24)$$

but where the M coefficient is a periodic function of time, being -2 when t is odd and $-\frac{1}{8}$ when t is even.[17]

---

[16] It may be noted that we can write this special periodic motion in the trick way

$$Q^*(t) = 50\frac{(1)^t + (-1)^t}{2} + 125\frac{(1)^t - (-1)^t}{2}$$

$$P^*(t) = 150\frac{(1)^t + (-1)^t}{2} + 75\frac{(1)^t - (-1)^t}{2} = 200 - Q^*(t)$$

where $(1)^t$ and $(-1)^t$ cancel each other out in the proper way depending upon whether t is even or odd.

[17] Generally, we find the M coefficients alternate, in one case being the ratio of the supply and demand curves' flatness on the left side of the YZWX box, and in the other

Mathematically, this introduction of coefficients which are periodic functions of time turns out to be the general case when the stability of a periodic motion is to be tested. But where in the region of non-linear dynamics Henri Poincaré, G. D. Birkhoff, van der Pol, and other mathematicians tread warily, we shall venture no further. However, the reader should verify that when Q starts out at any value greater than 150, the resulting motion spirals in toward the box in even-odd geometric progressions.

The above cases provide an introduction to the economics of dynamic processes. But as soon as we encounter models involving several periods of time or higher derivatives, the exact quantitative treatment becomes somewhat more complex—although still within the scope of elementary college mathematics.

(Thus, in the simplest model where the Acceleration Principle and the multiplier interact, we will encounter for $a = \frac{1}{2}$ and $\beta = 2$, the difference equation

$$y(t+2) = 1.5\,y(t+1) - y(t) \qquad\qquad (25)$$

and instead of its having for its solution simple exponential terms of the form M^t, we find that the answer leads to a pure sine wave of about 9 years' duration. If $a\beta < 1$, we get a sine wave which is multiplied by a dampening exponential factor; and if $a\beta > 1$, we get explosive oscillations.)

The Appendix provides a bird's eye survey of some aspects of the more complex analysis necessary if the economist is to follow closely recent work in business cycle, income, and value theory.

IV. CONCLUSION

The significance of dynamic analysis for economics may be briefly sketched, along with some indications of possible future trends in the field.

In the first place, the economist has no choice but to study dynamics; for otherwise there is little possibility of presenting a reasonably realistic description of such phenomena as speculation, cyclical fluctuations, and secular growth. In addition, dynamic process analysis is an enormously flexible mode of thought, both for pinning down the implications of various hypotheses and for investigating new possibilities.

---

case the corresponding ratio on the right-hand side of the box. So long as the geometric mean of the supply slopes is less than the geometric mean of the absolute demand slopes, the periodic motion will be stable.

Actually, it is so flexible a method that there are dangers involved in its use: the number of conceivable models is literally infinite and a lifetime may be spent in exploring possibilities; furthermore, by supplying the proper stage directions at the proper time, we can specify any sort of a sequence development desired and may find that there is almost no empirical content in the theory being expounded.[18]

Nonetheless, despite these possible pitfalls, dynamic analysis has produced many useful results. In the field of pure theory, the important problem of the *stability of equilibrium* is wholly a question of dynamics. For it involves the question of how a system behaves after it has been disturbed into a disequilibrium state.

As an example, let us consider the case of an agricultural or labor market characterized by a so-called "backward rising" supply curve. The higher the price, the smaller is the amount supplied. It used to be thought that this necessarily led to cumulative price instability because "a reduction in demand will reduce price, which will increase quantity, which will reduce price, and so forth indefinitely." This reasoning is quite wrong. If the supply curve is steeper than the demand curve, the market will be stable with the above-described tortoise-hare sequence being a convergent one.

The relevance of dynamics for the problem of stability of equilibrium will come as no surprise to anyone who thinks seriously about the matter. Less expected is the fact that knowledge about dynamic stability leads to information about the "comparative statical" behavior of a system. Thus, we can rule out the hypothesis that the marginal propensity to consume is constantly greater than one if we reject the assumption of instability of income determination. This alone tells us that the multiplier —a comparative-statics concept—is positive rather than negative.[19] This relation between comparative statics and dynamics I have elsewhere called the "correspondence principle."[20]

But it is probably in the field of business cycles proper that dynamic analysis has proved itself most indispensable. Implicit theoretical concepts have been sharpened by translation into dynamic terms, and useful distinctions have been made between exogenous, endogenous, and mixed cyclical theories.

Thus dynamic analysis is able to show that innovations may cause quasi-periodic oscillations even if they are not themselves distributed in

---

[18] An example of this is provided by the notion of a "self-generating" business cycle, during which "costs overtake revenues" and "dictate a downturn," etc.

[19] From dynamics we set up the hypothesis that $|a| < 1$, which implies $\frac{1}{1-a} > 0$.

[20] *Foundations of Economic Analysis*, Ch. IX, X.

a smooth oscillation. Even irregular random shocks may keep a cycle alive if the economic system's structure is not heavily "damped."

At the other extreme, dynamics can clear up a false difficulty that has been raised in connection with a self-generating cycle theory. It used to be thought that such a theory begged the question, by assuming the presence of the cycle whose existence was to be proved. But actually, a non-cyclical disturbance can be shown to be capable of starting off a repeating, self-perpetuating oscillation. And if indeed the system can be shown to perpetuate a cycle once started, it is only too easy to envisage, throughout the course of all history, disturbances sufficient to explain why the "first" cycles should have gotten started.

Dynamic process analysis also liberates economists from the necessity of having separate theories of the "turning-points" in addition to theories of cumulative upward and downward swings. Even a simple theory of inventory cycles, or acceleration-multipliers, can explain all four phases of an idealized cycle.[21]

At its best, dynamic analysis can enrich our understanding of possibilities without leading to credulity in new, over-narrow, monistic dogmas concerning the cyclical process. In the hands of an eclectic economist whose judgment stems from an immersion in history and statistics, dynamic analysis could lead to the hypothesis that the weighting of exogenous and endogenous factors is quite different for the so-called 50-year-long (Kondratieff) waves than it is for the "major cycles" which average slightly less than a decade in length, or for the shorter inventory-credit cycles, or for the cycles of the American construction industry.

But to explore further developments in this field would carry us over into the fields of econometrics and theory, and out of the present into the future.

---

[21] A fact which is overlooked by chastened prophets who, after every short-term downturn, utter plaintively, "But inventories did not seem high relative to sales."

Appendix

PROCESSES INVOLVING SEVERAL PERIODS

As soon as we leave the simpler cases, where today's variable depends only upon its value at one previous time period, the situation becomes a little more complicated. For example, if one combines the Acceleration Principle with the multiplier, or if one works out a theory of inventory cycle, or if one works with many countries in international trade—in all of these cases[22] national income turns out to depend on its own value at more than one previous period. In short, we end up with something like, say,

$$Y(t + 2) = 5Y(t + 1) - 6Y(t) + A \qquad (26)$$

instead of just

$$Y(t + 2) = 5Y(t + 1) + A$$

As before, we have a "steady-state" part, $\overline{Y}$, in addition to a "transient." This "steady-state" can be found statically by putting $\overline{Y}$ on both sides of the equation:

$$\overline{Y} = 5\overline{Y} - 6\overline{Y} + A$$

or

$$Y = \frac{1}{1 - 5 + 6} A = \tfrac{1}{2} A \qquad (27)$$

As before, the transient can be found by working with deviations from $\overline{Y}$, i.e., with $y(t) = Y(t) - \overline{Y}$; and as before we end up with a "reduced" or "homogeneous" difference equation possessing no constant term, A:

$$y(t + 2) = 5y(t + 1) - 6y(t) + 0 \qquad (28)$$

---

[22] L. A. Metzler, op. cit.; idem, "Nature and Stability of Inventory Cycles," Review of Economic Studies, August 1941, XXIII, pp. 113–129; F. Machlup, International Trade and the National Income Multiplier (Philadelphia, 1943); P. A. Samuelson, "Interactions between the Multiplier Analysis and the Principle of Acceleration," reprinted from the 1939 Review of Economic Statistics in Readings in Business Cycle Theory, pp. 261–269. For a fuller mathematical treatment of difference and differential equations, see P. A. Samuelson, Foundations of Economic Analysis, Mathematical Appendix B, and references cited there.

Of course, now it takes two starting or initial values to get the sequence going. But clearly if we know $Y(o)$ and $Y(1)$, we can also calculate $y(o)$ and $y(1)$. Our system can therefore be written in the form

$$\begin{cases} y(t+2) - 5y(t+1) + 6y(t) = o \\ y(o) = y_0 \\ y(1) = y_1 \end{cases} \tag{29}$$

Can we now expect the solution to this many-period equation to be of the simple geometric progression form $M^t K$? The answer is "not quite." Our system now will have *two* fundamental exponential responses, in much the way that striking a key on the piano will sound higher overtones as well as the key's own fundamental pitch. The quality of the final note depends upon the superposition of these different exponential sequences.

If three past periods were involved in our process, we could expect "three fundamental geometric progression responses"; and if our difference equation were of the nth order, we would have n geometric progression responses.

t	0	1	2	3	4	. . .	t	$t+1$	$t+2$	∞
$y_1(t)$	1	3	9	27	3^4	. . .	3^t	3^{t+1}	$3^t 3^2$	∞
$y_2(t)$	1	2	4	8	2^4	. . .	2^t	2^{t+1}	$2^t 2^2$	∞
$y_3(t)$	1	4	14	46	$3^4(2)-2^4$	. . .	$3^t 2-2^t$	$3^{t+1}2-2^{t+1}$	$+5y_3(t+1)-6y_3(t)$	∞

Perhaps the above numerical example will help make this clear. Consider

$$y(t+2) - 5y(t+1) + 6y(t) = o$$
$$y(o) = 1$$
$$y(1) = 3$$

Then we have the sequence shown in the first row of the above table. Obviously, $y_1(t) = 3^t(1)$ is a solution.

But consider

$$y(t+2) - 5y(t+1) + 6y(t) = o$$
$$y(o) = 1$$
$$y(1) = 2$$

Its solution turns out to be as given in the second row of the table.

Therefore, $2^t(1)$ is a solution to the difference equation as well as

$3^t(1)$. In fact if we start out in the third row with the initial conditions, $y(0) = 1$, $y(1) = 4$, it is not hard to show that the combined progressions

$$y(t) = 3^t(2) - 2^t(1)$$

also form a solution to (29).

How did we guess the fundamental exponential responses 2^t and 3^t? Why not 4^t? Why should there always be as many different fundamental responses as the number of periods in the difference equation? Why not either more or less?

To answer these questions, let us try a response of the form $y(t) = M^t K$, where K and M can be anything at all. Substituting, we find

$$M^{t+2} K - 5M^{t+1} K + 6M^t K = 0$$

or

$$M^t K [M^2 - 5M + 6] = 0 \qquad\qquad (30)$$

Now this equation can be satisfied only if the expression in brackets is zero, once we rule out the uninteresting case where K itself is zero. But the expression in brackets is a polynomial of the second degree in the unknown M. Such a polynomial or quadratic equation has two different roots or solutions, M_1 and M_2.

In this cooked-up case, it is easy to see that

$$M^2 - 5M + 6 = (M - 2)(M - 3) = 0$$

which can be equal to zero for the two cases

$$M_1 = 2$$
$$M_2 = 3$$

Therefore, either

$$M_1{}^t K_1 \text{ or } M_2{}^t K_2$$

is a solution. In fact, their sum

$$y(t) = M_1{}^t K_1 + M_2{}^t K_2$$

is also a solution of the difference equation, no matter what our choice of the two K's. This is very lucky, since we have two different initial conditions which have to be satisfied by an appropriate choice of K's. Specifically

$$y(0) = K_1 + K_2 = y_0$$
$$y(1) = M_1 K_1 + M_2 K_2 = y_1$$

so that

$$K_2 = y_0 - K_1$$

and

$$M_1 K_1 + M_2 y_0 - M_2 K_1 = y_1$$

or

$$K_1 = \frac{1}{M_1 - M_2} y_1 - \frac{M_2}{M_1 - M_2} y_0$$

$$K_2 = \frac{1}{M_2 - M_1} y_1 - \frac{M_1}{M_2 - M_1} y_0$$

To summarize:

(1) When given the difference equation

$$Y(t+2) + a_1 Y(t+1) + a_2 Y(t) = A$$
$$Y(0) = Y_0, \qquad Y(1) = Y_1 \qquad\qquad (31)$$

we solve for the stationary part by setting $Y(t) = Y(t+1) = Y(t+2) = \overline{Y}$ to get

$$\overline{Y} = \frac{1}{1 + a_1 + a_2} A \qquad\qquad (32)$$

(2) To this we add the "transient solution"

$$y(t) = Y(t) - \overline{Y} = M_1{}' K_1 + M_2{}' K_2 \qquad\qquad (33)$$

where $y(t)$ satisfies the difference equation

$$y(t+2) + a_1 y(t+1) + a_2 y(t) = 0$$
$$y(0) = y_0 = Y_0 - \overline{Y}$$
$$y(1) = y_1 = Y_1 - \overline{Y} \qquad\qquad (34)$$

and where M_1 and M_2 are roots of the quadratic equation in M

$$M^2 + a_1 M + a_2 = 0, \qquad\qquad (35)$$

or

$$M_1 = \frac{-a_1 + \sqrt{a_1{}^2 - 4a_2}}{2}, \qquad\qquad (36)$$

$$M_2 = \frac{-a_1 - \sqrt{a_1{}^2 - 4a_2}}{2},$$

and where the K's are defined in terms of the initial conditions, y_0 and y_1, as follows:[23]

$$K_1 = \frac{y_1 - M_2 y_0}{M_1 - M_2}$$

$$K_2 = \frac{y_1 - M_1 y_0}{M_2 - M_1} \qquad (37)$$

Fortunately, in most economic problems we need only know the value of the biggest M, because eventually that will dominate the final solution. Thus,

$$2^t(100) + 3^t(.01)$$

eventually differs by a negligible percentage from $3^t(.01)$.

Hence, regardless of the K's, we need usually only be sure that the largest root M is less than one in absolute value. That being the case, the equilibrium level must be stable and the transient terms must eventually die down.

It does not require much imagination to guess how the general case of n periods is to be handled. Given

$$Y(t+n) + a_1 Y(t+n-1) + \ldots + a_{n-1} Y(t+1) + a_n Y(t) = A \qquad (38)$$

we easily get the solution

$$Y(t) = \frac{1}{1 + a_1 + \ldots + a_n} A + \left[M_1{}^t K_1 + M_2{}^t K_2 + \ldots M_n{}^t K_n \right] \qquad (39)$$

where the M's are the n roots of the nth degree polynomial

$$M^n + a_1 M^{n-1} + \ldots + a_{n-1} M + a_n = (M - M_1)(M - M_2) \cdot \cdot \cdot (M - M_n) = 0 \quad (40)$$

and where the K's depend only on the initial condition.

If, and only if, the largest M is less than one in absolute value, the equilibrium will be stable and the disturbed system will always move back toward it.[24]

---

[23] The reader should verify that in the special case where $y(t+2) = y(t)$, our solution can be written

$$y(t) = \frac{(1)^t + (-1)^t}{2} y_0 + \frac{(1)^t - (-1)^t}{2} y_1$$

which looks similar to footnote 16.

[24] If two or more roots of the polynomial coincide—so that it contains repeated factors of the form $(M - M_1)^{1+s}$—our solutions of the form $M^t K$ will be too few. But the clue

THE MYSTERIOUS COMPLEX ROOTS

However, there is still a mathematical difficulty to be overcome. So simple a sequence as

$$x(t+2) = -x(t)$$
$$x(0) = x_0 \qquad\qquad (41)$$
$$x(1) = x_1$$

when we try the substitution $M^t K$, leads to the quadratic equation
$$M^2 = -1 \qquad\qquad (42)$$
which has no real roots at all. Or to put the matter differently, any geometric progression that begins with 1 and M will give the positive number M^2 for the next term, while our difference equation insists that the next term be negative.

Of course, the mathematician will say that $M^2 = -1$ has two "complex" or "imaginary" roots, $M = + \sqrt{-1}$ and $M = - \sqrt{-1}$, so that $M^2 = \sqrt{(-1)(-1)} = -1$. But as economists interested in the real world, what are imaginary numbers to us? The answer is that, like Voltaire's God, if they did not exist we would still find it convenient to invent them. And, like Mutt and Jeff, they always occur in pairs, with a plus and a minus term involving $\sqrt{-1}$. In pairs which can always be *combined* to form the real numbers that we require as practical men.

As a matter of fact, since $\sqrt{-1}$ raised to any even power is a real number, we may—by the use of the trick shown in note 24—write the solution to the above equation as

$$x(t) = x_0 \left\{ \frac{(1)^t + (-1)^t}{2} \right\} \left\{ \sqrt{-1} \right\}^t + x_1 \left\{ \frac{(1)^t - (-1)^t}{2} \right\} \left\{ -\sqrt{-1} \right\}^{t-1}$$
$$(43)$$

---

to the proper treatment is provided by watching what happens as M_2 gets closer and closer to M_1. Then in addition to $M_1{}^t K_1$, $\dfrac{M_2{}^t - M_1{}^t}{M_2 - M_1} K_3$ is also a solution. But as $M_2 \rightarrow M_1$, the latter expression becomes $t\, M_1{}^{t-1} = \dfrac{\partial}{\partial M} [M^t]_{M = M_1}$.

Therefore, in the general case of $s + 1$ repeated roots, we always make up for the s missing exponential terms by using expressions of the form

$$M_1{}^t, t M_1{}^{t-1}, t(t-1) M_1{}^{t-2}, \ldots, t(t-1) \ldots (t-s+1) M_1{}^{t-s} = \frac{\partial^s}{\partial M^s} [M^t]_{M = M_1}$$

or if more convenient,

$$M_1{}^t, t M_1{}^t, t^2 M_1{}^t, \ldots t^s M_1{}^t$$

Note that so long as $|M| < 1$, the powers of t will not affect the stability of the solution, since M^t will dominate.

For even t's, i.e., $t = 2T$, the second term is zero and the first term is $x_0 (-1)^T$; for odd t's, $t = 2T + 1$, the first term is zero, and the second term is $x_1 (-1)^T$. But combining the terms in brackets, we see that we can write

$$x(t) = (\sqrt{-1})^t K_1 + (-\sqrt{-1})^t K_2 \qquad (44)$$

where the K's are complex numbers of the form

$$K_1 = \tfrac{1}{2}(x_0 - \sqrt{-1}\, x_1)$$

$$K_2 = \tfrac{1}{2}(x_0 + \sqrt{-1}\, x_1) \qquad (45)$$

Note that K_1 and K_2 are Mutt and Jeff complex numbers, with $\sqrt{-1}$ having opposite signs—or as the mathematician would say, they are "conjugate complex numbers."

But there is still another way that our solution to (41) can be written, using the sine and cosine trigonometric functions. Let us try as a solution

$$x(t) = C_1 \cos 90°t + C_2 \sin 90°t \qquad (46)$$

Then

$$x(t + 2) = C_1 \cos (90°t + 180°) + C_2 \sin (90°t + 180°)$$

But adding 180° will always reverse the sign of the cosine and sine functions. Therefore, this satisfies our difference equation, once C_1 and C_2 have been determined so as to fit the initial conditions:

$$C_1 = x_0, C_2 = x_1$$

We have two expressions for the same solution:

$$x(t) = x_0 \cos 90°t + x_1 \sin 90°t \qquad (47)$$
$$= x_0 \frac{(1)^t + (-1)^t}{2} (\sqrt{-1})^t + x_1 \frac{(1)^t - (-1)^t}{2} (-\sqrt{-1})^{t-1}$$

This suggests that complex numbers are to be identified in a special way with the simple trigonometric functions. The sine and cosine functions provide a smooth way for having $(-1)^t$ go from $+1$ to -1 as t goes from 0 to 1. When $t = \tfrac{1}{2}$ or any fraction, imaginary numbers are involved—but always in pairs which combine to form real number solutions.

More precisely, wherever we have complex roots

$$M_1{}^t = (u + \sqrt{-1}\, v)^t$$
$$M_2{}^t = (u - \sqrt{-1}\, v)^t \tag{48}$$

we can write these as

$$(\sqrt{u^2 + v^2})^t \,(\cos \theta t \pm \sqrt{-1} \sin \theta t) \tag{49}$$

where

$$\cos \theta = \frac{u}{\sqrt{u^2 + v^2}}$$
$$\sin \theta = \frac{v}{\sqrt{u^2 + v^2}} \tag{50}$$

The K's will come in pairs so that all terms involving $\sqrt{-1}$ can cancel, and we finally end up with

$$(\sqrt{u^2 + v^2})^t \,(C_1 \cos \theta t + C_2 \sin \theta t) \tag{51}$$

For stability $|M| = \sqrt{u^2 + v^2}$, the "absolute value" or "modulus" of the complex roots, must be less than one. The relation between complex exponentials and the sine and cosine functions is further explored in the next section.

THE GENERAL THEORY OF DIFFERENTIAL EQUATIONS
WITH CONSTANT COEFFICIENTS

Whatever is true for difference equations holds perfectly well for differential equations, so long as we use e^{mt} instead of M^t, and use

$$\left[y(t), \frac{dy(t)}{dt}, \frac{d^2y(t)}{dt^2}, \ldots, \frac{d^ny(t)}{dt^n} \right]$$

wherever

$$[y(t), y(t+1), y(t+2), \ldots, y(t+n)]$$

appear.

Thus we saw earlier that

$$y(t+2) - 5y(t+1) + 6y(t) = 0$$
$$y(0) = 1$$
$$y(1) = 4$$

has the solution

$$y(t) = 3^t(2) - 2^t(1)$$

It follows, therefore, that

$$\frac{d^2y(t)}{dt^2} - 5\frac{dy(t)}{dt^2} + 6y(t) = 0$$

$$y(0) = 1$$

$$y'(0) = \left[\frac{d}{dt}y(t)\right]_{t=0} = 4$$

must have for its solution

$$y(t) = e^{3t}(2) - e^{2t}(1)$$

as the reader can verify.

Indeed, we always solve the general differential equation

$$\frac{d^n Y(t)}{dt^n} + a_1\frac{d^{n-1}Y(t)}{dt^{n-1}} + \ldots + a_{n-1}\frac{dY(t)}{dt} + a_n Y(t) = A$$

$$Y(0) = b_0$$

$$Y'(0) = b_1 \qquad\qquad (52)$$

$$\cdot\ \cdot\ \cdot\ \cdot\ \cdot$$

$$Y^{(n-1)}(0) = b_{n-1}$$

as follows:

First, we determine the stationary state level, by setting $Y(t) = \overline{Y}$, $\frac{d}{dt}\overline{Y} = 0 = \ldots = \frac{d^n}{dt^n}\overline{Y}$, to get

$$\overline{Y} = \frac{1}{a_n}A \qquad\qquad (53)$$

Then we work with deviations from the equilibrium level, $y(t) = Y(t) - \overline{Y}$. These transient terms which must be added to $\overline{Y}$ satisfy the "reduced" differential equation:

$$\frac{d^n y(t)}{dt^n} + a_1\frac{d^{n-1}y(t)}{dt^{n-1}} + \ldots + a_{n-1}\frac{dy(t)}{dt} + a_n y(t) = 0$$

$$y(0) = Y(0) - \overline{Y} = b_0 - \frac{A}{a_n} \qquad\qquad (54)$$

$$y'(0) = Y'(0) = b_1$$

$$\cdot\ \cdot\ \cdot\ \cdot\ \cdot\ \cdot\ \cdot\ \cdot$$

$$y^{(n-1)}(0) = Y^{(n-1)}(0) = b_{n-1}$$

Its solution is of the form

$$y(t) = e^{m_1 t}K_1 + e^{m_2 t}K_2 + \ldots + e^{m_n t}K_n \qquad\qquad (55)$$

where the substitution of $e^{mt} K$ into the differential equation shows that $(m_1, m_2, \ldots m_n)$ are to be the roots of the polynomial,

$$m^n + a_1 m^{n-1} + \ldots + a_{n-1} m + a_n = 0 \qquad (56)$$

The K's are determined by the initial conditions

$$\begin{aligned}
K_1 + \quad K_2 + \ldots + \quad K_n &= y(0) \\
m_1 K_1 + m_2 K_2 + \ldots + m_n K_n &= y'(0) \\
m_1^2 K_1 + m_2^2 K_2 + \ldots + m_n^2 K_n &= y''(0)
\end{aligned} \qquad (57)$$

$$\cdot \ \cdot \ \cdot \ \cdot \ \cdot \qquad \cdot \ \cdot \ \cdot \ \cdot$$

etc.

If all the roots are real and negative, the system is stable and the transient dies away. If some of the roots are repeated, the missing e^{mt} terms will be replaced by terms of the form te^{mt}, $t^2 e^{mt}$, . . ., $t^i e^{mt} = \dfrac{\partial^i}{\partial m^i} e^{mt}$, . . . and higher powers of t. These powers of t will not affect the stability of the system if $m < 0$.

But again, not all roots have to be real. Earlier we saw in equation (15) the case where the acceleration of capital depended inversely upon its own level and gave rise to pendulum-like oscillations rather than to exponential growth or decay. This was a relation of the type

$$\frac{d^2 y(t)}{dt^2} = -y(t) \qquad (58)$$

where the appropriate time units have been used to get rid of any numerical constants.

Obviously, neither e^t nor e^{-t} will do as a solution, since when differentiated twice, each of these gives rise to itself multiplied by $(1)^2$ or $(-1)^2 = 1$. What we need is some kind of a periodic or repeating function of time.[25]

A bold man would try $e^{\pm\sqrt{-1}t}$, since

$$\frac{d}{dt} e^{\pm\sqrt{-1}t} = \pm\sqrt{-1}\, e^{\pm\sqrt{-1}t}$$

$$\frac{d^2}{dt^2} e^{\pm\sqrt{-1}t} = \frac{d}{dt}\frac{d}{dt} e^{\pm\sqrt{-1}t} = +\sqrt{-1}\sqrt{-1}\, e^{\pm\sqrt{-1}t} = -e^{\pm\sqrt{-1}t}$$

But what in the real world is the meaning of e raised to an imaginary number? Let us take the magic series for e^t, given in footnote 10, and

[25] This follows from the earlier demonstration that capital will oscillate. We can further show the constancy of amplitude of these oscillations by the fact that $y''(t) = -y(t)$ implies $\dfrac{d}{dt}\left[\dfrac{y'^2 + y^2}{2}\right] = [y'(t) y''(t) + y'(t) y(t)] = 0$ or $y(t)^2 + y'(t)^2 = $ constant, and the oscillations can neither explode nor decay.

drop every other term, and then change the sign of every other term of what is left. This will give us two new functions, $f_1(t)$ and $f_2(t)$:

$$f_1(t) = 1 - \frac{t^2}{1 \cdot 2} + \frac{t^4}{4!} - \frac{t^6}{6!} + \cdot \cdot \cdot$$

$$(59)$$

$$f_2(t) = \frac{t}{1} - \frac{t^3}{3!} + \frac{t^5}{5!} - \frac{t^7}{7!} + \cdot \cdot \cdot$$

where n! stands for "n factorial" or $n(n-1) \ldots (3)(2)(1)$, and, so to speak,

$$e^{\pm \sqrt{-1}t} = f_1(t) \pm \sqrt{-1}\, f_2(t) \tag{60}$$

Obviously, differentiating either of these new functions twice will give us itself back again but with algebraic sign reversed. The reader should verify this and also that

$$\frac{d}{dt} f_2(t) = f_1(t), \frac{d}{dt} f_1(t) = - f_2(t)$$

$$f_1(0) = 1, \qquad\qquad f_2(0) = 0 \tag{61}$$

$$f_1'(0) = 0, \qquad\qquad f_2'(0) = 1$$

It follows that

$$y(t) = f_2(t)\, y(0) + f_1(t)\, y'(0)$$

is the solution to our system (58).

But from trigonometry, we know that the periodic function cos t has the same properties as $f_1(t)$, t being measured in terms of "radians"—i.e., in units equal to $360°/2\pi = 57.29°$. And sin t has the properties of $f_2(t)$. It can be shown that no other functions can have these properties.

This suggested to Euler one of the most "beautiful" relations in all mathematics:

$$e^{\pm \sqrt{-1}t} = \cos t \pm \sqrt{-1} \sin t \tag{62}$$

The patient reader can use this to verify that the complex numbers, m_1, m_2, K_1, and K_2, in the differential equation solution expressed in the form

$$y(t) = e^{(u+\sqrt{-1}v)t} (a + \sqrt{-1}\,\beta) + e^{(u-\sqrt{-1}v)t} (a -$$
$$\sqrt{-1}\beta) + \ldots \tag{63}$$

can always be grouped in pairs to give the real expression

$$y(t) = e^{ut} (C_1 \cos vt + C_2 \sin vt) \tag{64}$$

where $u < 0$ is the condition for stability, where the C's depend on the initial conditions, and where the period of oscillation is given by $2\pi/v$.

42

AN EXTENSION OF THE LECHATELIER PRINCIPLE

By Paul A. Samuelson

The vague and often teleological LeChatelier principle of thermodynamics can be formulated as an unambiguous mathematical theorem concerned with elements of the definite matrices associated with maximizing problems. It thus has found many applications in economic theory: e.g., in the study of how the constraints imposed by rationing diminish the price elasticity of a maximizing demander. The present paper shows that the LeChatelier principle can also be extended to Leontief-Metzler-Mosak systems by virtue of the special properties of their off-diagonal elements, and even though they do not have the symmetric and definite matrices characteristic of a maximum problem. Hence, the principle may be applicable to analysis of input-output, multisectoral Keynesian multiplier systems, and general demand analysis involving gross substitutes.

1

IN PHYSICS the principle of LeChatelier is used heuristically to predict qualitative effects like the following: Squeezing a balloon will decrease its volume more if you keep its temperature constant than it will if (by insulating it) you let the squeezing warm it up. Actually this heuristic principle reflects a mathematical theorem about matrices connected with definite quadratic forms.[1] And since quadratic forms of this type are intimately involved in economic maximizing problems, it is not surprising that the LeChatelier principle should have found many applications in theoretical economics. Thus, the demand for labor by a firm will be more elastic if you hold the *price* of its land constant than if you hold the *quantity* of its land constant (and this whether land and labor are complementary rather than substituting).

Aside from the positive definite matrices of maximizing type, there is another type of well-behaved matrix met in diverse applications of economic theory. I refer to the special Leontief input-output matrices, which in the field of Keynesian multisector analysis we call Metzler matrices, and which in the demand analysis of gross substitutes we call Mosak matrices. In the statistical literature these same matrices appear in slightly different form as Markoff transition probabilities. In the mathematical literature they are associated with the names of Minkowski and Frobenius; and they have repeatedly turned up in writings of the last eighty years dealing with networks.[2]

---

[1] See for example, P. A. Samuelson, *Foundations of Economic Analysis*, Cambridge, Mass.: Harvard University Press, 1947, Ch. III.

[2] See R. M. Solow, *Econometrica*, 21 (January, 1952), pp. 29–46, for discussion; also R. Dorfman, P. A. Samuelson, R. M. Solow, *Linear Programming and Economic*

There is no need for these matrices, which I shall call Minkowski matrices, to be definite or even symmetric. None the less we know they have many properties rather like those of definite matrices: thus, while their characteristic roots need not all be real, their stability still depends on a dominant real root; and just as the Gauss-Seidel iteration converges to the solution of linear equations with a definite symmetric matrix, so will the similar iteration applied to a Leontief system certainly converge.

I propose here to demonstrate that the LeChatelier principle, in addition to holding for definite matrices, also holds for matrices of Minkowski type.

2

To illustrate the matter, contemplate a statical Leontief system, whose total gross outputs (x_i) are determined by final consumptions (y_i) by the usual equations

$$x_i - \sum_{j=1}^{n} a_{ij}x_j = y_i \qquad (i = 1, \ldots, n)$$

or

(1) $$\sum_{j=1}^{n} A_{ij}x_j = y_i \qquad (i = 1, \ldots, n),$$

where for simplicity all the a's are taken to be positive and where units have been scaled so that the column sums have the "leakage" property

(2) $$1 - \sum_{j=1}^{n} a_{ij} = \sum_{j=1}^{n} A_{ij} > 0, \qquad (i = 1, \ldots, n).$$

Such a well-behaved system is known to satisfy the usual Hawkins-Simon conditions, and its inverse is known to consist of all positive elements

(3) $$A^{-1} = [A^{ij}] \text{ with } A^{ij} > 0 \text{ for all } (i,j).$$

It of course follows from this fact, and from common sense, that: An increase in final consumption of any good, say y_n or coal, must necessarily increase the total gross output of coal x_n — i.e., $A^{nn} > 0$.

The question arises: What can we say about the induced change in coal resulting from an increase in final coal consumed when other consumptions $y_2, \ldots, y_{n-1}$ are unchanged and when *instead of holding y_1, the consumption of iron, constant we instead hold iron's gross output x_1 constant*? By analogy with the established LeChatelier principle we would expect the resulting change, which we might label as A_1^{nn}, to have the following properties:

(4) $$0 < A_1^{nn} < A^{nn}.$$

Analysis, New York: McGraw-Hill, 1958, p. 256 ff. Important, as yet unpublished work by James Tobin on monetary theory suggested to me that these extensions would be of economic interest.

I.e., we should expect the resulting change in coal to be less when the total gross output of iron is held constant than when the final consumption of iron is held constant; but in either case we would expect the induced change in iron output to be positive.

This result turns out to be true, as will be easily proved. Indeed if for $k < i$ and j, we denote by A_k^{ij} the change in x_i induced by a change in y_j when the first k gross outputs are held constant, then the following more general theorem can be proved:

$$(5) \qquad 0 < A_{n-1}^{nn} < A_{n-2}^{nn} < \ldots < A_2^{nn} < A_1^{nn} < A^{nn} .$$

I.e., adding new auxiliary constraints to total outputs necessarily lessens the response of a good's output to a unit increase in its final consumption.

3

The extended LeChatelier principle uses the same Jacobi theorem on determinants employed to prove the original theorem.[3] If we denote cofactors of a matrix $[A_{ij}]$ by $[\Delta_{ij}]$, then Jacobi's identity is

$$(6) \qquad \Delta\Delta_{ii.jj} = \Delta_{ii}\Delta_{jj} - \Delta_{ij}\Delta_{ji}.$$

Setting $i = n, j = 1$, we get after a little manipulation

$$(7) \qquad 0 < A_1^{nn} = A^{nn} - \frac{A^{n1} A^{1n}}{A^{11}} < A^{nn} .$$

The last inequality follows from (3)'s fact that all A^{ij} are known to be positive. The other inequality follows from the fact that the inverse of $[A_1^{ij}]$ is the original Leontief matrix with the first row and first column deleted; and such a deletion leaves the leakage condition (2), and Hawkins-Simon conditions, intact.

Since $[A_1^{ij}]$ has the same formal properties as $[A^{ij}]$, we, in the same way as we derived (7), derive

$$(8) \qquad 0 < A_2^{nn} = A_1^{nn} - \frac{A_1^{n1} A_1^{1n}}{A_1^{22}} < A_1^{nn} < A^{nn} .$$

And by induction, we thus establish our basic theorem (5).

It should be noted that when the system is either decomposable or contains zeros among the a_{ij}, our strong equalities may have to be written in the safer form

$$(9) \qquad 0 < A_{n-1}^{nn} \leq A_{n-2}^{nn} \leq \ldots \leq A_1^{nn} \leq A^{nn} .$$

[3] See P. A. Samuelson, *Foundations of Economic Analysis*, p. 38, equation (43). (A mistake in sign marred the early printing.)

4

Even if a system is not, like the Leontief system, strictly linear with constant A_{ij} coefficients, the LeChatelier principle will still apply to its changes so long as its Jacobian has the well-behaved properties of a Minkowski matrix. Thus, consider the system

$$(10) \qquad y_i = A_i(x_1, \ldots, x_n) \qquad (i = 1,2, \ldots, n),$$

with

$$\left(\frac{\partial A_i(x_1, \ldots, x_n)}{\partial x_j} \right) = [A_{ij}];$$

$$A_{ii} > 0; A_{ij} < 0, i \neq j;$$

$$(11) \qquad \sum_{j=1}^{n} A_{ij} > 0 \qquad (i = 1,2, \ldots, n).$$

Evidently, (10) can then be uniquely inverted to give

$$(12) \qquad x_i = A^i(y_1, \ldots, y_n) \qquad (i = 1,2, \ldots, n),$$

with

$$(13) \qquad \left(\frac{\partial A^i(y_1, \ldots, y_n)}{\partial y_j} \right) = [A^{ij}] = [A_{ij}]^{-1},$$

$$A^{ij} > 0 \qquad (i, j = 1,2, \ldots, n).$$

Also, since all the principal minors of $[A_{ij}]$ are positive, (12) can be solved for $(y_1, \ldots, y_k; x_{k+1}, \ldots, x_n)$ in terms of the complementary independent variables $(x_1, \ldots, x_k; y_{k+1}, \ldots, y_n)$. Write this as

$$(14) \qquad \begin{aligned} y_i &= A_k^i(x_1, \ldots, x_k; \ldots, y_n) & (i = 1,2, \ldots, k), \\ x_i &= A_k^i(x_1, \ldots, x_k; \ldots, y_n) & (i = k+1, \ldots, n). \end{aligned}$$

In accordance with our earlier notation, the Jacobian matrix of (14) can be written as $[A_k^{ij}]$, only now these coefficients are not necessarily constants.

By exactly the same reasoning as was applied to the linear case, we may take as established for the general Minkowski case the fundamental LeChatelier principle

$$(15) \qquad 0 < A_{k+1}^{ii} < A_k^{ii}, \quad n \geq i > k + 1.$$

5

There is, though, one important difference between the linear and nonlinear case—both in the case of definite maximizing forms and Minkowski matrices. The LeChatelier principle is a *local* principle. It is a theorem on instantaneous derivatives. And from it we can be sure that, *in a neighborhood of a point*, x_n will be increased less by a change in y_n when some other x_j is constrained than when the corresponding y_j is constrained. Can the principle not also be proved *in the large*, so that it holds for *all finite movements* of y_n even in the nonlinear case?

When I first formulated the LeChatelier theorem twenty years ago, I had hopes of proving the non-local property. But for many years a proof eluded my most determined efforts. Finally it dawned on me that the theorem was *not* true in the large. This paradoxical result was confirmed by numerical counterexamples.

An example of this odd result would be the following: For a *small* squeeze of a balloon its volume contracts less when it is insulated than when its temperature is maintained; but if the balloon contained water near the anomalous 4°C temperature where water ceases to contract and begins to expand with cooling, a finite squeezing could be found which would reverse the expected relationships. In terms of economics, our paradox in the large could be illustrated by the following type of example: Near the critical point where labor and land go from being substitutes to being complements, as measured by the sign of off-diagonal elements in the profit Hessian matrix $[A_{ij}]$, we could find a clever counterexample in which the long-run arc elasticity of demand for labor was more *inelastic* than the short-run.[4]

It is not my present purpose to review known facts about the LeChatelier principle but to extend it to Minkowski matrices. These do have the strong one-signed condition on their off-diagonal terms sufficient to guarantee that the LeChatelier principle does hold in the large and not just locally. The proof is straightforward but rather lengthy and will only be sketched here.

What has to be proved is essentially the following:

THEOREM. *For any well-behaved Minkowski system satisfying* (11), *if*

$$X_n = A_{k+1}^n (X_1, \ldots, X_{k+1}; Y_{k+2}, \ldots, Y_n) = A_k^n (X_1, \ldots, X_k; Y_{k+1}, \ldots, Y_n),$$

then

$$(16) \quad A_{k+1}^n (X_1, \ldots, X_{k+1}; Y_{k+2}, \ldots, y_n) < A_k^n (X_1, \ldots, X_k; Y_{k+1}, \ldots, y_n)$$

for all $y_n > Y_n$.

Figure 1 shows what must not happen. A corresponds on the graph to (Y_n, X_n), with other variables of course being held constant in the background. In the neighborhood of A the broken "constrained" curve grows more slowly than the solid curve, in agreement with the general LeChatelier local principle. Above D, however, where the curves cross, the relationships

---

[4] These matters I have analyzed in Chapter 33 of this volume. I believe that M. McManus and Hendrik Houthakker have separately established similar conclusions.

are reversed. One would think that this necessarily involves a contradiction to the local LeChatelier principle at D. But this reasoning ignores the fact that the variables held constant along the two curves are *not* the same: a two dimensional graph gives only a two dimensional projection of a many-variable relationship. Actually, at any point such as D, there might be *more than one* broken curve, all but one corresponding to a configuration different from that indicated on the solid curve at that point. So long as the right one of the different broken curves cuts at D in the way demanded by the local LeChatelier principle, that principle has not been violated. Hence, we cannot in general rule out the phenomenon depicted in Figure 1.

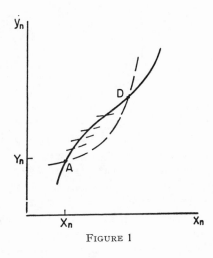

FIGURE 1

But if we could use both x_n and y_n as admissible prescribable independent variables and hold constant the same remaining variables in the background, then each point in the figure would truly determine exactly the same "state" of the system and D would represent a contradiction to the established local principle. Hence, we would have established (by contradiction) the truth of the LeChatelier principle in the large.

Now under what conditions can we be sure of being able to use x_n, along with y_n, as one of our admissible independent variables? Writing out the last equation of (14)

$$(17) \qquad x_n = A_k^n (x_1, \ldots, x_k; y_{k+1}, \ldots, y_n),$$

we know by the Implicit Function Theorem that we can solve this for y_{k+1} in terms of the remaining variables and thus use $(x_1, \ldots, x_k; x_n, y_{k+2}, \ldots, y_n)$ as independent variables in place of the independent variables in (14) provided

$$\frac{\partial A_k^n (x_1, \ldots, x_k; y_{k+1}, \ldots, y_n)}{\partial y_{k+1}} = A_k^{n,k+1} \neq 0 .$$

Actually, for well-behaved Minkowski systems

(18) $A_k^{n,i} > 0$ for all $n \geq i > k$.

Indeed, if we write out the $n \times n$ matrix $[A_k^{ij}]$ in partitioned form, we can be sure of the following pattern of signs

(19) $[A_k^{ij}] = \begin{bmatrix} \alpha & \beta \\ \gamma & \delta \end{bmatrix} = \left[\begin{array}{cccc:cccc} + & - & \ldots & - & - & - & \ldots & - \\ - & + & \ldots & - & - & - & \ldots & - \\ \cdot & & \cdot & & \cdot & & & \cdot \\ - & - & \ldots & + & - & - & \ldots & - \\ \hdashline + & + & \ldots & + & + & + & \ldots & + \\ \cdot & & \cdot & & \cdot & & & \cdot \\ + & + & \ldots & + & + & + & \ldots & + \end{array}\right]$

where α is a $k \times k$ matrix. For the present purpose we need only be assured of the positive pattern of signs in the lower right-hand corner δ, a fact that is mathematically demonstrable by use of the earlier Jacobi determinant theorem (but not now applied to a principal minor).[5]

The intuitive interpretation of these sign patterns can be naturally described from considering a Leontief system. Thus, consider a Leontief system and increase the prescribed consumption of any y such as y_n, while holding $(x_1, \ldots, x_k; y_{k+1}, \ldots, y_{n-1})$ constant. How much x_{k+1} will now be required? Certainly more than before since some of it will be needed now to provide needed new intermediate inputs. This establishes δ's positive pattern of signs.

Since at the same time the totals of $(x_1, \ldots, x_k)$ are held constant, the new needed amount of intermediate inputs of these goods will leave *less* for consumptions $(y_1, \ldots, y_k)$. This establishes β's negative pattern of signs.

Now imagine an increase in any x_1, holding $(x_2, \ldots, x_k; y_{k+1}, \ldots, y_n)$ constant. This will certainly necessitate more intermediate output of each of $(x_{k+1}, \ldots, x_n)$, and since their consumptions must still be met, we can be sure that the totals $(x_{k+1}, \ldots, x_n)$ must all grow. This establishes γ's positive pattern of signs.

But now the increase in x_1 will also force an increase in intermediate $(x_2, \ldots, x_k)$ and, since their totals are unchanged, will inevitably reduce $(y_2, \ldots, y_k)$ consumptions. This establishes the negative off-diagonal terms of α. Since, by the Hawkins-Simon condition, we know that not all of the

---

[5] Incidentally, if $[A_{ij}]$ is symmetric, so that $A = A^T$, then $\alpha = \alpha^T$, $\delta = \delta^T$, and $-\beta = \gamma^T$.

new x_1 is needed as intermediate input to produce itself as output, the positive diagonals of a are established.[6]

This completes the discussion of the fact that in the Minkowski realm we can derive the stronger non-local LeChatelier Principle—which is more than can be done in the *general* maximizing case.[7]

6

For the case of a positive definite $[A_{ij}]$, the following more general theorem on quadratic forms includes (9) as a special case:[8]

$$(20) \qquad \sum_{k+2}^{n} \sum_{k+2}^{n} A_{k+1}^{ij} z_i z_j \leqslant \sum_{k+2}^{n} \sum_{k+2}^{n} A_{k}^{ij} z_i z_j$$

for arbitrary z's.

Does this generalization of the LeChatelier principle hold for the Leontief-Minkowski case? The answer can be shown to be, No. If we restrict the z's to strictly positive values, however, (20) will be valid. The reason for this is to be found in the fact that for Leontief type matrices we can state a much stronger theorem than in the definite matrix case: namely, not only do the diagonal terms A_k^{ii} satisfy the LeChatelier principle but so also do the off-diagonal terms.

THEOREM. *If A_{ij} is a well-behaved matrix with the properties $A_{ij} < 0$ for $i \neq j$, and all principal minors of order 1 to n are positive then*

$$A_{k+1}^{ij} < A_{k}^{ij} < \ldots < A_{1}^{ij} < A^{ij}, \text{ for all } i,j > k+1.$$

The proof can again utilize Jacobi's theorem on determinants as in (5),

$$\Delta \Delta_{11 \cdot ij} = \Delta_{11} \Delta_{ij} - \Delta_{i1} \Delta_{1j},$$

---

[6] Since a is easily seen to be the inverse of the matrix made up of the first k rows and columns of $[A^{ij}]$, this means that the bills of goods represented by the nonnegative identity matrix are producible with the a coefficients. From property 3a of Dorfman *et al.*, *op. cit.*, p. 256, it follows that a satisfies the Hawkins-Simon and other well-behaved leakage properties of a Leontief system. Since δ is the inverse of the last $n - k$ rows and columns of $[A_{ij}]$, it of course has all the regularity properties of A^{-1} itself.

[7] In the special case of a Mosak-Hicks matrix with neglectable "income effects," the $[A_{ij}]$ matrix would be both symmetric-definite and Minkowski well-behaved. So, of course, there are many maximizing cases where the strong non-local principle will hold.

[8] This appears in the chapter of this volume that is entitled "The Structure of a Minimum Equilibrium System." It has also been discovered by Lawrence Klein in an as yet unpublished paper.

from which we find

$$\frac{\Delta_{11 \cdot ij}}{\Delta_{11}} = \frac{\Delta_{ij}}{\Delta} - \frac{\dfrac{\Delta_{i1}}{\Delta} \quad \dfrac{\Delta_{1j}}{\Delta}}{\dfrac{\Delta_{11}}{\Delta}}$$

or

$$A_1^{ij} = A^{ij} - \frac{A^{i1} A^{1j}}{A^{11}}.$$

Since the factors in the last term are known all to be positive, we have proved that $A_1^{ij} < A^{ij}$; and since the matrix A_1^{ij} has all the qualitative properties of A^{ij}, the general result of our theorem follows at once by induction.

An alternative proof would proceed from the well-known fact that decreasing an a_{rs} coefficient must lower all the terms in the inverse A^{ij}. By decreasing all the a coefficients in the same rows and columns, we go from A^{ij} to A_1^{ij}, A_2^{ij}, etc., being sure that we are always reducing these terms in the process. No similar result relating to off-diagonal complementarity terms holds in the case of definite matrices that arise from general extremum problems.

7

Now write $\Delta, \Delta_1, \Delta_2, \ldots, \Delta_{n-1}, \Delta_n = 1$ as the determinant of $[A_{ij}]$ when no rows and columns are omitted, when the first row and first column are omitted, when the first two rows and columns are omitted, ..., etc. It is well known that the good-behavior conditions (11) are sufficient to make all $\Delta_k > 0$. When the variables have been scaled so that $A_{ii} \leq 1$ and (2) or (11) holds, then it is also known that

(21) $0 < \Delta < \Delta_1 < \ldots < \Delta_{n-1} < 1.$

A good way to see this is through the realization that the diagonal elements of δ in (20) must all exceed unity. This fact, that $A_k^{ii} > 1$ for $n \geq i > k$, can be seen from the convergent series expansion $[A^{ij}] = I + a + a^2 + \ldots$, or from the economic fact that to get an extra consumption unit of y_i, you must produce it *and* some extra intermediate input of x_i.

Now consider the characteristic root of Δ_k with least real part, and call it λ_k. From the theory of Frobenius matrices, we know this to be real and positive. Then, necessarily

(22) $0 < \lambda < \lambda_1 < \ldots < \lambda_{n-1} < 1.$

Here, too, is a remarkable similarity to the known property of symmetric matrices—that the characteristic roots of the principal minor of a symmetric matrix separate those of the matrix itself.

Matching (21)'s inequalities on the principal minors of $[A_{ij}]$ are the following inequalities on the principal minors of $[A^{ij}]$ that must hold whenever $[A_{ij}]$ has been normalized so as to have diagonals no greater than unity:

$$(23) \qquad 1 < |A^{11}| < \begin{vmatrix} A^{11} & A^{12} \\ A^{21} & A^{22} \end{vmatrix} < \cdots < \begin{vmatrix} A^{11} & \cdots & A^{1n} \\ \vdots & & \vdots \\ A^{n1} & \cdots & A^{nn} \end{vmatrix}.$$

The truth of this follows from the fact that a ratio such as

$$\begin{vmatrix} A^{11} & \cdots & A^{1k} \\ \vdots & & \vdots \\ A^{k1} & \cdots & A^{kk} \end{vmatrix} \div \begin{vmatrix} A^{11} & \cdots & A^{1,k+1} \\ \vdots & & \vdots \\ A^{k+1,1} & \cdots & A^{k+1,k+1} \end{vmatrix}$$

equals a positive fractional diagonal coefficient like that of $[A_{ij}]$ or of a matrix like a of (19).

Although necessary, the inequalities (23) are not sufficient to make $[A^{ij}]$ the inverse of a well-behaved Minkowski matrix. Many such sets of sufficient conditions can be given. Thus, if a matrix $[B_{ij}]$ has an inverse with positive diagonals and negative off-diagonals, and if either it is known to have a positive determinant or a single row or column of all positive elements, then it definitely is the inverse of a well-behaved Minkowski system.

8

The following general LeChatelier principle for a minimizing process has no counterpart in the Minkowski case. Consider

$$(24) \qquad \underset{(x_1, \ldots, x_n)}{\text{Maximum}} A(x_1, \ldots, x_n) - \sum_1^n y_j x_j,$$

which for $[A_{ij}] = [\partial^2 A(x_1, \ldots, x_n)/\partial x_i \partial x_j]$ positive definite defines the equilibrium relations

$$(25) \qquad x_i = A^i(y_1, \ldots, y_n).$$

Suppose any auxiliary constraint

$$(26) \qquad \Phi(x_1, \ldots, x_n) = \text{constant}$$

is put on the maximum problem, which for $[y_i] = [Y_i]$ is consistent with

$$\Phi(A^1, \ldots, A^n) = \text{constant}.$$

Then let

$$(27) \qquad x_i = A^i_*(y_1, \ldots, y_n)$$

be the new equilibrium relations to (24) under constraint.

The general LeChatelier principle will assure us that

$$(28) \qquad \frac{\partial A^i(Y_1, \ldots, Y_n)}{\partial y_i} \geq \frac{\partial A^i_*(Y_1, \ldots, Y_n)}{\partial y_i} \geq 0.$$

This theorem can be proved by transforming variables so that Φ is a new variable of the type x_j, or by use of bordered determinants.[9]

There is no counterpart to the present phenomenon in the case of non-symmetric Minkowski systems. Indeed there is no formulation like (24) which even tells us how meaningfully to add a general auxiliary constraint to such a system.

9

In concluding, I have to point out that the LeChatelier principle as applied to extremum problems has the general property that it holds independently of the coordinate system. This is definitely not the case for a Minkowski system. Thus, taking a nonsingular transformation of the outputs in a Leontief system will generally not give us a set of algebraic equations which can be interpreted as a Leontief system. A new variable defined as a function of iron and coal does not behave like a new industry: the specification of the actual input-output processes as the yoccur in life is crucial. Mathematically $C^T A C$ has the definiteness properties of A when C is nonsingular and A is positive definite; but $C^T A C$ is not a Minkowski matrix just because A is—not even in the case where C is an orthogonal matrix.

There is another important difference between the case of the extremum problem's quadratic forms and the Leontief case. In the former case, as in (23)—(26), there is a perfect duality between the x's and the y's. Hence, just as there is a LeChatelier principle ordering the response of x's to y's under varying x constraints, so is there a completely analogous LeChatelier principle ordering the response of y's to x's under varying y constraints.

But in the case of a Leontief or Minkowski system, there is no such perfect dualism between the y's and the x's. Thus, while it is true that the inverse of a positive definite matrix is itself positive definite, it is most certainly not true that the inverse of a Minkowski matrix is itself a Minkowski matrix. Nevertheless, it can be shown that a LeChatelier principle must necessarily hold for the y responses of a Minkowski system as well as for its x responses.

This fact might have been expected, and proved, from the consideration that the inverse of a Minkowski matrix has the same one-signed-off-diagonal-term property that the matrix itself has. But it is perceived in its more general aspect from realizing the prosaic fact that the partial derivative $\partial y_i / \partial x_i$ is necessarily the reciprocal of the partial derivative $\partial x_i / \partial y_i$, it being understood that the same other independent variables are being held constant in the background.

[9] See *Foundations, op. cit.,* p. 37-8. There is no need for the constraint (39) there to be linear.

Thus, let subscripts denote other independent variables being held constant. Then

$$(29) \quad \left(\frac{\partial y_n}{\partial x_n}\right)_{x_1, \ldots, x_k, y_{k+1}, \ldots, y_{n-1}} = \frac{1}{\left(\frac{\partial x_n}{\partial y_n}\right)_{x_1, \ldots, x_k, y_{k+1}, \ldots, y_{n-1}}} = \frac{1}{A_k^{nn}}.$$

Then from the (8) or (15) LeChatelier relationship $A_{k+1}^{ii} < A_k^{ii}$, we get the completely dual relationship

$$(30) \quad \left(\frac{\partial y_n}{\partial x_n}\right)_{x_1, \ldots, x_{k+1}, y_{k+2}, \ldots, y_{n-1}} > \left(\frac{\partial y_n}{\partial x_n}\right)_{x_1, \ldots, x_k, y_{k+1}, \ldots, y_{n-1}}.$$

This says that the change in *any* y_n resulting from a change in its x_n is less when some other y_k is constrained than when that other x_k is constrained—which is completely parallel to the LeChatelier principle as applied to x responses. (I.e., the y's belong together in the same way that the x's do.)[10]

Massachusetts Institute of Technology

---

[10] Relation (15) implies (30) regardless of whether the off-diagonal terms of A and A^{-1} all have the same sign. But (15) does require that any pair A_{ij} and A_{ji} have the same sign, and the same holds for any pair A^{ij} and A^{ji}—a fact of significance for the economic theory of complementarity.

43

THE LE CHATELIER PRINCIPLE IN LINEAR PROGRAMMING[1]

Introduction and Summary

Often in pure or applied mathematics the equilibrium of a system can be defined by a minimum (or maximum) of some function (such as energy, cost, or profit). In *regular* or conventional problems studied in physics or economics, the minimum position has usually been defined by certain equalities on first (partial) derivatives and certain inequalities on second derivatives.

Linear programming represents a field in which the minimum position is *not* of this regular type, but instead is of a boundary or vertex type, defined by certain inequalities rather than equalities. Nonetheless, we often gain insight into the relations that hold in linear programming by following the heuristic practice of treating the problem as if it were of a regular type: for example, in the simple Koopmans transportation problem, the notion of using *potential differences* is suggested by the use of such a technique. I should like in this paper to describe one important property of regular minimum systems that carries over into the non-regular field of linear programming. A typical example is the following:

Consider the well-known linear-programming problem of finding the cheapest diet that realizes prescribed nutritional standards. What is the effect of raising the price (P_i) of any one food, say the ith? The mathe-

---

[1]This report was originally published as a research memorandum by the RAND Corporation, Santa Monica, California, on August 4, 1949. It gave rise to papers by Martin Beckmann and Martin J. Bailey in the *Review of Economic Studies*.

matical analogue of the physical principle associated with the name of Le Chatelier tells us that the quantity consumed of the ith good (x_i) will (if anything) go down. More difficult to establish is the following extension of the Le Chatelier principle: *For any small change in P_i, the decrease in x_i will be less every time we add a new constraint (nutritional or otherwise) to the system.*

By the principle of duality, these results tell us immediately that an increase in the nutritional requirement (C_j) of the jth nutrient will, if anything, raise the shadow price (y_j) of that nutrient.

Also, certain reciprocity relations are explored. The discussion is heuristic rather than rigorous.

The Le Chatelier Principle in Regular Problems

Since 1884, the literature of thermodynamics has given attention to the principle of Le Chatelier. Usually this is given vague and even mystical formulation, couched in teleological language reminiscent of Adam Smith's beneficent "invisible hand" that leads self-centered competition unwittingly to the social good. The following formulation is typical: "If the external conditions of a thermodynamic system are altered, the equilibrium of the system will tend to move in such a direction as to oppose the change in external conditions."[2]

The following are typical examples to illustrate what is meant by the critical word "oppose" in this definition. Increase the pressure (p) on a system, and, other things being equal, its volume (v) will contract; that is,

$$\Delta p \, \Delta v \leqq 0$$

Or increase the temperature of a system (T), and its so-called "entropy" (S) will increase. Mathematically, for given T and p, the equilibrium of the system can be defined as a minimum position of the following function:

$$\Phi = U(v, S) - TS - (-p)v$$

where U is the so-called "internal energy" of the system and Φ the so-called "thermodynamic potential function."

Stripped of all physical meaning, the Le Chatelier principle says that if, for fixed $P_1, P_2, \cdots, P_n$,

$$\Phi(x_1, \cdots, x_n) = U(x_1, \cdots, x_n) - \sum_1^n P_j x_j$$

is at a regular minimum so that the optimal x's can be written as

(1) $\qquad x_i = x_i(P_1, \cdots, P_n) \qquad\qquad (i = 1, 2, \cdots, n)$

[2]E. Fermi, *Thermodynamics* (New York: Dover Publications, 1937), p. 111.

then

(2) $\dfrac{\partial x_i}{\partial P_i} \geqq 0$ or $\Delta x_i \, \Delta P_i \geqq 0$

Similar problems arise in economics, Φ being profit, U being total revenue, $x_1, \cdots, x_n$ being the productive factors, and $P_1, \cdots, P_n$ their prices. Because profits are at a maximum rather than a minimum, the resulting theorem says: Any increase in the price of a productive factor will — other things being equal — cause a reduction in the amount used of that factor (or conceivably no change at all in the limit).

Mathematically, a regular minimum requires that Equations (1) be equivalent to

(1)′ $\dfrac{\partial \Phi}{\partial x_k} = 0 = \dfrac{\partial U}{\partial x_k}(x_1, \cdots, x_n) - P_k = 0$

with $[\partial^2 U/\partial x_i \, \partial x_k]$ a positive definite matrix. Consequently, after Equation (1)′ has been differentiated through by P_j and the system is solved, the required partial derivatives are given by the inverse matrix

(3) $\left[\dfrac{\partial x_i}{\partial P_j} \right] = \left[\dfrac{\partial^2 U}{\partial x_i \, \partial x_j} \right]^{-1}$

which must also be positive definite with plus diagonal elements of the form shown in (2).

If Φ were at a minimum subject to some constraints, then the x's would not be all independently variable, but by the use of bordered determinants the relation shown in (2) would still hold (it being understood that none of the constraints are permitted to involve P_i explicitly).

The Extended Le Chatelier Principle

Epstein[3] and other physicists have stated that there are really two different sets of phenomena that go under the name of Le Chatelier's principle. One is that described in my previous section, according to which an increase in external pressure means a decrease in the volume of a thermodynamic system. This holds true whether we insist that no heat be added or subtracted from the system (an "adiabatic" change), or whether we let heat change so as to keep the temperature unchanged (an "isothermal" change). Thus

$$\left(\frac{\partial v}{\partial p} \right)_{\substack{\text{entropy} \\ \text{constant}}} \leqq 0$$

$$\left(\frac{\partial v}{\partial p} \right)_{\substack{\text{temperature} \\ \text{constant}}} \leqq 0$$

[3] See P. S. Epstein, *Textbook of Thermodynamics* (New York: John Wiley, 1937), Ch. 21.

are each separate examples of the first form of the Le Chatelier principle.

The second form claims to tell us something about the *difference* between these terms. As we relax the requirements that entropy be constant, we release "secondary forces," and these act so as to "oppose" the initial change in external force pressure, so that the resulting change in volume is even greater. Thus, according to the second form of the principle,

$$\left(\frac{\partial v}{\partial p}\right)_{\text{temp.}} \leqq \left(\frac{\partial v}{\partial p}\right)_{\text{entropy}} \leqq 0$$

Expressed generally, this second principle claims that each time some constraint is added limiting the permissible changes in the variables of a system, the resulting change in x_1 from a change in P_i is less.

In words, all this is a little vague because who is to say whether holding entropy constant is more of a constraint than is holding temperature constant, or just what is meant by a "secondary force." Mathematically, though, all is definite.

Let $(x_1{}^0, x_2{}^0, \cdots, x_n{}^0)$ yield a minimum to

$$\Phi = U(x_1, \cdots, x_n) - \sum_1^n P_j x_j$$

subject to

$$G_i(x_1, \cdots, x_n) = G_i(x_1{}^0, \cdots, x_n{}^0) = 0 \quad (i = 1, 2, \cdots, m - 1)$$

Suppose that an extra constraint is put on the system as follows:

$$G_m(x_1, \cdots, x_n) = G_m(x_1{}^0, \cdots, x_n{}^0) = 0$$

For the same $(P_1, \cdots, P_n)$ this obviously has no effect on the equilibrium of our system since the constraint goes through the previous equilibrium point.

But now let us change P_i. The values of $(x_1, \cdots, x_i, \cdots, x_n)$ must all change. But if the new constraint is put on the system, the change in the x's will be a different one. Nonetheless, the change in x_i will still be in the same direction as in P_i, with or without the constraint — the first part of our principle. The second part tells us that the constrained change in x_i will be less than the unconstrained one; or the whole principle can be summarized as

(4)
$$\left(\frac{\partial x_i}{\partial P_i}\right)_{m-1 \text{ constraints}} \geqq \left(\frac{\partial x_i}{\partial P_i}\right)_{m \text{ constraints}} \geqq 0$$

or

(4)′
$$\left(\frac{\partial x_i}{\partial P_i}\right)_{\text{no constraints}} \geqq \left(\frac{\partial x_i}{\partial P_i}\right)_{1 \text{ constraint}} \geqq \cdots$$
$$\geqq \left(\frac{\partial x_i}{\partial P_i}\right)_{n-1 \text{ constraints}} \geqq 0$$

This can be proved by means of certain bordered determinants.[4] It is even simpler to redefine variables so that some x is constant along each of the constraints. The remaining x's are variable, and the equilibrium is defined by

$$(1)'' \qquad \frac{\partial \Phi}{\partial x_k} = \frac{\partial U}{\partial x_k} - P_k = 0$$

where the functions are new ones defined in terms of the new variables and where k ranges over all the unconstrained variables.

To show that adding one constraint always lowers the magnitude of response, let us number our variables so that the free ones are first $(x_1, \cdots, x_r)$, and so that our new constraint holds x_r constant. Then with only $(n - r)$ constraints,

$$(3)' \qquad \left(\frac{\partial x_i}{\partial P}\right)_{n-r} = \frac{D_{ii}}{D}$$

where

$$D = \begin{vmatrix} \dfrac{\partial^2 U}{\partial x_1} & \dfrac{\partial^2 U}{\partial x_1 \, \partial x_2} & \cdots & \dfrac{\partial^2 U}{\partial x_1 \, \partial x_2} \\[2ex] \dfrac{\partial^2 U}{\partial x_2 \, \partial x_1} & \cdot & & \cdot \\[2ex] \cdot & & & \cdot \\[1ex] \dfrac{\partial^2 U}{\partial x_r \, \partial x_1} & \cdots & & \dfrac{\partial^2 U}{\partial x_r} \end{vmatrix}$$

and D_{ij}, $D_{ij \cdot km}$, etc., are the usual symbols for cofactors, cofactors of cofactors, etc.

By a well-known theorem of determinants,

$$(3)'' \qquad \left(\frac{\partial x_i}{\partial P_i}\right)_{(n-r)+1} = \frac{D_{ii \cdot rr}}{D_{rr}} = \frac{D_{ii}}{D} - \frac{D_{ir} \, D_{ri}}{D \, D_{rr}}$$

and since D is symmetric and positive definite, it follows that the last term is positive and

$$(5) \qquad \left(\frac{\partial x_i}{\partial P_i}\right)_{n-r \text{ constraints}} \geqq \left(\frac{\partial x_i}{\partial P_i}\right)_{n-r \text{ constraints} + 1 \text{ constraint}}$$

which is the crucial part of our principle.

The Case of Linear Programming

None of these methods can be applied in the case of linear programming. No derivatives like $(1)'$ or $(1)''$ define the equilibrium of our

[4] See P. A. Samuelson, *Foundations of Economic Analysis* (Cambridge, Mass.: Harvard University Press, 1947), pp. 36–39. Some algebraic errors in sign have crept into the exposition, but they are neatly canceled out by minor errors of literary exposition.

system. It is tedious to calculate the x's which minimize

$$\Phi = P_1 x_1 + P_2 x_2 + \cdots + P_n x_n$$

subject to

(6)　　$a_{i1} x_1 + a_{i2} x_2 + \cdots + a_{in} x_n \geqq C_i$　　　　　$(i = 1, 2, \cdots, m \gtreqless n)$

$$x_1 \geqq 0, x_2 \geqq 0, \cdots, x_n \geqq 0$$

Nonetheless, we can predict in advance that an increase in a single P_i will, if anything, cause a reduction in x_i. Thus raising the price of spinach will never cause more of it to be prescribed in an optimal diet.

To prove this first form of Le Chatelier's principle, we cannot use determinants or definite quadratic forms. But by simple arithmetic we shall get the answer — as we could have done in the regular-minimum problem too.

Let our original P's be $(P_1, \cdots, P_n)$ and our new ones be $(P_1 + \Delta P_1, \cdots, P_n + \Delta P_n)$. Let the corresponding optimal x's be $(x_1, \cdots, x_n)$ and $(x_1 + \Delta x_1, \cdots, x_n + \Delta x_n)$. Then we can show that

(7)　　$\Delta x_1 \, \Delta P_1 + \Delta x_2 \, \Delta P_2 + \cdots + \Delta x_n \, \Delta P_n \leqq 0$

or, if only the ith P changes,

(7)′　　$\Delta x_i \, \Delta P_i \leqq 0$

This is so because

$$P_1 x_1 + \cdots + P_n x_n \leqq P_1 x_1{}^* + \cdots + P_n x_n{}^*$$

where $x_j{}^* = $ any other x's (including the set $x_j + \Delta x_j$) that satisfy the constraints; hence,

(8)　　$P_1 x_1 + \cdots + P_n x_n \leqq P_1 (x_1 + \Delta x_1) + \cdots + P_n (x_n + \Delta x_n)\cdot$

By similar reasoning about the second optimal position,

$$(P_1 + \Delta P_1)(x_1 + \Delta x_1) + \cdots + (P_n + \Delta P_n)(x_n + \Delta x_n)$$
$$\leqq (P_1 + \Delta P_1)(x_1{}^*) + \cdots + (P_n + \Delta P_n)(x_n{}^*)$$

and setting the arbitrary x^* equal to the previously optimal x's, we get

(9)　　$(P_1 + \Delta P_1)(x_1 + \Delta x_1) + \cdots + (P_n + \Delta P_n)(x_n + \Delta x_n)$
　　　　$\leqq (P_1 + \Delta P_1)x_1 + \cdots + (P_n + \Delta P_n)x_n$

Add (8) and (9), cancel terms, and transpose to get (7).

This shows that (7) — of which (2) is a special case — is a general truth for all minimum systems, and holds *in the large*, and not just for small changes or for instantaneous rates of change.

So much for the first part of the Le Chatelier principle.[5] Is the second part also still valid in linear programming? It is the purpose of this paper to show that the answer is yes.

Unfortunately, the second part of the principle is not so easily demonstrated as the first. The reason for this is not accidental but is intrinsic. The second part of the principle appears to be of a less fundamental character than the first. The first holds in the large — for changes in P_i of any size. We cannot assume from the previous proof that the second holds more than in the small — in some neighborhood of the previous equilibrium point. Thus, in the pressure-volume diagram of Figure 1, we demonstrate that the constant temperature curve TT will be steeper than the constant entropy curve SS in the neighborhood of E. We have not ruled out that the slopes may change elsewhere so as to

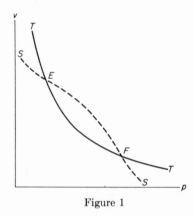

Figure 1

cause the curves actually to cross — so that for large increases in pressure the isothermal change may be less than the adiabatic change. Actually, in a simple thermodynamic system where the two variables P, v determine the system's "state," this is impossible.[6]

But I see no reason why this need be so for a general multivariable system of even the most regular behavior with respect to its second partial derivatives.[7] Certainly no purely arithmetic proof like that of the first part seems capable of demonstrating a similar result for the second part of the principle. For these reasons I confine myself to *terra firma* of small regions around the equilibrium points. As a long shot, I would

[5]This was proved in my paper, "Comparative Statics and the Logic of Economic Maximizing," *Review of Economic Studies*, Vol. XIV (1), No. 35 (1946), pp. 41–43, in connection with the Stigler diet problem. This paper is reproduced in the present volume as Chapter 6.

[6]At F, the curves must again look the way they do at E, which contradicts the assumption that they could ever cross.

[7]If *any* n of the $2n$ variables $(P_1, \cdots, P_n, x_1, \cdots, x_n)$ were uniquely to determine all of them, then the results would be true "in the large."

conjecture that a stronger result might hold in the large within the field of linear programming — but a single counterexample might disprove this extension of our theorem.

[*1965 Postscript:* Shortly after I wrote this, I proved that the Le Chatelier principle is indeed not true in the large: in any neighborhood where a complementarity term $\partial^2 U/\partial x_i \partial x_j$ changes sign, we can contrive a counterexample where a finite increase in P_i leads to a smaller finite change with fewer constraints than with more! The same is true in a linear programming model. All this is treated in my 1960 extension of the principle: in such a region, a point in the (p, v) diagram corresponds to more than one state of the system.]

Proof of Theorem

First, a rather remarkable relationship must be established. In the regular minimum problem where

$$\Phi = U(x_1, \cdots, x_n) - P_1 x_1 - \cdots - P_n x_n$$

is at a minimum when

$$\frac{\partial U}{\partial x_j} - P_j = 0 \qquad\qquad (j = 1, 2, \cdots, n)$$

it is easy to show that

(10) $$\left(\frac{\partial \Phi}{\partial P_i}\right)_{P\text{'s constant}} = -x_i$$

since

$$\left(\frac{\partial \Phi}{\partial P_i}\right)_{P\text{'s constant}} = \left[\sum_1^n \frac{\partial U}{\partial x_j}\frac{\partial x_j}{\partial P_i} - \sum_1^n P_j \frac{\partial x_j}{\partial P_i}\right] - x_i = [0] - x_i$$

If we add constraints to the problem, this same relationship (10) can still be shown to hold. We can also write (10) in the equivalent form

(10)′ $$\Phi(P_1, \cdots, P_i + \Delta P_i, \cdots, P_n) - \Phi(P_1, \cdots, P_i, \cdots, P_n)$$
$$= -\int_0^{\Delta P_i} x_i dP_i$$

where x_i is a function of the P's revealing how x_i changes so as always to be at an optimum.

This can also be written in terms of any two variable prices as

(10)″ $$\Phi(P_1, \cdots, P_i + \Delta P_i, \cdots, P_j + \Delta P_j, \cdots, P_n)$$
$$- \Phi(P_1, \cdots, P_i, \cdots, P_j, \cdots, P_n)$$
$$= -\int_0^{\Delta P_j} \int_0^{\Delta P_i} \frac{\partial x_i}{\partial P_j} dP_j\, dP_i$$

Since

(11) $$\frac{\partial^2 \Phi}{\partial P_j \, \partial P_i} = \frac{\partial^2 \Phi}{\partial P_i \, \partial P_j} = -\frac{\partial x_i}{\partial P_j}$$

it is obvious that the general reciprocity relation

(12) $$\frac{\partial x_i}{\partial P_j} = \frac{\partial x_j}{\partial P_i}$$

must always hold.

Also,

(13) $$\frac{\partial^2 \Phi}{\partial P_i^2} = -\frac{\partial x_i}{\partial P_i} \leqq 0$$

This gives us a new way of looking at the second part of our principle. Figure 2 shows $-\Phi$ plotted for each P_i in a neighborhood of the previous equilibrium, A.

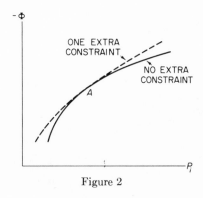

Figure 2

But now suppose that the system is under a new constraint that limits its departures from A. The lowest Φ will be not so low as that shown by our heavy curve; rather, it will look like our broken curve. The two curves are tangential, but obviously the unconstrained curve must be the more convex; and when we translate $-\dfrac{\partial^2 \Phi}{\partial P_i^2}$ into $+\dfrac{\partial x_i}{\partial P_i}$, this is the second part of our principle.

All this carries over into linear programming except that now we must be prepared for discontinuous and undefined derivatives. It still remains true that if we change an algebraic sign and define

(14) $$\Phi = +P_1 x_1 + P_2 x_2 + \cdots + P_n x_n$$

then

(15) $$\left(\frac{\partial \Phi}{\partial P_i} \right) = + x_i$$

at every point where this derivative exists. Actually, in linear programming vertex points are always optimal, and for some ranges of P_i we stay at one such point and then suddenly move over to another one as P_i changes further. Regarded as a function of P_i, any x is discontinuous, as shown in Figure 3. Any small change around the point A results in no change in x_i. The curve is discontinuous around B or C, but with the important property that anywhere between B and C is indifferently optimal. This follows from the convexity properties inherent in linear programming.

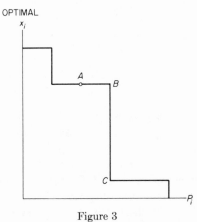

Figure 3

Note too that whereas the x's are discontinuous functions of the P's [or the a_{ij} and C's for that matter], the optimal Φ is nonetheless a continuous function of the P's. A discontinuity in one x must be just canceled out by discontinuities in all the remaining x's.

It is not really so surprising that a small change in a P will always result in a small change in Φ. Remember that the latter is optimal, and that by making no change in any x *at worst* we can move along a straight-line relationship between Φ and P_i. If Φ had a discontinuity at any point A, so that on one side of it the Φ's were k greater than at the point, we would have a contradiction — since along the feasible (but nonoptimal) straight line, Φ can be made arbitrarily close to its value at A. Thus, no jump is possible.

Moreover, if a right-hand derivative of Φ with respect to P_i exists anywhere, it must be less than the feasible value got when no x changes; or

$$\left(\frac{\partial \Phi}{\partial P_i}\right)_{\text{right-hand}} \leqq x_i$$

Also,

$$\left(\frac{\partial \Phi}{\partial P_i}\right)_{\text{left-hand}} \geqq x_i$$

Hence, wherever a true derivative exists, we must have equality as in (15).

Also, wherever the following double limit is uniquely defined as

$$\lim \Delta P_i \to 0 \; \frac{\Phi(P_1, \cdots, P_i + \Delta P_i, \cdots, P_j + \Delta P_j, \cdots)}{\Delta P_i \, \Delta P_j}$$
$$\lim \Delta P_j \to 0$$

$$\frac{- \; \Phi(P_1, \cdots, P_i + \Delta P_i, \cdots, P_j, \cdots)}{\Delta P_i \, \Delta P_j}$$

$$\frac{- \; \Phi(\cdots, P_i, \cdots, P_j + \Delta P_j, \cdots)}{\Delta P_i \, \Delta P_j}$$

$$\frac{+ \; \Phi(P_1, \cdots, P_i, \cdots, P_j, \cdots)}{\Delta P_i \, \Delta P_j}$$

$$= \frac{\partial^2 \Phi}{\partial P_i \, \partial P_j} = \frac{\partial^2 \Phi}{\partial P_j \, \partial P_i} = \frac{\partial x_i}{\partial P_j} = \frac{\partial x_j}{\partial P_i}$$

then our reciprocity relations must also hold. The common value in linear programming will always be zero. Where this double limit becomes indeterminate, then the x_i function is discontinuous in terms of P_j and at the same time the x_j function is discontinuous in terms of P_i.

Figure 4 shows Φ as a function of P_i. Instead of the smooth convex curve of Figure 2, we have straight lines with corners. The corners in Figure 4 correspond to the discontinuous steps in Figure 3.

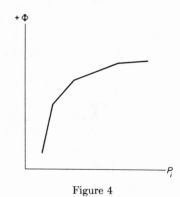

Figure 4

The surface of Φ plotted against P_i and P_j would consist of plane faces meeting in edges and also in corners or vertexes, where more than two faces meet. The contour lines of equal Φ are shown in Figure 5.

Figure 4's Φ as a function of P_i is the integral of Figure 3's x_i as a function of P_i. Despite all discontinuities, we can write

$$\Phi(P_1, \cdots, P_i + \Delta P_i, \cdots, P_n) - \Phi(P_1, \cdots, P_i, \cdots, P_n) = \int_0^{\Delta P_i} x_i \, dP_i$$

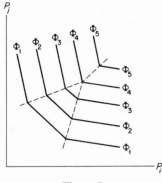

Figure 5

We can now see why an extra constraint will cause the change in x_i subsequent to a small change in P_i to be smaller in absolute value than when there is no constraint. Suppose the contrary were true. Then the minimum Φ achievable when we are under constraint would be less than that achievable when we are not so constrained — which is an absurdity. Figures 6*a* and 6*b* illustrate how the dotted-line constrained result must

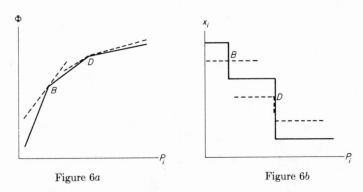

Figure 6*a*   Figure 6*b*

behave qualitatively with respect to the solid-line unconstrained results. The two curves may coincide, but the dotted curve of Φ can never pass below the solid curve. The reader may sketch the other possible types of behavior.

In every case for some small positive ΔP_i less than a preassigned size, we must have

$$(\Delta x_i)_{\text{unconstrained}} \leqq (\Delta x_i)_{\text{constrained}} \leqq 0$$

and for negative ΔP_i, the inequalities must all be reversed.

In conclusion, application to the dual problem can be indicated. By the above reasoning, the Le Chatelier principle tells us that

$$\Delta y_1 \, \Delta C_1 + \Delta y_2 \, \Delta C_2 + \cdots + \Delta y_m \, \Delta C_m \geqq 0$$

where Δy is the change in a shadow price and ΔC a change in the constant in one of our inequalities — such as a change in calories required of any diet. If we change only one C_1 — for example, our calorie requirements — then

$$\Delta y_1 \, \Delta C_1 \geqq 0$$

so that we know that the shadow price of that nutrient can only rise for an increase in the requirement. If now we add another food to the menu from which we can choose an optimal diet, the result will be to slow down (if anything) the rate at which the shadow price of calories will rise, which is the second part of our theorem.

44

Structure of a Minimum Equilibrium System

1. The functions met with in classical thermodynamics possess an abstract structure shared by equilibrium systems in quite diverse other fields — e.g., statics, economic theory, the recently developed mathematical theory of games and linear programming, etc.[1]) Given a set of numerical data on punch cards purporting to come from an equilibrium system sharing these properties, we should be able to determine whether such a supposition is tenable. Once the full empirical implications of the hypotheses embodied in the equilibrium theories have been elucidated, we can, if we wish, dispense with that theory except for mnemonic purposes.

By use of matrix notation, the present paper gives a brief but exhaustive summary of the properties of such systems, confining itself for simplicity to the *regular* case of unique and differentiable functions. Then it develops an exhaustive set of conditions that any finite set of observations must meet if the theory in question is not to be refuted.

2. Imagine that we are given a set of $2n$ variables that come in conjugate pairs (x_i, y_i). (In phenomenological thermodynamics these might be designated as generalized coordinates and generalized forces, such as entropy and temperature, volume and negative pressure, chemical mass and chemical potential, etc.)[2])

[1]) For the thermodynamic and economic interpretation of the mathematical relations here analyzed see such references as E. A. Guggenheim, *Thermodynamics* (Amsterdam, 1950); L. Tisza, "On the General Theory of Phase Transitions," in *Phase Transformations in Solids* (Wiley, 1951, N.Y.), pp. 1—37; P. A. Samuelson, *Foundations of Economic Analysis* (Cambridge, Mass. 1947), Ch. 3.

[2]) To avoid indeterminacy of scale, all extensive quantities can be thought of as expressed in ratio to the amount of an extensive variable, x_{n+1}, which is not included in this analysis.

There is assumed to exist n equilibrium conditions or equations of state between these $2n$ variables, defined as follows:

Axiom for a Regular Equilibrium System: Corresponding to prescribed values for n variables $(y_1, \ldots, y_n)$, values of the conjugate variables $(x_1, \ldots, x_n)$ are determined so as to provide a regular minimum to $F(x; y) = F(x_1, \ldots, x_n; y_1, \ldots, y_n) = Y(x_1, \ldots, x_n) - \sum_1^n y_j x_j$, so that

(1) $\partial F/\partial x_i = 0 = Y_i(x_1, \ldots, x_n) - y_i$ $(i = 1, \ldots, n)$

where subscripts to functions always stand for partial derivatives with respect to the indicated variables, and where the Hessian matrix of second derivatives of F and Y with respect to the x's is everywhere defined and is positive definite so as to insure a regular minimum.

Knowledge of the function Y above determines all properties of the equilibrium system. (In thermodynamics, Y is internal energy.) These regularity conditions of smoothness and convexity could be relaxed. But for the present it is sufficient to deduce the full implications of the regular case. We have immediately from the Axiom:

Theorem 1: Functions constraining a set of variables are equivalent to a regular equilibrium system, if and only if, they can be thrown into the form:

(2) $x_i = X^i(y_1, \ldots, y_n) \equiv X_i(y_1, \ldots, y_n)$ $(i = 1, \ldots, n)$,

where $X(y_1, \ldots, y_n)$ is an existent twice differentiable function, whose Hessian matrix of partial derivatives — which is also the symmetric Jacobian of the transformation (2) — must be positive definite.

The necessity part of this theorem follows immediately from the fact that the relations (1) can always be inverted by virtue of the fact that their Jacobian is postulated to be the non-singular matrix of a positive definite quadratic form. Equations (2) represent such inverse functions, and their Jacobian $[X_j^i] = [Y_{ij}]^{-1}$. Since the inverse of a symmetric matrix must be symmetric, our right to set $X^i = X_i$ is established and the integrability or symmetry conditions guarantee the existence of the function $X(y_1, \ldots, y_n) = \Sigma \int X_i \, dx_i$ independently of path, which is unique up to an inessential integration constant. Finally, because the inverse of a positive definite matrix must be positive definite, this stipulated property is indeed necessary.

The sufficiency part of the theorem can be most easily seen by recognizing the dualism between the x's and y's. If we interchanged the letters in (2), we should have a relation with all the properties of (1); call it (1)* and call (2)* the relation (1) with the labels interchanged. Then by the just proved necessary condition, it follows that (1)* implies (2)*, which is all that we need for our sufficiency proof of Theorem 1. This also shows the truth of

Corollary 1: The variables $(x_1, \ldots, x_n)$ and $(y_1, \ldots, y_n)$ are mutually conjugate: the same equilibrium system can be defined by the dual minimum problem,

$F^*(y; x) = X(y_1, \ldots, y_n) - \sum_1^n x_j y_j$, a minimum for prescribed x's.

3. The equilibrium conditions of (1), or (2), were seen to be n constraints among $2n$ variables. There are a vast number of ways of taking as prescribable variables n out of $2n$ variables, namely $(2n)!/(n!)^2$ permutations. But in the general case, there is no reason to believe that any n variables taken at random can be independently varied. Thus, in the simple case where $Y(x_1, x_2, \ldots) = \frac{1}{2}\sum x_j^2$, the equations of state are $x_i = y_i$, and the Hessians of Y and of X are the identity matrixes. Clearly for this system, the variables $(x_1, y_1, x_3, \ldots)$ cannot be independently varied.

In general, the only admissible sets that we can be sure of are those generated by the following rule: *Select one and only one member from each conjugate pair of variables.* Since there are two independent ways of selecting from each pair, there are obviously exactly 2^n such admissible sets of independently prescribable variables. If we follow the convention of suitably renumbering the variables, we can write any of the 2^n sets in one of the following $n + 1$ forms:

$(y_1, \ldots, y_n), (y_1, \ldots, y_{n-1}; x_n), \ldots, (y_1, \ldots, y_m; x_{m+1}, \ldots, x_n),$
$\ldots, (y_1; x_2, \ldots, x_n), (x_1, \ldots, x_n).$

The first and last of these are the "unmixed" sets of (1) and (2).

That the remaining "mixed" sets are admissible as independently prescribable follows from the fact that every principal minor of the definite Jacobians of (1) and (2) are necessarily definite and non-singular. This assures us that the first m equations of (1) can be solved explicitly for $(x_1, \ldots, x_m)$ in terms of $(y_1, \ldots, y_m; x_{m+1}, \ldots, x_n)$ since the crucial matrix of partial derivatives $[\partial y_i/\partial x_j]$ is the non-singular m rowed principal minor of $[Y_{ij}]$; with these x's solved for, we can substitute in the remaining $n - m$ equations of (1) to get $(y_{m+1}, \ldots, y_n)$ in terms of the same independent variables. (A dual similar argument could be made concerning the solvability for $(y_{m+1}, \ldots, y_n)$ of the last $n - m$ equations of (2).) Thus, by use of the Implicit Function Theorem — and by an extension of it that gives nowhere vanishing principal minors as sufficient conditions for uniqueness of our solutions in the large — we can deduce:

Theorem 2: For any of the 2^n admissible sets of n independent variables, consisting of one and only one member of each pair of conjugate variables, we can in regular systems — and only in such systems — determine unique and differentiable values of the remaining variables. After we have suitably renumbered the variables, we can write these relations as

$$(3) \quad \begin{aligned} x_i &= x^i(\bar{y}_1, \ldots, \bar{y}_m; \bar{x}_{m+1}, \ldots, \bar{x}_n) \quad (i = 1, \ldots, m) \\ y_i &= y^i(\bar{y}_1, \ldots, \bar{y}_m; \bar{x}_{m+1}, \ldots, \bar{x}_n) \quad (i = m+1, \ldots, n), \end{aligned}$$

$$0 \leqq m \leqq n$$

with the partitioned Jacobian matrix of skew-symmetric form

$$(4) \quad J_m = \begin{bmatrix} \dfrac{\partial x}{\partial \bar{y}}, & \dfrac{\partial x}{\partial \bar{x}} \\[2mm] \dfrac{\partial y}{\partial \bar{y}}, & \dfrac{\partial y}{\partial \bar{x}} \end{bmatrix} = \begin{bmatrix} Y_{xx}^{-1}, & -Y_{xx}^{-1} Y_{x\bar{x}} \\ Y_{\bar{x}x} Y_{xx}^{-1}, & Y_{\bar{x}\bar{x}} - Y_{\bar{x}x} Y_{xx}^{-1} Y_{x\bar{x}} \end{bmatrix}$$

$$= \begin{bmatrix} X_{\bar{y}\bar{y}} - X_{\bar{y}y} X_{yy}^{-1} X_{y\bar{y}}, & X_{\bar{y}y} X_{yy}^{-1} \\ -X_{yy}^{-1} X_{y\bar{y}}, & X_{yy}^{-1} \end{bmatrix} = \begin{bmatrix} Y_{xx}^{-1} & -Y_{xx}^{-1} Y_{x\bar{x}} \\ -X_{yy}^{-1} X_{y\bar{y}} & X_{yy}^{-1} \end{bmatrix}$$

$$= \begin{bmatrix} A & B \\ -B' & C \end{bmatrix}, \quad 0 \leqq m \leqq n,$$

Y_{xx} being understood to stand for the first m by m rows and columns of $[Y_{ij}], \ldots, X_{\bar{y}\bar{y}}$ for the last $n - m$ rows and columns of $[X_{ij}]$, etc.; and the symmetric diagonal blocks A and C being positive definite.[3])

In (3) the position of the semi-colon will serve to identify the value of m, except in the limiting cases where $m = 0$ or n, in which case we have the unmixed variables and equations of (1) and (2). To prove the various relations of (4), we make the appropriate matrix substitutions (or matrix premultiplications) in the differentials relation of (1) and (2)

(5)

$$\begin{bmatrix} Y_{xx} Y_{x\bar{x}} & -I_m & 0 \\ Y_{\bar{x}x} Y_{\bar{x}\bar{x}} & 0 & -I_{n-m} \end{bmatrix} \begin{bmatrix} dx \\ d\bar{x} \\ d\bar{y} \\ dy \end{bmatrix} = 0,$$

$$\begin{bmatrix} -I_m & 0 & X_{\bar{y}\bar{y}} & X_{\bar{y}v} \\ 0 & -I_{n-m} & X_{v\bar{y}} & X_{vv} \end{bmatrix} \begin{bmatrix} dx \\ d\bar{x} \\ d\bar{y} \\ dy \end{bmatrix} = 0,$$

to get the first row's relations of (4), which are seen to be dual forms. The next row of (4) immediately follows. The last form is important: it summarizes the facts that the diagonal blocks are symmetrical, but that the off-diagonal matrixes are skew-symmetric with $(\partial x/\partial \bar{x}) = -(\partial y/\partial \bar{y})'$. These properties follow from the symmetry relations $[Y_{ij}] = [Y_{ji}]$, while the definiteness of the positive blocks follows from the definiteness of $[Y_{ij}]$ and $[X_{ij}]$ and of the inverses of their principal minors.

To prove the converse part of the theorem — that the structure of (3) and (4) implies the structure of (1) or (2) — note that by the same routine substitutions by which (5) went into (4), but working in reverse, we find for the Jacobian of $(\bar{y}, y)$ in terms of $(x, \bar{x})$

---

[3]) If determinacy of scale has not been achieved by the device of the first footnote, then $Y(x_1, \ldots, x_n)$ will be a homogeneous function of order one, and its n^2 Hessian $[Y_{ij}]$ will be positive definite of rank $n - 1$. The functions (2) will then be determinate only in ratio and not in scale. For $m < n$, the functions (3) will be perfectly determinate, and can be shown to be homogeneous of order one in $[x_{m+1}, \ldots, x_n]$ alone, requiring C to be positive semi-definite of rank $(n - m - 1)$ with $[x_{m+1}, \ldots, x_n] C = 0$ and $[x_1, \ldots, x_n] = [x_{m+1}, \ldots, x_n] B'$.

$$(6) \qquad J_n = \begin{bmatrix} \dfrac{\partial \bar{y}}{\partial x}, & \dfrac{\partial \bar{y}}{\partial \bar{x}} \\[2ex] \dfrac{\partial y}{\partial x}, & \dfrac{\partial y}{\partial \bar{x}} \end{bmatrix} = \begin{bmatrix} A^{-1} & -A^{-1}B \\ -B'A^{-1} & C + B'A^{-1}B \end{bmatrix}$$

This is seen to be symmetric. It remains to show that independently of B, the positive definiteness of C and A will guarantee that this whole matrix is positive definite, and hence of the stipulated regular form $[Y_{ij}]$.

We make use of the easily demonstrable algebraic fact that any positive definite A^{-1} can be written in an infinity of different ways as $D'D$, where D is non-singular.

Now consider the quadratic form

$$Q = Q_1 + Q_2 = [z_1, \ldots, z_m, z_{m+1}, \ldots, z_n] J_n [z_1, \ldots, z_m, z_{m+1}, \ldots, z_n]'$$
$$= [z_{m+1}, \ldots, z_n] C [z_{m+1}, \ldots, z_n]'$$
$$+ [z_1, \ldots, z_n] \begin{bmatrix} D'D, & -D'(DB) \\ -(DB)'D, & (DB)'(DB) \end{bmatrix} \begin{bmatrix} z_1 \\ \vdots \\ z_n \end{bmatrix}$$
$$= [0, \ldots, 0, z_{m+1}, \ldots, z_n] C [0, \ldots, 0, z_{m+1}, \ldots, z_n]' + WW'$$

where $W = [z_1, \ldots, z_m] D' - [z_{m+1}, \ldots, z_n](DB)'$.

Q_1 is positive semi-definite because C was positive definite by hypothesis; Q_2 is a sum of squares and hence positive semi-definite. But for $z'z \neq 0$, where $Q_1 = 0$, $Q_2 > 0$ and where $Q_2 = 0$, $Q_1 > 0$; hence, Q is finally proved to be positive definite.

4. Returning now to the mixed relations (3), their skew-symmetry property warns us that, as they stand, these functions are not partial derivatives of any existent parent function. However, because of the special skew-symmetry between the off-diagonal blocks, it is clear that changing the algebraic sign of the two upper blocks will give us a symmetric matrix

$$(7) \qquad \begin{bmatrix} -A & -B \\ -B' & C \end{bmatrix}$$

which can be regarded as the second-derivative Hessian matrix of an existent function for each m. Hence

Theorem 3: Any regular equilibrium system in $2n$ conjugate variables has associated with it, for each of the 2^n admissible sets of independent variables, a characterizing function, which may be written

$$P(y_1, \ldots, y_m; x_{m+1}, \ldots, x_n) = \sum_1^m \int -x^i(y_1, \ldots, y_m; \ldots, x_n) dy_i$$

(8)

$$+ \sum_{m+1}^n \int y^i(y_1, \ldots, y_m; \ldots, x_n) dx_i$$

where the line integral is independent of path by virtue of the symmetry relations. In terms of the relevant characterizing function, we can rewrite equations (3)

(3)′
$$x_i = -\partial P(y_1, \ldots, y_m; \ldots, x_n)/\partial y_i, \quad i = 1, \ldots, m$$
$$y_i = +\partial P(y_1, \ldots, y_m; \ldots, x_n)/\partial x_i, \quad i = m + 1, \ldots, n.$$

Corollary 1: For $m = 0$, $P \equiv Y$; and for $m = n$, $P \equiv -X$; for all m and for values of the $2n$ variables satisfying the n equilibrium conditions,

(9) $$P(y_1, \ldots, y_m; x_{m+1}, \ldots, x_n) = Y - \sum_1^m y_j x_j = -X + \sum_{m+1}^n y_j x_j;$$

but these are not identities in the $2n$ variable space.

Corollary 2: For prescribed values of $(x_1, \ldots, x_m; y_{m+1}, \ldots, y_n)$ the expression

(10) $$F^m(x, \bar{x}; \bar{y}, y) = P(\bar{y}_1, \ldots, \bar{y}_m; \bar{x}_{m+1} \ldots, \bar{x}_n) + \sum_1^m x_i y_i - \sum_{m+1}^n x_i y_i$$

reaches a regular saddlepoint or minimax when, and only when, the remaining variables $(\bar{y}_1, \ldots, \bar{y}_m; \bar{x}_{m+1}, \ldots, \bar{x}_n)$ are in their regular equilibrium configuration; i.e., for an equilibrium position $(x_1^0, \ldots; \ldots, \bar{x}_n^0; \bar{y}_1^0, \ldots; \ldots y_n^0)$

(11) $$F^m(x^0, \bar{x}^0; \bar{y}, y^0) \leqq F^m(x^0, \bar{x}^0; \bar{y}^0, y^0) \leqq F^m(x^0, \bar{x}; \bar{y}^0, y^0)$$

with the inequalities valid for distinct points.

In classical thermodynamics these 2^n characterizing functions have a variety of notational descriptions and go by such names as internal energy, enthropy, enthalpy, Helmholtz free energy, Gibbs potential or free energy, etc. Knowledge of any one of them provides a succinct summary of all the regular equilibrium relations, and by use of the transformations of (6) and (4) we can in principle go from the properties of any one to the properties of any other.

The symmetry properties of (4) provides immediate proof of the existence of each of these characterizing functions described in theorem 3. To prove Corollary 1, we may use the properties of Legendre transformations or of differential geometry; but remaining within the limits of the present straightforward algebraic manipulation of Jacobian matrices, we make the equilibrium substitutions to get

$$Y - \sum_1^m y_j x_j = Y(x^1(\bar{y}_1, \ldots; \ldots, \bar{x}_n), \ldots; \ldots, \bar{x}_n) - \sum_1^m \bar{y}_j x^i(\bar{y}_1, \ldots; \ldots, \bar{x}_n)$$

and

(12)
$$\frac{\partial (Y - \sum_1^m y_j x_j)}{\partial \bar{y}_i} = \sum_1^m (Y_j - \bar{y}_j) x_i^j - x_i = 0 - x_i, \quad (i = 1, \ldots, m)$$

$$\frac{\partial (Y - \sum_1^m y_j x_j)}{\partial \bar{x}_i} = \sum_1^m (Y_j - \bar{y}_j) x_i^j + Y_i = 0 + y_i, \quad (i = m+1, \ldots, n)$$

which is seen to be identical with P if the inessential integration constant is appropriately adjusted. By using the dualism between Y and X, the relations of P to $-(X - \sum_{m+1}^n x_i y_i)$ shown in (9) are verified.

To prove the saddlepoint property of Corollary 2, we note the equivalence of

(13) $\quad \dfrac{\partial F^m}{\partial \bar{y}_i} = 0 \quad (i = 1, \ldots, m); \quad \dfrac{\partial F^m}{\partial \bar{x}_i} = 0 \quad (i = m+1, \ldots, n)$

to (3)′; and we note that in changing the algebraic signs in the upper blocks of (4), we achieve (7)'s symmetry but at the cost of making its upper diagonal block $-A = -Y_{xx}^{-1}$ be negative rather than positive definite. Together with the positive definiteness of $C = X_{yy}^{-1}$, this is sufficient for the saddle-point or minimax property.

This minimax property shows us that the notion of an unmixed set of conjugate variables $(y_1, \ldots, y_n)$ and $(x_1, \ldots, x_n)$ is not arbitrary. We are generally forced to group y_1 and y_2 together and are not free to interchange the x and y designations of y_1 and x_1. (Thus, entropy and volume belong together in a sense that temperature and volume do not; this we know from the mathematics as well as from the physics.) For if we link up admissible sets of conjugate variables without distinguishing which are x's and which are y's, the Jacobian (4) of the resulting transformation (3) will have a *determinable* number of rows and columns that yield skew-symmetry. Thus, m is a determinable number which can be verified to be 0 or n or to be in between. This enables us to find the proper way of dividing the $2n$ conjugate variables into two unmixed groups. Of course, which we call x and y has no mathematical significance because of the complete dualism between them. (In the singular case where whole rows and corresponding columns of J_m vanish, we shall later show that the exact size of m is indeterminable but indifferent, since the system then splits off into independent constellations.)

5. Theorem 3 and its corollaries each contains within itself, and is equivalent to, the previous theorems and Axiom. If any $2n$ variables can be labelled so that n of them can be expressed in terms of the remaining n by a transformation with the regular minimax properties of (11), such a system must have all the properties of a regular equilibrium system.

For each of the 2^n admissible sets of independent variables, there will be $n(n-1)/2$ symmetry or skew-symmetry relations. In thermodynamics these are called Maxwell relations, and any one complete set of them implies all the rest. Matrix notation and operations themselves constitute a most excellent mnemonic device; so the transformation of (4) and (6) represent an excellent substitute for the Bridgman[4]) and similar formulas by which partial derivatives of one set can be converted into partial derivatives of another. Given numerical coefficients, we can efficiently go from, say, J_6 to J_9, by the series of steps J_6, J_7, J_8, J_9, where at each stage the only needed operations are of the Gauss-Doolittle type convenient for desk and other calculators, namely $a - bc$, and $(a - bc)/d$. In practice, there is never need actually to renumber variables since the four partitioned matrices can always be represented by different colors for the numbers or by appropriate underlining.

[4]) P. W. Bridgman, A Condensed Collection of Thermodynamic Formulas (Harvard, 1925).

We might call a system a "regular variational system" if it satisfies all the symmetry equalities of a regular minimum system, whether or not it also has the definiteness properties on its Jacobians of a minimum. Before exploring further the inequalities implied by the minimum property itself, we first give a single minimum formulation that is capable of handling all admissible mixed cases simultaneously.

6. Our original axiom assures us that $F(x; y)$ attains a minimum if we set the x's at their optimal equilibrium values in terms of the y's as determined by the equilibrium relations (1) or (2). Thus, the minimum obtainable of F will depend only on the y's and we may write it as $F(y) \leq F(x; y)$, with the equality sign holding in equilibrium, and only then. It will be easily shown that $F(y) \equiv -X(y)$ for an appropriate choice of integration constant in the latter dual function to $Y(x)$. This suggests

Theorem 4: For any regular equilibrium system, we can find two mutually conjugate functions $Y(x_1, \ldots, x_n)$ and $X(y_1, \ldots, y_n)$, such that

$$(14) \quad N(x_1, \ldots, x_n; y_1, \ldots, y_n) = Y(x_1, \ldots, x_n) \\ + X(y_1, \ldots, y_n) - \sum_1^n x_i y_i$$

reaches a regular minimum value of zero if, and only if, the $2n$ variables are in their n equilibrium relations to each other. The Hessian matrices of Y and X will be positive definite everywhere and in the equilibrium configurations will be exact inverses of each other.

Note that this minimum formulation includes as special cases the dual minimum problems of the Axiom and Corollary 1. Note that it is the only formulation yet stated that treats both sides of the dual with perfect symmetry, and the only minimum formulation that handles all admissible mixed sets of variables. If the Y, X, and P functions are called "potentials," then $N(x; y)$, which is defined in the $2n$ space and not alone on the n-dimensional equilibrium locus, is in the nature of "superfluous or disequilibrium potential."

To prove theorem (4), we note that by $F(y)$'s definition,

$F(x; y) - F(y)$ does have the stipulated properties of $N(x; y)$. It remains to show that $X(y)$, as previously defined from (2), with its Hessian $[X_{ij}] = [Y_{ij}]^{-1}$, is for an appropriate choice of integration constant identical to $- F(y)$. But note that for $m = 0$, $P(y_1, \ldots, y_n)$, as defined already in (8), is identically $F(y_1, \ldots, y_n)$; and as shown in (9),

$$\frac{\partial F}{\partial y_i} = \frac{\partial P(y_1, \ldots, y_n)}{\partial y_i} = -x_i \quad (i = 1, \ldots, n)$$

which agrees with (2)'s definition of X. Hence, $X(y_1, \ldots, y_n) = - F(y_1, \ldots, y_n)$.

Corollary 1: The regular equilibrium is defined in terms of any admissible set of mixed variables by

(15)
$$\frac{\partial N}{\partial x_i} = 0 = Y_i(x_1, \ldots, x_n) - y_i \quad (i = 1, \ldots, m)$$

$$\frac{\partial N}{\partial y_i} = 0 = X_i(y_1, \ldots, y_n) - x_i \quad (i = m + 1, \ldots, n)$$

where the Hessian of N with respect to $(x_1, \ldots, x_m; y_{m+1}, \ldots, y_n)$ is positive definite being of the form

(16)
$$\begin{bmatrix} Y_{xx}^{-1} & 0 \\ 0 & X_{vv}^{-1} \end{bmatrix}$$

If we were to prescribe an inadmissible set of variables, involving both an x_i and y_i, then we would get -1 terms in the off-diagonal blocks of the Hessian matrix (16), and we could not infer that it has the positive definiteness properties needed for a minimum. Thus, in the case earlier mentioned where $x_i = y_i$, $N(x; y) = \frac{1}{2}\sum x_j^2 - \sum x_j y_j = \frac{1}{2}\sum(x_j - y_j)^2 + \frac{1}{2}\sum y_j^2$ and prescribing $(x_1, y_1, y_3, \ldots, y_n)$ and minimizing with respect to the remaining variables would give $N = \frac{1}{2}(x_1 - y_1)^2$, which need not vanish. This confirms that only 2^n sets of variables are generally independently variable.

It will be noted that (15) shows the first m equations of (1) and the last $(n - m)$ equations of (2) together to be equivalent to (1), or to (2), or to (3). Transforming the differentials of (15) by the usual methods will give us J_m in the next to the last form of (4), a form that treats both aspects of the dual with perfect symmetry. It will be noted that the P functions defined in (9) did not treat the dual functions Y and X perfectly symmetrically, there being a difference in algebraic sign. But we can split N up into two parts, so that

$$N(x; y) = (Y - \sum_1^m y_j x_j) - (-X + \sum_{m+1}^n y_j x_j)$$

(17) $$= -(Y - \sum_1^m y_j x_j) - (X - \sum_{m+1}^n y_j x_j)$$

(in equil.) $= P(y_1, \ldots, y_m; \ldots, x_n) - P(y_1, \ldots, y_m; \ldots, x_n)$

$$= P(y_1, \ldots, y_m; \ldots, x_n) + P^*(x_1, \ldots, x_m; \ldots, y_n)$$

where the definition of the functions P^*, mutually complementary to P, is obvious. Through the whole $2n$ space, P and P^* are independent of each other, even though they are complementary on the n-dimensional equilibrium locus.

The minimum formulation in terms of N immediately confirms that a set like $(y_1, \ldots, y_n; x_{m+1}, \ldots, x_n)$ is truly a mixed one, since generally $N - \sum_1^n x_j y_j$ can be resolved into two additive functions of n variables each in essentially one way only, as can be determined from the pattern of zeros in the $2n$ by $2n$ Hessian matrix of N. The singular case mentioned earlier, where $Y(x)$ and $X(y)$ can be each written as the sum of two functions involving no overlapping variables, is instantly revealed by the use of $N(x; y)$. Thus, if $Y(x_1, \ldots, x_n) = R(x_1, \ldots, x_r) + S(x_{r+1}, \ldots, x_n)$, X will be capable of a similar split and we are really dealing with two entirely independent sub-systems. That being the case, there is no mathematical way of relating x_1 to x_n in any sense different from the relating of x_1 to y_n.

Finally, it may be mentioned that the general minimum formulation in terms of N remains valid in irregular cases where some of the functions have corners with undefined partial derivatives, and where the equilibrium relations may not be unique or continuous. (Even the simplest case of phase equilibrium of a solid and liquid provides an "irregular" example where functions have a corner and partial derivatives are not defined.)

7. This exhausts the full empirical implications upon our observable functions. If someone specifies in detail any given

set of functions, we can in principle compute various sets of partial derivatives, test various of the symmetry relations, and various of the determinantal conditions for definiteness. However, suppose that the functions specified are purely empirical and not exactly represented by any finite combination of known mathematical formulas. We have a procedure for calculating the values of the equilibrium functions at any point. Also, we can approximate to various of their derivatives; however, unless we are given certain *a priori* bounds on the higher derivatives of the function, no matter how far we push our computations, we cannot strictly infer the goodness of our approximations and therefore cannot, strictly speaking, ever test a symmetry relation with complete rigor.

8. Fortunately, in applied sciences, we usually have at least vague notions concerning smoothness of higher derivatives, and we can therefore compute an expression like

$$(18) \quad \left\{ \frac{Y^2(x_1+h_1, x_2, \ldots) - Y^2(x_1, x_2, \ldots)}{h_1} \right. $$
$$\left. - \frac{Y^1(x_1, x_2+h_2, \ldots) - Y^1(x_1, x_2, \ldots)}{h_2} \right\} $$

for "small" h_1 and h_2, and decide whether it is sufficiently far from zero to refute the hypothesis that $\partial Y^2/\partial x_1 = \partial Y^1/\partial x_2$.

9. J. R. Hicks[5] has derived an interesting generalization of the above finite tests for integrability or symmetry. For this purpose, let us suppose that the $(Y^1, \ldots, Y^n)$ functions of the x's are indeed the partial derivatives of a function $Y(x_1, \ldots, x_n)$, which has continuous second partial derivatives. Then we can write various Taylor's expansions such as

$$Y(x_1^1, x_2^1, \ldots) - Y(x_1^2, x_2^2, \ldots) = \sum_1^n (x_j^1 - x_j^2) Y_j(\bar{x}_1, \bar{x}_2, \ldots) + 0$$
$$= \sum_1^n (x_j^1 - x_j^2) Y_j(x_1^2, x_2^2, \ldots) + R_2'$$
$$(19) \qquad = \sum_1^n (x_j^1 - x_j^2) Y_j(x_1^1, x_2^1, \ldots) - R_2''$$
$$= \sum_1^n (x_j^1 - x_j^2) \frac{Y_j(x_1^1, x_2^1, \ldots) + Y_j(x_1^2, x_2^2, \ldots)}{2} + R_3$$

[5] J. R. Hicks, *A Revision of Demand Theory* (Oxford, 1956), p. 126.

where $(\bar{x}_1, \bar{x}_2, \ldots)$ or $(\bar{x})$ represents a point intermediate between (x^1) and (x^2); where R_2' and R_2'' represent remainder terms involving second-degree or higher terms in $(x_j^1 - x_j^2)$; and where R_3 involves third-degree or higher terms in $(x_j^1 - x^2)$ because R_2' and $-R_2''$ can be shown to differ by terms of higher than the second degree.

Following Hicks, for the rest of this section I omit all terms of higher than second degree and state relations that the resulting approximations must satisfy. Of course

$$0 = [Y(x^1) - Y(x^2)] + [Y(x^2) - Y(x^3)] + [Y(x^3) - Y(x^1)]$$
$$= \tfrac{1}{2}\sum(x_j^1 - x_j^2)(y_j^1 + y_j^2) + \tfrac{1}{2}(x_j^2 - x_j^3)(y_j^2 + y_j^3) + \tfrac{1}{2}\sum(x_j^3 - x_j^1)(y_j^3 + y_j^1)$$
$$(20) \quad = \tfrac{1}{2}\sum(x_j^1 y_j^2 - \sum x_j^2 y_j^1) + \tfrac{1}{2}(\sum x_j^2 y_j^3 - \sum x_j^3 y_j^2) + \tfrac{1}{2}(\sum x_j^3 y_j^1 - x_j^1 y_j^3)$$

where the equilibrium substitutions $y_i = Y_i(x_1, \ldots, x_n)$ have been made.

This is a generalized integrability condition that any three near-by points must approximate to. This general Hicks condition includes as a special case the above relation (18); to see this set $(x^1) = (x_1, x_2, \ldots)$, $(x^2) = (x_1 + h_1, x_2, \ldots)$, $(x^3) = (x_1, x_2 + h_2, \ldots)$, and rearrange the resulting terms of (20) to get (18).

An obvious slight generalization of the Hicks reasoning will give us conditions that any 4, 5, 6, $\ldots$, or r distinct points must satisfy as they come close together.

Theorem 5: Any r nearby points observed from a regular, continuously smooth, minimum system must satisfy the finite equality

$$0 = \sum_{k=1}^{r}\left(Y(x^k) - Y(x^{k+1})\right) + \left(Y(x^r) - Y(x^1)\right)$$

$$(21) \quad = \sum_{k=1}^{r}\left(\tfrac{1}{2}\sum_{j=1}^{n}(x_j^k - x_j^{k+1})(y_j^k + y_j^{k+1})\right) + \tfrac{1}{2}\sum_{j=1}^{n}(x_j^r - x_j^1)(y_j^r + y_j^1) + R_3$$

$$= \tfrac{1}{2}\left((\sum_1^n x_j^1 y_j^2 - \sum x_j^2 y_j^1) + (\sum_1^n x_j^2 y_j^3 - \sum x^3 j^2) + \ldots \right.$$

$$\left. + (\sum_1^n x_j^r y_j^1 - \sum x_j^1 y_j^r)\right) + R_3$$

where R_3 involves terms of at least the third degree in $(x_j^i - x_j^k)$. By setting (x^1), (x^2), (x^3), (x^4) equal to $(x_1, x_2, \ldots)$,

$(x_1 + h_1, x_2, \ldots)$, $(x_1, x_2 + h_2, \ldots)$, $(x_1 + h_1'', x_2, \ldots)$, we can convert the above into the equality that must hold in the limit between the various more familiar finite approximations to

$$\frac{\partial^3 Y}{\partial x_1^2 \partial x_2} = \frac{\partial}{\partial x_1} \left(\frac{\partial^2 y}{\partial x_1 \partial x_2} \right) = \frac{\partial}{\partial x_2} \left(\frac{\partial^2 Y}{\partial x_1^2} \right), \text{ etc.;}$$

and still other special cases can be derived involving chains of any number of observations in excess of 2.

10. Equations (21) would be adequate tests for symmetry and for the variational (as distinct from minimum) aspect of the problem were it not for the fundamental methodological difficulty already mentioned in paragraph 7. Even if we could exactly calculate — free of all statistical or experimental error — any point on the n-dimensional equilibrium locus in the $2n$-dimensional space, nonetheless we could never be perfectly certain that an observed value for the bracketed expression in (18) did or did not refute integrability. If the bracketed test expression exactly equals zero, we cannot be sure that for still closer together points it will not turn out to differ from zero. If the test differs from zero, we cannot be sure that the difference is greater than the admissible remainder term R_3. Pragmatically, we may sidestep this methodological difficulty by hypothesizing *a priori* knowledge; or we may not care whether the equilibrium system is "really" variational, provided it behaves sufficiently like one for the purpose at hand.

The advantage of being able to convert a problem into variational form seems to be mainly mnemonic. Instead of having to record or remember n independent functions $Y_i(x_1, \ldots, x_n)$, we need only to know one function $Y(x_1, \ldots, x_n)$. Or it is enough to know everywhere the one function $\partial Y(x_1, \ldots, x_n)/\partial x_1$, with $\partial Y(\bar{x}_1, x_2, \ldots, x_n)/\partial x_2$ being only known everywhere in the subspace where $x = \bar{x}_1$; likewise $\partial Y(\bar{x}_1, \bar{x}_2, x_3, \ldots, x_n)/\partial x_3$ need be known only for varying $(x_3, \ldots, x_n)$ in the subspace where $(x_1, x_2) \equiv (\bar{x}_1, \bar{x}_2)$; ... finally $\partial Y(\bar{x}_1, \ldots, \bar{x}_{n-1}, x_n)/\partial x_n$ need be known only for varying x_n with the remaining variables fixed. (E.g. in a simple entropy, volume, absolute temperature, pressure system, knowledge everywhere of the pressure-volume-temperature "equations of state" need be supplemented by knowledge of the specific heat function at one temperature alone to define internal energy and all thermodynamic behavior everywhere.)

Also, a general one-to-one transformation of coordinates, as defined by $x_i = f^i(v_1, \ldots, v_n)$, will lead to new variables $w_1, \ldots, w_n$, conjugate to the v's and determined by the identity $dY = \sum_1^n w_j \, dv_j = \sum^n y_i \, dx_i = \sum_1^n [\sum_1^n Y_i(f^1, \ldots, f^n) f_j^i(v_1, \ldots, v_n)] \, dv_j$.

11. It turns out, however, that we can in principle give an exact test to refute the hypothesis that we have a minimum system. Given a set of finite observations, presumed free of statistical error or with known bounds on that error, we can specify exact inequalities that must be satisfied. Testing an *approximate equality* is in principle a methodologically different problem from the easier case of verifying or refuting an *inequality*. From this viewpoint it is desirable to reverse the usual relative treatment of a minimum and variational principle. In many discussions of classical mechanics, authors are satisfied to state a variational principle without being interested in whether the resulting conditions relate to "stationariness" or to the more difficult question of "definite minimization." From the standpoint of exact empirical refutation, it turns out to be conceptually much easier to test the hypothesis of definite minimization than to test the variational hypothesis. To repeat, this is because an inequality can be empirically refuted more easily than can an approximate equality.

12. Let us consider various distinct equilibrium positions $(x^1; y^1)$, $(x^2; y^2)$, $(x^3; y^3)$, ... Then by definition of the regular minimum

$$Y(x_1^1, x_1^1, \ldots) - \sum_1^n y_j^1 x_j^1 < Y(x_1^2, x_2^2, \ldots) - \sum_1^n y_j^1 x_j^2$$

or

(22) $$Y(x_1^1, x_2^1, \ldots) - Y(x_1^2, x_2^2, \ldots) < \sum_1^m (x_j^1 - x_j^2) y_j^1,$$

showing that R_2' in (19) is necessarily negative. Similarly for R_2''. Hence

(23) $$0 = [Y(x^1) - Y(x^2)] + [Y(x^2) - Y(x^1)] < \sum_1^n (x_j^1 - x_j^2)(y_j^1 - y_j^2);$$

or, letting $x_j^1 - x_j^2 = \Delta x_j$, $y_j^1 - y_j^2 = \Delta y_j$, we have holding between any two distinct equilibrium states

$$(24) \qquad \Delta x_1 \Delta y_1 + \Delta x_2 \Delta y_2 + \ldots + \Delta x_n \Delta y_n > 0.$$

In the special case where only one variable of any admissible set of prescribed parameters is allowed to change, we get

$$(25) \qquad 0 + \ldots + 0 + \Delta x_i \Delta y_i + 0 + \ldots + 0 > 0,$$

showing that conjugate variables must change in the same direction when no change takes place in at least one of every other pair or conjugate variables. (This is a weak form of the so-called Le Chatelier principle.)

If we have r observations, we can apply the above test (24) to each of the $r(r-1)/2$ pairs of observations. If any one of the inequalities fails to be satisfied, then the minimum hypothesis is refuted. However, if we have more than 2 observations, further independent inequalities must be satisfied.

From (22), we have

$$(26) \quad \sum_1^n y_j^1(x_j^1 - x_j^2) + \sum_1^n y_j^2(x_j^2 - x_j^3) + \sum_1^n y_j^3(x_j^3 - x_j^1) > 0$$
$$= [Y(x^1) - Y(x^2)] + [Y(x^2) - Y(x^3)] + [Y(x^3) - Y(x^1)]$$

a test that every triad of distinct points must satisfy. Reversing the order of the points, we get a second independent inequality binding the same triad.

Generally, for any circular chain of distinct points $(x^1; y^1)$, $(x^2; y^2)$, ..., $(x^r; y^r)$, $(x^{r+1}; y^{r+1}) \equiv (x^1; y^1)$, we have by similar reasoning

$$(27) \qquad \sum_{i=1}^r [\sum_j y_j^i(x_j^i - x_j^{i+1})] > 0 = \sum_{i=1}^r [Y(x_i) - Y(x_{i+1})].$$

Reversing the order of the points from $(1, 2, \ldots, r, 1)$ to $1, r, \ldots, 2, 1$ gives a similar relation

$$(28) \quad 0 > \sum_2^{r+1} [\sum_j y_j^i(x_j^i - x_j^{i-1})] = - \sum_1^r [\sum_j y_j^{i+1}(x_j^i - x_j^{i+1})].$$

By duality, we can infer relations just like (27) and (28), such as

$$(29) \qquad \sum_{i=1}^r [\sum_j x_j^i(y_j^i - y_j^{i-1})] < 0;$$

(29) can be derived directly from (28) by rearranging terms, and hence does not represent an independent condition.

The number of independent inequalities is equal to the number of distinct circular chains that can be formed from the finite given number of observations, r. If $r = 2$, we have a single condition, namely (24). If $r = 3$, we can form 3 independent pairings, and hence we have three chains of length two to provide us with inequalities. In addition, we have two independent chains of length three; viz. 123, 321. So altogether for $r = 3$, we have 5 independent inequalities to test.

Given any k points, we can make $N_k = (k-1)!$ circular chains involving all k elements. To prove this, note that $N_2 = 1$, because 12 and 21 are the same circular chain. Also, we go from a chain involving $12 \ldots k-1$ in some order to one involving $12 \ldots, k-1, k$ in some order by putting between *any* two adjacent numbers of the shorter chain the new element k. Since there are k such places to insert the new element, obviously there are k new chains of length k for each chain of length $k - 1$. Therefore, $N_k = kN_{k-1}$, a recursion relation yielding, with $N_2 = 1$, the unique solution $N_k = (k-1)!$

The total number of independent inequalities that any r empirically observed points must satisfy is the sum of all possible chain-inequalities of length $k \leq r$, and therefore equals in number

$$\binom{r}{2} N_2 + \binom{r}{3} N_3 + \ldots + \binom{r}{r} N_r = \binom{r}{2} 1 + \binom{r}{3} 2 + \binom{r}{4} 3! + \ldots$$

$$+ \binom{r}{r-1} (r-2)! + (r-1)! = \sum_{2}^{r} \binom{r}{k} (k-1)!$$

For $r = 2, 3, 4, 5$, we already have 1, 5, 20, 74 independent inequalities to be satisfied, and the number rises rapidly with r. (Incidentally, there are the same number of Hicksian equalities, of the type given in (21) that must be approximately satisfied for nearby points.)

This may all be summarized as follows.

Theorem 6: Any r distinct observations $(x^1; y^1), \ldots, (x^r; y^r)$ arising from a definite minimum system must satisfy $\sum_{2}^{r} \binom{r}{k} (k-1)!$ independent inequalities of the type

$$\sum_{i=1}^{k} [y_1 \Delta x_1 + y_2 \Delta x_2 + \ldots] > 0, \quad k \leqq r$$

where the summation is over a circular chain consisting of k distinct points and returning to the original point and where the superscripts in y_j^i and in $x_j^i - x_j^{i+1} = \Delta x_j$ have been omitted. Similar, but non-independent, dual relations involving Δy and x can be written.

13. Relations of the type given in Theorem 5 are necessary conditions: violation of any one of them could serve as a refutation of the hypothesis that we are dealing with a regular minimum system. (If we drop regularity assumptions, equalities must be added to the inequalities but otherwise the theorem is still valid.) The question naturally arises as to whether there can be any further necessary conditions beyond the ones already derived. That is, are these necessary conditions in some sense also sufficient conditions for a regular minimum system? The following answer can be given.

Theorem 7: Given n smoothly differentiable relations holding between $2n$ conjugate variables, namely $y_i = Y^i(x_1,...,x_n)$, $i = 1, 2, \ldots, n$, and if there can never arise for any finite number of observations a violation of any of the inequalities of Theorem 6, we are then assured that the system is a regular minimum one, with symmetric positive definite Jacobian matrix and all the other properties of such a system.

To prove this, consider a chain of m distinct points that lie along any simple closed path or contour in the n dimensional $(x_1, \ldots, x_n)$ space, with $1, 2, \ldots, m$ being arrayed by convention in counterclockwise order. Define $S_m = \sum_1^m [\sum_1^n y_j^{i+1}(x_j^i - x_j^{i+1})]$ and $s_m = \sum_1^m [\sum_1^n y^i(x_j^i - x_j^{i+1})]$. By (27) and (28) and our present hypothesis, it is to be true that S_m is positive and s_m is negative for any m. Now let the number of observations, m, along the same simple closed contour increase indefinitely in such a way as to make the distance between any two adjacent points go to zero in the limit. Then clearly from the definition of an integral as the limit of a sum,

$$\lim_{m \to \infty} S_m = \int \sum y_j \, dx_j = \lim_{m \to \infty} s_m$$

where the indicated line integral is taken counterclockwise around the specified simple closed contour and where $y_j = Y^j$ $(x_1, \ldots, x_n)$. Since this line integral is the limit of a sequence of positive numbers and at the same time is the limit of a sequence of negative numbers, its value is proved to be zero along any closed contour. Hence the expression $\sum y_j \, dx_j$ must be an exact differential $dY(x_1, \ldots, x_n)$, with $y_i = Y^i(x_i, \ldots, x_n) = Y_i(x_1, \ldots, x_n)$ and $Y^i_j = Y^j_i$. This proves the symmetry or variational aspect of the problem.

To prove the definiteness, we may consider the inequality that must hold between any pair of points; given our assumptions concerning differentiability, this may be written in the Taylor's expansion

$$0 < \sum_1^n \Delta y_j \Delta x_j = \sum_1^n \sum_1^n \bar{Y}_{ij} \Delta x_i \Delta x_j$$

where not all Δx_j are zero and where the second partial derivatives are evaluated at some point intermediate between the two points in question. Clearly at such a point the quadratic form made up of the Hessian matrix must be positive definite; and the same must be true of every observed point, else we could write down a contradiction to our finite inequality. This completes the proof.

The interpretation of this theorem is rather delicate. It shows that we can, by taking enough observations close enough together, always succeed in detecting any deviation of the facts from the regular minimum hypothesis. But it does not tell us how many observations will be necessary.[6] Therefore, no matter how many observations we may have examined, all of which satisfy all requisite inequalities, we cannot be sure but that still further observations might show a violation of the hypothesis. This is a common situation: methodologically, we can

[6] In *Economica*, February, 1953, p. 9 I posed the "open question" as to how many situations m might be needed to test the existence of an integrable field. Were $n = 2$, we know that $m = 2$ would be sufficient. For $n \geq 3$ is there a similar finite $m = \Phi(n)$ bound on the number of situations that might be needed to refute integrability? The question can now be closed by the statement: when there is definitely non-integrability, the closer the conditions for integrability are to being fulfilled, the larger must be the m needed to reveal that non-integrability; so there is no *a priori* finite bound on m possible.

refute a hypothesis with a finite number of observations, but we can never strictly "confirm" it in this way. Furthermore, the theorem does not tell us that, for fixed m, satisfying all the prescribed inequalities is all that can be required of the observations: i.e., it does not prove the non-existence of any further independent implications of the regular minimum hypothesis. I would conjecture, from various algebraic and geometric considerations, that no further independent inequalities can be prescribed; but this has not yet been proved.

14. This completes the program of characterization of the necessary and sufficient conditions for a system to have the structure of a regular minimum.[7]) A number of further problems may be briefly mentioned. First, the smoothness and uniqueness assumptions involved in the notion of "regularity" may be dropped, and investigations may be made of the resulting modifications in the theorems. With partial derivatives not being defined at sets of points, the Jacobian and Hessians of the first part of this paper will then not necessarily exist or be

---

[7]) The rather ambiguous principle of Le Chatelier, in its correct form

$$x_1^1(y_1, \ldots, y_n) \geqq x_1^1(y_1, \ldots, y_{n-1}; x_n) \geqq \ldots \geqq x_1^1(y_1; x_2, \ldots, x_n) \geqq 0$$

can be derived from our conditions, as can the equivalent dual form which says that $y_n^n(y_1, \ldots, y_m; \ldots, x_n)$ must be positive and non-decreasing with m. But adding the same finite positive $\varDelta y_1$ to each $(y_1, \ldots, y_m; x_{m+1}, \ldots, x_n)$, all of which correspond to the same initial equilibrium point, need not lead to the finite inequalities

$$x^1(y_1+\varDelta y_1, \ldots, y_n) \geqq x^1(y_1+\varDelta y_1, \ldots, y_{n-1}; x_n) \geqq \ldots \geqq x^1(y_1+\varDelta y_1; x_2, \ldots, x_n).$$

For sufficiently *small* changes in y_1 these finite inequalities must hold, but the proof is not immediate. For finite moves of any size, it is easy to give counterexamples that are nonetheless perfectly regular. This may be regarded as slightly paradoxical since it says that from any point in the (pressure, volume) diagram, there will be an isothermal line "flatter" than an adiabatic line; yet, the finite change in pressure in a system when you change its volume holding temperature constant, can turn out to be greater than the change in pressure resulting from an equal change in volume with entropy being held constant. The paradox is dispelled if one realizes that

$$\int_0^{\varDelta y_1} \{x_1^1(y_1 + t, \ldots, y_m; \ldots, x_n) - x_1^1(y_1 + t, \ldots, y_{m+1}; \ldots, x_n)\} dt$$

has an integral that starts out non-negative at $t = 0$ but which may become negative as the equilibrium points being compared become different ones. The last vestige of paradox disappears when we realize that regular systems need not admit of (p, v) as prescribable coordinates; hence, any point in this

invertable. Extensions of the Implicit Function Theorem and of the concept of one-to-one correspondence will lead to results, of which the regular systems constitute one special case. As far as the finite inequalities of the latter part of the paper are concerned, with the addition of equalities to the inequalities, they will all remain valid.

A second, quite different extension of the present program is to apply it to the study of regular systems involving an infinite number of variables or the equivalent. Thus, the differential equations of classical mechanics can be regarded as functional systems that are limiting cases involving an infinite number of variables. The question naturally arises as to an exhaustive summary of the necessary and sufficient conditions that the observable motions must satisfy if they are to have arisen from a regular variational system that is or is not a true minimum system. As far as I know, no one has yet carried through such a program in the full detail of the present examination of the simpler case of a finite number of functions of a finite number of variables. The present discussion shows some of the problems that will certainly be encountered in the more difficult realm of function spaces.

diagram may correspond to more than one physical state of the system.

A slight generalization of the Le Chatelier principle can be stated in terms of quadratic forms, namely

$$\sum_{1}^{r}\sum_{1}^{r} x_j^i(y_1, \ldots, y_m; \ldots, x_n) h_i h_j \geqq \sum_{1}^{r}\sum_{1}^{r} x_j^i(y_1, \ldots, y_k; \ldots x_n) h_i h_j$$

where $r \leqq k < m$. This is provable directly from the form of J_n in (6) and its dual.

APPENDIX

Axiomatic Basis For Equilibrium Relations in Classical Thermodynamics.

1. The formal mathematical analogy between classical thermodynamics and mathematic economic systems has now been explored. This does not warrant the commonly met attempt to find more exact analogies of physical magnitudes — such as entropy or energy — in the economic realm. Why should there be laws like the first or second laws of thermodynamics holding in the economic realm? Why should "utility" be literally identified with entropy, energy, or anything else? Why should a failure to make such a successful identification lead anyone to overlook or deny the mathematical isomorphism that does exist between minimum systems that arise in different disciplines?

In this Appendix, some of the special differences between the variables and relations that arise in thermodynamics and in economics will be briefly explored. This will involve giving a slightly unconventional axiomatic base for classical thermodynamics, or at least for that part which deals exclusively with equilibrium states and which might be called thermostatics.[1]

2. While in economics the variables (x_i, y_i) will usually be observable quantities of goods and their respective prices, in thermodynamics they will not all be as immediately observable as is the case of volume and (negative) pressure. Thus, (x_1, y_1) might correspond to "entropy" and "absolute temperature," which to early writers were not known, directly observable quantities. And a function like $Y(x_1, \ldots, x_n)$, which in economics might be easily measured as dollar revenue, in thermodynamics

[1] Such an axiomatic excursion departs from the usual Clausius formulation, in terms of the first and second laws. (Cf. also the work of Carnot, Kelvin, Gibbs, and Planck). It resembles a little the alternative axiomatic approach of C. Carathéodory, *Mathematische Annalen*, 67 (1909) pp. 355—86. See M. Born, *Natural Philosophy of Cause and Chance* (Oxford, 1949), Ch. V for a good account and for references.

might correspond to an internal energy function whose existence and properties have to be established by intricate reasoning.

Fig. 1 plots the properties of a simple system whose states can, for simplicity, be assumed to be determined by pressure and volume (p, v). The solid contours represent loci of equal "temperature" and as yet have no natural, preferred numbering on them corresponding to absolute temperature, t. Instead $T = T(v, p)$ represents any monotone numbering; and any renumbering $T' = f(T) = T'(v, p)$, with f an arbitrary monotone-increasing function, would be an equally good indicator of greater and smaller temperatures.

The broken contours represent "adiabatics" and represent loci of points that could be observed if the system were "insulated" from its environment by perfect non-conducting walls. I omit a good deal of explanatory matter needed to establish the exact nature of these two sets of contours, instead taking them as the given primitive concepts of the axiomatic system. Note that it would be premature to call the adiabatics "isentropes" since we do not yet have any entropy magnitude to be held constant. Yet we can give an arbitrary numbering to the adiabatics, written as $S = S(v, p)$ or as $S' = F(S) = S'(v, p)$, where again F is an arbitrary monotone-increasing function which will preserve the direction of the ordering.

3. The first task of our thermodynamic system is to define its own "canonical entropy and temperature" so that we can go from the arbitrary scaling of T and S to a privileged canonical temperature t and canonical entropy s; when this is done we shall be able to define an internal energy function $e = e(v, p)$ or $e = E(s, v)$.

Note that Fig. 1 is drawn with the special property of "proportional areas." Thus the shaded area A is to B as the area A' is to B'. And the same equal proportionality would be true of the appropriate curved parallelograms formed by any four thermal contours intersecting with any four adiabatics.

This equal proportionality of areas is not an accident: it is a fundamental regularity of nature, from which we can deduce the existence of an internal energy, a canonical temperature and canonical entropy.

4. In fact pick any thermal contour *aa* as the arbitrary origin for temperature and any other thermal contour *bb* as the arbitrary $t = 1$ level which will set the scale of one unit of canonical

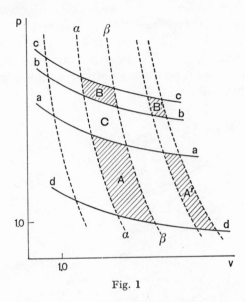

Fig. 1

temperature. We can now give a determinate number t to any arbitrarily given thermal contour by making its t the ratio of the algebraic area that it and any pair of adiabatics form with *aa* relative to the area formed by the unit temperature contour. Fig. 2. shows the resulting canonical temperature scaling for each contour. (Verify that *cc* corresponds to $t = 1.5$ because the area $C + B$ is one and a half times as great as the area C alone; of course $(C' + B')/B'$ gives the same ratio. And *dd* corresponds to $t = -2.0$ because the area A *below aa* is twice the absolute size of the area C.)

5. Having defined canonical t, we have no further use for T or T'. And we can now go from S or S' to canonical s, called entropy. This may be measured from *any* point selected as an arbitrary origin: thus the point northwest of A may be taken as zero origin, although it is to be understood that this entropy origin would not have to be at a point where $t = 0$.

Once the dimension of pressure is selected, the scale of s is not arbitrary. Suppose $\beta\beta$ has been selected just the proper distance from $\alpha\alpha$ as to make the area C (which has the dimension of pressure times volume) be exactly unity in area. Then $\beta\beta$ is given the designation $s = 1.0$ and every other adiabatic is given a unique s determined by the algebraic value of the area which it makes with aa, bb, and $\alpha\alpha$. (If the adiabatic is to the left of $\alpha\alpha$ we give it a negative entropy with magnitude proportional to appropriate absolute area. See Fig. 2 for illustrative s values.)

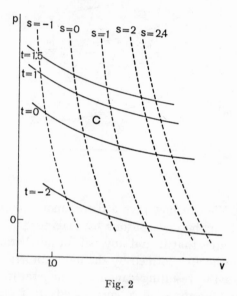

Fig. 2

6. Now that we have defined the functions $t = t(v,\ p)$ and $s = s(v,\ p)$, we can verify that the equal proportionality of area property implies that the line integral

(A1) $$t(v,\ p)\ ds(v,\ p) - p\,dv$$

must be independent of path and expressible as the exact differential $de(v,\ p)$ of an existent "canonical internal energy" function $e = e(v,\ p)$, which is arbitrary in its origin because of the constant of integration.

Because the canonical temperature t is arbitrary in its origin, transforming from t to $t + t_0$, would introduce an arbitrary linear entropy term $t_0(s - s_0)$ in our expression for canonical energy.

Within the realm of thermostatics, where we merely observe equilibrium states and make no measurements of "irreversible processes," we can never hope to remove this ambiguity in the definition of canonical internal energy.[2]) We can never hope to deduce the level of absolute zero, which characterizes the Kelvin scale. We cannot define the "efficiency" of an hypothetical Carnot cycle from knowledge of the isotherms and adiabatics alone. (In fact the present treatment never explicitly mentions "heat," inexact differentials like dQ, or exact differentials like dQ/t.)

7. Under our simplifying assumption that (v, p) are admissible state variables, we can rewrite internal energy e as a function of the pair of variables (s, v) to get $E(s, v)$ such that

(A2) $$dE(s, v) = t(s, v)ds - p(s, v)dv.$$

Here $E(s, v)$ corresponds precisely to my earlier $Y(x_1, x_2, \ldots)$; and it would be easy to show that the Gibbs potential $e - ts - (-p)v$, written as a function of t and $-p$, corresponds to the dual $X(y_1, y_2, \ldots)$. Corresponding to $P(y_1; x_2, \ldots)$ would be the Helmholtz free energy $e - ts$ written as a function of t and v.

8. All of the above implications of the equal-proportional areas axiom can be given brief mathematical summary[3]) in the case where all the functions have nice (overly strong) differentiability and regularity properties: in particular where any two $T(s, p)$ and $S(v, p)$ contours intersect in one and only one point so that these functions can be inverted to give $v = v(S, T)$ and $p = p(S, T)$ with smooth partial derivatives.

Suppose we know that indicators of temperature and entropy can be converted by determinate (save for arbitrary origin constants and scale constants) functions $t = f(T)$ and $s = F(S)$ to yield canonical temperature and energy; and that there exists a canonical internal energy function $e = E(s, v)$ with the Maxwell reciprocity or integrability property

---

[2]) This was noted by Carathéodory, *op. cit.*, p. 381. See also A. Landé, *Handbuch der Physik*, Band IX, 281—300 for a treatment related to the present one.

[3]) This and the next section can easily be skipped.

(A3)
$$\frac{\partial^2 E(s,\ v)}{\partial v \partial s} \equiv \frac{\partial^2 E(s,\ v)}{\partial s \partial v}.$$

From the form of the exact differential in (A2), this is equivalent to

(A4)
$$\frac{\partial t(s,\ v)}{\partial v} \equiv -\frac{\partial p(x,\ v)}{\partial s};$$

which in terms of arbitrary T and S and $f(T)$ and $F(S)$ becomes

(A5)
$$\frac{\left(\dfrac{\partial p}{\partial S}\right)_v}{\left(\dfrac{\partial T}{\partial v}\right)_s} \equiv f'(T)\,F'(S).$$

Now the left-hand side of this relation is a perfectly observable magnitude, being a function of $(v,\ p)$ or $(S,\ T)$ or any other two variables. Let us call it J. The equal-proportional area property — which is an integrability property in the large — is equivalent to saying that this observable left-hand expression J is truly a *product* of two separate functions. I.e., necessarily $\log J$ must be the sum of a function of T and a function of S, so that

(A6)
$$\frac{\partial^2 \log J(S,\ T)}{\partial S \partial T} \equiv 0$$

is a necessary and sufficient condition for the equal-proportional area property to hold.

An alternative functional equation which J must satisfy is

(A7)
$$\begin{vmatrix} J(S_1,\ T_1) & J(S_2,\ T_1) \\ J(S_1,\ T_2) & J(S_2,\ T_2) \end{vmatrix} \equiv 0$$

for all $(S_1,\ T_1)$ and $(S_2,\ T_2)$.

Both (A6) and (A7) are observable conditions which could be empirically verified.

Incidentally, by some manipulations of implicit function theory, it is easy to show that J is a certain Jacobian determinant, namely

$$(A8) \quad \frac{\left(\dfrac{\partial p}{\partial S}\right)_v}{\left(\dfrac{\partial T}{\partial v}\right)_S} = \frac{1}{\begin{vmatrix} \dfrac{\partial S}{\partial v} & \dfrac{\partial S}{\partial p} \\[2mm] \dfrac{\partial T}{\partial v} & \dfrac{\partial T}{\partial p} \end{vmatrix}} = \frac{\begin{vmatrix} \dfrac{\partial v}{\partial S} & \dfrac{\partial v}{\partial T} \\[2mm] \dfrac{\partial p}{\partial S} & \dfrac{\partial p}{\partial T} \end{vmatrix}}{} = \frac{\partial(v, p)}{\partial(S, T)} \equiv J(S, T).$$

9. Given the observable function $J(S, T)$, we can derive canonical temperature and entropy by simple integrations. Thus

$$(A9) \quad \begin{aligned} t = f(T) &= t_0 + \int_{T_0}^{T} f'(\tau)d\tau \\ &= t_0 + f'(T_0)\int_{T_0}^{T} \frac{J(S_0, \tau)}{J(S_0, T_0)} d\tau, \end{aligned}$$

where $t_0 = f(T_0)$ is an arbitrary origin constant and $f'(T_0)$ is an arbitrary scale constant. Also

$$(A10) \quad \begin{aligned} s = F(S) &= s_0 + \int_{S_0}^{S} F'(\sigma)d\sigma \\ &= s_0 + \int_{S_0}^{S} \frac{J(\sigma, T_0)}{f'(T_0)} d\sigma \end{aligned}$$

Because J has the remarkable multiplicative property, this $f(T)$ integral will be independent of the S_0 level and (A10)'s $F(S)$ integral will necessarily be independent of the T_0 level. Note that the origin of s is arbitrary, but the scale is definitely not.

Since the line integral $tds - pdv$ is independent of path, we can by a variety of alternative integrations calculate the canonical internal energy function $E(s, v)$, which is determinate except for an arbitrary linear term $t_0(s - s_0)$.

10. So far the discussion dealt with simple systems with only two degrees of freedom: e.g. a single homogeneous fluid. The existence of an absolute or Kelvin *temperature which is the same for all substances* shows that the equal-proportional area law must apply also to the interrelations of different bodies. Thus Fig. 3 shows that if two bodies are in respective equilibrium at $t = 0$ and at $t = 1$, then we can separately for each calculate the canonical temperatures $t_1 = \frac{1}{2}$ and $t_2 = \frac{1}{2}$ by our previously

described techniques of canonical temperatures. Then we can confidently predict — in advance of ever having made the experiment! — that the $t_1 = \frac{1}{2}$ and $t_2 = \frac{1}{2}$ contours will truly represent the same temperature and represent mutual equilibrium.

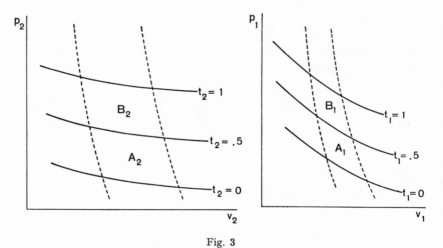

Fig. 3

This requires that the area relations $A_1/B_1 = A_2/B_2$ hold between different substances. (In fact this is the generalized form of our equal-proportional area axiom, from which all the other relations of thermostatics follow.)

11. There are far-reaching implications of the axiom. Thus, suppose two (or more) bodies are separated by *diathermous* walls (i.e. walls which require the bodies' mutual equilibrium to be at equal temperatures) and that these walls are also *elastic* (i.e. such as to require equal pressures at equilibrium). Then

(A11)
$$t_1(s_1, v_1) = t_2(s_2, v_2) = \ldots = t = f(T)$$
$$p_1(s_1, v_1) = p_2(s_2, v_2) = \ldots = p.$$

But in terms of the internal energies $E_i(s_i, v_i)$, this means

(A12)
$$\frac{\partial E_1(s_1, v_1)}{\partial s_1} = \frac{\partial E_2(s_2, v_2)}{\partial s_2} = \ldots = t$$
$$\frac{\partial E_1(s_1, v_1)}{\partial v_1} = \frac{\partial E_2(s_2, v_2)}{\partial v_2} = \ldots = -p,$$

which in turn is seen to be the necessary condition that $e = e_1 + e_2 + \ldots = E_1(s_1, v_1) + E_2(s_2, v_2) + \ldots$ be at a minimum subject to

(A13)
$$s_1 + s_2 + \ldots = s$$
$$v_1 + v_2 + \ldots = v;$$

and that the resulting minimized energy be a function of the total s and v respectively — namely

minimum $e = E(s_1 + s_2 + \ldots, v_1 + v_2 + \ldots) = E(s, v)$ with

(A14)
$$\frac{\partial E(S, v)}{\partial s} = t, \quad \frac{\partial E(s, v)}{\partial v} = -p,$$

where again an arbitrary linear term in total entropy $t_0(s - s_0)$ will be involved.[4])

For a true maximum, it is sufficient that each $E_i(v_i, s_i)$ have a positive definite Hessian matrix of second partial derivatives

$$H_i = \begin{bmatrix} \dfrac{\partial^2 E_i}{\partial s_i^2} & \dfrac{\partial^2 E_i}{\partial v_i \partial s_i} \\[3mm] \dfrac{\partial^2 E_i}{\partial s_i \partial v_i} & \dfrac{\partial^2 E_i}{\partial v_i^2} \end{bmatrix},$$

and then it will follow that the Hessian matrix of $E(s, v)$ is positive definite.[4a])

[4]) If the bodies are in thermal contact but separated by *rigid* walls, the pressure equality of (A12) is lost and the volumes $(v_1, v_2, \ldots)$ are separately specifiable: we then get $e = e_1 + e_2 + \ldots = E(s_1 + s_2 + \ldots, v_1, v_2 \ldots)$ in minimized form, with $\partial E / \partial v_i = -p_i$ and $\partial E / \partial s = t$.

[4a]) Many treatises on thermodynamics seem to be saying that $E(s, v)$ is at a minimum for prescribed s and v. Actually $E(s, v)$ is a determinate function of its arguments and is not free to be at a maximum or a minimum. It is the sum $E_1(s_1, v_1) + E_2(s_2, v_2)$ which has its (s_i, v_i) varied subject to fixed $s_1 + s_2$ and $v_1 + v_2$ until $E_1 + E_2$ is at a minimum. When the resulting optimal (s_i, v_i) are substituted into $E_1(s_1, v_1) + E_2(s_2, v_2)$ the result defines $E(s, v)$.

That the Gibbs free energy or potential is at a minimum for fixed t and p likewise requires careful statement. Write the expression $e - ts - (-p)v$, regarded as a function of t and p alone, as $G(t, p)$. Then $G(t, p)$ cannot be at a minimum for arbitrarily prescribed (t, p), nor at a maximum, nor anything else but at its determinate value. Rather it is $G(s, v; t, p) = E(s, v) - ts - (-p)v$ that is at a minimum with respect to (s, v) for prescribed (t, p). This can be shown to be a special case of the condition that $E_1 + E_2$ is at a minimum for prescribed $v_1 + v_2$ and $s_1 + s_2$. Think of s, v and E as belonging to one body, and hence write them as s_1, v_1, $E_1(s_1, v_1)$. Now consider a second body so large compared to the first that its temperature and pressure will be affected negligibly by

12. Note that in contrast to the Carathéodory-Born treatment, there was here no stipulation of any integrability conditions or inaccessibility conditions other than that of equal-proportional area. Once the $T_i = T_i(v_i, p_i)$ and $S_i = S_i(v_i, p_i)$ contours were specified and the equal-proportional area axiom of a single uniform canonical temperature was specified, then all the remaining relations of thermostatics logically followed.

13. Instead of minimizing total energy e for given total entropy s and total volume, with $t > 0$ we could have maximized entropy for given total energy and volume. Leaving thermostatics for true thermodynamics and actually observing the time changes of a given *isolated* system, we would actually find that total energy would remain constant and total entropy would increase in time. But within the realm of thermostatics — i.e. the study of equilibrium relations like (A11) — we would have no knowledge of this or interest in it.

14. The present formulation [5]) thus, seems to have turned the usual formulation upside down. Rather than begin with the first and second laws of thermodynamics and then deduce equilibrium relations and the existence of a universal absolute temperature, we have assumed a universal canonical temperature (with arbitrary origin) and have then deduced equilibrium relations and integrability conditions. We have assumed less than the first and second laws: and we deduce less. We deduce only thermostatic relations, deducing almost nothing about irreversible processes. (In the original definition of the adiabatics $S_i = S_i(v_i, p_i)$ there does lurk in the background an

---

the first. (A "heat and pressure bath.") Write its energy as $E_2(s_2, v_2) \equiv \bar{t}s_2 - (-\bar{p})v_2$, where $\bar{t}$ and $\bar{p}$ are fixed parameters. Now minimize $E_1(s_1, v_1) + E_2(s_2, v_2)$ subject to fixed $\bar{s} = s_1 + s_2$ and $\bar{v} = v_1 + v_2$ to get

Minimum $E_1(s_1, v_1) + E_2(s_2, v_2) = [E_1(s_1, v_1) - \bar{t}s_1 - (-\bar{p})v_1] + \bar{t}\bar{s} + (-\bar{p})\bar{v}$

$$= G_1(s_1, v_1; \bar{t}, \bar{p}) + \text{a constant.}$$

This last expression shows that minimizing the Gibbs G_1 is a special case of minimizing $E_1 + E_2$, the total of the observed system *and* its "environment."

[5]) The equal-proportional area property on which all this is based was suggested to me by an obvious extension of the reasoning of Maxwell's *Theory of Heat* (1871 edition), but I have not seen it explicitly alluded to in any twentieth century book. It is, however, so obvious and basic a property that it must have been rediscovered many times.

implicit reference to irreversible processes and *two-dimensional* "inaccessible neighboring states." But once the primitive notion of an adiabatic is assumed, all the rest is thermostatics.)

The Gibbs thermodynamics of heterogeneous substances has not been here discussed. But what was done here for $-\int p dv$ areas could also be done for $-\int \mu_i dM_i$ areas, where μ_i represents chemical potentials and M_i chemical masses; and it would seem that no new mathematical problems would be raised.

1965 POSTSCRIPT

The difference between the purely statical equilibrium relations in thermodynamics and the relations that depend upon the time sequence of events can be clarified further as follows:

1. The *isotherms* defined by empirical temperature $T(v, p)$, or canonical temperature $t(v, p)$, can be identified by purely statical observations of equilibrium (involving the so-called zeroth law of thermodynamics of Maxwell and later writers).

2. The adiabatics described by $S(v, p)$ or $s(v, p)$ do depend upon specification of the time sequence of events. Begin at (v^0, p^0) in equilibrium. Move the insulating wall to change the volume according to the actual time sequence, $v = v(t)$, $v(0) = v^0$. Let there be an observed concomitant time profile of pressure, $p = p(t)$, $p(0) = v^0$. Now slow down the movement of the wall by considering the movement $v = v(t/T) = v(t; T)$, where T is a positive constant. As $T \to 0$, the velocity of movement becomes "infinitely slow." For each fixed T, let the concomitant time profile of p be given by $p = p(t; T)$. Then it is an empirical fact (part of the second law of thermodynamics) that, in the limit as $T \to 0$, the parametric equations $[v = v(t/T),\ p = p(t; T)]$ define the adiabatic $S(v, p) = S(v^0, p^0)$. This frontier separates the (v, p) space into the points that are "accessible" from (v^0, p^0) by movements of the insulating wall and points that are not. The inaccessible points lie west and south of (v^0, p^0) in the figures, and the frontier goes from northwest to southeast. Note that no differentials or integrability conditions have been mentioned explicitly.

3. As in the text, the canonical temperature function $t(v, p)$ and canonical entropy function $s(v, p)$ can be defined by area properties alone. No time sequence need be involved, and only definite integrals of the form $\int I[v(u),\ p(u)]du$ need be evaluated, where $[v(u),\ p(u)]$ are any parametric representations of curves, having nothing to do with laboratory time sequences. Note that expressions like $(v,\ p)dp$ or $A(v,\ p)dp + B(v,\ p)dv$ can be avoided completely.

The same is true of the definition of canonical energy $e(v, p)$ since it is definable by the first-written integral alone, independently of the $[v(u),\ p(u)]$ path, by virtue of the postulated empirical property of proportional areas (which contained the statical part of the content of the first and second laws of thermodynamics). By convention, for an arbitrarily specified $(v^0,\ p^0)$, we may set $t(v^0,\ p^0) = 0$, $s(v^0,\ p^0) = 0$, $e(v^0,\ p^0) = 0$. By convention we may use any other $(v^1,\ p^1)$ at different temperature to set $t(v^1,\ p^1) = 1$ and fix the scale factor of canonical temperature and canonical entropy. The canonical energy is independent

684

of (v^1, p^1). In summary, by convention

$$t(v, p; v^0, p^0, v^1, p^1) = t(v, p)$$
$$s(v, p; v^0, p^0, v^1, p^1) = s(v, p)$$
$$e(v, p; v^0, p^0) = e(v, p)$$

4. Still we have no absolute origin for temperature, and different choices of p^0, v^0, and hence of the temperature origins, contribute to canonical energy an arbitrary linear term in entropy, namely $\theta(s - s^0)$, where θ is an arbitrary constant.

5. Now, following Joule, Mayer, and Helmholtz, we may consider the time sequence of events. Let the movable insulating wall be moved by the falling of a weight, which loses a definite amount of mechanical potential energy. Or let the falling weight turn a paddlewheel that causes (v, p) changes in the contained fluid; or let it generate electricity that changes (v, p) by passing through a resistance.

Then it is a brute fact (the time-phased first law of thermodynamics) that to go between any two points $(v^0, p^0; v^1, p^1)$, it takes the same change in the height of the weight (i.e., the same change in mechanical potential energy) regardless of the method used, the path followed, or the time elapsed.

We may observe this change in potential energy and depict it by the function $e^*(v, p; v^0, p^0) = e^*(v, p)$, with $e^*(v^0, p^0) = 0$.

6. This e^* function of mechanical energy must not be confused with the canonical interval energy function $e(v, p)$.

7. However, for movements between two points on the same adiabatic, e^* and e are identical, being calculated by the integral

$$e^*(v, \dot{p}) = e(v, p) = -\int_{v^0}^{v} p(V)dV$$

where $s[p(v), v] \equiv s(v^0, p^0)$. Note that no differentials or time motions $[p(t), v(t)]$ are needed to define this integral.

8. There is a fundamental empirical relationship between e^* and e that completes the theory, namely

$$\frac{e^*(v, p) - e(v, p)}{s(v, p)} = \theta \geq 0$$

This invariant θ defines for the first time an *absolute* or Kelvin temperature, which is a canonical temperature except for an origin constant. That θ depends on (v^0, p^0) and on its scaling point (v^1, p^1), as for example on the freezing and boiling point of water at 1 standard atmosphere, is shown by writing it as

$$(A15) \quad \theta(v^0, p^0; v^1, p^1) \underset{v, p}{\equiv} \frac{e^*(v, p; v^0, p^0) - e(v, p; v^0, p^0)}{s(v, p; v^0, p^0, v^1, p^1)} \geq 0$$

The contours defined in the (v^0, p^0) space by fixed (θ, v^1, p^1) are themselves isotherms. For no observable (v^0, p^0) has θ ever failed to be nonpositive, although absolute zero has been closely approached.

9. Note that the discussion has been completed (i) without mentioning any "heat" concept, (ii) without use of differentials, exact or inexact, (iii) with careful distinction of time-independent and time-phased sequences, including careful specification of the $T \rightarrow 0$ process by which "infinitely slow" movements are specified. Otherwise, concepts like "reversible, irreversible, natural, spontaneous, quasi-static" have been carefully avoided. No explicit mention of perpetual-motion machines or efficiency-of-cycles has been made.[1]

[1]Is this postulational basis redundant? Could introducing $e^*(v, p)$ before $e(v, p)$ have enabled us to deduce the proportional-area property, (A1), and (A15)? This can be expressed in the following way. Between any two adiabatics along the respective isotherms defined by $T_1 = T(v, p) \neq T_2 = T(v, p)$, calculate $A_1 = \int de^* + pdv$; and similarly A_2. Then the Carnot-Kelvin ratio A_1/A_2 would have to be independent of the adiabatic s chosen, and be a function of the empirical temperatures of the form $\theta(T_1)/\theta(T_2)$, where for each preassigned empirical temperature θ is uniquely defined except for scale. By giving θ an arbitrary positive numerical value at some chosen empirical temperature, for example at the triple point for water or at the freezing point of water at one standard atmosphere, we determine uniquely an absolute or Kelvin temperature. Such an absolute temperature must be a canonical temperature, but a special one which approaches zero as the coolest possible situations are observed. Note that the term "heat" has been avoided and any ill-defined heat concept has been avoided in defining the A_1/A_2 ratio. Briefly, $(de^* + pdv)/\theta(T)$ would have to be an exact differential, ds, where s is the definable canonical entropy.

PART VIII

Mathematical Investigations

45

CONDITIONS THAT THE ROOTS OF A POLYNOMIAL BE LESS THAN UNITY IN ABSOLUTE VALUE

By Paul A. Samuelson

Massachusetts Institute of Technology

1. Introduction. In econometric business cycle analysis, probability theory, and numerical mathematical computation the problem of convergence of repeated iterations arises. The solution of the difference equations defining such a process can in a wide variety of cases be shown to be stable in the sense of converging to a limit if a certain associated polynomial

$$(1) \qquad f(x) = p_0 x^n + p_1 x^{n-1} + \cdots + p_n = 0,$$

has roots whose moduli are all less than unity.

Thus, for "timeless" linear difference equation systems of the most general type, convertible into normal form,

$$(2) \qquad Q_i(t+1) = \sum_{j=1}^{n} a_{ij} Q_j(t), \qquad (i = 1, \cdots, n),$$

the polynomial is the characteristic or determinantal equation,

$$(3) \qquad f(x) = |\, a_{ij} - x\delta_{ij} \,| = 0,$$

which when expanded out is of the form (1). The roots of this equation, when multiplied by suitable polynomials in t, give the exact solution of the problem in the form

$$(4) \qquad Q(t) = \sum_{i=1}^{m} g_i(t) x_i^t,$$

where m is the number of distinct roots, and the g's are polynomials of degree one less than the multiplicity of the respective root. If complex roots occur, they do so in conjugate pairs and can be combined to form damped, undamped, or anti-damped harmonic terms. All terms go to zero as t approaches infinity if, and only if, the absolute value of each x is less than unity.

For non-linear systems the exact solution does not take this form, but in the neighborhood of an equilibrium point the roots of an associated polynomial, except in singular cases, do determine the stability of the system.

As far as the writer is aware, there does not appear in the literature an account of necessary and sufficient conditions for the roots of a polynomial to be less than unity in absolute value. This is in contrast to a related problem which arises in connection with the investigation of stability of dynamical systems defined by differential equations. These have associated with them a polynomial whose roots provide solutions in the form

$$(5) \qquad g_i(t)e^{x_i t},$$

or for non-linear systems infinite power series in such terms. It is required, therefore, to determine complete conditions under which the *real parts* of all roots must be negative.

This problem has been solved by Routh[1] in a manner which leaves little to be desired. Determinantal expression of his conditions in a slightly modified form was made by Hurwitz[2] who apparently was unaware of Routh's work, and by Frazer and Duncan[3] who were unaware of the Hurwitz results. A brief outline of Routh's mode of attack will prove instructive in dealing with the problem at hand.

2. Routhian analysis of sign of real parts of roots.

Routh realized that the condition that all coefficients be positive—the leading coefficient having been made so—was necessary, but not sufficient unless all the roots were real. But a "derived" equation of degree $n(n-1)/2$ whose roots equal the sums of the roots of the original equation taken two at a time has real roots which are simple sums of the real parts of those of the original equation. In consequence, it is necessary and sufficient that the coefficients of the original and the "derived" equation all be positive.

Thus, valid necessary and sufficient conditions are presented. However, they are disadvantageous from two points of view. First, they are not all independent, being $n(n+1)/2$ conditions in number, whereas only n are necessary. Secondly, despite several ingenious methods devised by Routh, it is not easy to compute them in the general case.

Recognizing these difficulties, he therefore began anew from an entirely different angle. Utilizing a theorem of Cauchy concerning the relationship between the behavior of a polynomial on a closed contour in the complex domain and the number of roots within that closed curve, he derived necessary and sufficient conditions, which may be written in the slightly more convenient determinantal form of Hurwitz and Frazer and Duncan as follows:

$$T_0 = p_0 > 0, \qquad T_1 = p_1 > 0, \qquad T_2 = \begin{vmatrix} p_1 & p_3 \\ p_0 & p_2 \end{vmatrix} > 0,$$

(6)
$$T_3 = \begin{vmatrix} p_1 & p_3 & p_5 \\ p_0 & p_2 & p_4 \\ 0 & p_1 & p_3 \end{vmatrix} > 0, \quad \cdots \quad T_s = \begin{vmatrix} p_1 & p_3 & \cdots & p_{2s-1} \\ p_0 & p_2 & \cdots & p_{2s-2} \\ 0 & p_1 & \cdots & p_{2s-3} \\ 0 & p_0 & \cdots\cdots \\ \cdots\cdots\cdots\cdots \\ 0 & 0 & \cdots & p_s \end{vmatrix} > 0.$$

---

[1] E. J. Routh, *A Treatise on the Stability of a Given State of Motion*, (London, 1877), Chaps. 2 and 3; *Advanced Rigid Dynamics*, 6th ed., London, 1905, Chap. 6.

[2] Hurwitz, *Math. Ann.*, Vol. 46 (1895), p. 521.

[3] R. A. Frazer and W. J. Duncan, *Royal Soc. Proc.*, Series A, Vol. 124 (1929), p. 642. Also R. A. Frazer, W. J. Duncan, and A. R. Collar, *Elementary Matrices*, Cambridge University Press, 1938, pp. 151–155.

The law of formation of these determinants is obvious. In the first row the odd p's starting with the first are listed. Within each column the p's diminish one unit at a time. Any p with negative subscript derived by this formula is treated as zero, and all p's of subscript higher than the degree of the equation are set equal to zero. With this convention, for p_0 made positive, complete and independent necessary conditions are that all principal minors of T_n formed by deleting successively the last row and column must be positive. These conditions are n in number and are independent.

3. Complete, independent, necessary and sufficient conditions. Corresponding to Routh's first attack on the problem, we might consider an equation of degree $n(n-1)/2$ whose roots equal the *products* two at a time of the original equation's. If this equation and the original equation have *real* roots less than unity in absolute value, our problem is solved. This is guaranteed if, and only if, two further transformed equations with roots equal to the squares minus unity of the roots of the original and derived equations respectively all have positive coefficients. These conditions are necessary and sufficient, but not independent, and cannot be easily computed in the general case. Therefore, I follow Routh's example and approach the problem from a different point of view.

When the roots of $f(x) = 0$ are plotted in the complex plane, they must all lie within the unit circle if their absolute values are to be less than unity, and conversely. We might therefore attempt to apply Cauchy's theorem. However, it is not necessary to do so. Routh has shown what the conditions are that there be no roots in the right-hand half-plane. Can we find a complex transformation of variables which carries the unit circle into the left-hand half-plane?

The answer is in the affirmative. The linear complex transformation

$$(7) \qquad\qquad x = \frac{z+1}{z-1}, \qquad z = \frac{x+1}{x-1}$$

will accomplish this. But after substituting for x its value in terms of z, we cease to have a polynomial but rather a rational function of z as follows:

$$(8) \qquad f(x) = f\left(\frac{z+1}{z-1}\right) = \frac{\sum\limits_{i=0}^{n} p_i(z+1)^{n-i}(z-1)^i}{(z-1)^n} = 0.$$

We need only consider the polynomial in the numerator, i.e.,

$$(9) \qquad\qquad \varphi(z) = \sum\limits_{0}^{n} \pi_i\, z^{n-i} = 0.$$

In order that the roots of the original equation be less than unity, in absolute value, it is necessary and sufficient that the real parts of the roots of equation (9) be negative. Once we determine the coefficients (π_i) in terms of the original p's, we can easily apply Routh's theorems. This yields $n+1$ necessary and sufficient conditions, all of which are independent.

Expanding the numerator of the right-hand side of (8) and collecting terms, the following explicit formulas for the π's are directly obtained:

$$(10) \qquad \pi_i = \sum_{j=0}^{n} p_j \sum_{k=0}^{m(i,j)} {}_{n-j}C_{i-k}(-1)^k \; {}_jC_k,$$

where

$$\qquad {}_vC_w = \frac{v!}{(v-w)!\,w!},$$

and

$m(i, j) = $ the smaller of i and j.

For fourth and higher degree equations literal substitution, while always possible, results in complicated expressions. It is preferable, therefore, to compute the π's numerically and then apply the conditions of (6) directly.

Other necessary conditions can be easily derived, but they will be dependent upon these. Thus, each π must be positive; but this is not, by itself, sufficient. Or, adding π_0 and π_n we find

$$(11) \qquad \pi_0 + \pi_n = p_0 + p_2 + p_4 + \cdots > 0,$$

i.e., the sum of the even p's must be positive. Similarly, still other linear sums of other π's will result in cancellation of certain of the p's. Except on special occasions there is probably no labor saved by utilizing conditions derived in this way.

One obvious but useful necessary condition will be stated without proof. If one forms polynomials from subsets of the coefficients of a given "stable" polynomial formed by arbitrary "cuts" which leave adjacent coefficients in unchanged order and introduce no gaps within each set, then the resulting polynomials will all be stable.

Special sufficiency conditions also can be developed. Carmichael[4] presents certain inequalities between the absolute values of the largest root and the coefficients of the original equation. For special problems these may be fruitfully applied.

4. Example. In conclusion I apply the conditions derived here to a well-known numerical equation determined statistically by Tinbergen[5] in the analysis of economic fluctuations. It is a fourth order difference equation with constant coefficients,

$$(12) \qquad Z_t - .398Z_{t-1} + .220Z_{t-2} - .013Z_{t-3} - .027Z_{t-4} = 0$$

---

[4] R. D. Carmichael, *Amer. Math. Soc. Bull.*, Vol. 24 (1918), pp. 286–296.

[5] J. Tinbergen, *Business Cycles in the United States, 1919–1932*, League of Nations, 1939, p. 140.

with the associated indicial equation

(13) $f(x) = x^4 - .398x^3 + .220x^2 - .013x - .027 = 0.$

Its roots have been computed and are known to be less than unity in absolute value. This may be verified by computing

$$
\begin{aligned}
\pi_0 &= & 0.782 &> 0 \\
\pi_1 &= & 3.338 &> 0 \\
\pi_2 &= & 5.398 &> 0 \\
\pi_3 &= & 4.878 &> 0 \\
\pi_4 &= & 1.604 &> 0 \\
T_2 &= & 14.204 &> 0 \\
T_3 &= & 43.177 &> 0
\end{aligned}
$$

(14)

To compute the same results by cross-multiplication the work is arranged as follows:

(15)

π_0	π_2	π_4
.782	5.398	1.604
π_1	π_3	
3.338	4.878	
$\pi_1\pi_2 - \pi_0\pi_3$	$\pi_3\pi_4 - 0$	
14.204	7.824	
$\pi_3(\pi_1\pi_2 - \pi_0\pi_3) - \pi_1\pi_3\pi_4$		
43.177		

It may be remarked that the presence of a negative coefficient anywhere in the table is an immediate indication of instability, and that there is no necessity to continue the computation until a negative sign appears in a leading coefficient. This fact often saves much labor.

46

A NOTE ON ALTERNATIVE REGRESSIONS

By PAUL A. SAMUELSON

IN THE JANUARY issue of this journal Mr. Elliott B. Woolley presented a method of determining a straight-line regression by minimizing the summed *absolute* values of the areas of rectangles formed by the projections of each observation upon the regression line.[1] The resulting line possesses the usual property of passing through the point of means, and its slope is a simple average of the elementary regression slopes derived by minimizing in each direction; it is the geometric mean of the elementary regression coefficients, each referred to the same axis, and has their algebraic sign. It should be pointed out that this is nothing other than Frisch's "diagonal" regression (cf. *Statistical Confluence Analysis . . .*), and a statistical parameter which has long appeared in the literature. In terms of a correlation surface it represents the major axis of the concentric ellipses of equal frequency.

While Mr. Woolley has made an interesting contribution in proving this "minimizing" property of the diagonal regression,[2] his further argument that it is to be preferred in any sense as a method of determining regression lines seems to require brief comment.

(a) The lack of consistency between the elementary regressions is a necessary property of a linear multivariate frequency surface. It is expressed in the purely formal statistical law of *regression towards the average*. The elementary regressions are not thereby "illogical."

(b) If the aim of the investigation is not simply a characterization of the properties of the multivariate distribution, but rather the search for a hypothetical "true" (in some sense) linear relationship, upon which has been superimposed a distribution of errors, then no definite method of determining the regression equation can be specified until some assumptions have been made concerning the nature of the disturbing causes. *These assumptions must be in the nature of postulates; by no possible method can they be determined inductively from an examination of the data, even in an infinitely large sample.* This last statement must be emphasized since some of the recent literature seems at first sight to suggest otherwise. This is because seemingly innocent, but in fact highly restrictive and often arbitrary, assumptions of "noncorrela-

---

[1] "The Method of Minimized Areas as a Basis for Correlation Analysis," ECONOMETRICA, Vol. 9, January, 1941, pp. 38–62; see also "Editorial Note," ECONOMETRICA, Vol. 9, July–October, 1941, p. 312.

[2] This holds only in the two variable case. The regression hyperplane which minimizes the sum of the absolute volumes of the parallelepipeds formed by the projections of an observation point upon the hyperplane is not equivalent to the "diagonal" regression plane when three or more variables are involved.

tion," etc., do succeed in determining allegedly "true" regressions or limits upon these. (Cf. the highly interesting treatment in T. Koopmans' *Linear Regression Analysis of Economic Time Series*.)

(c) Why then has Mr. Woolley argued in favor of the diagonal regression? Clearly because it is independent of the designation of one variable as independent and the other as dependent. It is consistent in his sense; namely, invariant under an interchange of variables. However, it is easy to show that an infinity of methods can be devised which have this property. Thus, minimizing the sum of the squares of the shortest distances between the points and the regression locus yields one such. Actually, minimizing any symmetric function of the residuals in all directions will do the same thing.

(d) There are various properties which a method of determining regression equations *might* desirably possess.

Property I. *For perfectly correlated variables the fitted curve should reduce to the correct equation.* All proposed methods possess this property.

Property II. *The fitted equation should be invariant under an interchange of variables.* An interchange of variables is a very special orthogonal transformation. (It represents a 90° rotation of axes followed by a reversal.) This suggests the following stronger condition:

Property III. *The fitted equation should be invariant under any orthogonal transformation of variables.* Another desirable property is the following:

Property IV. *The regression equation should be invariant under a simple dimensional or scale change in any of the variables.* A still stronger condition is implied in the following:

Property V. *The fitted equation should be invariant under any linear transformation of co-ordinates.* Of a different nature is the following condition:

Property VI. *The regression slope must depend only upon the correlation coefficient and ratios of standard deviations; i.e., it must be some function of the elementary regression coefficients alone.*

Still other properties could be enumerated, such as the obvious one that all coefficients should be symmetric functions of the observations, etc. But, are those listed consistent? Clearly, it is in principle impossible to satisfy Property V (unless the correlation is perfect). This means that *all* methods which yield a unique answer depend upon some privileged ("natural") choice of variables.

Properties I and VI together imply an alternative postulate: Property VII. *The fitted regression coefficient must be a (generalized) mean of the elementary regression coefficients, each related to the same axis.* For, when these are equal, Postulate I requires that the fitted coefficient be equal to the common true value.

The method of minimum perpendicular-squared-distances satisfies Properties I, II, III, and VI, but not IV. The proofs are obvious and are omitted. In the case of zero correlation with equal variance, it very properly breaks down, the regression coefficient becoming indeterminate. Near to this position the solution of the determining equation becomes increasingly sensitive, which should serve as a warning to the statistical computer.

The diagonal regression (in two variables) satisfies Properties I, II, IV, and VI, but not III. That it does not satisfy III is clear geometrically from the fact that a rotation of axes through any angle not a multiple of 90° will leave the rectangles whose summed areas are to be minimized in skewed positions relative to the new axes. Not only does the diagonal regression satisfy I, II, IV, and VI, but it is the *only* one which does so. This is proved simply as follows: Let B_{yx} be the fitted regression of y on x, b_{yx} and b_{xy} being the respective elementary regressions. Then by VI

(1) $$B_{yx} = f(b_{yx}, b_{xy}).$$

II requires that

$$B_{yx} = \frac{1}{B_{xy}}$$

or

(2) $$f(b_{yx}, b_{xy})f(b_{xy}, b_{yx}) \equiv 1.$$

Finally IV requires that

$$f(b_{yx}, b_{xy}) \equiv \frac{1}{\lambda} f\left(\lambda b_{yx}, \frac{b_{xy}}{\lambda}\right)$$

for all nonvanishing λ's; or

(3) $$f(b_{yx}, b_{xy}) \equiv \frac{f(b_{yx}b_{xy}, 1)}{b_{xy}} = \frac{h(b_{yx}b_{xy})}{b_{xy}}.$$

Substitution of (3) into (2) gives

$$h(v)h(v) \equiv v,$$

or

(4) $$h(b_{yx}b_{xy}) \equiv \pm \sqrt{b_{yx}b_{xy}}$$

and

(5) $$B_{yx} \equiv \pm \sqrt{\frac{b_{yx}}{b_{xy}}} \equiv \pm \frac{\sigma_y}{\sigma_x},$$

which is the diagonal regression. Properties I and VII are both corollaries.

(e) This and the following point are independent of the previous discussion, but relate to Mr. Woolley's paper. The reader of his paper will perhaps be interested to know that previous methods of curve fitting can be given a geometrical interpretation as minimizing areas. Thus the regression which minimizes the summed-perpendicular-squared-distances has the property of minimizing the sum of the areas of circles with radii equal to the distances from the line. (This illustrates its invariance under orthogonal transformation since a circle, unlike a quadrilateral, looks the same from all angles.) The elementary regressions are derived by minimizing the areas of circles whose centers lie at the projection of the observation upon the line and with radius equal to its distance from the line. Similarly, any weighted regression can be derived by averages of these respective circles or by the formation of ellipses whose principal axes are related to the weights involved.

(f) The minimizing property of the diagonal regression throws some light upon the ambiguity of sign necessarily involved when a square root is to be extracted. To each possible sign corresponds a different relative minimum of the function to be minimized. Choosing the sign of the correlation coefficient gives the lowest of these ($r \neq 0$). When r vanishes identically, both minimum positions take on equal values, and there is no way of choosing between them. (Taking their average by using the zero sign certainly has no sense since at this value the function to be minimized is infinite.) Unfortunately for *almost* zero correlation the solution of the equations, unlike the case mentioned in (d), gives no indication of proximity to indeterminacy.

Massachusetts Institute of Technology

47

A METHOD OF DETERMINING EXPLICITLY THE COEFFICIENTS OF THE CHARACTERISTIC EQUATION

By P. A. Samuelson

Massachusetts Institute of Technology

1. Introduction. When an investigator is interested in all of the latent roots of the characteristic equation of a matrix and not in its latent vectors, it is sometimes desirable to expand out the determinental equation in order to determine explicitly the polynomial coefficients $(p_1, p_2, \cdots, p_n)$ in the expression

$$(1) \qquad D(\lambda) = |\lambda I - a| = \lambda^n + p_1\lambda^{n-1} + \cdots + p_{n-1}\lambda + p_n.$$

This can be done in a variety of ways, all of which are necessarily somewhat tedious for high order matrices. Except for sign the coefficients are respectively the sum of a's principal minors of a given order. These can be computed efficiently by "pivotal" methods [1]. Alternatively through the utilization of the Cayley-Hamilton theorem, whereby a matrix satisfies its own characteristic equation, the p's appear as the solution of n linear equations [2, 3]. In a third method Horst has employed Newton's formula concerning the powers of roots to derive the p's as the solution of a triangular set of equations, the coefficients of the latter only being attained after considerable matrix multiplication [4]. A fourth method suggested to me by Professor E. Bright Wilson, Jr. of Harvard University, consists of evaluating $D(\lambda)$ for n values of λ, presumably by efficient "Doolittle" methods; to these n points, Lagrange's interpolation formula is applied to determine the n coefficients explicitly.

2. The New Method. The present paper describes a new computational method based upon well-known dynamical considerations. A single nth order differential equation can be converted into "normal" form, involving n first order differential equations. This is easily done by defining appropriate new variables. If the original nth order differential equation is written as

$$(2) \qquad X^{(n)}(t) + p_1 X^{(n-1)}(t) + \cdots + p_{n-1}X'(t) + p_n X = 0,$$

then the new normal system can be written as

$$(3) \qquad X'_i(t) = \sum_1^n b_{ij} X_j(t), \qquad (i = 1, \cdots n)$$

where

$$(4) \qquad [b_{ij}] = \begin{bmatrix} 0 & 1 & 0 & \cdots & 0 \\ 0 & 0 & 1 & \cdots & 0 \\ \cdots\cdots\cdots\cdots\cdots\cdots\cdots\cdots\cdots \\ 0 & 0 & 0 & \cdots & 1 \\ -p_n & -p_{n-1} & -p_{n-2} & \cdots & -p_1 \end{bmatrix}$$

is the so-called companion matrix to the polynomial in question.

The reverse process of going from a normal system in many variables to a single high order equation is not so simple. Yet it can be done, and in so doing we attain the required polynomial coefficients [5]. If

$$x'(t) = ax(t) \tag{5}$$

represents the normal system in matrix form, then symbolically

$$D\left(\frac{d}{dt}\right) X_1(t) = X_1^{(n)}(t) + p_1 X_1^{(n-1)}(t) + \cdots + p_{n-1} X_1'(t) + p_n X_1(t) \tag{6}$$

Because we wish to find out the expanded form of $D(\lambda)$, this relationship is of no use to us. Since similar matrices have the same characteristic equation, ours is the problem of finding a non-singular matrix C, such that

$$C^{-1}aC = b, \tag{7}$$

where b is of the form given in equation (4).

This problem can be approached from an elementary algebraic viewpoint. The relationships in (5) represent n linear equations between $2n$ variables, $[X_1(t), X_2(t), \cdots, X_n(t), X_1'(t), X_2'(t), \cdots, X_n'(t)]$. These are not sufficient to eliminate the $2(n-1)$ variables not involving the subscript 1. However, inasmuch as (5) holds for all values of t we may differentiate it repeatedly until we finally have the system of equations

$$
\begin{aligned}
-X_1^{(n)} + \cdots + a_{11} X_1^{(n-1)} + \cdots + a_{1n} X_n^{(n-1)} &= 0 \\
\cdots\cdots\cdots\cdots\cdots\cdots\cdots\cdots\cdots\cdots\cdots\cdots\cdots \\
-X_n^{(n)} + a_{n1} X_1^{(n-1)} + \cdots + a_{nn} X_n^{(n-1)} &= 0 \\
-X_1^{(n-1)} + \quad + a_{11} X_1^{(n-2)} + \cdots + a_{1n} X_n^{(n-2)} &= 0 \\
\cdots\cdots\cdots\cdots\cdots\cdots\cdots\cdots\cdots\cdots\cdots\cdots\cdots \\
-X_n^{(n-1)} + a_{n1} X_1^{(n-2)} + \cdots + a_{nn} X_n^{(n-2)} &= 0 \\
-X_1' + \cdots + a_{11} X_1 + \cdots + a_{1n} X_n &= 0 \\
\cdots\cdots\cdots\cdots\cdots\cdots\cdots\cdots\cdots\cdots\cdots\cdots\cdots \\
-X_n' + a_{n1} X_1 + \cdots + a_{nn} X_n &= 0
\end{aligned}
\tag{8}
$$

These are n^2 linear equations in $n^2 + n$ variables. We wish to eliminate all variables which have a subscript other than one; namely, $(X_2, \cdots, X_n, X_2', \cdots, X_n', \cdots, X_2^{(n)}, \cdots X_n^{(n)})$. These are $(n+1)(n-1) = n^2 - 1$ in number. We may utilize all but one of the n^2 equations to perform this elimination. The remaining equation after substitution will be the desired high order equation, and its coefficients are the polynomial coefficients.

Ordinarily one would solve all but one of the equations for the values of the variables to be eliminated. These would then be substituted into the remaining equation. Actually from the computational standpoint it is unnecessary to solve completely for any unknowns. The so-called "forward" solution of the usual Gauss-Doolittle technique automatically performs the elimination or substitution, without necessary recourse to a "back" solution for the values of the eliminated variables. These values are in any case of no interest.

There is no unique order in which the equations must be reduced. Indeed, when one order fails because a leading principal minor vanishes, we may switch to another. A suggested convenient order is given below. Let

$$\begin{bmatrix} a_{11} & a_{12} \cdots a_{1n} \\ a_{21} & a_{22} \cdots a_{2n} \\ \vdots & \vdots \quad \vdots \\ a_{n1} & a_{n2} \cdots a_{nn} \end{bmatrix} = \begin{bmatrix} a_{11} & R \\ S & M \end{bmatrix}; \qquad I = (\delta_{ij}), \qquad (i,j = 1, \cdots, n-1)$$

Then, consider the partitioned matrix

$$(9) \quad W = \begin{bmatrix} -I & M & 0 & \cdots & 0 & 0 & 0 & -S & 0 & \cdots & 0 \\ 0 & -I & M & \cdots & 0 & 0 & 0 & 0 & -S & \cdots & 0 \\ \cdots & \cdots & \cdots & & & & & \cdots & \cdots & & \\ 0 & 0 & 0 & \cdots & -I & M & 0 & 0 & 0 & \cdots & -S \\ 0 & 0 & 0 & \cdots & 0 & R & 0 & 0 & 0 & \cdots & -a_{11} \\ 0 & 0 & 0 & \cdots & R & 0 & 0 & 0 & 0 & \cdots & 0 \\ \cdots & \cdots & \cdots & & & & & \cdots & \cdots & & \\ 0 & 0 & R & \cdots & 0 & 0 & 0 & 1 & -a_{11} & \cdots & 0 \\ 0 & R & 0 & \cdots & 0 & 0 & 1 & -a_{11} & 0 & \cdots & 0 \end{bmatrix}$$

It is simply the matrix of the equations in (8) with the variables $(X_1, X_1', \cdots, X_1^{(n)})$ shifted over to the right-hand side, and with the equations in which the variable one leads off being placed at the bottom.

If the usual "forward" Doolittle technique is followed, then the final elements computed, corresponding to the elements in the lower right-hand box, are the coefficients $(1, p_1, p_2, \cdots, p_n)$. It is the present writer's experience that the Crout form [6], like Dwyer's [7] the last word in Doolittle abbreviation, is to be recommended, particularly since we are dealing with an asymmetrical matrix. A clerk masters its ritual in a few minutes, and the speeds achieved once the operations become mechanical are impressive.

For the trivial case of determining the coefficients corresponding to a two by two matrix the W matrix is of the form

$$(10) \quad \begin{bmatrix} -1 & a_{22} & 0 & 0 & -a_{21} & 0 \\ 0 & -1 & a_{22} & 0 & 0 & -a_{21} \\ 0 & 0 & a_{12} & 0 & 1 & -a_{11} \\ 0 & a_{12} & 0 & 1 & -a_{11} & 0 \end{bmatrix}$$

The Auxiliary Crout matrix becomes

$$(11) \quad \begin{bmatrix} -1 & a_{22} & 0 & 0 & -a_{21} & 0 \\ 0 & -1 & a_{22} & 0 & 0 & -a_{21} \\ 0 & 0 & a_{12} & 0 & 1 & -a_{11} \\ 0 & -a_{12} & a_{22} & 1 & (-a_{11} - a_{22}) & (-a_{12}a_{21} + a_{11}a_{22}) \end{bmatrix}$$

The answer in the lower right-hand box will immediately be recognized as the correct one. I have found it convenient to vary the precise Crout routine by dividing vertical columns by the "leading" diagonal element, rather than horizontal columns. This is a matter of indifference and saves some computations. As in the higher order cases, the presence of the identity matrix along the diagonal reduces most of the computations to mere copying. Actually the intelligent computer will soon notice that most of the copying may be eliminated since the numbers in question are to be added in later in other sums of products. After eliminating unknowns corresponding to the equations above the line on which (9) is written, there results the system

$$(12) \quad
\begin{bmatrix}
R & 0 & 0 & 0 & 0 & \cdots & 0 & 0 & 1 & -a_{11} \\
RM & 0 & 0 & 0 & 0 & \cdots & 0 & 1 & -a_{11} & -RS \\
RM^2 & 0 & 0 & 0 & 0 & \cdots & 1 & -a_{11} & -RS & -RMS \\
\cdot & & & & & & & & & \\
\cdot & & & & & & & & & \\
\cdot & & & & & & & & & \\
RM^{n-1} & 1 & -a_{11} & -RS & -RMS & \cdots & & \cdots & \cdots & -RM^{n-2}S
\end{bmatrix}$$

Thus, it would be simpler to start from this stage, avoiding unnecessary copying.

This remark shows that the present method is related to the Cayley-Hamilton methods described in [2] and [3], since the above set is derivable from the set

$$(13) \quad
\begin{bmatrix}
e_1' & A^0 & 1 & 0 & 0 & \cdots & 0 \\
e_1' & A^1 & 0 & 1 & 0 & \cdots & 0 \\
e_1' & A^2 & 0 & 0 & 1 & \cdots & 0 \\
\cdot & & & & & & \\
\cdot & & & & & & \\
\cdot & & & & & & \\
e_1' & A^n & 0 & 0 & 0 & \cdots & 1
\end{bmatrix}$$

The last named set appears in the Cayley-Hamilton method when the first row of the powers of the original matrix are used in setting up n equations to determine our n unknowns. Although related, the two methods are distinct since in the Cayley-Hamilton method one would arrive at a different set of equations after straightforward elimination of one variable, and since it would be shorter to dispense with the identity matrix used in the Aitken method in favor of the solution of a single set of equations by the usual Doolittle "back-solution."

The reader will easily see how the method may be modified to handle the more general case of determining the coefficients of

$$(14) \qquad D(\lambda) = |c\lambda + a| = 0,$$

where c and a are any matrices. The method also can be used to reduce a polynomial equation involving a determinant of the nth order, each of whose coefficients are of a given degree in λ, to a lower order determinant whose coefficients are of higher degree in λ.

The present method derives the p's as the algebraic solution of high order linear equations. It would therefore seem inferior to those methods which need only solve a system of n equations. However, two remarks are in order. The matrix of the high order system can be written down immediately without computation. Furthermore, most of the elements in the matrix are zeros, so that a mere counting of the equations is not a true indication of the labor involved.

3. Some comparsions between present method and other methods. Within the brief compass of the present work it is not possible to give an exhaustive appraisal of the comparative computational efficiencies of the methods mentioned. In general, a computing method is to be judged in terms of the number of multiplications that it involves, although other considerations such as the number of additions, the magnitude and sign of the numbers handled, the repetitiveness of the operations involved, the adaptability to punch card machinery, etc. are modifying factors. In this discussion the *power* of a method will be taken to be an inverse function of the number of multiplications that it involves.

It may be said first of all that inasmuch as the minimum number of multiplications involved in computing an nth order determinant is of the order of n^3, even with the most efficient "pivotal" methods, direct computation of the coefficients by principal minors involves, for sufficiently large n, computation of the order of n^4. The same is true of the Wilson method described above. The Horst method, and any other that requires the explicit n powers of an nth order matrix, also asymptotically requires multiplications of the order of n^4. This does not mean that the above three methods are equally powerful for small n, nor even asymptotically, since the coefficients of the n^4 term in the formula for the requisite number of multiplications may not be equal. In fact, Riersol [1] has shown that his method is better than Horst's for small n, but asymptotically less powerful.

It can also be shown that the Cayley-Hamilton methods which simply involve products of the powers of a matrix with row or column vectors are asymptotically more powerful than any of the above methods, the work only increasing as the cube of n. This is true whether the longer Aitken form of reduction is employed or whether the usual Doolittle back-solution is followed. The present method is also an efficient one in the sense that its requisite number of multiplications increases with the cube of n. For small values of n and asymptotically it can be shown to be more powerful than the Cayley-Hamilton method which uses the Aitken method of reduction, although in the limit as n becomes large the ratio of the powers of the two methods approaches unity.

It is of the greatest interest to compare the power of the new method with the shorter Doolittle C-H method. It can easily be shown that the coefficients of n^3 in the expressions giving the respective requisite number of multiplications differ in such a way as to make the C-H method more powerful after some value of n, the ratio of the respective powers approaching the limit 8/9. However, for low order matrices the new method is the more powerful. The reader may easily verify this for the case of a second order matrix. Below a sixth order matrix the present method seems to involve the smaller number of multiplications. For a sixth order matrix the two methods seem to involve the same number of multiplications (multiplications by unity not being counted). For matrices of the seventh order or higher the C-H method seems to be optimal.

As compared to an explicit evaluation of the coefficients by a straightforward computation of principal minors according to the fundamental definition of a determinant as the sum of signed products of elements, all of the methods discussed are efficient, since the work in the former increases faster than any power of n. However, for each of the methods discussed, in singular cases the method of reduction may fail so that modified procedures will be necessary. In actual practice such singularities will "almost never" be encountered. But in the neighborhood of such singular points the computations become extremely sensitive to any rounding off of digits. Consequently, it is from the nature of the case impossible ever to develop exact rules for the maximum error involved in any given calculation.

REFERENCES

[1] O. RIERSOL, "Recurrent Computations of all Principal Minors of a Determinant," *Annals of Math. Stat.*, Vol. 11 (1940), pp. 193–198.

[2] R. A. FRASER, W. J. DUNCAN, AND A. R. COLLAR, *Elementary Matrices*, pp. 141–142.

[3] M. M. FLOOD, "A Computational Procedure for the Method of Principal Components," *Psychometrika*, Vol. 5 (1940), pp. 169–172.

[4] P. HORST, "A Method for Determining the Coefficients of a Characteristic Equation," *Annals of Math. Stat.*, Vol. 5 (1935), pp. 83–84.

[5] F. R. MOULTON, *Differential Equations*, pp. 6–9.

[6] P. D. CROUT, "A Short Method for Evaluating Determinants and Solving Systems of Linear Equations with Real or Complex Coefficients," *American Institute of Electrical Engineers*, Vol. 60 (1941).

[7] P. S. DWYER, "The Solution of Simultaneous Equations," *Psychometrika*, Vol. 6 (1941), pp. 101–129.

48

FITTING GENERAL GRAM-CHARLIER SERIES

By Paul A. Samuelson

Massachusetts Institute of Technology

1. Introduction. Since the last part of the nineteenth century at least, it has been common to represent a probability distribution by means of a linear sum of terms consisting of a parent function and its successive derivatives. Usually the parent function is the Type A or normal curve, as discussed by Gram [1], Bruns [2], Charlier [3], and numerous others. In addition there have been generalizations in various directions: for example, the Type B expansion in terms of the Poisson parent function and its successive finite differences.

Unlike these two types, which have a definite probability interpretation, another generalization involves the use of other parent functions and their derivatives (or differences) to give an approximate representation of a given frequency curve. With this process is associated the names of Charlier, Carver [4], Roa [5], and many others. Two general methods by which the equating of moments of the fitted curve and the given distribution yield the appropriate coefficients have been given by Charlier and Carver respectively. An account of the latter's technique is more accessible to the average English speaking statistician.

It is the purpose of the present discussion to indicate how the Charlier method may be simplified, and can be used to replace the Carver method. In doing so, I am following up the oral suggestion made some years ago by Professor E. B. Wilson of Harvard, that repeated integration by parts will yield the requisite coefficients very simply. At the same time certain methods implicit in the work of Dr. A. C. Aitken [6] show how the use of a moment generating function can often lighten the algebraic analysis. There will also be a brief indication of analogous results for general finite difference parent families; and attention will be called to a troublesome historical blunder which has permeated the statistical literature.

2. Alternative methods. Avoiding the overburdened expression generating function, I shall consider parent functions, called $f(x)$, with the restrictive properties:

a) Moments of all order of $f(x)$ exist.

b) Derivatives of any required order exist with appropriate continuity.

c) There exist high order contact at the extremities of the distribution as defined below.

Mathematically,

a) $\int_{-\infty}^{\infty} x^k f(x) dx$ is finite for all positive integral values of k

and

c) $\lim_{x \to \pm\infty} x^j f^k(x) = 0$ for all positive integral values of j and k.

These conditions suffice for many statistically interesting cases, but where desirable they can be lightened. Thus, derivatives may only be defined "almost everywhere," and there may be finite instead of infinite limits to the distribution, etc.

Given an arbitrary frequency curve $F(x)$, we shall suppose it to be formally expanded in the series

(1) $F(x) \sim a_0 f(x) + a_1 f'(x) + a_2 f''(x) + \cdots + a_n f^n(x) + \cdots$.

For convenience in what follows, we shall assume that all distributions are given in terms of relative frequency so that the area under both f and F is equal to unity, so that a_0 may be taken as unity. The suppressed absolute frequency can clearly be restored at any time by multiplication of both sides with the appropriate constant. Also for algebraic convenience, many writers consider the slightly modified form of the expansion

$$F(x) \sim A_0 f(x) - \frac{A_1}{1!} f'(x) + \frac{A_2}{2!} f''(x) + \cdots \frac{(-1)^n A_n}{n!} f^n(x) + \cdots .$$

It is assumed without discussion that the first n coefficients in such a series are to be determined by equating the first n moments of each side.

I shall prove the two following identities:

(2) $$(-1)^n a_n = L_n(F) - \sum_0^{n-1} L_{n-j}(f)(-1)^j a_j ,$$

where

$$L_i(f^i) = \frac{\displaystyle\int_{-\infty}^{\infty} x^j f^i(x) dx}{j!} .$$

Alternatively

(3) $$A_n = \sum_{i=0}^{n} \binom{n}{i} \frac{d^i}{d\alpha^i} \left(\frac{1}{\displaystyle\int_{-\infty}^{\infty} f e^{\alpha x} \, dx} \right)_{\alpha=0} \int_{-\infty}^{\infty} x^{n-i} F(x) \, dx.$$

The first of these which I owe to Prof. Wilson is implicit in Charlier's work. The second which may fairly be attributed to Aitken may reduce the actual work in many special cases met in practice.

Both of these methods are closely related to the Charlier device of finding polynomials $S_n(x)$ with the bi-orthogonal property

$$\int_{-\infty}^{\infty} S_n(x) f^i(x) \, dx = 0, \qquad i \neq n.$$

The subscript indicates the degree of the polynomial. By means of n of the above relationships, the polynomials can be determined except for a factor of proportionality. By formal integration of both sides of our expansion we have the Charlier identity

$$a_n = \int_{-\infty}^{\infty} S_n(x)F(x)\,dx/\text{factor of proportionality}.$$

From a theoretical standpoint, this method leaves little to be desired; but in practice the algebraic work increases rapidly with the number of terms to be included in the series.

In the Carver method, the new parent function in question, as well as the function to be approximated, are both expanded in terms of the normal curve, thus almost doubling the numerical calculations. After some differentiation, the members of the Type A family are eliminated yielding in the process the required coefficients in terms of the new parent family. We shall see below how this method may be related to the three above.

3. Useful relationship. First, two simple identities may be presented:

$$L_j(f^i) = (-1)^i L_{j-i}(f), \quad j \geqq i$$
$$= 0 \qquad\qquad , \quad j < i.$$

Given the above assumptions of high contact, this follows immediately from repeated integration by parts.

Remembering that the reduced moments defined just above are the coefficients of the powers of α in the series expansion of the moment generating function

$$M(\alpha; f^i) = \int_{-\infty}^{\infty} e^{\alpha x} f^i(x)\,dx = L_0(f^i) + L_1(f^i)\alpha + L_2(f^i)\alpha^2 + \cdots$$

we have the useful Aitken identity

$$(4) \qquad\qquad M(\alpha; f^i) = (-1)^i M(\alpha; f)\alpha^i.$$

This, too, is the immediate consequence of repeated integration by parts.

4. Derivation of first method. Formally multiplying each side of (1) by $x^n/n!$ and integrating, we have the formal identity

$$L_n(F) = a_0 L_n(f) - a_1 L_{n-1}(f) + \cdots + (-1)^n a_n L_0(f).$$

This is a "triangular" system of linear equations in the unknown a's. It may be written in matrix terms

$$\begin{bmatrix} L_0(F) \\ L_1(F) \\ \cdot \\ \cdot \\ \cdot \end{bmatrix} = \begin{bmatrix} L_0(f) & 0 & 0 & \cdots \\ L_1(f) & L_0(f) & 0 & \cdots \\ L_2(f) & L_1(f) & L_0(f) & \cdots \\ \cdot & \cdot & \cdot & \\ \cdot & \cdot & \cdot & \end{bmatrix} \begin{bmatrix} a_0 \\ -a_1 \\ a_2 \\ -a_3 \\ \cdot \\ \cdot \end{bmatrix}.$$

The triangular matrix has the very special property that all of its elements are known as soon as the first column is given. For this reason, as we shall see, it is essentially equivalent to a simple sequence of numbers. This we shall call the *sequence property*. Because of this special form, the above system by simple rearrangement may be written in the modified form

$$\begin{bmatrix} L_0(F) & 0 & \cdots \\ L_1(F) & L_0(F) & \cdots \\ \cdot & \cdot & \\ \cdot & \cdot & \\ \cdot & \cdot & \end{bmatrix} = \begin{bmatrix} L_0(f) & 0 & \cdots \\ L_1(f) & L_0(f) & \cdots \\ \cdot & \cdot & \\ \cdot & \cdot & \\ \cdot & \cdot & \end{bmatrix} \begin{bmatrix} a_0 & 0 & 0 \cdots \\ -a_1 & a_0 & 0 \cdots \\ a_2 & -a_1 & a_0 \cdots \\ \cdot & \cdot & \cdot \\ \cdot & \cdot & \cdot \end{bmatrix}.$$

By appropriate definition of symbolism, this may be written in the simple matrix form:

$$L(F) = L(f)\, a(F, f),$$

since multiplication of two triangular, "sequence" matrices is commutative.

It is usually simplest to invert this triangular solution directly as in (2). But if necessary, we may express our answer in the equivalent form

(5) $$a(F, f) = L(F)\, L(f)^{-1},$$

where the inverse to any special triangular matrix, also possesses the sequence property.

If g is a second parent function with the properties of Section 2, we have the relationship

$$a(F, g) = a(F, f)\, a(f, g)$$

which follows directly from (5). This may be generalized to

$$a(f_1, f_2)\, a(f_2, f_3) \cdots a(f_{n-1}, f_n) = a(f_1, f_n).$$

If F itself is a parent function, we have

$$a(F, f)\, a(f, F) = a(F, F) = I$$

or

$$a(f, F) = a(F, f)^{-1}.$$

5. Relation to old methods. In terms of our notation, the Carver method seems to reduce to computing $a(F, f)$ by the relationship

$$a(F, f) = a(F, \phi)\, a(f, \phi)^{-1}$$

where ϕ is the Type A parent function. It involves a doubling of the work of coefficient determination. However, if only a few terms in the expansion are retained, this is of negligible importance.

The Charlier polynomials are clearly summed rows of the matrix product

$$L(f)^{-1} \cdot \begin{bmatrix} 1/1! & 0 & 0 & \cdots \\ 0 & x/1! & 0 & \cdots \\ 0 & 0 & x^2/2! & \cdots \\ \cdot & \cdot & \cdot & \\ \cdot & \cdot & \cdot & \\ \cdot & \cdot & \cdot & \end{bmatrix}.$$

To know the first n of these polynomials, it is not necessary to ⌄erive $n(n + 1)/2$ different coefficients. Because of the sequence property, it is only necessary to derive n elements of the first column of $L(f)^{-1}$. These can be expressed in terms of the reduced moments of f, as did Charlier; but the relationships are non-linear and algebraically become tedious for high n. They are better computed from sequence relationships.

The above discussion suggests that the bi-orthogonal relationship between a parent family and suitable polynomials has no deep significance. In particular, there is no essential relationship to least squares as in orthogonal expansions. It does, however, share one important property with orthogonal functions— determination of later coefficients does not affect the earlier ones. But this is a property of all triangular reductions, orthogonal expansions being only special cases of these.

6. Sequence properties. Ordinarily to derive the inverse of an n^2 matrix, n^2 equations must be solved. For our triangular matrices, we need only solve n equations for one column. To each triangular matrix $L(f)$ there corresponds a sequence $\{L_k(f)\}$, which is in fact the first column of the former. Similarly to $L(f)^{-1}$, there corresponds $\{\tilde{L}_k(f)\}$; the elements of the latter are defined by the n equations

$$L_0(f)\tilde{L}_0(f) = 1$$

$$L_0(f)\tilde{L}_1(f) + L_1(f)\tilde{L}_0(f) = 0$$

$$\cdots\cdots\cdots\cdots\cdots\cdots\cdots\cdots\cdots$$

$$\sum_0^n L_k(f)\tilde{L}_{n-k}(f) = 0$$

But these are precisely the equations involved in the formal inversion of any linear operator system of the form

$$(6) \qquad\qquad \sum_0^\infty c_k h^k y = z$$

where h is an operator which commutes with a constant, and for which $h^0 = 1$. z is a known function and y unknown. Thus h may be such operators as

$$x, \; d/dx, \; xd/dx, \; E, \; \Delta.$$

A particular solution of (6) is given by the formal expansion

$$y = \sum_0^\infty \tilde{c}_j h^j z$$

where the $\tilde{c}$'s bear the same relationship to the c's as do the $\tilde{L}$'s to the L's.

Such "reciprocal" sequences appear in many branches of applied mathematics. In particular, they arise in the inversion of a power series. If formally,

$$W(\alpha) = \sum_0^\infty S_k \alpha^k$$

then

$$\frac{1}{W(\alpha)} = \sum_0^\infty \tilde{S}_k \alpha^k.$$

Thus, to any triangular matrix with the sequence property, we can formally associate a function $W(\alpha)$ as well as a sequence of numbers. The calculus of multiplication of our triangular matrices clearly "corresponds" to the calculus of multiplication of functions, i.e. if the triangular matrices T_1, T_2, $\cdots T_n$ and $W_1(\alpha)$, $W_2(\alpha)$, $\cdots W_n(\alpha)$ correspond, and $T_n = T_1 \cdot T_2 \cdots T_{n-1}$; then

$$W_n(\alpha) = W_1(\alpha) W_2(\alpha) \cdots W_{n-1}(\alpha).$$

Also, $1/W_i(\alpha)$ corresponds to T_i^{-1}.

7. Moment generating functions. If only for the above reasons and no others, we should be tempted to consider the function formally defined by

$$\sum_0^\infty L_k(f) \alpha^k.$$

But this is precisely the expression for the familiar moment generating function, m. g. f.

$$M(\alpha; f) = \int_{-\infty}^\infty e^{\alpha x} f(x)\, dx = \sum_0^\infty L_k(f) \alpha^k.$$

In this way, the method of triangular matrices joins the method used by Aitken for the Type A family. If

$$F(x) \sim \sum_0^\infty a_i f^i(x),$$

and we formally equate moment generating functions of each side, we get

(7) $$M(\alpha; F) = M(\alpha; f) \sum_0^\infty (-1)^i a_i \alpha^i,$$

by means of the Aitken identity (4). Thus $(-1)^i a_i$ equals the coefficient of α^i in the formal expansion of

$$\frac{M(\alpha; F)}{M(\alpha; f)} = M(\alpha; F)M(\alpha; f)^{-1}.$$

Our relationship (2) follows immediately from (7); and by Taylor's expansion in α of $M(\alpha; f)^{-1}$, the identity (3) is quickly realized.

For many problems, the reciprocal of the m. g. f. of $f(x)$ is itself a simple function; to that our triangular equations may be inverted without solving linear equations. Thus where $F(x) = f(x + b)$, we immediately verify Taylor's expansion by use of familiar properties of the m. g. f. under shift of origin.

8. Finite difference expansions. Corresponding to integration by parts, we have the formula

$$\sum_{-\infty}^{\infty} W_i \nabla^k V_i = (-1) \sum_{-\infty}^{\infty} \Delta W_i \nabla^{k-1} V_i = (-1)^2 \sum_{-\infty}^{\infty} \Delta^2 W_i \nabla^{k-2} V_i , \quad \text{etc.},$$

provided "high contact" properties are assumed. ∇ and Δ are receding and advancing differences respectively. Recalling the familiar property of "reduced factorial" polynomials, ${}^k x$, we have

$$\sum_{-\infty}^{\infty} {}^j x \nabla^k f(x) = (-1)^k \sum_{-\infty}^{\infty} {}^{j-k} x f(x) \qquad\qquad j \geqq k$$

$$= 0 \qquad\qquad j < k,$$

or

$$Q_j(\nabla^k f) = (-1)^k Q_{j-k}(f) \qquad\qquad j \geqq k$$

$$= 0 \qquad\qquad j < k,$$

where

$$Q_j(g) = \sum_{-\infty}^{\infty} \frac{x(x - 1)(x - 2) \cdots (x - j + 1)}{j!} g(x).$$

In the expansion

$$F(x) \sim a_0 f(x) + a_1 \nabla f(x) + a_2 \nabla^2 f(x) + \cdots ,$$

the a's obey laws identical to (2) and (3) where reduced factorial moments are substituted for the reduced L moments, and the f. m. g. f.

$$\sum_{-\infty}^{\infty} f(x)(1 + \alpha)^x,$$

for the ordinary m. g. f.

9. Convergence. All of the above relationships are purely formal, without regard to convergence. The last is a difficult subject, and little discussed in the statistical literature, since applications of G-C series have been almost entirely concerned with empirical frequency curve fitting in which mathematical convergence does not enter. Actually in the scanty treatments of the subject there has arisen a confusion between the Type A *G-C* expansion, which equates moments, and the expansion of a function in orthogonal Hermite functions. These are not unrelated, but nevertheless they are distinct. This is well recognized in the purely mathematical literature, but hardly at all in the literature of statistics and physics.

The series differ by an irremovable factor of 2. If the Type A functions are written as

$$H_i(x)e^{-x^2},$$

then the Hermite functions will take the form

$$H_i(x)e^{-\frac{1}{2}x^2}.$$

where the *H*'s are Hermite polynomials suitably normalized. Unfortunately the *G-C* series often diverges when the *H* series converges. Thus, the statistically interesting Cauchy distribution can be expanded in an *H* series; but since it possesses no finite higher moments, the *G-C* series cannot even be defined.

It is not hard to show that the *G-C* expansion of *F* in terms of a Type A function $f(x)$, is equivalent to an *H* expansion of $Ff^{-\frac{1}{2}}$ in terms of the *H* family $f^{\frac{1}{2}}$. It is sufficient for convergence in the mean of the last expansion that $Ff^{-\frac{1}{2}}$ be of integrable square or belong to L^2. This means that the *G-C* type A expansion will be valid if $Ff^{-\frac{1}{2}}$ is well behaved, not simply if *F* is well behaved. For *F* a histogram as is often the case in practise, no difficulties of convergence arise, although rapid convergence may be another matter. Nevertheless, many well behaved *F*'s will not pass the more strict test. The reader is referred to the last five titles in the bibliography for mathematical discussions of this problem.

The above discussion holds only for the Type A expansion. There remains the very difficult problem of convergence conditions in the more general case. No immediate generalization suggests itself, except the application of the results of the "moment problem." However, this must be handled with delicacy, since the partial sums of the series may actually become negative over some range.

BIBLIOGRAPHY

References

[1] J. P. GRAM, "Ueber die Entwicklung reeler Functionen in Reihen mittelst der Methode der Kleinsten Quadrate," *Journal für die Reine und Angewandte Mathematik*, Vol. 94 (1882), pp. 41–73.

[2] H. BRUNS, *Wahrscheinlichkeitsrechnung und Kollektivmasslehre*, B. G. Teubner, Leipzig, 1906.

[3] C. V. L. CHARLIER, "Über die Darstellung willkürlicher Funktionen," *Arkiv för Matematik, Astronomi och Fysik (utgivet af k. svenska vetenskapsakademien)*, Vol. 2 (1905), 35 pp.

[4] H. C. CARVER, Chapter VII, *Handbook of Mathematical Statistics*, edited by H. L. Rietz, Cambridge, Massachusetts, 1924.

[5] EMETERIO ROA, "A number of new generating functions with application to statistics," 1923.

[6] A. C. AITKEN, *Statistical Mathematics*, London, 1939.
[7] V. ROMANOVSKY, "Generalisation of some Types of the Frequency Curves of Professor Pearson," *Biometrika*, Vol. 16 (1924), pp. 106–116.
[8] DUNHAM JACKSON, *Fourier Series and Orthogonal Polynomials*, (Carus Mathematical Monograph No. 6), The Mathematical Association of America, Oberlin, Ohio, 1941.
[9] E. H. HILDEBRANDT, "Systems of polynomials connected with the Charlier expansions and the Pearson differential and difference equations," *Annals of Math. Stat.*, Vol. II, 1931, pp. 379–439.

Further Literature

1. W. MYLLER-LEBEDEFF, "Die Theorie der Integralgleichungen in Anwendung auf einige Reihenentwicklungen," *Math. Annalen*, Vol. 64 (1907), pp. 388–416.
2. E. HILLE, "A class of reciprocal functions," *Annals of Math.*, Vol. 27 (1926), pp. 427–464. (Contains selected bibliography.)
3. M. H. STONE, "Developments in Hermite polynomials," *Annals of Math.*, Vol. 29 (1927), pp. 1–13.
4. W. E. MILNE, "On the degree of convergence of the Gram-Charlier series," *Trans. Amer. Math. Soc.*, Vol. 31 (1929), pp. 422–444.
5. *Bibliography on Orthogonal Polynomials*, National Research Council of the National Academy of Sciences, Washington, D. C., 1940.

712

49

A SIMPLE METHOD OF INTERPOLATION

By Paul A. Samuelson

Department of Economics and Social Science, Massachusetts Institute of Technology

Communicated July 8, 1943

I.—In many branches of statistics it is necessary to determine the coefficients of an nth degree polynomial, $f(x)$, from $n + 1$ observations, $(x_0, f_0; \ x_1, f_1; \ \ldots; \ x_n, f_n)$, and to determine readings from this polynomial. For this latter purpose recourse may be had to divided differences, Lagrange's interpolation formula,[1] Aitken's method of interpolation,[2] etc. However, where a number of readings are to be taken, or where the coefficients are of interest for their own sake, it is necessary to solve a system of linear equations

$$a_0 + x_0 a_1 + x_0^2 a_2 + \ldots + x_0^n a_n = f_0$$
$$\cdots \cdots \cdots \cdots \cdots \cdots \cdots \cdots \qquad \text{or } Va = f$$
$$a_n + x_n a_1 + x_n^2 a_2 + \ldots + x_n^n a_n = f_n$$

whose matrix is of the familiar Vandermonde form (x_i^j).

Now in the solution of nth order differential equations with constant coefficients and one-point boundary conditions, such as occur in electrical engineering and other fields of applied mathematics, the solutions can be written in the form of linear combinations of particular solutions, the coefficients being determined by the solution of a transposed Vandermonde set of linear equations.

By means of the Heaviside-Cauchy operational calculus (Laplace transform, etc.), the applied mathematician is able to avoid explicit inversion of such a system of equations. This suggests the possibility of lessening the calculations involved in interpolation by methods analogous to those used in solving differential equations; and upon examination it turns out that the resulting method seems admirably suited to numerical computation, with or without a modern calculating machine.

II.—For those interested simply in the procedure, we first describe the workings of the method, reserving to the last section the question of proof. The work is divided into three stages.

First, an auxiliary polynomial of the $(n + 1)$th degree is determined so that its leading coefficient is unity, and so that it vanishes at $(x_0, x_1, \ldots, x_n)$. Instead of working out its coefficients from the relations which must hold between the roots and coefficients of a polynomial, it is far simpler in practice to compute successively the partial products $\overset{r}{\underset{0}{\pi}}(x - x_i)$. The tabular arrangement in the numerical example suggests how this may be done expeditiously. We may write this polynomial as

$$P_{n+1}(x) = \overset{n}{\underset{0}{\pi}}(x - x_i) = x^{n+1} + b_1 x^n + \ldots + b_n x + b_{n+1}.$$

We associate with this, polynomials defined as follows

$$P_n(x) = x_n + b_1 x^{n-1} + \ldots + b_{n-1} x + b_n$$
$$\cdots \cdots \cdots \cdots \cdots \cdots \cdots \cdots \cdots \cdots$$
$$P_1(x) = x + b_1$$
$$P_0(x) = 1.$$

Each is derived from the preceding by dropping the last coefficient and lowering the power in each of the remaining terms.

In terms of the above, the unknown coefficients of $f(x)$ are given by the expressions

$$a_j = \frac{P_{n-j}(x_0)}{P_{n+1}'(x_0)} + \frac{P_{n-j}(x_1)}{P_{n+1}'(x)} + \ldots + \frac{P_{n-j}(x_n)}{P_{n+1}'(x_n)}. \qquad (1)$$
$$(j = 0, 1, 2, \ldots n)$$

The second stage of the numerical work consists of an evaluation of terms like $P_j(x_k)$ and $P_{n+1}'(x_k)$. This can be easily done by the familiar algebraic device of synthetic devision, which lends itself very well to machine calculation. From the definition of the P's, it follows that the partial remainders at each stage of synthetic division of P_{n+1} by x_k are, respectively, $P_0(x_k)$, $P_1(x_k)$, ..., $P_n(x_k)$, $P_{n+1}(x_k)$. Thus, all are calculated at once in the same operation. Moreover, by definition the last of these must in every case vanish, providing a check upon the accuracy of the previous work.

After the above terms have been calculated by synthetic division, a second synthetic division performed upon them gives in the penultimate position the required derivative $P_{n+1}'(x_k)$, in a manner familiar to all users of Horner's method.

The third stage consists simply of the summation indicated in equation (1). Some economies of keyboard or slide-rule settings can be realized if the indicated divisions are done all at once wherever possible.

The amount of effort required in the proposed method may be compared with other methods. To invert the linear equations directly would require multiplications of the order $2n^3/3$ if efficient Gauss-Doolittle methods are used. If advantage is taken of the Vandermonde form of the matrix as in the Aitken method, the calculations of a single reading seem to require multiplications and divisions of the order $3n^2/2$, and, of course, the coefficients of the polynomial are not derived.

The present method entails multiplications of the order of $3n^2$ plus n multiplications for each reading, where the method of synthetic division is used to derive the readings. If two readings are desired, the work is therefore about equal to the Aitken method, and for more than two readings it is very much less.

After using the method for awhile, one will learn how to effect certain economies of labor which need not be indicated here. Thus, if the abscissa points are all positive, as often occurs in practice, the occurrence of negative numbers in the calculations may be lessened by a reversal of signs, followed by a determination of $f(-x)$.

III.—The procedure may be illustrated by a simple numerical example. Suppose we are to fit a quadratic polynomial to the following three points $(-1, 4;\ 0, 1;\ 2, 7)$. Clearly the correct answer is given by $f(x) = 2x^2 - x + 1$. To achieve this by the present method, the coefficients of the partial products are computed in the following tabular arrangement.

$$
\begin{array}{rrrrcr}
1 & 1 & 0 & 0 & : & 0 \\
1 & 1 & 0 & 0 & : & -2 \\
1 & -1 & -2 & 0 & &
\end{array}
$$

Each element in a given row is computed from the elements of the preceding row by adding to the element directly above it the product of the element just northwest of it times the number in the preceding row just to the right of the colon. The last row of all gives the coefficients of the auxiliary cubic polynomial.

The second stage of the numerical work consists of dividing this polynomial in turn by $(x + 1)$, x, and $(x - 2)$, so as to calculate the partial remainders. Arranging the work as in synthetic division

$$
\begin{array}{rrrrl}
1 & -1 & -2 & 0 & \underline{|-1} \\
1 & -2 & 0 & 0 & \underline{|-1} \\
1 & -3 & +3 & &
\end{array}
$$

The second line gives the successive values of $P_i(-1)$. The last recorded item in the third row gives $P_3{}'(-1)$. If a modern calculating machine is used, only the final element in the third row need be copied.

This process is repeated for each of the roots, without however, having to recopy the starred first rows. Thus,

$$
\begin{array}{ccccc}
*1 & -1 & -2 & 0 & \underline{|0} \\
1 & -1 & -2 & 0 & \underline{|0} \\
1 & -1 & -2 & & \\
*1 & -1 & -2 & 0 & |2 \\
1 & +1 & 0 & 0 & |2 \\
1 & 3 & 6 & &
\end{array}
$$

The coefficients in each of the second rows is divided by the last element in the corresponding third row, and when arranged in order give us the inverse of V'.

$$
(V')^{-1} = \begin{bmatrix}
1/3 & -2/3 & 0 \\
-1/2 & 1/2 & 1 \\
1/6 & 1/6 & 0
\end{bmatrix}
$$

Premultiplying this by the row matrix $(f_0, f_1, \ldots, f_n)$, or in this case by $(4, 7, 1)$, the operations described in (1) are carried out, yielding the requisite solution $(2, -1, 1)$.

Two partial checks on the accuracy of the work may be mentioned. The divisors, being derivatives at simple roots of the auxiliary polynomial should oscillate in sign, with the last one being positive. Also, the sum of the elements in the last column of the inverse matrix should add up to unity, while the other columns should add up to zero. This provides a check upon all earlier operations. Of course, a final decisive check is provided by evaluating the resulting polynomial to verify that it does go through the prescribed points. This is best done by synthetic division.

IV.—To justify the method it is only necessary to show that the elements of the inverse of the transposed Vandermonde matrix are, in fact, equal to $P_{n-j}(x_i)/P_{n+1}'(x_i)$. This could be done directly by means of contour integration or by the elementary properties of symmetric functions. An indirect proof which lends itself readily to the generalization given below involves the fact that the expression above can easily be shown to give the coefficient of certain terms in the operational solution of differential equation systems. At the same time the classical non-operational solution yields the corresponding coefficients in the form of the inverse of the Vandermonde matrix. Since the classical and operational solutions can easily be shown to be identical, it follows that our theorem must be true.

This suggests a slightly more general method of interpolation in case we are to find a polynomial from a knowledge of its values, and the value of its derivatives up to some varying order, at a number of points. As in the above case, synthetic division, now carried to more rows, is utilized, and the work of fitting a polynomial of the same degree is only slightly increased.

The matrix of the equations which must be solved now takes the general partitioned form

$$
V' = \begin{bmatrix}
1 & 0 & & & & 1 & & & & & 1 & & & \\
x_0 & 1 & & & & x_1 & & & & & x_r & & & \\
x_0{}^2 & 2x_0 & & & & x_1{}^2 & & & & & & & & \\
\cdot & \cdot & \cdot & \cdot & \cdot & \cdot & & & & & & & & \\
x_0{}^j & (x_0{}^j)' & \cdots & (x_0{}^j)^{m_0-1} & & x_1{}^j & \cdots & (x_1{}^j)^{m_1-1} & & x_r{}^j & \cdots & (x_r{}^j)^{m_r-1} \\
\cdot & \cdot & \cdot & \cdot & \cdot & \cdot & & & & & & & & \\
x_0{}^n & nx_0{}^{n-1} & \cdots & \dfrac{n!x_0{}^{n-m_0+1}}{(n-m_0+1)!} & & x_1{}^n & & & & & & & &
\end{bmatrix}
$$

where $(x_s{}^j)^v = \dfrac{d^v}{dx^v}[x^j]_{x=x_s}$.

Then by precisely the same kind of proof as that sketched above, it can be shown that the inverse of this generalized Vandermonde matrix is given by

$$
(V')^{-1} = \left[\frac{1}{(m_i-k)!k!} \frac{d^{m_i-k}}{dx^{m_i-k}} \left\{ \frac{P_{n-j}(x)}{P_{n+1}(x)/(x-x_i)^{m_i}} \right\}_{x=x_i} \right]
$$

where

where $P_{n+1}(x) = \overset{r}{\underset{0}{\pi}} (x-x_j)^{m_j} = x^{n+1} + b_1 x^n + \cdots + b_{n+1}$

$P_n(x) = x^n + b_1 x^{n-1} + \cdots + b_n$

etc.

[1] Whittaker, E. T., and Robinson, G., *The Calculus of Observations*, Chap. II, Blackie and Son, Glasgow, 1932.

[2] Aitken, A. C., "On Interpolation by Iteration of Proportional Parts without the Use of Differences," *Proc. Edinburgh Mathematical Society Series*, **2**, No. 3, 56–76 1932.

50

EFFICIENT COMPUTATION OF THE LATENT VECTORS OF A MATRIX

By Paul A. Samuelson

Department of Economics and Social Science, Massachusetts Institute of Technology

Communicated July 8, 1943

In statistics, in quantum mechanics and in the study of dynamical oscillations it is often necessary to compute the latent roots and vectors of a matrix. A variety of methods are available for this purpose, involving direct algebraic computation, iteration and the application of perturbation-variation methods. It is the author's tentative conclusion from experience that the last two methods are excellent if only a few latent roots and vectors are desired, say those corresponding to the lowest or highest few roots, or if there exists some *a priori* familiarity with the data which permits very good initial guesses to be made. But in the general case of high order matrices both the iteration methods and the perturbation-variation methods become tedious, and so recourse must be had to direct algebraic computations.

A variety of methods are available under this heading, and the computer will choose between them not on the basis of their adequacy on constructed text-book examples, but in terms of a careful count of the number of calculations involved in each. Every method must involve the solution of a polynomial of the nth degree; but in addition, all of the methods known to the present writer seem to involve multiplications which increase with the fourth power of n, where the matrix involved is of order n by n. It is the purpose of this note to present, perhaps for the first time, a method which gives latent vectors as well as latent roots after multiplications which increase with the third power of n.

1. *Description of Procedure.* Let a be the n by n matrix in question, and let h be an arbitrary column vector. Form the matrix products $(h_0, h_1, h_2, \ldots, h_n)$ by means of the operations $[Ih, ah, a(ah), \ldots, a(a^{n-1}h)]$. Then in consequence of the Cayley-Hamilton theorem that a matrix satisfies its own characteristic equation, we derive the coefficients of the characteristic equation $(1, p_1, p_2, \ldots, p_n)$ by solution of the following n linear equations

$$[h_0, h_1, \ldots, h_{n-1}]\begin{bmatrix} p_{n-1} \\ p_{n-2} \\ \cdot \\ \cdot \\ \cdot \\ p_1 \end{bmatrix} = -h_n.$$

Then let the characteristic equation, $f_n(X) = \sum_0^n p_j X^{n-j} = 0$, be solved by any method for the latent roots $(X_1, X_2, \ldots, X_n)$, assumed for simplicity to be distinct. We now form new polynomials by the relations

$$f_{n-1}(X) = X^{n-1} + p_1 X^{n-2} + \ldots + p_{n-1}$$
$$f_{n-2}(X) = X^{n-2} + p_1 X^{n-3} + \ldots + p_{n-2}$$
$$\cdot$$
$$\cdot$$
$$\cdot$$
$$f_1(X) = X + p_1$$
$$f_0(X) = 1$$

where each is formed from the previous by dropping off the last term and lowering the degree of the remaining terms. Expressions of the form $f_i(X_j)$ are easily computed as partial remainders in the familiar process of synthetic division.

Then the n latent vectors of a, $(V_1, V_2, \ldots, V_n)$, can be shown to be given by the product of the following two square matrices

$$V = [h_0, h_1, h_2, \ldots, h_{n-1}] [f_{n-i}(X_j)]!. \tag{1}$$

Should the original column vector, h, have been a linear combination of less than n latent vectors, the above process will fail; however, the probability of this occurring is very small, and such occurrences can easily be detected and allowed for. There is no reason why complex latent roots and vectors cannot be handled in the above process. In the important special case where a is symmetrical, only real quantities will be involved, and a check upon the numerical computations is provided by the conjugate property $V_j'V_i = 0$, for $i \neq j$. When repeated roots are encountered, the modifications are relatively minor.

The labor involved in numerical processes of the above type is best reckoned in terms of the required number of multiplications. The method described here involves multiplications of the order $8n^3/3$, or about the equivalent of three square matrix multiplications. In addition, one nth degree polynomial must be solved. It will be noted that each latent vector can be determined independently of all the rest, once its corresponding latent root has been determined. Approximate values of a latent vector can be computed from the insertion of approximate roots in the process of synthetic division indicated above.

2. *Proof.* Consider the system of differential equations written in matrix form

$$DY(t) = aY(t).$$

If the latent roots are all distinct, it is known that the solution of these equations for initial values $Y(0) = h$ is unique and given by

$$Y_1(t) = c_{11} \exp X_1 t + c_{12} \exp X_2 t + \ldots + c_{1n} \exp X_n t$$
$$Y_2(t) = c_{21} \exp X_1 t + c_{22} \exp X_2 t + \ldots + c_{2n} \exp X_n t$$
$$\vdots$$
$$Y_n(t) = c_{n1} \exp X_1 t + c_{n2} \exp X_2 t + \ldots + c_{nn} \exp X_n t.$$

The $n^2 c$ coefficients are not all arbitrary, only n of them being dependent upon the initial conditions. Each column of the c's is equivalent to the appropriate latent vector, the initial conditions simply determining the factors of proportionality of the latent vectors.

Our task then is to compute the solution of such a set of differential equations; from this solution we can easily identify the appropriate latent vectors. Thus, we reverse the usual procedure in which the latent vectors are first algebraically computed as an aid in giving the solution of the differential equation system. The novelty of the present method consists in the recognition of this fact plus the specification of a speedy method of arriving at a particular solution of the differential equation system. It is fashionable to handle this last problem by means of the Heaviside-Cauchy operational calculus; a careful consideration of these techniques from a computational point of view will show their efficiency to be greatly overrated, involving in this case multiplications of the order n^4.

It is a commonplace that an nth order differential equation in one variable can be transformed into n first order equations. It is no less true that a system of the latter form can be converted into single equations of the nth order in each variable; for constant coefficient systems such as the one under consideration, the coefficients of the differential equation are in each case simply the coefficients of the characteristic equation; i.e.,

$$f_n(D) Y_j(t) = 0. \qquad (j = 1, \ldots, n).$$

If we can identify the appropriate initial conditions for each of the last equations, and then give the solution of each, we should end up with the required c coefficients indicated above. As for the appropriate initial conditions, if $Y(0) = h$, then by repeated use of the original differential equations, it becomes evident that

$$D^i Y(0) = a^i h = h_i.$$

It is a classical fact that the solution of an nth order differential equation for given initial conditions is given by the solution of a set of linear equations whose matrix is of the Vandermonde-Cauchy form

$$\begin{bmatrix} 1 & 1 & \cdots & 1 \\ X_1 & X_2 & \cdots & X_n \\ \cdot & \cdot & & \cdot \\ \cdot & \cdot & & \cdot \\ \cdot & \cdot & & \cdot \\ X_1^{n-1} & X_2^{n-1} & \cdots & X_n^{n-1} \end{bmatrix}$$

the transposed inverse of which is given by

$$\begin{bmatrix} \dfrac{P_{n-1}(X_1)}{P_n'(X_1)} & \dfrac{P_{n-1}(X_2)}{P_n'(X_2)} & \cdots & \dfrac{P_{n-1}(X_n)}{P_n'(X_n)} \\ \dfrac{P_{n-2}(X_1)}{P_n'(X_1)} & \dfrac{P_{n-2}(X_2)}{P_n'(X_2)} & \cdots & \dfrac{P_{n-2}(X_n)}{P_n'(X_n)} \\ \cdot & \cdot & & \cdot \\ \cdot & \cdot & & \cdot \\ \cdot & \cdot & & \cdot \\ \dfrac{1}{P_n'(X_1)} & \dfrac{1}{P_n'(X_2)} & \cdots & \dfrac{1}{P_n'(X_n)} \end{bmatrix}$$

Consequently the n by n c matrix, which is also the matrix made up of columns of latent vectors is given by equation (1) above, where the factors of proportionality $1/P_n'(X_i)$ have been omitted.

When repeated roots are encountered, a generalized Vandermonde determinant is involved whose inversion is easily effected if one simply pursues the close analogy between Vandermonde determinants and expansions in partial fractions.

If the same differential equations are to be solved for many different initial conditions, the above process may be repeated anew. Or a slight economy of effort may be achieved if the inverse of V is worked out once and for all so that the weightings of the different exponential terms can be easily determined by $V^{-1}h$. If the a matrix is symmetrical, the latent vector matrix will be orthogonal so that simple transposition will provide the inverse matrix, except for factors of proportionality.

51

A CONVERGENT ITERATIVE PROCESS

By Paul A. Samuelson

In applied mathematics it is often necessary to solve an implicit equation

$$G(X) - X = 0 \qquad (1)$$

by an iteration of the form

$$X_{t+1} = G(X_t). \qquad (2)$$

Let us suppose that

$$G(a) - a = 0;$$

then the above iteration will converge to a for all initial values, X_0, sufficiently close to a provided that $|G'(a)| < 1$.

Similarly, if $|G'(a)| > 1$, the iteration will diverge for initial values close to, but distinct from, a. This may be annoying in practice. Moreover, even if the process is convergent, an inordinately large number of whirls may be necessary to achieve a solution of given accuracy when $|G'(a)|$ is near to unity.

The following iteration is proposed to speed up convergence where convergence is slow and to guarantee convergence even in the unstable case.

$$Y_{t+1} = \frac{\{G[G(Y_t)]\}^2 - G(Y_t)G\{G[G(Y_t)]\}}{2G[G(Y_t)] - G(Y_t) - G\{G[G(Y_t)]\}} = F(Y_t) \qquad (3)$$

By the application of L'Hospital's rule it can be shown that

$$F(a) - a = 0$$

$$F'(a) = 0$$

if $G'(a) \neq 1$.

By classical reasoning it follows that the proposed iteration converges to a for all sufficiently close initial values Y_0. Moreover, the convergence is faster than that of any linear process.

The present method may be used with profit at the last stage of the usual iterative sequence. Because the solution is given as the ratio of two small differences, care must be taken in dropping digits. This, of course, is a property of many methods which attempt to squeeze the maximum of information out of a few iterations. The present method bears a close relationship to the Aitken* device for accelerating convergence of the Bernoulli approximation to the root of a polynomial; however, the analytical problems which are to be solved are not identical.

The motivation for the sequence (3) proceeds from recognition of the fact that in a close neighborhood of a the iteration is "almost linear" and can be approximated by the following function of time

$$X_t = a + Km^t \qquad (4)$$

---

* A. C. Aitken, "On Bernoulli's Numerical Solution of Algebraic Equations", *Proceedings of the Royal Society of Edinburgh*, 1926, Vol. 46, p. 289–305.

where $m = G'(a)$. Of course, a, m, and K are unknowns, but they may be determined from a knowledge of three values, X_t, X_{t+1}, X_{t+2} by substituting into (4) and solving the resulting three equations for a as in (3).

Our analysis admits of generalization in three different directions. First, we may consider iterations in many variables, interpreting the symbols in (1) as many variable vectors. Then in the neighborhood of a (vector) solution a, the vectors $(X_t - a)$ "almost" satisfy a linear difference equation in many variables

$$(X_{t+1} - a) = m(X_t - a) \tag{5}$$

where the matrix m is the Jacobian of the system at a. The sequence can be approximated by a sum of exponentials. From $(n + 2)$ observed vectors, the matrix of the system can be deduced, the exponential components, and finally an estimate of a. There is little of theoretical interest in this generalization, and its numerical application would be so tedious as to make its use impractical in most cases.

In our second generalization, we return to a one variable system and seek to accelerate convergence by taking account of the non-linear parts of the iteration process. If $G(X)$ admits of a formal power series development of the form $\sum_0^\infty b_i X^i$, then in a neighborhood of a there exists a formal solution of the non-linear difference equation system of the form

$$(X_t - a) = K_1 m^t + K_2 m^{2t} + K_3 m^{3t} + \cdots \tag{6}$$

where $m = G'(a)$ and the K's depend on the b's and the initial condition.

Our first method retained only the first term of (6). We now retain two terms and determine from four observed values $(X_t, X_{t+1}, X_{t+2}, X_{t+3})$ an estimate of a. These must almost satisfy a difference equation of the form

$$
\begin{aligned}
0 &= X_{t+3} + C_1 X_{t+2} + C_2 X_{t+1} + C_3 X_t = P(E) X_t \\
&= (E - 1)(E - m)(E - m^2) X_t \\
&= X_{t+3} - (1 + m + m^2) X_{t+2} + (m + m^2 + m^3) X_{t+1} - m^3 X_t
\end{aligned} \tag{7}
$$

where $E X_t = X_{t+1}$, etc.

With the X's known, we have a cubic equation in m. Once this has been solved, three values of X_t substituted into (6), give us enough equations to solve for a.

As an alternative method we can determine the coefficients by expanding the *perisymmetric* determinant,

$$
\begin{vmatrix}
\Delta X_t & \Delta X_{t+1} & 1 \\
\Delta X_{t+1} & \Delta X_{t+2} & E \\
\Delta X_{t+2} & \Delta X_{t+3} & E^2
\end{vmatrix} = 0,
$$

then finding the roots of this polynomial (one of which will be almost the square of the other); and finally substituting in (6) as before to get a.

The conditions under which this method can be profitably used remain to be investigated.

The third generalization concerns itself with speeding up the acceleration of iterative sequences which are already of great power—namely, those for which the linear term $G'(a)$ already vanishes. We have seen that $F(X_t)$ is such a process; the Newton-Raphson and many other common methods belong to this class.

For these processes, we may write our G in the form

$$G(X) = 0 + K(X - a)^2 + L(X - a)^3 + M(X - a)^4 + \cdots.$$

For initial values of X_0 close to a, the sequence X_t almost satisfies the quadratic difference equation

$$(X_{t+1} - a) = K(X_t - a)^2$$

where $K = G''(a)/2$ and a are unknowns. From three values, X_t, X_{t+1}, X_{t+2}, we can solve for a as follows

$$(X_{t+2} - a) = K(X_{t+1} - a)^2 = K^3(X_t - a)^4 = \frac{(X_{t+1} - a)^3 (X_t - a)^4}{(X_t - a)^6}$$

or

$$(X_{t+2} - a)(X_t - a)^2 - (X_t - a)^3 = 0.$$

This gives us a quadratic equation in a. The correct root can be easily selected. Thus, we have in effect defined a new iteration

$$Y_{t+1} = F_1(Y_t).$$

Intuitively, it is clear that F_1 is powerful in the sense that $F_1'(a) = 0$; tortuous investigation would be necessary to reveal whether a number of further derivatives do not necessarily vanish as well.

In conclusion, a few general remarks about the "power" of convergent methods may be in order. Linear sequences, for which $G'(a) \neq 0$, converge exponentially; i.e., if we drop no digits at each stage, our number of *correct digits* will asymptotically increase as a linear function of the number of iterations.

Quadratic iterations or second order iterations, those for which $G'(a) = 0$, $G''(a) \neq 0$, yield "correct digits" which increase in geometric progression with number of iterations N; i.e., asymptotically as 2^N. An iteration of the rth order (whose first non-vanishing derivative is the rth) has correct digits which increase with number of iterations as r^N.

If sufficiently many correct digits are wished, it will always save effort to replace a first order method by a higher order one, even if the latter involves more labor at each stage—provided that both methods involve a finite amount of work. A similar comparison between say a second order system and *any* higher order system is not possible. For a repeated 2nd order iteration equals a 4th order iteration; therefore, another 4th order iteration which involves more than twice the work of the given 2nd order iteration would not be profitable even when we wish great accuracy.

If enough correct digits are required, it would seem intuitively that an optimal choice between two methods (of which at least one is of order greater than one) would be to select that which maximizes $W(r) \log r$, where $W(r)$ is the amount of work required for each rth order iteration. However, in some cases, an optimal process might involve no "repeated" iterations of any order, but consist of a different set of rules at each stage.

MASSACHUSETTS INSTITUTE OF TECHNOLOGY.

ABSTRACTS OF PAPERS

The following five abstracts summarize Professor Samuelson's research in particular areas. They are reprinted as they were originally published in the *Bulletin of the American Mathematical Society*. The first three appeared in Vol. 52, No. 3 (March 1946) and the last two in Vol. 53, No. 3 (March 1947).

52

Generalization of the Laplace Transform for Difference Equations

The Laplace transformation has standardized operational methods in the field of ordinary differential equations. Its efficacy hinges on the fundamental relation $L(s; Df)_D = sL(s; f)_D - f(0)$ where $L(s; f)_D = \int_0^\infty \exp(-st)f(t)dt$. The Laplace transform has been applied to difference equations, but it is a clumsy tool there by virtue of the fact that it does *not* satisfy a similar fundamental relation with respect to the shifting operator E. One can easily verify that the linear functional $L(s; f)_E = \sum_0^\infty f(i)s^{-i-1}$ does have the fundamental property $L(s; Ef)_E = sL(s; f)_E - f(0)$. This generalized transform can also be easily inverted by the calculus of residues and extended by suitably defined "convolution." Consequently, after a table of "generalized" transform pairs has been drawn up, the solution of ordinary difference equations can be derived by operational methods *exactly* like those of differential equations. The most important of these transform pairs is $y(t) = t(t - 1)$, $\cdots$, $(t - n + 1)a^{t-n}$ and $\bar{y}(s) = (s - a)^{-n}(n - 1)!, |s| > |a|$. (Received February 1, 1946.)

53

Computation of Characteristic Vectors

Wayland has shown (Quarterly of Applied Mathematics vol. 2 (1945) p. 277) that the method of Danielewsky and the method of elimination are the two most efficient known ways of computing the coefficients of the characteristic equation. This note shows: (1) the Danielewsky reduction can be interpreted as a special case of the method of elimination; (2) the characteristic vectors of a companion matrix with simple roots are given by a Vandermonde matrix and its easily derived inverse; (3) the characteristic vectors of any matrix can therefore be derived with about $2n^3$ multiplications all told, by applying the Danielewsky transformations to the vectors of the corresponding companion matrix. (Received February 1, 1946.)

54

A Connection Between the Bernoulli and Newton Iterative Processes

By the Bernoulli method, the root of a polynomial $f(X) = \sum_0^n a_j X^{n-j}$ $= \prod_1^n (X - X_i) = 0$ is approximated by $Y_{t+1}/Y_t = (C_1 X_1^{t+1} + \cdots + C_n X_n^{t+1})/(C_1 X_1^t + \cdots + C_n X_n^t)$, where $\sum_0^n a_j Y_{t+n-j} = 0$, $Y_0 = b_0$, $\cdots$, $Y_{n-1} = b_{n-1}$, and the C's depend upon the X's and the b's. Weights w_k are sought such that $Z_{t+1}/Z_t = \sum_0^n w_k Y_{t+1-k}/\sum_0^n w_k Y_{t-k}$ is a good approximation to X_i, by virtue of the fact that coefficients of the *other* exponential terms are made to vanish. Clearly the w_k should be coefficients of $P(X)/(X - X_i)$ to give the exact root, X_i, in one step. If, instead, one uses the coefficients of $P(X)/(X - X_i^0)$, where X_i^0 is an approximate root, and sets $b_j = (X_i^0)^j$, then the newly calculated root $\bar{X}_i = Z_n/Z_{n-1} = X_i^0 - [f(X_i^0)/f'(X_i^0)]$, which is identical with the Newton approximation to a root. (Received February 1, 1946.)

55

Generalization of the Laplace Transform for Any Operator

Assume given any admissible operator h, such that the first-order linear equation $(h - s)y(t) = f(t)$ has a unique solution $F(t, s, b;f)_h$ for $t \geq t_0$, for arbitrary initial condition $y(t_0) = b$, and for $f(t)$ a sufficiently limited function. Examples of admissible operators are d/dt, E, td/dt, Δ, $5 + \Delta$, and so on, but not d^2/dt^2. By the generalized Laplace transform, $L(s;f)_h$, is meant a linear functional of f with the fundamental property that $L(s;hf)_h = sL(s;f)_h - f(t_0)$. Clearly $\int_{t_0}^{\infty} \exp - s(t - t_0) f(t)dt$, $\sum_{t_0}^{\infty} f(i)s^{-i-1+t_0}$, $\int_{t_0}^{\infty} t^{-s-1}t_0^s f(t)dt$, $\sum_{t_0}^{\infty} f(i)(1 + s)^{-i+t_0-1}$ are generalized L. T.'s for d/dt, E, td/dt, and Δ respectively. It may be verified that the appropriate expression is in every case given formally by $\lim_{t\to\infty} F(t, s, 0;f)F(t, s, 1;0)^{-1}$. Tables of transform pairs may be set up for practical use precisely like those of the usual Laplace transform. Regions of convergence must be determined for each different operator; however, in practice it is often possible to get the correct answer by proper "interpretation" even when convergence fails. (Received January 15, 1947.)

56

A Generalized Newton Iteration

An unknown simple root, A, of the equation $f(x) = 0$ can be approximated by a general iteration of the form $x_{t+1} = H(x_t)$, defined by the implicit relation $y(x_{t+1}) = G[x_{t+1} - x_t; f(x_t), f'(x_t), \cdots, f^{(n)}(x_t)] = 0$ where y is a solution of some differential equation system $y^{(n+1)} = g[y, y', \cdots, y^{(n)}]$ and $y^{(i)}(x_t) = f^{(i)}(x_t)$ for $i \leq n$. It can be shown that $H(A) = A$ and $H^{(i)}(A) = 0$, $i \leq n$, so that the iteration not only converges to the correct root for all sufficiently near initial approximations, but does so at an extremely rapid rate. Special cases include the Newton iteration (when $y'' = g \equiv 0$), numerous suggested high-order osculatory extrapolations, truncated Taylor series, inverse interpolation by means of derivatives, and other methods proposed in the literature — often without proof of convergence. (Received January 15, 1947.)

57

EXACT DISTRIBUTION OF CONTINUOUS VARIABLES IN SEQUENTIAL ANALYSIS

By PAUL A. SAMUELSON

SUMMARY

ONE of the most important wartime developments in statistical theory has been the field of "sequential analysis." Thanks largely to the work of Wald,[1] we can now improve greatly upon the "classical" methods that test hypotheses by means of samples of a *predetermined* size. Instead, we will cut down the work almost in half by letting the observations themselves decide whether we should, at any stage, come to a final decision or continue examining additional observations.

Because the results at any stage in sequential analysis depend upon the results at previous stages, some complex problems of conditional probability arise. For most practical purposes, it is not necessary to solve these problems. Also, in two important special cases, exact expressions for the relevant statistical distributions are available: (a) For the case where the likelihood ratio is an equally-spaced discrete variable; and (b) where we can neglect the "excess of the likelihood ratio" beyond the critical boundaries.[2] Useful limits are available for still other cases.

It may be of interest, nevertheless, to present general expressions for the exact sequential distribution (1) of the likelihood ratio, (2) of the power function, (3) of the probability of coming to a decision at the end of n observations, and (4) of the factorial moment-generating function of the latter probability distribution. Results will be given for only the continuous case; but by means of Stieltjes integrals, the same formulation will cover the discrete case, or more complicated mixed cases. Some of the relationships between sequential analysis and the classical probability problem of gambler's ruin are briefly developed.

* * *

1. Let $P_a(x)dx$ and $P_b(x)dx$ represent the probability distributions of x under two alternative hypotheses, H_a and H_b; and let $z = \log_e [P_b(x)/P_a(x)] = z(x)$. Then the Wald sequential procedure is to calcu-

---

[1] A. Wald, *Sequential Analysis*, New York, Wiley, 1947. See references there to earlier work. Also, see the fundamental paper, Walter Bartky, "Multiple Sampling with Constant Probability," *Annals of Mathematical Statistics*, Vol. 14 September, 1943, pp. 363–377.

[2] Wald, *op. cit.*, Appendix A.5; M. A. Girshick, "Contributions to the Theory of Sequential Analysis, II," *Annals of Mathematical Statistics*, Vol. 17, September, 1946, pp. 282–291.

late successively $Z_1 = z_1$, $Z_2 = z_1 + z_2$, $\cdots$, $Z_n = z_1 + z_2 + \cdots + z_n$, etc. If at any stage Z exceeds some specified constant, a, then H_a is rejected and H_b accepted; if at any stage Z is less than a negative constant, b, H_a is accepted and H_b rejected; if at any stage $b \leqq Z \leqq a$, then a new independent observation is drawn. The values of a and b are chosen in advance according to how often we are willing to tolerate rejecting H_a when it is really true, and rejecting H_b when it is true.

Whether H_a, H_b, or any other hypothesis is true, there will be a probability density distribution of z: $F(z)dz$. The frequency density of Z_1, $F_1(Z_1)$, is, of course, of exactly the same form $F(Z_1)dZ_1$. But the conditional distribution of $Z_2 = z_1 + z_2$ is no longer given by the simple "convolution," $F_2(Z_2) = F*F = \int_{-\infty}^{\infty} F(Z_2 - Z_1) F(Z_1)dZ_1$, and the usual theorems concerning cumulative sums (approach to normality so long as F has finite moments of given order, etc.) no longer hold. However, it is clear that $F_2(Z_2)$ is given by a "truncated" convolution, in which Z_1 never goes beyond the limits b and a; and more generally that $F_n(Z_n)dZ_n$ can be expressed in terms of $F_{n-1}(Z_{n-1})dZ_{n-1}$ in the form

$$F_2(Z_2) = \int_b^a F(Z_2 - Z_1)F_1(Z_1)dZ_1$$

$$= \int_b^a F(Z_2 - s)F_1(s)ds, \qquad -\infty < Z_2 < \infty,$$

$$F_n(Z_n) = \int_b^a F(Z_n - s)F_{n-1}(s)ds, \qquad -\infty < Z_n < \infty.$$

These iterated integrals can always be calculated numerically or otherwise. In connection with the random-walk problem, Kac[3] has suggested one possible expression which involves the "eigenvalues" and "eigenfunctions" of the homogeneous Fredholm integral equation $h(t) = \lambda \int_b^a F(t-s)h(s)ds$. However, particularly in the case of non-symmetrical frequency distributions—there seems to be little computational merit in this approach.

2. But suppose we ask for the frequency *density* of Z, regardless of the subscript showing when it occurs. Call this $g(Z)dZ$. This is arrived at by taking the sum of all F's, or namely by

(1) $g(Z) = F_1(Z) + F_2(Z) + \cdots + F_n(Z) + \cdots$.

Note that g, like the F's, represents a "frequency density"; it is not a "probability density" because its integral is different from unity.

    [3] M. Kac, "Random Walk in Presence of Absorbing Barriers," *Annals of Mathematical Statistics*, Vol. 16, March, 1945, pp. 62–67.

The whole turns out to be simpler than each of its parts. The function,' $g(Z)$, can be shown to satisfy a basic nonhomogeneous integral equation of the Fredholm type.

THEOREM 1: *The frequency density of any Z is uniquely defined by the relation*

$$(2) \qquad g(Z) = F(Z) + \int_b^a F(Z - s)g(s)ds.$$

If we substitute (1) into (2) the proof is immediate, once we verify that the probability character of the problem leads to rapid convergence of the infinite series in question.

However, (2) can be established directly by intuitive reasoning as follows. Any given value of Z can arise in only two ways: (a) by being observed as a first observation. In this case its frequency density is given by the first terms on the right-hand side of (2). But it may also be observed (b) as a result of a previously observed Z, provided that the previous Z lies within b and a. The second term on the right-hand side of (2) defines, in terms of the distribution of g between b and a, the frequency density of observing such a "repeat" Z.

3. A number of important properties of $g(Z)$ follow immediately from its definition by equation (2). These may be briefly indicated:

a. $\displaystyle\int_a^\infty g(Z)dZ$ is the power function.

b. $\displaystyle\int_{-\infty}^b g(Z)dZ = 1 - \int_a^\infty g(Z)dZ.$

c. Expected value of $n = E(n) = \displaystyle\int_{-\infty}^\infty g(Z)dZ = 1 + \int_b^a g(Z)dZ.$

d. $E(n) = \dfrac{\displaystyle\int_{-\infty}^b Zg(Z)dZ + \int_a^\infty Zg(Z)dZ}{\displaystyle\int_{-\infty}^\infty zF(z)d}.$

The first three follow immediately from the fundamental integral equation; the fourth can also be derived from (2), but follows more directly from the well-known Wald relation

$$E(n) = \frac{E(Z_n)}{E(z)}$$

which is to be replaced by

$$E(n) = \frac{E(Z_n{}^2)}{E(z^2)}$$

if $E(z) = 0$.

Wald's fundamental identity concerning characteristic functions can also be derived from the properties of the earlier indicated iterated truncated integrals. Also, let us define

$$_1g(t) = g(t), \qquad b \leqq t \leqq a,$$
$$= 0, \qquad b > t > a;$$
$$_2g(t) = g(t), \qquad b > t > a,$$
$$= 0, \qquad b \leqq t \leqq a;$$
$$g(t) = {}_1g(t) + {}_2g(t);$$

and similarly define $_1F(t)$ and $_2F(t)$. Then taking the "bilateral Laplace transform," or characteristic function of both sides of our integral equation gives us:

$$(3) \quad \int_{-\infty}^{\infty} e^{-pt}{}_1g(t)dt + \int_{-\infty}^{\infty} e^{-pt}{}_2g(t)$$
$$= \left[\int_{-\infty}^{\infty} e^{-pt}F(t)dt \right]\left[1 + \int_{-\infty}^{\infty} e^{-pt}{}_1g(t)dt \right].$$

By differentiating this identity with respect to p, the Wald formula for the average sample size can also be derived. Numerous other relationships between the moments, semi-invariants, and characteristic functions of F, $_1F$, $_2F$, G, $_1G$, $_2G$, F_2, $\cdots F_n$, $\cdots$ can also be readily derived.

4. The basic Fredholm integral equation (2) can be solved or approximated by a variety of well-known devices. But rather than go into these, it will be illuminating to generalize the relationship and to sketch briefly a derivation of the generating function of the probabilities of coming to a definite decision at stage 1, 2, 3, $\cdots$, n, $\cdots$. Call these probabilities P_1, P_2, $\cdots$, P_n, $\cdots$. As usual, let

$$\sum_1^{\infty} i^{[k]}P_i = \sum_1^{\infty} [i(i-1)\cdots(i-k+1)Pi]$$

be the kth factorial moment of the P's. Also, by definition

$$P_n = \int_{-\infty}^{b} F_n(Z_n)dZ_n + \int_a^{\infty} F_n(Z_n)dZ_n.$$

Intuitively, we can arrive at the first moment of the P's, or what is the same thing, the expected average sample size, by the following rather intricate reasoning. Suppose that we were to change our original frequency distribution $F(z)$ from one times F to some number just less than one times F', say $0.999F$, so that there is a little "leakage" of probability at each stage. Then P_1 would be reduced by about $1/1000$; P_2 would be reduced by about $2/1000$; P_3 by $3/1000$; and P_n by $n/1000$. Therefore, the change in $\sum_1^\infty P_i$ with respect to the leakage factor will be approximately proportionate to the first moment $\sum_1^\infty iP_i$.

This suggests the following basic theorem:

THEOREM 2. *The "generating" function of the probability of arriving at a decision at each stage is given by*

$$(4) \qquad G(\lambda) = \int_{-\infty}^{b} g(Z, \lambda)dZ + \int_{a}^{\infty} g(Z, \lambda)dZ,$$

where

$$(5) \qquad g(Z, \lambda) = \lambda F(Z) + \lambda \int_{b}^{a} F(Z - s)g(s, \lambda)ds$$

for $-\infty < Z < \infty$; *and consequently the probability distribution of the P's and its factorial moments are given by the following derivatives*

$$(6) \qquad P_i = \frac{G^{(i)}(0)}{i!}, \qquad i = 1, 2, \cdots,$$

$$\sum_1^\infty i^{[k]}P_i = G^{(k)}(1), \qquad k = 1, 2, \cdots.$$

To prove this we need only note that

$$(5) \qquad g(Z, \lambda) = \lambda F_1(Z) + \lambda^2 F_2(Z) + \cdots + \lambda^n F_n(Z) + \cdots$$

does satisfy the integral equation (5); and that consequently

$$G(\lambda) = \int_{-\infty}^{b} g(Z, \lambda)dZ + \int_{a}^{\infty} g(Z, \lambda)dZ = \sum_1^\infty P_i\lambda^i.$$

Actually, if we work with $g^*(Z) = g(Z, \lambda)/\lambda$ then g^* satisfies the more familiar Fredholm integral equation of the second kind with a parameter; namely

$$g^*(Z) = F(Z) + \lambda \int_{b}^{a} F(Z - s)g^*(s)ds.$$

This can be solved in terms of an ascending power series in λ; or by the Fredholm method as the ratio of two everywhere converging power series in λ; by "resolvent kernels"; and in still other ways. Where the first of these methods is practicable, it has the virtue of yielding the iterated integrals needed for the F_n's and the P_n's.

Note that Theorem 2 includes 1 as a special case.

5. If z can take on only equally-spaced integral values, our probability density F must be replaced by discrete probabilities of the form

$$\cdots, F(-2), F(-1), F(0), F(1), \cdots, F(i) \cdots.$$

Then our integrals are replaced by sums, our kernels by matrices, and we have corresponding to Theorem 2

(7)
$$g(i, \lambda) = \lambda F(i) + \lambda \sum_b^a F(i - j)g(j, \lambda), \qquad -\infty < i < \infty,$$

$$G(\lambda) = \sum_{-\infty}^{\infty} g(i, \lambda) - \sum_b^a g(i, \lambda).$$

Only between b and a need any simultaneous equations be solved, and there the g's are given in matrix terms by

(8)
$$[g(i, \lambda)] = [\delta_{ij} - \lambda F(i - j)]^{-1}[\lambda F(j)],$$

where the right-hand side is the ratio of two polynomials in λ of the same degree.

This result corresponds to the previous Girshick[4] solution of the equally-spaced discrete case, although the present derivation is a different one. It may also be remarked that the present approach helps to bring out the similarity between Bartky's special matrix methods and the general Wald theory.

6. In conclusion, the relationship between sequential analysis and the classical problem of "gambler's ruin" may be briefly sketched. Imagine two individuals, A and B, with initial money "fortunes" of size a and $|b| = -b$. In each game they wager so that B stands to win from A the algebraic amount z, with relative probability $F(z)dz$. Then at the end of n games A is ruined if $Z_n = z_1 + \cdots + z_n > a$; or B is ruined if $Z_n < b$; or if neither of these events occurs, a new game in the series is to be played until finally one of the players is ruined.

This classical probability problem, studied by Huygnens, James Bernoulli, Montmort, De Moivre, Lagrange, Laplace, Markoff, and others, was recognized by Barnard[5] to be formally equivalent to the Wald sequential-probability ratio test: A being ruined is equivalent to rejecting H_a, and B's ruin means H_b is rejected.

As Barnard has shown, the classical writers attacked this problem by studying a function not explicitly treated by Wald: namely, the

[4] Girshick, *op. cit.*

[5] G. A. Barnard, "Sequential Tests in Industrial Statistics," *Supplement to the Journal of the Royal Statistical Society*, Vol. 8, 1946, pp. 1–26.

probability—once Z has already reached the value X—of the final Z's being less than b, so that B is ruined. For the discrete case this function satisfies a fairly simple difference equation with easily prescribed boundary conditions. In the same discrete case, if we ask for $U_n(X)$, the probability of the above outcome in *exactly* n games, we are led to a corresponding partial-difference equation.

For brevity I shall confine my attention to the continuous case, to show the connection between this approach and the above integral equations which define the exact solution for the Wald process.

The integral equation

$$(2) \qquad g(Z) = F(Z) + \int_b^a F(Z - s)g(s)ds$$

is known from the Fredholm-Volterra theory to have an explicit solution of the form

$$(9) \qquad g(Z) = F(Z) + \int_b^a M(Z, X)F(X)dX$$

where the "resolvent kernel," $M(Z, X)$, satisfies either of the integral equations

$$M(Z, X) = F(Z - X) + \int_b^a F(Z - s)M(s, X)ds$$
$$(10)$$
$$= F(Z - X) + \int_a^b M(Z, s)F(s - X)ds.$$

Both of these relations could be given a simple, intuitive probability interpretation. Similar reasoning could also show that $M(Z, X)dZ$ is the probability—when already at X—of encountering a given final Z.

Let us now define

$$U(X) = \int_{-\infty}^b M(Z, X)dZ \quad \text{and} \quad V(X) = \int_a^\infty M(Z, X)dZ.$$

Then it is not too hard to show that $U(X)$ has the already described probability interpretation of the classical writers. Moreover, a single direct integration with respect to X of the first form of (10) will yield the following integral equations:

$$U(X) = \int_{-\infty}^b F(s - X)ds + \int_b^a F(s - X)U(s)ds,$$
$$(11)$$
$$V(X) = \int_a^\infty F(s - X)ds + \int_b^a F(s - X)U(s)ds = 1 - U(X).$$

To evaluate the exact distribution of n, the number of games or observations, we define $U(X, \lambda)$, $V(X, \lambda)$, $M(Z, X, \lambda)$, etc., by putting $\lambda F(Z)$ for $F(Z)$ in all of the above relations. Then by partial differentiation with respect to λ, as in Section 5, we can easily evaluate terms of the form $U_n(X)$, $V_n(X)$, and the higher moments and generating functions of such terms and of $P_n = U_n(0) + V_n(0)$. Other generalizations will immediately suggest themselves.

Massachusetts Institute of Technology

58

ITERATIVE COMPUTATION OF COMPLEX ROOTS

By P. A. Samuelson

1. In applied mathematics it is often necessary to evaluate complex roots of real polynomials, and in the study of oscillations it is frequently necessary to find the value of a polynomial for a number of complex arguments.[1] The present note points out that all this may be done by the same efficient methods as apply to the real variable problems—namely by synthetic division and by the classical methods of Newton, of "false position," and of generalized inverse interpolation. In addition there are set forth a few general considerations concerning iteration that are relevant to any comparison of the efficiencies of different methods that have been proposed. The recent method of Lin for finding complex roots is considered in some detail.

2. Let us consider a polynomial of the nth degree with real coefficients

$$f(x) = a_0 x^n + a_1 x^{n-1} + \cdots + a_n = \sum_0^n a_i x^{n-i}$$

Suppose we wish the value of $f(x_1)$ where x_1 is real. In the literature one occasionally encounters cases where such an answer is arrived at by calculating powers of x and then adding. But these are rare since it is almost universally realized that the work may be reduced by a factor of n if instead we take advantage of the remainder-factor theorem, and calculate $f(x_1)$ by synthetic division. This involves about n successive multiplications and additions, since

$$f(x) = (x - x_1)[a_0'x^{n-1} + a_1'x^{n-2} + \cdots + a_{n-1}'] + f(x_1)$$

where

(1)
$$a_0' = a_0,\ a_1' = x_1 a_0' + a_1,\ a_2' = x_1 a_1' + a_2 \cdots$$
$$a_n' = x_1 a_{n-1}' + a_n = f(x_1)$$

and this process is ideally adapted to modern desk calculating machines.

If x_1 is complex, the same procedure is valid. But now we shall have to multiply complex numbers at each stage; and this, of course quadruples the work. As a result, De Moivre's theorem is often invoked, and recourse is made to trigonometric tables. Almost nothing is more tedious, and it would be better to accept a quadrupling of the work of synthetic division—if no better method were available.

3. But actually, by a simple extension of the most elementary polynomial identities, it is easy to halve the labor of calculating $f(x)$ for a complex x_1. Furthermore, only real quantities are employed up to the final step. The number of multiplications is still double that required in the real variable case; but as we shall see again and again, even this extra labor is mostly an illusion—since

---

[1] The first 5 references deal with the problem of complex roots, while the last reference gives a convenient discussion of all the usual numerical methods.

we simultaneously evaluate both $f(x_1)$ and $f(x_1^*)$ where x_1^* is the complex conjugate of x_1.

By repeatedly dividing our polynomial by terms of the form, $(x - x_1)$, $(x - x_2)$, $(x - x_3)$, $\cdots$, etc., we arrive at a simple extension of the remainder-factor theorem; namely

(2) $f(x) = (x - x_1)(x - x_2) \cdots (x - x_r)f(x, x_r, x_{r-1}, \cdots, x_1) + R$

where $f(x, x_r, \cdots, x_1)$ is a polynomial of $(n - r)$ degree and where the remainder is a polynomial of $(r - 1)$ degree with the important property of having the same values as the original polynomial at each of the arguments $x = x_i$. That is,

$$f(x_i) = 0 + R(x_i, x_r, x_{r-1}, \cdots, x_1) \qquad (i = 1, 2, \cdots, r)$$

It may be noted that if s of the x_i's should be equal, then $(s - 1)$ of the derivatives of the remainder will have to equal the corresponding derivatives of the polynomial at such an x_i. It may also be remarked that the polynomial $f(x, x_r, \cdots, x_1)$ is the well-known Newtonian "divided difference of the rth order" of our original polynomial, and is a symmetric function of its arguments. Should all of the arguments turn out to be equal then instantaneous derivatives will enter the picture in a manner familiar to all students of interpolation.

We may apply this analysis to the problem of evaluating a polynomial for a complex number, x_1. We consider the real quadratic expression $x^2 + b_1 x + b_2 = (x - x_1)(x - x_1^*)$. We divide our polynomial by this quadratic expression, *encountering only real numbers in the process*, and arrive at a $(n - 2)$ degree quotient, $f(x, x_1, x_1^*)$, and a linear remainder; or

(3) $f(x) = (x^2 + b_1 x + b_2)[a_0'' x^{n-2} + \cdots + a_{n-2}''] + c_1'' x + c_0''.$

It follows that

(4) $f(x_1) = c_1'' x_1 + c_0'' = (c_1'' \operatorname{Re} x_1 + c_0'') + i(\operatorname{Im} x_1 c_1'')$

For efficient computation one may employ the useful mnemonic device of algebraic long division, or the equivalent relations, derived from equating coefficients of like powers of x on both sides of (3):

$$a_0'' = a_0$$
$$a_1'' = a_1 - b_1 a_0''$$
(5) $$a_2'' = a_2 - b_1 a_1'' - b_2 a_0''$$
$$a_3'' = a_3 - b_1 a_2'' - b_2 a_1''$$
$$\overline{a_{n-2}'' = a_{n-2} - b_1 a_{n-3}'' - b_2 a_{n-4}''}$$

and

(6) $$c_1'' = a_{n-1} - b_1 a_{n-2}'' - b_2 a_{n-3}''$$
$$c_0'' = a_n - 0 - b_2 a_{n-2}''$$

In all, these involve about $2n$ multiplications. This is twice that required for a real x, but $f(x_1^*)$ is computed along with $f(x_1)$.

As an illustration, one may consider the problem encountered in electrical and mechanical engineering of computing the complex impedance or transfer function of a differential equation with constant coefficients

$$f(d/dt)y(t) = e^{i\theta t}$$

whose steady-state solution is of the form

$$y(t) = [1/f(i\theta)]e^{i\theta t}$$

We calculate the remainder $c_1'' x + c_0''$, of $f(x)/(x^2 + \theta^2)$, and find

$$f(i\theta) = c_0'' + i(c_1'' \theta)$$

Here our complex number happens to be a pure imaginary and the work is halved, so that the example is rather a trivial one. But in the corresponding case of difference equations, met in many fields, where d/dt is replaced by the operator E, such that $Ey(t) = y(t + 1)$, we must evaluate terms of the form

$$y(t) = \frac{1}{f(\cos \theta + i \sin \theta)} [\cos \theta t + i \sin \theta t]$$

and here the efficiency of the present procedure is well illustrated.

4. Let us turn now to the problem of calculating complex or real roots of our polynomial. Two problems must always be distinguished: (1) that of determining *in the large* the general location of roots—by Graeffe's root-squaring method, Sturmian test functions, or general topological investigation of the transformation $y = f(x)$; and (2) improving the accuracy of a given root, or set of roots, once we have accomplished an approximate localization. It is primarily with this latter problem that most methods deal and with which this discussion will be primarily concerned.

The classical Newton method for calculating a real simple root is to use the iterative sequence (defined by replacing the function near a root by a tangential straight line)

(7) $$x_{t+1} = H(x_t) = x_t - [f(x_t)/f'(x_t)]$$

It is easy to show that this converges to a simple root, A, for all initial values x_0 sufficiently near to A. Moreover, as is well-known, $H'(A) = 0$ and the convergence is exceedingly rapid, the number of "correct decimal places" increasing asymptotically in a geometric rather than an arithmetic progression. Such "quadratic or second-order convergence" is always sure of being eventually more accurate than any "linear" iteration for which $|H'(A)| \neq 0$, and whose correct decimal places eventually increase in an arithmetic progression. [6]

This does not mean that an efficient method is necessarily always to be preferred to a less efficient one. Except in the problem of "prodigious calculation"— such as evaluating $\sqrt{2}$ to a thousand decimal places—an asymptotically inefficient method may be satisfactory. But in no case should we pass over a more efficient method unless there is some decided disadvantage in its application.

In the case of complex roots it is natural to consider using the same Newton method. In fact around the First World War, Edwin Bidwell Wilson used this method in aeronautical problems. But since then the method has come into disrepute, apparently for two quite different reasons. First, as we have seen, it is very time consuming to evaluate a polynomial for complex arguments by the conventional methods. The second objections do not relate peculiarly to the complex variable but are concerned with alleged inadequacies of Newton's method in the case of multiple roots or in the related case of closely clustered roots. Discussion of these second objections may be reserved for a later section.

By using the method just outlined, we may expeditiously evaluate $f(x_t)$ and $f'(x_t) = \sum_1^n a_{n-j} j x^{j-1}$. The work is double that for a real variable, but we approximate to two conjugate roots A, and A^*. In practice, even in the real variable case we need not work directly with the polynomial, $f'(x)$, but can calculate $f'(x_t)$ by a second synthetic division of $P(x)$ by $(x - x_t)$, the remainder c_1'' being the required derivative. A similar artifice can be followed in the complex variable case. For,

$$
\begin{aligned}
f(x) &= (x - x_t)f(x, x_t) + f(x_t) \\
&= (x - x_t)(x - x_t^*)f(x, x_t^*, x_t) + (x - x_t) f(x_t^*, x_t) + f(x_t) \\
f'(x_t) &= 0 + (x_t - x_t^*)f(x_t, x_t^*, x_t) + f(x_t, x_t^*) + 0 \\
&= (x_t - x_t^*)(c_2'''' - x_t^* c_3'''') + c_1''
\end{aligned}
$$

(8)

Our only task is to evaluate $f(x, x_t^*, x_t) = \sum_0^{n-2} a_j'' x^{n-j}$ for $x = x_t$. This too can be done by the method indicated for $f(x)$ itself; just as we can get (a_i') from (a_i), so we can get (a_i'''') from (a_i''). In short, by twice dividing $f(x)$ by $x^2 - (x_t + x_t^*)x + x_t x_t^*$, we are in a position to evaluate $f(x_t)$, $f'(x_t)$, $f(x_t^*)$, $f'(x_t^*)$. By more divisions by the same quadratic factor we can calculate higher derivatives. But since each such division reduces the degree of our polynomial by 2, we can apparently only hope to evaluate about half the non-vanishing higher derivatives of our polynomial by such methods.

Just as all parts of the proof of the convergence of the Newton method hold as well for complex as for real variables, so too the proof holds for the convergence of the even more ancient "rule of false position" method. In this method we replace the function by the straight line secant joining two of its points in the neighborhood of a root, and solve for a third better point. Thus, we have defined a difference equation of the second order.

(9)
$$
x_{t+2} = H(x_{t+1}, x_t) = \frac{x_t f(x_{t+1}) - x_{t+1} f(x_t)}{f(x_{t+1}) - f(x_t)}
$$

This is nothing but simple linear inverse interpolation. It is easy to verify by differentiation that in the neighborhood of any simple root, A, we have

(10)
$$
\frac{\partial H}{\partial x_{t+1}} (A, A) = 0 = \frac{\partial H}{\partial x_t} (A, A)
$$

so that the process must converge for all initial values x_0, x_1 sufficiently close to A. Moreover, the convergence is very rapid, again being asymptotically quadratic rather than linear.

As usually expounded in the text books, the rule of false position is used to interpolate between two values of $f(x)$ of opposite sign. This is unnecessary, and in fact undesirable: following the above iteration will lead to convergence to the true root by *extra*polation, a more efficient computational procedure.

Correctly applied, Newton's method and the rule of false position are about equally powerful and involve about the same amount of work. They are both much more efficient than the usually-taught Horner's method which proceeds one digit at a time, and which in order to diminish the roots of the polynomial by the appropriate numbers requires that *all* the derivatives of the function be calculated at *each* stage. Even with synthetic division, this involves a good deal of unnecessary work, especially after the very first stages. This is perceived in the more advanced treatments of the method (viz. Burnside and Panton's classical discussion); and it stems from the fact that Newton's method and the Rule of False Position quickly outrun single digit at a time accuracy, so that the practitioner of Horner's method soon feels that he is almost marking time.

The following numerical example is designed to bring into immediate play the relations which always hold after a number of whirls of any of the methods under discussion. The equation

$$f(x) = .001x^2 - x - .01 = 0$$

clearly has roots in the neighborhood of 1,000 and $-.01$. The correct larger root to 10 significant figures is 1,000.0099999 which could be determined by Newton's method with 3 whirls, or only a fraction of the work of the usual full Horner procedure.

5. The prevailing distrust of Newton's method, which dates back at least to Lagrange, seems to stem from its alleged inadequacies in the case of multiple roots. In such cases the denominator, $f'(x_t)$ is a very small number and the correction at each stage is the ratio of two very small numbers. Nonetheless, it can be shown that Newton's method does converge to a multiple root for all sufficiently close initial values; but the convergence is now slower, being linear rather than quadratic. In fact

(11) $$0 \neq H'(A) = (s - 1)/s$$

where s is the multiplicity of the root, A.

If we knew in advance that the sought for root was of multiplicity, s, we could solve for the root of $f^{(s-1)}(x) = 0$ by the efficient iteration

(12) $$x_{t+1} = x_t - [f^{(s-1)}(A)/f^{(s)}(A)]$$

But in numerical work, perfectly equal roots only occur as the result of some theoretical idealization of the empirical situation. We rarely can be sure in advance that the sought for root is multiple, so that the above artifice is not very useful.

In applied numerical work, we not infrequently do encounter the case of roots which cluster very close together. And it might be argued that this, rather than multiplicity of roots, provides a challenge to Newton's method, because in some near neighborhood of the root, the first derivative will vanish and cause the iteration to blow up. Consider as an illustration the simple examples $x^3 = 0$, and $x^3 = 1$. Newton's iteration, in the first case being $x_{t+1} = 2/3x_t$, has a domain of convergence of the whole complex plane. Here root multiplicity actually somewhat simplifies the problem of convergence in the large. But in the second example, $x = 0$ is a singular point of the iteration.

The difficulties arising from close or coincident roots are intrinsic. They show up in other methods than Newton's, both in locally efficient and inefficient procedures. Root squaring or other transformations cannot alter the basic qualitative topology of the problem in the large. Since there are neighborhoods of convergence around each root, there must always be watersheds to mark the no-man's frontier between each root's domain. What root squaring and other transformations can do is to help us to land in the convergence neighborhood of a particular root.

From a physical point of view we cannot always regard multiple or clustered roots as a nuisance; they may even be a positive advantage. Thus, if our problem is to locate a relative extremum (or stationary point) of $\int f(x)dx$, a multiple root means that the extremum value is nearly constant in a wide region near to the exact root, $x = A$. In still other applications, our concern is with the degree of closeness to which $|f(x)| = 0$, rather than $|x - A| = 0$, and the sequence $f(x_t)$ converges no less rapidly because of multiple roots; in fact, if one can use (12) or any other artifice to get x_t to converge with quadratic order to a multiple root, then $f(x_t)$ will converge with still higher order rapidity.

Often, too, where nature has clustered roots in a close array, it serves no useful purpose for man to try to unscramble them. For most practical purposes we may treat close roots as being multiple ones, especially since the constants in any empirical equation are subject to error. When the roots are close together, the separate identity of each becomes sensitive to slight changes in the data. This should not be taken to mean that the mathematical features of the total phenomena are "ill-conditioned"; it may be only the representation into particular components that is ambiguous.

6. Thus far, no explicit attention has been given to methods which approach a root with only linear convergence. Bernoulli's method of approximating to the largest root of a polynomial by means of a difference equation sequence is such a method. So too is the closely related Whittaker series method [7]. A popular variant of the Newton iteration is the simpler sequence, $x_{t+1} = x_t - f(x_t)/f'(B)$, where $f'(B)$ is the derivative evaluated at some fixed point near-by to the root, A. This is a special case of the sequence

(13) $x_{t+1} = x_t - [f(x_t)/R(x_t)]$

where R is some suitably defined function: e.g. R might be the slope of a secant. When $R(x) = f'(x)$, we have the Newton method; when $R(x)$ is a constant, we have the just mentioned variant of the Newton method. For local convergence, it is sufficient that

(14) $$| 1 - [f'(A)/R(A)] | < 1$$

But, unless $R(A) = f'(A)$, the convergence will be at best linear, and if A is a multiple root corresponding to an extremum of $f(x)$, then with $R \neq 0$ the process will not be convergent even for initial approximations arbitrarily close to A. Thus, when $R(x) \equiv f(b) \neq f'(A) = 0 \neq f''(A)$, there will be divergence of the sequence for all initial values on one side of A. However, for simple roots this sequence may behave almost as well during the first few iterations as an asymptotically more efficient method.

7. Lin [3, 4] has proposed a general method for evaluating a pair of real or complex roots. This method can be used to approximate a single real (or complex) root; or to approximate simultaneously several pairs of complex roots. There are conditions under which the method can be used to advantage; but nonetheless the method seems to lack two of the desirable properties of Newton's Method or the Method of False Position. First, it need not converge to a simple (or multiple) root even if the initial guesses are infinitesimally close to the correct values. Second, its convergence is at best linear rather than quadratic. There seem to be further difficulties inherent in the method when the roots of the polynomial happen to fall into special patterns and constellations. Also, rigorous conditions for convergence can be defined only in rather complicated terms, although simpler heuristic criteria may be suggested.

The essence of the Lin method is to set the right hand members of equation (6) to zero, and solve for a new, improved set of b's. In effect, the Lin method makes no use of the values of the remainder terms resulting from previous approximations to a root—since the method assumes the remainders are all zero. But, as the Newton method shows, it is the quantitative values of the remainder that permit the most precise estimate of the needed correction to the true root, so that a valuable part of our available information is being discarded.[2]

This may best be illustrated by examining the Lin method as applied to a single root. Given an approximate value, x_t, we seek a better approximation, x_{t+1}. Dividing $f(x)$ by $(x - x_t)$ gives

$$f(x) = (x - x_t)[a_0' x^{n-1} + a_1' x^{n-1} + \cdots + a_{n-1}'] + f(x_t)$$

where

$$f(x_t) = f(0) + x_t a_{n-1}'$$

Hence, rearranging terms and utilizing (6) according to Lin's technique, we find

(15) $$x_{t+1} = \frac{f(0)}{a_{n-1}'} = \frac{x_t a_{n-1}' - f(x_t)}{a_{n-1}'} = x_t - \frac{f(x_t)}{a_{n-1}'} = x_t - \frac{f(x_t)}{\dfrac{f(x_t) - f(0)}{x_t - 0}}$$

---

[2] The Hitchcock method [5] recognizes this fact; like Newton's method it involves two divisions of the polynomial by a trial quadratic factor, and correction of the quadratic factor by means of the remainder. Its convergence seems to be of a slower order than Newton's.

where

$$\frac{f(x_t) - f(0)}{x_t - 0} = \left(\frac{\Delta f}{\Delta x}\right)_{0,x_t} = R(x_t)$$

This has a simple graphical interpretation. It differs from the Newton method only in the denominator of the last term. Instead of drawing a line tangent to the curve through the point $[x_t, f(x_t)]$, we draw a line through that point with slope equal to that of the secant between $[0, f(0)]$ and $[x_t, f(x_t)]$. If the desired root A is small in absolute value, then this will not differ much from the Newton process or the Rule of False Position. The error, $(x_t - A)$ will ultimately behave like

$$(x_{t+1} - A) = [1 - \{f'(A)/R(A)\}](x_t - A) + \cdots$$

or nearly proportional to $[1 - \{f'(A)/R(A)\}]^t$.

For the Lin process to converge, it is not enough for $|x_0 - A|$ to be sufficiently small. In addition the equation must have been transformed so that $|A|$ is "small". Thus, if $f(x) = x^2 + a_1 x + a_2$, the Lin process will only converge to that root which is smallest in absolute value.

It would seem that in the more elaborate case where two roots are sought, convergence depends upon these two roots being "small"—not absolutely but in comparison with all other roots. Thus consider the cubic

$$(16) \quad \begin{aligned} x_3 + a_1 x^2 + a_2 x + a_3 &= (x^2 + B_1 x + B_2)(x + K) \\ &= x^3 + (B_1 + K)x^2 + (B_1 K + B_2)x + KB_2 \end{aligned}$$

where the coefficients may be real or complex. Suppose we guess an initial set of values $b_1(0)$, $b_2(0)$, which are near to B_1 and B_2. For what values of (B_1, B_2, K) will the resulting difference equation be convergent in a neighborhood of (B_1, B_2)?

Our iterative sequence for $b_1(t + 1)$, $b_2(t + 1)$ in terms of $b_1(t)$, $b_2(t)$ is from (16), (5), and (6) defined by

$$(17) \quad \begin{aligned} b_2(t + 1) &= \frac{a_3}{a_1} = \frac{KB_2}{B_1 + K - b(t)} \\ b_1(t + 1) &= \frac{a_2 - b_2 a_0''}{a_1''} = \frac{(B_2 + KB_1) - [KB_2/\{B_1 + K - b_1(t)\}]}{B_1 + K - b_1(t)} \end{aligned}$$

The second of these relations is a difference equation for $b_1(t)$ alone. Regardless of K, it has a stationary point for $b_1(t) = B_1$, and it will converge to B_1 for all initial values $b_1(0)$ sufficiently near to B_1, if at the point $b_1 = B_1$

$$(18) \quad \left|\frac{\partial b_1(t + 1)}{\partial b_1(t)}\right| = \left|\frac{B_2}{K_2} - \frac{B_1}{K}\right| < 1$$

The Lin process must therefore be divergent wherever the absolute value of the third root is small relative to the sum and products of the pair of roots sought. Doubtless a similar qualitative relation holds in the general case. Consequently it is only after certain preliminary transformations on the roots of the polynomial have been performed, that the method will enable us to locate certain specific roots; or only after other roots have been found, and have been used to reduce the degree of the equation.

7. In conclusion, I should like to point out that no mention has been made of the problem of rounding off errors. All of the enunciated theorems concerning convergence apply to the exact iterative sequence. In practice we must always round off, and even the most powerful method can be rendered nugatory by the manner in which we do so. In fact, the really powerful methods, as is well known, secure their power by squeezing the last bit of information out of every digit; there is therefore, always the danger that in rounding off we may throw out the baby along with the bath water, so as to end up with 0/0, or what is worse, with the ratio of one small random error to another such error. Rounding off errors can be thought of as "noise" impinging on our dynamic sequences. Much remains to be done in analyzing the effect of such shocks on different kinds of processes. The whole subject—of degree of convergence and of rounding error—acquires a new significance in the modern era of giant calculating machines.

REFERENCES

(1) SHARP, HENRY S.: A Comparison of Methods for Evaluating the Complex Roots of Quartic Equations, J. of Math. and Phys., **20** (1941), pp. 243–258.

(2) CORNOCK, A. F., AND HUGHES, JOAN M.: The Evaluation of the Complex Roots of Algebraic Equations, Philosophical Magazine, Seventh Series, **34** (1943), pp. 314–320.

(3) LIN, SHIH-NGE: A Method of Successive Approximations of Evaluating the Real and Complex Roots of Cubic and Higher-Order Equations, J. of Math. and Phys., **20** (1941), pp. 231–242.

(4) LIN, SHIH-NGE: A Method for Finding Roots of Algebraic Equations, J. of Math. and Phys., **22** (1943), pp. 60–77.

(5) HITCHCOCK, FRANK L.: An Improvement on the G. C. D. Method for Complex Roots, J. of Math. and Phys., **23** (1944), pp. 69–74.

(6) SAMUELSON, P. A.: A Convergent Iterative Process, J. of Math. and Phys., **24** (1945), pp. 131–134.

(7) WHITTAKER, E. T., AND ROBINSON, G.: The Calculus of Observations (3rd edition), Ch. VI.

MASSACHUSETTS INSTITUTE OF TECHNOLOGY

(Received December 15, 1948)

59

RAPIDLY CONVERGING SOLUTIONS TO INTEGRAL EQUATIONS

By Paul A. Samuelson

1. Suppose that for a given known kernel $K(x, z)$ and function $F(x, z)$, we wish to find the unknown solution, $U(x, z)$, defined by the Fredholm integral equation

$$(1) \qquad E(x, z) = F(x, z) + U(x, z) + \int_a^b K(x, s)U(s, z)\, ds = 0.$$

Important special cases met in practical applications often involve one or more of the following: $F(x, z)$ may be a function of the single variable x, often written $F = -f(x)$; the kernel K may involve a multiplicative parameter, λ, which is not explicitly shown here; K may vanish for $z > x$, and hence be of Volterra type with upper limit on the integral written as x rather than b; K may be of Poisson or Wiener type, of the form $K(x - z)$, with K vanishing for negative arguments. Throughout we assume that (1) does have a unique solution, which it will have for almost all K's, the only exception being when K happens to have an eigenvalue, $\lambda = 1$.

E as defined above is a measure of the error with which any arbitrary function inserted in place of the true solution U does satisfy the integral equation. E is a linear functional of each of the functions involved and for simplicity we can denote it by $E(F, U, K)$. It will be noted that the order of the functions is important, and that equating E to zero defines F explicitly in terms of the remaining two functions, whereas U is defined only implicitly in terms of the remaining two functions. To simplify notation, we write any integral of the form $\int_a^b K(x, s)U(s, z)\, ds$ as $K(x, z) \cdot U(x, z)$ or simply as $K \cdot U$. Similarly the definition of $K \cdot U \cdot W$ will be apparent.

If any approximation u to U were at hand, it would be natural to compute the error in satisfying (1), i.e. $E(F, u, K)$; and for many purposes, particularly where (1) is "ill-conditioned", it may be of more physical importance to know that E is small than that $u\text{-}U$ is small. Moreover, many of the usual methods for approximate iteration to a solution U try to utilize knowledge of E to get an improved approximation. Ways of speeding up such approximating sequences, so that they will converge more rapidly, will be developed below.

2. It can be easily verified by substitution that the solution U can be written down in terms of F by means of the reciprocal kernel to K, $k(x, z)$; i.e. as

$$(2) \qquad E(U, F, k) = 0$$

where k is defined by

$$(3) \qquad E(K, k, K) = 0 \text{ or } E(k, K, k) = 0.$$

Computationally it will pay to calculate this reciprocal kernel once and for all: (a) if many different problems are to be solved, involving a multitude of different F functions but always the same K; (b) if F is a function of x and z rather than of x alone, since in this case the conditions of (a) are realized; (c) if K is of the Poisson-Wiener type; (d) or if K happens to be of some special simple analytic form, yielding an easy recognizable solution.

Otherwise it will not usually pay to calculate the reciprocal kernel, just as it does not usually pay to calculate the inverse to a matrix if only one set of linear equations is to be inverted. This is because calculating or approximating the inverse of a matrix involves operations like multiplying a square matrix into a square matrix, which is n times as much work as to multiply a square matrix into a single vector of n components. Similarly, to compute a reciprocal kernel we must evaluate integrals of the form $A(x, z) \cdot B(x, z)$, which is of a higher dimensionality of work than to compute integrals of the form $A(x, z) \cdot B(x)$. However, as will be shown, any kind of an approximation to k can greatly accelerate the convergence to the true U solution.

3. A commonly used sequence of approximations to U is given by $U_0, U_1, \cdots, U_n$, where U_n satisfies the iteration

$$(4) \qquad U_{n+1} = -F - K \cdot U_n = U_n - E(F, U_n, K), \qquad U_0 \text{ arbitrary.}$$

If we set $U_0 = 0$, and calculate U_n as $\sum_1^n (U_i - U_{i-1})$, where these last differences satisfy a relation like (4) but without the F, then we have the Liouville-Neumann series; hence, for simplicity we can call (4) a Neumann sequence.

Provided our original problem has a solution, this sequence will either converge for all U_0 or else will diverge for almost all initial U_0. It is sufficient for convergence that K be of Volterra type, vanishing for $z > x$. Also, it is sufficient for convergence, but not necessary, that K be sufficiently small in absolute value so that its "norm," $N(K)$, satisfies

$$(5) \qquad N(K) = \max_x \int_a^b |K(x, s)| \, ds < 1,$$

where the so-defined norm can be shown to have the property

$$(6) \qquad N(A \cdot B) \leq N(A)N(B) \qquad \text{for all } A \text{ and } B.$$

Complete necessary and sufficient conditions for the convergence of (3) are that the eigenvalues of the associated homogeneous integral equation all satisfy the following inequality

$$(7) \qquad |\sigma^{-1}| = |m| < 1 \text{ where } E(0, V, -\sigma K) = 0, \qquad V \not\equiv 0.$$

The speed of asymptotic convergence to U will depend upon the smallness of the largest modulus of m. Note that if the Neumann sequence is defined as in (4) and is convergent, then a numerical error in iteration will be later self-correcting.

4. In many actual applications there is no reason why the norm of K or the dominating eigenvalue should be such as to make the Neumann iteration converge. Even if convergence is assured, as in the Volterra case, there is no guarantee that the convergence will be at all rapid. The reason is not hard to find: from the last expression in (4) it is apparent that the Neumann sequence does utilize the error, E, that comes from substituting an approximate U_n in (1). But it utilizes that error in rather an arbitrary way; at any point (x, z) we simply subtract E from U_n to get a new approximation, and such a procedure in no way suggests itself as being optimal.

However, if we had knowledge of the reciprocal kernel, k, it is easy to see what would be the correct way to utilize E. The expression

$$(8) \qquad U_{n+1} = U_n - E(F, U_n, K) - k \cdot E(F, U_n, K)$$

can by substitution be verified to give $U_{n+1} = U$ in one step regardless of U_n and regardless of the size of K. Hence, if we know any approximation to $k(x, z)$, which we may write as $j(x, z)$, then we should expect that using it in place of k in (8) will yield a modified Neumann sequence that is much more rapidly convergent than (4).

That this is rigorously the case can be seen by a different argument. Using any arbitrary function $j(x, z)$, which happens to be an approximation to $k(x, z)$ but need not be restricted to being so, we can add and subtract $j \cdot F$ to (1) and evaluate the resulting expression in terms of U; it turns out to give us a new integral equation for U

$$(9) \qquad 0 = (F + j \cdot F) + U + (j + K + j \cdot K) \cdot U$$
$$= E(F + j \cdot F, U, j + K + j \cdot K).$$

Now this is seen to be of exactly the same form as (1) but with a new known F and a new kernel

$$(10) \qquad j + K + j \cdot K = E(j, K, j).$$

Comparing (10) with the second form of (3), we see that if j were identical to the reciprocal kernel, k, the new kernel would vanish and (9) could provide an explicit solution to our problem. To the degree that j is close to k and almost satisfies (3), the new kernel will be very small, and hence applying the Neumann sequence (4) to the new equation (10), we arrive at the modified Neumann sequence in any of the equivalent forms

$$(11) \qquad U_{n+1} = -F - j \cdot F - (j + K + j \cdot K) \cdot U_n$$
$$= U_n - E(F + j \cdot F, U_n, j + K + j \cdot K)$$
$$= U_n - E(F, U_n, K) - j \cdot E(F, U_n, K).$$

Note that the last of these is precisely of the form (8) but with the j approximation to the reciprocal kernel used rather than k itself. Hence, the earlier argument of (8) for utilizing the error E has been confirmed.

The last expression in (11) is computationally the more convenient if F is a function of x alone and if only a few iterations are needed. This for two reasons: integrals of the form $j(x, z) \cdot U_n(x)$ are much less labor to compute than an integral of the form $j(x, z) \cdot K(x, z)$; also, the error of the original equation (1), $E(F, U_n, K)$ may be of intrinsic physical interest for its own sake. On the other hand, if F is a function of z as well as x and if many iterations are going to be needed, computing the new kernel once and for all will save the need to later evaluate integrals of the form $j \cdot E(x, z)$. Also, the new transformed equation will presumably have so small a kernel that it will be much better conditioned than (1) itself, and its error will already provide a very good approximation to $U - U_n$.

It goes without saying that we ought not to pick j with the singular property of making (9) not have a solution, as would be the case if the new kernel had an eigenvalue equal to unity. On the contrary, we wish to pick j near in some sense to k. As (9) and (10) show, a criterion for nearness of j to k is that $E(j, K, j)$ be everywhere small in absolute value so that its norm will be small and so that the $|m|$ of (7), defined for the new kernel, will be small and the convergence to U rapid.

5. Whether (4) or (11) is used and whether or not either is rapidly or slowly convergent or even divergent, after a number of iterations U_n primarily differs from U by a term proportional to $(m_1)^n$ where m_1 is the dominant root defined by a homogeneous equation of type (7). It can be shown to follow that we can usually speed up convergence by computing at a late stage of the iteration

$$(12) \qquad U \cong \frac{U_n U_{n+2} - U_{n+1}^2}{(U_{n+2} - U_{n+1}) - (U_{n+1} - U_n)}.$$

As far as I know, the exact conditions for convergence of this process and its speed of convergence have not been rigorously settled except in the case of a one-variable iteration, but there are intuitive reasons to expect this device to accelerate convergence. (See Aitken [1] and Samuelson [6].)

6. To apply the modified and generalized Neumann sequence (11), we need j, an approximation to K's reciprocal kernel, k; but we do not need to know j's own reciprocal, which might be called J, and which is an approximation to K itself. The way in which we get our j approximation is of no consequence for the above method. A good guess, or the similarity of this problem to another problem already solved, or the knowledge of the reciprocal kernel of K for some nearby parameter value, all these are possibilities. However, there is no reason why we cannot consider the problem of systematically improving on an approximation to the reciprocal kernel k itself, since it has been pointed out in (3) above that the problem of getting k is a special case of our general formulation—namely the case when F and K happen to be identical. Thus, our new modified sequence for k is given $k_0, k_1, k_2, \cdots, k_n, \cdots$, where

$$(11') \qquad k_{n+1} = k_n - E[K + j \cdot K, k_n, E(j, K, j)]$$
$$= k_n - E(K, k_n, K) - j \cdot E(K, k_n, K),$$

where the initial k_0 is arbitrary and may or may not be set equal to zero so as to give k_1 equal to j itself. The convergence of this sequence has already been discussed in connection with (11).

7. Like all convergent linear iterations that are not exact, the above process approaches the true k solution so as to give ultimately a number of additional correct decimal places proportional to the number of additional iterations. For many practical purposes this is good enough, especially if the accelerating device (12) is used after we have performed a number of linear iterations.

Nonetheless, a way immediately suggests itself to greatly speed up the convergence of the modified Neumann sequence (11)′. It will be recalled that its speed of convergence is conditioned upon our using for j the best known approximation to the true reciprocal kernel, k. But note that k_n in (11)′ is presumably a much closer approximation to k than k_0 or j. So it is natural to replace j in (11) by k_n itself, leading to the desired new sequence

$$(13) \qquad k_{n+1} = k_n - E(K, k_n, K) - k_n \cdot E(K, k_n, K).$$

This is no longer a linear iteration; i.e., k_{n+1} is a quadratic rather than a linear functional of k_n. Its convergence in a close neighborhood of k turns out to be more rapid than that of any linear iteration. This can be verified by an extension of the Liapunov stability theory to functionals: expanding the non-linear functional in a Taylor-like series in terms of functional derivatives around the true solution $k(x, z)$, we find that all linear terms vanish. From this it follows that asymptotically the number of correct decimal places grows in geometric progression with the number of iterations: i.e., $\log |k_n - k|$, for any x and z, ultimately diminishes like -2^n. This fact can be verified directly if we manipulate (13) into a verifiably equivalent form

$$(13') \qquad E(K, k_{n+1}, K) = -E(K, k_n, K) \cdot E(K, k_n, K)$$

with

$$N[E(K, k_{n+1}, ,K)] \leqq N[E(K, k_n, K)]^2$$

because of the property of (6). This means that the ultimate error is each time being squared, so that if we start out with a small enough error, convergence will be assured. (For the corresponding non-linear Newton-like iteration applied to inverting a finite matrix, see Frazer, Duncan, Collar [3]; by taking the limit of a large enough number of linear equations, the Fredholm integral equations can be shown to have all the same properties so that heuristically we may invent new methods and find proofs for them by extending to integral equations the various proposals made for matrices.)

The formulation (13′) enables us to give a sufficient condition for the neighborhood of convergence. For all k_0 with $N[E(K, k_0, K)] < 1$, convergence will be assured. This is of course not a necessary condition: a sequence that is going to converge may begin with a norm greater than unity; and for a transient period, its norm may actually grow rather than diminish.

One might at first think that a necessary and sufficient condition like that relating to the eigenvalue of (7) could be found, but it turns out that the problem of delineating the exact *region* of convergence of a non-linear iteration like that of (13) is theoretically a very delicate task. It has the pleasing quality of necessarily being locally convergent for all K provided we have a sufficiently close k_0 to k; moreover, the ultimate rate of local convergence is exceedingly rapid, as we have seen. But there has sometimes been observed a tendency for those iterations that are most powerful locally to have to pay the price of having a restricted domain in the large from which they will converge.

A little light on this problem of region of convergence is provided by recognizing that (13) is essentially a generalization to functions of infinitely many variables of the familiar Newton iteration, by which we find the root of an implicit equation by extrapolating along its tangent line at some approximate root and thereby inferring a better approximation where the tangent line intersects with the zero axis. Such an iteration is known to give rapid convergence of the second order in the neighborhood of any simple root.

To bring out the Newton analogy with the present problem, imagine that the implicit equation for k given by (3) referred to ordinary algebraic variables K and k, and that the integral of products could be interpreted as a simple product. This is not so far-fetched as might be the case, since in the special case where K happens to be independent of x and z, our problem becomes precisely of this type. We can write (3)

$$(3')\qquad 0 = E(K, k, K) = K + k + Kk = (1 + K)(1 + k) - 1,$$

or

$$0 = [1/(1 + k)] - (1 + K) = g(k), \qquad K \neq -1 \neq k.$$

Now applying the usual Newton-Raphson iteration (Whittaker and Robinson [9]), we have

$$
\begin{aligned}
(13'')\qquad k_{n+1} &= k_n - \frac{g(k_n)}{g'(k_n)} = k_n - \frac{[1/(1 + k_n)] - (1 + K)}{[-1/(1 + k_n)^2]} \\
&= k_n + (1 + k_n) - (1 + k_n)\{(1 + k_n)(1 + K)\} \\
&= k_n - E(K, k_n, K) - k_n E(K, k_n, K),
\end{aligned}
$$

which is seen to be of the same form as (13). Since (3') and (13'') refer to simple hyperbolas, it is easy to determine conditions for the neighborhood of convergence. In this simple case it turns out that the modified Neumann process (with $j = k_1$) and the Newton processes have exactly the same region of convergence, namely $|K + k_0 + Kk_0| < 1$. The reason for this special coincidence is the fact that in a one-variable problem, the norm sufficiency condition is also necessary: the norm must change in a monotonic way with each iteration, which is not at all true in the general case.

In practical applications there may be knowledge available that helps us to find an approximation (to the reciprocal kernel) which will serve as a satisfactory

j to insert in (11) or which can be used in (13) to get a more adequate approximation or a self-improving sequence of functions. It is just as well, however, to indicate how in theory we can always construct as close an approximation to k as we wish, even when we know little or nothing that helps us identify regions of convergence. Replace K by λK and consider moving from $\lambda = 0$ to $\lambda = 1$, which gives us our original problem. Now we know that for sufficiently small values of λ, the simple Neumann process will converge; hence we can calculate reciprocal kernels to λK, which we call k_λ, for all small λ. Moreover, it is known from the Fredholm theory that the eigenvalues of λK are isolated: therefore, in the complex plane for λ, there are only a finite number of eigenvalues in any finite circle including the origin. We can always construct a continuous path from 0 to 1 that avoids all such critical points. If we take sufficiently small steps along this path, we can certainly by the modified Neumann process, always find a convergent series for k_λ at every step; and proceeding in this way, we can finally find a convergent series for k itself. This is of course roundabout and would presumably be used rarely in practice, but it can always be done rigorously.

8. In conclusion, we can utilize the formulation (11) to classify a number of suggested methods of approximation in terms of what it is that they assume about K and j.

Case 1. If we put $j = 0$, we get the simple Neumann series (4). For this to be useful, the reciprocal kernel k must be almost zero, which obviously means that K itself must be almost zero. This checks with our derived stability conditions for convergence of the ordinary Neumann sequence.

Case 2. If we put j equal to a constant independently of x and z, we get the method attributed by Wagner [7] to Wiarda [9] and Bückner [2]. For this method to be optimal, k and K must not be too strongly dependent on x and z, as in the discussion of the Newton-Raphson problem. The average values $\bar{\bar{K}} = \int_a^b \int_a^b K(x, z)\, dz\, dx / (b - a)^2$ and $\bar{\bar{j}} = -\bar{\bar{K}}/(1 + \bar{\bar{K}})$ then recommend themselves for J and j, though to play it safe, convergence will be assured for sufficiently small $\bar{\bar{j}}$.

Case 3. If K, and k, are not too strongly dependent on z so that $K(x, z) \cong \bar{K}(x) = \int_a^b K(x, s)\, ds/(b - a)$, then we can easily solve for the reciprocal kernel to $\bar{K}(x)$ and set $j(x) = -\bar{K}(x) \Big/ \left(1 + \int_a^b \bar{K}(s)\, ds\right)$. Putting this in the modified Neumann sequence (11) gives us almost the same method as that recommended by Wagner [8]. However, as Dr. Wagner has kindly pointed out to me, there are some minor differences: for one thing, he found it most convenient for his problem to apply this procedure after several ordinary Neumann iterations had been performed, instead of from the beginning; also, in equation (8) of his paper, he uses the average value of his $\Delta^{(n)}(x)$, whereas I use its actual value at each x.

Case 4. If K and k are not too dependent on x, we can simply transpose the roles of x and z in Case 3 and define $j(z)$ in a corresponding fashion. The corresponding modified Neumann sequence can be defined easily.

Case 5. If we approximate K and k by the simple product of a function of x and a function of z, we get all of the previous cases as special cases. Thus, use the following estimates

(14)
$$K(x, z) \cong J(x, z) = A(x)B(z)$$

$$A(x) = \int_a^b K(x, s) \, ds, \qquad B(z) = \int_a^b K(s, z) \, ds \bigg/ \int_a^b \int_a^b K(x, z) \, dx \, dz.$$

By substitution or by consulting any text on integral equations, we can easily verify that the reciprocal kernel to a J of this form must be

(15) $\qquad j(x, z) = -qA(x)B(z) \quad$ where $\quad q = \left(1 + \int_a^b A(s)B(s) \, ds \right)^{-1}.$

Hence, we can easily define our modified Neumann sequence, and at each iteration this will involve only one quadrature of E rather than a new quadrature at each x. This Case 5 is clearly a generalization of all the previous cases, which emerge when A and B are given suitable constant values. As mentioned below, a further generalization would be possible in which J is written as the sum of a number of terms which are each products of a function of x and a function of z; the reciprocal kernel j can then be determined merely by solving a finite set of linear algebraic relations, whose coefficients are given by single quadratures. At the end of this paper, a numerical example is given to illustrate the general principles involved in the Neumann sequence and in Case 5.

It is to be noted that, even when K cannot be satisfactorily approximated by a product of functions of each variable, our problem can sometimes be converted into a new form in which this approximation is valid. Thus, $E(F + K \cdot F, U, K \cdot K) = 0$ can be easily verified to be equivalent to our original problem $E(F, U, K) = 0$. The new kernel $K \cdot K$ may be more capable of being closely approximated by a simple product; and should the approximation still not be adequate, we can convert our new problem into still a newer problem in exactly the same way just indicated. Provided all the eigenvalues of K exceed unity, except possibly for one simple real root, we can be sure that after a finite number of transformations our approximation will become adequate. Since integrals of the form $K \cdot K$ are laborious to compute, these transformations are not always to be recommended.

Case 6. If K has a very high peak along $x = z$, so too will k. If $K(x, z)$ can be approximated by $K(x)\delta(x - z)$, where δ refers to the Dirac impulse function with the property $\int_a^b K(x, s) \, ds = \int_a^b K(x)\delta(x - s) \, ds = K(x)$, then we set $j(x, z) = (-1 + c(x))\delta(x - z)$, where $c(x) = -1(1 + K(x))^{-1}$. This represents the interesting method recently proposed by Wagner [7]. Applying our norm condition to $E(j, K, j)$ in the usual fashion gives Wagner's sufficiency condition for convergence. It may be possible to extend this method by utilizing Dirac functions that depend upon terms like $x - g(z)$.

Case 7. Especially if K is symmetrical and positive definite, it may pay to approximate it by a function $J(x, z) = K(x, z)$ for $z \leqq x$, but which vanishes elsewhere. This approximation will then be of Volterra type, and even its simple Neumann series will be everywhere convergent so that its reciprocal kernel can be evaluated in terms of iterated integrals. Calling this reciprocal kernel j, we can proceed with the modified Neumann series; and from the known theory of similar iterations of definite matrixes, (von Mises and Pollaczek-Geiringer [4], Morris [5]) we can be sure the resulting sequence (11) will necessarily be convergent. Moreover, we can avoid calculating integrals of the type $J(x, z) \cdot A(x, z)$ involved in the calculation of the reciprocal kernel j, if we write and solve (11) in the verifiably equivalent form

$$(16) \qquad \{F + (K - J) \cdot U_n\} + U_{n+1} + J \cdot U_{n+1} = 0, \qquad n = 0, 1, \cdots.$$

Since we know that a Volterra J leads to a convergent ordinary Neumann series, we can in early iterations content ourselves with a few Neumann whirls of type (4), never calculating any integrals worse than of the form $J(x, z) \cdot A(x)$. Later we can strive for more accuracy. Or if we like, we can rather rapidly get approximate solutions to (16) by means of a net of approximating linear equations, whose matrix will be triangular and hence easily solved. Even if K is not symmetric, if it is everywhere negative and such as to make (4) convergent, then from the theory of Frobenius non-negative matrices, we can show that (16) is even more rapidly convergent.

Even if K is not symmetric or definite, we can always convert our problem into a new problem with this form. We calculate $\phi = \int_a^b E(F, U, K)^2 \, dx$ and seek U so as to minimize ϕ, leading to a new integral equation for U of the form (1) but with $F(x, z) + \int_a^b K(s, x)F(x, z) \, ds$ substituted for F, and the symmetric kernel $K(x, z) + K(z, x) + \int_a^b K(s, x)K(s, z) \, ds$ substituted for K. Note that it is $\delta(x - z) +$ the new kernel that is positive definite, and not necessarily the new kernel alone.

Case 8. Any Fredholm equations can be solved by using a finer and finer grid of linear approximations. We can think of the relevant rectangle of the (x, z) plane as being covered by a lattice of equally distant points, at each of which we evaluate K, and then proceed to set up and solve ordinary algebraic equations. This approximation to K can be written in terms of suitably defined Dirac functions and called J; its inverse, j, will also consist of certain defined Dirac functions, whose coefficients emerge from the solution of ordinary linear equations. Provided our norm condition is satisfied for j, we may remain content in most of the iterations with a rather coarse grid, going through more refined calculations with a finer grid only when it comes to evaluating the integrals in the expression $E(F, U_n, K)$, and only bothering with such refinement at a late stage in the iterations when the accuracy has some meaning.

Case 9. Needless to say, to the extent that we can interpolate for K by any one of the usual methods—such as polynomial interpolation, sums of exponentials, sums of products of functions of the form $\sum f_k(x)g_k(z)$, etc.—than a suitable

J and j can be defined and inserted into (11). The important thing is to utilize the information, which comes to us from simply checking how well our equation is satisfied, so as to best improve our estimate of the true solution.

9. A numerical example may be used to illustrate the general principles involved in the above discussion and also the special methods suggested in Case 5. Consider

(16)
$$U(x) = 1.5x + 1.5 - \int_0^1 (x + xs + s)U(s)\, ds \quad \text{or}$$

$$E(-1.5x - 1.5,\ U,\ x + xz + z) = 0$$

whose solution can be verified to be $U(x) = 1$. The first few Neumann iterations give $U_0(x) = 0$, $U_1(x) = 1.5x + 1.5$, $U_2(x) = -2x + .25 \cdots$, and this sequence can be easily shown to diverge in antidamped oscillations. (Actually the simple Neumann sequence with $C_n x + D_n$ fed into it at any stage gives back a similar linear expression but with new C_{n+1} and D_{n+1} coefficients. These new coefficients can be defined in terms of the old by simple linear relations:

$$C_{n+1} = 1.5 - \tfrac{5}{6}C_n - \tfrac{3}{2}D_n\,, \qquad D_{n+1} = 1.5 - \tfrac{1}{3}C_n - \tfrac{1}{2}D_n\,,$$

which can be verified to have a fixed point at $(C, D) = (0, 1)$. But by examining its 2 x 2 matrix, we find a characteristic root $\lambda = -(4 + \sqrt{19})/6$, which exceeds 1 in absolute value, so that the fixed point is unstable and even in its close vicinity we diverge away from it.)

We can easily apply the method of Case 5 to the modified Neumann sequence (11) with better results. For the case, $K(x, z) = x + xz + z$, we evaluate equations (14) and (15) as follows:

$$K = x + xz + z \cong J = A(x)B(z) = \tfrac{1}{5}(3x + 1)(3z + 1), \quad \text{where}$$

$$A(x) = \int_0^1 (x + xs + s)\, ds, \text{ etc.}$$

$$j(x, z) = -\tfrac{1}{12}(3x + 1)(3z + 1) \quad \text{with} \quad 12^{-1} = 1 + \int_0^1 A(s)B(s)\, ds.$$

The modified Neumann sequence (11) can now be written in the following form:

$$E_n(x) = -1.5x - 1.5 + U_n(x) + \int_0^1 (x + xs + s)U_n(s)\, ds$$

$$U_{n+1}(x) = U_n(x) - E_n(x) + \tfrac{1}{12}(3x + 1)\int_0^1 (3s + 1)E_n(s)\, ds.$$

The first few iterations yield the following $U_1 = 1.5x + 1.5$, $U_2 = \tfrac{3}{32}x + (1 - \tfrac{5}{96})$, $U_3 = \tfrac{3}{512}x + (1 - \tfrac{5}{1536})$, $\cdots$, which is seen to be rapidly convergent. Actually, if we had started with $U_0 = 0$, we should have gotten $U_1 = 1$, the exact answer, in a single step. This is because of the quite accidental fact that the Modified Neumann sequence gives us for $U_n = C_n x + D_n$ the *singular* linear iteration

$$C_{n+1} = 0 + \tfrac{1}{16}C_n + 0D_n, \qquad D_{n+1} = 1 - \tfrac{5}{144}C_n + 0D_n,$$

which is seen to have a *zero* characteristic root, and also a heavily damped $\lambda = \tfrac{1}{16}$. Another way of verifying convergence is to calculate (10)

$$E(K, j, K) = x + xz + z - \tfrac{1}{12}(3x + 1)(3z + 1)$$
$$- \tfrac{1}{12}(3z + 1) \int_0^1 (x + xs + s)(3s + 1) \, ds$$
$$= \tfrac{1}{24}(10x - 18xz + 9z - 5),$$

which, in absolute value never exceeds $\tfrac{5}{24}$ and whose norm is even less. For K such a simple polynomial in x and z, we can easily get the exact reciprocal kernel by trying a similar polynomial expression whose coefficients can be determined by substitution into (3) to be

$$k = \tfrac{4}{27} - \tfrac{2}{3}x - \tfrac{2}{3}z + 0xz,$$

so that the error in the j used in our Modified Neumann series is verified to be quite small and never to exceed $\tfrac{8}{27}$ at any point.

BIBLIOGRAPHY

1. A. C. AITKEN: Proceedings of the Royal Society of Edinburgh, **46**, 289 (1926).
2. H. BÜCKNER: Duke Mathematical Journal, **15**, 197 (1948).
3. R. A. FRAZER, W. J. DUNCAN AND A. R. COLLAR, "Elementary Matrices," (Cambridge Press, Cambridge, 1938), p. 120.
4. R. VON MISES AND H. POLLACZEK-GEIRINGER: Zeits. angew. Math. Mechanik, **9**, 58 (1929)
5. J. MORRIS: Journal of the Royal Aeronautical Society, **39**, 349 (1935).
6. P. A. SAMUELSON: Journal of Mathematics and Physics, **24**, 131 (1945).
7. C. WAGNER: Journal of Mathematics and Physics, **30**, 23 (1951).
8. C. WAGNER: Journal of Mathematics and Physics, **30**, 232 (1952).
9. G. WIARDA: "Integralgleichungen," (B. G. Teubner, Leipzig, Berlin, 1930), p. 120.
10. E. T. WHITTAKER AND G. ROBINSON: *The Calculus of Observations*, (Blackie, London, 1940), p. 84.

MASSACHUSETTS INSTITUTE OF TECHNOLOGY

(Received April 14, 1952)

CONTENTS

Volume II

Book Three

Trade, Welfare, and Fiscal Policy

Contents

Book Four

Economics and Public Policy

ACKNOWLEDGMENTS

The author, editor, and The M.I.T. Press wish to thank the publishers of the following essays for permission to reprint them here. The selections are arranged chronologically, with cross references in brackets to the chapter numbers used in this collection.

"A Note on Measurement of Utility," *The Review of Economic Studies*, Vol. IV, No. 2 (February 1937), pp. 155–161. [Chapter 20]

"Some Aspects of the Pure Theory of Capital," *The Quarterly Journal of Economics*, Vol. LI (May 1937), pp. 469–496. [Chapter 17]

"A Note on the Pure Theory of Consumer's Behaviour," *Economica*, Vol. V, No. 17 (February 1938), pp. 61–71. [Chapter 1]

"Welfare Economics and International Trade," *The American Economic Review*, Vol. XXVIII, No. 2 (June 1938), pp. 261–266. [Chapter 60]

"A Note on the Pure Theory of Consumer's Behaviour: An Addendum," *Economica*, Vol. V (August 1938), pp. 353–354. [Chapter 1]

"The Numerical Representation of Ordered Classifications and the Concept of Utility," *The Review of Economic Studies*, Vol. VI, No. 1 (October 1938), pp. 65–70. [Chapter 2]

"The Empirical Implications of Utility Analysis," *Econometrica*, Vol. 6, No. 4, (October 1938), pp. 344–356. [Chapter 3]

"The Rate of Interest under Ideal Conditions," *The Quarterly Journal of Economics*, Vol. LIII, No. 2 (February 1939), pp. 286–297. [Chapter 18]

"The End of Marginal Utility," *Economica*, Vol. VI (February 1939), pp. 86–87. [Chapter 4]

"The Gains from International Trade," *Canadian Journal of Economics and Political Science*, Vol. 5, No. 2 (May 1939), pp. 195–205. [Chapter 61]

"Interactions between the Multiplier Analysis and the Principle of Acceleration," *The Review of Economics and Statistics*, Vol. XXI, No. 2 (May 1939), pp. 75–78. Copyright 1939 by the President and Fellows of Harvard College. [Chapter 82]

Acknowledgments

"A Synthesis of the Principle of Acceleration and the Multiplier," *The Journal of Political Economy*, Vol. XLVII, No. 6 (December 1939), pp. 786–797. Copyright 1939 by the University of Chicago. [Chapter 83]

"The Theory of Pump-Priming Reëxamined," *The American Economic Review*, Vol. XXX, No. 3 (September 1940), pp. 492–506. [Chapter 85]

"Concerning Say's Law," abstract of a paper read to Econometric Society at New Orleans, December 1940, published in *Econometrica*, Vol. 9, No. 2 (April 1941), pp. 177–178. [Chapter 88]

"The Stability of Equilibrium: Comparative Statics and Dynamics," *Econometrica*, Vol. 9, No. 2 (April 1941), pp. 97–120. [Chapter 38]

"A Statistical Analysis of the Consumption Function," Appendix in A. H. Hansen, *Fiscal Policy and Business Cycles* (New York: W. W. Norton, 1941), pp. 250–260. [Chapter 87]

"Conditions that the Roots of a Polynomial Be Less than Unity in Absolute Value," *The Annals of Mathematical Statistics*, Vol. XXI, No. 3 (September 1941), pp. 360–364. [Chapter 45]

"Professor Pigou's Employment and Equilibrium," *The American Economic Review*, Vol. XXXI, No. 3 (September 1941), pp. 545–552. [Chapter 89]

With W. F. Stolper, "Protection and Real Wages," *The Review of Economic Studies*, Vol. IX, No. 1 (November 1941), pp. 58–73. [Chapter 66]

"A Note on Alternative Regressions," *Econometrica*, Vol. 10, No. 1 (January 1942), pp. 80–83. [Chapter 46]

"The Stability of Equilibrium: Linear and Nonlinear Systems," *Econometrica*, Vol. 10, No. 1 (January 1942), pp. 1–25. [Chapter 40]

"Constancy of the Marginal Utility of Income," in Lange *et al.*, eds., *Studies in Mathematical Economics and Econometrics, in Memory of Henry Schultz* (Chicago: University of Chicago Press, 1942), pp. 75–91. Copyright 1942 by the University of Chicago. [Chapter 5]

"Fiscal Policy and Income Determination," *The Quarterly Journal of Economics*, Vol. LVI, No. 4 (August 1942), pp. 575–605. [Chapter 86]

"The Business Cycle and Urban Development," in Guy Greer, ed., *The Problem of the Cities and Towns*, Conference on Urbanism, Harvard University, March 5–6, 1942, pp. 6–17. [Chapter 97]

"A Method of Determining Explicitly the Coefficients of the Characteristic Equation," *The Annals of Mathematical Statistics*, Vol. XIII, No. 4 (December 1942), pp. 424–429. [Chapter 47]

"Dynamics, Statics, and the Stationary States," essays in honor of Joseph Schumpeter, *The Review of Economics and Statistics*, Vol. XXV, No. 1 (February 1943), pp. 58–68. Copyright by the President and Fellows of Harvard College. [Chapter 19]

"Full Employment after the War," in S. E. Harris, ed., *Postwar Economic Problems* (New York: McGraw-Hill, 1943), pp. 27–53. Copyright 1943 by McGraw-Hill Book Co. [Chapter 108]

"Fitting General Gram-Charlier Series," *The Annals of Mathematical Statistics*, Vol. XIV, No. 2 (June 1943), pp. 179–187. [Chapter 48]

"A Fundamental Multiplier Identity," *Econometrica*, Vol. II, No. 3–4 (July–October 1943), pp. 221–226. [Chapter 90]

"Further Commentary on Welfare Economics," *The American Economic Review*, Vol. XXXIII, No. 3 (September 1943), pp. 605–607. [Chapter 76]

"A Simple Method of Interpolation," *Proceedings of the National Academy of Sciences*, Vol. 29, No. 11 (December 1943), pp. 397–401. [Chapter 49]

"Efficient Computation of the Latent Vectors of a Matrix," *Proceedings of the National Academy of Sciences*, Vol. 29, No. 11 (December 1943), pp. 393–397. [Chapter 50]

"The Relation between Hicksian Stability and True Dynamic Stability," *Econometrica*, Vol. 12, Nos. 3 and 4 (July–October 1944), pp. 256–257. [Chapter 39]

"The Effect of Interest Rate Increases on the Banking System," *The American Economic Review*, Vol. XXXV, No. 1 (March 1945), pp. 16–27. [Chapter 50]

"The Turn of the Screw," *American Economic Review*, Vol. XXXV, No. 4 (September 1945), pp. 674–676. [Chapter 96]

"A Convergent Iterative Process," *Journal of Mathematics and Physics*, Vol. XXIV, Nos. 3–4 (November 1945), pp. 131–134. [Chapter 51]

Book review of Jacob L. Mosak, *General Equilibrium Theory in International Trade* in *The American Economic Review*, Vol. XXXV, No. 5 (December 1945), pp. 943–945. [Chapter 63]

"Comparative Statics and the Logic of Economic Maximizing," *The Review of Economic Studies*, Vol. XIV (1), No. 35 (1946–1947), pp. 41–43. [Chapter 6]

"A Connection between the Bernoulli and Newton Iterative Processes," *Bulletin of the American Mathematical Society*, Vol. 52, No. 3 (March 1946), p. 239. [Chapter 54]

"Computation of Characteristic Vectors," *Bulletin of the American Mathematical Society*, Vol. 52, No. 3 (March 1946), pp. 239–240. [Chapter 53]

"Generalization of the Laplace Transform for Difference Equations," *Bulletin of the American Mathematical Society*, Vol. 52, No. 3 (March 1946), p. 240. [Chapter 52]

With C. C. Holt, "The Graphic Depiction of Elasticity of Demand," *The Journal of Political Economy*, Vol. LIV, No. 4 (August 1946), pp. 354–357. Copyright 1946 by the University of Chicago. [Chapter 7]

"A Generalized Newton Iteration," *Bulletin of the American Mathematical Society*, Vol. 53, No. 3 (March 1947), p. 283. [Chapter 56]

"Generalization of the Laplace Transform for Any Operator," *Bulletin of the American Mathematical Society*, Vol. 53, No. 3 (March 1947), pp. 283–284. [Chapter 55]

Acknowledgments

"Some Implications of 'Linearity'," *The Review of Economic Studies*, Vol. XV (2), No. 38 (1947–1948), pp. 88–90. [Chapter 8]

"The Simple Mathematics of Income Determination," in L. A. Metzler *et al.*, *Income, Employment and Public Policy: Essays in Honor of Alvin Hansen* (New York: W. W. Norton, 1948). [Chapter 91]

"Dynamic Process Analysis" for the American Economic Association's *A Survey of Contemporary Economics*, Vol. I, ed. by Howard Ellis (Philadelphia: Blakiston, 1948: Homewood, Illinois: Richard D. Irwin, 1952). [Chapter 41]

"Disparity in Postwar Exchange Rates," in Seymour Harris, ed., *Foreign Economic Policy for the United States* (Cambridge: Harvard University Press, 1948), pp. 397–412. Copyright 1948 by the President and Fellows of Harvard College. [Chapter 64]

"Exact Distribution of Continuous Variables in Sequential Analysis," *Econometrica*, Vol. 16, No. 2 (April 1948), pp. 191–198. [Chapter 57]

"International Trade and Equalisation of Factor Prices," *Economic Journal*, Vol. LVIII, No. 230 (June 1948), pp. 163–184. [Chapter 67]

"Consumption Theory in Terms of Revealed Preference," *Economica*, Vol. XV (November 1948), pp. 243–253. [Chapter 9]

"International Factor-Price Equalisation Once Again," *Economic Journal*, Vol. LIX, No. 234 (June 1949), pp. 181–197. [Chapter 68]

Book Review of Hla Myint, *Theories of Welfare Economics* in *Economica*, Vol. XVI (November 1949), pp. 371–374. [Chapter 79]

Market Mechanisms and Maximization, Part I: "The Theory of Comparative Advantage"; Part II: "The Cheapest-Adequate-Diet Problem"; and Part III: "Dynamics and Linear Programming"; published by the RAND Corporation, Parts I and II, March 28, 1949, and Part III, June 29, 1949. [Chapter 33]

"The Le Chatelier Principle in Linear Programming," published by the RAND Corporation, August 4, 1949. [Chapter 43]

"Evaluation of Real National Income," *Oxford Economic Papers* (New Series), Vol. II, No. 1 (Oxford, England: University Press, January 1950), pp. 1–29. [Chapter 77]

"Iterative Computation of Complex Roots," *Journal of Mathematics and Physics*, Vol. XXVII, No. 4 (January 1950), pp. 259–267. [Chapter 58]

"The Problem of Integrability in Utility Theory," *Economica*, Vol. XVII, No. 68 (November 1950), pp. 355–385. [Chapter 10]

"Probability and the Attempts to Measure Utility" (English and Japanese), *The Economic Review (Keizai Kenkyu)*, Vol. 1 (Tokyo: Hitotsubashi University, July 1950), pp. 167–173. [Chapter 12]

"Principles and Rules in Modern Fiscal Policy: A Neo-Classical Reformulation," in *Money, Trade and Economic Growth: Essays in Honor of John Henry Williams* (New York: Macmillan, 1951), pp. 157–176. [Chapter 98]

"Abstract of a Theorem Concerning Substitutability in Open Leontief Models," Chapter VII in Cowles Commission for Research in Economics, *Activity Analysis of Production and Allocation*, ed. by T. C. Koopmans (New York: Wiley, 1951). [Chapter 36]

"Economic Theory and Wages," in David McCord Wright, ed., *The Impact of the Union: Eight Economic Theorists Evaluate the Labor Union Movement* (New York: Harcourt, Brace, 1951), pp. 312–342. [Chapter 117]

"Schumpeter as a Teacher and Economic Theorist," *The Review of Economics and Statistics*, Vol. XXXIII, No. 2 (May 1951), pp. 98–103. Copyright 1951 by the President and Fellows of Harvard College. [Chapter 116]

"Comment," in *A Survey in Contemporary Economics*, Vol. II, ed. by B. F. Haley (Homewood, Ill.: Richard D. Irwin, 1952). [Chapter 81]

"A Comment on Factor Price Equalisation," *The Review of Economic Studies*, Vol. XIX (2), No. 49 (February 1952), pp. 121–122. [Chapter 69]

"Economic Theory and Mathematics: An Appraisal," *The American Economic Review*, Vol. XLII, No. 2 (May 1952), pp. 56–66. [Chapter 126]

"Spatial Price Equilibrium and Linear Programming," *The American Economic Review*, Vol. XLII, No. 3 (June 1952), pp. 283–303. [Chapter 72]

"The Transfer Problem and Transport Costs: The Terms of Trade When Impediments Are Absent," *Economic Journal*, Vol. LXII, No. 246 (June 1952), pp. 278–304. [Chapter 74]

"Probability, Utility, and the Independence Axiom," *Econometrica*, Vol. 20, No. 4 (October 1952), pp. 670–678. [Chapter 14]

"Rapidly Converging Solutions to Integral Equations," *Journal of Mathematics and Physics*, Vol. XXXI, No. 4 (January 1953), pp. 276–286. [Chapter 59]

"Consumption Theorems in Terms of Overcompensation rather than Indifference Comparisons," *Economica*, New Series, Vol. XX, No. 77 (February 1953), pp. 1–9. [Chapter 11]

"Prices of Factors and Goods in General Equilibrium," *The Review of Economic Studies*, Vol. XXI (1), No. 54 (1953–1954), pp. 1–20. [Chapter 70]

"Full Employment versus Progress and Other Economic Goals," Chapter XII of Max Millikan, ed., *Income Stabilization for a Developing Economy* (New Haven: Yale University Press, 1953). [Chapter 99]

With R. M. Solow, "Balanced Growth under Constant Returns to Scale," *Econometrica*, Vol. XXI, No. 3 (July 1953), pp. 412–424. [Chapter 24]

"The Transfer Problem and Transport Costs, II: Analysis of Effects of Trade Impediments," *Economic Journal*, Vol. LXIV, No. 254 (June 1954), pp. 264–289. [Chapter 75]

"The Pure Theory of Public Expenditure," *The Review of Economics and Statistics*, Vol. XXXVI, No. 4 (November 1964), pp. 387–389. Copyright 1954 by the President and Fellows of Harvard College. [Chapter 92]

"Some Psychological Aspects of Mathematics and Economics," *The Review of Economics and Statistics*, Vol. XXXVI, No. 4 (November 1954), pp. 380–382. Copyright 1954 by the President and Fellows of Harvard College. [Chapter 127]

Comment on "Professor Samuelson on Operationalism in Economic Theory," by Donald F. Gordon, in *The Quarterly Journal of Economics*, Vol. LXIX (May 1955), pp. 310–314. [Chapter 128]

"Linear Programming and Economic Theory," *Proceedings of the Second Symposium in Linear Programming* (Washington, D. C., National Bureau of Standards and U. S. Air Force, January 27–29, 1955), Vol. 1, pp. 251–272. [Chapter 34]

"The New Look in Tax and Fiscal Policy," Joint Committee on the Economic Report, 84th Congress, 1st Session, *Federal Tax Policy for Economic Growth and Stability*, November 9, 1955 (Washington: U. S. Government Printing Office, 1956), pp. 229–234. [Chapter 100]

"Diagrammatic Exposition of a Theory of Public Expenditure," *The Review of Economics and Statistics*, Vol. XXXVII, No. 4 (November 1955), pp. 350–356. Copyright 1955 by the President and Fellows of Harvard College. [Chapter 93]

"Social Indifference Curves," *The Quarterly Journal of Economics*, Vol. LXX, No. 1 (February 1956), pp. 1–22. [Chapter 78]

"Economic Forecasting and National Policy" in *The Employment Act Past and Future: A Tenth Anniversary Symposium*, edited by Gerhard Colm (Washington: National Planning Association, Special Report No. 41 (February 1956), pp. 130–134. [Chapter 101]

"Recent American Monetary Controversy," *Three Banks Review*, March 1956, pp. 1–21. [Chapter 109]

With R. M. Solow, "A Complete Capital Model Involving Heterogeneous Capital Goods," *The Quarterly Journal of Economics*, Vol. LXX (November 1956), pp. 537–562. [Chapter 25]

"The Economics of Eisenhower: A Symposium," *The Review of Economics and Statistics*, Vol. XXXVIII, No. 4 (November 1956), pp. 371–373. Copyright 1956 by the President and Fellows of Harvard College. [Chapter 110]

"Wages and Interest: A Modern Dissection of Marxian Economic Models," *The American Economic Review*, Vol. XLVII, No. 6 (December 1957), pp. 884–912. [Chapter 29]

"Intertemporal Price Equilibrium: A Prologue to the Theory of Speculation," *Weltwirtschaftliches Archiv*, Band 79, Heft 2 (Hamburg: Hoffmann & Campe Verlag, December 1957), pp. 181–219. [Chapter 73]

Book review of J. de V. Graaff, *Theoretical Welfare Economics* in *The Economic Journal*, Vol. 68, No. 271 (September 1958), pp. 539–541. [Chapter 80]

"Aspects of Public Expenditure Theories," *The Review of Economics and Statistics*, Vol. XL, No. 4 (November 1958), pp. 332–338. Copyright 1958 by the President and Fellows of Harvard College. [Chapter 94]

"Frank Knight's Theorem in Linear Programming," *Zeitschrift Für National-ökonomie*, Band XVIII, Heft 3 (1958), pp. 310–317. [Chapter 35]

"An Exact Consumption-Loan Model of Interest with or without the Social Contrivance of Money," *The Journal of Political Economy*, Vol. LXVI, No. 6 (December 1958), pp. 467–482. Copyright 1958 by the University of Chicago. [Chapter 21]

Book review of Torsten Gårdlund, *The Life of Knut Wicksell* in *The Review of Economics and Statistics*, Vol. XLI, No. 1 (February 1959), pp. 81–83. Copyright 1959 by the President and Fellows of Harvard College. [Chapter 120]

"A Modern Treatment of the Ricardian Economy: I. The Pricing of Goods and of Labor and Land Services," *The Quarterly Journal of Economics*, Vol. LXXIII, No. 1 (February 1959), pp. 1–35. [Chapter 31]

"What Economists Know," Chapter 7 in Daniel Lerner, ed., *The Human Meaning of the Social Sciences* (New York: Meridian Books, 1959), pp. 183–213. © Copyright by Meridian Books, Inc., 1959. [Chapter 121]

"A Modern Treatment of the Ricardian Economy: II. Capital and Interest Aspects of the Pricing Process," *The Quarterly Journal of Economics*, Vol. LXXIII, No. 2 (May 1959), pp. 217–231. [Chapter 32]

"Alvin Hansen and the Interactions between the Multiplier Analysis and the Principle of Acceleration," *The Review of Economics and Statistics*, Vol. XLI, No. 2, Part I (May 1959), pp. 183–184. Copyright 1959 by the President and Fellows of Harvard College. [Chapter 84]

"Reply" (Abba P. Lerner, "Consumption-Loan Interest and Money"), *The Journal of Political Economy*, Vol. LXVII, No. 5 (October 1959), pp. 518–522. Copyright 1959 by the University of Chicago. [Chapter 22]

"The St. Petersburg Paradox as a Divergent Double Limit," *International Economic Review*, Vol. 1, No. 1 (January 1960), pp. 31–37. [Chapter 15]

"Infinity, Unanimity, and Singularity: A Reply," *The Journal of Political Economy*, Vol. LXVIII, No. 1 (February 1960), pp. 76–83. Copyright 1960 by the University of Chicago. [Chapter 23]

With R. M. Solow, "Analytical Aspects of Anti-Inflation Policy," *The American Economic Review*, Vol. L, No. 2 (May 1960), pp. 177–194. [Chapter 102]

"American Economics," in Ralph E. Freeman, ed., *Postwar Economic Trends in the U.S.* (New York: Harpers, 1960), pp. 31–50. [Chapter 122 includes pp. 44–50 only]

"Harold Hotelling as Mathematical Economist," *American Statistician*, Vol. XIV, No. 3 (June 1960), pp. 21–25. [Chapter 118]

"Structure of a Minimum Equilibrium System," in Ralph W. Pfouts, ed., *Essays in Economics and Econometrics: A Volume in Honor of Harold Hotelling* (Chapel Hill: University of North Carolina Press, 1960), pp. 1–33. [Chapter 44]

"An Extension of the LeChatelier Principle," *Econometrica*, Vol. 28, No. 2 (April 1960), pp. 368–379. [Chapter 42]

"Efficient Paths of Capital Accumulation in Terms of the Calculus of Variations," in Kenneth J. Arrow, Samuel Karlin, and Patrick Suppes, eds., *Mathematical Methods in the Social Sciences, 1959* (Stanford: Stanford University Press, 1960), pp. 77–88. [Chapter 26]

"Reflections on Monetary Policy," *The Review of Economics and Statistics*, Vol. XLII, No. 3, Part 1 (August 1960), pp. 263–269. Copyright 1960 by the President and Fellows of Harvard College. [Chapter 103]

"Wages and Interest — A Modern Dissection of Marxian Economic Models: Reply," *The American Economic Review*, Vol. L, No. 4 (September 1960), pp. 719–721. [Chapter 30]

"Prospects and Policies for the 1961 American Economy," a Report to President-Elect Kennedy, Thursday, January 6, 1961. Reprinted as Chapter 3, "Economic Frontiers," in M. B. Schnapper, ed., *New Frontiers of the Kennedy Administration* (Washington, D.C: Public Affairs Press, 1961). [Chapter 111]

"The Evaluation of 'Social Income': Capital Formation and Wealth," Chapter 3 in F. A. Lutz and D. C. Hague, eds., *The Theory of Capital* (London: Macmillan, 1961), pp. 32–57. [Chapter 27]

"A New Theorem on Nonsubstitution," in *Money, Growth, and Methodology*, published in honor of Johan Åkerman, Vol. 20, Lund Social Science Studies (Lund, Sweden: CWK Gleerup, March 1961), pp. 407–423. [Chapter 37]

"Problems of the American Economy: An Economist's View," Stamp Memorial Lecture, delivered before the University of London on November 9, 1961 (London: The Athlone Press, 1962), pp. 1–30. [Chapter 123]

"Economists and the History of Ideas," (Presidential Address), *The American Economic Review*, Vol. LII, No. 1 (March 1962), pp. 1–18. [Chapter 113]

"Economic Policy for 1962," *The Review of Economics and Statistics*, Vol. XLIV, No. 1 (February 1962), pp. 3–6. Copyright 1962 by the President and Fellows of Harvard College. [Chapter 112]

Memorandum for The Royal Commission on Banking and Finance, Ottawa, Canada, October 19, 1962. [Chapter 104]

"Parable and Realism in Capital Theory: The Surrogate Production Function," *The Review of Economic Studies*, Vol. XXIX, No. 3 (June 1962), pp. 193–206. [Chapter 28]

"The Gains from International Trade Once Again," *The Economic Journal*, Vol. LXXII (December 1962), pp. 820–829. [Chapter 62]

"Stability and Growth in the American Economy," Wicksell Lectures 1962 (Stockholm: Alqvist and Wiksell, December 1962). [Chapter 124]

"Comment on Ernest Nagel's 'Assumptions in Economic Theory,'" *Papers and Proceedings of the American Economic Association*, December 29, 1962, pp. 231–236. [Chapter 129]

"Fiscal and Financial Policies for Growth," *Proceedings — A Symposium of Economic Growth*, sponsored by The American Bankers Association, Monday, February 25, 1963, Washington, D.C., pp. 78–100. [Chapter 105]

"Risk and Uncertainty: A Fallacy of Large Numbers," *Scientia*, 6th Series, 57th year (April–May 1963). [Chapter 16]

"Economic Thought and the New Industrialism," in Arthur M. Schlesinger, Jr., and Morton White, eds., *Paths of American Thought* (Boston: Houghton Mifflin Company, 1963), pp. 219–237. [Chapter 125]

"Modern Economic Realities and Individualism," *The Texas Quarterly*, Summer 1963, pp. 128–139. [Chapter 106]

"The Economic Role of Private Activity," in *A Dialogue on the Proper Economic Role of the State*, discussion given at Swarthmore, early 1963; Selected Papers No. 7, University of Chicago Graduate School of Business. [Chapter 107]

"Reflections on Central Banking," *The National Banking Review*, Vol. 1, No. 1 (September 1963), pp. 15–28. [Chapter 104]

"D. H. Robertson (1890–1963)", *The Quarterly Journal of Economics*, Vol. LXXVII, No. 4 (November 1963), pp. 517–536. [Chapter 119]

"The General Theory," and "A Brief Survey of Post-Keynesian Developments" in Robert Lekachman, ed., *Keynes' General Theory: Reports of Three Decades* (New York: St. Martin's Press, 1964), pp. 315–347. [Chapters 114 and 115]

"Theoretical Notes on Trade Problems," *The Review of Economics and Statistics*, Vol. XLVI, No. 2 (May 1964), pp. 145–154. Copyright 1964 by the President and Fellows of Harvard College. [Chapter 65]

"Equalization by Trade of the Interest Rate Along with the Real Wage," in *Trade, Growth, and the Balance of Payments*, essays in honor of Gottfried Haberler (Chicago: Rand McNally & Co., 1965), pp. 35–52. [Chapter 71]